Corporations

Corporations

Cases and Materials

Dalia Tsuk Mitchell
PROFESSOR OF LAW
THE GEORGE WASHINGTON UNIVERSITY LAW SCHOOL

CAROLINA ACADEMIC PRESS
Durham, North Carolina

Copyright © 2018
Dalia Tsuk Mitchell
All Rights Reserved.

ISBN 978-1-5310-0927-4
eISBN 978-1-53100-928-1
LCCN 2018933301

Carolina Academic Press, LLC
700 Kent Street
Durham, North Carolina 27701
Telephone (919) 489-7486
Fax (919) 493-5668
www.cap-press.com

Printed in the United States of America.

For Gabriella

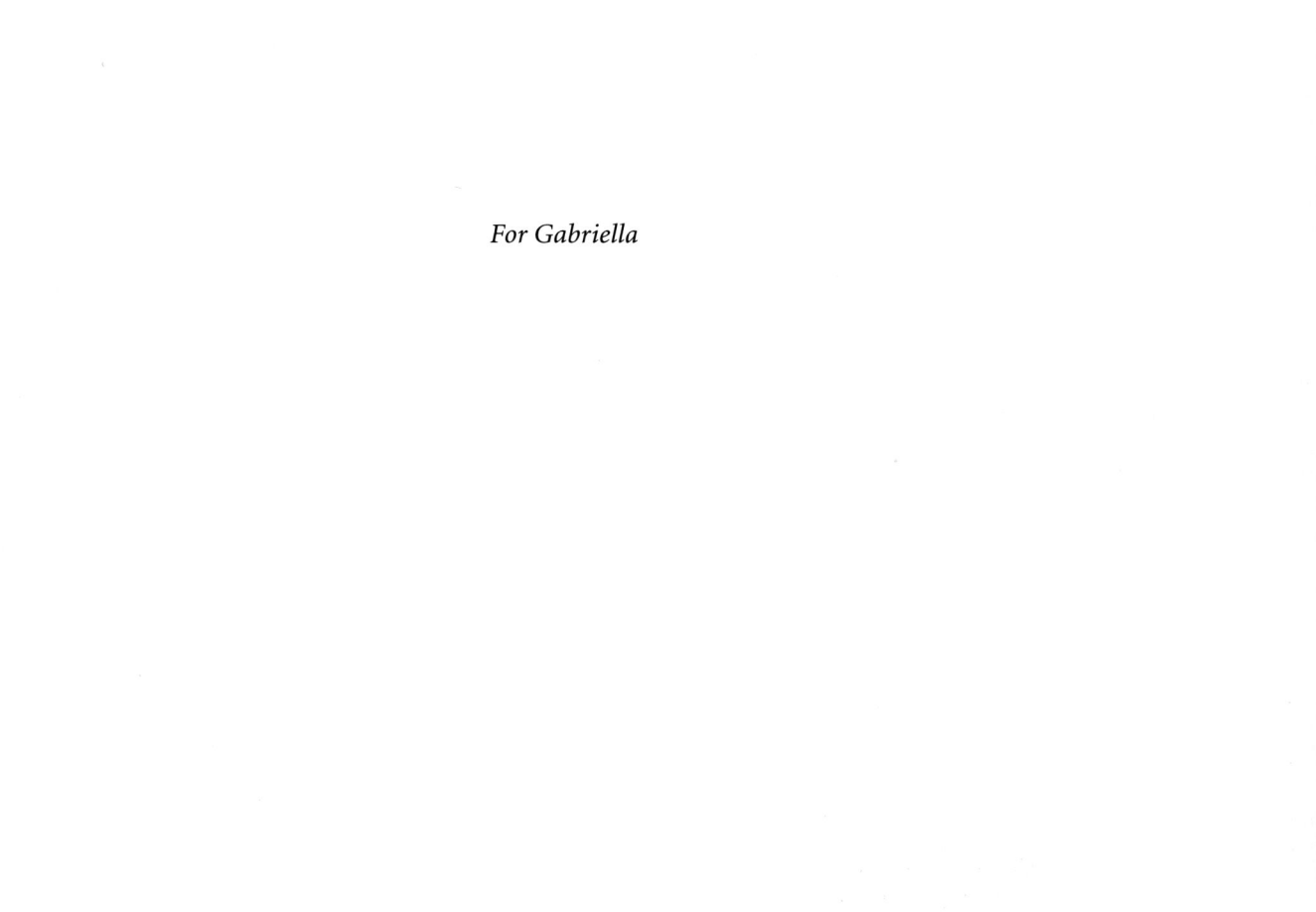

Contents

Table of Principal Cases	xiii
PART 1 · THE NATURE AND PURPOSE OF THE CORPORATION	
Section I · What is a Corporation?	3
Trustees of Dartmouth College v. Woodward	4
Liam Seamus O'Melinn, *Neither Contract nor Concession:*	
The Public Personality of the Corporation	16
Section II · The Corporation and the Community	21
Steinway v. Steinway & Sons	21
Dodge v. Ford Motor Co.	25
Dalia Tsuk Mitchell, *Corporations Without Labor: The Politics*	
of Progressive Corporate Law	34
A.P. Smith Mfg. Co. v. Barlow	36
Bell v. Maryland	42
Poletown Neighborhood Council v. City of Detroit	51
Charter Township of Ypsilanti v. General Motors Corporation	53
Section III · Ownership and Control	61
A. The Corporation and Other Business Forms	62
B. Limited Liability and Its Limits	65
Walkovszky v. Carlton	65
Kinney Shoe Corporation v. Polan	72
Sea-Land Services, Inc. v. The Pepper Source	77
Consolidated Rock Products Co. v. Du Bois	81
C. The Authority of the Board	86
Delaware General Corporation Law Section 141	86
Delaware General Corporation Law Section 142	90
Hoyt v. Thompson's Executor	90
Shlensky v. Wrigley	92
Grimes v. Donald	96
Section IV · The Corporation's Capital Structure	100
A. Debt	101
Simons v. Cogan	102
Metropolitan Life Insurance Company v. RJR Nabisco, Inc.	105

	Katz v. Oak Industries, Inc.	114
B. Preferred Stock		123
	Jedwab v. MGM Grand Hotels, Inc.	123
	In re Trados Incorporated Shareholder Litigation	128

Part 2 · The Duties of Directors, Officers and other Insiders

Section I · Derivative Litigation — 138

A. The Distinction Between Derivative and Direct Actions — 139
  Eisenberg v. The Flying Tiger Line, Inc. — 139
  Grimes v. Donald — 142
B. Security for Expenses — 144
  Baker v. MacFadden Publications, Inc.; Baker v. Boord — 144
C. Demand on the Board — 147
  Grimes v. Donald — 147
  Marx v. Akers — 151
  London v. Tyrrell — 160
D. The Role of Special Litigation Committees — 166
  Auerbach v. Bennett — 166
  Zapata Corporation v. Maldonado — 174
  In re Oracle Corp. Derivative Litigation — 182

Section II · The Duty of Care — 193

A. Directors' Negligence (The Duty to Act) — 194
  Francis v. United Jersey Bank — 194
  Senn v. Northwest Underwriters Inc. — 205
B. The Business Judgment Rule — 208
  Kamin v. American Express Company — 208
  Joy v. North — 212
C. The Business Judgment Rule and the Duty of Care — 216
  Smith v. Van Gorkom — 216
  Van Gorkom in context — 236

Section III · The Duty of Loyalty — 239

A. Interested Director Transactions — 240
  Meinhard v. Salmon — 241
  Bayer v. Beran — 246
  Delaware General Corporation Law Section 144 — 253
  Marciano v. Nakash — 255
  Benihana of Tokyo, Inc. v. Benihana, Inc. — 261
B. Corporate Opportunity — 266
  Broz v. Cellular Information Systems, Inc. — 266
  ALI Principles of Corporate Governance Section 5.05 — 276
  In re eBay, Inc. Shareholders Litigation — 278
C. Compensation and Waste — 282
  Lewis v. Vogelstein — 282

Section IV · Good Faith 295
    A. A New Framework 296
        Cede & Co. v. Technicolor, Inc. 296
        Cede v. Technicolor in context 306
        In re The Walt Disney Company Derivative Litigation,
        Brehm v. Eisner 307
    B. Good Faith and the Duty to Monitor 343
        In re Caremark International Inc. Derivative Litigation 343
        Stone v. Ritter 357
        In re Citigroup Inc. Shareholder Derivative Litigation 367
        In re China Agritech, Inc. Shareholder Derivative Litigation 387

Section V · The Federal Approach 404
    A. Rule 10b-5 406
        Halliburton Co. v. Erica P. John Fund, Inc. 406
        West v. Prudential Securities, Incorporated 419
    B. Insider Trading 423
        Securities and Exchange Commission v. Texas Gulf Sulphur Co. 424
        Dirks v. Securities and Exchange Commission 438
        United States v. O'Hagan 448
    C. Short-Swing Profits 457

Part 3 · Shareholders

Section I · Shareholders in Publicly Held Corporations 462
    Dalia Tsuk Mitchell, *Shareholders as Proxies: The Contours*
        of Shareholder Democracy 462
    A. Proxy and Consent Contests 464
        Rosenfeld v. Fairchild Engine and Airplane Corporation 466
        Campbell v. Loew's Incorporated 473
        Levin v. Metro-Goldwyn-Mayer, Inc. 483
        Blasius Industries, Inc. v. Atlas Corporation 492
        Andrew C. Houston, *Chancellor Allen's Jurisprudence:* Blasius
        and the Democratic Paradigm in Corporate Law 503
    B. Shareholders' Rights to Information 506
        Mills v. Electric Auto-Lite Co. 506
        TSC Industries, Inc. v. Northway, Inc. 512
        Virginia Bankshares, Inc. v. Sandberg 521
    C. Shareholder Proposals 533
        Dalia Tsuk Mitchell, *Shareholders as Proxies: The Contours*
            of Shareholder Democracy 533
        Amalgamated Clothing and Textile Workers Union v.
            Wal-Mart Stores, Inc. 541

American Federation of State, County & Municipal
  Employees (AFSCME), Employees Pension Plan v.
  American International Group, Inc. (AIG) 554
CA, Inc. v. AFSCME Employees Pension Plan 560

Section II · Shareholders in Closely Held Corporations 570
A. Shareholders' Voice and Exit Arrangements 571
  Ringling Bros.-Barnum & Bailey Combined Shows, Inc. v.
    Ringling 573
  Abercrombie v. Davies 580
  Lehrman v. Cohen 589
  Oceanic Exploration Company v. Grynberg 597
  Rosiny v. Schmidt 604
B. The Allocation of Power between Shareholders and Directors 618
  McQuade v. Stoneham 618
  Clark v. Dodge 625
  Galler v. Galler 628
C. Fiduciary Duties of Shareholders in Closely Held Corporations 635
  Donahue v. Rodd Electrotype Company of New England, Inc. 635
  Wilkes v. Springside Nursing Home, Inc. 645
  Smith v. Atlantic Properties, Inc. 652
  Brodie v. Jordan 656
  Jordan v. Duff and Phelps, Inc. 661
D. Remedies for Oppression 675
  Alaska Plastics, Inc. v. Coppock 675
  In the Matter of the Judicial Dissolution of Kemp & Beatley, Inc. 681

Section III · Controlling Shareholders 687
A. Controlling Shareholders' Fiduciary Duties 687
  Sinclair Oil Corporation v. Levien 687
  Anadarko Petroleum Corporation v. Panhandle
    Eastern Corporation 692
  Zahn v. Transamerica Corporation 699
B. Sale of Control 703
  Perlman v. Feldmann 703
  Essex Universal Corporation v. Yates 709

PART 4 · FUNDAMENTAL TRANSACTIONS

Section I · The De Facto Merger Doctrine 722
  Farris v. Glen Alden Corporation 723
  Hariton v. Arco Electronics, Inc. 729

Section II · Freeze-Out Mergers 730
  Weinberger v. UOP, Inc. 730

CONTENTS xi

Kahn v. M&F Worldwide Corp. 744
Coggins v. New England Patriots Football Club, Inc. 758
Glassman v. Unocal Exploration Corp. 765
Leader v. Hycor, Inc. 767

Section III · Tender Offers and Hostile Takeovers 772
    A. *Unocal / Revlon* Duties 774
        Unocal Corporation v. Mesa Petroleum Co. 774
        Unocal v. Mesa in context 783
        Moran v. Household International, Inc. 785
        Revlon, Inc. v. MacAndrews & Forbes Holdings, Inc. 792
        Paramount Communications, Inc. v. Time Incorporated 803
        Paramount Communications Inc. v. QVC Network Inc. 819
        Unitrin, Inc. v. American General Corp. 836
    B. Extending the *Unocal / Revlon* Approach 857
        Hilton Hotels Corporation v. ITT Corporation 858
        Omnicare, Inc. v. NCS Healthcare, Inc. 867
        Lyondell Chemical Company v. Ryan 890
    C. Anti-Takeover Legislation 896
        CTS Corporation v. Dynamics Corporation of America 896

Index 907

Table of Principal Cases

A
A.P. Smith Mfg. Co. v. Barlow, 55
Abercrombie v. Davies, 611
Alaska Plastics, Inc. v. Coppock, 706
Amalgamated Clothing and Textile Workers Union v. Wal-Mart Stores, Inc., 572
American Federation of State, County & Municipal Employees (AFSCME), Employees Pension Plan v. American International Group, Inc. (AIG), 584
Anadarko Petroleum Corporation v. Panhandle Eastern Corporation, 723
Auerbach v. Bennett, 196

B
Baker v. MacFadden Publications, Inc.; Baker v. Boord, 174
Bayer v. Beran, 277
Bell v. Maryland, 61
Benihana of Tokyo, Inc. v. Benihana, Inc., 292
Blasius Industries, Inc. v. Atlas Corporation, 523
Brodie v. Jordan, 687
Broz v. Cellular Information Systems, Inc., 296

C
CA, Inc. v. AFSCME Employees Pension Plan, 591
Campbell v. Loew's Incorporated, 509
Cede & Co. v. Technicolor, Inc., 327
Charter Township of Ypsilanti v. General Motors Corporation, 72
Clark v. Dodge, 656
Coggins v. New England Patriots Football Club, Inc., 787
Consolidated Rock Products Co. v. Du Bois, 100
CTS Corporation v. Dynamics Corporation of America, 927

D
Dirks v. Securities and Exchange Commission, 476
Dodge v. Ford Motor Co., 44
Donahue v. Rodd Electrotype Company of New England, Inc., 666

E
Eisenberg v. The Flying Tiger Line, Inc., 169
Essex Universal Corporation v. Yates, 740

F
Farris v. Glen Alden Corporation, 753
Francis v. United Jersey Bank, 224

G
Galler v. Galler, 659
Glassman v. Unocal Exploration Corp., 794
Grimes v. Donald, 115, 172, 177

H

Halliburton Co. v. Erica P. John Fund, Inc., 442
Hariton v. Arco Electronics, Inc., 758
Hilton Hotels Corporation v. ITT Corporation, 916
Hoyt v. Thompson's Executor, 109

I

In re Caremark International Inc. Derivative Litigation, 378
In re China Agritech, Inc. Shareholder Derivative Litigation, 422
In re Citigroup Inc. Shareholder Derivative Litigation, 401
In re eBay, Inc. Shareholders Litigation, 308
In re Oracle Corp Derivative Litigation, 212
In re The Walt Disney Company Derivative Litigation, 337
In re Trados Incorporated Shareholder Litigation, 158
In the Matter of the Judicial Dissolution of Kemp & Beatley, Inc., 712

J

Jedwab v. MGM Grand Hotels, Inc., 153
Jordan v. Duff and Phelps, Inc., 692
Joy v. North, 243

K

Kahn v. M&F Worldwide Corp., 774
Kamin v. American Express Company, 238
Katz v. Oak Industries, Inc., 144
Kinney Shoe Corporation v. Polan, 90

L

Leader v. Hycor, Inc., 797
Lehrman v. Cohen, 619
Levin v. Metro-Goldwyn-Mayer, Inc., 514
Lewis v. Vogelstein, 313
London v. Tyrrell, 190
Lyondell Chemical Company v. Ryan, 887

M

Marciano v. Nakash, 285
Marx v. Akers, 181
McQuade v. Stoneham, 649
Meinhard v. Salmon, 271
Metropolitan Life Insurance Company v. RJR Nabisco, Inc., 135
Mills v. Electric Auto-Lite Co., 537
Moran v. Household International, Inc., 814

O

Oceanic Exploration Company v. Grynberg, 627
Omnicare, Inc. v. NCS Healthcare, Inc., 894

P

Paramount Communications, Inc. v. Time Incorporated, 832
Paramount Communications Inc. v. QVC Network Inc., 848
Perlman v. Feldmann, 734
Poletown Neighborhood Council v. City of Detroit, 70

R

Revlon, Inc. v. MacAndrews & Forbes Holdings, Inc., 821
Ringling Bros.-Barnum & Bailey Combined Shows, Inc. v. Ringling, 604
Rosenfeld v. Fairchild Engine and Airplane Corporation, 502
Rosiny v. Schmidt, 634

S

Sea-Land Services, Inc. v. The Pepper Source, 95
Securities and Exchange Commission v. Texas Gulf Sulphur Co., 462

Senn v. Northwest Underwriters Inc., 236
Shlensky v. Wrigley, 111
Simons v. Cogan, 121
Sinclair Oil Corporation v. Levien, 718
Smith v. Atlantic Properties, Inc., 683
Smith v. Van Gorkom, 246
Steinway v. Steinway & Sons, 40
Stone v. Ritter, 392

T
Trustees of Dartmouth College v. Woodward, 4
TSC Industries, Inc. v. Northway, Inc., 543

U
United States v. O'Hagan, 485
Unitrin, Inc. v. American General Corp., 865
Unocal Corporation v. Mesa Petroleum Co., 803

V
Virginia Bankshares, Inc. v. Sandberg, 551

W
Walkovszky v. Carlton, 84
Weinberger v. UOP, Inc., 760
West v. Prudential Securities, Incorporated, 457
Wilkes v. Springside Nursing Home, Inc., 676

Z
Zahn v. Transamerica Corporation, 730
Zapata Corporation v. Maldonado, 204

Part 1

The Nature and Purpose of the Corporation

Part 1

The Nature and Purpose of the Corporation

Corporate law focuses, for the most part, on the relationship among directors, managers, and stockholders, the corporation's three statutory groups. But the corporation is more than a business form. In the course of the twentieth century, it has achieved political, social and cultural prominence in American and, indeed, world society. Legal theory played an important role in legitimating the different roles that corporations play. This Part 1 of the casebook explores the changing understandings of the nature of corporate entities, the purpose that corporations play in our society, as well as the unique characteristics of corporations. We begin in Section I by exploring the development of different theories addressing the nature of corporate entities—particularly, the grant theory, the entity theory, and the nexus of contracts theory. Section II offers examples of the different roles that corporations have played in our society, while Section III focuses on two unique characteristics of the corporate form and their relevance to doctrine: centralized management and limited liability. Section IV begins to introduce corporate finance with a short exploration of the relationship between corporations and financial constituencies other than the corporation's shareholders.

Section I

What is a Corporation?

Corporations have historically represented an anomaly to liberal legal thinkers who envisioned the world as sharply divided between state power and individual right holders, the ruler and the ruled. A corporation was both—an association of individual right holders, on the one hand, but an entity with state-like powers, on the other. For eighteenth-century thinkers, for example, the continued existence of corporations demonstrated the failure of liberal efforts to destroy the intermediate forms associated with medieval life. Early-nineteenth-century legal doctrine eased the tension by dividing corporations into two different entities—public corporations such as municipal associations that assimilated the role of the state, and private corporations such as business organizations that gradually assimilated the role of the individual in society (on the nature of corporate entities in liberal thought, see Gerald E. Frug, *The City as a Legal Concept*, 93 HARV. L. REV. 1059 (1980)).

Through the 1880s, private corporations were viewed as artificial entities (unlike real persons), created by a charter or a grant of the state with limited powers specified in their charters of incorporation. By the late nineteenth century, however, the fiction paradigm lost much of its credibility as states encouraged incorporation in their territories by reducing the requirement for a state charter into a mere formality. Instead of the fiction paradigm, legal scholars embraced the natural or real entity paradigms, describing corporations as distinct from their individual members, though, like them, they had real existence. The entity theory was an appropriate vision for the rapidly growing large business corporation with its multiplicity of ownership, complex financial structure, centralized managerial control and immortality. As such, this paradigm dominated corporate law at least through the 1970s when it was replaced by an economic theory of the firm that described corporations as nexuses of private contractual relationships. The following excerpts introduce you to these different paradigms. As you read them, consider the implications of these different theories for corporate law as well as federal regulation.

Trustees of Dartmouth College v. Woodward
17 U.S. 518 (1819)

MARSHALL, Chief Justice

... The single question now to be considered is, do the acts to which the verdict refers violate the constitution of the United States?

This court can be insensible neither to the magnitude nor delicacy of this question. The validity of a legislative act is to be examined; and the opinion of the highest law tribunal of a state is to be revised — an opinion which carries with it intrinsic evidence of the diligence, of the ability, and the integrity, with which it was formed. On more than one occasion, this court has expressed the cautious circumspection with which it approaches the consideration of such questions; and has declared, that in no doubtful case, would it pronounce a legislative act to be contrary to the constitution. But the American people have said, in the constitution of the United States, that "no state shall pass any bill of attainder, *ex post facto* law, or law impairing the obligation of contracts." In the same instrument, they have also said, "that the judicial power shall extend to all cases in law and equity arising under the constitution." On the judges of this court, then, is imposed the high and solemn duty of protecting, from even legislative violation, those contracts which the constitution of our country has placed beyond legislative control; and, however irksome the task may be, this is a duty from which we dare not shrink.

The title of the plaintiffs originates in a charter dated the 13th day of December, in the year 1769, incorporating twelve persons therein mentioned, by the name of "The Trustees of Dartmouth College," granting to them and their successors the usual corporate privileges and powers, and authorizing the trustees, who are to govern the college, to fill up all vacancies which may be created in their own body.

The defendant claims under three acts of the legislature of New Hampshire, the most material of which was passed on the 27th of June 1816, and is entitled, "an act to amend the charter, and enlarge and improve the corporation of Dartmouth College." Among other alterations in the charter, this act increases the number of trustees to twenty-one, gives the appointment of the additional members to the executive of the state, and creates a board of overseers, with power to inspect and control the most important acts of the trustees. This board consists of twenty-five persons. The president of the senate, the speaker of the house of representatives, of New Hampshire, and the governor and lieutenant-governor of Vermont, for the time being, are to be members *ex officio*. The board is to be completed by the governor and council of New Hampshire, who are also empowered to fill all vacancies which may occur. The acts of the 18th and 26th of December are supplemental to that of the 27th of June, and are principally intended to carry that act into effect. The majority of the trustees of the college have refused to accept this amended charter, and have brought this suit for the corporate property, which is in possession of a person holding by virtue of the acts which have been stated.

It can require no argument to prove, that the circumstances of this case constitute a contract. An application is made to the crown for a charter to incorporate a religious and literary institution. In the application, it is stated, that large contributions have been made for the object, which will be conferred on the corporation, as soon as it shall be created. The charter is granted, and on its faith the property is conveyed. Surely, in this transaction every ingredient of a complete and legitimate contract is to be found. The points for consideration are, 1. Is this contract protected by the constitution of the United States? 2. Is it impaired by the acts under which the defendant holds?

1. On the first point, it has been argued, that the word "contract," in its broadest sense, would comprehend the political relations between the government and its citizens, would extend to offices held within a state, for state purposes, and to many of those laws concerning civil institutions, which must change with circumstances, and be modified by ordinary legislation; which deeply concern the public, and which, to preserve good government, the public judgment must control. That even marriage is a contract, and its obligations are affected by the laws respecting divorces. That the clause in the constitution, if construed in its greatest latitude, would prohibit these laws. Taken in its broad, unlimited sense, the clause would be an unprofitable and vexatious interference with the internal concerns of a state, would unnecessarily and unwisely embarrass its legislation, and render immutable those civil institutions, which are established for purposes of internal government, and which, to subserve those purposes, ought to vary with varying circumstances. That as the framers of the constitution could never have intended to insert in that instrument, a provision so unnecessary, so mischievous, and so repugnant to its general spirit, the term

"contract" must be understood in a more limited sense. That it must be understood as intended to guard against a power, of at least doubtful utility, the abuse of which had been extensively felt; and to restrain the legislature in future from violating the right to property. That, anterior to the formation of the constitution, a course of legislation had prevailed in many, if not in all, of the states, which weakened the confidence of man in man, and embarrassed all transactions between individuals, by dispensing with a faithful performance of engagements. To correct this mischief, by restraining the power which produced it, the state legislatures were forbidden "to pass any law impairing the obligation of contracts," that is, of contracts respecting property, under which some individual could claim a right to something beneficial to himself; and that, since the clause in the constitution must in construction receive some limitation, it may be confined, and ought to be confined, to cases of this description; to cases within the mischief it was intended to remedy.

The general correctness of these observations cannot be controverted. That the framers of the constitution did not intend to restrain the states in the regulation of their civil institutions, adopted for internal government, and that the instrument they have given us, is not to be so construed, may be admitted. The provision of the constitution never has been understood to embrace other contracts, than those which respect property, or some object of value, and confer rights which may be asserted in a court of justice. It never has been understood to restrict the general right of the legislature to legislate on the subject of divorces. Those acts enable some tribunals, not to impair a marriage contract, but to liberate one of the parties, because it has been broken by the other. When any state legislature shall pass an act annulling all marriage contracts, or allowing either party to annul it, without the consent of the other, it will be time enough to inquire, whether such an act be constitutional.

The parties in this case differ less on general principles, less on the true construction of the constitution in the abstract, than on the application of those principles to this case, and on the true construction of the charter of 1769. This is the point on which the cause essentially depends. If the act of incorporation be a grant of political power, if it create a civil institution, to be employed in the administration of the government, or if the funds of the college be public property, or if the state of New Hampshire, as a government, be alone interested in its transactions, the subject is one in which the legislature of the state may act according to its own judgment, unrestrained by any limitation of its power imposed by the constitution of the United States.

But if this be a private eleemosynary institution, endowed with a capacity to take property, for objects unconnected with government, whose funds are bestowed by individuals, on the faith of the charter; if the donors have stipulated for the future disposition and management of those funds, in the manner prescribed by themselves; there may be more difficulty in the case, although neither the persons who have made these stipulations, nor those for whose benefit they were made, should be parties to the cause. Those who are no longer interested in the property, may yet retain such an interest in the preservation of their own arrangements, as to have a right to insist, that those arrangements shall be held sacred. Or, if they have themselves disappeared, it becomes a subject of serious and anxious inquiry, whether those whom they have legally empowered to represent them for ever, may not assert all the rights which they possessed, while in being; whether, if they be without personal representatives, who may feel injured by a violation of the compact, the trustees be not so completely their representatives, in the eye of the law, as to stand in their place, not only as respects the government of the college, but also as respects the maintenance of the college charter. It becomes then the duty of the court, most seriously to examine this charter, and to ascertain its true character.

From the instrument itself, it appears, that about the year 1754, the Rev. Eleazer Wheelock established, at his own expense, and on his own estate, a charity school for the instruction of Indians in the Christian religion. . . . Dr. Wheelock then applied to the crown for an act of incorporation; and represented the expediency of appointing those whom he had, by his last will, named as trustees in America, to be members of the proposed corporation. "In consideration of the premises," "for the education and instruction of the youth of the Indian tribes" . . . "and also of English youth, and any others," the charter was granted, and the trustees of Dartmouth College were, by that name, created a body corporate, with power, for the use of the said college, to acquire real and personal property, and to pay the president, tutors and other officers of the college, such salaries as they shall allow. . . .

. . . This charter was accepted, and the property, both real and personal, which had been contributed for the benefit of the college, was conveyed to, and vested in, the corporate body.

From this brief review of the most essential parts of the charter, it is apparent, that the funds of the college consisted entirely of private donations. It is, perhaps, not very important, who were the donors. The probability is, that the Earl of Dartmouth, and the other trustees in England, were, in fact, the largest contributors. Yet the legal conclusion, from the facts recited in the charter, would probably be, that Dr. Wheelock was the founder of the college. The origin of the institution was, undoubtedly, the Indian charity school, established by Dr. Wheelock, at his own expense. It was at his instance, and to enlarge this school, that contributions were solicited in England. The person soliciting these contributions was his agent; and the trustees, who received the money, were appointed by, and act under, his authority. It is not too much to say, that the funds were obtained by him, in trust, to be applied by him to the purposes of his enlarged school. The charter of incorporation was granted at his instance. The persons named by him, in his last will, as the trustees of his charity-school, compose a part of the corporation, and he is declared to be the founder of the college, and its president for life. . . . Dartmouth College is really endowed by private individuals, who have bestowed their funds for the propagation of the Christian religion among the Indians, and for the promotion of piety and learning generally. . . . It is then an eleemosynary, and so far as respects its funds, a private corporation.

Do its objects stamp on it a different character? Are the trustees and professors public officers, invested with any portion of political power, partaking in any degree in the administration of civil government, and performing duties which flow from the sovereign authority? That education is an object of national concern, and a proper subject of legislation, all admit. That there may be an institution, founded by government, and placed entirely under its immediate control, the officers of which would be public officers, amenable exclusively to government, none will deny. But is Dartmouth College such an institution? Is education altogether in the hands of government? Does every teacher of youth become a public officer, and do donations for the purpose of education necessarily become public property, so far that the will of the legislature, not the will of the donor, becomes the law of the donation? These questions are of serious moment to society, and deserve to be well considered.

Doctor Wheelock, as the keeper of his charity-school, instructing the Indians in the art of reading, and in our holy religion; sustaining them at his own expense, and on the voluntary contributions of the charitable, could scarcely be considered as a public officer, exercising any portion of those duties which belong to government; nor could the legislature have supposed, that his private funds, or those given by others, were subject to legislative management, because they were applied to the purposes of education. When, afterwards, his school was enlarged, and the liberal contributions made in England, and in America, enabled him to extend his care to the education of the youth of his own country, no change was wrought in his own character, or in the nature of his duties. Had he employed assistant-tutors with the funds contributed by others, or had the trustees in England established a school, with Dr. Wheelock at its head, and paid salaries to him and his assistants, they would still have been private tutors; and the fact, that they were employed in the education of youth, could not have converted them into public officers, concerned in the administration of public duties, or have given the legislature a right to interfere in the management of the fund. The trustees, in whose care that fund was placed by the contributors, would have been permitted to execute their trust, uncontrolled by legislative authority.

Whence, then, can be derived the idea, that Dartmouth College has become a public institution, and its trustees public officers, exercising powers conferred by the public for public objects? Not from the source whence its funds were drawn; for its foundation is purely private and eleemosynary—not from the application of those funds; for money may be given for education, and the persons receiving it do not, by being employed in the education of youth, become members of the civil government. Is it from the act of incorporation? Let this subject be considered.

A corporation is an artificial being, invisible, intangible, and existing only in contemplation of law. Being the mere creature of law, it possesses only those properties which the charter of its creation confers upon it, either expressly, or as incidental to its very existence. These are such as are supposed best calculated to effect the object for which it was created. Among the most important are immortality, and, if the expression may be allowed, individuality; properties, by which a perpetual succession of many persons are considered as the same, and may act as a single individual. They enable a corporation to manage its own affairs, and to hold property, without the perplexing intricacies, the hazardous and endless necessity, of perpetual conveyances for the purpose of transmitting it from hand to hand. It is chiefly for the purpose of clothing bodies of men, in succession, with these qualities and capacities, that corporations were invented, and are in use. By these means, a perpetual succession of individuals are capable of acting for the promotion of the particular object, like one immortal being. But this being does not share in the civil government of the country, unless that be the purpose for which it was created. Its immortality no more confers on it political power, or a political character, than immortality would confer such power or character on a natural person. It is no more a state instrument, than a natural person exercising the same powers would be. If, then, a natural person, employed by individuals in the education of youth, or for the government of a seminary in which youth is educated, would not become a public officer, or be considered as a member of the civil government, how is it, that this artificial being, created by law, for the purpose of being employed by the same individuals, for the same purposes, should become a part of the civil government of the country? Is it because its existence, its capacities, its powers, are given by law? Because the government has given it the power to take and to hold property, in a particular form, and for particular purposes, has the government a consequent right substantially to change that form, or to vary the purposes to which the property is to be applied? This principle has never been asserted or recognized, and is supported by no authority. Can it derive aid from reason?

The objects for which a corporation is created are universally such as the government wishes to promote. They are deemed beneficial to the country; and this benefit constitutes the consideration, and in most cases, the sole consideration of the grant. In most eleemosynary institutions, the object would be difficult, perhaps unattainable, without the aid of a charter of incorporation. Charitable or public-spirited individuals, desirous of making permanent appropriations for charitable or other useful purposes, find it impossible to effect their design securely and certainly, without an incorporating act. They apply to the government, state their beneficent object, and offer to advance the money necessary for its accomplishment, provided the government will confer on the instrument which is to execute their designs the capacity to execute them. The proposition is considered and approved. The benefit to the public is considered as an ample compensation for the faculty it confers, and the corporation is created. If the advantages to the public constitute a full compensation for the faculty it gives, there can be no reason for exacting a further compensation, by claiming a right to exercise over this artificial being, a power which changes its nature, and touches the fund, for the security and application of which it was created. There can be no reason for implying in a charter, given for a valuable consideration, a power which is not only not expressed, but is in direct contradiction to its express stipulations.

From the fact, then, that a charter of incorporation has been granted, nothing can be inferred, which changes the character of the institution, or transfers to the government any new power over it. The character of civil institutions does not grow out of their incorporation, but out of the manner in which they are formed, and the objects for which they are created. The right to change them is not founded on their being incorporated, but on their being the instruments of government, created for its purposes. The same institutions, created for the same objects, though not incorporated, would be public institutions, and, of course, be controllable by the legislature. The incorporating act neither gives nor prevents this control. Neither, in reason, can the incorporating act change the character of a private eleemosynary institution.

We are next led to the inquiry, for whose benefit the property given to Dartmouth College was secured? The counsel for the defendant have insisted, that the beneficial interest is in the people of New Hampshire. . . .

The particular interests of New Hampshire never entered into the mind of the donors, never constituted a motive for their donation. The propagation of the Christian religion among the savages, and the dissemination of useful knowledge among the youth of the country, were the avowed and the sole objects of their contributions. In these, New Hampshire would participate; but nothing particular or exclusive was intended for her. Even the site of the college was selected, not for the sake of New Hampshire, but because it was "most subservient to the great ends in view," and because liberal donations of land were offered by the proprietors, on condition that the institution should be there established. The real advantages from the location of the college, are, perhaps, not less considerable to those on the west, than to those on the east side of Connecticut river. The clause which constitutes the incorporation, and expresses the objects for which it was made, declares those objects to be the instruction of the Indians, "and also of English youth, and any others." So that the objects of the contributors, and the incorporating act, were the same; the promotion of Christianity, and of education generally, not the interests of New Hampshire particularly.

From this review of the charter, it appears, that Dartmouth College is an eleemosynary institution, incorporated for the purpose of perpetuating the application of the bounty of the donors, to the specified objects of that bounty; that its trustees or governors were originally named by the founder, and invested with the power of perpetuating themselves; that they are not public officers, nor is it a civil institution, participating in the administration of government; but a charity-school, or a seminary of education, incorporated for the preservation of its property, and the perpetual application of that property to the objects of its creation.

Yet a question remains to be considered, of more real difficulty, on which more doubt has been entertained, than on all that have been discussed. The founders of the college, at least, those whose contributions were in money, have parted with the property bestowed upon it, and their representatives have no interest in that property. The donors of land are equally without interest, so long as the corporation shall exist. Could they be found, they are unaffected by any alteration in its constitution, and probably regardless of its form, or even of its existence. The students are fluctuating, and no individual among our youth has a vested interest in the institution, which can be asserted in a court of justice. Neither the founders of the college, nor the youth for whose benefit it was founded, complain of the alteration made in its charter, or think themselves injured by it. The trustees alone complain, and the trustees have no beneficial interest to be protected. Can this be such a contract, as the constitution intended to withdraw from the power of state legislation? Contracts, the parties to which have a vested beneficial interest, and those only, it has been said, are the objects about which the constitution is solicitous, and to which its protection is extended.

The court has bestowed on this argument the most deliberate consideration, and the result will be stated. Dr. Wheelock, acting for himself, and for those who, at his solicitation, had made contributions to his school, applied for this charter, as the instrument which should enable him, and them, to perpetuate their beneficent intention. It was granted. An artificial, immortal being, was created by the crown, capable of receiving and distributing for ever, according to the will of the donors, the donations which should be made to it. On this being, the contributions which had been collected were immediately bestowed. These gifts were made, not indeed to make a profit for the donors, or their posterity, but for something, in their opinion, of inestimable value; for something which they deemed a full equivalent for the money with which it was purchased. The consideration for which they stipulated, is the perpetual application of the fund to its object, in the mode prescribed by themselves. Their descendants may take no interest in the preservation of this consideration. But in this respect their descendants are not their representatives; they are represented by the corporation. The corporation is the assignee of their rights, stands in their place, and distributes their bounty, as they would themselves have distributed it, had they been immortal. So, with respect to the students who are to derive learning from this source; the corporation is a trustee for them also. Their potential rights, which, taken distributively, are imperceptible, amount collectively to a most important interest. These are, in the aggregate, to be exercised, asserted and protected, by the corporation. They were as completely out of the donors, at the instant of their being vested in the corporation, and as incapable of being asserted by the students, as at present.

According to the theory of the British constitution, their parliament is omnipotent. To annul corporate rights might give a shock to public opinion, which that government has chosen to avoid; but its power is not questioned. Had parliament, immediately after the emanation of this charter, and the execution of those conveyances which followed it, annulled the instrument, so that the living donors would have witnessed the disappointment of their hopes, the perfidy of the transaction would have been universally acknowledged. Yet, then, as now, the donors would have no interest in the property; then, as now, those who might be students would have had no rights to be violated; then, as now, it might be said, that the trustees, in whom the rights of all were combined, possessed no private, individual, beneficial interests in the property confided to their protection. Yet the contract would, at that time, have been deemed sacred by all. What has since occurred, to strip it of its inviolability? Circumstances have not changed it. In reason, in justice, and in law, it is now, what it was in 1769.

This is plainly a contract to which the donors, the trustees and the crown (to whose rights and obligations New Hampshire succeeds) were the original parties. It is a contract made on a valuable consideration. It is a contract for the security and disposition of property. It is a contract, on the faith of which, real and personal estate has been conveyed to the corporation. It is, then, a contract within the letter of the constitution, and within its spirit also, unless the fact, that the property is invested by the donors in trustees, for the promotion of religion and education, for the benefit of persons who are perpetually changing, though the objects remain the same, shall create a particular exception, taking this case out of the prohibition contained in the constitution. . . .

On what safe and intelligible ground, can this exception stand? There is no expression in the constitution, no sentiment delivered by its contemporaneous expounders, which would justify us in making it. In the absence of all authority of this kind, is there, in the nature and reason of the case itself, that which would sustain a construction of the constitution, not warranted by its words? Are contracts of this description of a character to excite so little interest, that we must exclude them from the provisions of the constitution, as being unworthy of the attention of those who framed the instrument? Or does public policy so imperiously demand their remaining exposed to legislative alteration, as to compel us, or rather permit us, to say, that these words, which were introduced to give stability to contracts, and which in their plain import comprehend this contract, must yet be so construed as to exclude it?

Almost all eleemosynary corporations, those which are created for the promotion of religion, of charity or of education, are of the same character. The law of this case is the law of all. In every literary or charitable institution, unless the objects of the bounty be themselves incorporated, the whole legal interest is in trustees, and can be asserted only by them. The donors, or claimants of the bounty, if they can appear in court at all, can appear only to complain of the trustees. In all other situations, they are identified with, and personated by, the trustees; and their rights are to be defended and maintained by them. Religion, charity and education are, in the law of England, legatees or donees, capable of receiving bequests or donations in this form. They appear in court, and claim or defend by the corporation. Are they of so little estimation in the United States, that contracts for their benefit must be excluded from the protection of words, which in their natural import include them? Or do such contracts so necessarily require new modeling by the authority of the legislature, that the ordinary rules of construction must be disregarded, in order to leave them exposed to legislative alteration?

All feel, that these objects are not deemed unimportant in the United States. The interest which this case has excited, proves that they are not. The framers of the constitution did not deem them unworthy of its care and protection. They have, though in a different mode, manifested their respect for science, by reserving to the government of the Union the power "to promote the progress of science and useful arts, by securing for limited times, to authors and inventors, the exclusive right to their respective writings and discoveries." They have, so far, withdrawn science, and the useful arts, from the action of the state governments. Why then should they be supposed so regardless of contracts made for the advancement of literature, as to intend to exclude them from provisions, made for the security of ordinary contracts between man and man? No reason for making this supposition is perceived.

If the insignificance of the object does not require that we should exclude contracts respecting it from the protection of the constitution; neither, as we conceive, is the policy of leaving them subject to legislative alteration so apparent, as to require a forced construction of that instrument, in order to effect it. These eleemosynary institutions do not fill the place, which would otherwise be occupied by government, but that which would otherwise remain vacant. . . .

The opinion of the court, after mature deliberation, is, that this is a contract, the obligation of which cannot be impaired, without violating the constitution of the United States. This opinion appears to us to be equally supported by reason, and by the former decisions of this court.

2. We next proceed to the inquiry, whether its obligation has been impaired by those acts of the legislature of New Hampshire, to which the special verdict refers?

From the review of this charter, which has been taken, it appears that the whole power of governing the college, of appointing and removing tutors, of fixing their salaries, of directing the course of study to be pursued by the students, and of filling up vacancies created in their own body, was vested in the trustees. On the part of the crown, it was expressly stipulated, that this corporation, thus constituted, should continue for ever; and that the number of trustees should for ever consist of twelve, and no more. By this contract, the crown was bound, and could have made no violent alteration in its essential terms, without impairing its obligation.

By the revolution, the duties, as well as the powers, of government devolved on the people of New Hampshire. It is admitted, that among the latter was comprehended the transcendent power of parliament, as well as that of the executive department. It is too clear, to require the support of argument, that all contracts and rights respecting property, remained unchanged by the revolution. The obligations, then, which were created by the charter to Dartmouth College, were the same in the new, that they had been in the old government. The power of the government was also the same. A repeal of this charter, at any time prior to the adoption of the present constitution of the United States, would have been an extraordinary and unprecedented act of power, but one which could have been contested only by the restrictions upon the legislature, to be found in the constitution of the state. But the constitution of the United States has imposed this additional limitation, that the legislature of a state shall pass no act "impairing the obligation of contracts." . . .

It results from this opinion, that the acts of the legislature of New Hampshire, which are stated in the special verdict found in this cause, are repugnant to the constitution of the United States; and that the judgment on this special verdict ought to have been for the plaintiffs. The judgment of the state court must, therefore, be reversed.

Story, Justice

This is a cause of great importance, and as the very learned discussions, as well here, as in the state court, show, of no inconsiderable difficulty. There are two questions, to which the appellate jurisdiction of this court properly applies. 1. Whether the original charter of Dartmouth College is a contract, within the prohibitory clause of the constitution of the United States, which declares, that no state shall pass any "law impairing the obligation of contracts?" 2. If so, whether the legislative acts of New Hampshire of the 27th of June, and of the 18th and 27th of December 1816, or any of them, impair the obligations of that charter?

It will be necessary, however, before we proceed to discuss these questions, to institute an inquiry into the nature, rights and duties of aggregate corporations, at common law; that we may apply the principles, drawn from this source, to the exposition of this charter, which was granted emphatically with reference to that law.

An aggregate corporation, at common law, is a collection of individuals, united into one collective body, under a special name, and possessing certain immunities, privileges and capacities, in its collective character, which do not belong to the natural persons composing it. Among other things, it possesses the capacity of perpetual succession, and of acting by the collected vote or will of its component members, and of suing and being sued in all things touching its corporate rights and duties. It is, in short, an artificial person, existing in contemplation of law, and endowed with certain powers and franchises which, though they must be exercised through the medium of its natural members, are yet considered as subsisting in the corporation itself, as distinctly as if it were a real personage. Hence, such a corporation may sue and be sued by its own members, and may contract with them in the same manner, as with any strangers. A great variety of these corporations exist, in every country governed by the common law; in some of which, the corporate existence is perpetuated by new elections, made from time to time; and in others, by a continual accession of new members, without any corporate act. Some of these corporations are, from the particular purposes to which they are devoted, denominated spiritual, and some lay; and the latter are again divided into civil and eleemosynary corporations. It is unnecessary, in this place, to enter into any examination of civil corporations. Eleemosynary corporations are such as are constituted for the perpetual distribution of the free-alms and bounty of the founder, in such manner as he has directed; and in this class, are ranked hospitals for the relief of poor and impotent persons, and colleges for the promotion of learning and piety, and the support of persons engaged in literary pursuits.

Another division of corporations is into public and private. Public corporations are generally esteemed such as exist for public political purposes only, such as towns, cities, parishes and counties; and in many respects, they are so, although they involve some private interests; but strictly speaking, public corporations are such only as are founded by the government, for public purposes, where the whole interests belong also to the government. If, therefore, the foundation be private, though under the charter of the government, the corporation is private, however extensive the uses may be to which it is devoted, either by the bounty of the founder, or the nature and objects of the institution. For instance, a bank created by the government for its own uses, whose stock is exclusively owned by the government, is, in the strictest sense, a public corporation. So, an hospital created and endowed by the government for general charity. But a bank, whose stock is owned by private persons, is a private corporation, although it is erected by the government, and its objects and operations partake of a public nature. The same doctrine may be affirmed of insurance, canal, bridge and turnpike companies. In all these cases, the uses may, in a certain sense, be called public, but the corporations are private; as much so, indeed, as if the franchises were vested in a single person.

This reasoning applies in its full force to eleemosynary corporations. An hospital, founded by a private benefactor, is, in point of law, a private corporation, although dedicated by its charter to general charity. So, a college, founded and endowed in the same manner, although, being for the promotion of learning and piety, it may extend its charity to scholars from every class in the community, and thus acquire the character of a public institution. . . .

When a private eleemosynary corporation is thus created, by the charter of the crown, it is subject to no other control on the part of the crown, than what is expressly or implicitly reserved by the charter itself. Unless a power be reserved for this purpose, the crown cannot, in virtue of its prerogative, without the consent of the corporation, alter or amend the charter, or divest the corporation of any of its franchises, or add to them, or add to, or diminish, the number of the trustees, or remove any of the members, or change or control the administration of the charity, or compel the corporation to receive a new charter. This is the uniform language of the authorities, and forms one of the most stubborn, and well settled doctrines of the common law . . . .

In my judgment, it is perfectly clear, that any act of a legislature which takes away any powers or franchises vested by its charter in a private corporation, or its corporate officers, or which restrains or controls the legitimate exercise of them, or transfers them to other persons, without its assent, is a violation of the obligations of that charter. If the legislature mean to claim such an authority, it must be reserved in the grant. The charter of Dartmouth College contains no such reservation; and I am, therefore, bound to declare, that the acts of the legislature of New Hampshire, now in question, do impair the obligations of that charter, and are, consequently, unconstitutional and void.

Questions

1. What does it mean to say that the charter is a contract? If the charter is a contract, who are the parties? What is the consideration?

2. Why is the charter a private contract? What conclusions can we draw from the fact that the charter was deemed a private contract?

3. How does Chief Justice Marshall view the corporation? Does Justice Story share his vision?

4. Does the fact that Dartmouth College engaged in education affect its nature? Should it?

5. What are the implications of the decision as far as the state's ability to regulate corporate activities? Does the following provision of the Delaware General Corporation Law affect your answer?

> **394.** This chapter [the Delaware General Corporation Law] may be amended or repealed, at the pleasure of the General Assembly, but any amendment or repeal shall not take away or impair any remedy under this chapter against any corporation or its officers for any liability which shall have been previously incurred. This chapter and all amendments thereof shall be a part of the charter or certificate of incorporation of every corporation except so far as the same are inapplicable and inappropriate to the objects of the corporation.

6. What is the relationship between the Crown (or the state of New Hampshire) and the corporation? Is corporate theory in fact political theory? Consider this question as you read the following excerpt.

Liam Seamus O'Melinn, *Neither Contract nor Concession: The Public Personality of the Corporation*

74 Geo. Wash. L. Rev. 201 (2006) [footnotes omitted]

Dartmouth College received a royal charter in 1769, seven years before the Declaration of Independence severed the tie between Britain and thirteen of its North American colonies. In 1816, the legislature of New Hampshire attempted to add nine trustees to the number prescribed by the charter, to establish a board of overseers, and to change the name from Dartmouth College to Dartmouth University, all in order to seize effective control of the affairs of the college. The trustees appointed under the original charter sued to recover the corporate seal, but the Supreme Court of New Hampshire upheld the legislative alteration of the collegiate charter against their constitutional challenge. The United States Supreme Court reversed in a decision written by Chief Justice Marshall.

The Marshall opinion grounds its decision in the Contracts Clause of the Constitution and appears to use very literal contractual language. It also treats the corporation as an "artificial being." Why, then, does it not affirm either the contractual or the concession view of the corporation? The answer is that *Dartmouth College* is really an exercise in American constitutional theory based on the principle that a governor, whether of a state or a college, is a public servant who holds a position of trust. As applied to the state, this theory meant that the government of New Hampshire could not reconstitute the government of the college as if it owned the college outright. As applied to the trustees of the college, it meant that they did not themselves own collegiate property, but held it in trust for the use of Dartmouth's students, both current and future.

In ruling that New Hampshire's alteration of the charter violated the Contracts Clause, Justice Marshall imported the theory of the *social contract* to the law of the corporation. As Henry Monaghan observes, *Dartmouth College* did not decide that the college's charter was a contract as a matter of state law—it decided only that the college qualified for federal constitutional protection under the Contracts Clause. In so deciding, Marshall also affirmed what the concession theory would deny: the reality of the corporation as an entity apart from the state, and its corresponding entitlement to perpetual self-government. The contractual language of the *Dartmouth College* decision is the language of the social contract, and as Frank Easterbrook and Daniel Fischel—leading exponents of the "nexus of contracts" theory—point out, the social contract cannot be regarded as a "real" contract. Americans had long insisted that government was the result of a compact between the ruler and the people, and Marshall likewise ruled that the charter of Dartmouth College was the result of a compact between King George III and Eleazor Wheelock, the college's founder. The effect of this assertion was simply to deny that George III had created Dartmouth all by himself. Marshall's next step was the more general proposition that the corporation thus did not live at the sufferance of the sovereign. When Marshall made King George one of the signatories to the "contract" that created Dartmouth College, he was only repeating an argument that colonial Americans had made from the middle of the seventeenth century until the American Revolution: government is founded on a compact between ruler and people, making governors into trustees of the public interest and reminding them that they do not actually *own* the property that is commended to them for the benefit of the public. The first important result of the contractual reasoning, then, was to deny the concession theory, for just as Dartmouth College had not been created by the sovereign power, neither could it be dissolved or fundamentally altered at the will of the sovereign.

The second result was to move away from a contractual theory of corporate life by asserting that the trustees held a right to corporate governance. The collegiate charter may have been the result of a contract, but what *Dartmouth College* actually vindicated was a perpetual right of trustee government, a right that depended on corporate immortality. As Marshall put it, the college's founders contracted not merely for the application of their property to some immediate purpose, but also for "the constitution of the corporation," meaning that they contracted also to "retain forever the government of the literary institution they had formed in the hands of persons approved by themselves." To make any literal contractual understanding of the case still more difficult, Marshall proclaimed that the decision also constitutionalized the life of the college, the church, and the charity, noting that the Constitution thus did for all these enterprises what it had done for copyright and patent. In other words, the *Dartmouth College* decision marked out areas of public concern and pressed upon them the seal of public policy; the corporate seal for which the trustees sued was in this sense also the seal of public approval. Corporate law had been constitutionalized, and in the process, the corporation had become immortal, its trustees to form an eternal and self-perpetuating governing body invested with powers over matters of vital public significance.

As if it were not enough that the trustees had left the original contractors lost in the mists of time, the literal contractual language that appears in the opinion faces another great difficulty: King George III, one of the parties to the original Dartmouth "contract," was still alive in 1819, and—had he been asked and had he not been blind, deaf, and insane by this time—he would have denied vehemently that in issuing the Dartmouth charter he had entered into any contract. Indeed, British sovereigns had vigorously resisted the contractual theory of government that colonists had long urged on them, and King George had himself lost thirteen very important colonies as a result of the dispute.

With the benefit of just one semester of legal education, George III would also have had an excellent question to ask in rebuttal to the notion that the Dartmouth charter was a contract: where is the consideration? Given that he did not get anything in exchange for his grant of a corporate charter, there was no benefit to the promisor—only an obligation. According to Marshall, the consideration was the *public benefit* that would result from performance of the corporation's duties, a view that was quite consistent with the social contract argument. Alternatively, Justice Story's concurrence was at some pains to explain that detriment to the promisee could serve as consideration in lieu of benefit to the promisor, and Story insisted that Eleazor Wheelock had suffered detriment in the form of expense, labor, and foregone opportunity to incorporate somewhere other than in New Hampshire.

Each of these arguments presents a problem for proponents of the modern contractual explanation. Marshall's insistence that consideration could be found in the public benefit would make the *public* a party to the contract, a point strenuously resisted by those who consider the public—in the felicitous phrasing of Easterbrook and Fischel—as "strangers to the bargain."

The alternative argument, relying on detriment to the promisee to establish consideration, is liable to attack for a different reason. Detriment to the promisee furnishes consideration in the unusual case presented by *Hamer v. Sidway*, a chestnut in law schools' first year contracts courses. We should be wary to support frequent breach of contract claims against a promisor who *never* seemed to derive any promise of benefit from her bargains, yet this is the position in which the contractual view of *Dartmouth College* would place King George III. It seems reasonable to think that consideration was lacking in agreements by which the King always gave something valuable and never received anything of value in return.

Once again, these objections to the consideration argument point to the true significance of the case: *Dartmouth College* established the importance of perpetual internal corporate governance on the basis of the social contract, a position that had been frequently rejected by English monarchs. In his famous *Summary View of the Rights of British America*, a precursor to the Declaration of Independence, Thomas Jefferson used a similar argument to point out to King George III "that kings are the servants, not the proprietors of the people." An argument that begins with contract and ends with the sovereign as a servant of the public is a conventional statement of constitutional and political theory, but a very unconventional statement of contract law. Without siding with George III for a moment on the larger question of whether he should have been the colonists' owner or their servant, the language of contract in the *Dartmouth College* decision has much more to do with government by consent than with the expectations of contractors; the effect of the case was to remind both the government of New Hampshire and the Dartmouth College trustees that they were the servants of the college and not its owners.

A comparison with the New Hampshire decision that it reversed helps bring the nature of the Marshall opinion into sharper focus. As noted above, the Marshall decision is often criticized for its emphasis on the private nature of the corporation, for its resort to a concession or fiction theory of the kind that is used to justify corporate regulation, and for its emphasis on contract, property, and individual rights. It was the state court opinion, however, that spoke the language of fiction and individualism.

Chief Judge Richardson allowed that the trustees enjoyed individual rights under the charter, but held that because they had no property right in governing, they had no right of government at all. In order for the trustees to enjoy a right of government, they would need to have a property interest in the mission of the college, which was (ostensibly) to educate Indian youth, and he denied their entitlement to represent any interests other than their own. The court also indicated that the corporation was a fiction, a mere concession by the sovereign, and that resolving the case required looking beyond the fiction of corporate personality to the truly interested parties:

> In deciding a case like this, *where the complaint is that corporate rights have been unconstitutionally infringed, it is the duty of the court to strip off the forms and fictions with which the policy of the law has clothed those rights,* and look beyond that entangible [sic] creature of the law, the corporation, which *in form* possesses them, to the individuals and to the public, to whom, in *reality,* they belong, and who alone can be injured by a violation of them. *This action, therefore, though in form the complaint of the corporation, must be considered as in substance the complaint of the trustees themselves.*

The effect of this last sentence is to deny the representative character of the trustees—they might have spoken for themselves, but they did not speak for the corporation. It was also to deny the reality of the corporation itself, leaving it to inhabit the realm of fiction.

The individualism of the state court on the nature of the original incorporation of the college also provides an instructive contrast with Chief Justice Marshall's contractual reasoning. Judge Richardson insisted there was only one party to the creation—King George III. In his view, Dartmouth College was the result of an act of sovereign grace and nothing else. The creation of the college was a unilateral act of ordination, and the creator apparently had a power of perpetual superintendency. According to Richardson, the corporation was a creature of the state living at its sufferance.

The difference between the Richardson and Marshall opinions signals that a revolution in American law was beginning to challenge the proposition that corporations "have no souls." At the time that *Dartmouth College* was decided, the challenge was well under way; other organizations were leading the battle to establish that the American corporation did indeed have a soul, and foremost among them were churches.

Questions

1. Since *Trustees of Dartmouth College v. Woodward*, American law has considered the business corporation to be a private institution that, while subject to the same laws and regulations that govern individuals, is to be treated in the use of its assets and its behavior much like an individual human being; that is, it has the same kinds of liberty interests and privacy interests that a natural person has. In *Santa Clara County v. Southern Pacific Railroad Company* 118 U.S. 394 (1886), with hardly any discussion of the matter at all, the Supreme Court held that corporations enjoy essentially the same constitutional protections as individuals.

Citizens United v. Federal Election Commission 558 U.S. 310 (2010) and *Burwell v. Hobby Lobby Stores* 134 S.Ct. 2751 (2014) are two recent cases to address the matter. Citizens United, a non-profit organization seeking to broadcast and advertise a film critical of Hilary Clinton shortly before the 2008 Democratic primaries, challenged a federal statute that prohibited corporations from making "electioneering communication." The U.S. Supreme Court struck down the provision holding that the government cannot restrict political speech based on the speaker's corporate identity and thus cannot restrict independent expenditures for communications by non-profit corporations, for-profit corporations, labor unions, and other associations. Four years later, in *Hobby Lobby*, the Court held that "as applied to closely held corporations the Health and Human Services regulations imposing a contraceptive mandate violate the Religious Freedom Restoration Act." The majority opinion noted that "protecting the free-exercise rights of corporations . . . protects the religious liberty of the humans who own and control those companies."

Can you reconcile the Court's statement in *Hobby Lobby* with the Court's willingness, in *Citizens United*, to allow corporations to use their funds to influence elections irrespective of their investors' wishes? Does the Court embrace the same vision of the corporation in both?

2. As you began to see, state laws grant corporations privileges such as limited liability and immortality. Shouldn't that suggest that states can also regulate

corporations including their speech and religious freedom? Who or what is protected when constitutional rights are extended to entities such as corporations?

3. In recent decades, Delaware has endorsed the view that the purpose of corporations is to maximize shareholders wealth. Should the purpose of shareholder wealth maximization be relevant to decisions pertaining to federal and state regulation of corporate activities? Corporate speech? Do the opinions in *Citizens United* or *Hobby Lobby* promote such a purpose?

Section II

The Corporation and the Community

Steinway v. Steinway & Sons
40 N.Y.S. 718 (1896)

BEEKMAN, Judge

The plaintiff is a stockholder of the defendant corporation, Steinway & Sons, and brings this action against the trustees of the corporation for injunctive relief restraining the continuance of certain acts alleged to be ultra vires, or to involve wasteful, extravagant, and unnecessary expenditures, having no proper relation to the business of the corporation. An accounting is also asked for in respect to past transactions of this character, and the enforcement of a personal liability against the trustees to the corporation by reason of these alleged unlawful acts.

It is proper to state at the outset that the issues in this action do not involve any charge of fraud. It is not claimed that there was, nor does the evidence justify the slightest imputation of, bad faith on the part of any of the defendants. The inquiry, then, is largely limited to the question of corporate power, and the equities which bear upon the plaintiff's right to impeach the acts of which he complains. The evidence is so voluminous, and the range of inquiry has been so broad, covering, as it has, some 16 years — the entire period of the corporate existence of Steinway & Sons — that I shall not undertake to do more than to state my conclusions upon the proofs, although the entire record has been examined with the care which the importance of the questions involved has required.

The chief ground upon which plaintiff rests his complaint is the very large, and, as he claims, unnecessary, holdings of real estate by the corporation, and the extensive expenditure of money in developing the property for purposes having no immediate relation to the objects for which Steinway & Sons was incorporated. It appears that the company was incorporated in 1876, under the general manufacturing act of this state, for the purpose, as expressed in the certificate of incorporation, of manufacturing and selling pianofortes and other musical instruments. At that time the business was one of large proportions, which had for many years been conducted by the Steinway family as a co-partnership, and the change which was effected by the incorporation was one of form rather than of substance. It continued to be the same in its object and purposes, and under substantially the same ownership and control. The incorporators were the co-partners, the defendant William Steinway, and his brothers, C.F. Theodore Steinway and Albert Steinway, by whom all of the assets of the firm were transferred to the corporation in exchange for the greater part of the capital stock, which was fixed at $1,500,000. Among these assets were certain real estate in the city of New York, and some 400 acres of land, situate at Astoria, and within the limits of Long Island City, in Queens county. The principal factory and field of mechanical operation was in this city, but it was designed ultimately to transfer the entire manufacturing plant to Astoria, and it was with this purpose that the land at that place had been originally acquired. This policy thus inherited, and which has been continued by the corporation, was founded upon the theory that the growth and expansion of the business would require larger accommodations, which could not be obtained in the city of New York, and also that provision could be made for gathering together, as residents upon the property, the large number of employees in their service, under conditions and influences of exceptional advantage to them and their families, and thus promoting better and more permanent service on their part in their relations to the business. At the time this property was taken over, this policy was in course of execution. A portion of the manufacturing was carried on there, and some houses had been constructed in which employees of the company resided. Since then, other factory buildings have been erected and improvements made, so that at the present time the manufacturing part of the business of the corporation is almost exclusively located there; and a very large proportion of the employees live upon the property in proximity to their work, either in houses owned by the corporation or which they have acquired themselves by purchase from the corporation. For their benefit, the company has also, at a very moderate expenditure, contributed specific property and money towards the establishment of a church, a school, a free library, and a free bath—all agencies the usefulness of which, in the development of the best industrial results of a community, is fully recognized. The mass of these employees are skilled operatives, who have been permanently in the service of the company for many years, in harmonious relations with their employer, which have been practically uninterrupted by strikes or suspension of business for any cause. It may be fairly inferred from this that this policy of the company in dealing with its operatives has been a wise one, and, apart from its moral aspects, has materially contributed to the resources of the corporation. In connection with this general purpose, and also for the purpose of developing the remainder of this large tract, comprising in all about 400 acres, the trustees of the corporation have from time to time authorized the expenditure of money in regulating several streets or avenues running through the property, and in the construction of sewers and the supply of water. There is nothing in the proofs before me which reflects upon the wisdom of this, or which tends to show that the company has not realized a profitable return from the expenditure. At the time the property was taken over by the company upon its incorporation, it had been laid out as a part of the city in which it is, with streets and avenues, and had been subdivided into lots. Its character was thus fixed, and, assuming that the corporation had the right to hold that portion of it which was not necessary for its immediate needs and future wants, the propriety of these expenditures could not be assailed.

It is contended, however, on the part of the plaintiff, that all of the disbursements to which I have referred, saving only those immediately connected with the works and plant, were improper, and not within the competency of the trustees to sanction; that the corporation was actually engaged in an extensive land business, which was outside of its chartered powers; and that the contributions made towards the church, library, and kindred enterprises, to which I have referred, were likewise without authority in law.

The general rule of law, undoubtedly, is that a corporation must keep within the prescription of its charter. The difficulty, however, which arises, and which has given birth to the many decisions upon the subject, to some extent conflicting, is in the application of the rule to individual cases, so that the question is mainly one of construction. 27 Am. & Eng. Enc. Law, 355, where it is also said:

> "It may be stated as a general rule that the charter of a corporation, read in connection with the general laws applicable thereto, is the true measure of its powers, and a transaction manifestly beyond those powers is ultra vires; yet whatever, under the charter and general laws, reasonably construed, may fairly be considered as incidental to the purposes for which the corporation was created, is not to be taken as prohibited, but is as much granted as that which is expressed."

It is a question, therefore, in each case, of the logical relation of the act to the corporate purpose expressed in the charter. If that act is one which is lawful in itself, and not otherwise prohibited, is done for the purpose of serving corporate ends, and is reasonably tributary to the promotion of those ends, in a substantial, and not in a remote and fanciful, sense, it may fairly be considered within charter powers. The field of corporate action in respect to the exercise of incidental powers is thus, I think, an expanding one. As industrial conditions change, business methods must change with them, and acts become permissible which at an earlier period would not have been considered to be within corporate power. This, I think, tends to explain the difference found in the reported cases. In the absence of any more specific guide than the very general rule adverted to, it is plain that in many cases ample room will be found for such differences of opinion. I have been quite conscious of this in coming to the conclusion which I have reached, that the acts of the trustees of Steinway & Sons in providing, as they have done, for the physical, intellectual, and spiritual wants of their employees, under the circumstances of the case, were not ultra vires. The transfer of their manufactory to the Astoria site was a reasonable exercise of a conceded discretionary power, which cannot be criticized or questioned here. As, however, it involved also the transfer of a large number of operatives, whose well-being was essential to the proper and efficient performance of their work, and thus to the success of the corporation, a close and practical business relation subsisted between the provision made by the defendants for their employees and the object for which the corporation was organized. The district was sparsely settled, and it was desirable that the men should live within easy reach of their place of employment. It was also desirable (it may, I think, be said to have been necessary) to the success of the scheme that some provision should be made for the moral as well as the material needs of this new and isolated community, thus brought, by the exigencies of their employment, into a measure of social dependence upon their employer. It was also a part of the scheme, by this segregation of their employees, and surrounding them with healthful influences, to remove, or at least minimize, the temptation to participate in unreasonable strikes and agitations. It can hardly be doubted that such a policy as this, intelligently and liberally executed, might reasonably be expected to insure the continued and faithful services of a skilled and contented body of operatives. And so it seems to have turned out in this case. A large number of their men have for years been in the uninterrupted employment of the corporation. Nor has the arrangement been without incidental profit to the company, which has realized a pecuniary return, either in rentals or upon sales of dwellings, many of which have been purchased by the workmen.

In view of the situation which has been outlined, I am not prepared to hold that the very moderate expenditures or contributions of the company towards church, school, library, and baths were outside of its incidental powers. The scheme must be taken as a whole, and, from that point of view, every part of it was directly related to the legitimate objects of the corporation. Excluding from this large tract all that is now used or which may be needed in the future for corporate purposes, there still remains an extensive area, which, the plaintiff contends, should be disposed of. He has also criticized certain expenditures made upon this property, which have already been referred to, for regulating certain streets, sewering, and similar improvements. One answer to this seems to be that this land has always been held for sale, a large portion of it has been sold, and sales still continue to be made. Whether it was quite within the right of the trustees to acquire for the corporation land which was unnecessary for its purposes it is unnecessary to determine. The corporation is and has been doing all that the court could require it to do in transmuting it into money. The expenditures to which I have referred were advantageous to the property, such as at some time at least would have to be made, and tended to render the property salable. . . .

Complaint dismissed, with costs.

Questions

1. What according to the plaintiff did Steinway & Sons do wrong? Why would the company have engaged in this activity? Do you think that it was wrong to do so?

2. Steinway has left an impressive mark on Astoria ("Steinway Village"). In addition to building row houses for its employees, Steinway built a church, a public school, a library (with books from William Steinway's collection), a fire house, a post office,

an amusement park and bathing beach, as well as a network of streetcars, trolleys and trains to make the Village more accessible. The subway tunnel (known as "Steinway Tunnel"), linking Manhattan and Queens, was a project of Steinway railroad enterprise. For more, see RICHARD K. LIEBERMAN, STEINWAY AND SONS (Yale University Press, 1995).

Dodge v. Ford Motor Co.
204 Mich. 459 (1919)

The following facts are from the plaintiffs' brief:

The Ford Motor Company is a corporation, organized and existing under Act No. 232 of the Public Acts of 1903. . . .

The articles of association were executed June 16, 1903, and acknowledged on that day by the parties associating. In the articles the capital stock is fixed at the sum of $150,000, with 1,500 shares of the par value of $100 each. It is recited therein that the amount of capital stock subscribed is $100,000, and that said sum is actually paid in, $49,000 in cash and $51,000 in other property. The other property described is: Letters patent, issued and applied for, valued at $40,000; machinery and stock, $10,000; contracts for supplies, $1,000. Article II of the articles of association reads:

> The purpose or purposes of this corporation are as follows: To purchase, manufacture and placing on the market for sale of automobiles or the purchase, manufacture and placing [sic] on the market for sale of motors and of devices and appliances incident to their construction and operation.

The parties in the first instance associating, who signed the articles, included Henry Ford, whose subscription was for 255 shares, John F. Dodge, Horace E. Dodge, the plaintiffs, Horace H. Rackham and James Couzens, who each subscribed for 50 shares, and several other persons. The company began business in the month of June, 1903. In the year 1908, its articles were amended and the capital stock increased from $150,000 to $2,000,000, the number of shares being increased to 20,000; and in the certificate, made in November, 1908, evidencing the increase of capital stock, it was recited:

> "The total amount of stock, including such increase actually paid in, is the sum of two million ($2,000,000) dollars, of which one million eight hundred and fifty thousand ($1,850,000) dollars of the increase and fifty thousand ($50,000) dollars of the original capital stock not subscribed, has been paid in by the surrender of all the stockholders to the corporation of their respective claim and right to dividends duly declared by the board of directors of said corporation out of the surplus of said company to the amount of one million nine hundred thousand ($1,900,000) dollars."

"The amount of capital stock subscribed is the sum of two million ($2,000,000) dollars; the amount of said stock actually paid in at the date thereof is the sum of two million ($2,000,000) dollars, of which one hundred thousand ($100,000) dollars represents the capital stock originally subscribed and paid in, and one million nine hundred thousand ($1,900,000) dollars by surrender to the corporation by all stockholders of their claim to dividends duly declared by the board of directors payable out of surplus."

The business of the company continued to expand. The cars it manufactured met a public demand, and were profitably marketed, so that, in addition to regular quarterly dividends equal to 5 per cent monthly on the capital stock of $2,000,000, its board of directors declared and the company paid special dividends: December 13, 1911, $1,000,000; May 15, 1912, $2,000,000; July 11, 1912, $2,000,000; June 16, 1913, $10,000,000; May 14, 1914, $2,000,000; June 12, 1914, $2,000,000; July 6, 1914, $2,000,000; July 23, 1914, $2,000,000; August 23, 1914, $3,000,000; May 28, 1915, $10,000,000; October 13, 1915, $5,000,000, a total of $41,000,000 in special dividends. Sales and profits for several years were:

Year ending	
Sept. 30, 1910	18,664 cars, $4,521,509.51
Sept. 30, 1911	34,466 cars, $6,275,031.07
Sept. 30, 1912	68,544 cars, $13,057,312.24
Sept. 30, 1913	168,304 cars, $25,046,767.43
Sept. 30, 1914	248,307 cars, $30,338,454.63
July 31, 1915 (ten months)	264,351 cars, $24,641,423.17
July 31, 1916 (three years)	472,350 cars, $59,994,918.01

The surplus above capital stock was, September 30, 1912, $14,745,095.67, and was increased year by year to $28,124,173.68, $48,827,032.07, $59,135,770.66. July 31, 1916, it was $111,960,907.53. Originally, the car made by the Ford Motor Company sold for more than $900. From time to time, the selling price was lowered and the car itself improved until in the year ending July 31, 1916, it sold for $440. Up to July 31, 1916, it had sold 1,272,986 cars at a profit of $173,895,416.06. As the cars in use multiplied, sales of parts and or repairs increased, so that, in the year ending July 31, 1916, the gross profits from repairs and parts was $3,915,778.94; sales being more than $600,000 for each of the months of May, June, and July. For the year beginning August 1, 1916, the price of the car was reduced $80 to $360. . . .

From a mere assembling plant, the plant of the Ford Motor Company came to be a manufacturing plant, in which it made many of the parts of the car which in the beginning it had purchased from others. At no time has it been able to meet the demand for its cars or in a large way to enter upon the manufacture of motor trucks.

No special dividend having been paid after October, 1915 (a special dividend of $2,000,000 was declared in November, 1916, before the filing of the answers), the plaintiffs, who together own 2,000 shares, or one-tenth of the entire capital stock of the Ford Motor Company, on the 2d of November, 1916, filed in the circuit court for the county of Wayne, in chancery, their bill of complaint, which bill was later, upon leave granted, on April 26, 1917, amended, in which bill they charge that since 1914 they have not been represented on the board of directors of the Ford Motor Company, and that since that time the policy of the board of directors has been dominated and controlled absolutely by Henry Ford, the president of the company, who owns and for several years has owned 58 per cent of the entire capital stock of the company; that the directors of the company are Henry Ford, David H. Gray, Horace H. Rackham, F.L. Klingensmith, and James Couzens, and the executive officers Henry Ford, president, F.L. Klingensmith, treasurer, and Edsel B. Ford, son of Henry Ford, secretary; that after the filing of the original, and before the filing of the amended, bill, at the annual meeting of the stockholders, David H. Gray retired from the board of directors and Edsel B. Ford was elected and is acting as a director. Setting up that on the 31st of July, 1916, the end of its last fiscal year, the said Henry Ford gave out for publication a statement of the financial condition of the company . . . , that for a number of years a regular dividend, payable quarterly, equal to 5 per cent monthly upon the authorized capital stock, and the special dividends hereinbefore referred to, had been paid, it is charged that notwithstanding the earnings for the fiscal year ending July 31, 1916, the Ford Motor Company has not since that date declared any special dividends:

> "And the said Henry Ford, president of the company, has declared it to be the settled policy of the company not to pay in the future any special dividends, but to put back into the business for the future all of the earnings of the company, other than the regular dividend of five per cent (5%) monthly upon the authorized capital stock of the company—two million dollars ($2,000,000)."

This declaration of the future policy, it is charged in the bill, was published in the public press in the city of Detroit and throughout the United States in substantially the following language:

> "'My ambition,' declared Mr. Ford, 'is to employ still more men; to spread the benefits of this industrial system to the greatest possible number, to help them build up their lives and their homes. To do this, we are putting the greatest share of our profits back into the business.'"

It is charged further that the said Henry Ford stated to plaintiffs personally, in substance, that as all the stockholders had received back in dividends more than they had invested they were not entitled to receive anything additional to the regular dividend of 5 per cent a month, and that it was not his policy to have larger dividends declared in the future, and that the profits and earnings of the company would be put back into the business for the purpose of extending its operations and increasing the number of its employees, and that, inasmuch as the profits were to be represented by investment in plants and capital investment, the stockholders would have no right to complain. It is charged . . . that—

"the said Henry Ford, 'dominating and controlling the policy of said company, has declared it to be his purpose—and he has actually engaged in negotiations looking to carrying such purposes into effect—to invest millions of dollars of the company's money in the purchase of iron ore mines in the Northern Peninsula of Michigan or state of Minnesota; to acquire by purchase or have built ships for the purpose of transporting such ore to smelters to be erected on the River Rouge adjacent to Detroit in the county of Wayne and state of Michigan; and to construct and install steel manufacturing plants to produce steel products to be used in the manufacture of cars at the factory of said company; and by this means to deprive the stockholders of the company of the fair and reasonable returns upon their investment by way of dividends to be declared upon their stockholding interest in said company.'"

Setting up that the present invested assets of the company, exclusive of cash on hand, as of July 31, 1916, represented more than 30 times the present authorized capital of the company, and two and one-half times the maximum limit ($25,000,000) fixed by the laws of the state of Michigan for capitalization of such companies (now $50,000,000), it is charged that the present investment in capital and assets constitutes an unlawful investment of the earnings, and that the continued investment of earnings would be a continuation of such unlawful policy. . . .

[It is further charged that] by reason of the declared policy of said Henry Ford not to pay dividends and to continue the expansion of the business of said company, including the risks involved in various enterprises proposed to be carried on by said company, your orators' interest in said Ford Motor Company which is worth not less than $50,000,000, is practically limited to a valuation fixed by the dividends so regularly to be declared, which, as stated, amount to little more than one per cent upon the actual capital investment of the stockholders of the company in the business of said corporation and renders the disposition of your orators' stockholding interest in said corporation, except at a sacrifice, impossible. . . .

Plaintiffs ask for an injunction to restrain the carrying out of the alleged declared policy of Mr. Ford and the company, for a decree requiring the distribution to stockholders of at least 75 per cent of the accumulated cash surplus, and for the future that they be required to distribute all of the earnings of the company except such as may be reasonably required for emergency purposes in the conduct of the business.

The answer of the Ford Motor Company, which was filed November 28, 1916, admits most of the allegations in the plaintiffs' bill of complaint. . . .

The answer of Henry Ford is a repetition in many respects of the matter contained in the answer of the Ford Motor Company. . . .

The cause came on for hearing in open court on the 21st of May, 1917. A large volume of testimony was taken, with the result that a decree was entered December 5, 1917, in and by which it is decreed that within 30 days from the entry thereof the directors of the Ford Motor Company declare a dividend upon all of the shares of stock in an amount equivalent to one-half of, and payable out of, the accumulated cash surplus of said Ford Motor Company, on hand at the close of the fiscal year ending July 31, 1916, less the aggregate amount of the special dividends declared and paid after the filing of the bill and during the year ending July 31, 1917; the amount to be declared being $19,275,385.96. It was further decreed:

> "Third. The owning, holding or operating by the defendant, Ford Motor Company, of, and the using or appropriating or incurring obligations which might require or necessitate the using or appropriating of any funds or other property of said defendant, Ford Motor Company, for a smelting plant or blast furnace or furnaces of the kind or character which the proofs adduced herein show to be contemplated and now in course of construction on or near the River Rouge, and of any lands, buildings, machinery or equipment therefor, and other incident thereof, is without authority of law and is permanently and absolutely restrained and enjoined." ...

The limited dividend ordered is fixed with reference to the written demand of plaintiffs for the distribution of 50 per cent of the cash.

Defendants have appealed, plaintiffs have not appealed, from the decree ...

Ostrander, Chief Justice

The rule which will govern courts in deciding these questions is not in dispute. It is, of course, differently phrased by judges and by authors, and, as the phrasing in a particular instance may seem to lean for or against the exercise of the right of judicial interference with the actions of corporate directors, the context, or the facts before the court, must be considered. This court, in *Hunter v. Roberts, Throp & Co.* recognized the rule in the following language:

> "It is a well-recognized principle of law that the directors of a corporation, and they alone, have the power to declare a dividend of the earnings of the corporation, and to determine its amount. Courts of equity will not interfere in the management of the directors unless it is clearly made to appear that they are guilty of fraud or misappropriation of the corporate funds, or refuse to declare a dividend when the corporation has a surplus of net profits which it can, without detriment to its business, divide among its stockholders, and when a refusal to do so would amount to such an abuse of discretion as would constitute a fraud, or breach of that good faith which they are bound to exercise towards the stockholders." ...

To develop the points now discussed, and to a considerable extent they may be developed together as a single point, it is necessary to refer with some particularity to the facts.

When plaintiffs made their complaint and demand for further dividends, the Ford Motor Company had concluded its most prosperous year of business. The demand for its cars at the price of the preceding year continued. It could make and could market in the year beginning August 1, 1916, more than 500,000 cars. Sales of parts and repairs would necessarily increase. The cost of materials was likely to advance, and perhaps the price of labor; but it reasonably might have expected a profit for the year of upwards of $60,000,000. It had assets of more than $132,000,000, a surplus of almost $112,000,000, and its cash on hand and municipal bonds were nearly $54,000,000. Its total liabilities, including capital stock, was a little over $20,000,000. It had declared no special dividend during the business year except the October, 1915, dividend. It had been the practice, under similar circumstances, to declare larger dividends. Considering only these facts, a refusal to declare and pay further dividends appears to be not an exercise of discretion on the part of the directors, but an arbitrary refusal to do what the circumstances required to be done. These facts and others call upon the directors to justify their action, or failure or refusal to act. In justification, the defendants have offered testimony tending to prove, and which does prove, the following facts: It had been the policy of the corporation for a considerable time to annually reduce the selling price of cars, while keeping up, or improving, their quality. As early as in June, 1915, a general plan for the expansion of the productive capacity of the concern by a practical duplication of its plant had been talked over by the executive officers and directors and agreed upon; not all of the details having been settled, and no formal action of directors having been taken. The erection of a smelter was considered, and engineering and other data in connection therewith secured. In consequence, it was determined not to reduce the selling price of cars for the year beginning August 1, 1915, but to maintain the price and to accumulate a large surplus to pay for the proposed expansion of plant and equipment, and perhaps to build a plant for smelting ore. It is hoped, by Mr. Ford, that eventually 1,000,000 cars will be annually produced. The contemplated changes will permit the increased output.

The plan, as affecting the profits of the business for the year beginning August 1, 1916, and thereafter, calls for a reduction in the selling price of the cars. It is true that this price might be at any time increased, but the plan called for the reduction in price of $80 a car. The capacity of the plant, without the additions thereto voted to be made (without a part of them at least), would produce more than 600,000 cars annually. This number, and more, could have been sold for $440 instead of $360, a difference in the return for capital, labor, and materials employed of at least $48,000,000. In short, the plan does not call for and is not intended to produce immediately a more profitable business, but a less profitable one; not only less profitable than formerly, but less profitable than it is admitted it might be made. The apparent immediate effect will be to diminish the value of shares and the returns to shareholders.

It is the contention of plaintiffs that the apparent effect of the plan is intended to be the continued and continuing effect of it, and that it is deliberately proposed, not of record and not by official corporate declaration, but nevertheless proposed, to continue the corporation henceforth as a semi-eleemosynary institution and not as a business institution. In support of this contention, they point to the attitude and to the expressions of Mr. Henry Ford.

Mr. Henry Ford is the dominant force in the business of the Ford Motor Company. No plan of operations could be adopted unless he consented, and no board of directors can be elected whom he does not favor. One of the directors of the company has no stock. One share was assigned to him to qualify him for the position, but it is not claimed that he owns it. A business, one of the largest in the world, and one of the most profitable, has been built up. It employs many men, at good pay.

> "'My ambition,' said Mr. Ford, 'is to employ still more men, to spread the benefits of this industrial system to the greatest possible number, to help them build up their lives and their homes. To do this we are putting the greatest share of our profits back in the business.'"

> "With regard to dividends, the company paid sixty per cent on its capitalization of two million dollars, or $1,200,000, leaving $58,000,000 to reinvest for the growth of the company. This is Mr. Ford's policy at present, and it is understood that the other stockholders cheerfully accede to this plan."

He had made up his mind in the summer of 1916 that no dividends other than the regular dividends should be paid, "for the present."

> "Q. For how long? Had you fixed in your mind any time in the future, when you were going to pay?
>
> "A. No.
>
> "Q. That was indefinite in the future?
>
> "A. That was indefinite; yes, sir."

The record, and especially the testimony of Mr. Ford, convinces that he has to some extent the attitude towards shareholders of one who has dispensed and distributed to them large gains and that they should be content to take what he chooses to give. His testimony creates the impression, also, that he thinks the Ford Motor Company has made too much money, has had too large profits, and that, although large profits might be still earned, a sharing of them with the public, by reducing the price of the output of the company, ought to be undertaken. We have no doubt that certain sentiments, philanthropic and altruistic, creditable to Mr. Ford, had large influence in determining the policy to be pursued by the Ford Motor Company—the policy which has been herein referred to.

It is said by his counsel that—

> "Although a manufacturing corporation cannot engage in humanitarian works as its principal business, the fact that it is organized for profit does not prevent the existence of implied powers to carry on with humanitarian motives such charitable works as are incidental to the main business of the corporation."

And again:

"As the expenditures complained of are being made in an expansion of the business which the company is organized to carry on, and for purposes within the powers of the corporation as hereinbefore shown, the question is as to whether such expenditures are rendered illegal because influenced to some extent by humanitarian motives and purposes on the part of the members of the board of directors."

In discussing this proposition, counsel have referred to decisions such as *Hawes v. Oakland*; *Taunton v. Royal Ins. Co.*; *Henderson v. Bank of Australia*; *Steinway v. Steinway & Sons*; *People v. Hotchkiss*. These cases, after all, like all others in which the subject is treated, turn finally upon the point, the question, whether it appears that the directors were not acting for the best interests of the corporation. We do not draw in question, nor do counsel for the plaintiffs do so, the validity of the general proposition stated by counsel nor the soundness of the opinions delivered in the cases cited. The case presented here is not like any of them. The difference between an incidental humanitarian expenditure of corporate funds for the benefit of the employees, like the building of a hospital for their use and the employment of agencies for the betterment of their condition, and a general purpose and plan to benefit mankind at the expense of others, is obvious. There should be no confusion (of which there is evidence) of the duties which Mr. Ford conceives that he and the stockholders owe to the general public and the duties which in law he and his codirectors owe to protesting, minority stockholders. A business corporation is organized and carried on primarily for the profit of the stockholders. The powers of the directors are to be employed for that end. The discretion of directors is to be exercised in the choice of means to attain that end, and does not extend to a change in the end itself, to the reduction of profits, or to the nondistribution of profits among stockholders in order to devote them to other purposes.

There is committed to the discretion of directors, a discretion to be exercised in good faith, the infinite details of business, including the wages which shall be paid to employees, the number of hours they shall work, the conditions under which labor shall be carried on, and the price for which products shall be offered to the public.

It is said by appellants that the motives of the board members are not material and will not be inquired into by the court so long as their acts are within their lawful powers. As we have pointed out, and the proposition does not require argument to sustain it, it is not within the lawful powers of a board of directors to shape and conduct the affairs of a corporation for the merely incidental benefit of shareholders and for the primary purpose of benefiting others, and no one will contend that, if the avowed purpose of the defendant directors was to sacrifice the interests of shareholders, it would not be the duty of the courts to interfere.

We are not, however, persuaded that we should interfere with the proposed expansion of the business of the Ford Motor Company. In view of the fact that the selling price of products may be increased at any time, the ultimate results of the larger business cannot be certainly estimated. The judges are not business experts. It is recognized that plans must often be made for a long future, for expected competition, for a continuing as well as an immediately profitable venture. The experience of the Ford Motor Company is evidence of capable management of its affairs. It may be noticed, incidentally, that it took from the public the money required for the execution of its plan, and that the very considerable salaries paid to Mr. Ford and to certain executive officers and employees were not diminished. We are not satisfied that the alleged motives of the directors, in so far as they are reflected in the conduct of the business, menace the interests of shareholders. It is enough to say, perhaps, that the court of equity is at all times open to complaining shareholders having a just grievance.

Assuming the general plan and policy of expansion and the details of it to have been sufficiently, formally, approved at the October and November, 1917, meetings of directors, and assuming further that the plan and policy and the details agreed upon were for the best ultimate interest of the company and therefore of its shareholders, what does it amount to in justification of a refusal to declare and pay a special dividend or dividends? The Ford Motor Company was able to estimate with nicety its income and profit. It could sell more cars than it could make. Having ascertained what it would cost to produce a car and to sell it, the profit upon each car depended upon the selling price. That being fixed, the yearly income and profit was determinable, and, within slight variations, was certain.

There was appropriated—voted—for the smelter $11,325,000. As to the remainder voted, there is no available way for determining how much had been paid before the action of directors was taken and how much was paid thereafter; but assuming that the plans required an expenditure sooner or later of $9,895,000 for duplication of the plant, and for land and other expenditures $3,000,000, the total is $24,220,000. The company was continuing business, at a profit—a cash business. If the total cost of proposed expenditures had been immediately withdrawn in cash from the cash surplus (money and bonds) on hand August 1, 1916, there would have remained nearly $30,000,000.

Defendants say, and it is true, that a considerable cash balance must be at all times carried by such a concern. But, as has been stated, there was a large daily, weekly, monthly, receipt of cash. The output was practically continuous and was continuously, and within a few days, turned into cash. Moreover, the contemplated expenditures were not to be immediately made. The large sum appropriated for the smelter plant was payable over a considerable period of time. So that, without going further, it would appear that, accepting and approving the plan of the directors, it was their duty to distribute on or near the 1st of August, 1916, a very large sum of money to stockholders.

In reaching this conclusion, we do not ignore, but recognize, the validity of the proposition that plaintiffs have from the beginning profited by, if they have not lately, officially, participated in, the general policy of expansion pursued by this corporation. We do not lose sight of the fact that it had been, upon an occasion, agreeable to the plaintiffs to increase the capital stock to $100,000,000 by a stock dividend of $98,000,000. These things go only to answer other contentions now made by plaintiffs, and do not and cannot operate to estop them to demand proper dividends upon the stock they own. It is obvious that an annual dividend of 60 per cent upon $2,000,000, or $1,200,000, is the equivalent of a very small dividend upon $100,000,000, or more.

==The decree of the court below fixing and determining the specific amount to be distributed to stockholders is affirmed.== In other respects, except as to the allowance of costs, the said decree is reversed. Plaintiffs will recover interest at 5 per cent per annum upon their proportional share of said dividend from the date of the decree of the lower court. Appellants will tax the costs of their appeal, and two-thirds of the amount thereof will be paid by plaintiffs. No other costs are allowed.

Questions

1. What is *Dodge v. Ford* really about? (Who were the Dodge brothers and why do you suppose they wanted the money?) Is the court's discussion of corporate purpose necessary to the outcome? Would you have sued on the same cause of action as the Dodge brothers?

2. What is the difference between Steinway's actions and Ford's? Why, according to the court in *Dodge v. Ford*, are the cases different?

3. Could Ford have won the case and, if so, how?

4. What vision of the corporation does the court adopt in *Dodge v. Ford*? Is it similar to the one adopted by either Marshall or Story in *Trustees of Dartmouth College v. Woodward*? How does the court's vision of the corporation affect its evaluation of corporate purpose?

Perhaps the most important work on corporations published in the twentieth century was ADOLPH A. BERLE AND GARDINER C. MEANS, THE MODERN CORPORATION AND PRIVATE PROPERTY (1932). While most of the focus of modern corporate governance scholarship has been on Berle's and Means's observation that ownership and control had become separated in the public corporation (an observation made by Thorstein Veblen almost 30 years earlier), the following excerpt argues that Berle's and Means's principal concern was the power of the corporation and its corresponding obligation to society.

Dalia Tsuk Mitchell, *Corporations Without Labor: The Politics of Progressive Corporate Law*
151 U. Pa. L. Rev. 1861 (2003) [footnotes omitted]

On its face, *The Modern Corporation and Private Property* was "intended primarily to break ground on the relation which corporations bear to property." The statistical studies, which were carried out by Means, were intended to document the growing dispersion of stock ownership in large corporations, and hence, the rapid separation of ownership from control. These studies provided a background for the book's argument that the separation of ownership from control helped undermine traditional assumptions about the efficiency of competition over resources between self-interested individuals. According to Berle and Means, the divergence between managers' and shareholders' interests indicated that managerial use of shareholders' property might be both self-interested and inefficient.

Yet, as Berle's biographer indicated, "[b]y the spring of 1929, Berle discerned [another] significant trend in Means' research:" "American capitalism headed toward an oligarchical concentration of economic power." Means's statistical studies illustrated that some two hundred corporations, controlled by less than eighteen hundred men, administered over one-third of the national wealth. Thereafter, Berle and Means described the separation of ownership from control as a pressing matter not only because it could trigger market abuses of shareholders' interests, but also because multiple ownership created "tremendous aggregations of property," which made possible such buildups of power (in the hands of the control group). The possibility of mass concentration of power augmented the risk of inefficient uses of power and the potential adverse effect of corporations on the economy at large. The power that corporations could amass, and ways to tame it, became the book's underlying theme.

Power was "an elusive concept, for power [could] rarely be sharply segregated or clearly defined." As Scott Bowman explained, Berle described two dimensions of power: an internal dimension and an external one. The internal dimension focused on the power of corporations over individuals within them, specifically power over employment decisions: "the relation of the corporation to its workers, its plant organization and its technical problem of production." The external dimension emphasized corporations' impact on society at large, specifically corporations' power to control markets by administering prices, their capacity to accumulate capital and affect the economy, and their ability to shape the forces of production through the development of new technologies.

Both dimensions of power underlay Berle and Means's proclamation that the economic power of the modern corporation resembled the power of the sovereign state both in form and in substance. "The rise of the modern corporation," Berle and Means wrote in the last paragraph of *The Modern Corporation and Private Property*, "has brought a concentration of economic power which can compete on equal terms with the modern state. . . ." [I]n the future, [they suggested], the corporation could even supersede the state "as the dominant form of social organization." "The law of corporations," Berle and Means concluded, "might well be considered as a potential constitutional law for the new economic state, while business practice is increasingly assuming the aspect of economic statesmanship."

Having called attention to corporate power, as augmented by the separation of ownership from control, Berle and Means turned to the task of formulating a unified theme for the law of corporations. Specifically, they evaluated three ways to guarantee the responsible exercise of power. The first way—the application of strict property rules to passive ownership—would have required the control group to exercise corporate power "for the *sole* benefit of the security owners." Berle and Means feared that such an approach would have "the bulk of American industry . . . operated by trustees for the sole benefit of inactive and irresponsible security owners." The second way—application of strict contractual rules—would have invested in the control group uncurbed powers and seen security holders as having "agreed in advance to any losses which they may suffer by reason of such use." Berle and Means believed that such a scheme would create "a corporate oligarchy coupled with the probability of an era of corporate plundering." Rather than choosing traditional rules of property or contracts as the underlying theme of the modern law of corporations, Berle and Means settled on a third alternative, an alternative that offered "a wholly new concept of corporate activity." Shareholders, they argued, "by surrendering control and responsibility over the active property, have surrendered the right that the corporation should be operated in their sole interest[ ]—they have released the community from the obligation to protect them to the full extent implied in the doctrine of strict property rights."

According to Berle and Means, this tampering with the interests of the owners did not make the controlling group the beneficiary of corporate power. Rather, Berle and Means concluded that it had "cleared the way for the claims of a group far wider than either the owners or the control [group]." It had "placed the community in a position to demand that the modern corporation serve not [only] the owners or the control [group] but all society."

> Should the corporate leaders, for example, set forth a program comprising *fair wages, security to employees,* reasonable service to their public, and stabilization of business, all of which would divert a portion of the profits from the owners of passive property, and should the community generally accept such a scheme as a logical and human solution of industrial difficulties, *the interests of passive property owners would have to give way.*

Simply put, *The Modern Corporation and Private Property* announced that all publicly held business corporations were public trustees. Their power was to be exercised to satisfy the demands of the community.

A.P. Smith Mfg. Co. v. Barlow
13 N.J. 145 (1953)

JACOBS, Justice

The Chancery Division, in a well-reasoned opinion by Judge Stein, determined that a donation by the plaintiff, The A. P. Smith Manufacturing Company, to Princeton University was *intra vires*. Because of the public importance of the issues presented, the appeal duly taken to the Appellate Division has been certified directly to this court under Rule 1:5-1(a).

The company was incorporated in 1896 and is engaged in the manufacture and sale of valves, fire hydrants and special equipment, mainly for water and gas industries. Its plant is located in East Orange and Bloomfield and it has approximately 300 employees. Over the years the company has contributed regularly to the local community chest and on occasions to Upsala College in East Orange and Newark University, now part of Rutgers, the State University. On July 24, 1951 the board of directors adopted a resolution which set forth that it was in the corporation's best interests to join with others in the 1951 Annual Giving to Princeton University, and appropriated the sum of $1,500 to be transferred by the corporation's treasurer to the university as a contribution towards its maintenance. When this action was questioned by stockholders the corporation instituted a declaratory judgment action in the Chancery Division and trial was had in due course.

Mr. Hubert F. O'Brien, the president of the company, testified that he considered the contribution to be a sound investment, that the public expects corporations to aid philanthropic and benevolent institutions, that they obtain good will in the community by so doing, and that their charitable donations create favorable environment for their business operations. In addition, he expressed the thought that in contributing to liberal arts institutions, corporations were furthering their self-interest in assuring the free flow of properly trained personnel for administrative and other corporate employment. Mr. Frank W. Abrams, chairman of the board of the Standard Oil Company of New Jersey, testified that corporations are expected to acknowledge their public responsibilities in support of the essential elements of our free enterprise system. He indicated that it was not "good business" to disappoint "this reasonable and justified public expectation," nor was it good business for corporations "to take substantial benefits from their membership in the economic community while avoiding the normally accepted obligations of citizenship in the social community." Mr. Irving S. Olds, former chairman of the board of the United States Steel Corporation, pointed out that corporations have a self-interest in the maintenance of liberal education as the bulwark of good government. He stated that "Capitalism and free enterprise owe their survival in no small degree to the existence of our private, independent universities" and that if American business does not aid in their maintenance it is not "properly protecting the long-range interest of its stockholders, its employees and its customers." Similarly, Dr. Harold W. Dodds, President of Princeton University, suggested that if private institutions of higher learning were replaced by governmental institutions our society would be vastly different and private enterprise in other fields would fade out rather promptly. Further on he stated that "democratic society will not long endure if it does not nourish within itself strong centers of non-governmental fountains of knowledge, opinions of all sorts not governmentally or politically originated. If the time comes when all these centers are absorbed into government, then freedom as we know it, I submit, is at an end."

The objecting stockholders have not disputed any of the foregoing testimony nor the showing of great need by Princeton and other private institutions of higher learning and the important public service being rendered by them for democratic government and industry alike. Similarly, they have acknowledged that for over two decades there has been state legislation on our books which expresses a strong public policy in favor of corporate contributions such as that being questioned by them. Nevertheless, they have taken the position that (1) the plaintiff's certificate of incorporation does not expressly authorize the contribution and under common-law principles the company does not possess any implied or incidental power to make it, and (2) the New Jersey statutes which expressly authorize the contribution may not constitutionally be applied to the plaintiff, a corporation created long before their enactment. See R.S. 14:3–13, N.J.S.A.; R.S. 14:3–13.1 et seq., N.J.S.A.

In his discussion of the early history of business corporations Professor Williston refers to a 1702 publication where the author stated flatly that "The general intent and end of all civil incorporations is for better government." And he points out that the early corporate charters, particularly their recitals, furnish additional support for the notion that the corporate object was the public one of managing and ordering the trade as well as the private one of profit for the members. See 3 Select Essays on Anglo-American Legal History 201 (1909); 1 Fletcher, Corporations (rev. ed. 1931), 6. See also *Currie's Administrators v. Mutual Assurance Society*, 4 Hen. & M. 315, 347 (Va.Sup.Ct.App. 1809), where Judge Roane referred to the English corporate charters and expressed the view that acts of incorporation ought never to be passed "but in consideration of services to be rendered to the public." However, with later economic and social developments and the free availability of the corporate device for all trades, the end of private profit became generally accepted as the controlling one in all businesses other than those classed broadly as public utilities. Cf. Dodd, *For Whom Are Corporate Managers Trustees?*, 45 Harv. L. Rev. 1145, 1148 (1932). As a concomitant the common-law rule developed that those who managed the corporation could not disburse any corporate funds for philanthropic or other worthy public cause unless the expenditure would benefit the corporation. During the 19th Century when corporations were relatively few and small and did not dominate the country's wealth, the common-law rule did not significantly interfere with the public interest. But the 20th Century has presented a different climate. Berle and Means, *The Modern Corporation and Private Property* (1948). Control of economic wealth has passed largely from individual entrepreneurs to dominating corporations, and calls upon the corporations for reasonable philanthropic donations have come to be made with increased public support. In many instances such contributions have been sustained by the courts within the common-law doctrine upon liberal findings that the donations tended reasonably to promote the corporate objectives. See Cousens, *How Far Corporations May Contribute to Charity*, 35 Va. L. Rev. 401 (1949)....

When the wealth of the nation was primarily in the hands of individuals they discharged their responsibilities as citizens by donating freely for charitable purposes. With the transfer of most of the wealth to corporate hands and the imposition of heavy burdens of individual taxation, they have been unable to keep pace with increased philanthropic needs. They have therefore, with justification, turned to corporations to assume the modern obligations of good citizenship in the same manner as humans do. Congress and state legislatures have enacted laws which encourage corporate contributions, and much has recently been written to indicate the crying need and adequate legal basis therefor. In actual practice corporate giving has correspondingly increased. Thus, it is estimated that annual corporate contributions throughout the nation aggregate over 300 million dollars, with over 60 million dollars thereof going to universities and other educational institutions. Similarly, it is estimated that local community chests receive well over 40% of their contributions from corporations; these contributions and those made by corporations to the American Red Cross, to Boy Scouts and Girl Scouts, to 4-H Clubs and similar organizations have almost invariably been unquestioned.

During the first world war corporations loaned their personnel and contributed substantial corporate funds in order to insure survival; during the depression of the '30s they made contributions to alleviate the desperate hardships of the millions of unemployed; and during the second world war they again contributed to insure survival. They now recognize that we are faced with other, though nonetheless vicious, threats from abroad which must be withstood without impairing the vigor of our democratic institutions at home and that otherwise victory will be pyrrhic indeed. More and more they have come to recognize that their salvation rests upon sound economic and social environment which in turn rests in no insignificant part upon free and vigorous nongovernmental institutions of learning. It seems to us that just as the conditions prevailing when corporations were originally created required that they serve public as well as private interests, modern conditions require that corporations acknowledge and discharge social as well as private responsibilities as members of the communities within which they operate. Within this broad concept there is no difficulty in sustaining, as incidental to their proper objects and in aid of the public welfare, the power of corporations to contribute corporate funds within reasonable limits in support of academic institutions. But even if we confine ourselves to the terms of the common-law rule in its application to current conditions, such expenditures may likewise readily be justified as being for the benefit of the corporation; indeed, if need be the matter may be viewed strictly in terms of actual survival of the corporation in a free enterprise system. The genius of our common law has been its capacity for growth and its adaptability to the needs of the times. Generally courts have accomplished the desired result indirectly through the molding of old forms. Occasionally they have done it directly through frank rejection of the old and recognition of the new. But whichever path the common law has taken it has not been found wanting as the proper tool for the advancement of the general good. Cf. Holmes, The Common Law, 1, 5 (1951); Cardozo, Paradoxes of Legal Science, Hall, Selected Writings, 253 (1947).

In 1930 a statute was enacted in our State which expressly provided that any corporation could cooperate with other corporations and natural persons in the creation and maintenance of community funds and charitable, philanthropic or benevolent instrumentalities conducive to public welfare, and could for such purposes expend such corporate sums as the directors "deem expedient and as in their judgment will contribute to the protection of the corporate interests." Under the terms of the statute donations in excess of 1% of the capital stock required 10 days' notice to stockholders and approval at a stockholders' meeting if written objections were made by the holders of more than 25% of the stock; in 1949 the statute was amended to increase the limitation to 1% of capital and surplus. In 1950 a more comprehensive statute was enacted. In this enactment the Legislature declared that it shall be the public policy of our State and in furtherance of the public interest and welfare that encouragement be given to the creation and maintenance of institutions engaged in community fund, hospital, charitable, philanthropic, educational, scientific or benevolent activities or patriotic or civic activities conducive to the betterment of social and economic conditions; and it expressly empowered corporations acting singly or with others to contribute reasonable sums to such institutions, provided, however, that the contribution shall not be permissible if the donee institution owns more than 10% of the voting stock of the donor and provided, further, that the contribution shall not exceed 1% of capital and surplus unless the excess is authorized by the stockholders at a regular or special meeting. To insure that the grant of express power in the 1950 statute would not displace pre-existing power at common law or otherwise, the Legislature provided that the "act shall not be construed as directly or indirectly minimizing or interpreting the rights and powers of corporations, as heretofore existing, with reference to appropriations, expenditures or contributions of the nature above specified." It may be noted that statutes relating to charitable contributions by corporations have now been passed in 29 states.

The appellants contend that the foregoing New Jersey statutes may not be applied to corporations created before their passage. Fifty years before the incorporation of The A.P. Smith Manufacturing Company our Legislature provided that every corporate charter thereafter granted "shall be subject to alteration, suspension and repeal, in the discretion of the legislature." A similar reserved power was placed into our State Constitution in 1875, and is found in our present Constitution. In the early case of *Zabriskie v. Hackensack & New York Railroad Company*, the court was called upon to determine whether a railroad could extend its line, above objection by a stockholder, under a legislative enactment passed under the reserve power after the incorporation of the railroad. Notwithstanding the breadth of the statutory language and persuasive authority elsewhere (*Durfee v. Old Colony & Fall River Railroad Company*, 87 Mass. 230 (Sup.Jud.Ct. 1862)), it was held that the proposed extension of the company's line constituted a vital change of its corporate object which could not be accomplished without unanimous consent. See Lattin, A Primer on Fundamental Corporate Changes, 1 West.Res.L.Rev. 3, 7 (1949). The court announced the now familiar New Jersey doctrine that although the reserved power permits alterations in the public interest of the contract between the state and the corporation, it has no effect on the contractual rights between the corporation and its stockholders and between stockholders *inter se*. Unfortunately, the court did not consider whether it was not contrary to the public interest to permit the single minority stockholder before it to restrain the railroad's normal corporate growth and development as authorized by the Legislature and approved, reasonably and in good faith, by the corporation's managing directors and majority stockholders. Although the later cases in New Jersey have not disavowed the doctrine of the *Zabriskie* case, it is noteworthy that they have repeatedly recognized that where justified by the advancement of the public interest the reserved power may be invoked to sustain later charter alterations even though they affect contractual rights between the corporation and its stockholders and between stockholders *inter se*. . . .

State legislation adopted in the public interest and applied to pre-existing corporations under the reserved power has repeatedly been sustained by the United States Supreme Court above the contention that it impairs the rights of stockholders and violates constitutional guarantees under the Federal Constitution. . . . We are entirely satisfied that within the orbit of above authorities the legislative enactments found in R.S. 14:3–13, N.J.S.A., and N.J.S.A. 14:3–13.1 et seq. and applied to pre-existing corporations do not violate any constitutional guarantees afforded to their stockholders.

It seems clear to us that the public policy supporting the statutory enactments under consideration is far greater and the alteration of pre-existing rights of stockholders much lesser than in the cited cases sustaining various exercises of the reserve power. In encouraging and expressly authorizing reasonable charitable contributions by corporations, our State has not only joined with other states in advancing the national interest but has also specially furthered the interests of its own people who must bear the burdens of taxation resulting from increased state and federal aid upon default in voluntary giving. It is significant that in its enactments the State has not in anywise sought to impose any compulsory obligations or alter the corporate objectives. And since in our view the corporate power to make reasonable charitable contributions exists under modern conditions, even apart from express statutory provision, its enactments simply constitute helpful and confirmatory declarations of such power, accompanied by limiting safeguards.

In the light of all of the foregoing we have no hesitancy in sustaining the validity of the donation by the plaintiff. There is no suggestion that it was made indiscriminately or to a pet charity of the corporate directors in furtherance of personal rather than corporate ends. On the contrary, it was made to a preeminent institution of higher learning, was modest in amount and well within the limitations imposed by the statutory enactments, and was voluntarily made in the reasonable belief that it would aid the public welfare and advance the interests of the plaintiff as a private corporation and as part of the community in which it operates. We find that it was a lawful exercise of the corporation's implied and incidental powers under common-law principles and that it came within the express authority of the pertinent state legislation. As has been indicated, there is now widespread belief throughout the nation that free and vigorous non-governmental institutions of learning are vital to our democracy and the system of free enterprise and that withdrawal of corporate authority to make such contributions within reasonable limits would seriously threaten their continuance. Corporations have come to recognize this and with their enlightenment have sought in varying measures, as has the plaintiff by its contribution, to insure and strengthen the society which gives them existence and the means of aiding themselves and their fellow citizens. Clearly then, the appellants, as individual stockholders whose private interests rest entirely upon the well-being of the plaintiff corporation, ought not be permitted to close their eyes to present-day realities and thwart the long-visioned corporate action in recognizing and voluntarily discharging its high obligations as a constituent of our modern social structure.

The judgment entered in the Chancery Division is in all respects affirmed.

Questions

1. A New Jersey Statute "expressly provided that any corporation could cooperate with other corporations and natural persons in the creation and maintenance of community funds and charitable, philanthropic or benevolent instrumentalities conducive to public welfare, and could for such purposes expend such corporate sums as the directors 'deem expedient and as in their judgment will contribute to the protection of the corporate interests.'" Did the court rely upon this statute to determine the result in this case?

2. What is the relevance of a 1702 publication (cited by the court) to the case at hand? What about corporations' contributions to the war efforts both during World War I and World War II? Are they relevant?

3. As you learned, in THE MODERN CORPORATION AND PRIVATE PROPERTY, Adolf Berle (in collaboration with Gardiner Means) suggested that corporations were trustees for the community. Yet, Berle sought *certiorari* on behalf of the shareholders of Smith Mfg. Co. (it was denied). Can you think why?

Bell v. Maryland
378 U.S. 226 (1964)

BRENNAN, Justice

Petitioners, 12 Negro students, were convicted in a Maryland state court as a result of their participation in a "sit-in" demonstration at Hooper's restaurant in the City of Baltimore in 1960. The convictions were based on a record showing in summary that a group of 15 to 20 Negro students, including petitioners, went to Hooper's restaurant to engage in what their counsel describes as a "sit-in protest" because the restaurant would not serve Negroes. The "hostess," on orders of Mr. Hooper, the president of the corporation owning the restaurant, told them, "solely on the basis of their color," that they would not be served. Petitioners did not leave when requested to by the hostess and the manager; instead they went to tables, took seats, and refused to leave, insisting that they be served. On orders of Mr. Hooper the police were called, but they advised that a warrant would be necessary before they could arrest petitioners. Mr. Hooper then went to the police station and swore out warrants, and petitioners were accordingly arrested.

The statute under which the convictions were obtained was the Maryland criminal trespass law, § 577 of Art. 27 of the Maryland Code, 1957 edition, under which it is a misdemeanor to "enter upon or cross over the land, premises or private property of any person or persons in this State after having been duly notified by the owner or his agent not to do so." The convictions were affirmed by the Maryland Court of Appeals and we granted certiorari.

We do not reach the questions that have been argued under the Equal Protection and Due Process Clauses of the Fourteenth Amendment. It appears that a significant change has taken place in the applicable law of Maryland since these convictions were affirmed by the Court of Appeals. Under this Court's settled practice in such circumstances, the judgments must consequently be vacated and reversed and the case remanded so that the state court may consider the effect of the supervening change in state law.

Petitioners' convictions were affirmed by the Maryland Court of Appeals on January 9, 1962. Since that date, Maryland has enacted laws that abolish the crime of which petitioners were convicted. These laws accord petitioners a right to be served in Hooper's restaurant, and make unlawful conduct like that of Hooper's president and hostess in refusing them service because of their race....

It is clear from these enactments that petitioners' conduct in entering or crossing over the premises of Hooper's restaurant after being notified not to do so because of their race would not be a crime today; on the contrary, the law of Baltimore and of Maryland now vindicates their conduct and recognizes it as the exercise of a right, directing the law's prohibition not at them but at the restaurant owner or manager who seeks to deny them service because of their race....

Reversed and remanded.

DOUGLAS, Justice with whom GOLDBERG, Justice concurs as respects Parts II–V, for reversing and directing dismissal of the indictment

I

I reach the merits of this controversy. The issue is ripe for decision and petitioners, who have been convicted of asking for service in Hooper's restaurant, are entitled to an answer to their complaint here and now.

On this the last day of the Term, we studiously avoid decision of the basic issue of the right of public accommodation under the Fourteenth Amendment, remanding the case to the state court for reconsideration in light of an issue of state law....

The whole Nation has to face the issue; Congress is conscientiously considering it; some municipalities have had to make it their first order of concern; law enforcement officials are deeply implicated, North as well as South; the question is at the root of demonstrations, unrest, riots, and violence in various areas. The issue in other words consumes the public attention. Yet we stand mute, avoiding decision of the basic issue by an obvious pretense.

The clash between Negro customers and white restaurant owners is clear; each group claims protection by the Constitution and tenders the Fourteenth Amendment as justification for its action. Yet we leave resolution of the conflict to others, when, if our voice were heard, the issues for the Congress and for the public would become clear and precise. The Court was created to sit in troubled times as well as in peaceful days. . . .

For these reasons I reach the merits; and I vote to reverse the judgments of conviction outright.

II

The issue in this case, according to those who would affirm, is whether a person's "personal prejudices" may dictate the way in which he uses his property and whether he can enlist the aid of the State to enforce those "personal prejudices." With all respect, that is not the real issue. The corporation that owns this restaurant did not refuse service to these Negroes because "it" did not like Negroes. The reason "it" refused service was because "it" thought "it" could make more money by running a segregated restaurant.

In the instant case, G. Carroll Hooper, president of the corporate chain owning the restaurant here involved, testified concerning the episode that gave rise to these convictions. The reasons were wholly commercial ones:

> "I set at the table with him and two other people and reasoned and talked to him why my policy was not yet one of integration and told him that I had two hundred employees and half of them were colored. I thought as much of them as I did the white employees. I invited them back in my kitchen if they'd like to go back and talk to them. *I wanted to prove to them it wasn't my policy, my personal prejudice*, we were not, that I had valuable colored employees and I thought just as much of them. I tried to reason with these leaders, told them that *as long as my customers were the* [sic] *deciding who they want to eat with, I'm at the mercy of my customers. I'm trying to do what they want. If they fail to come in, these people are not paying my expenses, and my bills.* They didn't want to go back and talk to my colored employees because every one of them are in sympathy with me and that is we're in sympathy with what their objectives are, with what they are trying to abolish. . . ." (Italics added.)

Here, as in most of the sit-in cases before us, the refusal of service did not reflect "personal prejudices" but business reasons. Were we today to hold that segregated restaurants, whose racial policies were enforced by a State, violated the Equal Protection Clause, all restaurants would be on an equal footing and the reasons given in this and most of the companion cases for refusing service to Negroes would evaporate. Moreover, when corporate restaurateurs are involved, whose "personal prejudices" are being protected? The stockholders'? The directors'? The officers'? The managers'? The truth is, I think, that the corporate interest is in making money, not in protecting "personal prejudices." . . .

APPENDIX I TO OPINION OF MR. JUSTICE DOUGLAS.

In the sit-in cases involving eating places last Term and this Term, practically all restaurant or lunch counter owners whose constitutional rights were vindicated below are corporations. Only two out of the 20 before us are noncorporate, as Appendix III shows. Some of these corporations are small, privately owned affairs. Others are large, national or regional businesses with many stockholders:

S.H. Kress & Co., operating 272 stores in 30 States, its stock being listed on the New York Stock Exchange; McCrory Corporation, with 1,307 stores, its stock being listed on the New York Stock Exchange; J.J. Newberry Co., with 567 stores of which 371 serve food, its stock being listed on the New York Stock Exchange; F.W. Woolworth Co., with 2,130 stores, its stock also being listed on the New York Stock Exchange; Eckerd Drugs, having 17 stores with its stock traded over-the-counter. F.W. Woolworth has over 90,000 stockholders; J.J. Newberry about 8,000; McCrory over 24,000; S.H. Kress over 8,000; Eckerd Drugs about 1,000.

At the national level most "eating places," as Appendix IV shows, are individual proprietorships or partnerships. But a substantial number are corporate in form; and even though in numbers they are perhaps an eighth of the others, in business done they make up a much larger percentage of the total.

Those living in the Washington, D.C., metropolitan area know that it is true in that area—the hotels are incorporated; Howard Johnson Co., listed on the New York Stock Exchange, has 650 restaurants and over 15,000 stockholders; Hot Shoppes, Inc., has 4,900 stockholders; Thompson Co. (involved in *District of Columbia v. Thompson Co.*) has 50 restaurants in this country with over 1,000 stockholders and its stock is listed on the New York Stock Exchange; Peoples Drug Stores, with a New York Stock Exchange listing, has nearly 5,000 stockholders. See Moody's Industrial Manual (1963 ed.).

All the sit-in cases involve a contest in a criminal trial between Negroes who sought service and state prosecutors and state judges who enforced trespass laws against them. The corporate beneficiaries of these convictions, those whose constitutional rights were vindicated by these convictions, are not parties to these suits. The beneficiary in the present case was Hooper Food Co., Inc., a Maryland corporation; and as seen in Appendix IV, "eating places" in Maryland owned by corporations, though not a fourth in number of those owned by individuals or partnerships, do nearly as much business as the other two combined.

So far as the corporate owner is concerned, what constitutional right is vindicated? It is said that ownership of property carries the right to use it in association with such people as the owner chooses. The corporate owners in these cases—the stockholders—are unidentified members of the public at large, who probably never saw these petitioners, who may never have frequented these restaurants. What personal rights of theirs would be vindicated by affirmance? Why should a stockholder in Kress, Woolworth, Howard Johnson, or any other corporate owner in the restaurant field have standing to say that any associational rights personal to him are involved? Why should his interests—his associational rights—make it possible to send these Negroes to jail?

Who, in this situation, is the corporation? Whose racial prejudices are reflected in "its" decision to refuse service to Negroes? The racial prejudices of the manager? Of the stockholders? Of the board of directors?

The Court in *Santa Clara County v. Southern Pacific R. Co.*, 118 U.S. 394, interrupted counsel on oral argument to say, "The court does not wish to hear argument on the question whether the provision in the Fourteenth Amendment to the Constitution, which forbids a State to deny to any person within its jurisdiction the equal protection of the laws, applies to these corporations. We are all of opinion that it does." 118 U.S. at 396. Later the Court held that corporations are "persons" within the meaning of the Due Process Clause of the Fourteenth Amendment. *Minneapolis R. Co. v. Beckwith*, 129 U.S. 26, 28. While that view is the law today, it prevailed only over dissenting opinions. See the dissent of Mr. Justice Black in *Connecticut General Co. v. Johnson*, 303 U.S. 77, 85; and my dissent in *Wheeling Steel Corp. v. Glander*, 337 U.S. 562, 576. Mr. Justice Black said of that doctrine and its influence:

> ". . . of the cases in this Court in which the *Fourteenth Amendment* was applied during the first fifty years after its adoption, less than one-half of one per cent invoked it in protection of the negro race, and more than fifty per cent asked that its benefits be extended to corporations." *Connecticut General Co. v. Johnson*, 303 U.S., at 90.

A corporation, like any other "client," is entitled to the attorney-client privilege. A corporation is protected as a publisher by the Freedom of the Press Clause of the First Amendment. A corporation, over the dissent of the first Mr. Justice Harlan, was held entitled to protection against unreasonable searches and seizures by reason of the Fourth Amendment. On the other hand the privilege of self-incrimination guaranteed by the Fifth Amendment cannot be utilized by a corporation. "The constitutional privilege against self-incrimination is essentially a personal one, applying only to natural individuals."

We deal here, we are told, with personal rights—the rights pertaining to property. One need not share his home with one he dislikes. One need not allow another to put his foot upon his private domain for any reason he desire—whether bigoted or enlightened. In the simple agricultural economy that Jefferson extolled, the conflicts posed were highly personal. But how is a "personal" right infringed when a corporate chain store, for example, is forced to open its lunch counters to people of all races? How can that so-called right be elevated to a constitutional level? How is that corporate right more "personal" than the right against self-incrimination?

The revolutionary change effected by an affirmance in these sit-in cases would be much more damaging to an open and free society than what the Court did when it gave the corporation the sword and the shield of the Due Process and Equal Protection Clauses of the Fourteenth Amendment. Affirmance finds in the Constitution a corporate right to refuse service to anyone "it" chooses and to get the State to put people in jail who defy "its" will.

More precisely, affirmance would give corporate management vast dimensions for social planning.[1]

Affirmance would make corporate management the arbiter of one of the deepest conflicts in our society: corporate management could then enlist the aid of state police, state prosecutors, and state courts to force *apartheid* on the community they served, if *apartheid* best suited the corporate need; or, if its profits would be better served by lowering the barriers of segregation, it could do so.

Veblen, while not writing directly about corporate management and the racial issue, saw the danger of leaving fundamental, governmental decisions to the managers or absentee owners of our corporate enterprises:

"Absentee ownership and absentee management on this grand scale is immune from neighborly personalities and from sentimental considerations and scruples."

"It takes effect through the colorless and impersonal channels of corporation management, at the hands of businesslike officials whose discretion and responsibility extend no farther than the procuring of a reasonably large—that is to say the largest obtainable—net gain in terms of price. The absentee owners are removed out of all touch with the working personnel or with the industrial work in hand, except such remote, neutral and dispassionate contact by proxy as may be implied in the continued receipt of a free income; and very much the same is true for the business agents of the

---

1. The conventional claims of corporate management are stated in Ginzberg and Berg, Democratic Values and the Rights of Management (1963), pp. 153–154:

"The founding fathers, despite some differences of opinion among them, were of one mind when it came to fundamentals—the best guarantee of freedom was the retention by the individual of the broadest possible scope for decision-making. And early in the nation's history, when the Supreme Court decided that the corporation possessed many of the same rights as individuals, continuity was maintained in basic structure; the corporate owner as well as the individual had wide scope for decision-making. In recent decades, another extension of this trend became manifest. The agents of owner—the managers—were able to subsume for themselves the authorities inherent in ownership. The historical record, then, is clear. The right to do what one likes with his property lies at the very foundation of our historical experience. This is a basis for management's growing concern with the restrictions and limitations which have increasingly come to characterize an arena where the widest scope for individual initiative previously prevailed."

absentee owners, the investment-bankers and the staff of responsible corporation officials. Their relation to what is going on, and to the manpower by use of which it is going on, is a fiscal relation. As industry, as a process of workmanship and a production of the means of life, the work in hand has no meaning for the absentee owners sitting in the fiscal background of these vested interests. Personalities and tangible consequences are eliminated and the business of governing the rate and volume of the output goes forward in terms of funds, prices, and percentages." Absentee Ownership (1923), pp. 215–216.

The point is that corporate motives in the retail field relate to corporate profits, corporate prestige, and corporate public relations. Corporate motives have no tinge of an individual's choice to associate only with one class of customers, to keep members of one race from his "property," to erect a wall of privacy around a business in the manner that one is erected around the home.

At times a corporation has standing to assert the constitutional rights of its members, as otherwise the rights peculiar to the members as individuals might be lost or impaired. Thus in *NAACP v. Alabama,* the question was whether the N.A.A.C.P., a membership corporation, could assert on behalf of its members a right personal to them to be protected from compelled disclosure by the State of their affiliation with it. In that context we said the N.A.A.C.P. was "the appropriate party to assert these rights, because it and its members are in every practical sense identical." We felt, moreover, that to deny the N.A.A.C.P. standing to raise the question and to require it to be claimed by the members themselves "would result in nullification of the right at the very moment of its assertion." Those were the important reasons governing our decision, the adverse effect of disclosure on the N.A.A.C.P. itself being only a make-weight.

The corporate owners of a restaurant, like the corporate owners of streetcars, buses, telephones, and electric light and gas facilities, are interested in balance sheets and in profit and loss statements. "It" does not stand at the door turning Negroes aside because of "its" feelings of antipathy to black-skinned people. "It" does not have any associational rights comparable to the classic individual store owner at a country crossroads whose store, in the dichotomy of an Adam Smith, was indeed no different from his home. "It" has been greatly transformed, as Berle and Means, The Modern Corporation and Private Property (1932), made clear a generation ago; and "it" has also transformed our economy. Separation of power or control from beneficial ownership was part of the phenomenon of change:

> "This dissolution of the atom of property destroys the very foundation on which the economic order of the past three centuries has rested. Private enterprise, which has molded economic life since the close of the middle ages, has been rooted in the institution of private property. Under the feudal system, its predecessor, economic organization grew out of mutual obligations and privileges derived by various individuals from their relation to property

which no one of them owned. Private enterprise, on the other hand, has assumed an owner of the instruments of production with complete property rights over those instruments. Whereas the organization of feudal economic life rested upon an elaborate system of binding customs, the organization under the system of private enterprise has rested upon the self-interest of the property owner—a self-interest held in check only by competition and the conditions of supply and demand. Such self-interest has long been regarded as the best guarantee of economic efficiency. It has been assumed that, if the individual is protected in the right both to use his own property as he sees fit and to receive the full fruits of its use, his desire for personal gain, for profits, can be relied upon as an effective incentive to his efficient use of any industrial property he may possess."

"In the quasi-public corporation, such an assumption no longer holds. . . . it is no longer the individual himself who uses his wealth. Those in control of that wealth, and therefore in a position to secure industrial efficiency and produce profits, are no longer, as owners, entitled to the bulk of such profits. Those who control the destinies of the typical modern corporation own so insignificant a fraction of the company's stock that the returns from running the corporation profitably accrue to them in only a very minor degree. The stockholders, on the other hand, to whom the profits of the corporation go, cannot be motivated by those profits to a more efficient use of the property, since they have surrendered all disposition of it to those in control of the enterprise. The explosion of the atom of property destroys the basis of the old assumption that the quest for profits will spur the owner of industrial property to its effective use. It consequently challenges the fundamental economic principle of individual initiative in industrial enterprise." *Id.*, at 8–9.

By like token the separation of the atom of "property" into one unit of "management" and into another of "absentee ownership" has in other ways basically changed the relationship of that "property" to the public.

A corporation may exclude Negroes if "it" thinks "it" can make more money doing so. "It" may go along with community prejudices when the profit and loss statement will benefit; "it" is unlikely to go against the current of community prejudice when profits are endangered.[3]

---

3. The New York Times stated the idea editorially in an analogous situation on October 31, 1963. P. 32:

"When it comes to speaking out on business matters, Roger Blough, chairman of the United States Steel Corporation, does not mince words."

"Mr. Blough is a firm believer in freedom of action for corporate management, a position he made clear in his battle with the Administration last year. But he also has put some severe limits on the exercise of corporate responsibility, for he rejects the suggestion that U.S. Steel, the biggest employer in Birmingham, Ala., should use its economic influence to erase racial tensions. Mr. Blough feels that U.S. Steel has fulfilled its responsibilities by

Veblen stated somewhat the same idea in Absentee Ownership (1923), p. 107:

". . . the arts of business are arts of bargaining, effrontery, salesmanship, make-believe, and are directed to the gain of the business man at the cost of the community, at large and in detail. Neither tangible performance nor the common good is a business proposition. Any material use which his traffic may serve is quite beside the business man's purpose, except indirectly, in so far as it may serve to influence his clientele to his advantage."

By this standard the bus company could refuse service to Negroes if "it" felt "its" profits would increase once *apartheid* were allowed in the transportation field.

In the instant case, G. Carroll Hooper, president of the corporate chain owning the restaurant here involved, testified concerning the episode that gave rise to these convictions. His reasons were wholly commercial ones, as we have already seen.

There are occasions when the corporation is little more than a veil for man and wife or brother and brother; and disregarding the corporate entity often is the instrument for achieving a just result. But the relegation of a Negro customer to second-class citizenship is not just. Nor is fastening *apartheid* on America a worthy occasion for tearing aside the corporate veil.

APPENDIX III TO OPINION OF MR. JUSTICE DOUGLAS.

Corporate[1] Business Establishments Involved In The "Sit-in" Cases Before This Court During The 1962 Term And The 1963 Term. Reference (other than the record in each case): Moody's Industrial Manual (1963 ed.).

---

following a non-discriminatory hiring policy in Birmingham, and looks upon any other measures as both 'repugnant' and 'quite beyond what a corporation should do' to improve conditions."

"This hands-off strategy surely underestimates the potential influence of a corporation as big as U.S. Steel, particularly at the local level. It could, without affecting its profit margins adversely or getting itself directly involved in politics, actively work with those groups in Birmingham trying to better race relations. Steel is not sold on the retail level, so U.S. Steel has not been faced with the economic pressure used against the branches of national chain stores."

"Many corporations have belatedly recognized that it is in their own self-interest to promote an improvement in Negro opportunities. As one of the nation's biggest corporations, U.S. Steel and its shareholders have as great a stake in eliminating the economic imbalances associated with racial discrimination as any company. Corporate responsibility is not easy to define or to measure, but in refusing to take a stand in Birmingham, Mr. Blough appears to have a rather narrow, limited concept of his influence."

1. The only "sit-in" cases not involving a corporation are *Barr v. City of Columbia*, ante, p. 146, and *Daniels v. Virginia*, 374 U.S. 500. In *Barr*, the business establishment was the Taylor Street Pharmacy, which apparently is a partnership; in *Daniels*, it was the 403 Restaurant in Alexandria, Virginia, an individual proprietorship. [The names of the cases and corporations have been deleted — eds.]

Questions

1. Justice Douglas's opinion in *Bell v. Maryland* brings our discussion of changing definitions of the nature and purpose of corporate entities to bear upon the corporation's social and cultural duties. What vision of the corporation does Douglas endorse? Why?

2. Should corporations, unlike individuals, be subject to social duties we impose on sovereign states? Should corporations be subject to constitutional limitations simply because they are corporations? Should private entities be required to fulfill certain tasks typically reserved for the sovereign state? Consider these questions as you read the following two cases, both involving the impact of General Motors on communities in Michigan.

Poletown Neighborhood Council v. City of Detroit
304 N.W.2d 455 (Mich. 1981)

PER CURIAM

This case arises out of a plan by the Detroit Economic Development Corporation to acquire, by condemnation if necessary, a large tract of land to be conveyed to General Motors Corporation as a site for construction of an assembly plant. The plaintiffs, a neighborhood association and several individual residents of the affected area, brought suit. . . .

I

. . .

Plaintiffs-appellants do not challenge the declaration of the legislature that programs to alleviate and prevent conditions of unemployment and to preserve and develop industry and commerce are essential public purposes. Nor do they challenge the proposition that legislation to accomplish this purpose falls within the Constitutional grant of general legislative power to the legislature. . . .

What plaintiffs-appellants do challenge is the constitutionality of using the power of eminent domain to condemn one person's property to convey it to another private person in order to bolster the economy. They argue that whatever incidental benefit may accrue to the public, assembling land to General Motors' specifications for conveyance to General Motors for its uncontrolled use in profit making is really a taking for private use and not a public use because General Motors is the primary beneficiary of the condemnation.

The defendants-appellees contend, on the other hand, that the controlling public purpose in taking this land is to create an industrial site which will be used to alleviate and prevent conditions of unemployment and fiscal distress. The fact that it will be conveyed to and ultimately used by a private manufacturer does not defeat this predominant public purpose.

There is no dispute about the law. All agree that condemnation for a public use or purpose is permitted. All agree that condemnation for a private use or purpose is forbidden. Similarly, condemnation for a private use cannot be authorized whatever its incidental public benefit and condemnation for a public purpose cannot be forbidden whatever the incidental private gain. The heart of this dispute is whether the proposed condemnation is for the primary benefit of the public or the private user.

The Legislature has determined that governmental action of the type contemplated here meets a public need and serves an essential public purpose. The Court's role after such a determination is made is limited. . . .

In the court below, the plaintiffs-appellants challenged the necessity for the taking of the land for the proposed project. In this regard the city presented substantial evidence of the severe economic conditions facing the residents of the city and state, the need for new industrial development to revitalize local industries, the economic boost the proposed project would provide, and the lack of other adequate available sites to implement the project. . . .

In the instant case the benefit to be received by the municipality invoking the power of eminent domain is a clear and significant one and is sufficient to satisfy this Court that such a project was an intended and a legitimate object of the Legislature when it allowed municipalities to exercise condemnation powers even though a private party will also, ultimately, receive a benefit as an incident thereto.

The power of eminent domain is to be used in this instance primarily to accomplish the essential public purposes of alleviating unemployment and revitalizing the economic base of the community. The benefit to a private interest is merely incidental.

Our determination that this project falls within the public purpose, as stated by the Legislature, does not mean that every condemnation proposed by an economic development corporation will meet with similar acceptance simply because it may provide some jobs or add to the industrial or commercial base. If the public benefit was not so clear and significant, we would hesitate to sanction approval of such a project. The power of eminent domain is restricted to furthering public uses and purposes and is not to be exercised without substantial proof that the public is primarily to be benefited. Where, as here, the condemnation power is exercised in a way that benefits specific and identifiable private interests, a court inspects with heightened scrutiny the claim that the public interest is the predominant interest being advanced. Such public benefit cannot be speculative or marginal but must be clear and significant if it is to be within the legitimate purpose as stated by the Legislature. We hold this project is warranted on the basis that its significance for the people of Detroit and the state has been demonstrated. . . .

Questions

In 2004, the Supreme Court of Michigan's decision in *County of Wayne v. Hathcock* overruled *Poletown Neighborhood Council v. City of Detroit*. Wayne County sought to use the power of eminent domain to condemn nineteen parcels of land immediately south of Metropolitan Airport for the construction of a 1,300-acre business and technology park. The park was "intended to reinvigorate the struggling economy of southeastern Michigan by attracting businesses, particularly those involved in developing new technologies, to the area." Citing the dissenting opinion in *Poletown*, the Court concluded that a transfer of condemned property to private entity will be considered for "public use" when it possesses one of the following three characteristics: (1) where "public necessity of the extreme sort" requires collective action (for example, when the condemned property is required for the construction of "highways, railroads, canals, and other instrumentalities of commerce"); (2) where the property remains subject to public oversight after transfer to a private entity; and (3) where the property is selected because of "facts of independent public significance," rather than the interests of the private entity to which the property is eventually transferred (for example, a condemnation and resale of blighted housing).

In 2005, however, in *Kelo v. New London*, the United States Supreme Court upheld a condemnation of private homes for commercial development in New London, Connecticut. The city projected that the development plan would "create in excess of 1,000 jobs, . . . increase tax and other revenues, and . . . revitalize an economically distressed city, including its downtown and waterfront areas."

Do these different opinions about the meaning of "public use" endorse a particular vision of the role of corporations in society? Should they affect the demands we make on corporations? Does the factual background of each case (at the time of the facts in *Poletown*, unemployment in the City of Detroit was 18%, almost 30% among African Americans) affect your view of the role of the corporation or the correctness of the legal decisions in these cases? Consider these questions as you read the next case.

Charter Township of Ypsilanti v. General Motors Corporation
506 N.W.2d 556 (Mich. Ct. App. 1993)

Per Curiam

Defendant appeals from a February 9, 1993, order of the Washtenaw Circuit Court that enjoins defendant "from transferring the production of its Caprice sedan, and Buick and Cadillac [sic, Chevrolet] station wagons, from the Willow Run plant to any other facility." We reverse.

Defendant has operated two plants in Ypsilanti for a number of years. The Hydra-Matic plant employs approximately 9,000 workers and the Willow Run plant employs more than 4,000. In 1975, the township created an industrial development district for the Hydra-Matic plant. It did the same for Willow Run in 1977. Over the years the township granted defendant eleven tax abatements, eight at Hydra-Matic and three at Willow Run. That statute authorizes municipalities to establish plant rehabilitation and industrial development districts to encourage the creation and maintenance of jobs in the state. The act provides for tax exemptions for businesses that meet the requirements of the act. Two of the Willow Run abatements, for 1984 and 1988, are at issue in this case. On July 17, 1984, the township approved defendant's application for a twelve-year fifty percent abatement of personal property taxes on the corporation's $175 million investment for the introduction of a new car. The State Tax Commission later granted the exemption certificate. In April 1988, defendant announced that it would produce a new rear-wheel-drive vehicle, the Chevrolet Caprice, at Willow Run. Six months later, on October 7, 1988, defendant applied for a tax abatement for that project. The application was also for a twelve-year fifty percent abatement of personal property taxes on defendant's planned $75 million project. Following public hearings, the township approved that application, and the state tax commission issued an exemption certificate.

On December 18, 1991, defendant announced that it had decided to consolidate the work being done at Willow Run and Arlington, Texas, at Arlington. Defendant claims that the consolidation was necessary because of the company's record losses and because its Caprice sales, projected at 330,000 a year, had been running at about 275,000 a year and had slipped below 100,000 by late 1991.

The township commenced this action on April 29, 1992. The county joined voluntarily, while the state joined as an amicus curiae, but the trial court added the state as a party-plaintiff. The complaint alleged counts of breach of a contract created by the tax abatement statute, breach of a contract created by conduct, promissory estoppel, unjust enrichment, and misrepresentation.[1] Following a lengthy trial, the trial court found that the abatement statute and application did not create a contract between the township and the corporation. However, it did find that defendant was bound by promissory estoppel to retain production of the Caprice line in Willow Run, as long as the company produces that model. It concluded:

> There would be a gross inequity and patent unfairness if General Motors, having lulled the people of the Ypsilanti area into giving up millions of tax dollars which they so desperately need to educate their children and provide basic governmental services, is allowed to simply decide it will desert 4500 workers and their families because it thinks it can make these same cars cheaper somewhere else.

The trial court, relying on the background of defendant's negotiations for abatements and principally on a statement by Willow Run plant manager Harvey Williams at a public hearing, found that a promise had been made. Williams stated that "[u]pon completion of this project and favorable market demand, it will allow

---

1. The circuit court did not separately discuss the misrepresentation claim but incorporated it into its holding regarding promissory estoppel. A count for environmental nuisance was voluntarily dismissed without prejudice before trial. The unjust enrichment count was not discussed or decided by the trial court. The township considers that claim to be viable and preserved. We express no opinion concerning the claim or its viability, because neither point was decided below.

Willow Run to continue production and maintain continuous employment for our employees." The trial court ruled:

> In the context of this background, when the plant manager, in the prepared statement on behalf of General Motors stated that, subject to "favorable market demand," General Motors would "continue production and maintain continuous employment" at the Willow Run plant, *it was a promise*. The promise was clearly that if the Township granted the abatement, General Motors would make the Caprice at Willow Run and not just transfer that work somewhere else. [Emphasis added.]

A trial court's findings of fact in an equity action are reviewable under the clearly erroneous standard. A finding is clearly erroneous if the appellate court is left with a definite and firm conviction that a mistake has been made.

The elements of promissory estoppel are:

> A promise which the promisor should reasonably expect to induce action or forbearance on the part of the promisee or a third person and which does induce such action or forbearance is binding if injustice can be avoided only by enforcement of the promise. The remedy granted for breach may be limited as justice requires.

Promissory estoppel requires an actual, clear, and definite promise. Further, "reliance is reasonable only if it is induced by an actual promise." A determination that there was a promise will be overturned if it is clearly erroneous.[2]

The trial court's finding that defendant promised to keep Caprice and station wagon production at Willow Run is clearly erroneous. First, the mere fact that a corporation solicits a tax abatement and persuades a municipality with assurances of jobs cannot be evidence of a promise. The very purpose of tax abatement legislation is to induce companies to locate and to continue business enterprises in the municipality. Even the trial court recognized this when it stated, "Every time, the inducement to the township was the same—jobs will be created or preserved at that plant, and it should have been, for that was the ostensible purpose of the abatement."

Second, representations of job creation and retention are a statutory prerequisite. An applicant for an industrial facilities exemption certificate must, among other things, certify that "[c]ompletion of the facility is calculated to, and will *at the time of issuance of the certificate* have the reasonable likelihood to create employment, retain employment, prevent a loss of employment, or produce energy in the community in which the facility is situated." [Emphasis added.]

---

2. Plaintiffs' reliance on *Curry* is misplaced. It merely dealt with a situation in which there was a clear promise upon which the plaintiff detrimentally relied. *Curry*, rather than compelling a conclusion in plaintiffs' favor, points to why the doctrine does not apply to this case: the promise necessary to invoke the doctrine is distinguished from a statement of opinion or mere prediction of future events.

Third, the fact that a manufacturer uses hyperbole and puffery in seeking an advantage or concession does not necessarily create a promise. For example, statements such as "We're partners" and "We look forward to growing together" were found not to constitute a promise to keep a collective bargaining agreement in force for the foreseeable future so as to create by promissory estoppel a continuing duty of the employer to honor an expired agreement. Nor did exhortations for union concessions in order to keep a foundry open constitute promises under promissory estoppel to prevent a foundry from closing. Similarly, exhortations to its employees to increase productivity and assurances that a plant would not be closed, as long as it was profitable, did not establish by promissory estoppel an obligation on a steel company to keep open a plant.

Turning to the case at bar, almost all the statements the trial court cited as foundations for a promise were, instead, expressions of defendant's hopes or expectations of continued employment at Willow Run. The court summarized the corporation's concerted efforts to obtain abatements for Hydra-Matic between 1974 and 1981 as follows:

> Over the years, General Motors followed the example set in its first application and a course of conduct developed between General Motors and the township for the granting of tax abatements. Each time General Motors wanted an abatement to make a physical change in the plants, it would invite township officials to the plant for a briefing, a tour of the plant, and lunch. Then the formal application would be submitted and General Motors officials would appear at a public hearing before the entire Board, which would then approve the application. Each time, the Board was advised, in some specifics, of the impact of the improvements, and presumably the abatement, on production and employment levels in the plant.

The acts cited by the trial court were acts one would naturally expect a company to do in order to introduce and promote an abatement proposal to a municipality. The acts did not amount to a promise and, as course-of-conduct evidence, showed only efforts to take advantage of a statutory opportunity. They did not constitute assurances of continued employment. In any event, we note that the activity referred to by the trial court related to Hydra-Matic, not Willow Run.

The court cited the State Tax Commission's resolution regarding the 1984 Willow Run abatement in which the commission's approval "was based on its concern for economic development in Washtenaw County which results in increased job opportunities for unemployed and underemployed residents of our county." However, that was the commission's expectation, not defendant's promise.

In defendant's 1988 presentation, Russell Hughes, the Willow Run comptroller, recited background, including: "Since the '81, '82 time-frame you can see that we've been basically maintaining about five thousand employees each year in a very consistent pattern." However, Hughes made the statement by way of history, and not as an assurance of future employment.

The circuit court also cited plant manager Harvey Williams' prepared statement:

> General Motors selected Willow Run to build these new vehicles because of our reputation for high quality, our continued harmonious relationship and our spirit of all employees working together.
>
> ... We are asking the Board to accept our application and pass on it favorably. To join the corporation in the kind of relationship we have in the Township in assuring future investments in our plant.

However, that language is nearly identical to the puffery the federal court found not to constitute a promise in *Marine Transport Lines, Inc., supra*.

The trial court referred to the township assessor's remarks:

> Needless to say I recommend approval of the petition. Based on the past history in dealing with the people at General Motors, they've always done what they said they would do and they've kept the jobs there and they kept the plant operating as an operational facility.

Again, however, that was the assessor's evaluation, not defendant's promise.

The court quoted the State Tax Commission's resolution, which stated in part, "Where the facts indicate that positive results in gains in employment and taxes appear justified ... we will support all the local unit decisions." Once again, that was the commission's assessment, not defendant's promise of continuing employment.

Defendant's statement that the lower court principally relied on to find a promise was not sufficient to constitute a promise. Plant manager Williams stated:

> Good evening, my name is Harvey Williams and I am the plant manager of the Buick Oldsmobile Cadillac groups [sic] Willow Run plant.
>
> We are pleased to have this opportunity to appear before the Ypsilanti Township Board of Trustees. This application for an industrial facilities exemption certificate is for an investment totalling $75,000,000.00 for machinery and equipment. This will enable our plant to assemble a new full size car in the 1991 model year.
>
> This new rear wheel drive car is substantially larger then [sic] our current model. And specifically it will generate major booth, oven and conveyor changes in the paint shop and assembly line process, changes in the body, trim and chassis department. This change will also provide additional flexibility at our assembly plant. Essentially we would now have the capability to produce either front or rear wheel drive cars with minimum modifications to our facility. *Upon completion of this project and favorable market demand, it will allow Willow Run to continue production and maintain continuous employment for our employees.* ... [Emphasis added.]

Although the parties greatly dispute what the speaker meant by "favorable market demand" and even whether defendant should have been allowed to narrow it to Willow Run production, the fact is that the statement qualified defendant's expectation that the new abatement would allow it to continue production at the plant and maintain continuous employment for the employees. Again, even that statement was nothing more than the kind of hyperbole a corporation would use to obtain the tax abatement benefits afforded by the statute and willingly offered by the township. The trial court clearly erred in concluding that Williams' statement, and particularly the portion emphasized in the foregoing quotation, constituted a promise of continued Caprice and station wagon production at Willow Run as long as the company produces those vehicles.

Even if the finding of a promise could be sustained, reliance on the promise would not have been reasonable. "[T]he reliance interest protected by [Restatement] § 90 is reasonable reliance."

It has never been held that an abatement carries a promise of continued employment. Indeed, the history of this case shows that persons involved in the 1988 Willow Run abatement understood that defendant was not promising continued employment.

At a township board meeting in November 1988, Dillard Craiger, chairman of the Washtenaw County Board of Commissioners, opposed a tax break for Willow Run "unless a commitment was made by General Motors to remain operating at the present facility in Ypsilanti Township for that period of time thereby securing employment for the community." Craiger also complained that defendant had not given any commitments whatsoever. Outgoing Township Supervisor Ron Allen nevertheless endorsed defendant's request for tax relief, noting that "General Motors has never been overbearing or threatening" and cautioning "the Board not to take any action that would unravel the success that the Township has had [in dealing with General Motors] over the last several years." At a subsequent work session held on December 5, 1988, at least five of the seven board members—including new Township Supervisor Wesley Prater and Township Treasurer Ruth Ann Jamnick—decided to support the application.

At the public hearing at which plant manager Harvey Williams supposedly promised "continuous employment for our employees," plant comptroller Russell Hughes almost immediately warned that "[o]ne percent [market share] penetration that we lose at General Motors means ten thousand jobs for this corporation of our employees. In the assembly plant operation one percent means about twenty five hundred jobs throughout the US and all assembly plants."

Other speakers then took the floor, several of whom specifically pointed out that defendant had not committed itself to continue operating the Willow Run plant for any particular period of time. Washtenaw County Commission Chairman Craiger, after listening to plant manager Williams' presentation, restated in detail his admonition from the previous month:

> The plant has not given us any commitments in any way that they will not "outsource" production, they will not tell you how long they are going to

stay, they will not tell you that we only want it as long as we stay. Who knows, they might move tomorrow or two years from now and they will have been given three tax breaks with a hidden plan.

. . .

If Georgia or Alabama gives them a hundred percent [tax abatement], don't we have a right to bid on it? Don't we have that right, or should they just say, we're closing the plant because we got a better deal. . . . I would like to be able for them to tell us how long are they going to stay.

Others echoed this concern. A Mr. Smith referred to increases in his own property taxes and added: "I have eighteen years in and I'd like to see them stay here twelve years so I can retire, but they are not promising anything." Township Supervisor Prater, who chaired the meeting, then interjected a "point of clarification," explaining to Smith that "the abatement they are asking for is not on real estate tax, it's personal property tax." But Prater did not take issue with Smith's statement that no "promise" had been made, and Smith replied that "there should be some kind of proof by them that they are not going to . . . move out." Prater made no response. Other witnesses agreed with Smith that defendant had made no commitment to continue operations at Willow Run. Mr. Debs, president of the local union at the Willow Run plant, pointed out that "nobody can tell us what the sales are going to be" and that "no plant can stay open" if sales drop. A Mr. Alford remarked that "there were some legal issues there that cannot bind [Willow Run] or Hydra-Matic to giving jobs to Ypsilanti Township."

Defendant's representatives were not asked to respond to these comments, and no member of the township board took issue with them. Instead, Supervisor Prater urged the board to approve defendant's application. The township board then voted unanimously to approve a twelve-year abatement at Willow Run; the resolution contained no suggestion that approval was conditioned on a commitment to operate the plant for any particular period.

In short, defendant made no promises.

Reversed.

Questions

1. What are the social responsibilities of a corporation? To make a profit for the shareholders? To produce high quality and innovative goods and services? To provide meaningful jobs at good wages? To help build and support communities? What are the public policy implications of limiting the corporation's responsibility to its shareholders' wealth? What are the public policy implications of demanding greater responsibility to others? And what are the business and economic implications of each?

2. In 1983, the Pennsylvania legislature, in clear response to an attempt by Canadian business interests to acquire a major corporation operating within the state in a hostile takeover, passed the first of what has come to be known as "constituency"

statutes or "stakeholder" statutes. These statutes allow corporate directors to consider the interests of constituencies other than the shareholders when making business decisions. Other states soon followed, and constituency statutes now appear on the books of a majority of the states. Some of these apply only in a takeover context but others are drafted to apply more broadly. Only one (Ohio's) makes consideration of non-stockholder interests mandatory. Virtually all of these statutes either provide that they create no rights in these "other constituencies" or are silent as to whether such rights are created. In any event, none of the statutes provides a remedy for stakeholders if the board does not consider their interests. In light of these limitations (and mindful of the maxim that where there is a right, there is a remedy), what do you think the purpose of these statutes is?

3. In recent decades, there has been a significant increase in the amount of litigation attempting to hold corporations accountable for human rights violations (especially to hold parent companies liable for human rights violations committed by their overseas subsidiaries). In the 1980s, U.S. courts began using the Alien Tort Statute, a little-known provision of the Judiciary Act of 1789, to allow foreigners to bring suit for human rights violations committed abroad. In *Doe v. Unocal* 395 F.3d 932 (2002), Burmese villagers brought an action against Unocal for its complicity in human rights atrocities (including rape, torture, forced labor, and murder) that the Burmese government and military committed during the construction of the Yadana pipeline in Burma (now Myanmar). A three-judge panel for the Ninth Circuit held that Unocal might be found to have aided and abetted the Burmese government and military. According to the majority, evidence that Unocal provided practical assistance to the military in subjecting the villagers to forced labor and that it knew that forced labor was being used was sufficient to establish *actus reus* and *mens rea*, respectively. In a concurring opinion, Judge Reinhardt went further, suggesting that Unocal could be held liable either under the joint venture liability doctrine (imposing liability on any member of a joint venture for torts of its co-venturers) or under the agency liability doctrine (viewing the military as Unocal's agent). The Ninth Circuit decision was later vacated and an order for en banc rehearing issued. The case settled before the rehearing.

Recall the theories of corporations you have studied at the beginning of this Part. Which theory would be most helpful for an argument in favor of imposing liability on corporations under the Alien Tort Statute? Why? Can you think of additional, non-legal, means of constraining corporations abroad?

4. Many American corporations have moved their operations to other countries to reduce costs and increase profits. In most situations, these moves do not involve actionable human rights violations, but they might result in the exploitation of workers or the destruction of the environment in the countries in which they operate. Should we require U.S. corporations to abide by American labor and environmental standards even when they operate overseas? If not, why not?

5. After *Unocal*, several cases addressed the applicability of the Alien Tort Statute to foreign corporations. In *Kiobel v. Royal Dutch Petroleum Co.* 569 U.S. 108 (2013), Nigerian nationals residing in the United States filed suit under the Alien Tort Statute, alleging that Dutch, British, and Nigerian corporations "aided and abetted the Nigerian Government in committing violations of the law of nations in Nigeria." The Second Circuit Court of Appeals held that "the law of nations does not recognize corporate liability." Because the Alien Tort Statute provides jurisdiction only for violations of the law of nations, the court dismissed the suit. The U.S. Supreme Court granted certiorari and affirmed the Second Circuit's decision but did not resolve the question of corporate liability, holding only that the Alien Tort Statute does not extend to suits against foreign corporations when "all the relevant conduct took place outside the United States."

Five years later in *Jesner v. Arab Bank, PLC* (2018) the Supreme Court endorsed the Second Circuit approach in *Kiobel*, holding that "foreign corporations may not be defendants in suits brought under the Alien Tort Statute." (The case involved allegations by victims of terrorist attacks committed abroad against Arab Bank, PLC, a Jordanian financial institution with a branch in New York.)

Section III
Ownership and Control

The separation of ownership from control has been, perhaps, the most salient (if often inaccurate) characteristic of the modern publicly-held corporation. In the classical model of market relations, individuals owned and controlled the means of production, and competition between individual entrepreneurs was presumed to result in efficient distribution of market resources. Self-interest ensured economic efficiency. The separation of ownership from control in large public corporations challenged this assumption. Presumably without ownership interest, corporate managers had no incentive to increase the corporation's value, while the stockholders had no control over the affairs of the corporation. Beginning at the turn of the twentieth century, jurists turned to the separation of ownership from control to justify imposing fiduciary obligations on corporate management.

We will examine directors' and officers' fiduciary obligations in Part 2 of this casebook. In this Section III, we explore two unique characteristics of the modern corporation that are associated with the separation of ownership from control—limited liability for the corporation's presumed owners and centralized management under board structure. We begin with a brief discussion of the differences between corporations and other business forms.

A. The Corporation and Other Business Forms

There are four major business forms: sole proprietorships, partnerships, corporations, and, more recently, limited liability companies. Choosing a form means choosing a particular set of legal rules that apply to it. These rules address six different features: formation, owners' liability, transferability of ownership interest, continuity of existence, management, and taxation.

A *sole proprietorship* is the simplest form of business. The individual who decides to go into business owns the assets of the business and owes its liabilities in her individual capacity. The owner can hire others either to represent the business or work for the business, although the owner can also be the business's only employee and agent. There are no formal requirements to form or operate a sole proprietorship, although some businesses, like a retail liquor store, might need a special license to operate, and all businesses can operate only in those locations where zoning laws permit. The business's profits and losses belong to the owner and must be reported on the owner's individual tax return.

A *partnership*, or *general partnership* is defined as "an association of two or more persons to carry on as co-owners a business for profit" (Uniform Partnership Act section 6(1) (1914), Revised Uniform Partnership Act, section 101(6) (1996)). As co-owner, each partner has the right to participate in managing the partnership, and each can bind the partnership to obligations owed to third parties. All partners are also personally responsible for the obligations of the partnership. They are jointly liable for the partnership's contractual obligations and jointly and severally liable for its torts.

It should be obvious that because each partner has so much power and can expose the assets of others to risk, interests in a partnership are transferable only with the unanimous consent of the partners. (A partner can transfer her economic interest, but must retain her legal obligations.) Changes without unanimous consent result in the dissolution of the partnership. Each partner can cause dissolution by deciding to withdraw her interest. Death and bankruptcy of a partner will also bring about the dissolution of the partnership. Dissolution entails the death of the business, unless the partnership agreement allows for its continuation.

There are no formal requirements to create a partnership and, in fact, virtually all of the rules noted above can be altered by agreement. Even in the absence of a written agreement, individuals running a business together might be characterized as partners, and the rules applicable to partnerships in the particular jurisdiction will apply. It is thus highly advisable for individuals seeking to run a business together to hire a lawyer to write an agreement specifying their rights and obligations during the partnership's existence and in dissolution.

Finally, because the partnership is not a separate entity, it is not subject to taxation. Profits and losses from the partnership's operations flow through to the partners and are reported on their individual tax returns. The partnership only files an informational return showing how much tax the individual partners must pay on the partnership's income.

A *corporation* is considered a separate legal entity distinct from its owners. As a separate entity, the corporation owns its own assets and incurs its own liabilities. Unless a court chooses to ignore the existence of the corporation to treat it like a proprietorship or partnership (we will discuss these cases), the shareholders' liability is limited. Even if the corporation cannot pay its debts, the shareholders will only lose their investment. A creditor cannot reach the shareholders' pockets.

Corporations have centralized management. Under most state corporation laws, stockholders elect directors who select officers. The officers run the corporation, and the directors monitor their performance. In addition to electing directors, shareholders have statutory rights to vote to approve charter amendments and certain fundamental transactions such as merger. When asked by the management, they also vote to ratify transactions that are tainted with conflicts of interest. Beyond these statutory rights to approve or ratify transactions, shareholders do not participate in managing the affairs of the corporation (although as we will see, courts have allowed more flexibility in closely held corporations, where shareholders are often also officers and directors).

Shareholders can freely transfer their interests in the corporation (but, as we will see, shareholders in closely held corporations often limit the free transferability of shares by agreement or in provisions placed in the charter or by-laws). The transfer of ownership interests, or the death or bankruptcy of a shareholder, does not dissolve the corporation. Under most state corporation laws, in rare situations, a shareholder may sue to dissolve the corporation. But even in those situations where it is allowed, courts have fashioned remedies that would avoid dissolving the corporation. For all practical purposes, the corporation is in perpetual existence.

To form a corporation, the incorporators must file articles of incorporation with the secretary of state. The articles of incorporation, which are sometimes called the certificate of incorporation or charter, include information about the corporation, such as the corporate name, the number of authorized shares, and the name and address of each incorporator. The articles of incorporation might also include provisions about the allocation of power between directors, officers, and shareholders, or the power and purpose of the corporation. In addition to the articles of incorporation, a corporation will have bylaws, which set forth the details of the corporation's governance structure. The articles of incorporation cannot conflict with the corporation statute under which the corporation is organized, and the bylaws cannot conflict with either the statute or the articles.

As a separate entity, the corporation is taxed on its profits and can use losses from its business to offset them. When the profits are distributed to the shareholders as dividends, they are also taxed as income to the shareholders. This phenomenon is known as "double taxation." In 2003, Congress lowered the tax rate paid by shareholders for dividends received to a maximum of 15%, thus lessening the impact of double taxation.

A corporation that meets the requirements of Subchapter S of the Tax Code can elect to have the corporation's income taxed to the individual shareholders rather than the corporation, whether or not dividends were distributed.

As this short comparison between partnerships and corporations indicates, one of the most important features of the corporation is its limited liability, while one of the most important features of the partnership is its avoidance of double taxation. It thus should not surprise you that businessmen, their lawyers, and legislatures developed hybrid forms of business to allow investors to enjoy the significant features of both the corporation and the partnership.

For example, *limited partnerships* are partnerships in which one or more of the owners (called limited partners) has limited liability. The limited partnership must have at least one partner with unlimited liability (the general partner can be a corporation) who conducts the partnership. The limited partners cannot participate in managing the partnership affairs. Moreover, unlike shareholders, whose liability remains limited even when they participate in managing the affairs of the corporation, a limited partner who participates in the partnership's management might lose her limited liability.

A limited partnership survives the death, bankruptcy, or withdrawal of a limited partner, but dissolves with the withdrawal of a general partner. Most limited partnership agreements also provide that a limited partner can freely transfer her economic and governance interest. In the absence of such agreement, a limited partner can only transfer her economic interest.

A limited partnership is formed by filing of a certificate with the state. The certificate specifies the rights and duties of the partners and identifies the general partner.

Many states have recently adopted statutes allowing the creation of *limited liability partnerships* and *limited liability limited partnerships*. These are general and limited partnerships, respectively, in which the general partner can limit her liability to the amount of her investment. Despite such limitations, in both, the limited liability partnership and the limited liability limited partnership, the general partner will be liable for negligent acts committed by her or an employee under her supervision.

Both the limited liability partnership and the limited liability limited partnership are formed by filing a certificate with the state.

A *limited liability company* is also a relatively new form of business. It combines the benefits of the corporation and the partnership in one business form. The limited liability company's owners (called members) enjoy limited liability, and under most states' laws, the company can elect to use other characteristics of the corporation without incurring the burden of double taxation.

To form a limited liability company, the members must file articles of organization with the state. The articles include the name of the limited liability company and the address of its registered agent. Members also execute an operating agreement which establishes their rights and obligations. Under most state statutes, the operating agreement can override provisions in the articles of organization, although under some statutes, it cannot.

Limited liability companies are either member-managed (like partnerships) or manager-managed (like corporations). Under most state statutes, they can elect to have perpetual existence. Many statutes also allow for free transferability of interests in limited liability companies but, given variations among jurisdictions, it is advisable to include a provision governing the transferability of interests in the operating agreement.

B. Limited Liability and Its Limits

As the description of different business forms suggests, one of the most important characteristics of the corporation is its owners' limited liability. A common argument is that limited liability is a necessary characteristic of modern business. But there is evidence to suggest that the introduction of limited liability did not increase the number of incorporations. The cases below examine situations where the court disregards the corporate entity and imposes liability on the shareholders. As you read the cases, think about potential justifications for limited liability. Think also about the connections between any given liability regime and the different visions of the corporation (artificial entity, contractual vision, and natural/real entity) discussed in the previous Sections.

Walkovszky v. Carlton
18 N.Y.2d 414 (1966)

FULD, Judge

This case involves what appears to be a rather common practice in the taxicab industry of vesting the ownership of a taxi fleet in many corporations, each owning only one or two cabs.

The complaint alleges that the plaintiff was severely injured four years ago in New York City when he was run down by a taxicab owned by the defendant Seon Cab Corporation and negligently operated at the time by the defendant Marchese. The individual defendant, Carlton, is claimed to be a stockholder of 10 corporations, including Seon, each of which has but two cabs registered in its name, and it is implied that only the minimum automobile liability insurance required by law (in the amount of $10,000) is carried on any one cab. Although seemingly independent of one another, these corporations are alleged to be "operated . . . as a single entity, unit and enterprise" with regard to financing, supplies, repairs, employees and garaging, and all are named as defendants. The plaintiff asserts that he is also entitled to hold their stockholders personally liable for the damages sought because the multiple corporate structure constitutes an unlawful attempt "to defraud members of the general public" who might be injured by the cabs.

The defendant Carlton has moved, pursuant to CPLR 3211(a)7, to dismiss the complaint on the ground that as to him it "fails to state a cause of action." The court at Special Term granted the motion but the Appellate Division, by a divided vote, reversed, holding that a valid cause of action was sufficiently stated. The defendant Carlton appeals to us, from the nonfinal order, by leave of the Appellate Division on a certified question.

The law permits the incorporation of a business for the very purpose of enabling its proprietors to escape personal liability but, manifestly, the privilege is not without its limits. Broadly speaking, the courts will disregard the corporate form, or, to use accepted terminology, "pierce the corporate veil," whenever necessary "to prevent fraud or to achieve equity." In determining whether liability should be extended to reach assets beyond those belonging to the corporation, we are guided, as Judge Cardozo noted, by "general rules of agency." In other words, whenever anyone uses control of the corporation to further his own rather than the corporation's business, he will be liable for the corporation's acts "upon the principle of *respondeat superior* applicable even where the agent is a natural person." Such liability, moreover, extends not only to the corporation's commercial dealings but to its negligent acts as well.

In [*Mangan v. Terminal Transportation System*, 247 App. Div. 853 (1936)], the plaintiff was injured as a result of the negligent operation of a cab owned and operated by one of four corporations affiliated with the defendant Terminal. Although the defendant was not a stockholder of any of the operating companies, both the defendant and the operating companies were owned, for the most part, by the same parties. The defendant's name (Terminal) was conspicuously displayed on the sides of all of the taxis used in the enterprise and, in point of fact, the defendant actually serviced, inspected, repaired and dispatched them. These facts were deemed to provide sufficient cause for piercing the corporate veil of the operating company—the nominal owner of the cab which injured the plaintiff—and holding the defendant liable. The operating companies were simply instrumentalities for carrying on the business of the defendant without imposing upon it financial and other liabilities incident to the actual ownership and operation of the cabs.

In the case before us, the plaintiff has explicitly alleged that none of the corporations "had a separate existence of their own" and, as indicated above, all are named as defendants. However, it is one thing to assert that a corporation is a fragment of a larger corporate combine which actually conducts the business. It is quite another to claim that the corporation is a "dummy" for its individual stockholders who are in reality carrying on the business in their personal capacities for purely personal rather than corporate ends. Either circumstance would justify treating the corporation as an agent and piercing the corporate veil to reach the principal but a different result would follow in each case. In the first, only a larger *corporate* entity would be held financially responsible while, in the other, the stockholder would be personally liable. Either the stockholder is conducting the business in his individual capacity or he is not. If he is, he will be liable; if he is not, then, it does not matter—insofar as his personal liability is concerned—that the enterprise is actually being carried on by a larger "enterprise entity."

At this stage in the present litigation, we are concerned only with the pleadings and, since CPLR 3014 permits causes of action to be stated "alternatively or hypothetically," it is possible for the plaintiff to allege both theories as the basis for his demand for judgment. In ascertaining whether he has done so, we must consider the entire pleading, educing therefrom "'whatever can be implied from its statements by fair and reasonable intendment.'" Reading the complaint in this case most favorably and liberally, we do not believe that there can be gathered from its averments the allegations required to spell out a valid cause of action against the defendant Carlton.

The individual defendant is charged with having "organized, managed, dominated and controlled" a fragmented corporate entity but there are no allegations that he was conducting business in his individual capacity. Had the taxicab fleet been owned by a single corporation, it would be readily apparent that the plaintiff would face formidable barriers in attempting to establish personal liability on the part of the corporation's stockholders. The fact that the fleet ownership has been deliberately split up among many corporations does not ease the plaintiff's burden in that respect. The corporate form may not be disregarded merely because the assets of the corporation, together with the mandatory insurance coverage of the vehicle which struck the plaintiff, are insufficient to assure him the recovery sought. If Carlton were to be held individually liable on those facts alone, the decision would apply equally to the thousands of cabs which are owned by their individual drivers who conduct their businesses through corporations organized pursuant to section 401 of the Business Corporation Law and carry the minimum insurance required by subdivision 1 (par. [a]) of section 370 of the Vehicle and Traffic Law. These taxi owner-operators are entitled to form such corporations, and we agree with the court at Special Term that, if the insurance coverage required by statute "is inadequate for the protection of the public, the remedy lies not with the courts but with the Legislature." It may very well be sound policy to require that certain corporations must take out liability insurance which will afford adequate compensation to their potential tort victims. However, the responsibility for imposing conditions on the privilege of incorporation has been committed by the Constitution to the Legislature and it may not be fairly implied, from any statute, that the Legislature intended, without the slightest discussion or debate, to require of taxi corporations that they carry automobile liability insurance over and above that mandated by the Vehicle and Traffic Law.

This is not to say that it is impossible for the plaintiff to state a valid cause of action against the defendant Carlton. However, the simple fact is that the plaintiff has just not done so here. While the complaint alleges that the separate corporations were undercapitalized and that their assets have been intermingled, it is barren of any "sufficiently [particularized] statements" that the defendant Carlton and his associates are actually doing business in their individual capacities, shuttling their personal funds in and out of the corporations "without regard to formality and to suit their immediate convenience." Such a "perversion of the privilege to do business in a corporate form" would justify imposing personal liability on the individual stockholders. Nothing of the sort has in fact been charged, and it cannot reasonably or logically be inferred from the happenstance that the business of Seon Cab Corporation may actually be carried on by a larger corporate entity composed of many corporations which, under general principles of agency, would be liable to each other's creditors in contract and in tort.

In point of fact, the principle relied upon in the complaint to sustain the imposition of personal liability is not agency but fraud. Such a cause of action cannot withstand analysis. If it is not fraudulent for the owner-operator of a single cab corporation to take out only the minimum required liability insurance, the enterprise does not become either illicit or fraudulent merely because it consists of many such corporations. The plaintiff's injuries are the same regardless of whether the cab which strikes him is owned by a single corporation or part of a fleet with ownership fragmented among many corporations. Whatever rights he may be able to assert against parties other than the registered owner of the vehicle come into being not because he has been defrauded but because, under the principle of *respondeat superior*, he is entitled to hold the whole enterprise responsible for the acts of its agents.

In sum, then, the complaint falls short of adequately stating a cause of action against the defendant Carlton in his individual capacity.

The order of the Appellate Division should be reversed, with costs in this court and in the Appellate Division, the certified question answered in the negative and the order of the Supreme Court, Richmond County, reinstated, with leave to serve an amended complaint.

KEATING, Judge (dissenting)

The defendant Carlton, the shareholder here sought to be held for the negligence of the driver of a taxicab, was a principal shareholder and organizer of the defendant corporation which owned the taxicab. The corporation was one of 10 organized by the defendant, each containing two cabs and each cab having the "minimum liability" insurance coverage mandated by section 370 of the Vehicle and Traffic Law. The sole assets of these operating corporations are the vehicles themselves and they are apparently subject to mortgages.

From their inception these corporations were intentionally undercapitalized for the purpose of avoiding responsibility for acts which were bound to arise as a result of the operation of a large taxi fleet having cars out on the street 24 hours a day and engaged in public transportation. And during the course of the corporations' existence all income was continually drained out of the corporations for the same purpose.

The issue presented by this action is whether the policy of this State, which affords those desiring to engage in a business enterprise the privilege of limited liability through the use of the corporate device, is so strong that it will permit that privilege to continue no matter how much it is abused, no matter how irresponsibly the corporation is operated, no matter what the cost to the public. I do not believe that it is.

Under the circumstances of this case the shareholders should all be held individually liable to this plaintiff for the injuries he suffered. At least the matter should not be disposed of on the pleadings by a dismissal of the complaint. "If a corporation is organized and carries on business without substantial capital in such a way that the corporation is likely to have no sufficient assets available to meet its debts, it is inequitable that shareholders should set up such a flimsy organization to escape personal liability. The attempt to do corporate business without providing any sufficient basis of financial responsibility to creditors is an abuse of the separate entity and will be ineffectual to exempt the shareholders from corporate debts. It is coming to be recognized as the policy of law that shareholders should in good faith put at the risk of the business unencumbered capital reasonably adequate for its prospective liabilities. If capital is illusory or trifling compared with the business to be done and the risks of loss, this is a ground for denying the separate entity privilege."

In *Minton v. Cavaney,* 56 Cal. 2d 576 (1961), the Supreme Court of California had occasion to discuss this problem in a negligence case. The corporation of which the defendant was an organizer, director and officer operated a public swimming pool. One afternoon the plaintiffs' daughter drowned in the pool as a result of the alleged negligence of the corporation.

Justice Roger Traynor, speaking for the court, outlined the applicable law in this area. "The figurative terminology 'alter ego' and 'disregard of the corporate entity'," he wrote, "is generally used to refer to the various situations that are an abuse of the corporate privilege.... The equitable owners of a corporation, for example, are personally liable when they treat the assets of the corporation as their own and add or withdraw capital from the corporation at will...; when they hold themselves out as being personally liable for the debts of the corporation...; *or when they provide inadequate capitalization and actively participate in the conduct of corporate affairs.*"

Examining the facts of the case in light of the legal principles just enumerated, he found that "[it was] undisputed that there was no attempt to provide adequate capitalization. [The corporation] never had any substantial assets. It leased the pool that it operated, and the lease was forfeited for failure to pay the rent. Its capital was 'trifling compared with the business to be done and the risks of loss'."

It seems obvious that one of "the risks of loss" referred to was the possibility of drowning due to the negligence of the corporation. And the defendant's failure to provide such assets or any fund for recovery resulted in his being held personally liable. . . .

The policy of this State has always been to provide and facilitate recovery for those injured through the negligence of others. The automobile, by its very nature, is capable of causing severe and costly injuries when not operated in a proper manner. The great increase in the number of automobile accidents combined with the frequent financial irresponsibility of the individual driving the car led to the adoption of section 388 of the Vehicle and Traffic Law which had the effect of imposing upon the owner of the vehicle the responsibility for its negligent operation. It is upon this very statute that the cause of action against both the corporation and the individual defendant is predicated.

In addition the Legislature, still concerned with the financial irresponsibility of those who owned and operated motor vehicles, enacted a statute requiring minimum liability coverage for all owners of automobiles. The important public policy represented by both these statutes is outlined in section 310 of the Vehicle and Traffic Law. That section provides that: "The legislature is concerned over the rising toll of motor vehicle accidents and the suffering and loss thereby inflicted. The legislature determines that it is a matter of grave concern that motorists shall be financially able to respond in damages for their negligent acts, so that innocent victims of motor vehicle accidents may be recompensed for the injury and financial loss inflicted upon them."

The defendant Carlton claims that, because the minimum amount of insurance required by the statute was obtained, the corporate veil cannot and should not be pierced despite the fact that the assets of the corporation which owned the cab were "trifling compared with the business to be done and the risks of loss" which were certain to be encountered. I do not agree.

The Legislature in requiring minimum liability insurance of $10,000, no doubt, intended to provide at least some small fund for recovery against those individuals and corporations who just did not have and were not able to raise or accumulate assets sufficient to satisfy the claims of those who were injured as a result of their negligence. It certainly could not have intended to shield those individuals who organized corporations, with the specific intent of avoiding responsibility to the public, where the operation of the corporate enterprise yielded profits sufficient to purchase additional insurance. Moreover, it is reasonable to assume that the Legislature believed that those individuals and corporations having substantial assets would take out insurance far in excess of the minimum in order to protect those assets from depletion. Given the costs of hospital care and treatment and the nature of injuries sustained in auto collisions, it would be unreasonable to assume that the Legislature believed that the minimum provided in the statute would in and of itself be sufficient to recompense "innocent victims of motor vehicle accidents . . . for the injury and financial loss inflicted upon them."

The defendant, however, argues that the failure of the Legislature to increase the minimum insurance requirements indicates legislative acquiescence in this scheme to avoid liability and responsibility to the public. In the absence of a clear legislative statement, approval of a scheme having such serious consequences is not to be so lightly inferred.

The defendant contends that the court will be encroaching upon the legislative domain by ignoring the corporate veil and holding the individual shareholder. This argument was answered by Mr. Justice Douglas in *Anderson v. Abbot* where he wrote that: "In the field in which we are presently concerned, judicial power hardly oversteps the bounds when it refuses to lend its aid to a promotional project which would circumvent or undermine a legislative policy. To deny it that function would be to make it impotent in situations where historically it has made some of its most notable contributions. If the judicial power is helpless to protect a legislative program from schemes for easy avoidance, then indeed it has become a handy implement of high finance. *Judicial interference to cripple or defeat a legislative policy is one thing; judicial interference with the plans of those whose corporate or other devices would circumvent that policy is quite another.* Once the purpose or effect of the scheme is clear, once the legislative policy is plain, we would indeed forsake a great tradition to say we were helpless to fashion the instruments for appropriate relief." (Emphasis added.)

The defendant contends that a decision holding him personally liable would discourage people from engaging in corporate enterprise.

What I would merely hold is that a participating shareholder of a corporation vested with a public interest, organized with capital insufficient to meet liabilities which are certain to arise in the ordinary course of the corporation's business, may be held personally responsible for such liabilities. Where corporate income is not sufficient to cover the cost of insurance premiums above the statutory minimum or where initially adequate finances dwindle under the pressure of competition, bad times or extraordinary and unexpected liability, obviously the shareholder will not be held liable.

The only types of corporate enterprises that will be discouraged as a result of a decision allowing the individual shareholder to be sued will be those such as the one in question, designed solely to abuse the corporate privilege at the expense of the public interest.

For these reasons I would vote to affirm the order of the Appellate Division.

Questions

1. What were Carlton's reasons for operating 10 corporations, each of which had but two cabs?

2. Does it make sense, from a business perspective, to invest more capital in the companies as suggested by Judge Keating?

3. Judge Fuld's decision raises different theories to justify ignoring the corporation's separate entity and imposing liability on shareholders. What are those theories? What facts would a plaintiff have to prove in support of each theory? Who would be held liable under each theory?

4. Does Judge Keating offer different theories for imposing liability on shareholders? What is his disagreement with the majority?

Kinney Shoe Corporation v. Polan
939 F.2d 209 (4th Cir. 1991)

Chapman, Judge

Plaintiff-appellant Kinney Shoe Corporation ("Kinney") brought this action in the United States District Court for the Southern District of West Virginia against Lincoln M. Polan ("Polan") seeking to recover money owed on a sublease between Kinney and Industrial Realty Company ("Industrial"). Polan is the sole shareholder of Industrial. The district court found that Polan was not personally liable on the lease between Kinney and Industrial. Kinney appeals asserting that the corporate veil should be pierced, and we agree.

I

The district court based its order on facts which were stipulated by the parties. In 1984 Polan formed two corporations, Industrial and Polan Industries, Inc., for the purpose of re-establishing an industrial manufacturing business. The certificate of incorporation for Polan Industries, Inc. was issued by the West Virginia Secretary of State in November 1984. The following month the certificate of incorporation for Industrial was issued. Polan was the owner of both corporations. Although certificates of incorporation were issued, no organizational meetings were held, and no officers were elected.

In November 1984 Polan and Kinney began negotiating the sublease of a building in which Kinney held a leasehold interest. The building was owned by the Cabell County Commission and financed by industrial revenue bonds issued in 1968 to induce Kinney to locate a manufacturing plant in Huntington, West Virginia. Under the terms of the lease, Kinney was legally obligated to make payments on the bonds on a semi-annual basis through January 1, 1993, at which time it had the right to purchase the property. Kinney had ceased using the building as a manufacturing plant in June 1983.

The term of the sublease from Kinney to Industrial commenced in December 1984, even though the written lease was not signed by the parties until April 5, 1985. On April 15, 1985, Industrial subleased part of the building to Polan Industries for fifty percent of the rental amount due Kinney. Polan signed both subleases on behalf of the respective companies.

Other than the sublease with Kinney, Industrial had no assets, no income and no bank account. Industrial issued no stock certificates because nothing was ever paid in to this corporation. Industrial's only income was from its sublease to Polan Industries, Inc. The first rental payment to Kinney was made out of Polan's personal funds, and no further payments were made by Polan or by Polan Industries, Inc. to either Industrial or to Kinney.

Kinney filed suit against Industrial for unpaid rent and obtained a judgment in the amount of $166,400.00 on June 19, 1987. A writ of possession was issued, but because Polan Industries, Inc. had filed for bankruptcy, Kinney did not gain possession for six months. Kinney leased the building until it was sold on September 1, 1988. Kinney then filed this action against Polan individually to collect the amount owed by Industrial to Kinney. Since the amount to which Kinney is entitled is undisputed, the only issue is whether Kinney can pierce the corporate veil and hold Polan personally liable.

The district court held that Kinney had assumed the risk of Industrial's undercapitalization and was not entitled to pierce the corporate veil. Kinney appeals, and we reverse.

II

We have long recognized that a corporation is an entity, separate and distinct from its officers and stockholders, and the individual stockholders are not responsible for the debts of the corporation. This concept, however, is a fiction of the law "'and it is now well settled, as a general principle, that the fiction should be disregarded when it is urged with an intent not within its reason and purpose, and in such a way that its retention would produce injustices or inequitable consequences.'"

Piercing the corporate veil is an equitable remedy, and the burden rests with the party asserting such claim. A totality of the circumstances test is used in determining whether to pierce the corporate veil, and each case must be decided on its own facts. The district court's findings of facts may be overturned only if clearly erroneous.

Kinney seeks to pierce the corporate veil of Industrial so as to hold Polan personally liable on the sublease debt. The Supreme Court of Appeals of West Virginia has set forth a two prong test to be used in determining whether to pierce a corporate veil in a breach of contract case. This test raises two issues: first, is the unity of interest and ownership such that the separate personalities of the corporation and the individual shareholder no longer exist; and second, would an equitable result occur if the acts are treated as those of the corporation alone. *Laya v. Erin Homes, Inc.* Numerous factors have been identified as relevant in making this determination.*

---

* The following factors were identified in *Laya*:
 (1) commingling of funds and other assets of the corporation with those of the individual shareholders;
 (2) diversion of the corporation's funds or assets to noncorporate uses (to the personal uses of the corporation's shareholders);
 (3) failure to maintain the corporate formalities necessary for the issuance of or subscription to the corporation's stock, such as formal approval of the stock issue by the board of directors;
 (4) an individual shareholder representing to persons outside the corporation that he or she is personally liable for the debts or other obligations of the corporation;
 (5) failure to maintain corporate minutes or adequate corporate records;

The district court found that the two prong test of *Laya* had been satisfied. The court concluded that Polan's failure to carry out the corporate formalities with respect to Industrial, coupled with Industrial's gross undercapitalization, resulted in damage to Kinney. We agree.

It is undisputed that Industrial was not adequately capitalized. Actually, it had no paid in capital. Polan had put nothing into this corporation, and it did not observe any corporate formalities. As the West Virginia court stated in *Laya*, "[i]ndividuals who wish to enjoy limited personal liability for business activities under a corporate umbrella should be expected to adhere to the relatively simple formalities of creating and maintaining a corporate entity." This, the court stated, is "a relatively small price to pay for limited liability." Another important factor is adequate capitalization. "[G]rossly inadequate capitalization combined with disregard of corporate formalities, causing basic unfairness, are sufficient to pierce the corporate veil in order to hold the shareholder(s) actively participating in the operation of the business personally liable for a breach of contract to the party who entered into the contract with the corporation."

In this case, Polan bought no stock, made no capital contribution, kept no minutes, and elected no officers for Industrial. In addition, Polan attempted to protect his assets by placing them in Polan Industries, Inc. and interposing Industrial between

---

(6) identical equitable ownership in two entities;

(7) identity of the directors and officers of two entities who are responsible for supervision and management (a partnership or sole proprietorship and a corporation owned and managed by the same parties);

(8) failure to adequately capitalize a corporation for the reasonable risks of the corporate undertaking;

(9) absence of separately held corporate assets;

(10) use of a corporation as a mere shell or conduit to operate a single venture or some particular aspect of the business of an individual or another corporation;

(11) sole ownership of all the stock by one individual or members of a single family;

(12) use of the same office or business location by the corporation and its individual shareholder(s);

(13) employment of the same employees or attorney by the corporation and its shareholder(s);

(14) concealment or misrepresentation of the identity of the ownership, management or financial interests in the corporation, and concealment of personal business activities of the shareholders (sole shareholders do not reveal the association with a corporation, which makes loans to them without adequate security);

(15) disregard of legal formalities and failure to maintain proper arm's length relationships among related entities;

(16) use of a corporate entity as a conduit to procure labor, services or merchandise for another person or entity;

(17) diversion of corporate assets from the corporation by or to a stockholder or other person or entity to the detriment of creditors, or the manipulation of assets and liabilities between entities to concentrate the assets in one and the liabilities in another;

(18) contracting by the corporation with another person with the intent to avoid risk of nonperformance by use of the corporate entity; or the use of a corporation as a subterfuge for illegal transactions;

(19) the formation and use of the corporation to assume the existing liabilities of another person or entity.

Polan Industries, Inc. and Kinney so as to prevent Kinney from going against the corporation with assets. Polan gave no explanation or justification for the existence of Industrial as the intermediary between Polan Industries, Inc. and Kinney. Polan was obviously trying to limit his liability and the liability of Polan Industries, Inc. by setting up a paper curtain constructed of nothing more than Industrial's certificate of incorporation. These facts present the classic scenario for an action to pierce the corporate veil so as to reach the responsible party and produce an equitable result. Accordingly, we hold that the district court correctly found that the two prong test in *Laya* had been satisfied.

In *Laya*, the court also noted that when determining whether to pierce a corporate veil a third prong may apply in certain cases. The court stated:

> When, under the circumstances, it would be reasonable for that particular type of a party [those contract creditors capable of protecting themselves] entering into a contract with the corporation, for example, a bank or other lending institution, to conduct an investigation of the credit of the corporation prior to entering into the contract, such party will be charged with the knowledge that a reasonable credit investigation would disclose. If such an investigation would disclose that the corporation is grossly undercapitalized, based upon the nature and the magnitude of the corporate undertaking, such party will be deemed to have assumed the risk of the gross undercapitalization and will not be permitted to pierce the corporate veil.

The district court applied this third prong and concluded that Kinney "assumed the risk of Industrial's defaulting" and that "the application of the doctrine of 'piercing the corporate veil' ought not and does not [apply]." While we agree that the two prong test of *Laya* was satisfied, we hold that the district court's conclusion that Kinney had assumed the risk is clearly erroneous.

Without deciding whether the third prong should be extended beyond the context of the financial institution lender mentioned in *Laya*, we hold that, even if it applies to creditors such as Kinney, it does not prevent Kinney from piercing the corporate veil in this case. The third prong is permissive and not mandatory. This is not a factual situation that calls for the third prong, if we are to seek an equitable result. Polan set up Industrial to limit his liability and the liability of Polan Industries, Inc. in their dealings with Kinney. A stockholder's liability is limited to the amount he has invested in the corporation, but Polan invested nothing in Industrial. This corporation was no more than a shell — a transparent shell. When nothing is invested in the corporation, the corporation provides no protection to its owner; nothing in, nothing out, no protection. If Polan wishes the protection of a corporation to limit his liability, he must follow the simple formalities of maintaining the corporation. This he failed to do, and he may not relieve his circumstances by saying Kinney should have known better.

III

For the foregoing reasons, we hold that Polan is personally liable for the debt of Industrial, and the decision of the district court is reversed and this case is remanded with instructions to enter judgment for the plaintiff.

Reversed and remanded with instructions.

Questions

1. What are industrial revenue bonds and what is the transaction involved in this case?

2. What were Polan's business reasons for setting up the corporate structure as he did? Could Kinney Shoe Corporation have known these reasons?

3. What theory of liability does Judge Chapman use to justify imposing liability on Polan? Is it different or similar to any of the theories discussed in *Walkovszky v. Carlton*?

4. What are the three prongs of the test Judge Chapman adopts? How is each prong different from the other?

5. *Walkovszky* involved a tort creditor, while *Kinney Shoe Corporation* involved a contract creditor. From a policy standpoint, do these two types of creditors deserve different treatment? In which situations would you be more likely to impose liability on the shareholders in order to protect the creditor? One argument for different treatment points out that while individuals cannot protect themselves from tortious behavior, they can do so in contractual situations. They may examine books, records and formalities of the corporation before contracting and either withdraw from the transaction or negotiate for protective language in the contract if they are dissatisfied with what they see. Assuming no fraud by the corporation, one might ask why should society give claimants who failed to create contractual protection for themselves a second bite at the apple.

On the other hand, a tort claimant is in a very different situation. He or she cannot examine the books of the corporation or monitor its compliance with corporate formalities prior to the tort. Several commentators suggest that in the tort context, compliance with formalities should not be a significant factor in deciding whether to pierce. They believe undercapitalization is a more decisive consideration. Undercapitalization, however, is also a difficult concept. Again, assuming no fraud on the part of the corporate insiders, should a tort victim be compensated or not on the basis of this loosely defined and flexible concept? It seems that the disregard of the corporate existence by the insiders should essentially estop them from claiming the protection of that existence when corporate assets fail to satisfy claims against the corporation.

While it seems intuitive that it would be easier to pierce the veil in tort than in contract, empirical evidence suggests otherwise. In fact, piercing occurs more commonly in contract cases. Robert B. Thompson, *Piercing the Corporate Veil: An*

Empirical Study, 76 Cornell L. Rev. 1036 (1991). Can you think of any reason why this might be so?

Sea-Land Services, Inc. v. The Pepper Source
941 F.2d 519 (7th Cir. 1991)

Bauer, Chief Judge

This spicy case finds its origin in several shipments of Jamaican sweet peppers. Appellee Sea-Land Services, Inc. ("Sea-Land"), an ocean carrier, shipped the peppers on behalf of The Pepper Source ("PS"), one of the appellants here. PS then stiffed Sea-Land on the freight bill, which was rather substantial. Sea-Land filed a federal diversity action for the money it was owed. On December 2, 1987, the district court entered a default judgment in favor of Sea-Land and against PS in the amount of $86,767.70. But PS was nowhere to be found; it had been "dissolved" in mid-1987 for failure to pay the annual state franchise tax. Worse yet for Sea-Land, even had it not been dissolved, PS apparently had no assets. With the well empty, Sea-Land could not recover its judgment against PS. Hence the instant lawsuit.

In June 1988, Sea-Land brought this action against Gerald J. Marchese and five business entities he owns: PS, Caribe Crown, Inc., Jamar Corp., Salescaster Distributors, Inc., and Marchese Fegan Associates. Marchese also was named individually. Sea-Land sought by this suit to pierce PS's corporate veil and render Marchese personally liable for the judgment owed to Sea-Land, and then "reverse pierce" Marchese's other corporations so that they, too, would be on the hook for the $87,000. Thus, Sea-Land alleged in its complaint that all of these corporations "are alter egos of each other and hide behind the veils of alleged separate corporate existence for the purpose of defrauding plaintiff and other creditors." Not only are the corporations alter egos of each other, alleged Sea-Land, but also they are alter egos of Marchese, who should be held individually liable for the judgment because he created and manipulated these corporations and their assets for his own personal uses. (Hot on the heels of the filing of Sea-Land's complaint, PS took the necessary steps to be reinstated as a corporation in Illinois.)

In early 1989, Sea-Land filed an amended complaint adding Tie-Net International, Inc., as a defendant. Unlike the other corporate defendants, Tie-Net is not owned solely by Marchese: he holds half of the stock, and an individual named George Andre owns the other half. Sea-Land alleged that, despite this shared ownership, Tie-Net is but another alter ego of Marchese and the other corporate defendants, and thus it also should be held liable for the judgment against PS.

Through 1989, Sea-Land pursued discovery in this case, including taking a two-day deposition from Marchese. In December 1989, Sea-Land moved for summary judgment. In that motion—which, with the brief in support and the appendices, was about three inches thick—Sea-Land argued that it was "entitled to judgment as a matter of law, since the evidence including deposition testimony and exhibits in the appendix will show that piercing the corporate veil and finding the status of an alter ego is merited in this case." Marchese and the other defendants filed brief responses.

In an order dated June 22, 1990, the court granted Sea-Land's motion. The court discussed and applied the test for corporate veil-piercing explicated in *Van Dorn Co. v. Future Chemical and Oil Corp.*, 753 F.2d 565 (7th Cir. 1985). Analyzing Illinois law, we held in *Van Dorn* that a corporate entity will be disregarded and the veil of limited liability pierced when two requirements are met:

> [F]irst, there must be such unity of interest and ownership that the separate personalities of the corporation and the individual [or other corporation] no longer exist; and second, circumstances must be such that adherence to the fiction of separate corporate existence would sanction a fraud or promote injustice.

As for determining whether a corporation is so controlled by another to justify disregarding their separate identities, the Illinois cases, as we summarized them in *Van Dorn*, focus on four factors: "(1) the failure to maintain adequate corporate records or to comply with corporate formalities, (2) the commingling of funds or assets, (3) undercapitalization, and (4) one corporation treating the assets of another corporation as its own."

Following the lead of the parties, the district court in the instant case laid the template of *Van Dorn* over the facts of this case. The court concluded that both halves and all features of the test had been satisfied, and, therefore, entered judgment in favor of Sea-Land and against PS, Caribe Crown, Jamar, Salescaster, Tie-Net, and Marchese individually. These defendants were held jointly liable for Sea-Land's $87,000 judgment, as well as for post-judgment interest under Illinois law. From that judgment Marchese and the other defendants brought a timely appeal. . . .

The first and most striking feature that emerges from our examination of the record is that these corporate defendants are, indeed, little but Marchese's playthings. Marchese is the sole shareholder of PS, Caribe Crown, Jamar, and Salescaster. He is one of the two shareholders of Tie-Net. Except for Tie-Net, none of the corporations ever held a single corporate meeting. (At the handful of Tie-Net meetings held by Marchese and Andre, no minutes were taken.) During his deposition, Marchese did not remember any of these corporations ever passing articles of incorporation, bylaws, or other agreements. As for physical facilities, Marchese runs all of these corporations (including Tie-Net) out of the same, single office, with the same phone line, the same expense accounts, and the like. And how he does "run" the expense accounts! When he fancies to, Marchese "borrows" substantial sums of money from these corporations—interest free, of course. The corporations also "borrow" money from each other when need be, which left at least PS completely out of capital when the Sea-Land bills came due. What's more, Marchese has used the bank accounts of these corporations to pay all kinds of personal expenses, including alimony and child support payments to his ex-wife, education expenses for his children, maintenance of his personal automobiles, health care for his pet—the list goes on and on.

Marchese did not even have a personal bank account! (With "corporate" accounts like these, who needs one?)

And Tie-Net is just as much a part of this as the other corporations. On appeal, Marchese makes much of the fact that he shares ownership of Tie-Net, and that Sea-Land has not been able to find an example of funds flowing from PS to Tie-Net to the detriment of Sea-Land and PS's other creditors. So what? The record reveals that, in all material senses, Marchese treated Tie-Net like his other corporations: he "borrowed" over $30,000 from Tie-Net; money and "loans" flowed freely between Tie-Net and the other corporations; and Marchese charged up various personal expenses (including $460 for a picture of himself with President Bush) on Tie-Net's credit card. Marchese was not deterred by the fact that he did not hold all of the stock of Tie-Net; why should his creditors be?

In sum, we agree with the district court that there can be no doubt that the "shared control/unity of interest and ownership" part of the *Van Dorn* test is met in this case: corporate records and formalities have not been maintained; funds and assets have been commingled with abandon; PS, the offending corporation, and perhaps others have been undercapitalized; and corporate assets have been moved and tapped and "borrowed" without regard to their source. Indeed, Marchese basically punted this part of the inquiry before the district court by coming forward with little or no evidence in response to Sea-Land's extensively supported argument on these points. That fact alone was enough to do him in; opponents to summary judgment motions cannot simply rest on their laurels, but must come forward with specific facts showing that there is a genuine issue for trial. Regarding the elements that make up the first half of the *Van Dorn* test, Marchese and the other defendants have not done so. Thus, Sea-Land is entitled to judgment on these points.

The second part of the *Van Dorn* test is more problematic, however. "Unity of interest and ownership" is not enough; Sea-Land also must show that honoring the separate corporate existences of the defendants "would sanction a fraud or promote injustice." This last phrase truly is disjunctive:

> Although an intent to defraud creditors would surely play a part if established, the Illinois test does not require proof of such intent. Once the first element of the test is established, *either* the sanctioning of a fraud (intentional wrongdoing) or the promotion of injustice, will satisfy the second element.

Seizing on this, Sea-Land has abandoned the language in its two complaints that make repeated references to "fraud" by Marchese, and has chosen not to attempt to *prove* that PS and Marchese intended to defraud it—which would be quite difficult on summary judgment. Instead, Sea-Land has argued that honoring the defendants' separate identities would "promote injustice."

But what, exactly, does "promote injustice" mean, and how does one establish it on summary judgment? These are the critical, troublesome questions in this case. To start with, as the above passage from *Van Dorn* makes clear, "promote injustice" means something less than an affirmative showing of fraud—but how much less? In its one-sentence treatment of this point, the district court held that it was enough that "Sea-Land would be denied a judicially-imposed recovery." Sea-Land defends this reasoning on appeal, arguing that "permitting the appellants to hide behind the shield of limited liability would clearly serve as an injustice against appellee" because it would "impermissibly deny appellee satisfaction." But that cannot be what is meant by "promote injustice." The prospect of an unsatisfied judgment looms in every veil-piercing action; why else would a plaintiff bring such an action? Thus, if an unsatisfied judgment is enough for the "promote injustice" feature of the test, then *every* plaintiff will pass on that score, and *Van Dorn* collapses into a one-step "unity of interest and ownership" test.

Because we cannot abide such a result, we will undertake our own review of Illinois cases to determine how the "promote injustice" feature of the veil-piercing inquiry has been interpreted. In *Pederson*, a recent case from the Illinois court of appeals, the court offered the following summary: "Some element of unfairness, something akin to fraud or deception or the existence of a compelling public interest must be present in order to disregard the corporate fiction." . . .

Generalizing from these cases, we see that the courts that properly have pierced corporate veils to avoid "promoting injustice" have found that, unless it did so, some "wrong" beyond a creditor's inability to collect would result: the common sense rules of adverse possession would be undermined; former partners would be permitted to skirt the legal rules concerning monetary obligations; a party would be unjustly enriched; a parent corporation that caused a sub's liabilities and its inability to pay for them would escape those liabilities; or an intentional scheme to squirrel assets into a liability-free corporation while heaping liabilities upon an asset-free corporation would be successful. Sea-Land, although it alleged in its complaint the kind of intentional asset- and liability-shifting found in *Van Dorn*, has yet to come forward with evidence akin to the "wrongs" found in these cases. Apparently, it believed, as did the district court, that its unsatisfied judgment was enough. That belief was in error, and the entry of summary judgment premature. We, therefore, reverse the judgment and remand the case to the district court.

On remand, the court should require that Sea-Land produce, if it desires summary judgment, evidence and argument that would establish the kind of additional "wrong" present in the above cases. For example, perhaps Sea-Land could establish that Marchese, like Roth in *Van Dorn*, used these corporate facades to avoid its responsibilities to creditors; or that PS, Marchese, or one of the other corporations will be "unjustly enriched" unless liability is shared by all. Of course, Sea-Land is not required fully to prove intent to defraud, which it probably could not do on summary judgment anyway. But it is required to show the kind of injustice to merit the evocation of the court's essentially equitable power to prevent "injustice." It may well be that, after more of such evidence is adduced, no genuine issue of fact exists to prevent Sea-Land from reaching Marchese's other pet corporations for PS's debt. Or it may be that only a finder of fact will be able to determine whether fraud or "injustice" is involved here. In any event, the record as it currently stands is insufficient to uphold the entry of summary judgment.

Reversed and Remanded with instructions.

Questions

1. What theory or doctrine justified imposing liability on Marchese?

2. Why did the plaintiff sue Marchese's owned corporations? What theory or doctrine justified imposing liability on PS, Caribe Crown, Inc., Jamar Corp., Salescaster Distributors, Inc., and Marchese Fegan Associates?

3. What is the difference between this case and the previous cases in this Section? Whom does the court hold liable?

Consolidated Rock Products Co. v. Du Bois
312 U.S. 510 (1941)

DOUGLAS, Justice

This case involves questions as to the fairness under § 77B of the Bankruptcy Act, 48 Stat. 912, 11 U.S.C.A. § 207, of a plan of reorganization for a parent corporation (Consolidated Rock Products Co.) and its two wholly owned subsidiaries—Union Rock Co. and Consumers Rock and Gravel Co., Inc. The District Court confirmed the plan; the Circuit Court of Appeals reversed. We granted the petitions for certiorari because of the importance in the administration of the reorganization provisions of the Act of certain principles enunciated by the Circuit Court of Appeals.

The stock of Union and Consumers is held by Consolidated. Union has outstanding in the hands of the public $1,877,000 of 6% bonds secured by an indenture on its property, with accrued and unpaid interest thereon of $403,555—a total mortgage indebtedness of $2,280,555. Consumers has outstanding in the hands of the public $1,137,000 of 6% bonds secured by an indenture on its property, with accrued and unpaid interest thereon of $221,715—a total mortgage indebtedness of $1,358,715. Consolidated has outstanding 285,947 shares of no par value preferred stock and 397,455 shares of no par common stock.

The plan of reorganization calls for the formation of a new corporation to which will be transferred all of the assets of Consolidated, Union, and Consumers free of all claims. The securities of the new corporation are to be distributed as follows:

> Union and Consumers bonds held by the public will be exchanged for income bonds and preferred stock of the new company. For 50 per cent of the principal amounts of their claims, those bondholders will receive income bonds secured by a mortgage on all of the property of the new company; for the balance they will receive an equal amount of par value preferred stock. Their claims to accrued interest are to be extinguished, no

new securities being issued therefor. Thus Union bondholders for their claims of $2,280,555 will receive income bonds and preferred stock in the face amount of $1,877,000; Consumers bondholders for their claims of $1,358,715 will receive income bonds and preferred stock in the face amount of $1,137,000. Each share of new preferred stock will have a warrant for the purchase of two shares of new $2 par value common stock at prices ranging from $2 per share within six months of issuance, to $6 per share during the fifth year after issuance.

Preferred stockholders of Consolidated will receive one share of new common stock ($2 par value) for each share of old preferred or an aggregate of 285,947 shares of new common.

A warrant to purchase one share of new common for $1 within three months of issuance will be given to the common stockholders of Consolidated for each five shares of old common.

...

The bonds of Union and Consumers held by Consolidated, the stock of those companies held by Consolidated, and the intercompany claims (discussed hereafter) will be cancelled.

In 1929 when Consolidated acquired control of these various properties, they were appraised in excess of $16,000,000 and it was estimated that their annual net earnings would be $500,000. In 1931 they were appraised by officers at about $4,400,000, "exclusive of going concern, good will and current assets." The District Court did not find specific values for the separate properties of Consolidated, Union, or Consumers, or for the properties of the enterprise as a unit. The average of the valuations (apparently based on physical factors) given by three witnesses at the hearing before the master were $2,202,733 for Union as against a mortgage indebtedness of $2,280,555; $1,151,033 for Consumers as against a mortgage indebtedness of $1,358,715. Relying on similar testimony, Consolidated argues that the value of its property, to be contributed to the new company, is over $1,359,000, or exclusive of an alleged good will of $500,000, $859,784. These estimated values somewhat conflict with the consolidated balance sheet (as at June 30, 1938) which shows assets of $3,723,738.15 and liabilities (exclusive of capital and surplus) of $4,253,224.41. More important, the earnings record of the enterprise casts grave doubts on the soundness of the estimated values. No dividends were ever paid on Consolidated's common stock; and except for five quarterly dividends in 1929 and 1931, none on its preferred stock. For the eight and a half years from April 1, 1929, to September 30, 1937, Consolidated had a loss of about $1,200,000 before bond interest but after depreciation and depletion. And except for the year 1929, Consolidated had no net operating profit, after bond interest and amortization, depreciation and depletion, in any year down to September 30, 1937. Yet on this record the District Court found that the present fair value of all the assets of the several companies, exclusive of good will and going concern value, was in excess of the total bonded indebtedness, plus accrued and unpaid interest. And it also found that such value, including good will and going concern value, was insufficient to pay the bonded indebtedness plus accrued and unpaid interest and the liquidation preferences and accrued dividends on Consolidated preferred stock. It further found that the present fair value of the assets admittedly subject to the trust indentures of Union and Consumers was insufficient to pay the face amount, plus accrued and unpaid interest of the respective bond issues. In spite of that finding, the District Court also found that "it would be physically impossible to determine and segregate with any degree of accuracy or fairness properties which originally belonged to the companies separately"; that as a result of unified operation properties of every character "have been commingled and are now in the main held by Consolidated without any way of ascertaining what part, if any thereof, belongs to each or any of the companies separately"; and that, as a consequence, an appraisal "would be of such an indefinite and unsatisfactory nature as to produce further confusion."

The unified operation which resulted in that commingling of assets was pursuant to an operating agreement which Consolidated caused its wholly owned subsidiaries to execute in 1929. Under that agreement the subsidiaries ceased all operating functions and the entire management, operation and financing of the business and properties of the subsidiaries were undertaken by Consolidated. The corporate existence of the subsidiaries, however, was maintained and certain separate accounts were kept. Under this agreement Consolidated undertook, inter alia, to pay the subsidiaries the amounts necessary for the interest and sinking fund provisions of the indentures and to credit their current accounts with items of depreciation, depletion, amortization and obsolescence. Upon termination of the agreement the properties were to be returned and a final settlement of accounts made, Consolidated meanwhile to retain all net revenues after its obligations thereunder to the subsidiaries had been met. It was specifically provided that the agreement was made for the benefit of the parties, not "for the benefit of any third person." Consolidated's books as at June 30, 1938, showed a net indebtedness under that agreement to Union and Consumers of somewhat over $5,000,000. That claim was cancelled by the plan of reorganization, no securities being issued to the creditors of the subsidiaries therefor. The District Court made no findings as respects the amount or validity of that intercompany claim; it summarily disposed of it by concluding that any liability under the operating agreement was "not made for the benefit of any third parties and the bondholders are included in that category."

We agree with the Circuit Court of Appeals that it was error to confirm this plan of reorganization.

On this record no determination of the fairness of any plan of reorganization could be made. Absent the requisite valuation data, the court was in no position to exercise the "informed, independent judgment" which appraisal of the fairness of a plan of reorganization entails. There are two aspects of that valuation problem.

In the first place, there must be a determination of what assets are subject to the payment of the respective claims. This obvious requirement was not met. The status of the Union and Consumers bondholders emphasizes its necessity and importance. According to the District Court the mortgaged assets are insufficient to pay the mortgage debt. There is no finding, however, as to the extent of the deficiency or the amount of unmortgaged assets and their value. It is plain that the bondholders would have, as against Consolidated and its stockholders, prior recourse against any unmortgaged assets of Union and Consumers. The full and absolute priority rule . . . would preclude participation by the equity interests in any of those assets until the bondholders had been made whole. Here there are some unmortgaged assets, for there is a claim of Union and Consumers against Consolidated—a claim which according to the books of Consolidated is over $5,000,000 in amount. If that claim is valid, or even if it were allowed only to the extent of 25% of its face amount, then the entire assets of Consolidated would be drawn down into the estates of the subsidiaries. In that event Union and Consumers might or might not be solvent in the bankruptcy sense. But certainly it would render untenable the present contention of Consolidated and the preferred stockholders that they are contributing all of the assets of Consolidated to the new company in exchange for which they are entitled to new securities. On that theory of the case they would be making a contribution of only such assets of Consolidated, if any, as remained after any deficiency of the bondholders had been wholly satisfied.

. . . Consolidated makes some point of the difficulty and expense of determining the extent of its liability under the operating agreement and of the necessity to abide by the technical terms of that agreement in ascertaining that liability. But equity will not permit a holding company, which has dominated and controlled its subsidiaries, to escape or reduce its liability to those subsidiaries by reliance upon self-serving contracts which it has imposed on them. A holding company, as well as others in dominating or controlling positions . . . has fiduciary duties to security holders of its system which will be strictly enforced. . . . In this connection Consolidated cannot defeat or postpone the accounting because of the clause in the operating agreement that it was not made for the benefit of any third person. The question here is not a technical one as to who may sue to enforce that liability. It is merely a question as to the amount by which Consolidated is indebted to the subsidiaries and the proof and allowance of that claim. The subsidiaries need not be sent into state courts to have that liability determined. The bankruptcy court having exclusive jurisdiction over the holding company and the subsidiaries has plenary power to adjudicate all the issues pertaining to the claim. The intimations of Consolidated that there must be foreclosure proceedings and protracted litigation in state courts involve a misconception of the duties and powers of the bankruptcy court. The fact that Consolidated might have a strategic or nuisance value outside of § 77B does not detract from or impair the power and duty of the bankruptcy court to require a full accounting as a condition precedent to approval of any plan of reorganization. The fact that the claim might be settled, with the approval of the Court after full disclosure and notice to interested parties, does not justify the concealed compromise effected here through the simple expedient of extinguishing the claim.

So far as the ability of the bondholders of Union and Consumers to reach the assets of Consolidated on claims of the kind covered by the operation agreement is concerned, there is another and more direct route which reaches the same end. There has been a unified operation of those several properties by Consolidated pursuant to the operating agreement. That operation not only resulted in extensive commingling of assets. All management functions of the several companies were assumed by Consolidated. The subsidiaries abdicated. Consolidated operated them as mere departments of its own business. Not even the formalities of separate corporate organizations were observed, except in minor particulars such as the maintenance of certain separate accounts. In view of these facts, Consolidated is in no position to claim that its assets are insulated from such claims of creditors of the subsidiaries. To the contrary, it is well settled that where a holding company directly intervenes in the management of its subsidiaries so as to treat them as mere departments of its own enterprise, it is responsible for the obligations of those subsidiaries incurred or arising during its management. . . . We are not dealing here with a situation where other creditors of a parent company are competing with creditors of its subsidiaries. If meticulous regard to corporate forms, which Consolidated has long ignored, is now observed, the stockholders of Consolidated may be the direct beneficiaries. Equity will not countenance such a result. A holding company which assumes to treat the properties of its subsidiaries as its own cannot take the benefits of direct management without the burdens.

We have already noted that no adequate finding was made as to the value of the assets of Consolidated. In view of what we have said, it is apparent that a determination of that value must be made so that criteria will be available to determine an appropriate allocation of new securities between bondholders and stockholders in case there is an equity remaining after the bondholders have been made whole.

. . .

Affirmed.

Questions

1. The absolute priority rule, applicable in bankruptcy, requires that debts to creditors be paid first and what's left divided among the shareholders. What is the order in which creditors and shareholders of a subsidiary and its parent corporation (assume that both filed for bankruptcy) would be paid following an absolute priority rule? Do creditors of a subsidiary have a claim against its parent corporation?

2. What authority does Justice Douglas rely upon to allow the bondholders of Union and Consumers to reach the assets of Consolidated—state (corporate) law? the Bankruptcy Code? Does it make a difference? Could the interests of the bondholders be protected without substantive consolidation?

3. What about the creditors of the parent corporation? How should their claims and those of the subsidiaries' creditors be ordered? What if sorting out the value of the parent corporation and its subsidiaries is itself difficult (and thus expensive)?

C. The Authority of the Board

Section 141(a) of the Delaware Business Corporation Law, like every other state corporate law statute, provides that "The business and affairs of every corporation organized under this chapter shall be managed by or under the direction of a board of directors, except as may be otherwise provided in this chapter or in its certificate of incorporation." The board of directors is the supreme corporate authority. Regardless of who the particular directors are, the institution of the board is empowered by the state, not by the stockholders. Thus, neither directors nor stockholders have the power to change the role of the board absent the exceptions noted in the statute. The power of the board is almost absolute, checked by fiduciary obligation (and limited by certain provisions of the corporation law statute such as those governing the payment of dividends). One area in which the board's power is not absolute, however, is its ability to change its power. That is, while boards may (and do) delegate specialized tasks to committees, it is the board as a whole that has the ultimate responsibility for "the business and affairs of the corporation." As you will see, stockholders may alter this arrangement. Boards may not. Consider the implications of the foregoing when you read the material below.

Delaware General Corporation Law Section 141

(a) The business and affairs of every corporation organized under this chapter shall be managed by or under the direction of a board of directors, except as may be otherwise provided in this chapter or in its certificate of incorporation. If any such provision is made in the certificate of incorporation, the powers and duties conferred or imposed upon the board of directors by this chapter shall be exercised or performed to such extent and by such person or persons as shall be provided in the certificate of incorporation.

(b) The board of directors of a corporation shall consist of 1 or more members, each of whom shall be a natural person. The number of directors shall be fixed by, or in the manner provided in, the bylaws, unless the certificate of incorporation fixes the number of directors, in which case a change in the number of directors shall be made only by amendment of the certificate. Directors need not be stockholders unless so required by the certificate of incorporation or the bylaws. The certificate of incorporation or bylaws may prescribe other qualifications for directors. Each director shall hold office until such director's successor is elected and qualified or until such director's earlier resignation or removal. Any director may resign at any time upon notice given in writing or by electronic transmission to the corporation. A resignation is effective when the resignation is delivered unless the resignation specifies a later effective date or an effective date determined upon the happening of an event or events. A resignation which is conditioned upon the director failing to receive a specified vote for reelection as a director may provide that it is irrevocable. A majority of the total number of directors shall constitute a quorum for the transaction of business unless the certificate of incorporation or the bylaws require a greater number. Unless the certificate of incorporation provides otherwise, the bylaws may provide that a number less than a majority shall constitute a quorum which in no case shall be less than $1/3$ of the total number of directors. The vote of the majority of the directors present at a meeting at which a quorum is present shall be the act of the board of directors unless the certificate of incorporation or the bylaws shall require a vote of a greater number.

(c) (1) All corporations incorporated prior to July 1, 1996, shall be governed by this paragraph (c)(1) of this section, provided that any such corporation may by a resolution adopted by a majority of the whole board elect to be governed by paragraph (c)(2) of this section, in which case this paragraph (c)(1) of this section shall not apply to such corporation. All corporations incorporated on or after July 1, 1996, shall be governed by paragraph (c)(2) of this section. The board of directors may, by resolution passed by a majority of the whole board, designate 1 or more committees, each committee to consist of 1 or more of the directors of the corporation. The board may designate 1 or more directors as alternate members of any committee, who may replace any absent or disqualified member at any meeting of the committee. The bylaws may provide that in the absence or disqualification of a member of a committee, the member or members present at any meeting and not disqualified from voting, whether or not the member or members present constitute a quorum, may unanimously appoint another member of the board of directors to act at the meeting in the place of any such absent or disqualified member. Any such committee, to the extent provided in the resolution of the board of directors, or in the bylaws of the corporation, shall have and may exercise all the powers and authority of the board of directors in the management of the business and affairs of the corporation, and may authorize the seal of the corporation to be affixed to all papers which may require it; but no such committee shall have the power or authority in reference to amending the certificate of incorporation (except that a committee may, to the extent authorized in the resolution or resolutions providing for the issuance of shares of stock adopted by the board of directors as provided in § 151(a) of this title, fix the designations and any of the preferences or rights of such shares relating to dividends, redemption, dissolution, any distribution of assets of the corporation or the conversion into, or the exchange of such shares for, shares of any other class or classes or any other series of the same or any other class or classes of stock of the corporation or fix the number of shares of any series of stock or authorize the increase or decrease of the shares of any series), adopting an agreement of merger or consolidation under § 251, § 252, § 254, § 255, § 256, § 257, § 258, § 263 or § 264 of this title, recommending to the stockholders the sale, lease or exchange of all or substantially all of the corporation's property and assets, recommending to the stockholders a dissolution of the corporation or a revocation of a dissolution, or amending the bylaws of the corporation; and, unless the resolution, bylaws or certificate of incorporation expressly so provides, no such committee shall have the power or authority to declare a dividend, to authorize the issuance of stock or to adopt a certificate of ownership and merger pursuant to § 253 of this title.

(2) The board of directors may designate 1 or more committees, each committee to consist of 1 or more of the directors of the corporation. The board may designate 1 or more directors as alternate members of any committee, who may replace any absent or disqualified member at any meeting of the committee. The bylaws may provide that in the absence or disqualification of a member of a committee, the member or members present at any meeting and not disqualified from voting, whether or not such member or members constitute a quorum, may unanimously appoint another member of the board of directors to act at the meeting in the place of any such absent or disqualified member. Any such committee, to the extent provided in the resolution of the board of directors, or in the bylaws of the corporation, shall have and may exercise all the powers and authority of the board of directors in the management of the business and affairs of the corporation, and may authorize the seal of the corporation to be affixed to all papers which may require it; but no such committee shall have the power or authority in reference to the following matter: (i) approving or adopting, or recommending to the stockholders, any action or matter (other than the election or removal of directors) expressly required by this chapter to be submitted to stockholders for approval or (ii) adopting, amending or repealing any bylaw of the corporation. . . .

(d) The directors of any corporation organized under this chapter may, by the certificate of incorporation or by an initial bylaw, or by a bylaw adopted by a vote of the stockholders, be divided into 1, 2 or 3 classes; the term of office of those of the first class to expire at the first annual meeting held after such classification becomes effective; of the second class 1 year thereafter; of the third class 2 years thereafter; and at each annual election held after such classification becomes effective, directors shall be chosen for a full term, as the case may be, to succeed those whose terms expire. The certificate of incorporation or bylaw provision dividing the directors into classes may authorize the board of directors to assign members of the board already in office to such classes at the time such classification becomes effective. The certificate of incorporation may confer upon holders of any class or series of stock the right to elect 1 or more directors who shall serve for such term, and have such voting powers as shall be stated in the certificate of incorporation. The terms of office and voting powers of the directors elected separately by the holders of any class or series of stock may be greater than or less than those of any other director or class of directors. In addition, the certificate of incorporation may confer upon 1 or more directors, whether or not elected separately by the holders of any class or series of stock, voting powers greater than or less than those of other directors. Any such provision conferring greater or lesser voting power shall apply to voting in any committee, unless otherwise provided in the certificate of incorporation or bylaws. If the certificate of incorporation provides that

1 or more directors shall have more or less than 1 vote per director on any matter, every reference in this chapter to a majority or other proportion of the directors shall refer to a majority or other proportion of the votes of the directors.

(e) A member of the board of directors, or a member of any committee designated by the board of directors, shall, in the performance of such member's duties, be fully protected in relying in good faith upon the records of the corporation and upon such information, opinions, reports or statements presented to the corporation by any of the corporation's officers or employees, or committees of the board of directors, or by any other person as to matters the member reasonably believes are within such other person's professional or expert competence and who has been selected with reasonable care by or on behalf of the corporation.

(f) Unless otherwise restricted by the certificate of incorporation or bylaws, any action required or permitted to be taken at any meeting of the board of directors or of any committee thereof may be taken without a meeting if all members of the board or committee, as the case may be, consent thereto in writing, or by electronic transmission and the writing or writings or electronic transmission or transmissions are filed with the minutes of proceedings of the board, or committee. . . .

. . .

(i) Unless otherwise restricted by the certificate of incorporation or bylaws, members of the board of directors of any corporation, or any committee designated by the board, may participate in a meeting of such board, or committee by means of conference telephone or other communications equipment by means of which all persons participating in the meeting can hear each other, and participation in a meeting pursuant to this subsection shall constitute presence in person at the meeting. . . .

(k) Any director or the entire board of directors may be removed, with or without cause, by the holders of a majority of the shares then entitled to vote at an election of directors, except as follows:

(1) Unless the certificate of incorporation otherwise provides, in the case of a corporation whose board is classified as provided in subsection (d) of this section, stockholders may effect such removal only for cause; or

(2) In the case of a corporation having cumulative voting, if less than the entire board is to be removed, no director may be removed without cause if the votes cast against such director's removal would be sufficient to elect such director if then cumulatively voted at an election of the entire board of directors, or, if there be classes of directors, at an election of the class of directors of which such director is a part.

Whenever the holders of any class or series are entitled to elect 1 or more directors by the certificate of incorporation, this subsection shall apply, in respect to the removal without cause of a director or directors so elected, to the vote of the holders of the outstanding shares of that class or series and not to the vote of the outstanding shares as a whole.

Delaware General Corporation Law Section 142

(a) Every corporation organized under this chapter shall have such officers with such titles and duties as shall be stated in the bylaws or in a resolution of the board of directors which is not inconsistent with the bylaws and as may be necessary to enable it to sign instruments and stock certificates which comply with §§ 103(a)(2) and 158 of this title. One of the officers shall have the duty to record the proceedings of the meetings of the stockholders and directors in a book to be kept for that purpose. Any number of offices may be held by the same person unless the certificate of incorporation or bylaws otherwise provide.

(b) Officers shall be chosen in such manner and shall hold their offices for such terms as are prescribed by the bylaws or determined by the board of directors or other governing body. Each officer shall hold office until such officer's successor is elected and qualified or until such officer's earlier resignation or removal. Any officer may resign at any time upon written notice to the corporation. . . .

Hoyt v. Thompson's Executor
19 N.Y. 207 (1859)

COMSTOCK, Judge

. . . The first inquiry suggested by the facts stated is, whether the by-law of the company authorizing a quorum of five directors, including the president, to transact ordinary business was a valid regulation. We are clearly of opinion that it was. The charter of the company, it is true, declared that its powers should be exercised by a board of twenty-three directors, and it may well be conceded that in the absence of any different regulation, a majority of the whole number would be necessary to constitute a legal quorum for the transaction of any business whatever. But it would be a very extraordinary construction of the charter in this respect, to hold that the board of twenty-three directors, or a majority thereof, must meet and act whenever any corporate power was to be exercised, and that no delegation of authority could be made to subordinate agents, to committees, or to a quorum consisting of a smaller number. The board of directors of a corporation do not stand in the same relation to the corporate body which a private agent holds toward his principal. In the strict relation of principal and agent, all the authority of the latter is derived by delegation from the former, and if the power of substitution is not conferred in the appointment, it cannot exist at all. But in corporate bodies the powers of the board of directors are, in a very important sense, original and undelegated. The stockholders do not confer, nor can they revoke those powers. They are derivative only in the sense of being received from the State in the act of incorporation. The directors convened as a board are the primary possessors of all the powers which the charter confers, and like private principals they may delegate to agents of their own appointment the performance of any acts which they themselves can perform. The recognition of this principle is absolutely necessary in the affairs of every corporation whose powers are vested in a board of directors. Without it the most ordinary business could not be carried on, and the corporate powers could not be executed. It is upon this principle, not less than upon the express power contained in the charter to enact by-laws, that the by-law in question . . . rests. It was, in substance and effect, a regulation which constituted a subordinate agency to conduct the ordinary business of the corporation. The persons composing the agency would change according as the quorum of five or more directors attending the meetings might be constituted of different individuals. But if the board could delegate the power of transacting business to five or more individuals named, no doubt exists that the same authority might be imparted to a shifting quorum, composed of the same number. . . .

Questions

1. What does *Hoyt v. Thompson's Executor* tell us about the board's responsibilities?

2. What is the significance of *Hoyt*'s emphasis on centralized management to the development of the large publicly held corporation?

3. The dominant view during the nineteenth century was that stockholders were "the ultimately controlling power in the corporation." *Hoyt* was largely ignored by New York courts until the turn of the twentieth century when the tide changed and the dominant legal opinion equated the powers of the board of directors with the powers of the corporation. This change in legal opinion helped legitimate the entity theory of the corporation at the expense of the partnership-contract theory (about which you learned in Section I). It was also seen in changes in the allocation of power between shareholders, directors, and officers (more about that in Parts 2 & 3). Specifically, if shareholders were principals and directors their agents, not only would the directors be barred from delegating their power to subagents (officers), but any change in the agency relation would require a unanimous shareholder action. Given what you have learned thus far about the development of the modern public corporation, can you see why early twentieth century scholars rejected the agency theory? On the early twentieth century transformation, see MORTON J. HORWITZ, THE TRANSFORMATION OF AMERICAN LAW, 1870–1960: THE CRISIS OF LEGAL ORTHODOXY 65–107 (1992).

Beginning in the 1970s, corporate law scholars resurrected the agency theory. Michael C. Jensen and William H. Meckling offered an explanation of agency theory with respect to corporations in their 1976 article, "Theory of the Firm: Managerial Behavior, Agency Costs, and Ownership Structure." The article reintroduced the traditional rules of contracts into the study of firms and organizations, focusing on "the behavioral implications of the property rights specified in the contract between the owners and managers of the firm." Accordingly, "the relationship between the stockholders and manager of a corporate fit the definition of a pure agency relationship. . . ." *Theory of the Firm: Managerial Behavior, Agency Costs, and Ownership Structure*, 3 J. FIN. ECON. 305 (1976).

Writing about the economic concept of firms (rather than the legal concept of corporations), Jensen and Meckling did not distinguish between executives and directors. They lumped them together as managers. But corporate legal scholars were not troubled by such omission. Their application of Jensen and Meckling's theory of the firm to corporate law had a profound impact on the courts' understanding of the status of the board of directors in the last decades of the twentieth century. If the board is an independent agency, as *Hoyt* held, it is charged with the interests of the corporation. Seen as an agent of the shareholders, however, the board's obligations are deemed to extend only to the latter.

4. As we will see in Part 2, directors (and officers) are presumed to act in good faith, due care and in the best interests of the corporation. Unless a shareholder can rebut this presumption (known as the Business Judgment Rule), the court will not evaluate the board's decisions. As you read the following case, consider which view of the directors' role—the one expressed in *Hoyt* or the agency theory—better supports the business judgment rule.

Shlensky v. Wrigley
95 Ill. App. 2d 173 (Ill. 1968)

SULLIVAN, Justice

This is an appeal from a dismissal of plaintiff's amended complaint on motion of the defendants. The action was a stockholders' derivative suit against the directors for negligence and mismanagement. The corporation was also made a defendant. Plaintiff sought damages and an order that defendants cause the installation of lights in Wrigley Field and the scheduling of night baseball games.

Plaintiff is a minority stockholder of defendant corporation, Chicago National League Ball Club (Inc.), a Delaware corporation with its principal place of business in Chicago, Illinois. Defendant corporation owns and operates the major league professional baseball team known as the Chicago Cubs. The corporation also engages in the operation of Wrigley Field, the Cubs' home park, the concessionaire sales during Cubs' home games, television and radio broadcasts of Cubs' home games, the leasing of the field for football games and other events and receives its share, as visiting team, of admission moneys from games played in other National League stadia. The individual defendants are directors of the Cubs and have served for varying periods of years. Defendant Philip K. Wrigley is also president of the corporation and owner of approximately 80% Of the stock therein.

Plaintiff alleges that since night baseball was first played in 1935 nineteen of the twenty major league teams have scheduled night games. In 1966, out of a total of 1620 games in the major leagues, 932 were played at night. Plaintiff alleges that every member of the major leagues, other than the Cubs, scheduled substantially all of its home games in 1966 at night, exclusive of opening days, Saturdays, Sundays, holidays and days prohibited by league rules. Allegedly this has been done for the specific purpose of maximizing attendance and thereby maximizing revenue and income.

The Cubs, in the years 1961–65, sustained operating losses from its direct baseball operations. Plaintiff attributes those losses to inadequate attendance at Cubs' home games. He concludes that if the directors continue to refuse to install lights at Wrigley Field and schedule night baseball games, the Cubs will continue to sustain comparable losses and its financial condition will continue to deteriorate.

Plaintiff alleges that, except for the year 1963, attendance at Cubs' home games has been substantially below that at their road games, many of which were played at night.

Plaintiff compares attendance at Cubs' games with that of the Chicago White Sox, an American League club, whose weekday games were generally played at night. The weekend attendance figures for the two teams was similar; however, the White Sox week-night games drew many more patrons than did the Cubs' weekday games.

Plaintiff alleges that the funds for the installation of lights can be readily obtained through financing and the cost of installation would be far more than offset and recaptured by increased revenues and incomes resulting from the increased attendance.

==Plaintiff further alleges that defendant Wrigley has refused to install lights,== not because of interest in the welfare of the corporation but because of his personal opinions "that baseball is a 'daytime sport' and that the installation of lights and night baseball games will have a deteriorating effect upon the surrounding neighborhood." It is alleged that he has admitted that he is not interested in whether the Cubs would benefit financially from such action because of his concern for the neighborhood, and that he would be willing for the team to play night games if a new stadium were built in Chicago.

Plaintiff alleges that the other defendant directors, with full knowledge of the foregoing matters, have acquiesced in the policy laid down by Wrigley and have permitted him to dominate the board of directors in matters involving the installation of lights and scheduling of night games, even though they knew he was not motivated by a good faith concern as to the best interests of defendant corporation, but solely by his personal views set forth above. It is charged that the directors are acting for a reason or reasons contrary and wholly unrelated to the business interests of the corporation; that such arbitrary and capricious acts constitute mismanagement and waste of corporate assets, and that the directors have been negligent in failing to exercise reasonable care and prudence in the management of the corporate affairs. *[Claim]*

The question on appeal is whether plaintiff's amended complaint states a cause of action. It is plaintiff's position that fraud, illegality and conflict of interest are not the only bases for a stockholder's derivative action against the directors. Contrariwise, defendants argue that the courts will not step in and interfere with honest business judgment of the directors unless there is a showing of fraud, illegality or conflict of interest.

The cases in this area are numerous and each differs from the others on a factual basis. However, the courts have pronounced certain ground rules which appear in all cases and which are then applied to the given factual situation....

... In *Davis v. Louisville Gas & Electric Co.*, 16 Del.Ch. 157, 142 A. 654, a minority shareholder sought to have the directors enjoined from amending the certificate of incorporation. The court said on page 659:

> We have then a conflict in view between the responsible managers of a corporation and an overwhelming majority of its stockholders on the one hand and a dissenting minority on the other—a conflict touching matters of business policy, such as has occasioned innumerable applications to courts to intervene and determine which of the two conflicting views should prevail. The response which courts make to such applications is that it is not their function to resolve for corporations questions of policy and business management. The directors are chosen to pass upon such questions and their judgment *unless shown to be tainted with fraud* is accepted as final. The judgment of the directors of corporations enjoys the benefit of a presumption that it was formed in good faith and was designed to promote the best interests of the corporation they serve. (Emphasis supplied)

Similarly, the court in *Toebelman v. Missouri-Kansas Pipe Line Co.*, D.C., 41 F.Supp. 334, said at page 339:

> The general legal principle involved is familiar. Citation of authorities is of limited value because the facts of each case differ so widely. Reference may be made to the statement of the rule in *Helfman v. American Light & Traction Company*, 121 N.J.Eq. 1, 187 A. 540, 550, in which the Court stated the law as follows: 'In a purely business corporation ... the authority of the directors in the conduct of the business of the corporation must be regarded as absolute when they act within the law, and the court is without authority to substitute its judgment for that of the directors.'

Plaintiff argues that the allegations of his amended complaint are sufficient to set forth a cause of action under the principles set out in *Dodge v. Ford Motor Co.*, 204 Mich. 459, 170 N.W. 668. In that case plaintiff, owner of about 10% Of the outstanding stock, brought suit against the directors seeking payment of additional dividends and the enjoining of further business expansion. In ruling on the request for dividends the court indicated that the motives of Ford in keeping so much money in the corporation for expansion and security were to benefit the public generally and spread the profits out by means of more jobs, etc. The court felt that these were not only far from related to the good of the stockholders, but amounted to a change in the ends of the corporation and that this was not a purpose contemplated or allowed by the corporate charter....

From the authority relied upon in [*Ford*] it is clear that the court felt that there must be fraud or a breach of that good faith which directors are bound to exercise toward the stockholders in order to justify the courts entering into the internal affairs of corporations. This is made clear when the court refused to interfere with the directors decision to expand the business. . . .

Plaintiff in the instant case argues that the directors are acting for reasons unrelated to the financial interest and welfare of the Cubs. However, we are not satisfied that the motives assigned to Philip K. Wrigley, and through him to the other directors, are contrary to the best interests of the corporation and the stockholders. For example, it appears to us that the effect on the surrounding neighborhood might well be considered by a director who was considering the patrons who would or would not attend the games if the park were in a poor neighborhood. Furthermore, the long run interest of the corporation in its property value at Wrigley Field might demand all efforts to keep the neighborhood from deteriorating. By these thoughts we do not mean to say that we have decided that the decision of the directors was a correct one. That is beyond our jurisdiction and ability. We are merely saying that the decision is one properly before directors and the motives alleged in the amended complaint showed no fraud, illegality or conflict of interest in their making of that decision.

While all the courts do not insist that one or more of the three elements must be present for a stockholder's derivative action to lie, nevertheless we feel that unless the conduct of the defendants at least borders on one of the elements, the courts should not interfere. The trial court in the instant case acted properly in dismissing plaintiff's amended complaint.

We feel that plaintiff's amended complaint was also defective in failing to allege damage to the corporation. . . .

There is no allegation that the night games played by the other nineteen teams enhanced their financial position or that the profits, if any, of those teams were directly related to the number of night games scheduled. There is an allegation that the installation of lights and scheduling of night games in Wrigley Field would have resulted in large amounts of additional revenues and incomes from increased attendance and related sources of income. Further, the cost of installation of lights, funds for which are allegedly readily available by financing, would be more than offset and recaptured by increased revenues. However, no allegation is made that there will be a net benefit to the corporation from such action, considering all increased costs.

Plaintiff claims that the losses of defendant corporation are due to poor attendance at home games. However, it appears from the amended complaint, taken as a whole, that factors other than attendance affect the net earnings or losses. For example, in 1962, attendance at home and road games decreased appreciably as compared with 1961, and yet the loss from direct baseball operation and of the whole corporation was considerably less.

The record shows that plaintiff did not feel he could allege that the increased revenues would be sufficient to cure the corporate deficit. The only cost plaintiff was at all concerned with was that of installation of lights. No mention was made of operation and maintenance of the lights or other possible increases in operating costs of night games and we cannot speculate as to what other factors might influence the increase or decrease of profits if the Cubs were to play night home games.

... [P]laintiff's allegation that the minority stockholders and the corporation have been seriously and irreparably damaged by the wrongful conduct of the defendant directors is a mere conclusion and not based on well pleaded facts in the amended complaint.

Finally, we do not agree with plaintiff's contention that failure to follow the example of the other major league clubs in scheduling night games constituted negligence. Plaintiff made no allegation that these teams' night schedules were profitable or that the purpose for which night baseball had been undertaken was fulfilled. Furthermore, it cannot be said that directors, even those of corporations that are losing money, must follow the lead of the other corporations in the field. Directors are elected for their business capabilities and judgment and the courts cannot require them to forego their judgment because of the decisions of directors of other companies. Courts may not decide these questions in the absence of a clear showing of dereliction of duty on the part of the specific directors and mere failure to 'follow the crowd' is not such a dereliction.

For the foregoing reasons the order of dismissal entered by the trial court is affirmed.

Affirmed.

Questions

1. What is the difference, if any, between Ford's actions (described in *Dodge v. Ford*) and Wrigley's? Why did the court limit Ford's ability to pursue his plans but not Wrigley's?

2. What other courses of action could the plaintiff have pursued? Why did not he simply sell his shares?

We will explore the business judgment rule in Part 2 of this casebook. To conclude our discussion of the (statutorily) absolute power of the board, it is also important to consider important limits on such power, specifically, the board's inability to alter its role as discussed in the following case.

Grimes v. Donald
673 A.2d 1207 (Del. 1996)

VEASEY, Chief Justice

In this appeal we address the following issues: ... (2) a direct claim of alleged abdication by a board of directors of its statutory duty. ...

We hold that the Court of Chancery correctly dismissed this stockholder action for the failure to state a claim upon which relief can be granted where the plaintiff stockholder: (a) asserted a direct claim that the directors abdicated their statutory duty to manage or direct the management of the business and affairs of the corporation by entering various employment contracts (the "Agreements") with the chief executive officer ("CEO") providing that the CEO "shall be responsible for the general management of the affairs of the company" and further providing that the CEO can declare a constructive termination of the Employment Agreement for "unreasonable interference" by the Board with the CEO. . . .

I. The Facts

C.L. Grimes ("Grimes"), plaintiff below-appellant, appeals from the dismissal, for failure to state a claim, of his complaint against James L. Donald ("Donald") (the CEO) and the Board of Directors (the "Board") of DSC Communications Corporation ("DSC" or the "Company"). Grimes seeks a declaration of the invalidity of the Agreements between Donald and the Company. He also seeks an award of damages against Donald and other members of the Board. He alleges that the Board has breached its fiduciary duties by abdicating its authority, failing to exercise due care and committing waste. . . .

The Agreements, executed during 1990, are the focus of the complaint. The Employment Agreement provides that Donald "shall be responsible for the general management of the affairs of the company . . . ," and that Donald "shall report to the Board." The Employment Agreement runs until the earlier of Donald's 75th birthday or his termination (1) by reason of death or disability; (2) for cause; or (3) without cause. Under the Employment Agreement, Donald can declare a "Constructive Termination Without Cause" by the Company of his employment as a result of, *inter alia*, "unreasonable interference, in the good-faith judgment of . . . [Donald], by the Board or a substantial stockholder of the Company, in [Donald's] carrying out his duties and responsibilities under the [Employment] Agreement." A Constructive Termination Without Cause takes effect after delivery of notice by Donald and the failure by the Board to remedy such interference.

In the event of a Termination Without Cause, constructive or otherwise, Donald is entitled to the following:

> 1. Continued payment of his "Base Salary" at the level in effect immediately prior to termination for the remainder of his "Term of Employment," which, as stated, will be 6 1/2 years unless Donald dies or turns 75 first. In 1992, Donald's Base Salary exceeded $650,000.
>
> 2. Annual incentive awards for the remainder of the Term of Employment equal to the average of the three highest annual bonuses awarded to Donald during his last ten years as CEO. In 1992, such award allegedly equaled $300,000.

3. Medical benefits for Donald and his wife for life, as well as his children until the age of 23.

4. Continued participation in all employee benefit plans in which Donald is participating on the date of termination until the earlier of the expiration of the Term of Employment or the date on which he receives equivalent benefits from a subsequent employer.

5. Other (unidentified) benefits in accordance with DSC's plans and programs.

The Income Continuation Plan provides, *inter alia*, that after Base Salary payments cease under the Employment Agreement, Donald is entitled to receive, for the remainder of his life, annual payments equal to the average of the sum of his Base Salary plus bonuses in the three highest years, multiplied by 3%, multiplied by his years of service. Donald has also been awarded 200,000 "units" under the Long Term Incentive Plan. In the event of a Change of Control, as defined in the Incentive Plan, Donald will have the right to cash payments for his units, which Grimes alleges could total $60,000,000 at the stock price in effect at the time the complaint was filed.

[Grimes made a demand on the board, discussed in Part 2, *infra*, in which he demanded that the board terminate Donald's contract on the ground that it was an abdication of directorial duty to Donald. The board rejected Grimes' demand.]

II. Grimes Has Not Stated a Claim for Abdication of Directorial Duty.

. . .

C. Analysis of Grimes' Abdication Claim

In the case before us, the abdication claim fails as a matter of law. Grimes claims that the potentially severe financial penalties which the Company would incur in the event that the Board attempts to interfere in Donald's management of the Company will inhibit and deter the Board from exercising its duties under Section 141(a). The Court of Chancery assumed that, if a contract could have the practical effect of preventing a board from exercising its duties, it would amount to a *de facto* abdication of directorial authority. The Chancellor concluded, however, that Grimes has not set forth well-pleaded allegations which would establish such a situation. We agree.

Putting aside the payments which would result from a change of control, Grimes has pleaded, at most, that Donald would be entitled to $20 million in the event of a Constructive Termination. The Chancellor found, in light of the financial size of DSC reflected in the exhibits to the complaint, that this amount would not constitute a *de facto* abdication. Grimes contends, however, that the payments could amount to a *de facto* abdication in possible future circumstances. Such a set of facts has not been pleaded, is not before this Court, is based on speculation, and is not ripe for adjudication.

Directors may not delegate duties which lie "at the heart of the management of the corporation." *Chapin v. Benwood*. A court "cannot give legal sanction to agreements which have the effect of removing from directors in a very substantial way their duty to use their own best judgment on management matters." *Abercrombie v. Davies.* Distinguishing these cases, however, the Court of Chancery stated: "[U]nlike the agreements considered in *Abercrombie* and *Chapin*, the Donald Agreements do not formally preclude the DSC board from exercising its statutory powers and fulfilling its fiduciary duty." *Compare Rosenblatt v. Getty Oil Co.* (delegation to independent appraiser of responsibility to value oil and gas reserves as part of a merger agreement was proper exercise of business judgment).

With certain exceptions, "an informed decision to delegate a task is as much an exercise of business judgment as any other." *Rosenblatt.* Likewise, business decisions are not an abdication of directorial authority merely because they limit a board's freedom of future action. A board which has decided to manufacture bricks has less freedom to decide to make bottles. In a world of scarcity, a decision to do one thing will commit a board to a certain course of action and make it costly and difficult (indeed, sometimes impossible) to change course and do another. This is an inevitable fact of life and is not an abdication of directorial duty.

If the market for senior management, in the business judgment of a board, demands significant severance packages, boards will inevitably limit their future range of action by entering into employment agreements. Large severance payments will deter boards, to some extent, from dismissing senior officers. If an independent and informed board, acting in good faith, determines that the services of a particular individual warrant large amounts of money, whether in the form of current salary or severance provisions, the board has made a business judgment. That judgment normally will receive the protection of the business judgment rule unless the facts show that such amounts, compared with the services to be received in exchange, constitute waste or could not otherwise be the product of a valid exercise of business judgment.

The Board of DSC retains the ultimate freedom to direct the strategy and affairs of the Company. If Donald disagrees with the Board, the Company may or may not (depending on the circumstances) be required to pay him a substantial sum of money in order to pursue its chosen course of action. So far, we have only a rather unusual contract, but not a case of abdication. The Chancellor correctly dismissed the abdication claim.

Questions

1. Why, according to the court, didn't the board abdicate its duty in *Grimes v. Donald*? Do you find the argument persuasive? Given the agreement with Donald, will the board interfere with his judgment?

2. The dominant model of the board of large American public corporations is the monitoring board, composed largely of outside directors. The monitoring board model is predicated upon the assumption that the role of directors is to hire, compensate, and terminate the CEO and perhaps other senior officers, to provide a check on the corporation's auditing processes, to vote on conflict of interest transactions,

and to act on the most important (and therefore episodic) corporate decisions. The monitoring model contrasts with other board models such as a board that actually manages the corporation or a board that engages in strategic decisionmaking. The monitoring board model came under attack after the corporate scandals of 2002. Critics describe it as outmoded and ineffectual. Having read *Grimes v. Donald*, can you see why?

Section IV
The Corporation's Capital Structure

To understand the rules of American corporate governance, one must also understand the financial structure of the modern public corporation. As you will see in Part 2, modern finance theory has tremendously influenced the development of directors' and officers' fiduciary obligations in the second half of the twentieth century. These obligations, you will notice, are extended only to equity securities.

Equity financing is relatively simple. The corporation's articles of incorporation will describe the different classes of equity securities the corporation's board is authorized to issue, the number authorized for each class, as well as their preferences, limitations and rights (more when we discuss preferred stock). Once sold to shareholders, the securities are "issued and outstanding." If the securities are repurchased by the corporation, they are "issued but not outstanding" or, as they're typically called, "treasury stock." If the corporation must issue more stock than the articles authorize, the articles must be amended.

You have already seen in *Dodge v. Ford* that equity securities may receive dividends. Common shares typically also have voting rights, which grant shareholders some measure of control, however limited, over the corporation's board. If the company liquidates, the shareholders, as the residual claimants will receive distribution only after all other financial claims have been satisfied.

Given corporate law's focus on equity securities, it is important to stress that equity financing is rather limited and corporations regularly use other forms of financing—especially retained earnings and debt—to fund their operations and growth. In this Section IV, we focus on duties owed to holders of securities other than common stock, namely debt and preferred stock, and explore how and why corporate law has not extended fiduciary obligations to these investors. Some of the cases we discuss involve fundamental transactions. You need not worry about the technicalities of the transactions—you'll spend enough time on that in Part 4. Instead, focus on the courts' reasoning regarding the place of bondholders and preferred stockholders in the corporate structure.

A. Debt

Debt is a fixed claim to interest for a certain duration and principal. Companies use debt to finance their operations as well as expansion and development. Banks, institutional investors (i.e., mutual and pension funds, insurance companies) and individuals lend money to corporations. Banks set the detailed terms of the loan in a loan agreement, and their debt is typically secured. Individuals and institutions purchase bonds, debentures or notes. Publicly issued debt is typically not secured but can have different layers of priority—for example, senior and subordinated debentures. Publicly issued debt must meet the registration requirements promulgated under the Securities Act of 1933.

A bond, debenture, or note represents a promise by the borrowing institution to pay a set amount at a set date as well as interest at specific times. In addition, the borrowing corporation enters a contract called indenture with a trustee. The indenture includes different promises that run to the trustee, who enforces the borrower's obligations on behalf of the bondholders. Typically, an indenture specifies the amounts of money and future date of payment, the interest rate and the dates of interest payment, whether the debt is secured (and what is the security), and special covenants that the borrowing corporation accepted. These covenants typically ensure the preservation of the security or, if the debt is not secured, limit the ability of the borrowing corporation to incur more debt or engage in risky (or riskier) investments, require the corporation to maintain a certain net worth or equity to debt ratio, or limit its ability to distribute dividends to its stockholders. In addition, indentures address potential modifications to their terms, especially if the issuer merges into another corporation or sells all or substantially all of its assets. An indenture also typically specifies the duties and obligations of the trustee toward the borrowing corporation and the bondholders. In publicly issued bonds, the language of the indenture is usually standardized.

Lenders, bond and debenture holders (generally referred to as creditors) do not participate in corporate governance in the same way shareholders do. Their relationship with their corporation and their rights are governed by the indenture or loan agreement, and their remedy if the borrowing corporation defaults is a suit for enforcement of contract. By taking a security interest in a particular asset, by insisting on seniority, or by inserting restrictive covenants in the indenture or loan documents, lenders attempt to protect their investment. As you read the following cases, consider whether contractual terms offer adequate protection to debtholders. Consider also what alternative means (in addition to security and seniority) might be available to offer more protection to debtholders.

Simons v. Cogan
549 A.2d 300 (Del. 1988)

WALSH, Justice

This is an appeal from a decision of the Court of Chancery granting a motion to dismiss a class action brought by Louise Simons ("Simons"), a holder of convertible subordinated debentures, against the issuing corporation, Knoll International, Inc. ("Knoll"), its controlling shareholder, Marshall S. Cogan ("Cogan"), and other related corporate constituents. Simons' complaint asserted claims based on violations of fiduciary duty, breach of indenture and common law fraud. In granting the motion to dismiss, the Court of Chancery determined that the issuing corporation and its directors do not owe a fiduciary duty to the debenture holders. In addition, the court ruled that the restrictive provisions of the indenture agreement precluded a claim for breach of indenture. Finally, the court dismissed the fraud claim holding that Simons' complaint failed to plead facts constituting actionable fraud. We agree with the reasoning and holding of the Court of Chancery and accordingly affirm the judgment in all respects.

I

A brief recitation of the facts, consistent with the procedural setting of this appeal and based essentially on the allegations of the complaint, will suffice.

The transaction challenged in this case involves the merger of two related corporations, Hansac, Inc. ("Hansac") and Knoll.[1] The merger which was completed on January 22, 1987, left Knoll, the surviving corporation, as the wholly owned subsidiary of Knoll Holdings. The merger caused the minority shareholders of Knoll to be eliminated through a $12 cash tender offer.

Significantly, the merger also resulted in the execution of a supplemental indenture which eliminated the right of Knoll's convertible debenture holders to convert their debentures into shares of its common stock. The supplemental indenture, which was executed by Knoll and the indenture trustee, provided that in lieu of the right to convert into the common stock of Knoll, the debentures would be convertible into $12.00 cash for each $19.20 principal amount of debenture. An additional supplemental indenture was also executed increasing the interest rate on the debentures from 8 1/2 percent to 9 7/8 percent per annum.

Simons filed a class action on behalf of the holders of Knoll's convertible debentures asserting as a primary cause of action that the defendants, in terminating the

---

[1]. Hansac is a wholly owned subsidiary of GFI Nevada, Inc. ("GFI Nevada"). GFI Nevada is wholly owned by General Felt Industries, Inc. which is in turn wholly owned by Knoll International Holding, Inc. ("Knoll Holding"). Knoll Holding through its subsidiary GFI Nevada controls approximately 90.5 percent of the voting stock of Knoll. Marshall S. Cogan, an individual defendant, controls 51.5 percent of the voting interests of Knoll Holding giving him effective control of both Hansac and Knoll.

right to convert the debentures into the common stock of Knoll, breached a fiduciary duty to the debenture holders. In support of this claim the complaint essentially alleges: (1) Cogan, as the controlling shareholder of both Knoll and Hansac, unilaterally set the $12 conversion price without negotiating with a representative of the debenture holders; (2) there were conflicts of interest among Knoll's directors and no special committee of independent directors was formed to evaluate the transaction; (3) Knoll's directors did not seek other offers to acquire Knoll; and (4) the transaction was timed to take advantage of the 1986 low point in the trading price of Knoll's shares and debentures. Moreover, it is claimed that the $12 conversion price was unfair and inadequate....

II

The first issue presented in this appeal, whether the directors of the issuing corporation owe a fiduciary duty to the holders of convertible debentures, requires that we revisit a question addressed indirectly in an earlier opinion of this Court, *Harff v. Kerkorian*. [The court discusses the *Harff* case]....

Notwithstanding the clear inference of our holding in *Harff* [remanding the case for a trial on fraud, without addressing the Chancery Court's implication that convertible debenture holders might be owed extracontractual duties based on "special circumstances"], we deem it advisable to address directly the fiduciary claim asserted by Simons here and in the Court of Chancery. In order to determine whether a holder of a convertible debenture is owed a fiduciary duty by the issuing corporation and its directors we must begin our analysis with an examination of the nature of the interest or entitlement underlying a convertible debenture. A debenture represents a long term unsecured debt of the issuing corporation convertible into stock under certain specified conditions. A debenture is a credit instrument which does not devolve upon its holder an equity interest in the issuing corporation. Similarly, the convertibility feature of the debenture does not impart an equity element until conversion occurs. This distinction was noted by the Chancellor in *Harff*:

> "That a bond is convertible at the sole option of its holder into stock should no more affect its essential quality of being a bond than should the fact that cash is convertible into stock affect the nature of cash. Any bond, or any property, for that matter, is convertible into stock through the intermediate step of converting it to cash.... [C]ase law indicates that a convertible debenture is a bond and not an equity security until conversion occurs."

In sum, a convertible debenture represents a contractual entitlement to the repayment of a debt and does not represent an equitable interest in the issuing corporation necessary for the imposition of a trust relationship with concomitant fiduciary duties.

Simons argues that this traditional analysis has been softened by cases which have held that convertible debenture holders possess an interest in the underlying corporation sufficient to warrant the imposition of fiduciary duties. Typical of this expansive theory is *Green v. Hamilton Int'l Corp*. Interpreting the significance of the opinion in *Harff*, the court in *Green* reasoned:

> [*Harff*] supports two propositions relevant to the matter before this Court. First, under Delaware law, convertible debenture holders do not possess all the rights of shareholders with respect to actions taken by corporate directors or majority shareholders. Second, in certain circumstances, a holder of a convertible debenture is entitled to different treatment from a mere creditor of a corporation, and a cause of action for breach of fiduciary duty may lie under Delaware law apart from the express terms of an Indenture Agreement.
>
> . . .
>
> As holders of convertible debentures, plaintiffs were part of the entire community of interests in the corporation — creditors as well as stockholders to whom the fiduciary duties of directors and controlling shareholders run.

As previously indicated, we do not believe that our holding in *Harff* supports an inference that a fiduciary duty is owed to holders of convertible debentures. Nor are we persuaded by the reasoning in *Green*. In relying on an expectancy interest created by the conversion feature of the debenture, the *Green* court misperceives the type of interest required for the imposition of fiduciary duties under Delaware law. As this Court recently noted in *Anadarko Petroleum Corp. v. Panhandle Eastern Corp.*, a mere expectancy interest does not create a fiduciary relationship. Before a fiduciary duty arises, an existing property right or equitable interest supporting such a duty must exist. The obvious example is stock ownership. Until the debenture is converted into stock the convertible debenture holder acquires no equitable interest, and remains a creditor of the corporation whose interests are protected by the contractual terms of the indenture. . . .

The decision of the Court of Chancery dismissing Simons' complaint is affirmed.

Questions

1. You will study fiduciary duty closely in Part 2 of this casebook. For now, it is enough to know that to have a fiduciary duty to someone means that it is your responsibility to look after their interests. For directors and a corporation to have a fiduciary duty to stockholders means that it is to stockholder interests — and none other — that they are to look in considering business decisions.

2. What are the potential conflicts between bondholders and stockholders? What are the potential benefits to stockholders in having the corporation rely on debt financing?

3. What is Simons complaining about? Why does she think she is entitled to her conversion right? What other harm might she have suffered by the transaction between Knoll and Hansac?

4. The court concludes that fiduciary duties attach to a proprietary interest. Bondholders have a contractual relationship with their corporations and are thus not owed fiduciary obligations. Does the court explain why? Is the reasoning persuasive? Even if the reasoning itself is not, why do you think the court concludes that an equity (ownership) interest is required for a fiduciary duty to attach? Does the court explain this conclusion? Based upon what we've seen of the stockholder ownership concept, does this conclusion make sense? How do you think bonds differ from stock, and are these differences enough to justify the court's narrow focus of fiduciary duty? What alternatives are there to the court's approach? What problems do these alternatives present?

In the 1980s and 1990s, corporations began using debt to return value to their shareholders. Takeovers, stock buybacks, and leverage became management's principal techniques to satisfy stock price appreciation. The following case addresses a leveraged buyout (LBO). In an LBO, an acquiring corporation uses borrowed funds to purchase a target company, using the target company's assets as security. The borrowed funds are used to buy out the stockholders while the company becomes heavily leveraged, thus putting existing debt-holders at higher risk of default. Does (and should) the company have any duties to its debt-holders when engaging in an LBO? Consider this question as you read the case.

Metropolitan Life Insurance Company v. RJR Nabisco, Inc.
716 F. Supp. 1504 (S.D.N.Y. 1989)

WALKER, District Judge

I. INTRODUCTION

The corporate parties to this action are among the country's most sophisticated financial institutions, as familiar with the Wall Street investment community and the securities market as American consumers are with the Oreo cookies and Winston cigarettes made by defendant RJR Nabisco, Inc. (sometimes "the company" or "RJR Nabisco"). The present action traces its origins to October 20, 1988, when F. Ross Johnson, then the Chief Executive Officer of RJR Nabisco, proposed a $17 billion leveraged buy-out ("LBO") of the company's shareholders, at $75 per share.[1] Within a few days, a bidding war developed among the investment group led by Johnson and the investment firm of Kohlberg Kravis Roberts & Co. ("KKR"), and others. On December 1, 1988, a special committee of RJR Nabisco directors, established by

---

1. A leveraged buy-out occurs when a group of investors, usually including members of a company's management team, buy the company under financial arrangements that include little equity and significant new debt. The necessary debt financing typically includes mortgages or high risk/high yield bonds, popularly known as "junk bonds." Additionally, a portion of this debt is generally secured by the company's assets. Some of the acquired company's assets are usually sold after the transaction is completed in order to reduce the debt incurred in the acquisition.

the company specifically to consider the competing proposals, recommended that the company accept the KKR proposal, a $24 billion LBO that called for the purchase of the company's outstanding stock at roughly $109 per share.

. . . RJR Nabisco was also scheduled to assume roughly $19 billion of new debt. . . . [T]he merger was ultimately completed during the week of April 24, 1989.

Plaintiffs now allege, in short, that RJR Nabisco's actions have drastically impaired the value of bonds previously issued to plaintiffs by, in effect, misappropriating the value of those bonds to help finance the LBO and to distribute an enormous windfall to the company's shareholders. As a result, plaintiffs argue, they have unfairly suffered a multimillion dollar loss in the value of their bonds.

Although the numbers involved in this case are large, and the financing necessary to complete the LBO unprecedented the legal principles nonetheless remain discrete and familiar. Yet while the instant motions thus primarily require the Court to evaluate and apply traditional rules of equity and contract interpretation, plaintiffs do raise issues of first impression in the context of an LBO. At the heart of the present motions lies plaintiffs' claim that RJR Nabisco violated a restrictive covenant—not an explicit covenant found within the four corners of the relevant bond indentures, but rather an *implied* covenant of good faith and fair dealing—not to incur the debt necessary to facilitate the LBO and thereby betray what plaintiffs claim was the fundamental basis of their bargain with the company. The company, plaintiffs assert, consistently reassured its bondholders that it had a "mandate" from its Board of Directors to maintain RJR Nabisco's preferred credit rating. Plaintiffs ask this Court first to imply a covenant of good faith and fair dealing that would prevent the recent transaction, then to hold that this covenant has been breached, and finally to require RJR Nabisco to redeem their bonds.

RJR Nabisco defends the LBO by pointing to express provisions in the bond indentures that, *inter alia,* permit mergers and the assumption of additional debt. These provisions, as well as others that could have been included but were not, were known to the market and to plaintiffs, sophisticated investors who freely bought the bonds and were equally free to sell them at any time. Any attempt by this Court to create contractual terms *post hoc,* defendants contend, not only finds no basis in the controlling law and undisputed facts of this case, but also would constitute an impermissible invasion into the free and open operation of the marketplace.

For the reasons set forth below, this Court agrees with defendants. There being no express covenant between the parties that would restrict the incurrence of new debt, and no perceived direction to that end from covenants that are express, this Court will not imply a covenant to prevent the recent LBO and thereby create an indenture term that, while bargained for in other contexts, was not bargained for here and was not even within the mutual contemplation of the parties.

II. BACKGROUND

. . .

A. *The Parties*

Metropolitan Life Insurance Co. ("MetLife"), incorporated in New York, is a life insurance company . . . . MetLife's assets exceed $88 billion and its debt securities holdings exceed $49 billion. MetLife is a mutual company and therefore has no stockholders and is instead operated for the benefit of its policyholders. MetLife . . . owns $340,542,000 in principal amount of six separate RJR Nabisco debt issues . . . MetLife also owned 186,000 shares of RJR Nabisco common stock at the time this suit was filed.

. . .

RJR Nabisco, a Delaware corporation, is a consumer products holding company that owns some of the country's best known product lines . . . . KKR, a private investment firm, organizes funds through which investors provide pools of equity to finance LBOs.

B. *The Indentures*

The bonds implicated by this suit are governed by long, detailed indentures, which in turn are governed by New York contract law. No one disputes that the holders of public bond issues, like plaintiffs here, often enter the market after the indentures have been negotiated and memorialized. Thus, those indentures are often not the product of face-to-face negotiations between the ultimate holders and the issuing company. What remains equally true, however, is that underwriters ordinarily negotiate the terms of the indentures with the issuers. Since the underwriters must then sell or place the bonds, they necessarily negotiate in part with the interests of the buyers in mind. Moreover, these indentures were not secret agreements foisted upon unwitting participants in the bond market. No successive holder is required to accept or to continue to hold the bonds, governed by their accompanying indentures; indeed, plaintiffs readily admit that they could have sold their bonds right up until the announcement of the LBO. Instead, sophisticated investors like plaintiffs are well aware of the indenture terms and, presumably, review them carefully before lending hundreds of millions of dollars to any company.

Indeed, the prospectuses for the indentures contain a statement relevant to this action:

> The Indenture contains no restrictions on the creation of unsecured short-term debt by [RJR Nabisco] or its subsidiaries, no restriction on the creation of unsecured Funded Debt by [RJR Nabisco] or its subsidiaries which are not Restricted Subsidiaries, and no restriction on the payment of dividends by [RJR Nabisco].

. . .

1. The relevant Articles

A typical RJR Nabisco indenture contains thirteen Articles. At least four of them are relevant to the present motions and thus merit a brief review.

Article Three delineates the covenants of the issuer. Most important, it first provides for payment of principal and interest. . . . The Article also contains "negative pledge" and related provisions, which restrict mortgages or other liens on the assets of RJR Nabisco or its subsidiaries and seek to protect the bondholders from being subordinated to other debt.

Article Five describes various procedures to remedy defaults and the responsibilities of the Trustee. . . .

Article Nine governs the adoption of supplemental indentures. It provides, *inter alia,* that the Issuer and the Trustee can

> add to the covenants of the Issuer such further covenants, restrictions, conditions or provisions as its Board of Directors by Board Resolution and the Trustee shall consider to be for the protection of the holders of Securities, and to make the occurrence, or the occurrence and continuance, of a default in any such additional covenants, restrictions, conditions or provisions an Event of Default permitting the enforcement of all or any of the several remedies provided in this Indenture as herein set forth . . .

Article Ten addresses a potential "Consolidation, Merger, Sale or Conveyance," and explicitly sets forth the conditions under which the company can consolidate or merge into or with any other corporation. It provides explicitly that RJR Nabisco "may consolidate with, or sell or convey, all or substantially all of its assets to, or merge into or with any other corporation," so long as the new entity is a United States corporation, and so long as it assumes RJR Nabisco's debt. The Article also requires that any such transaction not result in the company's default under any indenture provision.

2. The elimination of restrictive covenants

In its Amended Complaint, MetLife lists the six debt issues on which it bases its claims. Indentures for two of those issues—the 10.25 percent Notes due in 1990, of which MetLife continues to hold $10 million, and the 8.9 percent Debentures due in 1996, of which MetLife continues to hold $50 million—once contained express covenants that, among other things, restricted the company's ability to incur precisely the sort of debt involved in the recent LBO. In order to eliminate those restrictions, the parties to this action renegotiated the terms of those indentures, first in 1983 and then again in 1985.

MetLife acquired $50 million principal amount of 10.25 percent Notes from Del Monte in July of 1975. To cover the $50 million, MetLife and Del Monte entered into a loan agreement. That agreement restricted Del Monte's ability, among other things, to incur the sort of indebtedness involved in the RJR Nabisco LBO. In 1979, R.J. Reynolds—the corporate predecessor to RJR Nabisco—purchased Del Monte and assumed its indebtedness. Then, in December of 1983, R.J. Reynolds requested MetLife to agree to deletions of those restrictive covenants in exchange for various guarantees from R.J. Reynolds. . . .

MetLife acquired the 8.9 percent Debentures from R.J. Reynolds in October of 1976 in a private placement. A promissory note evidenced MetLife's $100 million loan. That note, like the Del Monte agreement, contained covenants that restricted R.J. Reynolds' ability to incur new debt. In June of 1985, R.J. Reynolds announced its plans to acquire Nabisco Brands in a $3.6 billion transaction that involved the incurrence of a significant amount of new debt. R.J. Reynolds requested MetLife to waive compliance with these restrictive covenants in light of the Nabisco acquisition.

In exchange for certain benefits, MetLife agreed to exchange its 8.9 percent debentures—which *did* contain explicit debt limitations—for debentures issued under a public indenture—which contain no explicit limits on new debt. . . .

. . .

Solely for the purposes of these motions, the Court accepts various factual assertions advanced by plaintiffs: first, that RJR Nabisco actively solicited "investment grade" ratings for its debt; second, that it relied on descriptions of its strong capital structure and earnings record which included prominent display of its ability to pay the interest obligations on its long-term debt several times over; and third, that the company made express or implied representations not contained in the relevant indentures concerning its future creditworthiness . . . .

III. DISCUSSION

. . .

A. *Plaintiffs' Case Against the RJR Nabisco LBO*

1. Count One: The implied covenant

In their first count, plaintiffs assert that

> [d]efendant RJR Nabisco owes a continuing duty of good faith and fair dealing in connection with the contract [i.e., the indentures] through which it borrowed money from MetLife, Jefferson-Pilot and other holders of its debt, including a duty not to frustrate the purpose of the contracts to the debtholders or to deprive the debtholders of the intended object of the contracts—purchase of investment-grade securities.

> In the "buy-out," the [c]ompany breaches the duty [or implied covenant] of good faith and fair dealing by, *inter alia*, destroying the investment grade quality of the debt and transferring that value to the "buy-out" proponents and to the shareholders.

In effect, plaintiffs contend that express covenants were not necessary because an *implied* covenant would prevent what defendants have now done.

. . .

In contracts like bond indentures, "an implied covenant . . . derives its substance directly from the language of the Indenture, and 'cannot give the holders of Debentures any rights inconsistent with those set out in the Indenture.' [*Where*] *plaintiffs' contractual rights* [*have not been*] *violated, there can have been no breach of an implied covenant.*"

. . .

The appropriate analysis, then, is first to examine the indentures to determine "the fruits of the agreement" between the parties, and then to decide whether those "fruits" have been spoiled—which is to say, whether plaintiffs' contractual rights have been violated by defendants.

. . .

A review of the parties' submissions and the indentures themselves satisfies the Court that the substantive "fruits" guaranteed by those contracts and relevant to the present motions include the periodic and regular payment of interest and the eventual repayment of principal. According to a typical indenture, a default shall occur if the company either (1) fails to pay principal when due; (2) fails to make a timely sinking fund payment; (3) fails to pay within 30 days of the due date thereof any interest on the date; or (4) fails duly to observe or perform any of the express covenants or agreements set forth in the agreement. Plaintiffs' Amended Complaint nowhere alleges that RJR Nabisco has breached these contractual obligations; interest payments continue and there is no reason to believe that the principal will not be paid when due.

It is not necessary to decide that indentures like those at issue could never support a finding of additional benefits, under different circumstances with different parties. Rather, for present purposes, it is sufficient to conclude what obligation is *not* covered, either explicitly or implicitly, by these contracts held by these plaintiffs. Accordingly, this Court holds that the "fruits" of these indentures do not include an implied restrictive covenant that would prevent the incurrence of new debt to facilitate the recent LBO. To hold otherwise would permit these plaintiffs to straightjacket the company in order to guarantee their investment. These plaintiffs do not invoke an implied covenant of good faith to protect a legitimate, mutually contemplated benefit of the indentures; rather, they seek to have this Court create an additional benefit for which they did not bargain.

. . .

Plaintiffs argue in the most general terms that the fundamental basis of all these indentures was that an LBO along the lines of the recent RJR Nabisco transaction would never be undertaken, that indeed *no* action would be taken, intentionally or not, that would significantly deplete the company's assets. Accepting plaintiffs' theory, their fundamental bargain with defendants dictated that nothing would be done to jeopardize the extremely high probability that the company would remain able to make interest payments and repay principal over the 20 to 30 year indenture term—and perhaps by logical extension even included the right to ask a court "to make sure that plaintiffs had made a good investment." ... Plaintiffs' submissions ... remind the Court that a "fundamental basis" or a "fruit of an agreement" is often in the eye of the beholder, whose vision may well change along with the market, and who may, with hindsight, imagine a different bargain than the one he actually and initially accepted with open eyes.

The sort of unbounded and one-sided elasticity urged by plaintiffs would interfere with and destabilize the market. And this Court, like the parties to these contracts, cannot ignore or disavow the marketplace in which the contract is performed. Nor can it ignore the expectations of that market—expectations, for instance, that the terms of an indenture will be upheld, and that a court will not, *sua sponte,* add new substantive terms to that indenture as it sees fit. The Court has no reason to believe that the market, in evaluating bonds such as those at issue here, did not discount for the possibility that any company, even one the size of RJR Nabisco, might engage in an LBO heavily financed by debt. That the bonds did not lose any of their value until the October 20, 1988 announcement of a possible RJR Nabisco LBO only suggests that the market had theretofore evaluated the risks of such a transaction as slight.

The Court recognizes that the market is not a static entity, but instead involves what plaintiffs call "evolving understanding[s]." Just as the growing prevalence of LBO's has helped change certain ground rules and expectations in the field of mergers and acquisitions, so too it has obviously affected the bond market, a fact no one disputes. To support their argument that defendants have violated an implied covenant, plaintiffs contend that, since the October 20, 1988 announcement, the bond market has "stopped functioning." They argue that if they had "sold and abandoned the market [before October 20, 1988], the market, if everyone had the same attitude, would have disappeared." What plaintiffs term "stopped functioning" or "disappeared," however, are properly seen as natural responses and adjustments to market realities. Plaintiffs of course do not contend that no new issues are being sold, or that existing issues are no longer being traded or have become worthless.

To respond to changed market forces, new indenture provisions can be negotiated, ... There is no guarantee, of course, that companies like RJR Nabisco would accept such new covenants; parties retain the freedom to enter into contracts as they choose. But presumably, multi-billion dollar investors like plaintiffs have some say in the terms of the investments they make and continue to hold. And, presumably, companies like RJR Nabisco need the infusions of capital such investors are capable of providing.

Whatever else may be true about this case, it certainly does not present an example of the classic sort of form contract or contract of adhesion often frowned upon by courts. In those cases, what motivates a court is the strikingly inequitable nature of the parties' respective bargaining positions. Plaintiffs here entered this "liquid trading market," with their eyes open and were free to leave at any time. Instead they remained there notwithstanding its well understood risks.

Ultimately, plaintiffs cannot escape the inherent illogic of their argument. On the one hand, it is undisputed that investors like plaintiffs recognized that companies like RJR Nabisco strenuously opposed additional restrictive covenants that might limit the incurrence of new debt or the company's ability to engage in a merger. Furthermore, plaintiffs argue that they had no choice other than to accept the indentures as written, without additional restrictive covenants, or to "abandon" the market.

Yet on the other hand, plaintiffs ask this Court to imply a covenant that would have just that restrictive effect because, they contend, it reflects precisely the fundamental assumption of the market and the fundamental basis of their bargain with defendants. If that truly were the case here, it is difficult to imagine why an insistence on that term would have forced the plaintiffs to abandon the market. . . .

In the final analysis, plaintiffs offer no objective or reasonable standard for a court to use in its effort to define the sort of actions their "implied covenant" would permit a corporation to take, and those it would not. Plaintiffs say only that investors like themselves rely upon the "skill" and "good faith" of a company's board and management, and that their covenant would prevent the company from "destroy [ing] . . . the legitimate expectations of its long-term bondholders." As is clear from the preceding discussion, however, plaintiffs have failed to convince the Court that by upholding the explicit, bargained-for terms of the indenture, RJR Nabisco has either exhibited bad faith or destroyed plaintiffs' *legitimate,* protected expectations.

. . .

2. Count Five: In Equity

. . .

Third, plaintiffs advance a claim that remains based, their assertions to the contrary notwithstanding, on an alleged breach of a fiduciary duty. . . .

In the venerable case of *Meinhard v. Salmon*, 249 N.Y. 458, 164 N.E. 545 (1928), then Chief Judge Cardozo explained the obligations imposed on a fiduciary, and why those obligations are so special and rare:

> Many forms of conduct permissible in a workaday world for those acting at arm's length, are forbidden to those bound by fiduciary ties. A trustee is held to something stricter than the morals of the market place. Not honesty alone, but the punctilio of an honor the most sensitive, is then the standard of behavior. As to this there has developed a tradition that is unbending and inveterate. Uncompromising rigidity has been the attitude of courts of equity when petitioned to undermine the rule of undivided loyalty . . . Only thus has the level of conduct for fiduciaries been kept at a level higher than that trodden by the crowd.

Before a court recognizes the duty of a "punctilio of an honor the most sensitive," it must be certain that the complainant is entitled to more than the "morals of the market place," and the protections offered by actions based on fraud, state statutes or the panoply of available federal securities laws. This Court has concluded that the plaintiffs presently before it — sophisticated investors who are unsecured creditors — are not entitled to such additional protections.

Equally important, plaintiffs' position on this issue — that "A Company May Not Deliberately Deplete its Assets to the Injury of its Debtholders," provides no reasonable or workable limits, and is thus reminiscent of their implied covenant of good faith. Indeed, many indisputably legitimate corporate transactions would not survive plaintiffs' theory. With no workable limits, plaintiffs' envisioned duty would extend equally to trade creditors, employees, and every other person to whom the defendants are liable in any way. Of all such parties, these informed plaintiffs least require a Court's equitable protection; not only are they willing participants in a largely impersonal market, but they also possess the financial sophistication and size to secure their own protection.

. . .

III. CONCLUSION

For the reasons set forth above, the Court grants defendants summary judgment on Counts I and V, judgment on the pleadings for certain of the securities at issue in Count III, and dismisses for want of requisite particularity Counts II, III, and IX. All remaining motions made by the parties are denied in all respects. . . .

Questions

1. Why is MetLife complaining? How, if at all, did RJR Nabisco's obligations toward MetLife change? How did the LBO alter MetLife's position? What could have MetLife done *ex ante* to protect the value of its investment in RJR Nabisco?

2. Why does Judge Walker reject MetLife's argument regarding the implied covenant of good faith and fair dealing? Do you agree?

3. Between 1984 and 1988, "as a result of takeovers, buyouts, or defensive maneuvers by companies borrowing heavily to avoid a raid . . . [an estimated] $160 billion worth of bonds have been downgraded, clipping bondholders of at least $13 billion." Gary Hector, *The Bondholders Cold New World*, FORTUNE, February 27, 1989. What, if anything, can bondholders do to protect their investments?

In addition to being subject to interpretation, bond contracts, like other contracts, can be changed. When a borrowing corporation runs into financial difficulties, it might seek to lessen its debt obligations by convincing the bondholders to agree to certain modifications (lower interest rates, waive covenants, forgive default) to the indenture or even to exchange their bonds for different securities. Section 316 of the Trust Indenture Act of 1939 restricts the ability of corporations to alter certain bond terms without the consent of the individual bondholder. It provides that:

(a) . . . The indenture to be qualified—

(1) shall automatically be deemed (unless it is expressly provided therein that any such provision is excluded) to contain provisions authorizing

the holders of not less than a majority in principal amount of the indenture securities or if expressly specified in such indenture, of any series of securities at the time outstanding (A) to direct the time, method, and place of conducting any proceeding for any remedy available to such trustee, or exercising any trust or power conferred upon such trustee, under such indenture, or (B) on behalf of the holders of all such indenture securities, to consent to the waiver of any past default and its consequences; or

(2) may contain provisions authorizing the holders of not less than 75 per centum in principal amount of the indenture securities or if expressly specified in such indenture, of any series of securities at the time outstanding to consent on behalf of the holders of all such indenture securities to the postponement of any interest payment for a period not exceeding three years from its due date.

(b) Not withstanding any other provision of the indenture to be qualified, the right of any holder of any indenture security to receive payment of the principal of and interest on such indenture security, on or after the respective due dates expressed in such indenture security, or to institute suit for the enforcement of any such payment on or after such respective dates, shall not be impaired or affected without the consent of such holder . . . .

Is section 316(b) protective of the interests of debtholders? Could it encourage opportunistic behavior on the part of debtholders? Might it encourage holdouts? How might companies bypass its requirements? Consider this question as you read the following case.

Katz v. Oak Industries, Inc.
508 A.2d 873 (1986)

ALLEN, Chancellor

A commonly used word—seemingly specific and concrete when used in everyday speech—may mask troubling ambiguities that upon close examination are seen to derive not simply from casual use but from more fundamental epistemological problems. Few words more perfectly illustrate the deceptive dependability of language than the term "coercion" which is at the heart of the theory advanced by plaintiff as entitling him to a preliminary injunction in this case.

Plaintiff is the owner of long-term debt securities issued by Oak Industries, Inc. ("Oak"), a Delaware corporation; in this class action he seeks to enjoin the consummation of an exchange offer and consent solicitation made by Oak to holders of various classes of its long-term debt. As detailed below that offer is an integral part of a series of transactions that together would effect a major reorganization and recapitalization of Oak. The claim asserted is in essence, that the exchange offer is a coercive device and, in the circumstances, constitutes a breach of contract. This is the Court's opinion on plaintiff's pending application for a preliminary injunction.

I

The background facts are involved even when set forth in the abbreviated form the decision within the time period currently available requires.

Through its domestic and foreign subsidiaries and affiliated entities, Oak manufactures and markets component equipment used in consumer, industrial and military products (the "Components Segment"); produces communications equipment for use in cable television systems and satellite television systems (the "Communications Segment") and manufactures and markets laminates and other materials used in printed circuit board applications (the "Materials Segment"). During 1985, the Company has terminated certain other unrelated businesses. As detailed below, it has now entered into an agreement with Allied-Signal, Inc. for the sale of the Materials Segment of its business and is currently seeking a buyer for its Communications Segment.

Even a casual review of Oak's financial results over the last several years shows it unmistakably to be a company in deep trouble. During the period from January 1, 1982 through September 30, 1985, the Company has experienced unremitting losses from operations; on net sales of approximately $1.26 billion during that period it has lost over $335 million. As a result its total stockholders' equity has first shriveled (from $260 million on 12/31/81 to $85 million on 12/31/83) and then disappeared completely (as of 9/30/85 there was a $62 million deficit in its stockholders' equity accounts). Financial markets, of course, reflected this gloomy history.[2]

Unless Oak can be made profitable within some reasonably short time it will not continue as an operating company. Oak's board of directors, comprised almost entirely of outside directors, has authorized steps to buy the company time. In February, 1985, in order to reduce a burdensome annual cash interest obligation on its $230 million of then outstanding debentures, the Company offered to exchange such debentures for a combination of notes, common stock and warrants. As a result, approximately $180 million principal amount of the then outstanding debentures were exchanged. Since interest on certain of the notes issued in that exchange offer is payable in common stock, the effect of the 1985 exchange offer was to reduce to some extent the cash drain on the Company caused by its significant debt.

About the same time that the 1985 exchange offer was made, the Company announced its intention to discontinue certain of its operations and sell certain of its properties. Taking these steps, while effective to stave off a default and to reduce to some extent the immediate cash drain, did not address Oak's longer-range problems. Therefore, also during 1985 representatives of the Company held informal discussions with several interested parties exploring the possibility of an investment

---

2. The price of the company's common stock has fallen from over $30 per share on December 31, 1981 to approximately $2 per share recently. The debt securities that are the subject of the exchange offer here involved have traded at substantial discounts.

from, combination with or acquisition by another company. As a result of these discussions, the Company and Allied-Signal, Inc. entered into two agreements. The first, the Acquisition Agreement, contemplates the sale to Allied-Signal of the Materials Segment for $160 million in cash. The second agreement, the Stock Purchase Agreement, provides for the purchase by Allied-Signal for $15 million cash of 10 million shares of the Company's common stock together with warrants to purchase additional common stock.

The Stock Purchase Agreement provides as a condition to Allied-Signal's obligation that at least 85% of the aggregate principal amount of all of the Company's debt securities shall have tendered and accepted the exchange offers that are the subject of this lawsuit. Oak has six classes of such long term debt.[3] If less than 85% of the aggregate principal amount of such debt accepts the offer, Allied-Signal has an option, but no obligation, to purchase the common stock and warrants contemplated by the Stock Purchase Agreement. An additional condition for the closing of the Stock Purchase Agreement is that the sale of the Company's Materials Segment contemplated by the Acquisition Agreement shall have been concluded.

Thus, as part of the restructuring and recapitalization contemplated by the Acquisition Agreement and the Stock Purchase Agreement, the Company has extended an exchange offer to each of the holders of the six classes of its long-term debt securities. These pending exchange offers include a Common Stock Exchange Offer (available only to holders of the 9 ⅝% convertible notes) and the Payment Certificate Exchange Offers (available to holders of all six classes of Oak's long-term debt securities). The Common Stock Exchange Offer currently provides for the payment to each tendering note-holder of 407 shares of the Company's common stock in exchange for each $1,000 9 ⅝% note accepted. The offer is limited to $38.6 million principal amount of notes (out of approximately $83.9 million outstanding).

The Payment Certificate Exchange Offer is an any and all offer. Under its terms, a payment certificate, payable in cash five days after the closing of the sale of the Materials Segment to Allied-Signal, is offered in exchange for debt securities. The cash value of the Payment Certificate will vary depending upon the particular security tendered. In each instance, however, that payment will be less than the face amount of the obligation. The cash payments range in amount, per $1,000 of principal, from $918 to $655. These cash values however appear to represent a premium over the market prices for the Company's debentures as of the time the terms of the transaction were set.

---

3. The three classes of debentures are: 13.65% debentures due April 1, 2001, 10 ½% convertible subordinated debentures due February 1, 2002, and 11 ⅞% subordinated debentures due May 15, 1998. In addition, as a result of the 1985 exchange offer the company has three classes of notes which were issued in exchange for debentures that were tendered in that offer. Those are: 13.5% senior notes due May 15, 1990, 9 ⅝% convertible notes due September 15, 1991 and 11 ⅝% notes due September 15, 1990.

The Payment Certificate Exchange Offer is subject to certain important conditions before Oak has an obligation to accept tenders under it. First, it is necessary that a minimum amount ($38.6 million principal amount out of $83.9 total outstanding principal amount) of the 9 ⅝% notes be tendered pursuant to the Common Stock Exchange Offer. Secondly, it is necessary that certain minimum amounts of each class of debt securities be tendered, together with consents to amendments to the underlying indentures.[4] Indeed, under the offer one may not tender securities unless at the same time one consents to the proposed amendments to the relevant indentures.

The condition of the offer that tendering security holders must consent to amendments in the indentures governing the securities gives rise to plaintiff's claim of breach of contract in this case. Those amendments would, if implemented, have the effect of removing significant negotiated protections to holders of the Company's long-term debt including the deletion of all financial covenants. Such modification may have adverse consequences to debt holders who elect not to tender pursuant to either exchange offer.

Allied-Signal apparently was unwilling to commit to the $15 million cash infusion contemplated by the Stock Purchase Agreement, unless Oak's long-term debt is reduced by 85% (at least that is a condition of their obligation to close on that contract). Mathematically, such a reduction may not occur without the Company reducing the principal amount of outstanding debentures (that is the three classes outstanding notes constitute less than 85% of all long-term debt). But existing indenture covenants prohibit the Company, so long as any of its long-term notes are outstanding, from issuing any obligation (including the Payment Certificates) in exchange for any of the debentures. Thus, in this respect, amendment to the indentures is required in order to close the Stock Purchase Agreement as presently structured.

Restrictive covenants in the indentures would appear to interfere with effectuation of the recapitalization in another way. Section 4.07 of the 13.50% Indenture provides that the Company may not "acquire" for value any of the 9 ⅝% Notes or 11 ⅝% Notes unless it concurrently "redeems" a proportionate amount of the 13.50% Notes. This covenant, if unamended, would prohibit the disproportionate acquisition of the 9 ⅝% Notes that may well occur as a result of the Exchange Offers; in addition, it would appear to require the payment of the "redemption" price for the 13.50% Notes rather than the lower, market price offered in the exchange offer.

---

4. The holders of more than 50% of the principal amount of each of the 13.5% notes, the 9 ⅝% notes and the 11 ⅝% notes and at least 66 ⅔% of the principal amount of the 13.65% debentures, 10 ½% debentures, and 11 ⅞% debentures, must validly tender such securities and consent to certain proposed amendments to the indentures governing those securities.

In sum, the failure to obtain the requisite consents to the proposed amendments would permit Allied-Signal to decline to consummate both the Acquisition Agreement and the Stock Purchase Agreement.

. . .

II

Plaintiff's claim that the Exchange Offers and Consent Solicitation constitutes a threatened wrong to him and other holders of Oak's debt securities[6] appear to be summarized in paragraph 16 of his Complaint:

> The purpose and effect of the Exchange Offers is [1] to benefit Oak's common stockholders at the expense of the Holders of its debt securities, [2] to force the exchange of its debt instruments at unfair price and at less than face value of the debt instruments [3] pursuant to a rigged vote in which debt Holders who exchange, and who therefore have no interest in the vote, *must* consent to the elimination of protective covenants for debt Holders who do not wish to exchange.

As amplified in briefing on the pending motion, plaintiff's claim is that no free choice is provided to bondholders by the exchange offer and consent solicitation. Under its terms, a rational bondholder is "forced" to tender and consent. Failure to do so would face a bondholder with the risk of owning a security stripped of all financial covenant protections and for which it is likely that there would be no ready market. A reasonable bondholder, it is suggested, cannot possibly accept those risks and thus such a bondholder is coerced to tender and thus to consent to the proposed indenture amendments.

It is urged [that] this linking of the offer and the consent solicitation constitutes a breach of a contractual obligation that Oak owes to its bondholders to act in good faith. Specifically, plaintiff points to three contractual provisions from which it can be seen that the structuring of the current offer constitutes a breach of good faith. Those provisions (1) establish a requirement that no modification in the term of the various indentures may be effectuated without the consent of a stated percentage of bondholders; (2) restrict Oak from exercising the power to grant such consent with respect to any securities it may hold in its treasury; and (3) establish the price at which and manner in which Oak may force bondholders to submit their securities for redemption.

---

6. It is worthy of note that a very high percentage of the principal value of Oak's debt securities are owned in substantial amounts by a handful of large financial institutions. Almost 85% of the value of the 13.50% Notes is owned by four such institutions (one investment banker owns 55% of that issue); 69.1% of the 9 ⅝% Notes are owned by four financial institutions (the same investment banker owning 25% of that issue) and 85% of the 11 ⅝% Notes are owned by five such institutions. Of the debentures, 89% of the 13.65% debentures are owned by four large banks; and approximately 45% of the two remaining issues is owned by two banks.

III

. . .

This case does not involve the measurement of corporate or directorial conduct against that high standard of fidelity required of fiduciaries when they act with respect to the interests of the beneficiaries of their trust. Under our law—and the law generally—the relationship between a corporation and the holders of its debt securities, even convertible debt securities, is contractual in nature. Arrangements among a corporation, the underwriters of its debt, trustees under its indentures and sometimes ultimate investors are typically thoroughly negotiated and massively documented. The rights and obligations of the various parties are or should be spelled out in that documentation. The terms of the contractual relationship agreed to and not broad concepts such as fairness define the corporation's obligation to its bondholders.[7]

Thus, the first aspect of the pending Exchange Offers about which plaintiff complains—that "the purpose and effect of the Exchange Offers is to benefit Oak's common stockholders at the expense of the Holders of its debt"—does not itself appear to allege a cognizable legal wrong. It is the obligation of directors to attempt, within the law, to maximize the long-run interests of the corporation's stockholders; that they may sometimes do so "at the expense" of others (even assuming that a transaction which one may refuse to enter into can meaningfully be said to be at his expense) does not for that reason constitute a breach of duty. It seems likely that corporate restructurings designed to maximize shareholder values may in some instances have the effect of requiring bondholders to bear greater risk of loss and thus in effect transfer economic value from bondholders to stockholders. But if courts are to provide protection against such enhanced risk, they will require either legislative direction to do so or the negotiation of indenture provisions designed to afford such protection.

The second preliminary point concerns the limited analytical utility, at least in this context, of the word "coercive" which is central to plaintiff's own articulation of his theory of recovery. If, *pro arguendo*, we are to extend the meaning of the word coercion beyond its core meaning—dealing with the utilization of physical force to overcome the will of another—to reach instances in which the claimed coercion arises from an act designed to affect the will of another party by offering inducements to the act sought to be encouraged or by arranging unpleasant consequences for an alternative sought to be discouraged, then—in order to make the term legally meaningful at all—we must acknowledge that some further refinement is essential. Clearly some "coercion" of this kind is legally unproblematic. Parents may "coerce" a child to study with the threat of withholding an allowance; employers may "coerce"

---

7. To say that the broad duty of loyalty that a director owes to his corporation and ultimately its shareholders is not implicated in this case is not to say, as the discussion below reflects, that as a matter of contract law a corporation owes no duty to bondholders of good faith and fair dealing. Such a duty, however, is quite different from the congeries of duties that are assumed by a fiduciary.

regular attendance at work by either docking wages for time absent or by rewarding with a bonus such regular attendance. Other "coercion" so defined clearly would be legally relevant (to encourage regular attendance by corporal punishment, for example). Thus, for purposes of legal analysis, the term "coercion" itself—covering a multitude of situations—is not very meaningful. For the word to have much meaning for purposes of legal analysis, it is necessary in each case that a normative judgment be attached to the concept ("inappropriately coercive" or "wrongfully coercive", etc.). But, it is then readily seen that what is legally relevant is not the conclusory term "coercion" itself but rather the norm that leads to the adverb modifying it.

In this instance, assuming that the Exchange Offers and Consent Solicitation can meaningfully be regarded as "coercive" (in the sense that Oak has structured it in a way designed—and I assume effectively so—to "force" rational bondholders to tender), the relevant legal norm that will support the judgment whether such "coercion" is wrongful or not will, for the reasons mentioned above, be derived from the law of contracts. I turn then to that subject to determine the appropriate legal test or rule.

Modern contract law has generally recognized an implied covenant to the effect that each party to a contract will act with good faith towards the other with respect to the subject matter of the contract. The contractual theory for this implied obligation is well stated in a leading treatise:

> If the purpose of contract law is to enforce the reasonable expectations of parties induced by promises, then at some point it becomes necessary for courts to look to the substance rather than to the form of the agreement, and to hold that substance controls over form. What courts are doing here, whether calling the process "implication" of promises, or interpreting the requirements of "good faith", as the current fashion may be, is but a recognition that the parties occasionally have understandings or expectations that were so fundamental that they did not need to negotiate about those expectations. When the court "implies a promise" or holds that "good faith" requires a party not to violate those expectations, it is recognizing that sometimes silence says more than words, and it is understanding its duty to the spirit of the bargain is higher than its duty to the technicalities of the language. *Corbin on Contracts* (Kaufman Supp.1984), § 570.

It is this obligation to act in good faith and to deal fairly that plaintiff claims is breached by the structure of Oak's coercive exchange offer. Because it is an implied *contractual* obligation that is asserted as the basis for the relief sought, the appropriate legal test is not difficult to deduce. It is this: is it clear from what was expressly agreed upon that the parties who negotiated the express terms of the contract would have agreed to proscribe the act later complained of as a breach of the implied covenant of good faith—had they thought to negotiate with respect to that matter. If the answer to this question is yes, then, in my opinion, a court is justified in concluding that such act constitutes a breach of the implied covenant of good faith.

With this test in mind, I turn now to a review of the specific provisions of the various indentures from which one may be best able to infer whether it is apparent that the contracting parties—had they negotiated with the exchange offer and consent solicitation in mind—would have expressly agreed to prohibit contractually the linking of the giving of consent with the purchase and sale of the security.

IV

Applying the foregoing standard to the exchange offer and consent solicitation, I find first that there is nothing in the indenture provisions granting bondholders power to veto proposed modifications in the relevant indenture that implies that Oak may not offer an inducement to bondholders to consent to such amendments. Such an implication, at least where, as here, the inducement is offered on the same terms to each holder of an affected security, would be wholly inconsistent with the strictly commercial nature of the relationship.

Nor does the second pertinent contractual provision supply a ground to conclude that defendant's conduct violates the reasonable expectations of those who negotiated the indentures on behalf of the bondholders. Under that provision Oak may not vote debt securities held in its treasury. Plaintiff urges that Oak's conditioning of its offer to purchase debt on the giving of consents has the effect of subverting the purpose of that provision; it permits Oak to "dictate" the vote on securities which it could not itself vote.

The evident purpose of the restriction on the voting of treasury securities is to afford protection against the issuer voting as a bondholder in favor of modifications that would benefit it as issuer, even though such changes would be detrimental to bondholders. But the linking of the exchange offer and the consent solicitation does not involve the risk that bondholder interests will be affected by a vote involving anyone with a financial interest in the subject of the vote other than a bondholder's interest. That the consent is to be given concurrently with the transfer of the bond to the issuer does not in any sense create the kind of conflict of interest that the indenture's prohibition on voting treasury securities contemplates. Not only will the proposed consents be granted or withheld only by those with a financial interest to maximize the return on their investment in Oak's bonds, but the incentive to consent is equally available to all members of each class of bondholders. Thus the "vote" implied by the consent solicitation is not affected in any sense by those with a financial conflict of interest.

In these circumstances, while it is clear that Oak has fashioned the exchange offer and consent solicitation in a way designed to encourage consents, I cannot conclude that the offer violates the intendment of any of the express contractual provisions considered or, applying the test set out above, that its structure and timing breaches an implied obligation of good faith and fair dealing.

One further set of contractual provisions should be touched upon: Those granting to Oak a power to redeem the securities here treated at a price set by the relevant indentures. Plaintiff asserts that the attempt to force all bondholders to tender their securities at less than the redemption price constitutes, if not a breach of the redemption provision itself, at least a breach of an implied covenant of good faith and fair dealing associated with it. The flaw, or at least one fatal flaw, in this argument is that the present offer is not the functional equivalent of a redemption which is, of course, an act that the issuer may take unilaterally. In this instance it may happen that Oak will get tenders of a large percentage of its outstanding long-term debt securities. If it does, that fact will, in my judgment, be in major part a function of the merits of the offer (i.e., the price offered in light of the Company's financial position and the market value of its debt). To answer plaintiff's contention that the *structure* of the offer "forces" debt holders to tender, one only has to imagine what response this offer would receive if the price offered did not reflect a premium over market but rather was, for example, ten percent of market value. The exchange offer's success ultimately depends upon the ability and willingness of the issuer to extend an offer that will be a financially attractive alternative to holders. This process is hardly the functional equivalent of the unilateral election of redemption and thus cannot be said in any sense to constitute a subversion by Oak of the negotiated provisions dealing with redemption of its debt.

Accordingly, I conclude that plaintiff has failed to demonstrate a probability of ultimate success on the theory of liability asserted.

V

An independent ground for the decision to deny the pending motion is supplied by the requirement that a court of equity will not issue the extraordinary remedy of preliminary injunction where to do so threatens the party sought to be enjoined with irreparable injury that, in the circumstances, seems greater than the injury that plaintiff seeks to avoid. That principal has application here.

Oak is in a weak state financially. Its board, comprised of persons of experience and, in some instances, distinction, have approved the complex and interrelated transactions outlined above. It is not unreasonable to accord weight to the claims of Oak that the reorganization and recapitalization of which the exchange offer is a part may present the last good chance to regain vitality for this enterprise. I have not discussed plaintiff's claim of irreparable injury, although I have considered it. I am satisfied simply to note my conclusion that it is far outweighed by the harm that an improvidently granted injunction would threaten to Oak.

For the foregoing reasons plaintiff's application for a preliminary injunction shall be denied.

It is so ordered.

Questions

1. What causes workouts outside bankruptcy to fail? Why, when a company is in the vicinity of insolvency, would creditors hold out? Could an unsecured creditor benefit from holding out?

2. In *Unocal Corporation v. Mesa Petroleum Co.* (1985), the seminal takeover case you will see in Part 4 of this casebook, the Delaware Supreme Court empowered directors to protect their corporation's shareholders from tender offers that aim to benefit those who tender at the expense of those who do not, labeling such offers coercive. Why does Chancellor Allen not consider the offer in *Katz* coercive?

3. Given *Katz*'s holding, what, if anything, can unsecured creditors do *ex ante* to protect their interests? Should Congress modify the Trust Indenture Act's requirement of unanimous bondholder consent to accommodate the reality of the securities markets in the twenty-first century?

B. Preferred Stock

Jedwab v. MGM Grand Hotels, Inc.
509 A.2d 584 (Del. Ch. 1986)

ALLEN, Chancellor

MGM Grand Hotels, Inc., a Delaware corporation ("MGM Grand" or the "Company") that owns and operates resort hotels and gaming establishments in Las Vegas and Reno, Nevada, has entered into an agreement with Bally Manufacturing Corporation, also a Delaware corporation, ("Bally") contemplating a merger between a Bally subsidiary and the Company. On the effectuation of such merger, all classes of the Company's presently outstanding stock will be converted into the right to receive cash.

Defendant Kerkorian individually and through Tracinda Corporation, which he wholly owns, beneficially owns 69% of MGM Grand's issued and outstanding common stock and 74% of its only other class of stock, its Series A Redeemable Preferred Stock (the "preferred stock" or simply the "preferred"). Mr. Kerkorian took an active part in negotiating the proposed merger with Bally and agreed with Bally to vote his stock in favor of the merger. Since neither the merger agreement nor the Company's charter contains a provision conditioning such a transaction on receipt of approval by a greater than majority vote, Mr. Kerkorian's agreement to vote in favor of the merger assured its approval.

Neither Kerkorian nor any director or officer of MGM Grand is affiliated with Bally either as an owner of its stock, or as an officer or director. Nor, so far as the record discloses, has any such person had a business or social relationship with Bally or any director, officer or controlling person of Bally. Bally—at least prior to its obtaining an option on Kerkorian's shares as part of the negotiation of the agreement of merger—has owned no stock in MGM Grand.

Plaintiff is an owner of the Company's preferred stock. She brings this action as a class action on behalf of all owners of such stock other than Kerkorian and Tracinda and seeks to enjoin preliminarily and permanently the effectuation of the proposed merger. The gist of the theory urged as justifying the relief sought is that the effectuation of the proposed merger would constitute a breach of a duty to deal fairly with the preferred shareholders owed to such shareholders by Kerkorian, as a controlling shareholder of MGM Grand, and by the directors of the Company. The merger is said to constitute a wrong to the preferred shareholders principally in that it allegedly contemplates an unfair apportionment among the Company's shareholders of the total consideration to be paid by Bally upon effectuation of the merger. Pending is plaintiff's motion for a preliminary injunction.

I

Recitation of the relevant facts, as they appear at this preliminary stage, may helpfully be divided into two parts: the facts relating to the 1982 creation of the preferred stock on whose behalf this action is prosecuted and the more current events that have led to the proposed Bally merger, including the terms of that proposed transaction. Under plaintiff's theory, the circumstances surrounding the 1982 creation of the preferred stock are significant because those circumstances help to demonstrate the essential equivalence of the preferred and the common stock.

A. *The Creation of the Preferred Stock*

MGM Grand, through wholly-owned subsidiaries, owns and operates the MGM Grand Hotel-Las Vegas and the MGM Grand Hotel-Reno. Prior to May 30, 1980, the Company had been called Metro-Goldwyn-Mayer, Inc., and included both the present hotel business and a film production business now conducted through unrelated corporations.

The Company entered the hotel business in December, 1973, with the opening of its Las Vegas facility. That luxury hotel and casino now consists of some 2,800 guest rooms and a 62,500 square foot casino. In addition, tennis courts, swimming pools, restaurants, meeting rooms, shops and other facilities associated with a resort hotel are located on the hotel's 44-acre site. The Las Vegas hotel was very profitable from the outset and in May, 1978, the Company opened its Reno hotel which was constructed on a similarly large scale.

In November, 1980, tragedy struck at the MGM Grand Hotel-Las Vegas. That night a fire consumed the 25-story hotel and 84 lives were lost. The fire required the closing of the Las Vegas hotel for over 8 months and required almost total renovation of that facility. It gave rise as well to protracted litigation relating both to the personal injuries sustained in the fire and the loss of property by the Company. Hundreds of suits were brought against the Company seeking, in total, more than $650 million in compensatory damages and more than $2 billion in punitive damages. In addition, the Company was required to sue its property insurance carriers seeking recovery of losses occasioned by the fire.

Following the Las Vegas disaster there was a significant fall-off in the market value of MGM Grand's common stock. Closing the week of November 14, 1980, at 13 1/4, the price of the Company's common stock closed at 10 the following week and closed the week of December 12 at 7 1/2.

Apparently in response to the reduced price of the Company's stock and to the risks to stockholders' investment represented by the fire-related litigation claims, on April 1, 1982, the Company publicly offered to exchange one share of common stock for one share of a new class of stock, the Series A Redeemable Preferred Stock. The offer extended to a maximum of 10 million shares of the Company's then outstanding 32,500,000 shares. The offering document stated that Mr. Kerkorian (who at that time controlled very slightly in excess of 50% of the issued and outstanding common stock) would tender into the offer that number of shares equal to the total number tendered by all other shareholders, but in no event would he tender less than 5 million shares.

The preferred stock issued in connection with the 1982 exchange offer carries a cumulative $.44 annual dividend (the same dividend paid with respect to the common stock both at the time of the exchange offer and now), is **non-convertible, elects no directors unless dividends remain unpaid for six quarters, has a liquidation preference of $20 per share and carries a complex redemption right.** . . .

Through the exchange offer, 9,315,403 common shares were exchanged, including 5 million shares by Mr. Kerkorian and his corporation, Tracinda.

B. *Negotiation of the Proposed Merger*

On June 6, 1985, Tracinda and Kerkorian announced an intention to pursue a cash-out merger transaction that would eliminate the public common stockholders from the Company at $18 per share, but would leave the preferred stock in place. . . .

In August, 1985, the Drexel Burnham firm was engaged to explore alternatives to the Tracinda offer. That firm made a significant effort to instigate possible alternative deals—apparently some 50 firms were contacted, but the only indication of serious interest it apparently received was from Bally Manufacturing Corp.

In early November, 1985, Kerkorian, Stephen Silbert, his principal legal advisor, and representatives of Drexel Burnham met with Robert Mullane, the chairman and chief executive officer of Bally to discuss Bally's interest. At that meeting Bally apparently ultimately took the position that it thought all of the Company's equity was worth $440 million and said it would be willing to make a cash offer at that price for all the Company's stock—common and preferred.

It seems agreed by all parties that Bally made a total price offer and had no real input into the way in which that consideration would be divided among classes of MGM Grand's stock . . . , although its concurrence was obviously required. Kerkorian and Silbert had, however, discussed that question prior to the meeting, and Kerkorian had expressed the view that the common stock should get $18 a share since Tracinda had already announced an offer at that price.

Kerkorian, after discussions with his lawyer Silbert and with Drexel Burnham . . . apparently determined that $14 was the price that would be paid for the preferred. . . . However, a $14 per share price for the outstanding preferred, when added to an $18 price for all the common stock, would result in a cash price in excess of $440 million for all of the Company's stock. To solve this problem, Kerkorian agreed to take $12.24 per share for his common stock together with certain other property, including transfer of the exclusive rights to the name MGM Grand Hotels and certain contingent rights in litigation proceeds. . . .

II

Plaintiff claims that the proposed merger constitutes a breach of a fiduciary duty owed by the directors of MGM Grand and its controlling shareholder to the preferred stockholders. . . .

The main argument advanced by plaintiff is premised upon the assertion that the directors of a Delaware corporation have a duty in a merger transaction to negotiate and approve only a merger that apportions the merger consideration fairly among classes of the company's stock. To unfairly favor one class of stock over another is, on this view, a breach of the duty of loyalty that a director owes to the corporation and, by extension, that he owes equally to all of its shareholders. Asserting factually that under all the circumstances the two outstanding classes of MGM Grand's stock represent equivalent values, plaintiff contends that the proposed Bally merger which does not apportion the merger consideration equally breaches this duty. . . .

IV

. . .

A

Issue on the merits of claims alleged is first joined on the fundamental question whether the directors of MGM Grand owe *any* duty to the holders of the preferred stock other than the duty to accord to such holders the rights, powers and preferences set out in the certificate designating and defining the legal rights of the preferred. As I understand plaintiff's principal theories of liability each is premised upon the existence of a supervening fiduciary duty recognized in equity that requires directors and controlling shareholders to treat shareholders fairly. If there is no such duty insofar as preferred stockholders are concerned plaintiff's theories of liability would seem fatally flawed.

Defendants contend there is no broad duty of fidelity owed to preferred stock if that duty is understood to extend beyond the specific contractual terms defining the special rights, preferences or limitations of the preferred. In support of its position on this point defendants cite such cases as *Rothschild International Corp. v. Liggett Group, Inc.*; *Wood v. Coastal States Gas Corp.* and *Dart v. Kohlberg, Kravis, Roberts & Co.* Broadly speaking these cases apply the rule that "preferential rights are contractual in nature and therefore are governed by the express provisions of a company's certificate of incorporation" *Rothschild, supra.* Defendants restate this accepted principle as meaning "all rights of preferred shareholders are contractual in nature."[4] They then go on to argue (analogizing to the wholly contractual rights of bondholders—as to which no "fiduciary" duties extend) that the only duties directors have to preferred shareholders are those necessary to accord the preferred rights set out in their contract, i.e., the document designating the rights, preferences, etc., of their special stock.

The flaw in this argument lies in a failure to distinguish between "preferential" rights (and special limitations) on the one hand and rights associated with all stock on the other. At common law and in the absence of an agreement to the contrary all shares of stock are equal. Thus preferences and limitations associated with preferred stock exist only by virtue of an express provision (contractual in nature) creating such rights or limitations. But absent negotiated provision [sic] conferring rights on preference stock, it does not follow that no right exists. The point may be conclusively demonstrated by two examples. If a certificate designating rights, preferences, etc. of special stock contains *no* provision dealing with voting rights or *no* provision creating rights upon liquidation, it is not the fact that such stock has no voting rights or no rights upon liquidation. Rather, in such circumstances, the preferred stock has the same voting rights as common stock (8 Del.C. §212(a)); or the same rights to participate in the liquidation of the corporation as has such stock.

Thus, with respect to matters relating to preferences or limitations that distinguish preferred stock from common, the duty of the corporation and its directors is essentially contractual and the scope of the duty is appropriately defined by reference to the specific words evidencing that contract; where however the right asserted is not to a preference as against the common stock but rather a right shared equally with the common, the existence of such right and the scope of the correlative duty may be measured by equitable as well as legal standards.

With this distinction in mind the Delaware cases which frequently analyze rights of and duties towards preferred stock in legal (i.e., contractual) terminology may be made consistent with those cases that apply fiduciary standards to claims of preferred shareholders.

Accordingly, without prejudging the validity of any of plaintiff's liability theories, I conclude that her claim (a) to a "fair" allocation of the proceeds of the merger; (b) to have the defendants exercise appropriate care in negotiating the proposed merger and (c) to be free of overreaching by Mr. Kerkorian (as to the timing of the merger for his benefit) fairly implicate fiduciary duties and ought not be evaluated wholly from the point of view of the contractual terms of the preferred stock designations.

---

4. Certain language in the cases restating the principle quoted above would support defendants' interpretation. For example, in *Judah v. Delaware Trust Company* it is said: "Generally, the provisions of the certificate of incorporation govern the rights of preferred shareholders, the certificate... being interpreted in accordance with the law of contracts, with only those rights which are embodied in the certificate granted to preferred shareholders."

Questions

1. Unlike bonds, preferred stock is considered to be an equity security; that is, like common stock, it is only allowed to participate in the profits of the corporation, whether by dividends or upon dissolution, after all prior claimants have been paid. The difference between preferred stock and common stock is that preferred stock has the right to whatever "preferences" are designated in the corporation's certificate of incorporation. This means that, as far as those preferences are concerned, the preferred stock may take its share after everyone else but before the common stockholders. Thus, if the preferred stockholders are entitled, as they typically are, to preferred dividends (usually stated either as a set amount or a percentage of their designated par value), they are entitled to receive their dividends before any are paid on the common stock. Similarly, if the preferred are (as they typically are) entitled to a liquidation preference, they are entitled upon liquidation of the corporation to receive the amount of the preference stated in the certificate of incorporation before the common stockholders receive anything. As Chancellor Allen points out, in all respects in which the preferred stock does not have stated preferences (that is, the certificate of incorporation is silent as to preferences), it is to be treated in the same way as common stock. This mixture of preferences and parity creates the potential for conflicts of interest between the preferred stockholders and the common stockholders. Can you see how?

2. What is the Chancellor's solution for resolving the conflicts of interest between the preferred and common stock? Is it adequate? Does it even make sense? Do you suppose that preferences are always crystal clear, or might there be the same kinds of ambiguities that generally exist in contracts? If there are ambiguities, who is responsible (at least in the first instance) for interpreting them? Does the court's resolution instruct the corporation's board of directors as to the posture it is to take (fiduciary or arm's-length) in interpreting the preferred stock contract? Would each posture carry with it the same responsibilities? Would each be likely to lead to the same conclusions? If you think that the opinion doesn't adequately resolve the dilemma, what alternatives could you offer?

Consider all of this in the context of the following case.

In re Trados Incorporated Shareholder Litigation
2009 WL 2225958 (Del. Ch. 2009)

CHANDLER, Chancellor

This is a purported class action brought by a former stockholder of Trados Incorporated ("Trados," or the "Company") for breach of fiduciary duty arising out of a transaction whereby Trados became a wholly owned subsidiary of SDL, plc ("SDL"). Of the $60 million contributed by SDL, Trados' preferred stockholders received approximately $52 million. The remainder was distributed to the Company's executive officers pursuant to a previously approved bonus plan. Trados' common stockholders received nothing for their common shares.

Plaintiff contends that this transaction was undertaken at the behest of certain preferred stockholders that desired a transaction that would trigger their large liquidation preference and allow them to exit their investment in Trados. Plaintiff alleges that the Trados board favored the interests of the preferred stockholders, either at the expense of the common stockholders or without properly considering the effect of the merger on the common stockholders. Specifically, plaintiff alleges that the four directors designated by preferred stockholders had other relationships with preferred stockholders and were incapable of exercising disinterested and independent business judgment. Plaintiff further alleges that the two Trados directors who were also employees of the Company received material personal benefits as a result of the merger and were therefore also incapable of exercising disinterested and independent business judgment. . . .

As explained below, plaintiff has alleged facts sufficient, at this preliminary stage, to demonstrate that at least a majority of the members of Trados' seven member board were unable to exercise independent and disinterested business judgment in deciding whether to approve the merger. Accordingly, I decline to dismiss the breach of fiduciary duty claims arising out of the board's approval of the merger. . . .

I. Background

A. The Parties

Before the merger, Trados developed software and services used by businesses to make the translation of text and material into other languages more efficient. Founded in 1984 as a German entity, Trados moved to the United States in the mid-1990s with the hope of going public, and became a Delaware corporation in March 2000. To better position itself for the possibility of going public, Trados accepted investments from venture capital firms and other entities. As a result, preferred stockholders had a total of four designees on Trados' seven member board. Each of the seven members of Trados' board at the time of the board's approval of the merger is named as a defendant in this action.

David Scanlan was the board designee of, and a partner in, Wachovia Capital Partners, LLC ("Wachovia"). At the time of the merger, Wachovia owned 3,640,000 shares of Trados' Series A preferred stock (100% of that series) and 1,007,151 shares of Trados' Series BB preferred stock (approximately 24% of that series).

Lisa Stone was the board designee of Rowan Entities Limited and Rowan Nominees Limited RR (together, the "Rowan Entities"), transferees of Trados' preferred stock held by Hg Investment Managers Limited (collectively, "Hg"). Stone was a director and employee of both Hg Investment Managers Limited and the Rowan Entities. At the time of the merger, Hg owned 1,379,039 shares of Trados' common stock (approximately 4.3%), 2,014,302 shares of Trados' Series BB preferred stock (approximately 48.3% of that series), 5,333,330 shares of Trados' Series C preferred shares (all of that series), and 862,976 shares of Trados' Series D preferred stock (approximately 28.6% of that series).

Sameer Gandhi was a board designee of, and a partner in, several entities known as Sequoia. Sequoia owned 5,255,913 shares of Trados' Series E preferred stock (approximately 32% of that series).

Joseph Prang was also a board designee of Sequoia. Prang owned Mentor Capital Group LLC ("Mentor Capital"), which owned 263,810 shares of Trados' Series E preferred stock (approximately 1% of that series).

Wachovia, Hg, Sequoia, and Mentor combined owned approximately 51% of Trados' outstanding preferred stock. Plaintiff alleges that these preferred stockholders desired to exit their investment in Trados,

Two of the three remaining director defendants were employees of Trados. Jochen Hummel was acting President of Trados from April 2004 until September or October 2004, and was also the Company's chief technology officer. Joseph Campbell was Trados' CEO from August 23, 2004 until the merger. The remaining Trados director was Klaus-Dieter Laidig.

B. The Negotiations

In April 2004, the Trados board began to discuss a potential sale of the Company, and later formed a mergers and acquisitions committee, consisting of Stone, Gandhi, and Scanlan, to explore a sale or merger of Trados. Around the same time, the Company's President and CEO was terminated due to, among other issues, a perception by the rest of the board that Trados was underperforming. The board appointed Hummel as an interim President, but instructed him to consult with Gandhi and Scanlan before taking material action on behalf of the Company. In July 2004, Campbell was hired as the Company's CEO, effective August 23, 2004. Gandhi described Campbell as "a hard-nosed CEO whose task is to grow the company profitably or sell it." At the time Campbell joined Trados, however, the Company was losing money and had little cash to fund continuing operations. At a July 7, 2004 meeting, Trados' board determined that the fair market value of Trados' common stock was $0.10 per share.

In June 2004, Trados engaged JMP Securities, LLC, an investment bank, to assist in identifying potential alternatives for a merger or sale of the Company. By July 2004, JMP Securities had identified twenty seven potential buyers of Trados, and contacted seven of them, including SDL. By August 2004, JMP Securities had conducted discussions with SDL CEO Mark Lancaster, who made an acquisition proposal in the $40 million range. Trados informed Lancaster that it was not interested in a deal at that price, and Campbell formally terminated JMP Securities in September 2004.

In July 2004, Scanlan expressed concern that the executive officers of the Company might not have sufficient incentives to remain with the Company or pursue a potential acquisition of the Company, due to the high liquidation preference of the Company's preferred stock. The board instructed Scanlan to develop a bonus plan to address these concerns. This led to the December 2004 board approval of the

Management Incentive Plan (the "MIP"), which set a graduated compensation scale for the Company's management based on the price obtained for the Company in an acquisition.[5]

Trados' financial condition improved markedly during the fourth quarter of 2004, in part due to Campbell's efforts to reduce spending and bring in additional cash through debt financing. By the time of the December 2004 board meeting, Trados had arranged to borrow $2.5 million from Western Technology Investment, with the right to borrow an additional $1.5 million.

Despite the Company's improved performance, the board continued to work toward a sale of the Company. In December 2004, Gandhi reported to Sequoia Capital that the Company's performance was improving, but that Campbell's "mission is to architect an M&A event as soon as practicable." At a February 2, 2005 board meeting, Campbell presented positive financial results from the fourth quarter of 2004, including record revenue and profit from operations. As a result of its improved performance and the lack of an immediate need for cash, the board extended by six months the period during which it could obtain additional cash from Western Technology Investment.

In January 2005, SDL initiated renewed merger discussions with Campbell. Upon learning of SDL's interest, the Trados board expressed that it was not interested in any transaction involving less than a "60-plus" million dollar purchase price. Lancaster first discussed a transaction at $50 million, but later offered $60 million. At the February 2, 2005 meeting, the board instructed Campbell to continue negotiating with Lancaster under the general terms SDL proposed, including the $60 million price. In mid-February 2005, Campbell made inquiries with two other potential acquirers of Trados, but neither expressed any substantive interest.

. . .

By February 2005, Campbell and Lancaster agreed to the basic terms of a merger at $60 million. Trados then re-engaged JMP securities, which plaintiff alleges acted as little more than a "go-between." In April 2005, SDL and Trados signed the letter of intent for the merger at the $60 million price.

. . .

D. The Merger

The director defendants unanimously approved the merger, and on June 19, 2005 Trados and SDL entered into an Agreement and Plan of Merger. Of the $60 million

---

5. Under the MIP, management would receive 6% of the acquisition price for an acquisition between $30–40 million; 11% for an acquisition between $40–50 million; 13% for an acquisition between $50–90 million; 14% for an acquisition between $90–120 million; and 15% for an acquisition at or above $120 million. From that pool, Campbell would be entitled to 30%, Hummel to 12%, and James Budge to 10%. Plaintiff alleges that an investor described the MIP as "protection for the management team in case [some] shareholders want to sell [the company] at a price where the options/common shares are worthless."

merger price, approximately $7.8 million would go to management pursuant to the MIP, and the remainder would go to the preferred stockholders in partial satisfaction of their $57.9 million liquidation preference. Plaintiff alleges that the directors know both of these facts, and thus knew that the common shareholders would receive nothing in the merger. The merger was consummated on July 7, 2005.

Plaintiff alleges that Campbell and Hummel received benefits as a result of the merger. Campbell became a director of SDL and received $775,000 through the MIP, $1,315,000 in exchange for a non-compete agreement, and a $250,000 bonus. Campbell took $702,000 of his MIP compensation in SDL stock, and $73,000 in cash. Hummel became "SDL's general manager of Europe, the Middle East, and Asia (technology division)," and received $1,092,000 under the MIP, of which he took $436,800 in SDL stock and $655,200 in cash.

. . .

II. Analysis

. . .

C. Fiduciary Duty Claims

Count I of the Complaint asserts a claim that the director defendants breached their fiduciary duty of loyalty to Trados' common stockholders by approving the merger. Plaintiff alleges that there was no need to sell Trados at the time because the Company was well-financed, profitable, and beating revenue projections. Further, plaintiff contends, "in approving the Merger, the Director Defendants never considered the interest of the common stockholders in continuing Trados as a going concern, even though they were obliged to give priority to that interest over the preferred stockholders' interest in exiting their investment."

Directors of Delaware corporations are protected in their decision-making by the business judgment rule, which "is a presumption that in making a business decision the directors of a corporation acted on an informed basis, in good faith and in the honest belief that the action taken was in the best interests of the company." The rule reflects and promotes the role of the board of directors as the proper body to manage the business and affairs of the corporation.

. . .

Plaintiff's theory of the case is based on the proposition that, for purposes of the merger, the preferred stockholders' interests diverged from the interests of the common stockholders. Plaintiff contends that the merger took place at the behest of certain preferred stockholders, who wanted to exit their investment. Defendants contend that plaintiff ignores the "obvious alignment" of the interest of the preferred and common stockholders in obtaining the highest price available for the company. Defendants assert that because the preferred stockholders would not receive their entire liquidation preference in the merger, they would benefit if a higher price were obtained for the Company. Even accepting this proposition as true, however, it is not the case that the interests of the preferred and common stockholders were aligned with respect to the decision of whether to pursue a sale of the company or continue to operate the Company without pursuing a transaction at the time.

The merger triggered the $57.9 million liquidation preference of the preferred stockholders, and the preferred stockholders received approximately $52 million dollars as a result of the merger. In contrast, the common stockholders received nothing as a result of the merger, and lost the ability to ever receive anything of value in the future for their ownership interest in Trados. It would not stretch reason to say that this is the worst possible outcome for the common stockholders. The common stockholders would certainly be no worse off had the merger not occurred.

Taking, as I must, the well-pleaded facts in the Complaint in the light most favorable to plaintiff, it is reasonable to infer that the common stockholders would have been able to receive some consideration for their Trados shares at some point in the future had the merger not occurred. This inference is supported by plaintiff's allegations that the Company's performance had significantly improved and that the Company had secured additional capital through debt financing. Thus, it is reasonable to infer from the factual allegations in the Complaint that the interests of the preferred and common stockholders were not aligned with respect to the decision to pursue a transaction that would trigger the liquidation preference of the preferred and result in no consideration for the common stockholders.

Generally, the rights and preferences of preferred stock are contractual in nature. This Court has held that directors owe fiduciary duties to preferred stockholders as well as common stockholders where the right claimed by the preferred "is not to a preference as against the common stock but rather a right shared equally with the common." Where this is not the case, however, "generally it will be the duty of the board, where discretionary judgment is to be exercised, to prefer the interests of common stock—as the good faith judgment of the board sees them to be—to the interests created by the special rights, preferences, *etc.,* of preferred stock, where there is a conflict." Thus, in circumstances where the interests of the common stockholders diverge from those of the preferred stockholders, it is *possible* that a director could breach her duty by improperly favoring the interests of the preferred stockholders over those of the common stockholders. As explained above, the factual allegations in the Complaint support a reasonable inference that the interests of the preferred and common stockholders diverged with respect to the decision of whether to pursue the merger. Given this reasonable inference, plaintiff can avoid dismissal if the Complaint contains well-pleaded facts that demonstrate that the director defendants were interested or lacked independence with respect to this decision.

1. The Director Defendants' Approval of the Merger

Plaintiff has alleged facts that support a reasonable inference that Scanlan, Stone, Gandhi, and Prang, the four board designees of preferred stockholders, were interested in the decision to pursue the merger with SDL, which had the effect of triggering the large liquidation preference of the preferred stockholders and resulted in no consideration to the common stockholders for their common shares. Each of these four directors was designated to the Trados board by a holder of a significant number of preferred shares. While this, alone, may not be enough to rebut the presumption of the business judgment rule, plaintiff has alleged more. Plaintiff has alleged that Scanlan, Stone, Gandhi, and Prang each had an ownership or employment relationship with an entity that owned Trados preferred stock. Scanlan was a partner in Wachovia; Stone was a director, employee and part owner of Hg; Gandhi was a partner in several entities referred to as Sequoia; and Prang owned Mentor Capital. Plaintiff further alleges that each of these directors was dependent on the preferred stockholders for their livelihood. As detailed above, each of these entities owned a significant number of Trados' preferred shares, and together these entities owned approximately 51% of Trados' outstanding preferred stock. The allegations of the ownership and other relationships of each of Scanlan, Stone, Gandhi, and Prang to preferred stockholders, combined with the fact that each was a board designee of one of these entities, is sufficient, under the plaintiff-friendly pleading standard on a motion to dismiss, to rebut the business judgment presumption with respect to the decision to approve the merger with SDL.

. . .

Plaintiff has alleged facts that support a reasonable inference that a majority of the board was interested or lacked independence with respect to the decision to approve the merger. Accordingly, plaintiff has alleged sufficient facts to survive defendants' motion to dismiss the fiduciary duty claims based on the board's decision to approve the merger.

. . .

III. Conclusion

For the reasons set forth above, defendants' motion to dismiss is . . . denied . . .

Part 2

The Duties of Directors, Officers and other Insiders

Part 2

The Duties of Directors, Officers and other Insiders

The board of directors is the main actor in the corporate governance structure. The board is created by the state through its corporation statute and serves as a reminder of the public nature of the corporation. The bylaws or certificate of incorporation typically set the number of directors to be elected by the shareholders and the length of their terms (traditionally one year, but today, many corporations have staggered boards with longer terms). The board acts at meetings, typically by majority vote, and it can establish committees to act on its behalf. As a general matter, a corporation is to be managed by or under the direction of its board of directors. The board must act as a body, although some cases suggest that directors' behavior might be assessed individually.

While the legal power of the board is almost absolute, its power to act is circumscribed by federal regulation (and a few state corporate law provisions) and, more importantly, by its duties of care and loyalty—commonly referred to as the board's *fiduciary* duties (although, as we will see, the term can be misleading). These duties charge the board with the responsibility of exercising its absolute power in good faith, due care and the sole interest of the corporation. Stockholders have some (highly diluted) ability to ensure that the board complies with these duties through litigation (and, as you will see in Part 3, by the process of voting). The focus in this Part 2 will be on enforcement either through litigation or through processes created by legislatures or courts, conducted at the board level, designed to ensure independent review of the board's actions.

Section I begins with a unique enforcement mechanism—the derivative suit. The following sections examine the substance of directors' (and officers') duties—the duty of care (in Section II), the duty of loyalty (in Section III), and good faith (in Section IV). Section V concludes with the duties of insiders under the securities acts.

Section I
Derivative Litigation

The power of the board includes the power to decide when and against whom the corporation brings suit. But, as you will see in this Part 2, the board also owes significant duties to the corporation and its stockholders. This presents a potential problem. How are these duties to be enforced against directors if they control the corporation's litigation decisions? How likely is it that directors will cause the corporation to sue themselves? Even if the potential lawsuit is against only a few of the directors, will the remaining directors be willing to sue them? How do we get around this problem?

The answer is the derivative suit, which is an equitable action that may be brought by—and only by—one or more stockholders.[1] Derivative suits are, technically, two suits. First, the stockholder-plaintiff sues the corporation to compel it to bring suit against the directors. (This is why the captions of derivative suits typically are the plaintiff-stockholder versus the corporation rather than against the ultimate defendant in interest.) Second, the corporation actually brings the suit under the control of the stockholder plaintiff and his counsel. (Derivative suits can also be brought to compel the board to cause the corporation to bring suits against third parties, but the problems presented by this situation are minor in comparison to the ones involved when directors are defendants.) Obviously, allowing a stockholder to make what is, in effect, a corporate decision, takes the absolute power of the board and puts it in the hands of the stockholder—a stockholder who has not been chosen by any of the corporation's constituencies—to champion the corporation's cause. The result has been a number of rules determining when the stockholder-plaintiff may claim to herself this power. They are examined in each of the following subsections.

Subsection A begins by discussing the difference between derivative suits and suits brought by a stockholder to recover in her own right (direct suits). The following subsections examine two procedural aspects of derivative litigation, the security for expenses (Subsection B) and the demand (Subsection C) requirements. Subsection D concludes by exploring the circumstances under which the board may refuse demand and those in which it may dismiss the suit—both of which allow the board to retain or regain its power. The cases will likely be fully understood only after we discuss the duties of care, loyalty, and good faith, but it is important to introduce them at this stage.

---

1. There are a few cases granting convertible bondholders standing to bring derivative suits, and the ALI in its Principles of Corporate Governance has recommended this, but it remains rare.

A. The Distinction Between Derivative and Direct Actions

Eisenberg v. The Flying Tiger Line, Inc.
451 F.2d 267 (2d Cir. 1971)

KAUFMAN, Judge

Max Eisenberg, a resident of New York, "as stockholder of The Flying Tiger Line, Inc. [Flying Tiger], on behalf of himself and all other stockholders of said corporation similarly situated" commenced this action in the Supreme Court of the State of New York to enjoin the effectuation of a plan of reorganization and merger. Flying Tiger, a Delaware corporation with its principal place of business in California, removed the action to the District Court for the Eastern District of New York.

Flying Tiger pleaded several affirmative defenses and moved for an order to require Eisenberg to comply with New York Business Corporation Law § 627, which requires a plaintiff suing derivatively on behalf of a corporation to post security for the corporation's costs. Judge Travia granted the motion without opinion and afforded Eisenberg thirty days to post security in the sum of $35,000. Eisenberg did not comply, his action was dismissed and he appeals. We find Eisenberg's cause of action to be personal and not derivative within the meaning of § 627. We therefore reverse the dismissal.

In this action, Eisenberg is seeking to overturn a reorganization and merger which Flying Tiger effected in 1969. He charges that a series of corporate maneuvers were intended to dilute his voting rights. In order to achieve this end, he alleges, Flying Tiger in July 1969 organized a wholly owned Delaware subsidiary, the Flying Tiger Corporation ("FTC"). In August, FTC in turn organized a wholly owned subsidiary, FTL Air Freight Corporation ("FTL"). The three Delaware corporations then entered into a plan of reorganization, subject to stockholder approval, by which Flying Tiger merged into FTL and only FTL survived. A proxy statement dated August 11 was sent to stockholders, who approved the plan by the necessary two-thirds vote at the stockholders' meeting held on September 15.

Upon consummation of this merger Flying Tiger ceased as the operating company, FTL took over operations and Flying Tiger shares were converted into an identical number of FTC shares. Thereafter, FTL changed its name to "Flying Tiger Line, Inc.," for the obvious purpose of continuing without disruption the business previously conducted by Flying Tiger. The approximately 4,500,000 shares of the company traded on the New York and Pacific Coast stock exchanges are now those of the holding company, FTC, rather than those of the operating company, Flying Tiger. The effect of the merger is that business operations are now confined to a wholly owned subsidiary of a holding company whose stockholders are the former stockholders of Flying Tiger.

It is of passing interest that Eisenberg contends that the end result of this complex plan was to deprive minority stockholders of any vote or any influence over the affairs of the newly spawned company. Flying Tiger insists the plan was devised to bring about diversification without interference from the Civil Aeronautics Board, which closely regulates air carriers, and to better use available tax benefits. Even if any of these motives prove to be relevant, the alleged illegality is not relevant to the questions before this court. We are called on to decide, assuming Eisenberg's complaint is sufficient on its face, only whether he should have been required to post security for costs as a condition to prosecuting his action. . . .

We are told that if the gravamen of the complaint is injury to the corporation the suit is derivative, but "if the injury is one to the plaintiff as a stockholder and to him individually and not to the corporation," the suit is individual in nature and may take the form of a representative class action. This generalization is of little use in our case which is one of those "borderline cases which are more or less troublesome to classify." The essence of Eisenberg's claimed injury is that the reorganization has deprived him and fellow stockholders of their right to vote on the operating company affairs and that this right in no sense ever belonged to Flying Tiger itself. This right, he says, belonged to the stockholders *per se*. Flying Tiger notes, however, that the stockholders were harmed, if at all, only because their company was dissolved, and their vote can be restored only if that company is revived. It insists, therefore, that stockholders are affected only secondarily or derivatively because we must first breathe life back into their dissolved corporation before the stockholders can be helped.

Despite a leading New York case which would seem at first glance to support Flying Tiger's position, we find that its contention misses the mark by a wide margin in its failure to distinguish between derivative and non-derivative class actions. In *Gordon v. Elliman*, by a vote of 4 to 3, the Court of Appeals took an expansive view of the coverage of § 627's predecessor, General Corporation Law § 61-b. The majority held that an action to compel the payment of a dividend was derivative in nature and security for costs could be required. The test formulated by the majority was "whether the object of the lawsuit is to recover upon a chose in action belonging directly to the stockholders, or whether it is to compel the performance of corporate acts which good faith requires the directors to take in order to perform a duty which they owe to the corporation, and through it, to its stockholders." Pursuant to this test it is argued that, if Flying Tiger's directors had a duty not to merge the corporation, that duty was owed to the corporation and only derivatively to its stockholders. Both the 4–1 Appellate Division and the 4–3 Court of Appeals opinions evoked the quick and unanimous condemnation of commentators. Moreover, this test, "which appears to sweep away the distinction between a representative and a derivative action," in effect classifying all stockholder class actions as derivative, has been limited strictly to its facts by lower New York courts. In *Lazar* [*v. Knolls Cooperative Section No. 2, Inc.*], a stockholder sought to force directors to call a stockholders' meeting. The court stated security for costs could not be required where a plaintiff

> "does not challenge acts of the management on behalf of the corporation. He challenges the right of the present management to exclude him and other

stockholders from proper participation in the affairs of the corporation. He claims that the defendants are interfering with the plaintiff's rights and privileges as stockholders."

In substance, this is a similar to what Eisenberg challenges here.

The legislature also was concerned with the sweeping breadth of *Gordon*. In the recodification of corporate statutes completed in 1963, it added three words to the definition of derivative suits contained in §626. Suits are now derivative only if brought in the right of a corporation to procure a judgment "in its favor." This was to "forestall any such pronouncement in the future as that made by the Court of Appeals in *Gordon v. Elliman*." . . .

Eisenberg's position is even stronger than it would be in the ordinary merger case. In routine merger circumstances the stockholders retain a voice in the operation of the company, albeit a corporation other than their original choice. Here, however, the reorganization deprived him and other minority stockholders of any voice in the affairs of their previously existing operating company.

It is thus clear to us that *Gordon* is factually distinguishable from the instant case. Moreover, a close analysis of other New York cases, the amendment to §626 and the major treatises, lead us to conclude that *Gordon* has lost its viability as stating a broad principle of law.

Furthermore, we view as an objective of a requirement for security for costs the prevention of strike suits and collusive settlements. Where directors are sued for mismanagement, the risk of personal monetary liability is a strong motive for bringing the suit and inducing settlement. Here, no monetary damages are sought, and no individuals will be liable.

Perhaps the strongest string in Eisenberg's bow is one he helped to fashion when he made an investment some forty years ago in Central Zone Property Corp. In 1952 that New York corporation obtained stockholder approval to transfer its assets to a new Delaware corporation in return for the new company's stock. The stock was to be held by trustees in a voting trust, and the former stockholders received voting trust certificates. Eisenberg complained that this effectively deprived him of a voice in the operation of his company which would be run in the future by the trustees of the voting trust. The Court of Appeals agreed that New York law did not permit such a reorganization. *Eisenberg v. Central Zone Property Corp*. Although we have emphasized that we do not reach the merits of Eisenberg's present complaint, it is of some interest that security for costs was neither sought nor was it discussed in the *Central Zone* opinions, even though Eisenberg did not own five percent of the shares of the corporation. It was clear to all that the allegations of the complaint, quite similar in character to the instant one, stated a representative cause of action. We cannot conceive that the question of security for costs was not considered by the able counsel for the corporation or by the court, particularly since *Gordon* had been decided in the Appellate Division less than one year before the *Central Zone* decision in the Court of Appeals and extensive commentaries had already appeared. We believe Eisenberg's action should not have been dismissed for failure to post security pursuant to § 627.

Reversed.

Questions

1. What is Eisenberg's claim? How did the transaction dilute his control over Flying Tiger? Should the *de minimus* nature of any harm Eisenberg may have suffered be taken into consideration at this stage of the litigation or at the trial on the merits?

2. What is the difference between the test applied in *Gordon v. Elliman* and the test applied in *Eisenberg v. Flying Tiger Line, Inc.*? Note that the turn from the former to the latter represents a shift from a test in which direct suits were practically nonexistent to a much broader test allowing direct action by shareholders. Why do you think the court moved in this direction? What does it say about the court's view of the purpose of the corporation? Do you think that the rise of the securities class action in the 1960s had any effect on the court's view of the propriety of liberalized derivative suits?

Grimes v. Donald

673 A.2d 1207 (Del. 1996)

VEASEY, Chief Justice

In this appeal we address the following issues: (1) the distinction between a direct claim of a stockholder and a derivative claim....

We hold as follows: First, an abdication claim can be stated by a stockholder as a direct claim, as distinct from a derivative claim....

I. The Facts.

[The facts are as set forth in Part 1, *supra*.]

. . .

II. Grimes Has Not Stated a Claim for Abdication of Directorial Duty

... We agree that the Court of Chancery appropriately analyzed the abdication claim as a direct—as distinct from a derivative—claim.

Courts have long recognized that the same set of facts can give rise both to a direct claim and a derivative claim. The due care, waste and excessive compensation claims asserted here are derivative and will be considered as such. The abdication claim, however, is a direct claim. In order to reach this conclusion, we believe a further exploration of the distinction between direct and derivative claims is appropriate.

A. Distinction Between Direct and Derivative Claims, Generally

As the Court of Chancery has noted: "Although the tests have been articulated many times, it is often difficult to distinguish between a derivative and an individual action." The distinction depends upon "'the nature of the wrong alleged' and the relief, if any, which could result if plaintiff were to prevail." To pursue a direct action, the stockholder-plaintiff "must allege more than an injury resulting from a wrong to the corporation." The plaintiff must state a claim for "'an injury which is separate and distinct from that suffered by other shareholders,' . . . or a wrong involving a contractual right of a shareholder . . . which exists independently of any right of the corporation." *Moran v. Household Int'l, Inc.*

The American Law Institute ("ALI") *Principles of Corporate Governance: Analysis and Recommendations* (1992) ("*Principles*") is helpful in this instance. Section 7.01 of the *Principles* undertakes to state the common law with respect to the distinction between direct and derivative actions. *Id.* § 7.01, cmt. a. The Comment also discusses a situation relevant to the case *sub judice*:

> In some instances, actions that essentially involve the structural relationship of the shareholder to the corporation . . . may also give rise to a derivative action when the corporation suffers or is threatened with a loss. One example would be a case in which a corporate official knowingly acts in a manner that the certificate of incorporation [or the Delaware General Corporation Law] denied the official authority to do, thereby violating both specific restraints imposed by the shareholders [or the GCL] and the official's duty of care.

Id., cmt. c. The Comment further notes that, "courts have been more prepared to permit the plaintiff to characterize the action as direct when the plaintiff is seeking only injunctive or prospective relief." *Id.*, cmt. d.

With respect to the abdication claim, Grimes seeks only a declaration of the invalidity of the Agreements. Monetary recovery will not accrue to the corporation as a result. Chancellor Seitz illustrated this distinction in *Bennett*. The Court of Chancery there allowed the plaintiff-stockholder to proceed individually on his claim that stock was issued for an improper purpose and entrenchment; he proceeded derivatively on his claim that the stock was issued for an insufficient price.

Questions

1. Is the abdication claim in *Grimes v. Donald* similar to or different from the dilution claim in *Eisenberg v. Flying Tiger Line, Inc.*? Can you apply the *Eisenberg* test to *Grimes*?

2. Can you clearly state the test the court applied in *Grimes v. Donald* to distinguish between derivative and direct suits?

3. What does the court's underlying assumption about the corporation appear to be?

B. Security for Expenses

Baker v. MacFadden Publications, Inc.; Baker v. Boord
300 N.Y. 325 (1950)

Loughran, Chief Judge

In the above-entitled action of *Baker v. Boord*, stockholders of MacFadden Publications, Inc., a domestic corporation, assert derivatively a cause of action on its behalf for claimed misapplication of its funds and waste of its property by past directors and officers and other defendants. Judgment for an accounting and for damages is demanded. Upon appropriate allegations, MacFadden Publications, Inc., has been joined as a nominal defendant. We shall refer to that defendant as the corporation.

Section 61-b of the General Corporation Law was enacted in 1944. It makes in substance the following provision: In a stockholder's derivative action, the plaintiffs—unless they represent at least 5% of the corporation's shares or an aggregate of its shares having a value in excess of $50,000—must give security for the reasonable litigation expenses, including attorneys' fees, of all parties joined as defendants in the action. In the present case, the plaintiffs own approximately 4/1000ths of 1% of the stock of the corporation—an interest which at the commencement of this action had a market value of about $350. Hence the corporation was entitled to apply for the security authorized by section 61-b.

Upon such an application by the corporation, Special Term made an order which (1) fixed security in the sum of $40,000 and directed a bond therefor to be filed within sixty days; and (2) gave leave to the plaintiffs to move for a vacating of the order if within that time additional stockholders should join them in number sufficient to meet the requirements of section 61-b.

From that security order both the plaintiffs and the corporation appealed to the Appellate Division where the plaintiffs challenged the constitutionality of section 61-b, while the corporation made an attack upon the provision respecting the joinder of additional stockholders as parties plaintiff in the action. The corporation also appealed to the Appellate Division from an order made by Special Term in the above-entitled special proceeding of *Matter of Baker v. MacFadden Publications*. In that article 78 proceeding, the Special Term, upon a petition of the plaintiffs, had directed the corporation to allow them to inspect and copy its stock book and stockholders' list.

The Appellate Division (1) upheld section 61-b as a constitutional enactment; (2) modified on the law the security order by deleting the provision respecting the joinder of additional stockholders of the corporation as parties plaintiff in the action and affirmed that order as so modified; and (3) reversed on the law the order permitting the plaintiffs to inspect the corporation's stock book and stockholders' list and denied the petition for such inspection.

By permission of the Appellate Division, the plaintiffs—upon six questions certified—have appealed to us from the modification by that court of the security order. Besides, they have appealed here as of right from the order of that court denying their petition for inspection of the corporation's stock book and stockholders' list.

The first five of the six questions certified present issues in respect of the constitutionality of section 61-b which are now academic, since the validity of that section has already been finally adjudicated by us. The sixth question certified asks us to say whether Special Term was right in making the following provision a part of its security order: "Further ordered that, in the event that joinder in the action is effected by the plaintiffs of stockholders holding 5% of the outstanding shares of any class of stock of said MacFadden Publications, Inc., or shares of said MacFadden Publications, Inc. having a market value in excess of $50,000, plaintiffs may make application to vacate this order."

The Appellate Division struck out that provision for reasons clearly stated in its opinion as follows: "The time for determining the right of the corporation to security is when the action is instituted or when the motion for security is made. When the corporation's right to security is once determined and an order granted, the right is fixed and is not subject to defeasance by a change in the amount of stock that may subsequently be joined in the action. It is subject only to an increase or decrease in the amount of the security as it may subsequently prove to be inadequate or excessive in relation to the expenses of the corporation to be secured."

The construction thus put upon section 61-b fails to take proper account of a long-recognized rule of practice which for present purposes may be stated in this manner: The New York Supreme Court, so long as an action is pending before it, has power, for sufficient cause, to modify or vacate an order made in the course of the action. Section 61-b was not intended to declare an exception to that general rule. Hence, in our judgment, the Appellate Division was wrong in modifying the security order made by the Special Term.

We pass now to the appeal of the plaintiffs in the special proceeding from the order denying their petition for an examination of the corporation's stock book and stockholders' list. The plaintiffs sought that relief for the express purpose of inviting other stockholders to come into the derivative action as additional plaintiffs, in the hope of avoiding thereby the necessity of posting security. In denying that relief as matter of law, the Appellate Division said: "As the order for an examination of the stock book was sought and granted only in aid of the invalid provision of the security order, it must also be vacated."

This conclusion of the Appellate Division, of course, cannot here be accepted, since, as we now hold, the security order is entirely valid. The special proceeding, however, should be remitted to that court for decision of the questions of discretion that are involved therein.

In Matter of Baker v. MacFadden Publications, the order of the Appellate Division should be reversed, with costs in this court and in the Appellate Division, and the matter remitted to that court for determination, as it may be advised, of the questions of discretion that are therein involved.

In *Baker v. Boord*, the order of the Appellate Division should be reversed, with costs in this court and in the Appellate Division, and the order of Special Term affirmed. The sixth question certified is answered in the affirmative. The other questions certified are not answered.

Questions

1. Section 61-b, which is discussed in *Baker v. MacFadden Publications, Inc.*, was passed in 1944. $50,000 in 1944 is the equivalent of $707,361 in 2018 dollars. What do you think was the reasoning behind a statute requiring a stockholder with small number of shares (who presumably has no opportunity to influence the board's actions except by lawsuit) to post security for expenses but not requiring a stockholder with larger holdings (who presumably has greater influence with the board) to do the same? What are the policy reasons for and against the statute? In thinking about your answer, consider how much a small stockholder really has to gain by the time and expense of bringing litigation, especially when we have seen that derivative recovery goes to the corporation. Who do you suppose is the real party in interest? Does this suggest a reason underlying § 61-b?

2. Security for expenses legislation was adopted by many states as a response to the belief that some lawyers and shareholders with minimal holdings in a corporation were abusing derivative litigation. They were said to be engaging in *strike suits*; suits in the name of a corporation that were designed to result in settlements that gave plaintiffs' lawyers substantial attorneys' fees. The essence of these statutes was that if a plaintiff did not own at least a certain percentage of the corporate shares (often 5%) or hold shares of a value of a certain dollar amount (often $50,000), that plaintiff was subject, upon the motion of the corporation, to post a bond for the reasonable expenses, including the defendant's attorneys' fees, of the litigation. The percentage of shares held or their monetary value could be aggregated if there were more than one named plaintiff in order to reach the statutory thresholds.

3. Federal Rule of Civil Procedure 23.1, like the legislation in many states, gives courts greater control over derivative litigation, in part by prohibiting settlement without court approval.

Rule 23.1 Derivative Actions

(a) Prerequisites. This rule applies when one or more shareholders or members of a corporation or an unincorporated association bring a derivative action to enforce a right that the corporation or association may properly assert but has failed to enforce. The derivative action may not be maintained if it appears that the plaintiff does not fairly and adequately represent the interests of shareholders or members who are similarly situated in enforcing the right of the corporation or association.

(b) Pleading Requirements. The complaint must be verified and must: (1) allege that the plaintiff was a shareholder or member at the time of the transaction complained of, or that the plaintiff's share or membership later devolved on it by operation of law; (2) allege that the action is not a collusive one to confer jurisdiction that the court would otherwise lack; and (3) state with particularity: (A) any effort by the plaintiff to obtain the desired action from the directors or comparable authority and, if necessary, from the shareholders or members; and (B) the reasons for not obtaining the action or not making the effort.

(c) Settlement, Dismissal, and Compromise. A derivative action may be settled, voluntarily dismissed, or compromised only with the court's approval. Notice of a proposed settlement, voluntary dismissal, or compromise must be given to shareholders or members in the manner that the court orders.

4. Interestingly, Congress imposed even more restrictive limitations on securities class action suits under the Private Securities Litigation Reform Act of 1996. These limitations made it harder for plaintiffs to recover from corporations involved in the corporate scandals of 2002.

C. Demand on the Board

Grimes v. Donald
673 A.2d 1207 (Del. 1996)

VEASEY, Chief Justice

In this appeal we address the following issues: . . . (3) when a pre-suit demand in a derivative suit is required or excused; and (4) the consequences of demand by a stockholder and the refusal by the board to act on such a demand.

We hold that the Court of Chancery correctly dismissed this stockholder action for the failure to state a claim upon which relief can be granted where the plaintiff stockholder: . . . (b) made a pre-suit demand on the Board to abrogate the Agreements, the demand was refused, and the stockholder thereafter sought to assert other legal theories relating to the Agreements, arguing that demand was excused.

We hold as follows: . . . Second, when a stockholder demands that the board of directors take action on a claim allegedly belonging to the corporation and demand is refused, the stockholder may not thereafter assert that demand is excused with respect to other legal theories in support of the same claim, although the stockholder may have a remedy for wrongful refusal or may submit further demands which are not repetitious.

Accordingly, on the state of this record, we affirm the dismissal of this action by the Court of Chancery.

I. The Facts.

[Once again, the facts are as set forth in Part I.]

. . .

III. Grimes' Demand on the Board with Respect to the Derivative Claim Conceded that Demand Was Required.

The complaint alleges that Grimes made a pre-suit demand on the Board in the September 29, 1993, letter quoted above. In summary, the letter described the relevant provisions of the Donald Agreements and demanded that the Board "take immediate steps to abrogate" the cited sections of the Agreements. The Court of Chancery held that, by "making demand upon the board, plaintiff has in effect conceded that the board was in a position to consider and act upon his demand." Contending that demand was excused, Grimes later filed suit alleging waste, excessive compensation and due care claims arising out of the Agreements. But the Chancellor held that Grimes waived his right to argue that demand was excused with respect to these claims because he had already made demand that the agreements be abrogated as unlawful. We agree.

A. The Demand Requirement in Perspective

Because the prolix (43 page) complaint tends to confuse the issues in this case, it is appropriate to restate, as a matter of background, the Delaware jurisprudence relating to stockholder derivative litigation.

If a claim belongs to the corporation, it is the corporation, acting through its board of directors, which must make the decision whether or not to assert the claim. "[T]he derivative action impinges on the managerial freedom of directors." "[T]he demand requirement is a recognition of the fundamental precept that directors manage the business and affairs of the corporation."

A stockholder filing a derivative suit must allege either that the board rejected his pre-suit demand that the board assert the corporation's claim or allege with particularity why the stockholder was justified in not having made the effort to obtain board action. This is a "basic principle of corporate governance" and is a matter of substantive law embodied in the procedural requirements of Chancery Rule 23.1.

One ground for alleging with particularity that demand would be futile is that a "reasonable doubt" exists that the board is capable of making an independent decision to assert the claim if demand were made. The basis for claiming excusal would normally be that: (1) a majority of the board has a material financial or familial interest; (2) a majority of the board is incapable of acting independently for some other reason such as domination or control; or (3) the underlying transaction is not the product of a valid exercise of business judgment. If the stockholder cannot plead such assertions consistent with Chancery Rule 11, after using the "tools at hand" to obtain the necessary information before filing a derivative action, then the stockholder must make a pre-suit demand on the board.

The demand requirement serves a salutary purpose. First, by requiring exhaustion of intracorporate remedies, the demand requirement invokes a species of alternative dispute resolution procedure which might avoid litigation altogether. Second, if litigation is beneficial, the corporation can control the proceedings. Third, if demand is excused or wrongfully refused, the stockholder will normally control the proceedings.

The jurisprudence of *Aronson* [*v. Lewis*] and its progeny is designed to create a balanced environment which will: (1) on the one hand, deter costly, baseless suits by creating a screening mechanism to eliminate claims where there is only a suspicion expressed solely in conclusory terms; and (2) on the other hand, permit suit by a stockholder who is able to articulate particularized facts showing that there is a reasonable doubt either that (a) a majority of the board is independent for purposes of responding to the demand, or (b) the underlying transaction is protected by the business judgment rule.

Aronson introduced the term "reasonable doubt" into corporate derivative jurisprudence. Some courts and commentators have questioned why a concept normally present in criminal prosecution would find its way into derivative litigation. Yet the term is apt and achieves the proper balance. Reasonable doubt can be said to mean that there is a reason to doubt. This concept is sufficiently flexible and workable to provide the stockholder with "the keys to the courthouse" in an appropriate case where the claim is not based on mere suspicions or stated solely in conclusory terms.

B. Wrongful Refusal Distinguished from Excusal

Demand has been excused in many cases in Delaware under the *Aronson* test. The law regarding wrongful refusal is not as well developed, however. Although Delaware law does not require demand in every case because Delaware does have the mechanism of demand excusal, it is important that the demand process be meaningful. Therefore, a stockholder who makes a demand is entitled to know promptly what action the board has taken in response to the demand. A stockholder who makes a serious demand and receives only a peremptory refusal has the right to use the "tools at hand" to obtain the relevant corporate records, such as reports or minutes, reflecting the corporate action and related information in order to determine whether or not there is a basis to assert that demand was wrongfully refused. In no event may a corporation assume a position of neutrality and take no position in response to the demand.

If a demand is made, the stockholder has spent one — but only one — "arrow" in the "quiver." The spent "arrow" is the right to claim that demand is excused. The stockholder does not, by making demand, waive the right to claim that demand has been wrongfully refused.

Simply because the composition of the board provides no basis *ex ante* for the stockholder to claim with particularity and consistently with Rule 11 that it is reasonable to doubt that a majority of the board is either interested or not independent, it does not necessarily follow *ex post* that the board in fact acted independently, disinterestedly or with due care in response to the demand. A board or a committee of the board may appear to be independent, but may not always act independently. If a demand is made and rejected, the board rejecting the demand is entitled to the presumption of the business judgment rule unless the stockholder can allege facts with particularity creating a reasonable doubt that the board is entitled to the benefit of the presumption. If there is reason to doubt that the board acted independently or with due care in responding to the demand, the stockholder may have the basis *ex post* to claim wrongful refusal. The stockholder then has the right to bring the underlying action with the same standing which the stockholder would have had, *ex ante*, if demand had been excused as futile.

C. Application to This Case

In the case before the Court, plaintiff made a pre-suit demand. Later, however, plaintiff contended that demand was excused. Under the doctrine articulated by this Court in *Spiegel v. Buntrock*, plaintiff, by making a demand, waived his right to contest the independence of the board. As the Court of Chancery properly held, plaintiff may not bifurcate his theories relating to the same claim. Thus, demand having been made as to the propriety of the Agreements, it cannot be excused as to the claim that the Agreements constituted waste, excessive compensation or was the product of a lack of due care.

The Court of Chancery implicitly applied a test analogous to *res judicata* to determine whether Grimes' demand letter conceded that demand was required for all legal theories arising out of the set of facts described in the demand letter. We believe this to be a correct approach. The alternative claims raised in the complaint fit squarely within the same transactional rubric as the demand since all of the claims, however denominated, arise out of the Agreements. As the Court of Chancery stated: "There is little to recommend a process in which a shareholder seeks board consideration of only some aspects of a transaction or puts forward only selected theories for board consideration, while reserving other theories for judicial consideration. Such a process would be neither efficient nor fair." *Grimes*, 20 Del. J. Corp. L. at 772.

The same concerns are expressed in the Restatement (Second) of Judgments, which asserts that "fairness to the defendant, and sound judicial administration, require that at some point litigation over the particular controversy come to an end." RESTATEMENT (SECOND) OF JUDGMENTS § 19, cmt. a. (1980). Since the making of a pre-suit demand concedes that demand is required, the concession should apply "to all or any part of the transaction, or series of connected transactions, out of which the action [demand] arose." *Id.* § 24; see *Foltz v. Pullman, Inc.*

In *Spiegel*, this Court held that "[a] shareholder who makes a demand can no longer argue that demand is excused." Permitting a stockholder to demand action involving only one theory or remedy and to argue later that demand is excused as to other legal theories or remedies arising out of the same set of circumstances as set forth in the demand letter would create an undue risk of harassment.

In this case, the Board of DSC considered and rejected the demand. After investing the time and resources to consider and decide whether or not to take action in response to the demand, the Board is entitled to have its decision analyzed under the business judgment rule unless the presumption of that rule can be rebutted. *Spiegel.* Grimes cannot avoid this result by holding back or bifurcating legal theories based on precisely the same set of facts alleged in the demand.

Since Grimes made a pre-suit demand with respect to all claims arising out of the Agreements, he was required by Chancery Rule 23.1 to plead with particularity why the Board's refusal to act on the derivative claims was wrongful. The complaint recites the Board's rejection of Grimes' demand and proceeds to assert why Grimes disagrees with the Board's conclusion. The complaint generally asserts that the refusal could not have been the result of an adequate, good faith investigation since the Board decided not to act on the demand. Such conclusory, *ipse dixit*, assertions are inconsistent with the requirements of Chancery Rule 23.1. The complaint fails to include particularized allegations which would raise a reasonable doubt that the Board's decision to reject the demand was the product of a valid business judgment.

IV. Conclusion

Accordingly, the judgment of the Court of Chancery is affirmed.

Questions

1. What are the justifications for the demand requirement?

2. What will a plaintiff have to show to prove that demand was wrongfully refused? What will a plaintiff have to show to prove that demand should be excused? Which course of action would you recommend to a shareholder seeking to bring a derivative suit? Why?

3. Based upon what you know so far (and pending your study of the role and authority of special litigation committees below), what do you think are the chances for a plaintiff ever to reach the merits of a derivative suit? What, then, is the purpose of this equitable remedy? Consider this question as you read the following cases.

Marx v. Akers
88 N.Y.2d 189 (1996)

SMITH, Judge

Plaintiff commenced this shareholder derivative action against International Business Machines Corporation (IBM) and IBM's board of directors without first demanding that the board initiate a lawsuit. The amended complaint (complaint) alleges that the board wasted corporate assets by awarding excessive compensation to IBM's executives and outside directors. The issues raised on this appeal are whether the Appellate Division abused its discretion by dismissing plaintiff's complaint for failure to make a demand and whether plaintiff's complaint fails to state a cause of action. We affirm the order of the Appellate Division because we conclude that plaintiff was not excused from making a demand with respect to the executive compensation claim and that plaintiff has failed to state a cause of action for corporate waste in connection with the allegations concerning payments to IBM's outside directors.

Facts and Procedural History

The complaint alleges that during a period of declining profitability at IBM the director defendants engaged in self-dealing by awarding excessive compensation to the 15 outside directors on the 18-member board. Although the complaint identifies only one of the three inside directors as an IBM executive (defendant Akers is identified as a former chief executive officer of IBM), plaintiff also appears to allege that the director defendants violated their fiduciary duties to IBM by voting for unreasonably high compensation for IBM executives.

Defendants moved to dismiss the complaint for (1) failure to state a cause of action, and (2) failure to serve a demand on IBM's board to initiate a lawsuit based on the complaint's allegations. The Supreme Court dismissed, holding that plaintiff failed to establish the futility of a demand. Supreme Court concluded that excusing a demand here would render Business Corporation Law § 626(c) "virtually meaningless in any shareholders' derivative action in which all members of a corporate board are named as defendants." Having decided the demand issue in favor of defendants, the court did not reach the issue of whether plaintiff's complaint stated a cause of action.

The Appellate Division affirmed the dismissal, concluding that the complaint did not contain any details from which the futility of a demand could be inferred. The Appellate Division found that plaintiff's objections to the level of compensation were not stated with sufficient particularity in light of statutory authority permitting directors to set their own compensation.

Background

A shareholder's derivative action is an action "brought in the right of a domestic or foreign corporation to procure a judgment in its favor, by a holder of shares or of voting trust certificates of the corporation or of a beneficial interest in such shares or certificates" (Business Corporation Law § 626[a]). "Derivative claims against corporate directors belong to the corporation itself" (*Auerbach v. Bennett*).

> "The remedy sought is for wrong done to the corporation; the primary cause of action belongs to the corporation; recovery must enure to the benefit of the corporation. The stockholder brings the action, in behalf of others similarly situated, to vindicate the corporate rights and a judgment on the merits is a binding adjudication of these rights." (*Isaac v. Marcus*)

Business Corporation Law § 626(c) provides that in any shareholders' derivative action, "the complaint shall set forth with particularity the efforts of the plaintiff to secure the initiation of such action by the board or the reasons for not making such effort." Enacted in 1961, section 626(c) codified a rule of equity developed in early shareholder derivative actions requiring plaintiffs to demand that the corporation initiate an action, unless such demand was futile, before commencing an action on the corporation's behalf. The purposes of the demand requirement are to (1) relieve courts from deciding matters of internal corporate governance by providing corporate directors with opportunities to correct alleged abuses, (2) provide corporate boards with reasonable protection from harassment by litigation on matters clearly within the discretion of directors, and (3) discourage "strike suits" commenced by shareholders for personal gain rather than for the benefit of the corporation. "[T]he demand is generally designed to weed out unnecessary or illegitimate shareholder derivative suits."

By their very nature, shareholder derivative actions infringe upon the managerial discretion of corporate boards. "As with other questions of corporate policy and management, the decision whether and to what extent to explore and prosecute such [derivative] claims lies within the judgment and control of the corporation's board of directors." Consequently, we have historically been reluctant to permit shareholder derivative suits, noting that the power of courts to direct the management of a corporation's affairs should be "exercised with restraint."

In permitting a shareholder derivative action to proceed because a demand on the corporation's directors would be futile,

> "the object is for the court to chart the course for the corporation which the directors should have selected, and which it is presumed that they would have chosen if they had not been actuated by fraud or bad faith. Due to their misconduct, the court substitutes its judgment *ad hoc* for that of the directors in the conduct of its business."

Achieving a balance between preserving the discretion of directors to manage a corporation without undue interference, through the demand requirement, and permitting shareholders to bring claims on behalf of the corporation when it is evident that directors will wrongfully refuse to bring such claims, through the demand futility exception, has been accomplished by various jurisdictions in different ways. One widely cited approach to demand futility which attempts to balance these competing concerns has been developed by Delaware courts and applies a two-pronged test to each case to determine whether a failure to serve a demand is justified. At the other end of the spectrum is a universal demand requirement which would abandon particularized determinations in favor of requiring a demand in every case before a shareholder derivative suit may be filed.

The Delaware Approach

Delaware's demand requirement, codified in Delaware Chancery Court Rule 23.1, provides, in relevant part,

> "In a derivative action brought by 1 or more shareholders or members to enforce a right of a corporation . . . [the complaint shall allege] with particularity the efforts, if any, made by the plaintiff to obtain the action the plaintiff desires from the directors or comparable authority and the reasons for the plaintiff's failure to obtain the action or for not making the effort."

Interpreting Rule 23.1, the Delaware Supreme Court in *Aronson v. Lewis* developed a two-prong test for determining the futility of a demand. Plaintiffs must allege particularized facts which create a reasonable doubt that,

"(1) the directors are disinterested and independent and (2) the challenged transaction was otherwise the product of a valid exercise of business judgment. Hence, the Court of Chancery must make two inquiries, one into the independence and disinterestedness of the directors and the other into the substantive nature of the challenged transaction and the board's approval thereof."

The two branches of the *Aronson* test are disjunctive. Once director interest has been established, the business judgment rule becomes inapplicable and the demand excused without further inquiry. Similarly, a director whose independence is compromised by undue influence exerted by an interested party cannot properly exercise business judgment and the loss of independence also justifies the excusal of a demand without further inquiry. Whether a board has validly exercised its business judgment must be evaluated by determining whether the directors exercised procedural (informed decision) and substantive (terms of the transaction) due care.

The reasonable doubt threshold of Delaware's two-fold approach to demand futility has been criticized. The use of a standard of proof which is the heart of a jury's determination in a criminal case has raised questions concerning its applicability in the corporate context. The reasonable doubt standard has also been criticized as overly subjective, thereby permitting a wide variance in the application of Delaware law to similar facts (2 American Law Institute, Principles of Corporate Governance: Analysis and Recommendations § 7.03, Comment d, at 57 [1992]).

Universal Demand

A universal demand requirement would dispense with the necessity of making case-specific determinations and impose an easily applied bright line rule. The Business Law Section of the American Bar Association has proposed requiring a demand in all cases, without exception, and permits the commencement of a derivative proceeding within 90 days of the demand unless the demand is rejected earlier (Model Business Corporation Act § 7.42[1] [1995 Supp]). However, plaintiffs may file suit before the expiration of 90 days, even if their demand has not been rejected, if the corporation would suffer irreparable injury as a result.

The American Law Institute (ALI) has also proposed a "universal" demand. Section 7.03 of ALI's Principles of Corporate Governance would require shareholder derivative action plaintiffs to serve a written demand on the corporation *unless* a demand is excused because "the plaintiff makes a specific showing that irreparable injury to the corporation would otherwise result" (2 ALI, Principles of Corporate Governance: Analysis and Recommendations § 7.03[b], at 53–54 [1992]). Once a demand has been made and rejected, however, the ALI would subject the board's decision to "an elaborate set of standards that calibrates the deference afforded the decision of the directors to the character of the claim being asserted."

At least 11 States have adopted, by statute, the universal demand requirement proposed in the Model Business Corporation Act. Georgia, Michigan, Wisconsin, Montana, Virginia, New Hampshire, Mississippi, Connecticut, Nebraska and North

Carolina require shareholders to wait 90 days after serving a demand before filing a derivative suit unless the demand is rejected before the expiration of the 90 days, or irreparable injury to the corporation would result. Arizona additionally permits shareholders to file suit before the expiration of 90 days if the Statute of Limitations would expire during the 90-day period. Florida also appears to have adopted a universal demand requirement, although the statutory language does not track the Model Business Corporation Act. Florida's statute provides, "A complaint in a proceeding brought in the right of a corporation must be verified and allege with particularity the demand made to obtain action by the board of directors *and that the demand was refused or ignored.*" [Emphasis added.]

New York State has also considered and continues to consider implementing a universal demand requirement. However, even though bills to adopt a universal demand have been presented over three legislative sessions, the Legislature has yet to enact a universal demand requirement.

New York's Approach to Demand Futility

Although instructive, neither the universal demand requirement nor the Delaware approach to demand futility is adopted here. Since New York's demand requirement is codified in Business Corporation Law § 626(c), a universal demand may only be adopted by the Legislature. Delaware's approach, which resembles New York law in some respects, incorporates a "reasonable doubt" standard which, as we have already pointed out, has provoked criticism as confusing and overly subjective. An analysis of the *Barr* decision compels the conclusion that in New York, a demand would be futile if a complaint alleges with particularity that (1) a majority of the directors are interested in the transaction, or (2) the directors failed to inform themselves to a degree reasonably necessary about the transaction, or (3) the directors failed to exercise their business judgment in approving the transaction.

In *Barr v. Wackman*, we considered whether the plaintiff was excused from making a demand where the board of Talcott National Corporation (Talcott), consisting of 13 outside directors, a director affiliated with a related company and four interested inside directors, rejected a merger proposal involving Gulf & Western Industries (Gulf & Western) in favor of another proposal on allegedly less favorable terms for Talcott and its shareholders. The merger proposal, memorialized in a board-approved "agreement in principle," proposed exchanging one share of Talcott common stock for approximately $24 consisting of $17 in cash and 0.6 of a warrant to purchase Gulf & Western stock, worth approximately $7. This proposal was abandoned in favor of a cash tender offer for Talcott shares by Associates First Capital Corporation (a Gulf & Western subsidiary) at $20 per share—$4 less than proposed for the merger.

The plaintiff in *Barr* alleged that Talcott's board discarded the merger proposal after the four "controlling" inside directors received pecuniary and personal benefits from Gulf & Western in exchange for ceding control of Talcott on terms less favorable to Talcott's shareholders. As alleged in the complaint, these benefits included new and favorable employment contracts for nine Talcott officers, including five-year employment contracts for three of the controlling directors. In addition to his annual salary of $125,000 with Talcott, defendant Silverman (a controlling director) would allegedly receive $60,000 a year under a five-year employment contract with Associates First Capital, and an aggregate of $275,000 for the next five years in an arrangement with Associates First Capital to serve as a consultant. This additional compensation would be awarded to Silverman after control of Talcott passed to Associates First Capital and Gulf & Western. Plaintiff also alleged that Gulf & Western and Associates First Capital paid an excessive "finder's fee" of $340,000 to a company where Silverman's son was an executive vice-president. In addition to alleging that the controlling defendants obtained personal benefits, the complaint also alleged that Talcott's board agreed to sell a Talcott subsidiary at a net loss of $6,100,000 solely to accommodate Gulf & Western.

In *Barr*, we held that insofar as the complaint attacked the controlling directors' acts in causing the corporation to enter into a transaction for their own financial benefit, demand was excused because of the self-dealing, or self-interest of those directors in the challenged transaction. Specifically, we pointed to the allegation that the controlling directors "breached their fiduciary obligations to Talcott in return for personal benefits."

We also held in *Barr*, however, that as to the disinterested outside directors, demand could be excused even in the absence of their receiving any financial benefit from the transaction. That was because the complaint alleged that, by approving the terms of the less advantageous offer, those directors were guilty of a "breach of their duties of due care and diligence to the corporation." Their performance of the duty of care would have "put them on notice of the claimed self-dealing of the affiliated directors." The complaint charged that the outside directors failed "to do more than passively rubber-stamp the decisions of the active managers" resulting in corporate detriment. These allegations, the *Barr* Court concluded, also excused demand as to the charges against the disinterested directors.

Barr also makes clear that "[i]t is not sufficient ... merely to name a majority of the directors as parties defendant with conclusory allegations of wrongdoing or control by wrongdoers" to justify failure to make a demand. Thus, *Barr* reflects the statutory requirement that the complaint "shall set forth with particularity the ... reasons for not making such effort" (Business Corporation Law § 626[c]).

Unfortunately, various courts have overlooked the explicit warning that conclusory allegations of wrongdoing against each member of the board are not sufficient to excuse demand and have misinterpreted *Barr* as excusing demand whenever a majority of the board members who approved the transaction are named as defendants. As stated most recently, "[t]he rule is clear in this State that no demand is necessary if 'the complaint alleges acts for which a majority of the directors may be liable and plaintiff reasonably concluded that the board would not be responsive to a demand.'" The problem with such an approach is that it permits plaintiffs to frame their complaint in such a way as to automatically excuse demand, thereby allowing the exception to swallow the rule.

We thus deem it necessary to offer the following elaboration of *Barr*'s demand/futility standard. (1) Demand is excused because of futility when a complaint alleges with particularity that a majority of the board of directors is interested in the challenged transaction. Director interest may either be self-interest in the transaction at issue, or a loss of independence because a director with no direct interest in a transaction is "controlled" by a self-interested director. (2) Demand is excused because of futility when a complaint alleges with particularity that the board of directors did not fully inform themselves about the challenged transaction to the extent reasonably appropriate under the circumstances. The "long-standing rule" is that a director "does not exempt himself from liability by failing to do more than passively rubber-stamp the decisions of the active managers." (3) Demand is excused because of futility when a complaint alleges with particularity that the challenged transaction was so egregious on its face that it could not have been the product of sound business judgment of the directors.

The Current Appeal

Plaintiff argues that the demand requirement was excused both because the outside directors awarded themselves generous compensation packages and because of the acquiescence of the disinterested directors in the executive compensation schemes. The complaint states:

> "Plaintiff has made no demand upon the directors of IBM to institute this lawsuit because such demand would be futile. As set forth above, each of the directors authorized, approved, participated and/or acquiesced in the acts and transactions complained of herein and are liable therefor. Further, each of the Non-Employee [outside] Directors has received and retained the benefit of his excessive compensation and each of the other directors has received and retained the benefit of the incentive compensation described above. The defendants cannot be expected to vote to prosecute an action against themselves. Demand upon the company to bring action [*sic*] to redress the wrongs herein is therefore unnecessary."

Defendants argue that neither the Supreme Court nor the Appellate Division abused its discretion in holding that plaintiff's complaint did not set forth the futility of a demand with particularity.

As in *Barr*, we look to the complaint here to determine whether the allegations are sufficient and establish with particularity that demand would have been futile. Here, the plaintiff alleges that the compensation awarded to IBM's outside directors and certain IBM executives was excessive.

Defendants' motion to dismiss for failure to make a demand as to the allegations concerning the compensation paid to IBM's executive officers was properly granted. A board is not interested "in voting compensation for one of its members as an executive or in some other nondirectorial capacity, such as a consultant to the corporation," although "so-called 'back-scratching' arrangements, pursuant to which all directors vote to approve each other's compensation as officers or employees, do not constitute disinterested directors' action." Since only three directors are alleged to have received the benefit of the executive compensation scheme, plaintiff has failed to allege that a majority of the board was interested in setting executive compensation. Nor do the allegations that the board used faulty accounting procedures to calculate executive compensation levels move beyond "conclusory allegations of wrongdoing" which are insufficient to excuse demand. The complaint does not allege particular facts in contending that the board failed to deliberate or exercise its business judgment in setting those levels. Consequently, the failure to make a demand regarding the fixing of executive compensation was fatal to that portion of the complaint challenging that transaction.

However, a review of the complaint indicates that plaintiff also alleged that a majority of the board was self-interested in setting the compensation of outside directors because the outside directors comprised a majority of the board.

Directors are self-interested in a challenged transaction where they will receive a direct financial benefit from the transaction which is different from the benefit to shareholders generally. A director who votes for a raise in directors' compensation is always "interested" because that person will receive a personal financial benefit from the transaction not shared in by stockholders. Consequently, a demand was excused as to plaintiff's allegations that the compensation set for outside directors was excessive.

Corporate Waste

Our conclusion that demand should have been excused as to the part of the complaint challenging the fixing of directors' compensation does not end our inquiry. We must also determine whether plaintiff has stated a cause of action regarding director compensation, i.e., some wrong to the corporation. We conclude that plaintiff has not, and thus dismiss the complaint in its entirety.

Historically, directors did not receive any compensation for their work as directors. Thus, a bare allegation that corporate directors voted themselves excessive compensation was sufficient to state a cause of action. Many jurisdictions, including New York, have since changed the common-law rule by statute providing that a corporation's board of directors has the authority to fix director compensation unless the corporation's charter or bylaws provides otherwise. Thus, the allegation that directors have voted themselves compensation is clearly no longer an allegation which gives rise to a cause of action, as the directors are statutorily entitled to set those levels. Nor does a conclusory allegation that the compensation directors have set for themselves is excessive give rise to a cause of action.

"The courts will not undertake to review the fairness of official salaries, at the suit of a shareholder attacking them as excessive, unless wrongdoing and oppression or possible abuse of a fiduciary position are shown. However, the courts will take a hand in the matter at the instance of the corporation or of shareholders in extreme cases. A case of fraud is presented where directors increase their collective salaries so as to use up nearly the entire earnings of a company; where directors or officers appropriate the income so as to deprive shareholders of reasonable dividends, or perhaps so reduce the assets as to threaten the corporation with insolvency" (Fletcher, *Cyclopedia of Private Corporations*).

Thus, a complaint challenging the excessiveness of director compensation must—to survive a dismissal motion—allege compensation rates excessive on their face or other facts which call into question whether the compensation was fair to the corporation when approved, the good faith of the directors setting those rates, or that the decision to set the compensation could not have been a product of valid business judgment.

Applying the foregoing principles to plaintiff's complaint, it is clear that it must be dismissed. The complaint alleges that the directors increased their compensation rates from a base of $20,000 plus $500 for each meeting attended to a retainer of $55,000 plus 100 shares of IBM stock over a five-year period. The complaint also alleges that "[t]his compensation bears little relation to the part-time services rendered by the Non-Employee Directors or to the profitability of IBM. The board's responsibilities have not increased, its performance, measured by the company's earnings and stock price, has been poor yet its compensation has increased far in excess of the cost of living."

These conclusory allegations do not state a cause of action. There are no factually based allegations of wrongdoing or waste which would, if true, sustain a verdict in plaintiff's favor. Plaintiff's bare allegations that the compensation set lacked a relationship to duties performed or to the cost of living are insufficient as a matter of law to state a cause of action.

Accordingly, the order of the Appellate Division should be affirmed, with costs.

Questions

1. What are the differences, conceptual and real, between New York's approach to the demand requirement and Delaware's?

2. What is the purpose of the demand requirement according to the court?

3. The relationships among directors involve a great deal of psychological and sociological complexity. Does the formality of New York's approach properly account for such complexity? If not, are there other good reasons to support New York's approach?

London v. Tyrrell

2008 Del. Ch. LEXIS 75

CHANDLER, Chancellor

On October 31, 2007, plaintiffs Craig London and James Hunt filed their derivative complaint alleging that defendants Michael Tyrrell, Patrick Neven, and Walter Hupalo were harming the company in which all parties own shares. Specifically, plaintiffs allege that defendants have caused the company to issue stock options in contravention of an equity incentive plan by setting the exercise price of the issued options at an unfairly low value. On March 24, 2008, defendants moved to dismiss this complaint under Rules 9(b), 12(b)(6), and 23.1. Defendants argue that the plaintiffs have failed to meet the heightened pleading requirements of . . . demand futility and that the complaint otherwise fails to state a claim. Briefing on defendants' motion was completed on May 8, 2008. Although defendants have thrown nearly every rule in the book at plaintiffs' complaint in the hope of getting it dismissed, the complaint easily survives. For the reasons explained below in this Opinion, defendants' motion is denied.

I. Facts

In 1996, plaintiffs London and Hunt, defendants Neven and Hupalo, and others founded MA Federal, Inc., which does business as iGov ("iGov" or the "Company"). iGov is a government contracting firm that initially focused on participating in the reseller market for information technology hardware, primarily selling to federal military and civilian agencies. After nine years in the low margin, highly competitive reseller market, however, the Company decided to change its focus from product sales to the higher margin government services market. Consequently, since October 2005, iGov has competed for government services contracts, and has begun to reap the financial rewards of its shift in focus.

The facts pertinent to plaintiffs' claims occurred in 2006. At that time, iGov's board of directors consisted of London, Hunt, Neven, and Hupalo, and Tyrrell was the chief financial officer, having been brought to iGov by Neven the previous year. Plaintiffs allege that "[s]ometime in 2006, the Defendants secretly decided to implement an options plan at an unfair price to benefit themselves at the expense of the other stockholders." To allow defendants to value the stock of iGov and thus set the price of options, defendants caused the Company to retain Chessiecap Securities, Inc. ("Chessiecap"). Plaintiffs do not allege the precise time by which Chessiecap was retained, but they do allege that Cheesiecap's analysis valued the Company as of July 31, 2006. Despite the date of the valuation, Chessiecap did not deliver its initial draft until late September 2006 and did not offer its final draft until later that year. iGov used the Chessiecap valuation to set the price of the stock options granted in February and May 2007. Those options were granted pursuant to a plan that required the options' exercise price to be set with a value of at least 100% of the fair market value of the Company's stock as of the date of the grant.

Plaintiffs cite two problems with the options granted by defendants to themselves and others. First, the valuation on which the price of the options was based was fundamentally flawed because Tyrrell provided misleading and incomplete information to Chessiecap. Second, the options were granted in contravention of the stock option plan because the Chessiecap report valued the Company as of July 2006 but the options were not granted until February and May 2007.

A. *The Chessiecap Valuation*

Chessiecap was not the only financial institution receiving projections and information from Tyrrell in 2006. During that year, iGov was looking for a lender to provide it with an approximately $12 million line of credit. One of the potential lenders was Textron Financial ("Textron"). To induce Textron to provide the needed credit, Mr. Tyrrell kept Textron apprised of iGov's financial condition — creating and approving the financial information transmitted, which included monthly income statements, balance sheets, and updated forecasts for fiscal years 2006 and 2007. Moreover, Tyrrell frequently wrote to Textron, consistently boasting of how well iGov was performing.

Specifically, Tyrrell sent Textron a 2007 forecast projecting an EBITDA of over $3 million. That figure took into account the fact that iGov was likely to be awarded — but had not yet been awarded — a lucrative contract from the Department of Homeland Security ("DHS"). Tyrrell also highlighted iGov's future cost-cutting plans and predicted sustained profitability going forward. The complaint alleges that Textron granted the requested line of credit based on these assurances and projections.

Yet, the projections Tyrrell provided to Chessiecap were markedly different. First, after receiving a draft of the Chessiecap report that valued iGov at $5.5 million, defendants sought to revise the data given to Chessiecap because the $5.5 million figure was "probably on the high side." Second, defendants excluded from the projections given to Chessiecap any income from the DHS contract because that contract had not yet technically been awarded. Third, the defendants, in their revisions following the $5.5 million valuation, made material changes to the 2007 forecast based on decisions that were made after the valuation date of July 31, 2006. For example, based on the announcement on October 4, 2006 that iGov was going to shut down a subsidiary, the revenue projection for this unit went from $25,150,000 in the initial forecast to $0 in the revised forecast. Mr. Tyrrell also revised the projected revenue for another unit from $6 million to $900,000 because he thought that unit might be closed by the end of November. Moreover, although the revised forecast took account of negative events that occurred after July 31, 2006, it did not reflect positive developments that occurred after the valuation date, such as the award of a $7 million contract with the U.S. Patent and Trademark Office or the significant increase in profitability in another, preexisting contract. Moreover, in December 2006, DHS announced that iGov was the winning bidder for the contract, pending only the customary small business size protest period.

The revised forecast was allegedly never disclosed to Textron, and was allegedly never used by the Company in managing its business. Rather, plaintiffs allege, the revised forecast was purposely designed to suppress the value of the Company and only for use by Chessiecap. Based on this revised forecast, Chessiecap valued iGov at $4.7 million as of July 31, 2006. Chessiecap, of course, did not offer this valuation until late in the fall or winter of 2006. The Chessiecap final report was provided to plaintiffs on or around December 29, 2006. Thereafter, London and Hunt asked to be provided with the financial information that Chessiecap used to render its valuation. This information was provided on January 11, 2007, and five days later London objected to iGov's relying on the Chessiecap report, stating that the valuation was stale. One day later, on January 17, 2007, Hunt offered to buy all of Neven's shares at $28 per share and made clear that his offer applied to all shareholders. At the price offered by Hunt, iGov would be worth $20 million. His offer, however, was summarily rejected.

Two days after Hunt made this offer and three days after London criticized the Chessiecap valuation, Neven and Hupalo caused plaintiffs to be removed from the Board through a written consent. They also elected Tyrrell to the board by written consent. Thus, as of January 19, 2007, the defendants comprised the entire board of iGov. The new board contacted Chessiecap about the Hunt offer of $28 per share. Chessiecap responded by preparing an addendum—not by modifying its final report. In the addendum, Chessiecap stated simply that the Hunt "offer in no way affects or changes" the $4.7 million valuation as of July 31, 2006, and concluded that the value of iGov's common stock as of that July 31, 2006 valuation date was $4.92 per share. However, this per share price was calculated by including 65,000 shares and 300,000 options that were not outstanding as of July 31, 2006.[3]

B. *The Granting of the Options*

On January 30, 2007, the defendants held a telephonic meeting of the board of directors and unanimously voted to adopt the 2007 Equity Incentive Plan. This plan provides, in part, that the exercise price of an option "shall be not less than one hundred percent (100%) of the Fair Market Value of the Common Stock subject to the Option on the date the Option is granted." For stockholders holding more than ten percent of iGov's stock . . . the exercise price shall be "at least one hundred ten percent (110%) of the Fair Market Value of the Common Stock on the date of the grant." The director defendants authorized themselves to submit this plan to the stockholders for approval within twelve months.

In addition to adopting the Equity Incentive Plan, the defendants also voted unanimously to approve a resolution adopting the $4.92 per share price of the Chessiecap report "to be appropriate for purposes of determining the fair market value of the Company's Common Stock." With the price set, the defendants then approved the

---

3. These shares and options were presumably contemplated at the time the addendum was prepared, but were not actually approved until after the addendum was issued, on January 30, 2007.

grant of 300,000 options to sixteen employees pursuant to the Equity Incentive Plan. Among those 300,000 options were 80,000 for Tyrrell, 50,000 for Neven, and 50,000 for Hupalo. Finally, the defendants also authorized the sale of 65,000 additional shares to Tyrrell at the $4.92 per share price. The options were granted and the sale to Tyrrell was consummated on February 1, 2007.

As iGov had long anticipated, DHS had all-but-announced in December, and Tyrrell had long promised to shareholders and Textron, iGov announced on March 7, 2007 that it was officially awarded the contract with DHS. The second quarter results for fiscal year 2007 were available in April 2007, and iGov showed an operating income in excess of $1.4 million. Between this and the DHS contract, it seemed clear that iGov would outperform its own projections for 2007. Despite this, however, the defendants granted 25,000 options to another employee on May 30, 2007 priced at $4.92 per share. In their unanimous written consent authorizing the grant, the defendants justified using the $4.92 per share price because they "concluded that [since February 1, 2007] there ha[d] been no material changes affecting [iGov's] financial operations or prospects which would affect the [Chessiecap valuation opinion]."

II. Standard

Defendants have moved to dismiss the complaint pursuant to Rules 9(b), 12(b)(6), and 23.1. The standards governing such a motion are "familiar" to this Court. Under Rule 12(b)(6), a complaint may be dismissed where the plaintiff fails to state a claim upon which relief can be granted. In determining whether or not a complaint states such a claim, the Court must accept all well pleaded allegations as true and must draw all reasonable inferences in favor of the plaintiff. Of course, the Court neither heeds nor draws inferences from conclusory allegations.

Those general precepts of motions under Rule 12(b)(6) are augmented by Rules 9(b) and 23.1, which require particularized pleading where a complaint asserts allegations of fraud or derivative claims, respectively. This standard of particularity represents "a marked departure from the 'notice' pleading philosophy" of Rule 8 and makes pleading under Rules 9(b) and 23.1 "more onerous." Nevertheless, the burden remains on the movant to demonstrate that the plaintiff has not met the requirements of Rules 9(b), 12(b)(6), and 23.1.

III. Demand Futility

Defendants' primary argument charges that plaintiffs failed to make a demand on the board of directors and failed to adequately plead why demand would be futile. Rule 23.1 requires plaintiffs in a derivative suit to "allege with particularity the efforts, if any, made by plaintiff to obtain the action the plaintiff desires from the directors . . . [or] the reasons . . . for not making the effort." The purpose of the demand requirement has been explained elsewhere, and where, as here, the plaintiff alleges that demand would have been futile, the Court proceeds under the analysis of one of two decisions: *Aronson v. Lewis* (1984) or *Rales v. Blasband* (1993). Because the complaint here challenges a decision made by the current board of directors of the corporation on whose behalf the suit was filed, the *Aronson* test applies.[17] Under *Aronson,* a plaintiff demonstrates demand futility when "a reasonable doubt is created that: (1) the directors are disinterested and independent; or (2) the challenged transaction was otherwise the product of a valid exercise of business judgment." Here, plaintiffs have satisfied demand futility under both prongs.

A. *A Majority of the Board Was Interested in the Challenged Transactions*

Under the first prong of *Aronson*, demand will be excused where the plaintiff has alleged facts that create a reasonable doubt that a majority of the directors were disinterested. The Court has explained that there are two ways a director can be deemed "interested" in a transaction. The first occurs where a director received in the challenged transaction a benefit that was not generally shared with the other shareholders of the corporation and where that benefit is "of such subjective material significance to that particular director that it is reasonable to question whether that director objectively considered the advisability of the challenged transaction to the corporation and its shareholders." The second occurs where "a director stands on both sides of the challenged transaction." In that latter instance, the plaintiff need not show that the director received some sort of material benefit.

Defendants argue that plaintiffs have failed to satisfy the requirements of the first prong of *Aronson* because the complaint does not allege particularized facts that the options constituted a material benefit to each individual director defendant. This argument, however, ignores well settled law. Over ten years ago, in *Byrne v. Lord* (1995), this Court held that "[b]y alleging that each of the members of the Pace board has a financial interest in the challenged option plan, Plaintiffs have alleged facts that create a reasonable down [sic] as to whether the Pace board is independent and disinterested." Similarly, in *Lewis v. Vogelstein* (1997), former Chancellor Allen noted that directors who will receive stock options under a challenged transaction are interested in that transaction and ordinarily will have to prove its entire fairness. Finally, Vice Chancellor Lamb held earlier this year [*Weiss v. Swanson* (2008)] that "demand will be excused [where] all five directors to consider demand received at least some of the challenged option grants" because those directors "are not disinterested." None of those cases requires a showing that the options received by the director defendants constituted material benefits. Although the general rule holds that "demand is not excused simply because directors receive compensation from the company or an executive of the company," the receipt of stock options is different. Directors who have received the options plaintiffs seek to challenge "have a strong financial incentive to maintain the status quo by not authorizing any corrective action that would devalue their current holdings or cause them to disgorge improperly obtained profits." In

---

17. *See In re Bally's Grand Deriv. Litig.,* C.A. No. 14644, 1997 Del. Ch. LEXIS 77, 1997 WL 305803, at 3 (Del. Ch. June 4, 1997) (noting that the *Rales* test applies only "(1) where a business decision was made by the board of a company, but a majority of the directors making the decision have been replaced; (2) where the subject of the derivative suit is not a business decision of the board; [or] (3) where ... the decision being challenged was made by the board of a different corporation.").

sum, the defendants here stood on both sides of the transaction that plaintiffs are challenging; the defendants both granted and received the stock options. Demand is, therefore, excused under the first prong of *Aronson*.

B. *There is a Reasonable Doubt that the Challenged Transaction Was an Exercise of Valid Business Judgment*

In addition, the complaint contains sufficiently particularized allegations of fact to satisfy the second prong of *Aronson*. As the Court noted in *Weiss v. Swanson*, "[a]lthough . . . compensation decisions are typically protected by the business judgment rule, the rule applies to the directors' grant of options pursuant to a stockholder-approved plan only when the terms of the plan at issue are adhered to." The Court explained that this conclusion was compelled by its holding in *In re Tyson Foods, Inc. Consolidated Shareholder Litigation* (2007), where the Court made clear that "allegations in a complaint rebut the business judgment rule where they support an inference that the directors intended to violate the terms of stockholder-approved option plans."

Here, the Equity Incentive Plan under which the challenged options were granted requires that the exercise price of options be set at 100% or 110% of the stock's fair market value as of the date of the grant of the options. The complaint alleges particularized facts that lead to the reasonable inference that the defendants intentionally granted options in contravention of that fair market value requirement. It does so in two ways. First, the complaint alleges that the defendants intentionally gamed the Chessiecap valuation by withholding positive information about the Company while freely supplying the negative. In fact, the complaint alleges, after the first draft pegged iGov's value at $5.5 million, Tyrrell sent Chessiecap new numbers in order to depress the final valuation. Second, the complaint alleges that the directors intentionally violated the Equity Incentive Plan by pricing the options it granted in February and May of 2007 at the price Chessiecap said was fair as of July 2006. Plaintiffs have alleged that defendants knew Chessiecap was not provided with information of materially positive developments from the latter half of 2006 and, therefore, knew that the Chessiecap valuation could not possibly represent the fair market value of the Company as of February and May 2007.

The particularized facts of the complaint support an inference that the directors knowingly violated the Equity Incentive Plan. Consequently, under *Weiss* and *Tyson*, plaintiffs have also satisfied demand futility under the second prong of Aronson, and for this alternative reason defendants' motion to dismiss under Rule 23.1 is denied. Because plaintiffs have satisfied demand futility under both prongs of *Aronson* and defeated defendants Rule 23.1 motion, they have alleged sufficient facts to state a claim, and defendants' motion under Rule 12(b)(6) is likewise denied. . . .

V. Conclusion

For the reasons explained above, the complaint adequately pleads demand futility with particularity, does not need to plead the elements of fraud with particularity, and does indeed state a claim. As a result, defendants' motion to dismiss is denied.

Questions

1. Consider the following statement by the court: "Although the general rule holds that 'demand is not excused simply because directors receive compensation from the company or an executive of the company,' the receipt of stock options is different. Directors who have received the options plaintiffs seek to challenge 'have a strong financial incentive to maintain the status quo by not authorizing any corrective action that would devalue their current holdings or cause them to disgorge improperly obtained profits.'" What is unique about stock option compensation? Why does the court view stock options as different than other forms of compensation?

2. Directors typically are responsible for setting their own option compensation, although, for reasons we will discuss, they also typically submit their option plans for shareholder ratification. Leaving aside for the moment potential problems with the efficacy of shareholder ratification, doesn't the court's discussion in this case mean that a board that awards itself options will always fail the first prong of the *Aronson* test? Given the prevalence of option compensation for directors, is this a good result? Are there good reasons to put stock option compensation under greater scrutiny than other forms of directors' financial interests in the corporation?

D. The Role of Special Litigation Committees

Auerbach v. Bennett
47 N.Y.2d 619 (1979)

JONES, Judge

While the substantive aspects of a decision to terminate a shareholders' derivative action against defendant corporate directors made by a committee of disinterested directors appointed by the corporation's board of directors are beyond judicial inquiry under the business judgment doctrine, the court may inquire as to the disinterested independence of the members of that committee and as to the appropriateness and sufficiency of the investigative procedures chosen and pursued by the committee. In this instance, however, no basis is shown to warrant either inquiry by the court. Accordingly we hold that it was error to reverse the lower court's dismissal of the shareholders' derivative action.

In the summer of 1975 the management of General Telephone & Electronics Corporation, in response to reports that numerous other multinational companies had made questionable payments to public officials or political parties in foreign countries, directed that an internal preliminary investigation be made to ascertain whether that corporation had engaged in similar transactions. On the basis of the report of this survey, received in October, 1975, management brought the issue to the attention of the corporation's board of directors. At a meeting held on November 6 of that year the board referred the matter to the board's audit committee. The audit committee retained as its special counsel the Washington, D.C., law firm of Wilmer, Cutler & Pickering which had not previously acted as counsel to the corporation. With the assistance of such special counsel and Arthur Andersen & Co., the corporation's outside auditors, the audit committee engaged in an investigation into the corporation's worldwide operations, focusing on whether, in the period January 1, 1971 to December 31, 1975, corporate funds had been (1) paid directly or indirectly to any political party or person or to any officer, employee, shareholder or director of any governmental or private customer, or (2) used to reimburse any officer of the corporation or other person for such payments.

On March 4, 1976 the audit committee released its report which was filed with the Securities and Exchange Commission and disclosed to the corporation's shareholders in a proxy statement prior to the annual meeting of shareholders held in April, 1976. The audit committee reported that it had found evidence that in the period from 1971 to 1975 the corporation or its subsidiaries had made payments abroad and in the United States constituting bribes and kickbacks in amounts perhaps totaling more than 11 million dollars and that some of the individual defendant directors had been personally involved in certain of the transactions.

Almost immediately Auerbach, a shareholder in the corporation, instituted the present shareholders' derivative action on behalf of the corporation against the corporation's directors, Arthur Andersen & Co. and the corporation. The complaint alleged that in connection with the transactions reported by the audit committee defendants, present and former members of the corporation's board of directors and Arthur Andersen & Co., are liable to the corporation for breach of their duties to the corporation and should be made to account for payments made in those transactions.

On April 21, 1976 the board of directors of the corporation adopted a resolution creating a special litigation committee "for the purpose of establishing a point of contact between the Board of Directors and the Corporation's General Counsel concerning the position to be taken by the Corporation in certain litigation involving shareholder derivative claims on behalf of the Corporation against certain of its directors and officers" and authorizing that committee "to take such steps from time to time as it deems necessary to pursue its objectives including the retention of special outside counsel." The special committee comprised three disinterested directors who had joined the board after the challenged transactions had occurred. The board subsequently additionally vested in the committee "all of the authority of the Board of Directors to determine, on behalf of the Board, the position that the Corporation shall take with respect to the derivative claims alleged on its behalf" in the present and similar shareholder derivative actions.

The special litigation committee reported under date of November 22, 1976. It found that defendant Arthur Andersen & Co. had conducted its examination of the corporation's affairs in accordance with generally accepted auditing standards and in good faith and concluded that no proper interest of the corporation or its shareholders would be served by the continued assertion of a claim against it. The committee also concluded that none of the individual defendants had violated the New York State statutory standard of care, that none had profited personally or gained in any way, that the claims asserted in the present action are without merit, that if the action were allowed to proceed the time and talents of the corporation's senior management would be wasted on lengthy pretrial and trial proceedings, that litigation costs would be inordinately high in view of the unlikelihood of success, and that the continuing publicity could be damaging to the corporation's business. The committee determined that it would not be in the best interests of the corporation for the present derivative action to proceed, and, exercising the authority delegated to it, directed the corporation's general counsel to take that position in the present litigation as well as in pending comparable shareholders' derivative actions.

On December 17, 1976 the corporation and the four individual defendants who had been served moved for an order . . . dismissing the complaint or in the alternative for an order . . . for summary judgment. On January 7, 1977 Arthur Andersen & Co. made a similar motion. On May 13, 1977 Supreme Court, Special Term, granted the motions of all defendants and dismissed the complaint on the merits.

When it appeared that plaintiff Auerbach had no intention of appealing from the determination of Special Term, on June 13, 1977 Stanley Wallenstein, as executor of the estate of Ida S. Wallenstein, a stockholder of the corporation, filed and served a "Notice of Appeal" from the order and judgment of Special Term. On July 11, 1977 defendants moved in the Appellate Division to dismiss the purported Wallenstein appeal on the ground that he was not an aggrieved party. Thereupon Wallenstein cross-moved for an order . . . to intervene in the present action, *nunc pro tunc*, for the purpose of appealing from the judgment of Special Term pursuant to his notice of appeal dated June 13, 1977. Wallenstein predicated his right to intervene and to appeal on the grounds that Ida S. Wallenstein had been a stockholder of the corporation continuously from 1959 until her death in 1976 and that her estate, of which Stanley Wallenstein is sole executor, had continuously owned the corporate shares since her death, that in January, 1977 Wallenstein had commenced a shareholders' derivative action against the corporation, and that on May 24, 1977 the defendants in the Wallenstein action had moved for dismissal of that action on the ground that the order and judgment of Special Term in the present action was *res judicata* and resulted in collateral estoppel. On August 3, 1977 defendants' motion to dismiss the appeal and Wallenstein's cross motion for intervention were denied with leave to renew on argument of the appeal.

On August 7, 1978 the Appellate Division denied defendants' motion to dismiss the appeal, granted Wallenstein's cross motion for leave to intervene, and reversed the May 13, 1977 order of Special Term and denied defendants' motions for summary judgment. On October 12, 1978 that court granted defendants' motions for leave to appeal to our court. For the reasons stated below we now modify the order of the Appellate Division to the extent of reversing its reversal of the order of Special Term granting defendants summary judgment dismissing the complaint on the merits and reinstate the order of Special Term. We do not disturb those portions of the order at the Appellate Division which denied defendants' motion to dismiss the Wallenstein appeal and granted the cross motion for leave to intervene. . . .

As all parties and both courts below recognize, the disposition of this case on the merits turns on the proper application of the business judgment doctrine, in particular to the decision of a specially appointed committee of disinterested directors acting on behalf of the board to terminate a shareholders' derivative action. That doctrine bars judicial inquiry into actions of corporate directors taken in good faith and in the exercise of honest judgment in the lawful and legitimate furtherance of corporate purposes. "Questions of policy of management, expediency of contracts or action, adequacy of consideration, lawful appropriation of corporate funds to advance corporate interests, are left solely to their honest and unselfish decision, for their powers therein are without limitation and free from restraint, and the exercise of them for the common and general interests of the corporation may not be questioned, although the results show that what they did was unwise or inexpedient."

In this instance our inquiry, to the limited extent to which it may be pursued, has a two-tiered aspect. The complaint initially asserted liability on the part of defendants based on the payments made to foreign governmental customers and privately owned customers, some unspecified portions of which were allegedly passed on to officials of the customers, i.e., the focus was on first-tier bribes and kickbacks. Then subsequent to the service of the complaint there came the report of a special litigation committee, particularly appointed by the corporation's board of directors to consider the merits of the present and similar shareholders' derivative actions, and its determination that it would not be in the best interests of the corporation to press claims against defendants based on their possible first-tier liability. The motions for summary judgment were predicated principally on the report and determination of the special litigation committee and on the contention that this second-tier corporate action insulated the first-tier transactions from judicial inquiry and was itself subject to the shelter of the business judgment doctrine. The disposition at Special Term was predicated on this analysis; its decision focused on the actions of the special litigation committee, and the motions for summary judgment were granted on the ground that the business judgment doctrine precluded the courts from going back of the decision of the special litigation committee on behalf of the corporation not to pursue the claims alleged in the complaint. Similarly the reversal at the Appellate Division was based on that court's perception of the proper application of the business judgment rule to the actions and determination of the special litigation committee. We proceed on the same analysis, concluding, however, on the record before us, at variance with the Appellate Division, that the determination of the special litigation committee forecloses further judicial inquiry in this case.

It appears to us that the business judgment doctrine, at least in part, is grounded in the prudent recognition that courts are ill equipped and infrequently called on to evaluate what are and must be essentially business judgments. The authority and responsibilities vested in corporate directors both by statute and decisional law proceed on the assumption that inescapably there can be no available objective standard by which the correctness of every corporate decision may be measured, by the courts or otherwise. Even if that were not the case, by definition the responsibility for business judgments must rest with the corporate directors; their individual capabilities and experience peculiarly qualify them for the discharge of that responsibility. Thus, absent evidence of bad faith or fraud (of which there is none here) the courts must and properly should respect their determinations.

Derivative claims against corporate directors belong to the corporation itself. As with other questions of corporate policy and management, the decision whether and to what extent to explore and prosecute such claims lies within the judgment and control of the corporation's board of directors. Necessarily such decision must be predicated on the weighing and balancing of a variety of disparate considerations to reach a considered conclusion as to what course of action or inaction is best calculated to protect and advance the interests of the corporation. This is the essence of the responsibility and role of the board of directors, and courts may not intrude to interfere.

In the present case we confront a special instance of the application of the business judgment rule and inquire whether it applies in its full vigor to shield from judicial scrutiny the decision of a three-person minority committee of the board acting on behalf of the full board not to prosecute a shareholder's derivative action. The record in this case reveals that the board is a 15-member board, and that the derivative suit was brought against four of the directors. Nothing suggests that any of the other directors participated in any of the challenged first-tier transactions. Indeed the report of the audit committee on which the complaint is based specifically found that no other directors had any prior knowledge of or were in any way involved in any of these transactions. Other directors had, however, been members of the board in the period during which the transactions occurred. Each of the three director members of the special litigation committee joined the board thereafter.

The business judgment rule does not foreclose inquiry by the courts into the disinterested independence of those members of the board chosen by it to make the corporate decision on its behalf — here the members of the special litigation committee. Indeed the rule shields the deliberations and conclusions of the chosen representatives of the board only if they possess a disinterested independence and do not stand in a dual relation which prevents an unprejudicial exercise of judgment.

We examine then the proof submitted by defendants. It is not disputed that the members of the special litigation committee were not members of the corporation's board of directors at the time of the first-tier transactions in question. Howard Blauvelt, chairman of the board of Continental Oil Company, had been elected to the corporation's board of directors on October 9, 1975. Dr. John T. Dunlop, Lamont

University professor at the Graduate School of Business Administration of Harvard University had been elected to the board on April 21, 1976. James R. Barker, chairman of the board and chief executive officer of Moore McCormack Resources, Inc., was added as the third member of the committee when he was elected to the board on July 19, 1976. None of the three had had any prior affiliation with the corporation. Notwithstanding the vigorous and imaginative hypothesizing and innuendo of counsel there is nothing in this record to raise a triable issue of fact as to the independence and disinterested status of these three directors.

The contention of Wallenstein that any committee authorized by the board of which defendant directors were members must be held to be legally infirm and may not be delegated power to terminate a derivative action must be rejected. In the very nature of the corporate organization it was only the existing board of directors which had authority on behalf of the corporation to direct the investigation and to assure the co-operation of corporate employees, and it is only that same board by its own action—or as here pursuant to authority duly delegated by it—which had authority to decide whether to prosecute the claims against defendant directors. The board in this instance, with slight adaptation, followed prudent practice in observing the general policy that when individual members of a board of directors prove to have personal interests which may conflict with the interests of the corporation, such interested directors must be excluded while the remaining members of the board proceed to consideration and action. (Cf. Business Corporation Law, §713, which contemplates such situations and provides that the interested directors may nonetheless be included in the quorum count.) Courts have consistently held that the business judgment rule applies where some directors are charged with wrongdoing, so long as the remaining directors making the decision are disinterested and independent.

To accept the assertions of the intervenor and to disqualify the entire board would be to render the corporation powerless to make an effective business judgment with respect to prosecution of the derivative action. The possible risk of hesitancy on the part of the members of any committee, even if composed of outside, independent, disinterested directors, to investigate the activities of fellow members of the board where personal liability is at stake is an inherent, inescapable, given aspect of the corporation's predicament. To assign responsibility of the dimension here involved to individuals wholly separate and apart from the board of directors would, except in the most extraordinary circumstances, itself be an act of default and breach of the non-delegable fiduciary duty owed by the members of the board to the corporation and to its shareholders, employees and creditors. For the courts to preside over such determinations would similarly work an ouster of the board's fundamental responsibility and authority for corporate management.

We turn then to the action of the special litigation committee itself which comprised two components. First, there was the selection of procedures appropriate to the pursuit of its charge, and second, there was the ultimate substantive decision, predicated on the procedures chosen and the data produced thereby, not to pursue the claims advanced in the shareholders' derivative actions. The latter, substantive decision falls squarely within the embrace of the business judgment doctrine, involving as it did the weighing and balancing of legal, ethical, commercial, promotional, public relations, fiscal and other factors familiar to the resolution of many if not most corporate problems. To this extent the conclusion reached by the special litigation committee is outside the scope of our review. Thus, the courts cannot inquire as to which factors were considered by that committee or the relative weight accorded them in reaching that substantive decision—"the reasons for the payments, the advantages or disadvantages accruing to the corporation by reason of the transactions, the extent of the participation or profit by the respondent directors and the loss, if any, of public confidence in the corporation which might be incurred". Inquiry into such matters would go to the very core of the business judgment made by the committee. To permit judicial probing of such issues would be to emasculate the business judgment doctrine as applied to the actions and determinations of the special litigation committee. Its substantive evaluation of the problems posed and its judgment in their resolution are beyond our reach.

As to the other component of the committee's activities, however, the situation is different, and here we agree with the Appellate Division. As to the methodologies and procedures best suited to the conduct of an investigation of facts and the determination of legal liability, the courts are well equipped by long and continuing experience and practice to make determinations. In fact they are better qualified in this regard than are corporate directors in general. Nor do the determinations to be made in the adoption of procedures partake of the nuances or special perceptions or comprehensions of business judgment or corporate activities or interests. The question is solely how appropriately to set about to gather the pertinent data.

While the court may properly inquire as to the adequacy and appropriateness of the committee's investigative procedures and methodologies, it may not under the guise of consideration of such factors trespass in the domain of business judgment. At the same time those responsible for the procedures by which the business judgment is reached may reasonably be required to show that they have pursued their chosen investigative methods in good faith. What evidentiary proof may be required to this end will, of course, depend on the nature of the particular investigation, and the proper reach of disclosure at the instance of the shareholders will in turn relate inversely to the showing made by the corporate representatives themselves. The latter may be expected to show that the areas and subjects to be examined are reasonably complete and that there has been a good-faith pursuit of inquiry into such areas and subjects. What has been uncovered and the relative weight accorded in evaluating and balancing the several factors and considerations are beyond the scope of judicial concern. Proof, however, that the investigation has been so restricted in scope, so shallow in execution, or otherwise so *pro forma* or halfhearted as to constitute a pretext or sham, consistent with the principles underlying the application of the business judgment doctrine, would raise questions of good faith or conceivably fraud which would never be shielded by that doctrine.

In addition to the issue of the disinterested independence of the special litigation committee, addressed above, the disposition of the present appeal turns, then, on whether on defendants' motions for summary judgment predicated on the investigation and determination of the special litigation committee, Wallenstein by tender of evidentiary proof in admissible form has shown facts sufficient to require a trial of any material issue of fact as to the adequacy or appropriateness of the *modus operandi* of that committee or has demonstrated acceptable excuse for failure to make such tender. We conclude that the requisite showing has not been made on this record. . . .

On the submissions made by defendants in support of their motions, we do not find either insufficiency or infirmity as to the procedures and methodologies chosen and pursued by the special litigation committee. That committee promptly engaged eminent special counsel to guide its deliberations and to advise it. The committee reviewed the prior work of the audit committee, testing its completeness, accuracy and thoroughness by interviewing representatives of Wilmer, Cutler & Pickering, reviewing transcripts of the testimony of 10 corporate officers and employees before the Securities and Exchange Commission, and studying documents collected by and work papers of the Washington law firm. Individual interviews were conducted with the directors found to have participated in any way in the questioned payments, and with representatives of Arthur Andersen & Co. Questionnaires were sent to and answered by each of the corporation's nonmanagement directors. At the conclusion of its investigation the special litigation committee sought and obtained pertinent legal advice from its special counsel. The selection of appropriate investigative methods must always turn on the nature and characteristics of the particular subject being investigated, but we find nothing in this record that requires a trial of any material issue of fact concerning the sufficiency or appropriateness of the procedures chosen by this special litigation committee. Nor is there anything in this record to raise a triable issue of fact as to the good-faith pursuit of its examination by that committee. . . .

For the reasons stated the order of the Appellate Division should be modified, with costs to defendants, by reversing so much thereof as reversed the order of Supreme Court, and, as so modified, affirmed.

COOKE, Chief Judge (dissenting)

There should be an affirmance for the reasons set forth in the excellent analysis of Mr. Justice James D. Hopkins who wrote for a unanimous Appellate Division. In response to the majority opinion, a few remarks are added.

True, the "business judgment rule" is potentially applicable in these circumstances. But this case differs markedly from the typical situation in which that rule would be invoked. Here, the alleged wrongdoers are directors of the corporation. Of course, it would be most inappropriate to allow these interested directors to vote to preclude a shareholder's suit and thereby insulate themselves from liability. Hence, the lawsuit should be terminated only if a sufficient number of disinterested directors, in this case the special litigation committee, rendered a good faith, "unprejudiced exercise of judgment," determining that maintenance of the action would not be in the best interests of the corporation. . . .

In sum, to deny the intervenor an opportunity for pretrial disclosure is to mistakenly group this case with the typical case involving the business judgment rule. Since the business judgment rule is only conditionally applicable here, and since certain defendants as well as the members of the special litigation committee have the sole knowledge of the facts upon which its applicability turns, summary judgment should be withheld pending disclosure proceedings. The result reached by the majority not only effectively dilutes the substantive rule of law at issue, but may also render corporate directors largely unaccountable to the shareholders whose business they are elected to govern. . . .

Zapata Corporation v. Maldonado
430 A.2d 779 (Del. 1981)

QUILLEN, Justice

This is an interlocutory appeal from an order entered on April 9, 1980, by the Court of Chancery denying appellant-defendant Zapata Corporation's (Zapata) alternative motions to dismiss the complaint or for summary judgment. The issue to be addressed has reached this Court by way of a rather convoluted path.

In June, 1975, William Maldonado, a stockholder of Zapata, instituted a derivative action in the Court of Chancery on behalf of Zapata against ten officers and/or directors of Zapata, alleging, essentially, breaches of fiduciary duty. Maldonado did not first demand that the board bring this action, stating instead such demand's futility because all directors were named as defendants and allegedly participated in the acts specified. In June, 1977, Maldonado commenced an action in the United States District Court for the Southern District of New York against the same defendants, save one, alleging federal security law violations as well as the same common law claims made previously in the Court of Chancery.

By June, 1979, four of the defendant-directors were no longer on the board, and the remaining directors appointed two new outside directors to the board. The board then created an "Independent Investigation Committee" (Committee), composed solely of the two new directors, to investigate Maldonado's actions, as well as a similar derivative action then pending in Texas, and to determine whether the corporation should continue any or all of the litigation. The Committee's determination was stated to be "final, . . . not . . . subject to review by the Board of Directors and . . . in all respects . . . binding upon the Corporation."

Following an investigation, the Committee concluded, in September, 1979, that each action should "be dismissed forthwith as their continued maintenance is inimical to the Company's best interests...." Consequently, Zapata moved for dismissal or summary judgment in the three derivative actions. On January 24, 1980, the District Court for the Southern District of New York granted Zapata's motion for summary judgment, holding, under its interpretation of Delaware law, that the Committee had the authority, under the "business judgment" rule, to require the termination of the derivative action. Maldonado appealed that decision to the Second Circuit Court of Appeals.

On March 18, 1980, the Court of Chancery, in a reported opinion, the basis for the order of April 9, 1980, denied Zapata's motions, holding that Delaware law does not sanction this means of dismissal. More specifically, it held that the "business judgment" rule is not a grant of authority to dismiss derivative actions and that a stockholder has an individual right to maintain derivative actions in certain instances....

... As the Vice Chancellor noted, "it is the law of the State of incorporation which determines whether the directors have this power of dismissal". We limit our review in this interlocutory appeal to whether the Committee has the power to cause the present action to be dismissed.

We begin with an examination of the carefully considered opinion of the Vice Chancellor which states, in part, that the "business judgment" rule does not confer power "to a corporate board of directors to terminate a derivative suit". His conclusion is particularly pertinent because several federal courts, applying Delaware law, have held that the business judgment rule enables boards (or their committees) to terminate derivative suits, decisions now in conflict with the holding below.

As the term is most commonly used, and given the disposition below, we can understand the Vice Chancellor's comment that "the business judgment rule is irrelevant to the question of whether the Committee has the authority to compel the dismissal of this suit". Corporations, existing because of legislative grace, possess authority as granted by the legislature. Directors of Delaware corporations derive their managerial decision making power, which encompasses decisions whether to initiate, or refrain from entering, litigation, from 8 Del.C. § 141(a). This statute is the fount of directorial powers. The "business judgment" rule is a judicial creation that presumes propriety, under certain circumstances, in a board's decision. Viewed defensively, it does not create authority. In this sense the "business judgment" rule is not relevant in corporate decision making until after a decision is made. It is generally used as a defense to an attack on the decision's soundness. The board's managerial decision making power, however, comes from § 141(a). The judicial creation and legislative grant are related because the "business judgment" rule evolved to give recognition and deference to directors' business expertise when exercising their managerial power under § 141(a).

In the case before us, although the corporation's decision to move to dismiss or for summary judgment was, literally, a decision resulting from an exercise of the directors' (as delegated to the Committee) business judgment, the question of "business judgment", in a defensive sense, would not become relevant until and unless the decision to seek termination of the derivative lawsuit was attacked as improper. This question was not reached by the Vice Chancellor because he determined that the stockholder had an individual right to maintain this derivative action.

Thus, the focus in this case is on the power to speak for the corporation as to whether the lawsuit should be continued or terminated. As we see it, this issue in the current appellate posture of this case has three aspects: the conclusions of the Court below concerning the continuing right of a stockholder to maintain a derivative action; the corporate power under Delaware law of an authorized board committee to cause dismissal of litigation instituted for the benefit of the corporation; and the role of the Court of Chancery in resolving conflicts between the stockholder and the committee.

Accordingly, we turn first to the Court of Chancery's conclusions concerning the right of a plaintiff stockholder in a derivative action. We find that its determination that a stockholder, once demand is made and refused, possesses an independent, individual right to continue a derivative suit for breaches of fiduciary duty over objection by the corporation, as an absolute rule, is erroneous. The Court of Chancery relied principally upon *Sohland v. Baker*, for this statement of the Delaware rule. *Sohland* is sound law. But *Sohland* cannot be fairly read as supporting the broad proposition which evolved in the opinion below.

In *Sohland*, the complaining stockholder was allowed to file the derivative action in equity after making demand and after the board refused to bring the lawsuit. But the question before us relates to the power of the corporation by motion to terminate a lawsuit properly commenced by a stockholder without prior demand. No Delaware statute or case cited to us directly determines this new question and we do not think that *Sohland* addresses it by implication.

The language in *Sohland* relied on by the Vice Chancellor negates the contention that the case stands for the broad rule of stockholder right which evolved below. This Court therein stated that "a stockholder *may sue* in his own name for the purpose of enforcing corporate rights . . . in a proper case if the corporation on the demand of the stockholder refuses to bring suit." The Court also stated that "whether ['[t]he right of a stockholder to *file a bill* to litigate corporate rights'] exists necessarily depends on the facts of each particular case." Thus, the precise language only supports the stockholder's right to initiate the lawsuit. It does not support an absolute right to continue to control it. . . .

Moreover, *McKee v. Rogers*, stated "as a general rule" that "a stockholder cannot be permitted . . . to invade the discretionary field committed to the judgment of the directors and sue in the corporation's behalf when the managing body refuses. This rule is a well settled one."

The *McKee* rule, of course, should not be read so broadly that the board's refusal will be determinative in every instance. Board members, owing a well-established fiduciary duty to the corporation, will not be allowed to cause a derivative suit to be dismissed when it would be a breach of their fiduciary duty. Generally disputes pertaining to control of the suit arise in two contexts.

Consistent with the purpose of requiring a demand, a board decision to cause a derivative suit to be dismissed as detrimental to the company, after demand has been made and refused, will be respected unless it was wrongful. A claim of a wrongful decision not to sue is thus the first exception and the first context of dispute. Absent a wrongful refusal, the stockholder in such a situation simply lacks legal managerial power.

But it cannot be implied that, absent a wrongful board refusal, a stockholder can never have an individual right to initiate an action. For, as is stated in *McKee*, a "well settled" exception exists to the general rule.

> "[A] stockholder may sue in equity in his derivative right to assert a cause of action in behalf of the corporation, *without prior demand* upon the directors to sue, when it is apparent that a demand would be futile, that the officers are under an influence that sterilizes discretion and could not be proper persons to conduct the litigation."

This exception, the second context for dispute, is consistent with the Court of Chancery's statement below, that "[t]he stockholders' individual right to bring the action does not ripen, however, . . . unless he can show a demand to be futile."

These comments in *McKee* and in the opinion below make obvious sense. A demand, when required and refused (if not wrongful), terminates a stockholder's legal ability to initiate a derivative action. But where demand is properly excused, the stockholder does possess the ability to initiate the action on his corporation's behalf.

These conclusions, however, do not determine the question before us. Rather, they merely bring us to the question to be decided. It is here that we part company with the Court below. Derivative suits enforce corporate rights and any recovery obtained goes to the corporation. "The right of a stockholder to file a bill to litigate corporate rights is, therefore, solely for the purpose of preventing injustice where it is apparent that material corporate rights would not otherwise be protected." We see no inherent reason why the "two phases" of a derivative suit, the stockholder's suit to compel the corporation to sue and the corporation's suit, should automatically result in the placement in the hands of the litigating stockholder sole control of the corporate right throughout the litigation. To the contrary, it seems to us that such an inflexible rule would recognize the interest of one person or group to the exclusion of all others within the corporate entity. Thus, we reject the view of the Vice Chancellor as to the first aspect of the issue on appeal.

The question to be decided becomes: When, if at all, should an authorized board committee be permitted to cause litigation, properly initiated by a derivative stockholder in his own right, to be dismissed? As noted above, a board has the power to choose not to pursue litigation when demand is made upon it, so long as the decision is not wrongful. If the board determines that a suit would be detrimental to the company, the board's determination prevails. Even when demand is excusable, circumstances may arise when continuation of the litigation would not be in the corporation's best interests. Our inquiry is whether, under such circumstances, there is a permissible procedure under § 141(a) by which a corporation can rid itself of detrimental litigation. If there is not, a single stockholder in an extreme case might control the destiny of the entire corporation. This concern was bluntly expressed by the Ninth Circuit in *Lewis v. Anderson*: "To allow one shareholder to incapacitate an entire board of directors merely by leveling charges against them gives too much leverage to dissident shareholders." But, when examining the means, including the committee mechanism examined in this case, potentials for abuse must be recognized. This takes us to the second and third aspects of the issue on appeal.

Before we pass to equitable considerations as to the mechanism at issue here, it must be clear that an independent committee possesses the corporate power to seek the termination of a derivative suit. Section 141(c) allows a board to delegate all of its authority to a committee. Accordingly, a committee with properly delegated authority would have the power to move for dismissal or summary judgment if the entire board did.

Even though demand was not made in this case and the initial decision of whether to litigate was not placed before the board, Zapata's board, it seems to us, retained all of its corporate power concerning litigation decisions. If Maldonado had made demand on the board in this case, it could have refused to bring suit. Maldonado could then have asserted that the decision not to sue was wrongful and, if correct, would have been allowed to maintain the suit. The board, however, never would have lost its statutory managerial authority. The demand requirement itself evidences that the managerial power is retained by the board. When a derivative plaintiff is allowed to bring suit after a wrongful refusal, the board's authority to choose whether to pursue the litigation is not challenged although its conclusion — reached through the exercise of that authority — is not respected since it is wrongful. Similarly, Rule 23.1, by excusing demand in certain instances, does not strip the board of its corporate power. It merely saves the plaintiff the expense and delay of making a futile demand resulting in a probable tainted exercise of that authority in a refusal by the board or in giving control of litigation to the opposing side. But the board entity remains empowered under § 141(a) to make decisions regarding corporate litigation. The problem is one of member disqualification, not the absence of power in the board.

The corporate power inquiry then focuses on whether the board, tainted by the self-interest of a majority of its members, can legally delegate its authority to a committee of two disinterested directors. We find our statute clearly requires an affirmative answer to this question. As has been noted, under an express provision of the statute, § 141(c), a committee can exercise all of the authority of the board to the extent provided in the resolution of the board. Moreover, at least by analogy to our statutory section on interested directors, 8 Del.C. § 141, it seems clear that the Delaware statute is designed to permit disinterested directors to act for the board.

We do not think that the interest taint of the board majority is per se a legal bar to the delegation of the board's power to an independent committee composed of disinterested board members. The committee can properly act for the corporation to move to dismiss derivative litigation that is believed to be detrimental to the corporation's best interest.

Our focus now switches to the Court of Chancery which is faced with a stockholder assertion that a derivative suit, properly instituted, should continue for the benefit of the corporation and a corporate assertion, properly made by a board committee acting with board authority, that the same derivative suit should be dismissed as inimical to the best interests of the corporation.

At the risk of stating the obvious, the problem is relatively simple. If, on the one hand, corporations can consistently wrest bona fide derivative actions away from well-meaning derivative plaintiffs through the use of the committee mechanism, the derivative suit will lose much, if not all, of its generally-recognized effectiveness as an intra-corporate means of policing boards of directors. If, on the other hand, corporations are unable to rid themselves of meritless or harmful litigation and strike suits, the derivative action, created to benefit the corporation, will produce the opposite, unintended result.... It thus appears desirable to us to find a balancing point where bona fide stockholder power to bring corporate causes of action cannot be unfairly trampled on by the board of directors, but the corporation can rid itself of detrimental litigation.

As we noted, the question has been treated by other courts as one of the "business judgment" of the board committee. If a "committee, composed of independent and disinterested directors, conducted a proper review of the matters before it, considered a variety of factors and reached, in good faith, a business judgment that [the] action was not in the best interest of [the corporation]," the action must be dismissed. The issues become solely independence, good faith, and reasonable investigation. The ultimate conclusion of the committee, under that view, is not subject to judicial review.

We are not satisfied, however, that acceptance of the "business judgment" rationale at this stage of derivative litigation is a proper balancing point. While we admit an analogy with a normal case respecting board judgment, it seems to us that there is sufficient risk in the realities of a situation like the one presented in this case to justify caution beyond adherence to the theory of business judgment.

The context here is a suit against directors where demand on the board is excused. We think some tribute must be paid to the fact that the lawsuit was properly initiated. It is not a board refusal case. Moreover, this complaint was filed in June of 1975 and, while the parties undoubtedly would take differing views on the degree of litigation activity, we have to be concerned about the creation of an "Independent Investigation Committee" four years later, after the election of two new outside directors. Situations could develop where such motions could be filed after years of vigorous litigation for reasons unconnected with the merits of the lawsuit.

Moreover, notwithstanding our conviction that Delaware law entrusts the corporate power to a properly authorized committee, we must be mindful that directors are passing judgment on fellow directors in the same corporation and fellow directors, in this instance, who designated them to serve both as directors and committee members. The question naturally arises whether a "there but for the grace of God go I" empathy might not play a role. And the further question arises whether inquiry as to independence, good faith and reasonable investigation is sufficient safeguard against abuse, perhaps subconscious abuse. . . .

Whether the Court of Chancery will be persuaded by the exercise of a committee power resulting in a summary motion for dismissal of a derivative action, where a demand has not been initially made, should rest, in our judgment, in the independent discretion of the Court of Chancery. We thus steer a middle course between those cases which yield to the independent business judgment of a board committee and this case as determined below which would yield to unbridled plaintiff stockholder control. In pursuit of the course, we recognize that "[t]he final substantive judgment whether a particular lawsuit should be maintained requires a balance of many factors—ethical, commercial, promotional, public relations, employee relations, fiscal as well as legal." But we are content that such factors are not "beyond the judicial reach" of the Court of Chancery which regularly and competently deals with fiduciary relationships, disposition of trust property, approval of settlements and scores of similar problems. We recognize the danger of judicial overreaching but the alternatives seem to us to be outweighed by the fresh view of a judicial outsider. Moreover, if we failed to balance all the interests involved, we would in the name of practicality and judicial economy foreclose a judicial decision on the merits. At this point, we are not convinced that is necessary or desirable.

After an objective and thorough investigation of a derivative suit, an independent committee may cause its corporation to file a pretrial motion to dismiss in the Court of Chancery. The basis of the motion is the best interests of the corporation, as determined by the committee. The motion should include a thorough written record of the investigation and its findings and recommendations. Under appropriate Court supervision, akin to proceedings on summary judgment, each side should have an opportunity to make a record on the motion. As to the limited issues presented by the motion noted below, the moving party should be prepared to meet the normal burden under Rule 56 that there is no genuine issue as to any material fact and that the moving party is entitled to dismiss as a matter of law. The Court should apply a two-step test to the motion.

First, the Court should inquire into the independence and good faith of the committee and the bases supporting its conclusions. Limited discovery may be ordered to facilitate such inquiries. The corporation should have the burden of proving independence, good faith and a reasonable investigation, rather than presuming independence, good faith and reasonableness. If the Court determines either that the committee is not independent or has not shown reasonable bases for its conclusions, or, if the Court is not satisfied for other reasons relating to the process, including but not limited to the good faith of the committee, the Court shall deny the corporation's motion. If, however, the Court is satisfied under Rule 56 standards that the committee was independent and showed reasonable bases for good faith findings and recommendations, the Court may proceed, in its discretion, to the next step.

The second step provides, we believe, the essential key in striking the balance between legitimate corporate claims as expressed in a derivative stockholder suit and a corporation's best interests as expressed by an independent investigating committee. The Court should determine, applying its own independent business judgment, whether the motion should be granted. This means, of course, that instances could arise where a committee can establish its independence and sound bases for its good faith decisions and still have the corporation's motion denied. The second step is intended to thwart instances where corporate actions meet the criteria of step one, but the result does not appear to satisfy its spirit, or where corporate actions would simply prematurely terminate a stockholder grievance deserving of further consideration in the corporation's interest. The Court of Chancery of course must carefully consider and weigh how compelling the corporate interest in dismissal is when faced with a non-frivolous lawsuit. The Court of Chancery should, when appropriate, give special consideration to matters of law and public policy in addition to the corporation's best interests.

If the Court's independent business judgment is satisfied, the Court may proceed to grant the motion, subject, of course, to any equitable terms or conditions the Court finds necessary or desirable.

The interlocutory order of the Court of Chancery is reversed and the cause is remanded for further proceedings consistent with this opinion.

Questions

1. What is the role of the special committee? If the court maintains its discretion to review the decision of the special committee for compliance with the business judgment rule, what is the point of first deferring to the special committee?

2. What is the difference between a special committee making a decision regarding demand and the board making such a decision? Should the rule the court adopts in *Zapata Corporation v. Maldonado* with respect to decisions of the special litigation committee also apply to cases where the board refuses demand?

3. What is the relationship between the different rules applicable to derivative litigation and the role of the board and its centrality to corporate governance?

In re Oracle Corp. Derivative Litigation
824 A.2d 917 (Del. Ch. 2003)

STRINE, Vice Chancellor

In this opinion, I address the motion of the special litigation committee ("SLC") of Oracle Corporation to terminate this action, "the Delaware Derivative Action," and other such actions pending in the name of Oracle against certain Oracle directors and officers.... The SLC bears the burden of persuasion on this motion and must convince me that there is no material issue of fact calling into doubt its independence. This requirement is set forth in *Zapata Corp. v. Maldonado* and its progeny.

. . .

I. *Factual Background*
A. *Summary of the Plaintiffs' Allegations*

The Delaware Derivative Complaint centers on alleged insider trading by four members of Oracle's board of directors—Lawrence Ellison, Jeffrey Henley, Donald Lucas, and Michael Boskin (collectively, the "Trading Defendants"). Each of the Trading Defendants had a very different role at Oracle.

Ellison is Oracle's Chairman, Chief Executive Officer, and its largest stockholder, owning nearly twenty-five percent of Oracle's voting shares.... By virtue of his managerial position, Ellison has regular access to a great deal of information about how Oracle is performing on a week-to-week basis.

Henley is Oracle's Chief Financial Officer, Executive Vice President, and a director of the corporation. Like Ellison, Henley has his finger on the pulse of Oracle's performance constantly.

Lucas is a director who chairs Oracle's Executive Committee and its Finance and Audit Committee....

Boskin is a director, Chairman of the Compensation Committee, and a member of the Finance and Audit Committee....

Into early to mid-February, Oracle allegedly continued to assure the market that it would meet its December guidance. Then, on March 1, 2001, the company announced that rather than posting 12 cents per share in quarterly earnings and 25% license revenue growth as projected, the company's earnings for the quarter would be 10 cents per share and license revenue growth only 6%. The stock market reacted swiftly and negatively to this news, with Oracle's share price dropping as low as $15.75 before closing at $16.88—a 21% decline in one day. These prices were well below the above $30 per share prices at which the Trading Defendants sold in January 2001....

B. *The Plaintiffs' Claims in the Delaware Derivative Action*

The plaintiffs make two central claims in their amended complaint in the Delaware Derivative Action. First, the plaintiffs allege that the Trading Defendants breached their duty of loyalty by misappropriating inside information and using it as the basis for trading decisions....

Second, as to the other defendants—who are the members of the Oracle board who did not trade—the plaintiffs allege a *Caremark* violation, in the sense that the board's indifference to the deviation between the company's December guidance and reality was so extreme as to constitute subjective bad faith.

. . .

D. *The Formation of the Special Litigation Committee*

On February 1, 2002, Oracle formed the SLC in order to investigate the Delaware Derivative Action and to determine whether Oracle should press the claims raised by the plaintiffs, settle the case, or terminate it....

The SLC was granted full authority to decide these matters without the need for approval by the other members of the Oracle board.

E. *The Members of the Special Litigation Committee*

Two Oracle board members were named to the SLC. Both of them joined the Oracle board on October 15, 2001, more than a half a year after Oracle's 3Q FY 2001 closed. The SLC members also share something else: both are tenured professors at Stanford University.

Professor Hector Garcia-Molina is Chairman of the Computer Science Department at Stanford ... The other SLC member, Professor Joseph Grundfest, is the W.A. Franke Professor of Law and Business at Stanford University.... Like Garcia-Molina, Grundfest's appointment at Stanford was a homecoming, because he obtained his law degree and performed significant post-graduate work in economics at Stanford.

As will be discussed more specifically later, Grundfest also serves as a steering committee member and a senior fellow of the Stanford Institute for Economic Policy Research, and releases working papers under the "SIEPR" banner.

For their services, the SLC members were paid $250 an hour, a rate below that which they could command for other activities, such as consulting or expert witness testimony ... Garcia-Molina and Grundfest agreed to give up any SLC-related compensation if their compensation was deemed by this court to impair their impartiality.

F. *The SLC Members Are Recruited to the Board*

The SLC members were recruited to the board primarily by defendant Lucas, with help from defendant Boskin. The wooing of them began in the summer of 2001. Before deciding to join the Oracle board, Grundfest, in particular, did a good deal of due diligence. His review included reading publicly available information, among other things, the then-current complaint in the Federal Class Action.

Grundfest then met with defendants Ellison and Henley, among others, and asked them some questions about the Federal Class Action.... Grundfest received answers that were consistent enough with what he called the "exogenous" information about the case to form sufficient confidence to at least join the Oracle board. Grundfest testified that this did not mean that he had concluded that the claims in the Federal Class Action had no merit, only that Ellison's and Henley's explanations of their conduct were plausible. Grundfest did, however, conclude that these were reputable businessmen with whom he felt comfortable serving as a fellow director, and that Henley had given very impressive answers to difficult questions regarding the way Oracle conducted its financial reporting operations.

G. *The SLC's Advisors*

The most important advisors retained by the SLC were its counsel from Simpson Thacher & Bartlett LLP. Simpson Thacher had not performed material amounts of legal work for Oracle or any of the individual defendants before its engagement, and the plaintiffs have not challenged its independence.

National Economic Research Advisors ("NERA") was retained by the SLC to perform some analytical work. The plaintiffs have not challenged NERA's independence.

H. *The SLC's Investigation and Report*

The SLC's investigation was, by any objective measure, extensive. The SLC reviewed an enormous amount of paper and electronic records. SLC counsel interviewed seventy witnesses, some of them twice. SLC members participated in several key interviews, including the interviews of the Trading Defendants. . . .

During the course of the investigation, the SLC met with its counsel thirty-five times for a total of eighty hours. In addition to that, the SLC members, particularly Professor Grundfest, devoted many more hours to the investigation.

. . .

[T]aking into account all the relevant information sources, the SLC concluded that even Ellison and Henley—who were obviously the two Trading Defendants with the most access to inside information—did not possess material, non-public information. As to Lucas and Boskin, the SLC noted that they did not receive the weekly updates (of various kinds) that allegedly showed a weakening in Oracle's performance during 3Q FY 2001. As a result, there was even less of a basis to infer wrongdoing on their part.

. . .

For these and other reasons, the SLC concluded that the plaintiffs' allegations that the Trading Defendants had breached their fiduciary duty of loyalty by using inside information about Oracle to reap illicit trading gains were without merit. The SLC also determined that, consistent with this determination, there was no reason to sue the other members of the Oracle board who were in office as of 3Q FY 2001. Therefore, the SLC determined to seek dismissal of the Delaware Derivative Action and the other derivative actions.

. . .

III. *The Applicable Procedural Standard*

In order to prevail on its motion to terminate the Delaware Derivative Action, the SLC must persuade me that: (1) its members were independent; (2) that they acted in good faith; and (3) that they had reasonable bases for their recommendations. If the SLC meets that burden, I am free to grant its motion or may, in my discretion, undertake my own examination of whether Oracle should terminate and permit the suit to proceed if I, in my oxymoronic judicial "business judgment," conclude that procession is in the best interests of the company. This two-step analysis comes, of course, from *Zapata*.

IV. *Is the SLC Independent?*

A. *The Facts Disclosed in the Report*

In its Report, the SLC took the position that its members were independent. In support of that position, the Report noted several factors including:

- the fact that neither Grundfest nor Garcia-Molina received compensation from Oracle other than as directors;
- the fact that neither Grundfest nor Garcia-Molina were on the Oracle board at the time of the alleged wrongdoing;
- the fact that both Grundfest and Garcia-Molina were willing to return their compensation as SLC members if necessary to preserve their status as independent;
- the absence of any other material ties between Oracle, the Trading Defendants, and any of the other defendants, on the one hand, and Grundfest and Garcia-Molina, on the other; and
- the absence of any material ties between Oracle, the Trading Defendants, and any of the other defendants, on the one hand, and the SLC's advisors, on the other.

Noticeably absent from the SLC Report was any disclosure of several significant ties between Oracle or the Trading Defendants and Stanford University, the university that employs both members of the SLC. In the Report, it was only disclosed that:

- defendant Boskin was a Stanford professor;
- the SLC members were aware that Lucas had made certain donations to Stanford; and
- among the contributions was a donation of $50,000 worth of stock that Lucas donated to Stanford Law School after Grundfest delivered a speech to a venture capital fund meeting in response to Lucas's request. It happens that Lucas's son is a partner in the fund and that approximately half the donation was allocated for use by Grundfest in his personal research.

B. *The "Stanford" Facts that Emerged During Discovery*

In view of the modesty of these disclosed ties, it was with some shock that a series of other ties among Stanford, Oracle, and the Trading Defendants emerged during discovery. Although the plaintiffs have embellished these ties considerably beyond what is reasonable, the plain facts are a striking departure from the picture presented in the Report.

. . .

1. *Boskin*

Defendant Michael J. Boskin is the T.M. Friedman Professor of Economics at Stanford University. . . . During the 1970s, Boskin taught Grundfest when Grundfest was a Ph.D. candidate. Although Boskin was not Grundfest's advisor and although they do not socialize, the two have remained in contact over the years, speaking occasionally about matters of public policy.

Furthermore, both Boskin and Grundfest are senior fellows and steering committee members at the Stanford Institute for Economic Policy Research, which was previously defined as "SIEPR." . . .

[B]oth Boskin and Grundfest publish working papers under the SIEPR rubric and . . . SIEPR helps to publicize their respective works. . . .

2. *Lucas*

As noted in the SLC Report, the SLC members admitted knowing that Lucas was a contributor to Stanford. They also acknowledged that he had donated $50,000 to Stanford Law School in appreciation for Grundfest having given a speech at his request. About half of the proceeds were allocated for use by Grundfest in his research.

But Lucas's ties with Stanford are far, far richer than the SLC Report lets on. To begin, Lucas is a Stanford alumnus, having obtained both his undergraduate and graduate degrees there. By any measure, he has been a very loyal alumnus. . . .

. . . From his own personal funds, Lucas has contributed $4.1 million to Stanford, a substantial percentage of which has been donated within the last half-decade. Notably, Lucas has, among other things, donated $424,000 to SIEPR and approximately $149,000 to Stanford Law School. Indeed, Lucas is not only a major contributor to SIEPR, he is the Chair of its Advisory Board. At SIEPR's facility at Stanford, the conference center is named the Donald L. Lucas Conference Center.

From these undisputed facts, it is inarguable that Lucas is a very important alumnus of Stanford and a generous contributor to not one, but two, parts of Stanford important to Grundfest: the Law School and SIEPR. . . .

3. *Ellison*

There can be little doubt that Ellison is a major figure in the community in which Stanford is located. The so-called Silicon Valley has generated many success stories, among the greatest of which is that of Oracle and its leader, Ellison. One of the wealthiest men in America, Ellison is a major figure in the nation's increasingly important information technology industry. Given his wealth, Ellison is also in a position to make—and, in fact, he has made—major charitable contributions [including to Stanford].

. . .

During the time Ellison has been CEO of Oracle, the company itself has also made over $300,000 in donations to Stanford. . . .

Taken together, these facts suggest that Ellison (when considered as an individual and as the key executive and major stockholder of Oracle) had, at the very least, been involved in several endeavors of value to Stanford.

. . .

In order to buttress the argument that Stanford did not feel beholden to him, Ellison shared with the court the (otherwise private) fact that one of his children had applied to Stanford in October 2000 and was not admitted. If Stanford felt comfortable rejecting Ellison's child, the SLC contends, why should the SLC members hesitate before recommending that Oracle press insider trading-based fiduciary duty claims against Ellison?

But the fact remains that Ellison was still talking very publicly and seriously about the possibility of endowing a graduate interdisciplinary studies program at Stanford during the summer *after* his child was rejected from Stanford's undergraduate program.

C. The SLC's Argument

The SLC contends that even together, these facts regarding the ties among Oracle, the Trading Defendants, Stanford, and the SLC members do not impair the SLC's independence. In so arguing, the SLC places great weight on the fact that none of the Trading Defendants have the practical ability to deprive either Grundfest or Garcia-Molina of their current positions at Stanford. Nor, given their tenure, does Stanford itself have any practical ability to punish them for taking action adverse to Boskin, Lucas, or Ellison—each of whom, as we have seen, has contributed (in one way or another) great value to Stanford as an institution. As important, neither Garcia-Molina nor Grundfest are part of the official fundraising apparatus at Stanford; thus, it is not their on-the-job duty to be solicitous of contributors, and fundraising success does not factor into their treatment as professors.

In so arguing, the SLC focuses on the language of previous opinions of this court and the Delaware Supreme Court that indicates that a director is not independent only if he is dominated and controlled by an interested party, such as a Trading Defendant. The SLC also emphasizes that much of our jurisprudence on independence focuses on economically consequential relationships between the allegedly interested party and the directors who allegedly cannot act independently of that director. Put another way, much of our law focuses the bias inquiry on whether there are economically material ties between the interested party and the director whose impartiality is questioned, treating the possible effect on one's personal wealth as the key to the independence inquiry. Putting a point on this, the SLC cites certain decisions of Delaware courts concluding that directors who are personal friends of an interested party were not, by virtue of those personal ties, to be labeled non-independent. . . .

E. *The Court's Analysis of the SLC's Independence*

. . . [I]n my view, an emphasis on "domination and control" would serve only to fetishize much-parroted language, at the cost of denuding the independence inquiry of its intellectual integrity. Take an easy example. Imagine if two brothers were on a corporate board, each successful in different businesses and not dependent in any way on the other's beneficence in order to be wealthy. The brothers are brothers, they stay in touch and consider each other family, but each is opinionated and strong-willed. A derivative action is filed targeting a transaction involving one of the brothers. The other brother is put on a special litigation committee to investigate the case. If the test is domination and control, then one brother could investigate the other. Does any sensible person think that is our law? I do not think it is.

And it should not be our law. Delaware law should not be based on a reductionist view of human nature that simplifies human motivations on the lines of the least sophisticated notions of the law and economics movement. *Homo sapiens* is not merely *homo economicus.* We may be thankful that an array of other motivations exist that influence human behavior; not all are any better than greed or avarice, think of envy, to name just one. But also think of motives like love, friendship, and collegiality, think of those among us who direct their behavior as best they can on a guiding creed or set of moral values.

Nor should our law ignore the social nature of humans. To be direct, corporate directors are generally the sort of people deeply enmeshed in social institutions. Such institutions have norms, expectations that, explicitly and implicitly, influence and channel the behavior of those who participate in their operation. Some things are "just not done," or only at a cost, which might not be so severe as a loss of position, but may involve a loss of standing in the institution. In being appropriately sensitive to this factor, our law also cannot assume—absent some proof of the point—that corporate directors are, as a general matter, persons of unusual social bravery, who operate heedless to the inhibitions that social norms generate for ordinary folk.

For all these reasons, this court has previously held that the Delaware Supreme Court's teachings on independence can be summarized thusly:

> At bottom, the question of independence turns on whether a director is, *for any substantial reason,* incapable of making a decision with only the best interests of the corporation in mind. That is, the Supreme Court cases ultimately focus on impartiality and objectivity [*Parfi Holding AB v. Mirror Image Internet, Inc.*, 794 A. 2d 1211, 1232 (Del. Ch. 2001) . . .]

This formulation is wholly consistent with the teaching of *Aronson,* which defines independence as meaning that "a director's decision is based on the corporate merits of the subject before the board rather than extraneous considerations or influences." As noted by Chancellor Chandler recently, a director may be compromised if he is beholden to an interested person. Beholden in this sense does not mean just owing in the financial sense, it can also flow out of "personal or other relationships" to the interested party.

Without backtracking from these general propositions, it would be less than candid if I did not admit that Delaware courts have applied these general standards in a manner that has been less than wholly consistent. Different decisions take a different view about the bias-producing potential of family relationships, not all of which can be explained by mere degrees of consanguinity. Likewise, there is admittedly case law that gives little weight to ties of friendship in the independence inquiry. In this opinion, I will not venture to do what I believe to be impossible: attempt to rationalize all these cases in their specifics. Rather, I undertake what I understand to be my duty and what is possible: the application of the independence inquiry that our Supreme Court has articulated in a manner that is faithful to its essential spirit.

1. *The Contextual Nature of the Independence Inquiry Under Delaware Law*

In examining whether the SLC has met its burden to demonstrate that there is no material dispute of fact regarding its independence, the court must bear in mind the function of special litigation committees under our jurisprudence. Under Delaware law, the primary means by which corporate defendants may obtain a dismissal of a derivative suit is by showing that the plaintiffs have not met their pleading burden under the test of *Aronson v. Lewis,* or the related standard set forth in *Rales v. Blasband.* In simple terms, these tests permit a corporation to terminate a derivative suit if its board is comprised of directors who can impartially consider a demand.

Special litigation committees are permitted as a last chance for a corporation to control a derivative claim in circumstances when a majority of its directors cannot impartially consider a demand. By vesting the power of the board to determine what to do with the suit in a committee of independent directors, a corporation may retain control over whether the suit will proceed, so long as the committee meets the standard set forth in *Zapata.*

In evaluating the independence of a special litigation committee, this court must take into account the extraordinary importance and difficulty of such a committee's responsibility. It is, I daresay, easier to say no to a friend, relative, colleague, or boss who seeks assent for an act (*e.g.,* a transaction) that has not yet occurred than it would be to cause a corporation to sue that person. This is admittedly a determination of so-called "legislative fact," but one that can be rather safely made. Denying a fellow director the ability to proceed on a matter important to him may not be easy, but it must, as a general matter, be less difficult than finding that there is reason to believe that the fellow director has committed serious wrongdoing and that a derivative suit should proceed against him.

The difficulty of making this decision is compounded in the special litigation committee context because the weight of making the moral judgment necessarily falls on less than the full board. A small number of directors feels the moral gravity — and social pressures — of this duty alone.

For all these reasons, the independence inquiry is critically important if the special litigation committee process is to retain its integrity, a quality that is, in turn, essential to the utility of that process....

Thus, in assessing the independence of the Oracle SLC, I necessarily examine the question of whether the SLC can independently make the difficult decision entrusted to it: to determine whether the Trading Defendants should face suit for insider trading-based allegations of breach of fiduciary duty. An affirmative answer by the SLC to that question would have potentially huge negative consequences for the Trading Defendants, not only by exposing them to the possibility of a large damage award but also by subjecting them to great reputational harm. To have Professors Grundfest and Garcia-Molina declare that Oracle should press insider trading claims against the Trading Defendants would have been, to put it mildly, "news." Relatedly, it is reasonable to think that an SLC determination that the Trading Defendants had likely engaged in insider trading would have been accompanied by a recommendation that they step down as fiduciaries until their ultimate culpability was decided.

The importance and special sensitivity of the SLC's task is also relevant for another obvious reason: investigations do not follow a scientific process like an old-fashioned assembly line. The investigators' mindset and talent influence, for good or ill, the course of an investigation. Just as there are obvious dangers from investigators suffering from too much zeal, so too are dangers posed by investigators who harbor reasons not to pursue the investigation's targets with full vigor.

. . .

2. *The SLC Has Not Met Its Burden to Demonstrate the Absence of a Material Dispute of Fact About Its Independence*

Using the contextual approach I have described, I conclude that the SLC has not met its burden to show the absence of a material factual question about its independence. I find this to be the case because the ties among the SLC, the Trading Defendants, and Stanford are so substantial that they cause reasonable doubt about the SLC's ability to impartially consider whether the Trading Defendants should face suit. The concern that arises from these ties can be stated fairly simply, focusing on defendants Boskin, Lucas, and Ellison in that order, and then collectively.

As SLC members, Grundfest and Garcia-Molina were already being asked to consider whether the company should level extremely serious accusations of wrongdoing against fellow board members. As to Boskin, both SLC members faced another layer of complexity: the determination of whether to have Oracle press insider trading claims against a fellow professor at their university. Even though Boskin was in a different academic department from either SLC member, it is reasonable to assume that the fact that Boskin was also on faculty would — to persons possessing typical sensibilities and institutional loyalty—be a matter of more than trivial concern. Universities are obviously places of at-times intense debate, but they also see themselves as communities. In fact, Stanford refers to itself as a "community of scholars." To accuse a fellow professor—whom one might see at the faculty club or at interdisciplinary presentations of academic papers—of insider trading cannot be a small thing—even for the most callous of academics.

As to Boskin, Grundfest faced an even more complex challenge than Garcia-Molina. Boskin was a professor who had taught him and with whom he had maintained contact over the years. Their areas of academic interest intersected, putting Grundfest in contact if not directly with Boskin, then regularly with Boskin's colleagues.... Grundfest (I infer) would have more difficulty objectively determining whether Boskin engaged in improper insider trading than would a person who was not a fellow professor, had not been a student of Boskin, had not kept in touch with Boskin over the years, and who was not a senior fellow and steering committee member at SIEPR.

In so concluding, I necessarily draw on a general sense of human nature. It may be that Grundfest is a very special person who is capable of putting these kinds of things totally aside. But the SLC has not provided evidence that that is the case. In this respect, it is critical to note that I do not infer that Grundfest would be less likely to recommend suit against Boskin than someone without these ties. Human nature being what it is, it is entirely possible that Grundfest would in fact be tougher on Boskin than he would on someone with whom he did not have such connections. The inference I draw is subtly, but importantly, different. What I infer is that a person in Grundfest's position would find it difficult to assess Boskin's conduct without pondering his own association with Boskin and their mutual affiliations. Although these connections might produce bias in either a tougher or laxer direction, the key inference is that these connections would be on the mind of a person in Grundfest's position, putting him in the position of either causing serious legal action to be brought against a person with whom he shares several connections (an awkward thing) or not doing so (and risking being seen as having engaged in favoritism toward his old professor and SIEPR colleague).

The same concerns also exist as to Lucas. For Grundfest to vote to accuse Lucas of insider trading would require him to accuse SIEPR's Advisory Board Chair and major benefactor of serious wrongdoing—of conduct that violates federal securities laws. Such action would also require Grundfest to make charges against a man who recently donated $50,000 to Stanford Law School after Grundfest made a speech at his request.

And, for both Grundfest and Garcia-Molina, service on the SLC demanded that they consider whether an extremely generous and influential Stanford alumnus should be sued by Oracle for insider trading. Although they were not responsible for fundraising, as sophisticated professors they undoubtedly are aware of how important large contributors are to Stanford, and they share in the benefits that come from serving at a university with a rich endowment. A reasonable professor giving any thought to the matter would obviously consider the effect his decision might have on the University's relationship with Lucas, it being (one hopes) sensible to infer that a professor of reasonable collegiality and loyalty cares about the well-being of the institution he serves.

. . .

Before closing, it is necessary to address two concerns. The first is the undeniable awkwardness of opinions like this one. By finding that there exists too much doubt about the SLC's independence for the SLC to meet its *Zapata* burden, I make no finding about the subjective good faith of the SLC members, both of whom are distinguished academics at one of this nation's most prestigious institutions of higher learning. Nothing in this record leads me to conclude that either of the SLC members acted out of any conscious desire to favor the Trading Defendants or to do anything other than discharge their duties with fidelity. But that is not the purpose of the independence inquiry.

That inquiry recognizes that persons of integrity and reputation can be compromised in their ability to act without bias when they must make a decision adverse to others with whom they share material affiliations. To conclude that the Oracle SLC was not independent is not a conclusion that the two accomplished professors who comprise it are not persons of good faith and moral probity, it is solely to conclude that they were not situated to act with the required degree of impartiality. *Zapata* requires independence to ensure that stockholders do not have to rely upon special litigation committee members who must put aside personal considerations that are ordinarily influential in daily behavior in making the already difficult decision to accuse fellow directors of serious wrongdoing.

Finally, the SLC has made the argument that a ruling against it will chill the ability of corporations to locate qualified independent directors in the academy. This is overwrought. If there are 1,700 professors at Stanford alone, as the SLC says, how many must there be on the west coast of the United States, at institutions without ties to Oracle and the Trading Defendants as substantial as Stanford's? Undoubtedly, a corporation of Oracle's market capitalization could have found prominent academics willing to serve as SLC members, about whom no reasonable question of independence could have been asserted.

V. *Conclusion*

The SLC's motion to terminate is DENIED. IT IS SO ORDERED.

Questions

1. What are Vice-Chancellor Strine's concerns about the independence of the special litigation committee? Are they valid?

2. In situations not involving special litigation committees, the Delaware courts have refused to address how directors' social and personal relations might affect

their independence, limiting their investigation to questions of financial domination. Are there reasons to extend Strine's analysis to such situations, or should his analysis be limited to the independence of the special litigation committee (and, if so, why)?

Section II
The Duty of Care

The duty of care requires directors and officers to act in a responsible fashion. Like any tort-based duty, it is anchored in the concept of negligence, although, as we will see, mostly in a rhetorical fashion. What began, in the nineteenth and early twentieth century, as a tort concept has become by the 1980s a limited duty to be informed subsumed under the presumption business judgment rule.

Subsection A (Directors' Negligence) begins with *Francis v. United Jersey Bank* and *Senn v. Northwest Underwriters Inc.*, a New Jersey case and a Washington case, respectively, both of which explore directors' negligence. Although it is not included in this subsection, the seminal case addressing directors' negligence in Delaware was *Graham v. Allis-Chalmers Manufacturing Co.* (1963). *Graham* was the case in which the Delaware Supreme Court first espoused the existence of a director's duty to act with the care of a prudent person. (Up to the 1960s, the New York courts directed the formulation and development of the duty of care.)

Francis, *Senn*, and *Graham* involved directorial inaction. As Subsection B (The Business Judgment Rule) examines, challenges to directors' actions or decisions raise other questions, particularly the appropriate application of the presumption of the business judgment rule and how it changes the traditional negligence analysis. *Kamin v. American Express Company*, out of New York, and *Joy v. North*, out of the Second Circuit, examine the meaning of, and justifications for, the business judgment rule.

While the Delaware courts neglected to develop the doctrinal precepts of the duty of care before *Graham*, at the time that *Graham* was decided, they had already developed the business judgment rule independently of that duty. As Subsection C (The Business Judgment Rule and the Duty of Care) explores, after *Graham*, as the Delaware courts attempted to define the relationship between their developed business judgment rule and their underdeveloped duty-of-care jurisprudence, they lay the foundation for the obliteration of the latter, leading ultimately to the modern articulation of the duty of care, easily labeled "the dormant duty of care." We will return to the dormant duty of care in Section IV of this Part 2. For more on the development of the duty of care, see Dalia T. Mitchell, *Status Bound: The Twentieth Century Evolution of Directors' Liability*, 5 NYU J. L. & Bus. 63–151 (2009).

A. Directors' Negligence (The Duty to Act)

Francis v. United Jersey Bank
87 N.J. 15 (1981)

POLLOCK, Justice

The primary issue on this appeal is whether a corporate director is personally liable in negligence for the failure to prevent the misappropriation of trust funds by other directors who were also officers and shareholders of the corporation.

Plaintiffs are trustees in bankruptcy of Pritchard & Baird Intermediaries Corp. (Pritchard & Baird), a reinsurance broker or intermediary. Defendant Lillian P. Overcash is the daughter of Lillian G. Pritchard and the executrix of her estate. At the time of her death, Mrs. Pritchard was a director and the largest single shareholder of Pritchard & Baird. Because Mrs. Pritchard died after the institution of suit but before trial, her executrix was substituted as a defendant. United Jersey Bank is joined as the administrator of the estate of Charles Pritchard, Sr., who had been president, director and majority shareholder of Pritchard & Baird.

This litigation focuses on payments made by Pritchard & Baird to Charles Pritchard, Jr. and William Pritchard, who were sons of Mr. and Mrs. Charles Pritchard, Sr., as well as officers, directors and shareholders of the corporation. Claims against Charles, Jr. and William are being pursued in bankruptcy proceedings against them.

The trial court, sitting without a jury, characterized the payments as fraudulent conveyances within N.J.S.A. 25:2–10 and entered judgment of $10,355,736.91 plus interest against the estate of Mrs. Pritchard. The judgment includes damages from her negligence in permitting payments from the corporation of $4,391,133.21 to Charles, Jr. and $5,483,799.02 to William. . . .

. . . [T]he critical question is not whether the misconduct of Charles, Jr. and William should be characterized as fraudulent conveyances or acts of conversion. Rather, the initial question is whether Mrs. Pritchard was negligent in not noticing and trying to prevent the misappropriation of funds held by the corporation in an implied trust. A further question is whether her negligence was the proximate cause of the plaintiffs' losses. Both lower courts found that she was liable in negligence for the losses caused by the wrongdoing of Charles, Jr. and William. We affirm.

I

The matrix for our decision is the customs and practices of the reinsurance industry and the role of Pritchard & Baird as a reinsurance broker. Reinsurance involves a contract under which one insurer agrees to indemnify another for loss sustained under the latter's policy of insurance. Insurance companies that insure against losses arising out of fire or other casualty seek at times to minimize their exposure by sharing risks with other insurance companies. Thus, when the face amount of a policy is comparatively large, the company may enlist one or more insurers to participate in that risk. Similarly, an insurance company's loss potential and overall exposure may be reduced by reinsuring a part of an entire class of policies (*e.g.*, 25% of all of its fire insurance policies). The selling insurance company is known as a ceding company. The entity that assumes the obligation is designated as the reinsurer.

The reinsurance broker arranges the contract between the ceding company and the reinsurer. In accordance with industry custom before the Pritchard & Baird bankruptcy, the reinsurance contract or treaty did not specify the rights and duties of the broker. Typically, the ceding company communicates to the broker the details concerning the risk. The broker negotiates the sale of portions of the risk to the reinsurers. In most instances, the ceding company and the reinsurer do not communicate with each other, but rely upon the reinsurance broker. The ceding company pays premiums due a reinsurer to the broker, who deducts his commission and transmits the balance to the appropriate reinsurer. When a loss occurs, a reinsurer pays money due a ceding company to the broker, who then transmits it to the ceding company.

The reinsurance business was described by an expert at trial as having "a magic aura around it of dignity and quality and integrity." A telephone call which might be confirmed by a handwritten memorandum is sufficient to create a reinsurance obligation. Though separate bank accounts are not maintained for each treaty, the industry practice is to segregate the insurance funds from the broker's general accounts. Thus, the insurance fund accounts would contain the identifiable amounts for transmittal to either the reinsurer or the ceder. The expert stated that in general three kinds of checks may be drawn on this account: checks payable to reinsurers as premiums, checks payable to ceders as loss payments and checks payable to the brokers as commissions.

Messrs. Pritchard and Baird initially operated as a partnership. Later they formed several corporate entities to carry on their brokerage activities.... After the death of Charles, Sr. in 1973, only the remaining three directors continued to operate as the board. Lillian Pritchard inherited 72 of her husband's 120 shares in Pritchard & Baird, thereby becoming the largest shareholder in the corporation with 48% of the stock.

The corporate minute books reflect only perfunctory activities by the directors, related almost exclusively to the election of officers and adoption of banking resolutions and a retirement plan. None of the minutes for any of the meetings contain a discussion of the loans to Charles, Jr. and William or of the financial condition of the corporation. Moreover, upon instructions of Charles, Jr. that financial statements were not to be circulated to anyone else, the company's statements for the fiscal years beginning February 1, 1970, were delivered only to him.

Charles Pritchard, Sr. was the chief executive and controlled the business in the years following Baird's withdrawal. Beginning in 1966, he gradually relinquished control over the operations of the corporation. In 1968, Charles, Jr. became president and William became executive vice president. Charles, Sr. apparently became ill in 1971 and during the last year and a half of his life was not involved in the affairs of the business. He continued, however, to serve as a director until his death on December 10, 1973. Notwithstanding the presence of Charles, Sr. on the board until his death in 1973, Charles, Jr. dominated the management of the corporation and the board from 1968 until the bankruptcy in 1975.

Contrary to the industry custom of segregating funds, Pritchard & Baird commingled the funds of reinsurers and ceding companies with its own funds. All monies (including commissions, premiums and loss monies) were deposited in a single account. Charles, Sr. began the practice of withdrawing funds from the commingled account in transactions identified on the corporate books as "loans." As long as Charles, Sr. controlled the corporation, the "loans" correlated with corporate profits and were repaid at the end of each year. Starting in 1970, however, Charles, Jr. and William began to siphon ever-increasing sums from the corporation under the guise of loans. As of January 31, 1970, the "loans" to Charles, Jr. were $230,932 and to William were $207,329. At least by January 31, 1973, the annual increase in the loans exceeded annual corporate revenues. By October 1975, the year of bankruptcy, the "shareholders' loans" had metastasized to a total of $12,333,514.47.

The trial court rejected the characterization of the payments as "loans." No corporate resolution authorized the "loans," and no note or other instrument evidenced the debt. Charles, Jr. and William paid no interest on the amounts received. The "loans" were not repaid or reduced from one year to the next; rather, they increased annually.

The designation of "shareholders' loans" on the balance sheet was an entry to account for the distribution of the premium and loss money to Charles, Sr., Charles, Jr. and William. As the trial court found, the entry was part of a "woefully inadequate and highly dangerous bookkeeping system."

The "loans" to Charles, Jr. and William far exceeded their salaries and financial resources. If the payments to Charles, Jr. and William had been treated as dividends or compensation, then the balance sheets would have shown an excess of liabilities over assets. If the "loans" had been eliminated, the balance sheets would have depicted a corporation not only with a working capital deficit, but also with assets having a fair market value less than its liabilities. The balance sheets for 1970–1975, however, showed an excess of assets over liabilities. This result was achieved by designating the misappropriated funds as "shareholders' loans" and listing them as assets offsetting the deficits. Although the withdrawal of the funds resulted in an obligation of repayment to Pritchard & Baird, the more significant consideration is that the "loans" represented a massive misappropriation of money belonging to the clients of the corporation.

The "loans" were reflected on financial statements that were prepared annually as of January 31, the end of the corporate fiscal year. Although an outside certified public accountant prepared the 1970 financial statement, the corporation prepared only internal financial statements from 1971–1975. In all instances, the statements were simple documents, consisting of three or four 8H × 11 inch sheets.

The statements of financial condition from 1970 forward demonstrated:

	Working Capital Deficit	Shareholders' Loans	Net Brokerage Income
1970	$389,022	$509,941	$807,229
1971	not available	not available	not available
1972	$1,684,289	$1,825,911	$1,546,263
1973	$3,506,460	$3,700,542	$1,736,349
1974	$6,939,007	$7,080,629	$876,182
1975	$10,176,419	$10,298,039	$551,598

Those financial statements showed working capital deficits increasing annually in tandem with the amounts that Charles, Jr. and William withdrew as "shareholders' loans." In the last complete year of business (January 31, 1974, to January 31, 1975), "shareholders' loans" and the correlative working capital deficit increased by approximately $3,200,000.

The funding of the "loans" left the corporation with insufficient money to operate. Pritchard & Baird could defer payment on accounts payable because its clients allowed a grace period, generally 30 to 90 days, before the payment was due. During this period, Pritchard & Baird used the funds entrusted to it as a "float" to pay current accounts payable. By recourse to the funds of its clients, Pritchard & Baird not only paid its trade debts, but also funded the payments to Charles, Jr. and William. Thus, Pritchard & Baird was able to meet its obligations as they came due only through the use of clients' funds.

. . . This led ultimately to the filing in December, 1975, of an involuntary petition in bankruptcy and the appointments of the plaintiffs as trustees in bankruptcy of Pritchard & Baird.

Mrs. Pritchard was not active in the business of Pritchard & Baird and knew virtually nothing of its corporate affairs. She briefly visited the corporate offices in Morristown on only one occasion, and she never read or obtained the annual financial statements. She was unfamiliar with the rudiments of reinsurance and made no effort to assure that the policies and practices of the corporation, particularly pertaining to the withdrawal of funds, complied with industry custom or relevant law. Although her husband had warned her that Charles, Jr. would "take the shirt off my back," Mrs. Pritchard did not pay any attention to her duties as a director or to the affairs of the corporation.

After her husband died in December 1973, Mrs. Pritchard became incapacitated and was bedridden for a six-month period. She became listless at this time and started to drink rather heavily. Her physical condition deteriorated, and in 1978 she died. The trial court rejected testimony seeking to exonerate her because she "was old, was grief-stricken at the loss of her husband, sometimes consumed too much alcohol and was psychologically overborne by her sons." That court found that she was competent to act and that the reason Mrs. Pritchard never knew what her sons "were doing was because she never made the slightest effort to discharge any of her responsibilities as a director of Pritchard & Baird."

. . .

III

Individual liability of a corporate director for acts of the corporation is a prickly problem. Generally directors are accorded broad immunity and are not insurers of corporate activities. The problem is particularly nettlesome when a third party asserts that a director, because of nonfeasance, is liable for losses caused by acts of insiders, who in this case were officers, directors and shareholders. Determination of the liability of Mrs. Pritchard requires findings that she had a duty to the clients of Pritchard & Baird, that she breached that duty and that her breach was a proximate cause of their losses.

The New Jersey Business Corporation Act, which took effect on January 1, 1969, was a comprehensive revision of the statutes relating to business corporations. One section, N.J.S.A. 14A:6–14, concerning a director's general obligation . . . makes it incumbent upon directors to

> discharge their duties in good faith and with that degree of diligence, care and skill which ordinarily prudent men would exercise under similar circumstances in like positions. [N.J.S.A. 14A:6–14]

. . . Before the enactment of N.J.S.A. 14A:6–14, there was no express statutory authority requiring directors to act as ordinarily prudent persons under similar circumstances in like positions. Nonetheless, the requirement had been expressed in New Jersey judicial decisions.

A leading New Jersey opinion is *Campbell v. Watson*, which, like many early decisions on director liability, involved directors of a bank that had become insolvent. A receiver of the bank charged the directors with negligence that allegedly led to insolvency. In the opinion, Vice Chancellor Pitney explained that bank depositors have a right to

> rely upon the character of the directors and officers [and upon the representation] that they will perform their sworn duty to manage the affairs of the bank according to law and devote to its affairs the same diligent attention which ordinary, prudent, diligent men pay to their own affairs; and . . . such diligence and attention as experience has shown it is proper and necessary that bank directors should give to that business in order to reasonably protect the bank and its creditors against loss. [*Campbell v. Watson*]

Because N.J.S.A. 14A:6–14 is modeled in part upon section 717 of the New York statute, N.Y.Bus.Corp. Law § 717 (McKinney), we consider also the law of New York in interpreting the New Jersey statute.

Prior to the enactment of section 717, the New York courts, like those of New Jersey, had espoused the principle that directors owed that degree of care that a businessman of ordinary prudence would exercise in the management of his own affairs. In addition to requiring that directors act honestly and in good faith, the New York courts recognized that the nature and extent of reasonable care depended upon the type of corporation, its size and financial resources. Thus, a bank director was held to stricter accountability than the director of an ordinary business.[1]

In determining the limits of a director's duty, section 717 continued to recognize the individual characteristics of the corporation involved as well as the particular circumstances and corporate role of the director. Significantly, the legislative comment to section 717 states:

> The adoption of the standard prescribed by this section will allow the court to envisage the director's duty of care as a relative concept, depending on the kind of corporation involved, the particular circumstances and the corporate role of the director. [N.Y.Bus.Corp. Law § 717, comment (McKinney)]

. . .

As a general rule, a director should acquire at least a rudimentary understanding of the business of the corporation. Accordingly, a director should become familiar with the fundamentals of the business in which the corporation is engaged. Because directors are bound to exercise ordinary care, they cannot set up as a defense lack of the knowledge needed to exercise the requisite degree of care. If one "feels that he has not had sufficient business experience to qualify him to perform the duties of a director, he should either acquire the knowledge by inquiry, or refuse to act."

Directors are under a continuing obligation to keep informed about the activities of the corporation. Otherwise, they may not be able to participate in the overall management of corporate affairs. Directors may not shut their eyes to corporate misconduct and then claim that because they did not see the misconduct, they did not have a duty to look. The sentinel asleep at his post contributes nothing to the enterprise he is charged to protect.

Directorial management does not require a detailed inspection of day-to-day activities, but rather a general monitoring of corporate affairs and policies. Accordingly, a director is well advised to attend board meetings regularly. Indeed, a director who is absent from a board meeting is presumed to concur in action taken on a corporate matter, unless he files a "dissent with the secretary of the corporation within a reasonable time after learning of such action." N.J.S.A. 14A:6–13

---

1. The obligations of directors of banks involve some additional consideration because of their relationship to the public generally and directors in particular. Statutes impose certain requirements on bank directors. For example, directors of national banks must take an oath that they will diligently and honestly administer the affairs of the bank and will not permit violation of the banking laws. Moreover, they must satisfy certain requirements such as residence, citizenship, stockholdings and not serving as an investment banker. 12 U.S.C.A. §§ 77–78. *See generally* R. Barnett, *Responsibility & Liabilities of Bank Directors* (1980).

(Supp.1981–1982). Regular attendance does not mean that directors must attend every meeting, but that directors should attend meetings as a matter of practice. A director of a publicly held corporation might be expected to attend regular monthly meetings, but a director of a small, family corporation might be asked to attend only an annual meeting. The point is that one of the responsibilities of a director is to attend meetings of the board of which he or she is a member. That burden is lightened by N.J.S.A. 14A:6–7(2) (Supp.1981–1982), which permits board action without a meeting if all members of the board consent in writing.

While directors are not required to audit corporate books, they should maintain familiarity with the financial status of the corporation by a regular review of financial statements. In some circumstances, directors may be charged with assuring that bookkeeping methods conform to industry custom and usage. The extent of review, as well as the nature and frequency of financial statements, depends not only on the customs of the industry, but also on the nature of the corporation and the business in which it is engaged. Financial statements of some small corporations may be prepared internally and only on an annual basis; in a large publicly held corporation, the statements may be produced monthly or at some other regular interval. Adequate financial review normally would be more informal in a private corporation than in a publicly held corporation.

Of some relevance in this case is the circumstance that the financial records disclose the "shareholders' loans". Generally directors are immune from liability if, in good faith,

> they rely upon the opinion of counsel for the corporation or upon written reports setting forth financial data concerning the corporation and prepared by an independent public accountant or certified public accountant or firm of such accountants or upon financial statements, books of account or reports of the corporation represented to them to be correct by the president, the officer of the corporation having charge of its books of account, or the person presiding at a meeting of the board. [N.J.S.A. 14A:6–14]

The review of financial statements, however, may give rise to a duty to inquire further into matters revealed by those statements. Upon discovery of an illegal course of action, a director has a duty to object and, if the corporation does not correct the conduct, to resign.

In certain circumstances, the fulfillment of the duty of a director may call for more than mere objection and resignation. Sometimes a director may be required to seek the advice of counsel. One New Jersey case recognized the duty of a bank director to seek counsel where doubt existed about the meaning of the bank charter. The duty to seek the assistance of counsel can extend to areas other than the interpretation of corporation instruments. Modern corporate practice recognizes that on occasion a director should seek outside advice. A director may require legal advice concerning the propriety of his or her own conduct, the conduct of other officers and directors or the conduct of the corporation. In appropriate circumstances, a director would be "well advised to consult with regular corporate counsel (or his own legal adviser) at any time in which he is doubtful regarding proposed action...." Sometimes the duty of a director may require more than consulting with outside counsel. A director may have a duty to take reasonable means to prevent illegal conduct by co-directors; in any appropriate case, this may include threat of suit.

A director is not an ornament, but an essential component of corporate governance. Consequently, a director cannot protect himself behind a paper shield bearing the motto, "dummy director." The New Jersey Business Corporation Act, in imposing a standard of ordinary care on all directors, confirms that dummy, figurehead and accommodation directors are anachronisms with no place in New Jersey law. Similarly, in interpreting section 717, the New York courts have not exonerated a director who acts as an "accommodation." Thus, all directors are responsible for managing the business and affairs of the corporation.

The factors that impel expanded responsibility in the large, publicly held corporation may not be present in a small, close corporation. Nonetheless, a close corporation may, because of the nature of its business, be affected with a public interest. For example, the stock of a bank may be closely held, but because of the nature of banking the directors would be subject to greater liability than those of another close corporation. Even in a small corporation, a director is held to the standard of that degree of care that an ordinarily prudent director would use under the circumstances.

A director's duty of care does not exist in the abstract, but must be considered in relation to specific obligees. In general, the relationship of a corporate director to the corporation and its shareholders is that of a fiduciary. Shareholders have a right to expect that directors will exercise reasonable supervision and control over the policies and practices of a corporation. The institutional integrity of a corporation depends upon the proper discharge by directors of those duties.

While directors may owe a fiduciary duty to creditors also, that obligation generally has not been recognized in the absence of insolvency. With certain corporations, however, directors are seemed to owe a duty to creditors and other third parties even when the corporation is solvent. Although depositors of a bank are considered in some respects to be creditors, courts have recognized that directors may owe them a fiduciary duty. *See Campbell, supra.* Directors of nonbanking corporations may owe a similar duty when the corporation holds funds of others in trust....

The most striking circumstances affecting Mrs. Pritchard's duty as a director are the character of the reinsurance industry, the nature of the misappropriated funds and the financial condition of Pritchard & Baird. The hallmark of the reinsurance industry has been the unqualified trust and confidence reposed by ceding companies and reinsurers in reinsurance brokers. Those companies entrust money to reinsurance intermediaries with the justifiable expectation that the funds will be transmitted to the appropriate parties. Consequently, the companies could have assumed rightfully that Mrs. Pritchard, as a director of a reinsurance brokerage corporation, would not sanction the comingling and the conversion of loss and premium funds for the personal use of the principals of Pritchard & Baird.

As a reinsurance broker, Pritchard & Baird received annually as a fiduciary millions of dollars of clients' money which it was under a duty to segregate. To this extent, it resembled a bank rather than a small family business. Accordingly, Mrs. Pritchard's relationship to the clientele of Pritchard & Baird was akin to that of a director of a bank to its depositors. All parties agree that Pritchard & Baird held the misappropriated funds in an implied trust. That trust relationship gave rise to a fiduciary duty to guard the funds with fidelity and good faith.

As a director of a substantial reinsurance brokerage corporation, she should have known that it received annually millions of dollars of loss and premium funds which it held in trust for ceding and reinsurance companies. Mrs. Pritchard should have obtained and read the annual statements of financial condition of Pritchard & Baird. Although she had a right to rely upon financial statements prepared in accordance with N.J.S.A. 14A:6–14, such reliance would not excuse her conduct. The reason is that those statements disclosed on their face the misappropriation of trust funds.

From those statements, she should have realized that, as of January 31, 1970, her sons were withdrawing substantial trust funds under the guise of "Shareholders' Loans." The financial statements for each fiscal year commencing with that of January 31, 1970, disclosed that the working capital deficits and the "loans" were escalating in tandem. Detecting a misappropriation of funds would not have required special expertise or extraordinary diligence; a cursory reading of the financial statements would have revealed the pillage. Thus, if Mrs. Pritchard had read the financial statements, she would have known that her sons were converting trust funds. When financial statements demonstrate that insiders are bleeding a corporation to death, a director should notice and try to stanch the flow of blood.

In summary, Mrs. Pritchard was charged with the obligation of basic knowledge and supervision of the business of Pritchard & Baird. Under the circumstances, this obligation included reading and understanding financial statements, and making reasonable attempts at detection and prevention of the illegal conduct of other officers and directors. She had a duty to protect the clients of Pritchard & Baird against policies and practices that would result in the misappropriation of money they had entrusted to the corporation. She breached that duty.

IV

Nonetheless, the negligence of Mrs. Pritchard does not result in liability unless it is a proximate cause of the loss. Analysis of proximate cause requires an initial determination of cause-in-fact. Causation-in-fact calls for a finding that the defendant's act or omission was a necessary antecedent of the loss, *i.e.,* that if the defendant had observed his or her duty of care, the loss would not have occurred. Further, the plaintiff has the burden of establishing the amount of the loss or damages caused by the negligence of the defendant. Thus, the plaintiff must establish not only a breach of duty, "but in addition that the performance by the director of his duty would have avoided loss, and the amount of the resulting loss."

Cases involving nonfeasance present a much more difficult causation question than those in which the director has committed an affirmative act of negligence leading to the loss. Analysis in cases of negligent omissions calls for determination of the reasonable steps a director should have taken and whether that course of action would have averted the loss.

Usually a director can absolve himself from liability by informing the other directors of the impropriety and voting for a proper course of action. Conversely, a director who votes for or concurs in certain actions may be "liable to the corporation for the benefit of its creditors or shareholders, to the extent of any injuries suffered by such persons, respectively, as a result of any such action." N.J.S.A. 14A:6–12 (Supp.1981–1982). A director who is present at a board meeting is presumed to concur in corporate action taken at the meeting unless his dissent is entered in the minutes of the meeting or filed promptly after adjournment. N.J.S.A. 14:6–13. In many, if not most, instances an objecting director whose dissent is noted in accordance with N.J.S.A. 14:6–13 would be absolved after attempting to persuade fellow directors to follow a different course of action.

Even accepting the hypothesis that Mrs. Pritchard might not be liable if she had objected and resigned, there are two significant reasons for holding her liable. First, she did not resign until just before the bankruptcy. Consequently, there is no factual basis for the speculation that the losses would have occurred even if she had objected and resigned. Indeed, the trial court reached the opposite conclusion: "The actions of the sons were so blatantly wrongful that it is hard to see how they could have resisted any moderately firm objection to what they were doing." Second, the nature of the reinsurance business distinguishes it from most other commercial activities in that reinsurance brokers are encumbered by fiduciary duties owed to third parties. In other corporations, a director's duty normally does not extend beyond the shareholders to third parties.

In this case, the scope of Mrs. Pritchard's duties was determined by the precarious financial condition of Pritchard & Baird, its fiduciary relationship to its clients and the implied trust in which it held their funds. Thus viewed, the scope of her duties encompassed all reasonable action to stop the continuing conversion. Her duties extended beyond mere objection and resignation to reasonable attempts to prevent the misappropriation of the trust funds.

A leading case discussing causation where the director's liability is predicated upon a negligent failure to act is *Barnes v. Andrews*. In that case the court exonerated a figurehead director who served for eight months on a board that held one meeting after his election, a meeting he was forced to miss because of the death of his mother.

Writing for the court, Judge Learned Hand distinguished a director who fails to prevent general mismanagement from one such as Mrs. Pritchard who failed to stop an illegal "loan":

> When the corporate funds have been illegally lent, it is a fair inference that a protest would have stopped the loan, and that the director's neglect caused the loss. But when a business fails from general mismanagement, business incapacity, or bad judgment, how is it possible to say that a single director could have made the company successful, or how much in dollars he could have saved?

Pointing out the absence of proof of proximate cause between defendant's negligence and the company's insolvency, Judge Hand also wrote:

> The plaintiff must, however, go further than to show that [the director] should have been more active in his duties. This cause of action rests upon a tort, as much though it be a tort of omission as though it had rested upon a positive act. The plaintiff must accept the burden of showing that the performance of the defendant's duties would have avoided loss, and what loss it would have avoided.

. . .

In assessing whether Mrs. Pritchard's conduct was a legal or proximate cause of the conversion, "[l]egal responsibility must be limited to those causes which are so closely connected with the result and of such significance that the law is justified in imposing liability." Such a judicial determination involves not only considerations of causation-in-fact and matters of policy, but also common sense and logic. The act or the failure to act must be a substantial factor in producing the harm.

Within Pritchard & Baird, several factors contributed to the loss of the funds: comingling of corporate and client monies, conversion of funds by Charles, Jr. and William and dereliction of her duties by Mrs. Pritchard. The wrongdoing of her sons, although the immediate cause of the loss, should not excuse Mrs. Pritchard from her negligence which also was a substantial factor contributing to the loss. Her sons knew that she, the only other director, was not reviewing their conduct; they spawned their fraud in the backwater of her neglect. Her neglect of duty contributed to the climate of corruption; her failure to act contributed to the continuation of that corruption. Consequently, her conduct was a substantial factor contributing to the loss.

Analysis of proximate cause is especially difficult in a corporate context where the allegation is that nonfeasance of a director is a proximate cause of damage to a third party. Where a case involves nonfeasance, no one can say "with absolute certainty what would have occurred if the defendant had acted otherwise." Nonetheless, where it is reasonable to conclude that the failure to act would produce a particular result and that result has followed, causation may be inferred. We conclude that even if Mrs. Pritchard's mere objection had not stopped the depredations of her sons, her consultation with an attorney and the threat of suit would have deterred them. That conclusion flows as a matter of common sense and logic from the record. Whether in other situations a director has a duty to do more than protest and resign is best left to case-by-case determinations. In this case, we are satisfied that there was a duty to do more than object and resign. Consequently, we find that Mrs. Pritchard's negligence was a proximate cause of the misappropriations.

To conclude, by virtue of her office, Mrs. Pritchard had the power to prevent the losses sustained by the clients of Pritchard & Baird. With power comes responsibility. She had a duty to deter the depredation of the other insiders, her sons. She breached that duty and caused plaintiffs to sustain damages.

The judgment of the Appellate Division is affirmed.

Questions

1. What should Mrs. Pritchard have known about the corporation, and when?

2. What does the court think Mrs. Pritchard should have done under the circumstances? Do its expectations seem fair to you? Could she have stopped her sons? Does your answer to this question suggest something about the wisdom of boards composed of family members?

3. Why do you suppose the court holds Mrs. Pritchard liable? Can you state the elements required to prove a breach of the duty to monitor?

4. The case provides a directors' handbook. What does a director need to do in order to fulfill her duty of care?

5. What led the court to conclude that Mrs. Pritchard was liable to third parties (rather than the corporation's shareholders)? Do you think the case creates a general rule for such liability of directors? If so, what is that rule?

Senn v. Northwest Underwriters Inc.

875 P.2d 637 (Wash. App. 1994)

[Consumers Indemnity Company ("Consumers") was an insurance company that reimbursed car dealers for repairs done under warranty. Northwest Underwriters ("Underwriters") collected all premium payments from insured dealers on behalf of Consumers. Underwriters received a commission of 2% of each premium and received $60 for each claim paid and administered by Underwriters. All of Consumers' and Underwriters' stock was held by Cimoch, Inc., which in turn was owned by Norman and Mary Ann Cimoch. Norman and Mary Ann were directors of both Consumers and Underwriters. Norman was also president and chairman of both Consumers and Underwriters. Evidently, Norman diverted funds due to be paid by Underwriters to Consumers (under the Insured Service Contract (ISC) policy) to an account in Underwriters, retaining for himself substantial money. After Consumers went into receivership, the receiver brought an action against the Cimochs. Mary

Ann pleaded complete ignorance, much in the same way Mrs. Pritchard's representatives did.]

AGID, Judge

II. Cimoch's Liability for Underwriters' Defalcation

. . .

The final issue is whether Cimoch's breach was, as a matter of law, a proximate cause of Consumers' loss.

Proximate causation consists of two elements: cause in fact and legal causation. Cause in fact concerns the "but for" consequences of an act: those events the act produced in a direct, unbroken sequence, and which would not have resulted had the act not occurred. Legal causation rests on considerations of policy and common sense as to how far the defendant's responsibility for the consequences of its actions should extend. The question of legal causation is so intertwined with the question of duty that the former can be answered by addressing the latter.

We have already determined that Cimoch owed a statutory fiduciary duty to Consumers. We further hold that those same reasons of logic and public policy require that she be held liable for any damages flowing from a breach of that duty which is a cause in fact of the damage.

In determining the proper standard to apply to a case involving nonfeasance, we again turn to *Francis v. United Jersey Bank* for guidance. There, the court examined the scope of the duties of a director and held that, under the circumstances of that case, it extended beyond the duty to object, vote for the correct action and/or resign, actions which will normally absolve a director from liability. Because the conversions were "so blatantly wrongful" that the other directors would have had to stop if confronted and because the business owed a duty to third parties, the insureds, the Court held that Mrs. Pritchard's duties as a director "encompassed all reasonable action to stop the continuing conversion." The same factors are present here. The fraud was similarly blatant, and Consumers' directors, like those of Pritchard & Baird in the *Francis* case, owed a duty not only to the company but also to those it purported to insure. Thus, we conclude that Cimoch was required to take reasonable steps to stop the continuing course of conduct. She took none.[11]

---

11. We do not undertake to establish the extent and scope of an officer's or director's duty to prevent defalcations of other officers or directors. Because Cimoch failed entirely to take any action, that issue is not presented by this case. However, as the court in *Francis* noted, an individual in her position could be expected to do a number of things to prevent losses to the company to which she owes a duty. At a minimum, a director has a duty to make an objection to the other officers. She may also be required to resign in protest against those actions. In some instances, she may be required to consult with an attorney and even sue or threaten to sue the other directors in order to halt their activity. As the court noted in *Francis*, the determination of the extent of a director's duty to act is best left to a case-by-case determination.

We next address the question of cause in fact. Cimoch's liability is limited to the loss that was the "but for" consequence of her failure to act. The question, as phrased by Judge Learned Hand in *Barnes v. Andrews*, is whether "the performance of the defendant's duties would have avoided loss, and what loss it would have avoided." Where, as here, "the corporate funds have been illegally lent, it is a fair inference that a protest would have stopped the loan, and that the director's neglect caused the loss." Given the size of the diversion and Cimoch's substantial nonfeasance, the trial court properly inferred causation as a matter of law. Had Cimoch been even minimally involved in Consumers' affairs, she would have been on inquiry notice that funds were being diverted. Had she reviewed Consumers' records, she would have immediately discovered the diversion of ISC policy money because, instead of receiving approximately $300 for each warranty contract, Consumers was receiving only $20 per contract. This represents a 95 percent diversion of this portion of Consumers' insurance business and a 40 percent diversion of total ISC premiums. She also would have discovered that between June 1987 and September 1988, $30.3 million was paid by dealers for ISC insurance coverage, but Consumers only received $18 million.

Summary judgment is appropriate where no genuine issue of material fact exists and where the moving party is entitled to judgment as a matter of law. CR 56(c). In evaluating a motion for summary judgment, all reasonable inferences are to be construed against the moving party, and the motion should only be granted if, from all the evidence, reasonable persons could only reach one conclusion. Even viewing the evidence in the light most favorable to Cimoch, the diversion was so large that, had she discharged her duties as an officer and director, she would have noticed it and been in a position to take all reasonable actions to stop it.[12] Her failure to do so was a proximate cause of Consumers' loss, and summary judgment was properly granted.[13] . . .

Questions

1. Does it seem fair for the court to state, as it does in footnote 12, that causation will be inferred as a matter of law in cases of directorial inaction?

---

12. Because we hold that causation will be inferred as a matter of law where a fiduciary has a duty to inquire and act but fails to do so, there is no factual issue for a jury to resolve. The question of the extent of her liability would be a factual issue had she discovered the defalcation and taken some action. Only then would there be a question as to whether her action was appropriate and, if not, how much of the loss she could have prevented.

13. Cimoch further argues she is shielded from liability by the business judgment rule. She argues that even if a mistake was made in implementing the Reserve Program, the inference should be that it was made in good faith because of the similarity between it and another Consumers program. Again, Cimoch is confusing the issue of her personal liability for her breach of her own fiduciary duty with liability for the actions of Norman Cimoch. As discussed above, the pertinent issue in this case is Cimoch's liability for her own actions. Furthermore, as the Commissioner points out, the business judgment rule applies where a loss results from a decision or action by an officer or director, not "where the loss is the result of failure to exercise proper care, skill and diligence."

2. Are there circumstances in which it would be unreasonable to infer causation as a matter of law? What if the negligent director(s) were on the board of a large corporation with decentralized management structure? Do you think the court would take the same approach?

B. The Business Judgment Rule

Kamin v. American Express Company
383 N.Y.S.2d 807 (1st Dept. 1976)

GREENFIELD, Justice

In this stockholders' derivative action, the individual defendants, who are the directors of the American Express Company, move for an order dismissing the complaint for failure to state a cause of action, and alternatively, for summary judgment. . . .

The complaint is brought derivatively by two minority stockholders of the American Express Company, asking for a declaration that a certain dividend in kind is a waste of corporate assets, directing the defendants not to proceed with the distribution, or, in the alternative, for monetary damages. The motion to dismiss the complaint requires the Court to presuppose the truth of the allegations. It is the defendants' contention that, conceding everything in the complaint, no viable cause of action is made out.

After establishing the identity of the parties, the complaint alleges that in 1972 American Express acquired for investment 1,954,418 shares of common stock of Donaldson, Lufken and Jenrette, Inc. (hereafter DLJ), a publicly traded corporation, at a cost of $29.9 million. It is further alleged that the current market value of those shares is approximately $4.0 million. On July 28, 1975, it is alleged, the Board of Directors of American Express declared a special dividend to all stockholders of record pursuant to which the shares of DLJ would be distributed in kind. Plaintiffs contend further that if American Express were to sell the DLJ shares on the market, it would sustain a capital loss of $25 million, which could be offset against taxable capital gains on other investments. Such a sale, they allege, would result in tax savings to the company of approximately $8 million, which would not be available in the case of the distribution of DLJ shares to stockholders. It is alleged that on October 8, 1975 and October 16, 1975, plaintiffs demanded that the directors rescind the previously declared dividend in DLJ shares and take steps to preserve the capital loss which would result from selling the shares. This demand was rejected by the Board of Directors on October 17, 1975.

It is apparent that all the previously-mentioned allegations of the complaint go to the question of the exercise by the Board of Directors of business judgment in deciding how to deal with the DLJ shares. The crucial allegation which must be scrutinized to determine the legal sufficiency of the complaint is paragraph 19, which alleges:

> "19. All of the defendant Directors engaged in or acquiesced in or negligently permitted the declaration and payment of the Dividend in violation of the fiduciary duty owed by them to Amex to care for and preserve Amex's assets in the same manner as a man of average prudence would care for his own property."

Plaintiffs never moved for temporary injunctive relief, and did nothing to bar the actual distribution of the DLJ shares. The dividend was in fact paid on October 31, 1975. Accordingly, that portion of the complaint seeking a direction not to distribute the shares is deemed to be moot, and the Court will deal only with the request for declaratory judgment or for damages.

Examination of the complaint reveals that there is no claim of fraud or self-dealing, and no contention that there was any bad faith or oppressive conduct. The law is quite clear as to what is necessary to ground a claim for actionable wrongdoing.

> "In actions by stockholders, which assail the acts of their directors or trustees, courts will not interfere unless the powers have been illegally or unconscientiously executed; or unless it be made to appear that the acts were fraudulent or collusive, and destructive of the rights of the stockholders. Mere errors of judgment are not sufficient as grounds for equity interference, for the powers of those entrusted with corporate management are largely discretionary." *Leslie v. Lorillard*.

More specifically, the question of whether or not a dividend is to be declared or a distribution of some kind should be made is exclusively a matter of business judgment for the Board of Directors.

> "... Courts will not interfere with such discretion unless it be first made to appear that the directors have acted or are about to act in bad faith and for a dishonest purpose. It is for the directors to say, acting in good faith of course, when and to what extent dividends shall be declared.... The statute confers upon the directors this power, and the minority stockholders are not in a position to question this right, so long as the directors are acting in good faith...." *Liebman v. Auto Strop Co.*

Thus, a complaint must be dismissed if all that is presented is a decision to pay dividends rather than pursuing some other course of conduct. A complaint which alleges merely that some course of action other than that pursued by the Board of Directors would have been more advantageous gives rise to no cognizable cause of action. Courts have more than enough to do in adjudicating legal rights and devising remedies for wrongs. The directors' room rather than the courtroom is the appropriate forum for thrashing out purely business questions which will have an impact on profits, market prices, competitive situations, or tax advantages. As stated by Cardozo, J., when sitting at Special Term, the substitution of someone else's business judgment for that of the directors "is no business for any court to follow." *Holmes v. St. Joseph Lead Co.*

It is not enough to allege, as plaintiffs do here, that the directors made an imprudent decision, which did not capitalize on the possibility of using a potential capital loss to offset capital gains. More than imprudence or mistaken judgment must be shown.

> "Questions of policy of management, expediency of contracts or action, adequacy of consideration, lawful appropriation of corporate funds to advance corporate interests, are left solely to their honest and unselfish decision, for their powers therein are without limitation and free from restraint, and the exercise of them for the common and general interests of the corporation may not be questioned, although the results show that what they did was unwise or inexpedient." *Pollitz v. Wabash Railroad Co.*

Section 720(a)(1)(A) of the Business Corporation Law permits an action against directors for "the neglect of, or failure to perform, or other violation of his duties in the management and disposition of corporate assets committed to his charge." This does not mean that a director is chargeable with ordinary negligence for having made an improper decision, or having acted imprudently. The "neglect" referred to in the statute is neglect of duties (i.e., malfeasance or nonfeasance) and not misjudgment. To allege that a director "negligently permitted the declaration and payment" of a dividend without alleging fraud, dishonesty or nonfeasance, is to state merely that a decision was taken with which one disagrees.

Nor does this appear to a be a case in which a potentially valid cause of action is inartfully stated. The defendants have moved alternatively for summary judgment and have submitted affidavits under CPLR 3211(c), and plaintiffs likewise have submitted papers enlarging upon the allegations of the complaint. The affidavits of the defendants and the exhibits annexed thereto demonstrate that the objections raised by the plaintiffs to the proposed dividend action were carefully considered and unanimously rejected by the Board at a special meeting called precisely for that purpose at the plaintiffs' request. The minutes of the special meeting indicate that the defendants were fully aware that a sale rather than a distribution of the DLJ shares might result in the realization of a substantial income tax saving. Nevertheless, they concluded that there were countervailing considerations primarily with respect to the adverse effect such a sale, realizing a loss of $25 million, would have on the net income figures in the American Express financial statement. Such a reduction of net income would have a serious effect on the market value of the publicly traded American Express stock. This was not a situation in which the defendant directors totally overlooked facts called to their attention. They gave them consideration, and attempted to view the total picture in arriving at their decision. While plaintiffs contend that according to their accounting consultants the loss on the DLJ stock would still have to be charged against current earnings even if the stock were distributed, the defendants' accounting experts assert that the loss would be a charge against earnings only in the event of a sale, whereas in the event of distribution of the stock as a dividend, the proper accounting treatment would be to charge the loss only against surplus. While the chief accountant for the SEC raised some question as to the appropriate accounting treatment of this transaction, there was no basis for any action to be taken by the SEC with respect to the American Express financial statement.

The only hint of self-interest which is raised, not in the complaint but in the papers on the motion, is that four of the twenty directors were officers and employees of American Express and members of its Executive Incentive Compensation Plan. Hence, it is suggested, by virtue of the action taken earnings may have been overstated and their compensation affected thereby. Such a claim is highly speculative and standing alone can hardly be regarded as sufficient to support an inference of self-dealing. There is no claim or showing that the four company directors dominated and controlled the sixteen outside members of the Board. Certainly, every action taken by the Board has some impact on earnings and may therefore affect the compensation of those whose earnings are keyed to profits. That does not disqualify the inside directors, nor does it put every policy adopted by the Board in question. All directors have an obligation, using sound business judgment, to maximize income for the benefit of all persons having a stake in the welfare of the corporate entity. What we have here as revealed both by the complaint and by the affidavits and exhibits, is that a disagreement exists between two minority stockholders and a unanimous Board of Directors as to the best way to handle a loss already incurred on an investment. The directors are entitled to exercise their honest business judgment on the information before them, and to act within their corporate powers. That they may be mistaken, that other courses of action might have differing consequences, or that their action might benefit some shareholders more than others presents no basis for the superimposition of judicial judgment, so long as it appears that the directors have been acting in good faith. The question of to what extent a dividend shall be declared and the manner in which it shall be paid is ordinarily subject only to the qualification that the dividend be paid out of surplus (Business Corporation Law Section 510, subd. b). The Court will not interfere unless a clear case is made out of fraud, oppression, arbitrary action, or breach of trust. . . .

In this case it clearly appears that the plaintiffs have failed as a matter of law to make out an actionable claim. Accordingly, the motion by the defendants for summary judgment and dismissal of the complaint is granted.

Questions

1. Does the reason given by the American Express board for its action make sense? If you were a stockholder, how would you expect the American Express stock price to behave once the news of the DLJ price decline was public but before the financials were actually issued?

2. How might you see the board's decision as being in the best interest of the company and its stockholders? Does the case suggest any reason why the board

might have incentives to make a decision that is not in the best interest of the company and its stockholders?

3. Why do you think the court concluded that because the board was composed of a majority of outside directors, the board's decision was in the best interest of the company and its stockholders? Do you agree? Bernard Black and Sanjai Bhagat have used empirical evidence to demonstrate that independent directors make little if any difference in the actual financial performance of a corporation. Sanjai Bhagat and Bernard S. Black, *The Non-Correlation Between Board Independence and Long-Term Firm Performance*, 27 J. CORP. LAW 231 (2002). Their evidence suggests that independent boards may result in poorer corporate performance than do other kinds of boards. Lawrence Mitchell has explained these results in terms of economic sociology, and particularly the network-derived theory of structural holes, suggesting that corporations with independent boards have strong CEOs because the board is dependent upon the CEO for its information (which the CEO can control and manipulate), whereas in corporations with inside boards, the inside directors have their own independent ties into the networks of corporate officers which provide them with information sources independent of the CEO and also allow them to serve as information sources to outsiders on the board. Lawrence E. Mitchell, *Structural Holes, CEOs, and the Missing Link in Corporate Governance*, 70 BROOKLYN L. REV. 1313 (2005).

4. What does the standard of care appear to be? How does it compare with other standards of care with which you are familiar?

Joy v. North
692 F.2d 880 (2d Cir. 1982)

WINTER, Judge

. . .

A. The Liability of Corporate Directors and Officers and the Business Judgment Rule

While it is often stated that corporate directors and officers will be liable for negligence in carrying out their corporate duties, all seem agreed that such a statement is misleading. Whereas an automobile driver who makes a mistake in judgment as to speed or distance injuring a pedestrian will likely be called upon to respond in damages, a corporate officer who makes a mistake in judgment as to economic conditions, consumer tastes or production line efficiency will rarely, if ever, be found liable for damages suffered by the corporation. Whatever the terminology, the fact is that liability is rarely imposed upon corporate directors or officers simply for bad judgment and this reluctance to impose liability for unsuccessful business decisions has been doctrinally labeled the business judgment rule. Although the rule has suffered under academic criticism, it is not without rational basis.

First, shareholders to a very real degree voluntarily undertake the risk of bad business judgment. Investors need not buy stock, for investment markets offer an array of opportunities less vulnerable to mistakes in judgment by corporate officers. Nor need investors buy stock in particular corporations. In the exercise of what is genuinely a free choice, the quality of a firm's management is often decisive and information is available from professional advisors. Since shareholders can and do select among investments partly on the basis of management, the business judgment rule merely recognizes a certain voluntariness in undertaking the risk of bad business decisions.

Second, courts recognize that after-the-fact litigation is a most imperfect device to evaluate corporate business decisions. The circumstances surrounding a corporate decision are not easily reconstructed in a courtroom years later, since business imperatives often call for quick decisions, inevitably based on less than perfect information. The entrepreneur's function is to encounter risks and to confront uncertainty, and a reasoned decision at the time made may seem a wild hunch viewed years later against a background of perfect knowledge.

Third, because potential profit often corresponds to the potential risk, it is very much in the interest of shareholders that the law not create incentives for overly cautious corporate decisions. Some opportunities offer great profits at the risk of very substantial losses, while the alternatives offer less risk of loss but also less potential profit. Shareholders can reduce the volatility[5] of risk by diversifying their holdings. In the case of the diversified shareholder, the seemingly more risky alternatives may well be the best choice since great losses in some stocks will over time be offset by even greater gains in others.[6] Given mutual funds and similar forms of diversified investment, courts need not bend over backwards to give special protection to shareholders who refuse to reduce the volatility of risk by not diversifying. A rule which

---

5. For purposes of this opinion, "volatility" is "the degree of dispersion or variation of possible outcomes." Klein, *Business Organization and Finance* 147 (1980).

6. Consider the choice between two investments in an example adapted from Klein, *Business Organization and Finance* 147–49 (1980):

INVESTMENT A			INVESTMENT B		
Estimated Probability of Outcome	Outcome Profit or Loss	Value	Estimated Probability of Outcome	Outcome Profit or Loss	Value
.4	+15	6.0	.4	+6	2.4
.4	+1	.4	.4	+2	.8
.2	−13	−2.6	.2	+1	.2
1.0		3.8	1.0		3.4

Although A is clearly "worth" more than B, it is riskier because it is more volatile. Diversification lessens the volatility by allowing investors to invest in 20 or 200 A's which will tend to guarantee a total result near the value. Shareholders are thus better off with the various firms selecting investment A over B, although after the fact they will complain in each case of the 2.6 loss. If the courts did not abide by the business judgment rule, they might well penalize the choice of A in each such case and thereby unknowingly injure shareholders generally by creating incentives for management always to choose B.

penalizes the choice of seemingly riskier alternatives thus may not be in the interest of shareholders generally.

Whatever its merit, however, the business judgment rule extends only as far as the reasons which justify its existence. Thus, it does not apply in cases, *e.g.*, in which the corporate decision lacks a business purpose, is tainted by a conflict of interest, is so egregious as to amount to a no-win decision, or results from an obvious and prolonged failure to exercise oversight or supervision. Other examples may occur....

Questions

1. What assumptions underlie Judge Winter's reasoning? How valid or plausible are they?

2. What are the implications of Judge Winter's reasoning? For stockholders? For corporate law? For the market as a whole?

3. The facts of *Joy v. North* involved a bank making and continuing to extend improvident loans until the bank suffered losses exceeding ten percent of its capital. While there were undertones of conflict of interest (the chairman's son worked for the borrower), what other reasons might the bank have had to do this? What role do financial institutions play in coordinating American business? Are the risks involved the kinds of risks that shareholders voluntarily undertake?

4. In articulating a basis for the business judgment rule, courts often state that they are not business experts and therefore not equipped to second-guess business decisions. Is this a plausible justification? Are courts medical experts? They decide medical malpractice cases. Are they engineering experts? They decide engineering malpractice cases. Are they manufacturing experts? They decide products liability cases. Are they telecommunications experts, computer experts, economists? Yet they decide these and a wide variety of other cases that centrally involve disciplines in which judges are not experts. What makes business cases different?

5. Judge Winter's opinion is influenced by the Capital Asset Pricing Model, which was developed in second half of the twentieth century. In the 1950s, Harry Markowitz's portfolio theory suggested that investors could create "an efficient portfolio," that is, a portfolio that would achieve maximum return for any level of preferred risk by diversifying non-systematic risks. The portfolio, rather than individual corporations, became the focus of analysis. In the mid-1960s, William Sharpe and John Lintner's Capital Asset Pricing Model (CAPM) indicated that even systematic risks that affect the market as a whole could be diversified. Rather than study the fundamentals of companies in which they sought to invest, investors were told to study the historical performance of their companies' stock price in relation to the market.

The judiciary's embrace of CAPM happened concurrently with the development of mutual funds and the rapid growth in institutional investors' stock ownership. As Judge Winter reasoned, because rational shareholders would offset their exposure to business misfortunes by diversifying their portfolios (as modern finance theory dictated), corporate law did not need to protect them from such letdowns. For a short summary of the development of modern finance theory and CAPM, see Roberta Romano, *Corporate Law after the Revolution in Corporate Law*, 55 J. OF LEGAL ED. 342–59 (2005).

6. For Delaware's concurrence with Judge Winter's reasoning, see *Gagliardi v. Tri-Foods International, Inc.*, where Chancellor Allen reasoned that shareholders "can diversify the risks of their corporate investments." It was, "[t]hus in their economic interest for the corporation to accept in rank order all positive net present value investment projects available to the corporation, starting with the *highest risk adjusted rate of return first*." Given that making risky investments was in the rational investor's best interests, it was also:

> [I]n the shareholders' economic interest to offer sufficient protection to directors from liability for negligence, etc., to allow directors to conclude that, as a practical matter, there is no risk that, if they act in good faith and meet minimal proceduralist standards of attention, they can face liability as a result of a business loss.

Gagliardi v. TriFoods Int'l, Inc., 683 A.2d 1049 (Del. Ch. 1996).

7. CAPM relies upon the existence of an efficient market for stock, frequently referred to as an efficient capital market. Judge Winter's opinion assumes the substantial correctness of the Efficient Capital Market Hypothesis (ECMH). According to ECMH, with sufficiently wide market participation, sufficient numbers of shares, and sufficient information, capital markets will be efficient, that is, the price of a share of stock at any given point in time will be the "correct" price. There are three variations on ECMH: The strong form, which almost nobody accepts, holds that at any given time a stock's price will reflect all information known about a corporation, whether that information is publicly known or privately held. Note how obviously implausible this theory is — were it true, nobody could achieve better than average profits from investing in stock, not even those who trade on inside information. Since we know that insider trading can be profitable (if illegal), the strong form can't be right. The semi-strong form holds that the stock's price incorporates all past information about the company as well as all currently available public information. This is more plausible, especially in the computer age where instantaneous price information is available to almost everybody. Thus, as soon as news about a corporation becomes public, attentive traders can act immediately, and if they do so in sufficient numbers, this will affect the share price almost immediately in a way that will prevent any but the first informed from profiting on (or avoiding losses on) the news. Finally, there is the most plausible (indeed almost undeniable) version of the theory, the weak form, which says that all past information about a corporation is incorporated in its stock price. This version of the theory doesn't tell us much about the potential profits from trading, since gains are to be made in the future, not the past.

C. The Business Judgment Rule and the Duty of Care

Smith v. Van Gorkom
488 A.2d 858 (Del. 1985)

Horsey, Justice (for the majority)

This appeal from the Court of Chancery involves a class action brought by shareholders of the defendant Trans Union Corporation ("Trans Union" or "the Company"), originally seeking rescission of a cash-out merger of Trans Union into the defendant New T Company ("New T"), a wholly-owned subsidiary of the defendant, Marmon Group, Inc. ("Marmon"). Alternate relief in the form of damages is sought against the defendant members of the Board of Directors of Trans Union, New T, and Jay A. Pritzker and Robert A. Pritzker, owners of Marmon.

Following trial, the former Chancellor granted judgment for the defendant directors by unreported letter opinion dated July 6, 1982. Judgment was based on two findings: (1) that the Board of Directors had acted in an informed manner so as to be entitled to protection of the business judgment rule in approving the cash-out merger; and (2) that the shareholder vote approving the merger should not be set aside because the stockholders had been "fairly informed" by the Board of Directors before voting thereon. The plaintiffs appeal.

Speaking for the majority of the Court, we conclude that both rulings of the Court of Chancery are clearly erroneous. Therefore, we reverse and direct that judgment be entered in favor of the plaintiffs and against the defendant directors for the fair value of the plaintiffs' stockholdings in Trans Union....

We hold: (1) that the Board's decision, reached September 20, 1980, to approve the proposed cash-out merger was not the product of an informed business judgment; (2) that the Board's subsequent efforts to amend the Merger Agreement and take other curative action were ineffectual, both legally and factually; and (3) that the Board did not deal with complete candor with the stockholders by failing to disclose all material facts, which they knew or should have known, before securing the stockholders' approval of the merger.

The nature of this case requires a detailed factual statement. The following facts are essentially uncontradicted:

-A-

Trans Union was a publicly-traded, diversified holding company, the principal earnings of which were generated by its railcar leasing business. During the period here involved, the Company had a cash flow of hundreds of millions of dollars annually. However, the Company had difficulty in generating sufficient taxable income to offset increasingly large investment tax credits (ITCs)....

Beginning in the late 1960's, and continuing through the 1970's, Trans Union pursued a program of acquiring small companies in order to increase available taxable income. In July 1980, Trans Union Management prepared the annual revision of the

Company's Five Year Forecast. This report was presented to the Board of Directors at its July, 1980 meeting. The report projected an annual income growth of about 20%. The report also concluded that Trans Union would have about $195 million in spare cash between 1980 and 1985, "with the surplus growing rapidly from 1982 onward." The report referred to the ITC situation as a "nagging problem" and, given that problem, the leasing company "would still appear to be constrained to a tax breakeven." The report then listed four alternative uses of the projected 1982–1985 equity surplus: (1) stock repurchase; (2) dividend increases; (3) a major acquisition program; and (4) combinations of the above. The sale of Trans Union was not among the alternatives. The report emphasized that, despite the overall surplus, the operation of the Company would consume all available equity for the next several years, and concluded: "As a result, we have sufficient time to fully develop our course of action."

-B-

On August 27, 1980, Van Gorkom met with Senior Management of Trans Union. Van Gorkom reported on his lobbying efforts in Washington and his desire to find a solution to the tax credit problem more permanent than a continued program of acquisitions. Various alternatives were suggested and discussed preliminarily, including the sale of Trans Union to a company with a large amount of taxable income.

Donald Romans, Chief Financial Officer of Trans Union, stated that his department had done a "very brief bit of work on the possibility of a leveraged buy-out." This work had been prompted by a media article which Romans had seen regarding a leveraged buy-out by management. The work consisted of a "preliminary study" of the cash which could be generated by the Company if it participated in a leveraged buy-out. As Romans stated, this analysis "was very first and rough cut at seeing whether a cash flow would support what might be considered a high price for this type of transaction."

On September 5, at another Senior Management meeting which Van Gorkom attended, Romans again brought up the idea of a leveraged buy-out as a "possible strategic alternative" to the Company's acquisition program. Romans and Bruce S. Chelberg, President and Chief Operating Officer of Trans Union, had been working on the matter in preparation for the meeting. According to Romans: They did not "come up" with a price for the Company. They merely "ran the numbers" at $50 a share and at $60 a share with the "rough form" of their cash figures at the time. Their "figures indicated that $50 would be very easy to do but $60 would be very difficult to do under those figures." This work did not purport to establish a fair price for either the Company or 100% of the stock. It was intended to determine the cash flow needed to service the debt that would "probably" be incurred in a leveraged buy-out, based on "rough calculations" without "any benefit of experts to identify what the limits were to that, and so forth." These computations were not considered extensive and no conclusion was reached.

At this meeting, Van Gorkom stated that he would be willing to take $55 per share for his own 75,000 shares. He vetoed the suggestion of a leveraged buy-out by

Management, however, as involving a potential conflict of interest for Management. Van Gorkom, a certified public accountant and lawyer, had been an officer of Trans Union for 24 years, its Chief Executive Officer for more than 17 years, and Chairman of its Board for 2 years. It is noteworthy in this connection that he was then approaching 65 years of age and mandatory retirement.

For several days following the September 5 meeting, Van Gorkom pondered the idea of a sale. He had participated in many acquisitions as a manager and director of Trans Union and as a director of other companies. He was familiar with acquisition procedures, valuation methods, and negotiations; and he privately considered the pros and cons of whether Trans Union should seek a privately or publicly-held purchaser.

Van Gorkom decided to meet with Jay A. Pritzker, a well-known corporate takeover specialist and a social acquaintance. However, rather than approaching Pritzker simply to determine his interest in acquiring Trans Union, Van Gorkom assembled a proposed per share price for sale of the Company and a financing structure by which to accomplish the sale. Van Gorkom did so without consulting either his Board or any members of Senior Management except one: Carl Peterson, Trans Union's Controller. Telling Peterson that he wanted no other person on his staff to know what he was doing, but without telling him why, Van Gorkom directed Peterson to calculate the feasibility of a leveraged buy-out at an assumed price per share of $55. Apart from the Company's historic stock market price, and Van Gorkom's long association with Trans Union, the record is devoid of any competent evidence that $55 represented the per share intrinsic value of the Company.

Having thus chosen the $55 figure, based solely on the availability of a leveraged buy-out, Van Gorkom multiplied the price per share by the number of shares outstanding to reach a total value of the Company of $690 million. Van Gorkom told Peterson to use this $690 million figure and to assume a $200 million equity contribution by the buyer. Based on these assumptions, Van Gorkom directed Peterson to determine whether the debt portion of the purchase price could be paid off in five years or less if financed by Trans Union's cash flow as projected in the Five Year Forecast, and by the sale of certain weaker divisions identified in a study done for Trans Union by the Boston Consulting Group ("BCG study"). Peterson reported that, of the purchase price, approximately $50–80 million would remain outstanding after five years. Van Gorkom was disappointed, but decided to meet with Pritzker nevertheless.

Van Gorkom arranged a meeting with Pritzker at the latter's home on Saturday, September 13, 1980. Van Gorkom prefaced his presentation by stating to Pritzker: "Now as far as you are concerned, I can, I think, show how you can pay a substantial premium over the present stock price and pay off most of the loan in the first five years. * * * If you could pay $55 for this Company, here is a way in which I think it can be financed."

Van Gorkom then reviewed with Pritzker his calculations based upon his proposed price of $55 per share. Although Pritzker mentioned $50 as a more attractive figure, no other price was mentioned. However, Van Gorkom stated that to be sure that $55 was the best price obtainable, Trans Union should be free to accept any better offer. Pritzker demurred, stating that his organization would serve as a "stalking horse" for an "auction contest" only if Trans Union would permit Pritzker to buy 1,750,000 shares of Trans Union stock at market price which Pritzker could then sell to any higher bidder. After further discussion on this point, Pritzker told Van Gorkom that he would give him a more definite reaction soon.

On Monday, September 15, Pritzker advised Van Gorkom that he was interested in the $55 cash-out merger proposal and requested more information on Trans Union. Van Gorkom agreed to meet privately with Pritzker, accompanied by Peterson, Chelberg, and Michael Carpenter, Trans Union's consultant from the Boston Consulting Group. The meetings took place on September 16 and 17. Van Gorkom was "astounded that events were moving with such amazing rapidity."

On Thursday, September 18, Van Gorkom met again with Pritzker. At that time, Van Gorkom knew that Pritzker intended to make a cash-out merger offer at Van Gorkom's proposed $55 per share. Pritzker instructed his attorney, a merger and acquisition specialist, to begin drafting merger documents. There was no further discussion of the $55 price. However, the number of shares of Trans Union's treasury stock to be offered to Pritzker was negotiated down to one million shares; the price was set at $38—75 cents above the per share price at the close of the market on September 19. At this point, Pritzker insisted that the Trans Union Board act on his merger proposal within the next three days, stating to Van Gorkom: "We have to have a decision by no later than Sunday [evening, September 21] before the opening of the English stock exchange on Monday morning." Pritzker's lawyer was then instructed to draft the merger documents, to be reviewed by Van Gorkom's lawyer, "sometimes with discussion and sometimes not, in the haste to get it finished."

On Friday, September 19, Van Gorkom, Chelberg, and Pritzker consulted with Trans Union's lead bank regarding the financing of Pritzker's purchase of Trans Union. The bank indicated that it could form a syndicate of banks that would finance the transaction. On the same day, Van Gorkom retained James Brennan, Esquire, to advise Trans Union on the legal aspects of the merger. Van Gorkom did not consult with William Browder, a Vice-President and director of Trans Union and former head of its legal department, or with William Moore, then the head of Trans Union's legal staff.

On Friday, September 19, Van Gorkom called a special meeting of the Trans Union Board for noon the following day. He also called a meeting of the Company's Senior Management to convene at 11:00 a.m., prior to the meeting of the Board. No one, except Chelberg and Peterson, was told the purpose of the meetings. Van Gorkom did not invite Trans Union's investment banker, Salomon Brothers or its Chicago-based partner, to attend.

Of those present at the Senior Management meeting on September 20, only Chelberg and Peterson had prior knowledge of Pritzker's offer. Van Gorkom disclosed the offer and described its terms, but he furnished no copies of the proposed Merger Agreement. Romans announced that his department had done a second study which showed that, for a leveraged buy-out, the price range for Trans Union stock was between $55 and $65 per share. Van Gorkom neither saw the study nor asked Romans to make it available for the Board meeting.

Senior Management's reaction to the Pritzker proposal was completely negative. No member of Management, except Chelberg and Peterson, supported the proposal. Romans objected to the price as being too low; he was critical of the timing and suggested that consideration should be given to the adverse tax consequences of an all-cash deal for low-basis shareholders; and he took the position that the agreement to sell Pritzker one million newly-issued shares at market price would inhibit other offers, as would the prohibitions against soliciting bids and furnishing inside information to other bidders. Romans argued that the Pritzker proposal was a "lock up" and amounted to "an agreed merger as opposed to an offer." Nevertheless, Van Gorkom proceeded to the Board meeting as scheduled without further delay.

Ten directors served on the Trans Union Board, five inside (defendants Bonser, O'Boyle, Browder, Chelberg, and Van Gorkom) and five outside (defendants Wallis, Johnson, Lanterman, Morgan and Reneker). All directors were present at the meeting, except O'Boyle who was ill. Of the outside directors, four were corporate chief executive officers and one was the former Dean of the University of Chicago Business School. None was an investment banker or trained financial analyst. All members of the Board were well informed about the Company and its operations as a going concern. They were familiar with the current financial condition of the Company, as well as operating and earnings projections reported in the recent Five Year Forecast. The Board generally received regular and detailed reports and was kept abreast of the accumulated investment tax credit and accelerated depreciation problem.

Van Gorkom began the Special Meeting of the Board with a twenty-minute oral presentation. Copies of the proposed Merger Agreement were delivered too late for study before or during the meeting. He reviewed the Company's ITC and depreciation problems and the efforts theretofore made to solve them. He discussed his initial meeting with Pritzker and his motivation in arranging that meeting. Van Gorkom did not disclose to the Board, however, the methodology by which he alone had arrived at the $55 figure, or the fact that he first proposed the $55 price in his negotiations with Pritzker.

Van Gorkom outlined the terms of the Pritzker offer as follows: Pritzker would pay $55 in cash for all outstanding shares of Trans Union stock upon completion of which Trans Union would be merged into New T Company, a subsidiary wholly-owned by Pritzker and formed to implement the merger; for a period of 90 days, Trans Union could receive, but could not actively solicit, competing offers; the offer had to be acted on by the next evening, Sunday, September 21; Trans Union could only furnish to competing bidders published information, and not proprietary information; the offer was subject to Pritzker obtaining the necessary financing by October 10, 1980; if the financing contingency were met or waived by Pritzker, Trans Union was required to sell to Pritzker one million newly-issued shares of Trans Union at $38 per share.

Van Gorkom took the position that putting Trans Union "up for auction" through a 90-day market test would validate a decision by the Board that $55 was a fair price. He told the Board that the "free market will have an opportunity to judge whether $55 is a fair price." Van Gorkom framed the decision before the Board not as whether $55 per share was the highest price that could be obtained, but as whether the $55 price was a fair price that the stockholders should be given the opportunity to accept or reject.

Attorney Brennan advised the members of the Board that they might be sued if they failed to accept the offer and that a fairness opinion was not required as a matter of law.

Romans attended the meeting as chief financial officer of the Company. He told the Board that he had not been involved in the negotiations with Pritzker and knew nothing about the merger proposal until the morning of the meeting; that his studies did not indicate either a fair price for the stock or a valuation of the Company; that he did not see his role as directly addressing the fairness issue; and that he and his people "were trying to search for ways to justify a price in connection with such a [leveraged buy-out] transaction, rather than to say what the shares are worth." . . . Romans told the Board that, in his opinion, $55 was "in the range of a fair price," but "at the beginning of the range."

Chelberg, Trans Union's President, supported Van Gorkom's presentation and representations. He testified that he "participated to make sure that the Board members collectively were clear on the details of the agreement or offer from Pritzker;" that he "participated in the discussion with Mr. Brennan, inquiring of him about the necessity for valuation opinions in spite of the way in which this particular offer was couched;" and that he was otherwise actively involved in supporting the positions being taken by Van Gorkom before the Board about "the necessity to act immediately on this offer," and about "the adequacy of the $55 and the question of how that would be tested."

The Board meeting of September 20 lasted about two hours. Based solely upon Van Gorkom's oral presentation, Chelberg's supporting representations, Romans' oral statement, Brennan's legal advice, and their knowledge of the market history of the Company's stock, the directors approved the proposed Merger Agreement. However, the Board later claimed to have attached two conditions to its acceptance: (1) that Trans Union reserved the right to accept any better offer that was made during the market test period; and (2) that Trans Union could share its proprietary information with any other potential bidders. While the Board now claims to have reserved the right to accept any better offer received after the announcement of the Pritzker agreement (even though the minutes of the meeting do not reflect this), it is undisputed that the Board did not reserve the right to actively solicit alternate offers.

The Merger Agreement was executed by Van Gorkom during the evening of September 20 at a formal social event that he hosted for the opening of the Chicago Lyric Opera. Neither he nor any other director read the agreement prior to its signing and delivery to Pritzker.

On Monday, September 22, the Company issued a press release announcing that Trans Union had entered into a "definitive" Merger Agreement with an affiliate of the Marmon Group, Inc., a Pritzker holding company. Within 10 days of the public announcement, dissent among Senior Management over the merger had become widespread. Faced with threatened resignations of key officers, Van Gorkom met with Pritzker who agreed to several modifications of the Agreement. Pritzker was willing to do so provided that Van Gorkom could persuade the dissidents to remain on the Company payroll for at least six months after consummation of the merger.

Van Gorkom reconvened the Board on October 8 and secured the directors' approval of the proposed amendments—sight unseen. The Board also authorized the employment of Salomon Brothers, its investment banker, to solicit other offers for Trans Union during the proposed "market test" period.

The next day, October 9, Trans Union issued a press release announcing: (1) that Pritzker had obtained "the financing commitments necessary to consummate" the merger with Trans Union; (2) that Pritzker had acquired one million shares of Trans Union common stock at $38 per share; (3) that Trans Union was now permitted to actively seek other offers and had retained Salomon Brothers for that purpose; and (4) that if a more favorable offer were not received before February 1, 1981, Trans Union's shareholders would thereafter meet to vote on the Pritzker proposal.

It was not until the following day, October 10, that the actual amendments to the Merger Agreement were prepared by Pritzker and delivered to Van Gorkom for execution. As will be seen, the amendments were considerably at variance with Van Gorkom's representations of the amendments to the Board on October 8; and the amendments placed serious constraints on Trans Union's ability to negotiate a better deal and withdraw from the Pritzker agreement. Nevertheless, Van Gorkom proceeded to execute what became the October 10 amendments to the Merger Agreement without conferring further with the Board members and apparently without comprehending the actual implications of the amendments.

Salomon Brothers' efforts over a three-month period from October 21 to January 21 produced only one serious suitor for Trans Union—General Electric Credit Corporation ("GE Credit"), a subsidiary of the General Electric Company. However, GE Credit was unwilling to make an offer for Trans Union unless Trans Union first rescinded its Merger Agreement with Pritzker. When Pritzker refused, GE Credit terminated further discussions with Trans Union in early January.

In the meantime, in early December, the investment firm of Kohlberg, Kravis, Roberts & Co. ("KKR"), the only other concern to make a firm offer for Trans Union, withdrew its offer under circumstances hereinafter detailed.

On December 19, this litigation was commenced and, within four weeks, the plaintiffs had deposed eight of the ten directors of Trans Union, including Van Gorkom, Chelberg and Romans, its Chief Financial Officer. On January 21, Management's Proxy Statement for the February 10 shareholder meeting was mailed to Trans Union's stockholders. On January 26, Trans Union's Board met and, after a lengthy meeting, voted to proceed with the Pritzker merger. The Board also approved for mailing, "on or about January 27," a Supplement to its Proxy Statement. The Supplement purportedly set forth all information relevant to the Pritzker Merger Agreement, which had not been divulged in the first Proxy Statement.

On February 10, the stockholders of Trans Union approved the Pritzker merger proposal. Of the outstanding shares, 69.9% were voted in favor of the merger; 7.25% were voted against the merger; and 22.85% were not voted.

II

We turn to the issue of the application of the business judgment rule to the September 20 meeting of the Board.

The Court of Chancery concluded from the evidence that the Board of Directors' approval of the Pritzker merger proposal fell within the protection of the business judgment rule. The Court found that the Board had given sufficient time and attention to the transaction, since the directors had considered the Pritzker proposal on three different occasions, on September 20, and on October 8, 1980 and finally on January 26, 1981. On that basis, the Court reasoned that the Board had acquired, over the four-month period, sufficient information to reach an informed business judgment on the cash-out merger proposal. . . . We must disagree.

Under Delaware law, the business judgment rule is the offspring of the fundamental principle, codified in 8 Del.C. § 141(a), that the business and affairs of a Delaware corporation are managed by or under its board of directors. In carrying out their managerial roles, directors are charged with an unyielding fiduciary duty to the corporation and its shareholders. The business judgment rule exists to protect and promote the full and free exercise of the managerial power granted to Delaware directors. The rule itself "is a presumption that in making a business decision, the directors of a corporation acted on an informed basis, in good faith and in the honest belief that the action taken was in the best interests of the company." Thus, the party attacking a board decision as uninformed must rebut the presumption that its business judgment was an informed one.

The determination of whether a business judgment is an informed one turns on whether the directors have informed themselves "prior to making a business decision, of all material information reasonably available to them."

. . .

. . . We think the concept of gross negligence is also the proper standard for determining whether a business judgment reached by a board of directors was an informed one.

In the specific context of a proposed merger of domestic corporations, a director has a duty . . . along with his fellow directors, to act in an informed and deliberate manner in determining whether to approve an agreement of merger before submitting the proposal to the stockholders. Certainly in the merger context, a director may not abdicate that duty by leaving to the shareholders alone the decision to approve or disapprove the agreement. Only an agreement of merger satisfying the requirements of 8 Del.C. § 251(b) may be submitted to the shareholders under § 251(c). . . .

III

. . .

The issue of whether the directors reached an informed decision to "sell" the Company on September 20, 1980 must be determined only upon the basis of the information then reasonably available to the directors and relevant to their decision to accept the Pritzker merger proposal. This is not to say that the directors were precluded from altering their original plan of action, had they done so in an informed manner. What we do say is that the question of whether the directors reached an informed business judgment in agreeing to sell the Company, pursuant to the terms of the September 20 Agreement presents, in reality, two questions: (A) whether the directors reached an informed business judgment on September 20, 1980; and (B) if they did not, whether the directors' actions taken subsequent to September 20 were adequate to cure any infirmity in their action taken on September 20. We first consider the directors' September 20 action in terms of their reaching an informed business judgment.

-A-

On the record before us, we must conclude that the Board of Directors did not reach an informed business judgment on September 20, 1980 in voting to "sell" the Company for $55 per share pursuant to the Pritzker cash-out merger proposal. Our reasons, in summary, are as follows:

The directors (1) did not adequately inform themselves as to Van Gorkom's role in forcing the "sale" of the Company and in establishing the per share purchase price; (2) were uninformed as to the intrinsic value of the Company; and (3) given these circumstances, at a minimum, were grossly negligent in approving the "sale" of the Company upon two hours' consideration, without prior notice, and without the exigency of a crisis or emergency.

As has been noted, the Board based its September 20 decision to approve the cash-out merger primarily on Van Gorkom's representations. None of the directors, other than Van Gorkom and Chelberg, had any prior knowledge that the purpose of the meeting was to propose a cash-out merger of Trans Union. No members of Senior Management were present, other than Chelberg, Romans and Peterson; and the latter two had only learned of the proposed sale an hour earlier. Both general counsel Moore and former general counsel Browder attended the meeting, but were equally uninformed as to the purpose of the meeting and the documents to be acted upon.

Without any documents before them concerning the proposed transaction, the members of the Board were required to rely entirely upon Van Gorkom's 20-minute oral presentation of the proposal. No written summary of the terms of the merger was presented; the directors were given no documentation to support the adequacy of $55 price per share for sale of the Company; and the Board had before it nothing more than Van Gorkom's statement of his understanding of the substance of an agreement which he admittedly had never read, nor which any member of the Board had ever seen.

Under 8 Del.C. § 141(e), "directors are fully protected in relying in good faith on reports made by officers." . . . The term "report" has been liberally construed to include reports of informal personal investigations by corporate officers. However, there is no evidence that any "report," as defined under § 141(e), concerning the Pritzker proposal, was presented to the Board on September 20. Van Gorkom's oral presentation of his understanding of the terms of the proposed Merger Agreement, which he had not seen, and Romans' brief oral statement of his preliminary study regarding the feasibility of a leveraged buy-out of Trans Union do not qualify as § 141(e) "reports" for these reasons: The former lacked substance because Van Gorkom was basically uninformed as to the essential provisions of the very document about which he was talking. Romans' statement was irrelevant to the issues before the Board since it did not purport to be a valuation study. At a minimum for a report to enjoy the status conferred by § 141(e), it must be pertinent to the subject matter upon which a board is called to act, and otherwise be entitled to good faith, not blind, reliance. Considering all of the surrounding circumstances—hastily calling the meeting without prior notice of its subject matter, the proposed sale of the Company without any prior consideration of the issue or necessity therefor, the urgent time constraints imposed by Pritzker, and the total absence of any documentation whatsoever—the directors were duty bound to make reasonable inquiry of Van Gorkom and Romans, and if they had done so, the inadequacy of that upon which they now claim to have relied would have been apparent.

The defendants rely on the following factors to sustain the Trial Court's finding that the Board's decision was an informed one: (1) the magnitude of the premium or spread between the $55 Pritzker offering price and Trans Union's current market price of $38 per share; (2) the amendment of the Agreement as submitted on September 20 to permit the Board to accept any better offer during the "market test" period; (3) the collective experience and expertise of the Board's "inside" and "outside" directors; and (4) their reliance on Brennan's legal advice that the directors might be sued if they rejected the Pritzker proposal. We discuss each of these grounds *seriatim:*

(1)

A substantial premium may provide one reason to recommend a merger, but in the absence of other sound valuation information, the fact of a premium alone does not provide an adequate basis upon which to assess the fairness of an offering price. Here, the judgment reached as to the adequacy of the premium was based on a comparison between the historically depressed Trans Union market price and the amount of the Pritzker offer. Using market price as a basis for concluding that the premium adequately reflected the true value of the Company was a clearly faulty, indeed fallacious, premise, as the defendants' own evidence demonstrates.

The record is clear that before September 20, Van Gorkom and other members of Trans Union's Board knew that the market had consistently undervalued the worth of Trans Union's stock, despite steady increases in the Company's operating income in the seven years preceding the merger. The Board related this occurrence in large part to Trans Union's inability to use its ITCs as previously noted. Van Gorkom testified that he did not believe the market price accurately reflected Trans Union's true worth; and several of the directors testified that, as a general rule, most chief executives think that the market undervalues their companies' stock. Yet, on September 20, Trans Union's Board apparently believed that the market stock price accurately reflected the value of the Company for the purpose of determining the adequacy of the premium for its sale.

. . .

The parties do not dispute that a publicly-traded stock price is solely a measure of the value of a minority position and, thus, market price represents only the value of a single share. Nevertheless, on September 20, the Board assessed the adequacy of the premium over market, offered by Pritzker, solely by comparing it with Trans Union's current and historical stock price.

Indeed, as of September 20, the Board had no other information on which to base a determination of the intrinsic value of Trans Union as a going concern. As of September 20, the Board had made no evaluation of the Company designed to value the entire enterprise, nor had the Board ever previously considered selling the Company or consenting to a buy-out merger. Thus, the adequacy of a premium is indeterminate unless it is assessed in terms of other competent and sound valuation information that reflects the value of the particular business.

Despite the foregoing facts and circumstances, there was no call by the Board, either on September 20 or thereafter, for any valuation study or documentation of the $55 price per share as a measure of the fair value of the Company in a cash-out context. It is undisputed that the major asset of Trans Union was its cash flow. Yet, at no time did the Board call for a valuation study taking into account that highly significant element of the Company's assets.

We do not imply that an outside valuation study is essential to support an informed business judgment; nor do we state that fairness opinions by independent investment bankers are required as a matter of law. Often insiders familiar with the business of a going concern are in a better position than are outsiders to gather relevant information; and under appropriate circumstances, such directors may be fully protected in relying in good faith upon the valuation reports of their management. . . .

Here, the record establishes that the Board did not request its Chief Financial Officer, Romans, to make any valuation study or review of the proposal to determine the adequacy of $55 per share for sale of the Company. On the record before us: The Board rested on Romans' elicited response that the $55 figure was within a "fair price range" within the context of a leveraged buy-out. No director sought any further information from Romans. No director asked him why he put $55 at the bottom of his range. No director asked Romans for any details as to his study, the reason why it had been undertaken or its depth. No director asked to see the study; and no director asked Romans whether Trans Union's finance department could do a fairness study within the remaining 36-hour period available under the Pritzker offer.

. . .

The record also establishes that the Board accepted without scrutiny Van Gorkom's representation as to the fairness of the $55 price per share for sale of the Company—a subject that the Board had never previously considered. The Board thereby failed to discover that Van Gorkom had suggested the $55 price to Pritzker and, most crucially, that Van Gorkom had arrived at the $55 figure based on calculations designed solely to determine the feasibility of a leveraged buy-out. No questions were raised either as to the tax implications of a cash-out merger or how the price for the one million share option granted Pritzker was calculated.

We do not say that the Board of Directors was not entitled to give some credence to Van Gorkom's representation that $55 was an adequate or fair price. Under § 141(e), the directors were entitled to rely upon their chairman's opinion of value and adequacy, provided that such opinion was reached on a sound basis. Here, the issue is whether the directors informed themselves as to all information that was reasonably available to them. Had they done so, they would have learned of the source and derivation of the $55 price and could not reasonably have relied thereupon in good faith.

None of the directors, Management or outside, were investment bankers or financial analysts. Yet the Board did not consider recessing the meeting until a later hour that day (or requesting an extension of Pritzker's Sunday evening deadline) to give it time to elicit more information as to the sufficiency of the offer, either from inside Management (in particular Romans) or from Trans Union's own investment banker, Salomon Brothers, whose Chicago specialist in merger and acquisitions was known to the Board and familiar with Trans Union's affairs.

Thus, the record compels the conclusion that on September 20 the Board lacked valuation information adequate to reach an informed business judgment as to the fairness of $55 per share for sale of the Company.

(2)

This brings us to the post-September 20 "market test" upon which the defendants ultimately rely to confirm the reasonableness of their September 20 decision to accept the Pritzker proposal. In this connection, the directors present a two-part argument: (a) that by making a "market test" of Pritzker's $55 per share offer a condition of their September 20 decision to accept his offer, they cannot be found to have acted impulsively or in an uninformed manner on September 20; and (b) that the adequacy of the $17 premium for sale of the Company was conclusively established over the following 90 to 120 days by the most reliable evidence available—the marketplace. Thus, the defendants impliedly contend that the "market test" eliminated the need for the Board to perform any other form of fairness test either on September 20, or thereafter.

Again, the facts of record do not support the defendants' argument. There is no evidence: (a) that the Merger Agreement was effectively amended to give the Board freedom to put Trans Union up for auction sale to the highest bidder; or (b) that a public auction was in fact permitted to occur. The minutes of the Board meeting make no reference to any of this. Indeed, the record compels the conclusion that the directors had no rational basis for expecting that a market test was attainable, given the terms of the Agreement as executed during the evening of September 20. We rely upon the following facts which are essentially uncontradicted:

The Merger Agreement, specifically identified as that originally presented to the Board on September 20, has never been produced by the defendants, notwithstanding the plaintiffs' several demands for production before as well as during trial....

Van Gorkom states that the Agreement as submitted incorporated the ingredients for a market test by authorizing Trans Union to receive competing offers over the next 90-day period. However, he concedes that the Agreement barred Trans Union from actively soliciting such offers and from furnishing to interested parties any information about the Company other than that already in the public domain. Whether the original Agreement of September 20 went so far as to authorize Trans Union to receive competitive proposals is arguable. The defendants' unexplained failure to produce and identify the original Merger Agreement permits the logical inference that the instrument would not support their assertions in this regard....

The defendant directors assert that they "insisted" upon including two amendments to the Agreement, thereby permitting a market test: (1) to give Trans Union the right to accept a better offer; and (2) to reserve to Trans Union the right to distribute proprietary information on the Company to alternative bidders. Yet, the defendants concede that they did not seek to amend the Agreement to permit Trans Union to solicit competing offers.

. . .

The defendants attempt to downplay the significance of the prohibition against Trans Union's actively soliciting competing offers by arguing that the directors "understood that the entire financial community would know that Trans Union was for sale upon the announcement of the Pritzker offer, and anyone desiring to make a better offer was free to do so." Yet, the press release issued on September 22, with the authorization of the Board, stated that Trans Union had entered into "definitive agreements" with the Pritzkers; and the press release did not even disclose Trans Union's limited right to receive and accept higher offers. Accompanying this press release was a further public announcement that Pritzker had been granted an option to purchase at any time one million shares of Trans Union's capital stock at 75 cents above the then-current price per share.

Thus, notwithstanding what several of the outside directors later claimed to have "thought" occurred at the meeting, the record compels the conclusion that Trans Union's Board had no rational basis to conclude on September 20 or in the days immediately following, that the Board's acceptance of Pritzker's offer was conditioned on (1) a "market test" of the offer; and (2) the Board's right to withdraw from the Pritzker Agreement and accept any higher offer received before the shareholder meeting.

(3)

The directors' unfounded reliance on both the premium and the market test as the basis for accepting the Pritzker proposal undermines the defendants' remaining contention that the Board's collective experience and sophistication was a sufficient basis for finding that it reached its September 20 decision with informed, reasonable deliberation. . . .

(4)

. . .

We conclude that Trans Union's Board was grossly negligent in that it failed to act with informed reasonable deliberation in agreeing to the Pritzker merger proposal on September 20; and we further conclude that the Trial Court erred as a matter of law in failing to address that question before determining whether the directors' later conduct was sufficient to cure its initial error.

. . .

-B-

We now examine the Board's post-September 20 conduct for the purpose of determining first, whether it was informed and not grossly negligent; and second, if informed, whether it was sufficient to legally rectify and cure the Board's derelictions of September 20.

(1)

First, as to the Board meeting of October 8: Its purpose arose in the aftermath of the September 20 meeting: (1) the September 22 press release announcing that Trans Union "had entered into definitive agreements to merge with an affiliate of Marmon Group, Inc.;" and (2) Senior Management's ensuing revolt.

. . .

The press release made no reference to provisions allegedly reserving to the Board the rights to perform a "market test" and to withdraw from the Pritzker Agreement if Trans Union received a better offer before the shareholder meeting. The defendants also concede that Trans Union never made a subsequent public announcement stating that it had in fact reserved the right to accept alternate offers, the Agreement notwithstanding.

. . .

The public announcement of the Pritzker merger resulted in an "en masse" revolt of Trans Union's Senior Management. The head of Trans Union's tank car operations (its most profitable division) informed Van Gorkom that unless the merger were called off, fifteen key personnel would resign.

Instead of reconvening the Board, Van Gorkom again privately met with Pritzker, informed him of the developments, and sought his advice. Pritzker then made the following suggestions for overcoming Management's dissatisfaction: (1) that the Agreement be amended to permit Trans Union to solicit, as well as receive, higher offers; and (2) that the shareholder meeting be postponed from early January to February 10, 1981. In return, Pritzker asked Van Gorkom to obtain a commitment from Senior Management to remain at Trans Union for at least six months after the merger was consummated.

Van Gorkom then advised Senior Management that the Agreement would be amended to give Trans Union the right to solicit competing offers through January, 1981, if they would agree to remain with Trans Union. Senior Management was temporarily mollified; and Van Gorkom then called a special meeting of Trans Union's Board for October 8.

Thus, the primary purpose of the October 8 Board meeting was to amend the Merger Agreement, in a manner agreeable to Pritzker, to permit Trans Union to conduct a "market test." Van Gorkom understood that the proposed amendments were intended to give the Company an unfettered "right to openly solicit offers down through January 31." Van Gorkom presumably so represented the amendments to Trans Union's Board members on October 8. In a brief session, the directors approved Van Gorkom's oral presentation of the substance of the proposed amendments, the terms of which were not reduced to writing until October 10. But rather than waiting to review the amendments, the Board again approved them sight unseen and adjourned, giving Van Gorkom authority to execute the papers when he received them.

. . .

The next day, October 9, and before the Agreement was amended, Pritzker moved swiftly to off-set the proposed market test amendment. First, Pritzker informed Trans Union that he had completed arrangements for financing its acquisition and that the parties were thereby mutually bound to a firm purchase and sale arrangement. Second, Pritzker announced the exercise of his option to purchase one million shares of Trans Union's treasury stock at $38 per share—75 cents above the current market price. Trans Union's Management responded the same day by issuing a press release announcing: (1) that all financing arrangements for Pritzker's acquisition of Trans

Union had been completed; and (2) Pritzker's purchase of one million shares of Trans Union's treasury stock at $38 per share.

The next day, October 10, Pritzker delivered to Trans Union the proposed amendments to the September 20 Merger Agreement. Van Gorkom promptly proceeded to countersign all the instruments on behalf of Trans Union without reviewing the instruments to determine if they were consistent with the authority previously granted him by the Board. The amending documents were apparently not approved by Trans Union's Board until a much later date, December 2. The record does not affirmatively establish that Trans Union's directors ever read the October 10 amendments.

The October 10 amendments to the Merger Agreement did authorize Trans Union to solicit competing offers, but the amendments had more far-reaching effects. The most significant change was in the definition of the third-party "offer" available to Trans Union as a possible basis for withdrawal from its Merger Agreement with Pritzker. Under the October 10 amendments, a better *offer* was no longer sufficient to permit Trans Union's withdrawal. Trans Union was now permitted to terminate the Pritzker Agreement and abandon the merger only if, prior to February 10, 1981, Trans Union had either consummated a merger (or sale of assets) with a third party or had entered into a "definitive" merger agreement more favorable than Pritzker's and for a greater consideration—subject only to stockholder approval. Further, the "extension" of the market test period to February 10, 1981 was circumscribed by other amendments which required Trans Union to file its preliminary proxy statement on the Pritzker merger proposal by December 5, 1980 and use its best efforts to mail the statement to its shareholders by January 5, 1981. Thus, the market test period was effectively reduced, not extended.

In our view, the record compels the conclusion that the directors' conduct on October 8 exhibited the same deficiencies as did their conduct on September 20. The Board permitted its Merger Agreement with Pritzker to be amended in a manner it had neither authorized nor intended. The Court of Chancery, in its decision, overlooked the significance of the October 8–10 events and their relevance to the sufficiency of the directors' conduct. The Trial Court's letter opinion ignores: the October 10 amendments; the manner of their adoption; the effect of the October 9 press release and the October 10 amendments on the feasibility of a market test; and the ultimate question as to the reasonableness of the directors' reliance on a market test in recommending that the shareholders approve the Pritzker merger.

We conclude that the Board acted in a grossly negligent manner on October 8; and that Van Gorkom's representations on which the Board based its actions do not constitute "reports" under §141(e) on which the directors could reasonably have relied. Further, the amended Merger Agreement imposed on Trans Union's acceptance of a third party offer conditions more onerous than those imposed on Trans Union's acceptance of Pritzker's offer on September 20. After October 10, Trans Union could accept from a third party a better offer only if it were incorporated in a definitive agreement between the parties, and not conditioned on financing or on any other contingency.

The October 9 press release, coupled with the October 10 amendments, had the clear effect of locking Trans Union's Board into the Pritzker Agreement. Pritzker had thereby foreclosed Trans Union's Board from negotiating any better "definitive" agreement over the remaining eight weeks before Trans Union was required to clear the Proxy Statement submitting the Pritzker proposal to its shareholders.

(2)

Next, as to the "curative" effects of the Board's post-September 20 conduct, we review in more detail the reaction of Van Gorkom to the KKR proposal and the results of the Board-sponsored "market test."

The KKR proposal was the first and only offer received subsequent to the Pritzker Merger Agreement. The offer resulted primarily from the efforts of Romans and other senior officers to propose an alternative to Pritzker's acquisition of Trans Union. In late September, Romans' group contacted KKR about the possibility of a leveraged buy-out by all members of Management, except Van Gorkom. By early October, Henry R. Kravis of KKR gave Romans written notice of KKR's "interest in making an offer to purchase 100%" of Trans Union's common stock.

Thereafter, and until early December, Romans' group worked with KKR to develop a proposal. It did so with Van Gorkom's knowledge and apparently grudging consent. On December 2, Kravis and Romans hand-delivered to Van Gorkom a formal letter-offer to purchase all of Trans Union's assets and to assume all of its liabilities for an aggregate cash consideration equivalent to $60 per share. The offer was contingent upon completing equity and bank financing of $650 million, which Kravis represented as 80% complete. The KKR letter made reference to discussions with major banks regarding the loan portion of the buy-out cost and stated that KKR was "confident that commitments for the bank financing * * * can be obtained within two or three weeks." The purchasing group was to include certain named key members of Trans Union's Senior Management, excluding Van Gorkom, and a major Canadian company. Kravis stated that they were willing to enter into a "definitive agreement" under terms and conditions "substantially the same" as those contained in Trans Union's agreement with Pritzker. The offer was addressed to Trans Union's Board of Directors and a meeting with the Board, scheduled for that afternoon, was requested.

Van Gorkom's reaction to the KKR proposal was completely negative; he did not view the offer as being firm because of its financing condition. It was pointed out, to no avail, that Pritzker's offer had not only been similarly conditioned, but accepted on an expedited basis. Van Gorkom refused Kravis' request that Trans Union issue a press release announcing KKR's offer, on the ground that it might "chill" any other offer. Romans and Kravis left with the understanding that their proposal would be presented to Trans Union's Board that afternoon.

Within a matter of hours and shortly before the scheduled Board meeting, Kravis withdrew his letter-offer. He gave as his reason a sudden decision by the Chief Officer of Trans Union's rail car leasing operation to withdraw from the KKR purchasing group. Van Gorkom had spoken to that officer about his participation in the KKR proposal immediately after his meeting with Romans and Kravis. However, Van Gorkom denied any responsibility for the officer's change of mind.

At the Board meeting later that afternoon, Van Gorkom did not inform the directors of the KKR proposal because he considered it "dead." Van Gorkom did not contact KKR again until January 20, when faced with the realities of this lawsuit, he then attempted to reopen negotiations. KKR declined due to the imminence of the February 10 stockholder meeting.

GE Credit Corporation's interest in Trans Union did not develop until November; and it made no written proposal until mid-January. Even then, its proposal was not in the form of an offer. Had there been time to do so, GE Credit was prepared to offer between $2 and $5 per share above the $55 per share price which Pritzker offered. But GE Credit needed an additional 60 to 90 days; and it was unwilling to make a formal offer without a concession from Pritzker extending the February 10 "deadline" for Trans Union's stockholder meeting. As previously stated, Pritzker refused to grant such extension; and on January 21, GE Credit terminated further negotiations with Trans Union. Its stated reasons, among others, were its "unwillingness to become involved in a bidding contest with Pritzker in the absence of the willingness of [the Pritzker interests] to terminate the proposed $55 cash merger."

... Our review of the record compels a finding that confirmation of the appropriateness of the Pritzker offer by an unfettered or free market test was virtually meaningless in the face of the terms and time limitations of Trans Union's Merger Agreement with Pritzker as amended October 10, 1980.

(3)

. . .

Upon the basis of the foregoing, we hold that the defendants' post-September conduct did not cure the deficiencies of their September 20 conduct; and that, accordingly, the Trial Court erred in according to the defendants the benefits of the business judgment rule.

IV

Whether the directors of Trans Union should be treated as one or individually in terms of invoking the protection of the business judgment rule and the applicability of 8 Del.C. § 141(c) are questions which were not originally addressed by the parties in their briefing of this case. This resulted in a supplemental briefing and a second rehearing en banc on two basic questions: (a) whether one or more of the directors were deprived of the protection of the business judgment rule by evidence of an absence of good faith; and (b) whether one or more of the outside directors were entitled to invoke the protection of 8 Del.C. § 141(e) by evidence of a reasonable, good faith reliance on "reports," including legal advice, rendered the Board by certain inside directors and the Board's special counsel, Brennan.

The parties' response, including reargument, has led the majority of the Court to conclude: (1) that since all of the defendant directors, outside as well as inside, take a unified position, we are required to treat all of the directors as one as to whether they are entitled to the protection of the business judgment rule; and (2) that considerations of good faith, including the presumption that the directors acted in good faith, are irrelevant in determining the threshold issue of whether the directors as a Board exercised an informed business judgment. For the same reason, we must reject defense counsel's *ad hominem* argument for affirmance: that reversal may result in a multi-million dollar class award against the defendants for having made an allegedly uninformed business judgment in a transaction not involving any personal gain, self-dealing or claim of bad faith.

. . .

V

The defendants ultimately rely on the stockholder vote of February 10 for exoneration. The defendants contend that the stockholders' "overwhelming" vote approving the Pritzker Merger Agreement had the legal effect of curing any failure of the Board to reach an informed business judgment in its approval of the merger.

. . .

The settled rule in Delaware is that "where a majority of fully informed stockholders ratify action of even interested directors, an attack on the ratified transaction normally must fail." . . . The question of whether shareholders have been fully informed such that their vote can be said to ratify director action, "turns on the fairness and completeness of the proxy materials submitted by the management to the . . . shareholders." . . .

Applying this standard to the record before us, we find that Trans Union's stockholders were not fully informed of all facts material to their vote on the Pritzker Merger and that the Trial Court's ruling to the contrary is clearly erroneous. . . .

The burden must fall on defendants who claim ratification based on shareholder vote to establish that the shareholder approval resulted from a fully informed electorate. On the record before us, it is clear that the Board failed to meet that burden.

For the foregoing reasons, we conclude that the director defendants breached their fiduciary duty of candor by their failure to make true and correct disclosures of all information they had, or should have had, material to the transaction submitted for stockholder approval.

VI

To summarize: we hold that the directors of Trans Union breached their fiduciary duty to their stockholders (1) by their failure to inform themselves of all information reasonably available to them and relevant to their decision to recommend the Pritzker merger; and (2) by their failure to disclose all material information such as a reasonable stockholder would consider important in deciding whether to approve the Pritzker offer.

. . .

On remand, the Court of Chancery shall conduct an evidentiary hearing to determine the fair value of the shares represented by the plaintiffs' class, based on the intrinsic value of Trans Union on September 20, 1980. Such valuation shall be made in accordance with *Weinberger v. UOP*. Thereafter, an award of damages may be entered to the extent that the fair value of Trans Union exceeds $55 per share.

REVERSED and REMANDED for proceedings consistent herewith.

McNEILLY, Justice, dissenting

The majority opinion reads like an advocate's closing address to a hostile jury. And I say that not lightly. Throughout the opinion great emphasis is directed only to the negative, with nothing more than lip service granted the positive aspects of this case. . . . The majority has spoken and has effectively said that Trans Union's Directors have been the victims of a "fast shuffle" by Van Gorkom and Pritzker. . . .

Trans Union's Board of Directors consisted of ten men, five of whom were "inside" directors and five of whom were "outside" directors. The "inside" directors were Van Gorkom, Chelberg, Bonser, William B. Browder, Senior Vice-President-Law, and Thomas P. O'Boyle, Senior Vice-President-Administration. At the time the merger was proposed the inside five directors had collectively been employed by the Company for 116 years and had 68 years of combined experience as directors. The "outside" directors were A.W. Wallis, William B. Johnson, Joseph B. Lanterman, Graham J. Morgan and Robert W. Reneker. With the exception of Wallis, these were all chief executive officers of Chicago based corporations that were at least as large as Trans Union. The five "outside" directors had 78 years of combined experience as chief executive officers, and 53 years cumulative service as Trans Union directors.

The inside directors wear their badge of expertise in the corporate affairs of Trans Union on their sleeves. But what about the outsiders? Dr. Wallis is or was an economist and math statistician, a professor of economics at Yale University, dean of the graduate school of business at the University of Chicago, and Chancellor of the University of Rochester. Dr. Wallis had been on the Board of Trans Union since 1962. He also was on the Board of Bausch & Lomb, Kodak, Metropolitan Life Insurance Company, Standard Oil and others.

William B. Johnson is a University of Pennsylvania law graduate, President of Railway Express until 1966, Chairman and Chief Executive of I.C. Industries Holding Company, and member of Trans Union's Board since 1968.

Joseph Lanterman, a Certified Public Accountant, is or was President and Chief Executive of American Steel, on the Board of International Harvester, Peoples Energy, Illinois Bell Telephone, Harris Bank and Trust Company, Kemper Insurance Company and a director of Trans Union for four years.

Graham Morgan is a chemist, was Chairman and Chief Executive Officer of U.S. Gypsum, and in the 17 and 18 years prior to the Trans Union transaction had been involved in 31 or 32 corporate takeovers.

Robert Reneker attended University of Chicago and Harvard Business Schools. He was President and Chief Executive of Swift and Company, director of Trans Union since 1971, and member of the Boards of seven other corporations including U.S. Gypsum and the Chicago Tribune.

Directors of this caliber are not ordinarily taken in by a "fast shuffle". I submit they were not taken into this multi-million dollar corporate transaction without being fully informed and aware of the state of the art as it pertained to the entire corporate panorama of Trans Union. True, even directors such as these, with their business acumen, interest and expertise, can go astray. I do not believe that to be the case here. These men knew Trans Union like the back of their hands and were more than well qualified to make on the spot informed business judgments concerning the affairs of Trans Union including a 100% sale of the corporation. Lest we forget, the corporate world of then and now operates on what is so aptly referred to as "the fast track". These men were at the time an integral part of that world, all professional business men, not intellectual figureheads.

The majority of this Court holds that the Board's decision, reached on September 20, 1980, to approve the merger was not the product of an *informed* business judgment, that the Board's subsequent efforts to amend the Merger Agreement and take other curative action were *legally and factually* ineffectual, and that the Board did *not deal with complete candor* with the stockholders by failing to disclose all material facts, which they knew or should have known, before securing the stockholders' approval of the merger. I disagree. . . .

Van Gorkom in context

For most of the twentieth century, the business judgment rule was grounded in deference to directors' expert knowledge. This changed in the 1980s, a decade in which numerous corporations faced hostile takeovers. Seeking to protect directors' discretion to say no to hostile bidders, the Delaware courts focused their attention on the business judgment rule and its relationship to the duty of care. Take, for example, *Aronson v. Lewis* 473 A.2d 805 (Del. 1984), a case involving the question of demand futility. Having concluded that "demand can only be excused where facts are alleged with particularity which creates a reasonable doubt that the directors' action was entitled to the protections of the business judgment rule," the Delaware Supreme Court offered a definition of the business judgment rule. The court began by noting that:

> The business judgment rule is an acknowledgment of the managerial prerogatives of Delaware directors. . . . It is a presumption that in making a business decision the directors of a corporation acted on an informed basis, in good faith and in the honest belief that the action taken was in the best interests of the company. Absent an abuse of discretion, that judgment will be

respected by the courts. The burden is on the party challenging the decision to establish facts rebutting the presumption.

Following precedent, the court anchored the business judgment rule in "managerial prerogative" and emphasized that only disinterested directors could claim the protection of the rule. But the court went further. First, the court held that "to invoke the rule's protection directors have a duty to inform themselves, prior to making a business decision, of all material information reasonably available to them. Having become so informed, they must then act with requisite care in the discharge of their duties." As Lyman Johnson has pointed out, the "informed" element was not part of the business judgment rule doctrine until *Aronson* introduced it. In adding it, *Aronson* lay the foundation for the ultimate equation of the duty of care with the duty to be informed. Second, the court went on to declare that "while the Delaware cases use a variety of terms to describe the applicable standard of care, our analysis satisfies us that under the business judgment rule director liability is predicated upon concepts of gross negligence." The court noted that "the Delaware cases have not been precise in articulating the standard by which the exercise of business judgment is governed." Nonetheless it chose to characterize the cases as "hold[ing] that director liability is predicated on a standard which is less exacting than simple negligence." *See* Lyman Johnson, *The Modern Business Judgment Rule*, 55 Bus. L. 625 (1990–2000); Dalia Mitchell, *Status Bound: The Twentieth Century Evolution of Directors' Liability*, 5 NYU J. L. & Bus. 63 (2009).

Aronson v. Lewis altered the contours of the business judgment rule and duty of care. A year later in *Smith v. Van Gorkom*, 488 A. 2d 858 (Del. 1985), the Delaware Supreme court affirmed its own proclamation in *Aronson* that "under the business judgment rule director liability is predicated upon concepts of gross negligence." Moving even further, the court concluded that "the concept of gross negligence is also the proper standard for determining whether a business judgment reached by a board of directors was an informed one."

While limiting the scope of the duty of care, *Van Gorkom* remains the only Delaware case in recent memory to hold directors liable for breach of that duty. The opinion held the experienced and distinguished board of Trans Union Corporation liable for breach of the duty of care for too hastily approving a merger without sufficient outside evidence of the corporation's value, despite curative steps taken subsequently (and prior to the merger) by the board. *Van Gorkom* shocked both corporate lawyers and the corporate community more broadly out of a complacency that had developed regarding Delaware's stance in matters involving the duty of care. After all, hardly any lawyer could remember a time when a board had been held liable for such a breach. And the facts of *Van Gorkom* were not especially compelling. True, the Trans Union board had approved a merger with a corporation owned by Chicago real estate developer Jay Pritzker and his Marmon Group after a three-hour meeting, without prior notice, and without reading the merger agreement. But the board had spent quite a bit of time studying Trans Union's financial problems, including its historically depressed stock price, and considering the options for fixing it. Moreover, as the dissent pointed out, the directors were all highly experienced in business, were evenly divided between inside and outside directors, and the inside directors had a combined 116 years of experience with the company, with a total of 68 years of combined experience as directors. All but one of the outside directors was CEO of a major Chicago corporation of at least Trans Union's size, and together they had 78 years combined experience as corporate directors and 53 years combined experience with Trans Union. Moreover, they relied heavily on the advice and opinion of Van Gorkom, Trans Union's chair and CEO, who was both a lawyer and a CPA, had been an officer of Trans Union for 24 years, and its CEO for more than 17 years.

The court focused on several factors. First, in light of the magnitude of the transaction, the court considered the length of the meeting and the failure of the board to read the merger agreement prior to approving it inadequate behavior to fulfill the duty of care. The court was also deeply troubled by the board's reliance on Van Gorkom himself, hinting at a conflict of interest inhering in the fact that Van Gorkom was approaching retirement and held a substantial number of Trans Union shares (and thus presumably was interested in unloading them at a premium price, although the court never directly made this accusation). Reliance on a CEO (or lawyer or other professional) is, per Delaware General Corporation Law Section 141(e), perfectly appropriate, but under the statute, reliance must be on a "report." The court held Van Gorkom's information not to be a "report," because he was inadequately informed as to the "intrinsic value" of the company's stock, and the directors were held not entitled to rely upon it because they failed to ask questions that would elicit this information. Notwithstanding curative action subsequently taken by the board, including a market test designed to elicit interest from other bidders (which test the court discounted as flawed), the court relied largely on the failures of the first meeting at which the merger was approved to hold the directors liable for breach of their duty of care.

Why *Van Gorkom* and why in 1985? A number of reasons are plausible, but perhaps the most likely reason is that 1985 was a point during which the tender offer frenzy of the 1980s was well under way, bust-ups of established companies (with accompanying dislocations like layoffs) were occurring, and the strange new instrument of junk bond financing had been introduced in many of these transactions. Not only was there concern in the state houses (Pennsylvania passed the first statutory anti-takeover measure in 1983 in response to a particular hostile acquisition bid), but Congress had started to inquire into a number of aspects of this phenomenon as well. The Delaware court, likely fearing federal intervention and the loss of its franchise as corporate law's preeminent state (and the revenue that went with it), likely wanted to make a statement about its responsible regulation of corporate behavior. *Van Gorkom* was the result: it held directors liable for breach of the duty of care while narrowly defining the scope of that duty.

But even such limited assertion of responsibility was not long-lived. Shortly thereafter, the Delaware legislature enacted **Section 102(b)(7) of the Delaware General Corporation Law**, permitting corporations to include in their certificates of incorporation "A provision eliminating or limiting the personal liability of a director to the corporation or its stockholders for monetary damages for breach of fiduciary duty as a director, provided that such provision shall not eliminate or limit the liability of a director: (i) for any breach of the directors' duty of loyalty to the corporation or its stockholders; (ii) for acts or omissions not in good faith or which involve intentional misconduct or a knowing violation of law; (iii) under section 174 of this title [which deals with the payment of dividends]; or (iv) for any transaction from which the director derived an improper personal benefit . . . ." Corporate America calmed down, other states followed suit, and the charter amendment business picked up a great deal.

We will explore the implications of section 102(b)(7) in our discussion of good faith in Section IV. First, we turn to the duty of loyalty, the fiduciary duty.

Section III

The Duty of Loyalty

The duty of loyalty is corporate law's version of fiduciary duty. Fiduciary duties are duties of position or status. They exist in relations of power and dependency, that is, when one person cedes control of some aspect of his or her life to another who is empowered essentially to conduct that aspect of his or her life. The person who ceded control is relatively powerless to affect the conduct of the powerful person. Fiduciary duties allow some people to trust others (sometimes even unknown others) with the management of their personal business by backstopping that trust with the legal obligation of the fiduciary to act in the beneficiary's interest, and by providing legal redress to the beneficiary when the fiduciary fails to do so. Trustees have fiduciary obligations to the beneficiaries of trusts, agents to principals, lawyers to clients, parents to children, and directors and officers to the corporation and its shareholders.

In corporate law, the duty of loyalty requires that in discharging their duties, directors and officers put the interests of the corporation and its stockholders first. One might say that the law requires (except in the case of takeovers and mergers) that they put the interests of the corporation first, but in our current normative environment, it is probably more realistic to think of the duty as running in the interests of stockholders as well (although the duty of loyalty, like the duty of care is, with rare exceptions, enforceable only derivatively in the interest of the corporation).

The duty of loyalty is relevant to different types of conflicts. Subsection A begins by looking at a category of transactions known as interested director transactions (or self-dealing) and explores both the common law and statutory embodiments of the duty of loyalty in those situations. We then examine the corporate opportunity doctrine (Subsection B), and compensation and waste (Subsection C). The duties of controlling shareholders which bring together our analysis of the fiduciary duties of shareholders in closely-held corporations and our examination of the fiduciary duties of directors and officers will be treated in Part 3. The duty of loyalty also appears in the merger and takeover context, and we will address it in this context in Part 4.

A. Interested Director Transactions

In the nineteenth century, directors and officers, viewed as trustees or at least quasi-trustees, were prohibited from receiving benefits out of their fiduciary relationship with the corporation and its shareholders. Any contract between a director and his corporation was accordingly voidable at the request of the corporation or its shareholders. In 1880, summarizing the rule of law, Justice Field held:

> Directors of corporations, and all persons who stand in a fiduciary relation to other parties, and are clothed with power to act for them, are subject to this rule; they are not permitted to occupy a position which will conflict with the interest of parties they represent and are bound to protect. They cannot, as agents or trustees, enter into or authorize contracts on behalf of those for whom they are appointed to act, and then personally participate in the benefits.

Wardell v. R.R. Co., 103 U.S. 651 (1880).

Underlying the courts' strict rule — the sole interest rule derived from trust law — was an appreciation of the trust relationship between directors and their corporations, that is, the need to ensure that investors could trust that those who managed their money would not place themselves in a conflict-of-interest situation. In addition, the courts expressed an understanding of the nature of human relations; accordingly, directors could not be expected to scrutinize a contract with another board member. The rule applied to all situations where potential conflict existed, be it contracts between a director and the corporation, dealings between corporations with interlocking directorates (even when only a minority of the board members were common), or dealings between parent and subsidiary corporations.

In the first half of the twentieth century, the nineteenth century's understanding of the nature of human interactions gave way to the needs of business and managers, as courts rapidly moved away from a strict rule of prohibition to allow directors to engage in transactions and situations that had thus far been prohibited as violations of their duty of loyalty. A contract between a corporation and its director could be valid if a disinterested majority of the directors approved it and it was not "unfair or fraudulent." If a majority of the board was interested, the contract was voidable at the request of the corporation or its shareholders without regard to its fairness.

In the second half of the twentieth century, fairness became the standard for evaluating all self-dealing transactions (even those where a majority of the board members were interested). For more on this shift from trust to fairness, see Harold Marsh, Jr., *Are Directors Trustees?* 22 Bus. Law. 35 (1966).

Meinhard v. Salmon
249 N.Y. 458 (1928)

CARDOZO, Chief Judge

On April 10, 1902, Louisa M. Gerry leased to the defendant Walter J. Salmon the premises known as the Hotel Bristol at the northwest corner of Forty-Second street and Fifth avenue in the city of New York. The lease was for a term of 20 years, commencing May 1, 1902, and ending April 30, 1922. The lessee undertook to change the hotel building for use as shops and offices at a cost of $200,000. Alterations and additions were to be accretions to the land.

Salmon, while in course of treaty with the lessor as to the execution of the lease, was in course of treaty with Meinhard, the plaintiff, for the necessary funds. The result was a joint venture with terms embodied in a writing. Meinhard was to pay to Salmon half of the moneys requisite to reconstruct, alter, manage, and operate the property. Salmon was to pay to Meinhard 40 percent of the net profits for the first five years of the lease and 50 percent for the years thereafter. If there were losses, each party was to bear them equally. Salmon, however, was to have sole power to "manage, lease, underlet and operate" the building. There were to be certain pre-emptive rights for each in the contingency of death.

The two were coadventurers, subject to fiduciary duties akin to those of partners. As to this we are all agreed. The heavier weight of duty rested, however, upon Salmon. He was a coadventurer with Meinhard, but he was manager as well. During the early years of the enterprise, the building, reconstructed, was operated at a loss. If the relation had then ended, Meinhard as well as Salmon would have carried a heavy burden. Later the profits became large with the result that for each of the investors there came a rich return. For each the venture had its phases of fair weather and of foul. The two were in it jointly, for better or for worse.

When the lease was near its end, Elbridge T. Gerry had become the owner of the reversion. He owned much other property in the neighborhood, one lot adjoining the Bristol building on Fifth avenue and four lots on Forty-Second street. He had a plan to lease the entire tract for a long term to some one who would destroy the buildings then existing and put up another in their place. In the latter part of 1921, he submitted such a project to several capitalists and dealers. He was unable to carry it through with any of them. Then, in January, 1922, with less than four months of the lease to run, he approached the defendant Salmon. The result was a new lease to the Midpoint Realty Company, which is owned and controlled by Salmon, a lease covering the whole tract, and involving a huge outlay. The term is to be 20 years, but successive covenants for renewal will extend it to a maximum of 80 years at the will of either party. The existing buildings may remain unchanged for seven years. They are then to be torn down, and a new building to cost $3,000,000 is to be placed upon the site. The rental, which under the Bristol lease was only $55,000, is to be from $350,000 to $475,000 for the properties so combined. Salmon personally guaranteed the performance by the lessee of the covenants of the new lease until such time as the new building had been completed and fully paid for.

The lease between Gerry and the Midpoint Realty Company was signed and delivered on January 25, 1922. Salmon had not told Meinhard anything about it. Whatever his motive may have been, he had kept the negotiations to himself. Meinhard was not informed even of the bare existence of a project. The first that he knew of it was in February, when the lease was an accomplished fact. He then made demand on the defendants that the lease be held in trust as an asset of the venture, making offer upon the trial to share the personal obligations incidental to the guaranty. The demand was followed by refusal, and later by this suit. A referee gave judgment for the plaintiff, limiting the plaintiff's interest in the lease, however, to 25 per cent. The limitation was on the theory that the plaintiff's equity was to be restricted to one-half of so much of the value of the lease as was contributed or represented by the occupation of the Bristol site. Upon cross-appeals to the Appellate Division, the judgment was modified so as to enlarge the equitable interest to one-half of the whole lease. With this enlargement of plaintiff's interest, there went, of course, a corresponding enlargement of his attendant obligations. The case is now here on an appeal by the defendants.

Joint adventurers, like copartners, owe to one another, while the enterprise continues, the duty of the finest loyalty. Many forms of conduct permissible in a workaday world for those acting at arm's length, are forbidden to those bound by fiduciary ties. A trustee is held to something stricter than the morals of the market place. Not honesty alone, but the punctilio of an honor the most sensitive, is then the standard of behavior. As to this there has developed a tradition that is unbending and inveterate. Uncompromising rigidity has been the attitude of courts of equity when petitioned to undermine the rule of undivided loyalty by the "disintegrating erosion" of particular exceptions. Only thus has the level of conduct for fiduciaries been kept at a level higher than that trodden by the crowd. It will not consciously be lowered by any judgment of this court.

The owner of the reversion, Mr. Gerry, had vainly striven to find a tenant who would favor his ambitious scheme of demolition and construction. Baffled in the search, he turned to the defendant Salmon in possession of the Bristol, the keystone of the project. He figured to himself beyond a doubt that the man in possession would prove a likely customer. To the eye of an observer, Salmon held the lease as owner in his own right, for himself and no one else. In fact he held it as a fiduciary, for himself and another, sharers in a common venture. If this fact had been proclaimed, if the lease by its terms had run in favor of a partnership, Mr. Gerry, we may fairly assume, would have laid before the partners, and not merely before one of them, his plan of reconstruction. The pre-emptive privilege, or, better, the pre-emptive opportunity, that was thus an incident of the enterprise, Salmon appropriate to himself in secrecy and silence. He might have warned Meinhard that the plan had been submitted, and that either would be free to compete for the award. If he had done this, we do not need to say whether he would have been under a duty, if successful in the competition, to hold the lease so acquired for the benefit of a venture then about to end, and thus prolong by indirection its responsibilities and duties. The trouble about his conduct is that he excluded his coadventurer from any chance to compete, from any chance to enjoy the opportunity for benefit that had come to him alone by virtue of his agency. This chance, if nothing more, he was under a duty to concede. The price of its denial is an extension of the trust at the option and for the benefit of the one whom he excluded.

No answer is it to say that the chance would have been of little value even if seasonably offered. Such a calculus of probabilities is beyond the science of the chancery. Salmon, the real estate operator, might have been preferred to Meinhard, the woolen merchant. On the other hand, Meinhard might have offered better terms, or reinforced his offer by alliance with the wealth of others. Perhaps he might even have persuaded the lessor to renew the Bristol lease alone, postponing for a time, in return for higher rentals, the improvement of adjoining lots. We know that even under the lease as made the time for the enlargement of the building was delayed for seven years. All these opportunities were cut away from him through another's intervention. He knew that Salmon was the manager. As the time drew near for the expiration of the lease, he would naturally assume from silence, if from nothing else, that the lessor was willing to extend it for a term of years, or at least to let it stand as a lease from year to year. Not impossibly the lessor would have done so, whatever his protestations of unwillingness, if Salmon had not given assent to a project more attractive. At all events, notice of termination, even if not necessary, might seem, not unreasonably, to be something to be looked for, if the business was over and another tenant was to enter. In the absence of such notice, the matter of an extension was one that would naturally be attended to by the manager of the enterprise, and not neglected altogether. At least, there was nothing in the situation to give warning to any one that while the lease was still in being, there had come to the manager an offer of extension which he had locked within his breast to be utilized by himself alone. The very fact that Salmon was in control with exclusive powers of direction charged him the more obviously with the duty of disclosure, since only through disclosure could opportunity be equalized. If he might cut off renewal by a purchase for his own benefit when four months were to pass before the lease would have an end, he might do so with equal right while there remained as many years. He might steal a march on his comrade under cover of the darkness, and then hold the captured ground. Loyalty and comradeship are not so easily abjured.

Little profit will come from a dissection of the precedents. None precisely similar is cited in the briefs of counsel. What is similar in many, or so it seems to us, is the animating principle. Authority is, of course, abundant that one partner may not appropriate to his own use a renewal of a lease, though its term is to begin at the expiration of the partnership. The lease at hand with its many changes is not strictly a renewal. Even so, the standard of loyalty for those in trust relations is without the fixed divisions of a graduated scale. There is indeed a dictum in one of our decisions that a partner, though he may not renew a lease, may purchase the reversion if he acts openly and fairly. It is a dictum, and no more, for on the ground that he had acted slyly he was charged as a trustee. The holding is thus in favor of the conclusion that a purchase as well as a lease will succumb to the infection of secrecy and silence. Against the dictum in that case, moreover, may be set the opinion of Dwight, C., in *Mitchell v. Read*, where there is a dictum to the contrary. To say that a partner is free without restriction to buy in the reversion of the property where the business is conducted is to say in effect that he may strip the good will of its chief element of value, since good will is largely dependent upon continuity of possession. Equity refuses to confine within the bounds of classified transactions its precept of a loyalty that is undivided and unselfish. Certain at least it is that a "man obtaining his locus standi, and his opportunity for making such arrangements, by the position he occupies as a partner, is bound by his obligation to his copartners in such dealings not to separate his interest from theirs, but, if he acquires any benefit, to communicate it to them." Certain it is also that there may be no abuse of special opportunities growing out of a special trust as manager or agent. If conflicting inferences are possible as to abuse or opportunity, the trier of the facts must make the choice between them. There can be no revision in this court unless the choice is clearly wrong. It is no answer for the fiduciary to say "that he was not bound to risk his money as he did, or to go into the enterprise at all." "He might have kept out of it altogether, but if he went in, he could not withhold from his employer the benefit of the bargain." A constructive trust is, then, the remedial device through which preference of self is made subordinate to loyalty to others. Many and varied are its phases and occasions.

We have no thought to hold that Salmon was guilty of a conscious purpose to defraud. Very likely he assumed in all good faith that with the approaching end of the venture he might ignore his coadventurer and take the extension for himself. He had given to the enterprise time and labor as well as money. He had made it a success. Meinhard, who had given money, but neither time nor labor, had already been richly paid. There might seem to be something grasping in his insistence upon more. Such recriminations are not unusual when coadventurers fall out. They are not without their force if conduct is to be judged by the common standards of competitors. That is not to say that they have pertinency here. Salmon had put himself in a position in which thought of self was to be renounced, however hard the abnegation. He was much more than a coadventurer. He was a managing coadventurer. For him and for those like him the rule of undivided loyalty is relentless and supreme. A different question would be here if there were lacking any nexus of relation between the business conducted by the manager and the opportunity brought to him as an incident of management. For this problem, as for most, there are distinctions of degree. If Salmon had received from Gerry a proposition to lease a building at a location far removed, he might have held for himself the privilege thus acquired, or so we shall assume. Here the subject-matter of the new lease was an extension and enlargement of the subject-matter of the old one. A managing coadventurer appropriating the benefit of such a lease without warning to his partner might fairly expect to be reproached with conduct that was underhand, or lacking, to say the least, in reasonable candor, if the partner were to surprise him in the act of signing the new instrument. Conduct subject to that reproach does not receive from equity a healing benediction.

A question remains as to the form and extent of the equitable interest to be allotted to the plaintiff. The trust as declared has been held to attach to the lease which was in the name of the defendant corporation. We think it ought to attach at the option of the defendant Salmon to the shares of stock which were owned by him or were under his control. The difference may be important if the lessee shall wish to execute an assignment of the lease, as it ought to be free to do with the consent of the lessor. On the other hand, an equal division of the shares might lead to other hardships. It might take away from Salmon the power of control and management which under the plan of the joint venture he was to have from first to last. The number of shares to be allotted to the plaintiff should, therefore, be reduced to such an extent as may be necessary to preserve to the defendant Salmon the expected measure of dominion. To that end an extra share should be added to his half.

Subject to this adjustment, we agree with the Appellate Division that the plaintiff's equitable interest is to be measured by the value of half of the entire lease, and not merely by half of some undivided part. A single building covers the whole area. Physical division is impracticable along the lines of the Bristol site, the keystone of the whole. Division of interests and burdens is equally impracticable. Salmon, as tenant under the new lease, or as guarantor of the performance of the tenant's obligations, might well protest if Meinhard, claiming an equitable interest, had offered to assume a liability not equal to Salmon's, but only half as great. He might justly insist that the lease must be accepted by his coadventurer in such form as it had been given, and not constructively divided into imaginary fragments. What must be yielded to the one may be demanded by the other. The lease as it has been executed is single and entire. If confusion has resulted from the union of adjoining parcels, the trustee who consented to the union must bear the inconvenience. . . .

The judgment should be modified by providing that at the option of the defendant Salmon there may be substituted for a trust attaching to the lease a trust attaching to the shares of stock, with the result that one-half of such shares together with one additional share will in that event be allotted to the defendant Salmon and the other shares to the plaintiff, and as so modified the judgment should be affirmed with costs.

Questions

1. According to Cardozo, what did Salmon do wrong? What should Salmon have done?

2. What is Cardozo's definition of fiduciary duties? What would you advise a client in Salmon's position? Can you generalize a test to determine when a fiduciary breaches his or her trust?

3. Judge Andrews, in dissent, argued that the reason no duty was breached was that the arrangement in the case was a joint venture for a limited term, and that the new arrangement Salmon entered into was sufficiently different from the original lease so as not to constitute a partnership opportunity. Andrews doesn't deny the existence of a duty. Rather, he notes a range of duties, from that of good faith in a mere executory contract to the kind of duty Cardozo talks about in a true general partnership. Who has the better argument in the context of this business deal? Who has the better argument in terms of ensuring honorable business conduct more generally? As a matter of policy, whose argument would you choose as the groundwork for fiduciary law? Why?

4. Cardozo's decision seems emotionally charged. Why? The case involved two relatively wealthy men who established their deal, at least at the outset, at arm's length and had the opportunity to negotiate and specify its terms. Why did Cardozo feel so strongly about it? Where in Manhattan was the property located? What are its nearest landmarks? Think about (or look into the history of) the development of this part of New York. Is there anything in that history which might lead you to see Salmon's treatment of Meinhard as something more egregious than simple opportunism?

Bayer v. Beran
49 N.Y.S.2d 2 (1944)

SHIENTAG, Justice

These derivative stockholders' suits present for review two transactions upon which plaintiffs seek to charge the individual defendants, who are directors, with liability in favor of the corporate defendant, the Celanese Corporation of America. There are two causes of action alleging breach of fiduciary duty by the directors, one in connection with a program of radio advertising embarked upon by the corporation towards the end of 1941. . . . Before taking up the specific transactions complained of, I shall consider generally certain pertinent rules to be applied in determining the liability of directors of a business corporation such as is here involved.

Despite abuses that have developed in connection with the derivative stockholders' suit, abuses which should be dealt with promptly and effectively, it must be remembered that such an action is, at present, the only civil remedy that stockholders have for breach of fiduciary duty on the part of those entrusted with the management and direction of their corporations. We cannot therefore allow the prevailing mood of justifiable dissatisfaction with some of the temporary incidents of such suits to cause us to lose sight of certain deep-rooted, traditional concepts of the obligations of directors to their corporation and its stockholders.

Directors of a business corporation are not trustees and are not held to strict accountability as such. Nevertheless, their obligations are analogous to those of trustees. Directors are agents; they are fiduciaries. The fiduciary has two paramount obligations: responsibility and loyalty. Those obligations apply with equal force to the humblest agent or broker and to the director of a great and powerful corporation. They lie at the very foundation of our whole system of free private enterprise and are as fresh and significant today as when they were formulated decades ago. The responsibility—that is, the care and the diligence—required of an agent or of a fiduciary, is proportioned to the occasion. It is a concept that has, and necessarily so, a wide penumbra of meaning—a concept, however, which becomes sharpened in its practical application to the given facts of a situation.

The concept of loyalty, of constant, unqualified fidelity, has a definite and precise meaning. The fiduciary must subordinate his individual and private interests to his duty to the corporation whenever the two conflict. In an address delivered in 1934, Mr. Justice, now Chief Justice, Stone declared that the fiduciary principle of undivided loyalty was, in effect, "the precept as old as Holy Writ, that 'a man cannot serve two masters'. More than a century ago equity gave a hospitable reception to that principle and the common law was not slow to follow in giving it recognition. No thinking man can believe that an economy built upon a business foundation can long endure without loyalty to that principle." He went on to say that "The separation of ownership from management, the development of the corporate structure so as to vest in small groups control of resources of great numbers of small and uninformed investors, make imperative a fresh and active devotion to that principle if the modern world of business is to perform its proper function" . . . . [The court restates the business judgment rule and its justification.]

The "business judgment rule", however, yields to the rule of undivided loyalty. This great rule of law is designed "to avoid the possibility of fraud and to avoid the temptation of self-interest." It is "designed to obliterate all divided loyalties which may creep into a fiduciary relation. . . ." Thacher, J., in *City Bank Farmers Trust Co. v. Cannon*. "Included within its scope is every situation in which a trustee chooses to deal with another in such close relation with the trustee that possible advantage to such other person might influence, consciously or unconsciously, the judgment of the trustee. . . ." The dealings of a director with the corporation for which he is the fiduciary are therefore viewed "with jealousy by the courts." Such personal transactions of directors with their corporations, such transactions as may tend to produce a conflict between self-interest and fiduciary obligation, are, when challenged, examined with the most scrupulous care, and if there is any evidence of improvidence or oppression, any indication of unfairness or undue advantage, the transactions will be voided. "Their dealings with the corporation are subjected to rigorous scrutiny and where any of their contracts or engagements with the corporation are challenged the burden is on the director not only to prove the good faith of the transaction but also to show its inherent fairness from the viewpoint of the corporation and those interested therein."

While there is a high moral purpose implicit in this transcendent fiduciary principle of undivided loyalty, it has back of it a profound understanding of human nature and of its frailties. It actually accomplishes a practical, beneficent purpose. It tends to prevent a clouded conception of fidelity that blurs the vision. It preserves the free exercise of judgment uncontaminated by the dross of divided allegiance or self-interest. It prevents the operation of an influence that may be indirect but that is all the more potent for that reason. The law has set its face firmly against undermining "the rule of undivided loyalty by the 'disintegrating erosion' of particular exceptions." *Meinhard v. Salmon.*

The first, or "advertising", cause of action charges the directors with negligence, waste and improvidence in embarking the corporation upon a radio advertising program beginning in 1942 and costing about $1,000,000 a year. It is further charged that they were negligent in selecting the type of program and in renewing the radio contract for 1943. More serious than these allegations is the charge that the directors were motivated by a noncorporate purpose in causing the radio program to be undertaken and in expending large sums of money therefor. It is claimed that this radio advertising was for the benefit of Miss Jean Tennyson, one of the singers on the program, who in private life is Mrs. Camille Dreyfus, the wife of the president of the company and one of its directors; that it was undertaken to "further, foster and subsidize her career"; to "furnish a vehicle" for her talents.

Eliminating for the moment the part played by Miss Tennyson in the radio advertising campaign, it is clear that the character of the advertising, the amount to be expended therefor, and the manner in which it should be used, are all matters of business judgment and rest peculiarly within the discretion of the board of directors. Under the authorities previously cited, it is not, generally speaking, the function of a court of equity to review these matters or even to consider them. Had the wife of the president of the company not been involved, the advertising cause of action could have been disposed of summarily. Her connection with the program, however, makes it necessary to go into the facts in some detail.

Before 1942 the company had not resorted to radio advertising. While it had never maintained a fixed advertising budget, the company had, through its advertising department, spent substantial sums of money for advertising purposes. In 1941, for example, the advertising expense was $683,000, as against net sales for that year of $62,277,000 and net profits (before taxes) of $13,972,000. The advertising was at all times directed towards the creation of a consumer preference which would compel or induce the various trade elements linking the corporation to the consumer to label the corporation's products so that the consumer would know he was buying the material he wanted. The company had always claimed that its products, which it had called or labeled "Celanese", were different from rayon, chemically and physically; that its products had qualities, special and unique, which made them superior to rayon. The company had never called or designated its products as rayon.

As far back as ten years ago, a radio program was considered, but it did not seem attractive. In 1937, the Federal Trade Commission promulgated a rule, the effect of which was to require all celanese products to be designated and labeled rayon. The name "Celanese" could no longer be used alone. The products had to be called or labeled "rayon" or "celanese rayon". This gave the directors much concern. As one of them expressed it, "When we were compelled to put our product under the same umbrella with rayon rather than being left outside as a separate product, a thermoplastic such as nylon is, we believed we were being treated in an unfair manner and that it was up to us, however, to do the best we could to circumvent the situation in which we found ourselves.... All manner of things were considered but there seemed only one thing we could do. We could either multiply our current advertising and our method of advertising in the same mediums we had been using, or we could go into radio".

The directors, in considering the matter informally, but not collectively as a board, decided towards the end of 1941 to resort to the radio and to have the company go on the air with a dignified program of fine music, the kind of program which they felt would be in keeping with what they believed to be the beauty and superior quality of their products. The radio program was not adopted on the spur of the moment or at the whim of the directors. They acted after studies reported to them, made by the advertising department, beginning in 1939. A radio consultant was employed to advise as to time and station. An advertising agency of national repute was engaged to take charge of the formulation and production of the program. It was decided to expend about $1,000,000 a year, but the commitments were to be subject to cancellation every thirteen weeks, so that the maximum obligation of the company would be not more than $250,000.

So far, there is nothing on which to base any claim of breach of fiduciary duty. Some care, diligence and prudence were exercised by these directors before they committed the company to the radio program. It was for the directors to determine whether they would resort to radio advertising; it was for them to conclude how much to spend; it was for them to decide the kind of program they would use. It would be an unwarranted act of interference for any court to attempt to substitute its judgment on these points for that of the directors, honestly arrived at. The expenditure was not reckless or unconscionable. Indeed, it bore a fair relationship to the total amount of net sales and to the earnings of the company. The fact that the company had offers of more business than it could handle did not, in law, preclude advertising. Many corporations not now doing any business in their products because of emergency conditions advertise those products extensively in order to preserve the good will, the public interest, during the war period. The fact that the company's product may not now be identifiable did not bar advertising calculated to induce consumer demand for such identification. That a program of classical and semiclassical music was selected, rather than a variety program, or a news commentator program, furnishes no ground for legal complaint. True, variety programs have a wider popular appeal than do musicals, but it would be a very sad thing if the former were the only kind of radio programs to be used. Some of the largest industrial concerns in the country have recognized this and have maintained fine musical programs on the radio for many years.

Now we have to take up an unfortunate incident, one which cannot be viewed with the complacency displayed by some of the directors of the company. This is not a closely held family corporation. The Doctors Dreyfus and their families own about 135,000 shares of common stock, the other directors about 10,000 shares out of a total outstanding issue of 1,376,500 shares. Some of these other directors were originally employed by Dr. Camille Dreyfus, the president of the company. His wife, to whom he has been married for about twelve years, is known professionally as Miss Jean Tennyson and is a singer of wide experience.

Dr. Dreyfus, as was natural, consulted his wife about the proposed radio program; he also asked the advertising agency, that had been retained, to confer with her about it. She suggested the names of the artists, all stars of the Metropolitan Opera Company, and the name of the conductor, prominent in his field. She also offered her own services as a paid artist. All of her suggestions as to personnel were adopted by the advertising agency. While the record shows Miss Tennyson to be a competent singer, there is nothing to indicate that she was indispensable or essential to the success of the program. She received $500 an evening. It would be far-fetched to suggest that the directors caused the company to incur large expenditures for radio advertising to enable the president's wife to make $24,000 in 1942 and $20,500 in 1943.

Of course it is not improper to appoint relatives of officers or directors to responsible positions in a company. But where a close relative of the chief executive officer of a corporation, and one of its dominant directors, takes a position closely associated with a new and expensive field of activity, the motives of the directors are likely to be questioned. The board would be placed in a position where selfish, personal interests might be in conflict with the duty it owed to the corporation. That being so, the entire transaction, if challenged in the courts, must be subjected to the most rigorous scrutiny to determine whether the action of the directors was intended or calculated "to subserve some outside purpose, regardless of the consequences to the company, and in a manner inconsistent with its interests."

After such careful scrutiny I have concluded that, up to the present, there has been no breach of fiduciary duty on the part of the directors. The president undoubtedly knew that his wife might be one of the paid artists on the program. The other directors did not know this until they had approved the campaign of radio advertising and the general type of radio program. The evidence fails to show that the program was designed to foster or subsidize "the career of Miss Tennyson as an artist" or to "furnish a vehicle for her talents". That her participation in the program may have enhanced her prestige as a singer is no ground for subjecting the directors to liability, as long as the advertising served a legitimate and a useful corporate purpose and the company received the full benefit thereof.

The musical quality of "Celanese Hour" has not been challenged, nor does the record contain anything reflecting on Miss Tennyson's competence as an artist. There is nothing in the testimony to show that some other soprano would have enhanced the artistic quality of the program or its advertising appeal. There is no suggestion that the present program is inefficient or that its cost is disproportionate to what a program of that character reasonably entails. Miss Tennyson's contract with the advertising agency retained by the directors was on a standard form, negotiated through her professional agent. Her compensation, as well as that of the other artists, was in conformity with that paid for comparable work. She received less than any of the other artists on the program. Although she appeared with a greater regularity than any other singer, she received no undue prominence, no special build-up. Indeed, all of the artists were subordinated to the advertisement of the company and of its products. The company was featured. It appears also that the popularity of the program has increased since it was inaugurated.

It is clear, therefore, that the directors have not been guilty of any breach of fiduciary duty, in embarking upon the program of radio advertising and in renewing it. It is unfortunate that they have allowed themselves to be placed in a position where their motives concerning future decisions on radio advertising may be impugned. The free mind should be ever jealous of its freedom. "Power of control carries with it a trust or duty to exercise that power faithfully to promote the corporate interests, and the courts of this State will insist upon scrupulous performance of that duty." Thus far, that duty has been performed and with noteworthy success. The corporation has not, up to the present time, been wronged by the radio advertising attacked in the complaints.

It is urged that the expenditures were illegal because the radio advertising program was not taken up at any formal meeting of the board of directors, and no resolution approving it was adopted by the board or by the executive committee. The general rule is that directors acting separately and not collectively as a board cannot bind the corporation. There are two reasons for this: first, that collective procedure is necessary in order that action may be deliberately taken after an opportunity for discussion and an interchange of views; and second, that directors are the agents of the stockholders and are given by law no power to act except as a board. Liability may not, however, be imposed on directors because they failed to approve the radio program by resolution at a board meeting.

It is desirable to follow the regular procedure, prescribed by law, which is something more than what has, at times, thoughtlessly been termed red tape. Long experience has demonstrated the necessity for doing this in order to safeguard the interests of all concerned, particularly where, as here, the company has over 1,375,000 shares outstanding in the hands of the public, of which about 10% are held by the officers and directors.

But the failure to observe the formal requirements is by no means fatal. The directorate of this company is composed largely of its executive officers. It is a close, working directorate. Its members are in daily association with one another and their full time is devoted to the business of the company with which they have been connected for many years. In this respect it differs from the boards of many corporations of comparable size, where the directorate is made up of men of varied interests who meet only at stated, and somewhat infrequent, intervals.

The same informal practice followed in this transaction had been the customary procedure of the directors in acting on corporate projects of equal and greater magnitude. All of the members of the executive committee were available for daily consultation and they discussed and approved the plan for radio advertising. While a greater degree of formality should undoubtedly be exercised in the future, it is only just and proper to point out that these directors, with all their loose procedure, have done very well for the corporation. Under their administration the company has thrived and prospered. Its assets increased from $44,500,000 in 1935 to upwards of $103,000,000 in 1942. Its net profits, after taxes, doubled during that period, rising from $4,000,000 in 1935 to $8,000,000 in 1942; its net sales rose from $27,000,000 to upwards of $86,000,000; and its dividend disbursements to stockholders exceeded $29,500,000.

The expenditures for radio advertising, although made without resolution at a formal meeting of the board, were approved and authorized by the members individually, and may in no sense be considered to have been ultra vires. The resolution adopted by the board on July 6, 1943, with all of the directors present, except two who were resident in England, while expressly ratifying only the renewal of the broadcasting contract, may be deemed a ratification of all prior action taken in connection with the radio advertising. When this resolution was adopted, the Celanese Hour had been on the air to the knowledge of all the directors for eighteen months. Moreover, acceptance and retention of the benefits of the radio advertising, with full knowledge thereof, was as complete a ratification as would have resulted from any formal all-inclusive resolution. . . .

Questions

1. What is the rule of *Bayer v. Beran*? How is it different from the rule Cardozo applied in *Meinhard v. Salmon*?

2. With respect to the conflict of interest claim, who bore the burden of proof in *Bayer v. Beran*?

3. Do you agree with the court's reliance upon informal board action with subsequent ratification? Imagine yourself as a board member — what would you most

likely have done if presented, informally, with Dreyfus's plan? How would your behavior be likely to change, if at all, if he called a meeting well after the advertising program was in progress to ask you to ratify it? Is there a reason why board ratification of conflict transactions should be prohibited?

4. Jean Tennyson was a singer of some accomplishment. According to her obituary in the *Chicago Tribune* (March 20, 1991), the *Tribune* music critic covering her 1934 debut with the Chicago Lyric Opera as Mimi in *La Boheme* wrote, "Miss Tennyson ... justified herself both as a singer and personality of the operatic stage. She has a voice with both beauty and quality in it, one that takes the high ranges of the score with complete ease and gives warmth and vitality." According to *The New York Times* (March 19, 1991), she sang at La Scala and with the San Francisco Opera Company among others, and "she also sang on the CBS Radio program, 'Great Moments in Music' from 1942 to 1946" (the subject of this case). She appears to have had a keen interest in popularizing opera, renting a box at the Chicago Lyric Opera that she used exclusively for students who couldn't afford to attend on their own.

5. What are the differences between the trust and fairness standards of review?

6. Are there efficiencies in permitting self-dealing transactions? If so, do you expect that the same efficiency considerations would apply in all corporations or is there a difference, for example, between closely- and publicly-held corporations? If so, how might you structure different sets of rules to cover the different contexts? Consider these questions as you read the cases following section 144 below.

Delaware General Corporation Law Section 144

(a) No contract or transaction between a corporation and 1 or more of its directors or officers, or between a corporation and any other corporation, partnership, association, or other organization in which 1 or more of its directors or officers, are directors or officers, or have a financial interest, shall be void or voidable solely for this reason, or solely because the director or officer is present at or participates in the meeting of the board or committee which authorizes the contract or transaction, or solely because any such director's or officer's votes are counted for such purpose, if:

(1) The material facts as to the director's or officer's relationship or interest and as to the contract or transaction are disclosed or are known to the board of directors or the committee, and the board or committee in good faith authorizes the contract or transaction by the affirmative votes of a majority of the disinterested directors, even though the disinterested directors be less than a quorum; or

(2) The material facts as to the director's or officer's relationship or interest and as to the contract or transaction are disclosed or are known to the stockholders entitled to vote thereon, and the contract or transaction is specifically approved in good faith by vote of the stockholders; or

(3) The contract or transaction is fair as to the corporation as of the time it is authorized, approved or ratified, by the board of directors, a committee or the stockholders.

(b) Common or interested directors may be counted in determining the presence of a quorum at a meeting of the board of directors or of a committee which authorizes the contract or transaction.

The Delaware Supreme Court first addressed the effects of section 144 with respect to transactions in which directors or officers had a personal interest in *Fliegler v. Lawrence*, 361 A.2d 218 (1976). The case involved an option agreement between Agau Mines, Inc. (Agau), a publicly held corporation, and United States Antimony Corporation (USAC), a closely held corporation. Directors and officers of Agau owned a majority of the stock of USAC. The agreement, which the boards of Agau and USAC executed, gave Agau an option "to deliver 800,000 shares of its restricted investment stock for all authorized and issued shares of USAC." Six months after its execution, "the Agau board resolved to exercise the option, an action which was approved by majority vote of the shareholders," presumably in compliance with section 144(a)(2). A dissenting shareholder brought a derivative suit on behalf of Agau "to recover the 800,000 shares and for an accounting."

Viewing the transaction as a self-dealing transaction ("for it is clear that the individual defendants stood on both sides of the transaction in implementing and fixing the terms of the option agreement"), the court went on to address the effects of section 144 on the fairness standard of review. The defendant directors argued that "they have been relieved of the burden of proving fairness by reason of shareholder ratification of the Board's decision to exercise the option." Because the individual defendants held a majority of the shares voted, the court concluded that the directors did not factually establish their claim. More important, the court stressed that compliance with section 144 did not remove a transaction from judicial scrutiny. Rather, when its terms were met, an agreement in which a director or an officer had an interest would not be invalidated because of such involvement. Instead, it would be scrutinized under a test of fairness.

Turning to the transaction itself, the court carefully evaluated its substance, concluding that it was entirely fair to the corporation:

> Agau received properties which by themselves were clearly of substantial value. But more importantly, it received a promising, potentially self-financing and profit generating enterprise with proven markets and commercial capability which could well be expected to provide Agau at the very least with the cash it sorely needed to undertake further exploration and development of its own properties if not to stay in existence. For those reasons, we believe that the interest given to the USAC shareholders was a fair price to pay. Accordingly, we have no doubt but that this transaction was one

which at that time would have commended itself to an independent corporation in Agau's position.

Fliegler, in short, confirmed that section 144 merely removed "an 'interested director' cloud when its terms are met," leaving the courts to assess the substantive fairness of the transaction.

The following two cases offer interpretations of section 144 after *Fliegler*. As you read them, recall Cardozo's *punctilio of honor*. What is left of it, or of the standard of fairness, after these two cases? What is left of the duty of loyalty?

Marciano v. Nakash

535 A.2d 400 (Del. 1987)

WALSH, Justice

This is an appeal from a decision of the Court of Chancery which validated a claim in liquidation of Gasoline, Ltd. ("Gasoline"), a Delaware corporation, placed in custodial status pursuant to 8 Del.C. § 226 by reason of a deadlock among its board of directors. Fifty percent of Gasoline is owned by Ari, Joe, and Ralph Nakash (the "Nakashes") and fifty percent by Georges, Maurice, Armand and Paul Marciano (the "Marcianos"). The Vice Chancellor ruled that $2.5 million in loans made by the Nakashes faction to Gasoline were valid and enforceable debts of the corporation, notwithstanding their origin in self-dealing transactions. The Marcianos argue that the disputed debt is voidable as a matter of law but, in any event, the Nakashes failed to meet their burden of establishing full fairness. We conclude that the Vice Chancellor applied the proper standard for review of self-dealing transactions and the finding of full fairness is supported by the record. Accordingly, we affirm.

I

The factual basis underlying the contested loans was fully developed in the Court of Chancery. The liquidation proceeding marked the end of a joint venture launched in 1984 by the Marcianos and the Nakashes to market designer jeans and sportswear. Through a solely owned corporation called Guess? Inc. ("Guess"), the California based Marcianos had been engaged in the design and distribution of stylized jeans for several years. In 1983 they decided to form a separate division to market copies of Guess creations in a broader retail market. In order to secure financing and broaden market exposure the Marcianos entered into negotiations with the New York based Nakash brothers, the owners of Jordache Enterprises, Inc. a leading manufacturer of jeans. Ultimately, it was agreed that the Nakashes would receive fifty percent of the stock of Guess for a consideration of $4.7 million. As a result, the three Nakash brothers joined three of the Marcianos on the Guess board of directors.

Similarly, when Gasoline was formed, stock ownership and board composition was shared equally by the two families. Although corporate control and direction were equally divided, from an operational standpoint Gasoline functioned in New York under the Nakashes' operational guidance while the parent, Guess, continued under the primary attention of the Marcianos. Differences between the two factions quickly surfaced with resulting deadlocks at the director level of both Guess and Gasoline. The Marcianos filed an action, partly derivative, against Guess and the Nakashes in California followed by the Delaware proceeding in which the Marcianos sought the appointment of a custodian for Gasoline in addition to asserting derivative claims for diversion of corporate opportunities and assets arising out of the Nakashes' operation of Gasoline. Ultimately, the derivative aspect of the Delaware action was stayed in favor of the California proceedings and the Court of Chancery, after a court-ordered shareholder's meeting failed to resolve the director deadlock, appointed a custodian whose power was limited to resolving deadlocks on the Gasoline board.

The custodial arrangement failed to resolve the underlying policy differences between the two factions and neither group appeared willing to invest additional funds or provide guarantees to permit Gasoline to function as a viable commercial enterprise. In early 1987 the custodian advised the Court of Chancery that because of a lack of financing Gasoline had no prospects of continuation and recommended liquidation. A court-approved plan of liquidation authorized the custodian to sell the assets of Gasoline (with both the Marcianos and the Nakashes permitted to bid), pay all valid debts of the corporation and distribute the net proceeds to the shareholders. The determination of those debts, in particular the loan claims asserted by the Nakashes, was sharply disputed in the Court of Chancery and is the focus of this appeal.

The circumstances underlying the Nakashes' claim were determined by the Vice Chancellor following an evidentiary hearing. Prior to March, 1986, Gasoline had secured the necessary financing to support its inventory purchases from the Israel Discount Bank in New York. The bank advanced funds at one percent above prime rate secured by Gasoline's accounts receivable and the Nakashes' personal guarantee. Although requested to do so, the Marcianos were unwilling to participate in loan guarantees because of their dissatisfaction with the Nakashes' management. In response, the Nakashes withdrew their guarantees causing the Israel Discount Bank to terminate its outstanding loan of $1.6 million.

Without consulting the Marcianos, the Nakashes advanced approximately $2.3 million of their personal funds to Gasoline to enable the corporation to pay outstanding bills and acquire inventory. In June, 1986, the Nakashes arranged for U.F. Factors, an entity owned by them, to assume their personal loans and become Gasoline's lender. U.F. Factors charged interest at one percent over prime to which the Nakashes added one percent for their personal guarantees of the U.F. Factors loan. As of April 24, 1987, Gasoline's debt to U.F. Factors amounted to $2,575,000 of which $25,000 represented the Nakashes' guarantee fee. Another Nakash entity, Jordache Enterprises, also sought payment from Gasoline of two percent of the company's gross sales, or $30,000 for warehousing and invoicing services.

In November, 1986, the Nakashes had replaced the U.F. Factors loan, secured by a series of promissory notes executed by Gasoline, with a line of credit collateralized by Gasoline's assets including trademarks and copyrights. This action took place without the knowledge or consent of the custodian and was subsequently rescinded by the Nakashes. At the time of the court-ordered sale of assets, the Nakashes and their entities were general creditors of Gasoline. If allowed in full the Nakashes' claim will exhaust Gasoline's assets, leaving nothing for its shareholders.[1]

The parties agree that the loans made by the Nakashes to Gasoline were interested transactions. The Nakashes as officers of Gasoline executed the various documents which supported the loans and at the same time guaranteed those loans extended through their wholly owned entities. It is also not disputed that, given the control deadlock, the questioned transactions did not receive majority approval of Gasoline's directors or shareholders. The Marcianos argue that the loan transaction is voidable at the option of the corporation notwithstanding its fairness or the good faith of its participants. A review of this contention, rejected by the Court of Chancery, requires analysis of the concept of director self-dealing under Delaware law.

II

It is a long-established principle of Delaware corporate law that the fiduciary relationship between directors and the corporation imposes fundamental limitations on the extent to which a director may benefit from dealings with the corporation he serves. Thus, the "voting [for] and taking" of compensation may be deemed "constructively fraudulent" in the absence of shareholder ratification, or statutory or bylaw authorization. Perhaps the strongest condemnation of interested director conduct appears in *Potter v. Sanitary Co. of America*, a decision which the Marcianos advance as definitive of the rule of per se voidability. In *Potter* the Court of Chancery characterized transactions between corporations having common directors and officers "constructively fraudulent," absent shareholder ratification.

Support can also be found for the per se rule of voidability in this Court's decision in *Kerbs v. California Eastern Airways Inc*. The *Kerbs* court, in considering the validity of a profit sharing plan, ruled that the self-interest of the directors who voted on the plan caused the transaction to be voidable. The court concluded that the profit sharing plan was voidable based on the common law rule that the vote of an interested director will not be counted in determining whether the challenged action received the affirmative vote of a majority of the board of directors.

The principle of per se voidability for interested transactions, which is sometimes characterized as the common law rule, was significantly ameliorated by the 1967

---

1. The Nakashes used their $2.5 million claim as the basis for their liquidation bid ($1,000,101) for Gasoline's non-cash assets.

enactment of Section 144 of the Delaware General Corporation Law.[2] The Marcianos argue that section 144(a) provides the only basis for immunizing self-interested transactions and since none of the statute's component tests are satisfied the stricture of the common law per se rule applies. The Vice Chancellor agreed that the disputed loans did not withstand a section 144(a) analysis but ruled that the common law rule did not invalidate transactions determined to be intrinsically fair. We agree that section 144(a) does not provide the only validation standard for interested transactions.

It overstates the common law rule to conclude that relationship, alone, is the controlling factor in interested transactions. Although the application of the per se voidability rule in early Delaware cases resulted in the invalidation of interested transactions, the result was not dictated simply by a tainted relationship. Thus in *Potter*, the Court, while adopting the rule of voidability, emphasized that interested transactions should be subject to close scrutiny. Where the undisputed evidence tended to show that the transaction would advance the personal interests of the directors at the expense of stockholders, the stockholders, upon discovery, are entitled to disavow the transaction. Further, the court examined the motives of the defendant directors and the effect the transaction had on the corporation and its shareholders.

In other Delaware cases, decided before the enactment of section 144, interested director transactions were deemed voidable only after an examination of the fairness of a particular transaction *vis-à-vis* the nonparticipating shareholders and a determination of whether the disputed conduct received the approval of a noninterested majority of directors or shareholders. The latter test is now crystallized in the

---

2. Section 144 of Title 8 Del.C. now provides:

(a) No contract or transaction between a corporation and 1 or more of its directors or officers, or between a corporation and any other corporation, partnership, association, or other organization in which 1 or more of its directors or officers, are directors or officers, or have a financial interest, shall be void or voidable solely for this reason, or solely because the director or officer is present at or participates in the meeting of the board or committee which authorizes the contract or transaction, or solely because his or their votes are counted for such purpose, if:

(1) The material facts as to his relationship or interest and as to the contract or transaction are disclosed or are known to the board of directors or the committee, and the board or committee in good faith authorizes the contract or transaction by the affirmative votes of a majority of the disinterested directors, even though the disinterested directors be less than a quorum; or

(2) The material facts as to his relationship or interest and as to the contract or transaction are disclosed or are known to the shareholders entitled to vote thereon, and the contract or transaction is specifically approved in good faith by vote of the shareholders; or

(3) The contract or transaction is fair as to the corporation as of the time it is authorized, approved or ratified, by the board of directors, a committee or the shareholders.

(b) Common or interested directors may be counted in determining the presence of a quorum at a meeting of the board of directors or of a committee which authorizes the contract or transaction.

ratification criteria of section 144(a), although the non-quorum restriction of *Kerbs* has been superceded by the language of subparagraph (b) of section 144.

The Marcianos view compliance with section 144 as the sole basis for avoiding the per se rule of voidability. The Court of Chancery rejected this contention and we agree that it is not consonant with Delaware corporate law. This Court in *Fliegler v. Lawrence*, a post-section 144 decision, refused to view section 144 as either completely preemptive of the common law duty of director fidelity or as constituting a grant of broad immunity. As we stated in *Fliegler*: "It merely removes an 'interested director' cloud when its terms are met and provides against invalidation of an agreement 'solely' because such a director or officer is involved." In *Fliegler* this Court applied a two-tiered analysis: application of section 144 coupled with an intrinsic fairness test.

If section 144 validation of interested director transactions is not deemed exclusive, as *Fliegler* clearly holds, the continued viability of the intrinsic fairness test is mandated not only by fact situations, such as here present, where shareholder deadlock prevents ratification but also where shareholder control by interested directors precludes independent review. Indeed, if an independent committee of the board, contemplated by section 144(a)(1) is unavailable, the sole forum for demonstrating intrinsic fairness may be a judicial one. *See Merritt v. Colonial Foods, Inc.* In such situations the intrinsic fairness test furnishes the substantive standard against which the evidential burden of the interested directors is applied. It is this burden which was addressed by this Court in *Weinberger v. UOP, Inc.*:

> When directors of a Delaware corporation are on both sides of a transaction, they are required to demonstrate their utmost good faith and the most scrupulous inherent fairness of the bargain.
>
> . . .
>
> The requirement of fairness is unflinching in its demand that where one stands on both sides of a transaction, he has the burden of establishing its entire fairness, sufficient to pass the test of careful scrutiny by the courts.

This case illustrates the limitation inherent in viewing section 144 as the touchstone for testing interested director transactions. Because of the shareholder deadlock, even if the Nakashes had attempted to invoke section 144, it was realistically unavailable. The ratification process contemplated by section 144 presupposes the functioning of corporate constituencies capable of providing assents. Just as the statute cannot "sanction unfairness" neither can it invalidate fairness if, upon judicial review, the transaction withstands close scrutiny of its intrinsic elements.[3]

---

3. Although in this case none of the curative steps afforded under section 144(a) were available because of the director-shareholder deadlock, a non-disclosing director seeking to remove the cloud of interestedness would appear to have the same burden under section 144(a)(3), as under prior case law, of proving the intrinsic fairness of a questioned transaction which had been approved or ratified by the directors or shareholders. On the other hand, approval by fully-informed disinterested

III

On the issue of intrinsic fairness, the Court of Chancery concluded that the "U.F. Factors loans compared favorably with the terms available from unrelated lenders" and that the need for external financing had been clearly demonstrated. The Marcianos attack this ruling as factually and legally erroneous. Since the Vice Chancellor's factual findings were arrived at after an evidentiary hearing we are not free to reject them unless they are without record support or not the product of a logical deductive process. We find this standard to have been fully satisfied here.

Apart from the initial investment of $300,000 contributed equally by the Marcianos and the Nakashes, Gasoline's financial needs had been met through external borrowings. It is unnecessary to lay blame for the impasse which resulted in the Marcianos refusal to supply additional equity funding. It suffices to note that throughout 1985 and 1986, Gasoline was able to function only through cash advances from, and loans obtained by, the Nakashes, first through the Israel Discount Bank and later through U.F. Factors. During this period the evidence reflects the continued threat of bank overdrafts and inability to pay for purchases, particularly imported finished goods.

A finding of fairness is particularly appropriate in this case because the evidence indicates that the loans were made by the Nakashes with the *bona fide* intention of assisting Gasoline's efforts to remain in business. Directors who advance funds to a corporation in such circumstances do not forfeit their claims as creditors merely because of relationship. Further, in arranging for the loan, the interested directors were not depriving the corporation of a business opportunity but were instead providing a benefit for the corporation which was unavailable elsewhere.

The Marcianos argue that the Nakashes failed to demonstrate the full fairness of the loan transactions in two fundamental respects: the cost of the borrowings and the use of the funds. It is not disputed, however, that the direct financing by the Nakashes was essentially duplicative of the terms imposed by the Israel Discount Bank in an apparent arms-length transaction. We agree therefore with the Vice Chancellor that, on a comparative basis, the direct loans were favorable to Gasoline. . . .

We hold, therefore, that the Court of Chancery properly applied the intrinsic fairness test in determining the validity of the interested director transactions and its finding of full fairness is clearly supported by the record. Accordingly, the decision is affirmed.

Questions

1. Why isn't Delaware Section 144 applicable in *Marciano*?

---

directors under section 144(a)(1), or disinterested stockholders under section 144(a)(2), permits invocation of the business judgment rule and limits judicial review to issues of gift or waste with the burden of proof upon the party attacking the transaction.

2. The board of directors was deadlocked. Even if the terms of the Nakashes' loan were fair, why should their desire to lend money to the corporation override the Marcianos' desire to prevent this?

3. What is the potential effect of section 144 according to *Marciano*? How does the statute's definition of fairness differ, if at all, from the common law rule?

4. The court discusses fairness, both as a common law matter and in the context of the *Weinberger* decision (which is examined in Part 4). Is fairness a good test by which to evaluate self-dealing transactions? For example, assume a corporation that owns several parcels of developed real estate in a specific area and would like to acquire more. One director owns a piece of property that would be useful to the corporation and offers it for sale. The board, complying with Delaware General Corporation Law Section 144, hires an independent appraiser who gives a range of values for the property between $1,000,000 and $1,250,000 and otherwise does sufficient homework to satisfy the business judgment rule. Envision the negotiations between the independent directors (represented by the CEO) and the selling director. Do you think they would resemble negotiations between the CEO and a third party? If not, who benefits from the difference? Does this seem right?

5. We began with the proposition that fiduciary duty largely was about facilitating or backstopping trust. How does the fairness test affect a stockholder's ability to trust management?

Benihana of Tokyo, Inc. v. Benihana, Inc.
906 A.2d 114 (Del. 2006)

BERGER, Justice

. . .

Rocky Aoki founded Benihana of Tokyo, Inc. (BOT), and its subsidiary, Benihana, which own and operate Benihana restaurants in the United States and other countries. Aoki owned 100% of BOT until 1998, when he pled guilty to insider trading charges. In order to avoid licensing problems created by his status as a convicted felon, Aoki transferred his stock to the Benihana Protective Trust. The trustees of the Trust were Aoki's three children (Kana Aoki Nootenboom, Kyle Aoki and Kevin Aoki) and Darwin Dornbush (who was then the family's attorney, a Benihana director, and, effectively, the company's general counsel).

Benihana, a Delaware corporation, has two classes of common stock. There are approximately 6 million shares of Class A common stock outstanding. Each share has 1/10 vote and the holders of Class A common are entitled to elect 25% of the directors. There are approximately 3 million shares of Common stock outstanding. Each share of Common has one vote and the holders of Common stock are entitled to elect the remaining 75% of Benihana's directors. Before the transaction at issue,

BOT owned 50.9% of the Common stock and 2% of the Class A stock. The nine member board of directors is classified and the directors serve three-year terms.

In 2003, shortly after Aoki married Keiko Aoki, conflicts arose between Aoki and his children. In August, the children were upset to learn that Aoki had changed his will to give Keiko control over BOT. Joel Schwartz, Benihana's president and chief executive officer, also was concerned about this change in control. He discussed the situation with Dornbush, and they briefly considered various options, including the issuance of sufficient Class A stock to trigger a provision in the certificate of incorporation that would allow the Common and Class A to vote together for 75% of the directors.

The Aoki family's turmoil came at a time when Benihana also was facing challenges. Many of its restaurants were old and outmoded. Benihana hired WD Partners to evaluate its facilities and to plan and design appropriate renovations. The resulting Construction and Renovation Plan anticipated that the project would take at least five years and cost $56 million or more. . . . Benihana . . . retained Morgan Joseph & Co. to develop other financing options.

On January 9, 2004, after evaluating Benihana's financial situation and needs, Fred Joseph, of Morgan Joseph, met with Schwartz, Dornbush and John E. Abdo, the board's executive committee. Joseph expressed concern that Benihana would not have sufficient available capital to complete the Construction and Renovation Plan and pursue appropriate acquisitions. Benihana was conservatively leveraged, and Joseph discussed various financing alternatives, including bank debt, high yield debt, convertible debt or preferred stock, equity and sale/leaseback options.

The full board met with Joseph on January 29, 2004. He reviewed all the financing alternatives that he had discussed with the executive committee, and recommended that Benihana issue convertible preferred stock. Joseph explained that the preferred stock would provide the funds needed for the Construction and Renovation Plan and also put the company in a better negotiating position if it sought additional financing from Wachovia.

Joseph gave the directors a board book, marked "Confidential," containing an analysis of the proposed stock issuance (the Transaction). The book included, among others, the following anticipated terms: (i) issuance of $20,000,000 of preferred stock, convertible into Common stock; (ii) dividend of 6% +/− 0.5%; (iii) conversion premium of 20% +/− 2.5%; (iv) buyer's approval required for material corporate transactions; and (v) one to two board seats to the buyer. At trial, Joseph testified that the terms had been chosen by looking at comparable stock issuances and analyzing the Morgan Joseph proposal under a theoretical model.

The board met again on February 17, 2004, to review the terms of the Transaction. The directors discussed Benihana's preferences and Joseph predicted what a buyer likely would expect or require. . . .

Shortly after the February meeting, Abdo contacted Joseph and told him that BFC Financial Corporation was interested in buying the new convertible stock. In April 2005, Joseph sent BFC a private placement memorandum. Abdo negotiated with Joseph for several weeks. They agreed to the Transaction on the following basic terms: (i) $20 million issuance in two tranches of $10 million each, with the second tranche to be issued one to three years after the first; (ii) BFC obtained one seat on the board, and one additional seat if Benihana failed to pay dividends for two consecutive quarters; (iii) BFC obtained preemptive rights on any new voting securities; (iv) 5% dividend; (v) 15% conversion premium; (vi) BFC had the right to force Benihana to redeem the preferred stock in full after ten years; and (vii) the stock would have immediate "as if converted" voting rights. Joseph testified that he was satisfied with the negotiations, as he had obtained what he wanted with respect to the most important points.

On April 22, 2004, Abdo sent a memorandum to Dornbush, Schwartz and Joseph, listing the agreed terms of the Transaction. He did not send the memorandum to any other members of the Benihana board. Schwartz did tell Becker, Sturges, Sano, and possibly Pine that BFC was the potential buyer. At its next meeting, held on May 6, 2004, the entire board was officially informed of BFC's involvement in the Transaction. Abdo made a presentation on behalf of BFC and then left the meeting. Joseph distributed an updated board book, which explained that Abdo had approached Morgan Joseph on behalf of BFC, and included the negotiated terms. The trial court found that the board was not informed that Abdo had negotiated the deal on behalf of BFC. But the board did know that Abdo was a principal of BFC. After discussion, the board reviewed and approved the Transaction, subject to the receipt of a fairness opinion.

On May 18, 2004, after he learned that Morgan Joseph was providing a fairness opinion, Schwartz publicly announced the stock issuance. Two days later, Aoki's counsel sent a letter asking the board to abandon the Transaction and pursue other, more favorable, financing alternatives. The letter expressed concern about the directors' conflicts, the dilutive effect of the stock issuance, and its "questionable legality." Schwartz gave copies of the letter to the directors at the May 20 board meeting, and Dornbush advised that he did not believe that Aoki's concerns had merit. Joseph and another Morgan Joseph representative then joined the meeting by telephone and opined that the Transaction was fair from a financial point of view. The board then approved the Transaction.

During the following two weeks, Benihana received three alternative financing proposals. Schwartz asked Becker, Pine and Sturges to act as an independent committee and review the first offer. The committee decided that the offer was inferior and not worth pursuing. Morgan Joseph agreed with that assessment. Schwartz referred the next two proposals to Morgan Joseph, with the same result.

On June 8, 2004, Benihana and BFC executed the Stock Purchase Agreement. On June 11, 2004, the board met and approved resolutions ratifying the execution of the Stock Purchase Agreement and authorizing the stock issuance. Schwartz then reported on the three alternative proposals that had been rejected by the ad hoc committee and Morgan Joseph. On July 2, 2004, BOT filed this action against all of Benihana's directors, except Kevin Aoki, alleging breaches of fiduciary duties; and against BFC, alleging that it aided and abetted the fiduciary violations. Three months later, as the parties were filing their pre-trial briefs, the board again reviewed the Transaction. After considering the allegations in the amended complaint, the board voted once more to approve it. . . .

Discussion

. . .

A. Section 144(a)(1) Approval

Section 144 of the Delaware General Corporation Law provides a safe harbor for interested transactions, like this one, if "[t]he material facts as to the director's . . . relationship or interest and as to the contract or transaction are disclosed or are known to the board of directors . . . and the board . . . in good faith authorizes the contract or transaction by the affirmative votes of a majority of the disinterested directors . . . ." After approval by disinterested directors, courts review the interested transaction under the business judgment rule, which "is a presumption that in making a business decision, the directors of a corporation acted on an informed basis, in good faith and in the honest belief that the action taken was in the best interest of the company."

BOT argues that §144(a)(1) is inapplicable because, when they approved the Transaction, the disinterested directors did not know that Abdo had negotiated the terms for BFC. Abdo's role as negotiator is material, according to BOT, because Abdo had been given the confidential term sheet prepared by Joseph and knew which of those terms Benihana was prepared to give up during negotiations. We agree that the board needed to know about Abdo's involvement in order to make an informed decision. The record clearly establishes, however, that the board possessed that material information when it approved the Transaction on May 6, 2004 and May 20, 2004.

Shortly before the May 6 meeting, Schwartz told Becker, Sturges and Sano that BFC was the proposed buyer. Then, at the meeting, Abdo made the presentation on behalf of BFC. Joseph's board book also explained that Abdo had made the initial contact that precipitated the negotiations. The board members knew that Abdo is a director, vice-chairman, and one of two people who control BFC. Thus, although no one ever said, "Abdo negotiated this deal for BFC," the directors understood that he was BFC's representative in the Transaction. . . .

B. Abdo's alleged fiduciary violation

BOT next argues that the Court of Chancery should have reviewed the Transaction under an entire fairness standard because Abdo breached his duty of loyalty when he used Benihana's confidential information to negotiate on behalf of BFC. This argument starts with a flawed premise. The record does not support BOT's contention that Abdo used any confidential information against Benihana. Even without Joseph's comments at the February 17 board meeting, Abdo knew the terms a buyer could expect to obtain in a deal like this. Moreover, as the trial court found, "the negotiations involved give and take on a number of points" and Benihana "ended up where [it] wanted to be" for the most important terms. Abdo did not set the terms of the deal; he did not deceive the board; and he did not dominate or control the other directors' approval of the Transaction. In short, the record does not support the claim that Abdo breached his duty of loyalty.

C. Dilution of BOT's voting power

Finally, BOT argues that the board's primary purpose in approving the Transaction was to dilute BOT's voting control. BOT points out that Schwartz was concerned about BOT's control in 2003 and even discussed with Dornbush the possibility of issuing a huge number of Class A shares. Then, despite the availability of other financing options, the board decided on a stock issuance, and agreed to give BFC "as if converted" voting rights. . . .

It is settled law that, "corporate action . . . may not be taken for the sole or primary purpose of entrenchment." Here, however, the trial court found that "the primary purpose of the . . . Transaction was to provide what the directors subjectively believed to be the best financing vehicle available for securing the necessary funds to pursue the agreed upon Construction and Renovation Plan for the Benihana restaurants." That factual determination has ample record support, especially in light of the trial court's credibility determinations. . . .

Questions

1. What are the characteristics of the preferred stock issued in *Benihana of Tokyo, Inc. v. Benihana, Inc.*? How do they differ from the preferred stock you've learned about in Part 1 of this casebook? What difference if any does it make?

2. In *Benihana*, the court concludes that if directors follow the procedural requirements of section 144(a)(1), the standard of review shifts from fairness to business judgment. What are the implications of this conclusion as far as the directors' duty of loyalty? If you were a director of BOT, or a corporation in a similar situation, what would you have done to fulfill your duty?

B. Corporate Opportunity

Broz v. Cellular Information Systems, Inc.
673 A.2d 148 (Del. 1996)

VEASEY, Chief Justice

In this appeal, we consider the application of the doctrine of corporate opportunity. The Court of Chancery decided that the defendant, a corporate director, breached his fiduciary duty by not formally presenting to the corporation an opportunity which had come to the director individually and independent of the director's relationship with the corporation. Here the opportunity was not one in which the corporation in its current mode had an interest or which it had the financial ability to acquire, but, under the unique circumstances here, that mode was subject to change by virtue of the impending acquisition of the corporation by another entity.

We conclude that, although a corporate director may be shielded from liability by offering to the corporation an opportunity which has come to the director independently and individually, the failure of the director to present the opportunity does not necessarily result in the improper usurpation of a corporate opportunity. We further conclude that, if the corporation is a target or potential target of an acquisition by another company which has an interest and ability to entertain the opportunity, the director of the target company does not have a fiduciary duty to present the opportunity to the target company. Accordingly, the judgment of the Court of Chancery is reversed.

I. The Contentions of the Parties and the Decision Below

Robert F. Broz ("Broz") is the President and sole stockholder of RFB Cellular, Inc. ("RFBC"), a Delaware corporation engaged in the business of providing cellular telephone service in the Midwestern United States. At the time of the conduct at issue in this appeal, Broz was also a member of the board of directors of plaintiff below-appellee, Cellular Information Systems, Inc. ("CIS"). CIS is a publicly held Delaware corporation and a competitor of RFBC.

The conduct before the Court involves the purchase by Broz of a cellular telephone service license for the benefit of RFBC. The license in question, known as the Michigan-2 Rural Service Area Cellular License ("Michigan-2"), is issued by the Federal Communications Commission ("FCC") and entitles its holder to provide cellular telephone service to a portion of northern Michigan. CIS brought an action against Broz and RFBC for equitable relief, contending that the purchase of this license by Broz constituted a usurpation of a corporate opportunity properly belonging to CIS, irrespective of whether or not CIS was interested in the Michigan-2 opportunity at the time it was offered to Broz.

The principal basis for the contention of CIS is that PriCellular, Inc. ("PriCellular"), another cellular communications company which was contemporaneously engaged in an acquisition of CIS, was interested in the Michigan-2 opportunity. CIS contends that, in determining whether the Michigan-2 opportunity rightfully belonged to CIS, Broz was required to consider the interests of PriCellular insofar as those interests would come into alignment with those of CIS as a result of PriCellular's acquisition plans.

After trial, the Court of Chancery agreed with the contentions of CIS and entered judgment against Broz and RFBC. The court held that: (1) irrespective of the fact that the Michigan-2 opportunity came to Broz in a manner wholly independent of his status as a director of CIS, the Michigan-2 license was an opportunity that properly belonged to CIS; (2) due to an alignment of the interests of CIS and PriCellular arising out of PriCellular's efforts to acquire CIS, Broz breached his fiduciary duty by failing to consider whether the opportunity was one in which PriCellular would be interested; (3) despite the fact that CIS was aware of the opportunity and expressed no interest in pursuing it, Broz was required formally to present the transaction to the CIS board prior to seizing the opportunity for his own; and (4) absent formal presentation to the board, Broz' acquisition of Michigan-2 constituted an impermissible usurpation of a corporate opportunity. The trial court imposed a constructive trust on the agreement to purchase Michigan-2 and directed that the right to purchase the license be transferred to CIS. From this judgment, Broz and RFBC appeal. . . .

II. Facts

Broz has been the President and sole stockholder of RFBC since 1992. RFBC owns and operates an FCC license area, known as the Michigan-4 Rural Service Area Cellular License ("Michigan-4"). The license entitles RFBC to provide cellular telephone service to a portion of rural Michigan. Although Broz' efforts have been devoted primarily to the business operations of RFBC, he also served as an outside director of CIS at the time of the events at issue in this case. CIS was at all times fully aware of Broz' relationship with RFBC and the obligations incumbent upon him by virtue of that relationship.

In April of 1994, Mackinac Cellular Corp. ("Mackinac") sought to divest itself of Michigan-2, the license area immediately adjacent to Michigan-4. To this end, Mackinac contacted Daniels & Associates ("Daniels") and arranged for the brokerage firm to seek potential purchasers for Michigan-2. In compiling a list of prospects, Daniels included RFBC as a likely candidate. In May of 1994, David Rhodes, a representative of Daniels, contacted Broz and broached the subject of RFBC's possible acquisition of Michigan-2. Broz later signed a confidentiality agreement at the request of Mackinac, and received the offering materials pertaining to Michigan-2.

Michigan-2 was not, however, offered to CIS. Apparently, Daniels did not consider CIS to be a viable purchaser for Michigan-2 in light of CIS' recent financial difficulties. The record shows that, at the time Michigan-2 was offered to Broz, CIS had recently emerged from lengthy and contentious Chapter 11 proceedings. Pursuant to the Chapter 11 Plan of Reorganization, CIS entered into a loan agreement that substantially impaired the company's ability to undertake new acquisitions or to incur new debt. In fact, CIS would have been unable to purchase Michigan-2 without the approval of its creditors.

The CIS reorganization resulted from the failure of CIS' rather ambitious plans for expansion. From 1989 onward, CIS had embarked on a series of cellular license acquisitions. In 1992, however, CIS' financing failed, necessitating the liquidation of the company's holdings and reduction of the company's total indebtedness. During the period from early 1992 until the time of CIS' emergence from bankruptcy in 1994, CIS divested itself of some fifteen separate cellular license systems. CIS contracted to sell four additional license areas on May 27, 1994, leaving CIS with only five remaining license areas, all of which were outside of the Midwest.

On June 13, 1994, following a meeting of the CIS board, Broz spoke with CIS' Chief Executive Officer, Richard Treibick ("Treibick"), concerning his interest in acquiring Michigan-2. Treibick communicated to Broz that CIS was not interested in Michigan-2.[4] Treibick further stated that he had been made aware of the Michigan-2 opportunity prior to the conversation with Broz, and that any offer to acquire Michigan-2 was rejected. After the commencement of the PriCellular tender offer, in August of 1994, Broz contacted another CIS director, Peter Schiff ("Schiff"), to discuss the possible acquisition of Michigan-2 by RFBC. Schiff, like Treibick, indicated that CIS had neither the wherewithal nor the inclination to purchase Michigan-2. In late September of 1994, Broz also contacted Stanley Bloch ("Bloch"), a director and counsel for CIS, to request that Bloch represent RFBC in its dealings with Mackinac. Bloch agreed to represent RFBC, and, like Schiff and Treibick, expressed his belief that CIS was not at all interested in the transaction. Ultimately, all the CIS directors testified at trial that, had Broz inquired at that time, they each would have expressed the opinion that CIS was not interested in Michigan-2.[5]

On June 28, 1994, following various overtures from PriCellular concerning an acquisition of CIS, six CIS directors[6] entered into agreements with PriCellular to sell their shares in CIS at a price of $2.00 per share. These agreements were contingent upon, *inter alia*, the consummation of a PriCellular tender offer for all CIS shares at the same price. Pursuant to their agreements with PriCellular, the CIS directors also entered into a "standstill" agreement which prevented the directors from engaging in any transaction outside the regular course of CIS' business or incurring any new liabilities until the close of the PriCellular tender offer. On August 2, 1994,

---

4. In fact, during a deposition given in March of 1995, Treibick testified that he didn't "know who frankly was hawking [the Michigan-2 license] . . . at the time. . . . [W]e said forget it. It was not something we would have bought if they offered it to us for nothing."

5. We assume *arguendo* that informal contacts and individual opinions of board members are not a substitute for a formal process of presenting an opportunity to a board of directors. Nevertheless, in our view such a formal process was not necessary under the circumstances of this case in order for Broz to avoid liability. These contacts with individual board members do, however, tend to show that Broz was not acting surreptitiously or in bad faith.

6. All the members of the CIS board of directors except Broz and Bloch agreed to tender their shares to PriCellular.

PriCellular commenced a tender offer for all outstanding shares of CIS at $2.00 per share. The PriCellular tender offer mirrored the standstill agreements entered into by the CIS directors.

PriCellular's tender offer was originally scheduled to close on September 16, 1994. At the time the tender offer was launched, however, the source of the $106,000,000 in financing required to consummate the transaction was still in doubt. PriCellular originally planned to structure the transaction around bank loans. When this financing fell through, PriCellular resorted to a junk bond offering. PriCellular's financing difficulties generated a great deal of concern among the CIS insiders whether the tender offer was, in fact, viable. Financing difficulties ultimately caused PriCellular to delay the closing date of the tender offer from September 16, 1994 until October 14, 1994 and then again until November 9, 1994.

On August 6, September 6 and September 21, 1994, Broz submitted written offers to Mackinac for the purchase of Michigan-2. During this time period, PriCellular also began negotiations with Mackinac to arrange an option for the purchase of Michigan-2. PriCellular's interest in Michigan-2 was fully disclosed to CIS' chief executive, Treibick, who did not express any interest in Michigan-2, and was actually incredulous that PriCellular would want to acquire the license. Nevertheless, CIS was fully aware that PriCellular and Broz were bidding for Michigan-2 and did not interpose CIS in this bidding war.

In late September of 1994, PriCellular reached agreement with Mackinac on an option to purchase Michigan-2. The exercise price of the option agreement was set at $6.7 million, with the option remaining in force until December 15, 1994. Pursuant to the agreement, the right to exercise the option was not transferrable to any party other than a subsidiary of PriCellular. Therefore, it could not have been transferred to CIS. The agreement further provided that Mackinac was free to sell Michigan-2 to any party who was willing to exceed the exercise price of the Mackinac-PriCellular option contract by at least $500,000. On November 14, 1994, Broz agreed to pay Mackinac $7.2 million for the Michigan-2 license, thereby meeting the terms of the option agreement. An asset purchase agreement was thereafter executed by Mackinac and RFBC.

Nine days later, on November 23, 1994, PriCellular completed its financing and closed its tender offer for CIS. Prior to that point, PriCellular owned no equity interest in CIS. Subsequent to the consummation of the PriCellular tender offer for CIS, members of the CIS board of directors, including Broz, were discharged and replaced with a slate of PriCellular nominees. On March 2, 1995, this action was commenced by CIS in the Court of Chancery.

At trial in the Court of Chancery, CIS contended that the purchase of Michigan-2 by Broz constituted the impermissible usurpation of a corporate opportunity properly belonging to CIS. Thus, CIS asserted that Broz breached his fiduciary duty to CIS and its stockholders. CIS admits that, at the time the opportunity was offered to Broz, the board of CIS would not have been interested in Michigan-2, but CIS asserts that Broz usurped the opportunity nevertheless. CIS claims that Broz was required to look not just to CIS, but to the articulated business plans of PriCellular, to determine whether PriCellular would be interested in acquiring Michigan-2. Since Broz failed to do this and acquired Michigan-2 without first considering the interests of PriCellular in its capacity as a potential acquiror of CIS, CIS contends that Broz must be held to account for breach of fiduciary duty. . . .

[T]he court [below] held that:

> even though knowledge of the availability of the Michigan 2 RSA license and its associated assets came to Mr. Broz wholly independently of his role on the CIS board, that opportunity was within the core business interests of CIS at the relevant times; that at such time CIS would have had access to the financing necessary to compete for the assets that were for sale; and that the CIS board of directors were not asked to and thus did not consider whether such action would have been in the best interests of the corporation. In these circumstances I conclude that Mr. Broz as a director of CIS violated his duty of loyalty to CIS by seizing this opportunity without formally informing the CIS board fully about the opportunity and facts surrounding it and by proceeding to acquire rights for his benefit without the consent of the corporation.

. . .

IV. Application of the Corporate Opportunity Doctrine

The doctrine of corporate opportunity represents but one species of the broad fiduciary duties assumed by a corporate director or officer. A corporate fiduciary agrees to place the interests of the corporation before his or her own in appropriate circumstances. In light of the diverse and often competing obligations faced by directors and officers, however, the corporate opportunity doctrine arose as a means of defining the parameters of fiduciary duty in instances of potential conflict. The classic statement of the doctrine is derived from the venerable case of *Guth v. Loft, Inc.* In *Guth*, this Court held that:

> if there is presented to a corporate officer or director a business opportunity which the corporation is financially able to undertake, is, from its nature, in the line of the corporation's business and is of practical advantage to it, is one in which the corporation has an interest or a reasonable expectancy, and, by embracing the opportunity, the self-interest of the officer or director will be brought into conflict with that of the corporation, the law will not permit him to seize the opportunity for himself.*

---

* [*Guth v. Loft*, 5 A.2d 503 (1939), is the seminal Delaware case on corporate opportunity and involved defendant's attempted usurpation of plaintiff's opportunity to acquire the Pepsi-Cola Company.]

The corporate opportunity doctrine, as delineated by *Guth* and its progeny, holds that a corporate officer or director may not take a business opportunity for his own if: (1) the corporation is financially able to exploit the opportunity; (2) the opportunity is within the corporation's line of business; (3) the corporation has an interest or expectancy in the opportunity; and (4) by taking the opportunity for his own, the corporate fiduciary will thereby be placed in a position inimicable to his duties to the corporation. The Court in *Guth* also derived a corollary which states that a director or officer *may* take a corporate opportunity if: (1) the opportunity is presented to the director or officer in his individual and not his corporate capacity; (2) the opportunity is not essential to the corporation; (3) the corporation holds no interest or expectancy in the opportunity; and (4) the director or officer has not wrongfully employed the resources of the corporation in pursuing or exploiting the opportunity.

Thus, the contours of this doctrine are well established. It is important to note, however, that the tests enunciated in *Guth* and subsequent cases provide guidelines to be considered by a reviewing court in balancing the equities of an individual case. No one factor is dispositive and all factors must be taken into account insofar as they are applicable. Cases involving a claim of usurpation of a corporate opportunity range over a multitude of factual settings. Hard and fast rules are not easily crafted to deal with such an array of complex situations. As this Court noted in *Johnston v. Greene*, the determination of "[w]hether or not a director has appropriated for himself something that in fairness should belong to the corporation is 'a factual question to be decided by reasonable inference from objective facts.'" In the instant case, we find that the facts do not support the conclusion that Broz misappropriated a corporate opportunity.

We note at the outset that Broz became aware of the Michigan-2 opportunity in his individual and not his corporate capacity. As the Court of Chancery found, "Broz did not misuse proprietary information that came to him in a corporate capacity nor did he otherwise use any power he might have over the governance of the corporation to advance his own interests." This fact is not the subject of serious dispute. In fact, it is clear from the record that Mackinac did not consider CIS a viable candidate for the acquisition of Michigan-2. Accordingly, Mackinac did not offer the property to CIS. In this factual posture, many of the fundamental concerns undergirding the law of corporate opportunity are not present (*e.g.*, misappropriation of the corporation's proprietary information). The burden imposed upon Broz to show adherence to his fiduciary duties to CIS is thus lessened to some extent. *See Science Accessories Corp.* [*v. Summagraphics Corp.*], 425 A.2d at 964 (holding that because opportunity to purchase new technology was "an 'outside' opportunity not available to SAC, defendants' failure to disclose the concept to SAC and their taking it for themselves for purposes of competing with SAC cannot be found to be in breach of any agency fiduciary duty"). Nevertheless, this fact is not dispositive. The determination of whether a particular fiduciary has usurped a corporate opportunity necessitates a careful examination of the circumstances, giving due credence to the factors enunciated in *Guth* and subsequent cases.

We turn now to an analysis of the factors relied on by the trial court. First, we find that CIS was not financially capable of exploiting the Michigan-2 opportunity. Although the Court of Chancery concluded otherwise, we hold that this finding was not supported by the evidence. The record shows that CIS was in a precarious financial position at the time Mackinac presented the Michigan-2 opportunity to Broz. Having recently emerged from lengthy and contentious bankruptcy proceedings, CIS was not in a position to commit capital to the acquisition of new assets. Further, the loan agreement entered into by CIS and its creditors severely limited the discretion of CIS as to the acquisition of new assets and substantially restricted the ability of CIS to incur new debt.

The Court of Chancery based its contrary finding on the fact that PriCellular had purchased an option to acquire CIS' bank debt. Thus, the court reasoned, PriCellular was in a position to exercise that option and then waive any unfavorable restrictions that would stand in the way of a CIS acquisition of Michigan-2. The trial court, however, disregarded the fact that PriCellular's own financial situation was not particularly stable. PriCellular was unable to finance the acquisition of CIS through conventional bank loans and was forced to use the more risky mechanism of a junk bond offering to raise the required capital. Thus, the court's statement that "PriCellular had other sources of financing to permit the funding of that purchase" is clearly not free from dispute. Moreover, as discussed *infra*, the fact that PriCellular had available sources of financing is immaterial to the analysis. At the time that Broz was required to decide whether to accept the Michigan-2 opportunity, PriCellular had not yet acquired CIS, and any plans to do so were wholly speculative. Thus, contrary to the Court of Chancery's finding, Broz was not obligated to consider the contingency of a PriCellular acquisition of CIS and the related contingency of PriCellular thereafter waiving restrictions on the CIS bank debt. Broz was required to consider the facts only as they existed at the time he determined to accept the Mackinac offer and embark on his efforts to bring the transaction to fruition.

Second, while it may be said with some certainty that the Michigan-2 opportunity was within CIS' line of business, it is not equally clear that CIS had a cognizable interest or expectancy in the license.[7] Under the third factor laid down by this Court

---

7. The language in the *Guth* opinion relating to "line of business" is less than clear:
   Where a corporation is engaged in a certain business, and an opportunity is presented to it embracing an activity as to which it has fundamental knowledge, practical experience and *ability to pursue*, which, logically and naturally, is adaptable to its business *having regard for its financial position*, and *is consonant with its reasonable needs and aspirations for expansion*, it may properly be said that the opportunity is within the corporation's line of business.

Guth, 5 A.2d at 514 (emphasis supplied). This formulation of the definition of the term "line of business" suggests that the business strategy and financial well-being of the corporation are also relevant to a determination of whether the opportunity is within the corporation's line of business.

in *Guth*, for an opportunity to be deemed to belong to the fiduciary's corporation, the corporation must have an interest or expectancy in that opportunity. As this Court stated in *Johnston*, "[f]or the corporation to have an actual or expectant interest in any specific property, there must be some tie between that property and the nature of the corporate business." Despite the fact that the nature of the Michigan-2 opportunity was historically close to the core operations of CIS, changes were in process. At the time the opportunity was presented, CIS was actively engaged in the process of divesting its cellular license holdings. CIS' articulated business plan did not involve any new acquisitions. Further, as indicated by the testimony of the entire CIS board, the Michigan-2 license would not have been of interest to CIS even absent CIS' financial difficulties and CIS' then current desire to liquidate its cellular license holdings.[8] Thus, CIS had no interest or expectancy in the Michigan-2 opportunity.

Finally, the corporate opportunity doctrine is implicated only in cases where the fiduciary's seizure of an opportunity results in a conflict between the fiduciary's duties to the corporation and the self-interest of the director as actualized by the exploitation of the opportunity. In the instant case, Broz' interest in acquiring and profiting from Michigan-2 created no duties that were inimicable to his obligations to CIS. Broz, at all times relevant to the instant appeal, was the sole party in interest in RFBC, a competitor of CIS. CIS was fully aware of Broz' potentially conflicting duties. Broz, however, comported himself in a manner that was wholly in accord with his obligations to CIS. Broz took care not to usurp any opportunity which CIS was willing and able to pursue. Broz sought only to compete with an outside entity, PriCellular, for acquisition of an opportunity which both sought

---

Since we find that these considerations are decisive under the other factors enunciated by the Court in *Guth*, we do not reach the question of whether they are here relevant to a determination of the corporation's line of business.

8. At trial, each of the members of the CIS board testified to his belief that CIS would not have been interested in the Michigan-2 opportunity at the time it was presented to Broz. The Court of Chancery chose to disregard this testimony, holding that "the after the fact testimony of directors to the effect that they would not have been interested in pursuing this transaction had it been brought to the board, is not helpful to defendant, in my opinion, because most of them did not know at that time of PriCellular's interest in the property and how it related to PriCellular's plan for CIS." We disagree with the court's assessment. First, as discussed, *infra*, opportunity was presented. Thus, the fact the CIS directors were unaware of the future plans of PriCellular does not impact adversely on the weight to be ascribed to this particular evidence. Second, testimony of the CIS board is extremely helpful to establish the propriety of Broz' actions. As discussed, *infra*, Broz was not required to present this opportunity to the board. He was free to evaluate the situation and determine whether the opportunity was one properly belonging to CIS. Absent such formal presentation, however, this Court must make an after-the-fact assessment of an essentially stale factual scenario. In such a setting, the testimony of the directors who controlled the business and affairs of the corporation at the time the opportunity was allegedly usurped is relevant. . . . The Court of Chancery also held that "this sort of after the fact testimony is a very thin substitute for an informed board decision made at a meeting in 'real time' (*i.e.*, while the opportunity to act with effect continues)." While it is true that contemporaneous decisionmaking or unanimous written consent is required for board action (8 Del.C. § 141 (f)), in our view, this testimony of the CIS board was probative and should not have been wholly discounted.

to possess. Broz was not obligated to refrain from competition with PriCellular. Therefore, the totality of the circumstances indicates that Broz did not usurp an opportunity that properly belonged to CIS.

A. Presentation to the Board

In concluding that Broz had usurped a corporate opportunity, the Court of Chancery placed great emphasis on the fact that Broz had not formally presented the matter to the CIS board. The court held that "in such circumstances as existed at the latest after October 14, 1994 (date of PriCellular's option contract on Michigan 2 RSA) it was the obligation of Mr. Broz as a director of CIS to take the transaction to the CIS board for its formal action. . . ." In so holding, the trial court erroneously grafted a new requirement onto the law of corporate opportunity, *viz.*, the requirement of formal presentation under circumstances where the corporation does not have an interest, expectancy or financial ability.

The teaching of *Guth* and its progeny is that the director or officer must analyze the situation *ex ante* to determine whether the opportunity is one rightfully belonging to the corporation. If the director or officer believes, based on one of the factors articulated above, that the corporation is not entitled to the opportunity, then he may take it for himself. Of course, presenting the opportunity to the board creates a kind of "safe harbor" for the director, which removes the specter of a *post hoc* judicial determination that the director or officer has improperly usurped a corporate opportunity. Thus, presentation avoids the possibility that an error in the fiduciary's assessment of the situation will create future liability for breach of fiduciary duty. It is not the law of Delaware that presentation to the board is a necessary prerequisite to a finding that a corporate opportunity has not been usurped.

The numerous cases decided since *Guth* are in full accord with this view of the doctrine. . . .

Thus, we hold that Broz was not required to make formal presentation of the Michigan-2 opportunity to the CIS board prior to taking the opportunity for his own. In so holding, we necessarily conclude that the Court of Chancery erred in grafting the additional requirement of formal presentation onto Delaware's corporate opportunity jurisprudence.[10]

B. Alignment of Interests Between CIS and PriCellular

In concluding that Broz usurped an opportunity properly belonging to CIS, the Court of Chancery held that "[f]or practical business reasons CIS' interests with respect to the Mackinac transaction came to merge with those of PriCellular, even before the closing of its tender offer for CIS stock." Based on this fact, the trial court

---

10. Recognizing the interests the Court of Chancery sought to promote, however, we note that formal presentation to the board is often the preferred—or "safe"—approach, and we note that this litigation might have been unnecessary had this precaution been observed.

concluded that Broz was required to consider PriCellular's prospective, post-acquisition plans for CIS in determining whether to forego the opportunity or seize it for himself. Had Broz done this, the Court of Chancery determined that he would have concluded that CIS was entitled to the opportunity by virtue of the alignment of its interests with those of PriCellular.

We disagree. Broz was under no duty to consider the interests of PriCellular when he chose to purchase Michigan-2. As stated in *Guth*, a director's right to "appropriate [an] ... opportunity depends on the circumstances existing at the time it presented itself to him without regard to subsequent events." At the time Broz purchased Michigan-2, PriCellular had not yet acquired CIS. Any plans to do so would still have been wholly speculative. Accordingly, Broz was not required to consider the contingent and uncertain plans of PriCellular in reaching his determination of how to proceed.

Whether or not the CIS board would, at some time, have chosen to acquire Michigan-2 in order to make CIS a more attractive acquisition target for PriCellular or to enhance the synergy of any combined enterprise, is speculative. The trial court found this to be a plausible scenario and therefore found that, pursuant to the factors laid down in *Guth*, CIS had a valid interest or expectancy in the license. This speculative finding cuts against the statements made by CIS' Chief Executive and the entire CIS board of directors and ignores the fact that CIS still lacked the wherewithal to acquire Michigan-2, even if one takes into account the possible availability of PriCellular's financing. Thus, the fact of PriCellular's plans to acquire CIS is immaterial and does not change the analysis.

In reaching our conclusion on this point, we note that certainty and predictability are values to be promoted in our corporation law. Broz, as an active participant in the cellular telephone industry, was entitled to proceed in his own economic interest in the absence of any countervailing duty. The right of a director or officer to engage in business affairs outside of his or her fiduciary capacity would be illusory if these individuals were required to consider every potential, future occurrence in determining whether a particular business strategy would implicate fiduciary duty concerns. In order for a director to engage meaningfully in business unrelated to his or her corporate role, the director must be allowed to make decisions based on the situation as it exists at the time a given opportunity is presented. Absent such a rule, the corporate fiduciary would be constrained to refrain from exploiting any opportunity for fear of liability based on the occurrence of subsequent events. This state of affairs would unduly restrict officers and directors and would be antithetical to certainty in corporation law.

V. Conclusion

The corporate opportunity doctrine represents a judicially crafted effort to harmonize the competing demands placed on corporate fiduciaries in a modern business environment. The doctrine seeks to reduce the possibility of conflict between a director's duties to the corporation and interests unrelated to that role. In the instant case, Broz adhered to his obligations to CIS. We hold that the Court of Chancery erred as a matter of law in concluding that Broz had a duty formally to present the Michigan-2 opportunity to the CIS board. We also hold that the trial court erred in its application of the corporate opportunity doctrine under the unusual facts of this case, where CIS had no interest or financial ability to acquire the opportunity, but the impending acquisition of CIS by PriCellular would or could have caused a change in those circumstances.

Therefore, we hold that Broz did not breach his fiduciary duties to CIS. Accordingly, we reverse the judgment of the Court of Chancery holding that Broz diverted a corporate opportunity properly belonging to CIS and imposing a constructive trust.

Questions

1. How does Broz's failure to present the license to the entire board compare with Dr. Dreyfuss's actions in *Bayer v. Beran*? Does the court analyze both actions (or failures to act) similarly?

2. Do you agree with the court's conclusion that it was unnecessary for Broz to have formally presented the CIS opportunity to the board? How does this square, if at all, with the requirements of 8 Delaware General Corporation Law Section 144(a)(1)? Are there different considerations in this context that would justify the court's conclusion? What other policy considerations might underlie the court's relatively lenient treatment of Broz's actions?

3. What advice would you have given Broz had he asked you about bidding on Michigan-2 prior to having done so? How, if at all, will your advice differ if a director asked you about a self-dealing transaction? Consider the following:

ALI Principles of Corporate Governance Section 5.05

(a) *General Rule*. A director [§ 1.13] or senior executive [§ 1.33] may not take advantage of a corporate opportunity unless:

(1) The director or senior executive first offers the corporate opportunity to the corporation and makes disclosure concerning the conflict of interest [§ 1.14(a)] and the corporate opportunity [§ 1.14(b)];

(2) The corporate opportunity is rejected by the corporation; and

(3) Either:

(A) The rejection of the opportunity is fair to the corporation;

(B) The opportunity is rejected in advance, following such disclosure, by disinterested directors [§ 1.15], or, in the case of a senior executive who is not a director, by a disinterested superior, in a manner that satisfies the standards of the business judgment rule [§ 4.01(c)]; or

(C) The rejection is authorized in advance or ratified, following such disclosure, by disinterested shareholders [§ 1.16], and the rejection is not equivalent to a waste of corporate assets [§ 1.42].

(b) *Definition of a Corporate Opportunity.* For purposes of this Section, a corporate opportunity means:

(1) Any opportunity to engage in a business activity of which a director or senior executive becomes aware, either:

(A) In connection with the performance of functions as a director or senior executive, or under circumstances that should reasonably lead the director or senior executive to believe that the person offering the opportunity expects it to be offered to the corporation; or

(B) Through the use of corporate information or property, if the resulting opportunity is one that the director or senior executive should reasonably be expected to believe would be of interest to the corporation; or

(2) Any opportunity to engage in a business activity of which a senior executive becomes aware and knows is closely related to a business in which the corporation is engaged or expects to engage.

(c) *Burden of Proof.* A party who challenges the taking of a corporate opportunity has the burden of proof, except that if such party establishes that the requirements of Subsection (a)(3)(B) or (C) are not met, the director or the senior executive has the burden of proving that the rejection and the taking of the opportunity were fair to the corporation.

(d) *Ratification of Defective Disclosure.* A good faith but defective disclosure of the facts concerning the corporate opportunity may be cured if at any time (but no later than a reasonable time after suit is filed challenging the taking of the corporate opportunity) the original rejection of the corporate opportunity is ratified, following the required disclosure, by the board, the shareholders, or the corporate decisionmaker who initially approved the rejection of the corporate opportunity, or such decisionmaker's successor.

(e) *Special Rule Concerning Delayed Offering of Corporate Opportunities.* Relief based solely on failure to first offer an opportunity to the corporation under Subsection (a)(1) is not available if: (1) such failure resulted from a good faith belief that the business activity did not constitute a corporate opportunity, and (2) not later than a reasonable time after suit is filed challenging the taking of the corporate opportunity, the corporate opportunity is to the extent possible offered to the corporation and rejected in a manner that satisfies the standards of Subsection (a).

In re eBay, Inc. Shareholders Litigation
2004 Del. Ch. LEXIS 4 (2004)

CHANDLER, Chancellor

Shareholders of eBay, Inc. filed these consolidated derivative actions against certain eBay directors and officers for usurping corporate opportunities. Plaintiffs allege that eBay's investment banking advisor, Goldman Sachs Group, engaged in "spinning," a practice that involves allocating shares of lucrative initial public offerings of stock to favored clients. In effect, the plaintiff shareholders allege that Goldman Sachs bribed certain eBay insiders, using the currency of highly profitable investment opportunities—opportunities that should have been offered to, or provided for the benefit of, eBay rather than the favored insiders. Plaintiffs accuse Goldman Sachs of aiding and abetting the corporate insiders breach of their fiduciary duty of loyalty to eBay.

The individual eBay defendants, as well as Goldman Sachs, have moved to dismiss these consolidated actions for failure to state a claim.... For reasons I briefly discuss below, I deny ... the defendants' motions to dismiss.

I. Background Facts

The facts, as alleged in the complaint, are straightforward. In 1995, defendants Pierre M. Omidyar and Jeffrey Skoll founded nominal defendant eBay, a Delaware corporation, as a sole proprietorship. eBay is a pioneer in online trading platforms, providing a virtual auction community for buyers and sellers to list items for sale and to bid on items of interest. In 1998, eBay retained Goldman Sachs and other investment banks to underwrite an initial public offering of common stock. Goldman Sachs was the lead underwriter. The stock was priced at $18 per share. Goldman Sachs purchased about 1.2 million shares. Shares of eBay became immensely valuable during 1998 and 1999, rising to $175 per share in early April 1999. Around that time, eBay made a secondary offering, issuing 6.5 million shares of common stock at $170 per share for a total of $1.1 billion. Goldman Sachs again served as lead underwriter. Goldman Sachs was asked in 2001 to serve as eBay's financial advisor in connection with an acquisition by eBay of PayPal, Inc. For these services, eBay has paid Goldman Sachs over $8 million.

During this same time period, Goldman Sachs "rewarded" the individual defendants by allocating to them thousands of IPO shares, managed by Goldman Sachs, at the initial offering price. Because the IPO market during this particular period of time was extremely active, prices of initial stock offerings often doubled or tripled in a single day. Investors who were well connected, either to Goldman Sachs or to similarly situated investment banks serving as IPO underwriters, were able to flip these investments into instant profit by selling the equities in a few days or even in a few hours after they were initially purchased.

The essential allegation of the complaint is that Goldman Sachs provided these IPO share allocations to the individual defendants to show appreciation for eBay's business and to enhance Goldman Sachs' chances of obtaining future eBay business. In addition to co-founding eBay, defendant Omidyar has been eBay's CEO, CFO and President. He is eBay's largest stockholder, owning more than 23% of the company's equity. Goldman Sachs allocated Omidyar shares in at least forty IPOs at the initial offering price. Omidyar resold these securities in the public market for millions of dollars in profit. Defendant Whitman owns 3.3% of eBay stock and has been President, CEO and a director since early 1998. Whitman also has been a director of Goldman Sachs since 2001. Goldman Sachs allocated Whitman shares in over a 100 IPOs at the initial offering price. Whitman sold these equities in the open market and reaped millions of dollars in profit. Defendant Skoll, in addition to co-founding eBay, has served in various positions at the company, including Vice-President of Strategic Planning and Analysis and President. He served as an eBay director from December 1996 to March 1998. Skoll is eBay's second largest stockholder, owning about 13% of the company. Goldman Sachs has allocated Skoll shares in at least 75 IPOs at the initial offering price, which Skoll promptly resold on the open market, allowing him to realize millions of dollars in profit. Finally, defendant Robert C. Kagle has served as an eBay director since June 1997. Goldman Sachs allocated Kagle shares in at least 25 IPOs at the initial offering price. Kagle promptly resold these equities, and recorded millions of dollars in profit.

II. Analysis

. . .

B. Corporate Opportunity

Plaintiffs have stated a claim that defendants usurped a corporate opportunity of eBay. Defendants insist that Goldman Sachs' IPO allocations to eBay's insider directors were "collateral investments opportunities" that arose by virtue of the inside directors' status as wealthy individuals. They argue that this is not a corporate opportunity within the corporation's line of business or an opportunity in which the corporation had an interest or expectancy.[3] These arguments are unavailing.

First, no one disputes that eBay financially was able to exploit the opportunities in question. Second, eBay was in the business of investing in securities. The complaint alleges that eBay "consistently invested a portion of its cash on hand in marketable securities." According to eBay's 1999 10-K for example, eBay had more than $550 million invested in equity and debt securities. eBay invested more than $181 million in "short-term investments" and $373 million in "long-term investments." Thus, investing was "a line of business" of eBay. Third, the facts alleged in the complaint suggest that investing was integral to eBay's cash management strategies and a significant part of its business. Finally, it is no answer to say, as do defendants, that

---

3. See *Broz v. Cellular Info. Sys. Inc.* (listing factors to find corporate opportunity).

IPOs are risky investments. It is undisputed that eBay was never given an opportunity to turn down the IPO allocations as too risky.[4]

Defendants also argue that to view the IPO allocations in question as corporate opportunities will mean that every advantageous investment opportunity that comes to an officer or director will be considered a corporate opportunity. On the contrary, the allegations in the complaint in this case indicate that unique, below-market price investment opportunities were offered by Goldman Sachs to the insider defendants as financial inducements to maintain and secure corporate business. This was not an instance where a broker offered advice to a director about an investment in a marketable security. The conduct challenged here involved a large investment bank that regularly did business with a company steering highly lucrative IPO allocations to select insider directors and officers at that company, allegedly both to reward them for past business and to induce them to direct future business to that investment bank. This is a far cry from the defendants' characterization of the conduct in question as merely "a broker's investment recommendations" to a wealthy client.

Nor can one seriously argue that this conduct did not place the insider defendants in a position of conflict with their duties to the corporation. One can realistically characterize these IPO allocations as a form of commercial discount or rebate for past or future investment banking services. Viewed pragmatically, it is easy to understand how steering such commercial rebates to certain insider directors places those directors in an obvious conflict between their self-interest and the corporation's interest. It is noteworthy, too, that the Securities and Exchange Commission has taken the position that "spinning" practices violate the obligations of broker-dealers under the "Free-riding and Withholding Interpretation" rules.[5] As the SEC has explained, "the purpose of the interpretation is to protect the integrity of the public offering system by ensuring that members make a bona fide public distribution of 'hot issue' securities and do not withhold such securities for their own benefit or use the securities to reward other persons who are in a position to direct future business to the member."[6]

Finally, even if one assumes that IPO allocations like those in question here do not constitute a corporate opportunity, a cognizable claim is nevertheless stated on the common law ground that an agent is under a duty to account for profits obtained personally in connection with transactions related to his or her company. The complaint gives rise to a reasonable inference that the insider directors accepted a commission or gratuity that rightfully belonged to eBay but that was improperly diverted

---

4. Defendants' counsel implied at oral argument that these investments were so risky that defendants may have lost money on some or all of them. That is a factual assertion that certainly contradicts allegations in the complaint, but of course I may not consider it on a motion to dismiss.

5. See *Approval of Amendments to Free-riding and Withholding Interpretation*, NASD Notice 98-48, 1998 WL 1707944, at 1 (July 1998).

6. SEC Release No. 35059, Release No. 34-35059, 58 SEC Docket 451, 1994 WL 697640, at 1 (Dec. 7, 1994).

to them. Even if this conduct does not run afoul of the corporate opportunity doctrine, it may still constitute a breach of the fiduciary duty of loyalty. Thus, even if one does not consider Goldman Sachs' IPO allocations to these corporate insiders — allocations that generated millions of dollars in profit — to be a corporate, opportunity, the defendant directors were nevertheless not free to accept this consideration from a company, Goldman Sachs, that was doing significant business with eBay and that arguably intended the consideration as an inducement to maintaining the business relationship in the future.[8] . . .

III. Conclusion

For all of the above reasons, I deny the defendants' motions to dismiss the complaint in this consolidated action.

Questions

1. The practice of "spinning," described in the case, attracted a great deal of attention during the corporate scandals of 2002–03 when the investing public began to learn of the practice and its widespread nature. What, exactly, is wrong with spinning?

2. Why didn't the court simply decide the case on the agency theory it considered near the end? Is spinning really a corporate opportunity? What aspects of the corporate opportunity test does it satisfy? To what extent is this case really about corporate opportunity and to what extent is it a political reaction by the Delaware court to widespread public concern about the laxity of corporate governance rules?

3. Following a decade long attempts to regulate spinning, on September 29, 2010, the SEC approved FINRA (Financial Industry Regulatory Authority, Inc.) Rule 5131: New Issue Allocations and Distributions:

. . .

(b) Spinning

> (1) No member or person associated with a member may allocate shares of a new issue to any account in which an executive officer or director of a public company or a covered non-public company, or a person materially supported by such executive officer or director, has a beneficial interest:
>
>> (A) if the company is currently an investment banking services client of the member or the member has received compensation from the company for investment banking services in the past 12 months;
>>
>> (B) if the person responsible for making the allocation decision knows or has reason to know that the member intends to provide, or expects

---

8. RESTATEMENT (SECOND) OF AGENCY § 388 (1957).

to be retained by the company for, investment banking services within the next 3 months; or

(C) on the express or implied condition that such executive officer or director, on behalf of the company, will retain the member for the performance of future investment banking services.

. . .

C. Compensation and Waste

The problem of directors' and executives' compensation is one of the more intractable difficulties in fiduciary law. The problem is sufficiently hard when the board is deciding upon compensation for the CEO, who typically sits on the board and has a major role in selecting the candidates for director positions. The problem is compounded when we are dealing with the issue of compensation for directors themselves. Directors are not legally *entitled* to compensation although they are permitted to be compensated, and historically their compensation was, if any, quite modest, serving more as a gratuity acknowledging their attendance at meetings and participation in decision-making more than meaningful compensation. In more recent times, directors' compensation has grown to become substantial.

The difficulties that the directors' approval of their own compensation present are compounded when directors are compensated in anything other than cash. The use of stock options to compensate managers and directors is increasingly common, spurred on by a law passed by Congress in 1993 prohibiting corporations from deducting more than $1,000,000 in cash compensation for any single employee, and encouraged by the 1990s' bubble market. Thus, throughout the 1990s, we saw an enormous increase in managerial and directorial compensation in stock. Indeed, the average Fortune 1000 CEO receives more annually in stock options or stock than in cash. While such compensation must be disclosed, it obviously has the potential to present significant valuation problems. Consider Chancellor Allen's approach to the valuation problem in the following case.

Lewis v. Vogelstein
699 A.2d 327 (Del. Ch. 1997)

ALLEN, Chancellor

This shareholders' suit challenges a stock option compensation plan for the directors of Mattel, Inc., which was approved or ratified by the shareholders of the company at its 1996 Annual Meeting of Shareholders. Two claims are asserted.

First, and most interestingly, plaintiff asserts that the proxy statement that solicited shareholder proxies to vote in favor of the adoption of the 1996 Mattel Stock

Option Plan ("1996 Plan" or "Plan") was materially incomplete and misleading, because it did not include an estimated present value of the stock option grants to which directors might become entitled under the Plan. Thus, the first claim asserts that the corporate directors had, in the circumstances presented, a duty to disclose the present value of future options as estimated by some option-pricing formula, such as the Black-Scholes option-pricing model.

Second, it is asserted that the grants of options actually made under the 1996 Plan did not offer reasonable assurance to the corporation that it would receive adequate value in exchange for such grants, and that such grants represent excessively large compensation for the directors in relation to the value of their service to Mattel. For these reasons, the granting of the option is said to constitute a breach of fiduciary duty.

On this motion, this substantive liability theory is also pressed as an "entire fairness" claim. Plaintiff maintains that because the Plan constitutes a self-interested transaction by the incumbent directors, all of whom qualify for grants under the 1996 Plan, they must justify it as entirely fair in order to avoid liability for breach of loyalty, which it is said they cannot do. As shown below, this approach does not constitute a different claim than that stated above.

Pending is defendants' motion to dismiss the complaint for failure to state a claim upon which relief may be granted. . . .

For the reasons set forth below I conclude that there is no legal obligation for corporate directors who seek shareholder ratification of a plan of officer or director option grants, to make and disclose an estimate of present value of future options under a plan of the type described in the complaint. There is, therefore, no basis to conclude that failure to set forth such estimate constitutes a violation of any board obligation to set forth all material facts in connection with a ratification vote. Second, I conclude that the allegations of the complaint are not necessarily inconsistent with a conclusion that the 1996 Plan constitutes a waste of corporate assets. Thus, the complaint may not be dismissed as failing to state a claim.

I

The facts as they appear in the pleading are as follows. The Plan was adopted in 1996 and ratified by the company's shareholders at the 1996 annual meeting. It contemplates two forms of stock option grants to the company's directors: a one-time grant of options on a block of stock and subsequent, smaller annual grants of further options.

With respect to the one-time grant, the Plan provides that each outside director will qualify for a grant of options on 15,000 shares of Mattel common stock at the market price on the day such options are granted (the "one-time options"). The one-time options are alleged to be exercisable immediately upon being granted although they will achieve economic value, if ever, only with the passage of time. It is alleged that if not exercised, they remain valid for ten years.[2]

With respect to the second type of option grant, the Plan qualifies each director for a grant of options upon his or her re-election to the board each year (the "Annual Options"). The maximum number of options grantable to a director pursuant to the annual options provision depends on the number of years the director has served on the Mattel board. Those outside directors with five or fewer years of service will qualify to receive options on no more than 5,000 shares, while those with more than five years service will qualify for options to purchase up to 10,000 shares.[3] Once granted, these options vest over a four year period, at a rate of 25% per year. When exercisable, they entitle the holder to buy stock at the market price on the day of the grant. According to the complaint, options granted pursuant to the annual options provision also expire ten years from their grant date, whether or not the holder has remained on the board.

When the shareholders were asked to ratify the adoption of the Plan, as is typically true, no estimated present value of options that were authorized to be granted under the Plan was stated in the proxy solicitation materials.

II

As the presence of valid shareholder ratification of executive or director compensation plans importantly affects the form of judicial review of such grants, it is logical to begin an analysis of the legal sufficiency of the complaint by analyzing the sufficiency of the attack on the disclosures made in connection with the ratification vote.

A. Disclosure Obligation

I first note a preliminary point: The complaint's assertion is not simply that the ratification of the 1996 Plan by the Mattel shareholders was ineffective because it was defective. If that were the whole of plaintiff's theory, the effect of any defect in disclosure under it would be only to deny to the board the benefits that ratification bestows in such a case. The thrust of the allegation, however, is that in seeking ratification and in, allegedly, failing fully to disclose material facts, the board has committed an independent wrong. Despite the fact that shareholder approval was not

---

2. As to the term of the one-time options there exists a material dispute of relevant fact. The complaint alleges those options are valid for ten years. Defendants assert however that a reading of the Plan itself certainly establishes that in fact the options expire *sixty days after an outside director ceases to be a member of Mattel's board or in ten years whichever occurs first*. Thus, according to defendants, the value of the options only continues while the grantee is serving on the board and is, presumably, affected by their motivational effect. This fact if true would render these options very difficult to value under option pricing theory. The procedural setting of the motion requires me to assume that plaintiff's allegation is correct.

3. From a corporation law perspective one might defend as rational the greater incentive for longer serving directors; from a corporate governance perspective, however, the wisdom of this structure, which creates greater incentives to remain on the board, could sustain debate.

required for the authorization of this transaction and was sought only for its effect on the standard of judicial review, there is language in Delaware cases dealing with "fair process", suggesting that a misdisclosure may make available a remedy, even if the shareholder vote was not required to authorize the transaction and the transaction can substantively satisfy a fairness test.[5]

In all events, in this instance, the theory advanced is that the alleged non-disclosure itself breaches a duty of candor and gives rise to a remedy. The defect alleged is that *the shareholders were not told the present value of the compensation to the outside directors that the Plan contemplated i.e.*, the present value of the options that were authorized. It is alleged that the present value of the one-time options was as much as $180,000 per director and that that "fact" would be material to a Mattel shareholder in voting whether or not to ratify the board's action in adopting the 1996 Plan. According to plaintiff, the shareholders needed to have a specific dollar valuation of the options in order to decide whether to ratify the 1996 Plan. Such a valuation could, plaintiff suggests, be determined by application of formulas such as the widely-used option-pricing model first devised by Professors Fischer Black and Myron Scholes.[6] Plaintiff urges that this court should hold that because no such valuation was provided to the shareholders, the proxy statement failed to disclose material matter and was, therefore, defective.

B. Disclosure of Estimated Present Value of Options to be Granted

Estimates of option values are a species of "soft information" that would be derived from sources such as the specific terms of a plan (including when and for how long options are exercisable), historical information concerning the volatility of the securities that will be authorized to be optioned, and debatable assumptions about the future. Permissible and mandated disclosure of "soft information"— valuation opinions and projections most commonly — are problematic for federal and state disclosure law.[7] Such estimates are inherently more easily subject to

---

5. In fact in considering disclosure in the ratification context it may be useful to distinguish (1) innocently incomplete or defective (including negligent omission) disclosure, in which event the effect of failure to fully and adequately disclose material facts may be only to deny the ratification effect, from (2) knowing attempts to manipulate shareholders through deliberately false or misleading disclosures, in which event the additional subjective state component—the deliberate injury to the protected relationship—may justify not simply a denial of burden shifting but a separate remedy.

6. Fischer Black & Myron Scholes, *The Pricing of Options and Corporate Liabilities*, 81 J. Pol. Econ. 637 (1973).

7. In Delaware, for example, compare *Repairman's Service Corp. v. National Intergroup, Inc.* (holding that soft information such as projections and estimates of value need not, generally, be disclosed to shareholders); *In re Anderson, Clayton Shareholders Litig.* (stating that an appraisal of asset values need not be disclosed to shareholders in a proxy statement) and *Weinberger v. Rio Grande Indus.* (holding that pro forma financial projections need not be disclosed to shareholders because sufficient indicia of reliability for them was not established), the last two of which applied the materiality standard set forth in *Flynn v. Bass Bros. Enterp.*, with *Lynch v. Vickers Energy Corp.* (finding that an estimate of a target corporation's net asset value as calculated by the target management was

intentional manipulation or innocent error than data concerning historical facts. Such estimates raise threats to the quality and effectiveness of disclosure not raised by disclosure of historical data.

As the terms of the options granted under the 1996 Plan demonstrate, option-pricing models, when applied to executive or director stock options, are subject to special problems. Significant doubt exists whether the Black-Scholes option-pricing formula, or other, similar option-pricing models, provide a sufficiently reliable estimate of the value of options with terms such as those granted to the outside directors of Mattel.[8]

First, the Black-Scholes formula assumes that the options being valued are issued and publicly traded. Publicly-traded options have certain common characteristics that are important in assessing their value. The options granted to the Mattel directors under the Plan include restrictive terms that are different from those of typical, publicly-traded options and which may affect their value. Importantly, for instance, the directors' options are not assignable.

Second, the Black-Scholes model overstates the value of options that can be exercised at any time during their term because it does not take into account the cost-reducing effect of early exercise. The Mattel directors' one-time options are not options that are exercisable on a set date. They can be exercised at any time after the grant for a period, according to plaintiff, of up to ten years.

Third, the value of publicly-traded options and restricted options responds very differently to increased volatility of the price of the underlying stock. The volatility of the stock price is one of the important variables in the Black-Scholes formula. Publicly-traded options increase in value as the price volatility of the underlying stock increases. The value of options of the type granted to the Mattel directors, on the other hand, arguably decreases with increased volatility, because the holders are more likely to exercise the options early since they cannot be traded.

Plaintiff argues that option pricing techniques are sufficiently developed so that the Financial Accounting Standards Board ("FASB") requires that financial statements state a value of options granted to directors according to a stock-option pricing model. Thus, they assert, the same information should be given to shareholders by directors seeking ratification. There are salient differences, however, between

---

material to shareholders deciding whether to tender their shares to the majority shareholder). See generally Joel Seligman, *The SEC's Unfinished Soft Information Revolution*, 63 Fordham L. Rev. 1953 (1995) (providing a history of the SEC's treatment of "soft information").

8. For example, the term of such an option—a critical variable in estimating present value—is uncertain because it *expires when exercised, at any time during its life*, rather than at a fixed period at its maturity. *See also* footnote 2, regarding the dispute in this case concerning whether options terminate sixty days after any director ceases to be employed by Mattel. Such a provision would also make calculation of a present value of the option grant difficult since the probability of a directors' termination at any (or every) point during the ten year term is impossible to know and very hard to responsibly estimate. Thus, one of the vital components of an option-pricing formula, the life of the option, appears quite problematic in instances of this sort.

financial statement disclosure of an estimated value of stock options under a plan and disclosure for the purpose of shareholder ratification of adoption of the plan. For instance, financial statements are compiled at the end of the fiscal year, *when the value of the options granted can be assessed with greater certainty*, than is possible at the time the option plan is authorized or ratified since the market price at time of issue is known at that later point.

More broadly, it may be the case that good public policy recommends the disclosure to shareholders of estimates of present value (determined by one technique or another) of options that may be granted as compensation to senior officers and directors, when feasible techniques produce reliable estimates. But while it is unquestionably the case that corporation law plays an important part in the development of public policy in the area of directors' legal relations to corporations and shareholders, including disclosure law, it does not follow that the fiduciary duty of corporate directors is the appropriate instrument to determine and implement sound public policy with respect to this technical issue.

What makes good sense—good policy—in terms of *mandated corporate disclosure* concerning prospective option grants involves not simply the moral intuition that directors should be candid with shareholders with respect to relevant facts, but inescapably involves technical judgments concerning what is feasible and helpful in varying circumstances. Judgments concerning what disclosure, if any, of estimated present values of options should be mandated are best made at this stage of the science, not by a court under a very general materiality standard, but by an agency with finance expertise. An administrative agency—the Securities and Exchange Commission—has a technical staff, is able to hold public hearings, and can, thus, receive wide and expert input, and can specify forms of disclosure, if appropriate. It can propose rules for comment and can easily amend rules that do not work well in practice. As just one example, any option-pricing formula premised on the assumptions that underlie Professors Black and Scholes's model would be concerned with the expected volatility of the stock over the term of option. How that volatility is itself estimated would be a significant factor in any standardized disclosure regime. But this certainly is not the type of inquiry that the judicial process is designed optimally to address. Clearly, determining whether disclosure of estimates of the present value of options ought to be mandated, and how those values ought to be calculated, is not a subject that lends itself to the blunt instrument of duty of loyalty analysis.

In all events, for these reasons, I conclude that, given the tools currently used in financial analysis, a careful board or compensation committee may customarily be expected to consider whether expert estimates of the present value of option grants will be informative and reliable to itself or to shareholders. And if such estimates are deemed by the board, acting in good faith, to be reliable and helpful, the board may elect to disclose them to the shareholders, if it seeks ratification of its actions. But, such "soft information" estimates may be highly problematic and not helpful at all, as for example would likely be the case here, if the options terminate two months after the holder leaves Mattel's board, instead of continuing for ten years, as defendants assert.

While generally the materiality of "facts" omitted from a proxy statement is a question of fact unsuitable for determination on a motion to dismiss, nevertheless, I conclude that the allegations of failure to disclose estimated present value calculations fails to state a claim upon which relief may be granted. Where shareholder ratification of a plan of option compensation is involved, the duty of disclosure is satisfied by the disclosure or fair summary of all of the relevant terms and conditions of the proposed plan of compensation, together with any material extrinsic fact within the board's knowledge bearing on the issue. The directors' fiduciary duty of disclosure does not mandate that the board disclose one or more estimates of present value of options that may be granted under the plan. Such estimates may be an appropriate subject of disclosure where they are generated competently, and disclosed in a good faith effort to inform shareholder action, but no case is cited in which disclosure of such estimates has been mandated in order to satisfy the directors' fiduciary duty and I lack sufficient confidence to break that fresh ground. *Absent allegations of intentional manipulation,* where shareholder ratification of a plan of stock option compensation is sought, what may constitute appropriate disclosure respecting estimated present (or other) values of such options grantable under the plan is a subject better left to the judgment of the Securities and Exchange Commission and, subject to that regulatory regime, the judgment of the board seeking such approval.

III

Thus, concluding that the complaint does not state a claim for breach of any duty to fully disclose material facts to shareholders in connection with the board's request that the shareholders ratify the board's act of creating a directors' stock option plan, I turn to the motion to dismiss the complaint's allegation to the effect that the Plan, or grants under it, constitute a breach of the directors' fiduciary duty of loyalty. As the Plan contemplates grants to the directors that approved the Plan and who recommended it to the shareholders, we start by observing that it constitutes self-dealing that would ordinarily require that the directors prove that the grants involved were, in the circumstances, entirely fair to the corporation. However, it is the case that the shareholders have ratified the directors' action. That ratification is attacked only on the ground just treated. Thus, for these purposes I assume that the ratification was effective. The question then becomes what is the effect of informed shareholder ratification on a transaction of this type (*i.e.,* officer or director pay).

A. Shareholder Ratification Under Delaware Law

What is the effect under Delaware corporation law of shareholder ratification of an interested transaction? The answer to this apparently simple question appears less clear than one would hope or indeed expect. Four possible effects of shareholder ratification appear logically available: First, one might conclude that an effective shareholder ratification acts as a complete defense to any charge of breach of duty. Second, one might conclude that the effect of such ratification is to shift the substantive test on judicial review of the act from one of fairness that would otherwise be obtained (because the transaction is an interested one) to one of waste. Third, one might conclude that the ratification shifts the burden of proof of unfairness to plaintiff, but leaves that shareholder-protective test in place. Fourth, one might conclude (perhaps because of great respect for the collective action disabilities that attend shareholder action in public corporations) that shareholder ratification offers no assurance of assent of a character that deserves judicial recognition. Thus, under this approach, ratification on full information would be afforded no effect. Excepting the fourth of these effects, there are cases in this jurisdiction that reflect each of these approaches to the effect of shareholder voting to approve a transaction.

In order to state my own understanding I first note that by shareholder ratification I do not refer to every instance in which shareholders vote affirmatively with respect to a question placed before them. I exclude from the question those instances in which shareholder votes are a necessary step in authorizing a transaction. Thus the law of ratification as here discussed has no direct bearing on shareholder action to amend a certificate of incorporation or bylaws . . . nor does that law bear on shareholder votes necessary to authorize a merger, a sale of substantially all the corporation's assets, or to dissolve the enterprise. For analytical purposes one can set such cases aside.

1. Ratification generally: I start with principles broader than those of corporation law. Ratification is a concept deriving from the law of agency which contemplates the *ex post* conferring upon or confirming of the legal authority of an agent in circumstances in which the agent had no authority or arguably had no authority. To be effective, of course, the agent must fully disclose all relevant circumstances with respect to the transaction to the principal prior to the ratification. Beyond that, since the relationship between a principal and agent is fiduciary in character, the agent in seeking ratification must act not only with candor, but with loyalty. Thus an attempt to coerce the principal's consent improperly will invalidate the effectiveness of the ratification.[11]

Assuming that a ratification by an agent is validly obtained, what is its effect? One way of conceptualizing that effect is that it provides, after the fact, the grant of authority that may have been wanting at the time of the agent's act. Another might be to view the ratification as consent or as an estoppel by the principal to deny a lack of authority. In either event the effect of informed ratification is to validate or affirm the act of the agent as the act of the principal.

---

11. What constitutes an improper attempt to coerce consent and what constitutes fair conditions set by the agent would, like most fiduciary duty questions, be difficult to generalize about *ex ante*. For example a statement by an agent seeking ratification that unless this transaction is ratified the agent will exercise a legal power to terminate his agency would seem ordinarily within his power and not improper, but if he has arranged things so that the principal's interests are particularly vulnerable at that moment, he is arguably exploiting the relationship and improperly coercing consent.

Application of these general ratification principles to shareholder ratification is complicated by three other factors. First, most generally, in the case of shareholder ratification there is of course no single individual acting as principal, but rather a class or group of divergent individuals—the class of shareholders. This aggregate quality of the principal means that decisions to affirm or ratify an act will be subject to collective action disabilities; that some portion of the body doing the ratifying may in fact have conflicting interests in the transaction; and some dissenting members of the class may be able to assert more or less convincingly that the "will" of the principal is wrong, or even corrupt and ought not to be binding on the class. In the case of individual ratification these issues won't arise, assuming that the principal does not suffer from multiple personality disorder. Thus the collective nature of shareholder ratification makes it more likely that following a claimed shareholder ratification, nevertheless, there is a litigated claim on behalf of the principal that the agent lacked authority or breached its duty. The second, mildly complicating factor present in shareholder ratification is the fact that in corporation law the "ratification" that shareholders provide will often not be directed to lack of legal authority of an agent but will relate to the consistency of some authorized director action with the equitable duty of loyalty. Thus shareholder ratification sometimes acts not to confer legal authority—but as in this case—to affirm that action taken is consistent with shareholder interests. Third, when what is "ratified" is a director conflict transaction, the statutory law—in Delaware Section 144 of the Delaware General Corporation Law—may bear on the effect.[12]

2. Shareholder ratification: These differences between shareholder ratification of director action and classic ratification by a single principal, do lead to a difference in the effect of a valid ratification in the shareholder context. The principal novelty added to ratification law generally by the shareholder context, is the idea—no doubt analogously present in other contexts in which common interests are held—that, in addition to a claim that ratification was defective because of incomplete information or coercion, shareholder ratification is subject to a claim by a member of the class that the ratification is ineffectual (1) because a majority of those affirming the

---

12. Most jurisdictions have enacted statutes that appear to offer a procedural technique for removing courts from a fairness evaluation of the terms of director conflict transactions. Generally courts have given them a very narrow interpretation, however. In Delaware that statute enacted in 1967—Act of July 3, 1967, Ch. 50, 56 Del. Laws 151, 170 (1967) amended in 1969—is Section 144 of the DGCL. Early on it was narrowly held that compliance with that section simply removed the automatic taint of a director conflict transaction, but nevertheless left the transaction subject to substantive judicial review for fairness. *See Fliegler v. Lawrence* (involving claimed independent board action, not ratification by shareholders). This interpretation tended to be the general judicial response to these "safe-harbor" statutes. *See Cookies Food Prod., Inc. v. Lakes Warehouse Distrib.* (requiring directors who engage in self-dealing to prove that they have acted in good faith). *See also Cohen v. Ayers* (stating that under New York statutory law, in an unratified transaction involving interested directors the burden is on the directors to establish the fairness of the transaction, but where shareholder or disinterested-director ratification has occurred, the burden shifts to the challenger).

transaction had a conflicting interest with respect to it or (2) because the transaction that is ratified constituted a corporate waste. As to the second of these, it has long been held that shareholders may not ratify a waste except by a unanimous vote. The idea behind this rule is apparently that a transaction that satisfies the high standard of waste constitutes a *gift* of corporate property and no one should be forced against their will to make a gift of their property. In all events, informed, uncoerced, disinterested shareholder ratification of a transaction in which corporate directors have a material conflict of interest has the effect of protecting the transaction from judicial review except on the basis of waste.[13]

B. The Waste Standard

The judicial standard for determination of corporate waste is well developed. Roughly, a waste entails an exchange of corporate assets for consideration so disproportionately small as to lie beyond the range at which any reasonable person might be willing to trade. Most often the claim is associated with a transfer of corporate assets that serves no corporate purpose; or for which no consideration at all is received. Such a transfer is in effect a gift. If, however, there is *any substantial* consideration received by the corporation, and if there is a *good faith judgment* that in the circumstances the transaction is worthwhile, there should be no finding of waste, even if the fact finder would conclude *ex post* that the transaction was unreasonably risky. Any other rule would deter corporate boards from the optimal rational acceptance of risk, for reasons explained elsewhere. Courts are ill-fitted to attempt to weigh the "adequacy" of consideration under the waste standard or, *ex post,* to judge appropriate degrees of business risk.

C. Ratification of Officer or Director Option Grants

Let me turn now to the history of the Delaware law treating shareholder ratification of corporate plans that authorize the granting of stock options to corporate officers and directors. What is interesting about this law is that while it is consistent with the foregoing general treatment of shareholder ratification — *i.e.*, it appears to hold that informed, non-coerced ratification validates any such plan or grant, unless the plan is wasteful— in its earlier expressions, the waste standard used by the courts in fact was not a waste standard at all, but was a form of "reasonableness" or proportionality review.

1. Development of Delaware law of option compensation: It is fair to say I think that Delaware law took a skeptical or suspicious stance towards the innovation of stock option compensation as it developed in a major way following World War II. Such skepticism is a fairly natural consequence of the common law of director

---

13. Claims of breach of a duty of care seem difficult to relate to analysis under the waste standard. Duty of care analysis in this or other settings relate to deviations from ordinary care in the circumstances. Probably for this reason, it has been held, on authority, that ratification of a transaction that is thereafter made the subject of a breach of care claim is effective to defeat such a claim completely.

compensation[15] and of the experience that corporate law judges had over the decades with schemes to water stock or to divert investors funds into the hands of promoters or management.

The early Delaware cases on option compensation established that, even in the presence of informed ratification, in order for stock option grants to be valid a two part test had to be satisfied. First it was seen as necessary that the court conclude that the grant contemplates that the corporation will receive "sufficient consideration." "Sufficient consideration" as employed in the early cases does not seem like a waste standard: "Sufficient consideration to the corporation may be, *inter alia*, the retention of the services of an employee, or the gaining of the services of a new employee, *provided there is a reasonable relationship between the value of the services ... and the value of the options. ...*"

Secondly it was held early on that, in addition, the plan or the circumstances of the grant must include "conditions or the existence of circumstances *which may be expected to insure* that the contemplated consideration will in fact pass to the corporation." (emphasis added). Elsewhere the Supreme Court spoke of "circumstances which may reasonably be regarded as *sufficient to insure* that the corporation will receive that which it desires. ..."

This (1) weighing of the reasonableness of the relationship between the value of the consideration flowing both ways and (2) evaluating the sufficiency of the circumstances to insure receipt of the benefit sought, seem rather distant from the substance of a waste standard of judicial review. Indeed these tests seem to be a form of heightened scrutiny that is now sometimes referred to as an intermediate or proportionality review.

In all events, these tests were in fact operationally very problematic. Valuing an option grant (as part of a reasonable relationship test) is quite difficult, even under today's more highly developed techniques of financial analysis. This would be especially true where, as this case exemplifies, the options are tied to and conditioned upon a continued status as an officer or director. Even more problematic is valuing—or judicially reviewing a judgment of equivalency of value of—the future benefits that the corporation hopes to obtain from the option grant. There is no objective metric to gauge *ex ante* incentive effects of owning options by officers or directors.[17] Beyond this operational problem, the approach of these early option cases may be thought to raise the question, why was it necessary for the court reviewing a stock option grant to conclude that the circumstances "insure" that the corporation will

---

15. *See, e.g., Cahall v. Lofland*, Del. Ch. (directors serve without compensation unless it is explicitly authorized by its charter or by shareholders; director compensation where authorized is "scrutinized closely"; directors may not evaluate the value of their labor when it provides consideration for issuance of stock).

17. The benefits that Mattel contemplates receiving from the grant of options, according to its Proxy Statement, is to "attract, retain and reward ... directors" and "to strengthen the mutuality of interests between [the option-recipients] and the ... stockholders."

receive the benefits it seeks to achieve. In other contexts, even where interested transactions are involved, a fair (*i.e.*, valid and enforceable) contract might contemplate payment in exchange for a probability of corporation benefit. A corporation, for example, certainly could acquire from an officer or director at a fair price a property interest that had only prospective commercial value.

In *Beard v. Elster*, the Delaware Supreme Court relaxed slightly the general formulation of *Kerbs, et al.*,[19] and rejected the reading of *Kerbs* to the effect that the corporation had to have (or insure receipt of) *legally cognizable* consideration in order to make an option grant valid. The court also emphasized the effect that approval by an independent board or committee might have. It held that what was necessary to validate an officer or director stock option grant was a finding that a reasonable board could conclude from the circumstances that the corporation may reasonably expect to receive a proportionate benefit. A good faith determination by a disinterested board or committee to that effect, at least when ratified by a disinterested shareholder vote, entitled such a grant to business judgment protection (*i.e.*, classic waste standard). After *Beard*, judicial review of officer and director option grants sensibly focused in practice less on attempting independently to assess whether the corporation in fact would receive proportionate value, and more on the procedures used to authorize and ratify such grants. But *Beard* addressed only a situation in which an independent committee of the board functioned on the question.

2. Current law on ratification effect on option grants: A substantive question that remains however is whether in practice the waste standard that is utilized where informed shareholders ratify a grant of options adopted and recommended by a self-interested board *is* the classical waste test (*i.e.*, no consideration; gift; no person of ordinary prudence could possibly agree, etc.) or whether, in fact, it *is a species of intermediate review* in which the court assesses reasonableness in relationship to perceived benefits.

The Supreme Court has not expressly deviated from the "proportionality" approach to waste of its earlier decision, although in recent decades it has had few occasions to address the subject. In *Michelson v. Duncan*, a stock option case in which ratification had occurred, however, the court repeatedly referred to the relevant test where ratification had occurred as that of "gift or waste" and plainly meant by waste, the absence of *any consideration* ("... when there are issues of fact as to the *existence of consideration*, a full hearing is required regardless of shareholder ratification"). Issues of "sufficiency" of consideration or adequacy of assurance that a benefit or proportionate benefit would be achieved were not referenced.

---

19. "All stock option plans must ... contain conditions, or [the] surrounding circumstances [must be] such, that the corporation *may reasonably expect* to receive the contemplated benefit from the grant of options [, and] (2) there must be a reasonable relationship between the value of the benefit passing to the corporation and the value of the options granted." *Beard v. Elster* (emphasis added).

The Court of Chancery has interpreted the waste standard in the ratified option context as invoking not a proportionality or reasonableness test a la *Kerbs* but the traditional waste standard referred to in *Michelson*.

In according substantial effect to shareholder ratification these more recent cases are not unmindful of the collective action problem faced by shareholders in public corporations. These problems do render the assent that ratification can afford very different in character from the assent that a single individual may give. In this age in which institutional shareholders have grown strong and can more easily communicate, however, that assent, is, I think, a more rational means to monitor compensation than judicial determinations of the "fairness," or sufficiency of consideration, which seems a useful technique principally, I suppose, to those unfamiliar with the limitations of courts and their litigation processes. In all events, the classic waste standard does afford some protection against egregious cases or "constructive fraud." . . .

Before ruling on the pending motion to dismiss the substantive claim of breach of fiduciary duty, under a waste standard, I should make one other observation. The standard for determination of motions to dismiss is of course well established and understood. Where under any state of facts consistent with the factual allegations of the complaint the plaintiff would be entitled to a judgment, the complaint may not be dismissed as legally defective. It is also the case that in some instances "mere conclusions" may be held to be insufficient to withstand an otherwise well made motion. Since what is a "well pleaded" fact and what is a "mere conclusion" is not always clear, there is often and inevitably some small room for the exercise of informed judgment by courts in determining motions to dismiss under the appropriate test. Consider for example allegations that an arm's-length corporate transaction constitutes a waste of assets. Such an allegation is inherently factual and not easily amenable to determination on a motion to dismiss and indeed often not on a motion for summary judgment. Yet it cannot be the case that allegations of the facts of any (or every) transaction coupled with a statement that the transaction constitutes a waste of assets, necessarily states a claim upon which discovery may be had; such a rule would, in this area, constitute an undue encouragement to strike suits. Certainly some set of facts, if true, may be said as a matter of law not to constitute waste. For example, a claim that the grant of options on stock with a market price of say $5,000 to a corporate director, exercisable at a future time, if the optionee is still an officer or director of the issuer, constitutes a corporate waste, would in my opinion be subject to dismissal on motion, despite the contextual nature of judgments concerning waste. In some instances the facts alleged, if true, will be so far from satisfying the waste standard that dismissal is appropriate.

This is not such a case in my opinion. Giving the pleader the presumptions to which he is entitled on this motion, I cannot conclude that no set of facts could be shown that would permit the court to conclude that the grant of these options, particularly focusing upon the one-time options, constituted an exchange to which no reasonable person not acting under compulsion and in good faith could agree. In so concluding, I do not mean to suggest a view that these grants are suspect, only that one time option grants to directors of this size seem at this point sufficiently unusual to require the court to refer to evidence before making an adjudication of their validity and consistency with fiduciary duty. Thus, for that reason the motion to dismiss will be denied. It is so ordered.

Questions

1. What did the directors have to have known, or believed that they had known, at the time they asked for approval of the stock options? Would you accept compensation in any form as adequate if you didn't have a pretty good idea of what you thought you were getting? Even if the directors' beliefs about the value of the options are purely subjective, isn't that information itself material to stockholders?

2. If the court is correct regarding the value of the options, how could the directors have fulfilled their duty of care?

3. Commentators in favor of substantial stock options have argued that it aligns directors' interests with stockholders' interests in a manner that reduces agency problems in the corporate structure. But is it desirable for directors to be compensated in a manner that focuses them so closely on the stock price? What incentives does it create? How would you design a stock option plan that truly aligned managerial interests with stockholder interests and at the same time avoided the creation of incentives for managers to become obsessive about stock prices and even to manipulate their corporations' books?

4. In response to the financial crisis of 2008, Congress passed The Wall Street Reform and Consumer Protection Act of 2010, commonly referred to as "Dodd-Frank." Section 952 of the Act requires compensation committees of public companies to be fully independent, while section 951 requires companies periodically to conduct a shareholder advisory vote on executive compensation ("say on pay"). The Delaware courts have also taken a harsher stand on stock option plans, requiring disclosure of their features and value (*see, e.g., In re Tyson Foods*, C.A. No. 1106-CC (Del. Ch. Aug. 15, 2007)). Do you think these measures are sufficient to remedy or reverse the trend of rapidly growing executive compensation?

Section IV

Good Faith

The standard of good faith entered (or re-entered) judicial decisions in the 1990s, after, in response to *Smith v. Van Gorkom* (1985), the Delaware legislature enacted section 102(b)(7) of the DGCL. The added section allows corporations to include in their charters provisions that limit, or eliminate, the personal liability of directors for monetary damages for breaches of the duty of care. Other jurisdictions followed suit. Left out of these exculpatory provisions' reach were breaches of the duty of loyalty and actions not in good faith. Given the limited reach of the former, it was not long before the Delaware courts had to reckon with their definition of good faith, initially in cases involving the duty of care but ultimately in cases involving allegations of breach of the duty of loyalty.

As the cases below illustrate, section 102(b)(7) left the Delaware courts scrambling to reconfigure the duties of directors and officers. Suddenly, good faith became popular. In *Cede & Co. v. Technicolor*, Chancellor Allen stated the existence of a triad of duties—good faith, duty of care and duty of loyalty (and the Supreme Court of Delaware approved). *In re Disney Derivative Litigation* defined bad faith to mean conscious disregard of one's duties. *In re Caremark* held that only sustained or systematic failure of a director to exercise reasonable oversight will establish the lack of good faith required to find liability for breach of the duty to monitor. *Stone v. Ritter* revisited *Cede*'s triad of duty and concluded that good faith did not constitute a separate duty; rather, failure to act in good faith was a breach of the fiduciary duty of loyalty.

These cases addressed different aspects of directors' and officers' obligations, but their cumulative impact reached beyond the definition of good faith. As you read and try to make sense of the rapidly changing definitions of the standard of good faith, consider also what is left of directors' and officers' fiduciary obligations. We conclude our discussion by exploring *In re Citigroup Derivative Litigation* and *In re China Agritech Derivative Litigation* to assess when directors might be at risk of acting in bad faith.

A. A New Framework

Cede & Co. v. Technicolor, Inc.
634 A.2d 345 (Del. 1993)

Horsey, Justice

I. Nature of Case
Prior Proceedings
Summary of Principal Holdings

This appeal from final judgment of the Court of Chancery encompasses consolidated suits: a first-filed Delaware statutory appraisal proceeding (the "appraisal action"), and a later-filed shareholders' individual suit for rescissory damages for "fraud" and unfair dealing (the "personal liability action") brought by plaintiffs, Cinerama, Inc. ("Cinerama"), a New York corporation, and Cede & Co. ("Cede"), the owner of record. The actions stem from a 1982–83 cash-out merger in which

Technicolor, Incorporated ("Technicolor"), a Delaware corporation, was acquired by MacAndrews & Forbes Group, Incorporated ("MAF"), a Delaware corporation, through a merger with Macanfor Corporation ("Macanfor"), a wholly-owned subsidiary of MAF.[1] Under the terms of the tender offer and later cash-out merger, each shareholder of Technicolor (excluding MAF and its subsidiaries) was offered $23 cash per share.

Plaintiff Cinerama was at all times the owner of 201,200 shares of the common stock of Technicolor, representing 4.405 percent of the total shares outstanding. Cinerama did not tender its stock in the first leg of the MAF acquisition commencing November 4, 1982; and Cinerama dissented from the second stage merger, which was completed on January 24, 1983. After dissenting, Cinerama, in March 1983, petitioned the Court of Chancery for appraisal of its shares pursuant to 8 Del.C. § 262. In pretrial discovery during the appraisal proceedings, Cinerama obtained testimony leading it to believe that director misconduct had occurred in the sale of the company. In January 1986, Cinerama filed a second suit in the Court of Chancery against Technicolor, seven of the nine members of the Technicolor board at the time of the merger, MAF, Macanfor and Ronald O. Perelman ("Perelman"), MAF's Chairman and controlling shareholder. Cinerama's personal liability action encompassed claims for fraud, breach of fiduciary duty and unfair dealing, and included a claim for rescissory damages, among other relief. Cinerama also claimed that the merger was void *ab initio* for lack of unanimous director approval of repeal of a supermajority provision of Technicolor's charter. . . .

We also conclude that the trial court has erred as a matter of law in reformulating the business judgment rule's elements for finding director breach of duty of care in the context of an arms-length, third-party transaction lacking evidence of director bad faith or director self-dealing. The Chancellor has erroneously imposed on Cinerama, for purposes of rebutting the rule, a burden of proof of board lack of due care which is unprecedented. We refer to the Chancellor's holding that a shareholder plaintiff such as Cinerama must prove injury resulting from a *found* board breach of duty of care, to rebut the business judgment presumption. . . . Apart from the unresolved duty of loyalty issues, on the trial court's presumed findings of *board* breach of duty of care, we find the business judgment presumption accorded the Technicolor board action of October 29, 1982 to have been rebutted for board lack of due care. Therefore, we reverse and remand the personal liability action with instructions to the trial court to apply the entire fairness standard of review to the merger.

[The court discussed the facts leading up to the merger, detailing the failings of the board and individual members of the board both with respect to the duties of care and loyalty.]

---

1. Hereafter we refer to MAF and Macanfor, also a Delaware corporation, collectively as "MAF."

III. Application of the Business Judgment Rule

The pivotal question in this case is whether the Technicolor board's decision of October 29 to approve the plan of merger with MAF was protected by the business judgment rule or should be subject to judicial review for its entire fairness.

Principal Rulings Below/Issues on Appeal Duty of Loyalty

[Omitted.]

Duty of Care

Turning to the duty of care element of the rule, the court ruled that it was not sufficient for Cinerama to prove that the defendant directors had collectively, as a board, breached their duty of care. Cinerama was required to prove that it had suffered a monetary loss from such breach and to quantify that loss. The court expressed "grave doubts" that the Technicolor board "as a whole" had met that duty in approving the terms of the merger/sale of the company. The court, in effect, read into the business judgment presumption of due care the legal maxim that proof of negligence without proof of injury is not actionable. The court also reasoned that a judicial finding of director good faith and loyalty in a third-party, arms-length transaction should minimize the consequences of a board's *found* failure to exercise due care in a sale of a company. The Chancellor's rationale for subordinating the due care element of the business judgment rule, as applied to an arms-length, third-party transaction, was a belief that the rule, unless modified, would lead to draconian results. The Chancellor left no doubt that he was referring to this Court's decision in *Smith v. Van Gorkom*. He stated, "In all, plaintiff contends that this case presents a compelling case for another administration of the discipline applied by the Delaware Supreme Court in *Smith v. Van Gorkom*."

Issues on Appeal

This case raises at least three fundamental issues implicating the precepts and elements of the Delaware business judgment rule. Those issues are: . . . (3) whether a plaintiff should be required to establish injury from a proven claim of *board* lack of due care to rebut the rule for breach of the duty of care.

Parties' Contentions

Cinerama asserts that the Chancellor has committed fundamental errors of law in his formulation and application of the business judgment rule's requirements of director duty of loyalty *and* duty of care. Cinerama first contends that the Chancellor has placed upon a shareholder plaintiff burdens of proof for breach of . . . duty of care that [are] foreign to equity and to Delaware law. . . .

Defendants concede the novelty of the Chancellor's reformulation of the rule's duty of care elements for rebutting a business judgment standard of judicial review to require a shareholder plaintiff to establish harm or loss.[28] Defendants also concede the lack of any Delaware corporate law precedent for applying tort principles of liability to a fiduciary duty of care analysis. However, defendants assert that the Chancellor's requirement of proof of injury for a breach of the duty of care to be actionable, though novel, is "sound." . . .

Standard and Scope of Review

The principal issues raised involve the formulation and application of the duty of loyalty and duty of care standard of the business judgment rule. The formulation of the duty of loyalty and duty of care involves questions of law which are, of course, subject to *de novo* review by this Court. Assuming a correct formulation of the rule's elements, the trial court's findings upon application of the duty of loyalty or duty of care, being "fact dominated," are, on appeal, entitled to substantial deference unless clearly erroneous or not the product of a logical and deductive reasoning process.

Underlying Precepts and Elements of the Delaware Business Judgment Rule

Our starting point is the fundamental principle of Delaware law that the business and affairs of a corporation are managed by or under the direction of its board of directors. 8 Del.C. § 141(a). In exercising these powers, directors are charged with an unyielding fiduciary duty to protect the interests of the corporation and to act in the best interests of its shareholders.

The business judgment rule is an extension of these basic principles. The rule operates to preclude a court from imposing itself unreasonably on the business and affairs of a corporation. The rule, though formulated many years ago, was most recently restated by this Court as follows:

> The rule operates as both a procedural guide for litigants and a substantive rule of law. As a rule of evidence, it creates a "presumption that in making a business decision, the directors of a corporation acted on an informed basis [i.e., with due care], in good faith and in the honest belief that the action

---

28. In support of their argument that the Chancellor "properly applied" the business judgment rule, defendants state that the Chancellor's "approach to the question of director disinterest and independence is *firmly founded* in Delaware law" (emphasis added). However, in addressing the Chancellor's critical ruling that Cinerama retained the burden of proving all elements of its case, including damages, defendants make the flat concession that "no Delaware corporate decision appears to have addressed the precise question." Defendants conclude by stating that the Chancellor's placement of a burden of proof on Cinerama to establish that it has been *harmed* by the defendant directors' breach of duties seems "unexceptionable." Interestingly, defendants discuss the question of a shareholder's burden of proof of injury solely in the context of the Chancellor's formulation of the duty of loyalty and do not address the merits of the Chancellor's requirement of proof of injury in the context of a shareholder's claims for defendant directors' breach of their duty of care. Nowhere in defendants' briefing of the duty of care element of the business judgment rule do defendants address the legal correctness of the Chancellor's placing on Cinerama the burden of establishing harm to have resulted from the defendant directors' breach of their duty of care.

taken was in the best interest of the company." *Aronson v. Lewis*. The presumption initially attaches to a director-approved transaction within a board's conferred or apparent authority in the absence of any evidence of "fraud, bad faith, or self-dealing in the usual sense of personal profit or betterment."

Grobow v. Perot.

The rule posits a powerful presumption in favor of actions taken by the directors in that a decision made by a loyal and informed board will not be overturned by the courts unless it cannot be "attributed to any rational business purpose." Thus, a shareholder plaintiff challenging a board decision has the burden at the outset to rebut the rule's presumption. To rebut the rule, a shareholder plaintiff assumes the burden of providing evidence that directors, in reaching their challenged decision, breached any one of the *triads* of their fiduciary duty—good faith, loyalty or due care. If a shareholder plaintiff fails to meet this evidentiary burden, the business judgment rule attaches to protect corporate officers and directors and the decisions they make, and our courts will not second-guess these business judgments. If the rule is rebutted, the burden shifts to the defendant directors, the proponents of the challenged transaction, to prove to the trier of fact the "entire fairness" of the transaction to the shareholder plaintiff.

Under the entire fairness standard of judicial review, the defendant directors must establish to the *court's* satisfaction that the transaction was the product of both fair dealing *and* fair price. Further, in the review of a transaction involving a sale of a company, the directors have the burden of establishing that the price offered was the highest value reasonably available under the circumstances. . . .

V. Director and Board Duty of Care

Independent of our rulings under section IV, we find the Chancellor's restatement of the duty of care requirement of the rule and a shareholder plaintiff's burden of proof for rebuttal thereof, in the context of a good faith, arms-length sale of the company, to be erroneous as a matter of law. We adopt the court's presumed findings that the defendant directors were grossly negligent in failing to reach an informed decision when they approved the agreement of merger, and to have thereby breached their duty of care. Those findings are fully supported by the record. The formulation and application of the duty of care element of the rule, as applied to a third-party transaction, is explicated in [*Smith v. Van Gorkom*].

Applying *Van Gorkom* to the trial court's presumed findings of director *and* board gross negligence, we find the defendant directors, as a board, to have breached their duty of care by reaching an uninformed decision on October 29, 1982, to approve the sale of the company to MAF for a per-share sale price of $23. We hold that the plan of merger approved by the defendant directors on October 29, 1982, must, on remand, be reviewed for its entire fairness, applying *Weinberger*.

We think it patently clear that the question presented is not one of first impression, as the court below appears to have assumed. Applying controlling precedent of this Court, we hold that the record evidence establishes that Cinerama met its burden of proof for overcoming the rule's presumption of board duty of care in approving the sale of the company to MAF. The Chancellor's restatement of the rule—to require Cinerama to prove a proximate cause relationship between the Technicolor board's presumed breach of its duty of care *and* the shareholder's resultant loss—is contrary to well-established Delaware precedent, irreconcilable with *Van Gorkom*, and contrary to the tenets of *Unocal* and *Revlon, Inc. v. MacAndrews & Forbes Holdings*. More importantly, we think the court's restatement of the rule would lead to most unfortunate results, detrimental to goals of heightened and enlightened standards for corporate governance of Delaware corporations.

We also find the court to have committed error under *Weinberger* in apparently capping Cinerama's recoverable loss under an entire fairness standard of review at the fair value of a share of Technicolor stock on the date of approval of the merger. Under *Weinberger*'s entire fairness standard of review, a party may have a legally cognizable injury regardless of whether the tender offer and cash-out price is greater than the stock's fair value as determined for statutory appraisal purposes.

Director Duty of Care and Board Presumption of Care

The elements, formulation and application of the Delaware business judgment rule follow from the premise that shareholders of a public corporation delegate to their board of directors responsibility for managing the business enterprise. The General Assembly has codified that delegation of authority and mandate of management generally in 8 Del.C. § 141(a) and, specifically, in the context of a merger or sale of a company, in 8 Del.C. § 251.

The judicial presumption accorded director and board action which underlies the business judgment rule is "of paramount significance in the context of a derivative action." *Aronson*. As *Aronson* states, the presumption may only be invoked by directors who are found to be not only "disinterested" directors, but directors who have both adequately informed themselves before voting on the business transaction at hand *and* acted with the requisite care. There we also stated that, for the rule to apply and attach to a particular transaction, directors "have a duty to inform themselves, prior to making a business decision, of all material information reasonably available to them. Having become so informed, they must *then* act with requisite care in the discharge of their duties." (emphasis added).

The duty of the directors of a company to act on an informed basis, as that term has been defined by this Court numerous times, forms the duty of care element of the business judgment rule. Duty of care and duty of loyalty are the traditional hallmarks of a fiduciary who endeavors to act in the service of a corporation and its stockholders. Each of these duties is of equal and independent significance.

In decisional law of this Court applying the rule, preceding as well as following *Van Gorkom*, this Court has consistently given equal weight to the rule's requirements of duty of care and duty of loyalty. In those decisions we have defined a board's duty of care in a variety of settings. For example, we have stated that a director's duty of care requires a director to take an active and direct role in the context of a sale of a company from beginning to end. In a merger or sale, we have stated that the director's duty of care requires a director, before voting on a proposed plan of merger or sale, to inform himself and his fellow directors of all material information that is reasonably available to them.

We have also stated that the rule is premised on a presumption that the directors have severally met their duties of loyalty and that the directors have collectively, as a board, met their duty of care.[36]

Applying the rule, a trial court will not find a board to have breached its duty of care unless the directors individually and the board collectively have failed to inform themselves fully and in a deliberate manner before voting as a board upon a transaction as significant as a proposed merger or sale of the company. Only on such a judicial finding will a board lose the protection of the business judgment rule under the duty of care element and will a trial court be required to scrutinize the challenged transaction under an entire fairness standard of review.

The Chancellor held that "the questions of due care ... need not be addressed in this case, because even if a lapse of care is assumed, plaintiff is not entitled to a *judgment on this record*." Having assumed that the Technicolor board was grossly negligent in failing to exercise due care, the court avoided the business judgment rule's rebuttal by adding to the rule a requirement of proof of injury. The court then found that requirement not met and, indeed, injury not provable due to its earlier finding of fair value for statutory appraisal purposes. In this manner, the court avoided having to determine whether the board had failed to "satisfy its obligation to take reasonable steps in the sale of the enterprise to be adequately informed before it authorized the execution of the merger agreement."

The court found authority for its requirement of proof of injury in a seventy-year-old decision that none of the parties had relied on or felt pertinent. The trial court ruled:

---

36. In *Barkan*, this Court stated:
> ... a board's actions must be evaluated in light of relevant circumstances to determine if they were undertaken with due diligence [care] and good faith [loyalty]. If no breach of duty is found, the board's actions are entitled to the protections of the business judgment rule.

In *Moran*, this Court stated:
> The business judgment rule is a "presumption that in making a business decision the directors of a corporation acted on an informed basis, in good faith and in the honest belief that the action taken was in the best interests of the company."

because the board as a deliberative body was disinterested in the transaction and operating in good faith, plaintiff bears the burden to show that any such innocent, though regrettable, lapse was likely to have injured it.

In the absence of plaintiff's proof of injury, the court held that defendants were entitled to judgment "on all claims." The Chancellor concluded that the "fatal weakness in plaintiff's case" was plaintiff's failure to prove that it had been injured as a result of the defendant's negligence. The court put it this way:

> It is not the case, in my opinion, that *in an arms-length, third party merger* proof of a breach of the board's duty of care itself *entitles plaintiff to judgment*. Rather, in such a case, as in any case in which the gist of the claim is negligence, plaintiff bears the burden to establish that the negligence shown was the proximate cause of some injury to it and what that injury was.

On appeal, Cinerama contends: (1) that the court's assumed findings of the defendant directors' gross negligence in breach of their duty of care brought the case squarely under the control of this Court's rulings in *Van Gorkom* and, in the context of a sale of the company, under *Revlon*; and (2) that the Chancellor erred as a matter of law in invoking the tort principles implemented in *Barnes v. Andrews*, to grant defendants judgment on the record before the court. Cinerama's contentions are well taken, factually supported by the record and correct as a matter of law.

As defendants concede, this Court has never interposed, for purposes of the rule's rebuttal, a requirement that a shareholder asserting a claim of director breach of duty of care (*or* duty of loyalty) must prove not only a breach of such duty, but that an injury has resulted from the breach *and* quantify that injury at that juncture of the case. No Delaware court has, until this case, imposed such a condition upon a shareholder plaintiff. That should not be surprising. The purpose of a trial court's application of an entire fairness standard of review to a challenged business transaction is simply to shift to the defendant directors the burden of demonstrating to the court the entire fairness of the transaction to the shareholder plaintiff, applying *Weinberger* and its progeny. Requiring a plaintiff to show injury through unfair price would effectively relieve director defendants found to have breached their duty of care of establishing the entire fairness of a challenged transaction.

The Chancellor so ruled, notwithstanding finding from the record following trial that whether the Technicolor board exercised due care in approving the merger agreement was not simply a "close question" but one as to which he had "grave doubts." . . .

We adopt, as clearly supported by the record, the Chancellor's presumed findings of the directors' failure to reach an informed decision in approving the sale of the company. We disagree with the Chancellor's imposition on Cinerama of an additional burden, for overcoming the rule, of proving that the board's gross negligence caused any monetary loss to Cinerama. We turn to the court's reformulation of the rule's requirements for imposition of an entire fairness standard of review of the challenged transaction.

The question presented in this case is essentially the same as this Court was presented in *Van Gorkom*: whether the defendant directors, meeting as a board, satisfied the rule's presumption of board due care in meeting to consider for the first time a proposed sale of the company under terms negotiated exclusively by its chairman. We stated:

> In the specific context of a proposed merger of domestic corporations, a director has a duty under 8 Del.C. § 251(b), along with his fellow directors, to act in an informed and deliberate manner in determining whether to approve an agreement of merger before submitting the proposal to the stockholders. Certainly in the merger context, a director may not abdicate that duty by leaving to the shareholders alone the decision to approve or disapprove the agreement.

The Chancellor's Enlargement of the Rule to Require Cinerama to Prove Resultant Injury from the Board's Presumed Failure to Exercise Due Care

The trial court's presumed findings of fact of board breach of duty of care clearly brought the case under the controlling principles of *Van Gorkom* and its holding that the defendant board's breach of its duty of care required the transaction to be reviewed for its entire fairness. The Chancellor, without stating any reasons for finding *Van Gorkom* not to be controlling, chose instead to adopt the actionable negligence principles of *Barnes*.[38] Applying *Barnes*, the Court of Chancery concluded that Cinerama was not entitled to relief because it had failed to present evidence of injury caused by the defendants' negligence.

The Chancellor's reliance on *Barnes* is misguided.[39] While *Barnes* may still be "good law," *Barnes*, a tort action, does not control a claim for breach of fiduciary duty. In *Barnes*, the court found no actionable negligence or proof of loss—and granted

---

38. Cinerama asserts that it is a "mystery" how the court discovered the *Barnes* case and then based its decision on *Barnes*. *Barnes* was apparently not cited by any of the parties in the briefings below. Cinerama refers to *Barnes* as "obscure law" that has been cited but six times since 1924 and "never for the proposition relied upon by the Chancellor." Defendants make no adequate response.

39. In *Barnes*, the receiver of a failed corporation brought suit against Andrews, who was one of the corporation's former directors, for negligence in the performance of his duties. Andrews was charged with taking little, if any, active role as a director because he attended only part of one of two important board meetings. The court found Andrews to have been negligent in his inattention to his directorial duties but not liable for damages since plaintiff failed to prove that the company's insolvency actually resulted from Andrews' negligence rather than the negligence of his fellow directors. Then District Judge Learned Hand ruled:

> Therefore I cannot acquit Andrews of misprision in his office, though his integrity is unquestioned. The plaintiff must, however, go further than to show that he should have been more active in his duties. *This cause of action rests upon a tort,* as much though it be a tort of omission as though it had rested upon a positive act. The plaintiff must accept the burden of showing that the performance of the defendant's duties would have avoided the loss, and what loss it would have avoided.

Barnes (emphasis added).

defendant's motion for a nonsuit or grant of judgment for defendant on the merits. Here, the court was determining the appropriate standard of review of a business decision and whether it was protected by the judicial presumption accorded board action. The tort principles of *Barnes* have no place in a business judgment rule standard of review analysis.

To inject a requirement of proof of injury into the rule's formulation for burden shifting purposes is to lose sight of the underlying purpose of the rule. Burden shifting does not create *per se* liability on the part of the directors; rather, it is a procedure by which Delaware courts of equity determine under what standard of review director liability is to be judged. To require proof of injury as a component of the proof necessary to rebut the business judgment presumption would be to convert the burden shifting process from a threshold determination of the appropriate standard of review to a dispositive adjudication on the merits.

This Court has consistently held that the breach of the duty of care, without any requirement of proof of injury, is sufficient to rebut the business judgment rule. *See Mills*; *Van Gorkom*. In *Van Gorkom*, we held that although there was no breach of the duty of loyalty, the failure of the members of the board to adequately inform themselves represented a breach of the duty of care, which of itself was sufficient to rebut the presumption of the business judgment rule. *Van Gorkom*. A breach of either the duty of loyalty or the duty of care rebuts the presumption that the directors have acted in the best interests of the shareholders, and requires the directors to prove that the transaction was entirely fair. Cinerama clearly met its burden of proof for the purpose of rebutting the rule's presumption by showing that the defendant directors of Technicolor failed to inform themselves fully concerning all material information reasonably available prior to approving the merger agreement. Our basis for this conclusion is the Chancellor's own findings, enumerated above.

In sum, we find the Court of Chancery to have committed fundamental error in rewriting the Delaware business judgment rule's requirement of due care. The court has erroneously subordinated the due care element of the rule to the duty of loyalty element. The court has then injected into the duty of care element a burden of proof of resultant injury or loss. In this regard, we emphasize that the measure of any recoverable loss by Cinerama under an entire fairness standard of review is not necessarily limited to the difference between the price offered and the "true" value as determined under appraisal proceedings. Under *Weinberger*, the Chancellor may "fashion any form of equitable and monetary relief as may be appropriate, including rescissory damages." The Chancellor may incorporate elements of rescissory damages into his determination of fair price, if he considers such elements: (1) susceptible to proof; and (2) appropriate under the circumstances. *Id.* Thus, we must reverse and remand the case to the trial court with directions to apply the entire fairness standard of review to the challenged transaction....

Cede v. Technicolor in context

Cede & Co. v. Technicolor, Inc. is often cited for the proposition that good faith is a separate duty. As the Chancery Court noted, and the Supreme Court approved, to rebut the presumption of the business judgment rule, a plaintiff shareholder "assumes the burden of providing evidence that directors, in reaching their challenged decision, breached any one of the *triads* of their fiduciary duty—good faith, loyalty or due care." Indeed, *Cede* was the first case to reintroduce good faith. Yet, *Cede*'s significance (especially given *Stone v. Ritter*, which we discuss below) lies not in its definition of good faith but in its attempt to streamline the analysis of directors' duties (good faith, care and loyalty).

As we explored in the preceding sections, the duty of care and duty of loyalty are conceptually different. The duty of care is grounded in tort law; if it is breached, the corporation is entitled to damages for the harm caused as a result of the breach. In turn, the duty of loyalty is a fiduciary duty; if it is breached, the court must assess what would have been a fair result. The Delaware Supreme Court in *Cede* held, however, that unlike other duties of care, which require proof of duty, breach, causation, and damages in order for a plaintiff to recover, the corporate director's duty of care, like fiduciary duty, requires only proof of duty and breach before shifting the burden to the defendants to prove fairness.

While this is the rule, it does not necessarily make sense.

Think, for example, of the dispute in *Kamin v. American Express*, in which the issue involved was whether the American Express board had disposed of the DLJ stock in a reasonable manner. Of what relevance is the issue of fairness to the outcome? Try to restate the case as if the plaintiff had proved breach, and then apply the Delaware Court's rule in *Cede*. It doesn't make sense. And the reason it doesn't is that the Delaware court failed to perceive an important distinction between the duty of care and the duty of loyalty, the difference between "corrective justice" and "distributive justice." The purpose of corrective justice is to make a person whole for an injury she has suffered. Distributive justice, in turn, seeks to ensure that each person receives her due. This makes perfect sense in loyalty contexts, because loyalty cases always involve the claim that directors, officers, or controlling stockholders took a benefit from the corporation that was to the detriment of, or should have gone to, or been shared with, the stockholders.

So how come the Supreme Court of Delaware ruled as it did? *Cede* involved a merger, and the question of whether the stockholders received their due could be explored in two ways: either the defendants were not informed, hence the plaintiff was not paid what it was entitled to; or the defendant, due to a conflict of interest, sold the company for an unfair price. Both perspectives in *Cede* (and potentially in other mergers) will result in allowing the shareholder to recover her shares' fair price. If the issue is whether a plaintiff received a fair price, then the only relevance of the distinction is one of burden of proof, and it seems logical for Delaware to use the fiduciary rule of placing the burden of proof of fairness—of non-injury—on the defendants.

But, as Chancellor Allen, who wrote the Chancery court's decision in *Cede*, stressed, this is not always the case. Indeed, as the following cases illustrate, the Supreme Court of Delaware's insistence that it is muddled the jurisprudence of directors' (and officers') duties at a time where more clarity would have been particularly helpful.

In re The Walt Disney Company Derivative Litigation, Brehm v. Eisner
906 A.2d 27 (Del. 2006)

JACOBS, Justice

In August 1995, Michael Ovitz ("Ovitz") and The Walt Disney Company ("Disney" or the "Company") entered into an employment agreement under which Ovitz would serve as President of Disney for five years. In December 1996, only fourteen months after he commenced employment, Ovitz was terminated without cause, resulting in a severance payout to Ovitz valued at approximately $130 million.

In January 1997, several Disney shareholders brought derivative actions in the Court of Chancery, on behalf of Disney, against Ovitz and the directors of Disney who served at the time of the events complained of (the "Disney defendants"). The plaintiffs claimed that the $130 million severance payout was the product of fiduciary duty and contractual breaches by Ovitz, and breaches of fiduciary duty by the Disney defendants, and a waste of assets. After the disposition of several pretrial motions and an appeal to this Court, the case was tried before the Chancellor over 37 days between October 20, 2004 and January 19, 2005. In August 2005, the Chancellor handed down a well-crafted 174 page Opinion and Order, determining that "the director defendants did not breach their fiduciary duties or commit waste." The Court entered judgment in favor of all defendants on all claims alleged in the amended complaint.

The plaintiffs have appealed from that judgment, claiming that the Court of Chancery committed multitudinous errors. We conclude, for the reasons that follow, that the Chancellor's factual findings and legal rulings were correct and not erroneous in any respect. Accordingly, the judgment entered by the Court of Chancery will be affirmed.

I. THE FACTS

We next summarize the facts as found by the Court of Chancery that are material to the issues presented on this appeal. The critical events flow from what turned out to be an unfortunate hiring decision at Disney, a company that for over half a century has been one of America's leading film and entertainment enterprises.

In 1994 Disney lost in a tragic helicopter crash its President and Chief Operating Officer, Frank Wells, who together with Michael Eisner, Disney's Chairman and Chief Executive Officer, had enjoyed remarkable success at the Company's helm. Eisner temporarily assumed Disney's presidency, but only three months later, heart disease required Eisner to undergo quadruple bypass surgery. Those two events persuaded Eisner and Disney's board of directors that the time had come to identify a successor to Eisner.

Eisner's prime candidate for the position was Michael Ovitz, who was the leading partner and one of the founders of Creative Artists Agency ("CAA"), the premier talent agency whose business model had reshaped the entire industry. By 1995, CAA had 550 employees and a roster of about 1400 of Hollywood's top actors, directors, writers, and musicians. That roster generated about $150 million in annual revenues and an annual income of over $20 million for Ovitz, who was regarded as one of the most powerful figures in Hollywood.

Eisner and Ovitz had enjoyed a social and professional relationship that spanned nearly 25 years. Although in the past the two men had casually discussed possibly working together, in 1995, when Ovitz began negotiations to leave CAA and join Music Corporation of America ("MCA"), Eisner became seriously interested in recruiting Ovitz to join Disney. Eisner shared that desire with Disney's board members on an individual basis.[4]

A. Negotiation of the Ovitz Employment Agreement

Eisner and Irwin Russell, who was a Disney director and chairman of the compensation committee, first approached Ovitz about joining Disney. Their initial negotiations were unproductive, however, because at that time MCA had made Ovitz an offer that Disney could not match. The MCA-Ovitz negotiations eventually fell apart, and Ovitz returned to CAA in mid-1995. Business continued as usual, until Ovitz discovered that Ron Meyer, his close friend and the number two executive at CAA, was leaving CAA to join MCA. That news devastated Ovitz, who concluded that to remain with the company he and Meyer had built together was no longer palatable. At that point Ovitz became receptive to the idea of joining Disney. Eisner learned of these developments and re-commenced negotiations with Ovitz in earnest. By mid-July 1995, those negotiations were in full swing.

Both Russell and Eisner negotiated with Ovitz over separate issues and concerns. From his talks with Eisner, Ovitz gathered that Disney needed his skills and experience to remedy Disney's current weaknesses, which Ovitz identified as poor talent

---

4. The Disney board of directors at that time and at the time the Ovitz Employment Agreement was approved (the "old board") consisted of Eisner, Roy E. Disney, Stanley P. Gold, Sanford M. Litvack, Richard A. Nunis, Sidney Poitier, Irwin E. Russell, Robert A.M. Stern, E. Cardon Walker, Raymond L. Watson, Gary L. Wilson, Reveta F. Bowers, Ignacio E. Lozano, Jr., George J. Mitchell, and Stephen F. Bollenbach. The board of directors at the time Ovitz was terminated as President of Disney (the "new board") consisted of the persons listed above (other than Bollenbach), plus Leo J. O'Donovan and Thomas S. Murphy. Neither O'Donovan nor Murphy served on the old board.

relationships and stagnant foreign growth. Seeking assurances from Eisner that Ovitz's vision for Disney was shared, at some point during the negotiations Ovitz came to believe that he and Eisner would run Disney, and would work together in a relation akin to that of junior and senior partner. Unfortunately, Ovitz's belief was mistaken, as Eisner had a radically different view of what their respective roles at Disney should be.

Russell assumed the lead in negotiating the financial terms of the Ovitz employment contract. In the course of negotiations, Russell learned from Ovitz's attorney, Bob Goldman, that Ovitz owned 55% of CAA and earned approximately $20 to $25 million a year from that company. From the beginning Ovitz made it clear that he would not give up his 55% interest in CAA without "downside protection." Considerable negotiation then ensued over downside protection issues. During the summer of 1995, the parties agreed to a draft version of Ovitz's employment agreement (the "OEA") modeled after Eisner's and the late Mr. Wells' employment contracts. As described by the Chancellor, the draft agreement included the following terms:

> Under the proposed OEA, Ovitz would receive a five-year contract with two tranches of options. The first tranche consisted of three million options vesting in equal parts in the third, fourth, and fifth years, and if the value of those options at the end of the five years had not appreciated to $50 million, Disney would make up the difference. The second tranche consisted of two million options that would vest immediately if Disney and Ovitz opted to renew the contract.

The proposed OEA sought to protect both parties in the event that Ovitz's employment ended prematurely, and provided that absent defined causes, neither party could terminate the agreement without penalty. If Ovitz, for example, walked away, for any reason other than those permitted under the OEA, he would forfeit any benefits remaining under the OEA and could be enjoined from working for a competitor. Likewise, if Disney fired Ovitz for any reason other than gross negligence or malfeasance, Ovitz would be entitled to a non-fault payment (Non-Fault Termination or "NFT"), which consisted of his remaining salary, $7.5 million a year for unaccrued bonuses, the immediate vesting of his first tranche of options and a $10 million cash out payment for the second tranche of options.

As the basic terms of the OEA were crystallizing, Russell prepared and gave Ovitz and Eisner a "case study" to explain those terms. In that study, Russell also expressed his concern that the negotiated terms represented an extraordinary level of executive compensation. Russell acknowledged, however, that Ovitz was an "exceptional corporate executive" and "highly successful and unique entrepreneur" who merited "downside protection and upside opportunity." Both would be required to enable Ovitz to adjust to the reduced cash compensation he would receive from a public company, in contrast to the greater cash distributions and other perquisites more typically available from a privately held business. But, Russell did caution that Ovitz's salary would be at the top level for any corporate officer and significantly above that of the Disney CEO. Moreover, the stock options granted under the OEA would exceed the standards applied within Disney and corporate America and would "raise very strong criticism." Russell shared this original case study only with Eisner and Ovitz. He also recommended another, additional study of this issue.

To assist in evaluating the financial terms of the OEA, Russell recruited Graef Crystal, an executive compensation consultant, and Raymond Watson, a member of Disney's compensation committee and a past Disney board chairman who had helped structure Wells' and Eisner's compensation packages. Before the three met, Crystal prepared a comprehensive executive compensation database to accept various inputs and to conduct Black-Scholes analyses to output a range of values for the options.[8] Watson also prepared similar computations on spreadsheets, but without using the Black-Scholes method.

On August 10, Russell, Watson and Crystal met. They discussed and generated a set of values using different and various inputs and assumptions, accounting for different numbers of options, vesting periods, and potential proceeds of option exercises at various times and prices. After discussing their conclusions, they agreed that Crystal would memorialize his findings and fax them to Russell. Two days later, Crystal faxed to Russell a memorandum concluding that the OEA would provide Ovitz with approximately $23.6 million per year for the first five years, or $23.9 million a year over seven years if Ovitz exercised a two year renewal option.[9] Those sums, Crystal opined, would approximate Ovitz's current annual compensation at CAA.

During a telephone conference that same evening, Russell, Watson and Crystal discussed Crystal's memorandum and its assumptions. Their discussion generated additional questions that prompted Russell to ask Crystal to revise his memorandum to resolve certain ambiguities in the current draft of the employment agreement. But, rather than address the points Russell highlighted, Crystal faxed to Russell a new letter that expressed Crystal's concern about the OEA's $50 million option appreciation guarantee. Crystal's concern, based on his understanding of the current draft of the OEA, was that Ovitz could hold the first tranche of options, wait out the five-year term, collect the $50 million guarantee, and then exercise the in-the-money options and receive an additional windfall. Crystal was philosophically opposed to a pay package that would give Ovitz the best of both worlds-low risk and high return.

Addressing Crystal's concerns, Russell made clear that the guarantee would not function as Crystal believed it might. Crystal then revised his original letter, adjusting the value of the OEA (assuming a two year renewal) to $24.1 million per year.

---

8. The Black-Scholes method is a formula for option valuation that is widely used and accepted in the industry and by regulators.

9. In a later, revised memorandum, Crystal estimated that the two additional years would increase the value of the entire OEA to $24.1 million per year.

Up to that point, only three Disney directors—Eisner, Russell and Watson—knew the status of the negotiations with Ovitz and the terms of the draft OEA.

While Russell, Watson and Crystal were finalizing their analysis of the OEA, Eisner and Ovitz reached a separate agreement. Eisner told Ovitz that: (1) the number of options would be reduced from a single grant of five million to two separate grants, the first being three million options for the first five years and the second consisting of two million more options if the contract was renewed; and (2) Ovitz would join Disney only as President, not as a co-CEO with Eisner. After deliberating, Ovitz accepted those terms, and that evening Ovitz, Eisner, Sid Bass[10] and their families celebrated Ovitz's decision to join Disney.

Unfortunately, the celebratory mood was premature. The next day, August 13, Eisner met with Ovitz, Russell, Sanford Litvack (an Executive Vice President and Disney's General Counsel), and Stephen Bollenbach (Disney's Chief Financial Officer) to discuss the decision to hire Ovitz. Litvack and Bollenbach were unhappy with that decision, and voiced concerns that Ovitz would disrupt the cohesion that existed between Eisner, Litvack and Bollenbach. Litvack and Bollenbach were emphatic that they would not report to Ovitz, but would continue to report to Eisner. Despite Ovitz's concern about his "shrinking authority" as Disney's future President, Eisner was able to provide sufficient reassurance so that ultimately Ovitz acceded to Litvack's and Bollenbach's terms.

On August 14, Eisner and Ovitz signed a letter agreement (the "OLA"), which outlined the basic terms of Ovitz's employment, and stated that the agreement (which would ultimately be embodied in a formal contract) was subject to approval by Disney's compensation committee and board of directors. Russell called Sidney Poitier, a Disney director and compensation committee member, to inform Poitier of the OLA and its terms. Poitier believed that hiring Ovitz was a good idea because of Ovitz's reputation and experience. Watson called Ignacio Lozano, another Disney director and compensation committee member, who felt that Ovitz would successfully adapt from a private company environment to Disney's public company culture. Eisner also contacted each of the other board members by phone to inform them of the impending new hire, and to explain his friendship with Ovitz and Ovitz's qualifications.

That same day, a press release made the news of Ovitz's hiring public. The reaction was extremely positive: Disney was applauded for the decision, and Disney's stock price rose 4.4% in a single day, thereby increasing Disney's market capitalization by over $1 billion.

Once the OLA was signed, Joseph Santaniello, a Vice President and counsel in Disney's legal department, began to embody in a draft OEA the terms that Russell and Goldman had agreed upon and had been memorialized in the OLA. In the process, Santaniello concluded that the $50 million guarantee created negative tax

---

10. Sid Bass was one of Disney's largest individual shareholders.

implications for Disney, because it might not be deductible. Concluding that the guarantee should be eliminated, Russell initiated discussions on how to compensate Ovitz for this change. What resulted were several amendments to the OEA to replace the back-end guarantee. The (to-be-eliminated) $50 million guarantee would be replaced by: (i) a reduction in the option strike price from 115% to 100% of the Company's stock price on the day of the grant for the two million options that would become exercisable in the sixth and seventh year of Ovitz's employment; (ii) a $10 million severance payment if the Company did not renew Ovitz's contract; and (iii) an alteration of the renewal option to provide for a five-year extension, a $1.25 million annual salary, the same bonus structure as the first five years of the contract, and a grant of three million additional options. To assess the potential consequences of the proposed changes, Watson worked with Russell and Crystal, who applied the Black-Scholes method to evaluate the extended exercisability features of the options. Watson also generated his own separate analysis.

On September 26, 1995, the Disney compensation committee (which consisted of Messrs. Russell, Watson, Poitier and Lozano) met for one hour to consider, among other agenda items, the proposed terms of the OEA. A term sheet was distributed at the meeting, although a draft of the OEA was not. The topics discussed were historical comparables, such as Eisner's and Wells' option grants, and also the factors that Russell, Watson and Crystal had considered in setting the size of the option grants and the termination provisions of the contract. Watson testified that he provided the compensation committee with the spreadsheet analysis that he had performed in August, and discussed his findings with the committee. Crystal did not attend the meeting, although he was available by telephone to respond to questions if needed, but no one from the committee called. After Russell's and Watson's presentations, Litvack also responded to substantive questions. At trial Poitier and Lozano testified that they believed they had received sufficient information from Russell's and Watson's presentations to exercise their judgment in the best interests of the Company. The committee voted unanimously to approve the OEA terms, subject to "reasonable further negotiations within the framework of the terms and conditions" described in the OEA.

Immediately after the compensation committee meeting, the Disney board met in executive session. The board was told about the reporting structure to which Ovitz had agreed, but the initial negative reaction of Litvack and Bollenbach to the hiring was not recounted. Eisner led the discussion relating to Ovitz, and Watson then explained his analysis, and both Watson and Russell responded to questions from the board. After further deliberation, the board voted unanimously to elect Ovitz as President.

At its September 26, 1995 meeting, the compensation committee determined that it would delay the formal grant of Ovitz's stock options until further issues between Ovitz and the Company were resolved. That was done, and the committee met again, on October 16, 1995, to discuss stock option-related issues. The committee approved amendments to the Walt Disney Company 1990 Stock Incentive Plan (the "1990

Plan"), and also approved a new plan, known as the Walt Disney 1995 Stock Incentive Plan (the "1995 Plan"). Both plans were subject to further approval by the full board of directors and the shareholders. Both the amendment to the 1990 Plan and the Stock Option Agreement provided that in the event of a non-fault termination ("NFT"), Ovitz's options would be exercisable until the later of September 30, 2002 or twenty-four months after termination, but in no event later than October 16, 2005. After approving those Plans, the committee unanimously approved the terms of the OEA and the award of Ovitz's options under the 1990 Plan.

B. *Ovitz's Performance as President of Disney*

Ovitz's tenure as President of the Walt Disney Company officially began on October 1, 1995, the date that the OEA was executed. When Ovitz took office, the initial reaction was optimistic, and Ovitz did make some positive contributions while serving as President of the Company. By the fall of 1996, however, it had become clear that Ovitz was "a poor fit with his fellow executives." By then the Disney directors were discussing that the disconnect between Ovitz and the Company was likely irreparable and that Ovitz would have to be terminated.

The Court of Chancery identified three competing theories as to why Ovitz did not succeed:

> First, plaintiffs argue that Ovitz failed to follow Eisner's directives, especially in regard to acquisitions, and that generally, Ovitz did very little. Second, Ovitz contends Eisner's micromanaging prevented Ovitz from having the authority necessary to make the changes that Ovitz thought were appropriate. In addition, Ovitz believes he was not given enough time for his efforts to bear fruit. Third, the remaining defendants simply posit that Ovitz failed to transition from a private to a public company, from the "sell side to the buy side," and otherwise did not adapt to the Company culture or fit in with other executives. In the end, however, it makes no difference why Ovitz was not as successful as his reputation would have led many to expect, so long as he was not grossly negligent or malfeasant.

Although the plaintiffs attempted to show that Ovitz acted improperly (*i.e.*, with gross negligence or malfeasance) while in office, the Chancellor found that the trial record did not support those accusations. Rejecting the plaintiffs' first factual claim that Ovitz was insubordinate, the Court found that although many of Ovitz's efforts failed to produce results, that was because his efforts often reflected a philosophy opposite to "that held by Eisner, Iger, and Roth." That difference did not mean, however, "that Ovitz intentionally failed to follow Eisner's directives or that [Ovitz] was insubordinate."

The Chancellor also rejected the appellants' second claim-that Ovitz was a habitual liar. The Court found no evidence that Ovitz ever told a material falsehood or made any false or misleading disclosures during his tenure at Disney. Lastly, the Chancellor found that the record did not support, and often contradicted, the appellants' third claim—that Ovitz had violated the Company's policies relating to expenses and to reporting gifts he received while President of Disney.

Nonetheless, Ovitz's relationship with the Disney executives did continue to deteriorate through September 1996. In mid-September, Litvack, with Eisner's approval, told Ovitz that he was not working out at Disney and that he should start looking for a graceful exit from Disney and a new job. Litvack reported this conversation to Eisner, who sent Litvack back to Ovitz to make it clear that Eisner no longer wanted Ovitz at Disney and that Ovitz should seriously consider other opportunities, including one then developing at Sony. Ovitz responded by telling Litvack that he was not leaving and that if Eisner wanted him to leave Disney, Eisner could tell him that to his face.

On September 30, 1996, the Disney board met. During an executive session of that meeting, and in small group discussions where Ovitz was not present, Eisner told the other board members of the continuing problems with Ovitz's performance. On October 1, Eisner wrote a letter to Russell and Watson detailing Eisner's mounting difficulties with Ovitz, including Eisner's lack of trust of Ovitz and Ovitz's failures to adapt to Disney's culture and to alleviate Eisner's workload. Eisner's goal in writing this letter was to prevent Ovitz from succeeding him at Disney. Because of that purpose, the Chancellor found that the letter contained "a good deal of hyperbole to help Eisner unsell' Ovitz as his successor." Neither that letter nor its contents were shared with other members of the board.

Those interchanges set the stage for Ovitz's eventual termination as Disney's President.

C. *Ovitz's Termination at Disney*

After the discussions between Litvack and Ovitz, Eisner and Ovitz met several times. During those meetings they discussed Ovitz's future, including Ovitz's employment prospects at Sony. Eisner believed that because Ovitz had a good, longstanding relationship with many Sony senior executives, Sony would be willing to take Ovitz in "trade" from Disney. Eisner favored such a trade, which would not only remove Ovitz from Disney, but also would relieve Disney of any obligation to pay Ovitz under the OEA. Thereafter, in October 1996, Ovitz, with Eisner's permission, entered into negotiations with Sony. Those negotiations did not prove fruitful, however. On November 1, Ovitz wrote a letter to Eisner notifying him that the Sony negotiations had ended, and that Ovitz had decided to recommit himself to Disney with a greater dedication of his own energies and an increased appreciation of the Disney organization.

In response to this unwelcome news, Eisner wrote (but never sent) a letter to Ovitz on November 11, in which Eisner attempted to make it clear that Ovitz was no longer welcome at Disney.[24] Instead of sending that letter, Eisner met with Ovitz

---

24. As with his October 1 letter, Eisner did not share this letter or its contents with the board. The only director to receive the November 11 letter was Russell, who also did not share it with the other board members.

personally on November 13, and discussed much of what the letter contained. Eisner left that meeting believing that "Ovitz just would not listen to what he was trying to tell him and instead, Ovitz insisted that he would stay at Disney, going so far as to state that he would chain himself to his desk."

During this period Eisner was also working with Litvack to explore whether they could terminate Ovitz under the OEA for cause. If so, Disney would not owe Ovitz the NFT payment. From the very beginning, Litvack advised Eisner that he did not believe there was cause to terminate Ovitz under the OEA. Litvack's advice never changed.

At the end of November 1996, Eisner again asked Litvack if Disney had cause to fire Ovitz and thereby avoid the costly NFT payment. Litvack proceeded to examine that issue more carefully. He studied the OEA, refreshed himself on the meaning of "gross negligence" and "malfeasance," and reviewed all the facts concerning Ovitz's performance of which he was aware. Litvack also consulted Val Cohen, co-head of Disney's litigation department and Joseph Santaniello, in Disney's legal department. Cohen and Santaniello both concurred in Litvack's conclusion that no basis existed to terminate Ovitz for cause. Litvack did not personally conduct any legal research or request an outside opinion on the issue, because he believed that it "was not a close question, and in fact, Litvack described it as a no brainer." Eisner testified that after Litvack notified Eisner that he did not believe cause existed, Eisner "checked with almost anybody that [he] could find that had a legal degree, and there was just no light in that possibility. It was a total dead end from day one." Although the Chancellor was critical of Litvack and Eisner for lacking sufficient documentation to support his conclusion and the work they did to arrive at that conclusion, the Court found that Eisner and Litvack "did in fact make a concerted effort to determine if Ovitz could be terminated for cause, and that despite these efforts, they were unable to manufacture the desired result."[28]

Litvack also believed that it would be inappropriate, unethical and a bad idea to attempt to coerce Ovitz (by threatening a for-cause termination) into negotiating for a smaller NFT package than the OEA provided. The reason was that when pressed by Ovitz's attorneys, Disney would have to admit that in fact there was no cause, which could subject Disney to a wrongful termination lawsuit. Litvack believed that attempting to avoid legitimate contractual obligations would harm Disney's reputation as an honest business partner and would affect its future business dealings.

The Disney board next met on November 25. By then the board knew Ovitz was going to be fired, yet the only action recorded in the minutes concerning Ovitz was his renomination to a new three-year term on the board. Although that action was somewhat bizarre given the circumstances, Stanley Gold, a Disney director, testified

---

28. The Chancellor found Litvack's testimony on this issue especially persuasive because "in light of the hostile relationship between Litvack and Ovitz, I believe that if Litvack thought it were possible to avoid paying Ovitz the NFT payment, that out of pure ill-will, Litvack would have tried almost anything to avoid the payment."

that because Ovitz was present at that meeting, it would have been a "public hanging" not to renominate him. An executive session took place after the board meeting, from which Ovitz was excluded. At that session, Eisner informed the directors who were present that he intended to fire Ovitz by year's end, and that he had asked Gary Wilson, a board member and friend of Ovitz, to speak with Ovitz while Wilson and Ovitz were together on vacation during the upcoming Thanksgiving holiday.[30]

Shortly after the November 25 board meeting and executive session, the Ovitz and Wilson families left on their yacht for a Thanksgiving trip to the British Virgin Islands. Ovitz hoped that if he could manage to survive at Disney until Christmas, he could fix everything with Disney and make his problems go away. Wilson quickly dispelled that illusion, informing Ovitz that Eisner wanted Ovitz out of the Company. At that point Ovitz first began to realize how serious his situation at Disney had become. Reporting back his conversation with Ovitz, Wilson told Eisner that Ovitz was a "loyal friend and devastating enemy," and he advised Eisner to "be reasonable and magnanimous, both financially and publicly, so Ovitz could save face."

After returning from the Thanksgiving trip, Ovitz met with Eisner on December 3, to discuss his termination. Ovitz asked for several concessions, all of which Eisner ultimately rejected. Eisner told Ovitz that all he would receive was what he had contracted for in the OEA.

On December 10, the Executive Performance Plan Committee met to consider annual bonuses for Disney's most highly compensated executive officers. At that meeting, Russell informed those in attendance[33] that Ovitz was going to be terminated, but without cause.[34]

On December 11, Eisner met with Ovitz to agree on the wording of a press release to announce the termination, and to inform Ovitz that he would not receive any of the additional items that he requested. By that time it had already been decided that Ovitz would be terminated without cause and that he would receive his contractual NFT payment, but nothing more. Eisner and Ovitz agreed that neither Ovitz nor Disney would disparage each other in the press, and that the separation was to be undertaken with dignity and respect for both sides. After his December 11 meeting with Eisner, Ovitz never returned to Disney.

---

30. The Court of Chancery found that at least Eisner, Gold, Bowers, Watson, and Stem were present at that executive session. The Court also found that the record was in conflict as to whether any details of the NFT and the termination for cause question were discussed.

33. In attendance at that meeting were its members, Gold, Lozano, Poitier and Russell, although Poitier and Lozano attended by phone. Also in attendance were Eisner, Watson, Litvack, Santaniello, and another staff member, Marsha Reed.

34. The committee members also awarded a $7.5 million bonus to Ovitz for his services performed during fiscal year 1996, despite Ovitz's poor performance and the fact that the bonuses were discretionary. That bonus was later rescinded after more deliberate consideration, following Ovitz's termination.

Ovitz's termination was memorialized in a letter, dated December 12, 1996, that Litvack signed on Eisner's instruction. The board was not shown the letter, nor did it meet to approve its terms. A press release announcing Ovitz's termination was issued that same day. Before the press release was issued, Eisner attempted to contact each of the board members by telephone to notify them that Ovitz had been officially terminated. None of the board members at that time, or at any other time, objected to Ovitz's termination, and most, if not all, of them thought it was the appropriate step for Eisner to take. Although the board did not meet to vote on the termination, the Chancellor found that most, if not all, of the Disney directors trusted Eisner's and Litvack's conclusion that there was no cause to terminate Ovitz, and that Ovitz should be terminated without cause even though that involved making the costly NFT payment.[36]

A December 27, 1996 letter from Litvack to Ovitz, which Ovitz signed, memorialized the termination, accelerated Ovitz's departure date from January 31, 1997 to December 31, 1996, and informed Ovitz that he would receive roughly $38 million in cash and that the first tranche of three million options would vest immediately. By the terms of that letter agreement, Ovitz's tenure as an executive and a director of Disney officially ended on December 27, 1996. Shortly thereafter, Disney paid Ovitz what was owed under the OEA for an NFT, minus a holdback of $1 million pending final settlement of Ovitz's accounts. One month after Disney paid Ovitz, the plaintiffs filed this action.

II. SUMMARY OF APPELLANTS' CLAIMS OF ERROR

As noted earlier, the Court of Chancery rejected all of the plaintiff-appellants' claims on the merits and entered judgment in favor of the defendant-appellees on all counts. On appeal, the appellants claim that the adverse judgment rests upon multiple erroneous rulings and should be reversed, because the 1995 decision to approve the OEA and the 1996 decision to terminate Ovitz on a non-fault basis, resulted from various breaches of fiduciary duty by Ovitz and the Disney directors.

The appellants' claims of error are most easily analyzed in two separate groupings: (1) the claims against the Disney defendants and (2) the claims against Ovitz. The first category encompasses the claims that the Disney defendants breached their fiduciary duties to act with due care and in good faith by (1) approving the OEA, and specifically, its NFT provisions; and (2) approving the NFT severance payment to Ovitz upon his termination—a payment that is also claimed to constitute

---

36. Although neither the board nor the compensation committee voted on the matter, many directors believed that Eisner had the power to fire Ovitz on his own, and that he did not need to convene a board meeting to do so. Other directors believed that if a meeting was required to terminate Ovitz, then Litvack, as corporate counsel, would have so advised them and would have made sure that a meeting was called. Litvack believed that Eisner had the power to fire Ovitz on his own accord, and that no meeting was called, because it was unnecessary and because all the directors were up to speed and in agreement that Ovitz should be terminated.

corporate waste. It is notable that the appellants do *not* contend that the Disney defendants are directly liable as a consequence of those fiduciary duty breaches. Rather, appellants' core argument is indirect, *i.e.*, that those breaches of fiduciary duty deprive the Disney defendants of the protection of business judgment review, and require them to shoulder the burden of establishing that their acts were entirely fair to Disney. That burden, the appellants contend, the Disney defendants failed to carry.[37] The appellants claim that by ruling that the Disney defendants did not breach their fiduciary duty to act with due care or in good faith, the Court of Chancery committed reversible error in numerous respects.[38] Alternatively, the appellants claim that even if the business judgment presumptions apply, the Disney defendants are nonetheless liable, because the NFT payout constituted corporate waste and the Court of Chancery erred in concluding otherwise.

Falling into the second category are the claims being advanced against Ovitz. Appellants claim that Ovitz breached his fiduciary duties of care and loyalty to Disney by (i) negotiating for and accepting the NFT severance provisions of the OEA, and (ii) negotiating a full NFT payout in connection with his termination.[40] The appellants' position is that by concluding that Ovitz breached no fiduciary duty owed to Disney, the Court of Chancery reversibly erred in several respects.

---

37. The plaintiff-appellants appear to have structured their liability claim in this indirect way because Article Eleventh of the Disney Certificate of Incorporation contains an exculpatory provision modeled upon 8 Del. C. § 102(b)(7). That provision precludes a money damages remedy against the Disney directors for adjudicated breaches of their duty of care. For that reason the plaintiffs are asserting their due care claim as the basis for shifting the standard of review from business judgment to entire fairness, rather than as a basis for direct liability. Presumably for the sake of consistency the appellants are utilizing their good faith fiduciary claim in a like manner.

38. These claims are asserted against the Disney defendants in their capacity as directors. The appellants also advance, as an alternative claim, an argument that Disney defendants Eisner, Litvack and Russell, are liable in their separate capacity as officers who, unlike directors, are not protected by the business judgment rule or the exculpatory provision of the Disney charter. That alternative argument is procedurally barred, because it was not fairly presented to the Court of Chancery. Sup. Ct. R. 8. Indeed, the Chancellor noted in his Post-trial Opinion that the application of the business judgment to Eisner and Litvack was not contested, and that the "parties essentially treat both officers and directors as comparable fiduciaries, that is, subject to the same fiduciary duties and standards of substantive review." To the extent the argument is advanced against Russell, it also is not grounded in fact, because Russell was not an officer of Disney.

40. The claims against Ovitz, unlike those asserted against the Disney defendants, appear to be advanced as the basis for holding Ovitz liable directly, as distinguished from being used indirectly as a vehicle to shift the standard of review from business judgment to entire fairness. We use the qualifying term "appear," because we cannot ascertain with clarity, either from the appellants' briefs in this Court or in the Court of Chancery, the precise character of their liability argument. In the end, however, it does not matter, because our affirmance of the Chancellor's rulings render irrelevant the issue of whether appellants are asserting a claim of liability directly as a consequence of a breach of Ovitz's duty of loyalty and/or good faith, or indirectly as a consequence of his failure to prove the entire fairness of his actions.

In this Opinion we address these two groups of claims in reverse order. In Part 3, we analyze the claims relating to Ovitz. In Part 4, we address the claims asserted against the Disney defendants.

III. THE CLAIMS AGAINST OVITZ

The appellants argue that the Chancellor erroneously rejected their claims against Ovitz on two distinct grounds. We analyze them separately.

A. *Claims Based upon Ovitz's Conduct before Assuming Office at Disney*

First, appellants contend that the Court of Chancery erred by dismissing their claim, as a summary judgment matter, that Ovitz had breached his fiduciary duties to Disney by negotiating and entering into the OEA. On summary judgment the Chancellor determined that Ovitz had breached no fiduciary duty to Disney, because Ovitz did not become a fiduciary until he formally assumed office on October 1, 1995, by which time the essential terms of the NFT provision had been negotiated. Therefore, the Court of Chancery held, Ovitz's pre-October 1 conduct was not constrained by any fiduciary duty standard.

That ruling was erroneous, appellants argue, because even though Ovitz did not formally assume the title of President until October 1, 1995, he became a *de facto* fiduciary before then. As a result, the entire OEA negotiation process became subject to a fiduciary review standard. That conclusion is compelled, appellants urge, because Ovitz's substantial contacts with third parties, and his receipt of confidential Disney information and request for reimbursement of expenses before October 1, prove that Eisner and Disney had already vested Ovitz with at least apparent authority before his formal investiture in office. Therefore, summary judgment was inappropriate, not only for those reasons but also because before summary judgment was granted, Ovitz failed to produce his work files that would have established his *de facto* status. Lastly, appellants contend that even if Ovitz was not a fiduciary until October 1, he is still liable for negotiating the NFT provisions because the OEA was considerably revised after October 1 and did not become final until December 1995. At the very least, issues of fact concerning those revisions should have precluded summary judgment. . . .

. . . [T]he *de facto* officer argument lacks merit, both legally and factually. A *de facto* officer is one who actually assumes possession of an office under the claim and color of an election or appointment and who is actually discharging the duties of that office, but for some legal reason lacks *de jure* legal title to that office. Here, Ovitz did not assume, or purport to assume, the duties of the Disney presidency before October 1, 1995. In his post-trial Opinion, the Chancellor found as fact that all of Ovitz's pre-October 1 conduct upon which appellants rely to establish *de facto* officer status, represented Ovitz's preparations to assume the duties of President after he was formally in office. The record amply supports those findings.

Similarly unavailing is the appellants' alternative argument that even if Ovitz did not become a fiduciary until October 1, his negotiation of the OEA must nonetheless be measured by fiduciary standards, because the OEA did not become final until

December 1995, and because between October 1 and December 1995, substantial redrafting of the OEA had occurred. This argument lacks merit because the critical terms of Ovitz's employment that are at issue in this lawsuit were found to have been agreed to before Ovitz assumed office on October 1. The Chancellor further found that any changes negotiated after October 1 were not material. The appellants have not shown that those findings are clearly wrong.

B. *Claims Based upon Ovitz's Conduct During His Termination as President*

The appellants' second claim is that the Court of Chancery erroneously concluded that Ovitz breached no fiduciary duty, including his duty of loyalty, by receiving the NFT payment upon his termination as President of Disney. The Chancellor found:

> Ovitz did not breach his fiduciary duty of loyalty by receiving the NFT payment because he played no part in the decisions: (1) to be terminated and (2) that the termination would not be for cause under the OEA. Ovitz did possess fiduciary duties as a director and officer while these decisions were made, but by not improperly interjecting himself into the corporation's decisionmaking process nor manipulating that process, he did not breach the fiduciary duties he possessed in that unique circumstance. Furthermore, Ovitz did not "engage" in a transaction with the corporation — rather, the corporation imposed an unwanted transaction upon him.
>
> Once Ovitz was terminated without cause (as a result of decisions made entirely without input or influence from Ovitz), he was contractually entitled, without any negotiation or action on his part, to receive the benefits provided by the OEA for a termination without cause, benefits for which he negotiated at arm's length *before* becoming a fiduciary.

The appellants claim that these findings are reversible error, because the contemporaneous evidence shows that Ovitz was not fired but, rather, acted to "settle out his contract." In those circumstances, appellants urge, Ovitz had a fiduciary duty to convene a board meeting to consider terminating him for cause — a duty that he failed to observe. . . .

The record establishes overwhelmingly that Ovitz did not leave Disney voluntarily. Nor did Ovitz arrange beforehand with Eisner to structure his departure as a termination without cause. To be sure, the evidence upon which the appellants rely does show that Ovitz fought being forced out every step of the way, but in the end, Ovitz had no choice but to accept the inevitable. As the trial court found, "Ovitz did not 'engage' in a transaction with the corporation — rather, the corporation imposed an unwanted transaction upon him." Every witness with personal knowledge of the events confirmed the unilateral, involuntary nature of Ovitz's termination in credible and colorful detail. The Chancellor credited the testimony of those witnesses, and the appellants have not shown that the Court exercised its fact finding powers inappropriately. . . .

That brings us to the appellants' final Ovitz-related claim, which is that Ovitz breached a fiduciary duty to Disney by not convening a meeting of the Disney board to consider terminating him for cause. That argument is defective both legally and factually. The appellants cite no authority recognizing such a duty in these circumstances. That comes as no surprise, given the Chancellor's affirmation of Litvack's legal conclusion that no board action was required to terminate Ovitz and that no basis existed to terminate him for cause. The argument also fails factually because Ovitz never knew that a termination for cause was being considered. As the Court of Chancery stated:

> No reasonably prudent fiduciary in Ovitz's position would have unilaterally determined to call a board meeting to force the corporation's chief executive officer to reconsider his termination and the terms thereof, with that reconsideration for the benefit of shareholders and potentially to Ovitz's detriment.
>
> Furthermore, having just been terminated, no reasonably prudent fiduciary in Ovitz's shoes would have insisted on a board meeting to discuss and ratify his termination after being terminated by the corporation's *chief executive officer* (with guidance and assistance from the Company's general counsel). Just as Delaware law does not require directors-to-be to comply with their fiduciary duties, former directors owe no fiduciary duties, and after December 27, 1996, Ovitz could not breach a duty he no longer had.

The Court of Chancery determined that Ovitz did not breach any fiduciary duty that he owed to Disney when negotiating for, or when receiving severance payments under, the non-fault termination clause of the OEA. The Court made no error in arriving at that determination and we uphold it.[58]

IV. THE CLAIMS AGAINST THE DISNEY DEFENDANTS

We next turn to the claims of error that relate to the Disney defendants. Those claims are subdivisible into two groups: (A) claims arising out of the approval of the OEA and of Ovitz's election as President; and (B) claims arising out of the NFT severance payment to Ovitz upon his termination. We address separately those two categories and the issues that they generate.

A. *Claims Arising from the Approval of the OEA and Ovitz's Election as President*

As earlier noted, the appellants' core argument in the trial court was that the Disney defendants' approval of the OEA and election of Ovitz as President were not entitled to business judgment rule protection, because those actions were either grossly negligent or not performed in good faith. The Court of Chancery rejected

---

58. That determination stands independent of, and without regard to, whether the OEA and the NFT payout were properly approved, constituted a waste of assets or were otherwise the product of a breach of fiduciary duty by the Disney defendants. The appellants claim that the approval of the OEA and the NFT payout to Ovitz were legally improper on all these grounds. Those claims are addressed in Parts IV and V of this Opinion.

these arguments, and held that the appellants had failed to prove that the Disney defendants had breached any fiduciary duty.

For clarity of presentation we address the claimed errors relating to the fiduciary duty of care rulings separately from those that relate to the directors' fiduciary duty to act in good faith.

1. The Due Care Determinations

The plaintiff-appellants advance five contentions to support their claim that the Chancellor reversibly erred by concluding that the plaintiffs had failed to establish a violation of the Disney defendants' duty of care. The appellants claim that the Chancellor erred by: (1) treating as distinct questions whether the plaintiffs had established by a preponderance of the evidence either gross negligence or a lack of good faith; (2) ruling that the old board was not required to approve the OEA; (3) determining whether the old board had breached its duty of care on a director-by-director basis rather than collectively; (4) concluding that the compensation committee members did not breach their duty of care in approving the NFT provisions of the OEA; and (5) holding that the remaining members of the old board (*i.e.*, the directors who were not members of the compensation committee) had not breached their duty of care in electing Ovitz as Disney's President.

. . . We conclude that the Chancellor committed no error.

(a) TREATING DUE CARE AND BAD FAITH AS SEPARATE GROUNDS FOR DENYING BUSINESS JUDGMENT RULE REVIEW

This argument is best understood against the backdrop of the presumptions that cloak director action being reviewed under the business judgment standard. Our law presumes that "in making a business decision the directors of a corporation acted on an informed basis, in good faith, and in the honest belief that the action taken was in the best interests of the company." Those presumptions can be rebutted if the plaintiff shows that the directors breached their fiduciary duty of care or of loyalty or acted in bad faith. If that is shown, the burden then shifts to the director defendants to demonstrate that the challenged act or transaction was entirely fair to the corporation and its shareholders.

Because no duty of loyalty claim was asserted against the Disney defendants, the only way to rebut the business judgment rule presumptions would be to show that the Disney defendants had either breached their duty of care or had not acted in good faith. At trial, the plaintiff-appellants attempted to establish both grounds, but the Chancellor determined that the plaintiffs had failed to prove either.

The appellants' first claim is that the Chancellor erroneously (i) failed to make a "threshold determination" of gross negligence, and (ii) "conflated" the appellants' burden to rebut the business judgment presumptions, with an analysis of whether the directors' conduct fell within the 8 Del. C. § 102(b)(7) provision that precludes exculpation of directors from monetary liability "for acts or omissions not in good faith." The argument runs as follows: *Emerald Partners v. Berlin* (2001) required the Chancellor first to determine whether the business judgment rule presumptions were rebutted based upon a showing that the board violated its duty of care, *i.e.*, acted with gross negligence. If gross negligence were established, the burden would shift to the directors to establish that the OEA was entirely fair. Only if the directors failed to meet that burden could the trial court then address the directors' Section 102(b)(7) exculpation defense, including the statutory exception for acts not in good faith.

This argument lacks merit. To make the argument the appellants must ignore the distinction between (i) a determination of bad faith for the threshold purpose of rebutting the business judgment rule presumptions, and (ii) a bad faith determination for purposes of evaluating the availability of charter-authorized exculpation from monetary damage liability after liability has been established. Our law clearly permits a judicial assessment of director good faith for that former purpose. Nothing in *Emerald Partners* requires the Court of Chancery to consider only evidence of lack of due care (*i.e.* gross negligence) in determining whether the business judgment rule presumptions have been rebutted.

Even if the trial court's analytical approach were improper, the appellants have failed to demonstrate any prejudice. The Chancellor's determinations of due care and good faith were analytically distinct and were separately conducted, even though both were done for the purpose of deciding whether to apply the business judgment standard of review. Nowhere have the appellants shown that the result would have been any different had the Chancellor proceeded in the manner that they now advocate.

(b) RULING THAT THE FULL DISNEY BOARD WAS NOT REQUIRED TO CONSIDER AND APPROVE THE OEA

The appellants next challenge the Court of Chancery's determination that the full Disney board was not required to consider and approve the OEA, because the Company's governing instruments allocated that decision to the compensation committee. This challenge also cannot survive scrutiny.

As the Chancellor found, under the Company's governing documents the board of directors was responsible for selecting the corporation's officers, but under the compensation committee charter, the committee was responsible for establishing and approving the salaries, together with benefits and stock options, of the Company's CEO and President. The compensation committee also had the charter-imposed duty to "approve employment contracts, or contracts at will" for "all corporate officers who are members of the Board of Directors regardless of salary." That is exactly what occurred here. The full board ultimately selected Ovitz as President, and the compensation committee considered and ultimately approved the OEA, which embodied the terms of Ovitz's employment, including his compensation.

The Delaware General Corporation Law (DGCL) expressly empowers a board of directors to appoint committees and to delegate to them a broad range of responsibilities [8 Del. C. § 141(c)], which may include setting executive compensation. Nothing in the DGCL mandates that the entire board must make those decisions. At Disney, the responsibility to consider and approve executive compensation was allocated to the compensation committee, as distinguished from the full board. The Chancellor's ruling—that executive compensation was to be fixed by the compensation committee—is legally correct.

The appellants base their contrary argument upon their reading of this Court's opinion in *Brehm v. Eisner* (2000). A "central holding" of *Brehm*, which the appellants claim is the "law of the case," is that the Disney board had a duty to approve the OEA because of its materiality. The appellants misread *Brehm*. There, in upholding a dismissal of the complaint in a procedural setting where the complaint's well-pled allegations must be taken as true, we observed that "in this case the economic exposure of the corporation to the payout scenarios of the Ovitz contract was material, particularly given its large size, for purposes of the directors' decision-making process." Contrary to the appellant's position, that observation is not the law of the case, because in *Brehm* this Court was not addressing, and did not have before it, the question of whether it was the exclusive province of the full board (as distinguished from a committee of the board) to approve the terms of the contract. That issue did not arise until the trial, during which a complete record was made. Therefore, in deciding the issue of which body—the full board or the compensation committee—was empowered to approve the OEA, the Chancellor was not constrained by any pronouncement made in *Brehm*.[72]

---

72. The only arguably tenable "law of the case" contention might read *Brehm* to hold that the size of the NFT payout would be material to a decision maker, whether the decision maker is the full board or the compensation committee. Indeed, the appellants appear to suggest that argument in attacking as erroneous the Chancellor's determination that, even though the amount of the NFT payout was quite large, it was immaterial given the Company's size ($19 billion in revenues and over $3 billion in operating revenues) and the large amounts budgeted for a single feature film. If that is appellants' argument, it also reads too much into the *Brehm* decision, because our observation was based upon the facts as alleged in the complaint, not the facts as found by the Chancellor based upon a complete trial record. This argument also ignores our admonition therein that "[o]ne must also keep in mind that the size of executive compensation for a large public company in the current environment often involves huge numbers. This is particularly true in the entertainment industry where the enormous revenues from one 'hit' movie or enormous losses from a 'flop' place in perspective the compensation of executives whose genius or misjudgment, as the case may be, have contributed to the 'hit' or 'flop.'" In any event, the materiality or immateriality of the NFT payout, whether viewed from an *ex ante* or *ex post* perspective, is not legally germane to our analysis of the claims presented on this appeal, or to the result we reach here. For that reason we do not decide the issue of the materiality of the NFT payout.

(c) WHETHER THE BOARD MEMBERS' OBSERVANCE OF THEIR DUTY OF CARE SHOULD HAVE BEEN DETERMINED ON A DIRECTOR-BY-DIRECTOR BASIS OR COLLECTIVELY

In the Court of Chancery the appellants argued that the board had failed to exercise due care, using a director-by-director, rather than a collective analysis. In this Court, however, the appellants argue that the Chancellor erred in following that very approach. An about-face, the appellants now claim that in determining whether the board breached its duty of care, the Chancellor was legally required to evaluate the actions of the old board collectively.

We reject this argument, without reaching its merits, for two separate reasons. To begin with, the argument is precluded by Rule 8 of this Court, which provides that arguments not fairly presented to the trial court will not be considered by this Court. The appellants' "individual vs. collective" argument goes beyond being not fairly presented. It borders on being unfairly presented, since the appellants are taking the trial court to task for adopting the very analytical approach that they themselves used in presenting their position.

The argument also fails because nowhere do appellants identify how this supposed error caused them any prejudice. The Chancellor viewed the conduct of each director individually, and found that no director had breached his or her fiduciary duty of care (as members of the full board) in electing Ovitz as President or (as members of the compensation committee) in determining Ovitz's compensation. If, as appellants now argue, a due care analysis of the board's conduct must be made collectively, it is incumbent upon them to show how such a collective analysis would yield a different result. The appellants' failure to do that dooms their argument on this basis as well.

(d) HOLDING THAT THE COMPENSATION COMMITTEE MEMBERS DID NOT FAIL TO EXERCISE DUE CARE IN APPROVING THE OEA

The appellants next challenge the Chancellor's determination that although the compensation committee's decision-making process fell far short of corporate governance "best practices," the committee members breached no duty of care in considering and approving the NFT terms of the OEA...

The appellants advance five reasons why a reversal is compelled: (i) not all committee members reviewed a draft of the OEA; (ii) the minutes of the September 26, 1995 compensation committee meeting do not recite any discussion of the grounds for which Ovitz could receive a non-fault termination; (iii) the committee members did not consider any comparable employment agreements or the economic impact of extending the exercisability of the options being granted to Ovitz; (iv) Crystal did not attend the September 26, 1995 committee meeting, nor was his letter distributed to or discussed with Poitier and Lozano; and (v) Poitier and Lozano did not review the spreadsheets generated by Watson. These contentions amount essentially to an attack upon underlying factual findings that will be upheld where they result from the Chancellor's assessment of live testimony.

Although the appellants have balkanized their due care claim into several fragmented parts, the overall thrust of that claim is that the compensation committee approved the OEA with NFT provisions that could potentially result in an enormous payout, without informing themselves of what the full magnitude of that payout could be. Rejecting that claim, the Court of Chancery found that the compensation committee members were adequately informed. The issue thus becomes whether that finding is supported by the evidence of record. We conclude that it is.

In our view, a helpful approach is to compare what actually happened here to what would have occurred had the committee followed a "best practices" (or "best case") scenario, from a process standpoint. In a "best case" scenario, all committee members would have received, before or at the committee's first meeting on September 26, 1995, a spreadsheet or similar document prepared by (or with the assistance of) a compensation expert (in this case, Graef Crystal). Making different, alternative assumptions, the spreadsheet would disclose the amounts that Ovitz could receive under the OEA in each circumstance that might foreseeably arise. One variable in that matrix of possibilities would be the cost to Disney of a non-fault termination for each of the five years of the initial term of the OEA. The contents of the spreadsheet would be explained to the committee members, either by the expert who prepared it or by a fellow committee member similarly knowledgeable about the subject. That spreadsheet, which ultimately would become an exhibit to the minutes of the compensation committee meeting, would form the basis of the committee's deliberations and decision.

Had that scenario been followed, there would be no dispute (and no basis for litigation) over what information was furnished to the committee members or when it was furnished. Regrettably, the committee's informational and decision-making process used here was not so tidy. That is one reason why the Chancellor found that although the committee's process did not fall below the level required for a proper exercise of due care, it did fall short of what best practices would have counseled.

The Disney compensation committee met twice: on September 26 and October 16, 1995. The minutes of the September 26 meeting reflect that the committee approved the terms of the OEA (at that time embodied in the form of a letter agreement), except for the option grants, which were not approved until October 16—after the Disney stock incentive plan had been amended to provide for those options. At the September 26 meeting, the compensation committee considered a "term sheet" which, in summarizing the material terms of the OEA, relevantly disclosed that in the event of a non-fault termination, Ovitz would receive: (i) the present value of his salary ($1 million per year) for the balance of the contract term, (ii) the present value of his annual bonus payments (computed at $7.5 million) for the balance of the contract term, (iii) a $10 million termination fee, and (iv) the acceleration of his options for 3 million shares, which would become immediately exercisable at market price.

Thus, the compensation committee knew that in the event of an NFT, Ovitz's severance payment alone could be in the range of $40 million cash,[77] plus the value of the accelerated options. Because the actual payout to Ovitz was approximately $130 million, of which roughly $38.5 million was cash, the value of the options at the time of the NFT payout would have been about $91.5 million.[78] Thus, the issue may be framed as whether the compensation committee members knew, at the time they approved the OEA, that the value of the option component of the severance package could reach the $92 million order of magnitude if they terminated Ovitz without cause after one year. The evidentiary record shows that the committee members were so informed.

On this question the documentation is far less than what best practices would have dictated. There is no exhibit to the minutes that discloses, in a single document, the estimated value of the accelerated options in the event of an NFT termination after one year. The information imparted to the committee members on that subject is, however, supported by other evidence, most notably the trial testimony of various witnesses about spreadsheets that were prepared for the compensation committee meetings.

The compensation committee members derived their information about the potential magnitude of an NFT payout from two sources. The first was the value of the "benchmark" options previously granted to Eisner and Wells and the valuations by Watson of the proposed Ovitz options. Ovitz's options were set at 75% of parity with the options previously granted to Eisner and to Frank Wells. Because the compensation committee had established those earlier benchmark option grants to Eisner and Wells and were aware of their value, a simple mathematical calculation would have informed them of the potential value range of Ovitz's options. Also, in August and September 1995, Watson and Russell met with Graef Crystal to determine (among other things) the value of the potential Ovitz options, assuming different scenarios. Crystal valued the options under the Black-Scholes method, while Watson used a different valuation metric. Watson recorded his calculations and the resulting values on a set of spreadsheets that reflected what option profits Ovitz might receive, based upon a range of different assumptions about stock market price increases. Those spreadsheets were shared with, and explained to, the committee members at the September meeting.

---

77. The cash portion of the NFT payout after one year would be the sum of: (i) the present value of Ovitz's remaining salary over the life of the contract (4 years × $1 million/yr = $4 million, reduced to present value), plus (ii) the present value of his unpaid annual bonus payments ($7.5 million/yr × 4 years = $30 million, discounted to present value), plus (iii) $10 million cash for the second tranche of options. These amounts total $44 million before discounting the $34 million of annual salaries and bonuses to present value. The actual cash payment to Ovitz was $38.5 million, which, it would appear, reflects the then-present value of the $34 million of salaries and bonuses.

78. Or, if it is assumed that the compensation committee would have estimated the cash portion of an NFT payout after one year at $40 million, then the value of the option portion would have been $90 million.

The committee's second source of information was the amount of "downside protection" that Ovitz was demanding. Ovitz required financial protection from the risk of leaving a very lucrative and secure position at CAA, of which he was a controlling partner, to join a publicly held corporation to which Ovitz was a stranger, and that had a very different culture and an environment which prevented him from completely controlling his destiny. The committee members knew that by leaving CAA and coming to Disney, Ovitz would be sacrificing "booked" CAA commissions of $150 to $200 million—an amount that Ovitz demanded as protection against the risk that his employment relationship with Disney might not work out. Ovitz wanted at least $50 million of that compensation to take the form of an "up-front" signing bonus. Had the $50 million bonus been paid, the size of the option grant would have been lower. Because it was contrary to Disney policy, the compensation committee rejected the up-front signing bonus demand, and elected instead to compensate Ovitz at the "back end," by awarding him options that would be phased in over the five-year term of the OEA.

It is on this record that the Chancellor found that the compensation committee was informed of the material facts relating to an NFT payout. If measured in terms of the documentation that would have been generated if "best practices" had been followed, that record leaves much to be desired. The Chancellor acknowledged that, and so do we. But, the Chancellor also found that despite its imperfections, the evidentiary record was sufficient to support the conclusion that the compensation committee had adequately informed itself of the potential magnitude of the entire severance package, including the options, that Ovitz would receive in the event of an early NFT.

The OEA was specifically structured to compensate Ovitz for walking away from $150 million to $200 million of anticipated commissions from CAA over the five-year OEA contract term. This meant that if Ovitz was terminated without cause, the earlier in the contract term the termination occurred the larger the severance amount would be to replace the lost commissions. Indeed, because Ovitz was terminated after only one year, the total amount of his severance payment (about $130 million) closely approximated the lower end of the range of Ovitz's forfeited commissions ($150 million), less the compensation Ovitz received during his first and only year as Disney's President. Accordingly, the Court of Chancery had a sufficient evidentiary basis in the record from which to find that, at the time they approved the OEA, the compensation committee members were adequately informed of the potential magnitude of an early NFT severance payout.

Exposing the lack of merit in appellants' core due care claim enables us to address more cogently (and expeditiously) the appellants' fragmented subsidiary arguments. First, the appellants argue that not all members of the compensation committee reviewed the then-existing draft of the OEA. The Chancellor properly found that that was not required, because in this case the compensation committee was informed of the substance of the OEA.[79]

Second, appellants point out that the minutes of the September 26 compensation committee meeting recite no discussion of the grounds for which Ovitz could receive a non-fault termination. But the term sheet did include a description of the consequences of a not-for-cause termination, and the Chancellor found that although "no one on the committee recalled any discussion concerning the meaning of gross negligence or malfeasance," those terms "were not foreign to the board of directors, as the language was standard, and could be found, for example, in Eisner's, Wells', Katzenberg's and Roth's employment contracts."

Third, contrary to the appellants' position, the compensation committee members did consider comparable employment agreements. The Chancellor found, as Russell's extensive notes demonstrated, that the comparable historical option grants that Russell analyzed at the September 26 meeting were the grants to Eisner and Wells. The evidence also lays to rest the claim that the compensation committee members did not consider the economic impact of the extended exercisability of the options being granted to Ovitz. Russell and Crystal had assessed the value of those options using the Black-Scholes and other valuation methods during the two weeks preceding the September 26 compensation committee meeting. Russell summarized those analyses at that meeting, and (as earlier discussed) at the time the compensation committee members approved the OEA, they were informed of the magnitude of those values in the event of an NFT.

Fourth, the appellants stress that Crystal did not make a report in person to the compensation committee at its September 26 meeting. Although that is true, it is undisputed that Crystal was available by phone if the committee members had questions that could not be answered by those who were present. Moreover, Russell and Watson related the substance of Crystal's analysis and information to the committee. The Court of Chancery noted (and we agree) that although it might have been the better course of action, it was "not necessary for an expert to make a formal presentation at the committee meeting in order for the board to rely on that expert's analysis. . . ." Nor did the Chancellor find merit to the appellants' related argument that two committee members, Poitier and Lozano, were not entitled to rely upon the work performed by Russell, Watson and Crystal in August and September 1995, without having first seen all of the written materials generated during that process or having participated in the discussions held during that time. In reaching a contrary conclusion, the Chancellor found:

---

79. As the Court found, "the compensation committee was provided with a term sheet of the key terms of the OEA and a presentation was made by Russell (assisted by Watson), who had personal knowledge of the relevant information by virtue of his negotiations with Ovitz and discussions with Crystal."

The compensation committee reasonably believed that the analysis of the terms of the OEA was within Crystal's professional or expert competence, and together with Russell and Watson's professional competence in those same areas, the committee relied on the information, opinions, reports and statements made by Crystal, even if Crystal did not relay the information, opinions, reports and statements in person to the committee as a whole. Crystal's analysis was not so deficient that the compensation committee would have reason to question it. Furthermore, Crystal appears to have been selected with reasonable care, especially in light of his previous engagements with the Company in connection with past executive compensation contracts that were structurally, at least, similar to the OEA. For all these reasons, the compensation committee also is entitled to the protections of 8 Del. C. § 141(e) in relying upon Crystal.

The Chancellor correctly applied Section 141(e) in upholding the reliance of Lozano and Poitier upon the information that Crystal, Russell and Watson furnished to them. To accept the appellants' narrow reading of that statute would eviscerate its purpose, which is to protect directors who rely in good faith upon information presented to them from various sources, including "any other person as to matters the member reasonably believes are within such person's professional or expert competence and who has been selected with reasonable care by and on behalf of the corporation."

Finally, the appellants contend that Poitier and Lozano did not review the spreadsheets generated by Watson at the September 26 meeting. The short answer is that even if Poitier and Lozano did not review the spreadsheets themselves, Russell and Watson adequately informed them of the spreadsheets' contents. The Court of Chancery explicitly found, and the record supports, that Poitier and Lozano "were informed by Russell and Watson of all *material* information reasonably available, even though they were not privy to every conversation or document exchanged amongst Russell, Watson, Crystal, and Ovitz's representatives."

For these reasons, we uphold the Chancellor's determination that the compensation committee members did not breach their fiduciary duty of care in approving the OEA.

(e) HOLDING THAT THE REMAINING DISNEY DIRECTORS DID NOT FAIL TO EXERCISE DUE CARE IN APPROVING THE HIRING OF OVITZ AS THE PRESIDENT OF DISNEY

The appellants' final claim in this category is that the Court of Chancery erroneously held that the remaining members of the old Disney board[85] had not breached their duty of care in electing Ovitz as President of Disney. This claim lacks merit, because the arguments appellants advance in this context relate to a different

---

85. The remaining old board members were Bollenbach, Litvack, Roy Disney, Nunis, Stern, Walker, O'Donovan, Murphy, Gold, Bowers, Wilson and Mitchell.

subject—the approval of the OEA, which was the responsibility delegated to the compensation committee, not the full board.

... The only properly reviewable action of the entire board was its decision to elect Ovitz as Disney's President. In that context the sole issue, as the Chancellor properly held, is "whether [the remaining members of the old board] properly exercised their business judgment and acted in accordance with their fiduciary duties when they elected Ovitz to the Company's presidency." The Chancellor determined that in electing Ovitz, the directors were informed of all information reasonably available and, thus, were not grossly negligent. We agree.

The Chancellor found and the record shows the following: well in advance of the September 26, 1995 board meeting the directors were fully aware that the Company needed—especially in light of Wells' death and Eisner's medical problems—to hire a "number two" executive and potential successor to Eisner. There had been many discussions about that need and about potential candidates who could fill that role even before Eisner decided to try to recruit Ovitz. Before the September 26 board meeting Eisner had individually discussed with each director the possibility of hiring Ovitz, and Ovitz's background and qualifications. The directors thus knew of Ovitz's skills, reputation and experience, all of which they believed would be highly valuable to the Company. The directors also knew that to accept a position at Disney, Ovitz would have to walk away from a very successful business—a reality that would lead a reasonable person to believe that Ovitz would likely succeed in similar pursuits elsewhere in the industry. The directors also knew of the public's highly positive reaction to the Ovitz announcement, and that Eisner and senior management had supported the Ovitz hiring. Indeed, Eisner, who had long desired to bring Ovitz within the Disney fold, consistently vouched for Ovitz's qualifications and told the directors that he could work well with Ovitz.

The board was also informed of the key terms of the OEA (including Ovitz's salary, bonus and options). Russell reported this information to them at the September 26, 1995 executive session, which was attended by Eisner and all non-executive directors. Russell also reported on the compensation committee meeting that had immediately preceded the executive session. And, both Russell and Watson responded to questions from the board. Relying upon the compensation committee's approval of the OEA[89] and the other information furnished to them, the Disney directors, after further deliberating, unanimously elected Ovitz as President.

Based upon this record, we uphold the Chancellor's conclusion that, when electing Ovitz to the Disney presidency the remaining Disney directors were fully informed of all material facts, and that the appellants failed to establish any lack of due care on the directors' part.

---

89. Contrary to the appellants' assertion (made with no citation of authority), the remaining board members were entitled to rely upon the compensation committee's approval of the OEA, and upon Russell's report of the discussions that occurred at the compensation committee meeting, when considering whether to elect Ovitz as President of Disney. 8 Del. C. § 141(e).

2. The Good Faith Determinations

The Court of Chancery held that the business judgment rule presumptions protected the decisions of the compensation committee and the remaining Disney directors, not only because they had acted with due care but also because they had not acted in bad faith. That latter ruling, the appellants claim, was reversible error because the Chancellor formulated and then applied an incorrect definition of bad faith.

In its Opinion the Court of Chancery defined bad faith as follows:

> Upon long and careful consideration, I am of the opinion that the concept of *intentional dereliction of duty*, a *conscious disregard for one's responsibilities*, is an appropriate (although not the only) standard for determining whether fiduciaries have acted in good faith. Deliberate indifference and inaction *in the face of a duty to act* is, in my mind, conduct that is clearly disloyal to the corporation. It is the epitome of faithless conduct.

. . .

. . . Because of the increased recognition of the importance of good faith, some conceptual guidance to the corporate community may be helpful . . .

The precise question is whether the Chancellor's articulated standard for bad faith corporate fiduciary conduct—intentional dereliction of duty, a conscious disregard for one's responsibilitie—is legally correct. In approaching that question, we note that the Chancellor characterized that definition as "*an* appropriate (*although not the only*) standard for determining whether fiduciaries have acted in good faith." That observation is accurate and helpful, because as a matter of simple logic, at least three different categories of fiduciary behavior are candidates for the "bad faith" pejorative label.

The first category involves so-called "subjective bad faith," that is, fiduciary conduct motivated by an actual intent to do harm. That such conduct constitutes classic, quintessential bad faith is a proposition so well accepted in the liturgy of fiduciary law that it borders on axiomatic. We need not dwell further on this category, because no such conduct is claimed to have occurred, or did occur, in this case.

The second category of conduct, which is at the opposite end of the spectrum, involves lack of due care—that is, fiduciary action taken solely by reason of gross negligence and without any malevolent intent. In this case, appellants assert claims of gross negligence to establish breaches not only of director due care but also of the directors' duty to act in good faith. Although the Chancellor found, and we agree, that the appellants failed to establish gross negligence, to afford guidance we address the issue of whether gross negligence (including a failure to inform one's self of available material facts), without more, can also constitute bad faith. The answer is clearly no.

From a broad philosophical standpoint, that question is more complex than would appear, if only because (as the Chancellor and others have observed) "issues of good faith are (to a certain degree) inseparably and necessarily intertwined with the duties of care and loyalty. . . ." But, in the pragmatic, conduct-regulating legal realm which calls for more precise conceptual line drawing, the answer is that grossly negligent conduct, without more, does not and cannot constitute a breach of the fiduciary duty to act in good faith. The conduct that is the subject of due care may overlap with the conduct that comes within the rubric of good faith in a psychological sense,[104] but from a legal standpoint those duties are and must remain quite distinct. Both our legislative history and our common law jurisprudence distinguish sharply between the duties to exercise due care and to act in good faith, and highly significant consequences flow from that distinction.

The Delaware General Assembly has addressed the distinction between bad faith and a failure to exercise due care (*i.e.*, gross negligence) in two separate contexts. The first is Section 102(b)(7) of the DGCL, which authorizes Delaware corporations, by a provision in the certificate of incorporation, to exculpate their directors from monetary damage liability for a breach of the duty of care. That exculpatory provision affords significant protection to directors of Delaware corporations. The statute carves out several exceptions, however, including most relevantly, "for acts or omissions not in good faith. . . ." Thus, a corporation can exculpate its directors from monetary liability for a breach of the duty of care, but not for conduct that is not in good faith. To adopt a definition of bad faith that would cause a violation of the duty of care automatically to become an act or omission "not in good faith," would eviscerate the protections accorded to directors by the General Assembly's adoption of Section 102(b)(7).

A second legislative recognition of the distinction between fiduciary conduct that is grossly negligent and conduct that is not in good faith, is Delaware's indemnification statute, found at 8 Del. C. § 145. To oversimplify, subsections (a) and (b) of that statute permit a corporation to indemnify (*inter alia*) any person who is or was a director, officer, employee or agent of the corporation against expenses (including attorneys' fees), judgments, fines and amounts paid in settlement of specified actions, suits or proceedings, where (among other things): (i) that person is, was, or is threatened to be made a party to that action, suit or proceeding, and (ii) that person "acted in good faith and in a manner the person reasonably believed to be in or not opposed to the best interests of the corporation. . . ." Thus, under Delaware statutory law a director or officer of a corporation can be indemnified for liability (and litigation expenses) incurred by reason of a violation of the duty of care, but not for a violation of the duty to act in good faith.

---

104. An example of such overlap might be the hypothetical case where a director, because of subjective hostility to the corporation on whose board he serves, fails to inform himself of, or to devote sufficient attention to, the matters on which he is making decisions as a fiduciary. In such a case, two states of mind coexist in the same person: subjective bad intent (which would lead to a finding of bad faith) and gross negligence (which would lead to a finding of a breach of the duty of care). Although the coexistence of both states of mind may make them indistinguishable from a psychological standpoint, the fiduciary duties that they cause the director to violate — care and good faith — are legally separate and distinct.

Section 145, like Section 102(b)(7), evidences the intent of the Delaware General Assembly to afford significant protections to directors (and, in the case of Section 145, other fiduciaries) of Delaware corporations. To adopt a definition that conflates the duty of care with the duty to act in good faith by making a violation of the former an automatic violation of the latter, would nullify those legislative protections and defeat the General Assembly's intent. There is no basis in policy, precedent or common sense that would justify dismantling the distinction between gross negligence and bad faith.

That leaves the third category of fiduciary conduct, which falls in between the first two categories of (1) conduct motivated by subjective bad intent and (2) conduct resulting from gross negligence. This third category is what the Chancellor's definition of bad faith — intentional dereliction of duty, a conscious disregard for one's responsibilities — is intended to capture. The question is whether such misconduct is properly treated as a non-exculpable, non-indemnifiable violation of the fiduciary duty to act in good faith. In our view it must be, for at least two reasons.

First, the universe of fiduciary misconduct is not limited to either disloyalty in the classic sense (*i.e.*, preferring the adverse self-interest of the fiduciary or of a related person to the interest of the corporation) or gross negligence. Cases have arisen where corporate directors have no conflicting self-interest in a decision, yet engage in misconduct that is more culpable than simple inattention or failure to be informed of all facts material to the decision. To protect the interests of the corporation and its shareholders, fiduciary conduct of this kind, which does not involve disloyalty (as traditionally defined) but is qualitatively more culpable than gross negligence, should be proscribed. A vehicle is needed to address such violations doctrinally, and that doctrinal vehicle is the duty to act in good faith. The Chancellor implicitly so recognized in his Opinion, where he identified different examples of bad faith as follows:

> The good faith required of a corporate fiduciary includes not simply the duties of care and loyalty, in the narrow sense that I have discussed them above, but all actions required by a true faithfulness and devotion to the interests of the corporation and its shareholders. A failure to act in good faith may be shown, for instance, where the fiduciary intentionally acts with a purpose other than that of advancing the best interests of the corporation, where the fiduciary acts with the intent to violate applicable positive law, or where the fiduciary intentionally fails to act in the face of a known duty to act, demonstrating a conscious disregard for his duties. There may be other examples of bad faith yet to be proven or alleged, but these three are the most salient.

Those articulated examples of bad faith are not new to our jurisprudence. Indeed, they echo pronouncements our courts have made throughout the decades.

Second, the legislature has also recognized this intermediate category of fiduciary misconduct, which ranks between conduct involving subjective bad faith and gross negligence. Section 102(b)(7)(ii) of the DGCL expressly denies money damage exculpation for "acts or omissions not in good faith or which involve intentional misconduct or a knowing violation of law." By its very terms that provision distinguishes between "intentional misconduct" and a "knowing violation of law" (both examples of subjective bad faith) on the one hand, and "acts... not in good faith," on the other. Because the statute exculpates directors only for conduct amounting to gross negligence, the statutory denial of exculpation for "acts... not in good faith" must encompass the intermediate category of misconduct captured by the Chancellor's definition of bad faith.

For these reasons, we uphold the Court of Chancery's definition as a legally appropriate, although not the exclusive, definition of fiduciary bad faith. We need go no further. To engage in an effort to craft (in the Court's words) "a definitive and categorical definition of the universe of acts that would constitute bad faith"[112] would be unwise and is unnecessary to dispose of the issues presented on this appeal.

Having sustained the Chancellor's finding that the Disney directors acted in good faith when approving the OEA and electing Ovitz as President, we next address the claims arising out of the decision to pay Ovitz the amount called for by the NFT provisions of the OEA.

B. *Claims Arising from the Payment of the NFT Severance Payout to Ovitz*

The appellants advance three alternative claims (each accompanied by assorted subsidiary arguments) whose overall thrust is that even if the OEA approval was legally valid, the NFT severance payout to Ovitz pursuant to the OEA was not. Specifically, the appellants contend that: (1) only the full Disney board with the concurrence of the compensation committee—but not Eisner alone—was authorized to terminate Ovitz; (2) because Ovitz could have been terminated for cause, Litvack and Eisner acted without due care and in bad faith in reaching the contrary conclusion; and (3) the business judgment rule presumptions did not protect the new Disney board's acquiescence in the NFT payout, because the new board was not entitled to rely upon Eisner's and Litvack's contrary advice. Appellants urge that in rejecting these claims the Court of Chancery committed reversible error. We disagree.

1. Was Action by the New Board Required to Terminate Ovitz as the President of Disney?

The Chancellor determined that although the board as constituted upon Ovitz's termination (the "new board") had the authority to terminate Ovitz, neither that board nor the compensation committee was required to act, because Eisner also had, and properly exercised, that authority. The new board, the Chancellor found, was not required to terminate Ovitz under the company's internal documents. Without such a duty to act, the new board's failure to vote on the termination could not give

---

112. For the same reason, we do not reach or otherwise address the issue of whether the fiduciary duty to act in good faith is a duty that, like the duties of care and loyalty, can serve as an independent basis for imposing liability upon corporate officers and directors. That issue is not before us on this appeal.

rise to a breach of the duty of care or the duty to act in good faith. Because those are conclusions of law that rest upon the Chancellor's legal construction of Disney's governing instruments, our review of them is plenary.

Article Tenth of the Company's certificate of incorporation in effect at the termination plainly states that:

> The officers of the Corporation shall be chosen in such a manner, shall hold their offices for such terms and shall carry out such duties as are determined solely by the Board of Directors, subject to the right of the Board of Directors to remove any officer or officers at any time with or without cause.

Article IV of Disney's bylaws provided that the Board Chairman/CEO "shall, subject to the provisions of the Bylaws and the control of the Board of Directors, have general and active management, direction, and supervision over the business of the Corporation and over its officers. . . ." From these documents the Court of Chancery concluded (*inter alia*) that:

> 1) the board of directors has the sole power to elect the officers of the Company; . . . 3) the Chairman/CEO has "general and active management, direction and supervision over the business of the Corporation and over its officers," and that such management, direction and supervision is subject to the control of the board of directors; 4) the Chairman/CEO has the power to manage, direct and supervise the lesser officers and employees of the Company; 5) the board has the *right*, but not the *duty* to remove the officers of the Company with or without cause, and that right is non-exclusive; and 6) because that right is non-exclusive, and because the Chairman/CEO is affirmatively charged with the management, direction and supervision of the officers of the Company, together with the powers and duties incident to the office of chief executive, the Chairman/CEO, subject to the control of the board of directors, also possesses the *right* to remove the inferior officers and employees of the corporation.

The issue is whether the Chancellor's interpretation of these instruments, as giving the board and the Chairman/CEO concurrent power to terminate a lesser officer, is legally permissible. In two hypothetical cases there would be a clear answer. If the certificate of incorporation vested the power of removal exclusively in the board, then absent an express delegation of authority from the board, the presiding officer would have not have a concurrent removal power. If, on the other hand, the governing instruments expressly placed the power of removal in both the board and specified officers, then there would be concurrent removal power. This case does not fall within either hypothetical fact pattern, because Disney's governing instruments do not vest the removal power exclusively in the board, nor do they expressly give the Board Chairman/CEO a concurrent power to remove officers. Read together, the governing instruments do not yield a single, indisputably clear answer, and could reasonably be interpreted either way. For that reason, with respect to this specific issue, the governing instruments are ambiguous.

Where corporate governing instruments are ambiguous, our case law permits a court to determine their meaning by resorting to well-established legal rules of construction, which include the rules governing the interpretation of contracts. One such rule is that where a contract is ambiguous, the court must look to extrinsic evidence to determine which of the reasonable readings the parties intended.

Here, the extrinsic evidence clearly supports the conclusion that the board and Eisner understood that Eisner, as Board Chairman/CEO had concurrent power with the board to terminate Ovitz as President. In that regard, the Chancellor credited the testimony of new board members that Eisner, as Chairman and CEO, was empowered to terminate Ovitz without board approval or intervention; and also Litvack's testimony that during his tenure as general counsel, many Company officers were terminated and the board never once took action in connection with their terminations. Because Eisner possessed, and exercised, the power to terminate Ovitz unilaterally, we find that the Chancellor correctly concluded that the new board was not required to act in connection with that termination, and, therefore, the board did not violate any fiduciary duty to act with due care or in good faith.

As the Chancellor correctly held, the same conclusion is equally applicable to the compensation committee. The only role delegated to the compensation committee was "to establish and approve compensation for Eisner, Ovitz and other applicable Company executives and high paid employees." The committee's September 26, 1995 approval of Ovitz's compensation arrangements "included approval for the termination provisions of the OEA, obviating any need to meet and approve the payment of the NFT upon Ovitz's termination."

Because neither the new board nor the compensation committee was required to take any action that was subject to fiduciary standards, that leaves only the actions of Eisner and Litvack for our consideration. The appellants claim that in concluding that Ovitz could not be terminated "for cause," these defendants did not act with due care or in good faith. We next address that claim.

2. In Concluding that Ovitz Could Not Be Terminated for Cause, Did Litvack or Eisner Breach Any Fiduciary Duty?

It is undisputed that Litvack and Eisner (based on Litvack's advice) both concluded that if Ovitz was to be terminated, it could only be without cause, because no basis existed to terminate Ovitz for cause. The appellants argued in the Court of Chancery that the business judgment presumptions do not protect that conclusion, because by permitting Ovitz to be terminated without cause, Litvack and Eisner acted in bad faith and without exercising due care. Rejecting that claim, the Chancellor determined independently, as a matter of fact and law, that (1) Ovitz had not engaged in any conduct as President that constituted gross negligence or malfeasance-the standard for an NFT under the OEA; and (2) in arriving at that same conclusion in 1996,

Litvack and Eisner did not breach their fiduciary duty of care or their duty to act in good faith.

. . .

At the trial level, the appellants attempted to show, as a factual matter, that Ovitz's conduct as President met the standard for a termination for cause, because (i) Ovitz intentionally failed to follow Eisner's directives and was insubordinate, (ii) Ovitz was a habitual liar, and (iii) Ovitz violated Company policies relating to expenses and to reporting gifts he gave while President of Disney. The Court found the facts contrary to appellants' position. As to the first accusation, the Court found that many of Ovitz's efforts failed to produce results "often because his efforts reflected an opposite philosophy than that held by Eisner, Iger, and Roth. This does not mean that Ovitz intentionally failed to follow Eisner's directives or that he was insubordinate." As to the second, the Court found that:

> In the absence of any concrete evidence that Ovitz told a material falsehood during his tenure at Disney, plaintiffs fall back on alleging that Ovitz's disclosures regarding his earn-out with, and past income from, CAA, were false or materially misleading. As a neutral fact-finder, I find that the evidence simply does not support either of those assertions.

And, as to the third accusation, the Court found "that Ovitz was not in violation of The Walt Disney Company's policies relating to expenses or giving and receiving gifts." Accordingly, the appellants' claim that the Chancellor incorrectly determined that Ovitz could not legally be terminated for cause lacks any factual foundation.

Despite their inability to show factual or legal error in the Chancellor's determination that Ovitz could not be terminated for cause, appellants contend that Litvack and Eisner breached their fiduciary duty to exercise due care and to act in good faith in reaching that same conclusion. The Court of Chancery scrutinized the record to determine independently whether, in reaching their conclusion, Litvack and Eisner had separately exercised due care and acted in good faith. The Court determined that they had properly discharged both duties. Appellants' attack upon that determination lacks merit, because it is also without basis in the factual record.

After considering the OEA and Ovitz's conduct, Litvack concluded, and advised Eisner, that Disney had no basis to terminate Ovitz for cause and that Disney should comply with its contractual obligations. Even though Litvack personally did not want to grant a NFT to Ovitz, he concluded that for Disney to assert falsely that there was cause would be both unethical and harmful to Disney's reputation. As to Litvack, the Court of Chancery held:

> I do not intend to imply by these conclusions that Litvack was an infallible source of legal knowledge. Nevertheless, Litvack's less astute moments as a legal counsel do not impugn his good faith or preparedness in reaching his conclusions with respect to whether Ovitz could have been terminated for cause. . . .

. . .

In conclusion, Litvack gave the proper advice and came to the proper conclusions when it was necessary. He was adequately informed in his decisions, and he acted in good faith for what he believed were the best interests of the Company.

With respect to Eisner, the Chancellor found that faced with a situation where he was unable to work well with Ovitz, who required close and constant supervision, Eisner had three options: 1) keep Ovitz as President and continue trying to make things work; 2) keep Ovitz at Disney, but in a role other than as President; or 3) terminate Ovitz. The first option was unacceptable, and the second would have entitled Ovitz to the NFT, or at the very least would have resulted in a costly lawsuit to determine whether Ovitz was so entitled. After an unsuccessful effort to "trade" Ovitz to Sony, that left only the third option, which was to terminate Ovitz and pay the NFT. The Chancellor found that in choosing this alternative, Eisner had breached no duty and had exercised his business judgment:

> . . . I conclude that Eisner's actions in connection with the termination are, for the most part, consistent with what is expected of a faithful fiduciary. Eisner unexpectedly found himself confronted with a situation that did not have an easy solution. He weighed the alternatives, received advice from counsel and then exercised his business judgment in the manner he thought best for the corporation. Eisner knew all the material information reasonably available when making the decision, he did not neglect an affirmative duty to act (or fail to cause the board to act) and he acted in what he believed were the best interests of the Company, taking into account the cost to the Company of the decision and the potential alternatives. Eisner was not personally interested in the transaction in any way that would make him incapable of exercising business judgment, and I conclude that the plaintiffs have not demonstrated by a preponderance of the evidence that Eisner breached his fiduciary duties or acted in bad faith in connection with Ovitz's termination and receipt of the NFT.

These determinations rest squarely on factual findings that, in turn, are based upon the Chancellor's assessment of the credibility of Eisner and other witnesses. Even though the Chancellor found much to criticize in Eisner's "imperial CEO" style of governance, nothing has been shown to overturn the factual basis for the Court's conclusion that, in the end, Eisner's conduct satisfied the standards required of him as a fiduciary.

3. Were the Remaining Directors Entitled to Rely upon Eisner's and Litvack's Advice that Ovitz Could Not Be Fired for Cause?

The appellants' third claim of error challenges the Chancellor's conclusion that the remaining new board members could rely upon Litvack's and Eisner's advice that Ovitz could be terminated only without cause. The short answer to that challenge is that, for the reasons previously discussed, the advice the remaining directors received and relied upon was accurate. Moreover, the directors' reliance on that advice was found to be in good faith. Although formal board action was not necessary, the remaining directors all supported the decision to terminate Ovitz based on the information given by Eisner and Litvack. The Chancellor found credible the directors' testimony that they believed that Disney would be better off without Ovitz, and the appellants offer no basis to overturn that finding.

. . .

To summarize, the Court of Chancery correctly determined that the decisions of the Disney defendants to approve the OEA, to hire Ovitz as President, and then to terminate him on an NFT basis, were protected business judgments, made without any violations of fiduciary duty. Having so concluded, it is unnecessary for the Court to reach the appellants' contention that the Disney defendants were required to prove that the payment of the NFT severance to Ovitz was entirely fair.

V. THE WASTE CLAIM

The appellants' final claim is that even if the approval of the OEA was protected by the business judgment rule presumptions, the payment of the severance amount to Ovitz constituted waste. This claim is rooted in the doctrine that a plaintiff who fails to rebut the business judgment rule presumptions is not entitled to any remedy unless the transaction constitutes waste. The Court of Chancery rejected the appellants' waste claim, and the appellants claim that in so doing the Court committed error.

To recover on a claim of corporate waste, the plaintiffs must shoulder the burden of proving that the exchange was "so one sided that no business person of ordinary, sound judgment could conclude that the corporation has received adequate consideration." A claim of waste will arise only in the rare, "unconscionable case where directors irrationally squander or give away corporate assets." This onerous standard for waste is a corollary of the proposition that where business judgment presumptions are applicable, the board's decision will be upheld unless it cannot be "attributed to any rational business purpose."

The claim that the payment of the NFT amount to Ovitz, without more, constituted waste is meritless on its face, because at the time the NFT amounts were paid, Disney was contractually obligated to pay them. The payment of a contractually obligated amount cannot constitute waste, unless the contractual obligation is itself wasteful. Accordingly, the proper focus of a waste analysis must be whether the amounts required to be paid in the event of an NFT were wasteful *ex ante*.

Appellants claim that the NFT provisions of the OEA were wasteful because they incentivized Ovitz to perform poorly in order to obtain payment of the NFT provisions. The Chancellor found that the record did not support that contention:

> [T]erminating Ovitz and paying the NFT did not constitute waste because he could not be terminated for cause and because many of the defendants gave credible testimony that the Company would be better off without Ovitz, meaning that would be impossible for me to conclude that the termination

and receipt of NFT benefits result in "an exchange that is so one sided that no business person of ordinary, sound judgment could conclude that the corporation has received adequate consideration," or a situation where the defendants have "irrationally squandered or given away corporate assets." In other words, defendants did not commit waste.

That ruling is erroneous, the appellants argue, because the NFT provisions of the OEA were wasteful in their very design. Specifically, the OEA gave Ovitz every incentive to leave the Company before serving out the full term of his contract. The appellants urge that although the OEA may have induced Ovitz to join Disney as President, no contractual safeguards were in place to retain him in that position. In essence, appellants claim that the NFT provisions of the OEA created an irrational incentive for Ovitz to get himself fired.[139]

That claim does not come close to satisfying the high hurdle required to establish waste. The approval of the NFT provisions in the OEA had a rational business purpose: to induce Ovitz to leave CAA, at what would otherwise be a considerable cost to him, in order to join Disney.

The Chancellor found that the evidence does not support any notion that the OEA irrationally incentivized Ovitz to get himself fired.[141] Ovitz had no control over whether or not he would be fired, either with or without cause. To suggest that at the time he entered into the OEA Ovitz would engineer an early departure at the cost of his extraordinary reputation in the entertainment industry and his historical friendship with Eisner, is not only fanciful but also without proof in the record. Indeed, the Chancellor found that it was "patently unreasonable to assume that Ovitz intended to perform just poorly enough to be fired quickly, but not so poorly that he could be terminated for cause."

We agree. Because the appellants have failed to show that the approval of the NFT terms of the OEA was not a rational business decision, their waste claim must fail.

VI. CONCLUSION

For the reasons stated above, the judgment of the Court of Chancery is affirmed.

Questions

1. At the beginning of his decision in *Disney* (907 A.2d 693 (2005)) Chancellor Chandler announced that

---

139. The appellants also claim, because the Disney defendants had a rational basis to fire Ovitz for cause, the NFT payment to Ovitz constituted an unnecessary gift of corporate assets to Eisner's friend. Because we affirm the Court of Chancery's legal determination that no cause existed to terminate Ovitz, that claim lacks merit on its face.

141. Indeed, all the credible evidence supports the Chancellor's conclusion that Ovitz resisted, at every turn, all suggestions, communicated directly or indirectly by Eisner, that Ovitz leave Disney.

[u]nlike ideals of corporate governance, a fiduciary's duties do not change over time. How we understand those duties may evolve and become refined, but the duties themselves have not changed, except to the extent that fulfilling a fiduciary duty requires obedience to other positive law.

Now that you have studied the law of fiduciary duties, do you agree with this assessment?

2. Chancellor Chandler also commented that

[t]his Court strongly encourages directors and officers to employ best practices, as those practices are understood at the time a corporate decision is taken. But Delaware law does not—indeed, the common law cannot—hold fiduciaries liable for a failure to comply with the aspirational ideal of best practices, any more than a common-law court deciding a medical malpractice dispute can impose a standard of liability based on ideal—rather than competent or standard—medical treatment practices, lest the average medical practitioner be found inevitably derelict.

What do you think about the distinction between ideal and practice? As a practical matter, what is the significance of aspirational ideals if they are not enforced?

3. Chancellor Chandler concluded his introduction by noting, that

[e]ven where decision-makers act as faithful servants, however, their ability and the wisdom of their judgments will vary. The redress for failures that arise from faithful management must come from the markets, through the action of shareholders and the free flow of capital, and not from this Court. Should the Court apportion liability based on the ultimate outcome of decisions taken in good faith by faithful directors or officers, those decision-makers would necessarily take decisions that minimize risk, not maximize value. The entire advantage of the risk-taking, innovative, wealth-creating engine that is the Delaware corporation would cease to exist, with disastrous results for shareholders and society alike. That is why, under our corporate law, corporate decision-makers are held strictly to their fiduciary duties, but within the boundaries of those duties are free to act as their judgment and abilities dictate, free of *post hoc* penalties from a reviewing court using perfect hindsight. Corporate decisions are made, risks are taken, the results become apparent, capital flows accordingly, and shareholder value is increased.

Considering what you have studied thus far, do you agree that the market could redress managerial failures? What are the consequences of such assumptions—to the law of fiduciary duties? To corporations? To society?

4. In your view, were the directors fully informed when they made the decisions to hire Ovitz, and then fire him? What did they know? What might you have asked if you were in their place? Would asking the questions have influenced the ultimate

result of the board meeting? How would you advise directors as to their duty of care after *Disney*?

5. What is the difference between being fully informed and acting in good faith? How would you advise directors as to their duty to act in good faith after *Disney*?

6. Professor Griffith suggests that because "an ordinarily prudent person becomes an ordinarily prudent director only once we assume an element of loyalty ... the duty of loyalty is just a bet that some situations are likely to lead to careless or imprudent transactions for the corporation, which is to say that the duty of care is a motivating concern for the duty of loyalty." Sean J. Griffith, *Good Faith Business Judgment: A Theory of Rhetoric in Corporate Law Jurisprudence*, 55 Duke L.J. 1, 40 (2005). Having read *Disney* do you agree with this analysis?

B. Good Faith and the Duty to Monitor

In re Caremark International Inc. Derivative Litigation

698 A.2d 959 (Del. Ch. 1996)

Allen, Chancellor

Pending is a motion pursuant to Chancery Rule 23.1 to approve as fair and reasonable a proposed settlement of a consolidated derivative action on behalf of Caremark International, Inc. ("Caremark"). The suit involves claims that the members of Caremark's board of directors (the "Board") breached their fiduciary duty of care to Caremark in connection with alleged violations by Caremark employees of federal and state laws and regulations applicable to health care providers. As a result of the alleged violations, Caremark was subject to an extensive four year investigation by the United States Department of Health and Human Services and the Department of Justice. In 1994 Caremark was charged in an indictment with multiple felonies. It thereafter entered into a number of agreements with the Department of Justice and others. Those agreements included a plea agreement in which Caremark pleaded guilty to a single felony of mail fraud and agreed to pay civil and criminal fines. Subsequently, Caremark agreed to make reimbursements to various private and public parties. In all, the payments that Caremark has been required to make total approximately $250 million.

This suit was filed in 1994, purporting to seek on behalf of the company recovery of these losses from the individual defendants who constitute the board of directors of Caremark. The parties now propose that it be settled and, after notice to Caremark shareholders, a hearing on the fairness of the proposal was held on August 16, 1996.

A motion of this type requires the court to assess the strengths and weaknesses of the claims asserted in light of the discovery record and to evaluate the fairness and adequacy of the consideration offered to the corporation in exchange for the release of all claims made or arising from the facts alleged. The ultimate issue then is whether the proposed settlement appears to be fair to the corporation and its absent shareholders. In this effort the court does not determine contested facts, but evaluates the claims and defenses on the discovery record to achieve a sense of the relative strengths of the parties' positions. In doing this, in most instances, the court is constrained by the absence of a truly adversarial process, since inevitably both sides support the settlement and legally assisted objectors are rare. Thus, the facts stated hereafter represent the court's effort to understand the context of the motion from the discovery record, but do not deserve the respect that judicial findings after trial are customarily accorded.

Legally, evaluation of the central claim made entails consideration of the legal standard governing a board of directors' obligation to supervise or monitor corporate performance. For the reasons set forth below I conclude, in light of the discovery record, that there is a very low probability that it would be determined that the directors of Caremark breached any duty to appropriately monitor and supervise the enterprise. Indeed the record tends to show an active consideration by Caremark management and its Board of the Caremark structures and programs that ultimately led to the company's indictment and to the large financial losses incurred in the settlement of those claims. It does not tend to show knowing or intentional violation of law. Neither the fact that the Board, although advised by lawyers and accountants, did not accurately predict the severe consequences to the company that would ultimately follow from the deployment by the company of the strategies and practices that ultimately led to this liability, nor the scale of the liability, gives rise to an inference of breach of any duty imposed by corporation law upon the directors of Caremark.

I. Background

For these purposes I regard the following facts, suggested by the discovery record, as material. Caremark, a Delaware corporation with its headquarters in Northbrook, Illinois, was created in November 1992 when it was spun-off from Baxter International, Inc. ("Baxter") and became a publicly held company listed on the New York Stock Exchange. The business practices that created the problem pre-dated the spin-off. During the relevant period Caremark was involved in two main health care business segments, providing patient care and managed care services. As part of its patient care business, which accounted for the majority of Caremark's revenues, Caremark provided alternative site health care services. . . . Caremark's managed care services included prescription drug programs and the operation of multi-specialty group practices.

A. Events Prior to the Government Investigation

A substantial part of the revenues generated by Caremark's businesses is derived from third party payments, insurers, and Medicare and Medicaid reimbursement programs. The latter source of payments are subject to the terms of the Anti-Referral

Payments Law ("ARPL") which prohibits health care providers from paying any form of remuneration to induce the referral of Medicare or Medicaid patients. From its inception, Caremark entered into a variety of agreements with hospitals, physicians, and health care providers for advice and services, as well as distribution agreements with drug manufacturers, as had its predecessor prior to 1992. Specifically, Caremark did have a practice of entering into contracts for services (*e.g.*, consultation agreements and research grants) with physicians at least some of whom prescribed or recommended services or products that Caremark provided to Medicare recipients and other patients. Such contracts were not prohibited by the ARPL but they obviously raised a possibility of unlawful "kickbacks."

As early as 1989, Caremark's predecessor issued an internal "Guide to Contractual Relationships" ("Guide") to govern its employees in entering into contracts with physicians and hospitals. The Guide tended to be reviewed annually by lawyers and updated. Each version of the Guide stated as Caremark's and its predecessor's policy that no payments would be made in exchange for or to induce patient referrals. But what one might deem a prohibited *quid pro quo* was not always clear. Due to a scarcity of court decisions interpreting the ARPL, however, Caremark repeatedly publicly stated that there was uncertainty concerning Caremark's interpretation of the law.

To clarify the scope of the ARPL, the United States Department of Health and Human Services ("HHS") issued "safe harbor" regulations in July 1991 stating conditions under which financial relationships between health care service providers and patient referral sources, such as physicians, would *not* violate the ARPL. Caremark contends that the narrowly drawn regulations gave limited guidance as to the legality of many of the agreements used by Caremark that did not fall within the safeharbor. Caremark's predecessor, however, amended many of its standard forms of agreement with health care providers and revised the Guide in an apparent attempt to comply with the new regulations.

B. Government Investigation and Related Litigation

In August 1991, the HHS Office of the Inspector General ("OIG") initiated an investigation of Caremark's predecessor. Caremark's predecessor was served with a subpoena requiring the production of documents, including contracts between Caremark's predecessor and physicians (Quality Service Agreements ("QSAs")). Under the QSAs, Caremark's predecessor appears to have paid physicians fees for monitoring patients under Caremark's predecessor's care, including Medicare and Medicaid recipients. Sometimes apparently those monitoring patients were referring physicians, which raised ARPL concerns.

In March 1992, the Department of Justice ("DOJ") joined the OIG investigation and separate investigations were commenced by several additional federal and state agencies.[2]

C. Caremark's Response to the Investigation

During the relevant period, Caremark had approximately 7,000 employees and ninety branch operations. It had a decentralized management structure. By May 1991, however, Caremark asserts that it had begun making attempts to centralize its management structure in order to increase supervision over its branch operations.

The first action taken by management, as a result of the initiation of the OIG investigation, was an announcement that as of October 1, 1991, Caremark's predecessor would no longer pay management fees to physicians for services to Medicare and Medicaid patients. Despite this decision, Caremark asserts that its management, pursuant to advice, did not believe that such payments were illegal under the existing laws and regulations.

During this period, Caremark's Board took several additional steps consistent with an effort to assure compliance with company policies concerning the ARPL and the contractual forms in the Guide. In April 1992, Caremark published a fourth revised version of its Guide apparently designed to assure that its agreements either complied with the ARPL and regulations or excluded Medicare and Medicaid patients altogether. In addition, in September 1992, Caremark instituted a policy requiring its regional officers, Zone Presidents, to approve each contractual relationship entered into by Caremark with a physician.

Although there is evidence that inside and outside counsel had advised Caremark's directors that their contracts were in accord with the law, Caremark recognized that some uncertainty respecting the correct interpretation of the law existed. In its 1992 annual report, Caremark disclosed the ongoing government investigations, acknowledged that if penalties were imposed on the company they could have a material adverse effect on Caremark's business, and stated that no assurance could be given that its interpretation of the ARPL would prevail if challenged.

Throughout the period of the government investigations, Caremark had an internal audit plan designed to assure compliance with business and ethics policies. In addition, Caremark employed Price Waterhouse as its outside auditor. On February 8, 1993, the Ethics Committee of Caremark's Board received and reviewed an outside auditors report by Price Waterhouse which concluded that there were no material weaknesses in Caremark's control structure. Despite the positive findings of Price Waterhouse, however, on April 20, 1993, the Audit & Ethics Committee adopted a

---

2. In addition to investigating whether Caremark's financial relationships with health care providers were intended to induce patient referrals, inquiries were made concerning Caremark's billing practices, activities which might lead to excessive and medically unnecessary treatments for patients, potentially improper waivers of patient co-payment obligations, and the adequacy of records kept at Caremark pharmacies.

new internal audit charter requiring a comprehensive review of compliance policies and the compilation of an employee ethics handbook concerning such policies.

The Board appears to have been informed about this project and other efforts to assure compliance with the law. For example, Caremark's management reported to the Board that Caremark's sales force was receiving an ongoing education regarding the ARPL and the proper use of Caremark's form contracts which had been approved by in-house counsel. On July 27, 1993, the new ethics manual, expressly prohibiting payments in exchange for referrals and requiring employees to report all illegal conduct to a toll free confidential ethics hotline, was approved and allegedly disseminated.[5] The record suggests that Caremark continued these policies in subsequent years, causing employees to be given revised versions of the ethics manual and requiring them to participate in training sessions concerning compliance with the law.

During 1993, Caremark took several additional steps which appear to have been aimed at increasing management supervision. These steps included new policies requiring local branch managers to secure home office approval for all disbursements under agreements with health care providers and to certify compliance with the ethics program. In addition, the chief financial officer was appointed to serve as Caremark's compliance officer. In 1994, a fifth revised Guide was published.

D. Federal Indictments Against Caremark and Officers

On August 4, 1994, a federal grand jury in Minnesota issued a 47 page indictment charging Caremark, two of its officers (not the firm's chief officer), an individual who had been a sales employee of Genentech, Inc., and David R. Brown, a physician practicing in Minneapolis, with violating the ARPL over a lengthy period. According to the indictment, over $1.1 million had been paid to Brown to induce him to distribute Protropin, a human growth hormone drug marketed by Caremark.[6] The substantial payments involved started, according to the allegations of the indictment, in 1986 and continued through 1993. Some payments were "in the guise of research grants", and others were "consulting agreements." The indictment charged, for example, that Dr. Brown performed virtually none of the consulting functions described in his 1991 agreement with Caremark, but was nevertheless neither required to return the money he had received nor precluded from receiving future funding from Caremark. In addition the indictment charged that Brown received from Caremark

---

5. Prior to the distribution of the new ethics manual, on March 12, 1993, Caremark's president had sent a letter to all senior, district, and branch managers restating Caremark's policies that no physician be paid for referrals, that the standard contract forms in the Guide were not to be modified, and that deviation from such policies would result in the immediate termination of employment.

6. In addition to prescribing Protropin, Dr. Brown had been receiving research grants from Caremark as well as payments for services under a consulting agreement for several years before and after the investigation. According to an undated document from an unknown source, Dr. Brown and six other researchers had been providing patient referrals to Caremark valued at $6.55 for each $1 of research money they received.

payments of staff and office expenses, including telephone answering services and fax rental expenses.

Subsequently, five stockholder derivative actions were filed in this court and consolidated into this action. The original complaint, dated August 5, 1994, alleged, in relevant part, that Caremark's directors breached their duty of care by failing adequately to supervise the conduct of Caremark employees, or institute corrective measures, thereby exposing Caremark to fines and liability.

[Other indictments followed in response to which various amendments were made to the complaint herein.]

. . .

After each complaint was filed, defendants filed a motion to dismiss. According to defendants, if a settlement had not been reached in this action, the case would have been dismissed on two grounds. First, they contend that the complaints fail to allege particularized facts sufficient to excuse the demand requirement under Delaware Chancery Court Rule 23.1. Second, defendants assert that plaintiffs had failed to state a cause of action due to the fact that Caremark's charter eliminates directors' personal liability for money damages, to the extent permitted by law.

E. Settlement Negotiations

In September, following the announcement of the Ohio indictment, Caremark publicly announced that as of January 1, 1995, it would terminate all remaining financial relationships with physicians in its home infusion, hemophilia, and growth hormone lines of business.[9] In addition, Caremark asserts that it extended its restrictive policies to all of its contractual relationships with physicians, rather than just those involving Medicare and Medicaid patients, and terminated its research grant program which had always involved some recipients who referred patients to Caremark.

Caremark began settlement negotiations with federal and state government entities in May 1995. In return for a guilty plea to a single count of mail fraud by the corporation, the payment of a criminal fine, the payment of substantial civil damages, and cooperation with further federal investigations on matters relating to the OIG investigation, the government entities agreed to negotiate a settlement that would permit Caremark to continue participating in Medicare and Medicaid programs. On June 15, 1995, the Board approved a settlement ("Government Settlement Agreement") with the DOJ, OIG, U.S. Veterans Administration, U.S. Federal Employee Health Benefits Program, federal Civilian Health and Medical Program of the Uniformed Services, and related state agencies in all fifty states and the District of Columbia.[10] No senior officers or directors were charged with wrongdoing

---

9. On June 1, 1993, Caremark had stopped entering into new contractual agreements in those business segments.

10. The agreement, covering allegations since 1986, required a Caremark subsidiary to enter a guilty plea to two counts of mail fraud, and required Caremark to pay $29 million in criminal

in the Government Settlement Agreement or in any of the prior indictments. In fact, as part of the sentencing in the Ohio action on June 19, 1995, the United States stipulated that *no senior executive of Caremark participated in, condoned, or was willfully ignorant of wrongdoing in connection with the home infusion business practices.*

The federal settlement included certain provisions in a "Corporate Integrity Agreement" designed to enhance future compliance with law. The parties have not discussed this agreement, except to say that the negotiated provisions of the settlement of this claim are not redundant of those in that agreement.

Settlement negotiations between the parties in this action commenced in May 1995 as well, based upon a letter proposal of the plaintiffs, dated May 16, 1995.[12] These negotiations resulted in a memorandum of understanding ("MOU"), dated June 7, 1995, and the execution of the Stipulation and Agreement of Compromise and Settlement on June 28, 1995, which is the subject of this action.[13] The MOU, approved by the Board on June 15, 1995, required the Board to adopt several resolutions, discussed below, and to create a new compliance committee. The Compliance and Ethics Committee has been reporting to the Board in accord with its newly specified duties. . . .

F. The Proposed Settlement of this Litigation

In relevant part the terms upon which these claims asserted are proposed to be settled are as follows:

> 1. That Caremark, undertakes that it and its employees, and agents not pay any form of compensation to a third party in exchange for the referral of a patient to a Caremark facility or service or the prescription of drugs marketed or distributed by Caremark for which reimbursement may be sought from Medicare, Medicaid, or a similar state reimbursement program;
>
> 2. That Caremark, undertakes for itself and its employees, and agents not to pay to or split fees with physicians, joint ventures, any business combination in which Caremark maintains a direct financial interest, or other health care providers with whom Caremark has a financial relationship or interest, in exchange for the referral of a patient to a Caremark facility or service or the prescription of drugs marketed or distributed by Caremark for which

---

fines, $129.9 million relating to civil claims concerning payment practices, $3.5 million for alleged violations to the Controlled Substances Act, and $2 million, in the form of a donation, to a grant program set up by the Ryan White Comprehensive AIDS Resources Emergency Act. Caremark also agreed to enter into a compliance agreement with the HHS.

12. No government entities were involved in these separate, but concurrent negotiations.

13. Plaintiffs' initial proposal had both a monetary component, requiring Caremark's director-officers to relinquish stock options, and a remedial component, requiring management to adopt and implement several compliance related measures. The monetary component was subsequently eliminated.

reimbursement may be sought from Medicare, Medicaid, or a similar state reimbursement program;

3. That the full Board shall discuss all relevant material changes in government health care regulations and their effect on relationships with health care providers on a semi-annual basis;

4. That Caremark's officers will remove all personnel from health care facilities or hospitals who have been placed in such facility for the purpose of providing remuneration in exchange for a patient referral for which reimbursement may be sought from Medicare, Medicaid, or a similar state reimbursement program;

5. That every patient will receive written disclosure of any financial relationship between Caremark and the health care professional or provider who made the referral;

6. That the Board will establish a Compliance and Ethics Committee of four directors, two of which will be non-management directors, to meet at least four times a year to effectuate these policies and monitor business segment compliance with the ARPL, and to report to the Board semi-annually concerning compliance by each business segment; and

7. That corporate officers responsible for business segments shall serve as compliance officers who must report semi-annually to the Compliance and Ethics Committee and, with the assistance of outside counsel, review existing contracts and get advanced approval of any new contract forms.

II. Legal Principles

A. Principles Governing Settlements of Derivative Claims

As noted at the outset of this opinion, this Court is now required to exercise an informed judgment whether the proposed settlement is fair and reasonable in the light of all relevant factors. On an application of this kind, this Court attempts to protect the best interests of the corporation and its absent shareholders all of whom will be barred from future litigation on these claims if the settlement is approved. The parties proposing the settlement bear the burden of persuading the court that it is in fact fair and reasonable.

B. Directors' Duties To Monitor Corporate Operations

The complaint charges the director defendants with breach of their duty of attention or care in connection with the on-going operation of the corporation's business. The claim is that the directors allowed a situation to develop and continue which exposed the corporation to enormous legal liability and that in so doing they violated a duty to be active monitors of corporate performance. The complaint thus does not charge either director self-dealing or the more difficult loyalty-type problems arising from cases of suspect director motivation, such as entrenchment or sale of control contexts. The theory here advanced is possibly the most difficult theory in corporation law upon which a plaintiff might hope to win a judgment....

1. *Potential liability for directoral decisions*: Director liability for a breach of the duty to exercise appropriate attention may, in theory, arise in two distinct contexts. First, such liability may be said to follow *from a board decision* that results in a loss because that decision was ill advised or "negligent". Second, liability to the corporation for a loss may be said to arise from an *unconsidered failure of the board to act* in circumstances in which due attention would, arguably, have prevented the loss. The first class of cases will typically be subject to review under the director-protective business judgment rule, assuming the decision made was the product of a *process* that was *either* deliberately considered in good faith or was otherwise rational. What should be understood, but may not widely be understood by courts or commentators who are not often required to face such questions, is that compliance with a director's duty of care can never appropriately be judicially determined by reference to *the content of the board decision* that leads to a corporate loss, apart from consideration of the good faith *or* rationality of the process employed. That is, whether a judge or jury considering the matter after the fact, believes a decision substantively wrong, or degrees of wrong extending through "stupid" to "egregious" or "irrational", provides no ground for director liability, so long as the court determines that the process employed was either rational or employed in a *good faith* effort to advance corporate interests. To employ a different rule—one that permitted an "objective" evaluation of the decision—would expose directors to substantive second guessing by ill-equipped judges or juries, which would, in the long-run, be injurious to investor interests.[16] Thus, the business judgment rule is process oriented and informed by a deep respect for all *good faith* board decisions.

Indeed, one wonders on what moral basis might shareholders attack a *good faith* business decision of a director as "unreasonable" or "irrational." Where a director *in fact exercises a good faith effort to be informed and to exercise appropriate judgment*, he or she should be deemed to satisfy fully the duty of attention. If the shareholders thought themselves entitled to some other quality of judgment than such a director

---

16. The vocabulary of negligence while often employed, is not well-suited to judicial review of board attentiveness, especially if one attempts to look to the substance of the decision as any evidence of possible "negligence." Where review of board functioning is involved, courts leave behind as a relevant point of reference the decisions of the hypothetical "reasonable person", who typically supplies the test for negligence liability. It is doubtful that we want business men and women to be encouraged to make decisions as hypothetical persons of *ordinary* judgment and prudence might. The corporate form gets its utility in large part from its ability to allow diversified investors to accept greater investment risk. If those in charge of the corporation are to be adjudged personally liable for losses on the basis of a substantive judgment based upon what persons of ordinary or average judgment and average risk assessment talent regard as "prudent" "sensible" or even "rational", such persons will have a strong incentive at the margin to authorize less risky investment projects.

produces in the good faith exercise of the powers of office, then the shareholders should have elected other directors. Judge Learned Hand made the point rather better than can I. In speaking of the passive director defendant Mr. Andrews in *Barnes v. Andrews*, Judge Hand said:

> True, he was not very suited by experience for the job he had undertaken, but I cannot hold him on that account. After all it is the same corporation that chose him that now seeks to charge him.... Directors are not specialists like lawyers or doctors.... They are the general advisors of the business and if they faithfully give such ability as they have to their charge, it would not be lawful to hold them liable. Must a director guarantee that his judgment is good? Can a shareholder call him to account for deficiencies that their votes assured him did not disqualify him for his office? While he may not have been the Cromwell for that Civil War, Andrews did not engage to play any such role.

In this formulation Learned Hand correctly identifies, in my opinion, the core element of any corporate law duty of care inquiry: whether there was good faith effort to be informed and exercise judgment.

2. Liability for failure to monitor: The second class of cases in which director liability for inattention is theoretically possible entail circumstances in which a loss eventuates not from a decision but, from unconsidered inaction. Most of the decisions that a corporation, acting through its human agents, makes are, of course, not the subject of director attention. Legally, the board itself will be required only to authorize the most significant corporate acts or transactions: mergers, changes in capital structure, fundamental changes in business, appointment and compensation of the CEO, etc. As the facts of this case graphically demonstrate, ordinary business decisions that are made by officers and employees deeper in the interior of the organization can, however, vitally affect the welfare of the corporation and its ability to achieve its various strategic and financial goals. If this case did not prove the point itself, recent business history would. Recall for example the displacement of senior management and much of the board of Salomon, Inc.; the replacement of senior management of Kidder, Peabody following the discovery of large trading losses resulting from phantom trades by a highly compensated trader; or the extensive financial loss and reputational injury suffered by Prudential Insurance as a result of its junior officers' misrepresentations in connection with the distribution of limited partnership interests. Financial and organizational disasters such as these raise the question, what is the board's responsibility with respect to the organization and monitoring of the enterprise to assure that the corporation functions within the law to achieve its purposes?

Modernly this question has been given special importance by an increasing tendency, especially under federal law, to employ the criminal law to assure corporate compliance with external legal requirements, including environmental, financial, employee and product safety as well as assorted other health and safety regulations.

2 · THE DUTIES OF DIRECTORS, OFFICERS AND OTHER INSIDERS

In 1991, pursuant to the Sentencing Reform Act of 1984, the United States Sentencing Commission adopted Organizational Sentencing Guidelines which impact importantly on the prospective effect these criminal sanctions might have on business corporations. The Guidelines set forth a uniform sentencing structure for organizations to be sentenced for violation of federal criminal statutes and provide for penalties that equal or often massively exceed those previously imposed on corporations. The Guidelines offer powerful incentives for corporations today to have in place compliance programs to detect violations of law, promptly to report violations to appropriate public officials when discovered, and to take prompt, voluntary remedial efforts.

In 1963, the Delaware Supreme Court in *Graham v. Allis-Chalmers Mfg. Co.*, addressed the question of potential liability of board members for losses experienced by the corporation as a result of the corporation having violated the anti-trust laws of the United States. There was no claim in that case that the directors knew about the behavior of subordinate employees of the corporation that had resulted in the liability. Rather, as in this case, the claim asserted was that the directors *ought to have known* of it and if they had known they would have been under a duty to bring the corporation into compliance with the law and thus save the corporation from the loss. The Delaware Supreme Court concluded that, under the facts as they appeared, there was no basis to find that the directors had breached a duty to be informed of the ongoing operations of the firm. In notably colorful terms, the court stated that "absent cause for suspicion there is no duty upon the directors to install and operate a corporate system of espionage to ferret out wrongdoing which they have no reason to suspect exists." The Court found that there were no grounds for suspicion in that case and, thus, concluded that the directors were blamelessly unaware of the conduct leading to the corporate liability.[25]

How does one generalize this holding today? Can it be said today that, absent some ground giving rise to suspicion of violation of law, that corporate directors have no duty to assure that a corporate information gathering and reporting systems exists which represents a good faith attempt to provide senior management and the Board with information respecting material acts, events or conditions within the corporation, including compliance with applicable statutes and regulations? I certainly do not believe so. I doubt that such a broad generalization of the *Graham* holding would have been accepted by the Supreme Court in 1963. The case can be more narrowly interpreted as standing for the proposition that, absent grounds to suspect deception, neither corporate boards nor senior officers can be charged with wrongdoing simply for assuming the integrity of employees and the honesty of their dealings on the company's behalf.

---

25. Recently, the *Graham* standard was applied by the Delaware Chancery in a case involving Baxter. *In Re Baxter International, Inc. Shareholders Litig.*, Del. Ch., 654 A.2d 1268, 1270 (1995).

A broader interpretation of *Graham v. Allis-Chalmers*—that it means that a corporate board has no responsibility to assure that appropriate information and reporting systems are established by management—would not, in any event, be accepted by the Delaware Supreme Court in 1996, in my opinion. In stating the basis for this view, I start with the recognition that in recent years the Delaware Supreme Court has made it clear—especially in its jurisprudence concerning takeovers, from *Smith v. Van Gorkom* through *Paramount Communications v. QVC*—the seriousness with which the corporation law views the role of the corporate board. Secondly, I note the elementary fact that relevant and timely *information* is an essential predicate for satisfaction of the board's supervisory and monitoring role under Section 141 of the Delaware General Corporation Law. Thirdly, I note the potential impact of the federal organizational sentencing guidelines on any business organization. Any rational person attempting in good faith to meet an organizational governance responsibility would be bound to take into account this development and the enhanced penalties and the opportunities for reduced sanctions that it offers.

In light of these developments, it would, in my opinion, be a mistake to conclude that our Supreme Court's statement in *Graham* concerning "espionage" means that corporate boards may satisfy their obligation to be reasonably informed concerning the corporation, without assuring themselves that information and reporting systems exist in the organization that are reasonably designed to provide to senior management and to the board itself timely, accurate information sufficient to allow management and the board, each within its scope, to reach informed judgments concerning both the corporation's compliance with law and its business performance.

Obviously the level of detail that is appropriate for such an information system is a question of business judgment. And obviously too, no rationally designed information and reporting system will remove the possibility that the corporation will violate laws or regulations, or that senior officers or directors may nevertheless sometimes be misled or otherwise fail reasonably to detect acts material to the corporation's compliance with the law. But it is important that the board exercise a good faith judgment that the corporation's information and reporting system is in concept and design adequate to assure the board that appropriate information will come to its attention in a timely manner as a matter of ordinary operations, so that it may satisfy its responsibility.

Thus, I am of the view that a director's obligation includes a duty to attempt in good faith to assure that a corporate information and reporting system, which the board concludes is adequate, exists, and that failure to do so under some circumstances may, in theory at least, render a director liable for losses caused by noncompliance with applicable legal standards.[27] I now turn to an analysis of the claims

---

27. Any action seeking recover for losses would logically entail a judicial determination of proximate cause, since, for reasons that I take to be obvious, it could never be assumed that an adequate information system would be a system that would prevent all losses. I need not touch upon the

asserted with this concept of the directors duty of care, as a duty satisfied in part by assurance of adequate information flows to the board, in mind.

III. Analysis of Third Amended Complaint and Settlement

A. The Claims

On balance, after reviewing an extensive record in this case, including numerous documents and three depositions, I conclude that this settlement is fair and reasonable. In light of the fact that the Caremark Board already has a functioning committee charged with overseeing corporate compliance, the changes in corporate practice that are presented as consideration for the settlement do not impress one as very significant. Nonetheless, that consideration appears fully adequate to support dismissal of the derivative claims of director fault asserted, because those claims find no substantial evidentiary support in the record and quite likely were susceptible to a motion to dismiss in all events.

In order to show that the Caremark directors breached their duty of care by failing adequately to control Caremark's employees, plaintiffs would have to show either (1) that the directors knew or (2) should have known that violations of law were occurring and, in either event, (3) that the directors took no steps in a good faith effort to prevent or remedy that situation, and (4) that such failure proximately resulted in the losses complained of, although under *Cede & Co. v. Technicolor, Inc.* this last element may be thought to constitute an affirmative defense.

1. Knowing violation for statute: Concerning the possibility that the Caremark directors knew of violations of law, none of the documents submitted for review, nor any of the deposition transcripts appear to provide evidence of it. Certainly the Board understood that the company had entered into a variety of contracts with physicians, researchers, and health care providers and it was understood that some of these contracts were with persons who had prescribed treatments that Caremark participated in providing. The board was informed that the company's reimbursement for patient care was frequently from government funded sources and that such services were subject to the ARPL. But the Board appears to have been informed by experts that the company's practices while contestable, were lawful. There is no evidence that reliance on such reports was not reasonable. Thus, this case presents no occasion to apply a principle to the effect that knowingly causing the corporation to violate a criminal statute constitutes a breach of a director's fiduciary duty. It is not clear that the Board knew the detail found, for example, in the indictments arising from the Company's payments. But, of course, the duty to act in good faith to be informed cannot be thought to require directors to possess detailed information about all aspects of the operation of the enterprise. Such a requirement would simple [sic] be inconsistent with the scale and scope of efficient organization size in this technological age.

---

burden allocation with respect to a proximate cause issue in such a suit. Moreover, questions of waiver of liability under certificate provisions authorized by 8 Del.C. § 102(b)(7) may also be faced.

2. Failure to monitor: Since it does appears that the Board was to some extent unaware of the activities that led to liability, I turn to a consideration of the other potential avenue to director liability that the pleadings take: director inattention or "negligence". Generally where a claim of directorial liability for corporate loss is predicated upon ignorance of liability creating activities within the corporation, as in *Graham* or in this case, in my opinion only a sustained or systematic failure of the board to exercise oversight—such as an utter failure to attempt to assure a reasonable information and reporting system exits—will establish the lack of good faith that is a necessary condition to liability. Such a test of liability—lack of good faith as evidenced by sustained or systematic failure of a director to exercise reasonable oversight—is quite high. But, a demanding test of liability in the oversight context is probably beneficial to corporate shareholders as a class, as it is in the board decision context, since it makes board service by qualified persons more likely, while continuing to act as a stimulus to *good faith performance of duty* by such directors.

Here the record supplies essentially no evidence that the director defendants were guilty of a sustained failure to exercise their oversight function. To the contrary, insofar as I am able to tell on this record, the corporation's information systems appear to have represented a good faith attempt to be informed of relevant facts. If the directors did not know the specifics of the activities that lead to the indictments, they cannot be faulted.

The liability that eventuated in this instance was huge. But the fact that it resulted from a violation of criminal law alone does not create a breach of fiduciary duty by directors. The record at this stage does not support the conclusion that the defendants either lacked good faith in the exercise of their monitoring responsibilities or conscientiously permitted a known violation of law by the corporation to occur. The claims asserted against them must be viewed at this stage as extremely weak.

B. The Consideration for Release of Claim

The proposed settlement provides very modest benefits. Under the settlement agreement, plaintiffs have been given express assurances that Caremark will have a more centralized, active supervisory system in the future. Specifically, the settlement mandates duties to be performed by the newly named Compliance and Ethics Committee on an ongoing basis and increases the responsibility for monitoring compliance with the law at the lower levels of management. In adopting the resolutions required under the settlement, Caremark has further clarified its policies concerning the prohibition of providing remuneration for referrals. These appear to be positive consequences of the settlement of the claims brought by the plaintiffs, even if they are not highly significant. Nonetheless, given the weakness of the plaintiffs' claims the proposed settlement appears to be an adequate, reasonable, and beneficial outcome for all of the parties. Thus, the proposed settlement will be approved. . . .

Questions

1. Chancellor Allen began his analysis by noting that the duty to monitor (and duty of care more broadly) is "possibly the most difficult theory in corporation law upon which a plaintiff might hope to win a judgment." Why is this so?

2. What is the directors' duty to monitor after *Caremark*? Is it similar to the duty we saw in *Francis*? What standard does Chancellor Allen use to evaluate directors' actions or inactions?

3. Does *Caremark* make it harder or easier for directors to meet their obligations?

4. Do you agree with the court's conclusion? Think about yourself as a member of Caremark's board of directors. Based upon the decentralized structure of the corporation and your view of human nature, what would you know or at least expect? Human nature aside, what incentives did the corporation's structure create for employees? What might you have done as a Caremark employee? Should the board be held to have known this? If so, what measure of the duty of care remains after this opinion?

5. What is the relationship between the standard of good faith as *Caremark* defines it and the standard as it was defined in *Disney*? Consider the question as you read the following case.

Stone v. Ritter

911 A.2d 362 (Del. 2006)

HOLLAND, Justice

This is an appeal from a final judgment of the Court of Chancery dismissing a derivative complaint against fifteen present and former directors of AmSouth Bancorporation ("AmSouth"), a Delaware corporation. The plaintiffs-appellants, William and Sandra Stone, are AmSouth shareholders and filed their derivative complaint without making a pre-suit demand on AmSouth's board of directors (the "Board"). The Court of Chancery held that the plaintiffs had failed to adequately plead that such a demand would have been futile. The Court, therefore, dismissed the derivative complaint under Court of Chancery Rule 23.1.

The Court of Chancery characterized the allegations in the derivative complaint as a "classic *Caremark* claim," a claim that derives its name from *In re Caremark Int'l Deriv. Litig.* In *Caremark*, the Court of Chancery recognized that: "[g]enerally where a claim of directorial liability for corporate loss is predicated upon ignorance of liability creating activities within the corporation ... only a sustained or systematic failure of the board to exercise oversight—such as an utter failure to attempt to assure a reasonable information and reporting system exists—will establish the lack of good faith that is a necessary condition to liability."

In this appeal, the plaintiffs acknowledge that the directors neither "knew [n]or should have known that violations of law were occurring," *i.e.*, that there were no "red flags" before the directors. Nevertheless, the plaintiffs argue that the Court of Chancery erred by dismissing the derivative complaint which alleged that "the defendants had utterly failed to implement any sort of statutorily required monitoring, reporting or information controls that would have enabled them to learn of problems requiring their attention." The defendants argue that the plaintiffs' assertions are contradicted by the derivative complaint itself and by the documents incorporated therein by reference.

Consistent with our opinion in *In re Walt Disney Co. Deriv Litig*, we hold that *Caremark* articulates the necessary conditions for assessing director oversight liability. We also conclude that the *Caremark* standard was properly applied to evaluate the derivative complaint in this case. Accordingly, the judgment of the Court of Chancery must be affirmed.

FACTS

This derivative action is brought on AmSouth's behalf by William and Sandra Stone, who allege that they owned AmSouth common stock "at all relevant times." The nominal defendant, AmSouth, is a Delaware corporation with its principal executive offices in Birmingham, Alabama. During the relevant period, AmSouth's wholly-owned subsidiary, AmSouth Bank, operated about 600 commercial banking branches in six states throughout the southeastern United States and employed more than 11,600 people.

In 2004, AmSouth and AmSouth Bank paid $40 million in fines and $10 million in civil penalties to resolve government and regulatory investigations pertaining principally to the failure by bank employees to file "Suspicious Activity Reports" ("SARs"), as required by the federal Bank Secrecy Act ("BSA") and various anti-money-laundering ("AML") regulations. Those investigations were conducted by the United States Attorney's Office for the Southern District of Mississippi ("USAO"), the Federal Reserve, FinCEN and the Alabama Banking Department. No fines or penalties were imposed on AmSouth's directors, and no other regulatory action was taken against them.

The government investigations arose originally from an unlawful "Ponzi" scheme operated by Louis D. Hamric, II and Victor G. Nance. In August 2000, Hamric, then a licensed attorney, and Nance, then a registered investment advisor with Mutual of New York, contacted an AmSouth branch bank in Tennessee to arrange for custodial trust accounts to be created for "investors" in a "business venture." That venture (Hamric and Nance represented) involved the construction of medical clinics overseas. In reality, Nance had convinced more than forty of his clients to invest in promissory notes bearing high rates of return, by misrepresenting the nature and the risk of that investment. Relying on similar misrepresentations by Hamric and Nance, the AmSouth branch employees in Tennessee agreed to provide custodial accounts for the investors and to distribute monthly interest payments to each account upon receipt of a check from Hamric and instructions from Nance.

The Hamric-Nance scheme was discovered in March 2002, when the investors did not receive their monthly interest payments. Thereafter, Hamric and Nance became the subject of several civil actions brought by the defrauded investors in Tennessee and Mississippi (and in which AmSouth also was named as a defendant), and also the subject of a federal grand jury investigation in the Southern District of Mississippi. Hamric and Nance were indicted on federal money-laundering charges, and both pled guilty.

The authorities examined AmSouth's compliance with its reporting and other obligations under the BSA. On November 17, 2003, the USAO advised AmSouth that it was the subject of a criminal investigation. On October 12, 2004, AmSouth and the USAO entered into a Deferred Prosecution Agreement ("DPA") in which AmSouth agreed: first, to the filing by USAO of a one-count Information in the United States District Court for the Southern District of Mississippi, charging AmSouth with failing to file SARs; and second, to pay a $40 million fine. In conjunction with the DPA, the USAO issued a "Statement of Facts," which noted that although in 2000 "at least one" AmSouth employee suspected that Hamric was involved in a possibly illegal scheme, AmSouth failed to file SARs in a timely manner. In neither the Statement of Facts nor anywhere else did the USAO ascribe any blame to the Board or to any individual director.

On October 12, 2004, the Federal Reserve and the Alabama Banking Department concurrently issued a Cease and Desist Order against AmSouth, requiring it, for the first time, to improve its BSA/AML program. That Cease and Desist Order required AmSouth to (among other things) engage an independent consultant "to conduct a comprehensive review of the Bank's AML Compliance program and make recommendations, as appropriate, for new policies and procedures to be implemented by the Bank." KPMG Forensic Services ("KPMG") performed the role of independent consultant and issued its report on December 10, 2004 (the "KPMG Report").

Also on October 12, 2004, FinCEN and the Federal Reserve jointly assessed a $10 million civil penalty against AmSouth for operating an inadequate anti-money-laundering program and for failing to file SARs. In connection with that assessment, FinCEN issued a written Assessment of Civil Money Penalty (the "Assessment"), which included detailed "determinations" regarding AmSouth's BSA compliance procedures. FinCEN found that "AmSouth violated the suspicious activity reporting requirements of the Bank Secrecy Act," and that "[s]ince April 24, 2002, AmSouth has been in violation of the anti-money-laundering program requirements of the Bank Secrecy Act." Among FinCEN's specific determinations were its conclusions that "AmSouth's [AML compliance] program lacked adequate board and management oversight," and that "reporting to management for the purposes of monitoring and oversight of compliance activities was materially deficient." AmSouth neither admitted nor denied FinCEN's determinations in this or any other forum.

DEMAND FUTILITY AND DIRECTOR INDEPENDENCE

It is a fundamental principle of the Delaware General Corporation Law that "[t]he business and affairs of every corporation organized under this chapter shall be managed by or under the direction of a board of directors...." Thus, "by its very nature [a] derivative action impinges on the managerial freedom of directors." Therefore, the right of a stockholder to prosecute a derivative suit is limited to situations where either the stockholder has demanded the directors pursue a corporate claim and the directors have wrongfully refused to do so, or where demand is excused because the directors are incapable of making an impartial decision regarding whether to institute such litigation. Court of Chancery Rule 23.1, accordingly, requires that the complaint in a derivative action "allege with particularity the efforts, if any, made by the plaintiff to obtain the action the plaintiff desires from the directors [or] the reasons for the plaintiff's failure to obtain the action or for not making the effort."

In this appeal, the plaintiffs concede that "[t]he standards for determining demand futility in the absence of a business decision" are set forth in *Rales v. Blasband* (1993). To excuse demand under *Rales*, "a court must determine whether or not the particularized factual allegations of a derivative stockholder complaint create a reasonable doubt that, as of the time the complaint is filed, the board of directors could have properly exercised its independent and disinterested business judgment in responding to a demand." The plaintiffs attempt to satisfy the *Rales* test in this proceeding by asserting that the incumbent defendant directors "face a substantial likelihood of liability" that renders them "personally interested in the outcome of the decision on whether to pursue the claims asserted in the complaint," and are therefore not disinterested or independent.[12]

Critical to this demand excused argument is the fact that the directors' potential personal liability depends upon whether or not their conduct can be exculpated by the section 102(b)(7) provision contained in the AmSouth certificate of incorporation. Such a provision can exculpate directors from monetary liability for a breach of the duty of care, but not for conduct that is not in good faith or a breach of the duty of loyalty. The standard for assessing a director's potential personal liability for failing to act in good faith in discharging his or her oversight responsibilities has evolved beginning with our decision in *Graham v. Allis-Chalmers Manufacturing Company* (1963), through the Court of Chancery's *Caremark* decision to our most recent decision in *Disney* (2006). A brief discussion of that evolution will help illuminate the standard that we adopt in this case.

---

12. The fifteen defendants include eight current and seven former directors. The complaint concedes that seven of the eight current directors are outside directors who have never been employed by AmSouth. One board member, C. Dowd Ritter, the Chairman, is an officer or employee of AmSouth.

GRAHAM AND CAREMARK

Graham was a derivative action brought against the directors of Allis-Chalmers for failure to prevent violations of federal anti-trust laws by Allis-Chalmers employees. There was no claim that the Allis-Chalmers directors knew of the employees' conduct that resulted in the corporation's liability. Rather, the plaintiffs claimed that the Allis-Chalmers directors *should have known* of the illegal conduct by the corporation's employees. In *Graham*, this Court held that "*absent cause for suspicion* there is no duty upon the directors to install and operate a corporate system of espionage to ferret out wrongdoing which they have no reason to suspect exists."

In *Caremark*, the Court of Chancery reassessed the applicability of our holding in *Graham* when called upon to approve a settlement of a derivative lawsuit brought against the directors of Caremark International, Inc. The plaintiffs claimed that the Caremark directors should have known that certain officers and employees of Caremark were involved in violations of the federal Anti-Referral Payments Law. That law prohibits health care providers from paying any form of remuneration to induce the referral of Medicare or Medicaid patients. The plaintiffs claimed that the *Caremark* directors breached their fiduciary duty for having "allowed a situation to develop and continue which exposed the corporation to enormous legal liability and that in so doing they violated a duty to be active monitors of corporate performance."

In evaluating whether to approve the proposed settlement agreement in *Caremark*, the Court of Chancery narrowly construed our holding in *Graham* "as standing for the proposition that, absent grounds to suspect deception, neither corporate boards nor senior officers can be charged with wrongdoing simply for assuming the integrity of employees and the honesty of their dealings on the company's behalf." The *Caremark* Court opined it would be a "mistake" to interpret this Court's decision in *Graham* to mean that:

> corporate boards may satisfy their obligation to be reasonably informed concerning the corporation, without assuring themselves that information and reporting systems exist in the organization that are reasonably designed to provide to senior management and to the board itself timely, accurate information sufficient to allow management and the board, each within its scope, to reach informed judgments concerning both the corporation's compliance with law and its business performance.

To the contrary, the *Caremark* Court stated, "it is important that the board exercise a good faith judgment that the corporation's information and reporting system is in concept and design adequate to assure the board that appropriate information will come to its attention in a timely manner as a matter of ordinary operations, so that it may satisfy its responsibility." The *Caremark* Court recognized, however, that "the duty to act in good faith to be informed cannot be thought to require directors to possess detailed information about all aspects of the operation of the enterprise." The Court of Chancery then formulated the following standard for assessing the liability of directors where the directors are unaware of employee misconduct that results in the corporation being held liable:

> Generally where a claim of directorial liability for corporate loss is predicated upon ignorance of liability creating activities within the corporation, as in *Graham* or in this case, . . . only a sustained or systematic failure of the board to exercise oversight-such as an utter failure to attempt to assure a reasonable information and reporting system exists — will establish the lack of good faith that is a necessary condition to liability.

CAREMARK STANDARD APPROVED

As evidenced by the language quoted above, the *Caremark* standard for so-called "oversight" liability draws heavily upon the concept of director failure to act in good faith. That is consistent with the definition(s) of bad faith recently approved by this Court in its recent *Disney* decision, where we held that a failure to act in good faith requires conduct that is qualitatively different from, and more culpable than, the conduct giving rise to a violation of the fiduciary duty of care (i.e., gross negligence). In *Disney*, we identified the following examples of conduct that would establish a failure to act in good faith:

> A failure to act in good faith may be shown, for instance, where the fiduciary intentionally acts with a purpose other than that of advancing the best interests of the corporation, where the fiduciary acts with the intent to violate applicable positive law, or where the fiduciary intentionally fails to act in the face of a known duty to act, demonstrating a conscious disregard for his duties. There may be other examples of bad faith yet to be proven or alleged, but these three are the most salient.

The third of these examples describes, and is fully consistent with, the lack of good faith conduct that the *Caremark* court held was a "necessary condition" for director oversight liability, i.e., "a sustained or systematic failure of the board to exercise oversight — such as an utter failure to attempt to assure a reasonable information and reporting system exists. . . ."

Indeed, our opinion in *Disney* cited *Caremark* with approval for that proposition. Accordingly, the Court of Chancery applied the correct standard in assessing whether demand was excused in this case where failure to exercise oversight was the basis or theory of the plaintiffs' claim for relief.

It is important, in this context, to clarify a doctrinal issue that is critical to understanding fiduciary liability under *Caremark* as we construe that case. The phraseology used in *Caremark* and that we employ here — describing the lack of good faith as a "necessary condition to liability" — is deliberate. The purpose of that formulation is to communicate that a failure to act in good faith is not conduct that results, *ipso facto*, in the direct imposition of fiduciary liability.[29] The failure to act in good faith may result in liability because the requirement to act in good faith "is a subsidiary element[,]" i.e., a condition, "of the fundamental duty of loyalty."[30] It follows that because a showing of bad faith conduct, in the sense described in *Disney* and *Caremark*, is essential to establish director oversight liability, the fiduciary duty violated by that conduct is the duty of loyalty.

This view of a failure to act in good faith results in two additional doctrinal consequences. First, although good faith may be described colloquially as part of a "triad" of fiduciary duties that includes the duties of care and loyalty, the obligation to act in good faith does not establish an independent fiduciary duty that stands on the same footing as the duties of care and loyalty. Only the latter two duties, where violated, may directly result in liability, whereas a failure to act in good faith may do so, but indirectly. The second doctrinal consequence is that the fiduciary duty of loyalty is not limited to cases involving a financial or other cognizable fiduciary conflict of interest. It also encompasses cases where the fiduciary fails to act in good faith. As the Court of Chancery aptly put it in *Guttman*, "[a] director cannot act loyally towards the corporation unless she acts in the good faith belief that her actions are in the corporation's best interest."

We hold that *Caremark* articulates the necessary conditions predicate for director oversight liability: (a) the directors utterly failed to implement any reporting or information system or controls; *or* (b) having implemented such a system or controls, consciously failed to monitor or oversee its operations thus disabling themselves from being informed of risks or problems requiring their attention. In either case, imposition of liability requires a showing that the directors knew that they were not discharging their fiduciary obligations. Where directors fail to act in the face of a known duty to act, thereby demonstrating a conscious disregard for their responsibilities, they breach their duty of loyalty by failing to discharge that fiduciary obligation in good faith.

CHANCERY COURT DECISION

The plaintiffs contend that demand is excused under Rule 23.1 because AmSouth's directors breached their oversight duty and, as a result, face a "substantial likelihood of liability" as a result of their "utter failure" to act in good faith to put into place policies and procedures to ensure compliance with BSA and AML obligations. The Court of Chancery found that the plaintiffs did not plead the existence of "red flags"—"facts showing that the board ever was aware that AmSouth's internal controls were inadequate, that these inadequacies would result in illegal activity, and that the board chose to do nothing about problems it allegedly knew existed." In dismissing the derivative complaint in this action, the Court of Chancery concluded:

---

29. That issue, whether a violation of the duty to act in good faith is a basis for the direct imposition of liability, was expressly left open in *Disney*. We address that issue here.
30. *Guttman v. Huang*, 823 A.2d 492, 506 n.34 (Del. Ch. 2003).

This case is not about a board's failure to carefully consider a material corporate decision that was presented to the board. This is a case where information was not reaching the board because of ineffective internal controls. . . . With the benefit of hindsight, it is beyond question that AmSouth's internal controls with respect to the Bank Secrecy Act and anti-money laundering regulations compliance were inadequate. Neither party disputes that the lack of internal controls resulted in a huge fine — $50 million, alleged to be the largest ever of its kind. The fact of those losses, however, is not alone enough for a court to conclude that a majority of the corporation's board of directors is disqualified from considering demand that AmSouth bring suit against those responsible.

This Court reviews *de novo* a Court of Chancery's decision to dismiss a derivative suit under Rule 23.1.

REASONABLE REPORTING SYSTEM EXISTED

The KPMG Report evaluated the various components of AmSouth's longstanding BSA/AML compliance program. The KPMG Report reflects that AmSouth's Board dedicated considerable resources to the BSA/AML compliance program and put into place numerous procedures and systems to attempt to ensure compliance. According to KPMG, the program's various components exhibited between a low and high degree of compliance with applicable laws and regulations.

The KPMG Report describes the numerous AmSouth employees, departments and committees established by the Board to oversee AmSouth's compliance with the BSA and to report violations to management and the Board:

> BSA Officer. Since 1998, AmSouth has had a "BSA Officer" "responsible for all BSA/AML-related matters including employee training, general communications, CTR reporting and SAR reporting," and "presenting AML policy and program changes to the Board of Directors, the managers at the various lines of business, and participants in the annual training of security and audit personnel"[;]
>
> BSA/AML Compliance Department. AmSouth has had for years a BSA/AML Compliance Department, headed by the BSA Officer and comprised of nineteen professionals, including a BSA/AML Compliance Manager and a Compliance Reporting Manager;
>
> Corporate Security Department. AmSouth's Corporate Security Department has been at all relevant times responsible for the detection and reporting of suspicious activity as it relates to fraudulent activity, and William Burch, the head of Corporate Security, has been with AmSouth since 1998 and served in the U.S. Secret Service from 1969 to 1998; and
>
> Suspicious Activity Oversight Committee. Since 2001, the "Suspicious Activity Oversight Committee" and its predecessor, the "AML Committee," have actively overseen AmSouth's BSA/AML compliance program. The

Suspicious Activity Oversight Committee's mission has for years been to "oversee the policy, procedure, and process issues affecting the Corporate Security and BSA/AML Compliance Programs, to ensure that an effective program exists at AmSouth to deter, detect, and report money laundering, suspicious activity and other fraudulent activity."

The KPMG Report reflects that the directors not only discharged their oversight responsibility to establish an information and reporting system, but also proved that the system was designed to permit the directors to periodically monitor AmSouth's compliance with BSA and AML regulations. For example, as KPMG noted in 2004, AmSouth's designated BSA Officer "has made annual high-level presentations to the Board of Directors in each of the last five years." Further, the Board's Audit and Community Responsibility Committee (the "Audit Committee") oversaw AmSouth's BSA/AML compliance program on a quarterly basis. The KPMG Report states that "the BSA Officer presents BSA/AML training to the Board of Directors annually," and the "Corporate Security training is also presented to the Board of Directors."

The KPMG Report shows that AmSouth's Board at various times enacted written policies and procedures designed to ensure compliance with the BSA and AML regulations. For example, the Board adopted an amended bank-wide "BSA/AML Policy" on July 17, 2003 — four months before AmSouth became aware that it was the target of a government investigation. That policy was produced to plaintiffs in response to their demand to inspect AmSouth's books and records pursuant to section 220 and is included in plaintiffs' appendix. Among other things, the July 17, 2003, BSA/AML Policy directs all AmSouth employees to immediately report suspicious transactions or activity to the BSA/AML Compliance Department or Corporate Security.

COMPLAINT PROPERLY DISMISSED

In this case, the adequacy of the plaintiffs' assertion that demand is excused depends on whether the complaint alleges facts sufficient to show that the defendant *directors* are potentially personally liable for the failure of non-director bank *employees* to file SARs. Delaware courts have recognized that "[m]ost of the decisions that a corporation, acting through its human agents, makes are, of course, not the subject of director attention." Consequently, a claim that directors are subject to personal liability for employee failures is "possibly the most difficult theory in corporation law upon which a plaintiff might hope to win a judgment."

For the plaintiffs' derivative complaint to withstand a motion to dismiss, "only a sustained or systematic failure of the board to exercise oversight — such as an utter failure to attempt to assure a reasonable information and reporting system exists — will establish the lack of good faith that is a necessary condition to liability." As the *Caremark* decision noted:

Such a test of liability — lack of good faith as evidenced by sustained or systematic failure of a director to exercise reasonable oversight — is quite high. But, a demanding test of liability in the oversight context is probably beneficial to corporate shareholders as a class, as it is in the board decision context, since it makes board service by qualified persons more likely, while continuing to act as a stimulus to *good faith performance of duty* by such directors.

The KPMG Report—which the plaintiffs explicitly incorporated by reference into their derivative complaint—refutes the assertion that the directors "never took the necessary steps . . . to ensure that a reasonable BSA compliance and reporting system existed." KPMG's findings reflect that the Board received and approved relevant policies and procedures, delegated to certain employees and departments the responsibility for filing SARs and monitoring compliance, and exercised oversight by relying on periodic reports from them. Although there ultimately may have been failures by employees to report deficiencies to the Board, there is no basis for an oversight claim seeking to hold the directors personally liable for such failures by the employees.

With the benefit of hindsight, the plaintiffs' complaint seeks to equate a bad outcome with bad faith. The lacuna in the plaintiffs' argument is a failure to recognize that the directors' good faith exercise of oversight responsibility may not invariably prevent employees from violating criminal laws, or from causing the corporation to incur significant financial liability, or both, as occurred in *Graham*, *Caremark* and this very case. In the absence of red flags, good faith in the context of oversight must be measured by the directors' actions "to assure a reasonable information and reporting system exists" and not by second-guessing after the occurrence of employee conduct that results in an unintended adverse outcome. Accordingly, we hold that the Court of Chancery properly applied *Caremark* and dismissed the plaintiffs' derivative complaint for failure to excuse demand by alleging particularized facts that created reason to doubt whether the directors had acted in good faith in exercising their oversight responsibilities.

CONCLUSION

The judgment of the Court of Chancery is affirmed.

Questions

1. In footnote 12, the court notes that seven of the defendant directors are outside directors. Of what relevance is that fact to this case?

2. Think about the requirements necessary to find a breach of the duty of loyalty. What does the court's discussion of the duty to act in good faith, and its description of the failure to do so as constituting a breach of loyalty, add to the loyalty doctrine?

3. What does "good faith" mean? Do you think the board's actions here were sufficient to constitute good faith oversight of employees' activities?

4. Delaware law consistently notes that it is distinct and separate from the requirements of federal law, including the federal securities acts. Thus it is perfectly consistent with Delaware jurisprudence that it ignores federal law in this case.

Nonetheless, would the opinion have been better informed, and perhaps more in keeping with modern corporate governance standards, if the court had taken note of the internal controls requirement of section 404 of the Sarbanes-Oxley Act of 2002, and the extraordinary growth of internal control and reporting systems that have developed not only as a result of the disclosure requirements of this section but also as a means of improving corporate governance? Or do the court's statements in the *Disney* opinion regarding the differences between Delaware corporate governance law and best corporate governance practices sufficiently answer the question? Should they?

In re Citigroup Inc. Shareholder Derivative Litigation
964 A.2d 106 (Del. Ch. 2009)

CHANDLER, Chancellor

This is a shareholder derivative action brought on behalf of Citigroup Inc. ("Citigroup" or the "Company"), seeking to recover for the Company its losses arising from exposure to the subprime lending market. Plaintiffs, shareholders of Citigroup, brought this action against current and former directors and officers of Citigroup, alleging, in essence, that the defendants breached their fiduciary duties by failing to properly monitor and manage the risks the Company faced from problems in the subprime lending market and for failing to properly disclose Citigroup's exposure to subprime assets. Plaintiffs allege that there were extensive "red flags" that should have given defendants notice of the problems that were brewing in the real estate and credit markets and that defendants ignored these warnings in the pursuit of short term profits and at the expense of the Company's long term viability.

Plaintiffs further allege that certain defendants are liable to the Company for corporate waste for (1) allowing the Company to purchase $2.7 billion in subprime loans from Accredited Home Lenders in March 2007 and from Ameriquest Home Mortgage in September 2007; (2) authorizing and not suspending the Company's share repurchase program in the first quarter of 2007, which allegedly resulted in the Company buying its own shares at "artificially inflated prices;" (3) approving a multi-million dollar payment and benefit package for defendant Charles Prince, whom plaintiffs describe as largely responsible for Citigroup's problems, upon his retirement as Citigroup's CEO in November 2007; and (4) allowing the Company to invest in structured investment vehicles ("SIVs") that were unable to pay off maturing debt.

. . .

I. BACKGROUND

A. The Parties

Citigroup is a global financial services company whose businesses provide a broad range of financial services to consumers and businesses. Citigroup was incorporated in Delaware in 1988 and maintains its principal executive offices in New York, New York.

Defendants in this action are current and former directors and officers of Citigroup. The complaint names thirteen members of the Citigroup board of directors on November 9, 2007, when the first of plaintiffs' now-consolidated derivative actions was filed. Plaintiffs allege that a majority of the director defendants were members of the Audit and Risk Management Committee ("ARM Committee") in 2007 and were considered audit committee financial experts as defined by the Securities and Exchange Commission.

. . .

B. Citigroup's Exposure to the Subprime Crisis

Plaintiffs allege that since as early as 2006, defendants have caused and allowed Citigroup to engage in subprime lending that ultimately left the Company exposed to massive losses by late 2007. Beginning in late 2005, house prices, which many believe were artificially inflated by speculation and easily available credit, began to plateau, and then deflate. Adjustable rate mortgages issued earlier in the decade began to reset, leaving many homeowners with significantly increased monthly payments. Defaults and foreclosures increased, and assets backed by income from residential mortgages began to decrease in value. By February 2007, subprime mortgage lenders began filing for bankruptcy and subprime mortgages packaged into securities began experiencing increasing levels of delinquency. In mid-2007, rating agencies downgraded bonds backed by subprime mortgages.

Much of Citigroup's exposure to the subprime lending market arose from its involvement with collateralized debt obligations ("CDOs") — repackaged pools of lower rated securities that Citigroup created by acquiring asset-backed securities, including residential mortgage backed securities ("RMBSs"),[4] and then selling rights to the cash flows from the securities in classes, or tranches, with different levels of risk and return. Included with at least some of the CDOs created by Citigroup was a "liquidity put" — an option that allowed the purchasers of the CDOs to sell them back to Citigroup at original value.

According to plaintiffs, Citigroup's alleged $55 billion subprime exposure was in two areas of the Company's Securities & Banking Unit. The first portion totaled $11.7 billion and included securities tied to subprime loans that were being held until they could be added to debt pools for investors. The second portion included $43 billion of super-senior securities, which are portions of CDOs backed in part by RMBS collateral.[5]

By late 2007, it was apparent that Citigroup faced significant losses on its subprime-related assets, including the following as alleged by plaintiffs:

---

4. RMBSs are securities whose cash flows come from residential debt such as mortgages.
5. Rights to cash flows from CDOs are divided into tranches rated by credit risk, whereby the senior tranches are paid before the junior tranches.

October 1, 2007: Citigroup announced it would write-down approximately $1.4 billion on funded and unfunded highly leveraged finance commitments.

October 15, 2007: Citigroup issued a press release reporting a net income of $2.38 billion, a 57% decline from the Company's prior year results.

November 4, 2007: Citigroup announced significant declines on the fair value of the approximately $55 billion in the Company's U.S. subprime-related direct exposures, and estimated that further write downs would be between $8 and $11 billion.

November 6, 2007: Citigroup disclosed that it provided $7.6 billion of emergency financing to the seven SIVs the Company operated after they were unable to repay maturing debt. The SIVs drew on the $10 billion of so-called committed liquidity provided by Citigroup. On December 13, 2007 Citigroup bailed out seven of its affiliated SIVs by bringing $49 billion in assets onto its balance sheet and taking full responsibility for the SIVs' $49 billion worth of assets.

January 15, 2008: Citigroup announced it would take an additional $18.1 billion write-down for the fourth quarter 2007 and a quarterly loss of $9.83 billion. Citigroup also announced that the Company lowered its dividend to $0.32 per share, a 40% decline from the Company's previous dividend disbursement.

By March 2008, Citigroup shares traded below book value and the Company announced that it would lay off an additional 2,000 employees, bringing Citigroup's total layoff since the beginning of the subprime market crisis to more than 6,000.

July 18, 2008: Citigroup announced it lost $2.5 billion in the second quarter, largely caused by $7.2 billion of write-downs of Citigroup's investments in mortgages and other loans and by weakness in the consumer market.

Plaintiffs also allege that Citigroup was exposed to the subprime mortgage market through its use of SIVs. Banks can create SIVs by borrowing cash (by selling commercial paper) and using the proceeds to purchase loans; in other words, the SIVs sell short term debt and buy longer-term, higher yielding assets. According to plaintiffs, Citigroup's SIVs invested in riskier assets, such as home equity loans, rather than the low-risk assets traditionally used by SIVs.

The problems in the subprime market left Citigroup's SIVs unable to pay their investors. The SIVs held subprime mortgages that had decreased in value, and the normally liquid commercial paper market became illiquid. Because the SIVs could no longer meet their cash needs by attracting new investors, they had to sell assets at allegedly "fire sale" prices. In November 2007, Citigroup disclosed that it provided $7.6 billion of emergency financing to the seven SIVs the Company operated after they were unable to repay maturing debt. Ultimately, Citigroup was forced to bail out seven of its affiliated SIVs by bringing $49 billion in assets onto its balance sheet, notwithstanding that Citigroup previously represented that it would manage the SIVs on an arms-length basis.

C. Plaintiffs' Claims

Plaintiffs allege that defendants are liable to the Company for breach of fiduciary duty for (1) failing to adequately oversee and manage Citigroup's exposure to the problems in the subprime mortgage market, even in the face of alleged "red flags" and (2) failing to ensure that the Company's financial reporting and other disclosures were thorough and accurate. As will be more fully explained below, the "red flags" alleged in the eighty-six page Complaint are generally statements from public documents that reflect worsening conditions in the financial markets, including the subprime and credit markets, and the effects those worsening conditions had on market participants, including Citigroup's peers. By way of example only, plaintiffs' "red flags" include the following:

> *May 27, 2005:* Economist Paul Krugman of the *New York Times* said he saw "signs that America's housing market, like the stock market at the end of the last decade, is approaching the final, feverish stages of a speculative bubble."
>
> *May 2006:* Ameriquest Mortgage, one of the United States' leading wholesale subprime lenders, announced the closing of each of its 229 retail offices and reduction of 3,800 employees.
>
> *February 12, 2007:* ResMae Mortgage, a subprime lender, filed for bankruptcy. According to *Bloomberg,* in its Chapter 11 filing, ResMae stated that "[t]he subprime mortgage market has recently been crippled and a number of companies stopped originating loans and United States housing sales have slowed and defaults by borrowers have risen."
>
> *April 18, 2007:* Freddie Mac announced plans to refinance up to $20 billion of loans held by subprime borrowers who would be unable to afford their adjustable-rate mortgages at the reset rate.
>
> *July 10, 2007:* Standard and Poor's and Moody's downgraded bonds backed by subprime mortgages.
>
> *August 1, 2007:* Two hedge funds managed by Bear Stearns that invested heavily in subprime mortgages declared bankruptcy.
>
> *August 9, 2007:* American International Group, one of the largest United States mortgage lenders, warned that mortgage defaults were spreading beyond the subprime sector, with delinquencies becoming more common among borrowers in the category just above subprime.
>
> *October 18, 2007:* Standard & Poor's cut the credit ratings on $23.35 billion of securities backed by pools of home loans that were offered to borrowers during the first half of the year. The downgrades even hit securities rated

AAA, which was the highest of the ten investment-grade ratings and the rating of government debt.

Plaintiffs also allege that the director defendants and certain other defendants are liable to the Company for waste for: (1) allowing the Company to purchase $2.7 billion in subprime loans from Accredited Home Lenders in March 2007 and from Ameriquest Home Mortgage in September 2007; (2) authorizing and not suspending the Company's share repurchase program in the first quarter of 2007, which allegedly resulted in the Company buying its own shares at "artificially inflated prices;" (3) approving a multi-million dollar payment and benefit package for defendant Prince upon his retirement as Citigroup's CEO in November 2007; and (4) allowing the Company to invest in SIVs that were unable to pay off maturing debt.

. . .

III. THE MOTION TO DISMISS UNDER RULE 23.1

A. *The Legal Standard for Demand Excused*

The decision whether to initiate or pursue a lawsuit on behalf of the corporation is generally within the power and responsibility of the board of directors. This follows from the "cardinal precept of the General Corporation Law of the State of Delaware . . . that directors, rather than shareholders, manage the business and affairs of the corporation." Accordingly, in order to cause the corporation to pursue litigation, a shareholder must either (1) make a pre-suit demand by presenting the allegations to the corporation's directors, requesting that they bring suit, and showing that they wrongfully refused to do so, or (2) plead facts showing that demand upon the board would have been futile. Where, as here, a plaintiff does not make a pre-suit demand on the board of directors, the complaint must plead with particularity facts showing that a demand on the board would have been futile. The purpose of the demand requirement is not to insulate defendants from liability; rather, the demand requirement and the strict requirements of factual particularity under Rule 23.1 "exist[] to preserve the primacy of board decisionmaking regarding legal claims belonging to the corporation."

Under the familiar *Aronson* test, to show demand futility, plaintiffs must provide particularized factual allegations that raise a reasonable doubt that "(1) the directors are disinterested and independent [or] (2) the challenged transaction was otherwise the product of a valid exercise of business judgment." Where, however, plaintiffs complain of board inaction and do not challenge a specific decision of the board, there is no "challenged transaction," and the ordinary *Aronson* analysis does not apply. Instead, to show demand futility where the subject of the derivative suit is not a business decision of the board, a plaintiff must allege particularized facts that "create a reasonable doubt that, as of the time the complaint is filed, the board of directors could have properly exercised its independent and disinterested business judgment in responding to a demand."

. . .

... [A]s to the claims for waste . . . , plaintiffs allege that the approval of certain transactions did not constitute a valid exercise of business judgment under the second prong of the *Aronson* test. Plaintiffs allege that demand is futile as [to the other claims] . . . because the director defendants are not able to exercise disinterested business judgment in responding to a demand because their failure of oversight subjects them to a substantial likelihood of personal liability. According to plaintiffs, the director defendants face a substantial threat of personal liability because their conscious disregard of their duties and lack of proper supervision and oversight caused the Company to be overexposed to risk in the subprime mortgage market.

Demand is not excused solely because the directors would be deciding to sue themselves. Rather, demand will be excused based on a possibility of personal director liability only in the rare case when a plaintiff is able to show director conduct that is "so egregious on its face that board approval cannot meet the test of business judgment, and a substantial likelihood of director liability therefore exists."

B. Demand Futility Regarding Plaintiffs' Fiduciary Duty Claims

Plaintiffs' argument is based on a theory of director liability famously articulated by former-Chancellor Allen in *In re Caremark.* Before *Caremark,* in *Graham v. Allis-Chalmers Manufacturing Company,* the Delaware Supreme Court, in response to a theory that the Allis-Chalmers directors were liable because they should have known about employee violations of federal anti-trust laws, held that "absent cause for suspicion there is no duty upon the directors to install and operate a corporate system of espionage to ferret out wrongdoing which they have no reason to suspect exists." Over thirty years later, in the context of approval of a settlement of a class action, former-Chancellor Allen took the opportunity to revisit the duty to monitor under Delaware law. In *Caremark,* the plaintiffs alleged that the directors were liable because they should have known that certain officers and employees were violating the federal Anti-Referral Payments Law. In analyzing these claims, the Court began, appropriately, by reviewing the duty of care and the protections of the business judgment rule.

With regard to director liability standards, the Court distinguished between (1) "*a board decision* that results in a loss because that decision was ill advised or 'negligent'" and (2) "an *unconsidered failure of the board to act* in circumstances in which due attention would, arguably, have prevented the loss." In the former class of cases, director action is analyzed under the business judgment rule, which prevents judicial second guessing of the decision if the directors employed a rational process and considered all material information reasonably available — a standard measured by concepts of gross negligence. . . .

In the latter class of cases, where directors are alleged to be liable for a failure to monitor liability creating activities, the *Caremark* Court, in a reassessment of the holding in *Graham,* stated that while directors could be liable for a failure to monitor, "only a sustained or systematic failure of the board to exercise oversight — such as an utter failure to attempt to assure a reasonable information and reporting system exists-will establish the lack of good faith that is a necessary condition to liability."

In *Stone v. Ritter,* the Delaware Supreme Court approved the *Caremark* standard for director oversight liability and made clear that liability was based on the concept of good faith, which the *Stone* Court held was embedded in the fiduciary duty of loyalty and did not constitute a freestanding fiduciary duty that could independently give rise to liability. As the *Stone* Court explained:

> *Caremark* articulates the necessary conditions predicate for director oversight liability: (a) the directors utterly failed to implement any reporting or information system or controls; *or* (b) having implemented such a system or controls, consciously failed to monitor or oversee its operations thus disabling themselves from being informed of risks or problems requiring their attention. In either case, imposition of liability requires a showing that the directors knew that they were not discharging their fiduciary obligations. Where directors fail to act in the face of a known duty to act, thereby demonstrating a conscious disregard for their responsibilities, they breach their duty of loyalty by failing to discharge that fiduciary obligation in good faith.

Thus, to establish oversight liability a plaintiff must show that the directors *knew* they were not discharging their fiduciary obligations or that the directors demonstrated a *conscious* disregard for their responsibilities such as by failing to act in the face of a known duty to act. The test is rooted in concepts of bad faith; indeed, a showing of bad faith is a *necessary condition* to director oversight liability.

1. Plaintiffs' *Caremark* Allegations

Plaintiffs' theory of how the director defendants will face personal liability is a bit of a twist on the traditional *Caremark* claim. In a typical *Caremark* case, plaintiffs argue that the defendants are liable for damages that arise from a failure to properly monitor or oversee employee misconduct or violations of law. For example, in *Caremark* the board allegedly failed to monitor employee actions in violation of the federal Anti-Referral Payments Law; in *Stone,* the directors were charged with a failure of oversight that resulted in liability for the company because of employee violations of the federal Bank Secrecy Act.

In contrast, plaintiffs' *Caremark* claims are based on defendants' alleged failure to properly monitor Citigroup's *business risk,* specifically its exposure to the subprime mortgage market. In their answering brief, plaintiffs allege that the director defendants are personally liable under *Caremark* for failing to "make a good faith attempt to follow the procedures put in place or fail[ing] to assure that adequate and proper corporate information and reporting systems existed that would enable them to be fully informed regarding Citigroup's risk to the subprime mortgage market." Plaintiffs point to so-called "red flags" that should have put defendants on notice of the problems in the subprime mortgage market and further allege that the board should have been especially conscious of these red flags because a majority of the directors

(1) served on the Citigroup board during its previous Enron related conduct and (2) were members of the ARM Committee and considered financial experts.

Although these claims are framed by plaintiffs as *Caremark* claims, plaintiffs' theory essentially amounts to a claim that the director defendants should be personally liable to the Company because they failed to fully recognize the risk posed by subprime securities. When one looks past the lofty allegations of duties of oversight and red flags used to dress up these claims, what is left appears to be plaintiff shareholders attempting to hold the director defendants personally liable for making (or allowing to be made) business decisions that, in hindsight, turned out poorly for the Company. Delaware Courts have faced these types of claims many times and have developed doctrines to deal with them—the fiduciary duty of care and the business judgment rule. These doctrines properly focus on the decision-making process rather than on a substantive evaluation of the merits of the decision. This follows from the inadequacy of the Court, due in part to a concept known as hindsight bias, to properly evaluate whether corporate decision-makers made a "right" or "wrong" decision.

The business judgment rule "is a presumption that in making a business decision the directors of a corporation acted on an informed basis, in good faith and in the honest belief that the action taken was in the best interests of the company." The burden is on plaintiffs, the party challenging the directors' decision, to rebut this presumption. Thus, absent an allegation of interestedness or disloyalty to the corporation, the business judgment rule prevents a judge or jury from second guessing director decisions if they were the product of a rational process and the directors availed themselves of all material and reasonably available information. The standard of director liability under the business judgment rule "is predicated upon concepts of gross negligence."

Additionally, Citigroup has adopted a provision in its certificate of incorporation pursuant to 8 Del. C. § 102(b)(7) that exculpates directors from personal liability for violations of fiduciary duty, except for, among other things, breaches of the duty of loyalty or actions or omissions not in good faith or that involve intentional misconduct or a knowing violation of law. Because the director defendants are "exculpated from liability for certain conduct, 'then a serious threat of liability may only be found to exist if the plaintiff pleads a *non-exculpated* claim against the directors based on particularized facts.'" Here, plaintiffs have not alleged that the directors were interested in the transaction and instead root their theory of director personal liability in bad faith.

The Delaware Supreme Court has stated that bad faith conduct may be found where a director "intentionally acts with a purpose other than that of advancing the best interests of the corporation, . . . acts with the intent to violate applicable positive law, or . . . intentionally fails to act in the face of a known duty to act, demonstrating a conscious disregard for his duties." More recently, the Delaware Supreme Court held that when a plaintiff seeks to show that demand is excused because directors face a substantial likelihood of liability where "directors are exculpated from liability except for claims based on 'fraudulent,' 'illegal' or 'bad faith' conduct, a plaintiff must also plead particularized facts that demonstrate that the directors acted with scienter, *i.e.,* that they had 'actual or constructive knowledge' that their conduct was legally improper." A plaintiff can thus plead bad faith by alleging with particularity that a director *knowingly* violated a fiduciary duty or failed to act in violation of a *known* duty to act, demonstrating a *conscious* disregard for her duties.

Turning now specifically to plaintiffs' *Caremark* claims, one can see a similarity between the standard for assessing oversight liability and the standard for assessing a disinterested director's decision under the duty of care when the company has adopted an exculpatory provision pursuant to § 102(b)(7). In either case, a plaintiff can show that the director defendants will be liable if their acts or omissions constitute bad faith. A plaintiff can show bad faith conduct by, for example, properly alleging particularized facts that show that a director *consciously* disregarded an obligation to be reasonably informed about the business and its risks or *consciously* disregarded the duty to monitor and oversee the business.

The Delaware Supreme Court made clear in *Stone* that directors of Delaware corporations have certain responsibilities to implement and monitor a system of oversight; however, this obligation does not eviscerate the core protections of the business judgment rule—protections designed to allow corporate managers and directors to pursue risky transactions without the specter of being held personally liable if those decisions turn out poorly. Accordingly, the burden required for a plaintiff to rebut the presumption of the business judgment rule by showing gross negligence is a difficult one, and the burden to show bad faith is even higher. Additionally, as former-Chancellor Allen noted in *Caremark,* director liability based on the duty of oversight "is possibly the most difficult theory in corporation law upon which a plaintiff might hope to win a judgment." The presumption of the business judgment rule, the protection of an exculpatory § 102(b)(7) provision, and the difficulty of proving a *Caremark* claim together function to place an extremely high burden on a plaintiff to state a claim for personal director liability for a failure to see the extent of a company's business risk.

To the extent the Court allows shareholder plaintiffs to succeed on a theory that a director is liable for a failure to monitor business risk, the Court risks undermining the well settled policy of Delaware law by inviting Courts to perform a hindsight evaluation of the reasonableness or prudence of directors' business decisions. Risk has been defined as the chance that a return on an investment will be different that expected. The essence of the business judgment of managers and directors is deciding how the company will evaluate the trade-off between risk and return. Businesses—and particularly financial institutions—make returns by taking on risk; a company or investor that is willing to take on more risk can earn a higher return. Thus, in almost any business transaction, the parties go into the deal with the knowledge that, even if they have evaluated the situation correctly, the return could be different than they expected.

It is almost impossible for a court, in hindsight, to determine whether the directors of a company properly evaluated risk and thus made the "right" business decision. In any investment there is a chance that returns will turn out lower than expected, and generally a smaller chance that they will be far lower than expected. When investments turn out poorly, it is possible that the decision-maker evaluated the deal correctly but got "unlucky" in that a huge loss—the probability of which was very small—actually happened. It is also possible that the decision-maker improperly evaluated the risk posed by an investment and that the company suffered large losses as a result.

Business decision-makers must operate in the real world, with imperfect information, limited resources, and an uncertain future. To impose liability on directors for making a "wrong" business decision would cripple their ability to earn returns for investors by taking business risks. Indeed, this kind of judicial second guessing is what the business judgment rule was designed to prevent, and even if a complaint is framed under a *Caremark* theory, this Court will not abandon such bedrock principles of Delaware fiduciary duty law. With these considerations and the difficult standard required to show director oversight liability in mind, I turn to an evaluation of the allegations in the Complaint.

a. The Complaint Does Not Properly Allege Demand Futility for Plaintiffs' Fiduciary Duty Claims

In this case, plaintiffs allege that the defendants are liable for failing to properly monitor the risk that Citigroup faced from subprime securities. While it may be possible for a plaintiff to meet the burden under some set of facts, plaintiffs in this case have failed to state a *Caremark* claim sufficient to excuse demand based on a theory that the directors did not fulfill their oversight obligations by failing to monitor the business risk of the company.

The allegations in the Complaint amount essentially to a claim that Citigroup suffered large losses and that there were certain warning signs that could or should have put defendants on notice of the business risks related to Citigroup's investments in subprime assets. Plaintiffs then conclude that because defendants failed to prevent the Company's losses associated with certain business risks, they must have consciously ignored these warning signs or knowingly failed to monitor the Company's risk in accordance with their fiduciary duties. Such conclusory allegations, however, are not sufficient to state a claim for failure of oversight that would give rise to a substantial likelihood of personal liability, which would require particularized factual allegations demonstrating bad faith by the director defendants.

Plaintiffs do not contest that Citigroup had procedures and controls in place that were designed to monitor risk. Plaintiffs admit that Citigroup established the ARM Committee and in 2004 amended the ARM Committee charter to include the fact that one of the purposes of the ARM Committee was to assist the board in fulfilling its oversight responsibility relating to policy standards and guidelines for risk assessment and risk management. The ARM Committee was also charged with, among other things, (1) discussing with management and independent auditors the annual audited financial statements, (2) reviewing with management an evaluation of Citigroup's internal control structure, and (3) discussing with management Citigroup's major credit, market, liquidity, and operational risk exposures and the steps taken by management to monitor and control such exposures, including Citigroup's risk assessment and risk management policies. According to plaintiffs' own allegations, the ARM Committee met eleven times in 2006 and twelve times in 2007.

Plaintiffs nevertheless argue that the director defendants breached their duty of oversight either because the oversight mechanisms were not adequate or because the director defendants did not make a good faith effort to comply with the established oversight procedures. To support this claim, the Complaint alleges numerous facts that plaintiffs argue should have put the director defendants on notice of the impending problems in the subprime mortgage market and Citigroup's exposure thereto. Plaintiffs summarized some of these "red flags" in their answering brief as follows:

> the steady decline of the housing market and the impact the collapsing bubble would have on mortgages and subprime backed securities since as early as 2005;
>
> December 2005 guidance from the FASB staff—"The FASB staff is aware of loan products whose contractual features may increase the exposure of the originator, holder, investor, guarantor, or servicer to risk of nonpayment or realization.";
>
> the drastic rise in foreclosure rates starting in 2006;
>
> several large subprime lenders reporting substantial losses and filing for bankruptcy starting in 2006;
>
> billions of dollars in losses reported by Citigroup's peers, such as Bear Stearns and Merrill Lynch.

Plaintiffs argue that demand is excused because a majority of the director defendants face a substantial likelihood of personal liability because they were charged with management of Citigroup's risk as members of the ARM Committee and as audit committee financial experts and failed to properly oversee and monitor such risk. As explained above, however, to establish director oversight liability plaintiffs would ultimately have to prove bad faith conduct by the director defendants. Plaintiffs fail to plead any particularized factual allegations that raise a reasonable doubt that the director defendants acted in good faith.

The warning signs alleged by plaintiffs are not evidence that the directors consciously disregarded their duties or otherwise acted in bad faith; at most they evidence that the directors made bad business decisions. The "red flags" in the Complaint amount to little more than portions of public documents that reflected the worsening conditions in the subprime mortgage market and in the economy generally. Plaintiffs fail to plead "particularized facts suggesting that the Board was presented with 'red flags' alerting it to potential misconduct" at the Company. That the director defendants knew of signs of a deterioration in the subprime mortgage market, or even signs suggesting that conditions could decline further, is not sufficient to show that the directors were or should have been aware of any wrongdoing at the Company or were consciously disregarding a duty somehow to prevent Citigroup from suffering losses. Nothing about plaintiffs' "red flags" supports plaintiffs' conclusory allegation that "defendants have not made a good faith attempt to assure that adequate and proper corporate information and reporting systems existed that would enable them to be fully informed regarding Citigroup's risk to the subprime mortgage market." Indeed, plaintiffs' allegations do not even specify how the board's oversight mechanisms were inadequate or how the director defendants knew of these inadequacies and consciously ignored them. Rather, plaintiffs seem to hope the Court will accept the conclusion that since the Company suffered large losses, and since a properly functioning risk management system would have avoided such losses, the directors must have breached their fiduciary duties in allowing such losses.

Moving from such general ipse dixit syllogisms to the more specific, plaintiffs argue that the director defendants, and especially those nine directors who were on the board at the time, "should have been especially sensitive to the red flags in the marketplace in light of the Company's prior involvement in the Enron Corporation debacle and other financial scandals earlier in the decade." Plaintiffs also allege that the director defendants should have been especially alert to the dangers of transactions involving SIVs because SIVs were involved in Citigroup's transactions with Enron that resulted in liability for the Company. Plaintiffs allege that Citigroup helped finance transactions that allowed Enron to hide its true financial condition and resulted in Citigroup paying approximately $120 million in penalties and disgorgement as well as agreeing to new risk management procedures designed to prevent similar conduct.

Plaintiffs fail in their attempt to impose some sort of higher standard of liability on the director defendants that were on Citigroup's board at the time of its involvement with Enron. They have utterly failed to show how Citigroup's involvement with the financial scandals at Enron has any relevance to Citigroup's investments in subprime securities. Plaintiffs cite *McCall v. Scott* to support the proposition that directors who were on the board during previous misconduct should be sensitive to similar circumstances which had previously prompted investigations. That case, however, actually shows how plaintiffs' attempt to impose a higher standard on the directors because of the Enron scandal is inadequate. Unlike here, the plaintiffs in *McCall* alleged numerous specific instances of widespread, prevalent wrongdoing throughout the company and the mechanisms by which the wrongdoing came to the board's attention. The Sixth Circuit in *McCall* did *not,* as plaintiffs assert, hold that alleged prior, *unrelated* wrongdoing would make directors "sensitive to similar circumstances." Unlike plaintiffs' allegations about Enron, the prior "experience" referenced in *McCall* was an investigation and settlement for the *same type* of questionable billing practices before the Sixth Circuit. Plaintiffs have not shown how involvement with the Enron related scandals should have in any way put the director defendants on a heightened alert to problems in the subprime mortgage market. Additionally, the use of SIVs in the Enron related conduct would not serve to put the director defendants on any type of heightened notice to the unrelated use of SIVs in structuring transactions involving subprime securities.

The Complaint and plaintiffs' answering brief repeatedly make the conclusory allegation that the defendants have breached their duty of oversight, but nowhere do plaintiffs adequately explain what the director defendants actually did or failed to do that would constitute such a violation. Even while admitting that Citigroup had a risk monitoring system in place, plaintiffs seem to conclude that, because the director defendants (and the ARM Committee members in particular) were charged with monitoring Citigroup's risk, then they must be found liable because Citigroup experienced losses as a result of exposure to the subprime mortgage market. The only factual support plaintiffs provide for this conclusion are "red flags" that actually amount to nothing more than signs of continuing deterioration in the subprime mortgage market. These types of conclusory allegations are exactly the kinds of allegations that do not state a claim for relief under *Caremark*.

To recognize such claims under a theory of director oversight liability would undermine the long established protections of the business judgment rule. It is well established that the mere fact that a company takes on business risk and suffers losses — even catastrophic losses — does not evidence misconduct, and without more, is not a basis for personal director liability. That there were signs in the market that reflected worsening conditions and suggested that conditions may deteriorate even further is not an invitation for this Court to disregard the presumptions of the business judgment rule and conclude that the directors are liable because they did not properly evaluate business risk. What plaintiffs are asking the Court to conclude from the presence of these "red flags" is that the directors failed to see the extent of Citigroup's business risk and therefore made a "wrong" business decision by allowing Citigroup to be exposed to the subprime mortgage market.

This Court's recent decision in *American International Group, Inc. Consolidated Derivative Litigation* demonstrates the stark contrast between the allegations here and allegations that are sufficient to survive a motion to dismiss. In *AIG*, the Court faced a motion to dismiss a complaint that included "well-pled allegations of pervasive, diverse, and substantial financial fraud involving managers at the highest levels of AIG." In concluding that the complaint stated a claim for relief under Rule 12(b)(6), the Court held that the factual allegations in the complaint were sufficient to support an inference that AIG executives running those divisions knew of and approved much of the wrongdoing. The Court reasoned that huge fraudulent schemes were unlikely to be perpetrated without the knowledge of the executive in charge of that division of the company. Unlike the allegations in this case, the defendants in *AIG* allegedly failed to exercise reasonable oversight over pervasive *fraudulent* and *criminal* conduct. Indeed, the Court in *AIG* even stated that the complaint there supported the assertion that top AIG officials were leading a "criminal organization" and that "[t]he diversity, pervasiveness, and materiality of the alleged financial wrongdoing at AIG is extraordinary."

Contrast the *AIG* claims with the claims in this case. Here plaintiffs argue that the Complaint supports the reasonable conclusion that the director defendants acted in bad faith by failing to see the warning signs of a deterioration in the subprime mortgage market and failing to cause Citigroup to change its investment policy to limit its exposure to the subprime market. Director oversight duties are designed to ensure reasonable reporting and information systems exist that would allow directors to know about and prevent wrongdoing that could cause losses for the Company. There are significant differences between failing to oversee employee fraudulent or criminal conduct and failing to recognize the extent of a Company's business risk. Directors should, indeed must under Delaware law, ensure that reasonable information and reporting systems exist that would put them on notice of fraudulent or criminal conduct within the company. Such oversight programs allow directors to intervene and prevent frauds or other wrongdoing that could expose the company to risk of loss as a result of such conduct. While it may be tempting to say that directors have the same duties to monitor and oversee business risk, imposing *Caremark*-type duties on directors to monitor business risk is fundamentally different. Citigroup was in the business of taking on and managing investment and other business risks. To impose oversight liability on directors for failure to monitor "excessive" risk would involve courts in conducting hindsight evaluations of decisions at the heart of the business judgment of directors. Oversight duties under Delaware law are not designed to subject directors, even expert directors, to *personal liability* for failure to predict the future and to properly evaluate business risk.

Instead of alleging facts that could demonstrate bad faith on the part of the directors, by presenting the Court with the so called "red flags," plaintiffs are inviting the Court to engage in the exact kind of judicial second guessing that is proscribed by the business judgment rule. In any business decision that turns out poorly there will likely be signs that one could point to and argue are evidence that the decision was wrong. Indeed, it is tempting in a case with such staggering losses for one to think that they could have made the "right" decision if they had been in the directors' position. This temptation, however, is one of the reasons for the presumption against an objective review of business decisions by judges, a presumption that is no less applicable when the losses to the Company are large.

2. Plaintiffs' Disclosure Allegations

Plaintiffs argue that demand is excused as futile because the director defendants face a substantial likelihood of personal liability for violating their duty of disclosure and would therefore be unable to exercise independent and disinterested business judgment in responding to a demand. Plaintiffs allege that the director defendants violated their duty of disclosure by, among other things, failing to properly disclose the value of certain financial instruments, placing underperforming assets in SIVs without fully disclosing the risk that Citigroup might have to bring the assets back onto its balance sheet, and failing to properly account for guarantees, specifically the liquidity puts that allowed buyers of CDOs to sell the products back to Citigroup at face value. Plaintiffs argue that the "red flags" alleged in the Complaint lead to a reasonable inference that the director defendants, and particularly the ARM Committee members, knew that certain disclosures regarding the Company's exposure to subprime assets were misleading.

"[E]ven in the absence of a request for shareholder action, shareholders are entitled to honest communication from directors, given with complete candor and in good faith." When there is no request for shareholder action, a shareholder plaintiff can demonstrate a breach of fiduciary duty by showing that the directors "*deliberately* misinform[ed] shareholders about the business of the corporation, either directly or by a public statement." Citigroup's certificate of incorporation exculpates the director defendants from personal liability for violations of fiduciary duty except for, among other things, breaches of the duty of loyalty and acts or omissions not in good faith or that involve intentional misconduct or knowing violation of law. Thus, to show a substantial likelihood of liability that would excuse demand, plaintiffs must plead particularized factual allegations that "support the inference that the disclosure violation was made in bad faith, knowingly or intentionally." Additionally, directors of Delaware corporations are fully protected in relying in good faith on the reports of officers and experts.

The factual allegations in the Complaint are not sufficient to allow me to reasonably conclude that the director defendants face a substantial likelihood of liability that would prevent them from impartially considering a demand. This is so for at least three reasons. First, plaintiffs fail to allege with sufficient specificity the actual misstatements or omissions that constituted a violation of the board's duty of disclosure. The Complaint merely alleges, in general and conclusory terms, that the director defendants did not adequately disclose certain risks faced by the Company—for example, the risks posed by Citigroup's SIVs and the liquidity puts that allowed purchasers of CDOs to sell the instruments back to Citigroup at face value. The Complaint does not identify any actual disclosure that was misleading or any statement that was made misleading as a result of an omission of a material fact. Instead, plaintiffs allege, for instance, that the Citigroup board "abdicated its fiduciary duties by not disclosing information on the fair value of VIEs, CDOs and SIVs" and that "the ARM Committee abdicated its fiduciary duties ... to ensure the integrity of Citigroup's financial statements and financial reporting process, including earnings press releases and financial information provided to analysts and rating agencies."

In other words, the disclosure allegations in the complaint do not meet the stringent standard of factual particularity required under Rule 23.1. They fail to allege with particularity which disclosures were misleading, when the Company was obligated to make disclosures, what specifically the Company was obligated to disclose, and how the Company failed to do so. This information is critical because to establish a threat of director liability based on a disclosure violation, plaintiffs must plead facts that show that the violation was made knowingly or in bad faith, a showing that requires allegations regarding what the directors knew and when. Without knowing when and how the alleged disclosure violations occurred, it is impossible to determine if the directors made the misstatements or omissions knowingly or in bad faith. As a result, the disclosure allegations in the complaint do not meet the stringent requirements of factual particularity under Rule 23.1.

Second, the Complaint does not contain specific factual allegations that reasonably suggest sufficient board involvement in the preparation of the disclosures that would allow me to reasonably conclude that the director defendants face a substantial likelihood of personal liability. Plaintiffs do not allege facts suggesting that the director defendants prepared the financial statements or that they were directly responsible for the misstatements or omissions. The Complaint merely alleges that Citigroup's financial statements contained false statements and material omissions and that the director defendants reviewed the financial statements pursuant to their responsibilities under the ARM Committee charter. Thus, I am unable to reasonably conclude that the director defendants face a substantial likelihood of liability.

Third, and perhaps most importantly, the Complaint does not sufficiently allege that the director defendants had knowledge that any disclosures or omissions were false or misleading or that the director defendants acted in bad faith in not adequately informing themselves. Plaintiffs have not alleged particular facts showing that the director defendants were even aware of any misstatements or omissions. Instead, plaintiffs conclusorily assert that the members of the ARM Committee, as financial experts, knew the relevant accounting standards, knew or should have known the extent of the Company's exposure to the subprime mortgage market, and are therefore responsible for alleged false statements or omissions in Citigroup's financial statements. Instead of providing factual allegations regarding the knowledge or bad faith of the individual director defendants, the Complaint makes broad group allegations about the director defendants or the members of the ARM Committee. A determination of whether the alleged misleading statements or omissions were made with knowledge or in bad faith requires an analysis of the state of mind of the individual director defendants, and plaintiffs have not made specific factual allegations that would allow for such an inquiry. Plaintiffs' alleged "red flags," which amount to nothing more than indications of worsening economic conditions, do not support a reasonable inference that the director defendants approved or disseminated the financial disclosures knowingly or in bad faith. Merely alleging that there were signs of problems in the subprime mortgage market is not sufficient to show that the director defendants knew that Citigroup's disclosures were false or misleading. The allegations are not sufficiently specific to Citigroup or to the director defendants to meet the strict pleading requirements of Rule 23.1.

Although the members of the ARM Committee were charged with reviewing and ensuring the accuracy of Citigroup's financial statements under the ARM Committee charter, director liability is not measured by the aspirational standard established by the internal documents detailing a company's oversight system. Under our law, to establish liability for misstatements when the board is not seeking shareholder action, shareholder plaintiffs must show that the misstatement was made knowingly or in bad faith. Additionally, even board members who are experts are fully protected under § 141(e) in relying in good faith on the opinions and statements of the corporation's officers and employees who were responsible for preparing the company's financial statements. Plaintiffs' allegations that the members of the ARM Committee were financial experts and were aware of the "red flags" alleged in the Complaint do not support a reasonable inference that the director defendants' reliance on the officers and experts who prepared the financial statements was not in good faith.

Even accepting plaintiffs' allegations as true, the Complaint fails to plead with particularity facts that would lead to the reasonable inference that the director defendants made or allowed to be made any false statements or material omissions with knowledge or in bad faith. Accordingly, plaintiffs have failed to plead with particularity facts creating a reasonable doubt that the director defendants face a threat of personal liability that would render them incapable of exercising independent and disinterested business judgment in responding to a demand. Plaintiffs' disclosure claims are therefore dismissed pursuant to Rule 23.1

C. Demand Futility Allegations Regarding Plaintiffs' Waste Claims

Count III of the Complaint alleges that certain of the defendants are liable for waste for (1) approving the Letter Agreement dated November 4, 2007 between Citigroup and defendant Prince; (2) allowing the Company to purchase over $2.7 billion in subprime loans from Accredited Home Lenders at one of its "fire sales" in March 2007 and from Ameriquest Home Mortgage in September 2007; (3) approving the buyback of over $645 million worth of the Company's shares at artificially inflated prices pursuant to a repurchase program in early 2007; and (4) allowing the Company to invest in SIVs that were unable to pay off maturing debt.

Demand futility is analyzed under *Aronson* when plaintiffs have challenged board action or approval of a transaction. With regard to the claims based on the approval of the Letter Agreement and the repurchase of Citigroup stock, plaintiffs do not argue that a majority of the director defendants were not disinterested and independent. Rather, plaintiffs argue that demand is excused under the second prong of the *Aronson* analysis, which requires that the plaintiffs plead particularized factual allegations that raise a reasonable doubt at to whether "the challenged transaction was otherwise the product of a valid exercise of business judgment."

Delaware law provides stringent requirements for a plaintiff to state a claim for corporate waste, and to excuse demand on grounds of waste the Complaint must allege particularized facts that lead to a reasonable inference that the director defendants authorized "an exchange that is so one sided that no business person of ordinary, sound judgment could conclude that the corporation has received adequate consideration." The test to show corporate waste is difficult for any plaintiff to meet; indeed, "[t]o prevail on a waste claim ... the plaintiff must overcome the general presumption of good faith by showing that the board's decision was so egregious or irrational that it could not have been based on a valid assessment of the corporation's best interests."

1. Approval of the Stock Repurchase Program

Plaintiffs' claim for waste for the board's approval of the stock repurchase program falls far short of satisfying the standard for demand futility. Plaintiffs allege that "in spite of its prior buybacks below $50 per share and in spite of the Company's expanding losses and declining stock price, Citigroup repurchased 12.1 million shares during the first quarter of 2007 at an average price of $53.37." Plaintiffs then claim that at the time the buyback of Citigroup stock was halted, the stock was trading at $46 per share. Plaintiffs conclude that the director defendants "authorized and did not suspend the Company's share repurchase program, which resulted in the Company's buying back over $645 million worth of the Company's shares at artificially inflated prices."

Specifically, plaintiffs argue the following:

> As set forth in the Complaint, the Director Defendants recklessly failed to consider and account for the subprime lending crisis, the Company's exposure to falling CDO values by virtue of its liquidity puts, and the collective impact on the Company's billions in warehoused subprime loans. Consequently, the Director Defendants are not entitled to the presumption of business judgment and are liable for waste for approving the buyback of over $645 million worth of the Company's shares at artificially inflated prices pursuant to the repurchase program. Under the circumstances, the repurchase program should have been suspended, and would have saved the Company hundreds of millions of dollars. The magnitude of the Director Defendants' utter failure to properly inform themselves of the Company's dire straits has only been highlighted by the Company's recent historically low share prices.

To say the least, this argument demonstrates that the Complaint utterly fails to state a claim for waste for the board's approval of the stock repurchase. Plaintiffs seem to completely ignore the standard governing corporate waste under Delaware law — a standard that requires that plaintiffs plead facts overcoming the presumption of good faith by showing "an exchange that is so one sided that no business person of ordinary, sound judgment could conclude that the corporation has received adequate consideration." Plaintiffs attempted to meet this standard by alleging that the director defendants approved a repurchase of Citigroup stock *at the market price*. Other than a conclusory allegation, plaintiffs have alleged nothing that would explain how buying stock at the market price — the price at which presumably ordinary and rational businesspeople were trading the stock — could possibly be so one sided that no reasonable and ordinary business person would consider it adequate consideration. Again, plaintiffs merely allege "red flags" and then conclude that the board is liable for waste because Citigroup repurchased its stock before the stock dropped in price as a result of Citigroup's losses from exposure to the subprime market. In short, the

Complaint states no particularized facts that would lead to any inference that the board's approval of the stock repurchase constituted corporate waste. Accordingly, plaintiffs have not adequately alleged demand futility as to this claim pursuant to Rule 23.1.

2. Approval of the Letter Agreement

Plaintiffs allege that the board's approval of the November 4, 2007 letter agreement constituted corporate waste. Because approval of the letter was board action, demand is evaluated under the *Aronson* standard. Plaintiffs claim that demand is excused under the second prong of *Aronson* because the particularized factual allegations in the Complaint raise a reasonable doubt as to whether the approval was "the product of a valid exercise of business judgment."

The directors of a Delaware corporation have the authority and broad discretion to make executive compensation decisions. The standard under which the Court evaluates a waste claim is whether there was "an exchange of corporate assets for consideration so disproportionately small as to lie beyond the range at which any reasonable person might be willing to trade." It is also well settled in our law, however, that the discretion of directors in setting executive compensation is not unlimited. Indeed, the Delaware Supreme Court was clear when it stated that "there is an outer limit" to the board's discretion to set executive compensation, "at which point a decision of the directors on executive compensation is so disproportionately large as to be unconscionable and constitute waste."

According to plaintiffs' allegations, the November 4, 2007 letter agreement provides that Prince will receive $68 million upon his departure from Citigroup, including bonus, salary, and accumulated stockholdings. Additionally, the letter agreement provides that Prince will receive from Citigroup an office, an administrative assistant, and a car and driver for the lesser of five years or until he commences full time employment with another employer. Plaintiffs allege that this compensation package constituted waste and met the "so one sided" standard because, in part, the Company paid the multi-million dollar compensation package to a departing CEO whose failures as CEO were allegedly responsible, in part, for billions of dollars of losses at Citigroup. In exchange for the multi-million dollar benefits and perquisites package provided for in the letter agreement, the letter agreement contemplated that Prince would sign a non-compete agreement, a non-disparagement agreement, a non-solicitation agreement, and a release of claims against the Company. Even considering the text of the letter agreement, I am left with very little information regarding (1) how much additional compensation Prince actually received as a result of the letter agreement and (2) the real value, if any, of the various promises given by Prince. Without more information and taking, as I am required, plaintiffs' well pleaded allegations as true, there is a reasonable doubt as to whether the letter agreement meets the admittedly stringent "so one sided" standard or whether the letter agreement awarded compensation that is beyond the "outer limit" described by the Delaware Supreme Court. Accordingly, the Complaint has adequately alleged, pursuant to

Rule 23.1, that demand is excused with regard to the waste claim based on the board's approval of Prince's compensation under the letter agreement.

D. The Motion to Dismiss under Rule 12(b)(6)

The only claim as to which plaintiffs adequately pleaded demand futility is the claim for corporate waste for the board's approval of the letter agreement granting a multi-million dollar compensation package to Prince upon his departure as Citigroup's CEO. . . .

. . .

IV. CONCLUSION

Citigroup has suffered staggering losses, in part, as a result of the recent problems in the United States economy, particularly those in the subprime mortgage market. It is understandable that investors, and others, want to find someone to hold responsible for these losses, and it is often difficult to distinguish between a desire to blame *someone* and a desire to force those responsible to account for their wrongdoing. Our law, fortunately, provides guidance for precisely these situations in the form of doctrines governing the duties owed by officers and directors of Delaware corporations. This law has been refined over hundreds of years, which no doubt included many crises, and we must not let our desire to blame someone for our losses make us lose sight of the purpose of our law. Ultimately, the discretion granted directors and managers allows them to maximize shareholder value in the long term by taking risks without the debilitating fear that they will be held personally liable if the company experiences losses. This doctrine also means, however, that when the company suffers losses, shareholders may not be able to hold the directors personally liable.

. . . Defendants' motion to dismiss is denied as to the claim in Count III of the Complaint for waste for approval of the November 4, 2007 Prince letter agreement. All other claims in the complaint are dismissed for failure to adequately plead demand futility pursuant to Court of Chancery Rule 23.1.

An Order has been entered consistent with this Opinion.

Questions

1. According to Chancellor Chandler, the complaint did not raise a Caremark claim. Why? Do you agree with his analysis?

2. Given Citigroup's business, should its board of directors be subject to heightened duties, especially with respect to market risk?

3. What is the standard of good faith after *Citigroup*? How is it likely to be applied in cases involving the duty to monitor? What about cases involving directors' decisions?

In re China Agritech, Inc. Shareholder Derivative Litigation
2013 WL 2181514, 2013 Del. Ch. LEXIS 132

MEMORANDUM OPINION

Laster, Vice Chancellor

China Agritech, Inc. ("China Agritech" or the "Company") purportedly operates a fertilizer manufacturing business in China. According to lead plaintiff Albert Rish, China Agritech is a fraud that serves only to enrich its co-founders, defendants Yu Chang and Xiao Rong Teng. Rish has sued derivatively to recover damages resulting from (i) the Company's purchase of stock from a corporation owned by Chang and Teng, (ii) the suspected misuse of $23 million raised by the Company in a secondary offering, (iii) the mismanagement that occurred during a remarkable twenty-four month period that witnessed the terminations of two outside auditing firms and the resignations of six outside directors and two senior officers, and (iv) the Company's failure to make any federal securities filings since November 2010 and concomitant delisting by NASDAQ. Before filing suit, Rish used Section 220 of the General Corporation Law, 8 Del. C. § 220, to obtain books and records, and his complaint relies both on materials that the Company produced and on the glaring absence from the production of books and records that the Company should have readily possessed and provided.

The defendants have moved to dismiss pursuant to Rule 23.1, contending that the complaint fails to plead that demand was made on the board or would have been futile. The defendants also have moved to dismiss pursuant to Rule 12(b)(6), contending that the complaint fails to state a claim on which relief can be granted. Alternatively, the defendants argue that the litigation should be stayed. The motions are denied.

I. FACTUAL BACKGROUND

. . .

A. China Agritech

According to its public filings, China Agritech is a Delaware corporation that develops, manufactures, and markets environmentally friendly fertilizer products in the People's Republic of China. The Company accessed the domestic securities markets in February 2005 through a reverse merger with an inactive corporation that had retained its NASDAQ listing. "[U]sing a defunct Delaware corporation that happens to retain a public listing to evade the regulatory regime established by the federal securities laws is contrary to Delaware public policy." *Williams v. Calypso Wireless, Inc.*, 2012 WL 424880, at *1 n. 1 (Del. Ch. Feb. 8, 2012). . . .

Defendant Chang founded China Agritech. Chang has served as the Company's President, Chief Executive Officer, Secretary, and Chairman of the board since February 2005. He owns approximately 55% of China Agritech's outstanding common stock, holding 34.1% directly and another 20.8% beneficially through China Tailong

Group Limited. By virtue of his stock ownership and positions with the Company, Chang controls China Agritech.

Defendant Teng co-founded China Agritech. Teng has served as a director of the Company since June 2005. From February 3, 2005 until March 13, 2009, she served as the Company's Chief Operating Officer. She owns 1.68% of the Company's common stock directly.

In addition to the China Agritech stock that they hold individually, Chang and Teng own 85% and 15%, respectively, of Sammi Holdings Limited. This entity owns another 8.4% of the Company's outstanding common stock.

B. Problems With Internal Controls

In its Form 10-K for the year ending December 31, 2007, filed with the SEC on March 28, 2008, the Company disclosed that it "did not have in place the financial controls and procedures required to comply with U.S. financial reporting standards." The Company reiterated this disclosure....

In an effort to correct its control problems, the Company hired new executives and expanded its board. On October 22, 2008, defendant Yau-Sing Tang ("Y.Tang") joined China Agritech as its CFO and controller. On that same date, defendants Gene Michael Bennett, Lun Zhang Dai, and Hai Ling Zhang ("H.Zhang") became directors. The board then established an Audit Committee, a Compensation Committee, and a Nominating and Governance Committee (the "Governance Committee"), each populated with the new outside directors. Beginning with its Form 10-K for the year ending December 31, 2008, filed with the SEC on March 28, 2009, China Agritech disclosed that its internal controls and procedures were effective as of December 31, 2008.

C. The Yinlong Transaction

On February 12, 2009, Yinlong Industrial Co., Ltd. ("Yinlong") sold China Agritech the remaining 10% equity interest in China Agritech's otherwise 90% owned subsidiary, Pacific Dragon Fertilizers Co. Ltd. ("Pacific Dragon"). Chang and Teng owned 85% and 15%, respectively, of Yinlong's shares, making the deal an interested transaction. I refer to it as the "Yinlong Transaction."

China Agritech acquired the Pacific Dragon shares through a wholly owned subsidiary, China Tailong Holdings Company Ltd. ("Tailong"). China Agritech agreed to pay Yinlong $7,980,000 for the shares, with all but $1 million coming in the form of an interest-free promissory note from Tailong to Yinlong. The transaction closed on May 15, 2009. On the day of the closing, the parties entered into a supplemental purchase agreement. The supplemental purchase agreement amended the "settlement of the purchase consideration" to a cash payment of $1 million and the issuance of 1,745,000 restricted shares of China Agritech common stock.

. . .

Chang, Teng, Dai, Bennett, and H. Zhang comprised the board at the time of the Yinlong Transaction. Dai, Bennett, and H. Zhang comprised both the Audit Committee and the Governance Committee.

In March 2009, defendant Ming Gang Zhu became China Agritech's Chief Operating Officer, taking over from Teng. In December 2009, defendant Zheng Wang joined the board as a designee of a fund that invested in the Company. Because of her affiliation, the board did not consider her to be an independent director. It is not apparent which, if any, committees she joined.

In early January 2010, Charles Law became an outside director. He joined the Governance Committee and the Compensation Committee.

D. The $23 Million Offering

In April 2010, China Agritech announced a public offering of 1,243,000 shares of common stock, plus an underwriter's option on an additional 186,450 shares, which the underwriter exercised (the "Offering"). The stated purpose of the Offering was to finance the construction of distribution centers for China Agritech's fertilizer products. The Offering raised total gross proceeds of $23 million. According to the Complaint, the funds have not been used to construct distribution centers or for any other discernible business purpose, suggesting either that the funds have been misused or that the stated purpose was false. At the time of the Offering, Chang, Teng, Dai, Bennett, H. Zhang, Law, and Wang comprised the board.

E. The Material Weaknesses Return

In its Form 10-Q dated August 16, 2010, China Agritech disclosed that material weaknesses had again undermined its disclosure controls and procedures. . . .

In its Form 10-Q dated November 10, 2010, the Company claimed to have fixed its internal controls problem: "[M]anagement enhanced the supervision and review of the financial reporting process" and deemed that the "remediation steps correct[ed] the material weaknesses" previously identified. The November 2010 Form 10-Q was the last time that China Agritech made a federally mandated securities filing. Since then, China Agritech has posted occasional press releases on its website, but has not otherwise complied with its reporting obligations.

On November 13, 2010, three days after claiming that the material weaknesses were solved, the Company fired its outside auditor, Crowe Horwath LLP. The Audit Committee approved the termination. Dai, Bennett, and H. Zhang comprised the Audit Committee.

F. The Company Hires Ernst & Young.

Effective as of November 13, 2010, the Company hired Ernst & Young Hua Ming ("Ernst & Young") as its new outside auditor. On November 19, Dai's daughter, Lingziao Dai, was named head of China Agritech's internal audit department. She had served previously as China Agritech's Vice President of Finance since May 1, 2009.

Before approving the hiring of Ernst & Young, the Audit Committee considered that Ernst & Young had provided consulting services to the Company for its Sarbanes-Oxley Section 404 compliance effort from 2008 to 2010 and assisted the Company in testing its internal controls. The Audit Committee determined that the services did not impair Ernst & Young's ability to serve as the Company's independent auditor.

The Chairman of the Audit Committee, Bennett, confirmed to Ernst & Young that the Audit Committee had made this determination.

On December 15, 2010, Ernst & Young provided a letter to the Audit Committee describing matters which, if not appropriately addressed, could result in audit adjustments, significant deficiencies or material weaknesses, and delays in the filing of the Company's Form 10-K for 2010. Company management claimed to have addressed the issues, but Ernst & Young did not agree.

G. The McGee Report

While Ernst & Young was raising issues with Company management, Lucas McGee was investigating China Agritech. McGee is a self-described "consultant and private investor with more than ten years of business and finance experience throughout Asia, including China, Hong Kong and Vietnam." On February 3, 2011, McGee posted a report titled "China Agritech: A Scam" (the "McGee Report") on the investor website www.seekingalpha.com. McGee disclosed that he held a short position in the Company's stock and stood to profit from a decline in the Company's common stock price.

The McGee Report identified a series of alleged problems with the Company's business, including:

- *Factories are idle:* After visiting [China Agritech's] reported manufacturing facilities . . . we found virtually no manufacturing underway. The single exception was the facility in Pinggu County on the outskirts of Beijing, where the plant was not in operation on the Friday when we visited but local people told us that it has sporadically produced some liquid fertilizer over the last year. Plants in Bengbu, Anhui (supposedly the largest), Harbin, and Xinjiang were completely shuttered.

- *Harbin plant for sale:* The Harbin facility—supposedly a major manufacturing facility for the $100 million revenue business—whose name has never been officially changed in government documentation from "Pacific Dragon," had a sign hanging on the gates last summer reading "this factory is for sale." Although the [C]ompany gives an adjacent address for the facility . . . the registration documents with the local Administration of Industry and Commerce (AIC) have not been updated (a serious regulatory violation in China).

- *No contract with Sinochem:* A January [China Agritech] announcement states: "In May 2010, the Company signed a renewed contract supplying organic liquid compound fertilizers to Sinochem, China's largest fertilizer distributor." . . . But a manager with Sinochem told us that Sinochem has no contract with [China Agritech] and in fact has never bought or sold organic liquid fertilizers. . . .

- *[China Agritech] not permitted to make granular fertilizer:* [China Agritech] claims that most of its sales volume now derives from granular compound fertilizers. But government officials familiar with the [China Agritech] operation say that [China Agritech] has not received a license to manufacture granular compound fertilizer and does not sell any.

• *Unable to buy the product:* Although the [C]ompany has announced 21 regional distribution centers, we have not been able to locate any. We attempted ... to purchase at least one bottle of the [China Agritech] product but were disappointed. ...

• *Fictional Revenue:* [W]e have received an analysis of audited [China Agritech] revenues reported to the Chinese government for the year 2009 In its [third quarter 2010 10-Q], [China Agritech] claims that it has 100,000 metric tons of production capacity in Anhui, 50,000 metric tons in Harbin, and 50,000 tons in Xinjiang. But a total value of ... $3,000 in plant and equipment in Xinjiang would be insufficient to support 50,000 tons of production capacity. Indeed, when we visited the site of the Xinjiang plant, we found little more than a warehouse, shared with two other companies and demonstrating no activity.

Our early attempts to find the Xinjiang factory were unsuccessful. ... [A]fter searching the area and asking county officials, we were able to discover a factory bearing [China Agritech's] name along with the names of two other companies [at a different location than the registered address]. ... The facility, however, is idle and we were told by local people that there is no production activity there.

In Anhui, which [China Agritech] calls its principal production facility ... [w]e visited and found a small plant on a rutted road outside Bengbu, completely deserted.

The Beijing plant is larger, but plant staff said in our presence that the facility was idle. The [C]ompany would not allow us in, but we drove around the plant and saw a few people on site washing clothes but no evidence of production. Local government officials said that [China Agritech] had not been able to obtain a production license for granular fertilizer and that it produced a very small volume of liquid fertilizer.

• *No distribution centers:* In May 2010, [China Agritech] issued over 1.4 million new shares, raising just under $19 million for the construction of distribution centers. But we have not been able to find evidence that any distribution centers were actually built.

• *Mysterious suppliers:* The companies that [China Agritech] lists in its corporate materials as suppliers of raw materials ... cannot be found in any directory under possible Chinese names that would correspond to the transliterated names or under the alphabetic names. ...

• *Financial Anomalies:* We have done some analysis of financial reports that [China Agritech] has provided to [the SAIC]. ...

1. The Harbin company, Pacific Dragon, has cumulative losses since 1994 of over 4 million RMB. . . . There were no sales expenses at all, only administrative expenses. In short, the 2009 audit report . . . shows a dead company.

2. The Anhui facility has generated losses every year since its establishment in 2006. By the end of 2009, it had lost 3.89 million RMB. The company had zero cash on its books.

3. The Xinjiang company reports zero fixed assets, meaning that it owns no equipment for production. . . .

4. The Beijing facility has licensed registered capital of $20 million, but by the end of 2009 had received 88 million RMB, so only more than half of the legally required amount. But despite the missing capital, half of the registered capital was still sitting in the account in cash in 2009, indicating that the company had not purchased much, if any, equipment.

• *Money-losing compounds:* [Compound chemical fertilizers] earn slim or negative margins. In 2008, the compound fertilizer production volume showed negative growth, as raw materials prices soared and farmers limited consumption to manage their costs. . . .

McGee concluded that

China Agritech is not a currently functioning business that is manufacturing products. Instead it is, in our view, simply a vehicle for transferring shareholder wealth from outside investors into the pockets of the founders and inside management.

. . .

On February 4, 2011, the day after the McGee Report issued, the Company posted a press release on its website denying the allegations. On February 10, the Company issued a second press release in the form of an open letter from Chang to "Fellow Shareholders and Potential Investors" in which he contested key elements of the McGee Report. (the "Rebuttal Letter"). In the Rebuttal Letter, Chang asserted that the Company (i) had used the proceeds of the Offering to develop twenty-one distribution centers, which were "in operation," (ii) had a business relationship with SinoChem "for three years," and (iii) had "the necessary license for the production of all of its fertilizer products."

On February 10, 2011, Law resigned from the board. The remaining directors appointed X. Zhang to fill his seat.

H. The Company Fires Ernst & Young.

On March 8, 2011, Ernst & Young met with the Audit Committee to discuss potential violations of law, including the United States securities laws. The issues identified by Ernst & Young included goods delivery notes that appeared to be modified after the fact; time sheets and related data for the Harbin facility that appeared to be destroyed; material purchases apparently made without supporting official tax invoice or with duplicative official tax invoice; a tax notice from the Harbin City tax bureau that appeared to be falsified; and what appeared to be material undisclosed related party transactions.

Ernst & Young expressed concern about whether the firm could continue to rely on management's representations. Ernst & Young also noted that while Crowe Horwath had characterized a particular accounting issue as a significant control deficiency, Ernst & Young had determined that that the Company's treatment of the issue represented "a material accounting error that may require restatement of the Company's Forms 10-Q filed in 2010." Ernst & Young asked the Audit Committee to take "timely and appropriate action."

On March 10, 2011, the board formed a Special Investigation Committee (the "Special Committee") to investigate Ernst & Young's allegations. The original members of the Special Committee were Wang, Dai, Bennett, and H. Zhang. Because Dai, Bennett, and H. Zhang were members of the Audit Committee, they faced the awkward task of investigating, evaluating, and passing on the propriety of their own actions as members of the Audit Committee. Wang was the only member of the Special Committee who did not face the prospect of investigating her own actions, but she was also a director whom the board did not regard as independent.

On March 12, 2011, Company management drafted a press release stating that the Special Committee had been formed and explaining that the action was taken due to allegations "made by third parties" with respect to the Company and certain issues "identified in connection with the performance of the Company's year end audit." When the actual press release was issued, it omitted the phrase "identified in connection with the performance of the Company's year end audit." Ernst & Young immediately advised Company counsel that the deletion of the reference to audit issues was a material omission. Ernst & Young stated that it would resign if a corrective press release was not issued. No correction was made.

On March 14, 2011, Chang informed Ernst & Young that the Audit Committee had terminated its engagement. Ernst & Young had no prior notice regarding its potential termination and had no reason to believe its termination was under consideration before the dispute over the press release. Later that day, the Company issued a press release that claimed the termination

> was the result of [Ernst & Young] entering into a SOX 404 service agreement including performing the test of the Company's internal controls from 2008 through 2010. Recently, the public and the management team have raised doubts about this service agreement's impact on [Ernst & Young's] independence to act as the Company's auditor. In order to give the public fair and truthful financial results, the Board of Directors came to the above decision.

This claim was directly contrary to the determinations the Audit Committee made and Bennett conveyed to Ernst & Young in November 2010. Ernst & Young concluded that the press release "does not reflect the Company's actual reasons for terminating Ernst & Young . . . as the Company's auditors."

On March 15, 2011, Ernst & Young sent the Company a letter detailing its concerns about its termination and the accuracy of the Company's purported reasons. The letter noted that it was being sent to fulfill Ernst & Young's obligations "under Section 10A(b)(2) of the Securities Exchange Act of 1934," which requires an independent auditor to report directly to a company's board of directors if it believes an (i) "illegal act" has occurred that materially affects the issuer's financial statements and (ii) that management had not, either independently or as required by the board, yet taken "timely and appropriate remedial action."

Wang, the chair of the Special Committee, resigned from the board on March 15, 2011. She "was a Special Committee member only for one day." The other members of the Special Committee continued to serve. Bennett, the Chair of the Audit Committee, took over as Chair of the Special Committee.

On April 25, 2011, the remaining directors appointed defendant Kai Wai Sim to fill Wang's seat. On the same day, Bennett resigned from both the Audit Committee and Special Committee, although for the time being he remained a member of the board. Sim took over as Chair of the Special Committee. It is not clear whether Sim also took over as Chair of the Audit Committee. At that point, the members of the Audit Committee were Sim, Dai, and H. Zhang, and the members of the Special Committee were Sim, Dai, H. Zhang, and X. Zhang.

In April 2011, NASDAQ notified the Company that it would be delisted "based on public interest concerns and the Company's failure to file its 2010 form 10-K on time." China Agritech, Inc., Current Report (Form 8-K) (Apr. 18, 2011). The Company appealed the decision. In May 2011, NASDAQ denied the Company's appeal, and the Company's common stock was delisted on May 20.

On May 27, 2011, the Company announced that Zhu, the Company's COO, had resigned.

. . .

J. The Special Committee's "Findings"

On December 1, 2011, the Company issued a press release announcing that the Special Committee had completed its investigation. The Company noted that "[t]he investigation was subject to certain limitations," including that "[Ernst & Young] did not cooperate with the investigation . . . ." It is not clear what other limitations, if any, existed.

Without providing any details or explanation, the Company reported that according to the Special Committee, all was well. . . .

K. The Parade Of Resignations

On January 6, 2012, Rish filed this lawsuit. At the time, defendants Chang, Teng, Dai, Sim, Bennett, H. Zhang, and X. Zhang comprised the board (the "Demand Board"). Sim, Dai, H. Zhang, and X. Zhang served on the Special Committee, and Sim, H. Zhang, and X. Zhang served on the Audit Committee.

On January 14, 2012, Sim resigned from the board. His resignation became effective on January 25.

On January 16, 2012, Y. Tang resigned as CFO.

On March 13, 2012, H. Zhang and X. Zhang resigned from the board. Their resignations became effective on March 15.

On June 7, 2012, Bennett resigned from the board.

The resignations left Chang, Teng, and Dai as the only members of the board. To recapitulate, Chang and Teng are the Company's co-founders. Chang controls a mathematical majority of China Agritech's outstanding voting power, and he is the Company's President, CEO, Secretary, and Chairman of the Board. Dai's daughter heads up the Company's internal audit department.

At the Company's annual meeting on June 25, 2012, Chang, Teng, and Dai were reelected. Chang dominated the vote: Of the 7,080,620 shares voted, Chang owned all but 6,982.

II. LEGAL ANALYSIS

The defendants seek dismissal of the Complaint and the entry of judgment in their favor under Rule 23.1 and Rule 12(b)(6). Alternatively, they ask that the case be stayed. The motions are denied.

A. Rule 23.1

When a corporation suffers harm, the board of directors is the institutional actor legally empowered under Delaware law to determine what, if any, remedial action the corporation should take, including pursuing litigation against the individuals involved. . . .

In a derivative suit, a stockholder seeks to displace the board's authority over a litigation asset and assert the corporation's claim. . . . A stockholder whose litigation efforts are opposed by the corporation can accomplish this feat only by obtaining a judicial ruling establishing demand excusal or wrongful refusal.

. . .

Rish concedes that he did not make a litigation demand on the Demand Board, and the Company opposes his efforts to pursue litigation. Consequently, for Rish to obtain authority to move forward on behalf of China Agritech, his Complaint must "allege with particularity . . . the reasons . . . for not making the effort [to make a litigation demand]," Ch. Ct. R. 23.1, and this Court must determine based on those allegations that "demand is excused because the directors are incapable of making an impartial decision regarding whether to institute such litigation." . . .

The Delaware Supreme Court has established two tests for determining whether the allegations of a complaint sufficiently plead demand futility. . . . In *Aronson,* the seminal demand-futility decision, the Delaware Supreme Court crafted a specific two-part test that applies when a derivative plaintiff challenges an earlier board decision made by the same directors who remain in office at the time suit is filed. The Court of Chancery "must decide whether, under the particularized facts alleged, a reasonable doubt is created that: (1) the directors are disinterested and independent and (2) the challenged transaction was otherwise the product of a valid exercise of business judgment." The first of the two inquiries examines "the independence and disinterestedness of the directors" with respect to the decision that the derivative action would challenge. . . . If the underlying transaction was approved by a disinterested and independent board majority, then the court moves to the second inquiry: whether the plaintiff "has alleged facts with particularity which, if taken as true, support a reasonable doubt that the challenged transaction was the product of a valid exercise of business judgment." A plaintiff might allege sufficiently, for example, that the directors were grossly negligent in approving the transaction.

. . .

In *Rales,* the Delaware Supreme Court confronted a board whose members had not participated in the underlying decision that the derivative action would challenge, and therefore "the test enunciated in [*Aronson*] . . . [was] not implicated." In response, the Delaware Supreme Court framed a second and more comprehensive demand futility standard that asks "whether or not the particularized factual allegations of a derivative stockholder complaint create a reasonable doubt that, as of the time the complaint is filed, the board of directors could have properly exercised its independent and disinterested business judgment in responding to a demand." The Delaware Supreme Court envisioned that the *Rales* test would be used

> in three principal scenarios: (1) where a business decision was made by the board of a company, but a majority of the directors making the decision have been replaced; (2) where the subject of the derivative suit is not a business decision of the board; and (3) where . . . the decision being challenged was made by the board of a different corporation.

A director cannot consider a litigation demand under *Rales* if the director is interested in the alleged wrongdoing, not independent, or would face a "substantial likelihood" of liability if suit were filed. To show that a director faces a "substantial risk of liability," a plaintiff does not have to demonstrate a reasonable probability of success on the claim. . . . The plaintiff need only "make a threshold showing, through the allegation of particularized facts, that their claims have some merit." . . .

The *Aronson* and *Rales* have been described as complementary versions of the same inquiry. This case illustrates that reality. The fundamental question presented by the defendant's Rule 23.1 motion is whether the Demand Board could have validly considered a litigation demand. The Complaint challenges at least three events that involved actual decisions: the Yinlong Transaction, the terminations of the outside auditors, and the Special Committee's determination to take no action. Five of the seven members of the Demand Board were directors at the time those decisions were made. Because less than "a majority of the directors making the decision have been replaced," *Aronson* provides the demand futility standard for the five participating directors. *Rales* would provide the standard for the two remaining directors, but because the *Aronson* analysis establishes demand futility, I do not reach the *Rales* aspect. The outcome would be no different if *Rales* were used for all seven directors, because the *Rales* test asks whether a director would face a substantial risk of liability as a result of the litigation. To determine whether the participating directors would face a substantial risk of liability in litigation challenging their prior decisions, a reviewing court examines whether the directors had a personal interest in the decisions, were not independent with respect to the decisions, or otherwise would not enjoy the protections of the business judgment rule. Those are precisely the questions that *Aronson* asks.

The litigation also alleges a systematic lack of oversight at China Agritech. That challenge does not involve an actual board decision, so *Rales* governs. . . .

1. The Yinlong Transaction

To the extent the litigation challenges the Yinlong Transaction, it was futile under *Aronson* for Rish to make a litigation demand. The members of the Demand Board were Chang, Teng, Dai, Sim, Bennett, H. Zhang, and X. Zhang. Chang and Teng stood on both sides of the Yinlong Transaction, in which China Agritech purchased shares from an entity they owed. A director is deemed "interested" if he "has received, or is entitled to receive, a personal financial benefit from the challenged transaction which is not equally shared by the stockholders." "In such circumstances, a director cannot be expected to exercise his or her independent business judgment without being influenced by the adverse personal consequences resulting from the decision." Directors who have received the benefits of a challenged transaction "have a strong financial incentive to maintain the status quo by not authorizing any corrective action that would devalue their current holdings or cause them to disgorge improperly obtained profits. This creates an unacceptable conflict that restricts them from evaluating the litigation independently." . . .

Dai, Bennett, and H. Zhang were members of the Audit Committee when it approved the Yinlong Transaction. In a challenge to the Yinlong Transaction, Chang, Teng, and their fellow defendant directors would bear the burden of proving that the transaction was entirely fair. . . . The purchase price for the remaining 10% interest in Pacific Dragon that China Agritech acquired was set originally at $7.98 million. The day the transaction documents were signed, the Company issued an unsecured, interest-free promissory note for all but $1 million of the purchase price. At closing, the Company, through its subsidiary, "amended the settlement of the purchase consideration" to a $1 million cash payment plus 1,745,000 shares of the Company's common stock.... The litigation risk that the Audit Committee members would face in an entire fairness challenge to the Yinlong Transaction raises a reasonable doubt about their ability to disinterestedly consider a litigation demand.

Five of the seven members of the Demand Board therefore could not properly consider a litigation demand addressing the Yinlong Transaction. Demand is futile under *Aronson,* and I need not consider the remaining two directors under *Rales.*

2. Business Fraud

The Complaint more broadly contends that China Agritech is a fraud. Aspects of the fraud include failing to use the proceeds of the Offering for its stated purpose; not being able to produce basic documents essential to the Company's business, such as the original Chinese language contract with the Company's primary customer or a license to produce one of the Company's primary products; and repeated failures to maintain effective internal controls that prevented the Company from making public filings with the SEC since November 2010 and ultimately resulted in the delisting of the Company's common stock. Because this aspect of the Complaint challenges an ongoing failure of the board to provide oversight, *Rales* provides the test for evaluating demand futility.

The board of a Delaware corporation has a fiduciary obligation to adopt internal information and reporting systems that are "reasonably designed to provide to senior management and to the board itself timely, accurate information sufficient to allow management and the board, each within its scope, to reach informed judgments concerning both the corporation's compliance with law and its business performance." If a corporation suffers losses proximately caused by fraud or illegal conduct, and if the directors failed "to attempt in good faith to assure that a corporate information and reporting system, which the board concludes is adequate, exists," then there is a sufficient connection between the occurrence of the illegal conduct and board level action or conscious inaction to support liability. "[I]mposition of liability requires a showing that the directors knew that they were not discharging their fiduciary obligations." *Stone,* 911 A.2d at 370.

The burden on a plaintiff who seeks to establish liability under a failure-to-monitor theory "is quite high." *Caremark,* 698 A.2d at 971.

> Generally where a claim of directorial liability for corporate loss is predicated upon ignorance of liability creating activities within the corporation, as in *Graham* [*v. Allis-Chalmers Manufacturing Co.,* 188 A.2d 125 (Del.1963)] or in [the *Caremark* case itself], ... only a sustained or systematic failure of the board to exercise oversight—such as an utter failure to attempt to assure a reasonable information and reporting system exists—will establish the lack of good faith that is a necessary condition to liability.

Id.

. . .

During 2009 and 2010, the Company engaged in the Yinlong Transaction, conducted the Offering, disclosed a material weakness in its disclosure controls and procedures, claimed to have fixed the problem, terminated Crowe Horwath as its outside auditor, hired Ernst & Young as its new outside auditor, and named Dai's daughter as head of China Agritech's internal audit department. Yet there is no documentary evidence that the Audit Committee ever held a single meeting during this two year period. Then in 2011, Ernst & Young resigned and sent the Company a letter to fulfill Ernst & Young's obligations "under Section 10A(b)(2) of the Securities Exchange Act of 1934," which requires an independent auditor to report directly to a company's board of directors if it believes an (i) "illegal act" has occurred that materially affects the issuer's financial statements and (ii) that management had not, either independently or as required by the board, yet taken "timely and appropriate remedial action."

Discrepancies in the Company's public filings with governmental agencies reinforce the inference of an Audit Committee that existed in name only. During its time as a publicly listed entity in the United States, the federal securities laws mandated that the Company make periodic filings with the SEC. Regulatory requirements in China mandated that the Company make periodic filings with the State Administration for Industry and Commerce ("SAIC"). The Complaint alleges that in four of five years that the Company reported large profits in its filings with the SEC, the Company reported net losses to the SAIC. In the fifth year, the Company reported a large profit in its filings with the SEC, and one-fifth of that profit to the SAIC.

. . .

Although the Delaware state courts have not yet confronted the implications of dramatic divergences between U.S. and Chinese regulatory filings, the federal district courts have considered whether alleged divergences can support a claim of securities fraud under the Private Securities Litigation Reform Act and Federal Rule of Civil Procedure 9(b).... A federal court previously found that the "drastically different" figures China Agritech filed with the SEC and SAIC supported an inference of *scienter*. The SEC has pursued an enforcement action against an entity that filed financial statements claiming sales figures fifteen times higher than similar figures in financial statements filed with Chinese authorities....

Taken together, the factual allegations of the Complaint support a reasonable inference that the members of the Audit Committee acted in bad faith in the sense that they consciously disregarded their duties....

Because of their service on the Audit Committee, Dai, Bennett, and H. Zhang face a substantial risk of liability for knowingly disregarding their duty of oversight. These directors could not validly consider a litigation demand concerning the problems that occurred on their watch. Dai also could not validly consider a litigation demand for the additional reason that his daughter, Lingxiao Dai, served as Vice President of Finance from May 1, 2009 until November 19, 2010, and as head of the internal audit department thereafter. A director lacks independence when "the director is unable to base his or her decisions on the corporate merits of the issue before the board." ... A meaningful investigation into or litigation regarding China Agritech's lack of internal controls, financial reporting deficiencies, and potential violations of law would necessitate an investigation into Dai's daughter and could lead to a finding of wrongdoing against her. Close family relationships, like the parent-child relationship, create a reasonable doubt as to the independence of a director. ... Dai also cannot consider a demand that would place Chang or Teng at risk because his daughter's primary employment depends on the good wishes of the Company's controlling stockholders.

Bennett and H. Zhang's resignations further call into question their ability to consider a demand. ... Bennett was the Chair of the Audit Committee and Special Committee. As such, he was optimally positioned to represent the interests of the Company and its minority stockholders. Yet for reasons that are unclear at this point, Bennett resigned from both committees on April 25, 2011, shortly after the firing of the two outside auditors and Wang's resignation. On June 7, 2012, Bennett resigned from the board. At the pleading stage, when viewed in the context of the allegations of the Complaint as a whole, Bennett's resignation supports a reasonable inference that he could not meaningfully supervise Chang, which in turn contributes to an inference that he could not properly consider a litigation demand.

H. Zhang also was a member of the Audit Committee and Special Committee. Unlike Bennett, he continued to serve on both committees during the time when the Special Committee was conducting its investigation of the events surrounding the firing of the outside auditors. The Special Committee took no action as a result of its investigation, and the Company's description of the Committee's findings is hardly confidence inspiring. With respect to the McGee Report, the Company announced that "the Committee concluded that the allegations were either factually incorrect or that there were reasonable explanations as to their non-materiality." This cryptic statement leaves open the possibility that (i) some of the troubling allegations the McGee Report were correct, and (ii) the information could be deemed material. ...

The inferences drawn from Bennett and H. Zhang's resignations are necessarily fact-dependent. Their resignations were part of a parade of departures from the Company under highly suspicious circumstances. The Court's ability to draw such an inference on the facts alleged here does not suggest that an independent director's resignation typically would support either an inference of culpability or the inability to consider a demand.

Lastly, Chang could not validly consider a demand because he would face a substantial risk of liability in connection with the events of the 2009 through 2010 period. Chang was the Company's Chairman, CEO, and controlling stockholder. The disputes between the Company and Crowe Horwath and Ernst & Young pitted Chang and his management team against the outside auditors. Ernst & Young pointed the finger directly at Chang and his management team by advising the Audit Committee that it did not believe it could rely on management's statements. Ernst & Young also contended that it was senior management that made a materially misleading disclosure regarding Ernst & Young's termination. Chang's "potential culpability and the potential [adverse] consequences [to the Company] combine to raise reasonable doubt" as to whether he can disinterestedly consider a demand.

Chang, Dai, Bennett, and H. Zhang comprise a majority of the Demand Board. Demand is therefore futile under *Rales* for purposes of the *Caremark* claim, rendering it unnecessary to consider the other three directors.

3. The Termination of the Outside Auditors

To the extent the litigation challenges the termination of the outside auditors, demand is futile under *Aronson*. The particularized allegations of the Complaint . . . support a reasonable inference that both outside auditing firms raised serious issues about the Company's compliance with accounting requirements, and Ernst & Young took the additional step of questioning whether it could rely on management's representations and the Company's compliance with the law. The Audit Committee responded by terminating the firms and, in the case of Ernst & Young, permitting management to issue press releases that (i) failed to identify the outside auditors as the source of concern about the Company's financial statements and (ii) provided what can be regarded at the pleadings stage as pretextual grounds for Ernst & Young's termination. . . .

Chang could not properly consider a litigation demand regarding the termination of the Company's outside auditors because his role in management as the Company's CEO gives rise to a reasonable inference that he would face personal and professional risk in any litigation over the dispute, making him interested in the outcome.

The members of the Audit Committee could not properly consider a litigation demand regarding the termination of the Company's outside auditors because the allegations of the Complaint support a reasonable inference that they failed to act in good faith. The Complaint presents a pastiche of ongoing disputes between successive accountants and management, the doctoring of the initial press release about the delay of the 2010 10K to avoid mentioning audit issues, Chang's telephone call terminating Ernst & Young after the firm objected, the issuance of a second press release that can be viewed at the pleadings stage as containing pretextual excuses for the termination, Ernst & Young's formal objection "under Section 10A(b)(2) of the Securities Exchange Act of 1934," and Wang's immediate resignation after the Company received the letter. Taken together, the allegations support a reasonable inference that Chang wanted to get rid of Ernst & Young and that the Audit Committee rubberstamped his decision. At this stage of the litigation, Wang's hasty departure supports a reasonable inference that she questioned the propriety of the actions that the Audit Committee and management were contemplating and resigned in response. Dai, Bennett and H. Zhang could not properly consider a demand to institute litigation involving these matters. Dai could not properly consider a litigation demand regarding the termination of the Company's outside auditors for the additional reason that his daughter is the head of the Company's internal audit department, which gives rise to a reasonable inference that he is incapable of acting in a disinterested fashion with respect to an audit dispute.

Chang, Dai, Bennett, and H. Zhang comprise a majority of the Demand Board. They could not properly consider a litigation demand addressing the outside auditor terminations, rendering demand futile under *Aronson*. I need not consider the remaining directors.

4. The "Sham" Special Committee Investigation

To the extent the Complaint challenges what it describes as "a sham 'investigation' the sole purpose of which was to cover up defendants' breaches of fiduciary duties," demand is futile under *Aronson*. The Special Committee decided not to take any action with respect to the Audit Committee's termination of two successive outside auditors and the allegations made by Ernst & Young. The conscious decision not to take action was itself a decision. . . .

The actions of four of the seven members of the Demand Board were at issue in the Special Committee investigation: Chang, as a member of management, and Dai, Bennett, and H. Zhang, as members of the Audit Committee. For the reasons discussed in the preceding sections, these directors could not properly consider a demand under *Aronson* that asked them to assert litigation relating to the Audit Committee's termination of the outside auditors or management's related activities. A demand to assert litigation relating to the Special Committee's investigation implicates the same issues and creates the same problems for these individuals. Because these directors comprise a majority of the Demand Board, demand is futile under *Aronson*.

B. Rule 12(b)(6)

. . .

When a complaint alleges specific acts of fraud at a corporation, particularly acts suggesting widespread fraud, the complaint need not tie the fraud to each particular defendant to survive a Rule 12(b)(6) motion. . . .

Defendant Teng co-founded the Company and has served as a director throughout its existence. From February 3, 2005 until March 13, 2009, she served as the Company's COO. Defendant Y. Tang served as the Company's CFO and Controller from October 22, 2008 until January 16, 2012. Defendant Zhu served as the Company's COO from March 13, 2009 until May 27, 2011. Defendant Wang served as a director from December 2009 until March 14, 2011. Defendant Law served as a director of the Company from January 8, 2010 until February 10, 2011. During their tenures, the Company engaged in the Offering, suffered the problems that led to the terminations of Crowe Horwath and Ernst & Young, failed to file any periodic filings required by the federal securities laws, and was delisted by NASDAQ. For purposes of Rule 12(b)(6), it is reasonable to infer that Teng, Y. Tang, Zhu, Wang, and Law knew about the oversight problems and failed to stop them. At a later stage of the case, I will take into account Wang and Law's resignations, which could well serve to limit their potential liability for events described in the Complaint that post-date their board service. But because Wang and Law will remain in the case regardless as to certain claims, I will not attempt to parse the implications of their resignations at the pleadings stage.

Defendant X. Zhang served as a director from February 10, 2011, until his resignation on March, 15, 2012, and defendant Sim served as a director from April 25, 2011 until his resignation effective January 25, 2012. During this period, the Company failed to file any periodic filings required by the federal securities laws, and was delisted by NASDAQ. The Complaint supports a reasonable inference that oversight problems at the Company continued during this period and that X. Zhang and Sim knew about the problems and failed to stop them. The Complaint does not state a claim against X. Zhang or Sim for matters pre-dating their service on the board. As with Wang and Law, I will take into account their resignations at a later stage of the case.

C. Section 102(b)(7)

The defendants argue that the Complaint should be dismissed because it does not assert a claim for which the defendants could be held liable in light of the exculpatory provision in China Agritech's certificate of incorporation. Because the Complaint pleads claims that implicate the duty of loyalty, including its embedded requirement of good faith, the defendants cannot invoke the exculpatory provision as a defense at this stage.

The Complaint challenges the Yinlong Transaction, an interested transaction with a controlling stockholder where entire fairness provides the presumptive standard of review. . . .

The balance of the Complaint states claims that raise questions about whether the directors acted in good faith. A Section 102(b)(7) provision "can exculpate directors from monetary liability for a breach of the duty of care, but not for conduct that is not in good faith or a breach of the duty of loyalty." . . .

. . .

III. CONCLUSION

The Complaint has survived a motion to dismiss, and this action will not be stayed. The parties shall confer regarding a schedule for conducting discovery and bringing the matter to trial.

Questions

1. In assessing whether demand should have been excused, the court refers to the *Aronson* and *Rales* standards. What is the difference between the two standards?

2. Why are *Caremark* claims not exculpable under section 102(b)(7)? Should they be?

3. In what ways are the actions (or inactions) of the directors of China Agritech different from the actions or inactions of the directors in cases such as *Stone* or *Caremark*? What is unique about China Agritech? Why might the actions described in

this case amount to bad faith? Consider then-Chancellor Strine's bench ruling in *In re Puda Coal, Inc. Stockholders Litigation*, C.A. No. 6476-CS (Del. Ch. Feb. 6, 2013):

> ... [I]f you're going to have a company domiciled for purposes of its relations with its investors in Delaware and the assets and operations of that company are situated in China ..., in order for you to meet your obligation of good faith, you better have your physical body in China an awful lot. You better have in place a system of controls to make sure that you know that you actually own the assets. You better have the language skills to navigate the environment in which the company is operating. You better have retained accountants and lawyers who are fit to the task of maintaining a system of controls over a public company....
>
> ... Independent directors who step into these situations involving essentially the fiduciary oversight of assets in other parts of the world have a duty not to be dummy directors. I'm not mixing up care in the sense of negligence with loyalty here, in the sense of your duty of loyalty. I'm talking about the loyalty issue of understanding that if the assets are in Russia, if they're in Nigeria, if they're in the Middle East, if they're in China, that you're not going to be able to sit in your home in the U.S. and do a conference call four times a year and discharge your duty of loyalty. That won't cut it. That there will be special challenges that deal with linguistic, cultural and others in terms of the effort that you have to put in to discharge your duty of loyalty. There's no such thing as being a dummy director in Delaware, a shill, someone who just puts themselves up and represents to the investing public that they're a monitor. Because the only reason to have independent directors—remember, you don't pick them for their industry expertise. You pick them because of their independence and their ability to monitor the people who are managing the company....

Section V

The Federal Approach

As you saw in the previous sections, the Delaware courts often allude to the directors' duty to disclose, although the courts have yet to conclude that an independent duty to disclose exists under Delaware corporation law. For the most part, a duty to disclose is thus derived either from the directors' duty to act in good faith or from federal regulation addressing transactions in the primary and secondary markets. The primary market, in which the company issuing securities sells them to investors, is regulated by the Securities Act of 1933. The secondary market, where investors trade securities, is regulated by the Securities Exchange Act of 1934. Both acts were enacted after the crash of 1929 and rest on the assumption that government planning requires cooperation with big business, and that mandatory transparency and disclosure must underlie such cooperation.

An issuer of securities (a company) must register them with the SEC. When registering securities, the issuer must provide information about its finances and business. (This is the registration statement. The portion of the registration statement called the "prospectus" is delivered to purchasers of the issuer's securities.) The SEC does not evaluate the quality or worth of the security, only whether the registration statement includes the required information and whether the information appears to be accurate. It is important to note that the 1933 Act exempts some securities and some transactions from registration. The 1934 Act, in turn, is focused on secondary market transactions and matters such as securities fraud, insider trading, proxy solicitation and shareholder voting. The 1934 Act created the Securities and Exchange Commission (SEC) to administer the various securities laws.

Prior to the adoption of the Securities Acts of 1933 and 1934, securities fraud was a matter of state law. At common law, to prove fraud, the plaintiff had to show that the defendant, with *scienter*, *misrepresented* a *material* fact, that the plaintiff had relied upon the fact, and that the *misrepresentation* and *reliance caused injury* to the plaintiff. Loss was defined as the difference between what the plaintiff paid for the security and its actual worth. Proving reliance and causation in cases of securities fraud was almost impossible. For one thing, if the seller was simply silent, the plaintiff found it difficult to prove reliance. Moreover, because many factors affect the value of securities, it was rather difficult to prove what part of the loss was a result of the securities fraud.

The securities acts created different express private rights of action for private parties injured as a result of violations of the acts. Most important among them is Section 10(b) of the 1934 Act. It provides that:

> It shall be unlawful for any person, directly or indirectly, by the use of any means or instrumentality of interstate commerce or of the mails, or of any facility of any national securities exchange....
>
> > (b) To use or employ, in connection with the purchase or sale of any security registered on a national securities exchange or any security not so registered ... any manipulative or deceptive device or contrivance in contravention of such rules and regulations as the Commission may prescribe as necessary or appropriate in the public interest or for the protection of investors.

Section 10(b), which applies to any security, including securities of closely held corporations (about which you will learn in Part 3), requires the SEC to promulgate rules to implement it. Rule 10b-5, our focus in this section, states that:

> It shall be unlawful for any person, directly or indirectly, by the use of any means or instrumentality of interstate commerce, or of the mails or of any facility of any national securities exchange,
>
> > (a) To employ any device, scheme, or artifice to defraud,

(b) To make any untrue statement of a material fact or to omit to state a material fact necessary in order to make the statements made, in the light of the circumstances under which they were made, not misleading, or

(c) To engage in any act, practice, or course of business which operates or would operate as a fraud or deceit upon any person, in connection with the purchase or sale of any security.

A. Rule 10b-5

Halliburton Co. v. Erica P. John Fund, Inc.
134 S. Ct. 2398 (2014)

Chief Justice ROBERTS delivered the opinion of the Court.

Investors can recover damages in a private securities fraud action only if they prove that they relied on the defendant's misrepresentation in deciding to buy or sell a company's stock. In *Basic Inc. v. Levinson*, 485 U.S. 224, 108 S.Ct. 978, 99 L.Ed.2d 194 (1988), we held that investors could satisfy this reliance requirement by invoking a presumption that the price of stock traded in an efficient market reflects all public, material information—including material misstatements. In such a case, we concluded, anyone who buys or sells the stock at the market price may be considered to have relied on those misstatements.

We also held, however, that a defendant could rebut this presumption in a number of ways, including by showing that the alleged misrepresentation did not actually affect the stock's price—that is, that the misrepresentation had no "price impact." The questions presented are whether we should overrule or modify *Basic*'s presumption of reliance and, if not, whether defendants should nonetheless be afforded an opportunity in securities class action cases to rebut the presumption at the class certification stage, by showing a lack of price impact.

I

Respondent Erica P. John Fund, Inc. (EPJ Fund), is the lead plaintiff in a putative class action against Halliburton and one of its executives (collectively Halliburton) alleging violations of section 10(b) of the Securities Exchange Act of 1934, and Securities and Exchange Commission Rule 10b-5. According to EPJ Fund, between June 3, 1999, and December 7, 2001, Halliburton made a series of misrepresentations regarding its potential liability in asbestos litigation, its expected revenue from certain construction contracts, and the anticipated benefits of its merger with another company—all in an attempt to inflate the price of its stock. Halliburton subsequently made a number of corrective disclosures, which, EPJ Fund contends, caused the company's stock price to drop and investors to lose money.

EPJ Fund moved to certify a class comprising all investors who purchased Halliburton common stock during the class period. . . .

. . . Halliburton argued that class certification was inappropriate because the evidence . . . showed that none of its alleged misrepresentations had actually affected its stock price. By demonstrating the absence of any "price impact," Halliburton contended, it had rebutted *Basic*'s presumption that the members of the proposed class had relied on its alleged misrepresentations simply by buying or selling its stock at the market price. And without the benefit of the *Basic* presumption, investors would have to prove reliance on an individual basis, meaning that individual issues would predominate over common ones. The District Court declined to consider Halliburton's argument, holding that the *Basic* presumption applied and certifying the class under Rule 23(b)(3).

The Fifth Circuit affirmed. . . . While acknowledging that "Halliburton's price impact evidence could be used at the trial on the merits to refute the presumption of reliance," the court held that Halliburton could not use such evidence for that purpose at the class certification stage. . . .

We . . . granted certiorari . . . to resolve a conflict among the Circuits over whether securities fraud defendants may attempt to rebut the *Basic* presumption at the class certification stage with evidence of a lack of price impact. We also accepted Halliburton's invitation to reconsider the presumption of reliance for securities fraud claims that we adopted in *Basic*.

II

Halliburton urges us to overrule *Basic*'s presumption of reliance and to instead require every securities fraud plaintiff to prove that he actually relied on the defendant's misrepresentation in deciding to buy or sell a company's stock. Before overturning a long-settled precedent, however, we require "special justification," not just an argument that the precedent was wrongly decided. . . .

A

Section 10(b) of the Securities Exchange Act of 1934 and the Securities and Exchange Commission's Rule 10b-5 prohibit making any material misstatement or omission in connection with the purchase or sale of any security. Although section 10(b) does not create an express private cause of action, we have long recognized an implied private cause of action to enforce the provision and its implementing regulation. To recover damages for violations of section 10(b) and Rule 10b-5, a plaintiff must prove "(1) a material misrepresentation or omission by the defendant; (2) scienter; (3) a connection between the misrepresentation or omission and the purchase or sale of a security; (4) reliance upon the misrepresentation or omission; (5) economic loss; and (6) loss causation."

The reliance element "ensures that there is a proper connection between a defendant's misrepresentation and a plaintiff's injury." "The traditional (and most direct) way a plaintiff can demonstrate reliance is by showing that he was aware of a company's statement and engaged in a relevant transaction—*e.g.,* purchasing common stock—based on that specific misrepresentation."

In *Basic,* however, we recognized that requiring such direct proof of reliance "would place an unnecessarily unrealistic evidentiary burden on the Rule 10b-5 plaintiff who has traded on an impersonal market." That is because, even assuming an investor could prove that he was aware of the misrepresentation, he would still have to "show a speculative state of facts, *i.e.,* how he would have acted ... if the misrepresentation had not been made."

We also noted that "[r]equiring proof of individualized reliance" from every securities fraud plaintiff "effectively would ... prevent[] [plaintiffs] from proceeding with a class action" in Rule 10b-5 suits. If every plaintiff had to prove direct reliance on the defendant's misrepresentation, "individual issues then would ... overwhelm[] the common ones," making certification under Rule 23(b)(3) inappropriate.

To address these concerns, *Basic* held that securities fraud plaintiffs can in certain circumstances satisfy the reliance element of a Rule 10b-5 action by invoking a rebuttable presumption of reliance, rather than proving direct reliance on a misrepresentation. The Court based that presumption on what is known as the "fraud-on-the-market" theory, which holds that "the market price of shares traded on well-developed markets reflects all publicly available information, and, hence, any material misrepresentations." The Court also noted that, rather than scrutinize every piece of public information about a company for himself, the typical "investor who buys or sells stock at the price set by the market does so in reliance on the integrity of that price"—the belief that it reflects all public, material information. As a result, whenever the investor buys or sells stock at the market price, his "reliance on any public material misrepresentations ... may be presumed for purposes of a Rule 10b-5 action."

Based on this theory, a plaintiff must make the following showings to demonstrate that the presumption of reliance applies in a given case: (1) that the alleged misrepresentations were publicly known, (2) that they were material, (3) that the stock traded in an efficient market, and (4) that the plaintiff traded the stock between the time the misrepresentations were made and when the truth was revealed.

At the same time, *Basic* emphasized that the presumption of reliance was rebuttable rather than conclusive. Specifically, "[a]ny showing that severs the link between the alleged misrepresentation and either the price received (or paid) by the plaintiff, or his decision to trade at a fair market price, will be sufficient to rebut the presumption of reliance." So for example, if a defendant could show that the alleged misrepresentation did not, for whatever reason, actually affect the market price, or that a plaintiff would have bought or sold the stock even had he been aware that the stock's price was tainted by fraud, then the presumption of reliance would not apply. In either of those cases, a plaintiff would have to prove that he directly relied on the defendant's misrepresentation in buying or selling the stock.

B

Halliburton contends that securities fraud plaintiffs should *always* have to prove direct reliance and that the *Basic* Court erred in allowing them to invoke a presumption of reliance instead. According to Halliburton, the *Basic* presumption contravenes congressional intent and has been undermined by subsequent developments in economic theory. Neither argument, however, so discredits *Basic* as to constitute "special justification" for overruling the decision.

. . .

2

Halliburton's primary argument for overruling *Basic* is that the decision rested on two premises that can no longer withstand scrutiny. The first premise concerns what is known as the "efficient capital markets hypothesis." *Basic* stated that "the market price of shares traded on well-developed markets reflects all publicly available information, and, hence, any material misrepresentations." From that statement, Halliburton concludes that the *Basic* Court espoused "a robust view of market efficiency" that is no longer tenable, for "'overwhelming empirical evidence' now 'suggests that capital markets are not fundamentally efficient.'" To support this contention, Halliburton cites studies purporting to show that "public information is often not incorporated immediately (much less rationally) into market prices." . . .

Halliburton does not, of course, maintain that capital markets are *always* inefficient. Rather, in its view, *Basic*'s fundamental error was to ignore the fact that "efficiency is not a binary, yes or no question." The markets for some securities are more efficient than the markets for others, and even a single market can process different kinds of information more or less efficiently, depending on how widely the information is disseminated and how easily it is understood. Yet *Basic,* Halliburton asserts, glossed over these nuances, assuming a false dichotomy that renders the presumption of reliance both underinclusive and overinclusive: A misrepresentation can distort a stock's market price even in a generally inefficient market, and a misrepresentation can leave a stock's market price unaffected even in a generally efficient one.

Halliburton's criticisms fail to take *Basic* on its own terms. Halliburton focuses on the debate among economists about the degree to which the market price of a company's stock reflects public information about the company—and thus the degree to which an investor can earn an abnormal, above-market return by trading on such information. That debate is not new. Indeed, the *Basic* Court acknowledged it and declined to enter the fray, declaring that "[w]e need not determine by adjudication what economists and social scientists have debated through the use of sophisticated statistical analysis and the application of economic theory." To recognize the presumption of reliance, the Court explained, was not "conclusively to adopt any particular theory of how quickly and completely publicly available information is reflected in market price." The Court instead based the presumption on the fairly modest premise that "market professionals generally consider most publicly announced material statements about companies, thereby affecting stock market prices." *Basic*'s presumption of reliance thus does not rest on a "binary" view of market efficiency. Indeed, in making the presumption rebuttable, *Basic* recognized that market efficiency is a matter of degree and accordingly made it a matter of proof.

The academic debates discussed by Halliburton have not refuted the modest premise underlying the presumption of reliance. Even the foremost critics of the efficient-capital-markets hypothesis acknowledge that public information generally affects stock prices. . . . Debates about the precise *degree* to which stock prices accurately reflect public information are thus largely beside the point. . . . Even though the efficient capital markets hypothesis may have "garnered substantial criticism since *Basic*," Halliburton has not identified the kind of fundamental shift in economic theory that could justify overruling a precedent on the ground that it misunderstood, or has since been overtaken by, economic realities. . . .

Halliburton also contests a second premise underlying the *Basic* presumption: the notion that investors "invest 'in reliance on the integrity of [the market] price.'" . . . . Halliburton identifies a number of classes of investors for whom "price integrity" is supposedly "marginal or irrelevant." The primary example is the value investor, who believes that certain stocks are undervalued or overvalued and attempts to "beat the market" by buying the undervalued stocks and selling the overvalued ones. . . . If many investors "are indifferent to prices," Halliburton contends, then courts should not presume that investors rely on the integrity of those prices and any misrepresentations incorporated into them.

But *Basic* never denied the existence of such investors. As we recently explained, *Basic* concluded only that "it is reasonable to presume that *most* investors—knowing that they have little hope of outperforming the market in the long run based solely on their analysis of publicly available information—will rely on the security's market price as an unbiased assessment of the security's value in light of all public information." . . .

In any event, there is no reason to suppose that even Halliburton's main counterexample—the value investor—is as indifferent to the integrity of market prices as Halliburton suggests. Such an investor implicitly relies on the fact that a stock's market price will eventually reflect material information—how else could the market correction on which his profit depends occur? To be sure, the value investor "does not believe that the market price accurately reflects public information *at the time he transacts*." But to indirectly rely on a misstatement in the sense relevant for the *Basic* presumption, he need only trade stock based on the belief that the market price will incorporate public information within a reasonable period. The value investor also presumably tries to estimate *how* undervalued or overvalued a particular stock is, and such estimates can be skewed by a market price tainted by fraud.

. . .

III

Halliburton proposes two alternatives to overruling *Basic* that would alleviate what it regards as the decision's most serious flaws. The first alternative would require plaintiffs to prove that a defendant's misrepresentation actually affected the stock price—so-called "price impact"—in order to invoke the *Basic* presumption. It should not be enough, Halliburton contends, for plaintiffs to demonstrate the general efficiency of the market in which the stock traded. Halliburton's second proposed alternative would allow defendants to rebut the presumption of reliance with evidence of a *lack* of price impact, not only at the merits stage—which all agree defendants may already do—but also before class certification.

A

As noted, to invoke the *Basic* presumption, a plaintiff must prove that: (1) the alleged misrepresentations were publicly known, (2) they were material, (3) the stock traded in an efficient market, and (4) the plaintiff traded the stock between when the misrepresentations were made and when the truth was revealed. Each of these requirements follows from the fraud-on-the-market theory underlying the presumption. If the misrepresentation was not publicly known, then it could not have distorted the stock's market price. So too if the misrepresentation was immaterial—that is, if it would not have "been viewed by the reasonable investor as having significantly altered the 'total mix' of information made available,"—or if the market in which the stock traded was inefficient. And if the plaintiff did not buy or sell the stock after the misrepresentation was made but before the truth was revealed, then he could not be said to have acted in reliance on a fraud-tainted price.

The first three prerequisites are directed at price impact—"whether the alleged misrepresentations affected the market price in the first place." In the absence of price impact, *Basic*'s fraud-on-the-market theory and presumption of reliance collapse. The "fundamental premise" underlying the presumption is "that an investor presumptively relies on a misrepresentation so long as it was reflected in the market price at the time of his transaction." If it was not, then there is "no grounding for any contention that [the] investor[] indirectly relied on th[at] misrepresentation[] through [his] reliance on the integrity of the market price." . . .

Halliburton argues that since the *Basic* presumption hinges on price impact, plaintiffs should be required to prove it directly in order to invoke the presumption. Proving the presumption's prerequisites, which are at best an imperfect proxy for price impact, should not suffice.

Far from a modest refinement of the *Basic* presumption, this proposal would radically alter the required showing for the reliance element of the Rule 10b-5 cause of action. What is called the *Basic* presumption actually incorporates two constituent presumptions: First, if a plaintiff shows that the defendant's misrepresentation was public and material and that the stock traded in a generally efficient market, he is entitled to a presumption that the misrepresentation affected the stock price. Second, if the plaintiff also shows that he purchased the stock at the market price during the relevant period, he is entitled to a further presumption that he purchased the stock in reliance on the defendant's misrepresentation.

By requiring plaintiffs to prove price impact directly, Halliburton's proposal would take away the first constituent presumption. Halliburton's argument for doing so is the same as its primary argument for overruling the *Basic* presumption altogether: Because market efficiency is not a yes-or-no proposition, a public, material misrepresentation might not affect a stock's price even in a generally efficient market. But as explained, *Basic* never suggested otherwise; that is why it affords defendants an opportunity to rebut the presumption by showing, among other things, that the particular misrepresentation at issue did not affect the stock's market price. For the same reasons we declined to completely jettison the *Basic* presumption, we decline to effectively jettison half of it by revising the prerequisites for invoking it.

B

Even if plaintiffs need not directly prove price impact to invoke the *Basic* presumption, Halliburton contends that defendants should at least be allowed to defeat the presumption at the class certification stage through evidence that the misrepresentation did not in fact affect the stock price. We agree.

1

There is no dispute that defendants may introduce such evidence at the merits stage to rebut the *Basic* presumption. *Basic* itself "made clear that the presumption was just that, and could be rebutted by appropriate evidence," including evidence that the asserted misrepresentation (or its correction) did not affect the market price of the defendant's stock.

Nor is there any dispute that defendants may introduce price impact evidence at the class certification stage, so long as it is for the purpose of countering a plaintiff's showing of market efficiency, rather than directly rebutting the presumption. As EPJ Fund acknowledges, "[o]f course . . . defendants can introduce evidence at class certification of lack of price impact as some evidence that the market is not efficient."

After all, plaintiffs themselves can and do introduce evidence of the *existence* of price impact in connection with "event studies"—regression analyses that seek to show that the market price of the defendant's stock tends to respond to pertinent publicly reported events. In this case, for example, EPJ Fund submitted an event study of various episodes that might have been expected to affect the price of Halliburton's stock, in order to demonstrate that the market for that stock takes account of material, public information about the company. The episodes examined by EPJ Fund's event study included one of the alleged misrepresentations that form the basis of the Fund's suit. . . .

Defendants—like plaintiffs—may accordingly submit price impact evidence prior to class certification. What defendants may not do, EPJ Fund insists and the

Court of Appeals held, is rely on that same evidence prior to class certification for the particular purpose of rebutting the presumption altogether.

This restriction makes no sense, and can readily lead to bizarre results. Suppose a defendant at the certification stage submits an event study looking at the impact on the price of its stock from six discrete events, in an effort to refute the plaintiffs' claim of general market efficiency. All agree the defendant may do this. Suppose one of the six events is the specific misrepresentation asserted by the plaintiffs. All agree that this too is perfectly acceptable. Now suppose the district court determines that, despite the defendant's study, the plaintiff has carried its burden to prove market efficiency, but that the evidence shows no price impact with respect to the specific misrepresentation challenged in the suit. The evidence at the certification stage thus shows an efficient market, on which the alleged misrepresentation had no price impact. And yet under EPJ Fund's view, the plaintiffs' action should be certified and proceed as a class action (with all that entails), even though the fraud-on-the-market theory does not apply and common reliance thus cannot be presumed.

Such a result is inconsistent with *Basic*'s own logic. Under *Basic*'s fraud-on-the-market theory, market efficiency and the other prerequisites for invoking the presumption constitute an indirect way of showing price impact. As explained, it is appropriate to allow plaintiffs to rely on this indirect proxy for price impact, rather than requiring them to prove price impact directly, given *Basic* 's rationales for recognizing a presumption of reliance in the first place.

But an indirect proxy should not preclude direct evidence when such evidence is available. As we explained in *Basic*, "[a]ny showing that severs the link between the alleged misrepresentation and . . . the price received (or paid) by the plaintiff . . . will be sufficient to rebut the presumption of reliance" because "the basis for finding that the fraud had been transmitted through market price would be gone." And without the presumption of reliance, a Rule 10b-5 suit cannot proceed as a class action: Each plaintiff would have to prove reliance individually, so common issues would not "predominate" over individual ones, as required by Rule 23(b)(3). Price impact is thus an essential precondition for any Rule 10b-5 class action. While *Basic* allows plaintiffs to establish that precondition indirectly, it does not require courts to ignore a defendant's direct, more salient evidence showing that the alleged misrepresentation did not actually affect the stock's market price and, consequently, that the *Basic* presumption does not apply.

2

. . .

More than 25 years ago, we held that plaintiffs could satisfy the reliance element of the Rule 10b-5 cause of action by invoking a presumption that a public, material misrepresentation will distort the price of stock traded in an efficient market, and that anyone who purchases the stock at the market price may be considered to have done so in reliance on the misrepresentation. We adhere to that decision and decline to modify the prerequisites for invoking the presumption of reliance. But to maintain the consistency of the presumption with the class certification requirements of Federal Rule of Civil Procedure 23, defendants must be afforded an opportunity before class certification to defeat the presumption through evidence that an alleged misrepresentation did not actually affect the market price of the stock.

Because the courts below denied Halliburton that opportunity, we vacate the judgment of the Court of Appeals for the Fifth Circuit and remand the case for further proceedings consistent with this opinion.

It is so ordered.

. . .

Justice THOMAS, with whom Justice SCALIA and Justice ALITO join, concurring in the judgment

The implied Rule 10b-5 private cause of action is "a relic of the heady days in which this Court assumed common-law powers to create causes of action," . . . We have since ended that practice because the authority to fashion private remedies to enforce federal law belongs to Congress alone. Absent statutory authorization for a cause of action, "courts may not create one, no matter how desirable that might be as a policy matter." . . .

Basic Inc. v. Levinson, 485 U.S. 224, 108 S.Ct. 978, 99 L.Ed.2d 194 (1988), demonstrates the wisdom of this rule. *Basic* presented the question how investors must prove the reliance element of the implied Rule 10b-5 cause of action—the requirement that the plaintiff buy or sell stock in reliance on the defendant's misstatement—when they transact on modern, impersonal securities exchanges. Were the Rule 10b-5 action statutory, the Court could have resolved this question by interpreting the statutory language. Without a statute to interpret for guidance, however, the Court began instead with a particular policy "problem": for investors in impersonal markets, the traditional reliance requirement was hard to prove and impossible to prove as common among plaintiffs bringing 10b-5 class-action suits. With the task thus framed as "resol[ving]" that "problem" rather than interpreting statutory text, the Court turned to nascent economic theory and naked intuitions about investment behavior in its efforts to fashion a new, easier way to meet the reliance requirement. The result was an evidentiary presumption, based on a "fraud on the market" theory, that paved the way for class actions under Rule 10b-5.

Today we are asked to determine whether *Basic* was correctly decided. The Court suggests that it was, and that *stare decisis* demands that we preserve it. I disagree. Logic, economic realities, and our subsequent jurisprudence have undermined the foundations of the *Basic* presumption, and *stare decisis* cannot prop up the façade that remains. *Basic* should be overruled.

I

Understanding where *Basic* went wrong requires an explanation of the "reliance" requirement as traditionally understood.

"Reliance by the plaintiff upon the defendant's deceptive acts is an essential element" of the implied 10b-5 private cause of action. To prove reliance, the plaintiff must show "transaction causation," *i.e.*, that the specific misstatement induced "the investor's decision to engage in the transaction." Such proof "ensures that there is a proper 'connection between a defendant's misrepresentation and a plaintiff's injury'"—namely, that the plaintiff has not just lost money as a result of the misstatement, but that he was actually *defrauded* by it. . . . Without that connection, Rule 10b-5 is reduced to a "scheme of investor's insurance," because a plaintiff could recover whenever the defendant's misstatement distorted the stock price—regardless of whether the misstatement had actually tricked the plaintiff into buying (or selling) the stock in the first place. . . .

The "traditional" reliance element requires a plaintiff to "sho[w] that he was aware of a company's statement and engaged in a relevant transaction . . . based on that specific misrepresentation." But investors who purchase stock from third parties on impersonal exchanges (*e.g.*, the New York Stock Exchange) often will not be aware of any particular statement made by the issuer of the security, and therefore cannot establish that they transacted based on a specific misrepresentation. Nor is the traditional reliance requirement amenable to class treatment; the inherently individualized nature of the reliance inquiry renders it impossible for a 10b-5 plaintiff to prove that common questions predominate over individual ones, making class certification improper.

Citing these difficulties of proof and class certification, the *Basic* Court dispensed with the traditional reliance requirement in favor of a new one based on the fraud-on-the-market theory. The new version of reliance had two related parts.

First, *Basic* suggested that plaintiffs could meet the reliance requirement "'indirectly.'" The Court reasoned that "ideally, [the market] transmits information to the investor in the processed form of a market price." An investor could thus be said to have "relied" on a specific misstatement if (1) the market had incorporated that statement into the market price of the security, and (2) the investor then bought or sold that security "in reliance on the integrity of the [market] price," *i.e.*, based on his belief that the market price "reflect[ed]" the stock's underlying "value."

Second, *Basic* created a presumption that this "indirect" form of "reliance" had been proved. Based primarily on certain assumptions about economic theory and investor behavior, *Basic* afforded plaintiffs who traded in efficient markets an evidentiary presumption that both steps of the novel reliance requirement had been satisfied—that (1) the market *had* incorporated the specific misstatement into the market price of the security, and (2) the plaintiff *did* transact in reliance on the integrity of that price. A defendant was ostensibly entitled to rebut the presumption by putting forth evidence that either of those steps was absent.

II

Basic's reimagined reliance requirement was a mistake, and the passage of time has compounded its failings. First, the Court based both parts of the presumption of reliance on a questionable understanding of disputed economic theory and flawed intuitions about investor behavior. Second, *Basic*'s irebuttable presumption is at odds with our subsequent Rule 23 cases, which require plaintiffs seeking class certification to "affirmatively demonstrate" certification requirements like the predominance of common questions. Finally, *Basic*'s presumption that investors rely on the integrity of the market price is virtually irrebuttable in practice, which means that the "essential" reliance element effectively exists in name only.

A

Basic based the presumption of reliance on two factual assumptions. The first assumption was that, in a "well-developed market," public statements are generally "reflected" in the market price of securities. The second was that investors in such markets transact "in reliance on the integrity of that price." In other words, the Court created a presumption that a plaintiff had met the two-part, fraud-on-the-market version of the reliance requirement because, in the Court's view, "common sense and probability" suggested that each of those parts *would* be met.

In reality, both of the Court's key assumptions are highly contestable and do not provide the necessary support for *Basic*'s presumption of reliance. The first assumption—that public statements are "reflected" in the market price—was grounded in an economic theory that has garnered substantial criticism since *Basic*. The second assumption—that investors categorically rely on the integrity of the market price—is simply wrong.

1

The Court's first assumption was that "most publicly available information"—including public misstatements—"is reflected in [the] market price" of a security. The Court grounded that assumption in "empirical studies" testing a then-nascent economic theory known as the efficient capital markets hypothesis. Specifically, the Court relied upon the "semi-strong" version of that theory, which posits that the average investor cannot earn above-market returns (*i.e.,* "beat the market") in an efficient market by trading on the basis of publicly available information. . . . The upshot of the hypothesis is that "the market price of shares traded on well-developed markets [will] reflec[t] all publicly available information, and, hence, any material misrepresentations." At the time of *Basic,* this version of the efficient capital markets hypothesis was "widely accepted."

This view of market efficiency has since lost its luster. . . . As it turns out, even "well-developed" markets (like the New York Stock Exchange) do not uniformly incorporate information into market prices with high speed. "[F]riction in accessing public information" and the presence of "processing costs" means that "not all public information will be impounded in a security's price with the same alacrity, or perhaps with any quickness at all." ... For example, information that is easily digestible (merger announcements or stock splits) or especially prominent (Wall Street Journal articles) may be incorporated quickly, while information that is broadly applicable or technical (Securities and Exchange Commission filings) may be incorporated slowly or even ignored. ...

Further, and more importantly, "overwhelming empirical evidence" now suggests that even when markets do incorporate public information, they often fail to do so accurately.... "Scores" of "efficiency-defying anomalies"—such as market swings in the absence of new information and prolonged deviations from underlying asset values—make market efficiency "more contestable than ever." .... Such anomalies make it difficult to tell whether, at any given moment, a stock's price accurately reflects its value as indicated by all publicly available information. In sum, economists now understand that the price impact *Basic* assumed would happen reflexively is actually far from certain even in "well-developed" markets. Thus, *Basic*'s claim that "common sense and probability" support a presumption of reliance rests on shaky footing.

2

The *Basic* Court also grounded the presumption of reliance in a second assumption: that "[a]n investor who buys or sells stock at the price set by the market does so in reliance on the integrity of that price." In other words, the Court assumed that investors transact based on the belief that the market price accurately reflects the underlying "value" of the security. ...

The Court's rather superficial analysis does not withstand scrutiny. It cannot be seriously disputed that a great many investors do *not* buy or sell stock based on a belief that the stock's price accurately reflects its value. Many investors in fact trade for the opposite reason—that is, because they think the market has under- or overvalued the stock, and they believe they can profit from that mispricing. ... Indeed, securities transactions often take place because the transacting parties disagree on the security's value. ...

Other investors trade for reasons entirely unrelated to price—for instance, to address changing liquidity needs, tax concerns, or portfolio balancing requirements. ... These investment decisions—made with indifference to price and thus without regard for price "integrity"—are at odds with *Basic*'s understanding of what motivates investment decisions. In short, *Basic*'s assumption that all investors rely in common on "price integrity" is simply wrong.

The majority tries (but fails) to reconcile *Basic*'s assumption about investor behavior with the reality that many investors do not behave in the way *Basic* assumed. It first asserts that *Basic* rested only on the more modest view that "*most* investors" rely on the integrity of a security's market price. ... That gloss is difficult to square with *Basic*'s plain language: "An investor who buys or sells stock at the price set by the market does so in reliance on the integrity of that price." . . . In any event, neither *Basic* nor the majority offers anything more than a judicial hunch as evidence that even "most" investors rely on price integrity.

The majority also suggests that "there is no reason to suppose" that investors who buy stock they believe to be undervalued are "indifferent to the integrity of market prices." Such "value investor[s]," according to the majority, "implicitly rel[y] on the fact that a stock's market price will eventually reflect material information" and "presumably tr[y] to estimate *how* undervalued or overvalued a particular stock is" by reference to the market price. Whether the majority's unsupported claims about the thought processes of hypothetical investors are accurate or not, they are surely beside the point. Whatever else an investor believes about the market, he simply does not "rely on the integrity of the market price" if he does not believe that the market price accurately reflects public information *at the time he transacts*. That is, an investor cannot claim that a public misstatement induced his transaction by distorting the market price if he did not buy at that price while believing that it accurately incorporated that public information. For that sort of investor, *Basic*'s critical fiction falls apart.

B

Basic's presumption of reliance also conflicts with our more recent cases clarifying Rule 23's class-certification requirements. . . .

Basic permits plaintiffs to bypass that requirement of evidentiary proof. Under *Basic*, plaintiffs who invoke the presumption of reliance (by proving its predicates) are deemed to have met the predominance requirement of Rule 23(b)(3). . . . But, invoking the *Basic* presumption does not actually prove that individual questions of reliance will not overwhelm the common questions in the case. *Basic* still requires a showing that the *individual investor* bought or sold in reliance on the integrity of the market price and, crucially, permits defendants to rebut the presumption by producing evidence that individual plaintiffs do not meet that description. . . . Thus, by its own terms, *Basic* entitles defendants to ask each class member whether he traded in reliance on the integrity of the market price. That inquiry, like the traditional reliance inquiry, is inherently individualized; questions about the trading strategies of individual investors will not generate "common answers apt to drive the resolution of the litigation," . . . .

Basic thus exempts Rule 10b-5 plaintiffs from Rule 23's proof requirement. Plaintiffs who invoke the presumption of reliance are deemed to have shown predominance as a matter of law, even though the resulting rebuttable presumption leaves individualized questions of reliance in the case and predominance still unproved. . . .

For these reasons, *Basic* should be overruled in favor of the straightforward rule that "[r]eliance by the plaintiff upon the defendant's deceptive acts"—actual reliance, not the fictional "fraud-on-the-market" version—"is an essential element of the § 10(b) private cause of action."

. . .

Questions

1. To recover damages in a private securities fraud action under Rule 10b-5, a plaintiff must show scienter, materiality, reliance, and proximate cause. In *Basic v. Levinson*, 485 U.S. 224 (1988), the U.S. Supreme Court held that a plaintiff in misrepresentation cases could satisfy the reliance requirement by invoking the fraud-on-the-market theory, a theory grounded in the Efficient Capital Market Hypothesis (mentioned in our discussion of *Joy v. North*). As *Basic* explained, "the market price of shares traded on well-developed markets reflects all publicly available information, and, hence, any material misrepresentations," and rational investors buy and sell their shares on the market "in reliance on the integrity of the price." The market has changed since *Basic* was decided. Trading volumes and trading turnover have exploded, institutions have become considerably more active traders, and program trading, hedge funds in general, and activist hedge funds in particular, has risen. *Halliburton* came next.

2. What is Halliburton's claim? Why doesn't it accept *Basic*'s fraud-on-the-market theory?

3. What are the differences between the majority and concurring opinions? Do they just endorse different interpretations of ECMH?

4. Which investors are likely to benefit from the fraud-on-the-market theory? Why?

5. The question in *Halliburton* was "whether securities fraud defendants may attempt to rebut the *Basic* presumption at the class certification stage with evidence of a lack of price impact." What are the practical implications of the decision? What would be your advice to a plaintiff seeking to bring a securities fraud claim under *Basic*? Would it change after *Halliburton*?

West v. Prudential Securities, Incorporated
282 F.3d 935 (7th Cir. 2002)

EASTERBROOK, Judge

According to the complaint in this securities-fraud action, James Hofman, a stockbroker working for Prudential Securities, told 11 of his customers that Jefferson Savings Bancorp was "certain" to be acquired, at a big premium, in the near future. Hofman continued making this statement for seven months (repeating it to some clients); it was a lie, for no acquisition was impending. And if the statement had been the truth, then Hofman was inviting unlawful trading on the basis of material non-public information. He is a securities offender coming or going, as are any customers who traded on what they thought to be confidential information — if Hofman said what the plaintiffs allege, a subject still to be determined. What we must decide is whether the action may proceed, not on behalf of those who received Hofman's "news" in person but on behalf of *everyone* who bought Jefferson stock during the months when Hofman was misbehaving. The district judge certified such a class, invoking the fraud-on-the-market doctrine of *Basic, Inc. v. Levinson*. Prudential asks us to entertain an interlocutory appeal under Fed. R. Civ. P. 23(f). For two reasons, this is an appropriate case for such an appeal, which we now accept.

First, the district court's order marks a substantial extension of the fraud-on-the-market approach. *Basic* held that "[b]ecause most publicly available information is reflected in market price, an investor's reliance on any public material misrepresentations, therefore, may be presumed for purposes of a Rule 10b-5 action." The theme of *Basic* and other fraud-on-the-market decisions is that *public* information reaches professional investors, whose evaluations of that information and trades quickly influence securities prices. But Hofman did not release information to the public, and his clients thought that they were receiving and acting on non-public information; its value (if any) lay precisely in the fact that other traders did not know the news. No newspaper or other organ of general circulation reported that Jefferson was soon to be acquired. As plaintiffs summarize their position, their "argument in a nutshell is that it is unimportant for purposes of the fraud-on-the-market doctrine whether the information was 'publicly available' in the . . . sense that . . . the information was disseminated through a press release, or prospectus or other written format." Yet extending the fraud-on-the-market doctrine in this way requires not only a departure from *Basic* but also a novelty in fraud cases as a class—as another court of appeals remarked only recently in another securities suit, oral frauds have not been allowed to proceed as class actions, for the details of the deceit differ from victim to victim, and the nature of the loss also may be statement-specific. The appeal thus presents a novel and potentially important question of law.

Second, very few securities class actions are litigated to conclusion, so review of this novel and important legal issue may be possible only through the Rule 23(f) device. What is more, some scholars believe that the settlements in securities cases reflect high risk of catastrophic loss, which together with imperfect alignment of managers' and investors' interests leads defendants to pay substantial sums even when the plaintiffs have weak positions. . . . The strength of this effect has been debated, but its existence is established. The effect of a class certification in inducing settlement to curtail the risk of large awards provides a powerful reason to take an interlocutory appeal.

Because the parties' papers have developed their positions fully, and the district court has set a trial date less than two months away, we think it best to resolve the appeal promptly, and thus we turn to the merits.

Causation is the shortcoming in this class certification. *Basic* describes a mechanism by which public information affects stock prices, and thus may affect traders who did not know about that information. Professional investors monitor news about many firms; good news implies higher dividends and other benefits, which induces these investors to value the stock more highly, and they continue buying until the gains are exhausted. With many professional investors alert to news, markets are efficient in the sense that they rapidly adjust to all public information; if some of this information is false, the price will reach an incorrect level, staying there until the truth emerges. This approach has the support of financial economics as well as the imprimatur of the Justices: few propositions in economics are better established than the quick adjustment of securities prices to public information.

No similar mechanism explains how prices would respond to non-public information, such as statements made by Hofman to a handful of his clients. These do not come to the attention of professional investors or money managers, so the price-adjustment mechanism just described does not operate. Sometimes full-time market watchers can infer important news from the identity of a trader (when the corporation's CEO goes on a buying spree, this implies good news) or from the sheer volume of trades (an unprecedented buying volume may suggest that a bidder is accumulating stock in anticipation of a tender offer), but neither the identity of Hofman's customers nor the volume of their trades would have conveyed information to the market in this fashion. No one these days accepts the strongest version of the efficient capital market hypothesis, under which non-public information automatically affects prices. That version is empirically false: the public announcement of news (good and bad) has big effects on stock prices, which could not happen if prices already incorporated the effect of non-public information. Thus it is hard to see how Hofman's non-public statements could have caused changes in the price of Jefferson Savings stock. *Basic* founded the fraud-on-the-market doctrine on a causal mechanism with both theoretical and empirical power; for non-public information there is nothing comparable.

The district court did not identify any causal link between non-public information and securities prices, let alone show that the link is as strong as the one deemed sufficient (by a bare majority) in *Basic* (only four of the six Justices who participated in that case endorsed the fraud-on-the-market doctrine). Instead the judge observed that each side has the support of a reputable financial economist (Michael J. Barclay for the plaintiffs, Charles C. Cox for the defendant) and thought the clash enough by itself to support class certification and a trial on the merits. . . .

Because the record here does not demonstrate that non-public information affected the price of Jefferson Savings' stock, a remand is unnecessary. What the plaintiffs have going for them is that Jefferson's stock *did* rise in price (by about $5, or 20% of its trading price) during the months when Hofman was touting an impending acquisition, plus a model of demand-pull price increases offered by their expert. Barclay started with a model devised by another economist, in which trades themselves convey information to the market and thus affect price. See Joel Hasbrouck, *Measuring the Information Content of Stock Trades*, 46 J. Fin. 179 (1991). Hasbrouck's model assumes that some trades are by informed traders and some by uninformed traders, and that the market may be able to draw inferences about which is which. The model has not been verified empirically. Barclay approached the issue differently, assuming that *all* trades affect prices by raising demand even if no trader is well informed—as if there were an economic market in "Jefferson Savings stock" as there is in dill pickles or fluffy towels. Hofman's tips raised the demand for Jefferson Savings stock and curtailed the supply (for the tippees were less likely to sell their own shares); that combination of effects raised the stock's price. Yet investors do not want Jefferson Savings *stock* (as if they sought to paper their walls with beautiful certificates); they want monetary returns (at given risk levels), returns that are available from many financial instruments. One fundamental attribute of efficient markets is that *information*, not demand in the abstract, determines stock prices. There are so many substitutes for any one firm's stock that the effective demand curve is horizontal. It may shift up or down with new information but is not sloped like the demand curve for physical products. That is why institutional purchases (which can be large in relation to normal trading volume) do not elevate prices, while relatively small trades by insiders can have substantial effects; the latter trades convey information, and the former do not. Barclay, who took the view that the market for Jefferson Savings securities is efficient, did not explain why he departed from the normal understanding that information rather than raw demand determines securities prices.

Data may upset theory, and if Barclay had demonstrated that demand by itself elevates securities prices, then the courts would be required to attend closely. What Barclay did is inquire whether the price of Jefferson Savings stock rose during the period of additional demand by Hofman's customers. He gave an affirmative answer and stopped. Yet it is not possible to prove a relation between demand and price without considering *other* potential reasons. Was there perhaps some truthful Jefferson-specific information released to the market at the time? Did Jefferson perhaps move *with* the market? It rose relative to a basket of all financial institutions, but (according to Cox's report) not relative to a portfolio of Midwestern financial intermediaries. Several Missouri banks and thrifts similar to Jefferson Savings were acquired during the months in question, and these transactions conveyed some information about the probability of a deal involving Jefferson Savings. If the price of Jefferson Savings was doing just what one would have expected in the presence of this changing probability of acquisition, and the absence of any Hofman-induced trades, then the causal link between Hofman's statements and price has not been made out. By failing to test for and exclude other potential sources of price movement, Barclay undercut the power of the inference that he advanced.

Indeed, Barclay's report calls into question his belief that the market for Jefferson Savings stock is efficient, the foundation of the fraud-on-the-market doctrine. In an efficient market, how could *one* ignorant outsider's lie cause a long-term rise in price? Professional investors would notice the inexplicable rise and either investigate for themselves (discovering the truth) or sell short immediately, driving the price back down. In an efficient market, a lie told by someone with nothing to back up the statement (no professional would have thought Hofman a person "in the know") will self-destruct long before eight months have passed. Hofman asserted that an acquisition was imminent. That statement might gull people for a month, but after two or three months have passed the lack of a merger or tender offer puts the lie to the assertion;

professional investors then draw more astute inferences and the price effect disappears. That this did not occur implies either that Jefferson Savings was not closely followed by professional investors (and that the market therefore does not satisfy *Basic*'s efficiency requirement) or that something other than Hofman's statements explains these price changes.

The record thus does not support extension of the fraud-on-the-market doctrine to the non-public statements Hofman is alleged to have made about Jefferson Savings Bancorp. The order certifying a class is reversed.

Questions

1. According to Judge Easterbrook, "Information, not demand in the abstract," may determine stock prices. But isn't the fact that there is increased trading in a stock information that some people believe that the stock is undervalued, whether because of an impending transaction or otherwise? Easterbrook's opinion assumes that investors are rational, that the information that matters is that relating to the value of the corporation. But many economists have come to accept the increasingly obvious fact that investors are not rational. Stock prices move for many reasons. Irrational investors can simply jump into a rising market because it is rising, reinforcing a rise based on nothing. Day traders buy and sell stock solely on the basis of stock price movements. If investors were always (or even mostly) rational, what accounts for bull markets and market collapses?

2. Why were the plaintiffs trading? They knew they possessed nonpublic material information. Why should we care if they lost money because of Hofman's fraud if they were trying to capitalize on another kind of fraud?

3. What is the goal of section 10b-5? Is it meant to protect individual investors? Institutional ones? The market? Or simply to punish those who engage in securities fraud?

B. Insider Trading

At common law, a director or officer could sell her stock without disclosing material nonpublic information concerning the corporation that she had acquired through her position. *Goodwin v. Agassiz*, 186 N.E. 659 (Mass. 1933). On the other hand, a director or officer could not make a false statement or tell a half-truth about the securities, or prevent others from acquiring information about them.

The common law was eclipsed by section 10(b) of the 1934 Act and Rule 10b-5 promulgated thereunder. In *Cady Roberts*, the seminal 10b-5 case, which was a hearing before the SEC, a partner in the brokerage firm of Cady, Roberts, and Co. who was also a director of Curtis-Wright corporation, attended a board meeting and discovered that the corporation was about to cut its quarterly dividend. Allegedly believing that the information was public, he called Robert Gintel, a partner at Cady, Roberts, and Co. Gintel then sold Curtis-Wright stock from discretionary accounts over which he had authority. When the news actually became public, Gintel's clients avoided losses suffered by other stockholders (including those purchasing from Gintel). The Commission found Gintel's trading to be a violation of section 10(b) and Rule 10b-5. The bases for liability were the findings of (i) a special relationship giving one party access to material nonpublic information intended to be used solely for corporate purpose and (ii) the inherent unfairness of such a party trading on the basis of that information without first disclosing it.

There are two ways of looking at the special relationship requirement. On the one hand, the purpose of the requirement seems to derive from the common law of insider trading, as well as of fraud. Only when such relationship already existed could a buyer be held to have reasonably relied upon a seller's silence as an affirmation of the absence of material information affecting the object of the sale. On the other hand, it has been argued that the purpose of the requirement is solely to establish that defendant had access to material nonpublic information. By virtue of special access, a trader could enjoy advantages unavailable to others. In a securities market that assumes relatively equal access to information, such advantages seem unfair. As you read the following cases, try to assess which way of looking at the special relationship requirement each of them adopts. What are the consequences of adopting one approach and not the other?

Securities and Exchange Commission v. Texas Gulf Sulphur Co.

401 F.2d 833 (2d Cir. 1969)

WATERMAN, Judge

This action was commenced in the United States District Court for the Southern District of New York by the Securities and Exchange Commission (the SEC) pursuant to Sec. 21(e) of the Securities Exchange Act of 1934 (the Act), 15 U.S.C. § 78u(e), against Texas Gulf Sulphur Company (TGS) and several of its officers, directors and employees, to enjoin certain conduct by TGS and the individual defendants said to violate Section 10(b) of the Act, 15 U.S.C. Section 78j(b), and Rule 10b-5 (17 CFR 240.10b-5) (the Rule), promulgated thereunder, and to compel the rescission by the individual defendants of securities transactions assertedly conducted contrary to law. The complaint alleged (1) that defendants Fogarty, Mollison, Darke, Murray, Huntington, O'Neill, Clayton, Crawford, and Coates had either personally or through agents purchased TGS stock or calls thereon from November 12, 1963 through April 16, 1964 on the basis of material inside information concerning the results of TGS drilling in Timmins, Ontario, while such information remained undisclosed to the investing public generally or to the particular sellers; (2) that defendants Darke and Coates had divulged such information to others for use in purchasing TGS stock or calls[3] or recommended its purchase while the information was undisclosed to the public or to the sellers; that defendants Stephens, Fogarty, Mollison, Holyk, and Kline had accepted options to purchase TGS stock on Feb. 20, 1964 without disclosing the material information as to the drilling progress to either the Stock Option Committee or the TGS Board of Directors; and (4) that TGS issued a deceptive press release on April 12, 1964....

The Factual Setting

This action derives from the exploratory activities of TGS begun in 1957 on the Canadian Shield in eastern Canada. In March of 1959, aerial geophysical surveys were conducted over more than 15,000 square miles of this area by a group led by defendant Mollison, a mining engineer and a Vice President of TGS. The group included defendant Holyk, TGS's chief geologist, defendant Clayton, an electrical engineer and geophysicist, and defendant Darke, a geologist. These operations resulted in the detection of numerous anomalies, i.e., extraordinary variations in the conductivity of rocks, one of which was on the Kidd 55 segment of land located near Timmins, Ontario.

On October 29 and 30, 1963, Clayton conducted a ground geophysical survey on the northeast portion of the Kidd 55 segment which confirmed the presence of an anomaly and indicated the necessity of diamond core drilling for further evaluation. Drilling of the initial hole, K-55-1, at the strongest part of the anomaly was commenced on November 8 and terminated on November 12 at a depth of 655 feet.... This visual estimate convinced TGS that it was desirable to acquire the remainder of the Kidd 55 segment, and in order to facilitate this acquisition TGS President Stephens instructed the exploration group to keep the results of K-55-1 confidential and undisclosed even as to other officers, directors, and employees of TGS.... [T]he core of K-55-1 had been shipped to Utah for chemical assay which, when received in early December, revealed an average mineral content of 1.18% copper, 8.26% zinc, and 3.94% ounces of silver per ton over a length of 602 feet. These results were so remarkable that neither Clayton, an experienced geophysicist, nor four other TGS expert witnesses, had ever seen or heard of a comparable initial exploratory drill hole in a base metal deposit.... By March 27, 1964, TGS decided that the land acquisition program had advanced to such a point that the company might well resume drilling, and drilling was resumed on March 31.

During this period, from November 12, 1963 when K-55-1 was completed, to March 31, 1964 when drilling was resumed, certain of the individual defendants ... said to have received "tips" from them, purchased TGS stock or calls thereon. Prior to these transactions these persons had owned 1135 shares of TGS stock and possessed no calls; thereafter they owned a total of 8235 shares and possessed 12,300 calls.

---

3. A "call" is a negotiable option contract by which the bearer has the right to buy from the writer of the contract a certain number of shares of a particular stock at a fixed price on or before a certain agreed-upon date.

On February 20, 1964, also during this period, TGS issued stock options to 26 of its officers and employees whose salaries exceeded a specified amount. . . . At this time, neither the TGS Stock Option Committee nor its Board of Directors had been informed of the results of K-55-1, presumably because of the pending land acquisition program which required confidentiality. All of the foregoing defendants accepted the options granted them. . . .

Meanwhile, rumors that a major ore strike was in the making had been circulating throughout Canada. On the morning of Saturday, April 11, Stephens at his home in Greenwich, Conn. read in the New York Herald Tribune and in the New York Times unauthorized reports of the TGS drilling which seemed to infer a rich strike from the fact that the drill cores had been flown to the United States for chemical assay. Stephens immediately contacted Fogarty at his home in Rye, N. Y., who in turn telephoned and later that day visited Mollison at Mollison's home in Greenwich to obtain a current report and evaluation of the drilling progress. The following morning, Sunday, Fogarty again telephoned Mollison, inquiring whether Mollison had any further information and told him to return to Timmins with Holyk, the TGS Chief Geologist, as soon as possible "to move things along." With the aid of one Carroll, a public relations consultant, Fogarty drafted a press release designed to quell the rumors, which release, after having been channeled through Stephens and Huntington, a TGS attorney, was issued at 3:00 P.M. on Sunday, April 12, and which appeared in the morning newspapers of general circulation on Monday, April 13. It read in pertinent part as follows:

> NEW YORK, April 12—The following statement was made today by Dr. Charles F. Fogarty, executive vice president of Texas Gulf Sulphur Company, in regard to the company's drilling operations near Timmins, Ontario, Canada. Dr. Fogarty said:
>
> "During the past few days, the exploration activities of Texas Gulf Sulphur in the area of Timmins, Ontario, have been widely reported in the press, coupled with rumors of a substantial copper discovery there. These reports exaggerate the scale of operations, and mention plans and statistics of size and grade of ore that are without factual basis and have evidently originated by speculation of people not connected with TGS.
>
> The facts are as follows. TGS has been exploring in the Timmins area for six years as part of its overall search in Canada and elsewhere for various minerals—lead, copper, zinc, etc. During the course of this work, in Timmins as well as in Eastern Canada, TGS has conducted exploration entirely on its own, without the participation by others. Numerous prospects have been investigated by geophysical means and a large number of selected ones have been core-drilled. These cores are sent to the United States for assay and detailed examination as a matter of routine and on advice of expert Canadian legal counsel. No inferences as to grade can be drawn from this procedure.

Most of the areas drilled in Eastern Canada have revealed either barren pyrite or graphite without value; a few have resulted in discoveries of small or marginal sulphide ore bodies.

Recent drilling on one property near Timmins has led to preliminary indications that more drilling would be required for proper evaluation of this prospect. The drilling done to date has not been conclusive, but the statements made by many outside quarters are unreliable and include information and figures that are not available to TGS.

The work done to date has not been sufficient to reach definite conclusions and any statement as to size and grade of ore would be premature and possibly misleading. When we have progressed to the point where reasonable and logical conclusions can be made, TGS will issue a definite statement to its stockholders and to the public in order to clarify the Timmins project."

The release purported to give the Timmins drilling results as of the release date, April 12. From Mollison Fogarty had been told of the developments through 7:00 P.M. on April 10, and of the remarkable discoveries made up to that time, detailed supra, which discoveries, according to the calculations of the experts who testified for the SEC at the hearing, demonstrated that TGS had already discovered 6.2 to 8.3 million tons of proven ore having gross assay values from $26 to $29 per ton. TGS experts, on the other hand, denied at the hearing that proven or probable ore could have been calculated on April 11 or 12 because there was then no assurance of continuity in the mineralized zone.

The evidence as to the effect of this release on the investing public was equivocal and less than abundant. On April 13 the New York Herald Tribune in an article headnoted "Copper Rumor Deflated" quoted from the TGS release of April 12 and backtracked from its original April 11 report of a major strike but nevertheless inferred from the TGS release that "recent mineral exploratory activity near Timmins, Ontario, has provided preliminary favorable results, sufficient at least to require a step-up in drilling operations." Some witnesses who testified at the hearing stated that they found the release encouraging. On the other hand, a Canadian mining security specialist, Roche, stated that "earlier in the week [before April 16] we had a Dow Jones saying that they [TGS] didn't have anything basically" and a TGS stock specialist for the Midwest Stock Exchange became concerned about his long position in the stock after reading the release. The trial court stated only that "While, in retrospect, the press release may appear gloomy or incomplete, this does not make it misleading or deceptive on the basis of the facts then known." . . .

While drilling activity ensued to completion, TGC officials were taking steps toward ultimate disclosure of the discovery. On April 13, a previously-invited reporter for The Northern Miner, a Canadian mining industry journal, visited the drill site, interviewed Mollison, Holyk and Darke, and prepared an article which confirmed a 10 million ton ore strike. This report, after having been submitted to Mollison and returned to the reporter unamended on April 15, was published in the April 16 issue. A statement relative to the extent of the discovery, in substantial part drafted by Mollison, was given to the Ontario Minister of Mines for release to the Canadian media. Mollison and Holyk expected it to be released over the airways at 11 P.M. on April 15th, but, for undisclosed reasons, it was not released until 9:40 A.M. on the 16th. An official detailed statement, announcing a strike of at least 25 million tons of ore, based on the drilling data set forth above, was read to representatives of American financial media from 10:00 A.M. to 10:10 or 10:15 A.M. on April 16, and appeared over Merrill Lynch's private wire at 10:29 A.M. and, somewhat later than expected, over the Dow Jones ticker tape at 10:54 A.M.

Between the time the first press release was issued on April 12 and the dissemination of the TGS official announcement on the morning of April 16, the only defendants before us on appeal who engaged in market activity were Clayton and Crawford and TGS director Coates. Clayton ordered 200 shares of TGS stock through his Canadian broker on April 15 and the order was executed that day over the Midwest Stock Exchange. Crawford ordered 300 shares at midnight on the 15th and another 300 shares at 8:30 A.M. the next day, and these orders were executed over the Midwest Exchange in Chicago at its opening on April 16. Coates left the TGS press conference and called his broker son-in-law Haemisegger shortly before 10:20 A.M. on the 16th and ordered 2,000 shares of TGS for family trust accounts of which Coates was a trustee but not a beneficiary; Haemisegger executed this order over the New York and Midwest Exchanges, and he and his customers purchased 1500 additional shares.

During the period of drilling in Timmins, the market price of TGS stock fluctuated but steadily gained overall. On Friday, November 8, when the drilling began, the stock closed at 17 3/8; on Friday, November 15, after K-55-1 had been completed, it closed at 18. After a slight decline to 16 3/8 by Friday, November 22, the price rose to 20 7/8 by December 13, when the chemical assay results of K-55-1 were received, and closed at a high of 24 1/8 on February 21, the day after the stock options had been issued. It had reached a price of 26 by March 31, after the land acquisition program had been completed and drilling had been resumed, and continued to ascend to 30 1/8 by the close of trading on April 10, at which time the drilling progress up to then was evaluated for the April 12th press release. On April 13, the day on which the April 12 release was disseminated, TGS opened at 30 1/8, rose immediately to a high of 32 and gradually tapered off to close at 30 7/8. It closed at 30 1/4 the next day, and at 29 3/8 on April 15. On April 16, the day of the official announcement of the Timmins discovery, the price climbed to a high of 37 and closed at 36 3/8. By May 15, TGS stock was selling at 58 1/4.

I. The Individual Defendants

A. *Introductory*

... Rule 10b-5 was promulgated pursuant to the grant of authority given the SEC by Congress in Section 10(b) of the Securities Exchange Act of 1934 (15 U.S.C. § 78j(b). By that Act Congress purposed to prevent inequitable and unfair practices and to insure fairness in securities transactions generally, whether conducted face-to-face, over the counter, or on exchanges. The Act and the Rule apply to the transactions here, all of which were consummated on exchanges. ...

The essence of the Rule is that anyone who, trading for his own account in the securities of a corporation has "access, directly or indirectly, to information intended to be available only for a corporate purpose and not for the personal benefit of anyone" may not take "advantage of such information knowing it is unavailable to those with whom he is dealing," i.e., the investing public. Insiders, as directors or management officers are, of course, by this Rule, precluded from so unfairly dealing, but the Rule is also applicable to one possessing the information who may not be strictly termed an "insider" within the meaning of Sec.16(b) of the Act. Thus, anyone in possession of material inside information must either disclose it to the investing public, or, if he is disabled from disclosing it in order to protect a corporate confidence, or he chooses not to do so, must abstain from trading in or recommending the securities concerned while such inside information remains undisclosed. So, it is here no justification for insider activity that disclosure was forbidden by the legitimate corporate objective of acquiring options to purchase the land surrounding the exploration site; if the information was, as the SEC contends, material, its possessors should have kept out of the market until disclosure was accomplished.

B. *Material Inside Information*

An insider is not, of course, always foreclosed from investing in his own company merely because he may be more familiar with company operations than are outside investors. An insider's duty to disclose information or his duty to abstain from dealing in his company's securities arises only in "those situations which are essentially extraordinary in nature and which are reasonably certain to have a substantial effect on the market price of the security if [the extraordinary situation is] disclosed." Fleischer, *Securities Trading and Corporate Information Practices: The Implications of the Texas Gulf Sulphur Proceeding*, 51 Va.L.Rev. 1271, 1289.

Nor is an insider obligated to confer upon outside investors the benefit of his superior financial or other expert analysis by disclosing his educated guesses or predictions. The only regulatory objective is that access to material information be enjoyed equally, but this objective requires nothing more than the disclosure of basic facts so that outsiders may draw upon their own evaluative expertise in reaching their own investment decisions with knowledge equal to that of the insiders.

This is not to suggest, however, as did the trial court, that "the test of materiality must necessarily be a conservative one, particularly since many actions under Section 10(b) are brought on the basis of hindsight," in the sense that the materiality of facts is to be assessed solely by measuring the effect the knowledge of the facts would have upon prudent or conservative investors. As we stated in *List v. Fashion Park, Inc.*, 340 F.2d 457, 462, "The basic test of materiality . . . is whether a *reasonable* man would attach importance . . . in determining his choice of action in the transaction in question." This, of course, encompasses any fact ". . . which in reasonable and objective contemplation *might* affect the value of the corporation's stock or securities. . . ." Such a fact is a material fact and must be effectively disclosed to the investing public prior to the commencement of insider trading in the corporation's securities. The speculators and chartists of Wall and Bay Streets are also "reasonable" investors entitled to the same legal protection afforded conservative traders.[10] Thus, material facts include not only information disclosing the earnings and distributions of a company but also those facts which affect the probable future of the company and those which may affect the desire of investors to buy, sell, or hold the company's securities.

In each case, then, whether facts are material within Rule 10b-5 when the facts relate to a particular event and are undisclosed by those persons who are knowledgeable thereof will depend at any given time upon a balancing of both the indicated probability that the event will occur and the anticipated magnitude of the event in light of the totality of the company activity. Here, notwithstanding the trial court's conclusion that the results of the first drill core, K-55-1, were "too 'remote' . . . to have had any significant impact on the market, i.e., to be deemed material," knowledge of the possibility, which surely was more than marginal, of the existence of a mine of the vast magnitude indicated by the remarkably rich drill core located rather close to the surface (suggesting mineability by the less expensive open-pit method) within the confines of a large anomaly (suggesting an extensive region of mineralization) might well have affected the price of TGS stock and would certainly have been an important fact to a reasonable, if speculative, investor in deciding whether he should buy, sell, or hold. After all, this first drill core was "unusually good and . . . excited the interest and speculation of those who knew about it."

. . . Our survey of the facts found below conclusively establishes that knowledge of the results of the discovery hole, K-55-1, would have been important to a

---

10. The House of Representatives committee that reported out the bill which eventually became the Act did so with the observation that "no investor, *no speculator*, can safely buy and sell securities upon exchanges without having an intelligent basis for forming his judgment as to the value of the securities he buys or sells." H.R.Rep.No. 1383, 73d Cong., 2d Sess. (1934), p. 11. (Emphasis supplied.) Dr. Bellemore, the Texas Gulf defendants' expert witness, has written: "The intelligent speculator assumes that facts are available for a thorough analysis. The speculator then examines the facts to discover and evaluate the risks that are present. He then balances these risks against the apparent opportunities for capital gains and makes his decision accordingly. He is, to the best of his ability, taking calculated risks." BELLEMORE, INVESTMENTS: PRINCIPLES, PRACTICES AND ANALYSIS 4 (2d ed. 1962).

reasonable investor and might have affected the price of the stock.[12] On April 16, The Northern Miner, a trade publication in wide circulation among mining stock specialists, called K-55-1, the discovery hole, "one of the most impressive drill holes completed in modern times." ... Additional testimony revealed that the prices of stocks of other companies, albeit less diversified, smaller firms, had increased substantially solely on the basis of the discovery of good anomalies or even because of the proximity of their lands to the sites of a potentially major strike.

Finally, a major factor in determining whether the K-55-1 discovery was a material fact is the importance attached to the drilling results by those who knew about it. In view of other unrelated recent developments favorably affecting TGS, participation by an informed person in a regular stock-purchase program, or even sporadic trading by an informed person, might lend only nominal support to the inference of the materiality of the K-55-1 discovery; nevertheless, the timing by those who knew of it of their stock purchases and their purchases of *short-term* calls—purchases in some cases by individuals who had never before purchased calls or even TGS stock—virtually compels the inference that the insiders were influenced by the drilling results....

Our decision to expand the limited protection afforded outside investors by the trial court's narrow definition of materiality is not at all shaken by fears that the elimination of insider trading benefits will deplete the ranks of capable corporate managers by taking away an incentive to accept such employment. Such benefits, in essence, are forms of secret corporate compensation, derived at the expense of the uninformed investing public and not at the expense of the corporation which receives the sole benefit from insider incentives. Moreover, adequate incentives for corporate officers may be provided by properly administered stock options and employee purchase plans of which there are many in existence. In any event, the normal motivation induced by stock ownership, i.e., the identification of an individual with corporate progress, is ill-promoted by condoning the sort of speculative insider activity which occurred here; for example, some of the corporation's stock was sold at market in order to purchase short-term calls upon that stock, calls which would never be exercised to increase a stockholder equity in TGS unless the market price of that stock rose sharply.

The core of Rule 10b-5 is the implementation of the Congressional purpose that all investors should have equal access to the rewards of participation in securities

---

12. We do not suggest that material facts must be disclosed immediately; the timing of disclosure is a matter for the business judgment of the corporate officers entrusted with the management of the corporation within the affirmative disclosure requirements promulgated by the exchanges and by the SEC. Here, a valuable corporate purpose was served by delaying the publication of the K-55-1 discovery. We do intend to convey, however, that where a corporate purpose is thus served by withholding the news of a material fact, those persons who are thus quite properly true to their corporate trust must not during the period of non-disclosure deal personally in the corporation's securities or give to outsiders confidential information not generally available to all the corporation's stockholders and to the public at large.

transactions. It was the intent of Congress that all members of the investing public should be subject to identical market risks—which market risks include, of course the risk that one's evaluative capacity or one's capital available to put at risk may exceed another's capacity or capital. The insiders here were not trading on an equal footing with the outside investors. They alone were in a position to evaluate the probability and magnitude of what seemed from the outset to be a major ore strike; they alone could invest safely, secure in the expectation that the price of TGS stock would rise substantially in the event such a major strike should materialize, but would decline little, if at all, in the event of failure, for the public, ignorant at the outset of the favorable probabilities would likewise be unaware of the unproductive exploration, and the additional exploration costs would not significantly affect TGS market prices. Such inequities based upon unequal access to knowledge should not be shrugged off as inevitable in our way of life, or, in view of the congressional concern in the area, remain uncorrected.

We hold, therefore, that all transactions in TGS stock or calls by individuals apprised of the drilling results of K-55-1 were made in violation of Rule 10b-5. Inasmuch as the visual evaluation of that drill core (a generally reliable estimate though less accurate than a chemical assay) constituted material information, those advised of the results of the visual evaluation as well as those informed of the chemical assay traded in violation of law. The geologist Darke possessed undisclosed material information and traded in TGS securities. Therefore we reverse the dismissal of the action as to him and his personal transactions. The trial court also found that Darke, after the drilling of K-55-1 had been completed and with detailed knowledge of the results thereof, told certain outside individuals that TGS "was a good buy." These individuals thereafter acquired TGS stock and calls. . . .

As Darke's "tippees" are not defendants in this action, we need not decide whether, if they acted with actual or constructive knowledge that the material information was undisclosed, their conduct is as equally violative of the Rule as the conduct of their insider source, though we note that it certainly could be equally reprehensible.

[The court goes on to assess whether the other defendants traded on the basis of material inside information.]

C. When May Insiders Act?

. . .

Coates was absolved by the court below because his telephone order was placed shortly before 10:20 A.M. on April 16, which was after the announcement had been made even though the news could not be considered already a matter of public information. This result seems to have been predicated upon a misinterpretation of dicta in *Cady, Roberts*, where the SEC instructed insiders to "keep out of the market until the established procedures for public release of the information are *carried out* instead of hastening to execute transactions in advance of, and in frustration of, the objectives of the release," 40 SEC at 915 (emphasis supplied). The reading of a news release, which prompted Coates into action, is merely the first step in the process of dissemination required for compliance with the regulatory objective of providing all investors with an equal opportunity to make informed investment judgments. Assuming that the contents of the official release could instantaneously be acted upon,[18] at the minimum Coates should have waited until the news could reasonably have been expected to appear over the media of widest circulation, the Dow Jones broad tape, rather than hastening to insure an advantage to himself and his broker son-in-law.[19]

D. *Is an Insider's Good Faith a Defense Under 10b-5?*

Coates, Crawford and Clayton, who ordered purchases before the news could be deemed disclosed, claim, nevertheless, that they were justified in doing so because they honestly believed that the news of the strike had become public at the time they placed their orders. However, whether the case before us is treated solely as an SEC enforcement proceeding or as a private action,[20] proof of a specific intent to defraud is unnecessary. In an enforcement proceeding for equitable or prophylactic relief, the common law standard of deceptive conduct has been modified in the interests of broader protection for the investing public so that negligent insider conduct has become unlawful. A similar standard has been adopted in private actions for policy reasons which seem perfectly consistent with the broad Congressional design ". . . to insure the maintenance of fair and honest markets in . . . [securities] transactions."

Absent any clear indication of a legislative intention to require a showing of specific fraudulent intent, the securities laws should be interpreted as an expansion of the common law[21] both to effectuate the broad remedial design of Congress, and to

---

18. Although the only insider who acted after the news appeared over the Dow Jones broad tape is not an appellant and therefore we need not discuss the necessity of considering the advisability of a "reasonable waiting period" during which outsiders may absorb and evaluate disclosures, we note in passing that, where the news is of a sort which is not readily translatable into investment action, insiders may not take advantage of their advance opportunity to evaluate the information by acting immediately upon dissemination. In any event, the permissible timing of insider transactions after disclosures of various sorts is one of the many areas of expertise for appropriate exercise of the SEC's rule-making power, which we hope will be utilized in the future to provide some predictability of certainty for the business community.

19. The record reveals that news usually appears on the Dow Jones broad tape 2–3 minutes after the reporter completes dictation. Here, assuming that the Dow Jones reporter left the press conference as early as possible, 10:10 A.M., the 10–15 minute release (which took at least that long to dictate) could not have appeared on the wire before 10:22, and for other reasons unknown to us did not appear until 10:54. Indeed, even the abbreviated version of the release reported by Merrill Lynch over its private wire did not appear until 10:29. Coates, however, placed his call no later than 10:20.

20. The SEC seeks permanent injunctions restraining future proscribed activity by all the individual defendants and the corporation. The Commission also seeks court orders upon certain of the individual defendants that are essentially remedies of a private, rather than of a regulatory nature, court orders designed to have those individual defendants disgorge any profits they enjoyed from TGS stock transactions they or their "tippees" engaged in from November 12, 1963 to April 17, 1964.

21. Even at common law, the essentially private remedy of rescission which is sought here does not require more than a showing of negligence and frequently even less than that, see Restatement, Contracts, §476, comm. b (1932); and the common law concept of constructive fraud still available

insure uniformity of enforcement. Moreover, a review of other sections of the Act from which Rule 10b-5 seems to have been drawn suggests that the implementation of a standard of conduct that encompasses negligence as well as active fraud comports with the administrative and the legislative purposes underlying the Rule. Finally, we note that this position is not, as asserted by defendants, irreconcilable with previous language in this circuit because *"some form* of the traditional scienter requirement," sometimes defined as "fraud," is preserved. This requirement, whether it be termed lack of diligence, constructive fraud, or unreasonable or negligent conduct, remains implicit in this standard, a standard that promotes the deterrence objective of the Rule.

Thus, the beliefs of Coates, Crawford and Clayton that the news of the ore strike was sufficiently public at the time of their purchase orders are to no avail if those beliefs were not reasonable under the circumstances. . . .

E. *May Insiders Accept Stock Options without Disclosing Material Information to the Issuer?*

On February 20, 1964, defendants Stephens, Fogarty, Mollison, Holyk and Kline accepted stock options issued to them and a number of other top officers of TGS, although not one of them had informed the Stock Option Committee of the Board of Directors or the Board of the results of K-55-1, which information we have held was then material. The SEC sought rescission of these options. . . .

. . . [W]e believe that [Kline], a vice president, who had become the general counsel of TGS in January 1964, but who had been secretary of the corporation since January 1961, and was present in that capacity when the options were granted, and who was in charge of the mechanics of issuance and acceptance of the options, was a member of top management and under a duty before accepting his option to disclose any material information he may have possessed, and, as he did not disclose such information to the Option Committee we direct rescission of the option he received.[24] . . .

---

to private plaintiffs has been expanded from recklessness to include non-reckless negligent misrepresentations or omissions.

24. The options granted on February 20, 1964 to Mollison, Holyk, and Kline were ratified by the Texas Gulf directors on July 15, 1965 after there had been, of course, a full disclosure and after this action had been commenced. However, the ratification is irrelevant here, for we would hold with the district court that a member of top management, as was Kline, is required, before accepting a stock option, to disclose material inside information which, if disclosed, might affect the price of the stock during the period when the accepted option could be exercised . . . . [I]n a case where disclosure to the grantors of an option would seriously jeopardize corporate security, it could well be desirable, in order to protect a corporation from selling securities to insiders who are in a position to appreciate their true worth at a price which may not accurately reflect the true value of the securities and at the same time to preserve when necessary the secrecy of corporate activity, not to require that an insider possessed of undisclosed material information reject the offer of a stock option, but only to require that he abstain from exercising it until such time as there shall have been a full disclosure and, after the full disclosure, a ratification such as was voted here. However, as this suggestion was not presented to us, we do not consider it or make any determination with reference to it.

II. The Corporate Defendant

A. *Introductory*

At 3:00 P.M. on April 12, 1964, evidently believing it desirable to comment upon the rumors concerning the Timmins project, TGS issued the press release.... The SEC argued below and maintains on this appeal that this release painted a misleading and deceptive picture of the drilling progress at the time of its issuance, and hence violated Rule 10b-5(2).[25] ...

... The specific SEC allegation in its complaint is that this April 12 press release "... was materially false and misleading and was known by certain of defendant Texas Gulf's officers and employees, including defendants Fogarty, Mollison, Holyk, Darke and Clayton, to be materially false and misleading."

The specific relief the SEC seeks is, pursuant to Section 21(e) of Securities Exchange Act of 1934, 15 U.S.C. §78u(e), a permanent injunction restraining the issuance of any further materially false and misleading publicly distributed informative items.

B. *The "In Connection With..." Requirement.*

. . .

The dominant congressional purposes underlying the Securities Exchange Act of 1934 were to promote free and open public securities markets and to protect the investing public from suffering inequities in trading, including, specifically, inequities that follow from trading that has been stimulated by the publication of false or misleading corporate information releases.... [T]he House Committee ... stated:

> The idea of a free and open public market is built upon the theory that competing judgments of buyers and sellers as to the fair price of a security brings about a situation where the market price reflects as nearly as possible a just price. Just as artificial manipulation tends to upset the true function of an open market, so the hiding and secreting of important information obstructs the operation of the markets as indices of real value. *There cannot be honest markets without honest publicity.* Manipulation and dishonest practices of the market place thrive upon mystery and secrecy. The disclosure of information materially important to investors may not instantaneously be reflected in market value, but despite the intricacies of security values truth does find relatively quick acceptance on the market. That is why in many cases it is so carefully guarded. Delayed, inaccurate, and misleading reports are the tools of the unconscionable market operator and the

---

25. Rule 10b-5(2) provides in pertinent part:
 It shall be unlawful for any person, directly or indirectly, by the use of any means or instrumentality of interstate commerce ....
 (2) to make any untrue statement of a material fact or to omit to state a material fact necessary in order to make the statements made, in the light of the circumstances under which they were made, not misleading ....
in connection with the purchase or sale of any security.

recreant corporate official who speculate on inside information. Despite the tug of conflicting interests and the influence of popular groups, responsible officials of the leading exchanges have unqualifiedly recognized in theory at least the vital importance of *true and accurate corporate reporting as an essential cog in the proper functioning of the public exchanges.* Their efforts to bring about more adequate and prompt publicity have been handicapped by the lack of legal power and by the failure of certain banking and business groups to appreciate that a business that gathers its capital from the investing public has not the same right to secrecy as a small privately owned and managed business. It is only a few decades since men believed that the disclosure of a balance sheet was a disclosure of a trade secret. Today few people would admit the right of any company to solicit public funds without the disclosure of a balance sheet. (Emphasis supplied.) H.R.Rep.No. 1383, 73rd Cong., 2d Sess. 11 (1934).

. . . [I]t seems clear from the legislative purpose Congress expressed in the Act, and the legislative history of Section 10(b) that Congress when it used the phrase "in connection with the purchase or sale of any security" intended only that the device employed, whatever it might be, be of a sort that would cause reasonable investors to rely thereon, and, in connection therewith, so relying, cause them to purchase or sell a corporation's securities. There is no indication that Congress intended that the corporations or persons responsible for the issuance of a misleading statement would not violate the section unless they engaged in related securities transactions or otherwise acted with wrongful motives; indeed, the obvious purposes of the Act to protect the investing public and to secure fair dealing in the securities markets would be seriously undermined by applying such a gloss onto the legislative language. Absent a securities transaction by an insider it is almost impossible to prove that a wrongful purpose motivated the issuance of the misleading statement. The mere fact that an insider did not engage in securities transactions does not negate the possibility of wrongful purpose; perhaps the market did not react to the misleading statement as much as was anticipated or perhaps the wrongful purpose was something other than the desire to buy at a low price or sell at a high price. Of even greater relevance to the Congressional purpose of investor protection is the fact that the investing public may be injured as much by one's misleading statement containing inaccuracies caused by negligence as by a misleading statement published intentionally to further a wrongful purpose. We do not believe that Congress intended that the proscriptions of the Act would not be violated unless the makers of a misleading statement also participated in pertinent securities transactions in connection therewith, or unless it could be shown that the issuance of the statement was motivated by a plan to benefit the corporation or themselves at the expense of a duped investing public. . . .

The foregoing discussion demonstrates that Congress intended to protect the investing public in connection with their purchases or sales on Exchanges from being misled by misleading statements promulgated for or on behalf of corporations irrespective of whether the insiders contemporaneously trade in the securities of that corporation and irrespective of whether the corporation or its management have an ulterior purpose or purposes in making an official public release. Indeed, the Commission has been charged by Congress with the responsibility of policing all misleading corporate statements from those contained in an initial prospectus to those contained in a notice to stockholders relative to the need or desirability of terminating the existence of a corporation or of merging it with another. To render the Congressional purpose ineffective by inserting into the statutory words the need of proving, not only that the public may have been misled by the release, but also that those responsible were actuated by a wrongful purpose when they issued the release, is to handicap unreasonably the Commission in its work. . . .

More important, however, is the realization which we must again underscore at the risk of repetition, that the investing public is hurt by exposure to false or deceptive statements irrespective of the purpose underlying their issuance. It does not appear to be unfair to impose upon corporate management a duty to ascertain the truth of any statements the corporation releases to its shareholders or to the investing public at large. Accordingly, we hold that Rule 10b-5 is violated whenever assertions are made, as here, in a manner reasonably calculated to influence the investing public, e.g., by means of the financial media, if such assertions are false or misleading or are so incomplete as to mislead irrespective of whether the issuance of the release was motivated by corporate officials for ulterior purposes. . . .

C. Did the Issuance of the April 12 Release Violate Rule 10b-5?

Turning first to the question of whether the release was misleading, i.e., whether it conveyed to the public a false impression of the drilling situation at the time of its issuance . . . we cannot, from the present record, by applying the standard Congress intended, definitively conclude that it was deceptive or misleading to the reasonable investor, or that he would have been misled by it. Certain newspaper accounts of the release viewed the release as confirming the existence of preliminary favorable developments, and this optimistic view was held by some brokers, so it could be that the reasonable investor would have read between the lines of what appears to us to be an inconclusive and negative statement and would have envisioned the actual situation at the Kidd segment on April 12. On the other hand, in view of the decline of the market price of TGS stock from a high of 32 on the morning of April 13 when the release was disseminated to 29 3/8 by the close of trading on April 15, and the reaction to the release by other brokers, it is far from certain that the release was generally interpreted as a highly encouraging report or even encouraging at all. Accordingly, we remand this issue to the district court that took testimony and heard and saw the witnesses for a determination of the character of the release in the light of the facts existing at the time of the release, by applying the standard of whether the reasonable investor, in the exercise of due care, would have been misled by it. . . .

In the event that it is found that the statement was misleading to the reasonable investor it will then become necessary to determine whether its issuance resulted from a lack of due diligence. . . .

We hold only that, in an action for injunctive relief, the district court has the discretionary power under Rule 10b-5 and Section 10(b) to issue an injunction, if the misleading statement resulted from a lack of due diligence on the part of TGS. . . .

We conclude, then, that, having established that the release was issued in a manner reasonably calculated to affect the market price of TGS stock and to influence the investing public, we must remand to the district court to decide whether the release was misleading to the reasonable investor and if found to be misleading, whether the court in its discretion should issue the injunction the SEC seeks. . . .

Questions

1. In *SEC v. Texas Gulf Sulphur Co.*, the court extended Rule 10b-5 to cover "anyone in possession of material inside information." Does the relationship of such person to the corporation and its shareholders matter? Should it?

2. Of what relevance to the court's decision, if any, is the defendants' conduct?

3. Why should we protect against insider trading? Who is harmed? Is it accurate to describe shareholders in publicly held corporations, many of whom invest in diversified portfolios and therefore share a rational apathy, as victims? Some suggest that banning insider trading guarantees market efficiency and integrity. The idea is that insider trading impairs investors' trust in the market and thus impedes investment. But if one believes that stock price reflects all the available information about the stock, doesn't insider trading supply the market with non-public information? Some scholars have argued that insider trading is a positive good, enhancing market efficiency by moving the stock price in the right direction.

4. Could insider trading be an effective way of compensating, or at least motivating, officers and directors to discover or produce things materially important to the corporation?

Dirks v. Securities and Exchange Commission
463 U.S. 646 (1983)

POWELL, Justice

Petitioner Raymond Dirks received material nonpublic information from "insiders" of a corporation with which he had no connection. He disclosed this information to investors who relied on it in trading in the shares of the corporation. The question is whether Dirks violated the antifraud provisions of the federal securities laws by this disclosure.

I

In 1973, Dirks was an officer of a New York broker-dealer firm who specialized in providing investment analysis of insurance company securities to institutional investors. On March 6, Dirks received information from Ronald Secrist, a former officer of Equity Funding of America. Secrist alleged that the assets of Equity Funding, a diversified corporation primarily engaged in selling life insurance and mutual funds, were vastly overstated as the result of fraudulent corporate practices. Secrist also stated that various regulatory agencies had failed to act on similar charges made by Equity Funding employees. He urged Dirks to verify the fraud and disclose it publicly.

Dirks decided to investigate the allegations. He visited Equity Funding's headquarters in Los Angeles and interviewed several officers and employees of the corporation. The senior management denied any wrongdoing, but certain corporation employees corroborated the charges of fraud. Neither Dirks nor his firm owned or traded any Equity Funding stock, but throughout his investigation he openly discussed the information he had obtained with a number of clients and investors. Some of these persons sold their holdings of Equity Funding securities, including five investment advisers who liquidated holdings of more than $16 million.

While Dirks was in Los Angeles, he was in touch regularly with William Blundell, the Wall Street Journal's Los Angeles bureau chief. Dirks urged Blundell to write a story on the fraud allegations. Blundell did not believe, however, that such a massive fraud could go undetected and declined to write the story. He feared that publishing such damaging hearsay might be libelous.

During the 2-week period in which Dirks pursued his investigation and spread word of Secrist's charges, the price of Equity Funding stock fell from $26 per share to less than $15 per share. This led the New York Stock Exchange to halt trading on March 27. Shortly thereafter California insurance authorities impounded Equity Funding's records and uncovered evidence of the fraud. Only then did the Securities and Exchange Commission (SEC) file a complaint against Equity Funding[3] and only then, on April 2, did the Wall Street Journal publish a front-page story based largely on information assembled by Dirks. Equity Funding immediately went into receivership.[4]

The SEC began an investigation into Dirks' role in the exposure of the fraud. After a hearing by an Administrative Law Judge, the SEC found that Dirks had aided and abetted violations of § 17(a) of the Securities Act of 1933, 48 Stat. 84, as amended, 15

---

3. As early as 1971, the SEC had received allegations of fraudulent accounting practices at Equity Funding. Moreover, on March 9, 1973, an official of the California Insurance Department informed the SEC's regional office in Los Angeles of Secrist's charges of fraud. Dirks himself voluntarily presented his information at the SEC's regional office beginning on March 27.

4. A federal grand jury in Los Angeles subsequently returned a 105-count indictment against 22 persons, including many of Equity Funding's officers and directors. All defendants were found guilty of one or more counts, either by a plea of guilty or a conviction after trial.

U.S.C. § 77q(a),[5] § 10(b) of the Securities Exchange Act of 1934, 48 Stat. 891, 15 U.S.C. § 78j(b),[6] and SEC Rule 10b-5, 17 CFR § 240.10b-5 (1983),[7] by repeating the allegations of fraud to members of the investment community who later sold their Equity Funding stock. The SEC concluded: "Where 'tippees'—regardless of their motivation or occupation—come into possession of material 'corporate information that they know is confidential and know or should know came from a corporate insider,' they must either publicly disclose that information or refrain from trading." Recognizing, however, that Dirks "played an important role in bringing [Equity Funding's] massive fraud to light," the SEC only censured him.

Dirks sought review in the Court of Appeals for the District of Columbia Circuit. The court entered judgment against Dirks "for the reasons stated by the Commission in its opinion." . . .

In view of the importance to the SEC and to the securities industry of the question presented by this case, we granted a writ of certiorari. We now reverse.

---

5. Section 17(a), as set forth in 15 U.S.C. § 77q(a), provides:
"It shall be unlawful for any person in the offer or sale of any securities by the use of any means or instruments of transportation or communication in interstate commerce or by the use of the mails, directly or indirectly—
(1) to employ any device, scheme, or artifice to defraud, or
(2) to obtain money or property by means of any untrue statement of a material fact or any omission to state a material fact necessary in order to make the statements made, in the light of the circumstances under which they were made, not misleading, or
(3) to engage in any transaction, practice, or course of business which operates or would operate as a fraud or deceit upon the purchaser."

6. Section 10(b) provide
"It shall be unlawful for any person, directly or indirectly, by the use of any means or instrumentality of interstate commerce or of the mails, or of any facility of any national securities exchange—
. . .
(b) To use or employ, in connection with the purchase or sale of any security registered on a national securities exchange or any security not so registered, any manipulative or deceptive device or contrivance in contravention of such rules and regulations as the Commission may prescribe as necessary or appropriate in the public interest or for the protection of investors."

7. Rule 10b-5 provide
"It shall be unlawful for any person, directly or indirectly, by the use of any means or instrumentality of interstate commerce, or of the mails or of any facility of any national securities exchange,
(a) To employ any device, scheme, or artifice to defraud,
(b) To make any untrue statement of a material fact or to omit to state a material fact necessary in order to make the statements made, in the light of the circumstances under which they were made, not misleading, or
(c) To engage in any act, practice, or course of business which operates or would operate as a fraud or deceit upon any person, in connection with the purchase or sale of any security."

II

In the seminal case of *In re Cady, Roberts & Co.*, 40 S.E.C. 907 (1961), the SEC recognized that the common law in some jurisdictions imposes on "corporate 'insiders,' particularly officers, directors, or controlling stockholders" an "affirmative duty of disclosure . . . when dealing in securities." The SEC found that not only did breach of this common-law duty also establish the elements of a Rule 10b-5 violation, but that individuals other than corporate insiders could be obligated either to disclose material nonpublic information[12] before trading or to abstain from trading altogether. In *Chiarella*, we accepted the two elements set out in *Cady, Roberts* for establishing a Rule 10b-5 violation: "(i) the existence of a relationship affording access to inside information intended to be available only for a corporate purpose, and (ii) the unfairness of allowing a corporate insider to take advantage of that information by trading without disclosure." In examining whether Chiarella had an obligation to disclose or abstain, the Court found that there is no general duty to disclose before trading on material nonpublic information, and held that "a duty to disclose under § 10(b) does not arise from the mere possession of nonpublic market information." Such a duty arises rather from the existence of a fiduciary relationship.

Not "all breaches of fiduciary duty in connection with a securities transaction," however, come within the ambit of Rule 10b-5. There must also be "manipulation or deception." In an inside-trading case this fraud derives from the "inherent unfairness involved where one takes advantage" of "information intended to be available only for a corporate purpose and not for the personal benefit of anyone." Thus, an insider will be liable under Rule 10b-5 for inside trading only where he fails to disclose material nonpublic information before trading on it and thus makes "secret profits."

III

We were explicit in *Chiarella* in saying that there can be no duty to disclose where the person who has traded on inside information "was not [the corporation's] agent, . . . was not a fiduciary, [or] was not a person in whom the sellers [of the securities] had placed their trust and confidence." Not to require such a fiduciary relationship, we recognized, would "[depart] radically from the established doctrine that duty arises from a specific relationship between two parties" and would amount to "recognizing a general duty between all participants in market transactions to forgo actions based on material, nonpublic information." This requirement of a specific relationship between the shareholders and the individual trading on inside information has created analytical difficulties for the SEC and courts in policing tippees who trade on inside information. Unlike insiders who have independent

---

12. The SEC views the disclosure duty as requiring more than disclosure to purchasers or sellers: "Proper and adequate disclosure of significant corporate developments can only be effected by a public release through the appropriate public media, designed to achieve a broad dissemination to the investing public generally and without favoring any special person or group." *In re Faberge, Inc.*, 45 S.E.C. 249, 256 (1973).

fiduciary duties to both the corporation and its shareholders, the typical tippee has no such relationships.[14] In view of this absence, it has been unclear how a tippee acquires the *Cady, Roberts* duty to refrain from trading on inside information.

A

The SEC's position, as stated in its opinion in this case, is that a tippee "inherits" the *Cady, Roberts* obligation to shareholders whenever he receives inside information from an insider:

> "In tipping potential traders, Dirks breached a duty which he had assumed as a result of knowingly receiving confidential information from [Equity Funding] insiders. Tippees such as Dirks who receive non-public, material information from insiders become 'subject to the same duty as [the] insiders.' Such a tippee breaches the fiduciary duty which he assumes from the insider when the tippee knowingly transmits the information to someone who will probably trade on the basis thereof.... Presumably, Dirks' informants were entitled to disclose the [Equity Funding] fraud in order to bring it to light and its perpetrators to justice. However, Dirks—standing in their shoes—committed a breach of the fiduciary duty which he had assumed in dealing with them, when he passed the information on to traders."

This view differs little from the view that we rejected as inconsistent with congressional intent in *Chiarella*. In that case, the Court of Appeals agreed with the SEC and affirmed Chiarella's conviction, holding that "[a]nyone—corporate insider or not—who regularly receives material nonpublic information may not use that information to trade in securities without incurring an affirmative duty to disclose." *United States v. Chiarella*, 588 F.2d 1358, 1365 (CA2 1978) (emphasis in original). Here, the SEC maintains that anyone who knowingly receives nonpublic material information from an insider has a fiduciary duty to disclose before trading.[15]

---

14. Under certain circumstances, such as where corporate information is revealed legitimately to an underwriter, accountant, lawyer, or consultant working for the corporation, these outsiders may become fiduciaries of the shareholders. The basis for recognizing this fiduciary duty is not simply that such persons acquired nonpublic corporate information, but rather that they have entered into a special confidential relationship in the conduct of the business of the enterprise and are given access to information solely for corporate purposes. When such a person breaches his fiduciary relationship, he may be treated more properly as a tipper than a tippee. For such a duty to be imposed, however, the corporation must expect the outsider to keep the disclosed nonpublic information confidential, and the relationship at least must imply such a duty.

15. Apparently, the SEC believes this case differs from *Chiarella* in that Dirks' receipt of inside information from Secrist, an insider, carried Secrist's duties with it, while Chiarella received the information without the direct involvement of an insider and thus inherited no duty to disclose or abstain. The SEC fails to explain, however, why the receipt of non-public information from an insider automatically carries with it the fiduciary duty of the insider. As we emphasized in *Chiarella*, mere possession of nonpublic information does not give rise to a duty to disclose or abstain; only a specific relationship does that. And we do not believe that the mere receipt of information from an insider creates such a special relationship between the tippee and the corporation's shareholders.

In effect, the SEC's theory of tippee liability in both cases appears rooted in the idea that the antifraud provisions require equal information among all traders. This conflicts with the principle set forth in *Chiarella* that only some persons, under some circumstances, will be barred from trading while in possession of material nonpublic information. . . .

Imposing a duty to disclose or abstain solely because a person knowingly receives material nonpublic information from an insider and trades on it could have an inhibiting influence on the role of market analysts, which the SEC itself recognizes is necessary to the preservation of a healthy market.[17] It is commonplace for analysts to "ferret out and analyze information,"[18] and this often is done by meeting with and questioning corporate officers and others who are insiders. And information that the analysts obtain normally may be the basis for judgments as to the market worth of a corporation's securities. The analyst's judgment in this respect is made available in market letters or otherwise to clients of the firm. It is the nature of this type of information, and indeed of the markets themselves, that such information cannot be made simultaneously available to all of the corporation's stockholders or the public generally.

Apparently recognizing the weakness of its argument in light of *Chiarella*, the SEC attempts to distinguish that case factually as involving not "inside" information, but rather "market" information, i.e., "information originating outside the company and usually about the supply and demand for the company's securities." This Court drew no such distinction in *Chiarella* and, as the Chief Justice noted, "[i]t is clear that § 10(b) and Rule 10b-5 by their terms and by their history make no such distinction." 445 U.S., at 241, n. 1 (dissenting opinion). See ALI, Federal Securities Code § 1603, Comment (2)(j) (Prop. Off. Draft 1978).

17. The SEC expressly recognized that "[the] value to the entire market of [analysts'] efforts cannot be gainsaid; market efficiency in pricing is significantly enhanced by [their] initiatives to ferret out and analyze information, and thus the analyst's work redounds to the benefit of all investors." The SEC asserts that analysts remain free to obtain from management corporate information for purposes of "filling in the 'interstices in analysis.' . . ." But this rule is inherently imprecise, and imprecision prevents parties from ordering their actions in accord with legal requirements. Unless the parties have some guidance as to where the line is between permissible and impermissible disclosures and uses, neither corporate insiders nor analysts can be sure when the line is crossed.

18. On its facts, this case is the unusual one. Dirks is an analyst in a broker-dealer firm, and he did interview management in the course of his investigation. He uncovered, however, startling information that required no analysis or exercise of judgment as to its market relevance. Nonetheless, the principle at issue here extends beyond these facts. The SEC's rule — applicable without regard to any breach by an insider — could have serious ramifications on reporting by analysts of investment views.

Despite the unusualness of Dirks' "find," the central role that he played in uncovering the fraud at Equity Funding, and that analysts in general can play in revealing information that corporations may have reason to withhold from the public, is an important one. Dirks' careful investigation brought to light a massive fraud at the corporation. And until the Equity Funding fraud was exposed, the information in the trading market was grossly inaccurate. But for Dirks' efforts, the fraud might well have gone undetected longer.

B

The conclusion that recipients of inside information do not invariably acquire a duty to disclose or abstain does not mean that such tippees always are free to trade on the information. The need for a ban on some tippee trading is clear. Not only are insiders forbidden by their fiduciary relationship from personally using undisclosed corporate information to their advantage, but they also may not give such information to an outsider for the same improper purpose of exploiting the information for their personal gain. . . . Similarly, the transactions of those who knowingly participate with the fiduciary in such a breach are "as forbidden" as transactions "on behalf of the trustee himself." . . . Thus, the tippee's duty to disclose or abstain is derivative from that of the insider's duty. . . . As we noted in *Chiarella*, "[the] tippee's obligation has been viewed as arising from his role as a participant after the fact in the insider's breach of a fiduciary duty."

Thus, some tippees must assume an insider's duty to the shareholders not because they receive inside information, but rather because it has been made available to them *improperly*. And for Rule 10b-5 purposes, the insider's disclosure is improper only where it would violate his *Cady, Roberts* duty. Thus, a tippee assumes a fiduciary duty to the shareholders of a corporation not to trade on material nonpublic information only when the insider has breached his fiduciary duty to the shareholders by disclosing the information to the tippee and the tippee knows or should know that there has been a breach. . . . Tipping thus properly is viewed only as a means of indirectly violating the *Cady, Roberts* disclose-or-abstain rule.

C

In determining whether a tippee is under an obligation to disclose or abstain, it thus is necessary to determine whether the insider's "tip" constituted a breach of the insider's fiduciary duty. All disclosures of confidential corporate information are not inconsistent with the duty insiders owe to shareholders. In contrast to the extraordinary facts of this case, the more typical situation in which there will be a question whether disclosure violates the insider's *Cady, Roberts* duty is when insiders disclose information to analysts. . . . In some situations, the insider will act consistently with his fiduciary duty to shareholders, and yet release of the information may affect the market. For example, it may not be clear—either to the corporate insider or to the recipient analyst—whether the information will be viewed as material nonpublic information. Corporate officials may mistakenly think the information already has been disclosed or that it is not material enough to affect the market. Whether disclosure is a breach of duty therefore depends in large part on the purpose of the disclosure. This standard was identified by the SEC itself in *Cady, Roberts*: a purpose of the securities laws was to eliminate "use of inside information for personal advantage." Thus, the test is whether the insider personally will benefit, directly or indirectly, from his disclosure. Absent some personal gain, there has been no breach of duty to stockholders. And absent a breach by the insider, there is no derivative breach.[22] . . .

Determining whether an insider personally benefits from a particular disclosure, a question of fact, will not always be easy for courts. But it is essential, we think, to have a guiding principle for those whose daily activities must be limited and instructed by the SEC's inside-trading rules, and we believe that there must be a breach of the insider's fiduciary duty before the tippee inherits the duty to disclose or abstain. In contrast, the rule adopted by the SEC in this case would have no limiting principle.

IV

Under the inside-trading and tipping rules set forth above, we find that there was no actionable violation by Dirks. It is undisputed that Dirks himself was a stranger to Equity Funding, with no pre-existing fiduciary duty to its shareholders. He took no action, directly or indirectly, that induced the shareholders or officers of Equity Funding to repose trust or confidence in him. There was no expectation by Dirks' sources that he would keep their information in confidence. Nor did Dirks misappropriate or illegally obtain the information about Equity Funding. Unless the insiders breached their *Cady, Roberts* duty to shareholders in disclosing the nonpublic information to Dirks, he breached no duty when he passed it on to investors as well as to the Wall Street Journal.

It is clear that neither Secrist nor the other Equity Funding employees violated their *Cady, Roberts* duty to the corporation's shareholders by providing information to Dirks. The tippers received no monetary or personal benefit for revealing Equity Funding's secrets, nor was their purpose to make a gift of valuable information to Dirks. As the facts of this case clearly indicate, the tippers were motivated by a desire to expose the fraud. In the absence of a breach of duty to shareholders by the insiders, there was no derivative breach by Dirks. Dirks therefore could not have been "a participant after the fact in [an] insider's breach of a fiduciary duty." *Chiarella*, 445 U.S., at 230, n. 12.

---

22. An example of a case turning on the court's determination that the disclosure did not impose any fiduciary duties on the recipient of the inside information is *Walton v. Morgan Stanley & Co.*, 623 F.2d 796 (CA2 1980). There, the defendant investment banking firm, representing one of its own corporate clients, investigated another corporation that was a possible target of a takeover bid by its client. In the course of negotiations the investment banking firm was given, on a confidential basis, unpublished material information. Subsequently, after the proposed takeover was abandoned, the firm was charged with relying on the information when it traded in the target corporation's stock. For purposes of the decision, it was assumed that the firm knew the information was confidential, but that it had been received in arm's-length negotiations. In the absence of any fiduciary relationship, the Court of Appeals found no basis for imposing tippee liability on the investment firm.

V

We conclude that Dirks, in the circumstances of this case, had no duty to abstain from use of the inside information that he obtained. The judgment of the Court of Appeals therefore is reversed.

BLACKMUN, Justice with whom BRENNAN and MARSHALL, Justices join (dissenting)

The Court today takes still another step to limit the protections provided investors by § 10(b) of the Securities Exchange Act of 1934. The device employed in this case engrafts a special motivational requirement on the fiduciary duty doctrine. This innovation excuses a knowing and intentional violation of an insider's duty to shareholders if the insider does not act from a motive of personal gain. Even on the extraordinary facts of this case, such an innovation is not justified. . . .

II

A

No one questions that Secrist himself could not trade on his inside information to the disadvantage of uninformed shareholders and purchasers of Equity Funding securities . . . Secrist stood in a fiduciary relationship with these shareholders. . . .

The Court also acknowledges that Secrist could not do by proxy what he was prohibited from doing personally. But this is precisely what Secrist did. Secrist used Dirks to disseminate information to Dirks' clients, who in turn dumped stock on unknowing purchasers. Secrist thus intended Dirks to injure the purchasers of Equity Funding securities to whom Secrist had a duty to disclose. Accepting the Court's view of tippee liability, it appears that Dirks' knowledge of this breach makes him liable as a participant in the breach after the fact.

B

The Court holds, however, that Dirks is not liable because Secrist did not violate his duty; according to the Court, this is so because Secrist did not have the improper purpose of personal gain. In so doing, the Court imposes a new, subjective limitation on the scope of the duty owed by insiders to shareholders. The novelty of this limitation is reflected in the Court's lack of support for it. . . .

C

The fact that the insider himself does not benefit from the breach does not eradicate the shareholder's injury. . . . It makes no difference to the shareholder whether the corporate insider gained or intended to gain personally from the transaction; the shareholder still has lost because of the insider's misuse of nonpublic information. The duty is addressed not to the insider's motives,[10] but to his actions and their

---

10. Of course, an insider is not liable in a Rule 10b-5 administrative action unless he has the requisite scienter. He must know that his conduct violates or intend that it violate his duty. Secrist obviously knew and intended that Dirks would cause trading on the inside information and that Equity

consequences on the shareholder. Personal gain is not an element of the breach of this duty. . . .

III

. . .

Although Secrist's general motive to expose the Equity Funding fraud was laudable, the means he chose were not. Moreover, even assuming that Dirks played a substantial role in exposing the fraud, he and his clients should not profit from the information they obtained from Secrist. . . . As a citizen, Dirks had at least an ethical obligation to report the information to the proper authorities. The Court's holding is deficient in policy terms not because it fails to create a legal norm out of that ethical norm, but because it actually rewards Dirks for his aiding and abetting.

Dirks and Secrist were under a duty to disclose the information or to refrain from trading on it. I agree that disclosure in this case would have been difficult. I also recognize that the SEC seemingly has been less than helpful in its view of the nature of disclosure necessary to satisfy the disclose-or-refrain duty. The Commission tells persons with inside information that they cannot trade on that information unless they disclose; it refuses, however, to tell them how to disclose. . . . This seems to be a less than sensible policy, which it is incumbent on the Commission to correct. The Court, however, has no authority to remedy the problem by opening a hole in the congressionally mandated prohibition on insider trading, thus rewarding such trading. . . .

IV

In my view, Secrist violated his duty to Equity Funding shareholders by transmitting material nonpublic information to Dirks with the intention that Dirks would cause his clients to trade on that information. Dirks, therefore, was under a duty to make the information publicly available or to refrain from actions that he knew would lead to trading. Because Dirks caused his clients to trade, he violated § 10(b) and Rule 10b-5. Any other result is a disservice to this country's attempt to provide fair and efficient capital markets. I dissent.

Questions

1. Is the SEC's pursuit of Dirks justified? Could Dirks have disclosed the information in a more disinterested manner? Of what relevance, if any, is the fact that Blundell, the *Wall Street Journal* reporter, refused to investigate or write about the alleged scandal?

2. Tippee liability attaches, according to the Court, when the disclosing insider has made the information available for an improper purpose, that is, when the disclosing insider breaches his own fiduciary duty by disclosing the information and the tippee "knows or should know" that there is a breach. This makes tipping an indirect means of violating the disclose or abstain rule. So what's a tippee to do? How

---

Funding shareholders would be harmed. The scienter requirement addresses the intent necessary to support liability; it does not address the motives behind the intent.

does she know when the insider has breached his fiduciary duty? Why was Secrist absolved from liability?

3. What is the difference between the majority's and the dissent's understanding of Rule 10b-5 and its goals? Why limit a tippee's liability only to a known breach of fiduciary duty by the insider?

4. What is the role of financial analysts? Does the decision in *Dirks* undermine or support it?

United States v. O'Hagan
521 U.S. 642 (1997)

GINSBURG, Justice

This case concerns the interpretation and enforcement of § 10(b) and § 14(e) of the Securities Exchange Act of 1934, and rules made by the Securities and Exchange Commission pursuant to these provisions, Rule 10b-5 and Rule 14e-3(a). Two prime questions are presented. The first relates to the misappropriation of material, non-public information for securities trading; the second concerns fraudulent practices in the tender offer setting. In particular, we address and resolve these issues: (1) Is a person who trades in securities for personal profit, using confidential information misappropriated in breach of a fiduciary duty to the source of the information, guilty of violating § 10(b) and Rule 10b-5? (2) Did the Commission exceed its rulemaking authority by adopting Rule 14e-3(a), which proscribes trading on undisclosed information in the tender offer setting, even in the absence of a duty to disclose? Our answer to the first question is yes, and to the second question, viewed in the context of this case, no.

I

Respondent James Herman O'Hagan was a partner in the law firm of Dorsey & Whitney in Minneapolis, Minnesota. In July 1988, Grand Metropolitan PLC (Grand Met), a company based in London, England, retained Dorsey & Whitney as local counsel to represent Grand Met regarding a potential tender offer for the common stock of the Pillsbury Company, headquartered in Minneapolis. Both Grand Met and Dorsey & Whitney took precautions to protect the confidentiality of Grand Met's tender offer plans. O'Hagan did no work on the Grand Met representation. Dorsey & Whitney withdrew from representing Grand Met on September 9, 1988. Less than a month later, on October 4, 1988, Grand Met publicly announced its tender offer for Pillsbury stock.

On August 18, 1988, while Dorsey & Whitney was still representing Grand Met, O'Hagan began purchasing call options for Pillsbury stock. Each option gave him the right to purchase 100 shares of Pillsbury stock by a specified date in September 1988. Later in August and in September, O'Hagan made additional purchases of

Pillsbury call options. By the end of September, he owned 2,500 unexpired Pillsbury options, apparently more than any other individual investor. O'Hagan also purchased, in September 1988, some 5,000 shares of Pillsbury common stock, at a price just under $39 per share. When Grand Met announced its tender offer in October, the price of Pillsbury stock rose to nearly $60 per share. O'Hagan then sold his Pillsbury call options and common stock, making a profit of more than $4.3 million.

The Securities and Exchange Commission (SEC or Commission) initiated an investigation into O'Hagan's transactions, culminating in a 57-count indictment. The indictment alleged that O'Hagan defrauded his law firm and its client, Grand Met, by using for his own trading purposes material, nonpublic information regarding Grand Met's planned tender offer. According to the indictment, O'Hagan used the profits he gained through this trading to conceal his previous embezzlement and conversion of unrelated client trust funds. O'Hagan was charged with 20 counts of mail fraud, in violation of 18 U.S.C. § 1341; 17 counts of securities fraud, in violation of § 10(b) of the Securities Exchange Act of 1934 (Exchange Act), 48 Stat. 891, 15 U.S.C. § 78j(b), and SEC Rule 10b-5, 17 CFR § 240.10b-5 (1996); 17 counts of fraudulent trading in connection with a tender offer, in violation of § 14(e) of the Exchange Act, 15 U.S.C. § 78n(e), and SEC Rule 14e-3(a), 17 CFR § 240.14e-3(a) (1996); and 3 counts of violating federal money laundering statutes, 18 U.S.C. §§ 1956(a)(1)(B)(i), 1957. A jury convicted O'Hagan on all 57 counts, and he was sentenced to a 41-month term of imprisonment.

A divided panel of the Court of Appeals for the Eighth Circuit reversed all of O'Hagan's convictions. Liability under § 10(b) and Rule 10b-5, the Eighth Circuit held, may not be grounded on the "misappropriation theory" of securities fraud on which the prosecution relied. The Court of Appeals also held that Rule 14e-3(a) — which prohibits trading while in possession of material, nonpublic information relating to a tender offer — exceeds the SEC's § 14(e) rulemaking authority because the rule contains no breach of fiduciary duty requirement. The Eighth Circuit further concluded that O'Hagan's mail fraud and money laundering convictions rested on violations of the securities laws, and therefore could not stand once the securities fraud convictions were reversed....

Decisions of the Courts of Appeals are in conflict on the propriety of the misappropriation theory under § 10(b) and Rule 10b-5, and on the legitimacy of Rule 14e-3(a) under § 14(e). We granted certiorari, and now reverse the Eighth Circuit's judgment.

II

We address first the Court of Appeals' reversal of O'Hagan's convictions under § 10(b) and Rule 10b-5. Following the Fourth Circuit's lead, the Eighth Circuit rejected the misappropriation theory as a basis for § 10(b) liability. We hold, in accord with several other Courts of Appeals, that criminal liability under § 10(b) may be predicated on the misappropriation theory.

A

In pertinent part, § 10(b) of the Exchange Act provides:

"It shall be unlawful for any person, directly or indirectly, by the use of any means or instrumentality of interstate commerce or of the mails, or of any facility of any national securities exchange—

. . .

(b) To use or employ, in connection with the purchase or sale of any security registered on a national securities exchange or any security not so registered, any manipulative or deceptive device or contrivance in contravention of such rules and regulations as the [Securities and Exchange] Commission may prescribe as necessary or appropriate in the public interest or for the protection of investors." 15 U.S.C. § 78j(b).

The statute thus proscribes (1) using any deceptive device (2) in connection with the purchase or sale of securities, in contravention of rules prescribed by the Commission. The provision, as written, does not confine its coverage to deception of a purchaser or seller of securities; rather, the statute reaches any deceptive device used "in connection with the purchase or sale of any security."

Pursuant to its § 10(b) rulemaking authority, the Commission has adopted Rule 10b-5, which, as relevant here, provides:

"It shall be unlawful for any person, directly or indirectly, by the use of any means or instrumentality of interstate commerce, or of the mails or of any facility of any national securities exchange,

(a) To employ any device, scheme, or artifice to defraud, [or] . . .

(c) To engage in any act, practice, or course of business which operates or would operate as a fraud or deceit upon any person,

in connection with the purchase or sale of any security." 17 CFR § 240.10b-5 (1996).

. . .

Under the "traditional" or "classical theory" of insider trading liability, § 10(b) and Rule 10b-5 are violated when a corporate insider trades in the securities of his corporation on the basis of material, nonpublic information. Trading on such information qualifies as a "deceptive device" under § 10(b), we have affirmed, because "a relationship of trust and confidence [exists] between the shareholders of a corporation and those insiders who have obtained confidential information by reason of their position with that corporation." *Chiarella v. United States.* That relationship, we recognized, "gives rise to a duty to disclose [or to abstain from trading] because of the 'necessity of preventing a corporate insider from . . . taking unfair advantage of . . . uninformed . . . stockholders.'" The classical theory applies not only to officers, directors, and other permanent insiders of a corporation, but also to attorneys, accountants, consultants, and others who temporarily become fiduciaries of a corporation. *Dirks v. SEC.*

The "misappropriation theory" holds that a person commits fraud "in connection with" a securities transaction, and thereby violates § 10(b) and Rule 10b-5, when he misappropriates confidential information for securities trading purposes, in breach of a duty owed to the source of the information. Under this theory, a fiduciary's undisclosed, self-serving use of a principal's information to purchase or sell securities, in breach of a duty of loyalty and confidentiality, defrauds the principal of the exclusive use of that information. In lieu of premising liability on a fiduciary relationship between company insider and purchaser or seller of the company's stock, the misappropriation theory premises liability on a fiduciary-turned-trader's deception of those who entrusted him with access to confidential information.

The two theories are complementary, each addressing efforts to capitalize on nonpublic information through the purchase or sale of securities. The classical theory targets a corporate insider's breach of duty to shareholders with whom the insider transacts; the misappropriation theory outlaws trading on the basis of nonpublic information by a corporate "outsider" in breach of a duty owed not to a trading party, but to the source of the information. The misappropriation theory is thus designed to "protec[t] the integrity of the securities markets against abuses by 'outsiders' to a corporation who have access to confidential information that will affect th[e] corporation's security price when revealed, but who owe no fiduciary or other duty to that corporation's shareholders."

In this case, the indictment alleged that O'Hagan, in breach of a duty of trust and confidence he owed to his law firm, Dorsey & Whitney, and to its client, Grand Met, traded on the basis of nonpublic information regarding Grand Met's planned tender offer for Pillsbury common stock. This conduct, the Government charged, constituted a fraudulent device in connection with the purchase and sale of securities.[5]

B

We agree with the Government that misappropriation, as just defined, satisfies § 10(b)'s requirement that chargeable conduct involve a "deceptive device or contrivance" used "in connection with" the purchase or sale of securities. We observe, first, that misappropriators, as the Government describes them, deal in deception. A fiduciary who "[pretends] loyalty to the principal while secretly converting the principal's information for personal gain," "dupes" or defrauds the principal. . . .

---

5. The Government could not have prosecuted O'Hagan under the classical theory, for O'Hagan was not an "insider" of Pillsbury, the corporation in whose stock he traded. Although an "outsider" with respect to Pillsbury, O'Hagan had an intimate association with, and was found to have traded on confidential information from, Dorsey & Whitney, counsel to tender offeror Grand Met. Under the misappropriation theory, O'Hagan's securities trading does not escape Exchange Act sanction, as it would under [the dissent's reasoning], simply because he was associated with, and gained nonpublic information from, the bidder, rather than the target.

Deception through nondisclosure is central to the theory of liability for which the Government seeks recognition. As counsel for the Government stated in explanation of the theory at oral argument: "To satisfy the common law rule that a trustee may not use the property that [has] been entrusted [to] him, there would have to be consent. To satisfy the requirement of the Securities Act that there be no deception, there would only have to be disclosure."[6]

... [F]ull disclosure forecloses liability under the misappropriation theory: Because the deception essential to the misappropriation theory involves feigning fidelity to the source of information, if the fiduciary discloses to the source that he plans to trade on the nonpublic information, there is no "deceptive device" and thus no § 10(b) violation — although the fiduciary-turned-trader may remain liable under state law for breach of a duty of loyalty.[7]

We turn next to the § 10(b) requirement that the misappropriator's deceptive use of information be "in connection with the purchase or sale of [a] security." This element is satisfied because the fiduciary's fraud is consummated, not when the fiduciary gains the confidential information, but when, without disclosure to his principal, he uses the information to purchase or sell securities. The securities transaction and the breach of duty thus coincide. This is so even though the person or entity defrauded is not the other party to the trade, but is, instead, the source of the nonpublic information. A misappropriator who trades on the basis of material, nonpublic information, in short, gains his advantageous market position through deception; he deceives the source of the information and simultaneously harms members of the investing public.

The misappropriation theory targets information of a sort that misappropriators ordinarily capitalize upon to gain no-risk profits through the purchase or sale of securities. Should a misappropriator put such information to other use, the statute's prohibition would not be implicated. The theory does not catch all conceivable forms of fraud involving confidential information; rather, it catches fraudulent means of capitalizing on such information through securities transactions. ...

The misappropriation theory comports with § 10(b)'s language, which requires deception "in connection with the purchase or sale of any security," not deception of an identifiable purchaser or seller. The theory is also well-tuned to an animating purpose of the Exchange Act: to insure honest securities markets and thereby promote investor confidence. Although informational disparity is inevitable in the

---

6. Under the misappropriation theory urged in this case, the disclosure obligation runs to the source of the information, here, Dorsey & Whitney and Grand Met. Chief Justice Burger, dissenting in *Chiarella*, advanced a broader reading of § 10(b) and Rule 10b-5; the disclosure obligation, as he envisioned it, ran to those with whom the misappropriator trades. The Government does not propose that we adopt a misappropriation theory of that breadth.

7. Where, however, a person trading on the basis of material, nonpublic information owes a duty of loyalty and confidentiality to two entities or persons — for example, a law firm and its client — but makes disclosure to only one, the trader may still be liable under the misappropriation theory.

securities markets, investors likely would hesitate to venture their capital in a market where trading based on misappropriated nonpublic information is unchecked by law. An investor's informational disadvantage vis-à-vis a misappropriator with material, nonpublic information stems from contrivance, not luck; it is a disadvantage that cannot be overcome with research or skill.

In sum, considering the inhibiting impact on market participation of trading on misappropriated information, and the congressional purposes underlying § 10(b), it makes scant sense to hold a lawyer like O'Hagan a § 10(b) violator if he works for a law firm representing the target of a tender offer, but not if he works for a law firm representing the bidder. The text of the statute requires no such result. The misappropriation at issue here was properly made the subject of a § 10(b) charge because it meets the statutory requirement that there be "deceptive" conduct "in connection with" securities transactions.

C

... Vital to our decision that criminal liability may be sustained under the misappropriation theory, we emphasize, are two sturdy safeguards Congress has provided regarding scienter. To establish a criminal violation of Rule 10b-5, the Government must prove that a person "willfully" violated the provision.[12] Furthermore, a defendant may not be imprisoned for violating Rule 10b-5 if he proves that he had no knowledge of the Rule....

III

We consider next the ground on which the Court of Appeals reversed O'Hagan's convictions for fraudulent trading in connection with a tender offer, in violation of § 14(e) of the Exchange Act and SEC Rule 14e-3(a). A sole question is before us as to these convictions: Did the Commission, as the Court of Appeals held, exceed its rulemaking authority under § 14(e) when it adopted Rule 14e-3(a) without requiring a showing that the trading at issue entailed a breach of fiduciary duty? We hold that the Commission, in this regard and to the extent relevant to this case, did not exceed its authority.

The governing statutory provision, § 14(e) of the Exchange Act, reads in relevant part:

> "It shall be unlawful for any person ... to engage in any fraudulent, deceptive, or manipulative acts or practices, in connection with any tender offer.... The [SEC] shall, for the purposes of this subsection, by rules and regulations

---

12. In relevant part, § 32 of the Exchange Act, as set forth in 15 U.S.C. § 78ff(a), provides: "Any person who willfully violates any provision of this chapter ... or any rule or regulation thereunder the violation of which is made unlawful or the observance of which is required under the terms of this chapter ... shall upon conviction be fined not more than $1,000,000, or imprisoned not more than 10 years, or both ...; but no person shall be subject to imprisonment under this section for the violation of any rule or regulation if he proves that he had no knowledge of such rule or regulation."

define, and prescribe means reasonably designed to prevent, such acts and practices as are fraudulent, deceptive, or manipulative." 15 U.S.C. §78n(e).

. . .

Relying on § 14(e)'s rulemaking authorization, the Commission, in 1980, promulgated Rule 14e-3(a). That measure provides:

"(a) If any person has taken a substantial step or steps to commence, or has commenced, a tender offer (the 'offering person'), it shall constitute a fraudulent, deceptive or manipulative act or practice within the meaning of section 14(e) of the [Exchange] Act for any other person who is in possession of material information relating to such tender offer which information he knows or has reason to know is nonpublic and which he knows or has reason to know has been acquired directly or indirectly from:

(1) The offering person,

(2) The issuer of the securities sought or to be sought by such tender offer, or

(3) Any officer, director, partner or employee or any other person acting on behalf of the offering person or such issuer, to purchase or sell or cause to be purchased or sold any of such securities or any securities convertible into or exchangeable for any such securities or any option or right to obtain or to dispose of any of the foregoing securities, unless within a reasonable time prior to any purchase or sale such information and its source are publicly disclosed by press release or otherwise." 17 CFR § 240.14e-3(a) (1996).

As characterized by the Commission, Rule 14e-3(a) is a "disclose or abstain from trading" requirement.[15] The Second Circuit concisely described the rule's thrust:

"One violates Rule 14e-3(a) if he trades on the basis of material nonpublic information concerning a pending tender offer that he knows or has reason to know has been acquired 'directly or indirectly' from an insider of the offeror or issuer, or someone working on their behalf. Rule 14e-3(a) is a disclosure provision. It creates a duty in those traders who fall within its ambit to abstain or disclose, *without regard to whether the trader owes a pre-existing fiduciary duty* to respect the confidentiality of the information." *United States v. Chestman,* 947 F.2d 551, 557 (1991) (en banc) (emphasis added), cert. denied.

In the Eighth Circuit's view, because Rule 14e-3(a) applies whether or not the trading in question breaches a fiduciary duty, the regulation exceeds the SEC's § 14(e) rulemaking authority. . . .

---

15. The rule thus adopts for the tender offer context a requirement resembling the one Chief Justice Burger would have adopted in *Chiarella* for misappropriators under §10(b).

We need not resolve in this case whether the Commission's authority under § 14(e) to "define . . . such acts and practices as are fraudulent" is broader than the Commission's fraud-defining authority under § 10(b), for we agree with the United States that Rule 14e-3(a), as applied to cases of this genre, qualifies under § 14(e) as a "means reasonably designed to prevent" fraudulent trading on material, nonpublic information in the tender offer context.[17] A prophylactic measure, because its mission is to prevent, typically encompasses more than the core activity prohibited. . . . We hold, accordingly, that under § 14(e), the Commission may prohibit acts not themselves fraudulent under the common law or § 10(b), if the prohibition is "reasonably designed to prevent . . . acts and practices [that] are fraudulent."[18]

Because Congress has authorized the Commission, in § 14(e), to prescribe legislative rules, we owe the Commission's judgment "more than mere deference or weight." Therefore, in determining whether Rule 14e-3(a)'s "disclose or abstain from trading" requirement is reasonably designed to prevent fraudulent acts, we must accord the Commission's assessment "controlling weight unless [it is] arbitrary, capricious, or manifestly contrary to the statute." In this case, we conclude, the Commission's assessment is none of these. . . .

In sum, it is a fair assumption that trading on the basis of material, nonpublic information will often involve a breach of a duty of confidentiality to the bidder or target company or their representatives. The SEC, cognizant of the proof problem that could enable sophisticated traders to escape responsibility, placed in Rule 14e-3(a) a "disclose or abstain from trading" command that does not require specific proof of a breach of fiduciary duty. That prescription, we are satisfied, applied to this case, is a "means reasonably designed to prevent" fraudulent trading on material, nonpublic information in the tender offer context. . . . Therefore, insofar as it serves to prevent the type of misappropriation charged against O'Hagan, Rule 14e-3(a) is a proper exercise of the Commission's prophylactic power under § 14(e). . . .

IV

. . .

The judgment of the Court of Appeals for the Eighth Circuit is reversed, and the case is remanded for further proceedings consistent with this opinion.

---

17. We leave for another day, when the issue requires decision, the legitimacy of Rule 14e-3(a) as applied to "warehousing," which the Government describes as "the practice by which bidders leak advance information of a tender offer to allies and encourage them to purchase the target company's stock before the bid is announced." As we observed in *Chiarella*, one of the Commission's purposes in proposing Rule 14e-3(a) was "to bar warehousing under its authority to regulate tender offers." The Government acknowledges that trading authorized by a principal breaches no fiduciary duty. The instant case, however, does not involve trading authorized by a principal; therefore, we need not here decide whether the Commission's proscription of warehousing falls within its § 14(e) authority to define or prevent fraud.

18. The Commission's power under § 10(b) is more limited. (Rule 10b-5 may proscribe only conduct that § 10(b) prohibits).

It is so ordered.

SCALIA, Justice (concurring in part and dissenting in part)

I join Parts I, III, and IV of the Court's opinion. I do not agree, however, with Part II of the Court's opinion, containing its analysis of respondent's convictions under § 10(b) and Rule 10b-5. . . .

While the Court's explanation of the scope of § 10(b) and Rule 10b-5 would be entirely reasonable in some other context, it does not seem to accord with the principle of lenity we apply to criminal statutes (which cannot be mitigated here by the Rule, which is no less ambiguous than the statute). In light of that principle, it seems to me that the unelaborated statutory language: "[t]o use or employ, in connection with the purchase or sale of any security . . . any manipulative or deceptive device or contrivance," § 10(b), must be construed to require the manipulation or deception of a party to a securities transaction.

Questions

1. The misappropriation theory adopted in *O'Hagan* can be traced to Chief Justice Burger's dissent in *Chiarella v. U.S.* 445 U.S. 222 (1980). Burger wrote that "a person who has misappropriated non-public information has an absolute duty to disclose that information or to refrain from trading." Following that decision, the circuit courts split over the misappropriation theory, some adopted it, while others, like the Eighth Circuit, did not. Does Justice Ginsburg endorse Chief Justice Burger's position or does she alter it?

2. Justice Ginsburg's version of the misappropriation theory turns on a breach of fiduciary duty by the advantaged trader followed by a securities trade. She ties the breach to the trade by saying, *ipse dixit*, that the trade proves that the breach was "in connection with" the purchase or sale of securities. But what does the breach of fiduciary duty that led to O'Hagan's conviction have to do with his securities trades? True, the breach was taking information. But the harm caused by this breach has nothing whatsoever to do with securities trading, does it? The very fact that Dorsey & Whitney and Grand Met could have given O'Hagan permission to trade seems to demonstrate that the two aspects of O'Hagan's behavior are unrelated. After all, the integrity of the market and the contemporaneous traders would be no less damaged by O'Hagan's trading if he had permission to do it. How, if at all, can the majority's opinion be reconciled with a coherent policy against insider trading?

3. What is the relationship of the rule in *O'Hagan* to that in *Dirks*? Upon what reasons for banning insider trading is it based? Does it accomplish its purpose, or is the Court more concerned with getting the statute right than creating a coherent anti-fraud policy?

4. According to *O'Hagan* does the restriction on insider trading rest on moral or economic justifications?

C. Short-Swing Profits

Section 16(b) of the Securities Exchange Act of 1934 provides that profits realized by an insider "from any purchase and sale, or any sale and purchase," within less than six months, "shall inure to and be recoverable by the issuer." The purpose of this restriction is to prevent "the unfair use of information which may have been obtained by [the insider] by reason of his relationship to the issuer." There is no need to prove intention or unfair use. Liability attaches when such offsetting trades occur within six months. For purposes of section 16(b), insiders are officers, directors, and any person who is the beneficial owner of more than 10 percent of a class of equity securities of any corporation registered under section 12 of the Securities Exchange Act.

In order to allow efficient enforcement, individuals covered under section 16(b) are required under section 16(a) to file statements with the SEC disclosing their ownership interests and any changes to them. Initial statements have to be filed within 10 days after the person has become an insider, while updating statements have to be filed within 2 days after the change in ownership interest occurred.

Suit to recover short-swing profit can be brought by the issuer or any security holder in the name of the issuer, if the board refused or failed to bring suit sixty days after demand.

Part 3

Shareholders

Part 3

Shareholders

This part examines the shareholders' role in the modern corporation. As you saw in Part 2, corporations are run by their managers. The shareholders' role is typically limited to the election of directors. Shareholders also have statutory rights to vote on charter amendments and certain fundamental transactions such as mergers. And management might ask shareholders to ratify corporate transactions, especially when, as with executive stock option plans, they are tainted with conflicts of interest. Voting in large public corporations is conducted by proxy, which is a written authorization given by a shareholder to someone else, typically the corporation's management, to cast her vote at a shareholders' meeting. Proxies are typically solicited by the board. If the solicitation is successful, the board exercises the proxies to elect its own candidates, to make its proposed charter amendments, to engage in particular fundamental transactions, and to ratify its past decisions.

A shareholder seeking to challenge the actions of her corporation's management may engage in a proxy contest. This requires the shareholder to solicit proxies from other shareholders in competition with management. If the shareholder succeeds, she upsets management's plans, and may even oust the board and replace it with her own. But this is rare. The board almost always dominates the proxy process. First, the only votes that count are those cast in favor of the names on the proxy, which usually are proposed by management. Furthermore, management often proposes only one candidate for each seat. Finally, 60% of American firms have a staggered board, which means that only one-third of board seats are up for election each year. A shareholder could still submit her own proxy carrying a rival slate of candidates, and if she gets more votes, she wins. But unlike management, which has the right to use corporate funds to promote its slate, the shareholder has to incur her own cost of the proxy contest. This can amount to several millions of dollars. Not surprisingly, proxy contests rarely happen.

An individual shareholder might also demand that management include a shareholder proposal along with its proxy solicitation under rule 14a-8 of the Securities Exchange Act of 1934. But, as you will see, the SEC and the courts have limited the permissible scope of shareholder proposals. Most important, a board can refuse to include a proposal dealing with "ordinary business" activity. Furthermore, a shareholder proposal that is included and voted on has no binding force. It is legally nothing more than advice to the board, and the board can ignore it.

As you read the material in Section I of this Part 3, consider how the shareholders' limited role might affect their interest in the corporation's affairs beyond the limited interest in short-term wealth maximization. Because, for the most part, shareholders in publicly held corporations are only interested in the maximization of their wealth, should we limit their ability to participate in managing corporate affairs? Are there ways to encourage shareholders to take a more active role in the affairs of corporations in which they are invested? Are certain shareholders more likely to be active than others? Do we really want shareholders to be more active?

Section II will examine the role of shareholders in closely held corporations. As you will see, shareholders in closely-held corporations often play a more significant role in managing their corporation's affairs, and the courts have made legal changes that make it easier for them to do so. Section III will introduce you to the power of controlling shareholders and the duties that such power implies.

Section I

Shareholders in Publicly Held Corporations

Dalia Tsuk Mitchell, *Shareholders as Proxies: The Contours of Shareholder Democracy*

63 WASH. & LEE L. REV. 1563 (2006)

[footnotes omitted]

The turn of the twentieth century witnessed a dramatic growth in the scale of private business organizations. Increasing consumer demand, rising numbers of skilled and unskilled workers, and an expanding pool of capital made the creation of large enterprises possible, while corporate lawyers created a variety of legal devices to help their clients to increase the scope of their operations through cooperation and combinations. Trusts, holding companies, and mergers became common, even if often contested in state courts. The nineteenth-century corporation, which was subject to strict constraints on its powers as well as limitations on its capital structure, was replaced by larger and larger units. Between 1888 and 1893, New Jersey revised its general incorporation statute to eliminate restrictions on "capitalization and assets, mergers and consolidations, the issuance of voting stock, the purpose(s) of incorporation, and the duration and locale of business." Other states followed suit, enacting more enabling incorporation statutes (including Delaware which, by the second decade of the twentieth century, would become the revolution's leader). And corporations were quick to use the power that these enabling statutes granted them. . . .

The concentration of power in the trusts and large business corporations undermined nineteenth century democratic ideals. Progressives feared that corporations were wearing away the function of the individual producer and, with it, the nineteenth-century democratic and economic ideals. These ideals were the power of markets equally to distribute the rewards of individual industry and to help conform individual liberty to socially beneficial ends. For some, individual ownership of property and participation in the market economy were a means of cultivating social and political citizenship. They saw in the corporation's collective ownership a threat to the idea of "ordinary producers," who "shape[d] their world on equal footing." For others, private property was a means of constraining the exercise of public power. They saw in the concentration of power in a few corporations a threat to individual autonomy. Giant corporations obfuscated "the traditional relationships between individual liberty, competition and social utility," and made impossible assessment of the national wealth based on aggregations of individual valuations. . . .

The growth of business combinations and the resulting quest for capital also led to the issuance of more common stock to draw in the public investor. . . . [T]he 1920s witnessed the widest participation rate in the securities market, up to that point, of the small individual purchaser. . . .

. . . [J]ust as shareholding grew more dispersed, different changes in corporate law at the turn of the twentieth century eroded the individual shareholder's ability to participate in managing the affairs of the corporation. The erosion of the traditional *ultra vires* doctrine, which limited corporate activities to its prescribed charter powers, and the reintroduction of the idea that the power of the board of directors was "original and undelegated" rather than delegated from the shareholders, helped minimize shareholder authority. So did changing voting rules. Proxy voting—which was banned in the early nineteenth century—became, at the turn of the twentieth century, the norm, authorized either in a specific charter provision or a statutory provision; gradually it became a means by which voting power was taken away from the shareholder. Shareholders' ability to remove directors at will was eliminated. In addition, while in the nineteenth century a unanimous vote was required to effect fundamental corporate changes, at the turn of the twentieth century states gradually adopted statutes allowing a majority of the shareholders to sell corporate assets. By 1926, the common law rule of unanimous vote was abrogated by statute or the judiciary in almost every state. . . .

Theoretically, of course, even a small investor could overcome his or her "normal apathy" and launch a proxy contest to replace seated directors. But, as Berle and Means sarcastically pointed out, the only example of a shareholder who succeeded in a proxy contest in the early twentieth century was John D. Rockefeller in his fight with the management of the Standard Oil Company of Indiana. Rockefeller, who had owned 14.9% of Standard Oil for years, became displeased with the company's management and waged a proxy fight to replace it. As Berle and Means explained, he won because of his relatively large ownership stake, his ability to fund the fight, and his own standing in the community. He won his fight for control because he had control and he was wealthy.

Moreover, a variety of legal tools developed to remove even the possibility that a small shareholder would have a meaningful voice. Not only were rules banning corporations from owning stock in other corporations replaced with statutes allowing mergers and holding companies (as early as 1889 in New Jersey), but a pyramid-style structure of ownership (that is, holding stock of a corporation which owned a majority of the stock of a subsidiary) became common. By investing in a corporation with a line of subsidiaries, "each controlled through ownership of a majority of its stock by the company higher in the series," an investor could exercise control while having a very small ownership interest in the property so controlled. Beginning in the 1910s, restrictions on the voting rights of certain classes of shareholders also became common. "By issuing bonds and non-voting preferred stock" to public investors in the subsidiaries (rather than voting stock), an investor could exercise control by owning an even smaller percentage of the property. . . .

Furthermore, while non-voting preferred stock was longstanding, in the early decades of the twentieth century certain states, including Delaware and New York, enacted statutory provisions allowing corporations to issue common stock with different voting powers (including non-voting stock). Similarly, corporations began issuing conditional or contingent voting stock, that is, stock that could vote only on the occurrence of a particular event. And while the New York Stock Exchange viewed privileging one class of common stock over others with disfavor and refused to list new issues of non-voting common stock, a different legal device—voting trusts—was allowed. It often gave the trustees almost complete control over corporate affairs without any ownership interest.

All these legal mechanisms transformed the relationship between shareholders and their corporations. . . . Berle and Means concluded in *The Modern Corporation and Private Property*, that

> the usual stockholder has little power over the affairs of the enterprise and his vote, if he has one, is rarely capable of being used as an instrument of democratic control. The separation of ownership and control has become virtually complete. The bulk of the owners have in fact almost no control over the enterprise, while those in control hold only a negligible proportion of the total ownership.

A. Proxy and Consent Contests

For the most part, the shareholder's participation in corporate affairs is limited to the election of directors at the annual meeting (usually by proxy voting). Shareholders who disapprove of their corporation's management can attempt to solicit proxies and elect their own representatives to the board. Proxy contests are governed by state law, federal regulation, and each corporation's certificate of incorporation and by-laws. Questions as to the type of information that the proxy solicitation must disclose, fraud, revocability of proxies, shareholders' access to corporate information, and the time and place of the shareholder meeting are governed by this combination of state, federal, and private regulation.

Proxy contests were relatively common in the 1950s. Proxy specialists at the time identified different reasons for the rise of the proxy fight: "there [was] a lot of money around," and people thought it could be used to take over a going concern; some believed they could "put a stumbling concern back on its feet"; some were opportunists, "who move from one inviting situation to another, combining with each other in ever-changing alliances"; some wanted to sit on the board for business reasons; while some were "after outright control—as an investment, as a chance to wield power, or as a step toward liquidation." John C. Perham, *Revolt of the Stockholder: Proxy Fights Are Breaking Out Everywhere These Days*, Barron's National Business and Financial Weekly, Apr. 26, 1954.

By the 1970s, however, proxy contests fell into desuetude. State statutes, such as section 141(d) of the Delaware General Corporation Law, made it more difficult for an insurgent to gain control by conducting a proxy contest. They allowed corporations to adopt classified boards, eliminate cumulative voting, and adopt dual class stock plans. (Can you see how these devices make it more difficult to gain control of the board?) As you will see in the following cases, proxy contests were also extremely expensive. More important, perhaps, was the shareholders' rational apathy. As explained by lawyers and economists, a rational shareholder will compare the expected benefits of carefully considering the proxy material with the cost of doing so. Given the length and complexity of proxy statements, especially when there are multiple communications from different groups (as in a proxy contest), and given that most shareholders' holdings in the corporation are too small significantly to affect the vote's outcome, the average shareholder rationally will not choose to invest time and effort in making an informed voting decision and instead will either vote for the incumbent directors or sell her stock. A study of 71 proxy contests between 1962 and 1978 revealed that insurgents won a majority of the board in a mere 18 cases, and some seats (although not a majority) in 27 more cases.

Not surprisingly, perhaps, the 1970s and 1980s witnessed tender offers and hostile takeovers superseding the proxy contest as a means of gaining control of the corporation. (Given what you already know about the twin rights of voice and exit, can you think why this is so?) Between 1981 and 1985, only 40 proxy contests were conducted in which control was sought, as compared to more than 250 tender offers. Moreover, many of the proxy contests in that period were conducted in conjunction with tender offers.

Some scholars have suggested that several changes in the economy and corporate law might make the proxy contest more common in the future. The burst of the 1990s bubble tightened the credit market for acquisitions, courts allow directors to adopt a wide range of defenses against tender offers, and states have legislated protections against takeovers, all of which make hostile takeovers or even friendly tender offers more cumbersome; at the same time, the rise of institutional investors has corrected for the general shareholders' rational apathy (albeit not to the extent expected in the early 1990s). *See generally* Stephen M. Bainbridge, *Redirecting State Takeover Laws at Proxy Contests*, 1992 WISC. L. REV. 1071; Lucian Arye Bebchuk & Marcel Kahan, *A Framework for Analyzing Legal Policy Towards Proxy Contests* 78 CALIF. L. REV. 1073 (1990); Martin Lipton, *Corporate Control Transactions: Pills, Polls, and Professors Redux*, 69 U. CHI. L. REV. 1037 (2002). It is important to note, however, that many corporations have also amended their charters to include "proxy contest impediment" provisions, including provisions revoking the shareholders' rights to vote by written consent, provisions forbidding special shareholder meetings, and staggered board provisions. *See* Sharon Hannes, *Corporate Stagnation: Discussion and Reform Proposal*, 30 IOWA J. CORP. L. 51 (2004). (We will examine the courts' analysis of similar provisions in the takeover context in Part 4.)

The cases you will read below explore strategic aspects of the proxy contest, including whether the corporation can reimburse incumbent directors or the insurgents for expenses incurred during the contest, and who can use corporate facilities and employees to conduct the fight. While these are seemingly technical questions, because of the prohibitive costs of engaging in an attempt to oust incumbent directors, they might determine the results of the fight before it even begins.

Rosenfeld v. Fairchild Engine and Airplane Corporation
309 N.Y. 168 (1955)

FROESSEL, Judge

In a stockholder's derivative action brought by plaintiff, an attorney, who owns 25 out of the company's over 2,300,000 shares, he seeks to compel the return of $261,522, paid out of the corporate treasury to reimburse both sides in a proxy contest for their expenses. The Appellate Division has unanimously affirmed a judgment of an Official Referee dismissing plaintiff's complaint on the merits, and we agree. Exhaustive opinions were written by both courts below, and it will serve no useful purpose to review the facts again.

Of the amount in controversy $106,000 were spent out of corporate funds by the old board of directors while still in office in defense of their position in said contest; $28,000 were paid to the old board by the new board after the change of management following the proxy contest, to compensate the former directors for such of the remaining expenses of their unsuccessful defense as the new board found was fair and reasonable; payment of $127,000, representing reimbursement of expenses to members of the prevailing group, was expressly ratified by a 16 to 1 majority vote of the stockholders.

The essential facts are not in dispute, and, since the determinations below are amply supported by the evidence, we are bound by the findings affirmed by the

Appellate Division. The Appellate Division found that the difference between plaintiff's group and the old board "went deep into the policies of the company", and that among these Ward's contract was one of the "main points of contention". The Official Referee found that the controversy "was based on an understandable difference in policy between the two groups, at the very bottom of which was the Ward employment contract".

By way of contrast with the findings here, in *Lawyers' Adv. Co. v. Consolidated Ry. Lighting & Refrig. Co.*, 187 N.Y. 395, which was an action to recover for the cost of publishing newspaper notices not authorized by the board of directors, it was expressly found that the proxy contest there involved was "by one faction in its contest with another for the control of the corporation . . . a contest for the perpetuation of their offices and control". We there said by way of *dicta* that under *such* circumstances the publication of certain notices on behalf of the management faction was not a corporate expenditure which the directors had the power to authorize.

Other jurisdictions and our own lower courts have held that management may look to the corporate treasury for the reasonable expenses of soliciting proxies to defend its position in a bona fide policy contest.

It should be noted that plaintiff does not argue that the aforementioned sums were fraudulently extracted from the corporation; indeed, his counsel conceded that "the charges were fair and reasonable", but denied "they were legal charges which may be reimbursed for". This is therefore not a case where a stockholder challenges specific items, which, on examination, the trial court may find unwarranted, excessive or otherwise improper. Had plaintiff made such objections here, the trial court would have been required to examine the items challenged.

If directors of a corporation may not in good faith incur reasonable and proper expenses in soliciting proxies in these days of giant corporations with vast numbers of stockholders, the corporate business might be seriously interfered with because of stockholder indifference and the difficulty of procuring a quorum, where there is no contest. In the event of a proxy contest, if the directors may not freely answer the challenges of outside groups and in good faith defend their actions with respect to corporate policy for the information of the stockholders, they and the corporation may be at the mercy of persons seeking to wrest control for their own purposes, so long as such persons have ample funds to conduct a proxy contest. The test is clear. When the directors act in good faith in a contest over policy, they have the right to incur reasonable and proper expenses for solicitation of proxies and in defense of their corporate policies, and are not obliged to sit idly by. The courts are entirely competent to pass upon their *bona fides* in any given case, as well as the nature of their expenditures when duly challenged.

It is also our view that the members of the so-called new group could be reimbursed by the corporation for their expenditures in this contest by affirmative vote of the stockholders. With regard to these ultimately successful contestants, as the

Appellate Division below has noted, there was, of course, "no duty . . . to set forth the facts, with corresponding obligation of the corporation to pay for such expense." However, where a majority of the stockholders chose—in this case by a vote of 16 to 1—to reimburse the successful contestants for achieving the very end sought and voted for by them as owners of the corporation, we see no reason to deny the effect of their ratification nor to hold the corporate body powerless to determine how its own moneys shall be spent.

The rule then which we adopt is simply this: In a contest over policy, as compared to a purely personal power contest, corporate directors have the right to make reasonable and proper expenditures, subject to the scrutiny of the courts when duly challenged, from the corporate treasury for the purpose of persuading the stockholders of the correctness of their position and soliciting their support for policies which the directors believe, in all good faith, are in the best interests of the corporation. The stockholders, moreover, have the right to reimburse successful contestants for the reasonable and bona fide expenses incurred by them in any such policy contest, subject to like court scrutiny. That is not to say, however, that corporate directors can, under any circumstances, disport themselves in a proxy contest with the corporation's moneys to an unlimited extent. Where it is established that such moneys have been spent for personal power, individual gain or private advantage, and not in the belief that such expenditures are in the best interests of the stockholders and the corporation, or where the fairness and reasonableness of the amounts allegedly expended are duly and successfully challenged, the courts will not hesitate to disallow them.

The judgment of the Appellate Division should be affirmed, without costs.

DESMOND, Judge (concurring)

We granted leave to appeal in an effort to pass, and in the expectation of passing, on this question, highly important in modern-day corporation law: is it lawful for a corporation, on consent of a majority of its stockholders, to pay, out of its funds, the expenses of a "proxy fight," incurred by competing candidates for election as directors? Now that the appeal has been argued, I doubt that the question is presented by this record. . . .

Plaintiff asserts that it was illegal for the directors (unless by unanimous consent of stockholders) to expend corporate moneys in the proxy contest beyond the amounts necessary to give to stockholders bare notice of the meeting and of the matters to be voted on thereat. Defendants say that the proxy contest revolved around disputes over corporate policies and that it was, accordingly, proper not only to assess against the corporation the expense of serving formal notices and of routine proxy solicitation, but to go further and spend corporate moneys, on behalf of each group, thoroughly to inform the stockholders. The reason why that important question is, perhaps, not directly before us in this lawsuit is because, as the Appellate Division properly held, plaintiff failed "to urge liability as to specific expenditures". The cost of giving routinely necessary notice is, of course, chargeable to the corporation. It is just as clear, we think, that payment by a corporation of the expense of "proceedings by one faction in its contest with another for the control of the corporation" is *ultra vires*, and unlawful. Approval by directors or by a majority stock vote could not validate such gratuitous expenditures. Some of the payments attacked in this suit were, on their face, for lawful purposes and apparently reasonable in amount but, as to others, the record simply does not contain evidentiary bases for a determination as to either lawfulness or reasonableness. Surely, the burden was on plaintiff to go forward to some extent with such particularization and proof. It failed to do so, and so failed to make out a prima facie case. . . .

A final comment: since expenditures which do not meet that test of propriety are intrinsically unlawful, it could not be any answer to such a claim as plaintiff makes here that the stockholder vote which purported to authorize them was heavy or that the change in management turned out to be beneficial to the corporation.

The judgment should be affirmed, without costs.

VAN VOORHIS, Judge (dissenting)

. . .

No resolution was passed by the stockholders approving payment to the management group. It has been recognized that not all of the $133,966 in obligations paid or incurred by the management group was designed merely for information of stockholders. This outlay included payment for all of the activities of a strenuous campaign to persuade and cajole in a hard-fought contest for control of this corporation. It included, for example, expenses for entertainment, chartered airplanes and limousines, public relations counsel and proxy solicitors. However legitimate such measures may be on behalf of stockholders themselves in such a controversy, most of them do not pertain to a corporate function but are part of the familiar apparatus of aggressive factions in corporate contests. . . .

The Appellate Division acknowledged in the instant case that "It is obvious that the management group here incurred a substantial amount of needless expense which was charged to the corporation," but this conclusion should have led to a direction that those defendants who were incumbent directors should be required to come forward with an explanation of their expenditures under the familiar rule that, where it has been established that directors have expended corporate money for their own purposes, the burden of going forward with evidence of the propriety and reasonableness of specific items rests upon the directors. The complaint should not have been dismissed as against incumbent directors due to failure of plaintiff to segregate the specific expenditures which are *ultra vires*, but, once plaintiff had proved facts from which an inference of impropriety might be drawn, the duty of making an explanation was laid upon the directors to explain and justify their conduct.

The second ground assigned by the Appellate Division for dismissing the complaint against incumbent directors is stockholder ratification of reimbursement to the insurgent group. Whatever effect or lack of it this resolution had upon expenditures by the insurgent group, clearly the stockholders who voted to pay the insurgents entertained no intention of reimbursing the management group for their expenditures. The insurgent group succeeded as a result of arousing the indignation of these very stockholders against the management group; nothing in the resolution to pay the expenses of the insurgent group purported to authorize or ratify payment of the campaign expenses of their adversaries, and certainly no inference should be drawn that the stockholders who voted to pay the insurgents intended that the incumbent group should also be paid. Upon the contrary, they were removing the incumbents from control mainly for the reason that they were charged with having mulcted the corporation by a long-term salary and pension contract to one of their number, J. Carlton Ward, Jr. If these stockholders had been presented with a resolution to pay the expenses of that group, it would almost certainly have been voted down. The stockholders should not be deemed to have authorized or ratified reimbursement of the incumbents.

There is no doubt that the management was entitled and under a duty to take reasonable steps to acquaint the stockholders with essential facts concerning the management of the corporation, and it may well be that the existence of a contest warranted them in circularizing the stockholders with more than ordinarily detailed information. . . .

What expenses of the incumbent group should be allowed and what should be disallowed should be remitted to the trial court to ascertain, after taking evidence, in accordance with the rule that the incumbent directors were required to assume the burden of going forward in the first instance with evidence explaining and justifying their expenditures. Only such as were reasonably related to informing the stockholders fully and fairly concerning the corporate affairs should be allowed. The concession by plaintiff that such expenditures as were made were reasonable in amount does not decide this question. By way of illustration, the costs of entertainment for stockholders may have been, and it is stipulated that they were, at the going rates for providing similar entertainment. That does not signify that entertaining stockholders is reasonably related to the purposes of the corporation. The Appellate Division, as above stated, found that the management group incurred a substantial amount of needless expense. That fact being established, it became the duty of the incumbent directors to unravel and explain these payments.

Regarding the $127,556 paid by the new management to the insurgent group for their campaign expenditures, the question immediately arises whether that was for a corporate purpose. . . .

In considering this issue, as in the case of the expenses of the incumbents, we begin with the proposition that this court has already held that it is beyond the power of a corporation to authorize the expenditure of mere campaign expenses in a proxy contest. . . . We are called upon to decide whether to abandon the rule as previously established in this State and adopt the less strict doctrine of the State of Delaware.

... The case most frequently cited and principally relied upon from among these Delaware decisions is *Hall v. Trans-Lux Daylight Picture Screen Corp.* There the English case was followed of *Peel v. London & North Western Ry. Co.* which distinguished between expenses merely for the purpose of maintaining control, and contests over policy questions of the corporation. In the *Hall* case the issues concerned a proposed merger, and a proposed sale of stock of a subsidiary corporation. These were held to be policy questions, and payment of the management campaign expenses was upheld.

In our view, the impracticability of such a distinction is illustrated by the statement in the *Hall* case that "It is impossible in many cases of intracorporate contests over directors, to sever questions of policy from those of persons"....

That may be all very well, but the upshot of this reasoning is that inasmuch as it is generally impossible to distinguish whether "policy" or "personnel" is the dominant factor, any averments must be accepted at their face value that questions of policy are dominant. Nowhere do these opinions mention that the converse is equally true and more pervasive, that neither the "ins" nor the "outs" ever say that they have no program to offer to the shareholders, but just want to acquire or to retain control, as the case may be. In common experience, this distinction is unreal. ... As in political contests, aspirations for control are invariably presented under the guise of policy or principle....

The main question of "policy" in the instant corporate election, as is stated in the opinions below and frankly admitted, concerns the long-term contract with pension rights of a former officer and director, Mr. J. Carlton Ward, Jr. The insurgents' chief claim of benefit to the corporation from their victory consists in the termination of that agreement, resulting in an alleged actuarial saving of $350,000 to $825,000 to the corporation, and the reduction of other salaries and rent by more than $300,000 per year. The insurgents had contended in the proxy contest that these payments should be substantially reduced so that members of the incumbent group would not continue to profit personally at the expense of the corporation. If these charges were true, which appear to have been believed by a majority of the shareholders, then the disbursements by the management group in the proxy contest fall under the condemnation of the English and the Delaware rule.

These circumstances are mentioned primarily to illustrate how impossible it is to distinguish between "policy" and "personnel" ... but they also indicate that personal factors are deeply rooted in this contest. That is certainly true insofar as the former management group is concerned....

Some expenditures may concededly be made by a corporation represented by its management so as to inform the stockholders, but there is a clear distinction between such expenditures by management and by mere groups of stockholders. The latter are under no legal obligation to assume duties of managing the corporation. They may endeavor to supersede the management for any reason, regardless of whether it be advantageous or detrimental to the corporation but, if they succeed, that is not a determination that the company was previously mismanaged or that it may not be mismanaged in the future. A change in control is in no sense analogous to an adjudication that the former directors have been guilty of misconduct. The analogy of allowing expenses of suit to minority stockholders who have been successful in a derivative action based on misconduct of officers or directors, is entirely without foundation.

Insofar as a management group is concerned, it may charge the corporation with any expenses within reasonable limits incurred in giving widespread notice to stockholders of questions affecting the welfare of the corporation. Expenditures in excess of these limits are *ultra vires*. The corporation lacks power to defray them. The corporation lacks power to defray the expenses of the insurgents in their entirety. The insurgents were not charged with responsibility for operating the company. No appellate court case is cited from any jurisdiction holding otherwise. No contention is made that such disbursements could be made, in any event, without stockholder ratification; they could not be ratified except by unanimous vote if they were *ultra vires*. The insurgents, in this instance, repeatedly announced to the stockholders in their campaign literature that their proxy contest was being waged at their own personal expense. If reimbursement of such items were permitted upon majority stockholder ratification, no court or other tribunal could pass upon which types of expenditure were "needless", to employ the characterization of the Appellate Division in this case. Whether the insurgents should be paid would be made to depend upon whether they win the stockholders election and obtain control of the corporation. It would be entirely irrelevant whether the corporation is "benefited" by their efforts or by the outcome of such an election. The courts could not indulge in a speculative inquiry into that issue. That would truly be a matter of business judgment. In some instances corporations are better governed by the existing management and in others by some other group which supersedes the existing management. Courts of law have no jurisdiction to decide such questions, and successful insurgent stockholders may confidently be relied upon to reimburse themselves whatever may be the real merits of the controversy. The losers in a proxy fight may understand the interests of the corporation more accurately than their successful adversaries, and agitation of this character may ultimately result in corporate advantage even if there be no change in management. Nevertheless, under the judgment which is appealed from, success in a proxy contest is the indispensable condition upon which reimbursement of the insurgents depends. Adventurers are not infrequent who are ready to take advantage of economic recessions, reduction of dividends or failure to increase them, or other sources of stockholder discontent to wage contests in order to obtain control of well-managed corporations, so as to divert their funds through legal channels into other corporations in which they may be interested, or to discharge former officers and employees to make room for favored newcomers according to the fashion of political patronage, or for other objectives that are unrelated to the sound prosperity of the enterprise. The way is open and will be kept open for stockholders and groups of stockholders to contest corporate elections, but if the promoters of such movements choose to employ the costly modern media of mass persuasion, they should look for reimbursement to themselves and to the stockholders who are aligned with them. If the law be that they can be recompensed by the corporation in case of success, and only in that event, it will operate as a powerful incentive to persons accustomed to taking calculated risks to increase this form of high-powered salesmanship to such a degree that, action provoking reaction, stockholders' meetings will be very costly. To the financial advantages promised by control of a prosperous corporation, would be added the knowledge that the winner takes all insofar as the campaign expenses are concerned. To the victor, indeed, would belong the spoils.

The questions involved in this case assume mounting importance as the capital stock of corporations becomes more widely distributed. To an enlarged extent the campaign methods consequently come more to resemble those of political campaigns, but, as in the latter, campaign expenses should be borne by those who are waging the campaign and their followers, instead of being met out of the corporate or the public treasury. Especially is this true when campaign promises have been made that the expenses would not be charged to the corporation. . . .

Questions

1. What is the source of disagreement between the majority and the dissenting opinions?

2. The decision draws a distinction between a contest over policy and a personal power contest. Do you find the distinction persuasive?

3. Judge Desmond, concurring, stresses that "[s]ome of the payments attacked in this suit were, on their face, for lawful purposes and apparently reasonable in amount but, as to others, the record simply does not contain evidentiary bases for a determination as to either lawfulness or reasonableness." The court places the burden of proof on the complaining shareholders to show which payments were unreasonable. What is the likelihood that shareholders will be able to meet this burden?

4. The decision also draws a distinction between expenses directors incur during a proxy contest, for which they might be able to use corporate funds, and the expenses incurred by successful insurgents, which might be reimbursable upon the shareholders' approval. What do you think are the policy considerations or concerns underlying the court's distinction? Why wouldn't the successful insurgents' expenses be reimbursable without the shareholders' approval?

Campbell v. Loew's Incorporated
36 Del. Ch. 563 (1957)

SEITZ, Chancellor

This is the decision on plaintiff's request for a preliminary injunction to restrain the holding of a stockholders' meeting or alternatively to prevent the meeting from considering certain matters or to prevent the voting of certain proxies. Certain other relief is also requested....

Some background is in order if the many difficult and novel issues are to be understood. Two factions have been fighting for control of Loew's. One faction is headed by Joseph Tomlinson (hereafter "Tomlinson faction") while the other is headed by the President of Loew's, Joseph Vogel (hereafter "Vogel faction"). At the annual meeting of stockholders last February a compromise was reached by which each nominated six directors and they in turn nominated a thirteenth or neutral director. But the battle had only begun. Passing by much of the controversy, we come to the July 17–18 period of this year when two of the six Vogel directors and the thirteenth or neutral director resigned. A quorum is seven.

On the 19th of July the Tomlinson faction asked that a directors' meeting be called for July 30 to consider, inter alia, the problem of filling director vacancies. On the eve of this meeting one of the Tomlinson directors resigned. This left five Tomlinson directors and four Vogel directors in office. Only the five Tomlinson directors attended the July 30 meeting. They purported to fill two of the director vacancies and to take other action. This Court has now ruled that for want of a quorum the two directors were not validly elected and the subsequent action taken at that meeting was invalid.

On July 29, the day before the noticed directors' meeting, Vogel, as president, sent out a notice calling a stockholders' meeting for September 12 for the following purposes:

> 1. to fill director vacancies.
>
> 2. to amend the by-laws to increase the number of the board from 13 to 19; to increase the quorum from 7 to 10 and to elect six additional directors.
>
> 3. to remove Stanley Meyer and Joseph Tomlinson as directors and to fill such vacancies.

Still later, another notice for a September 12 stockholders' meeting as well as a proxy statement went out over the signature of Joseph R. Vogel, as president. It was accompanied by a letter from Mr. Vogel dated August 9, 1957, soliciting stockholder support for the matters noticed in the call of the meeting, and particularly seeking to fill the vacancies and newly created directorships with "his" nominees. Promptly thereafter, plaintiff began this action....

I believe it is appropriate first to consider those contentions made by plaintiff which concern the legality of the call of the stockholders' meeting for the purposes stated.

...

[The court concluded that Loew's bylaws authorized the president to call a special meeting of the stockholders to fill vacancies on the board and to amend the by-laws to enlarge the board of directors. The court further concluded that the by-laws granted the stockholders the right to elect directors to fill newly created directorships between annual meetings. Finally, the court concluded that, as a matter of Delaware corporation law, the stockholders have the power to remove directors for cause. The court then turned] to plaintiff's charges relating to procedural defects and to irregularities in proxy solicitation by the Vogel group....

I next consider plaintiff's contention that the charges against the two directors do not constitute "cause" as a matter of law.... [I]t charges that the two directors (Tomlinson and Meyer) failed to cooperate with Vogel in his announced program for rebuilding the company; that their purpose has been to put themselves in control; that they made baseless accusations against him and other management personnel and attempted to divert him from his normal duties as president by bombarding him with correspondence containing unfounded charges and other similar acts; that they moved into the company's building, accompanied by lawyers and accountants, and immediately proceeded upon a planned scheme of harassment. They called for many records, some going back twenty years, and were rude to the personnel. Tomlinson sent daily letters to the directors making serious charges directly and by means of innuendos and misinterpretations.

Are the foregoing charges, if proved, legally sufficient to justify the ouster of the two directors by the stockholders? I am satisfied that a charge that the directors desired to take over control of the corporation is not a reason for their ouster. Standing alone, it is a perfectly legitimate objective which is a part of the very fabric of corporate existence. Nor is a charge of lack of cooperation a legally sufficient basis for removal for cause.

The next charge is that these directors, in effect, engaged in a calculated plan of harassment to the detriment of the corporation. Certainly a director may examine books, ask questions, etc., in the discharge of his duty, but a point can be reached when his actions exceed the call of duty and become deliberately obstructive. In such a situation, if his actions constitute a real burden on the corporation then the stockholders are entitled to relief. The charges in this area made by the Vogel letter are legally sufficient to justify the stockholders in voting to remove such directors. In so concluding I of course express no opinion as to the truth of the charges.

I therefore conclude that the charge of "a planned scheme of harassment" as detailed in the letter constitutes a justifiable legal basis for removing a director.

I next consider whether the directors sought to be removed have been given a reasonable opportunity to be heard by the stockholders on the charges made.

The corporate defendant freely admits that it has flatly refused to give the five Tomlinson directors or the plaintiff a stockholders' list. Any doubt about the matter was removed by the statement of defendant's counsel in open court at the argument that no such list would be supplied. The Vogel faction has physical control of the corporate offices and facilities. By this action the corporation through the Vogel group has deliberately refused to afford the directors in question an adequate opportunity to be heard by the stockholders on the charges made. This is contrary to the legal requirements which must be met before a director can be removed for cause.

At the oral argument the defendant's attorney offered to mail any material which might be presented by the Tomlinson faction. This falls far short of meeting the requirements of the law when directors are sought to be ousted for cause. Nor does the granting of the statutory right to inspect and copy some 26,000 names fulfill the requirement that a director sought to be removed for cause must be afforded an opportunity to present his case to the stockholders before they vote.

When Vogel as president caused the notice of meeting to be sent, he accompanied it with a letter requesting proxies granting authority to vote for the removal of the two named directors. It is true that the proxy form also provided a space for the stockholder to vote against such removal. However, only the Vogel accusations accompanied the request for a proxy. Thus, while the stockholder could vote for or against removal, he would be voting with only one view-point presented. This violates every sense of equity and fair play in a removal for cause situation.

While the directors involved or some other group could mail a letter to the stockholders and ask for a proxy which would revoke the earlier proxy, this procedure does not comport with the legal requirement that the directors in question must be afforded an opportunity to be heard before the shareholders vote. This is not an ordinary proxy contest case and a much more stringent standard must be invoked, at least at the initial stage, where it is sought to remove a director for cause. This is so for several reasons. Under our statute the directors manage the corporation and each has a somewhat independent status during his term of office. This right could be greatly impaired if substantial safeguards were not afforded a director whose removal for cause is sought. The possibility of abuse is evident....

There seems to be an absence of cases detailing the appropriate procedure for submitting a question of director removal for cause for stockholder consideration. I am satisfied, however, that to the extent the matter is to be voted upon by the use of proxies, such proxies may be solicited only after the accused directors are afforded an opportunity to present their case to the stockholders. This means, in my opinion, that an opportunity must be provided such directors to present their defense to the stockholders by a statement which must accompany or precede the initial solicitation of proxies seeking authority to vote for the removal of such director for cause. If not provided then such proxies may not be voted for removal. And the corporation has a duty to see that this opportunity is given the directors at its expense. Admittedly, no such opportunity was given the two directors involved. Indeed, the corporation admittedly refused to supply them with a stockholders' list.

To require anything less than the foregoing is to deprive the stockholders of the opportunity to consider the case made by both sides before voting and would make a mockery of the requirement that a director sought to be removed for cause is entitled to an opportunity to be heard before the stockholders vote. See the persuasive language of the dissent in Auer v. Dressel. But in referring to the language of the dissent I do not thereby suggest that my conclusion here is necessarily contrary to the majority decision on this point.

I therefore conclude that the procedural sequence here adopted for soliciting proxies seeking authority to vote on the removal of the two directors is contrary to law. The result is that the proxy solicited by the Vogel group, which is based upon unilateral presentation of the facts by those in control of the corporate facilities, must be declared invalid insofar as they purport to give authority to vote for the removal of the directors for cause.

A preliminary injunction will issue restraining the corporation from recognizing or counting any proxies held by the Vogel group and others insofar as such proxies purport to grant authority to vote for the removal of Tomlinson and Meyer as directors of the corporation.

The Court emphasizes that it is considering only the proxy solicitation and use aspect of this problem and is considering those only where advance authority is given to vote in a particular way. I am not called upon to consider what procedural and substantive requirements must be met if the matter is raised for consideration by stockholders present in person at the meeting.

Plaintiff seeks a preliminary injunction restraining the defendant from using the corporate funds, employees and facilities for the solicitation of proxies for the Vogel group and from voting proxies so solicited. Plaintiff bases this request upon the contention that Vogel and his group, by calling the meeting and by using corporate funds and facilities, are usurping the authority of the board of directors. Plaintiff says that the president in effect is using his corporate authority and the corporate resources to deny the will of the board of directors and to maintain himself in office.

This brings the Court to an analysis of this most unusual aspect of this most unusual case. The by-laws provide for thirteen directors. Seven is a quorum. Due to four resignations there are now nine directors in office. Five of the nine are of the Tomlinson faction while the remaining four are of the Vogel faction. Since the Vogel faction will not attend directors' meetings, or at least will not attend directors meetings at which matters may possibly be considered which they do not desire to have considered, it follows that the Tomlinson faction is unable to muster a quorum of the board and thus is unable to take action on behalf of the board. In this setting, where a special stockholders' meeting for the election of directors is pending, it becomes necessary to determine the status of each faction in order to resolve the issues posed. And it must be kept in mind that this election can determine which faction will control the corporation.

We start with the basic proposition that the board of directors acting as a board must be recognized as the only group authorized to speak for "management" in the sense that under the statute they are responsible for the management of the corporation. . . . However, . . . Loew's board as such cannot act for want of a quorum. Thus, there is no board policy as such with respect to the matters noticed for stockholder consideration. I am nevertheless persuaded that at least where a quorum of directors is in office the majority thereof are not "outsiders" merely because they cannot procure the attendance of a quorum at a meeting. By this I mean that they are not like the customary opposition which is seeking to take control of corporate management. To hold otherwise would be to set a most undesirable legal precedent in connection with the allocation of corporate powers.

Since the Vogel group, being in physical possession of the records and facilities of the corporation, treated the request of the directors for a stockholders' list as though it were to be judged by standards applicable to a mere stockholder's request, I think they violated the duty owed such directors as directors. I need not decide how far the rights of such directors go but I am satisfied that they are not less than the rights of the four "in" directors insofar as the right to have a stockholders' list is concerned. The fact that Vogel, as president, had the power to call a stockholders' meeting to elect directors, and is, so to speak, in physical control of the corporation, cannot obscure the fact that the possible proxy fight is between two sets of directors. Vogel, as president, has no legal standing to make "his" faction the exclusive voice of Loew's in the forthcoming election.

On balance, I believe the conclusion on this point should not result in the absolute nullification of all proxies submitted by the Vogel group. However, I believe it does require that their use be made subject to terms. I say this because they should not be permitted to benefit merely because they have physical control of the corporate facilities when they represent less than a majority of the directors in office.

I conclude that the Vogel group should be enjoined from voting any proxies unless and until the Tomlinson board members are given a reasonable period to solicit proxies after a stockholders' list is made available to them without expense by the corporation. . . .

I next consider how these two groups should be classified for purposes of determining the rights of the Vogel group in connection with the use of corporate money and facilities for proxy solicitation at a stockholders' meeting duly called by the president. Basically, the stockholders are being asked whether they approve of a record made by one group and perhaps opposed by another. While the Tomlinson faction has five of the nine directors, it would be most misleading to have them represent to the stockholders that they are "management" in the sense that they have been responsible for the corporate policy and administration up to this stage. Resignations of directors have created the unusual situation now presented.

Viewing the situation in the light of what has just been said, it is apparent that the Vogel group is entitled to solicit proxies, not as representing a majority of the board, but as representing those who have been and are now responsible for corporate policy and administration. Whereas, the Tomlinson group, while not management in the sense that it is able on its own to take effective director action, is representative of the majority of the incumbent directors and is entitled to so represent to the stockholders if it decides to solicit proxies.

Since the stockholders will, in the event of a proxy fight, be asked to determine which group should run the corporation in the future, the Vogel faction, because it symbolizes existing policy, has sufficient status to justify the reasonable use of corporate funds to present its position to the stockholders. I am not called upon to decide whether the Tomlinson board members would also be entitled to have the corporation pay its reasonable charges for proxy solicitation.

Since I have concluded that the Vogel faction is entitled to expend reasonable sums of corporate funds in the solicitation of proxies, it follows that the request for a preliminary injunction against such use will be denied. The restraining order heretofore entered will be vacated to the extent that it prevents such expenditures.

I next consider whether the Vogel faction is entitled to use corporate facilities and employees in connection with its solicitation. Because such action would carry the intra-corporate strife even deeper within the corporation and because there is no practical way, if there is a proxy contest, to assure equal treatment for both factions in this area when only one is in physical control of such facilities and personnel, I conclude that the defendant should be preliminarily enjoined from using corporate facilities and personnel in soliciting proxies. I emphasize that this conclusion is based upon the corporate status of the two factions herein involved.

Plaintiff next claims that the Vogel group should be enjoined from voting any proxies obtained as a result of the material sent out by Vogel. He argues that Vogel's letter to the stockholders, the proxy statement and the form of proxy deceived and misled the stockholders into believing that the matters noticed for consideration by the stockholders were proposed by the company or its management, whereas the Vogel group is not authorized to speak as "management".

I should say preliminarily that I believe the proxy statement would have been more accurately informative had it contained a concise statement showing the factual situation which created the present status of the two groups. The proxy statement did receive S.E.C. clearance. However, that agency labored under a difficult burden since it did not know the legal rights and status of the Vogel group.

I turn now to the various factors which, according to plaintiff, show that the Vogel faction represented, contrary to fact, that it was soliciting proxies as management.

1. The letter of Mr. Vogel to the shareholders is reproduced on the letterhead of Loew's, Incorporated and comes from the "Office of the President".

I have already pointed out that this is not the case of a working majority of the board versus the president. Indeed, in this case Vogel's administration as president symbolizes one choice in the policy dispute. This dispute is evident from a reading of the material in its entirety. I therefore conclude that by sending the letter on Loew's stationery from the office of the president, Vogel, was not misleading the stockholders.

2. The notice of the special meeting is reproduced on the letterhead of Loew's, Incorporated, signed, by order of the president, by Irving H. Greenfield, Secretary.

The fact is that there was no misrepresentation when the notice of the special meeting was reproduced on Loew's letterhead and signed by the order of the president. I say this because the president was authorized as president to call such a meeting.

3. I assume that plaintiff had now abandoned this point which deals with the power to close the transfer books.

4. The proxy statement recites that "it is considered to be in the best interest of Loew's and the stockholders to remove . . . [Mr. Meyer and Mr. Thomlinson] as a director".

This is nothing more than a statement of belief of Vogel and his group. I cannot see how it is misleading.

5. The proxy material states that Loew's will bear all costs in connection with the solicitation of proxies; that Loew's will reimburse the brokerage houses for expenses incident to the solicitation of proxies; that Loew's has entered into contracts with certain firms to solicit proxies and has agreed to pay them a fee for their services, and that the costs to be paid by Loew's for proxy solicitation will be approximately $100,000.

Plaintiff is here saying in effect that Vogel's group was representing to the stockholders that the corporation would pay for the expenses of proxy solicitation for the Vogel group and thus leading the reader to believe that it was a management solicitation. First of all, such was the intention of the Vogel group and thus it did not constitute a misrepresentation as to their intention. But, in any event, I have now held that reasonable expenses of such solicitation are properly chargeable to the corporation and so no factual misrepresentation was involved. In any event, since the Vogel group was synonymous with management in the policy sense, I cannot see how a stockholder would be misled.

6. The proxy material states that the officers and employees of Loew's will solicit and request the return of proxies.

This is not a misrepresentation in the sense that it was contrary to the intention of the Vogel group. The Court has now determined that the officers and employees in such capacity, cannot solicit proxies. This does not mean that the representation is so material that it can be said to influence stockholders to the extent that the proxies should be voided.

7. The proxy statement is signed by Joseph R. Vogel, as president.

There is no merit to this contention. Vogel as president was certainly authorized to sign the statement in view of the fact that he had the authority to call the meeting.

8. The business reply envelope included with the proxy has on it that postage will be paid by the secretary of Loew's Inc., and is addressed to him in his official capacity. The permit on the envelope is Loew's permit.

The foregoing facts are true but I do not believe that they are so misleading as to void the proxies. After all, the Vogel group is soliciting proxies on the basis of its record in administering the corporation.

Plaintiff contends that in any event the cumulative effect of the various statements mentioned is to lead the ordinary reader to believe that the solicitation is by management.

Plaintiff recognizes that the proxy statement and the form of proxy both recite that "this proxy is solicited by the President and George L. Killion [of the Vogel group] who are members of the executive committee of Loew's, Inc., and in view of the circumstances, not by the management". However, he argues that the import of this statement is lost in the overall impact of the material. Since the meeting was validly called by the president, there was nothing misleading in the creation of the impression that the meeting and material were initiated by the company. I think the whole impact of the proxy material conveyed to the average reader the impression that there is a bitter fight between the president and his faction and another faction on the board.

While I have no doubt that it would have been better for the material to have contained a more explicit factual narrative of the status of the board personnel at the time of the proxy solicitation, I cannot believe that the overall result is so misleading as to justify this Court in concluding that the proxies may not be used for any purpose. This is particularly so in view of the statement made that it was not solicited by management. Indeed, I think the statement, which was apparently required by the S.E.C. may have been somewhat misleading in the sense that it may have suggested to the reader that the Vogel group was not responsible for the corporate policy up to that date. To this extent, it was more prejudicial to the Vogel group than the Tomlinson group, if a stockholder desired to vote for "management" in the policy sense.

Plaintiff's request that the Vogel group be enjoined from voting any proxies solicited under the material sent out by Vogel will be denied. This disposes of the issues raised in connection with the stockholders' meeting. . . .

Questions

1. *Campbell v. Loew*'s illustrates the different groups involved (or who might seek to be involved) in managing the corporation's affairs — directors, officers, shareholders — and the potential conflicts among them. In light of what you have learned in Part 2, who should determine how the corporation is run?

2. The court found that the shareholders have an inherent power to remove directors for cause. But if the directors are managing the shareholders' property ("other

people's money," as Louis Brandeis put it), why did the court insist on cause for removal prior to term? Shouldn't the shareholders, as presumed owners, be allowed to remove directors simply because they are not pleased with their performance? Wouldn't agency law give them such power? What are the difficulties associated with such an approach?

3. In determining that shareholders also had the inherent power, between annual meetings, not only to fill vacancies but also to fill newly created directorships, Chancellor Seitz announced that "[i]t would take a strong by-law language to warrant the conclusion that those adopting the by-laws intended to prohibit the stockholders from filling new directorships between annual meetings. No such strong language appears here and I do not think the implication is warranted in view of the subject matter." Does Chancellor Seitz's requirement accord with what you have already read about the way in which courts interpret corporations statutes and charters? Why is the shareholders' power to fill vacancies and newly created directorship so important so as to require "a strong by-law language" to alter it?

4. As you already studied (and as further discussed below), shareholders suffer from rational apathy. Who among the shareholders is thus likely to call a special meeting? Should this affect how we think about the power of shareholders to call meetings, remove directors for cause, and fill vacancies or new directorships?

5. Assuming the directors of both the Vogel group and the Tomlinson group were attempting to fulfill their duties to the corporation, is there any reason to think that one group should be entitled to use corporate funds and resources more than the other? Should it matter whether the dissident directors win or lose?

6. Loew's board divided in February 1957. President Joseph R. Vogel, in an attempt to avoid a proxy contest for control of this giant motion picture company, agreed to the removal of four company executives from the board of directors and their replacement by directors who were representative of the Tomlinson group and impartial banking interests that were holders of Loew's stock. *Battle over control of Loew's is Bared*, N.Y. TIMES, July 23, 1957. Tomlinson was the largest individual shareholder of the company. In retrospect, Vogel noted that "he thought Tomlinson's large stockholding would be an assurance of cooperation, but . . . events had shown Tomlinson's real ambition was to make Stanley Meyer president, himself board chairman, and Louis B. Mayer, 'the guiding spirit in all this—a paid adviser under contract to the studio.'" Louis B. Mayer, former production chief of Metro-Goldwyn-Mayer, Loew's production arm (about which you will read in the following case) was ousted from MGM in 1951. *Loew's Head Calls Vote to Oust Two Directors*, WASHINGTON POST AND TIMES HERALD, July 23, 1957.

In July 1957, Vogel called the special shareholders' meeting discussed in *Campbell v. Loew's* to remove Tomlinson and Meyer as directors. In response, the five dissident directors (by then a majority of the board) met and elected Mayer and Samuel J. Briskin to the board. They also resolved to forbid the expenditure of funds to solicit proxies or otherwise further the special stockholder meeting. Shortly after the meeting, Mayer described Vogel as "a nice man but not competent to run the company." The Vogel faction claimed the meeting was illegal (the required quorum was 7 directors) and charged that the dissident directors were engaged in "machinations" which had "virtually paralyzed the ability of the board of directors to function." In a more personal attack, Vogel proclaimed that "Mayer, who [had] been the conspirator behind the scenes, [was] now out in the open . . . . His program [had] simply shifted from obstruction to usurpation." *Battle over control of Loew's is Bared, supra*; *Mayer 'Elected' to Loew's Board*, N.Y. TIMES, July 31, 1957.

7. Given that many proxy fights over questions of policy also involve personal fights, should the courts attempt to determine which faction can use corporate funds and resources? Should all be barred from using such funds?

Levin v. Metro-Goldwyn-Mayer, Inc.
264 F. Supp. 797 (S.D.N.Y. 1967)

RYAN, District Judge

[As of January 5, 1967, 5,042,859 shares of 8,000,000 shares of MGM authorized common stock were outstanding. The stock is listed and traded on the New York Stock Exchange and the Pacific Coast Exchange. There are approximately 13,000 holders of MGM common stock; they are located throughout the United States and abroad.]

This action was filed by six stockholders of Metro-Goldwyn-Mayer, Inc. (MGM), a Delaware corporation with its principal place of business in New York. The defendants named are MGM and five of the thirteen members of its Board of Directors. [The five defendants named have been directors of MGM for many years — Robert H. O'Brien since 1957, Ira Guilden since 1958, Philip Roth since 1958, Benjamin Melniker since 1954, and George L. Killian since 1957.] They are part of present MGM corporate management; all of them serve as officers or as members of the Executive Committee.

Plaintiff, Philip Levin, is and has been a director of MGM since February, 1965 and all of the plaintiffs hold substantial blocks of MGM common stock. [Plaintiffs own 552,705 shares of MGM common stock, approximately 11% of the total outstanding shares, with a market value of nearly $20,000,000. Levin, one of the plaintiffs, also states by affidavit that he has other stockholders associated with him in the proxy contest who hold 127,150 shares of MGM common, with a market value of approximately $4,323,100.]

The present action flows from a conflict for corporate control between present management — called "the O'Brien group" and "the Levin group." Each group intends to nominate a slate of directors at the MGM stockholder annual meeting which is to be held on February 23, 1967; each has been actively soliciting proxies for this meeting. . . .

Plaintiffs complain of the manner, method and means employed by defendants in the solicitation of proxies for the coming annual meeting of MGM stockholders. Specifically, plaintiffs charged that the defendants, in connection with the proxy solicitation contest, have wrongfully committed MGM to pay for the services of specially retained attorneys, a public relations firm and proxy soliciting organizations, and, in addition, have improperly used the offices and employees of MGM in proxy solicitation and the good-will and business contacts of MGM to secure support for the present management. Plaintiffs, in their complaint, pray for temporary and permanent injunctive relief[5] against defendants' continuing this method of solicitation of proxies and against defendants' voting the proxies so obtained at the annual meeting. They also seek money damages of $2,500,000 on behalf of MGM from the individual defendants.

The temporary injunctive relief now sought is precisely the same injunctive relief prayed for as a final judgment in the complaint.

Although disapproving of the proxy solicitation methods of "the O'Brien group", and of certain financial and business policies applied in the conduct of corporate activities of MGM, Levin heretofore has described Robert H. O'Brien, the President and the Chief Executive Officer of MGM, as "able and dedicated." In a letter to MGM stockholders sent out in May, 1966, Levin wrote of the Directors — "I have never impugned the integrity of any of my fellow board members."

Plaintiffs' counsel during the presentation of their arguments have stated that no charge is made by plaintiffs that defendants or any of them or any one acting for them or on their behalf have made any false or fraudulent statements in their solicitation

---

5. The injunctive relief prayed for in the complaint is as follows:
"(a) That defendant MGM, its officers, agents, employees and attorneys, the individual defendants, and all others acting in concert with them or any of them, be permanently enjoined:
  (i) from using employees of MGM to solicit proxies, or from otherwise engaging in the aforesaid proxy contest;
  (ii) from soliciting proxies from exhibitors, distributors, producers and other persons with whom MGM has business relations, other than by proxy solicitation material addressed to stockholders generally;
  (iii) from using exhibitors, distributors, producers and other persons with whom MGM has business relations, in the solicitation of proxies;
  (iv) from voting at the Annual Meeting of Stockholders to be held February 23, 1967, or any adjournment thereof, any proxies obtained as a result of the unlawful solicitations and activities specified herein;
  (v) from using the funds or assets of MGM in the solicitation of proxies, the payment of legal fees or of any other expenses incident to the aforesaid proxy contest, including acts in opposition to plaintiff's proxy solicitations as well as litigation appertaining thereto.
(b) that, pending a final hearing, a temporary restraining order and preliminary injunction be issued in accordance with the above prayer."

of proxies. Plaintiffs make no charge of corruption in the conduct of the corporate affairs for direct personal gain or profit by any of the defendants.

Plaintiffs maintain the injunctive relief sought is required to prevent (1) the unlawful use of the corporate organization—its employees, good-will and offices and of corporate funds in the solicitation of proxies, (2) the retention of "the four top proxy-soliciting concerns and the passing of their bill for their services to the corporation rather than to the individuals" and (3) the employment at corporate expense of special counsel "for the sole and exclusive and no other purpose than the waging of a proxy contest on behalf of the individual defendants who have every right to pay for his valuable services" with their own private funds, particularly in view of the fact that regularly employed attorneys are available to represent the corporate interests of MGM.

Because of the nature of plaintiffs' allegations, we weigh the merits of this application for injunctive relief against the financial and business background of MGM. As of August 31, 1966, MGM had total assets of $251,132,000 and a gross income for its 1966 fiscal year of approximately $185,000,000. It is one of the major producers and distributors of motion pictures in the world and markets to exhibitors films produced by others as well as its own films. MGM has 31 branch distribution offices in the United States. It operates 49 theatres in foreign countries, and it licenses its feature productions and its "shorts" to local as well as network affiliated television stations. It operates a record manufacturing plant, pressing records for its own labels and for others and it produces and distributes records for itself and others. It also has a majority stockholding in one of the leading music publishing companies. MGM's gross revenue in the past fiscal year from music publishing and record distribution are stated to have been over $30,000,000. MGM owns and operates a motion picture producing studio in California and another in England, where feature films are produced by it, often involving expenditure of eight to ten million dollars on a single production. MGM is one of the "giants" in the entertainment industry.

Much has been said by the defendants of the need for expert knowledge in the entertainment field, in the specialized demands for financing, and in the management of an enterprise of the magnitude and diversity of MGM. This is undoubtedly required. Defendants point with unabashed pride to the results they have achieved in their direction of the affairs of MGM. We do not question that the successful operation of MGM has been accomplished in no small measure by diligent and intelligent application to corporate affairs and by the exercise of sound and informed business judgment. The decision as to the continuance of the present management, however, rests entirely with the stockholders. A court may not override or dictate on a matter of this nature to stockholders. When we speak of stockholders, we have especially in mind the large number of stockholders who are not firmly committed to or aligned with either of the two contesting groups; majority voting power is vested in them. It is the concern of the law and of the Court that they be fully and truthfully informed as to the merits of the contentions of those soliciting their proxy. It is equally important that the Court should not unnecessarily exercise its injunctive power in such matters lest such judicial action operate to unduly influence a stockholder's decision as to which faction should receive his proxy.

It is quite plain that the differences between "the O'Brien group" and "the Levin group" are much more than mere personality conflicts. These might readily be resolved by reasoning and hard-headed, profit-minded business men. There are definite business policies advocated by each group, so divergent that reconciliation does not seem possible. They appear so evident from the papers before us that detailed analysis would be a waste of time.[7] However, in such a situation the right of an independent stockholder to be fully informed is of supreme importance. The controlling question presented on this application is whether illegal or unfair means of communication, such as demand judicial intervention, are being employed by the present management. We find that they are not and conclude that the injunctive relief now sought should be denied.

The proxy statement filed by MGM under date of January 6, 1967, opens with the statement that "MGM will bear all cost in connection with the management solicitation of proxies." It discloses the purpose of the management to solicit proxies and "to request brokerage houses, custodians, nominees and others who hold stock in their names to solicit proxies from the persons who own such stock, pursuant to the rules of the New York Stock Exchange." It sets forth that MGM will reimburse them "for their out-of-pocket expenses and reasonable clerical expenses." It discloses the employment of Georgeson & Co. at $15,000 and Kissel-Blake Organization, Inc. at $5,000 for services and estimated out-of-pocket expenses. It informs the reader that "officers and regular employees of MGM and its subsidiaries" may request the return of proxies for which no additional compensation will be paid them. It advises that "Proxies may also be solicited in newspapers or other publications" and that the total

---

7. The fundamental policy differences between the contesting groups concern, among other matters:

a. The annual number of feature pictures MGM should produce; management policy would limit them to approximately 25 top productions (with cost per picture from $5,000,000 to $8,000,000) and the balance costing down to approximately $500,000; "the Levin group" policy advocates up to 50 top productions a year.

b. "The Levin" policy would provide for a slow release of pictures to TV showing; management would license to TV pictures of more recent release date.

c. Management and the independent accountants in setting rate of amortization of production costs have allocated part to later television licenses; Levin group would apply all of amortization to exhibitor or screen showings and at an earlier date than now used.

d. Levin policy would build up cash funds available for productions by reducing dividends, and thus reduce necessity for financing; present management policy is different.

e. Key personnel is presently engaged under 2 or 3 year contracts; Levin policy would make these agreements only for a year.

f. Management favors preemptive right to stockholders for general public cash offerings only; Levin policy would apply preemptive rights to all convertible offerings, options and private sale of stock.

g. Levin policy would support cumulative voting, which management opposes.

amount which it is estimated will be spent in the management solicitation is $125,000 "exclusive of amounts normally expended for a solicitation for an election of directors and costs represented by salaries and wages of regular employees and officers."

We do not find the amounts recited to be paid excessive, or the method of operation disclosed by MGM management to be unfair or illegal. It contravenes no federal statute or S.E.C. rule or regulation. It provides for orderly dissemination of information to the public investors and the methods and procedures outlined in the management proxy statement follow those set forth in "the Levin group" proxy statement issued under the auspices of "MGM Stockholder's Committee for Better Management." This "Levin group" statement discloses that R.A. Drennan & Co., Inc. has been hired at a fee (and reimbursement of expenses) not to exceed $17,000; that as of January 19, 1967 approximately $35,000 had been expended by the "Committee" and that it is estimated that the total expenditures for solicitation will amount to approximately $175,000; "all expenses will be paid by Philip J. Levin, his wife and corporations wholly owned by them." It is however noted that "no decision has yet been made as to whether reimbursement will be requested from the Company. However, if reimbursement from the Company is sought, it will be submitted to a vote of the stockholders."

We will next consider the other activities that plaintiffs would enjoin:

1. The use of corporate employees for proxy solicitation.

It is represented in defendants' affidavits that the use of MGM employees for proxy solicitation has been "extremely limited and moderate" and that "it is identical with the procedure we have followed at MGM for the past 15 years, even though no actual contest existed except in 1957 and this past year's special meeting." No statement has come from the plaintiffs to contradict this. Contrary to plaintiffs' unsupported statement that 9000 MGM employees are at work soliciting proxies, defendants have stated that the total number of employees who on their own time have consented to telephone shareholders to vote is less than 150. We do not find this an unreasonable situation under the circumstances. We are not informed as to whether these employees are themselves stockholders, but certainly a relationship of loyalty and friendly support between employees and management in a large corporation is not to be discouraged when viewed from a stockholder's point of view and absent even a suggestion of internal corrupt management.

Defendants state that following a custom of years standing the 31 branch managers in the United States and of the Canadian head office have received from management a letter requesting their aid in soliciting proxies. These letters conveyed copies of annual reports and information heretofore sent to stockholders. Plaintiffs have described the communications as "kits." We assume that they did contain pertinent information to inform the recipients of corporate factual history. No claim is made that there were threats of reprisal against the employees for failure to solicit proxies or that any such steps were taken, or that the "kits" contained false or misleading statements, with the intention they be repeated to stockholders to deceive or mislead. We find nothing inherently wrong or illegal in this procedure, nor can we say on the record before us that it is unreasonable or overreaching by management which should be enjoined.

2. MGM's use of more than one proxy solicitation concern upon the ground that a single firm is adequate for the purpose of getting material into the hands of stockholders.

The employment of two proxy solicitation firms and the fees agreed to be paid to them were fully disclosed in the MGM proxy statement. Georgeson & Co. is in charge of solicitation of proxies from stockholders directly; the Kissel-Blake Organization is directing its efforts to brokerage solicitation. Here again, defendants state without contradiction that "in every year since 1956, MGM has employed the firms of Georgeson & Co. and The Kissel-Blake Organization, Inc. to solicit proxies for its stockholders meetings." We do not find basis for injunctive relief in their employment, nor in the employment of Dudley King & Co. as a consultant in connection with corporate matters and stockholder relations. Of course, this Court may not forbid an independent supporter of management (Harry Brandt, who is not a party to this action) from engaging another proxy solicitation firm on his own responsibility.

3. The use of persons in business relationships with MGM in the solicitation of proxies for management, as a violation of the Securities Exchange Act of 1934.

There have been set forth in paid advertisements statements by actors, directors, writers and exhibitors supporting and expressing confidence in the present management. Defendants state these expressions have been unsolicited and spontaneous and "have been published by these persons [and] . . . paid for completely out of their own pockets without any direct or indirect promise of repayment by MGM." There is no proof to challenge this. Certainly, the defendants should not be expected to deny or contradict what they regard as well-deserved compliments graciously paid to them. Nor do we find the publication of such unsolicited individual advertisements a violation of the Act of 1934.

4. The further employment by MGM of a public relations firm.

It is undisputed that by contract entered into on April 28, 1966 and subject to a 30-day cancellation clause, MGM engaged the services of Thomas J. Deegan Company, Inc. Deegan is a recognized and reputable public relations firm. The engagement was long before the present proxy contest. The employment is neither unusual nor unreasonable. It does not afford ground for injunctive relief.

5. The employment out of corporate funds of the firm of Mr. Louis Nizer and his proxy associates.

The affidavits before us establish that the Nizer law firm for many years have been retained by MGM to handle a number of litigated matters. The competency of the firm and of Mr. Nizer is not questioned; their employment was justified in management's opinion; the importance of the matter to stockholders indicates the reasonableness of their engagement; the expense and fees charged may be objected to if believed to be excessive in amount. This engagement of counsel affords no support for injunctive relief.

The plaintiffs have failed to establish their right to the relief sought and there has been no showing of irreparable harm.

Motion denied.

Questions

1. Proxy fights are likely to occur when the insurgent believes her group can run the corporation more efficiently than the incumbents. However, if the insurgent tries to oust the incumbent board and loses, it has to bear its own costs. Given the informational disadvantage of the insurgent group, it seems that the rule adopted in the cases you've read would discourage many, potentially efficient proxy contests. Why does the court adopt such a rule? Why should the corporation's obligation to pay expenses turn on whether the insurgent group won or lost?

2. If proxy contests are supposed to be efficiency maximizing, why should either group be compensated for its expenses? Presumably, like any other rational actor, the insurgent and incumbent group should internalize the cost of their activities. Who are the beneficiaries of the rule adopted by the court?

3. Philip J. Levin was the largest individual shareholder of MGM (holding about 8% of the 2.5 million outstanding shares). Among the country's wealthiest real estate men (he was also a lawyer), with a personal net worth of more than $100 million, he developed 100 shopping centers on the East coast, as well as industrial parks and apartment complexes in New Jersey and Pennsylvania. He divided his time between a 106-acre estate near Mount Bethel in Warren Township, N.J., and an apartment in Manhattan. Alden Whitman, *Philip Levin, Head of Madison Square Garden, Dies*, N.Y. TIMES, August 4, 1971; Vincent Canby, *M-G-M Combatants Await Proxy Results*, N.Y. TIMES, May 25, 1966.

In February 1965, Levin became a member of the MGM's board and executive committee. But his tenure on the committee was short. In February 1966, he was replaced by Gen. Omar N. Bradley. Apparently, Levin was highly critical of Robert O'Brien's management. Shortly after he was replaced on the executive committee, Levin was quoted to say that "everyone and everything had to be cleared through Robert O'Brien, president and chief executive officer." According to Levin, MGM was "a one-man operation and a rubber-stamp board of directors that [was] rarely asked for judgment on important decisions." He thought "the company was licensing films to TV far too rapidly," and, more generally, was concerned about "the excessive expenses and costs of the company's operations." *Key M-G-M Holder Denies Stock Bid*, N.Y. TIMES, March 1, 1966.

Three weeks after he was ousted from the executive committee, Levin asked O'Brien for information covering all aspects of the company's operations. Vincent Canby, *Big M-G-M Holder Asks to See Books*, N.Y. TIMES, March 16, 1966. Fearing a potential proxy contest, the MGM board, in a meeting on April 15, 1966, approved three proposals (to be brought to a shareholder vote at the May shareholder meeting): "(1) to split the company's common stock two-for-one, (2) to increase the quarterly dividend by 25% to 25 cents a share, payable on the basis of the split shares, and (3) to increase the number of authorized common shares from 3 million to 8 million" (do you see how this could help protect incumbent directors against a proxy contest?). Levin and another director (who was about to resign from the board to take a position on another board) voted against the proposals. Vincent Canby, *M-G-M Proposes to Split Shares*, N.Y. TIMES, April 16, 1966. Levin's attempt to force the MGM board to present to the shareholders two separate proposals, one for a stock split, the other for an increase of the authorized shares, was turned down by the Federal District Court. *U.S. Court Rebuffs an M-G-M Dissident*, N.Y. TIMES, May 17, 1966. Levin then engaged in a proxy contest, but in their May meeting, the shareholders voted (albeit by a narrow margin) to approve the board's proposals. Levin's motion for a temporary restraining order to prevent the board from changing the certificate of incorporation in accordance with the approved proposals was denied. Leonard Sloane, *M-G-M Insurgent Loses Court Bid*, N.Y. TIMES, June 15, 1966.

In December of 1966, Levin notified the SEC of his intention to solicit proxies in an attempt to overthrow the incumbent directors at the February 23, 1967 shareholders' meeting. Robert E. Bedingfield, *M-G-M's Dissident Director Plans another Proxy Battle*, N.Y. TIMES, December 8, 1966. In preparation for the fight, Levin purchased additional stock, increasing his holdings in MGM to 10%. *Levin Increases M-G-M Holdings*, WASHINGTON POST, December 22, 1966. By January, Levin and his team (including his slate of directors and other supporters) collectively owned 13.5% of MGM's outstanding shares. In comparison, the incumbent directors collectively owned only 3.5% of MGM's stock. *M-G-M Proxy Bid Gains Intensity*, N.Y. TIMES, Jan. 10, 1967. By January 20, 1967, (a month before the shareholder meeting), Levin charged that "O'Brien had used company money to 'tip up' three of the largest proxy soliciting companies to hire three large law firms and a special public relations counsel, and had taken company personnel away from regular duties to solicit proxies." *Dissident Questions Use of M-G-M Funds*, N.Y. TIMES, Jan. 20, 1967.

The proxy battle gained much attention (including, apparently, a call by Senator John Sparkman, a friend of O'Brien, to 6 mutual funds with holdings in MGM to stay out of the fight, a call he retracted when Senator "Pete" Williams, a friend of Levin, urged him to do so. Drew Pearson, *M-G-M Lion Roars,* WASHINGTON POST, Feb. 13, 1967). Reporters followed the fight closely, describing it as the most important struggle of the decade. It was important, as Bosley Crowther for the *N.Y. Times* put it, "not only [because] this company is apparently flourishing like the green bay tree, but [because] it is generally regarded by knowledgeable people as having one of the coolest and shrewdest managements in the industry. If such a group can be knocked over by dissidents putting on the steam, any group can be knocked over—and that's a chilling thought, indeed." Bosley Crowther, *Gunfight at M-G-M Corral*, N.Y. TIMES, Feb 19, 1967.

Indeed, Robert O'Brien, an old New Dealer who once served on the SEC, dramatically improved MGM's business. When he took the company over in 1963, it had a loss of $35 million. By 1967, earnings had gone from a loss of $6.79 per share to a profit of $2.03 a share (accounting for a stock split), and dividends were increased. O'Brien's success had to do with his belief that the creators of films should be allowed free rein. While disasters sometimes happened, it turned out to be a very healthy policy, leading to growing interest on Wall Street in the film industry. O'Brien "kept his head—and Metro's. He has limited his old films for TV to licensing, not sales, a device that has had the effect of raising the price per picture and maintaining ownership as well." And he invested in major directors, including Stanley Kubrick, John Frankenheimer, Robert Aldrich, Roman Polanski, Antonioni and John Schlesinger. He had the courage to produce "Doctor Zhivago," which others in Hollywood were afraid to touch, and it turned out to be one of the best and most profitable movies of 1966, completing a full year on the screen a few weeks before the 1967 annual meeting. Richard L. Coe, *'Zhivago' Figures in Power Struggle*, WASHINGTON POST, Feb. 5, 1967; Drew Pearson, *M-G-M Lion Roars*, supra.

Moreover, as Crowther pointedly noted, companies like MGM (many of which were combating proxy contests) were "the owners of huge backlogs of old films that are worth millions for many years as products to be leased to television; and it could very well be that a prime interest of anyone trying to get control of one of those companies would be to get control of those old films, to spin them off, to make a lot of fast bucks from them, and also from the company's real estate. . . . Are these outsiders really trying to get in so they can run better companies and make better films, or are they simply looking for chances to reap fast harvests from their stocks?" In fact, Levin, who had not had any previous connection with the film world, was accused of eyeing MGM's big movie set outside Los Angeles where real estate values had skyrocketed. Bosley Crowther, *Gunfight at M-G-M Corral*, supra; Drew Pearson, *M-G-M Lion Roars*, supra.

But in the balance between management and insurgent, as a reporter for the *Washington Post* predicted after the court handed down its decision, "it is hard to think that the stockholders will vote this month to scratch a winning horse. When they chalk up their reasons for keeping the O'Brien slate, the success of 'Doctor Zhivago' will be up near the top." Richard L. Coe, *'Zhivago' Figures in Power Struggle*, supra.

On March 8, shortly before he was officially declared the loser in his bid to take control of MGM's board (he also lost his seat on the board), Levin filed the suit to void the election of directors which you read. When he lost the battle, he sold his MGM stock for a $21 million profit to Time Inc. and Edgar Bronfman of the

Seagrams liquor empire. At the time of his death, Levin was reportedly engaged in a struggle for effective control of Madison Square Garden Corporation, of which he was President and CEO (seeking to buy the shares owned by the trustees of the bankrupt Penn Central Transportation Company).

Twenty years separate *Levin* from the following case, *Blasius Industries, Inc. v. Atlas Corporation.* In that period, the idea that shareholders who disapprove of the way their corporations are run should simply sell their stock came to dominate corporate law and theory. *Blasius Industries, Inc. v. Atlas Corporation,* which involved a consent solicitation, attempted to redefine the boundaries of the shareholder's role in corporate affairs to adjust to this new way of thinking. As you read the case, think whether the court attempts to broaden or limit the power of shareholders.

Blasius Industries, Inc. v. Atlas Corporation
564 A.2d 651 (Del. Ch. 1988)

ALLEN, Chancellor

Two cases pitting the directors of Atlas Corporation against that company's largest (9.1%) shareholder, Blasius Industries, have been consolidated and tried together. Together, these cases ultimately require the court to determine who is entitled to sit on Atlas' board of directors. Each, however, presents discrete and important legal issues.

The first of the cases was filed on December 30, 1987. As amended, it challenges the validity of board action taken at a telephone meeting of December 31, 1987 that added two new members to Atlas' seven member board. That action was taken as an immediate response to the delivery to Atlas by Blasius the previous day of a form of stockholder consent that, if joined in by holders of a majority of Atlas' stock, would have increased the board of Atlas from seven to fifteen members and would have elected eight new members nominated by Blasius.

As I find the facts of this first case, they present the question whether a board acts consistently with its fiduciary duty when it acts, in good faith and with appropriate care, for the primary purpose of preventing or impeding an unaffiliated majority of shareholders from expanding the board and electing a new majority. For the reasons that follow, I conclude that, even though defendants here acted on their view of the corporation's interest and not selfishly, their December 31 action constituted an offense to the relationship between corporate directors and shareholders that has traditionally been protected in courts of equity. As a consequence, I conclude that the board action taken on December 31 was invalid and must be voided. . . .

The facts set forth below represent findings based upon a preponderance of the admissible evidence, as I evaluate it.

I

Blasius Acquires a 9% Stake in Atlas.

Blasius is a new stockholder of Atlas. It began to accumulate Atlas shares for the first time in July, 1987. On October 29, it filed a Schedule 13D with the Securities Exchange Commission disclosing that, with affiliates, it then owed 9.1% of Atlas' common stock. It stated in that filing that it intended to encourage management of Atlas to consider a restructuring of the Company or other transaction to enhance shareholder values. It also disclosed that Blasius was exploring the feasibility of obtaining control of Atlas, including instituting a tender offer or seeking "appropriate" representation on the Atlas board of directors.

Blasius has recently come under the control of two individuals, Michael Lubin and Warren Delano, who after experience in the commercial banking industry, had, for a short time, run a venture capital operation for a small investment banking firm. Now on their own, they apparently came to control Blasius with the assistance of Drexel Burnham's well noted junk bond mechanism. Since then, they have made several attempts to effect leveraged buyouts, but without success.

In May, 1987, with Drexel Burnham serving as underwriter, Lubin and Delano caused Blasius to raise $60 million through the sale of junk bonds. A portion of these funds were used to acquire a 9% position in Atlas. According to its public filings with the SEC, Blasius' debt service obligations arising out of the sale of the junk bonds are such that it is unable to service those obligations from its income from operations.

The prospect of Messrs. Lubin and Delano involving themselves in Atlas' affairs, was not a development welcomed by Atlas' management. Atlas had a new CEO, defendant Weaver, who had, over the course of the past year or so, overseen a business restructuring of a sort. Atlas had sold three of its five divisions. It had just announced (September 1, 1987) that it would close its once important domestic uranium operation. The goal was to focus the Company on its gold mining business. By October, 1987, the structural changes to do this had been largely accomplished. Mr. Weaver was perhaps thinking that the restructuring that had occurred should be given a chance to produce benefit before another restructuring (such as Blasius had alluded to in its Schedule 13D filing) was attempted, when he wrote in his diary on October 30, 1987:

> 13D by Delano & Lubin came in today. Had long conversation w/MAH & Mark Golden [of Goldman, Sachs] on issue. All agree we must dilute these people down by the acquisition of another Co. w/stock, or merger or something else.

The Blasius Proposal of a Leverage Recapitalization or Sale.

Immediately after filing its 13D on October 29, Blasius' representatives sought a meeting with the Atlas management. Atlas dragged its feet. A meeting was arranged for December 2, 1987 following the regular meeting of the Atlas board. Attending that meeting were Messrs. Lubin and Delano for Blasius, and, for Atlas, Messrs.

Weaver, Devaney (Atlas' CFO), Masinter (legal counsel and director) and Czajkowski (a representative of Atlas' investment banker, Goldman Sachs).

At that meeting, Messrs. Lubin and Delano suggested that Atlas engage in a leveraged restructuring and distribute cash to shareholders. In such a transaction, which is by this date a commonplace form of transaction, a corporation typically raises cash by sale of assets and significant borrowings and makes a large one time cash distribution to shareholders. The shareholders are typically left with cash and an equity interest in a smaller, more highly leveraged enterprise. Lubin and Delano gave the outline of a leveraged recapitalization for Atlas as they saw it.

Immediately following the meeting, the Atlas representatives expressed among themselves an initial reaction that the proposal was infeasible. On December 7, Mr. Lubin sent a letter detailing the proposal. In general, it proposed the following: (1) an initial special cash dividend to Atlas' stockholders in an aggregate amount equal to (a) $35 million, (b) the aggregate proceeds to Atlas from the exercise of option warrants and stock options, and (c) the proceeds from the sale or disposal of all of Atlas' operations that are not related to its continuing minerals operations; and (2) a special non-cash dividend to Atlas' stockholders of an aggregate $125 million principal amount of 7% Secured Subordinated Gold-Indexed Debentures. The funds necessary to pay the initial cash dividend were to principally come from (i) a "gold loan" in the amount of $35,625,000, repayable over a three to five year period and secured by 75,000 ounces of gold at a price of $475 per ounce, (ii) the proceeds from the sale of the discontinued Brockton Sole and Plastics and Ready-Mix Concrete businesses, and (iii) a then expected January, 1988 sale of uranium to the Public Service Electric & Gas Company.

Atlas Asks Its Investment Banker to Study the Proposal.

This written proposal was distributed to the Atlas board on December 9 and Goldman Sachs was directed to review and analyze it.

The proposal met with a cool reception from management. On December 9, Mr. Weaver issued a press release expressing surprise that Blasius would suggest using debt to accomplish what he characterized as a substantial liquidation of Atlas at a time when Atlas' future prospects were promising. He noted that the Blasius proposal recommended that Atlas incur a high debt burden in order to pay a substantial one time dividend consisting of $35 million in cash and $125 million in subordinated debentures. Mr. Weaver also questioned the wisdom of incurring an enormous debt burden amidst the uncertainty in the financial markets that existed in the aftermath of the October crash.

Blasius attempted on December 14 and December 22 to arrange a further meeting with the Atlas management without success. During this period, Atlas provided Goldman Sachs with projections for the Company. Lubin was told that a further meeting would await completion of Goldman's analysis. A meeting after the first of the year was proposed.

The Delivery of Blasius' Consent Statement.

On December 30, 1987, Blasius caused Cede & Co. (the registered owner of its Atlas stock) to deliver to Atlas a signed written consent (1) adopting a precatory resolution recommending that the board develop and implement a restructuring proposal, (2) amending the Atlas bylaws to, among other things, expand the size of the board from seven to fifteen members—the maximum number under Atlas' charter, and (3) electing eight named persons to fill the new directorships. Blasius also filed suit that day in this court seeking a declaration that certain bylaws adopted by the board on September 1, 1987 acted as an unlawful restraint on the shareholders' right, created by Section 228 of our corporation statute, to act through consent without undergoing a meeting.

threat of proxy contest

The reaction was immediate. Mr. Weaver conferred with Mr. Masinter, the Company's outside counsel and a director, who viewed the consent as an attempt to take control of the Company. They decided to call an emergency meeting of the board, even though a regularly scheduled meeting was to occur only one week hence, on January 6, 1988. The point of the emergency meeting was to act on their conclusion (or to seek to have the board act on their conclusion) "that we should add at least one and probably two directors to the board. . . ." A quorum of directors, however, could not be arranged for a telephone meeting that day. A telephone meeting was held the next day. At that meeting, the board voted to amend the bylaws to increase the size of the board from seven to nine and appointed John M. Devaney and Harry J. Winters, Jr. to fill those newly created positions. Atlas' Certificate of Incorporation creates staggered terms for directors; the terms to which Messrs. Devaney and Winters were appointed would expire in 1988 and 1990, respectively.

The Motivation of the Incumbent Board in Expanding the Board and Appointing New Members.

In increasing the size of Atlas' board by two and filling the newly created positions, the members of the board realized that they were thereby precluding the holders of a majority of the Company's shares from placing a majority of new directors on the board through Blasius' consent solicitation, should they want to do so. Indeed the evidence establishes that that was the principal motivation in so acting.

The conclusion that, in creating two new board positions on December 31 and electing Messrs. Devaney and Winters to fill those positions the board was principally motivated to prevent or delay the shareholders from possibly placing a majority of new members on the board, is critical to my analysis of the central issue posed by the first filed of the two pending cases. If the board in fact was not so motivated, but rather had taken action completely independently of the consent solicitation, which merely had an incidental impact upon the possible effectuation of any action authorized by the shareholders, it is very unlikely that such action would be subject to judicial nullification. The board, as a general matter, is under no fiduciary obligation to suspend its active management of the firm while the consent solicitation process goes forward.

There is testimony in the record to support the proposition that, in acting on December 31, the board was principally motivated simply to implement a plan to expand the Atlas board that preexisted the September, 1987 emergence of Blasius as an active shareholder. I have no doubt that the addition of Mr. Winters, an expert in mining economics, and Mr. Devaney, a financial expert employed by the Company, strengthened the Atlas board and, should anyone ever have reason to review the wisdom of those choices, they would be found to be sensible and prudent. I cannot conclude, however, that the strengthening of the board by the addition of these men was the principal motive for the December 31 action. As I view this factual determination as critical, I will pause to dilate briefly upon the evidence that leads me to this conclusion.

The evidence indicates that CEO Weaver was acquainted with Mr. Winters prior to the time he assumed the presidency of Atlas. When, in the fall of 1986, Mr. Weaver learned of his selection as Atlas' future CEO, he informally approached Mr. Winters about serving on the board of the Company. Winters indicated a willingness to do so and sent to Mr. Weaver a copy of his *curriculum vitae*. Weaver, however, took no action with respect to this matter until he had some informal discussion with other board members on December 2, 1987, the date on which Mr. Lubin orally presented Blasius' restructuring proposal to management. At that time, he mentioned the possibility to other board members. . . .

It is difficult to consider the timing of the activation of the interest in adding Mr. Winters to the board in December as simply coincidental with the pressure that Blasius was applying. The connection between the two events, however, becomes unmistakably clear when the later events of December 30 and 31 are focused upon. As noted above, on the 30th, Atlas received the Blasius consent which proposed to shareholders that they expand the board from seven to fifteen and add eight new members identified in the consent. It also proposed the adoption of a precatory resolution encouraging restructuring or sale of the Company. Mr. Weaver immediately met with Mr. Masinter. In addition to receiving the consent, Atlas was informed it had been sued in this court, but it did not yet know the thrust of that action. At that time, Messrs. Weaver and Masinter "discussed a lot of [reactive] strategies and Edgar [Masinter] told me we really got to put a program together to go forward with this consent. . . . we talked about taking no action. We talked about adding one board member. We talked about adding two board members. We talked about adding eight board members. And we did a lot of looking at other and various and sundry alternatives. . . ." They decided to add two board members and to hold an emergency board meeting that very day to do so. It is clear that the reason that Mr. Masinter advised taking this step immediately rather than waiting for the January 6 meeting was that he feared that the Court of Chancery might issue a temporary restraining order prohibiting the board from increasing its membership, since the consent solicitation had commenced. It is admitted that there was no fear that

Blasius would be in a position to complete a public solicitation for consents prior to the January 6 board meeting.

In this setting, I conclude that, while the addition of these qualified men would, under other circumstances, be clearly appropriate as an independent step, such a step was in fact taken in order to impede or preclude a majority of the shareholders from effectively adopting the course proposed by Blasius. Indeed, while defendants never forsake the factual argument that that action was simply a continuation of business as usual, they, in effect, admit from time to time this overriding purpose. For example, everyone concedes that the directors understood on December 31 that the effect of adding two directors would be to preclude stockholders from effectively implementing the Blasius proposal. . . .

. . . The timing of these events is, in my opinion, consistent only with the conclusion that Mr. Weaver and Mr. Masinter originated, and the board immediately endorsed, the notion of adding these competent, friendly individuals to the board, not because the board felt an urgent need to get them on the board immediately for reasons relating to the operations of Atlas' business, but because to do so would, for the moment, preclude a majority of shareholders from electing eight new board members selected by Blasius. As explained below, I conclude that, in so acting, the board was not selfishly motivated simply to retain power.

There was no discussion at the December 31 meeting of the feasibility or wisdom of the Blasius restructuring proposal. . . .

The January 6 Rejection of the Blasius Proposal.

On January 6, the board convened for its scheduled meeting. At that time, it heard a full report from its financial advisor concerning the feasibility of the Blasius restructuring proposal. . . .

After completing that presentation, Goldman Sachs concluded with its view that if Atlas implemented the Blasius restructuring proposal (i) a severe drain on operating cash flow would result, (ii) Atlas would be unable to service its long-term debt and could end up in bankruptcy, (iii) the common stock of Atlas would have little or no value, and (iv) since Atlas would be unable to generate sufficient cash to service its debt, the debentures contemplated to be issued in the proposed restructuring could have a value of only 20% to 30% of their face amount. Goldman Sachs also said that it knew of no financial restructuring that had been undertaken by a company where the company had no chance of repaying its debt, which, in its judgment, would be Atlas' situation if it implemented the Blasius restructuring proposal. Finally, Goldman Sachs noted that if Atlas made a meaningful commercial discovery of gold after implementation of the Blasius restructuring proposal, Atlas would not have the resources to develop the discovery.

The board then voted to reject the Blasius proposal. Blasius was informed of that action. The next day, Blasius caused a second, modified consent to be delivered to

Atlas. A contest then ensued between the Company and Blasius for the votes of Atlas' shareholders. The facts relating to that contest, and a determination of its outcome, form the subject of the second filed lawsuit to be now decided. That matter, however, will be deferred for the moment as the facts set forth above are sufficient to frame and decide the principal remaining issue raised by the first filed action: whether the December 31 board action, in increasing the board by two and appointing members to fill those new positions, constituted, in the circumstances, an inequitable interference with the exercise of shareholder rights.

II

Plaintiff attacks the December 31 board action as a selfishly motivated effort to protect the incumbent board from a perceived threat to its control of Atlas. Their conduct is said to constitute a violation of the principle, applied in such cases as *Schnell v. Chris Craft Industries*, Del.Supr., 285 A.2d 437 (1971), that directors hold legal powers subjected to a supervening duty to exercise such powers in good faith pursuit of what they reasonably believe to be in the corporation's interest. The December 31 action is also said to have been taken in a grossly negligent manner, since it was designed to preclude the recapitalization from being pursued, and the board had no basis at that time to make a prudent determination about the wisdom of that proposal, nor was there any emergency that required it to act in any respect regarding that proposal before putting itself in a position to do so advisedly.

Defendants, of course, contest every aspect of plaintiffs' claims. They claim the formidable protections of the business judgment rule.

They say that, in creating two new board positions and filling them on December 31, they acted without a conflicting interest (since the Blasius proposal did not, in any event, challenge *their* places on the board), they acted with due care (since they well knew the persons they put on the board and did not thereby preclude later consideration of the recapitalization), and they acted in good faith (since they were motivated, they say, to protect the shareholders from the threat of having an impractical, indeed a dangerous, recapitalization program foisted upon them). Accordingly, defendants assert there is no basis to conclude that their December 31 action constituted any violation of the duty of the fidelity that a director owes by reason of his office to the corporation and its shareholders.

Moreover, defendants say that their action was fair, measured and appropriate, in light of the circumstances. Therefore, even should the court conclude that some level of substantive review of it is appropriate under a legal test of fairness, or under the intermediate level of review authorized by *Unocal Corp. v. Mesa Petroleum Co.*, Del. Supr., 493 A.2d 946 (1985), defendants assert that the board's decision must be sustained as valid in both law and equity.

III

One of the principal thrusts of plaintiffs' argument is that, in acting to appoint two additional persons of their own selection, including an officer of the Company, to the board, defendants were motivated not by any view that Atlas' interest (or those of its shareholders) required that action, but rather they were motivated improperly, by selfish concern to maintain their collective control over the Company. That is, plaintiffs say that the evidence shows there was no policy dispute or issue that really motivated this action, but that asserted policy differences were pretexts for entrenchment for selfish reasons. If this were found to be factually true, one would not need to inquire further. The action taken would constitute a breach of duty.

In support of this view, plaintiffs point to the early diary entry of Mr. Weaver, to the lack of any consideration at all of the Blasius recapitalization proposal at the December 31 meeting, the lack of any substantial basis for the outside directors to have had any considered view on the subject by that time—not having had any view from Goldman Sachs nor seen the financial data that it regarded as necessary to evaluate the proposal—and upon what it urges is the grievously flawed, slanted analysis that Goldman Sachs finally did present.

While I am satisfied that the evidence is powerful, indeed compelling, that the board was chiefly motivated on December 31 to forestall or preclude the possibility that a majority of shareholders might place on the Atlas board eight new members sympathetic to the Blasius proposal, it is less clear with respect to the more subtle motivational question: whether the existing members of the board did so because they held a good faith belief that such shareholder action would be self-injurious and shareholders needed to be protected from their own judgment.

On balance, I cannot conclude that the board was acting out of a self-interested motive in any important respect on December 31. I conclude rather that the board saw the "threat" of the Blasius recapitalization proposal as posing vital policy differences between itself and Blasius. It acted, I conclude, in a good faith effort to protect its incumbency, not selfishly, but in order to thwart implementation of the recapitalization that it feared, reasonably, would cause great injury to the Company.

The real question the case presents, to my mind, is whether, in these circumstances, the board, even if it *is* acting with subjective good faith (which will typically, if not always, be a contestable or debatable judicial conclusion), may validly act for the principal purpose of preventing the shareholders from electing a majority of new directors. The question thus posed is not one of intentional wrong (or even negligence), but one of authority *as between the fiduciary and the beneficiary* (not simply legal authority, *i.e.*, as between the fiduciary and the world at large). [Agency Theory]

IV

It is established in our law that a board may take certain steps—such as the purchase by the corporation of its own stock—that have the effect of defeating a threatened change in corporate control, when those steps are taken advisedly, in good faith pursuit of a corporate interest, and are reasonable in relation to a threat to legitimate corporate interests posed by the proposed change in control. Does this rule—that the reasonable exercise of good faith and due care generally validates, in equity, the exercise of legal authority even if the act has an entrenchment effect—apply to action designed for the primary purpose of interfering with the effectiveness of a stockholder vote? Our authorities, as well as sound principles, suggest that the central importance of the franchise to the scheme of corporate governance, requires that, in this setting, that rule not be applied and that closer scrutiny be accorded to such transaction.

1. Why the deferential business judgment rule does not apply to board acts taken for the primary purpose of interfering with a stockholder's vote, even if taken advisedly and in good faith.

A. The question of legitimacy.

The shareholder franchise is the ideological underpinning upon which the legitimacy of directorial power rests. Generally, shareholders have only two protections against perceived inadequate business performance. They may sell their stock (which, if done in sufficient numbers, may so affect security prices as to create an incentive for altered managerial performance), or they may vote to replace incumbent board members.

It has, for a long time, been conventional to dismiss the stockholder vote as a vestige or ritual of little practical importance. It may be that we are now witnessing the emergence of new institutional voices and arrangements that will make the stockholder vote a less predictable affair than it has been. Be that as it may, however, whether the vote is seen functionally as an unimportant formalism, or as an important tool of discipline, it is clear that it is critical to the theory that legitimates the exercise of power by some (directors and officers) over vast aggregations of property that they do not own. Thus, when viewed from a broad, institutional perspective, it can be seen that matters involving the integrity of the shareholder voting process involve consideration not present in any other context in which directors exercise delegated power.

B. Questions of this type raise issues of the allocation of authority as between the board and the shareholders.

The distinctive nature of the shareholder franchise context also appears when the matter is viewed from a less generalized, doctrinal point of view. From this point of view, as well, it appears that the ordinary considerations to which the business judgment rule originally responded are simply not present in the shareholder voting context. That is, a decision by the board to act for the primary purpose of preventing the effectiveness of a shareholder vote inevitably involves the question who, as between the principal and the agent, has authority with respect to a matter of internal corporate governance. That, of course, is true in a very specific way in this case which deals with the question who should constitute the board of directors of the corporation, but it will be true in every instance in which an incumbent board seeks to thwart a shareholder majority. A board's decision to act to prevent the shareholders from creating a majority of new board positions and filling them does not involve the exercise of *the corporation's power* over its property, or with respect to *its* rights or obligations; rather, it involves allocation, between shareholders as a class and the board, of effective power with respect to governance of the corporation. This need not be the case with respect to other forms of corporate action that may have an entrenchment effect—such as the stock buybacks present in *Unocal*. . . . Action designed principally to interfere with the effectiveness of a vote inevitably involves a conflict between the board and a shareholder majority. Judicial review of such action involves a determination of the legal and equitable obligations of an agent towards his principal. This is not, in my opinion, a question that a court may leave to the agent finally to decide so long as he does so honestly and competently; that is, it may not be left to the agent's business judgment.

> 2. *What rule does apply: per se invalidity of corporate acts intended primarily to thwart effective exercise of the franchise or is there an intermediate standard?*

Plaintiff argues for a rule of *per se* invalidity once a plaintiff has established that a board has acted for the primary purpose of thwarting the exercise of a shareholder vote. . . .

A *per se* rule that would strike down, in equity, any board action taken for the primary purpose of interfering with the effectiveness of a corporate vote would have the advantage of relative clarity and predictability. It also has the advantage of most vigorously enforcing the concept of corporate democracy. The disadvantage it brings along is, of course, the disadvantage a *per se* rule always has: it may sweep too broadly.

In two recent cases dealing with shareholder votes, this court struck down board acts done for the primary purpose of impeding the exercise of stockholder voting power. In doing so, a *per se* rule was not applied. Rather, it was said that, in such a case, the board bears the heavy burden of demonstrating a compelling justification for such action.

In *Aprahamian v. HBO & Company*, Del.Ch., 531 A.2d 1204 (1987), the incumbent board had moved the date of the annual meeting on the eve of that meeting when it learned that a dissident stockholder group had or appeared to have in hand proxies representing a majority of the outstanding shares. The court restrained that action and compelled the meeting to occur as noticed, even though the board stated that it had good business reasons to move the meeting date forward, and that that action was recommended by a special committee. The court concluded as follows:

> The corporate election process, if it is to have any validity, must be conducted with scrupulous fairness and without any advantage being conferred or denied to any candidate or slate of candidates. In the interests of corporate democracy, those in charge of the election machinery of a corporation must be held to the highest standards of providing for and conducting corporate elections. The business judgment rule therefore does not confer any presumption of propriety on the acts of directors in postponing the annual

meeting. Quite to the contrary. When the election machinery appears, at least facially, to have been manipulated those in charge of the election have the burden of persuasion to justify their actions.

[The second case is *Phillips v. Insituform of North America, Inc.*, 1987 WL 16285 (Del. Ch. 1987)]. . . .

In my view, our inability to foresee now all of the future settings in which a board might, in good faith, paternalistically seek to thwart a shareholder vote, counsels against the adoption of a *per se* rule invalidating, in equity, every board action taken for the sole or primary purpose of thwarting a shareholder vote, even though I recognize the transcending significance of the franchise to the claims to legitimacy of our scheme of corporate governance. It may be that some set of facts would justify such extreme action. This, however, is not such a case.

3. Defendants have demonstrated no sufficient justification for the action of December 31 which was intended to prevent an unaffiliated majority of shareholders from effectively exercising their right to elect eight new directors.

The board was not faced with a coercive action taken by a powerful shareholder against the interests of a distinct shareholder constituency (such as a public minority). It was presented with a consent solicitation by a 9% shareholder. Moreover, here it had time (and understood that it had time) to inform the shareholders of its views on the merits of the proposal subject to stockholder vote. The only justification that can, in such a situation, be offered for the action taken is that the board knows better than do the shareholders what is in the corporation's best interest. While that premise is no doubt true for any number of matters, it is irrelevant (except insofar as the shareholders wish to be guided by the board's recommendation) when the question is who should comprise the board of directors. The theory of our corporation law confers power upon directors as the agents of the shareholders; it does not create Platonic masters. It may be that the Blasius restructuring proposal was or is unrealistic and would lead to injury to the corporation and its shareholders if pursued. Having heard the evidence, I am inclined to think it was not a sound proposal. The board certainly viewed it that way, and that view, held in good faith, entitled the board to take certain steps to evade the risk it perceived. It could, for example, expend corporate funds to inform shareholders and seek to bring them to a similar point of view. But there is a vast difference between expending corporate funds to inform the electorate and exercising power for the primary purpose of foreclosing effective shareholder action. A majority of the shareholders, who were not dominated in any respect, could view the matter differently than did the board. If they do, or did, they are entitled to employ the mechanisms provided by the corporation law and the Atlas certificate of incorporation to advance that view. They are also entitled, in my opinion, to restrain their agents, the board, from acting for the principal purpose of thwarting that action.

I therefore conclude that, even finding the action taken was taken in good faith, it constituted an unintended violation of the duty of loyalty that the board owed to the shareholders. I note parenthetically that the concept of an unintended breach of the duty of loyalty is unusual but not novel. That action will, therefore, be set aside by order of this court. . . .

Questions

1. What test does Chancellor Allen apply to board actions that interfere with the exercise of the stockholders' franchise? Is it different from the tests applied in cases involving breach of duty of care or loyalty?

2. How does Chancellor Allen see the relationship between directors and shareholders? Do you agree with his theory? Is it consistent with the roles of directors and shareholders discussed in the previous cases?

3. Does Allen's decision in *Blasius Industries v. Atlas Corporation* empower the individual shareholder to participate in managing her corporation's affairs?

4. What is Chancellor Allen's view of the twin rights of voice and exit? Which does he find more significant? What does this say about his vision of the role of the shareholders in the modern public corporation?

5. What does Chancellor Allen mean by the statement: "The shareholder franchise is the ideological underpinning upon which the legitimacy of directorial power rests"? The following excerpt attempts to examine this question.

Andrew C. Houston, *Chancellor Allen's Jurisprudence:* Blasius *and the Democratic Paradigm in Corporate Law*

17 Del. J. Corp. L. 843 (1992)

[footnotes omitted]

Blasius' legitimacy argument is brief, eloquent, and puzzling. It has two aspects: (1) the rejection of any functional explanation or justification of shareholder voting, and (2) the theory that shareholder voting is necessary to legitimate directorial power.

It is quite clear that *Blasius* rejects the view that the justification for shareholder voting for directors lies in its function in disciplining or controlling wayward or ineffective directors and managers. Indeed, *Blasius* appears to argue that the true justification for corporate voting is independent of any function that corporate voting plays in making the corporation operate more efficiently as an economic entity. . . .

The problem with this view, of course, is that *Blasius* does not, in fact, give any argument for it, and it is doubtful whether it is true. It is not easy to point to any general political or ethical theory that requires directors of corporations to be elected by shareholders. In our society, most people believe that only a *government* that enjoys the consent of the governed is legitimate, and most would agree that, as a practical matter, elections are the most effective means through which this consent can be demonstrated. This is necessary because governments are by nature public, all-inclusive bodies that exercise coercive force on citizens in a variety of ways. These characteristics do not necessarily apply to corporations because corporations, as opposed to governments, are inherently private and shareholder participation is voluntary.

Blasius implicitly suggests that for it to be legitimate for corporate directors to exercise power over "vast aggregations of property that they do not own," voting is required. However, it is hard to see why. Corporations that own large aggregations of property do so because people voluntarily capitalized them at the outset and voluntarily did business for and with them, causing that capital to grow. If the directors of such corporations were not elected, but were self-perpetuating, would this really pose an ethical or political problem? Of course, there might be a problem with the value of the corporation's shares if the corporation was not run in the shareholders' interests and the shareholders were unable to do anything about it. But to say that is to revert to the functional theory that *Blasius* rejects. . . .

While *Blasius* is not explicit about this, the legitimacy argument seems to appeal to an analogy between political and corporate bodies. Specifically, it appeals to an analogy between a central problem of political theory—how can it be justified for one person to rule over another—and a supposedly analogous corporate law problem—how can it be justified for one person to exercise control over another person's property. However, the value of this analogy is doubtful. The corporate law question is not quite as problematic as the political question. It is answered almost definitionally: If you want to conduct a business in the form of a large, publicly owned corporation, then these characteristics of control are inherent. This is pointed out by the difference between quasi-corporate forms of business where the board is self-perpetuating, which do not pose any ethical problems, and political bodies with self-perpetuating leaders, which many would view as ethically and politically problematic. . . .

It has been asserted above that there is no particular reason to see fundamental political or ethical values as factors in corporate law. Corporations are economic entities, created and sustained for economic reasons. The justification of particular features of corporate law lies in the realm of economics, specifically, in a functional view. This being the case, political metaphors are only marginally helpful in understanding corporate voting, though they are frequently used. A corporation is not a political body, and the reasons and rationale for its operation are completely distinct from that of a political body.

In particular, there is no reason to view corporations as analogous to democratic political societies, with the shareholders assuming the role of citizens and the directors that of an elected representative body. In any event, if political terminology must be used, it is inaccurate to view corporations as "democratic." "Plutocratic" would be a more apt description. After all, most of the constituencies that have an interest in corporate affairs, often larger than any one shareholder, do not and cannot vote unless they can also buy shares. And, of course, voting is proportional to shares owned, at least where the corporation follows the typical one vote/one share scheme.

If this theory is correct, then the democratic paradigm for corporate voting is misleading and should be abandoned. Moreover, any useful paradigm for contemplating corporate voting questions is likely to be a functional view, in which voting functions to make the corporation operate more efficiently. This raises the question of which functional paradigm to adopt. Clearly, that problem cannot be solved here. Instead, we can only sketch two alternative paradigms for corporate voting and suggest some of the considerations involved in choosing between them, or in developing other views.

One available paradigm is provided by the current academic literature which views relations between shareholders and directors as essentially one species of principal/agent relationship. This view envisions corporate voting as one of several means provided in corporate law for shareholder-principals to discipline or control director-agents. This principal/agent paradigm suggests that voting should exert constant and strict control over management and that it is evidence of a failure in the system if voting does not function in that way.

The second paradigm is quite different and is more consistent with the way in which our system of corporate elections, under which electoral challenges to directors are a comparative rarity, currently works. This paradigm analogizes shareholders and directors to two different branches of corporate government, the constitution of which establishes certain checks and balances. Under this paradigm, voting is a mechanism by which the powers of the directors, which otherwise are very sweeping, can in certain circumstances be restrained. However, this restraint may function only occasionally, in exceptional circumstances. Thus, this paradigm suggests rather different implications than the principal/agent paradigm. Under this paradigm, the fact that the shareholder vote rarely functions to replace existing directors and management does not evidence any failure of the system.

Choosing between these paradigms, one which represents the view of the shareholder rights movement and the other which adheres to the status quo, is likely to involve a number of competing considerations. Carrying into effect the principal/agent paradigm within the present institutional framework poses the threat of significant problems. Virtually all corporation statutes impose a requirement of annual shareholder meetings and director elections. Unlike many other rules, the pattern of annual elections cannot be varied by provisions of the certificate of incorporation. But vigorously contested annual elections would entail serious drains on both management and shareholder energies. They could also promote an extremely short time frame on management planning that could be deleterious to the long-term competitiveness of corporations. Thus, there are real, functional problems with the principal/agent paradigm.

On the other hand, the checks and balances paradigm also poses problems. First, this paradigm relegates voting to a position of comparatively little importance in the functioning of the corporation. If this is so, then we might wonder why so much voting is necessary. Put another way, if the corporation's annual elections will often be meaningless, as this paradigm suggests, one might ask why annual elections have to be held at all. Second, this paradigm suggests that shareholders' demands for greater influence on corporate policy through voting are simply misguided. But that answer is unlikely to satisfy shareholders who demand a larger role in corporate affairs.

The unsatisfactory nature of either paradigm suggests the need to develop a different vision of the role of corporate voting. . . .

B. Shareholders' Rights to Information

Proxy voting is the way most shareholders vote in publicly held corporations. SEC rules, promulgated under section 14(a) of the Securities and Exchange Act of 1934, govern proxy solicitations. These rules require the board, among other things, to make full disclosure when seeking the shareholders' vote for election of directors, approval of a transaction, or approval of amendments to the charter. (The rules also require periodic disclosure to the shareholders.) The following cases assess what full disclosure means in this context.

Mills v. Electric Auto-Lite Co.
396 U.S. 375 (1970)

HARLAN, Justice

This case requires us to consider a basic aspect of the implied private right of action for violation of § 14(a) of the Securities Exchange Act of 1934, recognized by this Court in *J.I. Case Co. v. Borak,* 377 U.S. 426 (1964). As in *Borak* the asserted wrong is that a corporate merger was accomplished through the use of a proxy statement that was materially false or misleading. The question with which we deal is what causal relationship must be shown between such a statement and the merger to establish a cause of action based on the violation of the Act.

I

Petitioners were shareholders of the Electric Auto-Lite Company until 1963, when it was merged into Mergenthaler Linotype Company. They brought suit on the day before the shareholders' meeting at which the vote was to take place on the merger, against Auto-Lite, Mergenthaler, and a third company, American Manufacturing Company, Inc. The complaint sought an injunction against the voting by Auto-Lite's management of all proxies obtained by means of an allegedly misleading proxy solicitation; however, it did not seek a temporary restraining order, and the voting went ahead as scheduled the following day. Several months later petitioners filed an amended complaint, seeking to have the merger set aside and to obtain such other relief as might be proper.

In Count II of the amended complaint, which is the only count before us,[2] petitioners predicated jurisdiction on § 27 of the 1934 Act, 15 U.S.C. § 78aa. They alleged that the proxy statement sent out by the Auto-Lite management to solicit shareholders' votes in favor of the merger was misleading, in violation of § 14(a) of the Act and SEC Rule 14a-9 thereunder. Petitioners recited that before the merger Merganthaler owned over 50% of the outstanding shares of Auto-Lite common stock, and had been in control of Auto-Lite for two years. American Manufacturing in turn owned about one-third of the outstanding shares of Mergenthaler, and for two years had been in voting control of Mergenthaler and, through it, of Auto-Lite. Petitioners charged that in light of these circumstances the proxy statement was misleading in that it told Auto-Lite shareholders that their board of directors recommended approval of the merger without also informing them that all 11 of Auto-Lite's directors were nominees of Mergenthaler and were under the "control and domination of Mergenthaler." Petitioners asserted the right to complain of this alleged violation both derivatively on behalf of Auto-Lite and as representatives of the class of all its minority shareholders.

On petitioners' motion for summary judgment with respect to Count II, the District Court for the Northern District of Illinois ruled as a matter of law that the claimed defect in the proxy statement was, in light of the circumstances in which the statement was made, a material omission. The District Court concluded, from its reading of the *Borak* opinion, that it had to hold a hearing on the issue whether there was "a causal connection between the finding that there has been a violation of the disclosure requirements of § 14(a) and the alleged injury to the plaintiffs" before it could consider what remedies would be appropriate.

After holding such a hearing, the court found that under the terms of the merger agreement, an affirmative vote of two-thirds of the Auto-Lite shares was required for approval of the merger, and that the respondent companies owned and controlled about 54% of the outstanding shares. Therefore, to obtain authorization of the merger, respondents had to secure the approval of a substantial number of the minority shareholders. At the stockholders' meeting, approximately 950,000 shares, out of 1,160,000 shares outstanding, were voted in favor of the merger. This included 317,000 votes obtained by proxy from the minority shareholders, votes that were "necessary and indispensable to the approval of the merger." The District Court concluded that a causal relationship had thus been shown, and it granted an interlocutory judgment in favor of petitioners on the issue of liability, referring the case to a master for consideration of appropriate relief.

The District Court made the certification required by 28 U.S.C. § 1292 (b), and respondents took an interlocutory appeal to the Court of Appeals for the Seventh Circuit. That court affirmed the District Court's conclusion that the proxy statement

---

2. In the other two counts, petitioners alleged common-law fraud and that the merger was *ultra vires* under Ohio law.

was materially deficient, but reversed on the question of causation. The court acknowledged that, if an injunction had been sought a sufficient time before the stockholders' meeting, "corrective measures would have been appropriate." However, since this suit was brought too late for preventive action, the courts had to determine "whether the misleading statement and omission caused the submission of sufficient proxies," as a prerequisite to a determination of liability under the Act. If the respondents could show, "by a preponderance of probabilities, that the merger would have received a sufficient vote even if the proxy statement had not been misleading in the respect found," petitioners would be entitled to no relief of any kind.

The Court of Appeals acknowledged that this test corresponds to the common-law fraud test of whether the injured party relied on the misrepresentation. However, rightly concluding that "[r]eliance by thousands of individuals, as here, can scarcely be inquired into," the court ruled that the issue was to be determined by proof of the fairness of the terms of the merger. If respondents could show that the merger had merit and was fair to the minority shareholders, the trial court would be justified in concluding that a sufficient number of shareholders would have approved the merger had there been no deficiency in the proxy statement. In that case respondents would be entitled to a judgment in their favor.

Claiming that the Court of Appeals has construed this Court's decision in *Borak* in a manner that frustrates the statute's policy of enforcement through private litigation, the petitioners then sought review in this Court. We granted certiorari, believing that resolution of this basic issue should be made at this stage of the litigation and not postponed until after a trial under the Court of Appeals' decision.

II

As we stressed in *Borak*, § 14(a) stemmed from a congressional belief that "[f]air corporate suffrage is an important right that should attach to every equity security bought on a public exchange." The provision was intended to promote "the free exercise of the voting rights of stockholders" by ensuring that proxies would be solicited with "explanation to the stockholder of the real nature of the questions for which authority to cast his vote is sought." The decision below, by permitting all liability to be foreclosed on the basis of a finding that the merger was fair, would allow the stockholders to be bypassed, at least where the only legal challenge to the merger is a suit for retrospective relief after the meeting has been held. A judicial appraisal of the merger's merits could be substituted for the actual and informed vote of the stockholders.

The result would be to insulate from private redress an entire category of proxy violations—those relating to matters other than the terms of the merger. Even outrageous misrepresentations in a proxy solicitation, if they did not relate to the terms of the transaction, would give rise to no cause of action under § 14(a). Particularly if carried over to enforcement actions by the Securities and Exchange Commission itself, such a result would subvert the congressional purpose of ensuring full and fair disclosure to shareholders.

Further, recognition of the fairness of the merger as a complete defense would confront small shareholders with an additional obstacle to making a successful challenge to a proposal recommended through a defective proxy statement. The risk that they would be unable to rebut the corporation's evidence of the fairness of the proposal, and thus to establish their cause of action, would be bound to discourage such shareholders from the private enforcement of the proxy rules that "provides a necessary supplement to Commission action."[5]

Such a frustration of the congressional policy is not required by anything in the wording of the statute or in our opinion in the *Borak* case. Section 14(a) declares it "unlawful" to solicit proxies in contravention of Commission rules, and SEC Rule 14a-9 prohibits solicitations "containing any statement which . . . is false or misleading with respect to any material fact, or which omits to state any material fact necessary in order to make the statements therein not false or misleading. . . ." Use of a solicitation that is materially misleading is itself a violation of law, as the Court of Appeals recognized in stating that injunctive relief would be available to remedy such a defect if sought prior to the stockholders' meeting. In *Borak*, which came to this Court on a dismissal of the complaint, the Court limited its inquiry to whether a violation of § 14(a) gives rise to "a federal cause of action for rescission or damages." Referring to the argument made by petitioners there "that the merger can be dissolved only if it was fraudulent or non-beneficial, issues upon which the proxy material would not bear," the Court stated: "But the causal relationship of the proxy material and the merger are questions of fact to be resolved at trial, not here. We therefore do not discuss this point further." In the present case there has been a hearing specifically directed to the causation problem. The question before the Court is whether the facts found on the basis of that hearing are sufficient in law to establish petitioners' cause of action, and we conclude that they are.

Where the misstatement or omission in a proxy statement has been shown to be "material," as it was found to be here, that determination itself indubitably embodies a conclusion that the defect was of such a character that it might have been considered important by a reasonable shareholder who was in the process of deciding

---

5. The Court of Appeals' ruling that "causation" may be negated by proof of the fairness of the merger also rests on a dubious behavioral assumption. There is no justification for presuming that the shareholders of every corporation are willing to accept any and every fair merger offer put before them; yet such a presumption is implicit in the opinion of the Court of Appeals. That court gave no indication of what evidence petitioners might adduce, once respondents had established that the merger proposal was equitable, in order to show that the shareholders would nevertheless have rejected it if the solicitation had not been misleading. Proof of actual reliance by thousands of individuals would, as the court acknowledged, not be feasible, see R. Jennings & H. Marsh, Securities Regulation, Cases and Materials 1001 (2d ed. 1968); and reliance on the *nondisclosure* of a fact is a particularly difficult matter to define or prove, see 3 L. Loss, Securities Regulation 1766 (2d ed. 1961). In practice, therefore, the objective fairness of the proposal would seemingly be determinative of liability. But, in view of the many other factors that might lead shareholders to prefer their current position to that of owners of a larger, combined enterprise, it is pure conjecture to assume that the fairness of the proposal will always be determinative of their vote.

how to vote.[6] This requirement that the defect have a significant *propensity* to affect the voting process is found in the express terms of Rule 14a-9, and it adequately serves the purpose of ensuring that a cause of action cannot be established by proof of a defect so trivial, or so unrelated to the transaction for which approval is sought, that correction of the defect or imposition of liability would not further the interests protected by § 14(a).

There is no need to supplement this requirement, as did the Court of Appeals, with a requirement of proof of whether the defect actually had a decisive effect on the voting. Where there has been a finding of materiality, a shareholder has made a sufficient showing of causal relationship between the violation and the injury for which he seeks redress if, as here, he proves that the proxy solicitation itself, rather than the particular defect in the solicitation materials, was an essential link in the accomplishment of the transaction. This objective test will avoid the impracticalities of determining how many votes were affected, and, by resolving doubts in favor of those the statute is designed to protect, will effectuate the congressional policy of ensuring that the shareholders are able to make an informed choice when they are consulted on corporate transactions. [7]

III

Our conclusion that petitioners have established their case by showing that proxies necessary to approval of the merger were obtained by means of a materially misleading solicitation implies nothing about the form of relief to which they may be entitled. We held in *Borak* that upon finding a violation the courts were "to be alert to provide such remedies as are necessary to make effective the congressional purpose," noting specifically that such remedies are not to be limited to prospective relief. In devising retrospective relief for violation of the proxy rules, the federal courts should consider the same factors that would govern the relief granted for any similar illegality or fraud. One important factor may be the fairness of the terms of the merger. Possible forms of relief will include setting aside the merger or granting other equitable relief, but, as the Court of Appeals below noted, nothing in the statutory

---

6. ... In this case, where the misleading aspect of the solicitation involved failure to reveal a serious conflict of interest on the part of the directors, the Court of Appeals concluded that the crucial question in determining materiality was "whether the minority shareholders were sufficiently alerted to the board's relationship to their adversary to be on their guard." 403 F.2d, at 434. An adequate disclosure of this relationship would have warned the stockholders to give more careful scrutiny to the terms of the merger than they might to one recommended by an entirely disinterested board. Thus, the failure to make such a disclosure was found to be a material defect "as a matter of law," thwarting the informed decision at which the statute aims, regardless of whether the terms of the merger were such that a reasonable stockholder would have approved the transaction after more careful analysis.

7. We need not decide in this case whether causation could be shown where the management controls a sufficient number of shares to approve the transaction without any votes from the minority. Even in that situation, if the management finds it necessary for legal or practical reasons to solicit proxies from minority shareholders, at least one court has held that the proxy solicitation might be sufficiently related to the merger to satisfy the causation requirement. . . .

policy "requires the court to unscramble a corporate transaction merely because a violation occurred." In selecting a remedy the lower courts should exercise "the sound discretion which guides the determinations of courts of equity," keeping in mind the role of equity as "the instrument for nice adjustment and reconciliation between the public interest and private needs as well as between competing private claims."

We do not read § 29(b) of the Act,[8] which declares contracts made in violation of the Act or a rule thereunder "void . . . as regards the rights of" the violator and knowing successors in interest, as requiring that the merger be set aside simply because the merger agreement is a "void" contract. This language establishes that the guilty party is precluded from enforcing the contract against an unwilling innocent party, but it does not compel the conclusion that the contract is a nullity, creating no enforceable rights even in a party innocent of the violation. . . . The interests of the victim are sufficiently protected by giving him the right to rescind; to regard the contract as void where he has not invoked that right would only create the possibility of hardships to him or others without necessarily advancing the statutory policy of disclosure.

. . . [A] determination of what relief should be granted in Auto-Lite's name must hinge on whether setting aside the merger would be in the best interests of the shareholders as a whole. In short, in the context of a suit such as this one, § 29(b) leaves the matter of relief where it would be under *Borak* without specific statutory language—the merger should be set aside only if a court of equity concludes, from all the circumstances, that it would be equitable to do so.

Monetary relief will, of course, also be a possibility. Where the defect in the proxy solicitation relates to the specific terms of the merger, the district court might appropriately order an accounting to ensure that the shareholders receive the value that was represented as coming to them. On the other hand, where, as here, the misleading aspect of the solicitation did not relate to terms of the merger, monetary relief might be afforded to the shareholders only if the merger resulted in a reduction of the earnings or earnings potential of their holdings. In short, damages should be recoverable only to the extent that they can be shown. If commingling of the assets and operations of the merged companies makes it impossible to establish direct injury from the merger, relief might be predicated on a determination of the fairness of the terms of the merger at the time it was approved. These questions, of course, are for decision in the first instance by the District Court on remand, and our singling out of some of the possibilities is not intended to exclude others. . . .

---

8. Section 29(b) provides in pertinent part: "Every contract made in violation of any provision of this chapter or of any rule or regulation thereunder . . . shall be void (1) as regards the rights of any person who, in violation of any such provision, rule, or regulation, shall have made . . . any such contract, and (2) as regards the rights of any person who, not being a party to such contract, shall have acquired any right thereunder with actual knowledge of the facts by reason of which the making . . . of such contract was in violation of any such provision, rule, or regulation. . . ." 15 U.S.C. § 78cc(b).

For the foregoing reasons we conclude that the judgment of the Court of Appeals should be vacated and the case remanded to that court for further proceedings consistent with this opinion.

It is so ordered.

[Dissenting opinion omitted.]

Questions

1. What are the different approaches to the question of causation adopted by the District Court, Court of Appeals and Supreme Court in *Mills v. Electric Auto-Lite Company*? What are the differences between them as a practical matter?

2. In light of the Supreme Court's interpretation of materiality in Rule 14a-9 and the remedies available to shareholders in situations such as *Mills*, what would you disclose to the shareholders if you were on the board of directors of a corporation about to engage in a merger?

3. In Part 4 you will learn that the common remedy for shareholders who oppose a merger is appraisal. The court in *Mills* suggests a wider range of available remedies. As a matter of policy, should shareholders be given additional remedies simply because a proxy statement omitted material information? On remand, the District Court held that the merger was unfair and awarded damages. The Seventh Circuit reversed, concluding that the merger was fair and hence that the plaintiff was not entitled to damages.

TSC Industries, Inc. v. Northway, Inc.
426 U.S. 438 (1976)

Marshall, Justice

The proxy rules promulgated by the Securities and Exchange Commission under the Securities Exchange Act of 1934 bar the use of proxy statements that are false or misleading with respect to the presentation or omission of material facts. We are called upon to consider the definition of a material fact under those rules, and the appropriateness of resolving the question of materiality by summary judgment in this case.

I

The dispute in this case centers on the acquisition of petitioner TSC Industries, Inc. by petitioner National Industries, Inc. In February 1969 National acquired 34% of TSC's voting securities by purchase from Charles E. Schmidt and his family. Schmidt, who had been TSC's founder and principal shareholder, promptly resigned along with his son from TSC's board of directors. Thereafter, five National nominees were placed on TSC's board; and Stanley R. Yarmuth, National's president and chief executive officer, became chairman of the TSC board, and Charles F. Simonelli, National's executive vice president, became chairman of the TSC executive committee. On October 16, 1969, the TSC board, with the attending National nominees abstaining, approved a proposal to liquidate and sell all of TSC's assets to National. The proposal in substance provided for the exchange of TSC common and Series 1 preferred stock for National Series B preferred stock and warrants.[1] On November 12, 1969, TSC and National issued a joint proxy statement to their shareholders, recommending approval of the proposal. The proxy solicitation was successful, TSC was placed in liquidation and dissolution, and the exchange of shares was effected.

This is an action brought by respondent Northway, a TSC shareholder, against TSC and National, claiming that their joint proxy statement was incomplete and materially misleading in violation of § 14(a) of the Securities Exchange Act of 1934 ... and Rules 14a-3 and 14a-9, promulgated thereunder. The basis of Northway's claim under Rule 14a-3 is that TSC and National failed to state in the proxy statement that the transfer of the Schmidt interests in TSC to National had given National control of TSC. The Rule 14a-9 claim, insofar as it concerns us, is that TSC and National omitted from the proxy statement material facts relating to the degree of National's control over TSC and the favorability of the terms of the proposal to TSC shareholders. ...

II

A

As we have noted on more than one occasion, § 14(a) of the Securities Exchange Act "was intended to promote 'the free exercise of the voting rights of stockholders' by ensuring that proxies would be solicited with 'explanation to the stockholder of the real nature of the questions for which authority to cast his vote is sought.'" In *Borak*, the Court held that § 14(a)'s broad remedial purposes required recognition ... of an implied private right of action for violations of the provision. And in *Mills*, ... we held that there was no need to demonstrate that the alleged defect in the proxy statement actually had a decisive effect on the voting. So long as the misstatement or omission was material, the causal relation between violation and injury is sufficiently established, we concluded, if "the proxy solicitation itself ... was an essential link in the accomplishment of the transaction." After *Mills,* then, the content given to the notion of materiality assumes heightened significance.[7]

---

1. Each share of TSC common stock brought .5 share of National Series B preferred stock and 1 1/2 National warrants. Each share of TSC Series 1 preferred stock brought .6 share of National Series B preferred stock and one National warrant. National Series B preferred stock is convertible into .75 share of National common stock. A National warrant entitles the holder to purchase one share of National common stock at a fixed price until October 1978.

7. Our cases have not considered, and we have no occasion in this case to consider, what showing of culpability is required to establish the liability under § 14(a) of a corporation issuing a materially misleading proxy statement, or of a person involved in the preparation of a materially misleading proxy statement.

B

The question of materiality, it is universally agreed, is an objective one, involving the significance of an omitted or misrepresented fact to a reasonable investor. Variations in the formulation of a general test of materiality occur in the articulation of just how significant a fact must be or, put another way, how certain it must be that the fact would affect a reasonable investor's judgment. . . .

C

In formulating a standard of materiality under Rule 14a-9, we are guided, of course, by the recognition in *Borak* and *Mills* of the Rule's broad remedial purpose. That purpose is not merely to ensure by judicial means that the transaction, when judged by its real terms, is fair and otherwise adequate, but to ensure disclosures by corporate management in order to enable the shareholders to make an informed choice. As an abstract proposition, the most desirable role for a court in a suit of this sort, coming after the consummation of the proposed transaction, would perhaps be to determine whether in fact the proposal would have been favored by the shareholders and consummated in the absence of any misstatement or omission. But as we recognized in *Mills*, such matters are not subject to determination with certainty. Doubts as to the critical nature of information misstated or omitted will be commonplace. And particularly in view of the prophylactic purpose of the Rule and the fact that the content of the proxy statement is within management's control, it is appropriate that these doubts be resolved in favor of those the statute is designed to protect.

We are aware, however, that the disclosure policy embodied in the proxy regulations is not without limit. Some information is of such dubious significance that insistence on its disclosure may accomplish more harm than good. The potential liability for a Rule 14a-9 violation can be great indeed, and if the standard of materiality is unnecessarily low, not only may the corporation and its management be subjected to liability for insignificant omissions or misstatements, but also management's fear of exposing itself to substantial liability may cause it simply to bury the shareholders in an avalanche of trivial information—a result that is hardly conducive to informed decisionmaking. Precisely these dangers are presented, we think, by the definition of a material fact adopted by the Court of Appeals in this case—a fact which a reasonable shareholder *might* consider important. . . .

The general standard of materiality that we think best comports with the policies of Rule 14a-9 is as follows: An omitted fact is material if there is a substantial likelihood that a reasonable shareholder would consider it important in deciding how to vote. This standard is fully consistent with *Mills*' general description of materiality as a requirement that "the defect have a significant *propensity* to affect the voting process." It does not require proof of a substantial likelihood that disclosure of the omitted fact would have caused the reasonable investor to change his vote. What the standard does contemplate is a showing of a substantial likelihood that, under all the circumstances, the omitted fact would have assumed actual significance in the deliberations of the reasonable shareholder. Put another way, there must be a substantial likelihood that the disclosure of the omitted fact would have been viewed by the reasonable investor as having significantly altered the "total mix" of information made available. . . .

III

The omissions found by the Court of Appeals to have been materially misleading as a matter of law involved two general issues—the degree of National's control over TSC at the time of the proxy solicitation, and the favorability of the terms of the proposed transaction to TSC shareholders.

A. *National's Control of TSC*

The Court of Appeals concluded that two omitted facts relating to National's potential influence, or control, over the management of TSC were material as a matter of law. First, the proxy statement failed to state that at the time the statement was issued, the chairman of the TSC board of directors was Stanley Yarmuth, National's president and chief executive officer, and the chairman of the TSC executive committee was Charles Simonelli, National's executive vice president. Second, the statement did not disclose that in filing reports required by the SEC, both TSC and National had indicated that National "may be deemed to be a 'parent' of TSC as that term is defined in the Rules and Regulations under the Securities Act of 1933." The Court of Appeals noted that TSC shareholders were relying on the TSC board of directors to negotiate on their behalf for the best possible rate of exchange with National. It then concluded that the omitted facts were material because they were "persuasive indicators that the TSC board was in fact under the control of National, and that National thus 'sat on both sides of the table' in setting the terms of the exchange."

We do not agree that the omission of these facts, when viewed against the disclosures contained in the proxy statement, warrants the entry of summary judgment against TSC and National on this record. Our conclusion is the same whether the omissions are considered separately or together.

The proxy statement prominently displayed the facts that National owned 34% of the outstanding shares in TSC, and that no other person owned more than 10%. It also prominently revealed that 5 out of 10 TSC directors were National nominees, and it recited the positions of those National nominees with National—indicating, among other things, that Stanley Yarmuth was president and a director of National, and that Charles Simonelli was executive vice president and a director of National. These disclosures clearly revealed the nature of National's relationship with TSC and alerted the reasonable shareholder to the fact that National exercised a degree of influence over TSC. In view of these disclosures, we certainly cannot say that the additional facts that Yarmuth was chairman of the TSC board of directors and Simonelli chairman of its executive committee were, on this record, so obviously important that reasonable minds could not differ on their materiality.

Nor can we say that it was materially misleading as a matter of law for TSC and National to have omitted reference to SEC filings indicating that National "may be deemed to be a parent of TSC." As we have already noted, both the District Court and the Court of Appeals concluded, in denying summary judgment on the Rule 14a-3 claim, that there was a genuine issue of fact as to whether National actually controlled TSC at the time of the proxy solicitation. We must assume for present purposes, then, that National did not control TSC. On that assumption, TSC and National obviously had no duty to state without qualification that control did exist. If the proxy statements were to disclose the conclusory statements in the SEC filings that National "may be deemed to be a parent of TSC," then it would have been appropriate, if not necessary, for the statement to have included a disclaimer of National control over TSC or a disclaimer of knowledge as to whether National controlled TSC. The net contribution of including the contents of the SEC filings accompanied by such disclaimers is not of such obvious significance, in view of the other facts contained in the proxy statement, that their exclusion renders the statement materially misleading as a matter of law.[15]

B. *Favorability of the Terms to TSC Shareholders*

The Court of Appeals also found that the failure to disclose two sets of facts rendered the proxy statement materially deficient in its presentation of the favorability of the terms of the proposed transaction to TSC shareholders. The first omission was of information, described by the Court of Appeals as "bad news" for TSC shareholders, contained in a letter from an investment banking firm whose earlier favorable opinion of the fairness of the proposed transaction was reported in the proxy statement. The second omission related to purchases of National common stock by National and by Madison Fund, Inc., a large mutual fund, during the two years prior to the issuance of the proxy statement.

1

The proxy statement revealed that the investment banking firm of Hornblower & Weeks-Hemphill, Noyes had rendered a favorable opinion on the fairness to TSC shareholders of the terms for the exchange of TSC shares for National securities. In that opinion, the proxy statement explained, the firm had considered, "among other things, the current market prices of the securities of both corporations, the high

---

15. We emphasize that we do not intend to imply that facts suggestive of control need be disclosed only if in fact there was control. If, for example, the proxy statement in this case had failed to reveal National's 34% stock interest in TSC and the presence of five National nominees on TSC's board, these omissions would have rendered the statement materially misleading as a matter of law, regardless of whether National can be said with certainty to have been in "control" of TSC. The reasons for this are twofold. First, to the extent that the existence of control was, at the time of the proxy statement's issuance, a matter of doubt to those responsible for preparing the statement, we would be unwilling to resolve that doubt against disclosure of facts so obviously suggestive of control. Second, and perhaps more to the point, even if National did not "control" TSC, its stock ownership and position on the TSC board make it quite clear that it enjoyed some influence over TSC, which would be of obvious importance to TSC shareholders.

redemption price of the National Series B preferred stock, the dividend and debt service requirements of both corporations, the substantial premium over current market values represented by the securities being offered to TSC stockholders, and the increased dividend income."

The Court of Appeals focused upon the reference to the "substantial premium over current market values represented by the securities being offered to TSC stockholders," and noted that any TSC shareholder could calculate the apparent premium by reference to the table of current market prices that appeared four pages later in the proxy statement. On the basis of the recited closing prices for November 7, 1969, five days before the issuance of the proxy statement, the apparent premiums were as follows. Each share of TSC Series 1 preferred, which closed at $12, would bring National Series B preferred stock and National warrants worth $15.23—for a premium of $3.23, or 27% of the market value of the TSC Series 1 preferred. Each share of TSC common stock, which closed at $13.25, would bring National Series B preferred stock and National warrants worth $16.19—for a premium of $2.94, or 22% of the market value of TSC common.

The closing price of the National warrants on November 7, 1969, was, as indicated in the proxy statement, $5.25. The TSC shareholders were misled, the Court of Appeals concluded, by the proxy statement's failure to disclose that in a communication two weeks after its favorable opinion letter, the Hornblower firm revealed that its determination of the fairness of the offer to TSC was based on the conclusion that the value of the warrants involved in the transaction would not be their current market price, but approximately $3.50. If the warrants were valued at $3.50 rather than $5.25, and the other securities valued at the November 7 closing price, the court figured, the apparent premium would be substantially reduced—from $3.23 (27%) to $1.48 (12%) in the case of the TSC preferred, and from $2.94 (22%) to $0.31 (2%) in the case of TSC common. "In simple terms," the court concluded: "TSC and National had received some good news and some bad news from the Hornblower firm. They chose to publish the good news and omit the bad news."

It would appear, however, that the subsequent communication from the Hornblower firm, which the Court of Appeals felt contained "bad news," contained nothing new at all. At the TSC board of directors meeting held on October 16, 1969, the date of the initial Hornblower opinion letter, Blancke Noyes, a TSC director and a partner in the Hornblower firm, had pointed out the likelihood of a decline in the market price of National warrants with the issuance of the additional warrants involved in the exchange, and reaffirmed his conclusion that the exchange offer was a fair one nevertheless. The subsequent Hornblower letter, signed by Mr. Noyes, purported merely to explain the basis of the calculations underlying the favorable opinion rendered in the October 16 letter. "In advising TSC as to the fairness of the offer from [National]," Mr. Noyes wrote, "we concluded that the warrants in question had a value of approximately $3.50." On its face, then, the subsequent letter from Hornblower does not appear to have contained anything to alter the favorable opinion rendered in the October 16 letter—including the conclusion that the securities being offered to TSC shareholders represented a "substantial premium over current market values."

The real question, though, is not whether the subsequent Hornblower letter contained anything that altered the Hornblower opinion in any way. It is, rather, whether the advice given at the October 16 meeting, and reduced to more precise terms in the subsequent Hornblower letter—that there might be a decline in the market price of the National warrants—had to be disclosed in order to clarify the import of the proxy statement's reference to "the substantial premium over current market values represented by the securities being offered to TSC stockholders." We note initially that the proxy statement referred to the substantial premium as but one of several factors considered by Hornblower in rendering its favorable opinion of the terms of exchange. Still, we cannot assume that a TSC shareholder would focus only on the "bottom line" of the opinion to the exclusion of the considerations that produced it.

TSC and National insist that the reference to a substantial premium required no clarification or supplementation, for the reason that there was a substantial premium even if the National warrants are assumed to have been worth $3.50. In reaching the contrary conclusion, the Court of Appeals, they contend, ignored the rise in price of TSC securities between early October 1969, when the exchange ratio was set, and November 7, 1969—a rise in price that they suggest was a result of the favorable exchange ratio's becoming public knowledge. When the proxy statement was mailed, TSC and National contend, the market price of TSC securities already reflected a portion of the premium to which Hornblower had referred in rendering its favorable opinion of the terms of exchange. Thus, they note that Hornblower assessed the fairness of the proposed transaction by reference to early October market prices of TSC preferred, TSC common, and National preferred. On the basis of those prices and a $3.50 value for the National warrants involved in the exchange, TSC and National contend that the premium was substantial. Each share of TSC preferred, selling in early October at $11, would bring National preferred stock and warrants worth $13.10—for a premium of $2.10, or 19%. And each share of TSC common, selling in early October at $11.63, would bring National preferred stock and warrants worth $13.25—for a premium of $1.62, or 14%. We certainly cannot say as a matter of law that these premiums were not substantial. And if, as we must assume in considering the appropriateness of summary judgment, the increase in price of TSC's securities from early October to November 7 reflected in large part the market's reaction to the terms of the proposed exchange, it was not materially misleading as a matter of law for the proxy statement to refer to the existence of a substantial premium.

There remains the possibility, however, that although TSC and National may be correct in urging the existence of a substantial premium based upon a $3.50 value for the National warrants and the early October market prices of the other securities involved in the transaction, the proxy statement misled the TSC shareholder to calculate a premium substantially in excess of that premium. The premiums apparent from early October market prices and a $3.50 value for the National warrants—19%

on TSC preferred and 14% on TSC common—are certainly less than those that would be derived through use of the November 7 closing prices listed in the proxy statement—27% on TSC preferred and 22% on TSC common. But we are unwilling to sustain a grant of summary judgment to Northway on that basis. To do so we would have to conclude as a matter of law, first, that the proxy statement would have misled the TSC shareholder to calculate his premium on the basis of November 7 market prices, and second, that the difference between that premium and that which would be apparent from early October prices and a $3.50 value for the National warrants was material. These are questions we think best left to the trier of fact.

2

The final omission that concerns us relates to purchases of National common stock by National and by Madison Fund, Inc., a mutual fund. Northway notes that National's board chairman was a director of Madison, and that Madison's president and chief executive, Edward Merkle, was employed by National pursuant to an agreement obligating him to provide at least one day per month for such duties as National might request. Northway contends that the proxy statement, having called the TSC shareholders' attention to the market prices of the securities involved in the proposed transaction, should have revealed substantial purchases of National common stock made by National and Madison during the two years prior to the issuance of the proxy statement. In particular, Northway contends that the TSC shareholders should, as a matter of law, have been informed that National and Madison purchases accounted for 8.5% of all reported transactions in National common stock during the period between National's acquisition of the Schmidt interests and the proxy solicitation. The theory behind Northway's contention is that disclosure of these purchases would have pointed to the existence, or at least the possible existence, of conspiratorial manipulation of the price of National common stock, which would have had an effect on the market price of the National preferred stock and warrants involved in the proposed transaction.

Before the District Court, Northway attempted to demonstrate that the National and Madison purchases were coordinated. The District Court concluded, however, that there was a genuine issue of fact as to whether there was coordination. Finding that a showing of coordination was essential to Northway's theory, the District Court denied summary judgment.

The Court of Appeals agreed with the District Court that "collusion is not conclusively established." But observing that "it is certainly suggested," the court concluded that the failure to disclose the purchases was materially misleading as a matter of law. The court explained:

> "Stockholders contemplating an offer involving preferred shares convertible to common stock and warrants for the purchase of common stock must be informed of circumstances which tend to indicate that the current selling price of the common stock involved may be affected by apparent market manipulations. It was for the shareholders to determine whether the

market price of the common shares was relevant to their evaluation of the convertible preferred shares and warrants, or whether the activities of Madison and National actually amounted to manipulation at all."

In short, while the Court of Appeals viewed the purchases as significant only insofar as they suggested manipulation of the price of National securities, and acknowledged the existence of a genuine issue of fact as to whether there was any manipulation, the court nevertheless required disclosure to enable the shareholders to decide whether there was manipulation or not.

The Court of Appeals' approach would sanction the imposition of civil liability on a theory that undisclosed information may *suggest* the existence of market manipulation, even if the responsible corporate officials knew that there was in fact no market manipulation. We do not agree that Rule 14a-9 requires such a result. Rule 14a-9 is concerned only with whether a proxy statement is misleading with respect to its presentation of material facts. If, as we must assume on a motion for summary judgment, there was no collusion or manipulation whatsoever in the National and Madison purchases—that is, if the purchases were made wholly independently for proper corporate and investment purposes, then by Northway's implicit acknowledgment they had no bearing on the soundness and reliability of the market prices listed in the proxy statement, and it cannot have been materially misleading to fail to disclose them.

That is not to say, of course, that the SEC could not enact a rule specifically requiring the disclosure of purchases such as were involved in this case, without regard to whether the purchases can be shown to have been collusive or manipulative. We simply hold that if liability is to be imposed in this case upon a theory that it was misleading to fail to disclose purchases suggestive of market manipulation, there must be some showing that there was in fact market manipulation.

IV

In summary, none of the omissions claimed to have been in violation of Rule 14a-9 were, so far as the record reveals, materially misleading as a matter of law, and Northway was not entitled to partial summary judgment. The judgment of the Court of Appeals is reversed, and the case is remanded for further proceedings consistent with this opinion.

It is so ordered.

The court in *TSC Industries, Inc. v. Northway Inc.* defined materiality in the following way: "An omitted fact is material if there is a substantial likelihood that a reasonable shareholder would consider it important in deciding how to vote." In light of the rational apathy of most shareholders, what sorts of things will a reasonable shareholder consider important in deciding how to vote? The following case further examines the subject.

Virginia Bankshares, Inc. v. Sandberg
501 U.S. 1083 (1991)

SOUTER, Justice

Section 14(a) of the Securities Exchange Act of 1934 authorizes the Securities and Exchange Commission (SEC) to adopt rules for the solicitation of proxies, and prohibits their violation. In *J.I. Case Co. v. Borak,* 377 U.S. 426 (1964), we first recognized an implied private right of action for the breach of § 14(a) as implemented by SEC Rule 14a-9, which prohibits the solicitation of proxies by means of materially false or misleading statements.

The questions before us are whether a statement couched in conclusory or qualitative terms purporting to explain directors' reasons for recommending certain corporate action can be materially misleading within the meaning of Rule 14a-9, and whether causation of damages compensable under § 14(a) can be shown by a member of a class of minority shareholders whose votes are not required by law or corporate bylaw to authorize the corporate action subject to the proxy solicitation. We hold that knowingly false statements of reasons may be actionable even though conclusory in form, but that respondents have failed to demonstrate the equitable basis required to extend the § 14(a) private action to such shareholders when any indication of congressional intent to do so is lacking.

I

In December 1986, First American Bankshares, Inc. (FABI), a bank holding company, began a "freeze-out" merger, in which the First American Bank of Virginia (Bank) eventually merged into Virginia Bankshares, Inc. (VBI), a wholly owned subsidiary of FABI. VBI owned 85% of the Bank's shares, the remaining 15% being in the hands of some 2,000 minority shareholders. FABI hired the investment banking firm of Keefe, Bruyette & Woods (KBW) to give an opinion on the appropriate price for shares of the minority holders, who would lose their interests in the Bank as a result of the merger. Based on market quotations and unverified information from FABI, KBW gave the Bank's executive committee an opinion that $42 a share would be a fair price for the minority stock. The executive committee approved the merger proposal at that price, and the full board followed suit.

Although Virginia law required only that such a merger proposal be submitted to a vote at a shareholders' meeting, and that the meeting be preceded by circulation of a statement of information to the shareholders, the directors nevertheless solicited proxies for voting on the proposal at the annual meeting set for April 21, 1987. In their solicitation, the directors urged the proposal's adoption and stated they had approved the plan because of its opportunity for the minority shareholders to achieve a "high" value, which they elsewhere described as a "fair" price, for their stock.

Although most minority shareholders gave the proxies requested, respondent Sandberg did not, and after approval of the merger she sought damages in the United

States District Court for the Eastern District of Virginia from VBI, FABI, and the directors of the Bank. She pleaded two counts, one for soliciting proxies in violation of § 14(a) and Rule 14a-9, and the other for breaching fiduciary duties owed to the minority shareholders under state law. Under the first count, Sandberg alleged, among other things, that the directors had not believed that the price offered was high or that the terms of the merger were fair, but had recommended the merger only because they believed they had no alternative if they wished to remain on the board. At trial, Sandberg invoked language from this Court's opinion in *Mills v. Electric Auto-Lite Co.*, 396 U.S. 375 (1970), to obtain an instruction that the jury could find for her without a showing of her own reliance on the alleged misstatements, so long as they were material and the proxy solicitation was an "essential link" in the merger process.

The jury's verdicts were for Sandberg on both counts, after finding violations of Rule 14a-9 by all defendants and a breach of fiduciary duties by the Bank's directors. The jury awarded Sandberg $18 a share, having found that she would have received $60 if her stock had been valued adequately. . . .

On appeal, the United States Court of Appeals for the Fourth Circuit affirmed the judgments, holding that certain statements in the proxy solicitation were materially misleading for purposes of the Rule, and that respondents could maintain their action even though their votes had not been needed to effectuate the merger. We granted certiorari because of the importance of the issues presented.

II

The Court of Appeals affirmed petitioners' liability for two statements found to have been materially misleading in violation of § 14(a) of the Act, one of which was that "The Plan of Merger has been approved by the Board of Directors because it provides an opportunity for the Bank's public shareholders to achieve a high value for their shares." Petitioners argue that statements of opinion or belief incorporating indefinite and unverifiable expressions cannot be actionable as misstatements of material fact within the meaning of Rule 14a-9, and that such a declaration of opinion or belief should never be actionable when placed in a proxy solicitation incorporating statements of fact sufficient to enable readers to draw their own, independent conclusions.

A

We consider first the actionability *per se* of statements of reasons, opinion, or belief. Because such a statement by definition purports to express what is consciously on the speaker's mind, we interpret the jury verdict as finding that the directors' statements of belief and opinion were made with knowledge that the directors did not hold the beliefs or opinions expressed, and we confine our discussion to statements so made. That such statements may be materially significant raises no serious question. The meaning of the materiality requirement for liability under § 14(a) was discussed at some length in *TSC Industries, Inc. v. Northway, Inc.*, 426 U.S. 438 (1976), where we held a fact to be material "if there is a substantial likelihood that a reasonable shareholder would consider it important in deciding how to vote." We think there is no room to deny that a statement of belief by corporate directors about a recommended course of action, or an explanation of their reasons for recommending it, can take on just that importance. Shareholders know that directors usually have knowledge and expertness far exceeding the normal investor's resources, and the directors' perceived superiority is magnified even further by the common knowledge that state law customarily obliges them to exercise their judgment in the shareholders' interest. Naturally, then, the shareowner faced with a proxy request will think it important to know the directors' beliefs about the course they recommend and their specific reasons for urging the stockholders to embrace it.

B

1

But, assuming materiality, the question remains whether statements of reasons, opinions, or beliefs are statements "with respect to . . . material fact[s]" so as to fall within the strictures of the Rule. Petitioners argue that we would invite wasteful litigation of amorphous issues outside the readily provable realm of fact if we were to recognize liability here on proof that the directors did not recommend the merger for the stated reason. . . .

Attacks on the truth of directors' statements of reasons or belief, however, need carry no such threats. Such statements are factual in two senses: as statements that the directors do act for the reasons given or hold the belief stated and as statements about the subject matter of the reason or belief expressed. . . . Reasons for directors' recommendations or statements of belief are . . . characteristically matters of corporate record subject to documentation, to be supported or attacked by evidence of historical fact outside a plaintiff's control. Such evidence would include not only corporate minutes and other statements of the directors themselves, but circumstantial evidence bearing on the facts that would reasonably underlie the reasons claimed and the honesty of any statement that those reasons are the basis for a recommendation or other action, a point that becomes especially clear when the reasons or beliefs go to valuations in dollars and cents.

It is no answer to argue, as petitioners do, that the quoted statement on which liability was predicated did not express a reason in dollars and cents, but focused instead on the "indefinite and unverifiable" term, "high" value, much like the similar claim that the merger's terms were "fair" to shareholders. The objection ignores the fact that such conclusory terms in a commercial context are reasonably understood to rest on a factual basis that justifies them as accurate, the absence of which renders them misleading. Provable facts either furnish good reasons to make a conclusory commercial judgment, or they count against it, and expressions of such judgments can be uttered with knowledge of truth or falsity just like more definite statements, and defended or attacked through the orthodox evidentiary process that either substantiates their underlying justifications or tends to disprove their existence. . . . In this case, whether $42 was "high," and the proposal "fair" to the minority shareholders, depended on whether provable facts about the Bank's assets, and about actual and potential levels of operation, substantiated a value that was above, below, or more or less at the $42 figure, when assessed in accordance with recognized methods of valuation.

Respondents adduced evidence for just such facts in proving that the statement was misleading about its subject matter and a false expression of the directors' reasons. Whereas the proxy statement described the $42 price as offering a premium above both book value and market price, the evidence indicated that a calculation of the book figure based on the appreciated value of the Bank's real estate holdings eliminated any such premium. The evidence on the significance of market price showed that KBW had conceded that the market was closed, thin, and dominated by FABI, facts omitted from the statement. There was, indeed, evidence of a "going concern" value for the Bank in excess of $60 per share of common stock, another fact never disclosed. However conclusory the directors' statement may have been, then, it was open to attack by garden-variety evidence, subject neither to a plaintiff's control nor ready manufacture, and there was no undue risk of open-ended liability or uncontrollable litigation in allowing respondents the opportunity for recovery on the allegation that it was misleading to call $42 "high."

This analysis comports with the holding that marked our nearest prior approach to the issue faced here, in *TSC Industries*. There, to be sure, we reversed summary judgment for a *Borak* plaintiff who had sued on a description of proposed compensation for minority shareholders as offering a "substantial premium over current market values." But we held only that on the case's undisputed facts the conclusory adjective "substantial" was not materially misleading as a necessary matter of law, and our remand for trial assumed that such a description could be both materially misleading within the meaning of Rule 14a-9 and actionable under § 14(a).

2

Under § 14(a), then, a plaintiff is permitted to prove a specific statement of reason knowingly false or misleadingly incomplete, even when stated in conclusory terms. In reaching this conclusion we have considered statements of reasons of the sort exemplified here, which misstate the speaker's reasons and also mislead about the stated subject matter (*e.g.*, the value of the shares). A statement of belief may be open to objection only in the former respect, however, solely as a misstatement of the psychological fact of the speaker's belief in what he says. In this case, for example, the Court of Appeals alluded to just such limited falsity in observing that "the jury was certainly justified in believing that the directors did not believe a merger at $42 per share was in the minority stockholders' interest but, rather, that they voted as they did for other reasons, *e.g.*, retaining their seats on the board."

The question arises, then, whether disbelief, or undisclosed belief or motivation, standing alone, should be a sufficient basis to sustain an action under § 14(a), absent proof by the sort of objective evidence described above that the statement also expressly or impliedly asserted something false or misleading about its subject matter.

We think that proof of mere disbelief or belief undisclosed should not suffice for liability under § 14(a), and if nothing more had been required or proven in this case, we would reverse for that reason.

On the one hand, it would be rare to find a case with evidence solely of disbelief or undisclosed motivation without further proof that the statement was defective as to its subject matter. While we certainly would not hold a director's naked admission of disbelief incompetent evidence of a proxy statement's false or misleading character, such an unusual admission will not very often stand alone, and we do not substantially narrow the cause of action by requiring a plaintiff to demonstrate something false or misleading in what the statement expressly or impliedly declared about its subject.

On the other hand, to recognize liability on mere disbelief or undisclosed motive without any demonstration that the proxy statement was false or misleading about its subject would authorize § 14(a) litigation confined solely to what one skeptical court spoke of as the "impurities" of a director's "unclean heart." . . . While it is true that the liability, if recognized, would rest on an actual, not hypothetical, psychological fact, the temptation to rest an otherwise nonexistent § 14(a) action on psychological enquiry alone would threaten just the sort of strike suits and attrition by discovery. . . . We therefore hold disbelief or undisclosed motivation, standing alone, insufficient to satisfy the element of fact that must be established under § 14(a).

C

Petitioners' fall-back position assumes the same relationship between a conclusory judgment and its underlying facts that we described in Part II-B-1. . . . [P]etitioners argue that even if conclusory statements of reason or belief can be actionable under § 14(a), we should confine liability to instances where the proxy material fails to disclose the offending statement's factual basis. There would be no justification for holding the shareholders entitled to judicial relief, that is, when they were given evidence that a stated reason for a proxy recommendation was misleading and an opportunity to draw that conclusion themselves.

The answer to this argument rests on the difference between a merely misleading statement and one that is materially so. While a misleading statement will not always lose its deceptive edge simply by joinder with others that are true, the true statements may discredit the other one so obviously that the risk of real deception drops to nil. Since liability under § 14(a) must rest not only on deceptiveness but materiality as well (*i.e.*, it has to be significant enough to be important to a reasonable investor deciding how to vote . . .), petitioners are on perfectly firm ground insofar as they argue that publishing accurate facts in a proxy statement can render a misleading proposition too unimportant to ground liability.

But not every mixture with the true will neutralize the deceptive. If it would take a financial analyst to spot the tension between the one and the other, whatever is misleading will remain materially so, and liability should follow. . . . The point of a proxy statement, after all, should be to inform, not to challenge the reader's critical wits. Only when the inconsistency would exhaust the misleading conclusion's capacity to influence the reasonable shareholder would a § 14(a) action fail on the element of materiality.

Suffice it to say that the evidence invoked by petitioners in the instant case fell short of compelling the jury to find the facial materiality of the misleading statement neutralized. The directors claim, for example, to have made an explanatory disclosure of further reasons for their recommendation when they said they would keep their seats following the merger, but they failed to mention what at least one of them admitted in testimony, that they would have had no expectation of doing so without supporting the proposal. And although the proxy statement did speak factually about the merger price in describing it as higher than share prices in recent sales, it failed even to mention the closed market dominated by FABI. None of these disclosures that the directors point to was, then, anything more than a half-truth, and the record shows that another fact statement they invoke was arguably even worse. The claim that the merger price exceeded book value was controverted, as we have seen already, by evidence of a higher book value than the directors conceded, reflecting appreciation in the Bank's real estate portfolio. Finally, the solicitation omitted any mention of the Bank's value as a going concern at more than $60 a share, as against the merger price of $42. There was, in sum, no more of a compelling case for the statement's immateriality than for its accuracy.

III

The second issue before us, left open in *Mills v. Electric Auto-Lite Co.,* is whether causation of damages compensable through the implied private right of action under § 14(a) can be demonstrated by a member of a class of minority shareholders whose votes are not required by law or corporate bylaw to authorize the transaction giving rise to the claim. . . .

. . . The *Mills* Court avoided the evidentiary morass that would have followed from requiring individualized proof that enough minority shareholders had relied upon the misstatements to swing the vote. Instead, it held that causation of damages by a material proxy misstatement could be established by showing that minority proxies necessary and sufficient to authorize the corporate acts had been given in accordance with the tenor of the solicitation, and the Court described such a causal relationship by calling the proxy solicitation an "essential link in the accomplishment of the transaction." In the case before it, the Court found the solicitation essential, as contrasted with one addressed to a class of minority shareholders without votes required by law or bylaw to authorize the action proposed, and left it for another day to decide whether such a minority shareholder could demonstrate causation.

In this case, respondents address *Mills*' open question by proffering two theories that the proxy solicitation addressed to them was an "essential link" under the *Mills* causation test. They argue, first, that a link existed and was essential simply because VBI and FABI would have been unwilling to proceed with the merger without the approval manifested by the minority shareholders' proxies, which would not have been obtained without the solicitation's express misstatements and misleading omissions. On this reasoning, the causal connection would depend on a desire to avoid bad shareholder or public relations, and the essential character of the causal link would stem not from the enforceable terms of the parties' corporate relationship, but from one party's apprehension of the ill will of the other.

In the alternative, respondents argue that the proxy statement was an essential link between the directors' proposal and the merger because it was the means to satisfy a state statutory requirement of minority shareholder approval, as a condition for saving the merger from voidability resulting from a conflict of interest on the part of one of the Bank's directors, Jack Beddow, who voted in favor of the merger while also serving as a director of FABI. . . . On this theory, causation would depend on the use of the proxy statement for the purpose of obtaining votes sufficient to bar a minority shareholder from commencing proceedings to declare the merger void. . . .

[The Court rejected both theories. As to the first theory, the Court said that:]

The same threats of speculative claims and procedural intractability are inherent in respondents' theory of causation linked through the directors' desire for a cosmetic vote. Causation would turn on inferences about what the corporate directors would have thought and done without the minority shareholder approval unneeded to authorize action. A subsequently dissatisfied minority shareholder would have virtual license to allege that managerial timidity would have doomed corporate action but for the ostensible approval induced by a misleading statement, and opposing claims of hypothetical diffidence and hypothetical boldness on the part of directors would probably provide enough depositions in the usual case to preclude any judicial resolution short of the credibility judgments that can only come after trial. Reliable evidence would seldom exist. Directors would understand the prudence of making a few statements about plans to proceed even without minority endorsement, and discovery would be a quest for recollections of oral conversations at odds with the official pronouncements, in hopes of finding support for *ex post facto* guesses about how much heat the directors would have stood in the absence of minority approval. The issues would be hazy, their litigation protracted, and their resolution unreliable. Given a choice, we would reject any theory of causation that raised such prospects, and we reject this one.[12] . . .

---

12. In parting company from us on this point, Justice Kennedy emphasizes that respondents in this particular case substantiated a plausible claim that petitioners would not have proceeded without minority approval. FABI's attempted freeze-out merger of a Maryland subsidiary had failed a year before the events in question when the subsidiary's directors rejected the proposal because of inadequate share price, and there was evidence of FABI's desire to avoid any renewal of adverse comment. The issue before us, however, is whether to recognize a theory of causation generally, and our decision against doing so rests on our apprehension that the ensuing litigation would be exemplified by cases far less tractable than this. Respondents' burden to justify recognition of causation beyond the scope of *Mills* must be addressed not by emphasizing the instant case but by

[As to the second theory, the Court noted that:]

This case does not, however, require us to decide whether § 14(a) provides a cause of action for lost state remedies, since there is no indication in the law or facts before us that the proxy solicitation resulted in any such loss. The contrary appears to be the case. Assuming the soundness of respondents' characterization of the proxy statement as materially misleading, the very terms of the Virginia statute indicate that a favorable minority vote induced by the solicitation would not suffice to render the merger invulnerable to later attack on the ground of the conflict. The statute bars a shareholder from seeking to avoid a transaction tainted by a director's conflict if, *inter alia*, the minority shareholders ratified the transaction following disclosure of the material facts of the transaction and the conflict. Assuming that the material facts about the merger and Beddow's interests were not accurately disclosed, the minority votes were inadequate to ratify the merger under state law, and there was no loss of state remedy to connect the proxy solicitation with harm to minority shareholders irredressable under state law. Nor is there a claim here that the statement misled respondents into entertaining a false belief that they had no chance to upset the merger until the time for bringing suit had run out.[14]

IV

The judgment of the Court of Appeals is reversed.

It is so ordered.

SCALIA, Justice (concurring in part and concurring in the judgment)

I

As I understand the Court's opinion, the statement "In the opinion of the Directors, this is a high value for the shares" would produce liability if in fact it was not a high value and the directors knew that. It would not produce liability if in fact it was not a high value but the directors honestly believed otherwise. The statement "The directors voted to accept the proposal *because* they believe it offers a high value" would not produce liability if in fact the directors' genuine motive was quite different—except that it would produce liability if the proposal in fact did not offer a high value and the directors knew that.

I agree with all of this. However, not every sentence that has the word "opinion" in it, or that refers to motivation for directors' actions, leads us into this psychic thicket. Sometimes such a sentence actually represents facts as facts rather than opinions—and in that event no more need be done than apply the normal rules for § 14(a) liability. I think that is the situation here. In my view, the statement at issue

---

confronting the risk inherent in the cases that could be expected to be characteristic if the causal theory were adopted.

14. Respondents do not claim that any other application of a theory of lost state remedies would avail them here. It is clear, for example, that no state appraisal remedy was lost through a § 14(a) violation in this case....

in this case is most fairly read as affirming *separately* both the fact of the directors' opinion *and* the accuracy of the facts upon which the opinion was assertedly based. It reads as follows:

> "The Plan of Merger has been approved by the Board of Directors because it provides an opportunity for the Bank's public shareholders to achieve a high value for their shares."

Had it read "because *in their estimation* it provides an opportunity, etc.," it would have set forth nothing but an opinion. As written, however, it asserts both that the board of directors acted for a particular reason *and* that that reason is correct. This interpretation is made clear by what immediately follows: "The price to be paid is about 30% higher than the [last traded price immediately before announcement of the proposal].... [T]he $42 per share that will be paid to public holders of the common stock represents a premium of approximately 26% over the book value.... [T]he bank earned $24,767,000 in the year ended December 31, 1986...." These are all facts that support—and that are obviously introduced for the *purpose* of supporting—the factual truth of the "because" clause, *i.e.*, that the proposal gives shareholders a "high value."

If the present case were to proceed, therefore, I think the normal § 14(a) principles governing misrepresentation of fact would apply....

STEVENS, Justice with whom MARSHALL, Justice joins (concurring in part and dissenting in part)

While I agree in substance with Parts I and II of the Court's opinion, I do not agree with the reasoning in Part III....

The case before us today involves a merger that has been found by a jury to be unfair, not fair. The interest in providing a remedy to the injured minority shareholders therefore is stronger, not weaker, than in *Mills*. The interest in avoiding speculative controversy about the actual importance of the proxy solicitation is the same as in *Mills*. Moreover, as in *Mills*, these matters can be taken into account at the remedy stage in appropriate cases. Accordingly, I do not believe that it constitutes an unwarranted extension of the rationale of *Mills* to conclude that because management found it necessary—whether for "legal or practical reasons"—to solicit proxies from minority shareholders to obtain their approval of the merger, that solicitation "was an essential link in the accomplishment of the transaction." In my opinion, shareholders may bring an action for damages under § 14(a) of the Securities Exchange Act of 1934 whenever materially false or misleading statements are made in proxy statements. That the solicitation of proxies is not required by law or by the bylaws of a corporation does not authorize corporate officers, once they have decided for whatever reason to solicit proxies, to avoid the constraints of the statute. I would therefore affirm the judgment of the Court of Appeals.

KENNEDY, Justice with whom MARSHALL, BLACKMUN, STEVENS, Justices join (concurring in part and dissenting in part)

I am in general agreement with Parts I and II of the majority opinion, but do not agree with the views expressed in Part III regarding the proof of causation required to establish a violation of § 14(a). With respect, I dissent from Part III of the Court's opinion.

. . .

II

. . .

B

The Court seems to assume, based upon the footnote in *Mills* reserving the question, that Sandberg bears a special burden to demonstrate causation because the public shareholders held only 15 percent of the stock of First American Bank of Virginia (Bank). Justice Stevens is right to reject this theory. Here, First American Bankshares, Inc. (FABI), and Virginia Bankshares, Inc. (VBI), retained the option to back out of the transaction if dissatisfied with the reaction of the minority shareholders, or if concerned that the merger would result in liability for violation of duties to the minority shareholders. The merger agreement was conditioned upon approval by two-thirds of the shareholders, and VBI could have voted its shares against the merger if it so decided. To this extent, the Court's distinction between cases where the "minority" shareholders could have voted down the transaction and those where causation must be proved by nonvoting theories is suspect. Minority shareholders are identified only by a *post hoc* inquiry. The real question ought to be whether an injury was shown by the effect the nondisclosure had on the entire merger process, including the period before votes are cast.

The Court's distinction presumes that a majority shareholder will vote in favor of management's proposal even if proxy disclosure suggests that the transaction is unfair to minority shareholders or that the board of directors or majority shareholder is in breach of fiduciary duties to the minority. If the majority shareholder votes against the transaction in order to comply with its state-law duties, or out of fear of liability, or upon concluding that the transaction will injure the reputation of the business, this ought not to be characterized as nonvoting causation. Of course, when the majority shareholder dominates the voting process, as was the case here, it may prefer to avoid the embarrassment of voting against its own proposal and so may cancel the meeting of shareholders at which the vote was to have been taken. For practical purposes, the result is the same: Because of full disclosure the transaction does not go forward and the resulting injury to minority shareholders is avoided. The Court's distinction between voting and nonvoting causation does not create clear legal categories.

III

Our decision in *Mills v. Electric Auto-Lite Co.* rested upon the impracticality of attempting to determine the extent of reliance by thousands of shareholders on alleged misrepresentations or omissions. A misstatement or an omission in a proxy statement does not violate § 14(a) unless "there is a substantial likelihood that a reasonable shareholder would consider it important in deciding how to vote." *TSC Industries, Inc. v. Northway, Inc.* If minority shareholders hold sufficient votes to defeat a management proposal and if the misstatement or omission is likely to be considered important in deciding how to vote, then there exists a likely causal link between the proxy violation and the enactment of the proposal; and one can justify recovery by minority shareholders for damages resulting from enactment of management's proposal.

If, for sake of argument, we accept a distinction between voting and nonvoting causation, we must determine whether the *Mills* essential link theory applies where a majority shareholder holds sufficient votes to force adoption of a proposal. The merit of the essential link formulation is that it rests upon the likelihood of causation and eliminates the difficulty of proof. Even where a minority lacks votes to defeat a proposal, both these factors weigh in favor of finding causation so long as the solicitation of proxies is an essential link in the transaction.

A

The Court argues that a nonvoting causation theory would "turn on 'hazy' issues inviting self-serving testimony, strike suits, and protracted discovery, with little chance of reasonable resolution by pretrial process." . . . Any causation inquiry under § 14(a) requires a court to consider a hypothetical universe in which adequate disclosure is made. Indeed, the analysis is inevitable in almost any suit when we are invited to compare what was with what ought to have been. The causation inquiry is not intractable. On balance, I am convinced that the likelihood that causation exists supports elimination of any requirement that the plaintiff prove the material misstatement or omission caused the transaction to go forward when it otherwise would have been halted or voted down. This is the usual rule under *Mills*, and the difficulties of proving or disproving causation are, if anything, greater where the minority lacks sufficient votes to defeat the proposal. A presumption will assist courts in managing a circumstance in which direct proof is rendered difficult.

B

There is no authority whatsoever for limiting § 14(a) to protecting those minority shareholders whose numerical strength could permit them to vote down a proposal. One of § 14(a)'s "chief purposes is 'the protection of investors.'" Those who lack the strength to vote down a proposal have all the more need of disclosure. The voting process involves not only casting ballots but also the formulation and withdrawal of proposals, the minority's right to block a vote through court action or the threat of adverse consequences, or the negotiation of an increase in price. The proxy rules support this deliberative process. These practicalities can result in causation sufficient to support recovery.

The facts in the case before us prove this point. Sandberg argues that had all the material facts been disclosed, FABI or the Bank likely would have withdrawn or revised the merger proposal. The evidence in the record, and more that might be available upon remand, meets any reasonable requirement of specific and nonspeculative proof.

FABI wanted a "friendly transaction" with a price viewed as "so high that any reasonable shareholder will accept it." Management expressed concern that the transaction result in "no loss of support for the bank out in the community, which was important." Although FABI had the votes to push through any proposal, it wanted a favorable response from the minority shareholders. Because of the "human element involved in a transaction of this nature," FABI attempted to "show those minority shareholders that [it was] being fair."

The theory that FABI would not have pursued the transaction if full disclosure had been provided and the shareholders had realized the inadequacy of the price is supported not only by the trial testimony but also by notes of the meeting of the Bank's board, which approved the merger. The inquiry into causation can proceed not by "opposing claims of hypothetical diffidence and hypothetical boldness," but through an examination of evidence of the same type the Court finds acceptable in its determination that directors' statements of reasons can lead to liability. Discussion at the board meeting focused upon matters such as "how to keep PR afloat" and "how to prevent adverse reac[tion]/perception," demonstrating the directors' concern that an unpopular merger proposal could injure the Bank. . . .

Though I would not require a shareholder to present such evidence of causation, this case itself demonstrates that nonvoting causation theories are quite plausible where the misstatement or omission is material and the damages sustained by minority shareholders is serious. . . .

I conclude that causation is more than plausible; it is likely, even where the public shareholders cannot vote down management's proposal. Causation is established where the proxy statement is an essential link in completing the transaction, even if the minority lacks sufficient votes to defeat a proposal of management. . . .

I would affirm the judgment of the Court of Appeals.

Questions

1. What theory of causation does Justice Souter adopt? Does it follow the *Mills* rationale? What are the concerns expressed by the dissenting / concurring Justices about this theory?

2. In balancing state law with federal securities regulation, which does Justice Souter privilege? Why?

3. What relief is available after *Virginia Bankshares* to a shareholder who believes that a proxy statement failed to disclose the unfairness of a transaction the shareholders were asked to approve?

C. Shareholder Proposals

Dalia Tsuk Mitchell, *Shareholders as Proxies: The Contours of Shareholder Democracy*
63 Wash. & Lee L. Rev. 1503–1578 (2006)

[footnotes omitted]

The main actors in the history of the SEC believed that its role was to promote capitalism.... [T]hey viewed government planning as required to guarantee the financial stability that could sustain capitalism....

Section 14 of the 1934 Act was meant to regulate proxy solicitation and eliminate the proxy abuse.... The section was not intended to empower shareholders, but only to "enhance management communication with stockholders within the framework of existing state corporation law." From 1934 through 1942, the SEC promulgated rules to encourage management to communicate with shareholders, as well as communication among stockholders themselves.

The SEC might have been successful in encouraging management to provide information to shareholders. But many corporations refused to refer to shareholders' proposed actions in their proxy solicitations. In 1939, Bethlehem Steel Corporation refused to include in its proxy solicitation a request from Lewis Gilbert for a shareholder vote on "moving the annual meeting site from Wilmington, Delaware to New York City, and to change the bylaws to allow stockholders to elect the auditors." When Gilbert notified the SEC, it advised Bethlehem Steel to postpone the scheduled meeting in order to give stockholders the opportunity to revoke their proxies. Bethlehem Steel "adjourned the meeting, and sent out a second proxy statement that made reference to Gilbert's proposed actions."

Shortly thereafter the SEC's Office of General Counsel undertook a study of the proxy regulations and, in 1942, suggested a number of changes.... [One of these changes] proposed adopting a rule requiring management to include proposals from security holders in its proxy solicitation, to allow shareholders to vote on these proposals, and, if management opposed the proposal, to allow the proponent to include 100-word supporting statement....

While they were not as vocal about it, business groups were ... opposed to the shareholder proposal rule and any other form of "further legitimizing shareholder activism." In various disparaging comments about the knowledge, intentions, and ability of small shareholders, business groups proclaimed that the rule would "allow 'crack-pots' to make virtually meaningless statements"; that it "would put 'dangerous weapons in the hands of the professional troublemaker'"; ... and that it would increase the length of the proxy statement, burden corporations with increased cost (at a time of war), and burden shareholders with too much information. Some went as far as to suggest that "shareholder participation was not really necessary at all."

Those businesses and business groups who were willing to support the rule wanted to limit the scope of shareholder democracy. They suggested imposing restrictions that would permit only shareholders who owned a certain amount of stock to include their proposals and limit the number of proposals that any shareholder could propose. They further suggested that shareholder proposals be limited to "proper subjects for shareholder action under state law, and not address the ordinary business activities under the purview of management." The final rule . . . endorsed the suggested limitation. It required management to include shareholder proposals in its proxy solicitation only when these proposals were "proper subjects for action by the security holders."

While it was willing to change the rule's requirement, the SEC was not willing to omit it. Proclaiming that it did not see how the shareholder proposal rule would burden corporations (even in times of war), the SEC included the shareholder proposal rule in its December 1942 release. [Chairman Ganson] Purcell and his team were simply keen on expanding the rights of shareholders, especially the small individual investor, or as they described her—the owner. For one thing, Purcell explained that:

> . . . [t]he rules are based on the fact that stockholders are the owners of their corporations and the stockholders' meetings are their meetings, and not the management's meetings. Anybody who approaches a stockholder and asks him for his proxy, must recognize that he is asking the stockholder to appoint him as the stockholder's agent. He should give the stockholder accurate information and must recognize his rights as the owner of the corporation.

There was little public pressure to enact the rule, but the SEC staff persisted. If early New Deal programs sought to empower organized groups such as labor unions, the shareholder proposal rule aimed at empowering small, disorganized shareholders in order to allow them to fight concentrated managerial power. As Milton Freeman, the draftsman of the shareholder proposal rule, explained in 1954, they envisioned the small shareholder who treated her investment as a long-term investment as the principal beneficiary of the rule. Holders of larger blocks of shares either had control or were able to launch a proxy fight if they wanted to gain control. If the 1934 act was designed to protect all individual shareholders, the shareholder proposal rule focused on those most vulnerable among the shareholders. In a world growing rapidly concerned about totalitarianism, Purcell and his team wanted to protect the individual investor against management and the control group. . . .

. . . [T]he battle for shareholder democracy did not end with the adoption of the December 1942 rules. . . .

. . . [B]eginning shortly after its adoption and well into the 1980s, the shareholder proposal rule, especially the definition of proper subjects and the qualification of the submitting shareholders, has gone through many cycles of interpretation and amendments (by the SEC and the courts). These changes corresponded to, and helped shape, changing visions of the shareholder's role in large corporations. . . .

... [In 1947, amendments to the proxy rules] formalized the role of the SEC's Division of Corporation Finance in reviewing shareholder proposals that corporations wanted to omit from their proxy statements. Before the amendment was adopted, the Third Circuit, in *SEC v. Transamerica*, formally established the SEC's authority to determine which shareholder proposals were "proper subjects." The Court accepted the SEC's position that shareholder proposals to change the location of the annual meeting, to require stockholder ratification of auditors, to require post-meeting disclosure of changes made to the by-laws, and to request the board to make a post-meeting report, were all proper subjects. . . .

While only 135 shareholder proposals (by 56 different proponents) were presented between 1943 and 1947, the American Society of Corporate Secretaries (founded in 1946) was keen on discouraging small shareholders from making proposals at annual meetings. In 1948, responding to the Society's fears that shareholder proposals would become a nuisance, the SEC made additional changes in the proxy rules. It allowed corporations to omit even "proper subject proposals" in three situations. First, corporations could omit proposals that were submitted primarily to enforce a personal claim or redress a personal grievance against the company or its management. Second, they could omit proposals if management had included a proposal from the security holder in a proxy solicitation related to the last two annual meetings and the security holder failed to attend the meeting or to present the proposal for action at the meeting. Finally, corporations could omit proposals if substantially the same proposal had been voted on at the last meeting and received less than three percent of the vote. Commissioner McConnaughey noted that these changes "were only designed to eliminate 'crackpot propositions without impeding consideration of opposition proposals that have at least debatable merit and are proper subjects for stockholder's action." No longer interested in encouraging the small individual shareholder to participate, the SEC aimed to protect management from its owners' presumed harassment.

This was also the gist of a more significant amendment that the SEC adopted in 1952. As if reflecting the vision of shareholder democracy that the shareholder proposal rule embraced, this amendment focused on internal corporate hierarchies or, more specifically, the appropriate roles of shareholders and managers. It codified the SEC practice of excluding from the scope of permissible shareholder proposals those primarily "for the purpose of promoting general economic, political, racial, religious, social or similar causes." The SEC did not see these as proper subjects for shareholder action. At the same time, the justification for the 1952 amendment seemed to follow the one offered for the 1948 amendments. The 1952 exclusion was predicated on the assumption that management became vulnerable to the shareholders.

The 1952 amendment followed discussions of a particular stockholder proposal, which James Peck, a founder of the Congress of Racial Equality, presented to the Greyhound Corporation in the fall of 1950. Peck wanted to require management to "consider the advisability of abolishing the segregated seating system in the

South." Peck had presented the proposal earlier, in March 1950, but it was rejected because it was not filed on time. In March 1951, the SEC advised Greyhound Corporation that it could omit the proposal because it involved "matters which [were] of a general political, social or economic nature" and thus not a proper subject for action by shareholders. While the SEC agreed that the proposal seemed relevant to Greyhound's business, it determined that Peck was not interested in solving a problem of relevance solely to the corporation, but in advancing a cause. The 1952 amendment was meant to codify this and similar SEC reactions. Despite opposition by civil rights groups, such the NAACP and the American Jewish Congress, the amendment was adopted. . . .

Even more damaging were the amendments the SEC introduced in 1954. Despite the fact that even when included in corporations' proxy materials, shareholder proposals never posed a threat to management, and, for the most part, were defeated on the floor, the SEC determined to stop the activities of such corporation gadflies like [Wilma] Soss and [Lewis] Gilbert. In 1934, Congress was concerned that the separation of ownership from control made the control group forget "that they were dealing with the savings of men and the making of profits became an impersonal thing." "When men do not know the victims of their aggression they are not always conscious of their wrongs," the House Report read. In 1947 the Third Circuit proclaimed that the proxy rules "created a mechanism to remind a firm's executives that a 'corporation is run for the benefit of its stockholders and not for that of its managers.'" But the 1954 amendments were predicated upon the "near opposite premise, recorded in the *SEC Minutes*, that a corporation should be permitted 'to omit any proposal which impinges upon the duties and functions of the management.'"

Generally, the issues which shareholder proposals from the 1940s through the 1950s raised fell under five categories: shareholder voting rights, matters concerning directors and officers, communication between managers and shareholders, directors and officers' compensation, and shareholders property interests.

Proposals addressing shareholders' voting rights included proposals requiring changing the location of the annual meeting, as well as proposals requiring cumulative voting for the election of directors. Proposals dealing with matters concerning directors and officers included proposals requiring that shareholders be allowed to nominate directors using the management proxy solicitation, proposals requiring that independent directors sit on the board, proposals requiring that women serve on boards (most of the latter proposals were introduced by Soss and her Federation of Women Shareholders), proposals requiring the elimination of staggered boards, and proposals requiring that shareholders be allowed to nominate and elect auditors. Proposals dealing with communication between management and the shareholders required the board to provide to the security holders financial reports throughout the year, and to submit post-meeting reports to the security holders. Proposals focusing on directors' and officers' compensation included proposals requiring changes in executive compensation (especially during a down cycle), proposals imposing a ceiling on executive compensation and employee pension funds, and proposals requiring a reduction in executive compensation when dividends were not distributed. Finally, proposals dealing with the shareholder's property interest included proposals that called for the distribution of dividends out of existing funds or that required preemptive rights for security holders.

As this short summary should indicate, shareholders did not abuse their power to introduce proposals. . . .

Still, in 1954, the SEC further limited the scope of permissible shareholder proposals. First, the 1954 amendments excluded proposals referring to ordinary business from the appropriate scope of shareholder action. Corporations could omit not only those proposals having to do with too general (economic, political, racial, religious, social) a matter, but also with a too narrow issue, that is, ordinary business.

With very little room to act, it is perhaps not surprising that some commentators suggested that shareholders focus their proposals (and action in the corporation) on "two areas of major importance to them . . . (a) the adequacy of earning results, and (b) the adequacy of the dividend policy." . . .

Furthermore, the 1954 amendments limited the right of the security holder to make a proposal even when the proposal's subject fit the divide between too narrow and too broad. The amendments allowed corporations to exclude a proposal that was submitted once within the previous three years, if it had failed to receive 3 percent of the vote. If the proposal was submitted twice within the previous three years, it could be excluded if it failed to receive 6 percent of the vote. If it was submitted three times, it could be excluded if it failed to receive 10 percent of the vote. The 1954 amendments also required security holders to notify corporations of their intent to include a proposal 60 days prior to the date on which the proxy solicitation material had been released the previous year. As proponents of shareholder democracy concluded, "[o]nly the Gilberts, the Federation of Women Shareholders in American Business, Inc., and a very few other representative proponents [were] able to operate effectively under the restrictive 1954 amendments . . . and even they [had to] resort to the seemingly devious tactic of changing proposals when a 3-6-10% favorable vote [could not] be obtained." . . .

Proponents of the shareholder proposal rule did not let go without a fight. In the 1970s, after more than twenty years in which the SEC had barred almost all social proposals, organized efforts to force corporations to act in a socially responsible way brought about a new interest in rule 14a-8.

The first organized effort was undertaken by the Project on Corporate Responsibility, which owned 12 shares of stock of General Motors. The Project, which was formed by four lawyers who were able to enlist Ralph Nader's support, asked GM's management to include nine proposals in the company's proxy solicitation. These proposals addressed product quality and safety, working conditions, environmental protection, and affirmative action (in selecting dealers). Ultimately, the Project on Corporate Responsibility was able to bring two proposals before the shareholders:

one seeking an increase in the size of the board, and the other seeking to improve the company's social impact by creating a "General Motors Shareholders Committee for Corporate Responsibility" "comprised of . . . persons appointed by General Motors, the United Auto Workers, and Campaign GM." While neither proposal gained sufficient votes (not even the three percent required for reintroduction the following year), their inclusion in the company's proxy constituted a major victory for advocates of social cause proposals.

Three months after the SEC permitted inclusion of the GM social responsibility proposal, Senator Edmund Muskie introduced the Corporate Participation Bill which sought to bar, *inter alia*, "exclusion of shareholder proposals 'on the ground that such proposal may involve economic, political, racial, religious, or similar issues, unless the matter or action proposed is not within the control of the issuer.'"

Shortly thereafter the DC Circuit handed down its decision in *Medical Committee for Human Rights v. SEC* (1970), reiterating the Third Circuit's 1947 statement: "A corporation is run for the benefit of the stockholders and not for that of its managers." The decision focused on the SEC letter of "no action" with respect to a proposal that the Medical Committee (as an owner of a few shares) wanted the board of the Dow Chemical Company to include in its proxy materials. The proposal requested the board "to adopt a resolution setting forth an amendment to the Composite Certificate of Incorporation . . . that napalm [should] not be sold to any buyer unless that buyer [gave] reasonable assurance that the substance [would] not be used on or against human beings." The board thought the proposal could be omitted, and the SEC announced that it would take no action on the matter. The DC Circuit saw things differently and remanded the case to the SEC for reconsideration. In a pointed comment about the role of the shareholder in the corporation, Judge Tamm wrote that

> [i]t could scarcely be argued that management is more qualified or more entitled to make these kinds of decisions than the shareholders who are the true beneficial owners of the corporation; and it seems equally implausible that an application of the proxy rules which permitted such a result could be harmonized with the philosophy of corporate democracy which Congress embodied in section 14(a). . . .

On appeal, the Supreme Court declared that the case was moot because the Company had included the proposal in a previous year and it failed to receive 3% of the votes. . . .

The pressure for change was mounting, sustained, in part, by the social unrest regarding the Vietnam War as well as civil rights that swept the country. Then, in September of 1972, the SEC amended rule 14a-8 to open the door, albeit not widely, for social purpose shareholder proposals. It substituted for the provision allowing exclusion of proposals intent on "promoting general economic, political, racial, religious, social or similar causes" a provision allowing omission if the proposal was "not significantly related to the business of the issuer or is not within the control of the issuer." . . .

In the following decade . . . social responsibility proposals became a "full-fledged phenomenon." . . . Church groups and institutional investors replaced the earlier "scattered shareholder campaigns" (such as the Medical Committee's campaign against Dow or even the influential Campaign GM). The Investor Responsibility Research Center, which was established in 1972 by a group of institutional investors who were trying to assess how to vote on these new resolutions, "counted 38 social responsibility resolutions coming to votes in 1973, 72 in 1974, 83 in 1975, and 133 in 1976."

Church groups' efforts focused on equal employment opportunities, plant closing, racism in South Africa, "activities in countries with controversial human rights records, energy conservation, nuclear power and nuclear weapons," as well military production. Church groups sponsored proposals to postpone mining in Puerto Rico because of environmental concerns as well as concerns to the health and well being of the people of Puerto Rico. They introduced proposals to withdraw operations from South Africa, as well as proposals to reform American manufacturers' practices of infant formula.

Other groups followed suit. In 1976, the American Jewish Congress turned to shareholder proposals in its campaign against the Arab nations' boycott of Israel. In the early 1980s antinuclear activists filed many proposals about the use of nuclear power. In 1983, Action on Smoking and Health filed 37 resolutions on smoking in airports and airplanes, while the American Jewish Congress organized "a major campaign to expose lobbying by companies in support of sales of Awacs planes to Saudi Arabia."

As to institutional investors, in 1987, the New York State Common Retirement Fund and TIAA-CREF engaged "campaigns to get companies to withdraw from South Africa, and New York City funds have stepped up their own South Africa divestment campaigns." Also in 1987, CREF, the Carpenters' union and the public pension funds of California and Wisconsin introduced a series of resolutions "against anti-takeover poison pill measures."

Although proponents of shareholder democracy celebrated the increased activity, the 1970s and 1980s vision of the shareholder's role in the corporation was very different from the one endorsed in earlier decades. While in 1983, the IRRC reported an increasing number of proposals from individual investors, for the most part, the vulnerable, individual investor had been displaced by advocacy groups and institutional investors as the focal point for legal and economic analysis.

Clearly, the participation of institutional investors helped bring about important changes. In 1982, Thomas Edwards, chairman of TIAA-CREF, commented that while institutional investors could not "out-vote management," "even the smallest institutional investors have improved the acoustics for change, whether management admits it or not." . . . [But] by shifting their attention to institutions, scholars and reformers helped eradicate the potential vulnerability of the individual investor from the academic imagination. . . .

Moreover, concerns about the rising numbers of shareholder proposals led the SEC to put additional hurdles before the individual investor. In 1983, for the first time in the rule's history, the SEC imposed "shareholder qualification standards." The 1983 amendments required that a proponent of a shareholder proposal owned "at least one percent or $1,000, whichever [was] less," of securities eligible to be voted at the meeting. The proponent had to "have owned those securities for at least one year prior to the meeting, and continue[e] to own them through the day on which the meeting [was] held." These amendments further restricted all shareholders "to one 14a-8 proposal per meeting."

After a decade of agitation against shareholder proposals, the American Society of Corporate Secretaries and other corporations finally had the upper hand. The SEC had expressed their articulated concerns, albeit unsupported by statistical data, about "abusive shareholders who purchased small amounts of stock from several companies as a means of buying a ticket to annual meetings, especially social activist shareholders." . . . [But] preventing shareholders' abuse could have been achieved by a more narrowly tailored exclusionary rule, focusing, for example, only on the duration of the investment. Moreover, the new amendments made it sufficiently more difficult for the shareholder to gain access to the proxy machine by changing the "voting percentages for resubmission" of proposals from 3% to 5% for the first resubmission, and from 6% to 8% for the second. In this context, requesting shareholders to have a particular equity interest seems to suggest that the SEC wanted to limit the individual shareholder access. Even AT&T commented that it did not "seem sensible to exclude a long-time shareholder interested in the corporation from participating in the proposal process because his shareholding is too small."

In qualifying shareholders according to their equity interest, the SEC also emphasized the vision of the shareholder as owner. Proponents of the shareholder proposal rule had often described shareholders as owners, but they did so in order to stress the vulnerability and different goals of the small shareholder. In turn, the 1983 rules were predicated upon the assumption that, as owners, all shareholders—large and small, institutional and individual—shared the common goal of maximizing their profits. Their participation in corporate affairs was to be limited to achieving this goal. . . . For the most part, [the SEC] assumed that shareholders would prefer to sell their stock than to participate in corporate affairs. The vision of the shareholder as participant converged with the view of the shareholder as investor to recreate the universal shareholder—an owner in search of profits.

Other 1983 amendments helped sustain this market based image of the relationship between shareholders, managers, and the corporation. For one thing, the SEC changed the rule allowing omission of proposals that were not significantly related to the issuer's business. It defined "not significantly related" as accounting for "less than five percent of the issuer's total assets . . . and for less than five percent of its net earnings and gross sales for the most recent fiscal year." Obsessed with economic markets, in the course of preparing the amendments, the SEC went as far as to challenge the necessity of "a federal regulatory scheme protecting shareholder's proposals."

In the year following the amendment "42% fewer proposals were recorded." While the numbers rebounded by 1987, in the decade that followed, shareholder social purpose proposals were displaced as the focus of debates about shareholder democracy and the role of the individual shareholder. . . . [C]orporate governance issues captured the attention of shareholders, especially institutional investors.

In the following case, a corporation sought to omit a shareholder proposal based on the argument that it dealt "with a matter relating to the company's ordinary business operations." As you read it, consider the court's explanation as to when a proposal does or does not relate to "ordinary business operations." What, in your opinion, influences the court's determination in the following case (and in the cases it describes)?

Amalgamated Clothing and Textile Workers Union v. Wal-Mart Stores, Inc.

821 F. Supp. 877 (S.D.N.Y. 1993)

Wood, Judge

On April 19, 1993, the court issued an Order enjoining defendant Wal-Mart Stores, Inc. ("Wal-Mart") from mailing out proxy material omitting plaintiffs' proposed resolution (the "Proposal") as amended by the court. The court's factual and legal findings are set forth below.

Plaintiffs, Wal-Mart shareholders, sought to enjoin the company from omitting their Proposal from proxy solicitation material the company plans to distribute in advance of Wal-Mart's June 4, 1993 annual meeting. Plaintiffs seek to submit to a shareholder vote a request for Wal-Mart's directors to prepare and distribute reports about Wal-Mart's equal employment opportunity ("EEO") and affirmative action policies, programs and data, along with a description of Wal-Mart's efforts to 1) publicize its EEO policies to suppliers, and 2) purchase goods and services from minority- and female-owned suppliers. Plaintiffs allege that Wal-Mart's omission of their proposal violates Securities and Exchange Commission ("SEC" or "Commission") Rule 14a-8.

Wal-Mart moves to dismiss the Amended Complaint. Wal-Mart asserts that it may exclude the proposal because it "deals with a matter relating to the conduct of [Wal-Mart's] ordinary business operations," an excludable category under Rule 14a-8(c)(7). Plaintiffs cross-move for summary judgment. The court treats the motions as cross-motions for summary judgment. The court denies Wal-Mart's motion and grants plaintiffs' motion for the reasons, and to the extent, set forth below.

I. Background

Plaintiff Amalgamated Clothing and Textile Workers Union ("ACTWU") is a labor union representing approximately 250,000 workers internationally. Plaintiffs National Council of Churches of Christ in the U.S.A., Unitarian Universalist Association and Literary Society of Saint Catherine of Sienna are religious organizations, which invest in socially responsible corporations as part of their religious missions. Each plaintiff believes that "issues concerning equal employment opportunity and affirmative action are important to shareholder value." Plaintiffs' stated ultimate goal is to improve Wal-Mart's EEO record and that of the discount retail store industry; to that end, they submit proposals, such as this one, to foster dialogue between plaintiffs and Wal-Mart and between plaintiffs and other shareholders. Under SEC Rule 14a-8(a)(1), plaintiffs, as owners of at least $1,000 worth of Wal-Mart stock, are eligible to submit proposals for inclusion in Wal-Mart's proxy material.

Wal-Mart operates a chain of retail stores throughout the United States. Wal-Mart is a Delaware corporation with its principal place of business in Bentonville, Arkansas. As a Delaware corporation, Wal-Mart is subject to Delaware corporate law pertaining to the use of shareholder proxies at annual meetings and is concurrently subject to the rules adopted by the SEC, which regulate the content and solicitation of proxies.

Plaintiff ACTWU submitted a proposal to Wal-Mart in 1991 that is substantially similar to the 1993 Proposal at issue here. In 1992, plaintiffs collectively submitted a revised proposal to Wal-Mart that is identical to the 1993 Proposal. Plaintiffs' resubmitted their 1992 proposal for inclusion in Wal-Mart's 1993 proxy material. Wal-Mart refused to include any of the proposals submitted by plaintiffs. The 1993 Proposal requests Wal-Mart's board of directors to prepare the following reports by September 1993:

> 1. A chart identifying employees according to their sex and race in each of the nine major EEOC defined job categories for 1990, 1991, 1992 listing either numbers or percentages in each category.

> 2. A summary description of Affirmative Action Programs to improve performance especially in job categories where women and minorities are under utilized and a description of major problems in meeting the company's goals and objectives in this area.

> 3. A description of steps taken to increase the number of managers who are qualified females and ethnic minorities.

> 4. A description of ways in which Wal-Mart publicizes our company's policies to merchandise suppliers and service providers to encourage forward action on their part as well.

5. A description of Wal-Mart's efforts to purchase goods and services from minority and female owned business enterprises.[4]

Plaintiffs envision a brief report, that could, in their view, range from the one page analysis produced by J.C. Penney as part of its annual report to a five page internal memorandum made available to shareholders of CIGNA Corporation.

II. Discussion A. Regulatory Framework

. . .

2. Shareholder Proposals

Under Delaware law, a shareholder in attendance at the annual meeting may offer a proposal for shareholder approval, as long as the proposal involves a proper subject on which shareholders may vote. "[T]he right of security holders to present proposals at the meeting, as distinguished from the right to include such proposals in management's proxy materials, turns upon state law." Unless the shareholders' proposed resolution is included in the proxy material, however, other shareholders would not have advance notice of the intention to make the proposal or have the ability to vote on the proposal via the proxy. . . .

3. Proxy Solicitations

. . .

Rule 14a-8(a) requires a company to include a shareholder's proposal in the company's proxy statement and provide shareholders with the opportunity to vote on the proposal by executing the proxy card. This ostensibly broad directive is limited by

---

4. The resolution is preceded by the following preamble:
WHEREAS, Wal-Mart is one of the nation's largest employers in what is rapidly becoming a service oriented job market for many Americans;
We believe the vast majority of Wal-Mart's customers are either women or members of a racial minority group.
By the beginning of the next century, the majority of new entrants to our nation's workforce will be women and/or minority group members.
We believe it makes good business sense for Wal-Mart to describe and publicize its employment standards which relate to its core customer groups and potential employees. By publicizing its standards, Wal-Mart will be an example to companies with whom it does business.
We share the concern stated by U.S. Labor Department Secretary Lynn Martin who has declared a new goal of challenging the "glass ceiling investigation to remedy this situation."
We believe a report containing basic information requested in this resolution keeps the issue high on management's agenda. It will also reaffirm our public commitment to non-discriminatory employment practices and equal economic opportunity and be responsive to the concerns of women and minorities. The format of the report requested is not important. Different companies use different styles and levels of detail in telling their story to shareholders. Bristol-Myers, Squibb and Travellers produced a magazine style report. Campbell Soup produced a four page document. GM discloses in its Public Interest Report.

thirteen content-based exceptions. Most relevant to this case is Rule 14a-8(c)(7), which permits a company to omit a shareholder proposal if "the proposal deals with a matter relating to the conduct of the ordinary business operations of the registrant." A shareholder proposal pertaining to "ordinary business operations" would be improper if raised at an annual meeting, because the law of most states (including Delaware) leaves the conduct of ordinary business operations to corporate directors and officers rather than the shareholders. As one court explained, "management cannot exercise its specialized talents effectively if corporate investors assert the power to dictate the minutiae of daily business decisions." The SEC adopted this exception to save management the cost and burden of including a proposal in proxy material that would be improper if raised by a shareholder at the annual meeting.

4. SEC Review of Intent to Omit Proposals

A company that objects to the inclusion of a proposal and wishes to omit it from the company's proxy statement must file with the SEC (1) a copy of the proposal, (2) any statement in support of the proposal submitted by the proponent, and (3) a statement of "the reasons why the [company] deems such omission to be proper in the particular case." The "burden of proof [is] upon the management to show that a particular security holder's proposal is not a proper one for inclusion in management's proxy material." . . .

In connection with its submission of the proposal and its objections, a company may ask the SEC to issue a "no-action" letter, in which the SEC staff informs the company whether the SEC believes the shareholder proposal may be omitted and opines on the SEC's enforcement position should the proposal be omitted. A company must notify the SEC of its intention to omit the proposal, but no response from the Commission or its staff is required before the company may mail out proxy material that omits the opposed shareholder proposal.

B. Standard for Court's Determination Whether a Proposal May Be Excluded as Pertaining to "Ordinary Business Operations"

Determining whether Wal-Mart may exclude plaintiffs' Proposal under the "ordinary business operations" exception requires the court to construe the meaning of the SEC's own rules. When a court interprets an administrative regulation, "the ultimate criterion" is the agency's interpretation of the regulation, which becomes of controlling weight unless that interpretation is "plainly erroneous or inconsistent with the regulation." . . . Thus before deciding whether Wal-Mart may omit the Proposal on the basis of the "ordinary business operations" exception, I must first examine how the SEC interprets Rule 14a-8(c)(7).

1. The SEC's Interpretive Release Standard

Both the present form of Rule 14a-8, which contains the phrase "ordinary business operations," and the SEC Interpretive Release that accompanied it, were adopted after a formal notice and comment rule-making period in 1976. The 1976 Release "established the principles by which [the Commission] intended the 'ordinary business' provision of Rule 14a-8 to be interpreted." ... Writing in January 1992, the SEC stated that "these principles are no less applicable today than when the Commission adopted them" in 1976.

The SEC issued the 1976 Interpretive Release to resolve previous interpretive difficulties over Rule 14a-8(c)(7)'s intended meaning. The Release states in pertinent part that

> the term "ordinary business operations" has been deemed on occasion to include certain matters which have significant policy, economic or other implications inherent in them. For instance, a proposal that a utility company not construct a proposed nuclear power plant has in the past been considered excludable.... In retrospect, however, it seems apparent that the economic and safety considerations attendant to nuclear power plants are of such magnitude that a determination whether to construct one is not an "ordinary" business matter. Accordingly, proposals of that nature as well as others having major implications be considered beyond the realm of an issuer's ordinary business operations, and future interpretive letters of the Commission's staff will reflect that view.
>
> ... Thus, where proposals involve business matters that are mundane in nature and do not involve any substantial policy or other considerations, the subparagraph may be relied upon to omit them.

2. Development of SEC Interpretation Through No-Action Letter Review Process

The general guidance provided to parties and the court by the 1976 Interpretive Release and state corporate law has been supplemented by the no-action letters issued by the SEC staff and the rare discretionary review of no-action letters provided by the full Commission. No-action letters can provide insight into the meaning of the term "ordinary business operations," because, unlike general interpretive releases, no-action letters address specific issues and build upon the SEC's "vast experience of daily contact with the practical workings of this rule." ... However, as the SEC itself maintains, the *ad hoc* nature of these letters means that courts cannot place them on a precedential par with formal rulemaking or adjudication. Before turning to how the SEC has applied Rule 14a-8(c)(7) to similar proposals through numerous no-action letters, the court will, therefore, address the extent to which it must defer to positions taken in no-action letters.

a. Deference Owed to No-Action Position

An individual no-action letter by itself is not an expression of agency interpretation to which the court must defer.... By responding to a company's request for a no-action letter, the "Commission and its staff do not purport in any way to issue 'rulings' or 'decisions' on shareholder proposals management indicates it intends to omit, and they do not adjudicate the merits of a management's posture concerning such a proposal."

The SEC staff reviews annually approximately 350 requests for no-action letters regarding shareholder proposals and over 6,700 proxy statements. . . . Time and staff constraints require the staff to evaluate a shareholder proposal as an indivisible whole; if one part of a multi-part proposal is excludable, the entire proposal is treated as excludable. . . . The administrative constraints on the SEC staff led the agency to express concern at its inability to enforce § 14(a) on its own through the informal no-action letter process, and it has acknowledged a need for its efforts to be supplemented by private enforcement in the courts.

However, although the court need not defer to an individual no-action position, courts have relied on the consistency of the SEC staff's position and reasoning on a given issue, or the lack of consistency, in determining whether a proposal that was deemed excludable by the SEC staff can in fact be omitted under Rule 14a-8(c)(7). . . .

In determining whether to defer to a position drawn from a series of no-action letters, courts must recognize that a change in SEC position does not necessarily reveal capricious action by the agency; changes in conditions and public perceptions justify changes in the SEC's construction of the "ordinary business operations" exception. The nature of the exception permits, if not requires, the SEC to reevaluate earlier positions "in light of new considerations, or changing conditions which indicate that its earlier views are no longer in keeping with the objectives of Rule 14a-8." The SEC has revised its position with respect to the inclusion of proposals on a number of issues formerly excludable under Rule 14a-8(c)(7) such as plant closings, tobacco production, cigarette advertising and all forms of senior executive and director compensation. . . . In announcing the change in the Commission's position on senior executive and director compensation, SEC Chairman Breeden stated that the "the level of public and shareholder concern . . . has become intense and widespread" and "dictates a reevaluation" of SEC policy. Thus, an SEC departure from a prior position must be considered in light of changing public and shareholder concerns. Having addressed the various considerations that help to determine the level of deference owed to no-action letters, the court now examines the SEC's interpretation of the "ordinary business operations" exception in its no-action letters dealing with similar EEO and affirmative action proposals.

b. SEC's No-Action Letter Position on Ordinary Business Operations

Although the SEC has been dealing with proposals like plaintiffs' since the mid-1970s, its treatment of these proposals has changed over time. Prior to 1983, the SEC took the position that proposals requesting reports on EEO data and policies could not be excluded, because the determination whether a *report* should be issued was matter of policy rather than ordinary business operations. . . . In 1983, the SEC changed its interpretation of the exception and determined that the *subject* of the report requested, rather than the fact that the information requested was in the form of a *report*, would determine the proposal's excludability under the "ordinary business operations" exception. . . .

Since 1983, the SEC has determined whether employment policy proposals must be included in proxy materials by examining whether the proposals relate to "day-to-day" employment matters and, therefore, are excludable as relating to "ordinary business operations," or whether the proposals relate to significant policy considerations and, therefore, are not excludable. Day-to-day employment matters have been interpreted as including matters concerning: employee health benefits, general compensation issues not focused on senior executives, management of the workplace, employee supervision, labor-management relations, employee hiring and firing, conditions of employment and employee training and motivation. . . . The SEC has also viewed a proposal requesting a company to hire contractors from within its service area as excludable under Rule 14a-8(c)(7). . . .

Despite the SEC's general view that employee hiring and firing and supplier decisions are related to a company's ordinary business operations, the SEC has until recently recognized that the issues of EEO and affirmative action raise policy considerations elevating them above the excludable day-to-day issues. Thus, in 1988, the SEC staff stated, and the full Commission affirmed, that AT&T may not exclude a shareholder proposal to phase out those aspects of AT&T's affirmative action program directed toward recruiting, employing or promoting individuals from any particular racial or ethnic group. *See American Telephone & Telegraph Co.*, SEC No-Action Letter, 1988 WL 235275 at 15 (Dec. 21. 1988). The staff stated that AT&T could not rely on the exception for "ordinary business operations" because the proposal involved "policy issues," described by the SEC staff as "the Company's affirmative action program, designed to assure equal employment opportunities for minority group members. . . ."

Similarly, on February 14, 1991, the SEC took the position that a proposal requesting the publication of EEO data and the adoption of an affirmative action program and a program for purchasing from vendors controlled by women and minorities was not excludable, because it related to "general policy decisions which are beyond the conduct of the Company's day-to-day operations." *V.F. Corp.*, SEC No-Action Letter, 1991 SEC No-Act. LEXIS 238 (Feb. 14, 1991).

In the same vein, on March 8, 1991 the SEC reviewed a proposal that was identical to a proposal plaintiff ACTWU submitted to Wal-Mart in 1991, and contained four of the five requests included in the 1993 Proposal at issue here. The SEC took the position that although the proposal "concerns employment and other matters that involve the Company's ordinary business operations, . . . questions with respect to equal employment opportunity and affirmative action involve policy decisions beyond those personnel matters that constitute the Company's ordinary course of business." *Dayton Hudson Corp.*, SEC No-Action Letter, 1991 SEC No-Act. LEXIS 428 (Mar. 8, 1991).

Thus, through March 1991, the SEC's no-action letters determined that companies could not exclude proposals requesting the information requested in plaintiffs' Proposal here. On April 4, 1991, however, the full Commission appeared to shift position, and voted 3–2 to reverse the staff position stated in a no-action letter issued to Capital Cities/ABC. The proposal there requested information quite similar to that requested here in plaintiffs' 1993 Proposal, although a notable difference is that in *Capital Cities/ABC*, the proposal requested a summary of timetables to implement affirmative action programs.[11] The divided Commission determined that the proposal was excludable because it "involves a request for detailed information on the composition of the company's work force, employment practices and policies, and the selection of program content." (Def. Ex. P at 1 [Letter from Secretary of SEC to General Counsel of Capital Cities/ABC] Apr. 4, 1991).

On April 10, 1991, six days after the Commission's decision in *Capital Cities/ABC*, the SEC staff issued Wal-Mart a no-action letter with respect to ACTWU's 1991 proposal, relying on the rationale of *Capital Cities/ABC*. The SEC's views on the issues raised in the 1991 proposal are unclear, because the staff based its conclusion partly on an erroneous characterization of the proposal. The SEC incorrectly construed the request that the board of directors publicize Wal-Mart's EEO and affirmative action policies to Wal-Mart's suppliers as requesting "detailed information on the . . . Company's practices and policies for selecting suppliers of goods and services."

After the Commission's decision in *Capital Cities/ABC*, the parties there reached a settlement whereby the shareholder proponents withdrew their petition for review of the Commission's action in the Court of Appeals for the District of Columbia Circuit. In exchange, Capital Cities/ABC agreed not to object to the shareholder proponents' request to vacate the Commission's April 4, 1991 letter. By letter dated July 15, 1991, the Commission agreed to vacate its earlier action, rendering the decision of no precedential value, according to Richard Y. Roberts, one of the SEC Commissioners. . . .

On April 10, 1992, the staff issued Wal-Mart a no-action letter with respect to plaintiffs' 1992 proposal, also relying on the rationale of *Capital Cities/ABC*, notwithstanding that the Commission had earlier vacated its decision in *Capital Cities/ABC*. The letter to Wal-Mart stated that the Division would not recommend an enforcement action to the SEC if Wal-Mart excluded plaintiffs' proposal from its 1992

---

11. The proposal in Capital Cities/ABC requested:
1) a breakdown by race and sex of all employees in each of the nine major EEOC job categories for 1988, 1989 and 1990 (equivalent to Proposal request in part 1);
2) a summary of affirmative action programs and timetables to implement these programs, and a description of major problems in meeting the goals of these programs (substantially similar to Proposal request in part 2 except for the reference to a timetable);
3) a description of the actions taken with the producers of television programming to increase the number of female and ethnic minority writers, producers and directors; (substantially similar to Proposal request in part 3); and
4) a description of the actions taken to ensure that the content of those programs is responsive to the concerns of women and minorities.

proxy materials because there appeared "some basis" for Wal-Mart's omission of the proposal, because the proposal "involves a request for detailed information on the composition of the Company's work-force, its employment practices and policies as well as its relationships with suppliers and other businesses." Wal-Mart, thereafter, omitted plaintiffs' proposal from its 1992 proxy materials.

In October 1992 the SEC staff expressed in more sweeping terms the view that companies could exclude EEO proposals, reversing the position it took in *AT&T* in 1988 and *Dayton Hudson* in 1991. See *Cracker Barrel Old Country Stores, Inc.*, No-Action Letter, 1992 SEC No-Act. LEXIS 984 (Oct. 13, 1992). The articulated reason for that decision was that the SEC found distinctions between policies implicating broad social issues and the conduct of day-to-day business simply too hard to draw as regards the employment of the general workforce. The shareholder proposal in *Cracker Barrel* was prompted by that company's announcement of a policy to discriminate against gay men and lesbians. The proposal asked the corporation (1) to include sexual orientation in its anti-discrimination policy, and (2) to enforce its amended policy. The SEC staff and later the Commission characterized the proposal as requesting that the directors "implement hiring policies relating to sexual orientation and incorporate such policies into the corporate employment policy statement." Based on this characterization of the proposal, the SEC staff explained:

> Notwithstanding the general view that employment matters concerning the workforce of the company are excludable as matters involving the conduct of day-to-day business, exceptions have been made in some cases where a proponent based an employment-related proposal on "social policy" concerns. In recent years, however, *the line between includable and excludable employment-related proposals based on social policy considerations has become increasingly difficult to draw*. The distinctions recognized by the staff are characterized by many as tenuous, without substance and effectively nullifying the application of the ordinary business exclusion to employment-related proposals.
>
> The Division has reconsidered the application of Rule 14a-8(c)(7) to employment-related proposals in light of these concerns and the staff's experience with these proposals in recent years. As a result, the Division has determined that *the fact that a shareholder proposal concerning a company's employment policies and practices for the general workforce is tied to a social issue will no longer be viewed as removing the proposal from the realm of ordinary business operations* of the registrant. Rather, determinations with respect to any such proposals are properly governed by the employment-based nature of the proposal.

On January 15, 1993, the Commission affirmed the Division's position that the proposal was excludable from the Company's proxy material, relying on Rule 14a-8(c)(7), without any further elaboration on the staff's rationale for its determination.

During 1993 the SEC staff issued several no-action letters on shareholder proposals involving employment-related matters. In each case, including those raising EEO issues, the staff decided that the proposal was excludable based on its view that the proposal was "principally directed at the Company's employment policies and practices which are matters relating to the conduct of ordinary business operations."

Thus, the SEC's current no-action position is that it can no longer continue to draw the lines between includable and excludable proposals that it drew in *AT&T, Ruddick Corp., V.F. Corp.* and *Dayton Hudson.* As a result, shareholder proposals involving EEO and affirmative action policies are now deemed excludable by the SEC because they relate to employment policies, and employment policies are viewed as ordinary business matters.

C. Whether Wal-Mart May Exclude Plaintiffs' Proposal

Having considered the SEC's formal interpretive guidelines for Rule 14a-8 and the SEC's application of those guidelines through the no-action letter process, the court turns to whether Wal-Mart carries its burden of showing that the Proposal may be excluded from management's proxy material because it falls within the "ordinary business operations" exception. Wal-Mart first contends that the court should defer to *Cracker Barrel* and the 1993 Wal-Mart no-action letter, which categorically reject the SEC's prior position on EEO and affirmative action proposals. It alternatively contends that the Proposal's request for "detailed" information about Wal-Mart's employee and supplier relations involves shareholders in the details of implementing rather than adopting corporate policy, and that the Proposal is thus excludable because the choice between ways to implement corporate policy is mundane in nature and does not involve substantial policy considerations.

1. Whether the Court Should Defer to the SEC's Cracker Barrel Position

The court does not defer to the SEC's position in *Cracker Barrel* and is not persuaded by its reasoning, because the reasoning in *Cracker Barrel* sharply deviates from the standard articulated in the 1976 Interpretive Release. The parties, the SEC and courts all agree that courts must defer to the 1976 Interpretive Release. . . . As discussed above, that Release interpreted Rule 14a-8(c)(7) as permitting the exclusion of "proposals that are mundane in nature and do not involve any substantial policy or other considerations."

Cracker Barrel fails to apply both parts of the Release's conjunctive standard. In *Cracker Barrel,* the Commission explicitly acknowledged that proposals in favor of or against the adoption of an EEO program continue to raise "social policy" issues, and it did not suggest any diminished public or shareholder interest in these social issues. It nonetheless took the position that the SEC's inability to continue to draw lines warranted an across-the-board rule that any proposal relating to employment matters is excludable because it relates to day-to-day business affairs, regardless of whether the proposal also involves a substantial policy consideration. This interpretation contravenes the 1976 Interpretive Release's explicit recognition that *all* proposals could be seen as involving some aspect of day-to-day business operations. That recognition underlay the Release's statement that the SEC's determination of whether a company may exclude a proposal should not depend on whether the proposal could be characterized as involving some day-to-day business matter. Rather, the proposal may be excluded only after the proposal is *also* found to raise no substantial policy consideration. *See 1976 Interpretive Release,* 41 Fed. Reg. at 52,998 (proposal requesting company not to construct nuclear power plant may not be excluded even though the proposal also relates to the mundane matters of the fuel mix and types of electrical generating methods), referring to *Potomac Electric Power Co.,* SEC No-Action Letter, 1976 SEC No-Act. LEXIS 622 (Mar. 5, 1976). The SEC did not follow the 1976 Interpretive Release standard in *Cracker Barrel* or in the 1993 no-action letter issued to Wal-Mart, in that the SEC focused only on whether employment policies generally involve day-to-day business matters.[13]

2. Whether Application of the 1976 Interpretive Release Standard Independently Permits Wal-Mart to Exclude the Proposal

Having concluded that deference is not owed to *Cracker Barrel* and the 1993 Wal-Mart no-action letter, the court considers whether Wal-Mart has carried its burden for excluding the Proposal under the standard articulated by the 1976 Interpretive Release and the corpus of SEC no-action letters that properly applied that standard . . .

Wal-Mart itself does not deny that equality and diversity in the workplace involve substantial policy considerations. Indeed, it would be difficult to sustain such a position in light of, among other things, the continual interest of Congress in employment discrimination since 1964, which was most recently underscored in the Civil Rights and Glass Ceiling Acts of 1991.

Rather, Wal-Mart argues that the Proposal would involve shareholders in dictating the *implementation* of a policy, albeit one of social import. Plaintiffs challenge that characterization of their Proposal. Regardless of whether the court characterizes the Proposal as seeking to *adopt* a policy or as seeking to *implement* a policy, the same inquiry guides the court: Does the proposal involve shareholders in dictating mundane matters that involve no substantial policy considerations? . . .

The Proposal seeks to identify general corporate policy regarding equal employment opportunities and efforts, if any, to promote those policies among its suppliers, on whom Wal-Mart may have some influence. As plaintiffs argue, the Proposal

---

13. This is not to say that the SEC cannot change its views with regard to what issues involve substantial policy considerations. If the SEC finds that the issues of EEO and affirmative action programs no longer implicate significant policy considerations, the 1976 Interpretive Release permits exclusion of proposals relating to them. No such change of view was expressed in *Cracker Barrel.*

Nor does the court suggest that the SEC may not abandon the 1976 Interpretive Release altogether, so long as, in doing so, it complies with appropriate procedures, which procedures need not be addressed here. The court's holding today is limited solely to the proposition that a court should not defer to a position taken by the SEC in a no-action letter that is inconsistent with an SEC interpretation offered in the context of formal notice and comment rulemaking.

does not involve shareholders in demanding, or monitoring compliance with, a specific timetable to accomplish plaintiffs' ultimate goal of improving Wal-Mart's EEO record. This aspect of the Proposal notably distinguishes it from the proposal considered in *Capital Cities/ABC* that the Commission found excludable. Plaintiffs' Proposal does not require Wal-Mart to gather any employee-related information that it does not already gather for the purpose of complying with government regulations. The Proposal states that the report should be prepared "at reasonable cost, omitting confidential information," and may be comparable to the one or two page reports produced by other companies in Wal-Mart's industry. The information about employees and policies toward suppliers requested in the Proposal is the same as the information the SEC considered appropriate in *Dayton Hudson*. . . . The Proposal thus generally involves a significant policy consideration and does not otherwise fall within the exception for proposals relating to the conduct of Wal-Mart's "ordinary business operations."

However, the court finds that a literal reading of the Proposal suggests that the requested report must contain every "step" Wal-Mart management has taken to increase the number of female and minority managers and state all the "ways" Wal-Mart publicizes its EEO and affirmative action policies. Such "steps" could range from formal policies announced by the board of directors and officers, to the individual acts of each supervisor who implements these policies, and to other personnel and purchasing actions that occur hundreds of times each business day. A request for this latter information is excludable because it involves the mundane matters of Wal-Mart's day-to-day business affairs that involve no substantial policy consideration. The court, therefore, finds that the Proposal may not be omitted from Wal-Mart's 1993 proxy material to the extent that plaintiffs agree to the inclusion of the following proposal as an alternative to paragraphs 1–5 of the Proposal they submitted to Wal-Mart:

> 1. A chart identifying employees according to their sex and race in each of the nine major EEOC defined job categories for 1990, 1991, and 1992, listing either numbers or percentages in each category.
>
> 2. A summary description of any Affirmative Action policies and programs to improve performances, including job categories where women and minorities are underutilized.
>
> 3. A description of any policies and programs oriented specifically toward increasing the number of managers who are qualified females and/or belong to ethnic minorities.
>
> 4. A general description of how Wal-Mart publicizes our company's Affirmative Action policies and programs to merchandise suppliers and service providers.
>
> 5. A description of any policies and programs favoring the purchase of goods and services from minority-and/or female-owned business enterprises.

In modifying the Proposal, the court notes the practice of the SEC staff to revise a proposal submitted to it to correct minor defects. These changes to the Proposal reflect a balance of the rights of shareholders to obtain information on an issue raising significant policy considerations and the right of management to run the day-to-day affairs of the corporation free from shareholder supervision.

III. Conclusion

To summarize, Congress delegated to the SEC the task of ensuring that shareholders are informed on all the major questions of policy to be raised at an annual meeting. The SEC continues to implement Congress's goals by providing shareholders with the right to communicate with other shareholders and with management through the dissemination of proxy material on matters of broad social import such as plant closings, tobacco production, cigarette advertising and executive compensation. The SEC cannot, in effect, eliminate this avenue of shareholder communication with management and other shareholders on a topic of broad social import simply because it finds the line between proper and improper issues for communication hard to draw, and still act consistently with the principles enunciated in the 1976 Interpretive Release. If the SEC wishes to amend its rules or the 1976 Interpretive Release, it may do so. Or if the SEC no longer considers EEO and affirmative action policies to have broad social import—if a shift in public concerns has diminished interest in these social issues—the SEC simply can so state, consistent with the 1976 Interpretive Release. The SEC's difficulties in drawing these lines do not excuse it or the courts from making these decisions, which Congress has entrusted to the SEC and, ultimately, to the courts. The court draws a line here between includable and excludable proposals that is consistent with the line previously drawn by the SEC and the courts between matters involving substantial policy considerations and matters involving only "ordinary business operations." When assessed in light of this standard, the Proposal is not excludable.

For all the reasons discussed above, the court concludes that Wal-Mart has not sustained its burden of establishing that it may omit plaintiffs' Proposal, as modified, from Wal-Mart's 1993 proxy solicitation material. The court, therefore, denies Wal-Mart's motion and grants plaintiffs' motion for summary judgment. As stated in the court's Order dated April 19, 1993, Wal-Mart is enjoined from omitting plaintiffs' Proposal, as amended, from Wal-Mart's 1993 proxy material.

Wal-Mart's time to file a notice of appeal or to request a stay of this court's Order contained herein pending appeal shall run from the issuance of this Opinion and Order.

So ordered.

While shareholder proposals in the 1970s and 1980s often dealt with questions of corporate policy, by the 1990s, the focus had shifted to corporate governance. Topics included executive compensation, confidential voting by shareholders, and removal of anti-takeover devices (such as poison pills). More recently, shareholders have tried to use shareholder proposals to change corporate bylaws in order to alter the allocation of power between shareholders and directors. As you read the following two cases, think about the excerpt you read at the beginning of this section about the disappearance of the individual investor. How, if at all, has our perception of the shareholder's role in the modern corporation changed in the course of the twentieth century?

American Federation of State, County & Municipal Employees (AFSCME), Employees Pension Plan v. American International Group, Inc. (AIG)

462 F.3d 121 (2006)

WESLEY, Circuit Judge

This case raises the question of whether a shareholder proposal requiring a company to include certain shareholder-nominated candidates for the board of directors on the corporate ballot can be excluded from the corporate proxy materials on the basis that the proposal "relates to an election" under Securities Exchange Act Rule 14a-8(i)(8) .... Complicating this question is not only the ambiguity of Rule 14a-8(i)(8) itself but also the fact that the Securities Exchange Commission (the "SEC" or "Commission") has ascribed two different interpretations to the Rule's language. The SEC's first interpretation was published in 1976, the same year that it last revised the election exclusion. The Division of Corporation Finance (the "Division"), the group within the SEC that handles investor disclosure matters and issues no-action letters, continued to apply this interpretation consistently for fifteen years until 1990, when it began applying a different interpretation, although at first in an ad hoc and inconsistent manner. The result of this gradual interpretive shift is the SEC's second interpretation, as set forth in its amicus brief to this Court. We believe that an agency's interpretation of an ambiguous regulation made at the time the regulation was implemented or revised should control unless that agency has offered sufficient reasons for its changed interpretation. Accordingly, we hold that a shareholder proposal that seeks to amend the corporate bylaws to establish a procedure by which shareholder-nominated candidates may be included on the corporate ballot does not relate to an election within the meaning of the Rule and therefore cannot be excluded from corporate proxy materials under that regulation.

Background

The American Federation of State, County & Municipal Employees ("AFSCME") is one of the country's largest public service employee unions. Through its pension plan, AFSCME holds 26,965 shares of voting common stock of American International Group ("AIG" or "Company"), a multi-national corporation operating in the insurance and financial services sectors. On December 1, 2004, AFSCME submitted to AIG for inclusion in the Company's 2005 proxy statement a shareholder proposal that, if adopted by a majority of AIG shareholders at the Company's 2005 annual meeting,[2] would amend the AIG bylaws to require the Company, under certain circumstances, to publish the names of shareholder-nominated candidates for director positions together with any candidates nominated by AIG's board of directors ("Proposal").[3] AIG sought the input of the Division regarding whether AIG could exclude the Proposal from its proxy statement under the election exclusion on the basis that it "relates to an election." The Division issued a no-action letter in which it indicated that it would not recommend an enforcement action against AIG should the Company exclude the Proposal from its proxy statement. Armed with the no-action letter, AIG then proceeded to exclude the Proposal from the Company's proxy statement. In response, AFSCME brought suit in the United States District Court for the Southern District of New York (Stanton, J.) seeking a court order compelling AIG to include the Proposal in its next proxy statement. The district court denied AFSCME's motion for a preliminary injunction, concluding that AFSCME's Proposal "on its face 'relates to an election.' Indeed, it relates to nothing else." After this Court denied AFSCME's motion for expedited appeal, the parties stipulated that the district court's opinion denying AFSCME's motion for a preliminary injunction "be deemed to contain the Court's complete findings of fact and conclusions of law with respect to all claims asserted by plaintiff in this action" and that it also "be deemed a final judgment

---

2. Delaware corporate law, which governs AIG's internal affairs, provides that shareholders have the power to amend bylaws by majority vote.

3. The AFSCME Proposal states in relevant part:
RESOLVED, pursuant to Section 6.9 of the By-laws (the "Bylaws") of American International Group Inc. ("AIG") and section 109(a) of the Delaware General Corporation Law, stockholders hereby amend the Bylaws to add section 6.10:

—"The Corporation shall include in its proxy materials for a meeting of stockholders the name, together with the Disclosure and Statement (both defined below), of any person nominated for election to the Board of Directors by a stockholder or group thereof that satisfies the requirements of this section 6.10 (the "Nominator"), and allow stockholders to vote with respect to such nominee on the Corporation's proxy card. Each Nominator may nominate one candidate for election at a meeting.

—To be eligible to make a nomination, a Nominator must:

(a) have beneficially owned 3 or more of the Corporation's outstanding common stock (the "Required Shares") for at least one year;

(b) provide written notice received by the Corporation's Secretary within the time period specified in section 1.11 of the Bylaws containing (i) with respect to the nominee, (A) the information required by Items 7(a), (b) and (c) of SEC Schedule 14A (such information is referred to herein as the "Disclosure") and (B) such nominee's consent to being named in the proxy statement and to serving as a director if elected; and (ii) with respect to the Nominator, proof of ownership of the Required Shares; and

(c) execute an undertaking that it agrees (i) to assume all liability of any violation of law or regulation arising out of the Nominator's communications with stockholders, including the Disclosure (ii) to the extent it uses soliciting material other than the Corporation's proxy materials, comply with all laws and regulations relating thereto.

—The Nominator shall have the option to furnish a statement, not to exceed 500 words, in support of the nominee's candidacy (the "Statement"), at the time the Disclosure is submitted to the Corporation's Secretary. The Board of Directors shall adopt a procedure for timely resolving disputes over whether notice of a nomination was timely given and whether the Disclosure and Statement comply with this section 6.10 and SEC Rules."

on the merits with respect to all claims asserted by plaintiff in this action." Pursuant to this joint stipulation, the district court entered final judgment denying plaintiff's claims for declaratory and injunctive relief and dismissing plaintiff's complaint.

Discussion

Rule 14a-8(i)(8), also known as "the town meeting rule," regulates what are referred to as "shareholders proposals," that is, "recommendation[s] or requirement[s] that the company and/or its board of directors take [some] action, which [the submitting shareholder(s)] intend to present at a meeting of the company's shareholders." If a shareholder seeking to submit a proposal meets certain eligibility and procedural requirements,[4] the corporation is required to include the proposal in its proxy statement and identify the proposal in its form of proxy, unless the corporation can prove to the SEC that a given proposal may be excluded based on one of thirteen grounds enumerated in the regulations. One of these grounds, Rule 14a-8(i)(8), provides that a corporation may exclude a shareholder proposal "[i]f the proposal relates to an election for membership on the company's board of directors or analogous governing body."

We must determine whether, under Rule 14a-8(i)(8), a shareholder proposal "relates to an election" if it seeks to amend the corporate bylaws to establish a procedure by which certain shareholders are entitled to include in the corporate proxy materials their nominees for the board of directors ("proxy access bylaw proposal"). "In interpreting an administrative regulation, as in interpreting a statute, we must begin by examining the language of the provision at issue." The relevant language here—"relates to an election"—is not particularly helpful. AFSCME reads the election exclusion as creating an obvious distinction between proposals addressing a particular seat in a particular election (which AFSCME concedes are excludable) and those, like AFSCME's proposal, that simply set the background rules governing elections generally (which AFSCME claims are not excludable). AFSCME's distinction rests on Rule 14a-8(i)(8)'s use of the article "an," which AFSCME claims "necessarily implies that the phrase 'relates to an election' is intended to relate to proposals that address *particular elections*, instead of simply 'elections' generally." It is at least plausible that the words "an election" were intended to narrow the scope of the election exclusion, confining its application to proposals relating to "a particular

---

4. "In order to be eligible to submit a proposal, [a shareholder] must have continuously held at least $2,000 in market value, or 1%, of the company's securities entitled to be voted on the proposal at the meeting for at least one year by the date [of the proposal's submission]." "Each shareholder may submit no more than one proposal to a company for a particular shareholders' meeting." "The proposal, including any accompanying supporting statement, may not exceed 500 words." The company's "principal executive offices" must have received the shareholder proposal "not less than 120 calendar days before the date of the company's proxy statement released to shareholders in connection with the previous year's annual meeting." "[I]f the company did not hold an annual meeting the previous year, or if the date of th[e present] year's annual meeting has been changed by more than 30 days from the date of the previous year's meeting, then the deadline is a reasonable time before the company begins to print and mail its proxy materials." [17 C.F.R. §240.14a-8.]

election *and not* elections generally." It is, however, also plausible that the phrase was intended to create a comparatively broader exclusion, one covering "a particular election *or* elections generally" since any proposal that relates to elections in general will necessarily relate to an election in particular. The language of Rule 14a-8(i)(8) provides no reason to adopt one interpretation over the other.

When the language of a regulation is ambiguous, we typically look for guidance in any interpretation made by the agency that promulgated the regulation in question.... We are aware of two statements published by the SEC that offer informal interpretations of Rule 14a-8(i)(8). The first is a statement appearing in the amicus brief that the SEC filed in this case at our request. The second interpretation is contained in a statement the SEC published in 1976, the last time the SEC revised the election exclusion. Neither of these interpretations has the force of law. But, while agency interpretations that lack the force of law do not warrant deference when they interpret ambiguous *statutes*, they do normally warrant deference when they interpret ambiguous *regulations*....

In its amicus brief, the SEC interprets Rule 14a-8(i)(8) as permitting the exclusion of shareholder proposals that "would result in contested elections." The SEC explains that "[f]or purposes of Rule 14a-8, a proposal would result in a contested election if it is a means either to campaign for or against a director nominee or to require a company to include shareholder-nominated candidates in the company's proxy materials." Under this interpretation, a proxy access bylaw proposal like AFSCME's would be excludable under Rule 14a-8(i)(8) because it "is a means to require AIG to include shareholder-nominated candidates in the company's proxy materials." However, that interpretation is plainly at odds with the interpretation the SEC made in 1976.

In that year, the SEC amended Rule 14a-8(i)(8) in an effort to clarify the purpose of the existing election exclusion. The SEC explained that "with respect to corporate elections, [] Rule 14a-8 is not the proper means for conducting campaigns or effecting reforms in elections of that nature [i.e., "corporate, political or other elections to office"], *since other proxy rules, including Rule 14a-11, are applicable thereto*." ... The district court opinion quoted the 1976 Statement but omitted the italicized language and concluded that shareholder proposals were not intended to be used to accomplish any type of election reform. Clearly, however, that cannot be what the 1976 Statement means. Indeed, when the SEC finally adopted the revision of Rule 14a-8(i)(8) four months after publication of the 1976 Statement, it explained that it was rejecting a previous proposed rule (which would have authorized the exclusion of proposals that "relate[] to a corporate, political or other election to office") in favor of the current version (which authorizes the exclusion of proposals that simply "relate[] to an election") so as to avoid creating "the erroneous belief that the Commission intended to expand the scope of the existing exclusion to cover proposals dealing with matters previously held not excludable by the Commission, such as cumulative voting rights, general qualifications for directors, and political contributions by the issuer." And yet, all three of these shareholder proposal topics—cumulative voting rights, general qualifications for directors, and political contributions—fit comfortably within the category "election reform."

In its amicus brief, the SEC places a slightly different gloss on the 1976 Statement than did the district court. The SEC reads the 1976 Statement as implying that the purpose of Rule 14a-8(i)(8) is to authorize the exclusion of proposals that seek to effect, not election reform in general, but only certain types of election reform, namely those to which "other proxy rules, including Rule 14a-11," are generally applicable. In 1976, Rule 14a-11 was essentially the equivalent of current Rule 14a-12, which requires certain disclosures where a solicitation is made "for the purpose of opposing" a solicitation by any other person "with respect to the election or removal of directors." The SEC reasons that, based on the 1976 Statement, "a proposal may be excluded pursuant to Rule 14a-8(i)(8) if it would result in an immediate election contest (e.g., by making a director nomination for a particular meeting) or would set up a process for shareholders to conduct an election contest in the future by requiring the company to include shareholder director nominees in the company's proxy materials for subsequent meetings."

We agree with the SEC that, based on the 1976 Statement, shareholder proposals can be excluded under the election exclusion if they would result in an immediate election contest. We understand the phrase "since other proxy rules, including Rule 14a-11, are applicable thereto" in the 1976 Statement to mean that under Rule 14a-8(i)(8), companies can exclude shareholder proposals dealing with those election-related matters that, if addressed in a proxy solicitation—the alternative to a shareholder proposal—would trigger Rule 14a-12, or the former Rule 14a-11. A proxy solicitation nominating a candidate for a specific election would be made "for the purpose of opposing" the company's proxy solicitation and therefore would clearly trigger Rule 14a-12. Accordingly, based on the 1976 Statement, a shareholder proposal seeking to contest management's nominees would be excludable under Rule 14a-8(i)(8).

By contrast, a proxy solicitation seeking to add a proxy access amendment to the corporate bylaws does not involve opposing solicitations dealing with "the election or removal of directors," and therefore Rule 14a-12, or, equivalently, the former Rule 14a-11, would not apply to a proposal seeking to accomplish the same end. Thus, we cannot agree with the second half of the SEC's interpretation of the 1976 Statement: that a proposal may be excluded under Rule 14a-8(i)(8) if it would simply establish a process for shareholders to wage a future election contest.

The 1976 Statement clearly reflects the view that the election exclusion is limited to shareholder proposals used to oppose solicitations dealing with an identified board seat in an upcoming election and rejects the somewhat broader interpretation that the election exclusion applies to shareholder proposals that would institute procedures making such election contests more likely. The SEC suggested as much when, four months after its 1976 Statement, it explained that the scope of the election exclusion does not cover shareholder proposals dealing with matters such as cumulative voting and general director requirements, both of which have the potential to increase the likelihood of election contests.

That the 1976 statement adopted this narrower view of the election exclusion finds further support in the fact that it was also the view that the Division adopted for roughly sixteen years following publication of the SEC's 1976 Statement. . . . It was not until 1990 that the Division first signaled a change of course by deeming excludable proposals that *might* result in contested elections, even if the proposal only purports to alter general procedures for nominating and electing directors.

Because the interpretation of Rule 14a-8(i)(8) that the SEC advances in its amicus brief—that the election exclusion applies to proxy access bylaw proposals—conflicts with the 1976 Statement, it does not merit the usual deference we would reserve for an agency's interpretation of its own regulations. . . . The SEC has not provided, nor to our knowledge has it or the Division ever provided, reasons for its changed position regarding the excludability of proxy access bylaw proposals. Although the SEC has substantial discretion to adopt new interpretations of its own regulations in light of, for example, changes in the capital markets or even simply because of a shift in the Commission's regulatory approach, it nevertheless has a "duty to explain its departure from prior norms." . . .

In its amicus submission, the SEC fails to so much as acknowledge a changed position, let alone offer a reasoned analysis of the change. The amicus brief is curiously silent on any Division action prior to 1990 and characterizes the intermittent post-1990 no-action letters which continued to apply the pre-1990 position as mere "mistake[s]." While we by no means wish to imply that the Commission or the Division cannot correct analytical errors following a refinement of their thinking, we have a difficult time accepting the SEC's characterization of a policy that the Division consistently applied for sixteen years as nothing more than a "mistake." Although we are willing to afford the Commission considerable latitude in explaining departures from prior interpretations, its reasoned analysis must consist of something more than *mea culpas*.

Accordingly, we deem it appropriate to defer to the 1976 Statement, which represents the SEC's interpretation of the election exclusion the last time the Rule was substantively revised. We therefore interpret the election exclusion as applying to shareholder proposals that relate to a particular election and not to proposals that, like AFSCME's, would establish the procedural rules governing elections generally.

In deeming proxy access bylaw proposals non-excludable under Rule 14a-8(i)(8), we take no side in the policy debate regarding shareholder access to the corporate ballot. There might be perfectly good reasons for permitting companies to exclude proposals like AFSCME's, just as there may well be valid policy reasons for rendering them non-excludable. However, Congress has determined that such issues are appropriately the province of the SEC, not the judiciary.

Conclusion

For the foregoing reasons, we reverse the judgment of the district court and remand the case for entry of judgment in favor of AFSCME.

Questions

1. Should shareholders have access to the ballot? Who are the shareholders who are likely to use such privilege? Who benefits?

2. Are federal proxy rules, explicitly Rule 14a-8, the appropriate means to address shareholder voting? Aren't the voting rights of shareholders governed by state corporation law?

3. In 2007, the SEC amended Rule 14a-8(i)(8) to allow corporations to exclude shareholder proposals "if the proposal relates to a nomination or an election for membership on the company's board of directors or analogous governing body or a procedure for such nomination or election." While the rule effectively overturned the result of *American Federation of State, County & Municipal Employees, Employees Pension Plan v. American International Group, Inc.*, it was not the final word on the matter.

The Dodd-Frank financial reform legislation of 2010 authorized the SEC to adopt rules setting the terms of proxy access. Rule 14a-11, promulgated shortly thereafter, mandated proxy access at all public companies. It was vacated in *Business Roundtable and Chamber of Commerce v. SEC*, 647 F.3d 1144 (D.C. Cir. 2011), but the U.S. Court of Appeals did not vacate amendments to Rule 14a-8 which allow shareholders to influence proxy access through "private ordering," that is, by proposing changes to the corporation's governing documents.

CA, Inc. v. AFSCME Employees Pension Plan
953 A.2d 227 (Del. 2008)

JACOBS, Justice

This proceeding arises from a certification by the United States Securities and Exchange Commission (the "SEC"), to this Court, of two questions of law pursuant to Article IV, Section 11(8) of the Delaware Constitution[1] and Supreme Court Rule 41. On June 27, 2008, the SEC asked this Court to address two questions of Delaware law regarding a proposed stockholder bylaw submitted by the AFSCME Employees Pension Plan ("AFSCME") for inclusion in the proxy materials of CA, Inc. ("CA" or the "Company") for CA's 2008 annual stockholders' meeting. This Court accepted

---

1. Article IV, § 11(8) was amended in 2007 to authorize this Court to hear and determine questions of law certified to it by ... the ... Securities and Exchange Commission .... This certification request is the first submitted by the SEC to this Court.

certification on July 1, 2008, and after expedited briefing, the matter was argued on July 9, 2008. This is the decision of the Court on the certified questions.

I. *FACTS*

CA is a Delaware corporation whose board of directors consists of twelve persons, all of whom sit for reelection each year. CA's annual meeting of stockholders is scheduled to be held on September 9, 2008. CA intends to file its definitive proxy materials with the SEC on or about July 24, 2008 in connection with that meeting.

AFSCME, a CA stockholder, is associated with the American Federation of State, County and Municipal Employees. On March 13, 2008, AFSCME submitted a proposed stockholder bylaw (the "Bylaw" or "proposed Bylaw") for inclusion in the Company's proxy materials for its 2008 annual meeting of stockholders. The Bylaw, if adopted by CA stockholders, would amend the Company's bylaws to provide as follows:

> RESOLVED, that pursuant to section 109 of the Delaware General Corporation Law and Article IX of the bylaws of CA, Inc., stockholders of CA hereby amend the bylaws to add the following Section 14 to Article II:
>
>> The board of directors shall cause the corporation to reimburse a stockholder or group of stockholders (together, the "Nominator") for reasonable expenses ("Expenses") incurred in connection with nominating one or more candidates in a contested election of directors to the corporation's board of directors, including, without limitation, printing, mailing, legal, solicitation, travel, advertising and public relations expenses, so long as (a) the election of fewer than 50% of the directors to be elected is contested in the election, (b) one or more candidates nominated by the Nominator are elected to the corporation's board of directors, (c) stockholders are not permitted to cumulate their votes for directors, and (d) the election occurred, and the Expenses were incurred, after this bylaw's adoption. The amount paid to a Nominator under this bylaw in respect of a contested election shall not exceed the amount expended by the corporation in connection with such election.

CA's current bylaws and Certificate of Incorporation have no provision that specifically addresses the reimbursement of proxy expenses. Of more general relevance, however, is Article SEVENTH, Section (1) of CA's Certificate of Incorporation, which tracks the language of 8 *Del. C.* § 141(a) and provides that:

> The management of the business and the conduct of the affairs of the corporation shall be vested in [CA's] Board of Directors.

It is undisputed that the decision whether to reimburse election expenses is presently vested in the discretion of CA's board of directors, subject to their fiduciary duties and applicable Delaware law.

On April 18, 2008, CA notified the SEC's Division of Corporation Finance (the "Division") of its intention to exclude the proposed Bylaw from its 2008 proxy materials. The Company requested from the Division a "no-action letter" stating that the Division would not recommend any enforcement action to the SEC if CA excluded the AFSCME proposal. CA's request for a no-action letter was accompanied by an opinion from its Delaware counsel, Richards Layton & Finger, P.A. ("RL & F"). The RL & F opinion concluded that the proposed Bylaw is not a proper subject for stockholder action, and that if implemented, the Bylaw would violate the Delaware General Corporation Law ("DGCL").

On May 21, 2008, AFSCME responded to CA's no-action request with a letter taking the opposite legal position. The AFSCME letter was accompanied by an opinion from AFSCME's Delaware counsel, Grant & Eisenhofer, P.A. ("G & E"). The G & E opinion concluded that the proposed Bylaw is a proper subject for shareholder action and that if adopted, would be permitted under Delaware law.

The Division was thus confronted with two conflicting legal opinions on Delaware law. Whether or not the Division would determine that CA may exclude the proposed Bylaw from its 2008 proxy materials would depend upon which of these conflicting views is legally correct. To obtain guidance, the SEC, at the Division's request, certified two questions of Delaware law to this Court. Given the short timeframe for the filing of CA's proxy materials, we concluded that "there are important and urgent reasons for an immediate determination of the questions certified," and accepted those questions for review on July 1, 2008.

II. *THE CERTIFIED QUESTIONS*

The two questions certified to us by the SEC are as follows:

1. Is the AFSCME Proposal a proper subject for action by shareholders as a matter of Delaware law?

2. Would the AFSCME Proposal, if adopted, cause CA to violate any Delaware law to which it is subject?

The questions presented are issues of law which this Court decides *de novo*.

III. *THE FIRST QUESTION*

A. *Preliminary Comments*

The first question presented is whether the Bylaw is a proper subject for shareholder action, more precisely, whether the Bylaw may be proposed and enacted by shareholders without the concurrence of the Company's board of directors. Before proceeding further, we make some preliminary comments in an effort to delineate a framework within which to begin our analysis.

First, the DGCL empowers both the board of directors and the shareholders of a Delaware corporation to adopt, amend or repeal the corporation's bylaws. 8 Del. C. § 109(a) relevantly provides that:

> After a corporation has received any payment for any of its stock, the power to adopt, amend or repeal bylaws shall be in the stockholders entitled to

vote . . . ; provided, however, any corporation may, in its certificate of incorporation, confer the power to adopt, amend or repeal bylaws upon the directors. . . . The fact that such power has been so conferred upon the directors . . . shall not divest the stockholders . . . of the power, nor limit their power to adopt, amend or repeal bylaws.

Pursuant to Section 109(a), CA's Certificate of Incorporation confers the power to adopt, amend or repeal the bylaws upon the Company's board of directors. Because the statute commands that that conferral "shall not divest the stockholders . . . of . . . nor limit" their power, both the board and the shareholders of CA, independently and concurrently, possess the power to adopt, amend and repeal the bylaws.

Second, the vesting of that concurrent power in both the board and the shareholders raises the issue of whether the stockholders' power is coextensive with that of the board, and vice versa. As a purely theoretical matter that is possible, and were that the case, then the first certified question would be easily answered. That is, under such a regime any proposal to adopt, amend or repeal a bylaw would be a proper subject for either shareholder or board action, without distinction. But the DGCL has not allocated to the board and the shareholders the identical, coextensive power to adopt, amend and repeal the bylaws. Therefore, how that power is allocated between those two decision-making bodies requires an analysis that is more complex.

Moving from the theoretical to this case, by its terms Section 109(a) vests in the shareholders a power to adopt, amend or repeal bylaws that is legally sacrosanct, *i.e.,* the power cannot be non-consensually eliminated or limited by anyone other than the legislature itself. If viewed in isolation, Section 109(a) could be read to make the board's and the shareholders' power to adopt, amend or repeal bylaws identical and coextensive, but Section 109(a) does not exist in a vacuum. It must be read together with 8 Del. C. § 141(a), which pertinently provides that:

> The business and affairs of every corporation organized under this chapter shall be managed by or under the direction of a board of directors, except as may be otherwise provided in this chapter or in its certificate of incorporation.

No such broad management power is statutorily allocated to the shareholders. Indeed, it is well-established that stockholders of a corporation subject to the DGCL may not directly manage the business and affairs of the corporation, at least without specific authorization in either the statute or the certificate of incorporation. Therefore, the shareholders' statutory power to adopt, amend or repeal bylaws is not coextensive with the board's concurrent power and is limited by the board's management prerogatives under Section 141(a).

Third, it follows that, to decide whether the Bylaw proposed by AFSCME is a proper subject for shareholder action under Delaware law, we must first determine: (1) the scope or reach of the shareholders' power to adopt, alter or repeal the bylaws of a Delaware corporation, and then (2) whether the Bylaw at issue here falls within that permissible scope. Where, as here, the proposed bylaw is one that limits director authority, that is an elusively difficult task. As one noted scholar has put it, "the efforts to distinguish by-laws that permissibly limit director authority from by-laws that impermissibly do so have failed to provide a coherent analytical structure, and the pertinent statutes provide no guidelines for distinction at all." The tools that are available to this Court to answer those questions are other provisions of the DGCL and Delaware judicial decisions that can be brought to bear on this question.

B. *Analysis*

1.

Two other provisions of the DGCL, 8 Del. C. §§ 109(b) and 102(b)(1), bear importantly on the first question and form the basis of contentions advanced by each side. Section 109(b), which deals generally with bylaws and what they must or may contain, provides that:

> The bylaws may contain any provision, not inconsistent with law or with the certificate of incorporation, relating to the business of the corporation, the conduct of its affairs, and its rights or powers or the rights or powers of its stockholders, directors, officers or employees.

And Section 102(b)(1), which is part of a broader provision that addresses what the certificate of incorporation must or may contain, relevantly states that:

> (b) In addition to the matters required to be set forth in the certificate of incorporation by subsection (a) of this section, the certificate of incorporation may also contain any or all of the following matters:
>
> (1) Any provision for the management of the business and for the conduct of the affairs of the corporation, and any provision creating, defining, limiting and regulating the powers of the corporation, the directors and the stockholders, or any class of the stockholders . . . . ; if such provisions are not contrary to the laws of this State. Any provision which is required or permitted by any section of this chapter to be stated in the bylaws may instead be stated in the certificate of incorporation.

AFSCME relies heavily upon the language of Section 109(b), which permits the bylaws of a corporation to contain "any provision . . . relating to the . . . rights or powers of its stockholders [and] directors. . . ." The Bylaw, AFSCME argues, "relates to" the right of the stockholders meaningfully to participate in the process of electing directors, a right that necessarily "includes the right to nominate an opposing slate."

CA argues, in response, that Section 109(b) is not dispositive, because it cannot be read in isolation from, and without regard to, Section 102(b)(1). CA's argument runs as follows: the Bylaw would limit the substantive decision-making authority of CA's board to decide whether or not to expend corporate funds for a particular purpose, here, reimbursing director election expenses. Section 102(b)(1) contemplates that any provision that limits the broad statutory power of the directors must be contained in the certificate of incorporation. Therefore, the proposed Bylaw can only be in CA's Certificate of Incorporation, as distinguished from its bylaws. Accordingly, the proposed bylaw falls outside the universe of permissible bylaws authorized by Section 109(b).

Implicit in CA's argument is the premise that *any* bylaw that in *any* respect might be viewed as limiting or restricting the power of the board of directors automatically falls outside the scope of permissible bylaws. That simply cannot be. That reasoning, taken to its logical extreme, would result in eliminating altogether the shareholders' statutory right to adopt, amend or repeal bylaws. Bylaws, by their very nature, set down rules and procedures that bind a corporation's board and its shareholders. In that sense, most, if not all, bylaws could be said to limit the otherwise unlimited discretionary power of the board. Yet Section 109(a) carves out an area of shareholder power to adopt, amend or repeal bylaws that is expressly inviolate. Therefore, to argue that the Bylaw at issue here limits the board's power to manage the business and affairs of the Company only begins, but cannot end, the analysis needed to decide whether the Bylaw is a proper subject for shareholder action. The question left unanswered is what is the scope of shareholder action that Section 109(b) permits yet does not improperly intrude upon the directors' power to manage corporation's business and affairs under Section 141(a).

It is at this juncture that the statutory language becomes only marginally helpful in determining what the Delaware legislature intended to be the lawful scope of the shareholders' power to adopt, amend and repeal bylaws. To resolve that issue, the Court must resort to different tools, namely, decisions of this Court and of the Court of Chancery that bear on this question. Those tools do not enable us to articulate with doctrinal exactitude a bright line that divides those bylaws that shareholders may unilaterally adopt under Section 109(b) from those which they may not under Section 141(a). They do, however, enable us to decide the issue presented in this specific case.

2.

It is well-established Delaware law that a proper function of bylaws is not to mandate how the board should decide specific substantive business decisions, but rather, to define the process and procedures by which those decisions are made. As the Court of Chancery has noted:

> Traditionally, the bylaws have been the corporate instrument used to set forth the rules by which the corporate board conducts its business. To this end, the DGCL is replete with specific provisions authorizing the bylaws to establish the procedures through which board and committee action is taken.... [T]here is a general consensus that bylaws that regulate the process by which the board acts are statutorily authorized.

* * *

. . . I reject International's argument that that provision in the Bylaw Amendments impermissibly interferes with the board's authority under § 141(a) to manage the business and affairs of the corporation. Sections 109 and 141, taken in totality, ... make clear that bylaws may pervasively and strictly regulate the process by which boards act, subject to the constraints of equity.

Examples of the procedural, process-oriented nature of bylaws are found in both the DGCL and the case law. For example, 8 Del. C. § 141(b) authorizes bylaws that fix the number of directors on the board, the number of directors required for a quorum (with certain limitations), and the vote requirements for board action. 8 Del. C. § 141(f) authorizes bylaws that preclude board action without a meeting. And, almost three decades ago this Court upheld a shareholder-enacted bylaw requiring unanimous board attendance and board approval for any board action, and unanimous ratification of any committee action. Such purely procedural bylaws do not improperly encroach upon the board's managerial authority under Section 141(a).

The process-creating function of bylaws provides a starting point to address the Bylaw at issue. It enables us to frame the issue in terms of whether the Bylaw is one that establishes or regulates a process for substantive director decision-making, or one that mandates the decision itself. Not surprisingly, the parties sharply divide on that question. We conclude that the Bylaw, even though infelicitously couched as a substantive-sounding mandate to expend corporate funds, has both the intent and the effect of regulating the process for electing directors of CA. Therefore, we determine that the Bylaw is a proper subject for shareholder action, and set forth our reasoning below.

Although CA concedes that "restrictive procedural bylaws (such as those requiring the presence of all directors and unanimous board consent to take action) are acceptable," it points out that even facially procedural bylaws can unduly intrude upon board authority. The Bylaw being proposed here is unduly intrusive, CA claims, because, by mandating reimbursement of a stockholder's proxy expenses, it limits the board's broad discretionary authority to decide whether to grant reimbursement at all. CA further claims that because (in defined circumstances) the Bylaw mandates the expenditure of corporate funds, its subject matter is necessarily substantive, not process-oriented, and, therefore falls outside the scope of what Section 109(b) permits.

Because the Bylaw is couched as a command to reimburse ("The board of directors shall cause the corporation to reimburse a stockholder"), it lends itself to CA's criticism. But the Bylaw's wording, although relevant, is not dispositive of whether or not it is process-related. The Bylaw could easily have been worded differently, to emphasize its process, as distinguished from its mandatory payment, component. By saying this we do not mean to suggest that this Bylaw's reimbursement component can be ignored. What we do suggest is that a bylaw that requires the expenditure of corporate funds does not, for that reason alone, become automatically deprived of its process-related character. A hypothetical example illustrates the point. Suppose that the directors of a corporation live in different states and at a considerable distance from the corporation's headquarters. Suppose also that the shareholders enact a bylaw that requires all meetings of directors to take place in person at the corporation's headquarters. Such a bylaw would be clearly process-related, yet it cannot be supposed that the shareholders would lack the power to adopt the bylaw because it would require the corporation to expend its funds to reimburse the directors' travel expenses. Whether or not a bylaw is process-related must necessarily be determined in light of its context and purpose.

The context of the Bylaw at issue here is the process for electing directors—a subject in which shareholders of Delaware corporations have a legitimate and protected interest. The purpose of the Bylaw is to promote the integrity of that electoral process by facilitating the nomination of director candidates by stockholders or groups of stockholders. Generally, and under the current framework for electing directors in contested elections, only board-sponsored nominees for election are reimbursed for their election expenses. Dissident candidates are not, unless they succeed in replacing at least a majority of the entire board. The Bylaw would encourage the nomination of non-management board candidates by promising reimbursement of the nominating stockholders' proxy expenses if one or more of its candidates are elected. In that the shareholders also have a legitimate interest, because the Bylaw would facilitate the exercise of their right to participate in selecting the contestants. The Court of Chancery has so recognized:

> [T]he unadorned right to cast a ballot in a contest for [corporate] office . . . is meaningless without the right to participate in selecting the contestants. As the nominating process circumscribes the range of choice to be made, it is a fundamental and outcome-determinative step in the election of officeholders. To allow for voting while maintaining a closed selection process thus renders the former an empty exercise.

* * *

The shareholders of a Delaware corporation have the right "to participate in selecting the contestants" for election to the board. The shareholders are entitled to facilitate the exercise of that right by proposing a bylaw that would encourage candidates other than board-sponsored nominees to stand for election. The Bylaw would accomplish that by committing the corporation to reimburse the election expenses of shareholders whose candidates are successfully elected. That the implementation of that proposal would require the expenditure of corporate funds will not, in and of itself, make such a bylaw an improper subject matter for shareholder action. Accordingly, we answer the first question certified to us in the affirmative.

That, however, concludes only part of the analysis. The DGCL also requires that the Bylaw be "not inconsistent with law." Accordingly, we turn to the second certified question, which is whether the proposed Bylaw, if adopted, would cause CA to violate any Delaware law to which it is subject.

IV. THE SECOND QUESTION

In answering the first question, we have already determined that the Bylaw does not facially violate any provision of the DGCL or of CA's Certificate of Incorporation. The question thus becomes whether the Bylaw would violate any common law rule or precept. Were this issue being presented in the course of litigation involving the application of the Bylaw to a specific set of facts, we would start with the presumption that the Bylaw is valid and, if possible, construe it in a manner consistent with the law. The factual context in which the Bylaw was challenged would inform our analysis, and we would "exercise caution [before] invalidating corporate acts based upon hypothetical injuries. . . ." The certified questions, however, request a determination of the validity of the Bylaw in the abstract. Therefore, in response to the second question, we must necessarily consider any possible circumstance under which a board of directors might be required to act. Under at least one such hypothetical, the board of directors would breach their fiduciary duties if they complied with the Bylaw. Accordingly, we conclude that the Bylaw, as drafted, would violate the prohibition, which our decisions have derived from Section 141(a), against contractual arrangements that commit the board of directors to a course of action that would preclude them from fully discharging their fiduciary duties to the corporation and its shareholders.

This Court has previously invalidated contracts that would require a board to act or not act in such a fashion that would limit the exercise of their fiduciary duties. In *Paramount Communications, Inc. v. QVC Network, Inc.*, we invalidated a "no shop" provision of a merger agreement with a favored bidder (Viacom) that prevented the directors of the target company (Paramount) from communicating with a competing bidder (QVC) the terms of its competing bid in an effort to obtain the highest available value for shareholders. We held that:

> The No-Shop Provision could not validly define or limit the fiduciary duties of the Paramount directors. To the extent that a contract, or a provision thereof, purports to require a board to act or not act in such a fashion as to limit the exercise of fiduciary duties, it is invalid and unenforceable. [. . .] [T]he Paramount directors could not contract away their fiduciary obligations. Since the No-Shop Provision was invalid, Viacom never had any vested contract rights in the provision.

Similarly, in *Quickturn Design Systems, Inc. v. Shapiro,* the directors of the target company (Quickturn) adopted a "poison pill" rights plan that contained a so-called "delayed redemption provision" as a defense against a hostile takeover bid, as part of which the bidder (Mentor Graphics) intended to wage a proxy contest to replace the target company board. The delayed redemption provision was intended to deter that effort, by preventing any newly elected board from redeeming the poison pill for six months. This Court invalidated that provision, because it would "impermissibly deprive any newly elected board of both its statutory authority to manage the corporation under 8 Del. C. § 141(a) and its concomitant fiduciary duty pursuant to that statutory mandate." We held that:

> One of the most basic tenets of Delaware corporate law is that the board of directors has the ultimate responsibility for managing the business and affairs of a corporation. [. . .] The Quickturn certificate of incorporation contains no provision purporting to limit the authority of the board in any way. The Delayed Redemption Provision, however, would prevent a newly elected board of directors from *completely* discharging its fundamental management duties to the corporation and its stockholders for six months. While the Delayed Redemption Provision limits the board of directors' authority in only one respect, the suspension of the Rights Plan, it nonetheless restricts the board's power in an area of fundamental importance to the shareholders negotiating a possible sale of the corporation. Therefore, we hold that the Delayed Redemption Provision is invalid under Section 141(a), which confers upon any newly elected board of directors *full* power to manage and direct the business and affairs of a Delaware corporation.

Both *QVC* and *Quickturn* involved binding contractual arrangements that the board of directors had voluntarily imposed upon themselves. This case involves a binding bylaw that the shareholders seek to impose involuntarily on the directors in the specific area of election expense reimbursement. Although this case is distinguishable in that respect, the distinction is one without a difference. The reason is that the internal governance contract—which here takes the form of a bylaw—is one that would also prevent the directors from exercising their full managerial power in circumstances where their fiduciary duties would otherwise require them to deny reimbursement to a dissident slate. That this limitation would be imposed by a majority vote of the shareholders rather than by the directors themselves, does not, in our view, legally matter.

AFSCME contends that it is improper to use the doctrine articulated in *QVC* and *Quickturn* as the measure of the validity of the Bylaw. Because the Bylaw would remove the subject of election expense reimbursement (in circumstances as defined by the Bylaw) entirely from the CA's board's discretion (AFSCME argues), it cannot fairly be claimed that the directors would be precluded from discharging their fiduciary duty. Stated differently, AFSCME argues that it is unfair to claim that the Bylaw prevents the CA board from discharging its fiduciary duty where the effect of the Bylaw is to relieve the board entirely of those duties in this specific area.

That response, in our view, is more semantical than substantive. No matter how artfully it may be phrased, the argument concedes the very proposition that renders the Bylaw, as written, invalid: the Bylaw mandates reimbursement of election expenses in circumstances that a proper application of fiduciary principles could preclude. That such circumstances could arise is not far fetched. Under Delaware law, a board may expend corporate funds to reimburse proxy expenses "[w]here the controversy is concerned with a question of policy as distinguished from personnel o[r] management." But in a situation where the proxy contest is motivated by personal or petty concerns, or to promote interests that do not further, or are adverse to, those of the corporation, the board's fiduciary duty could compel that reimbursement be denied altogether.

It is in this respect that the proposed Bylaw, as written, would violate Delaware law if enacted by CA's shareholders. As presently drafted, the Bylaw would afford CA's directors full discretion to determine what *amount* of reimbursement is appropriate, because the directors would be obligated to grant only the "reasonable" expenses of a successful short slate. Unfortunately, that does not go far enough, because the Bylaw contains no language or provision that would reserve to CA's directors their full power to exercise their fiduciary duty to decide whether or not it would be appropriate, in a specific case, to award reimbursement at all.

* * *

In arriving at this conclusion, we express no view on whether the Bylaw as currently drafted, would create a better governance scheme from a policy standpoint. We decide only what is, and is not, legally permitted under the DGCL. That statute, as currently drafted, is the expression of policy as decreed by the Delaware legislature. Those who believe that CA's shareholders should be permitted to make the proposed Bylaw as drafted part of CA's governance scheme, have two alternatives. They may seek to amend the Certificate of Incorporation to include the substance of the Bylaw; *or* they may seek recourse from the Delaware General Assembly.

Accordingly, we answer the second question certified to us in the affirmative.

Questions

1. How does the court reconcile sections 109 and 141 of the DGCL? Do you find the solution satisfactory?

2. The shareholder proposal rule was enacted in the early 1940s, at a time when American jurists celebrated the ideal of American democracy as a shield against totalitarianism. Given the political and economic changes since, does the rule have a role in today's corporate law?

Section II
Shareholders in Closely Held Corporations

While there is no single definition of close corporations, most courts, legislatures, and commentators generally agree that close corporations share the following characteristics: "(i) a relatively small number of persons hold shares; (ii) those shareholders tend to have a substantial portion of their wealth invested in the corporation; (iii) those shareholders are intimately involved in the management of the corporation; and (iv) the shareholders seek to restrict membership in the corporation." Many closely held corporations are relatively small local businesses, but some are multinational (e.g., Bechtel, Hallmark, Mars Candy). Moreover, the first industrial corporations either were closely held or unincorporated. In the late nineteenth century, only railroad stocks traded on the markets in any volume, and typically the common stock was held by a control group.

The particular characteristics of a closely held corporation make it very different from the publicly held corporation, which, as we have seen, is characterized by a separation between ownership and control. Shareholders in a publicly held corporation are presumed to be passive investors, they rarely participate in managing the corporation, and the readily available market for their shares has made it very simple to enter and exit the corporation. As we already have seen, shareholders in publicly held corporations have diversified portfolios and often care little, if at all, about the activities of their corporations. Their main goal is wealth maximization. Shareholders in closely held corporations often know each other (and typically are either family members or friends before they form the corporation). They often invest most of their wealth in the corporation, sit on its board, and serve as officers of the corporation. Their main sources of income are salaries and profits from the corporation. They care deeply about the corporation's activities.

Despite these fundamental differences, the law governing publicly held corporations applies to closely held corporations. But beginning in the 1960s, courts began to modify traditional rules to accommodate the special needs of shareholders in closely held corporations. By the second half of the twentieth century, almost every state revised its corporation laws to allow closely held corporations to opt into a set of modified rules, more adapted to their shareholders' needs. As you read the cases in this section, think about what these needs are and how they could be protected in the corporation's charter or bylaws, or in an agreement among the shareholders. Think also about the judicial response to conflicts among shareholders in closely held corporations. Should the law of closely held corporations follow the doctrines adopted in the context of publicly held corporations or, for example, those adopted in the context of partnerships?

A. Shareholders' Voice and Exit Arrangements

Given their interpersonal and financial ties to the corporation, shareholders in closely held corporations often attempt to guarantee their control. They might do so by creating special voting and liquidation rights, by entering agreements to control the composition of the board, and even by prescribing the power of the board.

The standard voting rule entitles each share to one vote for each open directorship (and as you already saw, different classes of shares might have different voting rights). Typically, directors are elected by a plurality of the votes cast. If any shareholder (or group of shareholders) controls more than 50% of the shares, they will be able to elect the entire board of directors. To guarantee that minority shareholders will have representation on the board, a closely held corporation might adopt an alternative voting method—cumulative voting. Under this method, each share receives one vote for each open directorship, but the shareholder can cumulate her votes and allocate them however she sees fit. She can, for example, cast all the votes for one director. The following formula determines how many shares will be required to elect a given number of directors under cumulative voting:

$$X = \frac{(s) \times (d)}{D+1} + 1$$

Where:
X = minimum number of shares required to elect the desired number of directors
s = Total number of shares to be voted at the meeting
d = Number of directors the shareholder desires to elect
D = Total number of directors to be elected

As should be obvious, a controlling faction might be able to manipulate even cumulative voting either by limiting the number of directors to be elected in any given election (for example, by creating a staggered board), or by decreasing the size of the board. But some commentators have challenged the premise of cumulative voting more broadly, by suggesting that it is likely to create factions on the board and impede efficient management.

Another method of guaranteeing minority representation on the board (and one that is less easily manipulated) is class voting. A corporation can have different classes of shares (for example, corresponding to the number of shareholders in a closely held corporation), each entitled to elect a certain number of directors. Different classes of shares might also have different dividend or liquidation rights.

While cumulative voting and class voting are used to increase the voting power of minority shareholders, shareholders in closely held corporations might also enter shareholder agreements in an attempt to control the manner in which the shares will be voted. Typically, these agreements include voting trusts, irrevocable proxies, and pooling agreements.

A voting trust is created when shareholders execute a trust agreement by which they convey the legal title to their shares to a trustee (or group of trustees). The trustee becomes the legal owner of the shares, and the shareholders are the beneficiaries of the trust. In exchange for their shares, the shareholders receive voting trust certificates. Typically, these certificates entitle the shareholders to the dividends paid on the underlying stock. The trust agreement defines the scope of the trustee's voting rights (for example, the trustee might be limited to voting for the election of directors, but not other matters). Voting trusts are regulated by statute, and must follow certain formal requirements.

Traditionally, courts were suspicious of voting trusts, because they viewed the trusts as separating the shareholders' voting power from their economic interests in the corporation. They thus required strict adherence to the statute regulating trusts. Over time, however, courts recognized the need for flexible shareholder arrangements, especially in closely held corporations, and became less stringent in their interpretations of the statutes.

An irrevocable proxy transfers the shareholder's voting rights to a proxy, usually for a period of time. Because irrevocable proxies separate the vote from the stock, the courts have treated them, too, with suspicion, and were reluctant to enforce them unless they were "coupled with an interest." An interest might exist when a shareholder borrows money and secures the loan by granting the lender an irrevocable proxy. Why is there an interest in this situation? To appreciate the answer, we need to remember that shareholders owe no duty to the corporation or the other shareholders. But the law assumes that when they exercise their voting rights, they will vote in their own economic interest and that their (aggregate) economic interest is also the economic interest of the corporation. Without an economic interest, a holder of an irrevocable proxy might exercise the vote in a matter detrimental to the corporation. (As you read this explanation, you should think back to the voting trust— What is the interest of a trustee of a voting trust?)

Vote pooling agreements are contractual arrangements which, like voting trusts and irrevocable proxies, seek to bind some of the shareholders to vote together on certain or all issues. (Like the other two arrangements, pooling agreements have been treated with suspicion.) Typically, a pooling agreement will include an agreement to vote for the other shareholder or shareholders to be on the board, an agreement to confer with other shareholders and to abide by certain dispute resolution mechanisms, restrictions on the transferability of shares, and a buy-sell agreement. You will encounter each of these provisions in the cases you read in this subsection. The following subsection will address additional provisions that might be included in pooling agreements and that have raised their own policy concerns, such as an agreement to appoint certain shareholders as officers, an agreement about dividends, or an agreement about employment and compensation.

Ringling Bros.-Barnum & Bailey Combined Shows, Inc. v. Ringling
53 A.2d 441 (Del. 1947)

PEARSON, Justice

The Court of Chancery was called upon to review an attempted election of directors at the 1946 annual stockholders meeting of the corporate defendant. The pivotal questions concern an agreement between two of the three present stockholders, and particularly the effect of this agreement with relation to the exercise of voting rights by these two stockholders. At the time of the meeting, the corporation had outstanding 1000 shares of capital stock held as follows: 315 by petitioner Edith Conway Ringling; 315 by defendant Aubrey B. Ringling Haley (individually or as executrix and legatee of a deceased husband); and 370 by defendant John Ringling North. The purpose of the meeting was to elect the entire board of seven directors. The shares could be voted cumulatively. Mrs. Ringling asserts that by virtue of the operation of an agreement between her and Mrs. Haley, the latter was bound to vote her shares for an adjournment of the meeting, or in the alternative, for a certain slate of directors. Mrs. Haley contends that she was not so bound for reason that the agreement was invalid, or at least revocable.

The two ladies entered into the agreement in 1941. It makes like provisions concerning stock of the corporate defendant and of another corporation, but in this case, we are concerned solely with the agreement as it affects the voting of stock of the corporate defendant. The agreement recites that each party was the owner "subject only to possible claims of creditors of the estates of Charles Ringling and Richard Ringling, respectively" (deceased husbands of the parties), of 300 shares of the capital stock of the defendant corporation; that in 1938 these shares had been deposited under a voting trust agreement which would terminate in 1947, or earlier, upon the elimination of certain liability of the corporation; that each party also owned 15 shares individually; that the parties had "entered into an agreement in April 1934 providing for joint action by them in matters affecting their ownership of stock and interest in" the corporate defendant; that the parties desired "to continue to act jointly in all matters relating to their stock ownership or interest in" the corporate defendant (and the other corporation). The agreement then provides as follows:

> "Now, Therefore, in consideration of the mutual covenants and agreements hereinafter contained the parties hereto agree as follows:
>
> . . .
>
> 2. In exercising any voting rights to which either party may be entitled by virtue of ownership of stock or voting trust certificates held by them in either of said corporation, each party will consult and confer with the other and the parties will act jointly in exercising such voting rights in accordance with such agreement as they may reach with respect to any matter calling for the exercise of such voting rights.
>
> 3. In the event the parties fail to agree with respect to any matter covered by paragraph 2 above, the question in disagreement shall be submitted for arbitration to Karl D. Loos, of Washington, D. C. as arbitrator and his decision thereon shall be binding upon the parties hereto. Such arbitration shall be exercised to the end of assuring for the respective corporations good management and such participation therein by the members of the Ringling family as the experience, capacity and ability of each may warrant. The parties may at any time by written agreement designate any other individual to act as arbitrator in lieu of said Loos. . . ."

The Mr. Loos mentioned in the agreement is an attorney and has represented both parties since 1937, and, before and after the voting trust was terminated in late 1942, advised them with respect to the exercise of their voting rights. At the annual meetings in 1943 and the two following years, the parties voted their shares in accordance with mutual understandings arrived at as a result of discussions. In each of these years, they elected five of the seven directors. Mrs. Ringling and Mrs. Haley each had sufficient votes, independently of the other, to elect two of the seven directors. By both voting for an additional candidate, they could be sure of his election regardless of how Mr. North, the remaining stockholder, might vote.[1]

Some weeks before the 1946 meeting, they discussed with Mr. Loos the matter of voting for directors. They were in accord that Mrs. Ringling should cast sufficient votes to elect herself and her son; and that Mrs. Haley should elect herself and her husband; but they did not agree upon a fifth director. The day before the meeting, the discussions were continued, Mrs. Haley being represented by her husband since she could not be present because of illness. In a conversation with Mr. Loos, Mr. Haley indicated that he would make a motion for an adjournment of the meeting for sixty days, in order to give the ladies additional time to come to an agreement about their voting. On the morning of the meeting, however, he stated that because of something Mrs. Ringling had done, he would not consent to a postponement. Mrs. Ringling then made a demand upon Mr. Loos to act under the third paragraph of the agreement "to arbitrate the disagreement" between her and Mrs. Haley in connection with the manner in which the stock of the two ladies should be voted. At the opening of the meeting, Mr. Loos read the written demand and stated that he determined and directed that the stock of both ladies be voted for an adjournment of sixty days. Mrs. Ringling then made a motion for adjournment and voted for it. Mr. Haley, as proxy for his wife, and Mr. North voted against the motion. Mrs. Ringling (herself or through her attorney, it is immaterial which,) objected to the voting of Mrs. Haley's stock in any manner other than in accordance with Mr. Loos' direction. The chairman ruled that the stock could not be voted contrary to such direction, and declared the motion for adjournment had carried. Nevertheless, the meeting proceeded to the election of directors. Mrs. Ringling stated that she would continue in the meeting "but without prejudice to her position with respect to the voting of the stock and the fact that adjournment had not been taken." Mr. Loos directed Mrs. Ringling to cast her votes

---

1. Each lady was entitled to cast 2205 votes (since each had the cumulative voting rights of 315 shares, and there were 7 vacancies in the directorate). The sum of the votes of both is 4410, which is sufficient to allow 882 votes for each of 5 persons. Mr. North, holding 370 shares, was entitled to cast 2590 votes, which obviously cannot be divided so as to give to more than two candidates as many as 882 votes each. It will be observed that in order for Mrs. Ringling and Mrs. Haley to be sure to elect five directors (regardless of how Mr. North might vote) they must act together in the sense that their combined votes must be divided among five different candidates and at least one of the five must be voted for by both Mrs. Ringling and Mrs. Haley.

>   882 for Mrs. Ringling,
>   882 for her son, Robert, and
>   441 for a Mr. Dunn, who had been a member of the board for several years.

She complied. Mr. Loos directed that Mrs. Haley's votes be cast

>   882 for Mrs. Haley,
>   882 for Mr. Haley, and
>   441 for Mr. Dunn.

Instead of complying, Mr. Haley attempted to vote his wife's shares

>   1103 for Mrs. Haley, and
>   1102 for Mr. Haley.
>   Mr. North voted his shares
>   864 for a Mr. Woods,
>   863 for a Mr. Griffin, and
>   863 for Mr. North.

The chairman ruled that the five candidates proposed by Mr. Loos, together with Messrs. Woods and North, were elected. The Haley-North group disputed this ruling insofar as it declared the election of Mr. Dunn; and insisted that Mr. Griffin, instead, had been elected. A directors' meeting followed in which Mrs. Ringling participated after stating that she would do so "without prejudice to her position that the stockholders' meeting had been adjourned and that the directors' meeting was not properly held." Mr. Dunn and Mr. Griffin, although each was challenged by an opposing faction, attempted to join in voting as directors for different slates of officers. Soon after the meeting, Mrs. Ringling instituted this proceeding.

The Vice-Chancellor determined that the agreement to vote in accordance with the direction of Mr. Loos was valid as a "stock pooling agreement" with lawful objects and purposes, and that it was not in violation of any public policy of this state. He held that where the arbitrator acts under the agreement and one party refuses to comply with his direction, "the Agreement constitutes the willing party . . . an implied agent possessing the irrevocable proxy of the recalcitrant party for the purpose of casting the particular vote." It was ordered that a new election be held before a master, with the direction that the master should recognize and give effect to the agreement if its terms were properly invoked.

Before taking up defendants' objections to the agreement, let us analyze particularly what it attempts to provide with respect to voting, including what functions and powers it attempts to repose in Mr. Loos, the "arbitrator". The agreement recites that the parties desired "to continue to act jointly in all matters relating to their stock ownership or interest in" the corporation. The parties agreed to consult and confer with each other in exercising their voting rights and to act jointly—that is, concertedly; unitedly; towards unified courses of action—in accordance with such agreement as they might reach. Thus, so long as the parties agree for whom or for what their shares shall be voted, the agreement provides no function for the arbitrator. His role is limited to situations where the parties fail to agree upon a course of action. In such cases, the agreement directs that "the question in disagreement shall be submitted for arbitration" to Mr. Loos "as arbitrator and his decision thereon shall be binding upon the parties." These provisions are designed to operate in aid of what appears to be a primary purpose of the parties, "to act jointly" in exercising their voting rights, by providing a means for fixing a course of action whenever they themselves might reach a stalemate.

Should the agreement be interpreted as attempting to empower the arbitrator to carry his directions into effect? Certainly there is no express delegation or grant of power to do so, either by authorizing him to vote the shares or to compel either party to vote them in accordance with his directions. The agreement expresses no other function of the arbitrator than that of deciding questions in disagreement which prevent the effectuation of the purpose "to act jointly." The power to enforce a decision does not seem a necessary or usual incident of such a function. Mr. Loos is not a party to the agreement. It does not contemplate the transfer of any shares or interest in shares to him, or that he should undertake any duties which the parties might compel him to perform. They provided that they might designate any other individual to act instead of Mr. Loos. The agreement does not attempt to make the arbitrator a trustee of an express trust. What the arbitrator is to do is for the benefit of the parties, not for his own benefit. Whether the parties accept or reject his decision is no concern of his, so far as the agreement or the surrounding circumstances reveal. We think the parties sought to bind each other, but to be bound only to each other, and not to empower the arbitrator to enforce decisions he might make.

From this conclusion, it follows necessarily that no decision of the arbitrator could ever be enforced if both parties to the agreement were unwilling that it be enforced, for the obvious reason that there would be no one to enforce it. Under the agreement, something more is required after the arbitrator has given his decision in order that it should become compulsory: at least one of the parties must determine that such decision shall be carried into effect. Thus, any "control" of the voting of the shares, which is reposed in the arbitrator, is substantially limited in action under the agreement in that it is subject to the overriding power of the parties themselves.

The agreement does not describe the undertaking of each party with respect to a decision of the arbitrator other than to provide that it "shall be binding upon the parties". It seems to us that this language, considered with relation to its context and the situations to which it is applicable, means that each party promised the other to exercise her own voting rights in accordance with the arbitrator's decision. The agreement is silent about any exercise of the voting rights of one party by the other. The language with reference to situations where the parties arrive at an understanding as to voting plainly suggests "action" by each, and "exercising" voting rights by each, rather than by one for the other. There is no intimation that this method should be different where the arbitrator's decision is to be carried into effect. Assuming that a power in each party to exercise the voting rights of the other might be a relatively more effective or convenient means of enforcing a decision of the arbitrator than would be available without the power, this would not justify implying a delegation of the power in the absence of some indication that the parties bargained for that means. The method of voting actually employed by the parties tends to show that they did not construe the agreement as creating powers to vote each other's shares; for at meetings prior to 1946 each party apparently exercised her own voting rights, and at the 1946 meeting, Mrs. Ringling, who wished to enforce the agreement, did not attempt to cast a ballot in exercise of any voting rights of Mrs. Haley. We do not find enough in the agreement or in the circumstances to justify a construction that either party was empowered to exercise voting rights of the other.

Having examined what the parties sought to provide by the agreement, we come now to defendants' contention that the voting provisions are illegal and revocable. They say that the courts of this state have definitely established the doctrine "that there can be no agreement, or any device whatsoever, by which the voting power of stock of a Delaware corporation may be irrevocably separated from the ownership of the stock, except by an agreement which complies with Section 18" of the Corporation Law, Rev. Code 1935, § 2050, and except by a proxy coupled with an interest. . . . The statute reads, in part, as follows:

> "Sec.18. Fiduciary Stockholders; Voting Power of; Voting Trusts:—Persons holding stock in a fiduciary capacity shall be entitled to vote the shares so held, and persons whose stock is pledged shall be entitled to vote, unless in the transfer by the pledgor on the books of the corporation he shall have expressly empowered the pledgee to vote thereon, in which case only the pledgee, or his proxy may represent said stock and vote thereon.
>
> One or more stockholders may by agreement in writing deposit capital stock of an original issue with or transfer capital stock to any person or persons, or corporation or corporations authorized to act as trustee, for the purpose of vesting in said person or persons, corporation or corporations, who may be designated Voting Trustee or Voting Trustees, the right to vote thereon for any period of time determined by such agreement, not exceeding ten years, upon the terms and conditions stated in such agreement. Such agreement may contain any other lawful provisions not inconsistent with said purpose. . . . Said Voting Trustees may vote upon the stock so issued or transferred during the period in such agreement specified; stock standing in the names of such Voting Trustees may be voted either in person or by proxy, and in voting said stock, such Voting Trustees shall incur no responsibility as stockholder, trustee or otherwise, except for their own individual malfeasance."

In our view, neither the cases nor the statute sustain the rule for which the defendants contend. Their sweeping formulation would impugn well-recognized means by which a shareholder may effectively confer his voting rights upon others while retaining various other rights. For example, defendants' rule would apparently not permit holders of voting stock to confer upon stockholders of another class, by the device of an amendment of the certificate of incorporation, the exclusive right to vote during periods when dividends are not paid on stock of the latter class. The broad prohibitory meaning which defendants find in Section 18 seems inconsistent with their concession that proxies coupled with an interest may be irrevocable, for the statute contains nothing about such proxies. The statute authorizes, among other things, the deposit or transfer of stock in trust for a specified purpose, namely, "vesting" in the transferee "the right to vote thereon" for a limited period; and prescribes numerous requirements in this connection. Accordingly, it seems reasonable to infer that to establish the relationship and accomplish the purpose which the statute authorizes, its requirements must be complied with. But the statute does not purport to deal with agreements whereby shareholders attempt to bind each other as to how they shall vote their shares. Various forms of such pooling agreements, as they are sometimes called, have been held valid and have been distinguished from voting trusts. We think the particular agreement before us does not violate Section 18 or constitute an attempted evasion of its requirements, and is not illegal for any other reason. Generally speaking, a shareholder may exercise wide liberality of judgment in the matter of voting, and it is not objectionable that his motives may be for personal profit, or determined by whims or caprice, so long as he violates no duty owed his fellow shareholders. The ownership of voting stock imposes no legal duty to vote at all. A group of shareholders may, without impropriety, vote their respective shares so as to obtain advantages of concerted action. They may lawfully contract with each other to vote in the future in such way as they, or a majority of their group, from time to time determine. Reasonable provisions for cases of failure of the group to reach a determination because of an even division in their ranks seem unobjectionable. The provision here for submission to the arbitrator is plainly designed as a deadlock-breaking measure, and the arbitrator's decision cannot be enforced unless at least one of the parties (entitled to cast one-half of their combined votes) is willing that it be enforced. We find the provision reasonable. It does not appear that the agreement enables the parties to take any unlawful advantage of the outside shareholder, or of any other person. It offends no rule of law or public policy of this state of which we are aware.

Legal consideration for the promises of each party is supplied by the mutual promises of the other party. The undertaking to vote in accordance with the arbitrator's decision is a valid contract. The good faith of the arbitrator's action has not been challenged and, indeed, the record indicates that no such challenge could be supported. Accordingly, the failure of Mrs. Haley to exercise her voting rights in accordance with his decision was a breach of her contract. It is no extenuation of the breach that her votes were cast for two of the three candidates directed by the arbitrator. His directions to her were part of a single plan or course of action for the voting of the shares of both parties to the agreement, calculated to utilize an advantage of joint action by them which would bring about the election of an additional director. The actual voting of Mrs. Haley's shares frustrates that plan to such an extent that it should not be treated as a partial performance of her contract.

Throughout their argument, defendants make much of the fact that all votes cast at the meeting were by the registered shareholders. The Court of Chancery may, in a review of an election, reject votes of a registered shareholder where his voting of them is found to be in violation of rights of another person.... It seems to us that upon the application of Mrs. Ringling, the injured party, the votes representing Mrs. Haley's shares should not be counted. Since no infirmity in Mr. North's voting has been demonstrated, his right to recognition of what he did at the meeting should be considered in granting any relief to Mrs. Ringling; for her rights arose under a contract to which Mr. North was not a party. With this in mind, ==we have concluded that the election should not be declared invalid, but that effect should be given to a rejection of the votes representing Mrs. Haley's shares.== No other relief seems appropriate in this proceeding. Mr. North's vote against the motion for adjournment was sufficient to defeat it. With respect to the election of directors, the return of the inspectors should be corrected to show a rejection of Mrs. Haley's votes, and to declare the election of the six persons for whom Mr. North and Mrs. Ringling voted.

This leaves one vacancy in the directorate. The question of what to do about such a vacancy was not considered by the court below and has not been argued here. For this reason, and because an election of directors at the 1947 annual meeting (which presumably will be held in the near future) may make a determination of the question unimportant, we shall not decide it on this appeal. If a decision of the point appears important to the parties, any of them may apply to raise it in the Court of Chancery, after the mandate of this court is received there.

An order should be entered directing a modification of the order of the Court of Chancery in accordance with this opinion.

Questions

1. Mr. Haley voted his wife's stock against Loos's decision. What difference did it make in the ultimate composition of the board? Why did it matter to Mr. and Mrs. Haley? Why does Mrs. Haley appeal the Vice-Chancellor's decision?

2. How does the Delaware Supreme Court characterize the agreement between Haley and Ringling? Why does the court reject the Vice-Chancellor's characterization of the agreement? What are the policy considerations that motivate the court?

3. What is the court's definition of a voting trust?

Abercrombie v. Davies
130 A.2d 338 (Del. 1957)

SOUTHERLAND, Chief Justice

The pertinent facts are as follows:

American Independent Oil Company ("American") is a Delaware corporation. It was formed to develop an oil concession in the Kuwait-Saudi Arabian neutral zone. The organizers were James S. Abercrombie, Sunray Oil Corporation ("Sunray"),

Phillips Petroleum Company ("Phillips"), Ralph K. Davies, Signal Oil and Gas Company ("Signal"), The Hancock Oil Company ("Hancock"), The Globe Oil and Refining Company ("Globe"), Lario Oil and Gas Company ("Lario"), Ashland Oil & Refining Company ("Ashland"), Deep Rock Oil Corporation ("Deep Rock"), and Allied Oil Company (later acquired by Ashland). The organizers subscribed in varying proportions to American's original issue of stock. Additional stock was later issued, and there are now outstanding 150,000 shares.

The organization agreement provided that the Board of Directors of American should consist of one director for each 5,000 shares held, and that the directors should be elected by cumulative voting. In effect, each stockholder has been permitted to name the director or directors to represent on the board his or its interests. Davies represents his own interest and is president of the corporation. At all times the number of directors has been fifteen. No one stockholder holds a majority of stock, and no one stockholder is represented by more than four directors. Obviously, smooth functioning of such a board was dependent either upon substantial harmony among the interests represented on it or upon an effective coalition of the interests of a majority.

On March 30, 1950, six of the stockholders took steps to form such a coalition. On that date an agreement was executed between eight individuals designated "Agents", and the six stockholders—Davies, Ashland, Globe, Lario, Hancock and Signal. These stockholders hold about 54 1/2% of the shares. They are represented on the board by eight of the fifteen directors. The Agents named in the agreement were at the time the eight directors representing these six stockholders.

The obvious purpose of the agreement was to achieve effective control of the board and thus control of corporate policy. The motive for the agreement, according to the defendants, was to prevent acquisition of control by Phillips, which was the largest single stockholder, holding about one-third of the stock. In the view we take of the case, only the purpose is material.

The Agents' Agreement is an unusual one. In effect, it transfers voting control of the stock of the six stockholders to the eight Agents for a period of ten years (subject to termination by seven of the Agents). The Agents are to be, as far as possible identical with the directors. The agreement of seven of the eight is required to vote the stock and elaborate provisions are added for the choice of an arbitrator to resolve disagreements. Somewhat similar provisions attempt to control the action of the directors. A more detailed examination of the agreement will later be made. At the moment we note that the majority of the board secured by this agreement (eight of the fifteen) comprised Davies, the two Signal directors, the two Hancock directors, the director representing Globe and Lario, and the two Ashland directors.

The effective control thus sought to be achieved apparently lasted until December 9, 1954. On that date a meeting of the Board of Directors was held in Chicago. A resolution was adopted calling a special meeting of the board for December 16, to consider and take action upon certain amendments to the by-laws and other matters. This resolution was adopted by a vote of nine to six. This majority consisted of Abercrombie, the four Phillips directors, the Sunray director, the Deep Rock director, and the two Ashland directors. The minority consisted of Davies and the Globe, Lario, Hancock and Signal directors. The nature of the action to be considered at the proposed meeting was such as to indicate to the minority that the control of the board set up by the Agents' Agreement was seriously threatened. The Ashland directors, it was charged, had violated the Agents' Agreement. Counter moves were made by Davies. Litigation was instituted in California by Davies, Signal, Hancock, Globe and Lario against Ashland and its two directors. American, named as a defendant, was preliminarily enjoined from recognizing any action taken at a board meeting of December 16, and Ashland was enjoined from violating the Agents' Agreement.

In the meantime, the suit below was filed by Abercrombie, Phillips and Sunray against the other shareholders and the Agents. Davies, Signal, Hancock, Lario, Globe and six of the Agents appeared and answered. Plaintiffs filed a motion for summary judgment. Several contentions arose out of the hearings on this motion. The Chancellor made the following rulings of law:

(1) Certain provisions of the Agents' Agreement attempting to control directorate action are invalid on their face;

(2) The agreement is not a voting trust;

(3) The provisions respecting stockholder action are severable from the illegal provisions, and constitute a valid stockholders' pooling agreement.

Both sides appeal. All of the issues argued below have been presented here.

We turn to an analysis of the Agents' Agreement.

Paragraph 1 provides in part:

"Upon the signing of this Agreement, or as soon thereafter as it may be possible for them to do so, by those whose certificates may be pledged or deposited, as hereinafter referred to, the Shareholders will deliver to the Agents the certificate or certificates representing all the shares of American Independent Oil Company now owned or controlled by them, said certificates to be endorsed in blank or attached to a stock power endorsed in blank. Said Agents will give to each depositing Shareholder a proper receipt for all certificates so delivered."

The certificates and stock powers are to be deposited in escrow in a bank or trust company, subject to withdrawal at any time by any seven of the agents.

Paragraph 2 sets forth a method of dealing with a possible increase in the number of Agents "(or in case a Voting Trust shall have been created, the number of Trustees)".

Paragraph 3 provides in part:

"During the term of this Agreement the Agents or their successors shall have the sole and exclusive voting power of the stock subject to this

Agreement. The Shareholders shall deliver to the Agents and shall keep in effect during the life of this Agreement proxies giving said Agents or their successors jointly and each of them severally, with full power of substitution to any or all of them, the power to vote the stock at all regular and special meetings of the stockholders and to vote for, do or assent or consent to any act or proceeding which the Shareholders of said corporation might or could vote for, do or assent or consent to."

Paragraph 3 also provides:

"The vote of the Agents shall always be exercised as a unit, on any matter on which a vote of the stockholders is called for, as any seven of said Agents shall direct and determine. If any seven Agents fail to agree on any such matter, then the question in disagreement shall be submitted for arbitration to some disinterested person (i.e., one having no financial interest in American Independent Oil Company), chosen by the affirmative vote of seven of the Agents, as sole arbitrator."

Then follow provisions for the choice of an arbitrator if seven Agents fail to agree upon the matter, and for the enforcement of his decision.

Then follow two paragraphs dealing with control of directorate action. These are the provisions held invalid by the Chancellor as an unlawful attempt to strip the directors of their statutory right and duty to manage the corporate affairs.

Paragraph 3 then concludes:

"In the event a Voting Trust is established as provided in Paragraph 7 hereof, the provisions of the two preceding subparagraphs shall remain in effect, substituting the words 'Trustee' or 'Trustees' for the words 'Agent' or 'Agents' wherever those words occur in said two subparagraphs."

Paragraph 4 provides for filling a vacancy in the position of Agent. As to the corporate shareholders, the successor is to be named by the shareholder that the Agent was representing. As to Davies, his successor is to be named by the majority of the remaining Agents. Each corporate shareholder has the right to remove its Agent or Agents at any time without cause.

Paragraphs 6 and 7 provide:

"6. Except as herein otherwise provided, the proxies to be given hereunder shall not be revoked and the powers herein delegated to said Agents shall be irrevocable during a period of ten years from and after the date of said Agreement. This Agreement, however, shall terminate if any seven of the Agents hereunder declare in writing that the Agreement is terminated. Unless the Agents by unanimous vote otherwise determine, this Agreement shall also terminate if and when less than 50% of the outstanding shares of American Independent Oil Company remain subject to this Agreement. Upon the termination of said Agreement the certificates representing all of the shares so held under this Agreement and then remaining in escrow or in the hands of said Agents or their successors shall be returned or assigned to the parties then entitled thereto, upon surrender to said Agents of the receipts given for said certificates.

7. Any seven of said Agents may at any time withdraw said stock certificates from escrow and transfer said stock to the persons then acting as Agents, as trustees to be held under a voting trust. The parties agree, upon the written request of seven of said Agents to execute a voting trust agreement substantially in the form attached hereto marked Exhibit "A", the persons then acting as Agents to be Trustees, and the Shareholders parties hereto to be Beneficiaries thereunder. The parties do hereby constitute any one of said Agents their attorney in fact to execute said voting trust agreement for them and in their names, in the event any of them should be unable, or should fail or refuse to sign said voting trust agreement upon the written request of seven of said Agents. Upon the execution of said voting trust agreement the Shareholders will surrender to said Agents the receipts given for said certificates."

This agreement, plaintiffs assert, is invalid on its face. Among other contentions they say that in substance, though not in form, it is a voting trust, and that it is void because it does not comply with the provisions of our voting trust statute. Defendants reply that it is not, and was not intended to be, a voting trust, and is a mere pooling agreement of the kind recognized as legal in Delaware by the decision in *Ringling Bros.-Barnum & Bailey Combined Shows v. Ringling,* 29 Del. Ch. 610, 53 A.2d 441.

The General Corporation Law, 8 Del.C. § 218, provides in part:

"(a) One or more stockholders may by agreement in writing deposit capital stock of an original issue with or transfer capital stock to any person or persons, or corporation or corporations authorized to act as trustee, for the purpose of vesting in such person or persons, corporation or corporations, who may be designated voting trustee or voting trustees, the right to vote thereon for any period of time determined by such agreement, not exceeding ten years, upon the terms and conditions stated in such agreement. Such agreement may contain any other lawful provisions not inconsistent with said purpose. After the filing of a copy of such agreement in the principal office of the corporation in the State of Delaware, which copy shall be open to the inspection of any stockholder of the corporation or any beneficiary of the trust under said agreement daily during business hours, certificates of stock shall be issued to the voting trustees to represent any stock of an original issue so deposited with them, and any certificates of stock so transferred to the voting trustees shall be surrendered and cancelled and new certificates therefor shall be issued to the voting trustees, and in the certificates so issued it shall appear that they are issued pursuant to such agreement, and in the entry of such voting trustees as owners of such stock in the proper books of the issuing corporation that fact shall also be noted. The voting trustees may vote upon the stock so issued or transferred during the period in such agreement specified."

This statute was enacted in 1925. Prior to its passage there was no Delaware decision declaring that voting trusts were lawful at common law—a question upon which the decisions in other states were in disagreement. . . . [I]n Delaware, as in New York, voting trusts derive their validity solely from the statute. . . . The statute lays down for voting trusts "the law of their life"; compliance with its provisions is mandatory. Voting trusts not so complying are illegal. . . .

. . . If any stockholders' agreement provided for joint or concerted voting is so drawn as in effect to occupy the field reserved for the statutory voting trust, it is illegal, whatever mechanics may be devised to attain the result. The provisions of the instrument determine its legal effect, and if they clearly create a voting trust, any intention of the parties to the contrary is immaterial.

A review of the Delaware decisions upon the subject of voting trusts shows that our courts have indicated that one essential feature that characterizes a voting trust is the separation of the voting rights of the stock from the other attributes of ownership. . . .

When we apply these tests to the Agents' Agreement we find: (1) that the voting rights of the pooled stock have been divorced from the beneficial ownership, which is retained by the stockholders; (2) that the voting rights have been transferred to fiduciaries denominated Agents; (3) that the transfer of such rights is, through the medium of irrevocable proxies, effective for a period of ten years; (4) that all voting rights in respect of all the stock are pooled in the Agents as a group, through the device of proxies running to the agents jointly and severally, and no stockholder retains the right to vote his or its shares; and (5) that on its face the agreement has for its principal object voting control of American.

These elements, under our decisions, are the elements of a voting trust.

We find one other significant circumstance.

Paragraph 7 of the Agents' Agreement gives any seven of the eight agents the power to withdraw the stock from escrow and to transform the Agreement into a formal voting trust. Any one of the agents is authorized to sign the voting trust agreement for any shareholder who fails to do so upon the request of any seven of the agents. A form of a voting trust agreement is attached as an exhibit to the Agents' Agreement. A comparison of this form with the provisions of the Agents' Agreement shows that upon the execution of the Voting Trust Agreement the scheme of control functions just as it functions under the Agents' Agreement. Without pausing for a detailed analysis, we note that Paragraphs 2, 4, 5 and 6 of the Agents' Agreement are paralleled (in some cases almost verbatim) by Paragraphs 2, 5, 8 and 10, respectively, of the Voting Trust Agreement. Paragraph 3 of the Agents' Agreement is paralleled in part by Paragraph 3 of the Voting Trust Agreement. The provisions of Paragraph 3 of the Agents' Agreement controlling directorate action remain in effect as part of the Voting Trust Agreement.

Thus the only significant changes made in transforming the Agents' Agreement into a Voting Trust Agreement are the provisions formalizing the trust, viz.: (1) the Agents become Trustees—a change of name and nothing more; (2) the stock with irrevocable stock powers running to the Agents becomes stock registered in their names as Trustees; and (3) voting trust certificates instead of receipts are issued to the stockholders.

To sum up: the substance of the voting trust already existed; the transformation added only the special mechanics that the statute requires.

Now, the provisions of the statute that were not complied with are the requirement that the shares be transferred on the books and the requirement that a copy of the agreement shall be filed in the corporation's principal office in Delaware. The effect was to create a secret voting trust. The provision respecting the filing of a copy in the principal office in Delaware "open to the inspection of any stockholder . . . or any beneficiary of the trust" is a provision obviously for the benefit of all stockholders and of all beneficiaries of the trust, who are entitled to know where voting control of a corporation resides. And the provision for transfer of the stock on the corporate books necessarily serves, though perhaps only incidentally, a similar purpose with respect to the officers and directors. If the validity of a stockholders' pooling agreement of the kind here presented were to be sustained, the way is clear for the creation of secret voting trusts. The statute clearly forbids them.

The Chancellor took the contrary view. He held the Agents' Agreement not to be a voting trust because (1) title to the stock did not pass to the Agents, and (2) because the Agents are in fact the agents and are subject to the directions of their principals.

The failure to transfer the stock on the books is not a sufficient reason in this case for holding the Agents' Agreement not a voting trust. It is an indication that the parties did not intend to create a voting trust; but that subjective intention is unimportant. The stock here was endorsed in blank and delivered to the agents for deposit in escrow with irrevocable proxies. Transfer of the stock on the books is not essential to effect an irrevocable transfer of voting rights to fiduciaries, divorced from the other attributes of the stock, in order to secure voting control, as the Agents' Agreement demonstrates. It is such a transfer that is the characteristic feature of a voting trust.[1]

The fact that the Agents are subject to control by their respective principals does not prevent the agreement from constituting a voting trust. The stock is voted by the Agents as a group. No one stockholder retains complete control over the voting of its stock. It cannot vote its own stock directly; all it can do is to direct its Agent how to vote on a decision to be made by the Agents as a group. The stock of any corporate stockholder may at any time be voted against its will by the vote of the seven other

---

1. The relationship between the "irrevocable proxy" to fiduciaries and the voting trust is so close that one writer has said: "To achieve irrevocable proxies the voting trust was developed."

agents. The control of the agents rests upon the provisions that they are severally chosen by the respective stockholders and each may be removed and replaced by the stockholder he represents. In effect, these provisions come to this: that each corporate stockholder participating in the agreement reserves the right to name and remove the fiduciary or fiduciaries representing him. Such a provision is not inconsistent with a voting trust. In fact, the scheme is carried forward to the voting trust set out as "Exhibit A" to the Agents' Agreement. See Paragraphs 3 and 5, paralleling Paragraphs 3 and 4 of the Agents' Agreement. And the alleged continuing control of the Agent by the stockholder clearly would not exist in the event of the death, removal or resignation of Davies in his capacity of Agent. In that case his successor, whether Agent or Trustee, is named by a majority of the remaining Agents or Trustees, as the case may be, and his estate has no control whatever over the Agent so named.

Defendants stress the contention that the parties to the Agents' Agreement did not intend to create a voting trust. As above noted, the intent that governs is the intent derived from the instrument itself. A desire to avoid the legal consequences of the language used is immaterial. Additional arguments (1) that the fiduciaries vested with voting rights are called agents instead of trustees, and (2) that title to the stock did not pass to the agents, have already been noticed.

In support of their argument that the Agents' Agreement creates only a stockholders' pooling agreement and not a voting trust, defendants lean heavily on the decision of this Court in *Ringling Bros.-Barnum & Bailey Combined Shows v. Ringling,* 29 Del. Ch. 610, 53 A.2d 441. That case involved a true pooling agreement, far short of a voting trust. Two stockholders agreed to act jointly in exercising their voting rights. There was no deposit of the stock with irrevocable stock powers conferring upon a group of fiduciaries exclusive voting powers over the pooled stock. Indeed, the Supreme Court (modifying the decision below) held that the agreement did not provide, either expressly or impliedly, for a proxy to either stockholder to vote the other's shares. The *Ringling* case is clearly distinguishable on the facts.

And although the case recognizes the validity of various forms of pooling agreements, it does not announce, as defendants appear to think, an unrestricted and uncritical approval of all agreements between stockholders relating to the voting of their stock. Not all pooling agreements are lawful. . . .

Defendants would push the general statements of the *Ringling* case to unwarranted lengths. They quote extensively from that part of the opinion which deals with the scope of the voting trust statute. Among other things, the Court said:

> "But the statute does not purport to deal with agreements whereby stockholders attempt to bind each other as to how they shall vote their shares."

We gather that defendants go so far as to say that a pooling agreement may assume any form whatever without running afoul of the voting trust statute. Thus, if we understand defendants' argument, a pooling agreement may, through the medium of fiduciaries with exclusive voting powers, lawfully accomplish substantially the same purposes as a voting trust and thus avoid compliance with § 218. We disagree. Obviously, as a pooling agreement in substance and purpose approaches more and more nearly the substance and purpose of the statute, there comes a point at which, if the statute is not complied with, the agreement is illegal. A pooling agreement may not escape the statutory controls by calling the trustees agents and giving to the stockholders receipts instead of voting trust certificates. If this were not so, stockholders could, through the device of an agreement such as the one before us, accept for themselves the chief benefits of the statute: unified voting control through fiduciaries for an appreciable period of time; and escape its burdens: the requirements for making an open record of the matter, and the limitations in respect of time. If the agreement before us is upheld, what is there to prevent a similar agreement for 15 years — or 25 years?

Although the general language of the *Ringling* case, if read literally, may seem to lend some support to the position of the defendants, we do not think that it should be carried so far as to permit the result urged by them in this case. . . .

For the foregoing reasons, we are compelled to disagree with the holding of the Chancellor upon the question discussed. We are of opinion that the Agents' Agreement is void as an illegal voting trust.

Our conclusion upon this question makes it unnecessary to discuss any of the other questions raised on the appeal.

The cause is remanded to the Court of Chancery of New Castle County, with instructions to vacate paragraphs (2) to (5) inclusive of the order of October 24, 1956, and to enter a further order consistent with this opinion, with such provisions for injunctive relief, if any, as the Chancellor may determine to be appropriate.

Questions

1. What is the difference between the agreement in *Ringling Bros. v. Ringling* and the agreement in *Abercrombie v. Davies*? Didn't the shareholders in *Abercrombie* do exactly what the *Ringling* court told them to do to create a valid agreement?

2. What is the court's test to determine whether an agreement is a voting trust? Is it the same test applied in *Ringling*?

3. What policy considerations influenced the court's ruling in *Abercrombie*?

Lehrman v. Cohen

222 A.2d 800 (Del. 1966)

HERRMANN, Justice

The primary problem presented on this appeal involves the applicability of the Delaware Voting Trust Statute.[1] Other questions involve the legality of stock having voting power but no dividend or liquidation rights except repayment of par value, and an alleged unlawful delegation of directorial duties and powers.

These are the material facts:

Giant Food Inc. (hereinafter the "Company") was incorporated in Delaware in 1935 by the defendant N. M. Cohen and Samuel Lehrman, deceased father of the plaintiff Jacob Lehrman. From its inception, the Company was controlled by the Cohen and Lehrman families, each of which owned equal quantities of the voting stock, designated Class AC (held by the Cohen family) and Class AL (held by the Lehrman family) common stock. The two classes of stock have cumulative voting rights and each is entitled to elect two members of the Company's four-member board of directors.

Over the years, as may have been expected, there were differences of opinion between the Cohen and Lehrman families as to operating policies of the Company. Samuel Lehrman died in 1949; each of his children inherited part of his stock in the Company; but a dispute arose among the children regarding an *inter vivos* gift of certain shares made to the plaintiff by his father shortly before his death. To eliminate the Lehrman family dispute and its possible disruption of the affairs of the Company, an arrangement was made which settled the dispute and permitted the plaintiff to acquire all of the outstanding Class AL stock, thereby vesting in him voting

---

1. 8 Del.C. § 218 provides in part as follows:

   "§ 218. Voting trusts

   (a) One or more stockholders may by agreement in writing deposit capital stock of an original issue with or transfer capital stock to any person or persons, or corporation or corporations authorized to act as trustee, for the purpose of vesting in such person or persons, corporation or corporations, who may be designated voting trustee or voting trustees, the right to vote thereon for any period of time determined by such agreement, not exceeding ten years, upon the terms and conditions stated in such agreement. Such agreement may contain any other lawful provisions not inconsistent with said purpose. After the filing of a copy of such agreement in the principal office of the corporation in the State of Delaware, which copy shall be open to the inspection of any stockholder of the corporation or any beneficiary of the trust under said agreement daily during business hours, certificates of stock shall be issued to the voting trustees to represent any stock of an original issue so deposited with them, and any certificates of stock so transferred to the voting trustees shall be surrendered and cancelled and new certificates therefor shall be issued to the voting trustees, and in the certificates so issued it shall appear that they are issued pursuant to such agreement, and in the entry of such voting trustees as owners of such stock in the proper books of the issuing corporation that fact shall also be noted. The voting trustees may vote upon the stock so issued or transferred during the period in such agreement specified. . . ."

power equal to that held by the Cohen family. The arrangement involved repurchase by the Company of the stock held by the plaintiff's brothers and sister, their relinquishment of any claim to the stock gift, and an equalizing surrender of certain stock by the Cohens to the Company for retirement. An essential part of the arrangement, upon the insistence of the Cohens, was the establishment of a fifth directorship to obviate the risk of deadlock which would have continued if the equal division of voting power between AL and AC stock were continued.

To implement the arrangement, on December 31, 1949, the Company's certificate of incorporation was amended, *inter alia*, to create a third class of voting stock, designated Class AD common stock, entitled to elect the fifth director. Article Fourth of the amendment to the certificate of incorporation provided for the issuance of one share of Class AD stock, having a par value of $10 and the following rights and powers:

> "The holder of Class AD common stock shall be entitled to all of the rights and privileges pertaining to common stock without any limitations, prohibitions, restrictions or qualifications except that the holder of said Class AD stock shall not be entitled to receive any dividends declared and paid by the corporation, shall not be entitled to share in the distribution of assets of the corporation upon liquidation or dissolution either partial or final, except to the extent of the par value of said Class AD common stock, and in the election of Directors shall have the right to vote for and elect one of the five Directors hereinafter provided for.
>
> The corporation shall have the right, at any time, to redeem and call in the Class AD stock by paying to the holder thereof the par value of said stock, provided however, that such redemption or call shall be authorized and directed by the affirmative vote of four of the five Directors hereinafter provided for."[2]

By resolution of the board of directors, the share of Class AD stock was issued forthwith to the defendant Joseph B. Danzansky, who had served as counsel to the Company since 1944. All corporate action regarding the creation and the issuance of the Class AD stock was accomplished by the unanimous vote of the AC and AL

---

2. Article Fourth of the amendment also co-related the Class AL and the Class AC stock as follows:
> "The holders of Class AL common stock shall be entitled to all of the rights and privileges pertaining to common stock without any limitations, prohibitions, restrictions, or qualifications except that the holder or holders of said Class AL common stock, in the election of Directors, shall have the right to vote for and elect two of the five Directors hereinafter provided for.
> The holders of Class AC common stock shall be entitled to all of the rights and privileges pertaining to common stock without any limitations, prohibitions, restrictions, or qualifications except that the holder or holders of said Class AC common stock, in the election of Directors, shall have the right to vote for and elect two of the five Directors hereinafter provided for."

stockholders and of the board of directors. In April 1950, pursuant to the arrangement, Danzansky voted his share of AD stock to elect himself as the Company's fifth director; and he served as such until the institution of this action in 1964. During that entire period, the AC and AL stock have been voted to elect two directors each. From 1950 through 1964, Danzansky regularly attended board meetings, raised and discussed general items of business, and voted on all issues as they came before the board. He was not obliged to break any deadlock among the directors prior to October 1, 1964 because no such deadlock arose before that date.

Beginning in December 1959, 200,000 shares of non-voting common stock of the Company were sold in a public issue for over $3,000,000. Each prospectus published in connection with the public issue contained the following statement:

> "Common Stock AD is not a participating stock, and the only purpose for the provision and issuance of such stock is to prevent a deadlock in case the Directors elected by the Common Stock AC and the Directors elected by the Common Stock AL cannot reach an agreement."

Similarly, a letter on behalf of the Company to the Commissioner of Internal Revenue, dated July 15, 1959, contained the following statement:

> "As can be seen from the enclosed certified copy of the stock provisions of the certificate of Incorporation, as amended, the Class AD common stock is not a participating stock, the only purpose for the provision and issuance of such a stock being to prevent a deadlock in case the AC and AL Directors cannot reach an agreement."

From the outset and until October 1, 1964, the defendant N. M. Cohen was president of the Company. On that date, a resolution was adopted at the Company's annual stockholders' meeting to give Danzansky a fifteen year executive employment contract at an annual salary of $67,600, and options for 25,000 shares of the non-voting common stock of the Company. The AC and AD stock were voted in favor and the AL stock was voted against the resolution. At a directors meeting held the same day, Danzansky was elected president of the Company by a 3–2 vote, the two AL directors voting in opposition. On December 11, 1964, Danzansky resigned as director and voted his share of AD stock to elect as the fifth director, Millard F. West, Jr., a former AL director and investment banker whose firm was one of the underwriters of the public issue of the Company's stock. The newly constituted board ratified the election of Danzansky as president; and, on January 27, 1965, after the commencement of this action and after a review and report by a committee consisting of the new AD director and one AL director, Danzansky's employment contract was approved and adopted with certain modifications.

The plaintiff brought this action on December 11, 1964, basing it upon two claims: The First Claim charges that the creation, issuance, and voting of the one share of Class AD stock resulted in an arrangement illegal under the law of this State for the reasons hereinafter set forth. The Second Claim, addressed to the events of October 1, 1964, charges that the election of Danzansky as president of the Company and his employment contract violated the terms of the 1959 deadlock-breaking arrangement, as made between the holders of the AC and AL stock, and constituted breaches of contract and fiduciary duty. The plaintiff and the defendants filed cross-motions for summary judgment as to the First Claim. The Court of Chancery, after considering the contentions now before us and discussed *infra,* granted summary judgment in favor of the defendants and denied the plaintiff's motion for summary judgment. The plaintiff appeals.

I

The plaintiff's primary contention is that the Class AD stock arrangement is, in substance and effect, a voting trust; that, as such, it is illegal because not limited to a ten year period as required by the Voting Trust Statute. The defendants deny that the AD stock arrangement constitutes a disguised voting trust; but they concede that if it is, the arrangement is illegal for violation of the Statute. Thus, issue is clearly joined on the point.

The criteria of a voting trust under our decisions have been summarized by this Court in *Abercrombie v. Davies,* 36 Del.Ch. 371, 130 A.2d 338 (1957). The tests there set forth, accepted by both sides of this cause as being applicable,[3] are as follows: (1) the voting rights of the stock are separated from the other attributes of ownership; (2) the voting rights granted are intended to be irrevocable for a definite period of time; and (3) the principal purpose[4] of the grant of voting rights is to acquire voting control of the corporation.

Adopting and applying these tests, the plaintiff says, as to the first element, that the AD arrangement provides for a divorcement of voting rights from beneficial ownership of the AC and AL stock; that the creation and issuance of the share of AD stock is tantamount to a pooling by the AC and AL stockholders of a portion of their voting stock and giving it to a trustee, in the person of the AD stockholder, to vote for the election of the fifth director; that after the creation of the AD stock, the AC and AL stockholders each hold but 40% of the voting power, and the AD stockholder holds the controlling balance of 20%; that the AD stock has no property rights except the right to a return of the $10 paid as the par value; and that, therefore, there has been a transfer of the voting rights devoid of any participating property rights. So runs the argument of the plaintiff in support of his contention that the first of the *Abercrombie* criteria for a voting trust is met.

---

3. While the tests and criteria set forth in the *Abercrombie* case prevail, its facts are entirely different. There, several stockholders, each representing a minority interest, agreed to place their stock in escrow for a period of ten years, in exchange for stock receipts, for the purpose of acquiring voting control of the corporation. Agents were appointed and, by irrevocable proxies, the agents were given joint and several voting rights and sole power of decision; no stockholder retained the right to vote his own stock. On those facts, an attempt having been thus made to separate the vote from the stock, this Court held that the stockholders had created a voting trust subject to the controls and limitations of §218.

4. It is noteworthy, in this connection, that in *Abercrombie,* this Court distinguished between purpose and motive, stating that it considered only purpose to be material (130 A.2d 338, 341).

The contention is unacceptable. The AD arrangement did not separate the voting rights of the AC or the AL stock from the other attributes of ownership of those classes of stock. Each AC and AL stockholder retains complete control over the voting of his stock; each can vote his stock directly; no AL or AC stockholder is divested of his right to vote his stock as he sees fit; no AL or AC stock can be voted against the shareholder's wishes; and the AL and AC stock continued to elect two directors each.

The AD stock arrangement, as we view it, became a part of the capitalization of the Company. The fact that there is but a single share, or that the par value is nominal, is of no legal significance; the one share and the $10 par value might have been multiplied many times over, with the same consequence. It is true that the creation of the separate class of AD stock may have diluted the voting *power* which had previously existed in the AC and AL stock—the usual consequence when additional voting stock is created—but the creation of the new class did not divest and separate the voting *rights* which remain vested in each AC and AL shareholder, together with the other attributes of the ownership of that stock. The fallacy of the plaintiff's position lies in his premise that since the voting power of the AC and AL stock was reduced by the creation of the AD stock, the percentage of reduction became the *res* of a voting trust. In any recapitalization involving the creation of additional voting stock, the voting power of the previously existing stock is diminished; but a voting trust is not necessarily the result.

Since the holders of the Class AC and Class AL stock of the Company did not separate the voting rights from the other attributes of ownership of those classes when they created the Class AD stock, the first *Abercrombie* test of a voting trust is not met.

This conclusion disposes of the second and third *Abercrombie* tests, i.e., that the voting rights granted are irrevocable for a definite period of time, and that the principal object of the grant of voting rights is voting control of the corporation. Having held that the AC and AL stockholders have not divested themselves of their voting rights, although they may have diluted their voting powers, we do not reach the remaining *Abercrombie* tests, both of which assume the divestiture of voting rights.

In the final analysis, the essence of the question raised by the plaintiff in this connection is this: Is the substance and purpose of the AD stock arrangement sufficiently close to the substance and purpose of § 218 to warrant its being subjected to the restrictions and conditions imposed by that Statute? The answer is negative not only for the reasons above stated, but also because § 218 regulates trusts and pooling agreements amounting to trusts, not other and different types of arrangements and undertakings possible among stockholders. . . . The AD stock arrangement is neither a trust nor a pooling agreement.

We hold, therefore, that the Class AD stock arrangement is not controlled by the Voting Trust Statute.

II

The plaintiff's second point is that even if the Class AD stock arrangement is not a voting trust in substance and effect, the AD stock is illegal, nevertheless, because the creation of a class of stock having voting rights only, and lacking any substantial participating proprietary interest in the corporation, violates the public policy of this State as declared in § 218.

The fallacy of this argument is twofold: First, it is more accurate to say that what the law has disfavored, and what the public policy underlying the Voting Trust Statute means to control, is the separation of the vote from the stock—not from the stock ownership.... Clearly, the AD stock arrangement is not violative of that public policy. Secondly, there is nothing in § 218, either expressed or implied, which requires that all stock of a Delaware corporation must have both voting rights and proprietary interests. Indeed, public policy to the contrary seems clearly expressed by 8 Del.C. § 151(a)[5] which authorizes, in very broad terms, such voting powers and participating rights as may be stated in the certificate of incorporation. Non-voting stock is specifically authorized by § 151(a); and in the light thereof, consistency does not permit the conclusion, urged by the plaintiff, that the present public policy of this State condemns the separation of voting rights from beneficial stock ownership....

We conclude that the plaintiff's contention in this regard cannot withstand the force and effect of § 151(a). In our view, that Statute permits the creation of stock having voting rights only, as well as stock having property rights only. The voting powers and the participating rights of the Class AD stock being specified in the Company's certificate of incorporation, we are of the opinion that the Class AD stock is legal by virtue of § 151(a)....

We are told that if the AD stock arrangement is allowed thus to stand, our Voting Trust Statute will become a "dead letter" because it will be possible to evade and circumvent its purpose simply by issuing a class of non-participating voting stock, as was done here. We have three negative reactions to this argument:

First, it presupposes a divestiture of the voting rights of the AC and AL stock— an untenable supposition as has been stated. Secondly, it fails to take into account the main purpose of a Voting Trust Statute: to avoid secret, uncontrolled combinations of stockholders formed to acquire voting control of the corporation to the possible detriment of non-participating shareholders.... It may not be said that the AD stock arrangement contravenes that purpose. Finally on this point, if we misconceive the legislative intent, and if the AD stock arrangement in this case reveals a loophole

---

5. 8 Del.C. § 151(a) provides:
"§ 151. Classes and series of stock; rights, etc.
(a) Every corporation may issue one or more classes of stock or one or more series of stock within any class thereof, any or all of which classes may be of stock with par value or stock without par value, with such voting powers, full or limited, or without voting powers and in such series and with such designations, preferences and relative, participating, optional or other special rights, and qualifications, limitations or restrictions thereof, as shall be stated and expressed in the certificate of incorporation or of any amendment thereto, or in the resolution or resolutions providing for the issue of such stock adopted by the board of directors pursuant to authority expressly vested in it by the provisions of the certificate of incorporation or of any amendment thereto...."

in § 218 which should be plugged, it is for the General Assembly to accomplish — not for us to attempt by interstitial judicial legislation.

III

The plaintiff advances yet another reason for invalidating the AD stock. The essence of this argument is that the only function of that class of stock is to break directorial deadlocks; that the issuance of the AD stock is merely a technical device to permit that result; that, as such, it is illegal because it permits the AC and AL directors of the Company to delegate their statutory duties to the AD director as an arbitrator.

We see nothing inherently wrong or contrary to the public policy of this State, as plaintiff seems to suggest, about a device, otherwise lawful, designed by the stockholders of a corporation to break deadlocks of directors. The plaintiff says in this connection, that if public policy sanctioned such device, our General Corporation Law would provide for it. The fallacy of this argument lies in the assumption that legislative silence is a dependable indicator of public policy. We know of no reason either under our statutes or our decisions, which would prevent the stockholders of a Delaware corporation from protecting themselves and their corporation, by a plan otherwise lawful, against the paralyzing and often fatal consequences of a stalemate in the directorate of the corporation. We hold, therefore, that the AD stock arrangement had a proper purpose.

As to the means adopted for the accomplishment of that purpose, we find the AD stock arrangement valid by virtue of § 141(a) of the Delaware Corporation Law which provides:

> "The business of every corporation organized under the provisions of this chapter shall be managed by a board of directors, except as hereinafter or in its certificate of incorporation otherwise provided."

The AD stock arrangement was created by the unanimous action of the stockholders of the Company by amendment to the certificate of incorporation. The stockholders thereby provided how the business of the corporation is to be managed, as is their privilege and right under § 141(a). It was this stockholder action which delegated to the AD director whatever powers and duties he possesses; they were not delegated to him by his fellow directors, either out of their own powers and duties, or otherwise.

It is settled, of course, as a general principle, that directors may not delegate their duty to manage the corporate enterprise. But there is no conflict with that principle where, as here, the delegation of duty, if any, is made not by the directors but by stockholder action under § 141(a), via the certificate of incorporation.

In our judgment, therefore, the AD stock arrangement is not invalid on the ground that it permits the AC and AL directors of the Company to delegate their statutory duties to the AD director.

On this point, the plaintiff relies mainly upon the Chancery Court decision in *Abercrombie v. Davies,* 35 Del.Ch. 599, 611, 123 A.2d 893 (1956). There, in considering an agreement requiring all eight directors to submit a disputed question to an arbitrator if seven were unable to agree, the Chancery Court stated that legal sanction may not be accorded to an agreement, at least when made by less than all the stockholders, which takes from the board of directors the power of determining substantial management policy. The plaintiff's reliance is misplaced, because, *inter alia,* the *Abercrombie* arrangement was not created by the certificate of incorporation, within the authority of § 141(a). . . .

Our conclusions upon these questions make it unnecessary to discuss the defendants' contentions that the plaintiff's action is barred by the principles of estoppel, laches, acquiescence and ratification.

Finding no error in the judgment below, it is affirmed.

Questions

1. What is the definition of a voting trust that the Supreme Court of Delaware adopts in *Lehrman v. Cohen*? Is it similar to or different from the one adopted in *Ringling Bros. v. Ringling*?

2. Is the decision in *Lehrman* privileging form or substance?

3. What are the policy considerations underlying the decision?

4. What do you think of Danzansky's conduct?

5. The last part of the decision dealt with the power of shareholders in closely held corporations actively to participate in managing the affairs of the corporation. We will return to this topic in the following section.

6. As you will learn in Part 4 of the casebook, the decision in *Lehrman* served as important precedent in the development of the poison pill—an antitakeover device. The Delaware Supreme Court in *Moran v. Household International* relied on *Lehrman* to justify the board's power to create poison pills, which give shareholders voting rights separate from economic interest.

7. Giant Food began a new era in American history. Until 1935, most food stores were small and had high markups. Giant founders, Nehemiah M. Cohen and Samuel Lehrman, replaced high markups with high volume—a novel approach at the time. They believed that a large self-service store that would sell a lot of goods could keep prices low and still make profit. They opened the first Giant store in February 1936 on Georgia Avenue in Washington, D.C. Within a year, Washington area food prices were down 35%. The first store outside Washington was opened in Arlington, Virginia, in 1941. In the 1950s, Giant Food added automatic doors, mechanized checkouts, and open display cases for meat and frozen food, setting standards for supermarkets across the nation. By 1959, with 53 Giant stores, the company began computerizing its customer data, inventory, and the like. In 1962 it opened its first Food/Drug combination.

After the Supreme Court of Delaware refused to invalidate the AD stock, Lehrman continued to sit on the Giant board, and Giant was enormously successful under Danzansky's leadership. (The company is now owned by Ahold Delhaize, a multinational corporation headquartered in the Netherlands.) The Lehrmans didn't suffer financially either. In 1993, *The Washington Post* reported that Sam Lehrman was building "what may be the largest house in Washington" (but raising a hue and cry among the neighbors in his quiet part of town). At the time, he and Israel Cohen were the company's two voting shareholders.

Oceanic Exploration Company v. Grynberg
428 A.2d 1 (Del. 1981)

QUILLEN, Justice

This appeal comes before this Court on a challenge to an interlocutory order. Notwithstanding the stage of the proceedings, however, the case already has a lengthy legal history in the Court of Chancery and has been the subject of two lengthy opinions by the Vice Chancellor. . . . We rely heavily on the opinions below for the statement of the facts and the statement of the issues before us.

Plaintiffs, individually and as trustees, are the owners of 76 per cent of the outstanding stock of the defendant Oceanic Exploration Company (Oceanic). In particular, the beneficial ownership of the stock interest is with Jack J. Grynberg and members of his family, the majority shareholder group. On February 10, 1976, plaintiffs entered into a written agreement whereby 51 per cent of the company's stock was placed into a "voting trust agreement" which gave their voting rights in the stock to others. The "voting trust agreement" was to expire four years later on February 9, 1980.

On June 2, 1976 this "voting trust agreement" was "amended," again by written instrument, as a result of which all of plaintiffs' stock, 76 per cent of the company's stock, totaling some 5,222,558 shares, was placed in this trust. The "Amendment to Voting Trust Agreement and Purchase Option Agreement" took the form of an agreement between the depositing shareholders and the corporation. It was not signed by the voting trustees. The June 2 instrument also added to the "voting trust agreement" an option in favor of the corporation which gave it the right for a period of 5 years to purchase "all or any part" of plaintiffs' stock. The term of the trust was amended to correspond with the option period ending 5 years from June 2, 1976. The purchase price under the option was fixed at $2.87 per share (or one-half of the then current market price of the stock) for the first year, with this price increasing by 10 per cent on each anniversary date thereafter for the term of the option. The agreement further provides that during the term of the option plaintiffs may not "sell, hypothecate, pledge or otherwise encumber said shares of their interests therein." The "amendment" also required Grynberg to resign as a Director and Chairman of the Board and from positions with subsidiaries, to release the company from an employment contract, and to agree not to compete with the company to a substantial extent. It further recited a general plan for the internal management of the company including a proposal to enlarge the Board of Directors. The voting trustees were to possess and be entitled "to exercise all stockholders' rights of every kind." It is fair to say that the "amendment" radically changed the nature of the agreement. Indeed, in substance it was not the same agreement.

Basically this lawsuit, filed on October 26, 1976, involves plaintiffs' attempt to have the "voting trust agreement and purchase option agreement" declared void so as to regain control of the corporation. The pre-trial attack thus far has had several prongs.

The plaintiffs first moved for summary judgment on the theory that the agreements were invalid because they imposed an illegal restraint on their right to alienate their stock interests. The Court below rejected this attack at the summary judgment stage. It is not presently before us.

Some twenty-one months after the filing of the complaint, on July 11, 1978, by a second motion for partial summary judgment, plaintiffs mounted a threefold attack upon the validity of the trust. They took the position that, first, the June 2 agreement was invalid since it attempted, not within two years prior to the time of the expiration of the February agreement, to extend the duration of a voting trust in violation of 8 Del.C. § 218(b).[1] Second, they argued that no voting trust was validly constituted by the June 2 agreement since it called for a deposit of some shares into the trust which, at the time, were held by others as a pledge of security for debts of the corporation. Thus, the statutory requirement for a deposit of the stock could not occur.[2] Third, plaintiffs took the position that even if the first two impediments could be overcome, they, comprising all the settlors, nonetheless effectively terminated any voting trust by a letter of revocation sent by them to the corporation and the defendant voting trustees under date of October 15, 1976.

---

1. 8 Del. C. § 218(b) provides:
"(b) At any time within 2 years prior to the time of expiration of any voting trust agreement as originally fixed or as last extended as provided in this subsection, 1 or more beneficiaries of the trust under the voting trust agreement may, by written agreement and with the written consent of the voting trustee or trustees, extend the duration of the voting trust agreement for an additional period not exceeding 10 years from the expiration date of the trust as originally fixed or as last extended, as provided in this subsection. . . ."

2. 8 Del.C. § 218(a) provides:
"(a) One or more stockholders may by agreement in writing deposit capital stock of an original issue with or transfer capital stock to any person or persons, or corporation or corporations authorized to act as trustee, for the purpose of vesting in such person or persons, corporation or corporations, who may be designated voting trustee, or voting trustees, the right to vote thereon for any period of time determined by such agreement, not exceeding 10 years, upon the terms and conditions stated in such agreement. . . . [C]ertificates of stock shall be issued to the voting trustee or trustees to represent any stock of an original issue so deposited with him or them. . . . The voting trustee or trustees may vote the stock so issued or transferred during the period specified in the agreement. . . ."

VC opinion

The Vice Chancellor found the "voting trust" portion of the agreement was governed by 8 Del.C. §218 and that the June 2 "extension" agreement was invalid in that it was executed in violation of extension restrictions of §218(b). As noted, extensions under the statute are only permitted within the last two years of the term of the voting trust.

The Vice Chancellor went on to hold that, since the June 2 agreement on its face showed the majority of the covered shares were pledged and thus were incapable of being deposited in the trust, the terms of the agreement violated the mandatory certificate deposit provisions of 8 Del.C. §218(a). Thus, for this additional reason, the Vice Chancellor concluded the June 2 agreement failed to create a valid statutory voting trust of the shares described therein. . . .

Oceanic brings this appeal arguing: (1) the June 2 agreement is not a §218 voting trust; (2) the June 2 agreement is validated by §218(e); and (3) the June 2 agreement must be validated by general principles of equity. The plaintiffs counter that the statutory provisions relating to voting trusts govern this case and the Trial Court should be affirmed.

Some financial background is necessary to understand the appeal. "By February 1976, Oceanic was in deep financial trouble, several large loans were overdue, and, as to one such loan, Morgan Guaranty Trust Company of New York had filed suit for recovery. It was at this point that the original voting trust concept was suggested and put into effect. Without going into the contested details at this point, it is sufficient to note that with the surrender of voting control of the corporation to three outside directors by means of the voting trust, Morgan Guaranty Trust Company withdrew its lawsuit and extended the loan."

While the Vice Chancellor found it unnecessary to go into the facts surrounding the execution of the June 2 document, it should be noted generally that the background facts and the reasons for the execution of that document are hotly contested and indeed constitute the heart of the dispute between the opposing sides, at least factually. The company says that, despite the February agreement, Grynberg remained in control and the financial situation worsened. As summarized in the appellants' brief, the company was on the brink of bankruptcy, was failing to meet its obligations, was facing a renewal of the Morgan suit, and was threatened by a minority shareholder suit. It was in this atmosphere, the company says, that Grynberg and his family, fully advised, entered the June 2 agreement relinquishing control and granting the option in exchange for valuable benefits including indemnity for large liabilities. Having reaped the benefit of the contract debt elimination and stock resurrection, the company says Grynberg now seeks to escape his legitimate burden under the contract.

Plaintiffs' view is different. They say they were given 24 hours notice to agree to changes in the February agreement on the fraudulent representations that a partner in a Greek venture was willing to purchase a certain interest in a Greek concession, sufficient to solve the company's financial crisis, if the amendments were made. This fraudulent inducement appears to be the major contention of the original complaint.

The Vice Chancellor, with customary precision, isolated a threshold question, namely: Is the "voting trust agreement" here governed by § 218? He concluded that it was and, in so doing, as a matter of law, voided the trust for the reasons noted above, thereby eliminating the conflicting factual equities argued by the parties as to the voting trust. He did not disturb at this stage the option in the June 2 agreement. We are unable to agree to that disposition and therefore we are compelled to reverse. But we do not do so with ease and we candidly find our position difficult to express and regretfully perhaps less clear than the view so positively expressed below. Stated as directly and simply as possible, there are prominent facts which weigh against our conclusion. The February and June agreements were expressly labeled "VOTING TRUST AGREEMENT" and "AMENDMENT TO VOTING TRUST AGREEMENT AND PURCHASE OPTION AGREEMENT" and both were filed in the registered office of the corporation in Delaware as required by § 218(a). The description used and action taken by the parties thus brings the role of statute directly into play.

While the statute, § 218(a) and (b) does not expressly state it is exclusive, the case law rather pointedly supports the view that § 218 of the Delaware General Corporation Law provides the exclusive method for creating voting trusts of stock of a Delaware corporation. . . .

But our decision can neither rest blindly on the form elected by the parties to the June agreement without regard to the substance of the whole contract nor on the exclusivity of the statute without regard to its scope or intended purpose. Deciding the case on such bases would constitute an abstraction divorced from the facts of the case and the intent of the law. The term voting trust as used in our law is a concept which flows from our statute and is specifically defined by our statute and case law. See, e.g., *Abercrombie,* 130 A.2d at 344. Case comment as to statutory exclusivity has to be related to that definition. In determining the applicability of § 218(a) and (b), the test is whether the substance and purpose of the stock arrangement is "sufficiently close to the substance and the purpose of [the statute] to warrant its being subject to the restrictions and conditions imposed by that statute". *Lehrman v. Cohen,* Del.Supr., 222 A.2d 800, 806 (1966). As did the Vice Chancellor, we take a frontal tack and direct our attention to the same threshold question. Is the voting trust arrangement here governed by § 218(a) and (b)?

Without attempting to resolve factual disputes, we note the defendant alleges, with some record support, evidence of the following factors:

(1) The final overall contract is one of internal corporate reorganization with integrated portions of which the voting trust is merely one.

(2) The final contract here, including the voting trust feature, is an agreement between the majority shareholder group and the corporation.

(3) While the voting trust portion of the contract is important, it is basically an enforcement provision to a purchase option agreement involving the sale of the majority interest and incidents connected with such sale such as change in management and an agreement not to compete.

(4) The contract is open and notorious within the corporation. Not only was the contract with the corporation itself and not only did it occasion fundamental changes in corporate management but it was prominently featured and positively represented in the proxy statement dated October 14, 1976 and in the 1975 annual report. The operations of the company and the involvement of minority shareholders, officers and employees proceeded in reliance on the contract.

(5) The contract serves a valid corporate purpose, being designed to end financial hardship, and perhaps to end financial ruin.

(6) The contract has been significantly performed by the corporation, its officers and employees.

(7) A substantial benefit has been conferred on the depositing majority shareholder group.

(8) The contemplated benefit to the corporation and the minority shareholders remains largely executory.

(9) The party seeking a declaration that the agreement is void is the depositing majority shareholder group itself.

In such a factual setting, if established or substantially established at trial, we do not find that the Vice Chancellor should be legally prohibited from specifically enforcing the "voting trust agreement" in issue here as a consequence of the statutory provisions contained in § 218(a) and (b).[5] Our reasons are simple: statutory language, statutory purpose and public policy.

First, even viewed historically, § 218, from its original enactment in 1925, was designed to regulate agreements by "[o]ne or more stockholders". Not all trusts of

---

5. Obviously, on the defendant's version of the facts, the equities lie totally in the defendant's favor. We have considered several other possible legal approaches on the possibility that the defendant would prevail in the factual disputes. For example, consideration was given to recognizing the general intent of the parties to form a valid voting trust and permitting the Vice Chancellor to frame the precise mechanics; but this approach seems to run counter to both our voting trust law and our rather strict law of contract reformation.... Moreover, in the statutory voting trust area, our courts have not generally, nor specifically with relation to illegal time extensions or inability to make stock deposits, been inclined to weigh equities or characterize the illegality as merely *malum prohibitum*. Finally, equitable principles of restitution, estoppel and unclean hands are not particularly helpful in face of case law declaring non-complying voting trusts regulated by the statute to be void. While we are not here called upon to foreclose and do not foreclose consideration of any such approach, all of these indirect approaches seem to us an attempt to hide the real issue which is consequently disclosed and emphasized. Is the "voting trust agreement" in this case the type of agreement the General Assembly intended to regulate in § 218(a) and (b)? Thus, as indicated, we take the frontal approach and address that issue directly.

corporate stock which, either expressly or by implication, give voting rights to a trustee are voting trusts. As was noted in *Fixman v. Diversified Industries, Inc.*, Del. Ch., 1 Del.J. Corp.Law 171, 178–79 (1975), the statutory language contemplates an association of stockholders whether it be created by way of individual agreements or joint agreements. The Court of Chancery defined a voting trust in *Peyton v. William C. Peyton Corp.,* Del.Ch., 194 A. 106, 111 (1937), *rev'd on other grounds*, Del. Supr., 7 A.2d 737 (1939) in the following manner:

> "A voting trust as commonly understood is a device whereby two or more persons owning stock with voting powers, divorce the voting rights thereof from the ownership, retaining to all intents and purposes the latter in themselves and transferring the former to trustees in whom the voting rights of all the depositors in the trust are pooled."

This definition has been adopted in several cases. Regulation of voting trusts is directed to a class of trusts created to unify voting. . . . "At the bottom of a voting trust is an agreement among stockholders. . . ."

Thus, the voting trust statute was not intended to be all inclusive in the sense that it was designed to apply to every set of facts in which voting rights are transferred to trustees incident to or as part of the assignment of other stockholder rights. Rather, a voting trust is a stockholder pooling arrangement with the criteria that voting rights are separated out and irrevocably assigned for a definite period of time to voting trustees for control purposes while other attributes of ownership are retained by the depositing stockholders. *Lehrman,* 222 A.2d at 805. . . . While we do not suggest that the mere fact that the corporation is a party removes a trust from the statute, we do find that the final contract in issue here, with its multi-faceted aspects including a stock purchase option agreement running from an already unified majority shareholder group to the corporation may be so foreign to the stockholder voting trust agreement to which the language used by the General Assembly was directed that it is beyond the contemplated scope of the statute. Given the scope of this agreement it may be that the voting rights are not separated from the other retained attributes of ownership. In short, the agreement here may not be a voting trust as that term is used in our law.

Second, our case law makes it clear that the main purpose of a voting trust statute is "to avoid secret, uncontrolled combinations of stockholders formed to acquire control of the corporation to the possible detriment of non-participating shareholders." *Lehrman,* 222 A.2d at 807. The contract involved in this case, given the factual contentions of the defendants, may be so far divorced from that purpose that it makes the contemplated regulation unnecessary and irrelevant.

Third, it is important to recognize there has been a significant change from the days of our original 1925 statute. Voting trusts were viewed with "disfavor" or "looked upon . . . with indulgence" by the courts. Other contractual arrangements interfering with stock ownership, such as irrevocable proxies, were viewed with suspicion. The desire for flexibility in modern society has altered such restrictive thinking. The trend of liberalization was markedly apparent in the 1967 changes to our own § 218.

Voting or other agreements and irrevocable proxies were given favorable treatment and restrictive judicial interpretations as to the absolute voiding of voting trusts for terms beyond the statutory limit were changed by statute.[8] The trend was not to extend the voting trust restrictions beyond the class of trust being regulated and beyond the reasons for statutory regulation. That public policy cannot be ignored here.

Thus we are faced with a "voting trust agreement" which: (1) may not fit into the situation contemplated by the language of the restrictive statute, (2) may have little, if any, connection with the purpose for which the statute was enacted, and (3) may have no evil or improper aspects under any current ascertainable public policy. Given such circumstances, we are hard pressed to see why § 218(a) and (b) should be a legal bar to a factual inquiry and a discretionary consideration by the Court of Chancery of full enforcement of the contract in this case. We conclude the Vice Chancellor erred in holding the voting trust aspect of the contract in this case to be, as a matter of law, a § 218(a) and (b) voting trust.

The interlocutory order of the Court of Chancery is reversed and the case is remanded.

Questions

1. What was the purpose of the agreement in question in *Oceanic v. Grynberg*? Why was it modified?

2. What is the definition of a voting trust that the court adopts in *Oceanic*? What are the court's policy considerations?

3. What is the significance of the list of factors the court examines in concluding that the agreement in question was not a voting trust? Which, if any of them, has relevance to the policy concerns courts (and the Delaware Supreme Court in this decision) have expressed with respect to voting trusts?

4. After *Oceanic v. Grynberg*, when is a voting trust not a voting trust?

---

8. 8 Del.C. § 218(c), (d) and (e) provide:

"(c) An agreement between 2 or more stockholders, if in writing and signed by the parties thereto, may provide that in exercising any voting rights, the shares held by them shall be voted as provided by the agreement, or as the parties may agree, or as determined in accordance with a procedure agreed upon by them. No such agreement shall be effective for a term or [sic] more than 10 years, but, at any time within 2 years prior to the time of the expiration of such agreement, the parties may extend its duration for as many additional periods, each not to exceed 10 years, as they may desire.

(d) The validity of any such voting trust or other voting agreement, otherwise lawful, shall not be affected during a period of 10 years from the date when it was created or last extended by the fact that under its terms it will or may last beyond the 10 year period.

(e) This section shall not be deemed to invalidate any voting or other agreement among stockholders or any irrevocable proxy which is not otherwise illegal."

5. Note the court's self-consciousness in holding as it does. It states with respect to the Chancellor's holding: "We are unable to agree to that disposition and therefore we are compelled to reverse. But we do not do so with ease and we candidly find our position difficult to express and regretfully perhaps less clear than the view so positively expressed below. Stated as directly and simply as possible, there are prominent facts which weigh against our conclusion." Given this admission, wouldn't it have been more appropriate for the court to have explicitly overruled prior case law? If a court can't give clear reasoning for its conclusion (and admits it), is the decision really legitimate?

6. After *Lehrman v. Cohen* and *Oceanic v. Grynberg*, what is left of section 218?

The following case deals with a buy-sell provision in an agreement among shareholders. As you read the case, think about the importance of such provisions. Think also about the appropriate method of valuing stock in closely held corporations.

Rosiny v. Schmidt
185 A.D.2d 727 (N.Y. 1992)

[Facts have been taken from the dissenting opinion: In 1941, Charles L. McGuire, Theodore A. Schmidt and Max Levy became shareholders in C.L. McGuire & Co., Inc., pursuant to an agreement apparently drafted by the law firm of Lindenaur and Rosiny. Edward Rosiny, the plaintiffs' father, was a member of that firm. C.L. McGuire & Co. operated an automobile repair business in a building located at 14–16 West End Avenue in Manhattan ("the premises"). In 1957, an opportunity arose to purchase the premises, and Ched Realty was formed for that purpose. The initial shareholders of Ched were Edward Rosiny, who owned 20 shares; and Charles McGuire and Theodore Schmidt, who owned 10 shares apiece. Edward Rosiny was one of the incorporators, and his law office was listed as the address to be used by the Secretary of State for service of process.

On January 24, 1957, the shareholders entered into an agreement which provided as here pertinent that none of them could sell or transfer their shares without first offering the remaining shareholders the option to purchase at the price of $100 per share or the book value thereof, and in such case the purchasing shareholders would also have to pay back the corporation's loan indebtedness to the retiring shareholder. Upon the death of any shareholder, the representative of his estate was required to offer his shares for sale to the remaining shareholders under the same terms, and the offeree shareholders were obligated to purchase the shares. The automobile repair business continued to operate on the premises until it ceased to do business in 1963.

The original shareholders continued their ownership in Ched until 1964, when plaintiffs' father Edward Rosiny transferred his 20 shares to his wife, Annabelle Rosiny. There is no documentation or testimony to show that there was formal compliance with the provision of the original agreement that the shares had to be offered to the other shareholders before a transfer could be made to a third party. Nevertheless, Charles McGuire and Theodore Schmidt executed a new agreement on October 19, 1964, with Annabelle Rosiny, who signed it as the holder of 20 shares. The 1964 agreement differed from the initial agreement in that the offering price for the sale of shares was modified to provide that "any real property owned by the corporation shall be evaluated at the then fair market value of such real property in place and instead of the value ascribed thereto on the books of the corporation."

The next change in the Ched shareholders arose from the death of Theodore Schmidt. The Surrogate found that while it was "not definitively established" that Edward Rosiny represented Theodore Schmidt's widow Jeannette Priddy (then Schmidt) with regard to her husband's estate or his interest in Ched, four letters on Edward Rosiny's legal stationery dealing with Schmidt's interest in Ched were introduced in evidence. A new shareholders' agreement executed on June 10, 1971, listed Jeannette Schmidt as owner of the shares previously held by her husband. The 1971 agreement differed from the 1964 agreement in that the price at which the shares had to be offered reverted back to the 1957 provision of "book value" which, I note, was not defined in any of the shareholders' agreements, past or future. When Edward Rosiny forwarded the new agreement to Jeannette Priddy, he wrote: "Also enclosed please find Certificate No. 7 for ten shares of stock of Ched Realty Corp. issued to you. The same is in replacement of the shares of stock of said firm heretofore owned by your late husband, Gus, which you inherited as the sole legatee under his will."

At this point in relating the background to the instant litigation, it is important to identify Jacob Kwalwasser, Ched's accountant. Kwalwasser was a friend of the plaintiffs, Allen and Frank Rosiny, and their parents, Edward and Annabelle Rosiny, since the 1940s, and was a distant relative of the Rosiny family. He performed accounting services for Edward and Annabelle Rosiny, and from the 1970s until his death in 1985, he managed Ched, collecting rents, and paying bills and taxes. He negotiated a lease with Ched's only tenant, and that lease was drafted by Allen Rosiny. Frank Rosiny drafted Kwalwasser's will, and either the plaintiffs' law firm, Rosiny & Rosiny, or Frank Rosiny individually, was the attorney for the executrix of Kwalwasser's estate. The Surrogate concluded that Kwalwasser's "primary allegiance was to plaintiffs' family," rather than to Charles McGuire and Jeannette Priddy.

The heart of this dispute had its genesis in the following events which occurred in 1981. At that time, Allen Rosiny was 36 years old. He had been practicing law for 11 years, after graduating Harvard Law School with honors, and he had been an associate in several prestigious law firms from 1970 to 1979. Frank Rosiny was 41 years old. He had been practicing law for 17 years, after graduating Columbia Law School, and he was formerly a partner at a prestigious law firm. By contrast, Charles McGuire was 80 years old. He had a grade school education, had been retired for 17 years, and had been drinking liquor at the rate of a bottle a day for some years. His mental condition was "not good." Jeannette Priddy was 74 years old. She had a partial high school education, had worked as a waitress, and a bookkeeper, and was preoccupied with the death of her second husband, Harry Priddy, on April 25, 1981.

In the spring of 1981, Kwalwasser telephoned Allen Rosiny and asked if Allen or Frank would be interested in acquiring their mother's shares of Ched stock if the consent of the other shareholders (Priddy and McGuire) could be obtained. Allen testified that Kwalwasser made this suggestion "for income tax reasons, my mother being a very high marginal rate, it would make sense to shift that income [then $2,400 annually] from my mother to my brother and I [sic]." Allen and Frank Rosiny each paid their mother $10,000 for a one-quarter interest in Ched. Jeannette Priddy and Charles McGuire apparently trusted Kwalwasser and the Rosinys, because without seeking legal advice, they agreed to the stock transfers. At Kwalwasser's request, Allen Rosiny drew up a new agreement whereby he and Frank each became the owner of 10 shares of Ched. The new agreement incorporated the provisions of the 1971 agreement in all essential respects, including the stock transfer provisions.]

Memorandum Decision

Order, Surrogate's Court, Bronx County (Lee Holzman, S.), entered on or about November 19, 1990, which, after a non-jury trial, *inter alia,* dismissed the complaint and granted the defendants' counterclaim for a declaratory judgment to the extent of declaring that the plaintiffs have no right, pursuant to a shareholders' agreement dated June 30, 1981, to purchase shares held by the defendants' decedents at the time of their deaths and that said shares may pass pursuant to the terms of the decedents' wills, modified, on the law and the facts, the complaint is reinstated and judgment is awarded thereon to the plaintiffs directing specific performance of the 1981 agreement, the defendants' counterclaim for a declaratory judgment is denied, and the order is otherwise affirmed, without costs.

The Surrogate erred in concluding that the post-mortem buyout provision of the 1981 Ched shareholders' agreement was unenforceable.

The record fails to support the defendants' initial contention that the agreement was unconscionable. "A determination of unconscionability generally requires a showing that the contract was both procedurally and substantively unconscionable when made—i.e., 'some showing of an "absence of meaningful choice on the part of one of the parties together with contract terms which are unreasonably favorable to the other party."'" . . .

Central to the defendants' claim of unconscionability is the fact that at the time the 1981 agreement was entered into, the plaintiffs were young attorneys and the defendants' decedents, McGuire and Priddy, were elderly and less educated. The record, however, reveals that this was the fourth Ched shareholders' agreement and the only one to which the plaintiffs were signatories. With the exception of one agreement in 1964 which contained a market value-based post-mortem buyout provision, which was later discarded, the others all provided for a book value formula to determine the value of a decedent's shares.

Priddy, a former bookkeeper who was later an office manager, was a signatory to a 1971 agreement wherein the shareholders agreed to return to a book value formula after the 1964 agreement, signed by her husband and containing a fair market value approach, was abandoned. McGuire, who ran a successful business for many years, executed not only the 1981 agreement but also three others containing book value buyout provisions. He had been a party to the 1964 agreement containing the thereafter rejected market value-based formula and the subsequent 1971 agreement returning to the book value approach. In fact the 1941 shareholders' agreement of C.L. McGuire & Co., Inc., to which McGuire and Priddy's first husband, Theodore Schmidt, were parties, contained such a book value buyout provision. Neither of the plaintiffs, nor either of their parents whose interest in Ched they succeeded, were party to that agreement.

The 1981 agreement is simple and straightforward, and provides that shareholders will not, during their lifetime, "sell, assign, transfer, pledge or hypothecate either all or any part" of their stock unless it is first offered to the other shareholders. The parties agreed that "[t]he price at which said stock shall be offered for sale shall be the book value thereof as of the last day of the month immediately preceding the date of the said offer or $200 per share, whichever amount is greater." With regard to post-mortem transfers, the agreement provided for the surviving shareholders to buy the decedents' shares at the same price applicable to transfers during their lifetime.

Any claim that the Rosinys or the accountant Kwalwasser exerted deceptive or high-pressured tactics to induce the decedents to sign the 1981 agreement is not borne out by the record. Nor were the plaintiffs the draftsmen of the 1981 agreement as the defendants allege. The 1981 agreement contained the identical post-mortem buyout provision as the 1971 agreement, and was only changed to reflect the plaintiffs as the new owners of their mother's shares, a change to which the decedents consented.

Nor does the record support the implication that because of the disparity in age and educational background, the decedents were deceived by the young attorneys. There is nothing to indicate that the decedents were unaware of the provisions of the 1981 agreement they signed, particularly since they executed an agreement with the identical buyout provision ten years earlier, an agreement to which the plaintiffs were not parties. It may not nor should it be presumed that because one is of a certain advanced age that a contract is void or even voidable.

While the $200 per share buyout provision pertains to shares worth considerably more, "the validity of the restriction on transfer does not rest on any abstract notion of intrinsic fairness of price. To be invalid, more than mere disparity between option price and current value of the stock must be shown."

"[W]hen parties set down their agreement in a clear, complete document, their writing should as a rule be enforced according to its terms." Moreover, "a mistake, as to the legal effect of an agreement, or as to the legal results of an act, cannot avail to defeat a specific performance."

Also to be noted is that the 1981 agreement provided for its termination by the sale of the property or by the voluntary or involuntary dissolution of the corporation. Priddy and McGuire owned fifty percent of the shares in Ched and had the option of selling the property or dissolving the corporation. In fact, both options were considered by the decedents. In 1987, a broker had a potential buyer for the property. At a subsequent shareholders' meeting held at McGuire's home, where both McGuire and Priddy's interests were represented by counsel and family members, Priddy's representatives agreed to have an appraisal made of the property before a sale was seriously considered. However, an appraisal was never obtained. Priddy's attorney thereafter wrote to McGuire's attorneys suggesting the dissolution of Ched but the parties never followed through. Despite representation by counsel, neither Priddy nor McGuire opted to sell the property or dissolve the corporation during the seven years following their execution of the 1981 agreement, of which their counsel were aware.

In sum, the record fails to support the absence of meaningful choice on the decedents' part in executing the 1981 agreement. Accordingly, the agreement was not unconscionable.

Nor is there support in the record for the conclusion that there was no meeting of the minds with respect to the term "book value." The dissent maintains that while the plaintiffs understood the meaning of the term when they signed the 1981 agreement, Priddy and McGuire did not, as demonstrated by "surrounding circumstances." However, these circumstances demonstrate that Priddy and McGuire had signed a 1971 agreement containing the identical buyout provision after rejecting a fair market value approach contained in an earlier agreement. The return to the use of "book value," an unambiguous term, from fair market value, as well as the use of this term in previous agreements, evinces a meeting of the minds as to this term of the agreement.

The defendants further maintain that the plaintiffs, as attorneys and fellow shareholders in a closely held corporation, owed a fiduciary duty to the decedents and that they breached this duty by failing to discuss the efficacy of the buyout provision with them. As the Surrogate found, the proof supports the plaintiffs' position that they did not act as attorneys for the decedents in any Ched transaction.

While it is true that in a close corporation, shareholders must deal in good faith in the conduct of the affairs of the corporation, we are unaware of any dictate requiring one shareholder to explain a provision of a shareholders' agreement to another, particularly when the latter signed previous agreements containing the identical provision in question and the former did not. As of 1981, there had been virtually no contact between the plaintiffs and McGuire and they had never met Priddy. More importantly, as the Surrogate noted, the corporation did not engage in the type of business where there was a close working relationship among shareholders. No fiduciary duty is created by a shareholders' agreement containing a mandatory buyout provision.

The fact that the plaintiffs are attorneys and the decedents were not, does not of itself lead to the conclusion that any advantage was obtained by undue influence. It is not apparent from the positions they held that the plaintiffs possessed the power to induce the decedents to act against their own interest or that any control was exercised by them. Both Priddy and McGuire "were possessed of ordinary intelligence, could read and write, and had an opportunity to examine, or to have examined," the agreement.

Both had been represented by counsel. Those counsel were aware of the 1981 agreement and had reviewed it. Those counsel had actively advised their clients. Those counsel explored the possibility of dissolution proceedings for Ched. Those counsel considered a potential sale of the Ched real estate when a substantial offer was made by a broker representing a prospective purchaser. Those counsel were aware that Allen Rosiny was about to, and then had put up $40,000 of his own money to secure refinancing of a Ched mortgage which had come due, with no contribution by Priddy or McGuire. In these circumstances, the dissent's observations about fiduciary obligations are simply inapposite.

The dissent further finds that the buyout provision was abrogated by the conduct of the shareholders over the years and cites to the plaintiffs and their mother's succession to their shares without complying with the buyout provision. Contrary to the conclusion reached by the dissent, there was no violation of previous shareholders' agreements when the plaintiffs and their mother before them came into possession of their shares. The shareholders' agreements specifically provided that shareholders could modify the agreements by executing a superseding agreement. Every transfer of Ched stock was effected by formal compliance with the superseding agreement provision of the shareholders' agreements.

To establish abandonment of a contract by conduct, it must be shown that the conduct is mutual, positive, unequivocal, and inconsistent with the intent to be bound. The party who asserts abandonment has the burden of establishing it since the termination of a contract is not presumed. The defendants have failed to establish an intent to abandon the buyout provision of the shareholders' agreement.

In conclusion, the post-mortem buyout provision of the 1981 agreement is enforceable and the plaintiffs are entitled to specific performance of its terms.

We have considered the parties' remaining contentions and find them to be without merit.

CARRO, Justice (dissenting)

... It does not require a great deal of acumen to understand the significance of what occurred when Jeannette Priddy and Charles McGuire executed the new shareholders' agreement on June 30, 1981. At the time the agreement was signed, Priddy's and McGuire's interests were each worth in excess of $42,000* and gaining in value.

---

* The appraised fair market value of the premises owned by Ched was $235,000 as of June 30, 1981, and the mortgage balance was approximately $66,000. Dividing the $169,000 difference by 40, the number of outstanding shares, results in a per share price of $4,225.

But while the shares were gaining in *market* value, their *book* value was decreasing because of declared yearly depreciation of the premises on Ched's books. Thus, when the 1981 agreement was signed, Ched had a negative book value, and each share was redeemable for $200 upon the death of a shareholder. The death-buyout provision might be considered not oppressive with respect to the 1971 shareholders' agreement, even assuming that the parties understood the significance of book value, because the parties were of roughly equal age. But with the replacement of Annabelle Rosiny by her two sons as shareholders, the 1971 agreement underwent a substantial change, and became grossly one-sided, for the Rosinys, approximately 40 years younger, were virtually guaranteed to outlive Priddy and McGuire, and thus enjoy an unconscionable windfall. When the Surrogate asked Allen Rosiny whether he as a lawyer would ever advise a client in the position of McGuire or Priddy to consent to the 1981 agreement, he contended that he did not understand the questions, or evaded their significance, and never responded directly.

Returning to the chronology of events, on September 27, 1986 Mary Jane Lidaka, an attorney for Mrs. Priddy, wrote to Allen Rosiny requiring information regarding the net value and corporate assets and liabilities of Ched. Allen Rosiny forwarded to Ms. Lidaka the U.S. income tax return for the corporation for the year 1985. It appears that Mrs. Priddy had been exploring the possibility of transferring her shares in Ched to her two sons while retaining the right to receive the income. It further appears that she was advised by Ms. Lidaka that she could not effectuate a transfer without first offering the shares to the other shareholders.

In January, 1987, Cushman & Wakefield indicated that it had a buyer who was willing to purchase the premises that Ched owned for $1,250,000. As a result of this offer, a shareholders' meeting was held at Charles McGuire's home in the Bronx on January 31, 1987. Mrs. Priddy did not attend the meeting, but her son Ted, her son-in-law Bob Robinson (who was a real estate broker) and her attorney attended the meeting on her behalf. Both of the plaintiffs were present, as well as Mr. McGuire, his daughter, and his attorney. A letter dated February 4, 1987 from Mrs. Priddy's attorney to Mr. Robinson contains the opinion that "Frank was particularly abrupt and argumentative" and "Allen was equally evasive, but more pleasant." Plaintiffs testified that they did not express an opinion relative to the Cushman & Wakefield offer, and this is consistent with the statement in the February 4, 1987 letter of Mrs. Priddy's attorney that he did not know their position on the offer. The witnesses who testified about the events at this meeting confirmed that Mr. Robinson suggested that an appraisal be obtained for the property, and when the Rosinys refused to contribute toward the cost of an appraisal, it was agreed that he would either obtain it at no cost to the corporation, or any cost would be shared by Mrs. Priddy and Mr. McGuire. The outcome of the meeting was a general agreement that if Cushman & Wakefield made any further inquiries of Allen Rosiny, he would refer them to the attorney for Mr. McGuire, and the parties would await the appraisal before taking any further action. The appraisal was never obtained, and Cushman & Wakefield did not take any additional action toward effecting a sale of the premises. The attorney for Mrs. Priddy apparently believed that the plaintiffs had some hidden agenda, and in a February 5, 1987 letter to the attorney for Mr. McGuire stated that he was "exploring the possibility of a judicial dissolution of the corporation if the stockholders cannot agree to sell the property at a reasonable price."

The last communication between the plaintiffs and the other shareholders prior to their respective deaths related to satisfying an obligation of approximately $38,000 owed to Goldome Bank which was secured by a mortgage on Ched's real property. In December, 1987, Allen Rosiny was able to obtain a commercial loan from Banco Central to pay the Goldome obligation by promising to use the bank for Ched's accounts and by opening an account in the sum of $40,000 in his own name in that bank, and then assigning the account as security for the loan. Allen Rosiny testified that the other shareholders signed the necessary documents in connection with the loan only after their attorneys were assured that they would not be personally liable for the loan, and that he would not have used his own funds as security for the loan if he had known that the other shareholders did not intend to honor the provisions of the 1981 agreement.

Charles McGuire died on June 19, 1988, and Jeannette Priddy died on July 25, 1988. Allen Rosiny advised their estate representatives that Ched had a negative book value and referred them to the 1981 agreement for the purchase price, which was specified in the agreement as "the book value thereof ... or $200.00 per share, whichever amount is greater." When the estate representatives protested that the agreement was unconscionable (the fair market value was then $41,500 per share), the plaintiffs commenced the instant litigation to compel the estates to transfer the shares for $200 apiece. By December 1989, the premises had increased in value to $2,500,000, and each share was worth over $60,000.

It may be noted, since this is an action in equity, that aside from the Ched stock, the defendant estates are meager; neither deceased shareholder had any other stock, bonds or real estate, except for the residences in which they respectively lived. It bears repeating that the plaintiffs' mother, Annabelle Rosiny, was permitted by the deceased shareholders to obtain ownership of 20 shares, without reference to the buyout provisions of the agreement then in force. Likewise, in 1981 the plaintiffs obtained ownership of their 10 share interests without a word of protest from the deceased shareholders, or any reference to the buyout provisions of the agreement then in force. Nevertheless, the plaintiffs find nothing unconscionable in their obtaining nearly the entire corpus of the decedents' estates, worth over $800,000 at the time of their deaths, for $4,000. The Surrogate disagreed, and so do I.

At trial, Jeannette Priddy's son and Charles McGuire's daughter testified in support of their respective positions that their parents were unsophisticated, that they had trusted the Rosinys, and that they had not understood that they could not freely leave their interests in Ched to their children upon their deaths. Jeannette Priddy's son testified that his mother had worked as a waitress, that his father had worked as an automobile mechanic until he retired in the early 1960's, that his parents had moved 80 miles away from New York in 1964, that his mother continued to reside in this residence until her death and that she became a widow for the second time in 1981. He conceded that his mother had also worked as a bookkeeper prior to her marriage in 1925, and had corresponded with at least two attorneys about her interest in Ched. He nevertheless maintained that his mother had only met in person with an attorney on one occasion, and that she believed that only a lifetime transfer of her interest in Ched was restricted. His mother had indicated on more than one occasion that she intended to leave her interest in Ched to her two sons. A letter from his mother to her other son is consistent with this contention.

Charles McGuire's daughter had lived with him in his house in the Bronx for over 40 years. She testified that after his wife had died, and during the 1970's until the early 1980's, he often drank a bottle of alcohol a day, and was frequently drunk. On one occasion he told her that he would sign anything that the Rosinys sent. She recalled that Frank Rosiny had assured her father that everything would be okay when her father appeared concerned at the shareholders' meeting that was held in his home in January, 1987.

Two of the central issues presented in this case concern the doctrine of unconscionability, and whether there was a breach of a fiduciary relationship which existed among the parties. The Surrogate stated the plaintiffs' position on these issues as follows:

> Plaintiffs' interpretation of the proof is that their lack of involvement with the other shareholders precludes applying any principle of law based upon an attorney/client relationship. Turning around the admonition that the sins of the fathers may be visited upon their sons, they assert that even if their father had at one time or another acted as the attorney for the other shareholders, which they are not willing to concede, this has no bearing on their obligation to the other shareholders. The plaintiffs contend that the doctrine of unconscionability is inapplicable because their lack of involvement in the events leading up to the signing of the 1981 agreement precludes finding the existence of high pressure tactics and that without such a finding there was no procedural unfairness which must be established together with substantive unfairness before an agreement can be held to be unconscionable. Their final argument is that the other shareholders, at least by 1986 or 1987 when they obtained independent counsel relative to the affairs of the corporation, eventually had to have been apprised as to the meaning of the option provisions and that their estates should be estopped from not honoring these provisions when they had remained mute during their lifetimes and permitted Allen Rosiny, in reliance upon the provisions of the agreement, to use his own funds as security for a corporate obligation.

In analyzing the various actions and shifting relations among the parties past and present, it is apparent that insofar as their interests were adverse, the Rosiny family and their friend and accountant Jacob Kwalwasser were aligned on one side, while Theodore A. Schmidt, Jeannette Priddy and Charles McGuire stood on the other. The plaintiffs' attempt to distance themselves from the consequences of any actions of Kwalwasser and their predecessors in interest prior to 1981 simply does not withstand analysis in the circumstances presented herein.

It is well established in New York that fellow shareholders in a closely held corporation owe each other, and where applicable their estates, those duties and responsibilities found in fiduciary relationships, which include "a duty to deal fairly, in good faith, and with loyalty." "[I]n a close corporation, the relationship between the shareholders vis-à-vis each other is akin to that between partners [citations omitted]. The law exacts a high degree of fidelity and good faith in dealings between partners in the conduct of the affairs of the partnership. The same obligations are likewise applicable to shareholders in a close corporation."

... Even in the absence of a fiduciary relationship, where one party to a transaction deals from a position of "weakness, dependence, or trust justifiably reposed, unfair advantage in a transaction is rendered probable, there the burden is shifted, the transaction is presumed void, and it is incumbent upon the stronger party to show affirmatively that no deception was practiced, no undue influence was used, and that all was fair, open, voluntary and well understood. This doctrine is well settled."

These rules are closely related to the salutary and far-reaching principle that he who seeks equity [such as specific performance of a contract] must do equity. . . .

Evaluation of the underlying facts in this case . . . confirms the correctness of the Surrogate's conclusion that ordering specific performance of the 1981 agreement according to its literal terms would be inequitable, unduly harsh and oppressive upon the defendants, and unjust. Neither of the elderly lay shareholders was represented by counsel at the time the agreement was entered into, presumably because they trusted Kwalwasser, and the plaintiffs, whose father had served them as a counselor and advisor for more than 30 years. During the period from 1957 to 1988 none of the parties had adhered to the buyout provisions of the several shareholders' agreements in Ched. The practice prior to 1988 was that of permitting transfers within one's family without involving the right of first refusal that the other shareholders had. When Jeannette Priddy's first husband, Theodore Schmidt, died, Edward Rosiny wrote to her that the decision whether she should retain the Ched stock held by her husband was hers to make, and he later sent her a stock certificate "in replacement of the ten shares of stock of said firm heretofore owned by your late husband, Gus, which you inherited as the sole legatee under his will." These communications were sent on Edward Rosiny's legal stationery, and I note that plaintiff Frank Rosiny was listed thereon as a member of the firm. Thus it was the Rosinys who led Mrs. Priddy to conclude, as she expressed in a letter dated November 14, 1986, in which she discussed the inadequacy of the offering price on the Ched property, that when she died her sons would inherit her interest in Ched. The Rosinys should thereby be estopped from enforcing the death buyout provision of the 1981 agreement.

A closely related issue is whether the buyout provisions carried forward in the several agreements were effectively abrogated by the conduct of the parties during the thirty years of Ched's existence. "The rule is recognized that stockholders may by consent or by acts and conduct repeal or accomplish the modification or abrogation of a by-law, as fully and effectively as if done by them by formal action, and the by-law is deemed to have been repealed or modified, as the case may be; likewise, non-usage of a by-law, continuing for a considerable length of time, and acquiesced therein, will work its abrogation." . . . Application of this principle is particularly appropriate in this case because it would be inequitable to allow the Rosinys to enforce the buyout provisions when they, and their mother before them, succeeded to ownership of their Ched shares without adherence to those provisions.

Alternatively, even if we were to assume the continued viability of the buyout provisions despite the long history of their having been ignored, I would agree with the Surrogate's conclusion that there was no meeting of the minds as to the meaning of "book value," which as previously noted, was never defined in any of the agreements. Allen Rosiny conceded that he knew what book value meant when he signed the 1981 agreement, and it is clear from the surrounding circumstances that the now deceased shareholders did not know the meaning of book value when they signed the 1981 agreement. There was simply no imaginable reason for Priddy and McGuire to have considered plaintiffs as natural objects of their bounty, and both had expressed a desire that their Ched shares be inherited by their respective children. As articulated by the Surrogate:

> It defies common sense that the elderly decedents knowingly and reasonably entered into an agreement which would require their estates to sell for $2,000 their respective interests in the corporation which were worth in the neighborhood of $40,000 at the time the agreement was signed. Under all of the circumstances of this case, the court finds that the plaintiffs reasonably believed that book value meant one thing while the decedents reasonably believed it meant another thing and, consequently, the lack of agreement as to this essential term results in a determination that no contract was ever created relative to the sale of shares upon the death of a shareholder.

The Surrogate's analysis is consistent with contract principles governing the legal consequences of mistakes as to the meaning given to words and expressions. As stated in Corbin on Contracts [1950] § 104:

> A much more common form of mistake is as to the meaning of words and expressions. Both parties know with accuracy the words used but understand them differently. Either party may inadvertently or ignorantly use words that by common usage do not express his meaning and intention. Either party may inadvertently or ignorantly give to another's words a meaning that the other did not intend or that may not accord with common usage. In such a case there is a misunderstanding of the terms used in making a contract, a misunderstanding that prevents a "meeting of the minds," that is, prevents a true agreement. Nevertheless, there may be a valid contract in spite of such a lack of true agreement. . . .

If one of the parties gave a meaning to the language that is not the only reasonable one under the circumstances, and the other expressed his assent knowing that the first party was giving it this meaning, that is the meaning that the court should adopt, and there is a contract accordingly. But if the parties had materially different meanings, and neither one knew or had reason to know the meaning of the other, there is no contract.

Either evaluation of the understanding of the parties should result in a determination in the defendants' favor. The only reasonable interpretation of "book value" from McGuire and Priddy's standpoint was that book value was equivalent to market value, and the Rosinys, both experienced attorneys, had every reason to know or at least suspect that such was the decedents' understanding. Thus, if there was a contractual agreement as to the meaning of book value, that meaning should be deemed equivalent to market value. On the other hand, if the Rosinys did not know or have reason to know that Priddy and McGuire understood book value as equivalent to market value, there was no meeting of the minds, and no contract with respect to the provisions here at issue. There is simply no basis for our disturbing the conclusions of the fact-finding court in this regard, because before doing so it should appear "obvious that the court's conclusions could not be reached under any fair interpretation of the evidence." That cannot be said in this case. . . .

Finally, the plaintiffs argue that at least in 1986 or 1987, the decedents could have dissolved the corporation, and that as a consequence of their not having done so, their estates should be estopped from claiming that the death buyout provision is unenforceable. This contention ignores the unique procedural history and fiduciary relationships developed over the years, the various equitable principles set forth at length earlier in this opinion, which clearly favor the defendants, and unjustifiably presumes that the aged and unsophisticated decedents had reason to believe that the plaintiffs would seek to strictly enforce against their estates a buyout provision that had been consistently ignored by all the shareholders over a period of 30 years.

The majority has reversed virtually every factual finding and legal conclusion reached by the Surrogate in his extensive and thoughtful opinion, and in its place has constructed a scenario which is at odds with the evidence, and contrary to experience and common sense. The majority minimizes Priddy's and McGuire's lack of financial sophistication by pointing out that Priddy was once a bookkeeper (sometime before 1925), and an officer manager sometime thereafter, and McGuire ran a successful business for many years (he was an automobile mechanic and his business was repairing automobiles). That McGuire was afflicted with alcoholism, consuming a bottle of liquor daily when he signed the 1981 agreement, is ignored, implying that this circumstance also is of little significance.

The majority imputes to the decedents open-eyed knowledge of the legal significance of the 1981 agreement because "book value" is an unambiguous term. Interestingly, the first case cited by the majority in support of this proposition generally equates "book value" with "actual value", that is, the value of assets less liabilities in connection therewith. Significantly, Frank Rosiny testified that he did not know Ched's book value in 1981, and Allen Rosiny testified with regard to his knowledge of Ched's book value, that "it was not knowledge that I had in '81 *or indeed could have had prior to Mr. Kwalwasser's death* [in 1985]." (Emphasis added.) Are decedents to be faulted then for believing in 1981 that the book value of Ched's property bore at least a reasonable relationship to its actual value?

To be sure, "book value" has a literal definition as "the value of something as shown by the books of account of the business owning it". But the central aspect of "book value" as pertinent to this case is its ordinary relationship to actual or market value, and whether there is anything in the record that would have led the decedents to suspect the extraordinary circumstance that Ched had a negative book value while its only asset had a substantial and increasing market value. The changes in past agreements from book value to fair market value and back to book value, far from demonstrating Priddy's and McGuire's understanding of the financial significance of those terms, rather suggest their understanding that the terms were almost interchangeable, and more procedural than substantive. I note that a recent New York Times article, reporting on the deficit of the Mutual Benefit Life Insurance Company, stated that "[t]he deficit is blamed on heavy investment in real estate, which is currently valued at about 20 percent less than book value." On the west coast, the Los Angeles Times reported the book value to market value ratio of "the best performing companies in California." Of the 25 companies listed in the article, only *one* had a book value more than 4% lower than its market value.

The majority finds that the record does not demonstrate that high pressure tactics were used to induce the decedents to sign the 1981 agreement, but that claim was not advanced by the defendants. The majority also finds no evidence of deception by the accountant Kwalwasser, but his deception and breach of trust are patent. As Ched's manager and accountant from the 1970's until 1985, Kwalwasser surely was in a fiduciary relationship with Priddy and McGuire; yet it was he who suggested to Priddy and McGuire that they permit the younger Rosinys to acquire their mother's shares, thus practically guaranteeing that the Rosinys would eventually enjoy an unconscionable windfall at the expense of Priddy's and McGuire's heirs. Kwalwasser, of all people, surely was aware that Ched had a negative book value in 1981, and it is a virtual certainty that he neither advised the decedents of this circumstance, nor of its significance.

In *Meinhard v Salmon,* then Chief Judge Cardozo enunciated these ringing phrases that reverberate in our equity jurisprudence to this day:

> Many forms of conduct permissible in a workaday world for those acting at arm's length, are forbidden to those bound by fiduciary ties. A trustee is held to something stricter than the morals of the market place. Not honesty alone, but the punctilio of an honor the most sensitive, is then the standard of behavior. As to this there has developed a tradition that is unbending and inveterate. Uncompromising rigidity has been the attitude of courts of equity

when petitioned to undermine the rule of undivided loyalty by the "disintegrating erosion" of particular exceptions. Only thus has the level of conduct for fiduciaries been kept at a level higher than that trodden by the crowd. It will not consciously be lowered by any judgment of this court.

The determination rendered by this court today is not, in my view, faithful to these precepts. To the contrary, these precepts, and those stated by Pomeroy as quoted earlier in this opinion, point ineluctably toward an affirmance in this case, thus giving the Priddy and McGuire heirs that which any fair-minded person must conclude is rightfully theirs.

It is hornbook law that "[i]n the general juristic sense, equity means the power to meet the moral standards of justice in a particular case by a tribunal having discretion to mitigate the rigidity of the application of strict rules of law so as to adapt the relief to the circumstances of the particular case." Can it truly be said that this court has vindicated the moral standards of justice by giving due recognition to the Surrogate's equity power in this case? I think not. One of our great contemporary teachers of jurisprudence posited that justice could best be defined by reflecting on what actions so violated principles of fairness, equity and morality that they provoked a "sense of injustice". It seems to me fitting to borrow Justice Stewart's famous test for obscenity — "I know it when I see it" — set forth in his concurrence in *Jacobellis v. Ohio,* in expressing the sense of injustice that I not only see in the result reached herein, but feel deep within.

I would accordingly affirm the Surrogate's order entered November 19, 1990, which declared that plaintiffs have no right under the 1981 agreement to purchase the shares at issue for a total sum of $4,000, and that those shares should instead pass pursuant to the terms of the wills of the decedents.

Questions

1. Who has the better doctrinal argument in *Rosiny v. Schmidt* — the majority or the dissenting opinion?

2. Assuming that the majority was doctrinally correct, was the outcome just? Does law always serve justice? Should the courts, as the dissent seems to suggest, seek to achieve justice?

3. Is there anything further that Priddy's and Schmidt's estates can do to realize their gains?

4. Frank Rosiny was, for a time, chair of the New York State and American Bar Association's ethics committees. In January 1993, he published an article in the *New York State Bar Journal* defending the legal profession as a noble one in the face of significant public criticism and predicting greater public approval of lawyers in the future.

B. The Allocation of Power between Shareholders and Directors

As you saw in Part 2, directors and officers run the corporation. But in closely held corporations, as we already noticed, shareholders are more active in management. Should they also be able to dispense with corporate formalities and even supersede or bind the board? This question is addressed in the following cases. As you will see, the courts' responses have changed over time. At least in part, different visions of the corporation influenced this transformation. We see in the sequence from *McQuade v. Stoneham* to *Galler v. Galler* a progression from viewing the corporation as an entity created by the state and thus publicly regulated to viewing the corporation as the private property of the shareholders. As you read these cases, consider the policy implications of thinking about close corporations as public entities in contrast to thinking about them as private property.

McQuade v. Stoneham
263 N.Y. 323 (1934)

POUND, Chief Judge

The action is brought to compel specific performance of an agreement between the parties, entered into to secure the control of National Exhibition Company, also called the Baseball Club (New York Nationals or "Giants"). This was one of Stoneham's enterprises which used the New York polo grounds for its home games. McGraw was manager of the Giants. McQuade was at the time the contract was entered into a city magistrate. He resigned December 8, 1930.

Defendant Stoneham became the owner of 1,306 shares, or a majority of the stock of National Exhibition Company. Plaintiff and defendant McGraw each purchased 70 shares of his stock. Plaintiff paid Stoneham $50,338.10 for the stock he purchased. As a part of the transaction the agreement in question was entered into. It was dated May 21, 1919. Some of its pertinent provisions are

"VIII. The parties hereto will use their best endeavors for the purpose of continuing as directors of said Company and as officers thereof the following:

Directors:

Charles A. Stoneham,

John J. McGraw,

Francis X. McQuade,

with the right to the party of the first part [Stoneham] to name all additional directors as he sees fit.

Officers:

Charles A. Stoneham, President,

John J. McGraw, Vice-President,

Francis X. McQuade, Treasurer.

IX. No salaries are to be paid to any of the above officers or directors, except as follows:

President	$45,000
Vice-President	7,500
Treasurer	7,500

X. There shall be no change in said salaries, no change in the amount of capital, or the number of shares, no change or amendment of the by-laws of the corporation or any matters regarding the policy of the business of the corporation or any matters which may in anywise affect, endanger or interfere with the rights of minority stockholders, excepting upon the mutual and unanimous consent of all of the parties hereto. . . .

XIV. This agreement shall continue and remain in force so long as the parties or any of them or the representative of any, own the stock referred to in this agreement, to wit, the party of the first part, 1,166 shares, the party of the second part 70 shares and the party of the third part 70 shares, except as may otherwise appear by this agreement. . . ."

In pursuance of this contract Stoneham became president and McGraw vice-president of the corporation. McQuade became treasurer. In June, 1925, his salary was increased to $10,000 a year. He continued to act until May 2, 1928, when Leo J. Bondy was elected to succeed him. The board of directors consisted of seven men. The four outside of the parties hereto were selected by Stoneham and he had complete control over them. At the meeting of May 2, 1928, Stoneham and McGraw refrained from voting, McQuade voted for himself and the other four voted for Bondy. Defendants did not keep their agreement with McQuade to use their best efforts to continue him as treasurer. On the contrary, he was dropped with their entire acquiescence. At the next stockholders' meeting he was dropped as a director although they might have elected him.

The courts below have refused to order the reinstatement of McQuade, but have given him damages for wrongful discharge, with a right to sue for future damages.

The cause for dropping McQuade was due to the falling out of friends. McQuade and Stoneham had disagreed. The trial court has found in substance that their numerous quarrels and disputes did not affect the orderly and efficient administration of the business of the corporation; that plaintiff was removed because he had antagonized the dominant Stoneham by persisting in challenging his power over the corporate treasury and for no misconduct on his part. The court also finds that plaintiff was removed by Stoneham for protecting the corporation and its minority stockholders. We will assume that Stoneham put him out when he might have retained him, merely in order to get rid of him.

Defendants say that the contract in suit was void because the directors held their office charged with the duty to act for the corporation according to their best judgment and that any contract which compels a director to vote to keep any particular person in office and at a stated salary is illegal. Directors are the exclusive executive representatives of the corporation, charged with administration of its internal affairs and the management and use of its assets. They manage the business of the corporation. "An agreement to continue a man as president is dependent upon his continued loyalty to the interests of the corporation." So much is undisputed.

Plaintiff contends that the converse of this proposition is true and that an agreement among directors to continue a man as an officer of a corporation is not to be broken so long as such officer is loyal to the interests of the corporation and that, as plaintiff has been found loyal to the corporation, the agreement of defendants is enforceable.

Although it has been held that an agreement among stockholders whereby it is attempted to divest the directors of their power to discharge an unfaithful employee of the corporation is illegal as against public policy, it must be equally true that the stockholders may not, by agreement among themselves, control the directors in the exercise of the judgment vested in them by virtue of their office to elect officers and fix salaries. Their motives may not be questioned so long as their acts are legal. The bad faith or the improper motives of the parties does not change the rule. Directors may not by agreements entered into as stockholders abrogate their independent judgment.

Stockholders may, of course, combine to elect directors. That rule is well settled. As Holmes, C.J., pointedly said: "If stockholders want to make their power felt, they must unite. There is no reason why a majority should not agree to keep together." The power to unite is, however, limited to the election of directors and is not extended to contracts whereby limitations are placed on the power of directors to manage the business of the corporation by the selection of agents at defined salaries.

The minority shareholders whose interests McQuade says he has been punished for protecting, are not, aside from himself, complaining about his discharge. He is not acting for the corporation or for them in this action. It is impossible to see how the corporation has been injured by the substitution of Bondy as treasurer in place of McQuade. As McQuade represents himself in this action and seeks redress for his own wrongs, "we prefer to listen to [the corporation and the minority stockholders] before any decision as to their wrongs."

It is urged that we should pay heed to the morals and manners of the market place to sustain this agreement and that we should hold that its violation gives rise to a cause of action for damages rather than base our decision on any outworn notions of public policy. Public policy is a dangerous guide in determining the validity of a contract and courts should not interfere lightly with the freedom of competent parties to make their own contracts. We do not close our eyes to the fact that such agreements, tacitly or openly arrived at, are not uncommon, especially in close corporations where the stockholders are doing business for convenience under a corporate organization. We know that majority stockholders, united in voting trusts, effectively manage the business of a corporation by choosing trustworthy directors to reflect their policies in the corporate management. Nor are we unmindful that McQuade has, so the court has found, been shabbily treated as a purchaser of stock from Stoneham. We have said: "A trustee is held to something stricter than the morals of the market place," but Stoneham and McGraw were not trustees for McQuade as an individual. ==Their duty was to the corporation and its stockholders, to be exercised according to their unrestricted lawful judgment.== They were under no legal obligation to deal righteously with McQuade if it was against public policy to do so.

The courts do not enforce mere moral obligations, nor legal ones either, unless someone seeks to establish rights which may be waived by custom and for convenience. We are constrained by authority to hold that a contract is illegal and void so far as it precludes the board of directors, at the risk of incurring legal liability, from changing officers, salaries or policies or retaining individuals in office, except by consent of the contracting parties. On the whole, such a holding is probably preferable to one which would open the courts to pass on the motives of directors in the lawful exercise of their trust.

A further reason for reversal exists. At the time the contract was made the plaintiff was a city magistrate. He complains that the defendant Stoneham breached the contract by failure "to use his best endeavors" for the purpose of continuing him as a director and treasurer of the corporation which Stoneham controlled. The plaintiff resigned as city magistrate after the commencement of this action. He has recovered a judgment for "the amount of the salary of the treasurer of the National Exhibition Company at the rate of $10,000 per year from the second day of May, 1928, to the date of the entry of this decree."

The Inferior Criminal Courts Act provides that no "city magistrate shall engage in any other business, profession or hold any other public office or shall serve as the representative of any political party for any assembly, aldermanic, senatorial or congressional district in the executive committee or other governing body of any political party organization or political party association. No city magistrate shall engage in any other business or profession or act as referee, or receiver, but each of said justices and magistrates shall devote his whole time and capacity, so far as the public interest demands, to the duties of his office. . . ." The contract contemplated that the plaintiff should hold an executive office at a stipulated and substantial salary. The by-laws of the corporation impose upon the treasurer regular duties as the fiscal agent of the corporation and provide in addition that "he shall perform such other duties, as shall be, from time to time assigned to him by the board of directors or the president, or as may be required by these by-laws." If the performance of regular duties in the management of a business corporation for a substantial remuneration does not constitute "engaging in a business" then these words are futile and meaningless. . . .

The judgment of the Appellate Division and that of the Trial Term should be reversed and the complaint dismissed, with costs in all courts.

Lehman, Judge (concurring)

I concur in the decision of the court on the second ground stated in the opinion. I desire to state the reasons why I do not accept the first ground.

The defendant Stoneham owned the majority stock of the corporation and could exercise the control of the corporation which the holder of the majority stock possesses. He could choose the directors of the corporation who in turn would elect the officers and determine the corporate policies. The agreement between the defendant Stoneham, the plaintiff, McQuade, and McGraw provided, in effect, that, in consideration of the sale by Stoneham of part of his majority stock, the power of control which Stoneham had previously exercised should be shared with McQuade and McGraw and, specifically, that mutual assurance should be given that this power of control would be used in concert to continue each of the three parties to the contract as directors and officers of the corporation at stipulated salaries and to preclude change without common consent in "matters regarding the policy of the business of the corporation or any matters which may in any wise affect, endanger or interfere with the rights of minority stockholders."

We have said: "An ordinary agreement, among a minority in number, but a majority in shares, for the purpose of obtaining control of the corporation by the election of particular persons as directors is not illegal." *Manson v. Curtis*. We are agreed that, if the contract had provided only for the election of directors, it would not have been illegal. Its vice, if any, is inherent in the provisions intended to give assurance that the directors so elected would act according to the prearranged design of the stockholders in apportioning the corporate offices and emoluments of such offices among the majority stockholders.

The corporate charter and statutory provisions fix the manner in which the corporate affairs must be conducted. The majority stockholders do not own the corporation nor have they unlimited power of control. Their corporate powers are conferred by the charter and may be exercised only in the field defined by the charter. They act at stockholders' meetings in relation to matters which may be decided at such meetings. There, the directors are chosen by the vote of the holders of a majority of the stock, but the stockholders have no power, except as provided by charter or statute, to divest directors of any of their functions or direct them in the exercise of their functions. The directors are constituted managers of the corporate affairs. They determine the corporate policies, they elect the corporate officers. In the functioning of the corporate machinery the power of control of the holders of the majority stock is, as in such matters, exhausted with the election of the directors. When elected the directors must act in behalf of the corporation, not in behalf of any group of stockholders. It would constitute a wrong to the corporation and its minority stockholders if the directors were permitted to transfer their powers and functions to the holders of a majority of the stock or to bind themselves to accept direction from any persons not vested with power of control by law.

There can, I think, be no doubt that shareholders owning a majority of the corporate stock may combine to obtain and exercise any control which a single owner of such stock could exercise. What may lawfully be done by an individual may ordinarily be lawfully done by a combination, but no combination is legal if formed to accomplish an illegal object. No such combination or agreement may "contravene any express charter or statutory provision or contemplate any fraud, oppression or wrong against other stockholders or other illegal object." *Manson v. Curtis.*

In [*Manson v. Curtis*] we held invalid, on that ground, an agreement for the selection "of directors who should remain passive or mechanical to the will and word" of one of the parties to the agreement. Now it is said that, for the same reason, this agreement must be held unenforceable, though here the agreement contemplated no restriction upon the powers of the board of directors, and no dictation or interference by stockholders except in so far as concerns the election and remuneration of officers and the adhesion by the corporation to established policies.

It seems difficult to reconcile such a decision with the statements in the opinion in *Manson v. Curtis* that "it is not illegal or against public policy for two or more stockholders owning the majority of the shares of stock to unite upon a course of corporate policy or action, or upon the officers whom they will elect," and that "shareholders have the right to combine their interests and voting powers to secure such control of the corporation and the adoption of and adhesion by it to a specific policy and course of business." Obviously a combination intended to effect the election of certain officers and to obtain control of the corporation and adhesion by it to a specific policy and course of business can accomplish its ends only to the extent that directors will bow to the will of those who united to elect them. The directors have the power and the duty to act in accordance with their own best judgment so long as they remain directors. The majority stockholders can compel no action by the directors, but at the expiration of the term of office of the directors the stockholders have the power to replace them with others whose actions coincide with the judgment or desires of the holders of a majority of the stock. The theory that directors exercise in all matters an independent judgment in practice often yields to the fact that the choice of directors lies with the majority stockholders and thus gives the stockholders a very effective control of the action by the board of directors. In truth the board of directors may check the arbitrary will of those who would otherwise completely control the corporation, but cannot indefinitely thwart their will.

A contract which destroys this check contravenes "express charter or statutory provisions" and is, therefore, illegal. A contract which merely provides that stockholders shall in combination use their power to achieve a legitimate purpose is not illegal. They may join in the election of directors who, in their opinion, will be in sympathy with the policies of the majority stockholders and who, in the choice of executive officers, will be influenced by the wishes of the majority stockholders. The directors so chosen may not act in disregard of the best interests of the corporation and its minority stockholders, but with that limitation they may and, in practice, usually are swayed by the wishes of the majority. Otherwise there would be no continuity of corporate policy and no continuity in management of corporate affairs.

The contract now under consideration provides, in a narrow field, for corporate action within these limitations. Its purpose and intent is to fix the manner in which control vested in the stockholders shall be exercised. It is not designed to create a control which is itself illegal. True it does contemplate that the parties will, as directors, vote to place each other in specified offices. If this represented a corrupt bargain intended to despoil the corporation, it would be an illegal combination, but there is no evidence or finding that it had such purpose or result. Neither the corporation nor any minority stockholders are complaining and the findings establish that the arrangement resulted in protection which the minority stockholders would not otherwise have had and that it was repudiated by defendant (Stoneham) because such protection proved irksome to him. It does constrain the parties while acting as directors to vote for officers in a predetermined manner, but there is no suggestion that such vote would not accord with their best judgment and be in the interests of the corporation. It is subject to the implied condition that the officers so elected will be loyal to the corporation. It binds the directors only in a matter where freedom is a fiction rather than a fact. If this contract is unenforceable and contrary to public policy, then every purchase of a substantial block of stock upon the promise of the majority stockholders that the purchaser will be elected a director and officer of the corporation is likewise against public policy.

We have said: "The law requires of the majority of the stockholders the utmost good faith in their control and management of the corporation as regards the minority, and in this respect the majority stand in much the same attitude towards the minority that the directors sustain towards all the stockholders." *Farmers L. & T. Co. v. New York & Northern Ry. Co.* The courts should and do enforce the rule of good faith towards all stockholders. No group of stockholders may use their power to wrong others. No director may repudiate his trust to exercise his best judgment. A contract calculated to deprive the corporation and its minority stockholders of statutory safeguards constitutes such a wrong. So, too, does a contract by directors to repudiate their trust. A contract which merely provides for the election of fit officers and adhesion to particular policy determined in advance constitutes an agreement by which men in combination exercise a power which could be lawfully exercised if lodged in a single man. It is legal if designed to protect legitimate interests without wrong to others. Public policy should be governed by facts, not abstractions. The contract is, in my opinion, valid. It is unenforceable only because it resulted in an employment which was itself illegal.

Questions

1. Why did McQuade invest in the Giants? What did he hope to get out of the investment? Consider the fact that the annual salary of a city magistrate at the turn

of the twentieth century was roughly equivalent to the size of McQuade's investment in the Giants. What does this tell you about McQuade's goals?

2. Why did the court refuse to enforce the contract? What policy considerations support the majority opinion?

3. What is the nature of the corporate entity according to the majority?

4. What is Judge Lehman's approach? On what grounds does he disagree with the majority? What policy considerations support his position?

Clark v. Dodge
269 N.Y. 410 (1936)

CROUCH, Judge.

The action is for the specific performance of a contract between the plaintiff, Clark, and the defendant Dodge, relating to the affairs of the two defendant corporations.... The defendant then moved ... to dismiss the complaint.... We shall deal, therefore, with the questions here presented in the light of the facts most favorable to plaintiff appearing in the pleadings only.

Those facts, briefly stated, are as follows: The two corporate defendants are New Jersey corporations manufacturing medicinal preparations by secret formulae. The main office, factory, and assets of both corporations are located in the State of New York. In 1921, and at all times since, Clark owned 25 per cent and Dodge 75 per cent of the stock of each corporation. Dodge took no active part in the business, although he was a director and, through ownership of their qualifying shares, controlled the other directors of both corporations. He was the president of Bell & Company, Inc., and nominally general manager of Hollings-Smith Company, Inc. The plaintiff, Clark, was a director and held the offices of treasurer and general manager of Bell & Company, Inc., and also had charge of the major portion of the business of Hollings-Smith Company, Inc. The formulae and methods of manufacture of the medicinal preparations were known to him alone. Under date of February 15, 1921, Dodge and Clark, the sole owners of the stock of both corporations, entered into a written agreement under seal, which after reciting the stock ownership of both parties, the desire of Dodge that Clark should continue in the efficient management and control of the business of Bell & Company, Inc., so long as he should "remain faithful, efficient and competent to so manage and control the said business"; and his further desire that Clark should not be the sole custodian of a specified formula but should share his knowledge thereof and of the method of manufacture with a son of Dodge, provided, in substance, as follows: That Dodge during his lifetime and, after his death, a trustee to be appointed by his will, would so vote his stock and so vote as a director that the plaintiff (a) should continue to be a director of Bell & Company, Inc. and (b) should continue as its general manager so long as he should be "faithful, efficient and competent"; (c) should during his life receive one-fourth of the net income of the corporations either by way of salary or dividends; and (d) that no unreasonable or incommensurate salaries should be paid to other officers or agents which would so reduce the net income as materially to affect Clark's profits. Clark on his part agreed to disclose the specified formula to the son and to instruct him in the details and methods of manufacture; and further, at the end of his life to bequeath his stock—if no issue survived him—to the wife and children of Dodge.

It was further provided that the provisions in regard to the division of net profits and the regulation of salaries should also apply to the Hollings-Smith Company.

The complaint alleges due performance of the contract by Clark and breach thereof by Dodge in that he has failed to use his stock control to continue Clark as a director and as general manager, and has prevented Clark from receiving his proportion of the income, while taking his own, by causing the employment of incompetent persons at excessive salaries, and otherwise.

The relief sought is reinstatement as director and general manager and an accounting by Dodge and by the corporations for waste and for the proportion of net income due plaintiff, with an injunction against further violations.

The only question which need be discussed is whether the contract is illegal as against public policy within the decision in *McQuade v. Stoneham,* upon the authority of which the complaint was dismissed by the Appellate Division.

"The business of a corporation shall be managed by its board of directors." That is the statutory norm. Are we committed by the *McQuade* case to the doctrine that there may be no variation, however slight or innocuous, from that norm, where salaries or policies or the retention of individuals in office are concerned? There is ample authority supporting that doctrine, and something may be said for it, since it furnishes a simple, if arbitrary, test. Apart from its practical administrative convenience, the reasons upon which it is said to rest are more or less nebulous. Public policy, the intention of the Legislature, detriment to the corporation, are phrases which in this connection mean little. Possible harm to bona fide purchasers of stock or to creditors or to stockholding minorities have more substance; but such harms are absent in many instances. If the enforcement of a particular contract damages nobody—not even, in any perceptible degree, the public—one sees no reason for holding it illegal, even though it impinges slightly upon the broad provision of [the statute]. Damage suffered or threatened is a logical and practical test, and has come to be the one generally adopted by the courts. Where the directors are the sole stockholders, there seems to be no objection to enforcing an agreement among them to vote for certain people as officers. There is no direct decision to that effect in this court, yet there are strong indications that such a rule has long been recognized. The opinion in *Manson v. Curtis* closed its discussion by saying: "The rule that all the stockholders by their universal consent may do as they choose with the corporate concerns and assets, provided the interests of creditors are not affected, because they are the complete owners of the corporation, cannot be invoked here." That was because all the stockholders were not parties to the agreement there in question. So, where the public was not affected, "the parties in interest, might, by their original agreement of incorporation, limit their respective rights and powers," even where there was a conflicting statutory standard. "Such corporations were little more (though not quite the same as) than chartered partnerships." *Ripin v. U.S. Woven Label Co.,* 205 N.Y. 442, 447. In *Lorillard v. Clyde,* 86 N.Y. 384, and again in *Drucklieb v. Harris,* 209 N.Y. 211, where the questioned agreements were entered into by all the stockholders of small corporations about to be organized, the fact that the agreements conflicted to some extent with the statutory duty of the directors to manage the corporate affairs was thought not to render the agreements illegal as against public policy, though it was said they might not be binding upon the directors of the corporation when organized. Cf. Lehman, J., dissenting opinion in the *McQuade* case. The rule recognized in *Manson v. Curtis,* and quoted above, was thus stated by Blackmar, J., in *Kassel v. Empire Tinware Co.,* 178 App. Div. 176, 180: "As the parties to the action are the complete owners of the corporation, there is no reason why the exercise of the power and discretion of the directors cannot be controlled by valid agreement between themselves, provided that the interests of creditors are not affected." . . .

Except for the broad dicta in the *McQuade* opinion, we think there can be no doubt that the agreement here in question was legal and that the complaint states a cause of action. There was no attempt to sterilize the board of directors, as in the *Manson* and *McQuade* cases. The only restrictions on Dodge were (a) that as a stockholder he should vote for Clark as a director—a perfectly legal contract; (b) that as director he should continue Clark as general manager, so long as he proved faithful, efficient and competent—an agreement which could harm nobody; (c) that Clark should always receive as salary or dividends one-fourth of the "net income." For the purposes of this motion, it is only just to construe that phrase as meaning whatever was left for distribution after the directors had in good faith set aside whatever they deemed wise; (d) that no salaries to other officers should be paid, unreasonable in amount or incommensurate with services rendered—a beneficial and not a harmful agreement.

If there was any invasion of the powers of the directorate under that agreement, it is so slight as to be negligible; and certainly there is no damage suffered by or threatened to any body. The broad statements in the *McQuade* opinion, applicable to the facts there, should be confined to those facts.

The judgment of the Appellate Division should be reversed and the order of the Special Term affirmed, with costs in this court and in the Appellate Division.

Questions

1. What vision of the corporation did the court adopt in *Clark v. Dodge*? How does it differ from the one adopted in *McQuade v. Stoneham*? How does this vision affect the court's analysis of the shareholders' ability to bind directors?

2. The corporations involved in *Clark v. Dodge* were incorporated in New Jersey, but the court applied New York law. This seems to violate the well-established internal affairs doctrine, holding that legal disputes involving the internal affairs of a corporation are to be determined based on the law of the state of incorporation. Why do you think the court applied New York law?

3. Compare the court's description of the contract at the beginning of its analysis with its description at the end of the case. What are the differences? Why do you suppose the court varied its description of the contract?

Galler v. Galler
32 Ill. 2d 16 (1964)

UNDERWOOD, Justice

Plaintiff, Emma Galler, sued in equity for an accounting and for specific performance of an agreement made in July, 1955, between plaintiff and her husband, of one part, and defendants, Isadore A. Galler and his wife, Rose, of the other. Defendants appealed from a decree of the superior court of Cook County granting the relief prayed. The First District Appellate Court reversed the decree and denied specific performance, affirming in part the order for an accounting, and modifying the order awarding master's fees. That decision is appealed here on a certificate of importance.

There is no substantial dispute as to the facts in this case. From 1919 to 1924, Benjamin and Isadore Galler, brothers, were equal partners in the Galler Drug Company, a wholesale drug concern. In 1924 the business was incorporated under the Illinois Business Corporation Act, each owning one half of the outstanding 220 shares of stock. In 1945 each contracted to sell 6 shares to an employee, Rosenberg, at a price of $10,500 for each block of 6 shares, payable within 10 years. They guaranteed to repurchase the shares if Rosenberg's employment were terminated, and further agreed that if they sold their shares, Rosenberg would receive the same price per share as that paid for the brothers' shares. Rosenberg was still indebted for the 12 shares in July, 1955, and continued to make payments on account even after Benjamin Galler died in 1957 and after the institution of this action by Emma Galler in 1959. Rosenberg was not involved in this litigation either as a party or as a witness, and in July of 1961, prior to the time that the master in chancery hearings were concluded, defendants Isadore and Rose Galler purchased the 12 shares from Rosenberg. A supplemental complaint was filed by the plaintiff, Emma Galler, asserting an equitable right to have 6 of the 12 shares transferred to her and offering to pay the defendants one half of the amount that the defendants paid Rosenberg. The parties have stipulated that pending disposition of the instant case, these shares will not be voted or transferred. For approximately one year prior to the entry of the decree by the chancellor in July of 1962, there were no outstanding minority shareholder interests.

In March, 1954, Benjamin and Isadore, on the advice of their accountant, decided to enter into an agreement for the financial protection of their immediate families and to assure their families, after the death of either brother, equal control of the corporation. In June, 1954, while the agreement was in the process of preparation by an attorney-associate of the accountant, Benjamin suffered a heart attack. Although he resumed his business duties some months later, he was again stricken in February, 1955, and thereafter was unable to return to work. During his brother's illness, Isadore asked the accountant to have the shareholders' agreement put in final form in order to protect Benjamin's wife, and this was done by another attorney employed in the accountant's office. On a Saturday night in July, 1955, the accountant brought the agreement to Benjamin's home, and 6 copies of it were executed there by the two brothers and their wives. The accountant then collected all signed copies of the agreement and informed the parties that he was taking them for safe keeping. Between the execution of the agreement in July, 1955, and Benjamin's death in December, 1957, the agreement was not modified. Benjamin suffered a stroke late in July, 1955, and on August 2, 1955, Isadore and the accountant and a notary public brought to Benjamin for signature two powers of attorney which were retained by the accountant after Benjamin executed them with Isadore as a witness. The plaintiff did not read the powers and she never had them. One of the powers authorized the transfer of Benjamin's bank account to Emma and the other power enabled Emma to vote Benjamin's 104 shares. Because of the state of Benjamin's health, nothing further was said to him by any of the parties concerning the agreement. It appears from the evidence that some months after the agreement was signed, the defendants Isadore and Rose Galler and their son, the defendant, Aaron Galler, sought to have the agreements destroyed. The evidence is undisputed that defendants had decided prior to Benjamin's death they would not honor the agreement, but never disclosed their intention to plaintiff or her husband.

On July 21, 1956, Benjamin executed an instrument creating a trust naming his wife as trustee. The trust covered, among other things, the 104 shares of Galler Drug Company stock and the stock certificates were endorsed by Benjamin and delivered to Emma. When Emma presented the certificates to defendants for transfer into her name as trustee, they sought to have Emma abandon the 1955 agreement or enter into some kind of a noninterference agreement as a price for the transfer of the shares. Finally, in September, 1956, after Emma had refused to abandon the shareholders' agreement, she did agree to permit defendant Aaron to become president for one year and agreed that she would not interfere with the business during that year. The stock was then reissued in her name as trustee. During the year 1957 while Benjamin was still alive, Emma tried many times to arrange a meeting with Isadore to discuss business matters but he refused to see her.

Shortly after Benjamin's death, Emma went to the office and demanded the terms of the 1955 agreement be carried out. Isadore told her that anything she had to say could be said to Aaron, who then told her that his father would not abide by the agreement. He offered a modification of the agreement by proposing the salary continuation payment but without her becoming a director. When Emma refused to modify the agreement and sought enforcement of its terms, defendants refused and this suit followed.

During the last few years of Benjamin's life both brothers drew an annual salary of $42,000. Aaron, whose salary was $15,000 as manager of the warehouse prior to September, 1956, has since the time that Emma agreed to his acting as president drawn an annual salary of $20,000. In 1957, 1958, and 1959 a $40,000 annual dividend was paid. Plaintiff has received her proportionate share of the dividend.

The July, 1955, agreement in question here, entered into between Benjamin, Emma, Isadore and Rose, recites that Benjamin and Isadore each own 47 1/2% of the issued and outstanding shares of the Galler Drug Company, an Illinois corporation, and that Benjamin and Isadore desired to provide income for the support and maintenance of their immediate families. No reference is made to the shares then being purchased by Rosenberg. The essential features of the contested portions of the agreement are substantially as set forth in the opinion of the Appellate Court: (2) that the bylaws of the corporation will be amended to provide for a board of four directors; that the necessary quorum shall be three directors; and that no directors' meeting shall be held without giving ten days notice to all directors. (3) The shareholders will cast their votes for the above named persons (Isadore, Rose, Benjamin and Emma) as directors at said special meeting and at any other meeting held for the purpose of electing directors. (4, 5) In the event of the death of either brother his wife shall have the right to nominate a director in place of the decedent. (6) Certain annual dividends will be declared by the corporation. The dividend shall be $50,000 payable out of the accumulated earned surplus in excess of $500,000. If 50% of the annual net profits after taxes exceeds the minimum $50,000, then the directors shall have discretion to declare a dividend up to 50% of the annual net profits. If the net profits are less than $50,000, nevertheless the minimum $50,000 annual dividend shall be declared, providing the $500,000 surplus is maintained. Earned surplus is defined. (9) The certificates evidencing the said shares of Benjamin Galler and Isadore Galler shall bear a legend that the shares are subject to the terms of this agreement. (10) A salary continuation agreement shall be entered into by the corporation which shall authorize the corporation upon the death of Benjamin Galler or Isadore Galler, or both, to pay a sum equal to twice the salary of such officer, payable monthly over a five-year period. Said sum shall be paid to the widow during her widowhood, but should be paid to such widow's children if the widow remarries within the five-year period. (11, 12) The parties to this agreement further agree and hereby grant to the corporation the authority to purchase, in the event of the death of either Benjamin or Isadore, so much of the stock of Galler Drug Company held by the estate as is necessary to provide sufficient funds to pay the federal estate tax, the Illinois inheritance tax and other administrative expenses of the estate. If as a result of such purchase from the estate of the decedent the amount of dividends to be received by the heirs is reduced, the parties shall nevertheless vote for directors so as to give the estate and heirs the same representation as before (2 directors out of 4, even though they own less stock), and also that the corporation pay an additional benefit payment equal to the diminution of the dividends. In the event either Benjamin or Isadore decides to sell his shares he is required to offer them first to the remaining shareholders and then to the corporation at book value, according each six months to accept the offer.

The Appellate Court found the 1955 agreement void because "the undue duration, stated purpose and substantial disregard of the provisions of the Corporation Act outweigh any considerations which might call for divisibility" and held that "the public policy of this state demands voiding this entire agreement".

While the conduct of defendants towards plaintiff was clearly inequitable, the basically controlling factor is the absence of an objecting minority interest, together with the absence of public detriment. . . .

The power to invalidate the agreements on the grounds of public policy is so far reaching and so easily abused that it should be called into action to set aside or annul the solemn engagement of parties dealing on equal terms only in cases where the corrupt or dangerous tendency clearly and unequivocally appears upon the face of the agreement itself or is the necessary inference from the matters which are expressed, and the only apparent exception to this general rule is to be found in those cases where the agreement, though fair and unobjectionable on its face, is a part of a corrupt scheme and is made to disguise the real nature of the transaction. . . .

At this juncture it should be emphasized that we deal here with a so-called close corporation. Various attempts at definition of the close corporation have been made. . . . For our purposes, a close corporation is one in which the stock is held in a few hands, or in a few families, and wherein it is not at all, or only rarely, dealt in by buying or selling. Moreover, it should be recognized that shareholder agreements similar to that in question here are often, as a practical consideration, quite necessary for the protection of those financially interested in the close corporation. While the shareholder of a public-issue corporation may readily sell his shares on the open market should management fail to use, in his opinion, sound business judgment, his counterpart of the close corporation often has a large total of his entire capital invested in the business and has no ready market for his shares should he desire to sell. He feels, understandably, that he is more than a mere investor and that his voice should be heard concerning all corporate activity. Without a shareholder agreement, specifically enforceable by the courts, insuring him a modicum of control, a large minority shareholder might find himself at the mercy of an oppressive or unknowledgeable majority. Moreover, as in the case at bar, the shareholders of a close corporation are often also the directors and officers thereof. With substantial shareholding interests abiding in each member of the board of directors, it is often quite impossible to secure, as in the large public-issue corporation, independent board judgment free from personal motivations concerning corporate policy. For these and other reasons too voluminous to enumerate here, often the only sound basis for protection is afforded by a lengthy, detailed shareholder agreement securing the rights and obligations of all concerned.

As the preceding review of the applicable decisions of this court points out, there has been a definite, albeit inarticulate, trend toward eventual judicial treatment of the close corporation as *sui generis*. Several shareholder-director agreements that have technically "violated" the letter of the Business Corporation Act have nevertheless been upheld in the light of the existing practical circumstances, i.e., no apparent public injury, the absence of a complaining minority interest, and no apparent prejudice to creditors. However, we have thus far not attempted to limit these decisions as applicable only to close corporations and have seemingly implied that general considerations regarding judicial supervision of all corporate behavior apply.

The practical result of this series of cases, while liberally giving legal efficacy to particular agreements in special circumstances notwithstanding literal "violations" of statutory corporate law, has been to inject much doubt and uncertainty into the thinking of the bench and corporate bar of Illinois concerning shareholder agreements. . . .

It is therefore necessary, we feel, to discuss the instant case with the problems peculiar to the close corporation particularly in mind.

It would admittedly facilitate judicial supervision of corporate behavior if a strict adherence to the provisions of the Business Corporation Act were required in all cases without regard to the practical exigencies peculiar to the close corporation. However, courts have long ago quite realistically, we feel, relaxed their attitudes concerning statutory compliance when dealing with close corporate behavior, permitting "slight deviations" from corporate "norms" in order to give legal efficacy to common business practice. . . . This attitude is illustrated by the following language in *Clark* v. *Dodge*: "Public policy, the intention of the Legislature, detriment to the corporation, are phrases which in this connection [the court was discussing a shareholder-director agreement whereby the directors pledged themselves to vote for certain people as officers of the corporation] mean little. Possible harm to bona fide purchasers of stock or to creditors or to stockholding minorities have more substance; but such harms are absent in many instances. If the enforcement of a particular contract damages nobody—not even, in any perceptible degree, the public—one sees no reason for holding it illegal, even though it impinges slightly on the broad provisions of [the relevant statute providing that the business of a corporation shall be managed by its board of directors.]. Damage suffered or threatened is a logical and practical test, and has come to be the one generally adopted by the courts.

Again, "As the parties to the action are the complete owners of the corporation, there is no reason why the exercise of the power and discretion of the directors cannot be controlled by valid agreement between themselves, provided that the interests of creditors are not affected." *Clark v. Dodge*. . . .

This court has recognized, albeit *sub silentio*, the significant conceptual differences between the close corporation and its public-issue counterpart in, among other cases, *Kantzler v. Bensinger,* 214 Ill. 589, where an agreement quite similar to the one under attack here was upheld. Where, as in *Kantzler* and here, no injury to a minority interest appears, no fraud or apparent injury to the public or creditors is present, and no clearly prohibitory statutory language is violated, we can see no valid reason for precluding the parties from reaching any arrangements concerning the management of the corporation which are agreeable to all.

Perhaps, as has been vociferously advanced, a separate comprehensive statutory scheme governing the close corporation would best serve here. . . .

At any rate, however, the courts can no longer fail to expressly distinguish between the close and public-issue corporation when confronted with problems relating to either. What we do here is to illuminate this problem—before the bench, corporate bar, and the legislature, in the context of a particular fact situation. To do less would be to shirk our responsibility, to do more would, perhaps be to invade the province of the legislative branch.

We now, in the light of the foregoing, turn to specific provisions of the 1955 agreement.

The Appellate Court correctly found many of the contractual provisions free from serious objection, and we need not prolong this opinion with a discussion of them here. That court did, however, find difficulties in the stated purpose of the agreement as it relates to its duration, the election of certain persons to specific offices for a number of years, the requirement for the mandatory declaration of stated dividends (which the Appellate Court held invalid), and the salary continuation agreement.

Since the question as to the duration of the agreement is a principal source of controversy, we shall consider it first. The parties provided no specific termination date, and while the agreement concludes with a paragraph that its terms "shall be binding upon and shall inure to the benefits of" the legal representatives, heirs and assigns of the parties, this clause is, we believe, intended to be operative only as long as one of the parties is living. It further provides that it shall be so construed as to carry out its purposes, and we believe these must be determined from a consideration of the agreement as a whole. Thus viewed, a fair construction is that its purposes were accomplished at the death of the survivor of the parties. While these life spans are not precisely ascertainable, and the Appellate Court noted Emma Galler's life expectancy at her husband's death was 26.9 years, we are aware of no statutory or public policy provision against stockholder's agreements which would invalidate this agreement on that ground. . . . While defendants argue that the public policy evinced by the legislative restrictions upon the duration of voting trust agreements should be applied here, this agreement is not a voting trust, but as pointed out by the dissenting justice in the Appellate Court, is a straight contractual voting control agreement which does not divorce voting rights from stock ownership. . . . [T]he policy against agreements in which stock ownership and voting rights are separated, is inapplicable to voting control agreements. . . . While limiting voting trusts in 1947 to a maximum duration of 10 years, the legislature has indicated no similar policy regarding straight voting agreements although these have been common since prior to 1870. In view of the history of decisions of this court generally upholding, in the absence of fraud or prejudice to minority interests or public policy, the right of stockholders to agree among themselves as to the manner in which their stock will be voted, we do not regard the period of time within which this agreement may remain effective as rendering the agreement unenforceable.

The clause that provides for the election of certain persons to specified offices for a period of years likewise does not require invalidation. In *Kantzler v. Bensinger,* 214 Ill. 589, this court upheld an agreement entered into by all the stockholders providing that certain parties would be elected to the offices of the corporation for a fixed period. In *Faulds v. Yates,* 57 Ill. 416, we upheld a similar agreement among the majority stockholders of a corporation, notwithstanding the existence of a minority which was not before the court complaining thereof.

We turn next to a consideration of the effect of the stated purpose of the agreement upon its validity. The pertinent provision is: "The said Benjamin A. Galler and Isadore A. Galler desire to provide income for the support and maintenance of their immediate families." Obviously, there is no evil inherent in a contract entered into for the reason that the persons originating the terms desired to so arrange their property as to provide post-death support for those dependent upon them. Nor does the fact that the subject property is corporate stock alter the situation so long as there exists no detriment to minority stock interests, creditors or other public injury. It is, however, contended by defendants that the methods provided by the agreement for implementation of the stated purpose are, as a whole, violative of the Business Corporation Act to such an extent as to render it void *in toto.*

The terms of the dividend agreement require a minimum annual dividend of $50,000, but this duty is limited by the subsequent provision that it shall be operative only so long as an earned surplus of $500,000 is maintained. It may be noted that in 1958, the year prior to commencement of this litigation, the corporation's net earnings after taxes amounted to $202,759 while its earned surplus was $1,543,270, and this was increased in 1958 to $1,680,079 while earnings were $172,964. The minimum earned surplus requirement is designed for the protection of the corporation and its creditors, and we take no exception to the contractual dividend requirements as thus restricted.

The salary continuation agreement is a common feature, in one form or another, of corporate executive employment. It requires that the widow should receive a total benefit, payable monthly over a five-year period, aggregating twice the amount paid her deceased husband in one year. This requirement was likewise limited for the protection of the corporation by being contingent upon the payments being income tax-deductible by the corporation. The charge made in those cases which have considered the validity of payments to the widow of an officer and shareholder in a corporation is that a gift of its property by a noncharitable corporation is in violation of the rights of its shareholders and *ultra vires.* Since there are no shareholders here other than the parties to the contract, this objection is not here applicable, and its effect, as limited, upon the corporation is not so prejudicial as to require its invalidation. . . .

Accordingly, the judgment of the Appellate Court is reversed, except insofar as it relates to fees, and is, as to them affirmed. The cause is remanded to the circuit court of Cook County with directions to proceed in accordance herewith.

Affirmed in part and reversed in part, and remanded with directions.

Questions

1. What did Emma want? She was promised all the financial benefits guaranteed in the agreement. Why does she insist on enforcing its other provisions?

2. Does *Galler v. Galler* offer a different vision of the corporation than *Clark v. Dodge*?

C. Fiduciary Duties of Shareholders in Closely Held Corporations

Donahue v. Rodd Electrotype Company of New England, Inc.

367 Mass. 578 (1975)

TAURO, Chief Justice

The plaintiff, Euphemia Donahue, a minority stockholder in the Rodd Electrotype Company of New England, Inc. (Rodd Electrotype), a Massachusetts corporation, brings this suit against the directors of Rodd Electrotype, Charles H. Rodd, Frederick I. Rodd and Mr. Harold E. Magnuson, against Harry C. Rodd, a former director, officer, and controlling stockholder of Rodd Electrotype and against Rodd Electrotype (hereinafter called defendants). The plaintiff seeks to rescind Rodd Electrotype's purchase of Harry Rodd's shares in Rodd Electrotype[2] and to compel Harry Rodd "to repay to the corporation the purchase price of said shares, $36,000, together with interest from the date of purchase." The plaintiff alleges that the defendants caused the corporation to purchase the shares in violation of their fiduciary duty to her, a minority stockholder of Rodd Electrotype.[4]

---

2. In her original bill of complaint, the plaintiff alleged numerous breaches of the fiduciary duties owed to her by the individual defendants in their respective capacities as controlling stockholders and directors. Essentially, she contended that the individual defendants were diverting Rodd Electrotype assets for the benefit of the Rodd family. She requested injunctive relief and restitution of misappropriated funds. At the trial in the Superior Court, the plaintiff's counsel stipulated orally that the only transaction challenged in this suit was the purchase of Harry Rodd's stock by Rodd Electrotype.

4. In form, the plaintiff's bill of complaint presents, at least in part, a derivative action, brought on behalf of the corporation, and, in the words of the bill, "on behalf of . . . [the] stockholders" of Rodd Electrotype. Yet, the plaintiff's bill, in substance, was one seeking redress because of alleged breaches of the fiduciary duty owed *to her*, a minority stockholder, by the controlling stockholders.

The trial judge, after hearing oral testimony, dismissed the plaintiff's bill on the merits. He found that the purchase was without prejudice to the plaintiff and implicitly found that the transaction had been carried out in good faith and with inherent fairness. The Appeals Court affirmed with costs. The case is before us on the plaintiff's application for further appellate review. . . .

The evidence may be summarized as follows: In 1935, the defendant, Harry C. Rodd, began his employment with Rodd Electrotype, then styled the Royal Electrotype Company of New England, Inc. (Royal of New England). At that time, the company was a wholly-owned subsidiary of a Pennsylvania corporation, the Royal Electrotype Company (Royal Electrotype). Mr. Rodd's advancement within the company was rapid. The following year he was elected a director, and, in 1946, he succeeded to the position of general manager and treasurer.

In 1936, the plaintiff's husband, Joseph Donahue (now deceased), was hired by Royal of New England as a "finisher" of electrotype plates. His duties were confined to operational matters within the plant. Although he ultimately achieved the positions of plant superintendent (1946) and corporate vice president (1955), Donahue never participated in the "management" aspect of the business.

In the years preceding 1955, the parent company, Royal Electrotype, made available to Harry Rodd and Joseph Donahue shares of the common stock in its subsidiary, Royal of New England. Harry Rodd took advantage of the opportunities offered to him and acquired 200 shares for $20 a share. Joseph Donahue, at the suggestion of Harry Rodd, who hoped to interest Donahue in the business, eventually obtained fifty shares in two twenty-five share lots priced at $20 a share. The parent company at all times retained 725 of the 1,000 outstanding shares. One Lawrence W. Kelley owned the remaining twenty-five shares.

In June of 1955, Royal of New England purchased all 725 of its shares owned by its parent company. The total price amounted to $135,000. Royal of New England remitted $75,000 of this total in cash and executed five promissory notes of $12,000 each, due in each of the succeeding five years. Lawrence W. Kelley's twenty-five shares were also purchased at this time for $1,000. A substantial portion of Royal of New England's cash expenditures was loaned to the company by Harry Rodd, who mortgaged his house to obtain some of the necessary funds.

The stock purchases left Harry Rodd in control of Royal of New England. Early in 1955, before the purchases, he had assumed the presidency of the company. His

---

We treat the bill of complaint (as have the parties) as presenting a proper cause of suit in the personal right of the plaintiff. The defendants have not demurred to the plaintiff's bill of complaint. The case was tried on the plaintiff's theory. The evidence introduced was consistent with litigation of the personal right presented in the bill. The issue of the duty owed by controlling stockholders to minority stockholders was sufficiently before the trial court. The issue was raised and argued fully on appeal. In this instance we prefer substance over form and decide the case on this basis.

200 shares gave him a dominant eighty per cent interest. Joseph Donahue, at this time, was the only minority stockholder.

Subsequent events reflected Harry Rodd's dominant influence. In June, 1960, more than a year after the last obligation to Royal Electrotype had been discharged, the company was renamed the Rodd Electrotype Company of New England, Inc. In 1962, Charles H. Rodd, Harry Rodd's son (a defendant here), who had long been a company employee working in the plant, became corporate vice president. In 1963, he joined his father on the board of directors. In 1964, another son, Frederick I. Rodd (also a defendant), replaced Joseph Donahue as plant superintendent. By 1965, Harry Rodd had evidently decided to reduce his participation in corporate management. That year, Charles Rodd succeeded him as president and general manager of Rodd Electrotype.

From 1959 to 1967, Harry Rodd pursued what may fairly be termed a gift program by which he distributed the majority of his shares equally among his two sons and his daughter, Phyllis E. Mason. Each child received thirty-nine shares. Two shares were returned to the corporate treasury in 1966.

We come now to the events of 1970 which form the grounds for the plaintiff's complaint. In May of 1970, Harry Rodd was seventy-seven years old. The record indicates that for some time he had not enjoyed the best of health and that he had undergone a number of operations. His sons wished him to retire. Mr. Rodd was not averse to this suggestion. However, he insisted that some financial arrangements be made with respect to his remaining eighty-one shares of stock. A number of conferences ensued. Harry Rodd and Charles Rodd (representing the company) negotiated terms of purchase for forty-five shares which, Charles Rodd testified, would reflect the book value and liquidating value of the shares.

A special board meeting convened on July 13, 1970. As the first order of business, Harry Rodd resigned his directorship of Rodd Electrotype. The remaining incumbent directors, Charles Rodd and Mr. Harold E. Magnuson (clerk of the company and a defendant and defense attorney in the instant suit), elected Frederick Rodd to replace his father. The three directors then authorized Rodd Electrotype's president (Charles Rodd) to execute an agreement between Harry Rodd and the company in which the company would purchase forty-five shares for $800 a share ($36,000).

The stock purchase agreement was formalized between the parties on July 13, 1970. Two days later, a sale pursuant to the July 13 agreement was consummated. At approximately the same time, Harry Rodd resigned his last corporate office, that of treasurer.

Harry Rodd completed divestiture of his Rodd Electrotype stock in the following year. As was true of his previous gifts, his later divestments gave equal representation to his children. Two shares were sold to each child on July 15, 1970, for $800 a share. Each was given ten shares in March, 1971. Thus, in March, 1971, the shareholdings in Rodd Electrotype were apportioned as follows: Charles Rodd, Frederick Rodd and Phyllis Mason each held fifty-one shares; the Donahues[8] held fifty shares.

A special meeting of the stockholders of the company was held on March 30, 1971. At the meeting, Charles Rodd, company president and general manager, reported the tentative results of an audit conducted by the company auditors and reported generally on the company events of the year. For the first time, the Donahues learned that the corporation had purchased Harry Rodd's shares. According to the minutes of the meeting, following Charles Rodd's report, the Donahues raised questions about the purchase. They then voted against a resolution, ultimately adopted by the remaining stockholders, to approve Charles Rodd's report. Although the minutes of the meeting show that the stockholders unanimously voted to accept a second resolution ratifying all acts of the company president (he executed the stock purchase agreement) in the preceding year, the trial judge found, and there was evidence to support his finding, that the Donahues did not ratify the purchase of Harry Rodd's shares.

A few weeks after the meeting, the Donahues, acting through their attorney, offered their shares to the corporation on the same terms given to Harry Rodd. Mr. Harold E. Magnuson replied by letter that the corporation would not purchase the shares and was not in a financial position to do so.[10] This suit followed.

In her argument before this court, the plaintiff has characterized the corporate purchase of Harry Rodd's shares as an unlawful distribution of corporate assets to controlling stockholders. She urges that the distribution constitutes a breach of the fiduciary duty owed by the Rodds, as controlling stockholders, to her, a minority stockholder in the enterprise, because the Rodds failed to accord her an equal opportunity to sell her shares to the corporation. The defendants reply that the stock purchase was within the powers of the corporation and met the requirements of good faith and inherent fairness imposed on a fiduciary in his dealings with the corporation. They assert that there is no right to equal opportunity in corporate stock purchases for the corporate treasury. For the reasons hereinafter noted, we agree with the plaintiff and reverse the decree of the Superior Court. However, we limit the applicability of our holding to "close corporations," as hereinafter defined. Whether the holding should apply to other corporations is left for decision in another case, on a proper record.

A. *Close Corporations.* In previous opinions, we have alluded to the distinctive nature of the close corporation, but have never defined precisely what is meant by a close corporation. There is no single, generally accepted definition. Some

---

8. Joseph Donahue gave his wife, the plaintiff, joint ownership of his fifty shares in 1962. In 1968, they transferred five shares to their son, Dr. Robert Donahue. On Joseph Donahue's death, the plaintiff became outright owner of the forty-five share block. This was the ownership pattern which obtained in March, 1971.

10. Between 1965 and 1969, the company offered to purchase the Donahue shares for amounts between $2,000 and $10,000 ($40 to $200 a share). The Donahues rejected these offers.

commentators emphasize an "integration of ownership and management." Others focus on the number of stockholders and the nature of the market for the stock. In this view, close corporations have few stockholders; there is little market for corporate stock.... We accept aspects of both definitions. We deem a close corporation to be typified by: (1) a small number of stockholders; (2) no ready market for the corporate stock; and (3) substantial majority stockholder participation in the management, direction and operations of the corporation.

As thus defined, the close corporation bears striking resemblance to a partnership. Commentators and courts have noted that the close corporation is often little more than an "incorporated" or "chartered" partnership.... The stockholders "clothe" their partnership "with the benefits peculiar to a corporation, limited liability, perpetuity and the like." In essence, though, the enterprise remains one in which ownership is limited to the original parties or transferees of their stock to whom the other stockholders have agreed, in which ownership and management are in the same hands, and in which the owners are quite dependent on one another for the success of the enterprise. Many close corporations are "really partnerships between two or three people who contribute their capital, skills, experience and labor." Just as in a partnership, the relationship among the stockholders must be one of trust, confidence and absolute loyalty if the enterprise is to succeed. Close corporations with substantial assets and with more numerous stockholders are no different from smaller close corporations in this regard. All participants rely on the fidelity and abilities of those stockholders who hold office. Disloyalty and self-seeking conduct on the part of any stockholder will engender bickering, corporate stalemates, and, perhaps, efforts to achieve dissolution....

In *Helms v. Duckworth,* 101 U.S. App. D.C. 390 (1957), the United States Court of Appeals for the District of Columbia Circuit had before it a stockholders' agreement providing for the purchase of the shares of a deceased stockholder by the surviving stockholder in a small "two-man" close corporation. The court held the surviving stockholder to a duty "to deal fairly, honestly, and openly with ... [his] fellow stockholders." Judge Burger, now Chief Justice Burger, writing for the court, emphasized the resemblance of the two-man close corporation to a partnership: "In an intimate business venture such as this, stockholders of a close corporation occupy a position similar to that of joint adventurers and partners. While courts have sometimes declared stockholders 'do not bear toward each other that same relation of trust and confidence which prevails in partnerships,' this view ignores the practical realities of the organization and functioning of a small 'two-man' corporation organized to carry on a small business enterprise in which the stockholders, directors, and managers are the same persons" (footnotes omitted).

Although the corporate form provides the above-mentioned advantages for the stockholders (limited liability, perpetuity, and so forth), it also supplies an opportunity for the majority stockholders to oppress or disadvantage minority stockholders. The minority is vulnerable to a variety of oppressive devices, termed "freeze-outs," which the majority may employ.... In particular, the power of the board of directors, controlled by the majority, to declare or withhold dividends and to deny the minority employment is easily converted to a device to disadvantage minority stockholders. . . .

The minority can, of course, initiate suit against the majority and their directors. Self-serving conduct by directors is proscribed by the director's fiduciary obligation to the corporation. However, in practice, the plaintiff will find difficulty in challenging dividend or employment policies. Such policies are considered to be within the judgment of the directors. This court has said: "The courts prefer not to interfere . . . with the sound financial management of the corporation by its directors, but declare as a general rule that the declaration of dividends rests within the sound discretion of the directors, refusing to interfere with their determination unless a plain abuse of discretion is made to appear." Judicial reluctance to interfere combines with the difficulty of proof when the standard is "plain abuse of discretion" or bad faith, to limit the possibilities for relief. Although contractual provisions in an "agreement of association and articles of organization or in bylaws" have justified decrees in this jurisdiction ordering dividend declarations, generally, plaintiffs who seek judicial assistance against corporate dividend or employment policies do not prevail. . . .

Thus, when these types of "freeze-outs" are attempted by the majority stockholders, the minority stockholders, cut off from all corporation-related revenues, must either suffer their losses or seek a buyer for their shares. Many minority stockholders will be unwilling or unable to wait for an alteration in majority policy. Typically, the minority stockholder in a close corporation has a substantial percentage of his personal assets invested in the corporation. The stockholder may have anticipated that his salary from his position with the corporation would be his livelihood. Thus, he cannot afford to wait passively. He must liquidate his investment in the close corporation in order to reinvest the funds in income-producing enterprises.

At this point, the true plight of the minority stockholder in a close corporation becomes manifest. He cannot easily reclaim his capital. In a large public corporation, the oppressed or dissident minority stockholder could sell his stock in order to extricate some of his invested capital. By definition, this market is not available for shares in the close corporation. In a partnership, a partner who feels abused by his fellow partners may cause dissolution by his "express will . . . at any time" and recover his share of partnership assets and accumulated profits. If dissolution results in a breach of the partnership articles, the culpable partner will be liable in damages. By contrast, the stockholder in the close corporation or "incorporated partnership" may achieve dissolution and recovery of his share of the enterprise assets only by compliance with the rigorous terms of the applicable chapter of the General Laws. . . .

Thus, in a close corporation, the minority stockholders may be trapped in a disadvantageous situation. No outsider would knowingly assume the position of the disadvantaged minority. The outsider would have the same difficulties. To cut losses, the minority stockholder may be compelled to deal with the majority. This is the capstone of the majority plan. Majority "freeze-out" schemes which withhold dividends are designed to compel the minority to relinquish stock at inadequate prices.... When the minority stockholder agrees to sell out at less than fair value, the majority has won.

Because of the fundamental resemblance of the close corporation to the partnership, the trust and confidence which are essential to this scale and manner of enterprise, and the inherent danger to minority interests in the close corporation, we hold that stockholders[17] in the close corporation owe one another substantially the same fiduciary duty in the operation of the enterprise[18] that partners owe to one another. In our previous decisions, we have defined the standard of duty owed by partners to one another as the "utmost good faith and loyalty." Stockholders in close corporations must discharge their management and stockholder responsibilities in conformity with this strict good faith standard. They may not act out of avarice, expediency or self-interest in derogation of their duty of loyalty to the other stockholders and to the corporation.

We contrast this strict good faith standard with the somewhat less stringent standard of fiduciary duty to which directors and stockholders of all corporations must adhere in the discharge of their corporate responsibilities. Corporate directors are held to a good faith and inherent fairness standard of conduct and are not "permitted to serve two masters whose interests are antagonistic." "Their paramount duty is to the corporation, and their personal pecuniary interests are subordinate to that duty." ...

The more rigorous duty of partners and participants in a joint adventure, here extended to stockholders in a close corporation, was described by then Chief Judge Cardozo of the New York Court of Appeals in *Meinhard v. Salmon*, 249 N.Y. 458 (1928): "Joint adventurers, like copartners, owe to one another, while the enterprise continues, the duty of the finest loyalty. Many forms of conduct permissible in a workaday world for those acting at arm's length, are forbidden to those bound by fiduciary ties.... Not honesty alone, but the punctilio of an honor the most sensitive, is then the standard of behavior."

Application of this strict standard of duty to stockholders in close corporations is a natural outgrowth of the prior case law. In a number of cases involving close corporations, we have held stockholders participating in management to a standard of fiduciary duty more exacting than the traditional good faith and inherent

---

17. We do not limit our holding to majority stockholders. In the close corporation, the minority may do equal damage through unscrupulous and improper "sharp dealings" with an unsuspecting majority....

18. We stress that the strict fiduciary duty which we apply to stockholders in a close corporation in this opinion governs *only* their actions relative to the operations of the enterprise and the effects of that operation on the rights and investments of other stockholders. We express no opinion as to the standard of duty applicable to transactions in the shares of the close corporation when the corporation is not a party to the transaction....

fairness standard because of the trust and confidence reposed in them by the other stockholders. . . .

. . . [W]e have imposed a duty of loyalty more exacting than that duty owed by a director to his corporation or by a majority stockholder to the minority in a public corporation because of facts particular to the close corporation in the cases. In the instant case, we extend this strict duty of loyalty to all stockholders in close corporations. The circumstances which justified findings of relationships of trust and confidence in these particular cases exist universally in modified form in all close corporations. Statements in other cases . . . which suggest that stockholders of a corporation do not stand in a relationship of trust and confidence to one another will not be followed in the close corporation context.

B. *Equal Opportunity in a Close Corporation.* Under settled Massachusetts law, a domestic corporation, unless forbidden by statute, has the power to purchase its own shares. . . . An agreement to reacquire stock "[is] enforceable, subject, at least, to the limitations that the purchase must be made in good faith and without prejudice to creditors and stockholders." . . . When the corporation reacquiring its own stock is a close corporation, the purchase is subject to the additional requirement, in the light of our holding in this opinion, that the stockholders, who, as directors or controlling stockholders, caused the corporation to enter into the stock purchase agreement, must have acted with the utmost good faith and loyalty to the other stockholders.

To meet this test, if the stockholder whose shares were purchased was a member of the controlling group, the controlling stockholders must cause the corporation to offer each stockholder an equal opportunity to sell a ratable number of his shares to the corporation at an identical price.[24] Purchase by the corporation confers substantial benefits on the members of the controlling group whose shares were purchased. These benefits are not available to the minority stockholders if the corporation does not also offer them an opportunity to sell their shares. The controlling group may not, consistent with its strict duty to the minority, utilize its control of the corporation to obtain special advantages and disproportionate benefit from its share ownership. . . .

The benefits conferred by the purchase are twofold: (1) provision of a market for shares; (2) access to corporate assets for personal use. By definition, there is no ready market for shares of a close corporation. The purchase creates a market for shares which previously had been unmarketable. It transforms a previously illiquid investment into a liquid one. If the close corporation purchases shares only from a member of the controlling group, the controlling stockholder can convert his shares into cash at a time when none of the other stockholders can. Consistent with its strict fiduciary

---

24. Of course, a close corporation may purchase shares from one stockholder without offering the others an equal opportunity if all other stockholders give advance consent to the stock purchase arrangements through acceptance of an appropriate provision in the articles of organization, the corporate by-laws, or a stockholder's agreement. Similarly, all other stockholders may ratify the purchase. . . .

duty, the controlling group may not utilize its control of the corporation to establish an exclusive market in previously unmarketable shares from which the minority stockholders are excluded. . . .

The purchase also distributes corporate assets to the stockholder whose shares were purchased. Unless an equal opportunity is given to all stockholders, the purchase of shares from a member of the controlling group operates as a *preferential* distribution of assets. In exchange for his shares, he receives a percentage of the contributed capital and accumulated profits of the enterprise. The funds he so receives are available for his personal use. The other stockholders benefit from no such access to corporate property and cannot withdraw their shares of the corporate profits and capital in this manner unless the controlling group acquiesces. Although the purchase price for the controlling stockholder's shares may seem fair to the corporation and other stockholders under the tests established in the prior case law, the controlling stockholder whose stock has been purchased has still received a relative advantage over his fellow stockholders, inconsistent with his strict fiduciary duty — an opportunity to turn corporate funds to personal use.

The rule of equal opportunity in stock purchases by close corporations provides equal access to these benefits for all stockholders. We hold that, in any case in which the controlling stockholders have exercised their power over the corporation to deny the minority such equal opportunity, the minority shall be entitled to appropriate relief. . . .

C. *Application of the Law to this Case*. We turn now to the application of the learning set forth above to the facts of the instant case.

The strict standard of duty is plainly applicable to the stockholders in Rodd Electrotype. Rodd Electrotype is a close corporation. Members of the Rodd and Donahue families are the sole owners of the corporation's stock. In actual numbers, the corporation, immediately prior to the corporate purchase of Harry Rodd's shares, had six stockholders. The shares have not been traded, and no market for them seems to exist. Harry Rodd, Charles Rodd, Frederick Rodd, William G. Mason (Phyllis Mason's husband), and the plaintiff's husband all worked for the corporation. The Rodds have retained the paramount management positions.

Through their control of these management positions and of the majority of the Rodd Electrotype stock, the Rodds effectively controlled the corporation. In testing the stock purchase from Harry Rodd against the applicable strict fiduciary standard, we treat the Rodd family as a single controlling group. We reject the defendants' contention that the Rodd family cannot be treated as a unit for this purpose. From the evidence, it is clear that the Rodd family was a close-knit one with strong community of interest. Harry Rodd had hired his sons to work in the family business, Rodd Electrotype. As he aged, he transferred portions of his stock holdings to his children. Charles Rodd and Frederick Rodd were given positions of responsibility in the business as he withdrew from active management. In these circumstances, it is realistic to assume that appreciation, gratitude, and filial devotion would prevent the younger Rodds from opposing a plan which would provide funds for their father's retirement.

Moreover, a strong motive of interest requires that the Rodds be considered a controlling group. When Charles Rodd and Frederick Rodd were called on to represent the corporation in its dealings with their father, they must have known that further advancement within the corporation and benefits would follow their father's retirement and the purchase of his stock. The corporate purchase would take only forty-five of Harry Rodd's eighty-one shares. The remaining thirty-six shares were to be divided among Harry Rodd's children in equal amounts by gift and sale. Receipt of their portion of the thirty-six shares and purchase by the corporation of forty-five shares would effectively transfer full control of the corporation to Frederick Rodd and Charles Rodd, if they chose to act in concert with each other or if one of them chose to ally with his sister. Moreover, Frederick Rodd was the obvious successor to his father as director and corporate treasurer when those posts became vacant after his father's retirement. Failure to complete the corporate purchase (in other words, impeding their father's retirement plan) would have delayed, and perhaps have suspended indefinitely, the transfer of these benefits to the younger Rodds. They could not be expected to oppose their father's wishes in this matter. Although the defendants are correct when they assert that no express agreement involving a quid pro quo — subsequent stock gifts for votes from the directors — was proved, no express agreement is necessary to demonstrate the identity of interest which disciplines a controlling group acting in unison.

On its face, then, the purchase of Harry Rodd's shares by the corporation is a breach of the duty which the controlling stockholders, the Rodds, owed to the minority stockholders, the plaintiff and her son. The purchase distributed a portion of the corporate assets to Harry Rodd, a member of the controlling group, in exchange for his shares. The plaintiff and her son were not offered an equal opportunity to sell their shares to the corporation. In fact, their efforts to obtain an equal opportunity were rebuffed by the corporate representative. As the trial judge found, they did not, in any manner, ratify the transaction with Harry Rodd.

Because of the foregoing, we hold that the plaintiff is entitled to relief. Two forms of suitable relief are set out hereinafter. The judge below is to enter an appropriate judgment. The judgment may require Harry Rodd to remit $36,000 with interest at the legal rate from July 15, 1970, to Rodd Electrotype in exchange for forty-five shares of Rodd Electrotype treasury stock. This, in substance, is the specific relief requested in the plaintiff's bill of complaint. Interest is manifestly appropriate. A stockholder, who, in violation of his fiduciary duty to the other stockholders, has obtained assets from his corporation and has had those assets available for his own use, must pay for that use. . . . In the alternative, the judgment may require Rodd Electrotype to purchase all of the plaintiff's shares for $36,000 without interest. In the circumstances of this case, we view this as the equal opportunity which the plaintiff should have received. Harry Rodd's retention of thirty-six shares, which were to be sold and given to his children within a year of the Rodd Electrotype purchase, cannot disguise the fact that the corporation acquired one hundred per cent of that portion of his holdings (forty-five shares) which he did not intend his children to own. The plaintiff is entitled to have one hundred per cent of her forty-five shares similarly purchased.

The final decree, in so far as it dismissed the bill as to Harry C. Rodd, Frederick I. Rodd, Charles H. Rodd, Mr. Harold E. Magnuson and Rodd Electrotype Company of New England, Inc., and awarded costs, is reversed. The case is remanded to the Superior Court for entry of judgment in conformity with this opinion.

So ordered.

WILKINS, Justice (concurring)

I agree with much of what the Chief Justice says in support of granting relief to the plaintiff. However, I do not join in any implication . . . that the rule concerning a close corporation's purchase of a controlling stockholder's shares applies to all operations of the corporation as they affect minority stockholders. That broader issue, which is apt to arise in connection with salaries and dividend policy, is not involved in this case. The analogy to partnerships may not be a complete one.

Questions

1. Why did the Rodd family decide to have the corporation repurchase Harry Rodd's shares? What benefits did Harry Rodd and his family receive from the corporation's repurchase of his shares? What benefits, if any, did the corporation receive?

2. What is the harm suffered by Ms. Donahue? She remains, after the repurchase, a minority shareholder of Rodd Electrotype, but now has a higher percentage of the corporation's outstanding shares. Is she harmed at all as long as the corporation paid a fair price for the shares?

3. The Massachusetts court seems to equate the fiduciary duties of shareholders in a closely held corporation to those of partners. Does the equation make sense? What reasons might exist to justify treating shareholders in closely held corporations and partners differently?

4. What alternative grounds could the Massachusetts court have used to impose liability on the majority shareholder in this case?

Wilkes v. Springside Nursing Home, Inc.

370 Mass. 842 (1976)

HENNESSEY, Chief Justice

On August 5, 1971, the plaintiff (Wilkes) filed a bill in equity for declaratory judgment in the Probate Court for Berkshire County, naming as defendants T. Edward Quinn (Quinn), Leon L. Riche (Riche), the First Agricultural National Bank of Berkshire County and Frank Sutherland MacShane as executors under the will of

Lawrence R. Connor (Connor), and the Springside Nursing Home, Inc. (Springside or the corporation). Wilkes alleged that he, Quinn, Riche and Dr. Hubert A. Pipkin (Pipkin)[4] entered into a partnership agreement in 1951, prior to the incorporation of Springside, which agreement was breached in 1967 when Wilkes's salary was terminated and he was voted out as an officer and director of the corporation. Wilkes sought, among other forms of relief, damages in the amount of the salary he would have received had he continued as a director and officer of Springside subsequent to March, 1967.

A judge of the Probate Court referred the suit to a master, who, after a lengthy hearing, issued his final report in late 1973. Wilkes's objections to the master's report were overruled after a hearing, and the master's report was confirmed in late 1974. A judgment was entered dismissing Wilkes's action on the merits. We granted direct appellate review. On appeal, Wilkes argued in the alternative that (1) he should recover damages for breach of the alleged partnership agreement; and (2) he should recover damages because the defendants, as majority stockholders in Springside, breached their fiduciary duty to him as a minority stockholder by their action in February and March, 1967.

We conclude that the master's findings were warranted by the evidence and that his report was properly confirmed. However, we reverse so much of the judgment as dismisses Wilkes's complaint and order the entry of a judgment substantially granting the relief sought by Wilkes under the second alternative set forth above.

A summary of the pertinent facts as found by the master is set out in the following pages. It will be seen that, although the issue whether there was a breach of the fiduciary duty owed to Wilkes by the majority stockholders in Springside was not considered by the master, the master's report and the designated portions of the transcript of the evidence before him supply us with a sufficient basis for our conclusion.

In 1951 Wilkes acquired an option to purchase a building and lot located on the corner of Springside Avenue and North Street in Pittsfield, Massachusetts, the building having previously housed the Hillcrest Hospital. Though Wilkes was principally engaged in the roofing and siding business, he had gained a reputation locally for profitable dealings in real estate. Riche, an acquaintance of Wilkes, learned of the option, and interested Quinn (who was known to Wilkes through membership on the draft board in Pittsfield) and Pipkin (an acquaintance of both Wilkes and Riche) in joining Wilkes in his investment. The four men met and decided to participate jointly in the purchase of the building and lot as a real estate investment which, they believed, had good profit potential on resale or rental.

The parties later determined that the property would have its greatest potential for profit if it were operated by them as a nursing home. Wilkes consulted his

---

4. Dr. Pipkin transferred his interest in Springside to Connor in 1959 and is not a defendant in this action.

attorney, who advised him that if the four men were to operate the contemplated nursing home as planned, they would be partners and would be liable for any debts incurred by the partnership and by each other. On the attorney's suggestion, and after consultation among themselves, ownership of the property was vested in Springside, a corporation organized under Massachusetts law.

Each of the four men invested $1,000 and subscribed to ten shares of $100 par value stock in Springside.[6] At the time of incorporation it was understood by all of the parties that each would be a director of Springside and each would participate actively in the management and decision making involved in operating the corporation.[7] It was, further, the understanding and intention of all the parties that, corporate resources permitting, each would receive money from the corporation in equal amounts as long as each assumed an active and ongoing responsibility for carrying a portion of the burdens necessary to operate the business.

The work involved in establishing and operating a nursing home was roughly apportioned, and each of the four men undertook his respective tasks.[8] Initially, Riche was elected president of Springside, Wilkes was elected treasurer, and Quinn was elected clerk.[9] Each of the four was listed in the articles of organization as a director of the corporation.

At some time in 1952, it became apparent that the operational income and cash flow from the business were sufficient to permit the four stockholders to draw money from the corporation on a regular basis. Each of the four original parties initially received $35 a week from the corporation. As time went on the weekly return to each was increased until, in 1955, it totalled $100.

In 1959, after a long illness, Pipkin sold his shares in the corporation to Connor, who was known to Wilkes, Riche and Quinn through past transactions with Springside in his capacity as president of the First Agricultural National Bank of Berkshire County. Connor received a weekly stipend from the corporation equal to that received

---

6. On May 2, 1955, and again on December 23, 1958, each of the four original investors paid for and was issued additional shares of $100 par value stock, eventually bringing the total number of shares owned by each to 115.

7. Wilkes testified before the master that, when the corporate officers were elected all four men "were ... guaranteed directorships." Riche's understanding of the parties' intentions was that they all wanted to play a part in the management of the corporation and wanted to have some "say" in the risks involved; that, to this end, they all would be directors; and that "unless you [were] a director and officer you could not participate in the decisions of [the] enterprise."

8. Wilkes took charge of the repair, upkeep and maintenance of the physical plant and grounds; Riche assumed supervision over the kitchen facilities and dietary and food aspects of the home; Pipkin was to make himself available if and when medical problems arose; and Quinn dealt with the personnel and administrative aspects of the nursing home, serving informally as a managing director. Quinn further coordinated the activities of the other parties and served as a communication link among them when matters had to be discussed and decisions had to be made without a formal meeting.

9. Riche held the office of president from 1951 to 1963; Quinn served as president from 1963 on, as clerk from 1951 to 1967, and as treasurer from 1967 on; Wilkes was treasurer from 1951 to 1967.

by Wilkes, Riche and Quinn. He was elected a director of the corporation but never held any other office. He was assigned no specific area of responsibility in the operation of the nursing home but did participate in business discussions and decisions as a director and served additionally as financial adviser to the corporation.

In 1965 the stockholders decided to ==sell a portion of the corporate property to Quinn w==ho, in addition to being a stockholder in Springside, possessed an interest in another corporation which desired to operate a rest home on the property. Wilkes was successful in prevailing on the other stockholders of Springside to procure a higher sale price for the property than Quinn apparently anticipated paying or desired to pay. After the sale was consummated, the relationship between Quinn and Wilkes began to deteriorate.

The bad blood between Quinn and Wilkes affected the attitudes of both Riche and Connor. As a consequence of the strained relations among the parties, Wilkes, in January of 1967, gave notice of his intention to sell his shares for an amount based on an appraisal of their value. In February of 1967 a directors' meeting was held and the board exercised its right to establish the salaries of its officers and employees.[10] A schedule of payments was established whereby Quinn was to receive a substantial weekly increase and Riche and Connor were to continue receiving $100 a week. Wilkes, however, was left off the list of those to whom a salary was to be paid. The directors also set the annual meeting of the stockholders for March, 1967.

At the annual meeting in March, Wilkes was not reelected as a director, nor was he reelected as an officer of the corporation. He was further informed that neither his services nor his presence at the nursing home was wanted by his associates.

The meetings of the directors and stockholders in early 1967, the master found, were used as a vehicle to force Wilkes out of active participation in the management and operation of the corporation and to cut off all corporate payments to him. Though the board of directors had the power to dismiss any officers or employees for misconduct or neglect of duties, there was no indication in the minutes of the board of directors' meeting of February, 1967, that the failure to establish a salary for Wilkes was based on either ground. The severance of Wilkes from the payroll resulted not from misconduct or neglect of duties, but because of the personal desire of Quinn, Riche and Connor to prevent him from continuing to receive money from the corporation. Despite a continuing deterioration in his personal relationship with his associates, Wilkes had consistently endeavored to carry on his responsibilities to the corporation in the same satisfactory manner and with the same degree of competence he had previously shown. Wilkes was at all times willing to carry on his

---

10. The by-laws of the corporation provided that the directors, subject to the approval of the stockholders, had the power to fix the salaries of all officers and employees. This power, however, up until February, 1967, had not been exercised formally; all payments made to the four participants in the venture had resulted from the informal but unanimous approval of all the parties concerned.

responsibilities and participation if permitted so to do and provided that he receive his weekly stipend.

1. We turn to Wilkes's claim for damages based on a breach of fiduciary duty owed to him by the other participants in this venture. In light of the theory underlying this claim, we do not consider it vital to our approach to this case whether the claim is governed by partnership law or the law applicable to business corporations. This is so because, as all the parties agree, Springside was at all times relevant to this action, a close corporation as we have recently defined such an entity in *Donahue v. Rodd Electrotype Co. of New England, Inc.,* 367 Mass. 578, 585–586 (1975).

In *Donahue,* we held that "stockholders in the close corporation owe one another substantially the same fiduciary duty in the operation of the enterprise that partners owe to one another." As determined in previous decisions of this court, the standard of duty owed by partners to one another is one of "utmost good faith and loyalty." Thus, we concluded in *Donahue,* with regard to "their actions relative to the operations of the enterprise and the effects of that operation on the rights and investments of other stockholders," "[s]tockholders in close corporations must discharge their management and stockholder responsibilities in conformity with this strict good faith standard. They may not act out of avarice, expediency or self-interest in derogation of their duty of loyalty to the other stockholders and to the corporation."

In the *Donahue* case we recognized that one peculiar aspect of close corporations was the opportunity afforded to majority stockholders to oppress, disadvantage or "freeze out" minority stockholders. In *Donahue* itself, for example, the majority refused the minority an equal opportunity to sell a ratable number of shares to the corporation at the same price available to the majority. The net result of this refusal, we said, was that the minority could be forced to "sell out at less than fair value," since there is by definition no ready market for minority stock in a close corporation.

"Freeze outs," however, may be accomplished by the use of other devices. One such device which has proved to be particularly effective in accomplishing the purpose of the majority is to deprive minority stockholders of corporate offices and of employment with the corporation. This "freeze-out" technique has been successful because courts fairly consistently have been disinclined to interfere in those facets of internal corporate operations, such as the selection and retention or dismissal of officers, directors and employees, which essentially involve management decisions subject to the principle of majority control. As one authoritative source has said, "[M]any courts apparently feel that there is a legitimate sphere in which the controlling [directors or] shareholders can act in their own interest even if the minority suffers."

The denial of employment to the minority at the hands of the majority is especially pernicious in some instances. A guaranty of employment with the corporation may have been one of the "basic reason[s] why a minority owner has invested capital in the firm." The minority stockholder typically depends on his salary as the principal return on his investment, since the "earnings of a close corporation . . . are distributed in major part in salaries, bonuses and retirement benefits."[13] Other non-economic interests of the minority stockholder are likewise injuriously affected by barring him from corporate office. Such action severely restricts his participation in the management of the enterprise, and he is relegated to enjoying those benefits incident to his status as a stockholder. In sum, by terminating a minority stockholder's employment or by severing him from a position as an officer or director, the majority effectively frustrate the minority stockholder's purposes in entering on the corporate venture and also deny him an equal return on his investment.

The *Donahue* decision acknowledged, as a "natural outgrowth" of the case law of this Commonwealth, a strict obligation on the part of majority stockholders in a close corporation to deal with the minority with the utmost good faith and loyalty. On its face, this strict standard is applicable in the instant case. The distinction between the majority action in *Donahue* and the majority action in this case is more one of form than of substance. Nevertheless, we are concerned that untempered application of the strict good faith standard enunciated in *Donahue* to cases such as the one before us will result in the imposition of limitations on legitimate action by the controlling group in a close corporation which will unduly hamper its effectiveness in managing the corporation in the best interests of all concerned. The majority, concededly, have certain rights to what has been termed "selfish ownership" in the corporation which should be balanced against the concept of their fiduciary obligation to the minority.

Therefore, when minority stockholders in a close corporation bring suit against the majority alleging a breach of the strict good faith duty owed to them by the majority, we must carefully analyze the action taken by the controlling stockholders in the individual case. It must be asked whether the controlling group can demonstrate a legitimate business purpose for its action. In asking this question, we acknowledge the fact that the controlling group in a close corporation must have some room to maneuver in establishing the business policy of the corporation. It must have a large measure of discretion, for example, in declaring or withholding dividends, deciding whether to merge or consolidate, establishing the salaries of corporate officers, dismissing directors with or without cause, and hiring and firing corporate employees.

When an asserted business purpose for their action is advanced by the majority, however, we think it is open to minority stockholders to demonstrate that the same legitimate objective could have been achieved through an alternative course of action less harmful to the minority's interest. If called on to settle a dispute, our courts must weigh the legitimate business purpose, if any, against the practicability of a less harmful alternative.

Applying this approach to the instant case it is apparent that the majority stockholders in Springside have not shown a legitimate business purpose for severing

---

13. We note here that the master found that Springside never declared or paid a dividend to its stockholders.

Wilkes from the payroll of the corporation or for refusing to reelect him as a salaried officer and director. The master's subsidiary findings relating to the purpose of the meetings of the directors and stockholders in February and March, 1967, are supported by the evidence. There was no showing of misconduct on Wilkes's part as a director, officer or employee of the corporation which would lead us to approve the majority action as a legitimate response to the disruptive nature of an undesirable individual bent on injuring or destroying the corporation. On the contrary, it appears that Wilkes had always accomplished his assigned share of the duties competently, and that he had never indicated an unwillingness to continue to do so.

It is an inescapable conclusion from all the evidence that the action of the majority stockholders here was a designed "freeze out" for which no legitimate business purpose has been suggested. Furthermore, we may infer that a design to pressure Wilkes into selling his shares to the corporation at a price below their value well may have been at the heart of the majority's plan.[14]

In the context of this case, several factors bear directly on the duty owed to Wilkes by his associates. At a minimum, the duty of utmost good faith and loyalty would demand that the majority consider that their action was in disregard of a longstanding policy of the stockholders that each would be a director of the corporation and that employment with the corporation would go hand in hand with stock ownership; that Wilkes was one of the four originators of the nursing home venture; and that Wilkes, like the others, had invested his capital and time for more than fifteen years with the expectation that he would continue to participate in corporate decisions. Most important is the plain fact that the cutting off of Wilkes's salary, together with the fact that the corporation never declared a dividend, assured that Wilkes would receive no return at all from the corporation. . . .

Therefore our order is as follows: So much of the judgment as dismisses Wilkes's complaint and awards costs to the defendants is reversed. The case is remanded to the Probate Court for Berkshire County for further proceedings concerning the issue of damages. Thereafter a judgment shall be entered declaring that Quinn, Riche and Connor breached their fiduciary duty to Wilkes as a minority stockholder in Springside, and awarding money damages therefor. Wilkes shall be allowed to recover from Riche, the estate of T. Edward Quinn and the estate of Lawrence R. Connor, ratably, according to the inequitable enrichment of each, the salary he would have received had he remained an officer and director of Springside. In considering the issue of damages the judge on remand shall take into account the extent to which any remaining corporate funds of Springside may be diverted to satisfy Wilkes's claim.

So ordered.

---

14. This inference arises from the fact that Connor, acting on behalf of the three controlling stockholders, offered to purchase Wilkes's shares for a price Connor admittedly would not have accepted for his own shares.

Questions

1. The Massachusetts court in *Wilkes v. Springside Nursing Home, Inc.* stated that it did not matter whether it applied partnership law or corporate law in resolving the question before it. Do you agree? Is there another doctrinal regime that the court could have used to resolve the dispute without reference either to partnership law or to corporate law? Why do you suppose the court did not use this alternative?

2. The court refers to the majority's right of "selfish ownership." Is such right consistent with the fiduciary duty imposed in *Donahue v. Rodd Electrotype Company of New England, Inc.*? Is such right recognized under partnership law?

3. What are the differences and similarities between the rule adopted in *Wilkes* and the role that the Business Judgment Rule plays in determining the fiduciary duties of directors and officers?

Smith v. Atlantic Properties, Inc.

12 Mass. App. Ct. 201 (1981)

CUTTER, Justice

In December, 1951, Dr. Louis E. Wolfson agreed to purchase land in Norwood for $350,000, with an initial cash payment of $50,000 and a mortgage note of $300,000 payable in thirty-three months. Dr. Wolfson offered a quarter interest each in the land to Mr. Paul T. Smith, Mr. Abraham Zimble, and William H. Burke. Each paid to Dr. Wolfson $12,500, one quarter of the initial payment. Mr. Smith, an attorney, organized the defendant corporation (Atlantic) in 1951 to operate the real estate. Each of the four subscribers received twenty-five shares of stock. Mr. Smith included, both in the corporation's articles of organization and in its by-laws, a provision reading, "No election, appointment or resolution by the Stockholders and no election, appointment, resolution, purchase, sale, lease, contract, contribution, compensation, proceeding or act by the Board of Directors or by any officer or officers shall be valid or binding upon the corporation until effected, passed, approved or ratified by an affirmative vote of eighty (80%) per cent of the capital stock issued outstanding and entitled to vote." This provision (hereafter referred to as the 80% provision) was included at Dr. Wolfson's request and had the effect of giving to any one of the four original shareholders a veto in corporate decisions.

Atlantic purchased the Norwood land. Some of the land and other assets were sold for about $220,000. Atlantic retained twenty-eight acres on which stood about twenty old brick or wood mill-type structures, which required expensive and constant repairs. After the first year, Altantic became profitable and showed a profit every year prior to 1969, ranging from a low of $7,683 in 1953 to a high of $44,358 in 1954. The mortgage was paid by 1958 and Atlantic has incurred no long-term debt thereafter. Salaries of about $25,000 were paid only in 1959 and 1960. Dividends in the total amount of $10,000 each were paid in 1964 and 1970. By 1961, Atlantic had about $172,000 in retained earnings, more than half in cash.

For various reasons, which need not be stated in detail, disagreements and ill will soon arose between Dr. Wolfson, on the one hand, and the other stockholders as a group.[3] Dr. Wolfson wished to see Atlantic's earnings devoted to repairs and possibly some improvements in its existing buildings and adjacent facilities. The other stockholders desired the declaration of dividends. Dr. Wolfson fairly steadily refused to vote for any dividends. Although it was pointed out to him that failure to declare dividends might result in the imposition by the Internal Revenue Service of a penalty under the Internal Revenue Code, I.R.C. § 531 et seq. (relating to unreasonable accumulation of corporate earnings and profits), Dr. Wolfson persisted in his refusal to declare dividends. The other shareholders did agree over the years to making at least the most urgent repairs to Atlantic's buildings, but did not agree to make all repairs and improvements which were recommended in a 1962 report by an engineering firm retained by Atlantic to make a complete estimate of all repairs and improvements which might be beneficial.

The fears of an Internal Revenue Service assessment of a penalty tax were soon realized. Penalty assessments were made in 1962, 1963, and 1964. These were settled by Dr. Wolfson for $11,767.71 in taxes and interest. Despite this settlement, Dr. Wolfson continued his opposition to declaring dividends. The record does not indicate that he developed any specific and definitive schedule or plan for a series of necessary or desirable repairs and improvements to Atlantic's properties. At least none was proposed which would have had a reasonable chance of satisfying the Internal Revenue Service that expenditures for such repairs and improvements constituted "reasonable needs of the business," I.R.C. § 534(c), a term which includes (see I.R.C. § 537) "the reasonably anticipated needs of the business." Predictably, despite further warnings by Dr. Wolfson's shareholder colleagues, the Internal Revenue Service assessed further penalty taxes for the years 1965, 1966, 1967, and 1968. These taxes were upheld by the United States Tax Court in *Atlantic Properties, Inc. v. Commissioner of Int. Rev.*, 62 T.C. 644 (1974), and on appeal in 519 F.2d 1233 (1st Cir. 1975)....

On January 30, 1967, the shareholders, other than Dr. Wolfson, initiated this proceeding in the Superior Court, later supplemented to reflect developments after the original complaint. The plaintiffs sought a court determination of the dividends to be paid by Atlantic, the removal of Dr. Wolfson as a director, and an order that Atlantic be reimbursed by him for the penalty taxes assessed against it and related expenses. The case was tried before a justice of the Superior Court (jury waived) in September and October, 1979.

---

3. At least one cause of ill will on Dr. Wolfson's part may have been the refusal of the other shareholders to consent to his transferring his shares in Atlantic to the Louis E. Wolfson Foundation, a charitable foundation created by Dr. Wolfson.

The trial judge made findings (but in more detail) of essentially the facts outlined above and concluded that Dr. "Wolfson's obstinate refusal to vote in favor of . . . dividends was . . . caused more by his dislike for other stockholders and his desire to avoid additional tax payments than . . . by any genuine desire to undertake a program for improving . . . (Atlantic) property." She also determined that Dr. Wolfson was liable to Atlantic for taxes and interest amounting to "$11,767.11 plus interest from the commencement of this action, plus $35,646.14 plus interest from August 11, 1975," the date of the First Circuit decision affirming the second penalty tax assessment. The latter amount includes an attorney's fee of $7,500 in the Federal tax cases. She also ordered the directors of Atlantic to declare "a reasonable dividend at the earliest practical date and reasonable dividends annually thereafter consistent with good business practice." In addition, the trial judge directed that jurisdiction of the case be retained in the Superior Court "for a period of five years to (e)nsure compliance." Judgment was entered pursuant to the trial judge's order. After the entry of judgment, Dr. Wolfson and Atlantic filed a motion for a new trial and to amend the judge's findings. This motion, after hearing, was denied, and Dr. Wolfson and Atlantic claimed an appeal from the judgment and the former from the denial of the motion. The plaintiffs . . . requested payment of their attorneys' fees in this proceeding and filed supporting affidavits. The motion was denied, and the plaintiffs appealed.

1. The trial judge, in deciding that Dr. Wolfson had committed a breach of his fiduciary duty to other stockholders, relied greatly on broad language in *Donahue v. Rodd Electrotype Co.*, 367 Mass. 578, 586–597, 328 N.E.2d 505 (1975) in which the Supreme Judicial Court afforded to a minority stockholder in a close corporation equality of treatment (with members of a controlling group of shareholders) in the matter of the redemption of shares. The court relied on the resemblance of a close corporation to a partnership and held that "stockholders in the close corporation owe one another substantially the same fiduciary duty in the operation of the enterprise that partners owe to one another" (footnotes omitted). That standard of duty, the court said, was the "utmost good faith and loyalty." The court went on to say that such stockholders "may not act out of avarice, expediency or self-interest in derogation of their duty of loyalty to the other stockholders and to the corporation." Similar principles were stated in *Wilkes v. Springside Nursing Home, Inc.*, 370 Mass. 842, 848–852, 353 N.E.2d 657 (1976), but with some modifications, mentioned in the margin, of the sweeping language of the *Donahue* case. . . .

In . . . *Donahue* . . . the court recognized that cases may arise in which, in a close corporation, majority stockholders may ask protection from a minority stockholder. Such an instance arises in the present case because Dr. Wolfson has been able to exercise a veto concerning corporate action on dividends by the 80% provision (in Atlantic's articles or organization and by-laws) already quoted. The 80% provision may have substantially the effect of reversing the usual roles of the majority and the minority shareholders. The minority, under that provision, becomes an ad hoc controlling interest.[6]

... In the present case, Dr. Wolfson testified that he requested the inclusion of the 80% provision "in case the people (the other shareholders) whom I knew, but not very well, ganged up on me." The possibilities of shareholder disagreement on policy made the provision seem a sensible precaution.[8] A question is presented, however, concerning the extent to which such a veto power possessed by a minority stockholder may be exercised as its holder may wish, without a violation of the "fiduciary duty" referred to in ... *Donahue* ... as modified in the Wilkes case.

The decided cases in Massachusetts do little to answer this question. The most pertinent guidance is probably found in the *Wilkes* case, essentially to the effect that in any judicial intervention in such a situation there must be a weighing of the business interests advanced as reasons for their action (a) by the majority or controlling group and (b) by the rival persons or group. It would obviously be appropriate, before a court-ordered solution is sought or imposed, for both sides to attempt to reach a sensible solution of any incipient impasse in the interest of all concerned after consideration of all relevant circumstances.

2. With respect to the past damage to Atlantic caused by Dr. Wolfson's refusal to vote in favor of any dividends, the trial judge was justified in finding that his conduct went beyond what was reasonable. The other stockholders shared to some extent responsibility for what occurred by failing to accept Dr. Wolfson's proposals with much sympathy, but the inaction on dividends seems the principal cause of the tax penalties. Dr. Wolfson had been warned of the dangers of an assessment under the Internal Revenue Code, I.R.C. § 531 et seq. He had refused to vote dividends in any amount adequate to minimize that danger and had failed to bring forward, within the relevant taxable years, a convincing, definitive program of appropriate improvements which could withstand scrutiny by the Internal Revenue Service. Whatever may have been the reason for Dr. Wolfson's refusal to declare dividends (and even if

---

6. The majority shareholders, in the event of a deadlock, at least may seek dissolution of the corporation if forty percent of the voting power can be mustered, whereas a single stockholder with only twenty-five percent of the stock may not do so. See G.L. c. 156B, § 99(b), as amended by St.1969, c. 392, § 23.

8. Dr. Wolfson himself had discovered the business opportunity which led to the formation of Atlantic, had made the initial $50,000 payment which made possible the Norwood land purchase, and had given the other shareholders an opportunity to share with him in what looked like a probably profitable enterprise. It was reasonably foreseeable that there might be differences of opinion between Dr. Wolfson, a man with substantial income likely to be in a high income tax bracket, and less affluent shareholders on such matters of policy as dividend declarations, salaries, and investment in improvements in the property. The other shareholders, two of whom were attorneys, should have known that it was as open to Dr. Wolfson reasonably to exercise the veto provided to him by the 80% provision in favor of a policy of reinvestment of earnings in Atlantic's properties, which would probably avoid taxes and increase the value of the corporate assets, as it was for them (possessed of the same veto) to use reasonably their voting power in favor of a more generous dividend and salary policy.

in any particular year he may have gained slight, if any, tax advantage from withholding dividends) we think that he recklessly ran serious and unjustified risks of precisely the penalty taxes eventually assessed, risks which were inconsistent with any reasonable interpretation of a duty of "utmost good faith and loyalty." The trial judge (despite the fact that the other shareholders helped to create the voting deadlock and despite the novelty of the situation) was justified in charging Dr. Wolfson with the out-of-pocket expenditure incurred by Atlantic for the penalty taxes and related counsel fees of the tax cases.[10] . . . .

Questions

1. What did Dr. Wolfson do wrong? Why aren't the other shareholders at fault for refusing his plans for the corporation?

2. Given *Wilkes*' conclusion that shareholders have "certain rights to . . . 'selfish ownership,'" which selfish ownership rights should the court embrace — the majority's or the minority's?

3. What is left of *Wilkes*' test after *Smith v. Atlantic Properties, Inc.*?

Brodie v. Jordan

447 Mass. 866 (S.J. Ct. Mass. 2006)

Cowin, Justice

In this case we are asked to consider the appropriate remedy for a "freeze-out" of a minority shareholder by the majority shareholders in a close corporation. The plaintiff, Mary M. Brodie, is a shareholder in Malden Centerless Grinding Co., Inc. (Malden). The defendants, Robert J. Jordan and David J. Barbuto (collectively, defendants), are the corporation's two other shareholders. The plaintiff brought suit, claiming that the defendants had "frozen her out" from participation in the company, refused her access to company information, and denied her any economic benefit from her shares. After a jury-waived trial, a judge in the Superior Court found that the defendants had breached their fiduciary duty to the plaintiff. As a remedy, the judge ordered that the defendants purchase the plaintiff's shares in the corporation at a price equal to her share of the corporation's net assets, as valuated by a court-appointed expert, plus prejudgment interest.

A divided Appeals Court affirmed, with the majority upholding both the finding of a breach of fiduciary duty and the remedy imposed. The dissenting judge agreed that a breach of fiduciary duty had been established, but maintained that the forced

---

10. We do not now suggest that the standard of "utmost good faith and loyalty" may require some relaxation when applied to a minority ad hoc controlling interest, created by some device, similar to the 80% provision, designed in part to protect the selfish interests of a minority shareholder. This seems to us a difficult area of the law best developed on a case by case basis.

buyout overcompensated the plaintiff and unfairly punished the defendants. We granted the defendants' application for further appellate review limited to the propriety of the remedy. We conclude that, at least on this record, it was error to order a buyout.

1. *Background.* Malden is a Massachusetts corporation that operates a small machine shop and produces metal objects such as ball bearings. The plaintiff's now deceased husband, Walter S. Brodie (Walter), was one of the founding members of the company and served as its president from 1979 to 1992. Barbuto has been a shareholder, a director, and the treasurer of the company since its formation. Jordan has been an employee of the company since 1975 and a shareholder, director, and officer since 1984; he is the one responsible for the day-to-day operation of the business. Beginning in 1984, Walter, Barbuto, and Jordan each held one-third of the shares of the corporation and all three served as directors. By 1988, however, Walter was no longer involved in the company's day-to-day operation and only met with Barbuto and Jordan two to three times each year. After Walter and the defendants began to disagree over various management issues, Walter made a number of requests that the company purchase his shares, but those requests were rejected. Neither the articles of organization nor any corporate bylaw obligated Malden or the defendants to purchase the stock of a shareholder.

The corporation has not paid any dividends to shareholders since 1989. As an employee, Jordan receives a salary at a rate set by the board of directors (Barbuto and himself). Jordan participates in a profit-sharing plan made available by the corporation and has the use of a company vehicle. Barbuto received director's fees from the corporation until 1998. He owns the building that houses Malden's corporate offices and receives rent from the corporation. Barbuto also owns a separate corporation, Barco Engineering, Inc., which is a customer of Malden and for which Malden regularly performs services on an open credit account. Walter received compensation from the company prior to 1992, and was paid a consultant's fee in 1994 and 1995. However, neither Walter nor the plaintiff appears to have received any compensation or other money from the corporation since 1995.

In 1992, Walter was voted out as president and director of Malden, and Jordan was elected president. Walter died in 1997. The plaintiff was appointed Walter's executrix and inherited his one-third interest in Malden. She attended a Malden shareholders' meeting in July, 1997, at which she nominated herself, through counsel, as a director, but Barbuto and Jordan voted against her election. At this same meeting, the plaintiff asked Jordan and Barbuto to perform a valuation of the company so that she could ascertain the value of her shares, but such a valuation was never performed.

In 1998, the plaintiff filed the instant suit. Prior to and since that time, the defendants failed to provide her with various financial and operational company information that she requested. At the time of trial, the defendants had failed to hold an annual shareholder's meeting for the previous five years, and the plaintiff had not participated in any company decision-making.

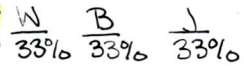

2. *Discussion.* The parties do not dispute that Malden is a close corporation as defined in *Donahue v. Rodd Electrotype Co. of New England, Inc.* (1975), in that it has "(1) a small number of stockholders; (2) no ready market for the corporate stock; and (3) substantial majority stockholder participation in the management, direction and operations of the corporation." "[S]tockholders in [a] close corporation owe one another substantially the same fiduciary duty in the operation of the enterprise that partners owe to one another," that is, a duty of "utmost good faith and loyalty."

Majority shareholders in a close corporation violate this duty when they act to "freeze out" the minority. We have defined freeze-outs by way of example:

> "The squeezers [those who employ the freeze-out techniques] may refuse to declare dividends; they may drain off the corporation's earnings in the form of exorbitant salaries and bonuses to the majority shareholder-officers and perhaps to their relatives, or in the form of high rent by the corporation for property leased from majority shareholders . . . ; they may deprive minority shareholders of corporate offices and of employment by the company; they may cause the corporation to sell its assets at an inadequate price to the majority shareholders. . . ."

. . . What these examples have in common is that, in each, the majority frustrates the minority's reasonable expectations of benefit from their ownership of shares.

We have previously analyzed freeze-outs in terms of shareholders' "reasonable expectations" both explicitly and implicitly. See *Bodio v. Ellis* (1987) (thwarting minority shareholder's "rightful expectation" as to control of close corporation was breach of fiduciary duty); *Wilkes v. Springside Nursing Home, Inc.* (1976) (denying minority shareholders employment in corporation may "effectively frustrate [their] purposes in entering on the corporate venture"). A number of other jurisdictions, either by judicial decision or by statute, also look to shareholders' "reasonable expectations" in determining whether to grant relief to an aggrieved minority shareholder in a close corporation.[3] . . . As discussed *infra*, we believe that this mode of analysis is useful at both the liability and the remedy stages of freeze-out litigation.

In the present case, the Superior Court judge properly analyzed the defendants' liability in terms of the plaintiff's reasonable expectations of benefit. The judge found that the defendants had interfered with the plaintiff's reasonable expectations by excluding her from corporate decision-making, denying her access to company information, and hindering her ability to sell her shares in the open market.[4] In addition,

---

3. Although these jurisdictions, unlike Massachusetts, afford minority shareholders a statutory cause of action for majority "oppression," "[t]he standards used to determine a breach of fiduciary duty are often the same as used to define oppression."

4. As the Superior Court judge acknowledged, the defendants gave the plaintiff full permission to sell her stock to a third party. The judge concluded, however, that by refusing to perform a valuation of the company, the defendants prevented the plaintiff from determining the value of her shares.

the judge's findings reflect a state of affairs in which the defendants were the only ones receiving any financial benefit from the corporation. The Appeals Court determined that the findings were warranted, and the defendants have not sought further appellate review with respect to liability. Thus, the only question before us is whether, on this record, the plaintiff was entitled to the remedy of a forced buyout of her shares by the majority. We conclude that she was not so entitled.

a. *Remedies for freeze-out of minority shareholder.* The proper remedy for a freeze-out is "to restore [the minority shareholder] as nearly as possible to the position [s]he would have been in had there been no wrongdoing." *Zimmerman v. Bogoff* (1988). Because the wrongdoing in a freeze-out is the denial by the majority of the minority's reasonable expectations of benefit, it follows that the remedy should, to the extent possible, restore to the minority shareholder those benefits which she reasonably expected, but has not received because of the fiduciary breach.

If, for example, a minority shareholder had a reasonable expectation of employment by the corporation and was terminated wrongfully, the remedy may be reinstatement, back pay, or both. Similarly, if a minority shareholder has a reasonable expectation of sharing in company profits and has been denied this opportunity, she may be "entitled to participate in the favorable results of operations to the extent that those results have been wrongly appropriated by the majority." *Crowley v. Communications for Hosps., Inc.* (1991) (ordering, in derivative action brought by frozen-out minority, that majority return wrongly appropriated funds to corporation and distribute them as dividend to shareholders). The remedy should neither grant the minority a windfall nor excessively penalize the majority. Rather, it should attempt to reset the proper balance between the majority's "concede[d] . . . rights to what has been termed 'selfish ownership,'" *Wilkes v. Springside Nursing Home, Inc.* and the minority's reasonable expectations of benefit from its shares.

b. *The Superior Court judge's remedy.* Courts have broad equitable powers to fashion remedies for breaches of fiduciary duty in a close corporation, and their choice of a particular remedy is reviewed for abuse of discretion. Here, the Superior Court judge ordered the defendants to buy out the plaintiff at the price of an expert's estimate of her share of the corporation, a remedy that no Massachusetts appellate court has previously authorized.[5] The problem with this remedy is that it placed the plaintiff in a significantly *better* position than she would have enjoyed absent the wrongdoing, and well exceeded her reasonable expectations of benefit from her shares.

---

5. The remedy in *Donahue v. Rodd Electrotype Co. of New England, Inc.* is readily distinguishable. There, the majority had caused the corporation to purchase majority shareholders' stock at a favorable price while denying minority shareholders the same opportunity. We held that, to comply with its fiduciary duties, the majority had to either rescind the sale of its own shares to the corporation or cause the corporation to purchase the minority's shares on the same terms. Here, there is no allegation that Malden purchased the defendants' shares without giving the plaintiff a similar opportunity.

One of the defining aspects of a close corporation is "the absence of a ready market for corporate stock." In this case, it is undisputed that neither the articles of organization nor any corporate bylaw obligates Malden or the defendants to purchase the plaintiff's shares. Thus, there is nothing in the background law, the governing rules of this particular close corporation, or any other circumstance that could have given the plaintiff a reasonable expectation of having her shares bought out.

In ordering the defendants to purchase the plaintiff's stock at the price of her share of the company, the judge created an artificial market for the plaintiff's minority share of a close corporation—an asset that, by definition, has little or no market value. Thus, the remedy had the perverse effect of placing the plaintiff in a position superior to that which she would have enjoyed had there been no wrongdoing.

The remedy of a forced buyout may be an appealing one for a court of equity in that it results in a "clean break" between acrimonious parties. Yet this rationale would require a forced share purchase in virtually every freeze-out case, given that resort to litigation is itself an indication of the inability of shareholders to work together.[6] In any event, no matter how expedient a forced buyout may be as a solution, the remedy for a breach of fiduciary duty must be proportional to the breach. Other remedies are available to compensate and protect minority shareholders without radically transforming the nature of their asset or arbitrarily increasing its value.[7]

c. *Considerations on remand.* As we have indicated, the remedy for the defendants' breach of fiduciary duty is one that protects the plaintiff's reasonable expectations of benefit from the corporation and that compensates her for their denial in the past. An evidentiary hearing is appropriate to determine her reasonable expectations of ownership; whether such expectations have been frustrated; and, if so, the means by which to vindicate the plaintiff's interests. For breaches visited upon the plaintiff resulting in deprivations that can be quantified, money damages will be the appropriate remedy.[8] Prospective injunctive relief may be granted to ensure that the plaintiff is allowed to participate in company governance, and to enjoy financial or other benefits from the business, to the extent that her ownership interest justifies.

---

6. In past decisions of this court and the Appeals Court, antagonistic shareholders in a close corporation often have been required to continue their business relationship. . . .

7. We have considered the cases from other jurisdictions cited by the plaintiff in which buyout was considered an appropriate remedy for majority shareholder misconduct. In most of these States, statutes authorize the more drastic remedy of involuntary dissolution, and thus courts have understandably inferred the power to order the lesser remedy of a buyout. In Massachusetts, by contrast, minority shareholders have no statutory right to involuntary dissolution of a corporation due to majority misconduct. To the extent that any cases have held that, even in the absence of statutory authorization, forced buyout is a remedy generally available to an aggrieved minority shareholder in a close corporation, we decline to follow them.

8. It is not clear what pecuniary damages, if any, the plaintiff may have incurred as a result of the defendants' conduct. To the extent that the plaintiff has suffered compensable harm, the judge on remand should make findings and enter a money judgment accordingly.

In devising a remedy that grants the plaintiff her reasonable expectations of benefit from stock ownership in Malden, the judge may consider the fact that the plaintiff has received no economic benefit from her shares. If the defendants have denied the plaintiff any return on her investment while "drain[ing] off the corporation's earnings" for themselves, the judge may consider, among other possibilities, the propriety of compelling the declaration of dividends.

3. *Conclusion.* That part of the judgment of the Superior Court awarding the plaintiff $94,500 plus prejudgment interest is reversed; in all other respects the judgment is affirmed. The case is remanded to the Superior Court for proceedings consistent with this opinion.

So ordered.

Questions

1. The court in *Brodie v. Jordan* cites both *Donahue v. Rodd Electrotype Company of New England, Inc.* and *Wilkes v. Springside Nursing Home, Inc.* to support its conclusions. In what ways does *Brodie* follow both (or either of) these cases? In what ways does it deviate from their rulings?

2. What remedy should the court fashion on remand?

3. Is it efficient, or even reasonably practicable, to insist that the parties continue together in a business relationship? Who benefits from this?

4. What is left of the fiduciary duties that shareholders in closely held corporations owe each other after *Brodie*?

Jordan v. Duff and Phelps, Inc.
815 F.2d 429 (7th Cir. 1987)

EASTERBROOK, Judge

... This case contains two wrinkles. First, it involves the acquisition of a closely held corporation by a public corporation. Second, the investor in the closely held corporation was an employee, and he was offered shares to cement his loyalty to the firm; yet he quit (and was compelled by a shareholders' agreement to sell his shares) for reasons unrelated to the value of the stock. The parties hotly contest the effects of these facts. ...

I

...

Duff and Phelps, Inc. evaluates the risk and worth of firms and their securities. It sells credit ratings, investment research, and financial consulting services to both the firms under scrutiny and potential investors in them. Jordan started work at Duff &

Phelps in May 1977 and was viewed as a successful securities analyst. In 1981 the firm offered Jordan the opportunity to buy some stock. By November 1983 Jordan had purchased 188 of the 20,100 shares outstanding. He was making installment payments on another 62 shares. Forty people other than Jordan held stock in Duff & Phelps.

Jordan purchased his stock at its "book value" (the accounting net worth of Duff & Phelps, divided by the number of shares outstanding). Before selling him any stock, Duff & Phelps required Jordan to sign a "Stock Restriction and Purchase Agreement" (the Agreement). This provided in part:

> Upon the termination of any employment with the Corporation ... for any reason, including resignation, discharge, death, disability or retirement, the individual whose employment is terminated or his estate shall sell to the Corporation, and the Corporation shall buy, all Shares of the Corporation then owned by such individual or his estate. The price to be paid for such Shares shall be equal to the adjusted book value (as hereinafter defined) of the Shares on the December 31 which coincides with, or immediately precedes, the date of termination of such individual's employment.

Duff & Phelps enforced this restriction with but a single exception. During 1983 the board of directors of Duff & Phelps adopted a resolution—of which Jordan did not learn until 1984—allowing employees fired by the firm to keep their stock for five years. The resolution followed the discharge of Carol Franchik, with whom Claire Hansen, the (married) chairman of the board, had been having an affair. When Franchik threatened suit, the board allowed her to keep her stock.

While Jordan was accumulating stock, Hansen, the chairman of the board, was exploring the possibility of selling the firm. Between May and August 1983 Hansen and Francis Jeffries, another officer of Duff & Phelps, negotiated with Security Pacific Corp., a bank holding company. The negotiators reached agreement on a merger, in which Duff & Phelps would be valued at $50 million, but a higher official within Security Pacific vetoed the deal on August 11, 1983. As of that date, Duff & Phelps had no irons in the fire.

Jordan, however, was conducting a search of his own—for a new job. Jordan's family lived near Chicago, the headquarters of Duff & Phelps, and Jordan's wife did not get along with Jordan's mother. The strain between the two occasionally left his wife in tears. He asked Duff & Phelps about the possibility of a transfer to the firm's only branch office, in Cleveland, but the firm did not need Jordan's services there. Concluding that it was time to choose between his job and his wife, Jordan chose his wife and started looking for employment far away from Chicago. His search took him to Houston, where Underwood Neuhaus & Co., a broker-dealer in securities, offered him a job at a salary ($110,000 per year) substantially greater than his compensation ($67,000) at Duff & Phelps. Jordan took the offer on the spot during an interview in Houston, but Underwood would have allowed Jordan to withdraw this oral acceptance.

On November 16, 1983, Jordan told Hansen that he was going to resign and accept employment with Underwood. Jordan did not ask Hansen about potential mergers; Hansen did not volunteer anything. Jordan delivered a letter of resignation, which Duff & Phelps accepted the same day. By mutual agreement, Jordan worked the rest of the year for Duff & Phelps even though his loyalties had shifted. He did this so that he could receive the book value of the stock as of December 31, 1983—for under the Agreement a departure in November would have meant valuation as of December 31, 1982. Jordan delivered his certificates on December 30, 1983, and the firm mailed him a check for $23,225, the book value (at $123.54 per share) of the 188 shares of stock. Jordan surrendered, as worthless under the circumstances, the right to buy the remaining 62 shares.

Before Jordan cashed the check, however, he was startled by the announcement on January 10, 1984, of a merger between Duff & Phelps and a subsidiary of Security Pacific. Under the terms of the merger Duff & Phelps would be valued at $50 million. If Jordan had been an employee on January 10, had quickly paid for the other 62 shares, and the merger had closed that day, he would have received $452,000 in cash and the opportunity to obtain as much as $194,000 more in "earn out" (a percentage of Duff & Phelps's profits to be paid to the former investors—an arrangement that keeps the employees' interest in the firm keen and reduces the buyer's risk if profits fall short). Jordan refused to cash the check and demanded his stock back; Duff & Phelps told him to get lost. He filed this suit in March 1984, asking for damages measured by the value his stock would have had under the terms of the acquisition.

The public announcement on January 10 explained that the boards of the two firms had reached an agreement in principle on January 6. The definitive agreement was signed on March 23. Because Security Pacific is a bank holding company, the acquisition required the approval of the Board of Governors of the Federal Reserve. The Fed granted approval, but with a condition so onerous that the firms abandoned the transaction. The Fed objected to Security Pacific's acquisition of Duff & Phelps's credit rating business. The agreement was formally cancelled on January 9, 1985. Duff & Phelps quickly asked the district court to dismiss Jordan's suit, on the ground that he could not establish damages. Jordan responded by amending his complaint, with Judge Hart's permission, to ask for rescission rather than damages.

Throughout 1985 Duff & Phelps continued looking for a partner; finding none, it decided to dance with itself. The firm's management formed an "Employee Stock Ownership Trust," which was able to borrow $40 million against the security of the firm's assets and business. The Trust acquired Duff & Phelps through a new firm, Duff Research, Inc. This transaction occurred in December 1985. The employees at the time, together with Carol Franchik, received cash, notes, and beneficial interests in the Trust. Jordan asserts that the package was worth almost $2,000 per share, or $497,000 if he had held 250 shares in December 1985.

Defendants' second motion for summary judgment maintained that information about negotiations looking toward a merger is immaterial as a matter of law. The information Jordan says should have been disclosed before he departed includes: (1) the negotiations through August 11, 1983, with Security Pacific; (2) the decision by the board of Duff & Phelps on November 14, 1983, to seek bids for the firm; (3) miscellaneous conversations between Hansen and employees of Security Pacific during the fall of 1983, which Jordan says may have been renewed overtures; (4) the serious negotiations during December 1983 between Duff & Phelps and Security Pacific, after the manager who nixed the deal on August 11 changed his mind; (5) the board's decision to allow Franchik to keep her stock; and (6) the formal settlement agreement signed by Franchik on December 21, 1983. Duff & Phelps, on the other hand, believes that Jordan quit on November 16, 1983, that nothing after that date matters, and that nothing before that date needed to be revealed.

Judge Leinenweber concluded that the agreement in principle approved on January 6, 1984, was the first thing that needed to be disclosed. Because Jordan sold his stock no later than December 31, Duff & Phelps did not violate any duty to disclose. . . . The court stated: "When at least one of the parties to acquisition negotiations is a publicly-traded company, an agreement in principal [sic] to the acquisition by both corporations must occur before either corporation has a duty to disclose the fact of negotiations to a stockholder." The district judge allowed that the negotiators may have settled the terms of the deal before December 31 but continued: "Although the *negotiators* may have agreed before December 31, 1983, the *corporations* did not agree until action by their Boards of Directors or other authorized agents."

Judge Leinenweber also concluded that even if wronged, Jordan is not entitled to relief. He is not entitled to rescission because he is not employed by Duff & Phelps, and the Agreement ties ownership to employment. (The Franchik exception, according to the court, was at most a breach of the Agreement; because the Agreement was an arrangement among the shareholders, only unanimous consent could modify it.) He is not entitled to damages because the Security Pacific deal fell through.

II

. . . Most people are free to buy and sell stock on the basis of valuable private knowledge without informing their trading partners. Strangers transact in markets all the time using private information that might be called "material" and, unless one has a duty to disclose, both may keep their counsel. . . . The ability to make profits from the possession of information is the principal spur to create the information, which the parties and the market as a whole may find valuable. The absence of a duty to disclose may not justify a lie about a material fact, but Duff & Phelps did not lie to Jordan. It simply remained silent when Jordan quit and tendered the stock, and it offered the payment required by the Agreement. . . .

. . . The "duty" in question is the fiduciary duty of corporate law. Close corporations buying their own stock, like knowledgeable insiders of closely held firms buying from outsiders, have a fiduciary duty to disclose material facts. . . .

Because the fiduciary duty is a standby or off-the-rack guess about what parties would agree to if they dickered about the subject explicitly, parties may contract with greater specificity for other arrangements. . . . We may assume that duties concerning the timing of disclosure by an otherwise-silent firm also may be the subject of contract. . . . But we need not decide how far contracts can redefine obligations to disclose. Jordan was an employee at will; he signed no contract.

The stock was designed to bind Duff & Phelps's employees loyally to the firm. The buy-sell agreement tied ownership to employment. Understandably Duff & Phelps did not want a viper in its nest, a disgruntled employee remaining only in the hope of appreciation of his stock. So there could have been reason to divorce the employment decision from the value of the stock. Perhaps it would have been rational for each employee to agree with Duff & Phelps to look to salary alone in deciding whether to stay. A contractual agreement that the firm had no duty to disclose would have uncoupled the investment decision from the employment decision, leaving whoever was in the firm on the day of a merger to receive a surprise appreciation. Some might lose by leaving early; some might reap a windfall by buying just before the announcement; all might think it wise to have as little as possible said in the interim.

Yet an explicit agreement to make all employment decisions in ignorance of the value of the stock might not have been in the interests of the firm or its employees. Duff & Phelps was trying to purchase loyalty by offering stock to its principal employees. The package of compensation contained salary and the prospect of appreciation of the stock. Perhaps it paid a lower salary than, say, Underwood Neuhaus & Co., because its package contained a higher component of gain from anticipated appreciation in the stock. It is therefore unwarranted to say that the implicit understanding between Jordan and Duff & Phelps should be treated as if it had such a no-duty clause; we are not confident that this is the clause firms and their employees regularly would prefer. Duff & Phelps has not identified any firm that adopted such a clause explicitly, and the absence of explicit clauses counsels caution in creating implicit exceptions to the general fiduciary duty.

The course of dealing between Jordan and Duff & Phelps suggests that the firm did not demand that employees decide whether to stay or go without regard to the value of the stock. It apparently informed Jordan what the book value was expected to be on December 31, 1983, so that Jordan could decide whether to leave in November (receiving the value as of December 31, 1982) or stay for another six weeks. The firm did not demand that Jordan depart as soon as it learned he had switched loyalties; it allowed employees to time their departures to obtain the maximum advantage from their stock. The Agreement did not ensure that employees disregard the value of the stock when deciding what to do, and neither did the usual practice at Duff & Phelps. So the possibility that a firm could negotiate around the fiduciary duty does not assist Duff & Phelps; it did not obtain such an agreement, express or implied.

The closest Duff & Phelps came is the provision in the Agreement fixing the price of the stock at book value. Yet although the Agreement fixed the price to be paid those who quit, it did not establish the terms on which anyone would leave. . . . Jordan, though, exercised choice about the date on which the formula would be triggered. He could have remained at Duff & Phelps; his decision to depart was affected by his wife's distress, his salary, his working conditions, the enjoyment he received from the job, and the value of his stock. The departure of such an employee is an investment decision as much as it is an employment decision. It is not fanciful to suppose that Mrs. Jordan would have found her mother in law a whole lot more tolerable if she had known that Jordan's stock might shortly be worth 20 times book value.

The securities acts apply to investment decisions, even those made indirectly or bound up with other decisions, such as employment or entrepreneurship. . . . The position of this court that § 10(b) and cognate provisions of the securities laws were designed exclusively to protect passive investors was rejected. There must be an "investment" decision, to be sure, but Jordan unavoidably made one. That he took the value of stock into account is evident from the timing of his departure. A few thousand dollars' increase in book value led the Jordans to stay in Chicago an extra six weeks. How long would they have stayed for the prospect of another $620,000?

Our dissenting colleague concludes that all of this is beside the point because Hansen could have said, on receiving Jordan's letter on November 16: "In a few weeks we will pull off a merger that would have made your stock 20 times more valuable. It's a shame you so foolishly resigned. But even if you hadn't resigned, we would have fired you, the better to engross the profits of the merger for ourselves. So long, sucker." This would have been permissible, under our colleague's interpretation, because Jordan was an employee at will and therefore could have been fired at any time, even the day before the merger, for any reason—including the desire to deprive Jordan of a share of the profits. The ability to fire Jordan enabled the firm to "call" his shares, at book value, on whim. On this view, it is foolish to say that Duff & Phelps had a duty to disclose, because disclosure would have been no use to Jordan. (Perhaps this is really an argument about "causation" rather than "duty," but the terminology is unimportant.) But Duff & Phelps itself does not press this argument, and in civil litigation an appellate court ought not put words in a party's mouth and use them as the grounds on which to decide. The district court has not had an opportunity to address such a claim, and Jordan has not been asked to respond to it. Perhaps Duff & Phelps does not want to establish a reputation for shoddy dealing; as our dissenting brother observes, a firm's desire to preserve its reputation is a powerful inducement to treat its contractual partners well. To attribute to a litigant an argument that it will take every possible advantage is to assume that the party wishes to dissipate its reputation, and the assumption is unwarranted.

More than that, a person's status as an employee "at will" does not imply that the employer may discharge him for every reason. Illinois, where Jordan was employed, has placed some limits on the discharge of at-will employees. We do not disparage the utility of at-will contracts. . . . But employment at will is still a contractual relation, one in which a particular duration ("at will") is implied in the absence of a contrary expression. The silence of the parties may make it necessary to imply other terms—those we are confident the parties would have bargained for if they had signed a written agreement. One term implied in every written contract and therefore, we suppose, every unwritten one, is that neither party will try to take opportunistic advantage of the other. "[T]he fundamental function of contract law (and recognized as such at least since Hobbes's day) is to deter people from behaving opportunistically toward their contracting parties, in order to encourage the optimal timing of economic activity and to make costly self-protective measures unnecessary."

Employment creates occasions for opportunism. A firm may fire an employee the day before his pension vests, or a salesman the day before a large commission becomes payable. Cases of this sort may present difficult questions about the reasons for the decision (was it opportunism, or was it a decline in the employee's performance?). The difficulties of separating opportunistic conduct from honest differences of opinion about an employee's performance on the job may lead firms and their employees to transact on terms that keep such disputes out of court—which employment at will usually does. But no one, not even Professor Epstein, doubts that an *avowedly opportunistic discharge is a breach of contract,* although the employment is at-will.... The element of good faith dealing implied in a contract "is not an enforceable legal duty to be nice or to behave decently in a general way." It is not a version of the Golden Rule, to regard the interests of one's contracting partner the same way you regard your own. An employer may be thoughtless, nasty, and mistaken. Avowedly opportunistic conduct has been treated differently, however.

The stock component in Jordan's package induced him to stick around and work well. Such an inducement is effective only if the employee reaps the rewards of success as well as the penalties of failure. We do not suppose for a second that if Jordan had not resigned on November 16, the firm could have fired him on January 9 with a little note saying: "Dear Mr. Jordan: There will be a lucrative merger tomorrow. You have been a wonderful employee, but in order to keep the proceeds of the merger for ourselves, we are letting you go, effective this instant. Here is the $23,000 for your shares." Had the firm fired Jordan for this stated reason, it would have broken an implied pledge to avoid opportunistic conduct. It may well be that Duff & Phelps could have fired Jordan without the slightest judicial inquiry; it does not follow that an opportunistic discharge would have allowed Duff & Phelps to cash out the stock on the eve of its appreciation. ... [A]n opportunistic discharge would not necessarily allow Duff & Phelps to buy back the stock. As a result, Jordan's employment at will, the essential ingredient of our colleague's argument that Jordan waived the duty to disclose, does not establish that the firm had no duties concerning the stock.

The timing of the sale and the materiality of the information Duff & Phelps withheld on November 16 are for the jury to determine. Our dissenting colleague stresses that businesses would be shocked to learn that they must disclose valuable corporate information to fickle employees. If disclosure is unthinkable, however, Jordan may have trouble establishing that Duff & Phelps acted with intent to defraud, a necessary element of a case under Rule 10b-5. . . .

III

[As to remedy, Judge Easterbrook determines that rescission was not available because Jordan's "employment was a quid pro quo for ownership of the stock," and it was "too late to restore his employment for 1984–86, and he [had] not offered to go back to work at Duff & Phelps if he [won] the case." Judge Easterbrook suggested that Jordan might be able to claim damages based on the assessment of Security Pacific as to the value of Duff & Phelps, but he also stated that Jordan might not be able to establish causation—that is, that "on learning of the negotiations with Security Pacific he would have dropped plans to go to Houston, and that even after the disappointment of the Fed's action that scuttled the deal with Security Pacific Jordan would have stuck around until the end of 1985, finally receiving the payment from the LBO. . . . These and all related issues [were] left for the district court on remand."]

Posner, Judge (dissenting)

A corporate employee at will quit, owning shares that he had agreed to sell back to the corporation at book value. The agreement was explicit that his status as a shareholder conferred no job rights on him. Nevertheless the court holds that the corporation had, as a matter of law, a duty, enforceable by proceedings under Rule 10b-5 of the Securities Exchange Act, to volunteer to the employee information about the corporation's prospects that might have led him to change his mind about quitting, although as an employee at will he had no right to change his mind. I disagree with this holding. The terms of the stockholder agreement show that there was no duty of disclosure, and since there was no duty there was no violation of Rule 10b-5.

The plaintiff, a young man named Jordan, had gone to work for Duff and Phelps as a financial analyst. He had no employment contract; he was an employee at will. . . . As a junior executive he was permitted to buy modest quantities of stock in the company, which was (and is) closely held. He agreed that if he left the company, whether voluntarily or involuntarily, he would sell back his stock at its book value on the December 31 preceding or coinciding with the end of his employment.

After working for Duff and Phelps for six and a half years Jordan had accumulated about one percent of the company's stock. His stock had a book value on December 31, 1983, of $23,000 (I round all dollar figures to the nearest $1,000). Earlier in 1983 Jordan had decided to leave Chicago because his mother, who also lived in Chicago, didn't get along with his wife. After Duff and Phelps declined to move him to its only other office (Cleveland), he began to explore the possibility of leaving the firm. On November 11, 1983, he accepted a job in Houston, Texas, at a substantially higher salary than his salary at Duff and Phelps ($110,000 versus $67,000). On November 14 he told Hansen, the chief executive officer of Duff and Phelps, that he was quitting, and on November 16 handed him a letter of resignation. At Jordan's request, Hansen agreed that the resignation would not take effect till the end of the year, so that Jordan would get a higher price for his stock. Both men believed that the book value of the stock would be higher on December 31, 1983, than it had been on December 31, 1982, the relevant date if Jordan's resignation took effect before the end of the year.

Hansen did not reveal to Jordan that in the summer he and Jeffries (the other principal officer of Duff and Phelps) had negotiated with some executives at Security Pacific Corporation to sell Duff and Phelps to Security Pacific for $50 million; that had the deal gone through Jordan's stock would have been worth $640,000 rather than $23,000; that the deal had been nixed in August by higher levels of Security Pacific's management; but that the episode had so encouraged Hansen that at a meeting of the board of directors of Duff and Phelps on November 14 (just before Jordan came to him with the news that he was leaving) he had sought and obtained authority to make active efforts to sell the company.

Negotiations between Duff and Phelps and Security Pacific resumed in December. On December 30, Jordan, who knew nothing of the negotiations, delivered his shares to Duff and Phelps, as his agreement with the company required him to do. The resumed negotiations were successful, and resulted in an announcement in January (1984) that Security Pacific would buy Duff and Phelps for $50 million, contingent on regulatory approval. Shortly afterward Duff and Phelps sent Jordan a check for $23,000 in payment for his stock. Rather than cash the check Jordan brought this suit, seeking damages equal to the value of his stock if he hadn't quit Duff and Phelps and if the deal with Security Pacific went through. It didn't go through. It collapsed the following January when the Federal Reserve Board refused to approve it except on conditions that Security Pacific found too onerous. Jordan amended his complaint, dropping the claim for damages and asking instead for rescission of the sale of his stock to Duff and Phelps. Almost a year later, Duff and Phelps reorganized, and its shareholders exchanged their stock for a combination of cash, notes, and pension rights that Jordan believes to be worth about $40 million.

Rule 10b-5 forbids "fraud or deceit" in the sale or purchase of corporate securities. Jordan does not argue that Duff and Phelps made any misleading statements. He makes nothing of the fact that when he told Hansen he was quitting, Hansen said that the firm had a good potential for growth and that Jordan's shares would rise in value if he stayed. The target of the complaint is not misrepresentation or even misleading half-truths; it is Hansen's omission to tell Jordan that he should think twice about quitting since the company might soon be sold at a price that would increase the value of Jordan's stock almost 30-fold. The statement that Hansen failed to make may have been material, since it might have caused Jordan to change his mind about resigning. I say "may have been material" rather than "was material" because Hansen need not have allowed Jordan to change his mind about resigning. But I shall pass this point and assume materiality, in order to reach the more fundamental question, which is duty. "One who fails to disclose material information prior to the consummation of a transaction commits fraud only when he is under a duty to do so." . . .

My brethren find such a duty implicit in the fiduciary relationship between a closely held corporation and its shareholders. By this approach, what should be the beginning of analysis becomes its end. A publicly held corporation is a fiduciary of its shareholders, too; yet if Duff and Phelps had been publicly held it would have had no duty to tell Jordan about the company's prospects of being sold. . . . Thus the mere existence of a fiduciary relationship between a corporation and its shareholders does not require disclosure of material information to the shareholders. A further inquiry is necessary, and here must focus on the particulars of Jordan's relationship with Duff and Phelps.

The cases do not establish an automatic duty to disclose, even on the part of closely held corporations. . . . *Kohler v. Kohler Co.,* 319 F.2d 634, 638 (7th Cir. 1963), says that the duty "must be fashioned case by case as particular facts dictate." The court found no duty in that case. *Michaels v. Michaels,* 767 F.2d 1185, 1192–93, 1197–98 (7th Cir. 1985), did find a duty, and it is the case most like the present one factually, because it involved a shareholder who, like Jordan, was also an employee. But his status as a shareholder, unlike Jordan's, was not contingent on his remaining an employee. The contingent nature of Jordan's status as a shareholder has a twofold significance. First, it raises a question about the applicability of the majority's rule requiring disclosure "in the course of negotiating to purchase stock." One may doubt whether there was any real negotiation in this case, for once Jordan resigned he was contractually obligated to sell back his stock at a predetermined price. Second, and more important, the contingent nature of Jordan's status as a shareholder negates the existence of a right to be informed and hence a duty to disclose. This point is central to my dissent and has now to be explained.

Jordan's deal with Duff and Phelps required him to surrender his stock at book value if he left the company. It didn't matter whether he quit or was fired, retired or died; the agreement is explicit on these matters. My brethren hypothesize "implicit parts of the relations between Duff & Phelps and its employees." But those relations are totally defined by (1) the absence of an employment contract, which made Jordan an employee at will; (2) the shareholder agreement, which has no "implicit parts" that bear on Duff and Phelps' duty to Jordan, and explicitly ties his rights as a shareholder to his status as an employee at will; (3) a provision in the stock purchase agreement between Jordan and Duff and Phelps (signed at the same time as the shareholder agreement) that "nothing herein contained shall confer on the Employee any right to be continued in the employment of the Corporation." There is no occasion to speculate about "the implicit understanding" between Jordan and Duff and Phelps. The parties left nothing to the judicial imagination. The effect of the shareholder and stock purchase agreements (which for simplicity I shall treat as a single "stockholder agreement"), against a background of employment at will, was to strip Jordan of any contractual protection against what happened to him, and indeed against worse that might have happened to him. Duff and Phelps points out that it would not have had to let Jordan withdraw his resignation had he gotten wind of the negotiations with Security Pacific and wanted to withdraw it. On November 14

Hansen could have said to Jordan, "I accept your resignation effective today; we hope to sell Duff and Phelps for $50 million but have no desire to see you participate in the resulting bonanza. You will receive the paltry book value of your shares as of December 31, 1982." The "nothing herein contained" provision in the stockholder agreement shows that this tactic is permitted. Equally, on November 14, at the board meeting before Hansen knew that Jordan wanted to quit, the board could have decided to fire Jordan in order to increase the value of the deal with Security Pacific to the remaining shareholders.

These possibilities eliminate any inference that the stockholder agreement obligated Duff and Phelps to inform Jordan about the company's prospects. Under the agreement, if Duff and Phelps didn't want to give him the benefit of the information all it had to do to escape any possible liability was to give [Jordan] the information and then fire him. . . .

My brethren correctly observe that, "Because the fiduciary duty is a standby or off-the-rack guess about what parties would agree to if they dickered about the subject explicitly, parties may contract with greater specificity for other arrangements." But, they add, "we need not decide how far contracts can redefine obligations to disclose. Jordan was an employee at will; he signed no contract." It is true that he signed no contract of employment, but he signed a stockholder agreement that defined his rights as a shareholder "with greater specificity." The agreement entitled Duff and Phelps to terminate Jordan as shareholder, subject only to a duty to buy back his shares at book value. The arrangement that resulted (call it "shareholder at will") is incompatible with an inference that Duff and Phelps undertook to keep him abreast of developments affecting the value of the firm.

The majority states that "the absence of explicit clauses counsels caution in creating implicit exceptions to the general fiduciary duty." A similar caution was not evident when this circuit in *Flamm* adopted the "price and structure" rule. That rule allows a publicly held corporation to withhold material information from its shareholders until a corporate transaction is firmed up. Its premise is that the shareholders are compensated for being kept in ignorance, by the prospect of greater gains than if the information were disclosed. Ignorance will cause some shareholders to sell their shares before the transaction takes place, and thus to be losers after the fact; but on average the winners will outnumber the losers; so the shareholders can be assumed to have consented in advance to surrender their right to be informed. The grounds for an inference that Jordan surrendered his right to be informed are stronger. His stockholder agreement, read in light of his status as an employee at will (a status the agreement emphatically declined to modify), waived either explicitly or by implication every pertinent right he might otherwise have had, except to the book value of his shares on the December 31 preceding or coinciding with the end of his employment. Since the company had a right to deprive him of any participation in the profits from a sale of the company, a duty to reveal to him information about the value of the company would have been empty. If Hansen had wanted Jordan to stay he would have told him about the rosy prospects for selling Duff and Phelps. Evidently

Hansen didn't care whether Jordan stayed or not, so he didn't tell him. He could have fired him, or told him and then fired him—possibilities that make my brethren's statement that Jordan "could have remained at Duff & Phelps" highly ambiguous.

Since receipt of the information would have conferred no right on Jordan to benefit from the information, how can the parties be thought to have intended Duff and Phelps to have an enforceable duty to disclose the information to him? There is no duty to give shareholders information that they have no right to benefit from. . . . By signing the stockholder agreement Jordan gave Duff and Phelps in effect an option . . . to buy back his stock at any time at a fixed price. The grant of the option denied Jordan the right to profit from any information that the company might have about its prospects but prefer not to give him. If Hansen had known of the rule of law that my brethren adopt today, he could have avoided liability simply by telling Jordan that, come what may, December 30 would be Jordan's last day working for Duff and Phelps. Failure to disclose would be immaterial because Jordan could not act on the disclosure. Only because Hansen failed to make Jordan's resignation effective immediately (a generous gesture, which we have given Hansen cause to regret), as he could have done without violating any contractual obligation, is he held to have violated a duty of disclosure.

The case would be different if Jordan had had an employment contract or if he had had the right to retain his stock after ceasing to be an employee. Then a right to information about the prospects of the company would have been meaningful. Such a right is not meaningful when the employee has no right to act on it. That was Jordan's position. The company could have told him everything yet still have prevented him from benefiting from the information, by firing him.

Was Jordan a fool to have become a shareholder of Duff and Phelps on such disadvantageous terms as I believe he agreed to? (If so, that might be a reason for doubting whether those were the real terms.) He was not. Few business executives in this country have contractual entitlements to earnings, bonuses, or even retention of their jobs. They would rather take their chances on their employer's good will and interest in reputation, and on their own bargaining power and value to the firm, than pay for contract rights that are difficult and costly to enforce. If Jordan had had greater rights as a shareholder he would have had a lower salary; when he went to work for a new employer in Houston and received no stock rights he got a higher salary.

I go further: Jordan was protected by Duff and Phelps' own self-interest from being exploited. The principal asset of a service company such as Duff and Phelps is good will. It is a product largely of its employees' efforts and skills. If Jordan were a particularly valuable employee, so that the firm would be worth less without him, Hansen, desiring as he did to sell the firm for the highest possible price, would have told him about the prospects for selling the company. If Jordan was not a particularly valuable employee—if his departure would not reduce the value of the firm—there was no reason why he should participate in the profits from the sale of the firm, unless perhaps he had once been a particularly valuable employee but had ceased to be so.

That possibility might, but did not, lead him to negotiate for an employment contract, or for stock rights that would outlast his employment. By the type of agreement that he made with Duff and Phelps, Jordan gambled that he was and would continue to be such a good employee that he would be encouraged to stay long enough to profit from the firm's growth. The relationship that the parties created aligned their respective self-interests better than the legal protections that the court devises today.

My brethren are well aware that Duff and Phelps faced market constraints against exploiting its employee shareholders, but seem to believe that this implies that the company also assumed contractual duties. Businessmen, however, are less enthusiastic about contractual duties than lawyers are, so it is incorrect to infer from the existence of market constraints against exploitation that the parties also imposed a contractual duty against exploitation. Contractual obligation is a source of uncertainty and cost, and is therefore an expensive way of backstopping market forces. That is why employment at will is such a common form of employment relationship. It is strange to infer that firms invariably assume a legal obligation not to do what is not in their self-interest to do, and stranger to suppose — in the face of an explicit disclaimer — that by "allow[ing] employees to time their departures to obtain the maximum advantage from their stock," Duff and Phelps obligated itself to allow them to do this.

Having earlier in its opinion tried to get mileage out of the fact that Jordan "signed no [employment] contract," the majority later tries to get additional mileage from the observation that employment at will is a "contractual relation." This is the kind of legal half-truth that should make us thankful that our opinions are not subject to Rule 10b-5. Employment at will is a voluntary relationship, and thus contractual in the sense in which the word contract is used in the expression "freedom of contract." And the relationship can provide a framework for contracting: if Duff and Phelps had not paid Jordan his agreed-on wage after he had earned it, he could have sued the company for breach of contract. But the only element of employment at will that is relevant to this case is that employment at will is terminable at will, meaning that the employer can fire the employee without worrying about legal sanctions and likewise the employee can quit without worrying about them. Freedom of contract includes freedom not to contract. . . .

The majority's view that "the silence of the parties" is an invitation to judges to "imply other terms — those we [judges] are confident the parties would have bargained for if they had signed a written agreement" is doubly gratuitous. The parties did not want their relationship dragged into court and there made over by judges. And the parties were not silent. The stockholder agreement provides that Jordan's rights under it do not give him any employment tenure.

The inroads that the majority opinion makes on freedom of contract are not justified by its quotation from my academic writings concerning the purpose of contract law (which presupposes an agreement that the parties regard as legally enforceable) or by the possibility that corporations will exploit their junior executives, which may well be the least urgent problem facing our nation. The majority's statement that "one term implied in every written contract and therefore, we suppose, every unwritten one, is that neither party will try to take opportunistic advantage of the other" confuses the underlying rationale of contract law with the actual requirements of that law, and is anyway irrelevant since the parties decided not to subject the relevant parts of their relationship to the law of contracts and not to give Jordan any contractual protections against being fired. There was no "implied pledge to avoid opportunistic conduct" any more than there were "implicit parts of the relations" giving rise to contractual obligations. . . .

And if Duff and Phelps had fired Jordan (or refused to let him withdraw his resignation), this would not necessarily have been opportunistic. One might equally well say . . . that by trying to stick around merely to participate in an unexpectedly lucrative sale of Duff and Phelps, Jordan would have been the opportunist. The majority says that "understandably Duff & Phelps did not want a viper in its nest, a disgruntled employee remaining only in the hope of appreciation of his stock." I call that "viper" an opportunist. . . .

The issue of Duff and Phelps' duty to Jordan is a little more complicated than I have portrayed it. A resolution passed at the November 14 meeting of Duff and Phelps' board of directors provided that any employee who was terminated involuntarily could retain his stock for up to five years. If treated as an amendment to Jordan's stockholder agreement, the resolution would have prevented Duff and Phelps from forcing him to give up his stock by converting his voluntary termination into an involuntary one. There is a question, however, whether the resolution was effective without all the shareholders' consent. Moreover, another provision of the same resolution weakens Jordan's position: "If an employee voluntarily resigns (or gives notice of resignation) from the Corporation, the employee shall sell to the Corporation and the Corporation shall buy all of the Corporation's common stock then owned by the employee at book value." Jordan gave notice of resignation on November 14; and, under the resolution, having given notice he was obligated to sell his stock back to the company at book value.

I would understand, though might not agree, if the majority thought that the issue whether Duff and Phelps had a duty to disclose is unclear enough to warrant a trial. I cannot understand its holding that the duty exists as a matter of law. If, as appears, the holding is that just because Jordan was a shareholder Duff and Phelps had a duty to disclose material information to him, it is inconsistent with the basic premise of the "price and structure" rule (that premise being that a corporation isn't always required to disclose to its shareholders inside information regarding the prospects for selling the corporation), with the proposition seemingly endorsed by the majority that a duty of disclosure can be waived by its beneficiary, with the even more fundamental proposition that duty is a function of circumstances, and with the terms of the stockholder agreement in this case and of the employment relationship to which that agreement was expressly linked. If the holding is, instead, that the duty to disclose wells up from the complex of implied parts of relations, implied understandings, implied pledges, usual practices, and other particulars of the relationship between the parties (that is, if the discussion of these things in the majority opinion is anything more than rebuttal of this dissent), then I do not see how the duty can be thought a matter of law, to be imposed by this court without the benefit of a jury's or a trial judge's findings. . . .

Although my principal disagreement is with the majority's holding about duty to disclose, I also have reservations about the majority's discussion of causation and damages. . . .

Questions

1. What does Judge Easterbrook mean by fiduciary duties being an "off-the-rack" guess at what parties would agree to if they negotiated about such duties? Thinking back to your readings in Part 2, do you agree with his characterization of fiduciary duties?

2. Does Judge Posner accept Easterbrook's test? What is his dissenting argument?

3. What is the underlying policy rationale for Easterbrook's approach? Does Judge Posner accept this rationale?

4. What is the difference between Easterbrook's and Posner's approaches? Which one makes more sense? Why?

D. Remedies for Oppression

Alaska Plastics, Inc. v. Coppock

621 P.2d 270 (Alaska 1980)

CONNOR, Justice

The issue in this case involves the rights of a minority shareholder in a close corporation who allegedly has been deprived of benefits accorded other shareholders. The trial judge concluded that the corporation was obligated to buy the minority shareholder's stock at its fair value. We have concluded that this remedy is not available on the present record as a matter of law. Accordingly, we remand to the superior court to determine whether, based upon adequate findings of fact and conclusions of law, a remedy more appropriate to the alleged facts is available.

Those facts which the parties have stipulated to or which appear to be undisputed in the record are summarized below.

In 1961 the three individual appellants, Ralph Stefano, C. Harold Gillam, and Robert Crow formed a corporation known as Alaska Plastics and began to produce foam insulation at a building they bought in Fairbanks. Each of the three incorporators held 300 shares of stock. In 1970 Crow was divorced and, as part of a property settlement, gave his former wife, Patricia Muir, 150 shares or a one-sixth interest in the corporation.[1] From the time of incorporation until this lawsuit, Stefano, Gillam and Crow have been the only directors and officers of Alaska Plastics.

Stefano conceded at trial that the corporation forgot to notify Muir of annual shareholders meetings in 1971 and 1974. It was also undisputed that Muir was not notified of a shareholders meeting in 1972. According to Muir's testimony she was told of the 1973 shareholders meeting about three hours before the meeting was held.

In 1971 and 1972, Stefano, Gillam and Crow held the shareholders meetings in Seattle. It appears from Stefano's testimony that he and Gillam also brought their wives to these meetings at company expense, but he conceded that there was no business purpose for doing so.

In 1971, Stefano, Gillam and Crow voted themselves each a $3,000 annual director's fee. Although director's fees were apparently paid from 1971 through 1974, the three directors have never authorized Alaska Plastics to pay dividends. In 1974 the three board members also authorized an annual salary of $30,000 a year for Gillam, who was then employed as general manager of Alaska Plastics. Muir testified that she has never received any money from the corporation.

At the 1974 board meeting Stefano, Gillam and Crow also decided to offer Muir $15,000 for her shares and on May 1, 1974, Stefano wrote Muir informing her of the corporation's offer. Thinking the firm's offer was too low, Muir retained a lawyer who wrote the corporation expressing her concern both regarding the offered price and regarding the corporation's failure to inform Muir of shareholders meetings. In July, 1974, Muir's lawyer made a further demand on the corporation to inspect the books and records of the corporation. Gillam apparently advised Muir where the firm kept its books and told her they could be made available. An accountant employed by Muir did investigate the company's books and estimated that the shares might have a value somewhere between $23,000 and $40,000. Muir also ordered an appraisal of Alaska Plastics' Fairbanks property.

Later that same year, at a special director's meeting in October, 1974, the three board members agreed to make a $50,000 offer for Broadwater Industries, a firm located near Palmer that made a type of plastic foam insulation similar to that produced by Alaska Plastics at their Fairbanks plant. The purchase was apparently accomplished at some time between October and the next shareholders meeting, which was held on April 25, 1975. Muir testified that she was never consulted about the purchase and first learned about it at the 1975 meeting. At that meeting, however, she did not dissent from a shareholder vote ratifying all the acts of the directors and officers for the previous year.

Broadwater Industries was subsequently renamed Valley Plastics and is now a wholly-owned subsidiary of Alaska Plastics. The directors and officers of Valley Plastics are Stefano, Gillam and Crow.

---

1. At the time this action was filed Muir had remarried and assumed the name of Patricia Coppock. She has since that time resumed using her maiden name.

At the 1975 shareholders meeting, Muir offered her stock to the corporation for $40,000. In June, 1975, the board raised its offer to $20,000, which Muir again rejected.

Shortly after these negotiations failed, Alaska Plastics' Fairbanks plant, which was not insured, burned to the ground. The fire caused a total loss. Since the fire, Alaska Plastics has ceased production from Fairbanks and the corporation has not made an attempt to resume production in Fairbanks. All the remaining manufacturing and sales of Alaska Plastics are accomplished through its subsidiary, Valley Plastics. The fire, in effect, turned Alaska Plastics into a holding company for its affiliate.

About a year after the fire, in 1976, Stefano, acting as an individual, made a further offer of $20,000 to Muir, but the purchase never took place. Further attempts by the parties to negotiate a purchase or settlement failed and a lawsuit was filed in October 1976.

An amended complaint alleges ten separate causes of action, and prays for relief both in the name of the corporation and individually for Muir. After trial, the case was submitted to an advisory jury on two issues. The first issue was whether Stefano, when he acted as an individual, breached a contract to purchase Muir's shares. The jury found no contract. The second issue was whether the corporation's offer to buy Muir's shares was "equitable." The jury found that the corporation's offer of $15,000 in 1974 was not equitable, and determined that a fair offer would have been $32,000. Following the jury's verdict, the trial judge issued a judgment which states in part:

> "[T]he continued retention by Plaintiff of one-sixth of the shares in Alaska Plastics, Inc. following the offer on April 1974 was oppressive to Plaintiff and . . . an appropriate remedy would be to direct the transfer of Plaintiff's shares to Alaska Plastics, Inc. in exchange for a fair and equitable value. . . ."

A total judgment was entered against the three individual appellants and Alaska Plastics for $52,314, which represented $32,000 for the value of the shares, $5,200 for attorney's fees, and $15,144 in interest and costs. Muir was in turn required to convey her shares to Alaska Plastics. Both sides subsequently filed appeals.

I. Shareholder Remedies

In a corporation with publicly traded stock, dissatisfied shareholders can sell their stock on the market, recover their assets, and invest elsewhere. In a close corporation there is not likely to be a ready market for the corporation's shares. The corporation itself, or one of the other individual shareholders of the corporation, who are likely to provide the only market, may not be interested in buying out another shareholder. If they are interested, majority shareholders who control operate policy are in a unique position to "squeeze out" a minority shareholder at an unreasonably low price.

From a dissatisfied shareholder's point of view, the most successful remedy is likely to be a requirement that the corporation buy his or her shares at their fair value. Ordinarily, there are four ways in which this can occur. First, there may be a provision in the articles of incorporation or by-laws that provide for the purchase of shares by the corporation, contingent upon the occurrence of some event, such as the death of a shareholder or transfer of shares. Second, the shareholder may petition the court for involuntary dissolution of the corporation. Third, upon some significant change in corporate structure, such as a merger, the shareholder may demand a statutory right of appraisal. Finally, in some circumstances, a purchase may be justified as an equitable remedy upon a finding of a breach of a fiduciary duty between directors and shareholders and the corporation or other shareholders.

It does not appear from the record that there is any provision in the articles of incorporation or by-laws which would allow Muir to force Alaska Plastics to purchase her shares. Muir has not suggested that there is such provision, and we, therefore, do not consider the availability of this first method.

As to the second method, Alaska's corporation code provides in AS 10.05.540(2) that a shareholder may bring an action to liquidate the assets of a corporation upon a showing that "the acts of the directors or those in control of the corporation are illegal, oppressive or fraudulent...." A shareholder may also seek liquidation when "corporate assets are being misapplied or wasted." AS 10.05.540(4). Upon a liquidation of assets all creditors and the cost of liquidation must be paid and the remainder distributed among all the shareholders "according to their respective rights and interests." AS 10.05.561. There is no indication whether Muir would have received more or less than the $32,000 price for her shares ordered by the court if Alaska Plastics had been liquidated.

Liquidation is an extreme remedy. In a sense, forced dissolution allows minority shareholders to exercise retaliatory oppression against the majority. Absent compelling circumstances, courts often are reluctant to order involuntary dissolution.[5] As a result, courts have recognized alternative remedies based upon their inherent equitable powers. Thus in *Baker* [*v. Commercial Body Builders, Inc.*, 264 Ore. 614, 507 P.2d 387 (1973)], interpreting a statute substantially similar to AS 10.05.540, the court authorized numerous alternative remedies for oppressive or fraudulent conduct by the majority. Among those would be:

> "an order requiring the corporation or a majority of its stockholders to purchase the stock of the minority stockholders at a price to be determined according to a specified formula or at a price determined by the court to be a fair and reasonable price." (footnote omitted).

. . .

We are persuaded by *Baker* and conclude that Muir's request in her amended complaint for liquidation, although not actively pursued, could justify the trial court's order as an equitable remedy less drastic than liquidation. To prevail on this basis, Muir must establish on remand that the acts of Stefano, Gillam and Crow were "illegal, oppressive or fraudulent," AS 10.05.540(2), or alternatively, constituted a waste or misapplication of corporate assets. AS 10.05.540(4). Because the trial court did

---

5. However, courts in other jurisdictions have ordered dissolution of profitable, closely held corporations where there has been a breakdown in the relationship of shareholders....

not reach the issue, we express no opinion here on whether Muir has satisfied the statutory standards of AS 10.05.540.

The third method of forcing a corporation to purchase a minority shareholder's shares is a statutory appraisal remedy, which may be available under the Alaska Business Corporation Act in two circumstances where there is some fundamental corporate change. The remedy is available upon the merger or consolidation with another corporation, AS 10.05.417, or upon a sale of substantially all of the corporation's assets. AS 10.05.447. There is no suggestion that either statute is applicable in this case. . . .

We turn, then, to the fourth possibility by which a minority shareholder may force a corporation to purchase his or her shares. Two leading cases have concluded that transactions by one group of shareholders that enable it to derive some special benefit not shared in common by all shareholders should be subject to close judicial scrutiny. The Massachusetts Supreme Judicial Court concluded that shareholders in closely held corporations owe one another a fiduciary duty:

> "Because of the fundamental resemblance of the close corporation to the partnership, the trust and confidence which are essential to this scale and manner of enterprise, and the inherent danger to minority interests in the close corporation, we hold that stockholders in the close corporation owe one another substantially the same fiduciary duty in the operation of the enterprise that partners owe to one another. In our previous decisions, we have defined the standard of duty owed by partners to one another as the 'utmost good faith and loyalty.'" (footnotes and citations omitted).

Donahue v. Rodd Electrotype Co., 367 Mass. 578 (1975). . . .

We believe that *Donahue* . . . correctly state[s] the law applicable to the relationship between shareholders in closely held corporations, or between those holding a controlling block of stock, and minority shareholders. We do not believe, though, that the existence and breach of a fiduciary duty among corporate shareholders supports the appraisal remedy ordered by the trial court in this case.

The trial judge made no findings of fact or conclusions of law, but the basis for his decision is clear from extensive discussions that took place prior to instructing the jury and the form of the judge's final order. The court concluded that once the corporation made an offer to Muir it was under an obligation to purchase her stock at a "fair" price, regardless of what price the corporation had initially offered. Had Muir actually sold the stock at an unfairly low price, she might have brought an action to set the transaction aside. The existence of a fiduciary duty between shareholders would justify careful scrutiny and shifting the burden onto the defendants to show that the transaction was fair. In this case, however, Muir rejected both of the corporation's offers. We are not aware of any authority which would allow a court to order specific performance on the basis of an unaccepted offer, particularly on terms totally different from those offered. Such a rule would place a court in the impossible position of making and enforcing contracts between unwilling parties.

Donahue . . . suggest[s] the appropriate form of a remedy in this case, however. In *Donahue*, one of the controlling shareholders caused the corporation to purchase forty-five of his shares, but then refused to buy an equal number of shares held by a minority shareholder. The court first noted the benefit that a shareholder in a close corporation gained by forcing the corporation to buy his shares.

> "The benefits conferred by the purchase are twofold: (1) provision of a market for shares; (2) access to corporate assets for personal use. By definition, there is no ready market for shares of a close corporation. The purchase creates a market for shares which previously had been unmarketable. It transforms a previously illiquid investment into a liquid one."

Donahue v. Rodd Electrotype Co. The court then went on to conclude that where a controlling shareholder took advantage of such a special benefit, the fiduciary duty owed to other shareholders required that the corporation offer such a benefit equally:

> "The rule of equal opportunity in stock purchases by close corporations provides equal access to these benefits for all stockholders."

Id. . . .

As we read Muir's complaint, the essence of her action is that Stefano, Gillam and Crow enjoyed benefits from the corporation which should have been shared equally with her. None of the other shareholders of Alaska Plastics have sold their stock to the corporation so it would not be appropriate to order the corporation to purchase Muir's stock. Unlike *Donahue*, this was not one of the benefits which the majority received and which they did not share with Muir. There was evidence, however, that the corporation paid Stefano, Gillam and Crow "director's fees." Gillam received a substantial salary. The corporation apparently paid some of the personal expenses of the directors' wives. Regardless of how the corporation labels these expenditures, if they were not made for the reasonable value of services rendered to the corporation, some portion of these payments might be characterized as constructive dividends. . . . [I]f so the excluded shareholder must participate equally in the payments received by other shareholders.

We express no opinion as to whether Muir has shown that these payments were a distribution of dividends, whether she was deprived of other corporate benefits which she should have shared in equally with the other three shareholders, or whether the majority shareholders violated AS 10.05.540. The case must be remanded to the trial court to make appropriate findings of fact and conclusions of law based upon the present record. . . .

The case is remanded to the superior court for further proceedings in accordance with this opinion.

Questions

1. Has Muir sued the right defendant?

2. Where does the court get its power to order the corporation to purchase Muir's shares?

3. How does the court distinguish Muir's claim from the one involved in *Donahue v. Rodd Electrotype Company of New England, Inc.*?

In the Matter of the Judicial Dissolution of Kemp & Beatley, Inc.
64 N.Y.2d 63 (1984)

COOKE, Chief Judge

When the majority shareholders of a close corporation award *de facto* dividends to all shareholders except a class of minority shareholders, such a policy may constitute "oppressive actions" and serve as a basis for an order made pursuant to section 1104-a of the Business Corporation Law dissolving the corporation. In the instant matter, there is sufficient evidence to support the lower courts' conclusion that the majority shareholders had altered a long-standing policy to distribute corporate earnings on the basis of stock ownership, as against petitioners only. Moreover, the courts did not abuse their discretion by concluding that dissolution was the only means by which petitioners could gain a fair return on their investment.

I

The business concern of Kemp & Beatley, incorporated under the laws of New York, designs and manufactures table linens and sundry tabletop items. The company's stock consists of 1,500 outstanding shares held by eight shareholders. Petitioner Dissin had been employed by the company for 42 years when, in June 1979, he resigned. Prior to resignation, Dissin served as vice-president and a director of Kemp & Beatley. Over the course of his employment, Dissin had acquired stock in the company and currently owns 200 shares.

Petitioner Gardstein, like Dissin, had been a long-time employee of the company. Hired in 1944, Gardstein was for the next 35 years involved in various aspects of the business including material procurement, product design, and plant management. His employment was terminated by the company in December 1980. He currently owns 105 shares of Kemp & Beatley stock.

Apparent unhappiness surrounded petitioners' leaving the employ of the company. Of particular concern was that they no longer received any distribution of the company's earnings. Petitioners considered themselves to be "frozen out" of the company; whereas it had been their experience when with the company to receive a distribution of the company's earnings according to their stockholdings, in the form of either dividends or extra compensation, that distribution was no longer forthcoming.

Gardstein and Dissin, together holding 20.33% of the company's outstanding stock, commenced the instant proceeding in June 1981, seeking dissolution of Kemp & Beatley pursuant to section 1104-a of the Business Corporation Law. Their petition alleged "fraudulent and oppressive" conduct by the company's board of directors such as to render petitioners' stock "a virtually worthless asset." Supreme Court referred the matter for a hearing, which was held in March 1982.

Upon considering the testimony of petitioners and the principals of Kemp & Beatley, the referee concluded that "the corporate management has by its policies effectively rendered petitioners' shares worthless, and . . . the only way petitioners can expect any return is by dissolution". Petitioners were found to have invested capital in the company expecting, among other things, to receive dividends or "bonuses" based upon their stock holdings. Also found was the company's "established buy-out policy" by which it would purchase the stock of employee shareholders upon their leaving its employ.

The involuntary-dissolution statute (Business Corporation Law, § 1104-a) permits dissolution when a corporation's controlling faction is found guilty of "oppressive action" toward the complaining shareholders. The referee considered oppression to arise when "those in control" of the corporation "have acted in such a manner as to defeat those expectations of the minority stockholders which formed the basis of [their] participation in the venture." The expectations of petitioners that they would not be arbitrarily excluded from gaining a return on their investment and that their stock would be purchased by the corporation upon termination of employment, were deemed defeated by prevailing corporate policies. Dissolution was recommended in the referee's report, subject to giving respondent corporation an opportunity to purchase petitioners' stock.

The Supreme Court confirmed the referee's report. It, too, concluded that due to the corporation's new dividend policy petitioners had been prevented from receiving any return on their investments. Liquidation of the corporate assets was found the only means by which petitioners would receive a fair return. The court considered judicial dissolution of a corporation to be "a serious and severe remedy." Consequently, the order of dissolution was conditioned upon the corporation's being permitted to purchase petitioners' stock. The Appellate Division affirmed, without opinion.

At issue in this appeal is the scope of section 1104-a of the Business Corporation Law. Specifically, this court must determine whether the provision for involuntary dissolution when the "directors or those in control of the corporation have been guilty of . . . oppressive actions toward the complaining shareholders" was properly applied in the circumstances of this case. We hold that it was, and therefore affirm.

II

Judicially ordered dissolution of a corporation at the behest of minority interests is a remedy of relatively recent vintage in New York. Historically, this State's courts were considered divested of equity jurisdiction to order dissolution, as statutory prescriptions were deemed exclusive. . . .

Minority shareholders were granted standing in the absence of statutory authority to seek dissolution of corporations when controlling shareholders engaged in certain egregious conduct. Predicated on the majority shareholders' fiduciary obligation to treat all shareholders fairly and equally, to preserve corporate assets, and to fulfill their responsibilities of corporate management with "scrupulous good faith," the courts' equitable power can be invoked when "it appears that the directors and majority shareholders 'have so palpably breached the fiduciary duty they owe to the minority shareholders that they are disqualified from exercising the exclusive discretion and the dissolution power given to them by statute.'" True to the ancient principle that equity jurisdiction will not lie when there exists a remedy at law, the courts have not entertained a minority's petition in equity when their rights and interests could be adequately protected in a legal action, such as by a shareholder's derivative suit.

Supplementing this principle of judicially ordered equitable dissolution of a corporation, the Legislature has shown a special solicitude toward the rights of minority shareholders of closely held corporations by enacting section 1104-a of the Business Corporation Law.[1] That statute provides a mechanism for the holders of at least 20% of the outstanding shares of a corporation whose stock is not traded on a securities market to petition for its dissolution "under special circumstances". The circumstances that give rise to dissolution fall into two general classifications: mistreatment of complaining shareholders, or misappropriation of corporate assets by controlling shareholders, directors or officers.

Section 1104-a describes three types of proscribed activity: "illegal", "fraudulent", and "oppressive" conduct. The first two terms are familiar words that are commonly

---

1. The statute provides:
"§ 1104-a. Petition for judicial dissolution under special circumstances
(a) The holders of twenty percent or more of all outstanding shares of a corporation, other than a corporation registered as an investment company under an act of congress entitled 'Investment Company Act of 1940', no shares of which are listed on a national securities exchange or regularly quoted in an over-the-counter market by one or more members of a national or an affiliated securities association, who are entitled to vote in an election of directors may present a petition of dissolution on one or more of the following grounds:
   (1) The directors or those in control of the corporation have been guilty of illegal, fraudulent or oppressive actions toward the complaining shareholders;
   (2) The property or assets of the corporation are being looted, wasted, or diverted for non-corporate purposes by its directors, officers or those in control of the corporation.
(b) The court, in determining whether to proceed with involuntary dissolution pursuant to this section, shall take into account:
   (1) Whether liquidation of the corporation is the only feasible means whereby the petitioners may reasonably expect to obtain a fair return on their investment; and
   (2) Whether liquidation of the corporation is reasonably necessary for the protection of the rights and interests of any substantial number of shareholders or of the petitioners."

understood at law. The last, however, does not enjoy the same certainty gained through long usage. As no definition is provided by the statute, it falls upon the courts to provide guidance.

The statutory concept of "oppressive actions" can, perhaps, best be understood by examining the characteristics of close corporations and the Legislature's general purpose in creating this involuntary-dissolution statute. It is widely understood that, in addition to supplying capital to a contemplated or ongoing enterprise and expecting a fair and equal return, parties comprising the ownership of a close corporation may expect to be actively involved in its management and operation.

As a leading commentator in the field has observed: "Unlike the typical shareholder in a publicly held corporation, who may be simply an investor or a speculator and cares nothing for the responsibilities of management, the shareholder in a close corporation is a co-owner of the business and wants the privileges and powers that go with ownership. His participation in that particular corporation is often his principal or sole source of income. As a matter of fact, providing employment for himself may have been the principal reason why he participated in organizing the corporation. He may or may not anticipate an ultimate profit from the sale of his interest, but he normally draws very little from the corporation as dividends. In his capacity as an officer or employee of the corporation, he looks to his salary for the principal return on his capital investment, because earnings of a close corporation, as is well known, are distributed in major part in salaries, bonuses and retirement benefits." O'Neal, Close Corporations.

Shareholders enjoy flexibility in memorializing these expectations through agreements setting forth each party's rights and obligations in corporate governance. In the absence of such an agreement, however, ultimate decision-making power respecting corporate policy will be reposed in the holders of a majority interest in the corporation. A wielding of this power by any group controlling a corporation may serve to destroy a stockholder's vital interests and expectations.

As the stock of closely held corporations generally is not readily salable, a minority shareholder at odds with management policies may be without either a voice in protecting his or her interests or any reasonable means of withdrawing his or her investment. This predicament may fairly be considered the legislative concern underlying the provision at issue in this case; inclusion of the criteria that the corporation's stock not be traded on securities markets and that the complaining shareholder be subject to oppressive actions supports this conclusion.

Defining oppressive conduct as distinct from illegality in the present context has been considered in other forums. The question has been resolved by considering oppressive actions to refer to conduct that substantially defeats the "reasonable expectations" held by minority shareholders in committing their capital to the particular enterprise. This concept is consistent with the apparent purpose underlying the provision under review. A shareholder who reasonably expected that ownership in the corporation would entitle him or her to a job, a share of corporate earnings, a place in corporate management, or some other form of security, would be oppressed in a very real sense when others in the corporation seek to defeat those expectations and there exists no effective means of salvaging the investment.

Given the nature of close corporations and the remedial purpose of the statute, this court holds that utilizing a complaining shareholder's "reasonable expectations" as a means of identifying and measuring conduct alleged to be oppressive is appropriate. A court considering a petition alleging oppressive conduct must investigate what the majority shareholders knew, or should have known, to be the petitioner's expectations in entering the particular enterprise. Majority conduct should not be deemed oppressive simply because the petitioner's subjective hopes and desires in joining the venture are not fulfilled. Disappointment alone should not necessarily be equated with oppression.

Rather, oppression should be deemed to arise only when the majority conduct substantially defeats expectations that, objectively viewed, were both reasonable under the circumstances and were central to the petitioner's decision to join the venture. It would be inappropriate, however, for us in this case to delineate the contours of the courts' consideration in determining whether directors have been guilty of oppressive conduct. As in other areas of the law, much will depend on the circumstances in the individual case.

The appropriateness of an order of dissolution is in every case vested in the sound discretion of the court considering the application. Under the terms of this statute, courts are instructed to consider both whether "liquidation of the corporation is the only feasible means" to protect the complaining shareholder's expectation of a fair return on his or her investment and whether dissolution "is reasonably necessary" to protect "the rights or interests of any substantial number of shareholders" not limited to those complaining. Implicit in this direction is that once oppressive conduct is found, consideration must be given to the totality of circumstances surrounding the current state of corporate affairs and relations to determine whether some remedy short of or other than dissolution constitutes a feasible means of satisfying both the petitioner's expectations and the rights and interests of any other substantial group of shareholders.

By invoking the statute, a petitioner has manifested his or her belief that dissolution may be the only appropriate remedy. Assuming the petitioner has set forth a prima facie case of oppressive conduct, it should be incumbent upon the parties seeking to forestall dissolution to demonstrate to the court the existence of an adequate, alternative remedy. A court has broad latitude in fashioning alternative relief, but when fulfillment of the oppressed petitioner's expectations by these means is doubtful, such as when there has been a complete deterioration of relations between the parties, a court should not hesitate to order dissolution. Every order of dissolution, however, must be conditioned upon permitting any shareholder of the corporation to elect to purchase the complaining shareholder's stock at fair value.

One further observation is in order. The purpose of this involuntary dissolution statute is to provide protection to the minority shareholder whose reasonable expectations in undertaking the venture have been frustrated and who has no adequate means of recovering his or her investment. It would be contrary to this remedial purpose to permit its use by minority shareholders as merely a coercive tool. Therefore, the minority shareholder whose own acts, made in bad faith and undertaken with a view toward forcing an involuntary dissolution, give rise to the complained-of oppression should be given no quarter in the statutory protection.

III

There was sufficient evidence presented at the hearing to support the conclusion that Kemp & Beatley had a long-standing policy of awarding *de facto* dividends based on stock ownership in the form of "extra compensation bonuses." Petitioners, both of whom had extensive experience in the management of the company, testified to this effect. Moreover, both related that receipt of this compensation, whether as true dividends or disguised as "extra compensation", was a known incident to ownership of the company's stock understood by all of the company's principals. Finally, there was uncontroverted proof that this policy was changed either shortly before or shortly after petitioners' employment ended. Extra compensation was still awarded by the company. The only difference was that stock ownership was no longer a basis for the payments; it was asserted that the basis became services rendered to the corporation. It was not unreasonable for the fact finder to have determined that this change in policy amounted to nothing less than an attempt to exclude petitioners from gaining any return on their investment through the mere recharacterization of distributions of corporate income. Under the circumstances of this case, there was no error in determining that this conduct constituted oppressive action within the meaning of section 1104-a of the Business Corporation Law.

Nor may it be said that Supreme Court abused its discretion in ordering Kemp & Beatley's dissolution, subject to an opportunity for a buy-out of petitioners' shares. After the referee had found that the controlling faction of the company was, in effect, attempting to "squeeze-out" petitioners by offering them no return on their investment and increasing other executive compensation, respondents, in opposing the report's confirmation, attempted only to controvert the factual basis of the report. They suggested no feasible, alternative remedy to the forced dissolution. In light of an apparent deterioration in relations between petitioners and the governing shareholders of Kemp & Beatley, it was not unreasonable for the court to have determined that a forced buy-out of petitioners' shares or liquidation of the corporation's assets was the only means by which petitioners could be guaranteed a fair return on their investments.

Accordingly, the order of the Appellate Division should be modified, with costs to petitioners-respondents, by affirming the substantive determination of that court but extending the time for exercising the option to purchase petitioners-respondents' shares to 30 days following this court's determination.

Order modified, with costs to petitioners-respondents, in accordance with the opinion herein and, as so modified, affirmed.

Questions

1. How does the court define oppression in *Matter of Kemp & Beatley, Inc.*? What is the rationale supporting its definition?

2. How does the court balance the majority's legitimate exercise of its "right of selfish ownership" with the need to protect the minority from oppression?

Section III

Controlling Shareholders

Since the rise of the modern public corporation, courts and legal scholars have given much attention to the fiduciary duties of controlling shareholders toward the corporation and its minority shareholders. As you read the cases in this Section III, think about the doctrinal and policy reasons for imposing fiduciary duties on shareholders because of their ownership interest. Why and when, if at all, should the controlling shareholder be allowed to exercise her right of selfish ownership?

A. Controlling Shareholders' Fiduciary Duties

Sinclair Oil Corporation v. Levien

280 A.2d 717 (Del. 1971)

WOLCOTT, Chief Justice

This is an appeal by the defendant, Sinclair Oil Corporation (hereafter Sinclair), from an order of the Court of Chancery in a derivative action requiring Sinclair to account for damages sustained by its subsidiary, Sinclair Venezuelan Oil Company (hereafter Sinven), organized by Sinclair for the purpose of operating in Venezuela, as a result of dividends paid by Sinven, the denial to Sinven of industrial development, and a breach of contract between Sinclair's wholly-owned subsidiary, Sinclair International Oil Company, and Sinven.

Sinclair, operating primarily as a holding company, is in the business of exploring for oil and of producing and marketing crude oil and oil products. At all times relevant to this litigation, it owned about 97% of Sinven's stock. The plaintiff owns about 3000 of 120,000 publicly held shares of Sinven. Sinven, incorporated in 1922, has been engaged in petroleum operations primarily in Venezuela and since 1959 has operated exclusively in Venezuela.

Sinclair nominates all members of Sinven's board of directors. The Chancellor found as a fact that the directors were not independent of Sinclair. Almost without exception, they were officers, directors, or employees of corporations in the Sinclair complex. By reason of Sinclair's domination, it is clear that Sinclair owed Sinven a fiduciary duty. Sinclair concedes this.

The Chancellor held that because of Sinclair's fiduciary duty and its control over Sinven, its relationship with Sinven must meet the test of intrinsic fairness. The standard of intrinsic fairness involves both a high degree of fairness and a shift in the burden of proof. Under this standard the burden is on Sinclair to prove, subject to careful judicial scrutiny, that its transactions with Sinven were objectively fair.

Sinclair argues that the transactions between it and Sinven should be tested, not by the test of intrinsic fairness with the accompanying shift of the burden of proof, but by the business judgment rule under which a court will not interfere with the judgment of a board of directors unless there is a showing of gross and palpable overreaching. A board of directors enjoys a presumption of sound business judgment, and its decisions will not be disturbed if they can be attributed to any rational business purpose. A court under such circumstances will not substitute its own notions of what is or is not sound business judgment.

We think, however, that Sinclair's argument in this respect is misconceived. When the situation involves a parent and a subsidiary, with the parent controlling the transaction and fixing the terms, the test of intrinsic fairness, with its resulting shifting of the burden of proof, is applied. The basic situation for the application of the rule is the one in which the parent has received a benefit to the exclusion and at the expense of the subsidiary. . . .

A parent does indeed owe a fiduciary duty to its subsidiary when there are parent-subsidiary dealings. However, this alone will not evoke the intrinsic fairness standard. This standard will be applied only when the fiduciary duty is accompanied by self-dealing—the situation when a parent is on both sides of a transaction with its subsidiary. Self-dealing occurs when the parent, by virtue of its domination of the subsidiary, causes the subsidiary to act in such a way that the parent receives something from the subsidiary to the exclusion of, and detriment to, the minority stockholders of the subsidiary.

We turn now to the facts. The plaintiff argues that, from 1960 through 1966, Sinclair caused Sinven to pay out such excessive dividends that the industrial development of Sinven was effectively prevented, and it became in reality a corporation in dissolution.

From 1960 through 1966, Sinven paid out $108,000,000 in dividends ($38,000,000 in excess of Sinven's earnings during the same period). The Chancellor held that Sinclair caused these dividends to be paid during a period when it had a need for large amounts of cash. Although the dividends paid exceeded earnings, the plaintiff concedes that the payments were made in compliance with 8 Del.C. § 170, authorizing payment of dividends out of surplus or net profits. However, the plaintiff attacks these dividends on the ground that they resulted from an improper motive—Sinclair's need for cash. The Chancellor, applying the intrinsic fairness standard, held that Sinclair did not sustain its burden of proving that these transactions were intrinsically fair to the minority stockholders of Sinven.

Since it is admitted that the dividends were paid in strict compliance with 8 Del.C. § 170, the alleged excessiveness of the payments alone would not state a cause of action. Nevertheless, compliance with the applicable statute may not, under all circumstances, justify all dividend payments. If a plaintiff can meet his burden of proving that a dividend cannot be grounded on any reasonable business objective, then the courts can and will interfere with the board's decision to pay the dividend.

Sinclair contends that it is improper to apply the intrinsic fairness standard to dividend payments even when the board which voted for the dividends is completely dominated....

We do not accept the argument that the intrinsic fairness test can never be applied to a dividend declaration by a dominated board, although a dividend declaration by a dominated board will not inevitably demand the application of the intrinsic fairness standard. If such a dividend is in essence self-dealing by the parent, then the intrinsic fairness standard is the proper standard. For example, suppose a parent dominates a subsidiary and its board of directors. The subsidiary has outstanding two classes of stock, X and Y. Class X is owned by the parent and Class Y is owned by minority stockholders of the subsidiary. If the subsidiary, at the direction of the parent, declares a dividend on its Class X stock only, this might well be self-dealing by the parent. It would be receiving something from the subsidiary to the exclusion of and detrimental to its minority stockholders. This self-dealing, coupled with the parents' fiduciary duty, would make intrinsic fairness the proper standard by which to evaluate the dividend payments.

Consequently it must be determined whether the dividend payments by Sinven were, in essence, self-dealing by Sinclair. The dividends resulted in great sums of money being transferred from Sinven to Sinclair. However, a proportionate share of this money was received by the minority shareholders of Sinven. Sinclair received nothing from Sinven to the exclusion of its minority stockholders. As such, these dividends were not self-dealing. We hold therefore that the Chancellor erred in applying the intrinsic fairness test as to these dividend payments. The business judgment standard should have been applied.

We conclude that the facts demonstrate that the dividend payments complied with the business judgment standard and with 8 Del.C. § 170. The motives for causing the declaration of dividends are immaterial unless the plaintiff can show that the dividend payments resulted from improper motives and amounted to waste. The plaintiff contends only that the dividend payments drained Sinven of cash to such an extent that it was prevented from expanding.

The plaintiff proved no business opportunities which came to Sinven independently and which Sinclair either took to itself or denied to Sinven. As a matter of fact, with two minor exceptions which resulted in losses, all of Sinven's operations have been conducted in Venezuela, and Sinclair had a policy of exploiting its oil properties located in different countries by subsidiaries located in the particular countries.

From 1960 to 1966 Sinclair purchased or developed oil fields in Alaska, Canada, Paraguay, and other places around the world. The plaintiff contends that these were all opportunities which could have been taken by Sinven. The Chancellor concluded that Sinclair had not proved that its denial of expansion opportunities to Sinven was intrinsically fair. He based this conclusion on the following findings of fact. Sinclair made no real effort to expand Sinven. The excessive dividends paid by Sinven resulted in so great a cash drain as to effectively deny to Sinven any ability to expand. During this same period Sinclair actively pursued a company-wide policy of developing through its subsidiaries new sources of revenue, but Sinven was not permitted to participate and was confined in its activities to Venezuela.

However, the plaintiff could point to no opportunities which came to Sinven. Therefore, Sinclair usurped no business opportunity belonging to Sinven. Since Sinclair received nothing from Sinven to the exclusion of and detriment to Sinven's minority stockholders, there was no self-dealing. Therefore, business judgment is the proper standard by which to evaluate Sinclair's expansion policies.

Since there is no proof of self-dealing on the part of Sinclair, it follows that the expansion policy of Sinclair and the methods used to achieve the desired result must, as far as Sinclair's treatment of Sinven is concerned, be tested by the standards of the business judgment rule. Accordingly, Sinclair's decision, absent fraud or gross overreaching, to achieve expansion through the medium of its subsidiaries, other than Sinven, must be upheld.

Even if Sinclair was wrong in developing these opportunities as it did, the question arises, with which subsidiaries should these opportunities have been shared? No evidence indicates a unique need or ability of Sinven to develop these opportunities. The decision of which subsidiaries would be used to implement Sinclair's expansion policy was one of business judgment with which a court will not interfere absent a showing of gross and palpable overreaching. No such showing has been made here.

Next, Sinclair argues that the Chancellor committed error when he held it liable to Sinven for breach of contract.

In 1961 Sinclair created Sinclair International Oil Company (hereafter International), a wholly owned subsidiary used for the purpose of coordinating all of Sinclair's foreign operations. All crude purchases by Sinclair were made thereafter through International.

On September 28, 1961, Sinclair caused Sinven to contract with International whereby Sinven agreed to sell all of its crude oil and refined products to International at specified prices. The contract provided for minimum and maximum quantities and prices. The plaintiff contends that Sinclair caused this contract to be breached in two respects. Although the contract called for payment on receipt, International's payments lagged as much as 30 days after receipt. Also, the contract required International to purchase at least a fixed minimum amount of crude and refined products from Sinven. International did not comply with this requirement.

Clearly, Sinclair's act of contracting with its dominated subsidiary was self-dealing. Under the contract Sinclair received the products produced by Sinven, and of course the minority shareholders of Sinven were not able to share in the receipt of these products. If the contract was breached, then Sinclair received these products to the detriment of Sinven's minority shareholders. We agree with the Chancellor's finding that the contract was breached by Sinclair, both as to the time of payments and the amounts purchased.

Although a parent need not bind itself by a contract with its dominated subsidiary, Sinclair chose to operate in this manner. As Sinclair has received the benefits of this contract, so must it comply with the contractual duties.

Under the intrinsic fairness standard, Sinclair must prove that its causing Sinven not to enforce the contract was intrinsically fair to the minority shareholders of Sinven. Sinclair has failed to meet this burden. Late payments were clearly breaches for which Sinven should have sought and received adequate damages. As to the quantities purchased, Sinclair argues that it purchased all the products produced by Sinven. This, however, does not satisfy the standard of intrinsic fairness. Sinclair has failed to prove that Sinven could not possibly have produced or someway have obtained the contract minimums. As such, Sinclair must account on this claim.

Finally, Sinclair argues that the Chancellor committed error in refusing to allow it a credit or setoff of all benefits provided by it to Sinven with respect to all the alleged damages. The Chancellor held that setoff should be allowed on specific transactions, e.g., benefits to Sinven under the contract with International, but denied an over all setoff against all damages claimed. We agree with the Chancellor, although the point may well be moot in view of our holding that Sinclair is not required to account for the alleged excessiveness of the dividend payments.

We will therefore reverse that part of the Chancellor's order that requires Sinclair to account to Sinven for damages sustained as a result of dividends paid between 1960 and 1966, and by reason of the denial to Sinven of expansion during that period. We will affirm the remaining portion of that order and remand the cause for further proceedings.

Questions

1. What is the court's doctrinal justification for imposing fiduciary duties on Sinclair? Does it make sense? Does it also justify granting Sinclair the presumption of the Business Judgment Rule?

2. Is there anything new about the court's definition of self-dealing? Consider the circumstances under which interested director transactions are questioned, corporate opportunities challenged, and compensation tested. Are they judged by the standard of self-dealing that the court articulated in *Sinclair Oil Corporation v. Levien*?

Anadarko Petroleum Corporation v. Panhandle Eastern Corporation
545 A.2d 1171 (Del. 1988)

WALSH, Justice

This is an appeal from a decision of the Court of Chancery granting summary judgment against Anadarko Petroleum Corporation ("Anadarko") in its suit against three of its former directors and its former parent, Panhandle Eastern Corporation ("Panhandle"), for an alleged breach of fiduciary duty in modifying certain contracts, the so-called disputed agreements, between Anadarko and Panhandle. The lawsuit arises from a spin-off of Panhandle's wholly-owned subsidiary, Anadarko, through a stock dividend. After the stock dividend was declared but prior to the date of distribution, Panhandle and the Anadarko board of directors approved the disputed agreements. Anadarko argues that the disputed agreements are voidable because they are unfair and were approved in violation of fiduciary duties owed to the prospective stockholders of Anadarko. The Court of Chancery ruled as a matter of law that the former directors of Anadarko owed a fiduciary duty only to the parent corporation, Panhandle, at the time the disputed agreements were approved. Further, because Anadarko's claims with respect to the validity of the disputed agreements were premised on the existence of a fiduciary duty owed to the prospective stockholders of Anadarko, the court granted summary judgment against Anadarko.

This appeal presents a novel issue: whether a corporate parent and directors of a wholly-owned subsidiary owe fiduciary duties to the prospective stockholders of the subsidiary after the parent declares its intention to spin-off the subsidiary. We conclude that prior to the date of distribution the interests held by Anadarko's prospective stockholders were insufficient to impose fiduciary obligations on the parent and the subsidiary's directors. Accordingly, we affirm the decision of the Court of Chancery.

I

Panhandle, through its subsidiaries, Panhandle Eastern Pipeline Company ("Pipeline") and Trunkline Gas Company ("Trunkline"), is engaged in the pipeline transportation of natural gas. Prior to September, 1986, another Panhandle subsidiary Anadarko Production Company ("Production") through its subsidiary Anadarko was engaged in the exploration and production of crude oil and natural gas.

On August 20, 1986, Panhandle's board of directors voted unanimously to effect a spin-off of Panhandle's production and exploration assets by distributing one share of Anadarko common stock for each issued and outstanding share of Panhandle stock held of record on September 12, 1986. The date for distribution of the stock dividend was set at October 1, 1986. To advise Panhandle's shareholders and the market place of the impending spin-off, Panhandle and Anadarko issued an Information Statement for Anadarko Common Stock ("Information Statement") dated August 29, 1986. Further, on September 18, 1986, Panhandle furnished a list of its stockholders of record as of September 12, to Anadarko's transfer agent to facilitate the distribution of the stock dividend.

In order to enhance the value of the spin-off, representatives of Panhandle and Anadarko met with representatives of the New York Stock Exchange for the avowed purpose of creating a market for Anadarko stock prior to the date of distribution. The New York Stock Exchange approved the application and trading began in Anadarko stock on September 8, 1986. From September 8, 1986, to October 1, 1986, Panhandle and Anadarko stock were traded in essentially three forms. First, Panhandle's stock was traded the "regular way" reflecting the combined value of Panhandle and Anadarko. A share of Panhandle traded the regular way included a due bill which required the seller to deliver to the buyer the Anadarko stock dividend if and when it was distributed. Second, Panhandle stock was traded "ex-distribution." This form of trading reflected only the value of Panhandle, with the seller retaining the right to the Anadarko stock dividend. Finally, trading in Anadarko stock was effected on a "when-issued" basis, reflecting the value of Anadarko as an independent entity. Between September 8 and October 1, approximately three million shares of Anadarko shares were traded on a when-issued basis; one million of Panhandle shares were sold on an ex-distribution basis; and more than five million shares of Panhandle were traded the regular way.

Following board approval of the spin-off dividend, Panhandle began restructuring existing contracts between Panhandle and Anadarko. Initially an effort was made to modify the existing contracts through negotiations between the operating staffs of Anadarko and Panhandle. On September 11, Anadarko's board approved modifications to a prior "take or pay" agreement, requiring Anadarko to reduce the advance price of gas sold to Panhandle on a short term basis. After failing to modify the remaining agreements through negotiations, on September 30, 1986, Anadarko's board of directors met to resolve all the outstanding impasse issues relating to the spin-off.

Five of the then seven Anadarko directors participated in the September 30 board meeting. Only one director, James T. Rodgers ("Rodgers"), was not affiliated with Panhandle or one of its subsidiaries. At the meeting Rodgers was joined by Robert J. Allison, Jr., ("Allison") a director of both Anadarko and Panhandle, in protesting the terms of the disputed agreements as being unfair to Anadarko. Further, the board was advised by Anadarko's General Counsel that it owed a fiduciary duty to

Anadarko's prospective stockholders which would be breached if the board approved the unfair contracts.

The disputed agreements were approved by Anadarko's board by a 3–2 vote. (Rodgers voted against all of the modifications and Allison voted against five and abstained on one). Following the approval of the agreements the three inside directors[1] resigned, effective October 1, 1986, and were replaced by four new directors. The newly constituted board reviewed the disputed agreements and based on an opinion by outside counsel that the contracts were unfair and voidable, the board voted unanimously to rescind the agreements.[2]

II

The linchpin of Anadarko's attack on the terms of the disputed agreements is the claim that the agreements were crafted adversely to Anadarko's interests by entities who were in a fiduciary relationship to Anadarko's prospective shareholders. This assertion assumes significance because if such a relationship exists Panhandle and its designated directors are required to demonstrate the entire fairness of the disputed agreements.

It is a basic principle of Delaware General Corporation Law that directors are subject to the fundamental fiduciary duties of loyalty and disinterestedness. Specifically, directors cannot stand on both sides of the transaction nor derive any personal benefit through self-dealing. However, in a parent and wholly-owned subsidiary context, the directors of the subsidiary are obligated only to manage the affairs of the subsidiary in the best interests of the parent and its shareholders. *See Sinclair Oil Corporation v. Levien*, 280 A.2d at 720. . . .

---

1. The three inside directors R.D. Hunsucker, R.C. Dixon, and R.L. O'Shields were the majority votes in approving the disputed agreements and constitute the individual defendants in this case. R.D. Hunsucker was Panhandle's president and chief executive officer; R.L. O'Shields was chairman of Panhandle's board of directors; and R.C. Dixon was an officer and director of two Panhandle subsidiaries, Pipeline and Trunkline.

2. A detailed review of the disputed agreements is not required for an understanding of the issues presented on this appeal. Essentially, Anadarko alleges that the disputed agreements:
> (1) require Anadarko to reduce its price of gas to Trunkline to $2.21/mm Btu for a fixed period, without any consideration and without the protection of the termination clause that Trunkline had made available in contracts with other producers; (2) require Anadarko to settle Panhandle's monetary obligations for past contractual nonperformance for less than ten cents on the dollar and further permanently reduce the price of Anadarko's gas to Trunkline; (3) require Anadarko to indemnify Panhandle against liability for Panhandle's breach of its obligations to third parties under a stipulation and agreement with the Federal Energy Regulatory Commission; (4) grant Panhandle contractual rights amounting to an exclusive option to take or refuse gas from Anadarko's most valuable gas reserve (Matagorda Island Blocks 622 and 623) and thereby expose Anadarko to the serious risk of uncompensated drainage during the term of the option; and (5) require Anadarko to indemnify Panhandle for potential liability to Sonatrach, the state-owned petroleum company of Algeria, in the amount of several billion dollars.

Anadarko acknowledges that a parent does not owe a fiduciary duty to its wholly owned subsidiary. However, Anadarko argues that Panhandle's actions relating to the spin-off have established a class of stockholders to whom fiduciary duties are owed. Specifically Anadarko contends that by setting a record date for the dividend distribution and by establishing a market for Anadarko shares to be traded on a when-issued basis, Panhandle has created a fiduciary relationship with the prospective shareholders of Anadarko. As a result, Panhandle and the inside directors of Anadarko have assumed responsibility for demonstrating that the agreements are entirely fair to Anadarko's new shareholders—a formidable burden in view of the obvious one-sidedness of the agreements.

Anadarko first argues that record ownership passed to Anadarko's prospective stockholders as of September 12, the record date for the stock dividend. The argument follows that as record owners, the prospective stockholders of Anadarko were owed fiduciary duties by Panhandle and Anadarko's former directors. In support of this argument, Anadarko relies on the fact that the disputed agreements were approved after the record date and that a stock ledger had been prepared and delivered to a transfer agent. We do not view the passing of the record date and preparation of a stock ledger as determinative of the nature of the relationship.

Anadarko correctly states that Delaware law provides that the "stock ledger shall be the only evidence as to who are the stockholders entitled to examine the stockledger, . . . or the books of the corporation, or to vote in person or by proxy at any meeting of the stockholders." 8 Del.C. §219(c). The stock ledger referred to in section 219 and in the cases interpreting it, refer to a listing of present stockholders of existing entities. In this case the stock ledger relied on by Anadarko was not a list of Anadarko stockholders but was instead a list of Panhandle stockholders as of September 12. As the Chancery Court noted, the preparation of the stock list and the subsequent delivery to the transfer agent was done merely to facilitate the stock distribution plan for October 1, 1986 and did not serve to pass record ownership to Panhandle's stockholders. Thus, the existence of a stock ledger containing the names of Panhandle's stockholders as of September 12, who had an expectation of becoming Anadarko shareholders at a future specified date, does not provide a valid basis to impose fiduciary duties on Panhandle and Anadarko's former directors.

Anadarko's next argument presents a more substantial issue, i.e., whether beneficial ownership of Anadarko stock passed to Panhandle's stockholders of record and to those who purchased Anadarko stock on a when-issued basis. Anadarko relies on two assertions in support of its beneficial ownership argument; first, Panhandle's stockholders of record had a vested contractual right to the dividend of Anadarko stock; and second, the trading in Anadarko stock prior to the date of distribution created a beneficial interest distinct from Panhandle's legal interest in Anadarko.[3]

---

3. In support of its argument that Anadarko's prospective stockholders were beneficial owners, Anadarko also relies, by analogy, on section 16(a) of the Securities Exchange Act of 1934, under which the Securities and Exchange Commission has ruled that beneficial ownership of a dividend

The general rule regarding the vesting of cash dividends is that a contractual right of the stockholder to the dividend becomes fixed upon the declaration of the dividend. Thus, upon a valid declaration of a dividend the corporation becomes indebted to the stockholder, and the stockholder may recover the declared amount in an action, *ex contractu*, against the corporation. However, the same rule does not extend to stock dividends.

In the context of a stock dividend, the nature of the res distributed and the shareholders' right to and interest in the dividend are less certain. The value of the underlying asset to be distributed, i.e., a proportionate interest in the equity of the corporation, may fluctuate between the date of declaration and date of distribution as a result of market forces and/or management decisions. Thus, the corresponding right to the stock dividend is not compromised by foreseeable changes in the inherent value of the underlying corporation. Given the inherent risk of possible change in equity value, the stock interest held by Anadarko's prospective stockholders does not support the conclusion that a separate class of beneficial stockholders has been created by the declaration of the spin-off dividend.

Anadarko next argues that a distinct beneficial interest was created in Anadarko stock as a result of trading on the New York Stock Exchange in Anadarko and Panhandle stock. Anadarko contends that individuals who bought Anadarko stock on a when-issued basis acquired an interest in Anadarko and not in Panhandle. Similarly, individuals who sold their Panhandle stock on an ex-distribution basis relinquished ownership of Panhandle but retained an interest in Anadarko. The result, as Anadarko contends, is that a beneficial interest in Anadarko was created that was distinct from Panhandle's stockholders' interest in Panhandle individually and as the parent corporation of Anadarko. While we agree that a distinct interest was created by providing a market for Anadarko stock prior to distribution, we conclude that the interest does not rise to the level of a beneficial interest for purposes of imposing fiduciary duties on Panhandle and Anadarko's former directors.

The concept of "beneficial ownership" of stock, though somewhat inexact, is contextually defined, and has become a term of art for purposes of establishing fiduciary duties under Delaware law. As applied in this case, beneficial ownership contemplates a separation of legal and equitable ownership. Under this concept, the equitable or beneficial owner possesses an economic interest in the subject property distinct from legal ownership or control. . . .

The separation of legal and equitable ownership is lacking in this case. Until the date of distribution, both legal and equitable title remained with Panhandle as the parent of a wholly owned subsidiary. As noted by the Vice Chancellor, Panhandle

---

stock is acquired on the record date. We are not persuaded by this argument. The definition of "beneficial ownership" under the 1934 act facilitates the broad disclosure function of section 16(a). This expansive definition does not comport with the rationale and purpose of establishing fiduciary duties under Delaware corporate law, and thus will not be adopted in this case.

continued as Anadarko's record owner and, as such, had voting control of Anadarko stock until the date of distribution. The question of beneficial ownership, however, is less clear and requires an examination of the expectancy interest held by Anadarko's prospective stockholders.

The nature and scope of the expectancy interest held by Anadarko's prospective stockholders is addressed in the Information Statement issued prior to the spin-off of Anadarko. Regarding Panhandle's relationship with Anadarko the Information Statement clearly states that it can be expected that the companies will enter into agreements concluding long-term negotiations providing for adjustments to the terms of certain gas purchase and related contracts. Further, the Information Statement specifically provides:

> These adjustments will include, among other things: (1) the settlement by the Company of claims for "take-or-pay" payments for prior periods; (2) interim price reductions under, and a procedure for the renegotiation of all gas purchase contracts between Anadarko and Trunkline involved in Trunkline's program to obtain price and volume relief on a long-term basis; (3) the implementation of new or amended contracts covering gas produced by Pan Eastern from Matagorda Island Blocks 622 and 623; (4) the implementation of new arrangements with respect to the Kansas intrastate pipeline system of Production (which will remain a subsidiary of PEC) providing, among other things, for the renegotiation of all gas purchase agreements between Production and Anadarko effective April 1988; and (5) amendments to certain gas processing and other contracts.

Significantly, the Information Statement concludes that the adjusted gas purchase agreements will likely result in "contractual terms as to price, 'take or pay' obligations and other matters" which are not as favorable to Anadarko as the terms of its present contracts with Panhandle.

Through the Information Statement, Anadarko's prospective stockholders were thus on notice that Panhandle continued to exercise both legal and equitable ownership of Anadarko and that this ownership would be used to effect contractual arrangements between the two companies. Indeed the contractual modifications complained of in this case were the subject of specific comment in the Information Statement. Panhandle's stockholders and those who purchased Anadarko stock on a when-issued basis could not reasonably expect a continuation of the status quo nor did they have any assurance of a protected financial interest in Anadarko prior to the date of distribution. It cannot be claimed, therefore, that Panhandle purported to act in a fiduciary role to protect Anadarko's prospective stockholders from the risk that changes would occur prior to the distribution date.

Finally, Anadarko argues that as of the record date for distribution, September 12, 1986, Panhandle and Anadarko's directors held Anadarko stock in trust for the prospective stockholders of Anadarko. Specifically, Anadarko contends that as trustees,

Panhandle and the Anadarko board had a general fiduciary duty to preserve the value of the corpus of the trust, i.e., the Anadarko stock. . . .

In order for a trust relationship to exist there must be evidence of an intention on the part of the grantor to separate legal and equitable title to the subject of the trust. As previously discussed, this division of interests does not exist in this case. To the contrary, Panhandle, through its actions and public disclosures in the Information Statement, has indicated its intention that Anadarko would continue to be its wholly owned subsidiary until the date of distribution. . . .

We hold, therefore, that the Court of Chancery properly concluded that a fiduciary relationship did not exist between Panhandle and Anadarko's prospective stockholders. Accordingly, the decision granting summary judgment is affirmed.

ON MOTION FOR REARGUMENT OR REHEARING EN BANC

Anadarko seeks reargument on related contentions. First, Anadarko argues that by relying on the Information Statement to support the conclusion that a fiduciary relationship did not exist between Anadarko's directors and its prospective stockholders, this Court has implicitly recognized the proposition that disclosure can relieve a director of the duty of loyalty. Second, Anadarko contends that if disclosure can relieve a director of the duty of loyalty, it is important for this Court, upon reconsideration, to establish a clear test for adequacy of disclosure. Finally, Anadarko seeks the opportunity to litigate the factual adequacy of disclosure upon remand to the Court of Chancery.

Contrary to Anadarko's claims, the ruling in the principal opinion, when confined to its specific facts, is not inconsistent with a director's duty of loyalty nor does it stand for the proposition that disclosure is a substitute for loyalty. As the opinion makes clear, under the circumstances of this case the corporate parent's ownership interest was not legally divisible before the date of distribution for purposes of imposing fiduciary duties on Anadarko's former directors. The relevant inquiry is thus twofold: to whom is the fiduciary duty owed and at what time. Our ruling is specifically confined to Anadarko's claim that, under Delaware corporate law, a fiduciary relationship existed between Anadarko's board and its prospective stockholders prior to the issue date of the expected shares. We have concluded that the duty of loyalty arises only upon establishment of the underlying relationship.

Finally, we note that the viability of Anadarko's claim of nondisclosure, assertable as a federal cause of action, is not before us. Our ruling is confined to claims against corporate directors arising out of an alleged fiduciary relationship.

Given the narrow confines of our holding we find no basis for reargument. Accordingly, the motion for reargument is denied.

Questions

1. Who has the potential to be harmed by Panhandle's restructuring of the contracts? Recall the Efficient Capital Markets Hypothesis. According to the hypothesis, and given full disclosure by Panhandle, should there be any cause for concern?

2. How could a shareholder of Anadarko self-protect? Should she be required to do so?

3. The court refers to the fact that directors of a wholly owned subsidiary owe fiduciary duties only to its parent and to the parent's shareholders. Why should that be the case? Doesn't this negate the separate entity theory of the corporation?

4. What duties do the directors of the parent corporation have? How is this case different from *Sinclair Oil Corporation v. Levien*?

Zahn v. Transamerica Corporation
162 F.2d 36 (3d Cir. 1947)

BIGGS, Judge

Zahn, a holder of Class A common stock of Axton-Fisher Tobacco Company, a corporation of Kentucky, sued Transamerica Corporation, a Delaware company, on his own behalf and on behalf of all stockholders similarly situated, in the District Court of the United States for the District of Delaware. His complaint as amended asserts that Transamerica caused Axton-Fisher to redeem its Class A stock at $80.80 per share on July 1, 1943, instead of permitting the Class A stockholders to participate in the assets on the liquidation of their company in June, 1944. He alleges in brief that if the Class A stockholders had been allowed to participate in the assets on liquidation of Axton-Fisher and had received their respective shares of the assets, he and the other Class A stockholders would have received $240 per share instead of $80.80. Zahn takes the position that he has two separate causes of action, one based on the Class A shares which were not turned back to the company for redemption; another based on the shares which were redeemed.[1] He prayed the court below to direct Transamerica to pay over to the shareholders who had not surrendered their stock the liquidation value and to pay over to those shareholders who had surrendered their stock the liquidation value less $80.80. Transamerica filed a motion to dismiss. The court below granted the motion holding that Zahn had failed to state a cause of action. He appealed.

The facts follow as appear from the pleadings, which recite provisions of Axton-Fisher's charter. Prior to April 30, 1943, Axton-Fisher had authorized and outstanding three classes of stock, designated respectively as preferred stock, Class A stock

---

[1]. The plaintiff was originally the holder of 235 shares of Class A stock purchased on four occasions between July 23 and August 10, 1943, inclusive. Between August 2 and August 20, 1943, the plaintiff surrendered for redemption 215 shares and retained 20 shares.

and Class B stock. Each share of preferred stock had a par value of $100 and was entitled to cumulative dividends at the rate of $6 per annum and possessed a liquidation value of $105 plus accrued dividends. The Class A stock, specifically described in the charter as a "common" stock, was entitled to an annual cumulative dividend of $3.20 per share. If further funds were made available by action of the board of directors by way of dividends, the Class A stock and the Class B stock were entitled to share equally therein. Upon liquidation of the company and the payment of the sums required by the preferred stock, the Class A stock was entitled to share with the Class B stock in the distribution of the remaining assets, but the Class A stock was entitled to receive twice as much per share as the Class B stock.[2]

Each share of Class A stock was convertible at the option of the shareholder into one share of Class B stock. All or any of the shares of Class A stock were callable by the corporation at any quarterly dividend date upon sixty days' notice to the shareholders, at $60 per share with accrued dividends.[3] The voting rights were vested in the Class B stock but if there were four successive defaults in the payment of quarterly dividends, the class or classes of stock as to which such defaults occurred gained voting rights equal share for share with the Class B stock. By reason of this provision the Class A stock had possessed equal voting rights with the Class B stock since on or about January 1, 1937.

On or about May 16, 1941, Transamerica purchased 80,160 shares of Axton-Fisher's Class B common stock. This was about 71.5% of the outstanding Class B stock and about 46.7% of the total voting stocks of Axton-Fisher. By August 15, 1942, Transamerica owned 5,332 shares of Class A stock and 82,610 shares of Class B stock. By

---

2. The charter provides as follows:
"In the event of the dissolution, liquidation, merger or consolidation of the corporation, or sale of substantially all its assets, whether voluntary or involuntary, there shall be paid to the holders of the preferred stock then outstanding $105 per share, together with all unpaid accrued dividends thereon, before any sum shall be paid to or any assets distributed among the holders of the Class A common stock and/or the holders of the Class B common stock. After such payment to the holders of the preferred stock, and all unpaid accrued dividends on the Class A common stock shall have been paid, then all remaining assets and funds of the corporation shall be divided among and paid to the holders of the Class A common stock and to the holders of the Class B common stock in the ratio of 2 to 1; that is to say, there shall be paid upon each share of Class A common stock twice the amount paid upon each share of Class B common stock, in any such event."

3. The charter provides as follows:
"The whole or any part of the Class A common stock of the corporation at the option of the Board of Directors, may be redeemed on any quarterly dividend payment date by paying therefor in cash Sixty dollars ($60.00) per share and all unpaid and accrued dividends thereon at the date fixed for such redemption, upon sending by mail to the registered holders of the Class A common stock at least sixty (60) days' notice of the exercise of such option. If at any time the Board of Directors shall determine to redeem less than the whole amount of Class A common stock then outstanding, the particular stock to be so redeemed shall be determined in such manner as the Board of Directors shall prescribe; provided, however, that no holder of Class A common stock shall be preferred over any other holder of such stock."

March 31, 1943, the amount of Class A stock of Axton-Fisher owned by Transamerica had grown to 30,168 shares or about 66 2/3% of the total amount of this stock outstanding, and the amount of Class B stock owned by Transamerica had increased to 90,768 shares or about 80% of the total outstanding. Additional shares of Class B stock were acquired by Transamerica after April 30, 1943, and Transamerica converted the Class A stock owned by it into Class B stock so that on or about the end of May, 1944 Transamerica owned virtually all of the outstanding Class B stock of Axton-Fisher. Since May 16, 1941, Transamerica had control of and had dominated the management, directorate, financial policies, business and affairs of Axton-Fisher. Since the date last stated Transamerica had elected a majority of the board of directors of Axton-Fisher. These individuals are in large part officers or agents of Transamerica.

In the fall of 1942 and in the spring of 1943 Axton-Fisher possessed as its principal asset leaf tobacco which had cost it about $6,361,981. This asset was carried on Axton-Fisher's books in that amount. The value of leaf tobacco had risen sharply and, to quote the words of the complaint, 'unbeknown to the public holders of . . . Class A common stock of Axton-Fisher, but known to Transamerica, the market value of . . . [the] tobacco had, in March and April of 1943, attained the huge sum of about $20,000,000.'

The complaint then alleges the gist of the plaintiff's grievance, viz., that Transamerica, knowing of the great value of the tobacco which Axton-Fisher possessed, conceived a plan to appropriate the value of the tobacco to itself by redeeming the Class A stock at the price of $60 a share plus accrued dividends, the redemption being made to appear as if "incident to the continuance of the business of Axton-Fisher as a going concern," and thereafter, the redemption of the Class A stock being completed, to liquidate Axton-Fisher; that this would result, after the disbursal of the sum required to be paid to the preferred stock, in Transamerica gaining for itself most of the value of the warehouse tobacco. The complaint further alleges that in pursuit of this plan Transamerica, by a resolution of the Board of Directors of Axton-Fisher on April 30, 1943, called the Class A stock at $60 and, selling a large part of the tobacco to Phillip-Morris Company, Ltd., Inc., together with substantially all of the other assets of Axton-Fisher, thereafter liquidated Axton-Fisher, paid off the preferred stock and pocketed the balance of the proceeds of the sale. Warehouse receipts representing the remainder of the tobacco were distributed to the Class B stockholders.

Assuming as we must that the allegations of the complaint are true, it will be observed that agents or representatives of Transamerica constituted Axton-Fisher's board of directors at the times of the happening of the events complained of, and that Transamerica was Axton-Fisher's principal and controlling stockholder at such times. . . .

The circumstances of the case at bar are *sui generis*. . . .

It is appropriate to emphasize at this point that the right to call the Class A stock for redemption was confided by the charter of Axton-Fisher to the directors and not to the stockholders of that corporation. We must also re-emphasize . . . that there is a radical difference when a stockholder is voting strictly as a stockholder and when voting as a director; that when voting as a stockholder he may have the legal right to vote with a view of his own benefits and to represent himself only; but that when he votes as a director he represents all the stockholders in the capacity of a trustee for them and cannot use his office as a director for his personal benefit at the expense of the stockholders.

Two theories are presented on one of which the case at bar must be decided: One, vigorously asserted by Transamerica . . . is that the board of directors of Axton-Fisher, whether or not dominated by Transamerica, the principal Class B stockholder, at any time and for any purpose, might call the Class A stock for redemption; the other, asserted with equal vigor by Zahn, is that the board of directors of Axton-Fisher as fiduciaries were not entitled to favor Transamerica, the Class B stockholder, by employing the redemption provisions of the charter for its benefit. . . .

The difficulty in accepting Transamerica's contentions in the case at bar is that the directors of Axton-Fisher, if the allegations of the complaint be accepted as true, were the instruments of Transamerica, were directors voting in favor of their special interest, that of Transamerica, could not and did not exercise an independent judgment in calling the Class A stock, but made the call for the purpose of profiting their true principal, Transamerica. In short a puppet-puppeteer relationship existed between the directors of Axton-Fisher and Transamerica.

The act of the board of directors in calling the Class A stock, an act which could have been legally consummated by a disinterested board of directors, was here effected at the direction of the principal Class B stockholder in order to profit it. Such a call is voidable in equity at the instance of a stockholder injured thereby. It must be pointed out that under the allegations of the complaint there was no reason for the redemption of the Class A stock to be followed by the liquidation of Axton-Fisher except to enable the Class B stock to profit at the expense of the Class A stock. As has been hereinbefore stated the function of the call was confided to the board of directors by the charter and was not vested by the charter in the stockholders of any class. It was the intention of the framers of Axton-Fisher's charter to require the board of directors to act disinterestedly if that body called the Class A stock, and to make the call with a due regard for its fiduciary obligations. If the allegations of the complaint be proved, it follows that the directors of Axton-Fisher, the instruments of Transamerica, have been derelict in that duty. Liability which flows from the dereliction must be imposed upon Transamerica which, under the allegations of the complaint, constituted the board of Axton-Fisher and controlled it. . . .

As has been stated the plaintiff has endeavored to set up a "First Cause of Action" and a "Second Cause of Action" in his complaint. The first cause of action is based upon his ownership of shares of Class A stock not surrendered by him to

Axton-Fisher for redemption and is asserted not only on his own behalf but also on behalf of other Class A stockholders retaining their stock. The second cause of action is asserted by him on his own behalf and on behalf of other Class A stockholders in respect to the value of the stock which was surrendered for redemption. The two alleged separate causes of action, however, are in reality one. In our opinion, if the allegations of the complaint be proved, Zahn may maintain his cause of action to recover from Transamerica the value of the stock retained by him as that shall be represented by its aliquot share of the proceeds of Axton-Fisher on dissolution. It is also our opinion that he may maintain a cause of action to recover the difference between the amount received by him for the shares already surrendered and the amount which he would have received on liquidation of Axton-Fisher if he had not surrendered his stock. . . .

The judgment will be reversed.

Questions

1. For whom were the directors of Axton-Fisher Tobacco Company trustees? As directors, could they have taken the interests of owners of Class B stock into account? If they had to choose between Class A and Class B, whose interest should they have considered?

2. What should Zahn have inferred once Axton-Fisher Tobacco Company announced that it would redeem the Class A stock. What should he have done?

3. The court concluded that Zahn is entitled to the value of his stock in liquidation as if he had not surrendered his stock. Is this the remedy you would have fashioned? Is it fair?

B. Sale of Control

Perlman v. Feldmann
219 F.2d 173 (2nd Cir. 1955)

CLARK, Chief Judge

This is a derivative action brought by minority stockholders of Newport Steel Corporation to compel accounting for, and restitution of, allegedly illegal gains which accrued to defendants as a result of the sale in August, 1950, of their controlling interest in the corporation. The principal defendant, C. Russell Feldmann, who represented and acted for the others, members of his family,[1] was at that time not only the dominant stockholder, but also the chairman of the board of directors and the

---

1. The stock was not held personally by Feldmann in his own name, but was held by the members of his family and by personal corporations. The aggregate of stock thus had amounted to 33% of the outstanding Newport stock and gave working control to the holder. The actual sale included

president of the corporation. Newport, an Indiana corporation, operated mills for the production of steel sheets for sale to manufacturers of steel products, first at Newport, Kentucky, and later also at other places in Kentucky and Ohio. The buyers, a syndicate organized as Wilport Company, a Delaware corporation, consisted of end-users of steel who were interested in securing a source of supply in a market becoming ever tighter in the Korean War. Plaintiffs contend that the consideration paid for the stock included compensation for the sale of a corporate asset, a power held in trust for the corporation by Feldmann as its fiduciary. This power was the ability to control the allocation of the corporate product in a time of short supply, through control of the board of directors; and it was effectively transferred in this sale by having Feldmann procure the resignation of his own board and the election of Wilport's nominees immediately upon consummation of the sale.

The present action represents the consolidation of three pending stockholders' actions in which yet another stockholder has been permitted to intervene. Jurisdiction below was based upon the diverse citizenship of the parties. Plaintiffs argue here, as they did in the court below, that in the situation here disclosed the vendors must account to the non-participating minority stockholders for that share of their profit which is attributable to the sale of the corporate power. Judge Hincks denied the validity of the premise, holding that the rights involved in the sale were only those normally incident to the possession of a controlling block of shares, with which a dominant stockholder, in the absence of fraud or foreseeable looting, was entitled to deal according to his own best interests. Furthermore, he held that plaintiffs had failed to satisfy their burden of proving that the sales price was not a fair price for the stock per se. Plaintiffs appeal from these rulings of law which resulted in the dismissal of their complaint.

The essential facts found by the trial judge are not in dispute. Newport was a relative newcomer in the steel industry with predominantly old installations which were in the process of being supplemented by more modern facilities. Except in times of extreme shortage Newport was not in a position to compete profitably with other steel mills for customers not in its immediate geographical area. Wilport, the purchasing syndicate, consisted of geographically remote end-users of steel who were interested in buying more steel from Newport than they had been able to obtain during recent periods of tight supply. The price of $20 per share was found by Judge Hincks to be a fair one for a control block of stock, although the over-the-counter market price had not exceeded $12 and the book value per share was $17.03. But this finding was limited by Judge Hincks' statement that "[w]hat value the block would have had if shorn of its appurtenant power to control distribution of the corporate product, the evidence does not show." It was also conditioned by his earlier ruling that the burden was on plaintiffs to prove a lesser value for the stock.

55,552 additional shares held by friends and associates of Feldmann, so that a total of 37% of the Newport stock was transferred.

Both as director and as dominant stockholder, Feldmann stood in a fiduciary relationship to the corporation and to the minority stockholders as beneficiaries thereof. . . .

It is true, as defendants have been at pains to point out, that this is not the ordinary case of breach of fiduciary duty. We have here no fraud, no misuse of confidential information, no outright looting of a helpless corporation. But on the other hand, we do not find compliance with that high standard which we have just stated and which we and other courts have come to expect and demand of corporate fiduciaries. In the often-quoted words of Judge Cardozo: "Many forms of conduct permissible in a workaday world for those acting at arm's length, are forbidden to those bound by fiduciary ties. A trustee is held to something stricter than the morals of the market place. Not honesty alone, but the punctilio of an honor the most sensitive, is then the standard of behavior. As to this there has developed a tradition that is unbending and inveterate. Uncompromising rigidity has been the attitude of courts of equity when petitioned to undermine the rule of undivided loyalty by the 'disintegrating erosion' of particular exceptions." *Meinhard v. Salmon.* The actions of defendants in siphoning off for personal gain corporate advantages to be derived from a favorable market situation do not betoken the necessary undivided loyalty owed by the fiduciary to his principal.

The corporate opportunities of whose misappropriation the minority stockholders complain need not have been an absolute certainty in order to support this action against Feldmann. If there was possibility of corporate gain, they are entitled to recover. . . .

This rationale is equally appropriate to a consideration of the benefits which Newport might have derived from the steel shortage. In the past Newport had used and profited by its market leverage by operation of what the industry had come to call the "Feldmann Plan." This consisted of securing interest-free advances from prospective purchasers of steel in return for firm commitments to them from future production. The funds thus acquired were used to finance improvements in existing plants and to acquire new installations. In the summer of 1950 Newport had been negotiating for cold-rolling facilities which it needed for a more fully integrated operation and a more marketable product, and Feldmann plan funds might well have been used toward this end.

Further, as plaintiffs alternatively suggest, Newport might have used the period of short supply to build up patronage in the geographical area in which it could compete profitably even when steel was more abundant. Either of these opportunities was Newport's, to be used to its advantage only. Only if defendants had been able to negate completely any possibility of gain by Newport could they have prevailed. It is true that a trial court finding states: "Whether or not, in August, 1950, Newport's position was such that it could have entered into 'Feldmann Plan' type transactions to procure funds and financing for the further expansion and integration of its steel facilities and whether such expansion would have been desirable for Newport, the evidence does not show." This, however, cannot avail the defendants, who—contrary to the ruling below—had the burden of proof on this issue, since fiduciaries always have the burden of proof in establishing the fairness of their dealings with trust property.

Defendants seek to categorize the corporate opportunities which might have accrued to Newport as too unethical to warrant further consideration. It is true that reputable steel producers were not participating in the gray market brought about by the Korean War and were refraining from advancing their prices, although to do so would not have been illegal. But Feldmann plan transactions were not considered within this self-imposed interdiction; the trial court found that around the time of the Feldmann sale Jones & Laughlin Steel Corporation, Republic Steel Company, and Pittsburgh Steel Corporation were all participating in such arrangements. In any event, it ill becomes the defendants to disparage as unethical the market advantages from which they themselves reaped rich benefits.

We do not mean to suggest that a majority stockholder cannot dispose of his controlling block of stock to outsiders without having to account to his corporation for profits or even never do this with impunity when the buyer is an interested customer, actual or potential, for the corporation's product. But when the sale necessarily results in a sacrifice of this element of corporate good will and consequent unusual profit to the fiduciary who has caused the sacrifice, he should account for his gains. So in a time of market shortage, where a call on a corporation's product commands an unusually large premium, in one form or another, we think it sound law that a fiduciary may not appropriate to himself the value of this premium. Such personal gain at the expense of his coventurers seems particularly reprehensible when made by the trusted president and director of his company. In this case the violation of duty seems to be all the clearer because of this triple role in which Feldmann appears, though we are unwilling to say, and are not to be understood as saying, that we should accept a lesser obligation for any one of his roles alone.

Hence to the extent that the price received by Feldmann and his codefendants included such a bonus, he is accountable to the minority stockholders who sue here. And plaintiffs, as they contend, are entitled to a recovery in their own right, instead of in right of the corporation (as in the usual derivative actions), since neither Wilport nor their successors in interest should share in any judgment which may be rendered. Defendants cannot well object to this form of recovery, since the only alternative, recovery for the corporation as a whole, would subject them to a greater total liability.

The case will therefore be remanded to the district court for a determination of the question expressly left open below, namely, the value of defendants' stock without the appurtenant control over the corporation's output of steel. We reiterate that on this issue, as on all others relating to a breach of fiduciary duty, the burden of proof must rest on the defendants. Judgment should go to these plaintiffs and those whom they represent for any premium value so shown to the extent of their respective stock interests.

The judgment is therefore reversed and the action remanded for further proceedings pursuant to this opinion.

Swan, Judge (dissenting)

With the general principles enunciated in the majority opinion as to the duties of fiduciaries I am, of course, in thorough accord. But, as Mr. Justice Frankfurter stated . . . , "to say that a man is a fiduciary only begins analysis; it gives direction to further inquiry. To whom is he a fiduciary? What obligations does he owe as a fiduciary? In what respect has he failed to discharge these obligations?" My brothers' opinion does not specify precisely what fiduciary duty Feldmann is held to have violated or whether it was a duty imposed upon him as the dominant stockholder or as a director of Newport. Without such specification I think that both the legal profession and the business world will find the decision confusing and will be unable to foretell the extent of its impact upon customary practices in the sale of stock.

The power to control the management of a corporation, that is, to elect directors to manage its affairs, is an inseparable incident to the ownership of a majority of its stock, or sometimes, as in the present instance, to the ownership of enough shares, less than a majority, to control an election. Concededly a majority or dominant shareholder is ordinarily privileged to sell his stock at the best price obtainable from the purchaser. In so doing he acts on his own behalf, not as an agent of the corporation. If he knows or has reason to believe that the purchaser intends to exercise to the detriment of the corporation the power of management acquired by the purchase, such knowledge or reasonable suspicion will terminate the dominant shareholder's privilege to sell and will create a duty not to transfer the power of management to such purchaser. The duty seems to me to resemble the obligation which everyone is under not to assist another to commit a tort rather than the obligation of a fiduciary. But whatever the nature of the duty, a violation of it will subject the violator to liability for damages sustained by the corporation. Judge Hincks found that Feldmann had no reason to think that Wilport would use the power of management it would acquire by the purchase to injure Newport, and that there was no proof that it ever was so used. Feldmann did know, it is true, that the reason Wilport wanted the stock was to put in a board of directors who would be likely to permit Wilport's members to purchase more of Newport's steel than they might otherwise be able to get. But there is nothing illegal in a dominant shareholder purchasing from his own corporation at the same prices it offers to other customers. That is what the members of Wilport did, and there is no proof that Newport suffered any detriment therefrom.

My brothers say that "the consideration paid for the stock included compensation for the sale of a corporate asset," which they describe as "the ability to control the allocation of the corporate product in a time of short supply, through control of the board of directors; and it was effectively transferred in this sale by having Feldmann procure the resignation of his own board and the election of Wilport's nominees immediately upon consummation of the sale." The implications of this are not clear to me. If it means that when market conditions are such as to induce users of a corporation's product to wish to buy a controlling block of stock in order to be able to purchase part of the corporation's output at the same mill list prices as are offered to other customers, the dominant stockholder is under a fiduciary duty not to sell his stock, I cannot agree. For reasons already stated, in my opinion Feldmann was not proved to be under any fiduciary duty as a stockholder not to sell the stock he controlled.

Feldmann was also a director of Newport. Perhaps the quoted statement means that as a director he violated his fiduciary duty in voting to elect Wilport's nominees to fill the vacancies created by the resignations of the former directors of Newport. As a director Feldmann was under a fiduciary duty to use an honest judgment in acting on the corporation's behalf. A director is privileged to resign, but so long as he remains a director he must be faithful to his fiduciary duties and must not make a personal gain from performing them. Consequently, if the price paid for Feldmann's stock included a payment for voting to elect the new directors, he must account to the corporation for such payment, even though he honestly believed that the men he voted to elect were well qualified to serve as directors. He can not take pay for performing his fiduciary duty. There is no suggestion that he did do so, unless the price paid for his stock was more than its value. So it seems to me that decision must turn on whether finding 120 and conclusion 5 of the district judge are supportable on the evidence. They are set out in the margin.[1]

Judge Hincks went into the matter of valuation of the stock with his customary care and thoroughness. He made no error of law in applying the principles relating to valuation of stock. Concededly a controlling block of stock has greater sale value than a small lot. While the spread between $10 per share for small lots and $20 per share for the controlling block seems rather extraordinarily wide, the $20 valuation was supported by the expert testimony of Dr. Badger, whom the district judge said he could not find to be wrong. I see no justification for upsetting the valuation as clearly erroneous. Nor can I agree with my brothers that the $20 valuation "was limited" by the last sentence in finding 120. The controlling block could not by any possibility be shorn of its appurtenant power to elect directors and through them to control distribution of the corporate product. It is this "appurtenant power" which gives a controlling block its value as such block. What evidence could be adduced to show the value of the block "if shorn" of such appurtenant power, I cannot conceive, for it cannot be shorn of it.

The opinion also asserts that the burden of proving a lesser value that $20 per share was not upon the plaintiffs but the burden was upon the defendants to prove that the stock was worth that value. Assuming that this might be true as to the defendants who were directors of Newport, they did show it, unless finding 120 be set aside. Furthermore, not all the defendants were directors; upon what theory the plaintiffs

---

1. "[Finding 120]: The 398,927 shares of Newport stock sold to Wilport as of August 31, 1950, had a fair value as a control block of $20 per share. What value the block would have had if shorn of its appurtenant power to control distribution of the corporate product, the evidence does not show."

"[Conclusion 5]: Even if Feldmann's conduct in cooperating to accomplish a transfer of control to Wilport immediately upon the sale constituted a breach of a fiduciary duty to Newport, no part of the moneys received by the defendants in connection with the sale constituted profits for which they were accountable to Newport."

should be relieved from the burden of proof as to defendants who were not directors, the opinion does not explain.

The final conclusion of my brothers is that the plaintiffs are entitled to recover in their own right instead of in the right of the corporation. This appears to be completely inconsistent with the theory advanced at the outset of the opinion, namely, that the price of the stock "included compensation for the sale of a corporate asset." If a corporate asset was sold, surely the corporation should recover the compensation received for it by the defendants. Moreover, if the plaintiffs were suing in their own right, Newport was not a proper party. . . .

I would affirm the judgment on appeal.

Questions

1. What are the doctrinal grounds for the majority opinion in *Perlman v. Feldmann*? What duty did Feldmann violate?

2. According to the majority, what harm was inflicted on the corporation and its minority shareholders?

3. Under the majority view, could Feldmann have ever disposed of his shares at a premium?

4. If control is a corporate asset, who owns it?

Essex Universal Corporation v. Yates

305 F.2d 572 (2d Cir. 1962)

LUMBARD, Chief Judge

This appeal from the district court's summary judgment in favor of the defendant raises the question whether a contract for the sale of 28.3 per cent of the stock of a corporation is, under New York law, invalid as against public policy solely because it includes a clause giving the purchaser an option to require a majority of the existing directors to replace themselves, by a process of seriatim resignation, with a majority designated by the purchaser. Despite the disagreement evidenced by the diversity of our opinions, my brethren and I agree that such a provision does not on its face render the contract illegal and unenforceable, and thus that it was improper to grant summary judgment. Judge Friendly would reject the defense of illegality without further inquiry concerning the provision itself (as distinguished from any contention that control could not be safely transferred to the particular purchaser). Judge Clark and I are agreed that on remand, which must be had in any event to consider other defenses raised by the pleadings, further factual issues may be raised by the parties upon which the legality of the clause in question will depend; we disagree, however, on the nature of those factual issues, as our separate opinions reveal. Accordingly, the grant of summary judgment is reversed and the case is remanded for trial of the question of the legality of the contested provision and such further proceedings as may be proper on the other issues raised by the pleadings.

Since we are in agreement on certain preliminary questions, this opinion constitutes the opinion of the court up to the point where it is indicated that it thenceforth states only my individual views.

The defendant Herbert J. Yates, a resident of California, was president and chairman of the board of directors of Republic Pictures Corporation, a New York corporation which at the time relevant to this suit had 2,004,190 shares of common stock outstanding. Republic's stock was listed and traded on the New York Stock Exchange. In August 1957, Essex Universal Corporation, a Delaware corporation owning stock in various diversified businesses, learned of the possibility of purchasing from Yates an interest in Republic. Negotiations proceeded rapidly, and on August 28 Yates and Joseph Harris, the president of Essex, signed a contract in which Essex agreed to buy, and Yates agreed "to sell or cause to be sold" at least 500,000 and not more than 600,000 shares of Republic stock. The price was set at eight dollars a share, roughly two dollars above the then market price on the Exchange. Three dollars per share was to be paid at the closing on September 18, 1957 and the remainder in twenty-four equal monthly payments beginning January 31, 1958. The shares were to be transferred on the closing date, but Yates was to retain the certificates, endorsed in blank by Essex, as security for full payment. In addition to other provisions not relevant to the present motion, the contract contained the following paragraph:

"6. Resignations.

Upon and as a condition to the closing of this transaction if requested by Buyer at least ten (10) days prior to the date of the closing:

(a) Seller will deliver to Buyer the resignations of the majority of the directors of Republic.

(b) Seller will cause a special meeting of the board of directors of Republic to be held, legally convened pursuant to law and the by-laws of Republic, and simultaneously with the acceptance of the directors' resignations set forth in paragraph 6(a) immediately preceding will cause nominees of Buyer to be elected directors of Republic in place of the resigned directors."

Before the date of the closing, as provided in the contract, Yates notified Essex that he would deliver 566,223 shares, or 28.3 per cent of the Republic stock then outstanding, and Essex formally requested Yates to arrange for the replacement of a majority of Republic's directors with Essex nominees pursuant to paragraph 6 of the contract. This was to be accomplished by having eight of the fourteen directors resign seriatim, each in turn being replaced by an Essex nominee elected by the others; such a procedure was in form permissible under the charter and by-laws of Republic, which empowered the board to choose the successor of any of its members who might resign.

On September 18, the parties met as arranged for the closing at Republic's office in New York City. Essex tendered bank drafts and cashier's checks totalling $1,698,690, which was the 37 1/2 per cent of the total price of $4,529,784 due at this time. The drafts and checks were payable to one Benjamin C. Cohen, who was Essex' banker and had arranged for the borrowing of the necessary funds. Although Cohen was prepared to endorse these to Yates, Yates upon advice of his lawyer rejected the tender as "unsatisfactory" and said, according to his deposition testimony, "Well, there can be no deal. We can't close it."

... Essex seeks damages of $2,700,000, claiming that at the time of the aborted closing the stock was in actuality worth more than $12.75 a share. Yates' answer raised a number of defenses, but the motion for summary judgment now before us was made and decided only on the theory that the provision in the contract for immediate transfer of control of the board of directors was illegal *per se* and tainted the entire contract. We have no doubt, and the parties agree, that New York law governs. ...

On the face of the contract the sale of stock and the transfer of director control are but two aspects of a single transaction; the provision for the latter in paragraph 6 states that it is to be "a condition to the closing of this transaction." A matter so practically important as achieving immediate rather than deferred acquisition of control over the day-to-day operations of the corporation in which Essex was making such a substantial investment cannot be dismissed as a mere "incidental provision."

The terms of the contract thus express the unwillingness of Essex to pay the agreed price if Yates did not bring about the transfer of directorships, and surely no court would have forced it to make payment in that event. Since Yates could thus not have chosen to excise the hypothetically illegal term of the contract to make the provision for the sale of stock enforceable, it would be unjust to allow Essex the option of waiving it to make the sale enforceable should it suit its purposes to do so.

We are strongly influenced by those New York cases holding invalid agreements to sell stock because accompanied by illegal agreements for the transfer of management control, even though they contain no indication that the issue of separability was explicitly raised. Accordingly, we hold the provision regarding directors inseparable from the sale of shares, and proceed to a consideration of its legality.

Up to this point my brethren and I are in agreement. The following analysis is my own, except insofar as the separate opinions of Judges Clark and Friendly may indicate agreement.

It is established beyond question under New York law that it is illegal to sell corporate office or management control by itself (that is, accompanied by no stock or insufficient stock to carry voting control). The same rule apparently applies in all jurisdictions where the question has arisen. The rationale of the rule is indisputable: persons enjoying management control hold it on behalf of the corporation's stockholders, and therefore may not regard it as their own personal property to dispose of as they wish.[3] Any other rule would violate the most fundamental principle of corporate democracy, that management must represent and be chosen by, or at least with the consent of, those who own the corporation.

Essex was, however, contracting with Yates for the purchase of a very substantial percentage of Republic stock. If, by virtue of the voting power carried by this stock, it could have elected a majority of the board of directors, then the contract was not a simple agreement for the sale of office to one having no ownership interest in the corporation, and the question of its legality would require further analysis. Such stock voting control would incontestably belong to the owner of a majority of the voting stock, and it is commonly known that equivalent power usually accrues to the owner of 28.3% of the stock. For the purpose of this analysis, I shall assume that Essex was contracting to acquire a majority of the Republic stock, deferring consideration of the situation where, as here, only 28.3% is to be acquired.

Republic's board of directors at the time of the aborted closing had fourteen members divided into three classes, each class being "as nearly as may be" of the same size. Directors were elected for terms of three years, one class being elected at each annual shareholder meeting on the first Tuesday in April. Thus, absent the immediate replacement of directors provided for in this contract, Essex as the hypothetical new majority shareholder of the corporation could not have obtained managing control in the form of a majority of the board in the normal course of events until April 1959, some eighteen months after the sale of the stock. The first question before us then is whether an agreement to accelerate the transfer of management control, in a manner legal in form under the corporation's charter and by-laws, violates the public policy of New York.

There is no question of the right of a controlling shareholder under New York law normally to derive a premium from the sale of a controlling block of stock. In other words, there was no impropriety *per se* in the fact that Yates was to receive more per share than the generally prevailing market price for Republic stock.

The next question is whether it is legal to give and receive payment for the immediate transfer of management control to one who has achieved majority share control but would not otherwise be able to convert that share control into operating control for some time. I think that it is.

Of course under some circumstances controlling shareholders transferring immediate control may be compelled to account to the corporation for that part of the consideration received by them which exceeds the fair value of the block of stock sold, as well as for the injury which they may cause to the corporation. In *Gerdes v. Reynolds*, 28 N.Y.S.2d 622 (N.Y.County Sup.Ct. 1941), the purchasers of control of an investment company proceeded immediately to loot the corporation of its assets, and the court

---

3. The cases have made no distinction between contracts by directors or officers to resign and contracts by persons who in actuality control the actions of officers or directors to procure their resignations, and of course none should exist.

required the sellers to account on the theory that the circumstances of the sale put them on notice of the buyers' evil intentions. The court found the price paid grossly in excess of the calculable fair value of a controlling interest in the corporation, and found the differential to be payment for the immediate control which, foreseeably, the buyers used to the detriment of the corporation and its other shareholders. . . .

In *Perlman v. Feldmann,* this court, in a decision based only nominally on Indiana law, went beyond this rule to hold liable controlling shareholders who similarly sold immediate control even in the absence of illegitimate activity on the part of the purchasers. Our theory was basically that the controlling shareholders in selling control to a potential customer had appropriated to their personal benefit a corporate asset: the premium which the company's product could command in a time of market shortage. . . .

A fair generalization from these cases may be that a holder of corporate control will not, as a fiduciary, be permitted to profit from facilitating actions on the part of the purchasers of control which are detrimental to the interests of the corporation or the remaining shareholders. There is, however, no suggestion that the transfer of control over Republic to Essex carried any such threat to the interests of the corporation or its other shareholders.

Our examination of the New York cases discussed thus far gives us no reason to regard as impaired the holding of the early case of *Barnes v. Brown,* 80 N.Y. 527 (1880), that a bargain for the sale of a majority stock interest is not made illegal by a plan for immediate transfer of management control by a program like that provided for in the Essex-Yates contract. Judge Earl wrote:

> "[The seller] had the right to sell out all his stock and interest in the corporation, . . . and when he ceased to have any interest in the corporation, it was certainly legitimate and right that he should cease to control it. . . . It was simply the mode of transferring the control of the corporation to those who by the policy of the law ought to have it, and I am unable to see how any policy of the law was violated, or in what way, upon the evidence, any wrong was thereby done to anyone."

To be sure, in *Barnes v. Brown* no term of the contract of sale *required* the seller to effectuate the immediate replacement of directors, as did paragraph 6 of the Essex-Yates contract, but Judge Earl stated that "I shall assumed that it was the understanding and a part of the scheme that he should do so." Although the court might have decided the case by pointing out that under the parol evidence rule either party could have ignored what was at best a collateral oral agreement for the replacement of directors and enforced the written contract for the sale of the stock as it read, it chose not to do so but explicitly upheld the legality of the transfer of directorships.

Given this principle that it is permissible for a seller thus to choose to facilitate immediate transfer of management control, I can see no objection to a contractual provision requiring him to do so as a condition of the sale. Indeed, a New York court has upheld an analogous contractual term requiring the board of directors to elect the nominees of the purchasers of a majority stock interest to officerships. *San Remo Copper Mining Co. v. Moneuse,* 133 N.Y.S. 509 (1st Dept. 1912). The court said that since the purchaser was about to acquire "absolute control" of the corporation, "it certainly did not destroy the validity of the contract that by one of its terms defendant was to be invested with this power of control at once, upon acquiring the stock, instead of waiting for the next annual meeting." . . .

The easy and immediate transfer of corporate control to new interests is ordinarily beneficial to the economy and it seems inevitable that such transactions would be discouraged if the purchaser of a majority stock interest were required to wait some period before his purchase of control could become effective. Conversely it would greatly hamper the efforts of any existing majority group to dispose of its interest if it could not assure the purchaser of immediate control over corporation operations. I can see no reason why a purchaser of majority control should not ordinarily be permitted to make his control effective from the moment of the transfer of stock.

Thus if Essex had been contracting to purchase a majority of the stock of Republic, it would have been entirely proper for the contract to contain the provision for immediate replacement of directors. Although in the case at bar only 28.3 per cent of the stock was involved, it is commonly known that a person or group owning so large a percentage of the voting stock of a corporation which, like Republic, has at least the 1,500 shareholders normally requisite to listing on the New York Stock Exchange, is almost certain to have share control as a practical matter. If Essex was contracting to acquire what in reality would be equivalent to ownership of a majority of stock, i.e., if it would as a practical certainty have been guaranteed of the stock voting power to choose a majority of the directors of Republic in due course, there is no reason why the contract should not similarly be legal. Whether Essex was thus to acquire the equivalent of majority stock control would, if the issue is properly raised by the defendants, be a factual issue to be determined by the district court on remand.

Because 28.3 per cent of the voting stock of a publicly owned corporation is usually tantamount to majority control, I would place the burden of proof on this issue on Yates as the party attacking the legality of the transaction. Thus, unless on remand Yates chooses to raise the question whether the block of stock in question carried the equivalent of majority control, it is my view that the trial court should regard the contract as legal and proceed to consider the other issues raised by the pleadings. If Yates chooses to raise the issue, it will, on my view, be necessary for him to prove the existence of circumstances which would have prevented Essex from electing a majority of the Republic board of directors in due course. It will not be enough for Yates to raise merely hypothetical possibilities of opposition by the other Republic shareholders to Essex' assumption of management control. Rather, it will be necessary for him to show that, assuming neutrality on the part of the retiring management, there was at the time some concretely foreseeable reason why Essex' wishes would not have prevailed in shareholder voting held in due course. In other words, I would require him to show that there was at the time of the contract some other organized block of stock of sufficient size to outvote the block Essex was buying, or else some circumstance making it likely that enough of the holders of the remaining Republic stock would band together to keep Essex from control.

Reversed and remanded for further proceedings not inconsistent with the judgment of this court.

CLARK, Judge (concurring)

Since *Barnes v. Brown,* 80 N.Y. 527, teaches us that not all contracts like the one before us are necessarily illegal, summary judgment seems definitely improper and the action should be remanded for trial. But particularly in view of our lack of knowledge of corporate realities and the current standards of business morality, I should prefer to avoid too precise instructions to the district court in the hope that if the action again comes before us the record will be generally more instructive on this important issue than it now is. I share all the doubts and questions stated by my brothers in their opinions and perhaps have some additional ones of my own. My concern is lest we may be announcing abstract moral principles which have little validity in daily business practice other than to excuse a defaulting vendor from performance of his contract of sale. Thus for fear of a possible occasional contract inimical to general stockholder interest we may be condemning out of hand what are more often normal and even desirable business relationships. As at present advised I would think that the best we can do is to consider each case on its own facts and with the normal presumption that he who asserts illegality must prove it.

I add that while New York law may render unlawful an agreement for the naked transfer of corporate office, the record before us does not present such a situation and there is no ground for declaring the present agreement void on its face. Surely an otherwise unlawful sale of office should not become lawful simply on the simultaneous transfer of a few shares of stock. But such formalistic niceties are not involved here, and in any event such an approach would raise factual questions to be resolved only by trial. Further I am constrained to point out that I do not believe a district court determination as to whether or not "working control" was transferred to the vendee can or should affect the outcome of this case. The contract provides for transfer of 28.3 per cent of the outstanding stock and effective control of the board of directors, and there is no evidence at this stage that the vendor's power to transfer control of the board was to be secured unlawfully, as for example, by bribe or duress. Surely in the normal course of events a management which has behind it 28.3 per cent of the stock has working control, absent perhaps a pitched proxy battle which might unseat it. But the court cannot foresee such an unlikely event or predict its outcome; thus it is difficult to see what further evidence on the question of control could be adduced. My conclusion that there is no reason to declare this contract illegal on its face would remain unaffected by any hypothetical findings on "control." . . .

FRIENDLY, Judge (concurring)

Chief Judge Lumbard's thoughtful opinion illustrates a difficulty, inherent in our dual judicial system, which has led at least one state to authorize its courts to answer questions about its law that a Federal court may ask. Here we are forced to decide a question of New York law, of enormous importance to all New York corporations and their stockholders, on which there is hardly enough New York authority for a really informed prediction what the New York Court of Appeals would decide on the facts here presented, yet too much for us to have the freedom used to good effect in *Perlman v. Feldmann*. . . .

I have no doubt that many contracts, drawn by competent and responsible counsel, for the purchase of blocks of stock from interests thought to "control" a corporation although owning less than a majority, have contained provisions like paragraph 6 of the contract *sub judice*. However, developments over the past decades seem to me to show that such a clause violates basic principles of corporate democracy. To be sure, stockholders who have allowed a set of directors to be placed in office, whether by their vote or their failure to vote, must recognize that death, incapacity or other hazard may prevent a director from serving a full term, and that they will have no voice as to his immediate successor. But the stockholders are entitled to expect that, in that event, the remaining directors will fill the vacancy in the exercise of their fiduciary responsibility. A mass seriatim resignation directed by a selling stockholder, and the filling of vacancies by his henchmen at the dictation of a purchaser and without any consideration of the character of the latter's nominees, are beyond what the stockholders contemplated or should have been expected to contemplate. This seems to me a wrong to the corporation and the other stockholders which the law ought not countenance, whether the selling stockholder has received a premium or not. Right in this Court we have seen many cases where sudden shifts of corporate control have caused serious injury. . . . To hold the seller for delinquencies of the new directors only if he knew the purchaser was an intending looter is not a sufficient sanction. The difficulties of proof are formidable even if receipt of too high a premium creates a presumption of such knowledge, and, all too often, the doors are locked only after the horses have been stolen. Stronger medicines are needed—refusal to enforce a contract with such a clause, even though this confers an unwarranted benefit on a defaulter, and continuing responsibility of the former directors for negligence of the new ones until an election has been held. Such prophylactics are not contraindicated, as Judge Lumbard suggests, by the conceded desirability of preventing the dead hand of a former 'controlling' group from continuing to dominate the board after a sale, or of protecting a would-be purchaser from finding himself without a majority of the board after he has spent his money. A special meeting of stockholders to replace a board may always be called, and there could be no objection to making the closing of a purchase contingent on the results of such an election. I perceive some of the difficulties of mechanics such a procedure presents, but I have enough confidence in the ingenuity of the corporate bar to believe these would be surmounted.

Hence, I am inclined to think that if I were sitting on the New York Court of Appeals, I would hold a provision like Paragraph 6 violative of public policy save when it was entirely plain that a new election would be a mere formality—i.e., when the seller owned more than 50% of the stock. . . .

Chief Judge Lumbard's proposal goes part of the way toward meeting the policy problem I have suggested. Doubtless proceeding from what, as it seems to me, is the only justification in principle for permitting even a majority stockholder to condition a sale on delivery of control of the board—namely that in such a case a vote of the stockholders would be a useless formality, he sets the allowable bounds at the line where there is "a practical certainty" that the buyer would be able to elect his nominees and, in this case, puts the burden of disproving that on the person claiming illegality.

Attractive as the proposal is in some respects, I find difficulties with it. One is that I discern no sufficient intimation of the distinction in the New York cases, or even in the writers, who either would go further in voiding such a clause, or believe the courts have not yet gone that far. To strike down such a condition only in cases falling short of the suggested line accomplishes little to prevent what I consider the evil; in most instances a seller will not enter into a contract conditioned on his "delivering" a majority of the directors unless he has good reason to think he can do that. When an issue does arise, the "practical certainty" test is difficult to apply. The existence of such certainty will depend not merely on the proportion of the stock held by the seller but on many other factors—whether the other stock is widely or closely held, how much of it is in "street names," what success the corporation has experienced, how far its dividend policies have satisfied its stockholders, the identity of the purchasers, the presence or absence of cumulative voting, and many others. Often, unless the seller has nearly 50% of the stock, whether he has "working control" can be determined only by an election; groups who thought they had such control have experienced unpleasant surprises in recent years. Judge Lumbard correctly recognizes that, from a policy standpoint, the pertinent question must be the buyer's prospects of election, not the seller's—yet this inevitably requires the court to canvass the likely reaction of stockholders to a group of whom they know nothing and seems rather hard to reconcile with a position that it is "right" to insert such a condition if a seller has a larger proportion of the stock and "wrong" if he has a smaller. At the very least the problems and uncertainties arising from the proposed line of demarcation are great enough, and its advantages small enough, that in my view a Federal court would do better simply to overrule the defense here, thereby accomplishing what is obviously the "just" result in this particular case, and leave the development of doctrine in this area to the State, which has primary concern for it.

I would reverse the grant of summary judgment and remand for consideration of defenses other than a claim that the inclusion of paragraph 6 *ex mero motu* renders the contract void.

Questions

1. Judge Lumbard seems to go out of his way not to hold the contract illegal. Why? What are the differences between his and the concurring opinions?

2. Does the decision encourage or constrain sales of control? Does it simply write into law an already existing norm?

3. Based on what you already know about the shareholder's role in the corporation, does the contract examined in *Essex v. Yates* harm anyone? If not, what is the reason to invalidate it?

Part 4

Fundamental Transactions

Part 4

Fundamental Transactions

Introduction

In this part, we explore fundamental transactions, specifically mergers and hostile takeovers. Mergers have their origin in the sale of assets transaction, which follows other sales transactions. In a typical sale of assets transaction, the acquiring corporation buys all or substantially all of the target corporation's assets. The parties determine the consideration for the assets as well as which liabilities the buyer agrees to assume (and certain liabilities attach by law).

The acquiring corporation might choose to purchase the company's stock instead of its assets. If the target company is a wholly owned subsidiary of another corporation, the transaction typically proceeds as a sale of assets transaction. If this is not the case, the acquiring corporation may purchase less than all of a target's shares and force the remaining shareholders to sell, either by a "freeze-out" merger or a statutory short-form merger. In either event, unlike a buyer in an asset sale, a buyer of stock accepts ownership of the company with all of its assets and liabilities.

A merger is a magical occurrence. As a transaction, it involves the automatic disappearance of one corporation and the wholesale absorption of its assets and liabilities into another simply upon the filing of a certificate of merger in the secretary of state's office in the state of incorporation (or states of incorporation, in the case of mergers between two corporations of different states). Unlike the sale of assets transaction, no bills of sale or assumptions of liabilities are signed. Simply file the magic papers and the deal is done. The stock of the disappearing or "acquired" corporation remains not as a claim on the residual assets of the surviving or "acquiring" corporation, but merely as evidence of the stockholder's right to receive the consideration promised by the surviving corporation as the price of the merger. This can be cash, stock, or any other lawful form of consideration.

Because the surviving corporation, as a matter of law, must assume the liabilities of the disappearing corporation, a common practice has been for mergers to be done as "triangular mergers," in which the surviving corporation sets up a shell subsidiary into which the "acquired" company merges (a forward triangular merger) or which merges into the "acquired" company (a reverse triangular merger). The latter is typically done for tax reasons when it is necessary for the "acquired" company to maintain its corporate existence (in order to maintain tax loss carry-forwards, for example).

A merger is negotiated and approved by the corporations' boards of directors and by a required percentage of the corporations' shareholders (typically a majority under the statute but sometimes a higher percentage if required by the corporation's charter or bylaws). If the merger is so approved, shareholders of the "acquired" company who object to the merger have no choice but to give up their stock. They are required to go along with the will of the majority. They do have available to them a remedy known as appraisal rights (or dissenters' rights), which allows them to petition the court to value the shares and, if the court values the shares at a higher price than the merger consideration, to receive that higher price (and if at a lower price, the lower price—appraisal proceedings are not, at least in theory, riskless to the dissenting shareholder). But they have no right to hold on to their stock.

When a merger occurs between unrelated corporations, is clearly designated as such, and the procedures for a merger are followed, there is very little question about the legal consequences. Fiduciary difficulties arise when there is a preexisting relationship between the corporations, as we will see in Section II of this Part 4. But, first, we must confront the question of *whether* a merger has actually occurred.

Section I
The De Facto Merger Doctrine

The question as to whether a transaction constitutes a merger arises out of the variety of ways that corporate law presents of achieving the same economic result by using different legal processes. One way of accomplishing a merger is to comply with the merger statute, so assume that Greenacres Corporation merges into Blackacres Corporation (for simplicity's sake let's assume they're both Delaware corporations), and that the Greenacres stockholders receive Blackacres common stock as consideration for the merger. We have a merger, with Blackacres owning all of the assets and owing all of the liabilities both of itself and Greenacres, and Greenacres shareholders now remaining as shareholders of Blackacres (along with Blackacres' preexisting shareholders).

Now assume instead that Greenacres sells all of its assets (and transfers all of its liabilities) to Blackacres. Blackacres pays for these assets in Blackacres common stock. After the transaction, the board of Greenacres elects to dissolve Greenacres and distribute all of its assets (now consisting of Blackacres common stock) to Greenacre's stockholders. What, if any, is the economic difference between this sale of assets and the merger described above? Should they be treated differently as a legal matter? The following cases address these differences. As you read them, think about the policy reasons that justify the courts' approaches. Who benefits and who is hurt? Is one transaction more efficient than the other?

Farris v. Glen Alden Corporation
143 A.2d 25 (Pa. 1958)

COHEN, Justice

We are required to determine on this appeal whether, as a result of a "Reorganization Agreement" executed by the officers of Glen Alden Corporation and List Industries Corporation, and approved by the shareholders of the former company, the rights and remedies of a dissenting shareholder accrue to the plaintiff.

Glen Alden is a Pennsylvania corporation engaged principally in the mining of anthracite coal and lately in the manufacture of air conditioning units and firefighting equipment. In recent years the company's operating revenue has declined substantially, and in fact, its coal operations have resulted in tax loss carryovers of approximately $14,000,000. In October 1957, List, a Delaware holding company owning interests in motion picture theaters, textile companies and real estate, and to a lesser extent, in oil and gas operations, warehouses and aluminum piston manufacturing, purchased through a wholly owned subsidiary 38.5% of Glen Alden's outstanding stock. This acquisition enabled List to place three of its directors on the Glen Alden board.

On March 20, 1958, the two corporations entered into a "reorganization agreement," subject to stockholder approval, which contemplated the following actions:

1. Glen Alden is to acquire all of the assets of List, excepting a small amount of cash reserved for the payment of List's expenses in connection with the transaction. These assets include over $8,000,000 in cash held chiefly in the treasuries of List's wholly owned subsidiaries.

2. In consideration of the transfer, Glen Alden is to issue 3,621,703 shares of stock to List. List in turn is to distribute the stock to its shareholders at a ratio of five shares of Glen Alden stock for each six shares of List stock. In order to accomplish the necessary distribution, Glen Alden is to increase the authorized number of its shares of capital stock from 2,500,000 shares to 7,500,000 shares without according pre-emptive rights to the present shareholders upon the issuance of any such shares.

3. Further, Glen Alden is to assume all of List's liabilities including a $5,000,000 note incurred by List in order to purchase Glen Alden stock in 1957, outstanding stock options, incentive stock options plans, and pension obligations.

4. Glen Alden is to change its corporate name from Glen Alden Corporation to List Alden Corporation.

5. The present directors of both corporations are to become directors of List Alden.

6. List is to be dissolved and List Alden is to then carry on the operations of both former corporations.

Two days after the agreement was executed notice of the annual meeting of Glen Alden to be held on April 11, 1958, was mailed to the shareholders together with a proxy statement analyzing the reorganization agreement and recommending its approval as well as approval of certain amendments to Glen Alden's articles of incorporation and bylaws necessary to implement the agreement. At this meeting the holders of a majority of the outstanding shares (not including those owned by List), voted in favor of a resolution approving the reorganization agreement.

On the day of the shareholders' meeting, plaintiff, a shareholder of Glen Alden, filed a complaint in equity against the corporation and its officers seeking to enjoin them temporarily until final hearing, and perpetually thereafter, from executing and carrying out the agreement.

The gravamen of the complaint was that the notice of the annual shareholders' meeting did not conform to the requirements of the Business Corporation Law, 15 P.S. § 2852-1 et seq., in three respects: (1) It did not give notice to the shareholders that the true intent and purpose of the meeting was to effect a merger or consolidation of Glen Alden and List; (2) It failed to give notice to the shareholders of their right to dissent to the plan of merger or consolidation and claim fair value for their shares; and (3) It did not contain copies of the text of certain sections of the Business Corporation Law as required.[3]

By reason of these omissions, plaintiff contended that the approval of the reorganization agreement by the shareholders at the annual meeting was invalid and unless the carrying out of the plan were enjoined, he would suffer irreparable loss by being deprived of substantial property rights.

The defendants answered admitting the material allegations of fact in the complaint but denying that they gave rise to a cause of action because the transaction complained of was a purchase of corporate assets as to which shareholders had no rights of dissent or appraisal. For these reasons the defendants then moved for judgment on the pleadings.[5]

---

3. The proxy statement included the following declaration: "Appraisal Rights. In the opinion of counsel, the shareholders of neither Glen Alden nor List Industries will have any rights of appraisal or similar rights of dissenters with respect to any matter to be acted upon at their respective meetings."

5. Counsel for the defendants concedes that if the corporation is required to pay the dissenting shareholders the appraised fair value of their shares, the resultant drain of cash would prevent Glen Alden from carrying out the agreement. On the other hand, plaintiff contends that if the shareholders had been told of their rights as dissenters, rather than specifically advised that they had no such rights, the resolution approving the reorganization agreement would have been defeated.

The court below concluded that the reorganization agreement entered into between the two corporations was a plan for a *de facto* merger, and that therefore the failure of the notice of the annual meeting to conform to the pertinent requirements of the merger provisions of the Business Corporation Law rendered the notice defective and all proceedings in furtherance of the agreement void. Wherefore, the court entered a final decree denying defendants' motion for judgment on the pleadings, entering judgment upon plaintiff's complaint and granting the injunctive relief therein sought. This appeal followed.

When use of the corporate form of business organization first became widespread, it was relatively easy for courts to define a "merger" or a "sale of assets" and to label a particular transaction as one or the other. But prompted by the desire to avoid the impact of adverse, and to obtain the benefits of favorable, government regulations, particularly federal tax laws, new accounting and legal techniques were developed by lawyers and accountants which interwove the elements characteristic of each, thereby creating hybrid forms of corporate amalgamation. Thus, it is no longer helpful to consider an individual transaction in the abstract and solely by reference to the various elements therein determine whether it is a "merger" or a "sale." Instead, to determine properly the nature of a corporate transaction, we must refer not only to all the provisions of the agreement, but also to the consequences of the transaction and to the purposes of the provisions of the corporation law said to be applicable. We shall apply this principle to the instant case.

Section 908, subd. A of the Pennsylvania Business Corporation Law provides:

> "If any shareholder of a domestic corporation which becomes a party to a plan of merger or consolidation shall object to such plan of merger or consolidation . . . such shareholder shall be entitled to . . . [the fair value of his shares upon surrender of the share certificate or certificates representing his shares]." Act of May 5, 1933, P.L. 364, as amended, 15 P.S. § 2852-908, subd. A.[6]

This provision had its origin in the early decision of this Court in *Lauman v. Lebanon Valley R.R. Co.* There a shareholder who objected to the consolidation of his company with another was held to have a right in the absence of statute to treat the consolidation as a dissolution of his company and to receive the value of his shares upon their surrender.

The rationale of the Lauman case, and of the present section of the Business Corporation Law based thereon, is that when a corporation combines with another so as to lose its essential nature and alter the original fundamental relationships of the

---

6. Furthermore, section 902, subd. B provides that notice of the proposed merger and of the right to dissent thereto must be given the shareholders. "There shall be included in, or enclosed with . . . notice [of meeting of shareholders to vote on plan of merger] a copy or a summary of the plan of merger or plan of consolidation, as the case may be, and . . . a copy of subsection A of section 908 and of subsections B, C and D of section 515 of this act."

shareholders among themselves and to the corporation, a shareholder who does not wish to continue his membership therein may treat his membership in the original corporation as terminated and have the value of his shares paid to him.

Does the combination outlined in the present "reorganization" agreement so fundamentally change the corporate character of Glen Alden and the interest of the plaintiff as a shareholder therein, that to refuse him the rights and remedies of a dissenting shareholder would in reality force him to give up his stock in one corporation and against his will accept shares in another? If so, the combination is a merger within the meaning of section 908, subd. A of the corporation law.

If the reorganization agreement were consummated plaintiff would find that the "List Alden" resulting from the amalgamation would be quite a different corporation than the "Glen Alden" in which he is now a shareholder. Instead of continuing primarily as a coal mining company, Glen Alden would be transformed, after amendment of its articles of incorporation, into a diversified holding company whose interests would range from motion picture theaters to textile companies, Plaintiff would find himself a member of a company with assets of $169,000,000 and a long-term debt of $38,000,000 in lieu of a company one-half that size and with but one-seventh the long-term debt.

While the administration of the operations and properties of Glen Alden as well as List would be in the hands of management common to both companies, since all executives of List would be retained in List Alden, the control of Glen Alden would pass to the directors of List; for List would hold eleven of the seventeen directorships on the new board of directors.

As an aftermath of the transaction plaintiff's proportionate interest in Glen Alden would have been reduced to only two-fifths of what it presently is because of the issuance of an additional 3,621,703 shares to List which would not be subject to preemptive rights. In fact, ownership of Glen Alden would pass to the stockholders of List who would hold 76.5% of the outstanding shares as compared with but 23.5% retained by the present Glen Alden shareholders.

Perhaps the most important consequence to the plaintiff, if he were denied the right to have his shares redeemed at their fair value, would be the serious financial loss suffered upon consummation of the agreement. While the present book value of his stock is $38 a share after combination it would be worth only $21 a share. In contrast, the shareholders of List who presently hold stock with a total book value of $33,000,000 or $7.50 a share, would receive stock with a book value of $76,000,000 or $21 a share.

Under these circumstances it may well be said that if the proposed combination is allowed to take place without right of dissent, plaintiff would have his stock in Glen Alden taken away from him and the stock of a new company thrust upon him in its place. He would be projected against his will into a new enterprise under terms not of his own choosing. It was to protect dissident shareholders against just such a result that this Court one hundred years ago in the Lauman case, and the legislature thereafter in section 908, subd. A, granted the right of dissent. And it is to accord that protection to the plaintiff that we conclude that the combination proposed in the case at hand is a merger within the intendment of section 908, subd. A.

Nevertheless, defendants contend that the 1957 amendments to sections 311 and 908 of the corporation law preclude us from reaching this result and require the entry of judgment in their favor. Subsection F of section 311 dealing with the voluntary transfer of corporate assets provides: "The shareholders of a business corporation which acquires by sale, lease or exchange all or substantially all of the property of another corporation by the issuance of stock, securities or otherwise shall not be entitled to the rights and remedies of dissenting shareholders. . . ." Act of July 11, 1957, P.L. 711, § 1, 15 P.S. § 2852-311, subd. F.

And the amendment to section 908 reads as follows: "The right of dissenting shareholders . . . shall not apply to the purchase by a corporation of assets whether or not the consideration therefor be money or property, real or personal, including shares or bonds or other evidences of indebtedness of such corporation. The shareholders of such corporation shall have no right to dissent from any such purchase."

Defendants view these amendments as abridging the right of shareholders to dissent to a transaction between two corporations which involves a transfer of assets for a consideration even though the transfer has all the legal incidents of a merger. They claim that only if the merger is accomplished in accordance with the prescribed statutory procedure does the right of dissent accrue. In support of this position they cite to us the comment on the amendments by the Committee on Corporation Law of the Pennsylvania Bar Association, the committee which originally drafted these provisions. The comment states that the provisions were intended to overrule cases which granted shareholders the right to dissent to a sale of assets when accompanied by the legal incidents of a merger.

Whatever may have been the intent of the *committee*, there is no evidence to indicate that the *legislature* intended the 1957 amendments to have the effect contended for. But furthermore, the language of these two provisions does not support the opinion of the committee and is inapt to achieve any such purpose. The amendments of 1957 do not provide that a transaction between two corporations which has the effect of a merger but which includes a transfer of assets for consideration is to be exempt from the protective provisions of sections 908, subd. A and 515. They provide only that the shareholders of a corporation which acquires the property or purchases the assets of another corporation, *without more*, are not entitled to the right to dissent from the transaction. So, as in the present case, when as part of a transaction between two corporations, one corporation dissolves, its liabilities are assumed by the survivor, its executives and directors take over the management and control of the survivor, and, as consideration for the transfer, its stockholders acquire a majority of the shares of stock of the survivor, then the transaction is no longer simply a purchase of assets or acquisition of property to which sections 311, subd. F and 908, subd. C apply, but a merger governed by section 908, subd. A of the corporation law. To divest shareholders of their right of dissent under such circumstances would require express language which is absent from the 1957 amendments.

Even were we to assume that the combination provided for in the reorganization agreement is a "sale of assets" to which section 908, subd. A does not apply, it would avail the defendants nothing; we will not blind our eyes to the realities of the transaction. Despite the designation of the parties and the form employed, Glen Alden does not in fact acquire List, rather, List acquires Glen Alden, and under section 311, subd. D[8] the right of dissent would remain with the shareholders of Glen Alden.

We hold that the combination contemplated by the reorganization agreement, although consummated by contract rather than in accordance with the statutory procedure, is a merger within the protective purview of sections 908, subd. A and 515 of the corporation law. The shareholders of Glen Alden should have been notified accordingly and advised of their statutory rights of dissent and appraisal. The failure of the corporate officers to take these steps renders the stockholder approval of the agreement at the 1958 shareholders' meeting invalid. The lower court did not err in enjoining the officers and directors of Glen Alden from carrying out this agreement. . . .

Questions

1. Why did the parties structure the deal as a sale of assets?

2. The court in this case wrote:

> "The rationale of the *Lauman* case, and of the present section of the Business Corporation Law based thereon, is that when a corporation combines with another so as to lose its essential nature and alter the original fundamental relationships of the shareholders among themselves and to the corporation," the shareholders have the right to dissent and have their shares appraised by the court.

What is "the essential nature" of the corporation?

3. How were the "original fundamental relationships of the shareholders among themselves and to the corporation" changed?

4. What was the "serious financial loss" that the plaintiff would suffer from the transaction?

5. What are the practical consequences of the court's decision? Consider that as you compare it to the following case—from Delaware.

---

8. "If any shareholder of a business corporation which sells, leases or exchanges all or substantially all of its property and assets otherwise than (1) in the usual and regular course of its business, (2) for the purpose of relocating its business, or (3) in connection with its dissolution and liquidation, shall object to such sale, lease or exchange and comply with the provisions of section 515 of this act, such shareholder shall be entitled to the rights and remedies of dissenting shareholders as therein provided."

Hariton v. Arco Electronics, Inc.
188 A.2d 123 (Del. 1963)

SOUTHERLAND, Chief Justice

This case involves a sale of assets under § 271 of the corporation law, 8 Del. C. . . . [The question] may be stated as follows:

> A sale of assets is effected under § 271 in consideration of shares of stock of the purchasing corporation. The agreement of sale embodies also a plan to dissolve the selling corporation and distribute the shares so received to the stockholders of the seller, so as to accomplish the same result as would be accomplished by a merger of the seller into the purchaser. Is the sale legal?

The facts are these:

The defendant Arco and Loral Electronics Corporation, a New York corporation, are both engaged, in somewhat different forms, in the electronic equipment business. In the summer of 1961 they negotiated for an amalgamation of the companies. As of October 27, 1961, they entered into a "Reorganization Agreement and Plan." The provisions of this Plan pertinent here are in substance as follows:

> 1. Arco agrees to sell all its assets to Loral in consideration (inter alia) of the issuance to it of 283,000 shares of Loral.
>
> 2. Arco agrees to call a stockholders meeting for the purpose of approving the Plan and the voluntary dissolution.
>
> 3. Arco agrees to distribute to its stockholders all the Loral shares received by it as a part of the complete liquidation of Arco.

At the Arco meeting all the stockholders voting (about 80%) approved the Plan. It was thereafter consummated.

Plaintiff, a stockholder who did not vote at the meeting, sued to enjoin the consummation of the Plan on the grounds (1) that it was illegal, and (2) that it was unfair. The second ground was abandoned. Affidavits and documentary evidence were filed, and defendant moved for summary judgment and dismissal of the complaint. The Vice Chancellor granted the motion and plaintiff appeals.

The question before us we have stated above. Plaintiff's argument that the sale is illegal runs as follows:

> The several steps taken here accomplish the same result as a merger of Arco into Loral. In a "true" sale of assets, the stockholder of the seller retains the right to elect whether the selling company shall continue as a holding company. Moreover, the stockholder of the selling company is forced to accept an investment in a new enterprise without the right of appraisal granted under the merger statute. § 271 cannot therefore be legally combined with a dissolution proceeding under § 275 and a consequent distribution of the purchaser's stock. Such a proceeding is a misuse of the power granted under § 271, and a *de facto* merger results.

The foregoing is a brief summary of plaintiff's contention.

Plaintiff's contention that this sale has achieved the same result as a merger is plainly correct. . . . Accepting it as correct, we noted [in an earlier case] that this result is made possible by the overlapping scope of the merger statute and section 271. . . .

We now hold that the reorganization here accomplished through §271 and a mandatory plan of dissolution and distribution is legal. This is so because the sale-of-assets statute and the merger statute are independent of each other. They are, so to speak, of equal dignity, and the framers of a reorganization plan may resort to either type of corporate mechanics to achieve the desired end. This is not an anomalous result in our corporation law. . . .

Plaintiff concedes, as we read his brief, that if the several steps taken in this case had been taken separately they would have been legal. That is, he concedes that a sale of assets, followed by a separate proceeding to dissolve and distribute, would be legal, even though the same result would follow. This concession exposes the weakness of his contention. To attempt to make any such distinction between sales under §271 would be to create uncertainty in the law and invite litigation.

We are in accord with the Vice Chancellor's ruling, and the judgment below is affirmed.

Section II

Freeze-Out Mergers

When mergers and other fundamental transactions occur between unrelated corporations, they are treated for the most part like any other third-party transaction, and the acquiring corporation owes no fiduciary obligations to the shareholders of the acquired corporation. If, however, the bidder owns some stake in the target or, more significantly, owns a controlling stake in, or is a director or officer (or group of directors or officers) of, the target, the bidder might owe fiduciary obligations toward the shareholders of the acquired corporation. The following cases focus on the obligations of certain fiduciaries in the context of mergers. As you read these cases, consider how they fit into the analysis of the duty of loyalty we saw in Part 2 of this casebook.

Weinberger v. UOP, Inc.
457 A.2d 701 (Del. 1983)

MOORE, Justice

This post-trial appeal was reheard en banc from a decision of the Court of Chancery. It was brought by the class action plaintiff below, a former shareholder of UOP,

Inc., who challenged the elimination of UOP's minority shareholders by a cash-out merger between UOP and its majority owner, The Signal Companies, Inc. Originally, the defendants in this action were Signal, UOP, certain officers and directors of those companies, and UOP's investment banker, Lehman Brothers Kuhn Loeb, Inc.[3] The present Chancellor held that the terms of the merger were fair to the plaintiff and the other minority shareholders of UOP. Accordingly, he entered judgment in favor of the defendants.

Numerous points were raised by the parties, but we address only the following questions presented by the trial court's opinion:

1) The plaintiff's duty to plead sufficient facts demonstrating the unfairness of the challenged merger;

2) The burden of proof upon the parties where the merger has been approved by the purportedly informed vote of a majority of the minority shareholders;

3) The fairness of the merger in terms of adequacy of the defendants' disclosures to the minority shareholders;

4) The fairness of the merger in terms of adequacy of the price paid for the minority shares and the remedy appropriate to that issue;

. . .

In ruling for the defendants, the Chancellor re-stated his earlier conclusion that the plaintiff in a suit challenging a cash-out merger must allege specific acts of fraud, misrepresentation, or other items of misconduct to demonstrate the unfairness of the merger terms to the minority. We approve this rule and affirm it.

The Chancellor also held that even though the ultimate burden of proof is on the majority shareholder to show by a preponderance of the evidence that the transaction is fair, it is first the burden of the plaintiff attacking the merger to demonstrate some basis for invoking the fairness obligation. We agree with that principle. However, where corporate action has been approved by an informed vote of a majority of the minority shareholders, we conclude that the burden entirely shifts to the plaintiff to show that the transaction was unfair to the minority. But in all this, the burden clearly remains on those relying on the vote to show that they completely disclosed all material facts relevant to the transaction.

Here, the record does not support a conclusion that the minority stockholder vote was an informed one. Material information, necessary to acquaint those shareholders with the bargaining positions of Signal and UOP, was withheld under circumstances amounting to a breach of fiduciary duty. We therefore conclude that this merger does not meet the test of fairness, at least as we address that concept, and no burden thus shifted to the plaintiff by reason of the minority shareholder vote. Accordingly, we reverse and remand for further proceedings consistent herewith.

---

3. Shortly before the last oral argument, the plaintiff dismissed Lehman Brothers from the action. Thus, we do not deal with the issues raised by the plaintiff's claims against this defendant.

In considering the nature of the remedy available under our law to minority shareholders in a cash-out merger, we believe that it is, and hereafter should be, an appraisal under 8 Del. C. § 262 as hereinafter construed. . . . But to give full effect to section 262 within the framework of the General Corporation Law we adopt a more liberal, less rigid and stylized, approach to the valuation process than has heretofore been permitted by our courts. While the present state of these proceedings does not admit the plaintiff to the appraisal remedy per se, the practical effect of the remedy we do grant him will be co-extensive with the liberalized valuation and appraisal methods we herein approve for cases coming after this decision.

Our treatment of these matters has necessarily led us to a reconsideration of the business purpose rule. . . . For the reasons hereafter set forth we consider that the business purpose requirement of these cases is no longer the law of Delaware.

I

The facts found by the trial court, pertinent to the issues before us, are supported by the record, and we draw from them as set out in the Chancellor's opinion.

Signal is a diversified, technically based company operating through various subsidiaries. Its stock is publicly traded on the New York, Philadelphia and Pacific Stock Exchanges. UOP, formerly known as Universal Oil Products Company, was a diversified industrial company engaged in various lines of business, including petroleum and petro-chemical services and related products, construction, fabricated metal products, transportation equipment products, chemicals and plastics, and other products and services including land development, lumber products and waste disposal. Its stock was publicly held and listed on the New York Stock Exchange.

In 1974 Signal sold one of its wholly-owned subsidiaries for $420,000,000 in cash. While looking to invest this cash surplus, Signal became interested in UOP as a possible acquisition. Friendly negotiations ensued, and Signal proposed to acquire a controlling interest in UOP at a price of $19 per share. UOP's representatives sought $25 per share. In the arm's length bargaining that followed, an understanding was reached whereby Signal agreed to purchase from UOP 1,500,000 shares of UOP's authorized but unissued stock at $21 per share.

This purchase was contingent upon Signal making a successful cash tender offer for 4,300,000 publicly held shares of UOP, also at a price of $21 per share. This combined method of acquisition permitted Signal to acquire 5,800,000 shares of stock, representing 50.5% of UOP's outstanding shares. The UOP board of directors advised the company's shareholders that it had no objection to Signal's tender offer at that price. Immediately before the announcement of the tender offer, UOP's common stock had been trading on the New York Stock Exchange at a fraction under $14 per share.

The negotiations between Signal and UOP occurred during April 1975, and the resulting tender offer was greatly oversubscribed. However, Signal limited its total purchase of the tendered shares so that, when coupled with the stock bought from UOP, it had achieved its goal of becoming a 50.5% shareholder of UOP.

Although UOP's board consisted of thirteen directors, Signal nominated and elected only six. Of these, five were either directors or employees of Signal. The sixth, a partner in the banking firm of Lazard Freres & Co., had been one of Signal's representatives in the negotiations and bargaining with UOP concerning the tender offer and purchase price of the UOP shares.

However, the president and chief executive officer of UOP retired during 1975, and Signal caused him to be replaced by James V. Crawford, a long-time employee and senior executive vice president of one of Signal's wholly-owned subsidiaries. Crawford succeeded his predecessor on UOP's board of directors and also was made a director of Signal.

By the end of 1977 Signal basically was unsuccessful in finding other suitable investment candidates for its excess cash, and by February 1978 considered that it had no other realistic acquisitions available to it on a friendly basis. Once again its attention turned to UOP.

The trial court found that at the instigation of certain Signal management personnel, including William W. Walkup, its board chairman, and Forrest N. Shumway, its president, a feasibility study was made concerning the possible acquisition of the balance of UOP's outstanding shares. This study was performed by two Signal officers, Charles S. Arledge, vice president (director of planning), and Andrew J. Chitiea, senior vice president (chief financial officer). Messrs. Walkup, Shumway, Arledge and Chitiea were all directors of UOP in addition to their membership on the Signal board.

==Arledge and Chitiea concluded that it would be a good investment for Signal to acquire the remaining 49.5% of UOP shares at any price up to $24 each.== Their report was discussed between Walkup and Shumway who, along with Arledge, Chitiea and Brewster L. Arms, internal counsel for Signal, constituted Signal's senior management. In particular, they talked about the proper price to be paid if the acquisition was pursued, purportedly keeping in mind that as UOP's majority shareholder, Signal owed a fiduciary responsibility to both its own stockholders as well as to UOP's minority. It was ultimately agreed that a meeting of Signal's executive committee would be called to propose that Signal acquire the remaining outstanding stock of UOP through a cash-out merger in the range of $20 to $21 per share.

The executive committee meeting was set for February 28, 1978. As a courtesy, UOP's president, Crawford, was invited to attend, although he was not a member of Signal's executive committee. On his arrival, and prior to the meeting, Crawford was asked to meet privately with Walkup and Shumway. He was then told of Signal's plan to acquire full ownership of UOP and was asked for his reaction to the proposed price range of $20 to $21 per share. Crawford said he thought such a price would be "generous", and that it was certainly one which should be submitted to UOP's minority shareholders for their ultimate consideration. He stated, however, that Signal's 100% ownership could cause internal problems at UOP. He believed that employees would have to be given some assurance of their future place in a fully-owned Signal subsidiary. Otherwise, he feared the departure of essential personnel. Also, many of UOP's key employees had stock option incentive programs which would be wiped out by a merger. Crawford therefore urged that some adjustment would have to be made, such as providing a comparable incentive in Signal's shares, if after the merger he was to maintain his quality of personnel and efficiency at UOP.

Thus, Crawford voiced no objection to the $20 to $21 price range, nor did he suggest that Signal should consider paying more than $21 per share for the minority interests. Later, at the executive committee meeting the same factors were discussed, with Crawford repeating the position he earlier took with Walkup and Shumway. Also considered was the 1975 tender offer and the fact that it had been greatly oversubscribed at $21 per share. For many reasons, Signal's management concluded that the acquisition of UOP's minority shares provided the solution to a number of its business problems.

Thus, it was the consensus that a price of $20 to $21 per share would be fair to both Signal and the minority shareholders of UOP. Signal's executive committee authorized its management "to negotiate" with UOP "for a cash acquisition of the minority ownership in UOP, Inc., with the intention of presenting a proposal to [Signal's] board of directors . . . on March 6, 1978". Immediately after this February 28, 1978 meeting, Signal issued a press release stating:

> The Signal Companies, Inc. and UOP, Inc. are conducting negotiations for the acquisition for cash by Signal of the 49.5 per cent of UOP which it does not presently own, announced Forrest N. Shumway, president and chief executive officer of Signal, and James V. Crawford, UOP president.
>
> Price and other terms of the proposed transaction have not yet been finalized and would be subject to approval of the boards of directors of Signal and UOP, scheduled to meet early next week, the stockholders of UOP and certain federal agencies.

The announcement also referred to the fact that the closing price of UOP's common stock on that day was $14.50 per share.

Two days later, on March 2, 1978, Signal issued a second press release stating that its management would recommend a price in the range of $20 to $21 per share for UOP's 49.5% minority interest. This announcement referred to Signal's earlier statement that "negotiations" were being conducted for the acquisition of the minority shares.

Between Tuesday, February 28, 1978 and Monday, March 6, 1978, a total of four business days, Crawford spoke by telephone with all of UOP's non-Signal, i.e., outside, directors. Also during that period, Crawford retained Lehman Brothers to render a fairness opinion as to the price offered the minority for its stock. He gave two reasons for this choice. First, the time schedule between the announcement and the board meetings was short (by then only three business days) and since Lehman Brothers had been acting as UOP's investment banker for many years, Crawford felt that it would be in the best position to respond on such brief notice. Second, James W. Glanville, a long-time director of UOP and a partner in Lehman Brothers, had acted as a financial advisor to UOP for many years. Crawford believed that Glanville's familiarity with UOP, as a member of its board, would also be of assistance in enabling Lehman Brothers to render a fairness opinion within the existing time constraints.

Crawford telephoned Glanville, who gave his assurance that Lehman Brothers had no conflicts that would prevent it from accepting the task. Glanville's immediate personal reaction was that a price of $20 to $21 would certainly be fair, since it represented almost a 50% premium over UOP's market price. Glanville sought a $250,000 fee for Lehman Brothers' services, but Crawford thought this too much. After further discussions Glanville finally agreed that Lehman Brothers would render its fairness opinion for $150,000.

During this period Crawford also had several telephone contacts with Signal officials. In only one of them, however, was the price of the shares discussed. In a conversation with Walkup, Crawford advised that as a result of his communications with UOP's non-Signal directors, it was his feeling that the price would have to be the top of the proposed range, or $21 per share, if the approval of UOP's outside directors was to be obtained. But again, he did not seek any price higher than $21.

Glanville assembled a three-man Lehman Brothers team to do the work on the fairness opinion. These persons examined relevant documents and information concerning UOP, including its annual reports and its Securities and Exchange Commission filings from 1973 through 1976, as well as its audited financial statements for 1977, its interim reports to shareholders, and its recent and historical market prices and trading volumes. In addition, on Friday, March 3, 1978, two members of the Lehman Brothers team flew to UOP's headquarters in Des Plaines, Illinois, to perform a "due diligence" visit, during the course of which they interviewed Crawford as well as UOP's general counsel, its chief financial officer, and other key executives and personnel.

As a result, the Lehman Brothers team concluded that "the price of either $20 or $21 would be a fair price for the remaining shares of UOP". They telephoned this impression to Glanville, who was spending the weekend in Vermont.

On Monday morning, March 6, 1978, Glanville and the senior member of the Lehman Brothers team flew to Des Plaines to attend the scheduled UOP directors meeting. Glanville looked over the assembled information during the flight. The two had with them the draft of a "fairness opinion letter" in which the price had been left blank. Either during or immediately prior to the directors' meeting, the two-page "fairness opinion letter" was typed in final form and the price of $21 per share was inserted.

On March 6, 1978, both the Signal and UOP boards were convened to consider the proposed merger. Telephone communications were maintained between the two meetings. Walkup, Signal's board chairman, and also a UOP director, attended UOP's meeting with Crawford in order to present Signal's position and answer any questions that UOP's non-Signal directors might have. Arledge and Chitiea, along with Signal's other designees on UOP's board, participated by conference telephone. All of UOP's outside directors attended the meeting either in person or by conference telephone.

First, Signal's board unanimously adopted a resolution authorizing Signal to propose to UOP a cash merger of $21 per share as outlined in a certain merger agreement and other supporting documents. This proposal required that the merger be approved by a majority of UOP's outstanding minority shares voting at the stockholders meeting at which the merger would be considered, and that the minority shares voting in favor of the merger, when coupled with Signal's 50.5% interest would have to comprise at least two-thirds of all UOP shares. Otherwise the proposed merger would be deemed disapproved.

UOP's board then considered the proposal. Copies of the agreement were delivered to the directors in attendance, and other copies had been forwarded earlier to the directors participating by telephone. They also had before them UOP financial data for 1974–1977, UOP's most recent financial statements, market price information, and budget projections for 1978. In addition they had Lehman Brothers' hurriedly prepared fairness opinion letter finding the price of $21 to be fair. Glanville, the Lehman Brothers partner, and UOP director, commented on the information that had gone into preparation of the letter.

Signal also suggests that the Arledge-Chitiea feasibility study, indicating that a price of up to $24 per share would be a "good investment" for Signal, was discussed at the UOP directors' meeting. The Chancellor made no such finding, and our independent review of the record, detailed *infra*, satisfies us by a preponderance of the evidence that there was no discussion of this document at UOP's board meeting. Furthermore, it is clear beyond peradventure that nothing in that report was ever disclosed to UOP's minority shareholders prior to their approval of the merger.

After consideration of Signal's proposal, Walkup and Crawford left the meeting to permit a free and uninhibited exchange between UOP's non-Signal directors. Upon their return a resolution to accept Signal's offer was then proposed and adopted. While Signal's men on UOP's board participated in various aspects of the meeting, they abstained from voting. However, the minutes show that each of them "if voting would have voted yes".

On March 7, 1978, UOP sent a letter to its shareholders advising them of the action taken by UOP's board with respect to Signal's offer. This document pointed out, among other things, that on February 28, 1978 "both companies had announced negotiations were being conducted".

Despite the swift board action of the two companies, the merger was not submitted to UOP's shareholders until their annual meeting on May 26, 1978. In the notice of that meeting and proxy statement sent to shareholders in May, UOP's management and board urged that the merger be approved. The proxy statement also advised:

The price was determined after *discussions* between James V. Crawford, a director of Signal and Chief Executive Officer of UOP, and officers of Signal which took place during meetings on February 28, 1978, and in the course of several subsequent telephone conversations. (Emphasis added.)

In the original draft of the proxy statement the word "negotiations" had been used rather than "discussions." However, when the Securities and Exchange Commission sought details of the "negotiations" as part of its review of these materials, the term was deleted and the word "discussions" was substituted. The proxy statement indicated that the vote of UOP's board in approving the merger had been unanimous. It also advised the shareholders that Lehman Brothers had given its opinion that the merger price of $21 per share was fair to UOP's minority. However, it did not disclose the hurried method by which this conclusion was reached.

As of the record date of UOP's annual meeting, there were 11,488,302 shares of UOP common stock outstanding, 5,688,302 of which were owned by the minority. At the meeting only 56%, or 3,208,652, of the minority shares were voted. Of these, 2,953,812, or 51.9% of the total minority, voted for the merger, and 254,840 voted against it. When Signal's stock was added to the minority shares voting in favor, a total of 76.2% of UOP's outstanding shares approved the merger while only 2.2% opposed it.

By its terms the merger became effective on May 26, 1978, and each share of UOP's stock held by the minority was automatically converted into a right to receive $21 cash.

II

A

A primary issue mandating reversal is the preparation by two UOP directors, Arledge and Chitiea, of their feasibility study for the exclusive use and benefit of Signal. This document was of obvious significance to both Signal and UOP. Using UOP data, it described the advantages to Signal of ousting the minority at a price range of $21–$24 per share. Mr. Arledge, one of the authors, outlined the benefits to Signal:

Purpose of the Merger

1) Provides an outstanding investment opportunity for Signal—(Better than any recent acquisition we have seen.)

2) Increases Signal's earnings.

3) Facilitates the flow of resources between Signal and its subsidiaries—(Big factor—works both ways.)

4) Provides cost savings potential for Signal and UOP.

5) Improves the percentage of Signal's 'operating earnings' as opposed to 'holding company earnings'.

6) Simplifies the understanding of Signal.

7) Facilitates technological exchange among Signal's subsidiaries.

8) Eliminates potential conflicts of interest.

Having written those words, solely for the use of Signal, it is clear from the record that neither Arledge nor Chitiea shared this report with their fellow directors of UOP. We are satisfied that no one else did either. This conduct hardly meets the fiduciary standards applicable to such a transaction. While Mr. Walkup, Signal's chairman of the board and a UOP director, attended the March 6, 1978 UOP board meeting and testified at trial that he had discussed the Arledge-Chitiea report with the UOP directors at this meeting, the record does not support this assertion. Perhaps it is the result of some confusion on Mr. Walkup's part. In any event Mr. Shumway, Signal's president, testified that he made sure the Signal outside directors had this report prior to the March 6, 1978 Signal board meeting, but he did not testify that the Arledge-Chitiea report was also sent to UOP's outside directors.

Mr. Crawford, UOP's president, could not recall that any documents, other than a draft of the merger agreement, were sent to UOP's directors before the March 6, 1978 UOP meeting. Mr. Chitiea, an author of the report, testified that it was made available to Signal's directors, but to his knowledge it was not circulated to the outside directors of UOP. He specifically testified that he "didn't share" that information with the outside directors of UOP with whom he served.

None of UOP's outside directors who testified stated that they had seen this document. The minutes of the UOP board meeting do not identify the Arledge-Chitiea report as having been delivered to UOP's outside directors. This is particularly significant since the minutes describe in considerable detail the materials that actually were distributed. While these minutes recite Mr. Walkup's presentation of the Signal offer, they do not mention the Arledge-Chitiea report or any disclosure that Signal considered a price of up to $24 to be a good investment. If Mr. Walkup had in fact provided such important information to UOP's outside directors, it is logical to assume that these carefully drafted minutes would disclose it. The post-trial briefs of Signal and UOP contain a thorough description of the documents purportedly available to their boards at the March 6, 1978, meetings. Although the Arledge-Chitiea report is specifically identified as being available to the Signal directors, there is no mention of it being among the documents submitted to the UOP board. Even when queried at a prior oral argument before this Court, counsel for Signal did not claim that the Arledge-Chitiea report had been disclosed to UOP's outside directors. Instead, he chose to belittle its contents. This was the same approach taken before us at the last oral argument.

Actually, it appears that a three-page summary of figures was given to all UOP directors. Its first page is identical to one page of the Arledge-Chitiea report, but this dealt with nothing more than a justification of the $21 price. Significantly, the contents of this three-page summary are what the minutes reflect Mr. Walkup told the UOP board. However, nothing contained in either the minutes or this three-page summary reflects Signal's study regarding the $24 price.

The Arledge-Chitiea report speaks for itself in supporting the Chancellor's finding that a price of up to $24 was a "good investment" for Signal. It shows that a return on the investment at $21 would be 15.7% versus 15.5% at $24 per share. This was a difference of only two-tenths of one percent, while it meant over $17,000,000 to the minority. Under such circumstances, paying UOP's minority shareholders $24 would have had relatively little long-term effect on Signal, and the Chancellor's findings concerning the benefit to Signal, even at a price of $24, were obviously correct.

Certainly, this was a matter of material significance to UOP and its shareholders. Since the study was prepared by two UOP directors, using UOP information for the exclusive benefit of Signal, and nothing whatever was done to disclose it to the outside UOP directors or the minority shareholders, a question of breach of fiduciary duty arises. This problem occurs because there were common Signal-UOP directors participating, at least to some extent, in the UOP board's decision-making processes without full disclosure of the conflicts they faced.[7]

B

In assessing this situation, the Court of Chancery was required to:

> examine what information defendants had and to measure it against what they gave to the minority stockholders, in a context in which 'complete candor' is required. In other words, the limited function of the Court was to determine whether defendants had disclosed all information in their possession germane to the transaction in issue. And by 'germane' we mean, for present purposes, information such as a reasonable shareholder would consider important in deciding whether to sell or retain stock. . . .
>
> . . . Completeness, not adequacy, is both the norm and the mandate under present circumstances.

This is merely stating in another way the long-existing principle of Delaware law that these Signal designated directors on UOP's board still owed UOP and its shareholders an uncompromising duty of loyalty. The classic language of *Guth v. Loft, Inc.*, Del. Supr., 23 Del. Ch. 255 (1939), requires no embellishment:

> A public policy, existing through the years, and derived from a profound knowledge of human characteristics and motives, has established a rule that demands of a corporate officer or director, peremptorily and inexorably, the most scrupulous observance of his duty, not only affirmatively to protect the

---

7. Although perfection is not possible, or expected, the result here could have been entirely different if UOP had appointed an independent negotiating committee of its outside directors to deal with Signal at arm's length. Since fairness in this context can be equated to conduct by a theoretical, wholly independent, board of directors acting upon the matter before them, it is unfortunate that this course apparently was neither considered nor pursued. Particularly in a parent-subsidiary context, a showing that the action taken was as though each of the contending parties had in fact exerted its bargaining power against the other at arm's length is strong evidence that the transaction meets the test of fairness.

interests of the corporation committed to his charge, but also to refrain from doing anything that would work injury to the corporation, or to deprive it of profit or advantage which his skill and ability might properly bring to it, or to enable it to make in the reasonable and lawful exercise of its powers. The rule that requires an undivided and unselfish loyalty to the corporation demands that there shall be no conflict between duty and self-interest.

Given the absence of any attempt to structure this transaction on an arm's length basis, Signal cannot escape the effects of the conflicts it faced, particularly when its designees on UOP's board did not totally abstain from participation in the matter. There is no "safe harbor" for such divided loyalties in Delaware. When directors of a Delaware corporation are on both sides of a transaction, they are required to demonstrate their utmost good faith and the most scrupulous inherent fairness of the bargain. The requirement of fairness is unflinching in its demand that where one stands on both sides of a transaction, he has the burden of establishing its entire fairness, sufficient to pass the test of careful scrutiny by the courts.

There is no dilution of this obligation where one holds dual or multiple directorships, as in a parent-subsidiary context. *Levien v. Sinclair Oil Corp.* Thus, individuals who act in a dual capacity as directors of two corporations, one of whom is parent and the other subsidiary, owe the same duty of good management to both corporations, and in the absence of an independent negotiating structure, or the directors' total abstention from any participation in the matter, this duty is to be exercised in light of what is best for both companies. The record demonstrates that Signal has not met this obligation.

C

The concept of fairness has two basic aspects: fair dealing and fair price. The former embraces questions of when the transaction was timed, how it was initiated, structured, negotiated, disclosed to the directors, and how the approvals of the directors and the stockholders were obtained. The latter aspect of fairness relates to the economic and financial considerations of the proposed merger, including all relevant factors: assets, market value, earnings, future prospects, and any other elements that affect the intrinsic or inherent value of a company's stock. However, the test for fairness is not a bifurcated one as between fair dealing and price. All aspects of the issue must be examined as a whole since the question is one of entire fairness. However, in a non-fraudulent transaction we recognize that price may be the preponderant consideration outweighing other features of the merger. Here, we address the two basic aspects of fairness separately because we find reversible error as to both.

D

Part of fair dealing is the obvious duty of candor. . . . Moreover, one possessing superior knowledge may not mislead any stockholder by use of corporate information to which the latter is not privy. Delaware has long imposed this duty even upon persons who are not corporate officers or directors, but who nonetheless are privy to matters of interest or significance to their company. With the well-established

Delaware law on the subject, and the Court of Chancery's findings of fact here, it is inevitable that the obvious conflicts posed by Arledge and Chitiea's preparation of their "feasibility study", derived from UOP information, for the sole use and benefit of Signal, cannot pass muster.

The Arledge-Chitiea report is but one aspect of the element of fair dealing. How did this merger evolve? It is clear that it was entirely initiated by Signal. The serious time constraints under which the principals acted were all set by Signal. It had not found a suitable outlet for its excess cash and considered UOP a desirable investment, particularly since it was now in a position to acquire the whole company for itself. For whatever reasons, and they were only Signal's, the entire transaction was presented to and approved by UOP's board within four business days. Standing alone, this is not necessarily indicative of any lack of fairness by a majority shareholder. It was what occurred, or more properly, what did not occur, during this brief period that makes the time constraints imposed by Signal relevant to the issue of fairness.

The structure of the transaction, again, was Signal's doing. So far as negotiations were concerned, it is clear that they were modest at best. Crawford, Signal's man at UOP, never really talked price with Signal, except to accede to its management's statements on the subject, and to convey to Signal the UOP outside directors' view that as between the $20–$21 range under consideration, it would have to be $21. The latter is not a surprising outcome, but hardly arm's length negotiations. Only the protection of benefits for UOP's key employees and the issue of Lehman Brothers' fee approached any concept of bargaining.

As we have noted, the matter of disclosure to the UOP directors was wholly flawed by the conflicts of interest raised by the Arledge-Chitiea report. All of those conflicts were resolved by Signal in its own favor without divulging any aspect of them to UOP.

This cannot but undermine a conclusion that this merger meets any reasonable test of fairness. The outside UOP directors lacked one material piece of information generated by two of their colleagues, but shared only with Signal. True, the UOP board had the Lehman Brothers' fairness opinion, but that firm has been blamed by the plaintiff for the hurried task it performed, when more properly the responsibility for this lies with Signal. There was no disclosure of the circumstances surrounding the rather cursory preparation of the Lehman Brothers' fairness opinion. Instead, the impression was given UOP's minority that a careful study had been made, when in fact speed was the hallmark, and Mr. Glanville, Lehman's partner in charge of the matter, and also a UOP director, having spent the weekend in Vermont, brought a draft of the "fairness opinion letter" to the UOP directors' meeting on March 6, 1978 with the price left blank. We can only conclude from the record that the rush imposed on Lehman Brothers by Signal's timetable contributed to the difficulties under which this investment banking firm attempted to perform its responsibilities. Yet, none of this was disclosed to UOP's minority.

Finally, the minority stockholders were denied the critical information that Signal considered a price of $24 to be a good investment. Since this would have meant over $17,000,000 more to the minority, we cannot conclude that the shareholder vote was an informed one. Under the circumstances, an approval by a majority of the minority was meaningless.

Given these particulars and the Delaware law on the subject, the record does not establish that this transaction satisfies any reasonable concept of fair dealing, and the Chancellor's findings in that regard must be reversed.

E

. . .

The plaintiff has not sought an appraisal, but rescissory damages of the type contemplated by *Lynch v. Vickers Energy Corp.* In view of the approach to valuation that we announce today, we see no basis in our law for *Lynch II*'s exclusive monetary formula for relief. On remand the plaintiff will be permitted to test the fairness of the $21 price by the standards we herein establish, in conformity with the principle applicable to an appraisal—that fair value be determined by taking "into account all relevant factors" [see 8 Del. C. §262(h)]. In our view this includes the elements of rescissory damages if the Chancellor considers them susceptible of proof and a remedy appropriate to all the issues of fairness before him. To the extent that *Lynch II* purports to limit the Chancellor's discretion to a single remedial formula for monetary damages in a cash-out merger, it is overruled.

While a plaintiff's monetary remedy ordinarily should be confined to the more liberalized appraisal proceeding herein established, we do not intend any limitation on the historic powers of the Chancellor to grant such other relief as the facts of a particular case may dictate. The appraisal remedy we approve may not be adequate in certain cases, particularly where fraud, misrepresentation, self-dealing, deliberate waste of corporate assets, or gross and palpable overreaching are involved. Under such circumstances, the Chancellor's powers are complete to fashion any form of equitable and monetary relief as may be appropriate, including rescissory damages. Since it is apparent that this long completed transaction is too involved to undo, and in view of the Chancellor's discretion, the award, if any, should be in the form of monetary damages based upon entire fairness standards, i.e., fair dealing and fair price. . . .

III

Finally, we address the matter of business purpose. The defendants contend that the purpose of this merger was not a proper subject of inquiry by the trial court. The plaintiff says that no valid purpose existed—the entire transaction was a mere subterfuge designed to eliminate the minority. . . .

The requirement of a business purpose is new to our law of mergers and was a departure from prior case law. . . .

In view of the fairness test which has long been applicable to parent-subsidiary mergers, . . . the expanded appraisal remedy now available to shareholders, and the broad discretion of the Chancellor to fashion such relief as the facts of a given case may dictate, we do not believe that any additional meaningful protection is afforded minority shareholders by the business purpose requirement.... Accordingly, such requirement shall no longer be of any force or effect.

The judgment of the Court of Chancery, finding both the circumstances of the merger and the price paid the minority shareholders to be fair, is reversed. The matter is remanded for further proceedings consistent herewith. Upon remand the plaintiff's post-trial motion to enlarge the class should be granted.

Reversed and Remanded

Questions

1. What are the practical implications of the court's conclusion that "while a plaintiff's monetary remedy ordinarily should be confined to the more liberalized appraisal proceeding herein established, we do not intend any limitation on the historic powers of the Chancellor to grant such other relief as the facts of a particular case may dictate"?

2. What did the Signal directors do wrong? What should they have done?

3. How does *Weinberger v. UOP* fit in the discussion of the duty of loyalty in Part 2? How does it fit in the discussion of the duties of controlling shareholders in Part 3?

4. *Weinberger* remains the decisive case about the dual components of the fairness standard of review—fair dealing and fair price, process and substance. Yet, its analysis left unanswered the question as to whether one component carried more weight than the other. On its face, the court gave equal weight to both (despite earlier cases that seemed to prioritize substantive fairness). Yet, it was unclear what standard of review would apply if a disinterested, independent body such as a majority of the disinterested directors approved the transaction. Would the shareholder plaintiff have to show that the transaction was unfair, as earlier cases seemed to suggest, or would the transaction be protected under the presumption of the business judgment rule? The court indicated its expectations as far as conduct (i.e., independent negotiation) but refrained from commenting on the implications. (The court did hold that an informed vote by a majority of the disinterested shareholders would shift the burden to the plaintiff shareholder to prove the unfairness of the transaction.)

Cases immediately following *Weinberger* continued to use the fairness standard of review when a majority of the independent directors or a majority of the disinterested shareholders approved the merger. Such independent approval, however, permitted burden shifting. As the Supreme Court of Delaware held in *Kahn v. Lynch Communications Systems, Inc.*, 638 A.2d 1110, 1117 (Del. 1994), once the defendant directors demonstrated that the transaction was either negotiated by a "truly independent, fully informed" and free to negotiate special committee, or ratified by a majority of the minority shareholders, the burden would shift to the plaintiffs to demonstrate that the transaction was entirely unfair. (An independent committee negotiating "with what could be considered a quick surrender" or under threats from the controlling shareholder would not meet such requirements and the burden would not be shifted.)

But such an approach was not without its critics. In *In re Cox Communications, Inc. Shareholders Litigation*, 879 A.2d 604 (2005), then Vice-Chancellor Strine, concerned about plaintiff lawyers misusing litigation over fairness gratuitously to raise the price offered to shareholders in cash out mergers, recommended a standard-altering approach. Careful not to deviate from precedent, Strine recommended that the court allow the invocation of the business judgment rule if both an independent special committee negotiating at arm's length and the majority of the disinterested (minority) shareholders approved the cash out merger. Given that the business judgment rule made the transaction almost insusceptible to challenge, Strine was confident that his recommended approach would motivate directors to use both processes. Thus it "would promote the universal use of a transactional structure that is very favorable to minority stockholders — one that deploys an active, disinterested negotiating agent to bargain for the minority coupled with an opportunity for the minority to freely decide whether to accept or reject their agent's work product." At the same time, it would dissuade plaintiff lawyers from misusing derivative litigation.

Almost a decade later, then-Chancellor Strine was offered an opportunity to turn his suggestion into law in deciding *In re M&F Worldwide Corporation Shareholders Litigation* (2002). On appeal, the Supreme Court of Delaware endorsed. Its decision follows below.

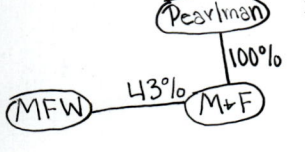

Kahn v. M&F Worldwide Corp.

88 A.3d 635 (Del. 2013)

HOLLAND, Justice

This is an appeal from a final judgment entered by the Court of Chancery in a proceeding that arises from a 2011 acquisition by MacAndrews & Forbes Holdings, Inc. ("M & F" or "MacAndrews & Forbes") — a 43% stockholder in M & F Worldwide Corp. ("MFW") — of the remaining common stock of MFW (the "Merger"). From the outset, M & F's proposal to take MFW private was made contingent upon two stockholder-protective procedural conditions. First, M & F required the Merger to be negotiated and approved by a special committee of independent MFW directors (the "Special Committee"). Second, M & F required that the Merger be approved by a majority of stockholders unaffiliated with M & F. The Merger closed in December 2011, after it was approved by a vote of 65.4% of MFW's minority stockholders.

The Appellants initially sought to enjoin the transaction. They withdrew their request for injunctive relief after taking expedited discovery, including several depositions. The Appellants then sought post-closing relief against M & F, Ronald O. Perelman, and MFW's directors (including the members of the Special Committee) for breach of fiduciary duty. Again, the Appellants were provided with extensive discovery. The Defendants then moved for summary judgment, which the Court of Chancery granted.

. . .

FACTS

MFW and M & F

MFW is a holding company incorporated in Delaware. Before the Merger that is the subject of this dispute, MFW was 43.4% owned by MacAndrews & Forbes, which in turn is entirely owned by Ronald O. Perelman. MFW had four business segments. Three were owned through a holding company, Harland Clarke Holding Corporation ("HCHC"). . . . The fourth segment, which was not part of HCHC, was Mafco Worldwide Corporation, a manufacturer of licorice flavorings.

The MFW board had thirteen members. They were: Ronald Perelman, Barry Schwartz, William Bevins, Bruce Slovin, Charles Dawson, Stephen Taub, John Keane, Theo Folz, Philip Beekman, Martha Byorum, Viet Dinh, Paul Meister, and Carl Webb. Perelman, Schwartz, and Bevins were officers of both MFW and MacAndrews & Forbes. Perelman was the Chairman of MFW and the Chairman and CEO of MacAndrews & Forbes; Schwartz was the President and CEO of MFW and the Vice Chairman and Chief Administrative Officer of MacAndrews & Forbes; and Bevins was a Vice President at MacAndrews & Forbes.

The Taking MFW Private Proposal

In May 2011, Perelman began to explore the possibility of taking MFW private. At that time, MFW's stock price traded in the $20 to $24 per share range. MacAndrews & Forbes engaged a bank, Moelis & Company, to advise it. After preparing valuations based on projections that had been supplied to lenders by MFW in April and May 2011, Moelis valued MFW at between $10 and $32 a share.

On June 10, 2011, MFW's shares closed on the New York Stock Exchange at $16.96. The next business day, June 13, 2011, Schwartz sent a letter proposal ("Proposal") to the MFW board to buy the remaining MFW shares for $24 in cash. The Proposal stated, in relevant part:

> The proposed transaction would be subject to the approval of the Board of Directors of the Company [*i.e.*, MFW] and the negotiation and execution of mutually acceptable definitive transaction documents. It is our expectation that the Board of Directors will appoint a special committee of independent directors to consider our proposal and make a recommendation to the Board of Directors. *We will not move forward with the transaction unless it is approved by such a special committee. In addition, the transaction will be subject to a non-waivable condition requiring the approval of a majority of the shares of the Company not owned by M & F or its affiliates* . . . .
>
> . . . In considering this proposal, you should know that in our capacity as a stockholder of the Company we are interested only in acquiring the shares of the Company not already owned by us and that in such capacity we have

no interest in selling any of the shares owned by us in the Company nor would we expect, in our capacity as a stockholder, to vote in favor of any alternative sale, merger or similar transaction involving the Company. If the special committee does not recommend or the public stockholders of the Company do not approve the proposed transaction, such determination would not adversely affect our future relationship with the Company and we would intend to remain as a long-term stockholder.

. . .

In connection with this proposal, we have engaged Moelis & Company as our financial advisor and Skadden, Arps, Slate, Meagher & Flom LLP as our legal advisor, and we encourage the special committee to retain its own legal and financial advisors to assist it in its review.

MacAndrews & Forbes filed this letter with the U.S. Securities and Exchange Commission ("SEC") and issued a press release disclosing substantially the same information.

The Special Committee Is Formed

The MFW board met the following day to consider the Proposal. At the meeting, Schwartz presented the offer on behalf of MacAndrews & Forbes. Subsequently, Schwartz and Bevins, as the two directors present who were also directors of MacAndrews & Forbes, recused themselves from the meeting, as did Dawson, the CEO of HCHC, who had previously expressed support for the proposed offer.

The independent directors then invited counsel from Willkie Farr & Gallagher—a law firm that had recently represented a Special Committee of MFW's independent directors in a potential acquisition of a subsidiary of MacAndrews & Forbes—to join the meeting. The independent directors decided to form the Special Committee, and resolved further that:

> [T]he Special Committee is empowered to: (i) make such investigation of the Proposal as the Special Committee deems appropriate; (ii) evaluate the terms of the Proposal; (iii) negotiate with Holdings [*i.e.,* MacAndrews & Forbes] and its representatives any element of the Proposal; (iv) negotiate the terms of any definitive agreement with respect to the Proposal (it being understood that the execution thereof shall be subject to the approval of the Board); (v) report to the Board its recommendations and conclusions with respect to the Proposal, including a determination and *recommendation as to whether the Proposal is fair and in the best interests of the stockholders of the Company other than Holdings* and its affiliates and should be approved by the Board; and (vi) determine to elect not to pursue the Proposal. . . .
>
> . . . [T]he Board shall not approve the Proposal without a prior favorable recommendation of the Special Committee. . . .

... [T]he Special Committee [is] empowered to retain and employ legal counsel, a financial advisor, and such other agents as the Special Committee shall deem necessary or desirable in connection with these matters. ...

The Special Committee consisted of Byorum, Dinh, Meister (the chair), Slovin, and Webb. The following day, Slovin recused himself because, although the MFW board had determined that he qualified as an independent director under the rules of the New York Stock Exchange, he had "some current relationships that could raise questions about his independence for purposes of serving on the Special Committee."

ANALYSIS

What Should Be the Review Standard?

Where a transaction involving self-dealing by a controlling stockholder is challenged, the applicable standard of judicial review is "entire fairness," with the defendants having the burden of persuasion. In other words, the defendants bear the ultimate burden of proving that the transaction with the controlling stockholder was entirely fair to the minority stockholders. In *Kahn v. Lynch Communication Systems, Inc.*, however, this Court held that in "entire fairness" cases, the defendants may shift the burden of persuasion to the plaintiff if either (1) they show that the transaction was approved by a well-functioning committee of independent directors; or (2) they show that the transaction was approved by an informed vote of a majority of the minority stockholders.

This appeal presents a question of first impression: what should be the standard of review for a merger between a controlling stockholder and its subsidiary, where the merger is conditioned *ab initio* upon the approval of both an independent, adequately-empowered Special Committee that fulfills its duty of care, and the uncoerced, informed vote of a majority of the minority stockholders. The question has never been put directly to this Court.

. . .

The Court of Chancery held that the consequence should be that the business judgment standard of review will govern going private mergers with a controlling stockholder that are conditioned *ab initio* upon (1) the approval of an independent and fully-empowered Special Committee that fulfills its duty of care and (2) the uncoerced, informed vote of the majority of the minority stockholders.

The Court of Chancery rested its holding upon the premise that the common law equitable rule that best protects minority investors is one that encourages controlling stockholders to accord the minority both procedural protections. A transactional structure subject to both conditions differs fundamentally from a merger having only one of those protections, in that:

> By giving controlling stockholders the opportunity to have a going private transaction reviewed under the business judgment rule, a strong incentive is created to give minority stockholders much broader access to the transactional structure that is most likely to effectively protect their interests. ...

That structure, it is important to note, is critically different than a structure that uses only *one* of the procedural protections. The "or" structure does not replicate the protections of a third-party merger under the DGCL approval process, because it only requires that one, and not both, of the statutory requirements of director and stockholder approval be accomplished by impartial decisionmakers. The "both" structure, by contrast, replicates the arm's-length merger steps of the DGCL by "requir[ing] two independent approvals, which it is fair to say serve independent integrity-enforcing functions."

Before the Court of Chancery, the Appellants acknowledged that "this transactional structure is the optimal one for minority shareholders." Before us, however, they argue that neither procedural protection is adequate to protect minority stockholders, because "possible ineptitude and timidity of directors" may undermine the special committee protection, and because majority-of-the-minority votes may be unduly influenced by arbitrageurs that have an institutional bias to approve virtually any transaction that offers a market premium, however insubstantial it may be. Therefore, the Appellants claim, these protections, even when combined, are not sufficient to justify "abandon[ing]" the entire fairness standard of review.

With regard to the Special Committee procedural protection, the Appellants' assertions regarding the MFW directors' inability to discharge their duties are not supported either by the record or by well-established principles of Delaware law. As the Court of Chancery correctly observed:

> Although it is possible that there are independent directors who have little regard for their duties or for being perceived by their company's stockholders (and the larger network of institutional investors) as being effective at protecting public stockholders, the court thinks they are likely to be exceptional, and certainly our Supreme Court's jurisprudence does not embrace such a skeptical view.

Regarding the majority-of-the-minority vote procedural protection, as the Court of Chancery noted, "plaintiffs themselves do not argue that minority stockholders will vote against a going private transaction because of fear of retribution." Instead, as the Court of Chancery summarized, the Appellants' argued as follows:

> [Plaintiffs] just believe that most investors like a premium and will tend to vote for a deal that delivers one and that many long-term investors will sell out when they can obtain most of the premium without waiting for the ultimate vote. But that argument is not one that suggests that the voting decision is not voluntary, it is simply an editorial about the motives of investors and does not contradict the premise that a majority-of-the-minority condition gives minority investors a free and voluntary opportunity to decide what is fair for themselves.

Business Judgment Review Standard Adopted

We hold that business judgment is the standard of review that should govern mergers between a controlling stockholder and its corporate subsidiary, where the merger is conditioned *ab initio* upon both the approval of an independent, adequately-empowered Special Committee that fulfills its duty of care; and the uncoerced, informed vote of a majority of the minority stockholders. We so conclude for several reasons.

First, entire fairness is the highest standard of review in corporate law. It is applied in the controller merger context as a substitute for the dual statutory protections of disinterested board and stockholder approval, because both protections are potentially undermined by the influence of the controller. However, as this case establishes, that undermining influence does not exist in every controlled merger setting, regardless of the circumstances. The simultaneous deployment of the procedural protections employed here create a countervailing, offsetting influence of equal — if not greater — force. That is, where the controller irrevocably and publicly disables itself from using its control to dictate the outcome of the negotiations and the shareholder vote, the controlled merger then acquires the shareholder-protective characteristics of third-party, arm's-length mergers, which are reviewed under the business judgment standard.

Second, the dual procedural protection merger structure optimally protects the minority stockholders in controller buyouts. As the Court of Chancery explained:

> [W]hen these two protections are established up-front, a potent tool to extract good value for the minority is established. From inception, the controlling stockholder knows that it cannot bypass the special committee's ability to say no. And, the controlling stockholder knows it cannot dangle a majority-of-the-minority vote before the special committee late in the process as a deal-closer rather than having to make a price move.

Third, and as the Court of Chancery reasoned, applying the business judgment standard to the dual protection merger structure;

> . . . is consistent with the central tradition of Delaware law, which defers to the informed decisions of impartial directors, especially when those decisions have been approved by the disinterested stockholders on full information and without coercion. Not only that, the adoption of this rule will be of benefit to minority stockholders because it will provide a strong incentive for controlling stockholders to accord minority investors the transactional structure that respected scholars believe will provide them the best protection, a structure where stockholders get the benefits of independent, empowered negotiating agents to bargain for the best price and say no if the agents believe the deal is not advisable for any proper reason, plus the critical ability to determine for themselves whether to accept any deal that their negotiating agents recommend to them. A transactional

structure with both these protections is fundamentally different from one with only one protection.

Fourth, the underlying purposes of the dual protection merger structure utilized here and the entire fairness standard of review both converge and are fulfilled at the same critical point: price. Following *Weinberger v. UOP, Inc.*, this Court has consistently held that, although entire fairness review comprises the dual components of fair dealing and fair price, in a non-fraudulent transaction "price may be the preponderant consideration outweighing other features of the merger." The dual protection merger structure requires two price-related pretrial determinations: first, that a fair price was achieved by an empowered, independent committee that acted with care; and, second, that a fully-informed, uncoerced majority of the minority stockholders voted in favor of the price that was recommended by the independent committee.

The New Standard Summarized

To summarize our holding, in controller buyouts, the business judgment standard of review will be applied *if and only if:* (i) the controller conditions the procession of the transaction on the approval of both a Special Committee and a majority of the minority stockholders; (ii) the Special Committee is independent; (iii) the Special Committee is empowered to freely select its own advisors and to say no definitively; (iv) the Special Committee meets its duty of care in negotiating a fair price; (v) the vote of the minority is informed; and (vi) there is no coercion of the minority.

If a plaintiff that can plead a reasonably conceivable set of facts showing that any or all of those enumerated conditions did not exist, that complaint would state a claim for relief that would entitle the plaintiff to proceed and conduct discovery. If, after discovery, triable issues of fact remain about whether either or both of the dual procedural protections were established, or if established were effective, the case will proceed to a trial in which the court will conduct an entire fairness review.

This approach is consistent with *Weinberger, Lynch* and their progeny. A controller that employs and/or establishes only one of these dual procedural protections would continue to receive burden-shifting within the entire fairness standard of review framework. Stated differently, unless *both* procedural protections for the minority stockholders are established *prior to trial,* the ultimate judicial scrutiny of controller buyouts will continue to be the entire fairness standard of review.

Having articulated the circumstances that will enable a controlled merger to be reviewed under the business judgment standard, we next address whether those circumstances have been established as a matter of undisputed fact and law in this case.

Dual Protection Inquiry

. . .

The Special Committee Was Independent

The Appellants do not challenge the independence of the Special Committee's Chairman, Meister. They claim, however, that the three other Special Committee members—Webb, Dinh, and Byorum—were beholden to Perelman because of their prior business and/or social dealings with Perelman or Perelman-related entities.

The Appellants first challenge the independence of Webb. They urged that Webb and Perelman shared a "longstanding and lucrative business partnership" between 1983 and 2002 which included acquisitions of thrifts and financial institutions, and which led to a 2002 asset sale to Citibank in which Webb made "a significant amount of money." The Court of Chancery concluded, however, that the fact of Webb having engaged in business dealings with Perelman nine years earlier did not raise a triable fact issue regarding his ability to evaluate the Merger impartially. We agree.

Second, the Appellants argued that there were triable issues of fact regarding Dinh's independence. The Appellants demonstrated that between 2009 and 2011, Dinh's law firm, Bancroft PLLC, advised M & F and Scientific Games (in which M & F owned a 37.6% stake), during which time the Bancroft firm earned $200,000 in fees. The record reflects that Bancroft's limited prior engagements, which were inactive by the time the Merger proposal was announced, were fully disclosed to the Special Committee soon after it was formed. The Court of Chancery found that the Appellants failed to proffer any evidence to show that compensation received by Dinh's law firm was material to Dinh, in the sense that it would have influenced his decisionmaking with respect to the M & F proposal. The only evidence of record, the Court of Chancery concluded, was that these fees were "*de minimis*" and that the Appellants had offered no contrary evidence that would create a genuine issue of material fact.

The Court of Chancery also found that the relationship between Dinh, a Georgetown University Law Center professor, and M & F's Barry Schwartz, who sits on the Georgetown Board of Visitors, did not create a triable issue of fact as to Dinh's independence. No record evidence suggested that Schwartz could exert influence on Dinh's position at Georgetown based on his recommendation regarding the Merger. Indeed, Dinh had earned tenure as a professor at Georgetown before he ever knew Schwartz.

The Appellants also argue that Schwartz's later invitation to Dinh to join the board of directors of Revlon, Inc. "illustrates the ongoing personal relationship between Schwartz and Dinh." There is no record evidence that Dinh expected to be asked to join Revlon's board at the time he served on the Special Committee. Moreover, the Court of Chancery noted, Schwartz's invitation for Dinh to join the Revlon board of directors occurred months after the Merger was approved and did not raise a triable fact issue concerning Dinh's independence from Perelman. We uphold the Court of Chancery's findings relating to Dinh.

Third, the Appellants urge that issues of material fact permeate Byorum's independence and, specifically, that Byorum "had a business relationship with Perelman from 1991 to 1996 through her executive position at Citibank." The Court of Chancery concluded, however, the Appellants presented no evidence of the nature of Byorum's interactions with Perelman while she was at Citibank. Nor was there evidence that after 1996 Byorum had an ongoing economic relationship with Perelman that was material to her in any way. Byorum testified that any interactions she had with Perelman while she was at Citibank resulted from her role as a senior executive, because Perelman was a client of the bank at the time. Byorum also testified that she had no business relationship with Perelman between 1996 and 2007, when she joined the MFW Board.

The Appellants also contend that Byorum performed advisory work for Scientific Games in 2007 and 2008 as a senior managing director of Stephens Cori Capital Advisors ("Stephens Cori"). The Court of Chancery found, however, that the Appellants had adduced no evidence tending to establish that the $100,000 fee Stephens Cori received for that work was material to either Stephens Cori or to Byorum personally. Stephens Cori's engagement for Scientific Games, which occurred years before the Merger was announced and the Special Committee was convened, was fully disclosed to the Special Committee, which concluded that "it was not material, and it would not represent a conflict." We uphold the Court of Chancery's findings relating to Byorum as well.

To evaluate the parties' competing positions on the issue of director independence, the Court of Chancery applied well-established Delaware legal principles. To show that a director is not independent, a plaintiff must demonstrate that the director is "beholden" to the controlling party "or so under [the controller's] influence that [the director's] discretion would be sterilized." Bare allegations that directors are friendly with, travel in the same social circles as, or have past business relationships with the proponent of a transaction or the person they are investigating are not enough to rebut the presumption of independence.

A plaintiff seeking to show that a director was not independent must satisfy a materiality standard. The court must conclude that the director in question had ties to the person whose proposal or actions he or she is evaluating that are sufficiently substantial that he or she could not objectively discharge his or her fiduciary duties. Consistent with that predicate materiality requirement, the existence of some financial ties between the interested party and the director, without more, is not disqualifying. The inquiry must be whether, applying a subjective standard, those ties were *material*, in the sense that the alleged ties could have affected the impartiality of the individual director.

The Appellants assert that the materiality of any economic relationships the Special Committee members may have had with Mr. Perelman "should not be decided on summary judgment." But Delaware courts have often decided director independence as a matter of law at the summary judgment stage. In this case, the Court of Chancery noted, that despite receiving extensive discovery, the Appellants did "nothing . . . to compare the actual circumstances of the [challenged directors] to the ties [they] contend affect their impartiality" and "fail[ed] to proffer any real evidence of their economic circumstances."

. . .

The Court of Chancery found that to the extent the Appellants claimed the Special Committee members, Webb, Dinh, and Byorum, were beholden to Perelman based on prior economic relationships with him, the Appellants never developed or proffered evidence showing the materiality of those relationships:

> Despite receiving the chance for extensive discovery, the plaintiffs have done nothing . . . to compare the actual economic circumstances of the directors they challenge to the ties the plaintiffs contend affect their impartiality. In other words, the plaintiffs have ignored a key teaching of our Supreme Court, requiring a showing that a specific director's independence is compromised by factors material to her. As to each of the specific directors the plaintiffs challenge, the plaintiffs fail to proffer any real evidence of their economic circumstances.

The record supports the Court of Chancery's holding that none of the Appellants' claims relating to Webb, Dinh or Byorum raised a triable issue of material fact concerning their individual independence or the Special Committee's collective independence.

The Special Committee Was Empowered

It is undisputed that the Special Committee was empowered to hire its own legal and financial advisors, and it retained Willkie Farr & Gallagher LLP as its legal advisor. After interviewing four potential financial advisors, the Special Committee engaged Evercore Partners ("Evercore"). The qualifications and independence of Evercore and Willkie Farr & Gallagher LLP are not contested.

Among the powers given the Special Committee in the board resolution was the authority to "report to the Board its recommendations and conclusions with respect to the [Merger], including a determination and recommendation as to whether the Proposal is fair and in the best interests of the stockholders . . . ." The Court of Chancery also found that it was "undisputed that the [S]pecial [C]ommittee was empowered not simply to 'evaluate' the offer, like some special committees with weak mandates, but to negotiate with [M & F] over the terms of its offer to buy out the noncontrolling stockholders. This negotiating power was accompanied by the clear authority to say no definitively to [M & F]" and to "make that decision stick." MacAndrews & Forbes promised that it would not proceed with any going private proposal that did not have the support of the Special Committee. Therefore, the Court of Chancery concluded, "the MFW committee did not have to fear that if it bargained too hard, MacAndrews & Forbes could bypass the committee and make a tender offer directly to the minority stockholders."

The Court of Chancery acknowledged that even though the Special Committee had the authority to negotiate and "say no," it did not have the authority, as a practical matter, to sell MFW to other buyers. MacAndrews & Forbes stated in its announcement that it was not interested in selling its 43% stake. Moreover, under Delaware law, MacAndrews & Forbes had no duty to sell its block, which was large enough, again as a practical matter, to preclude any other buyer from succeeding unless MacAndrews & Forbes decided to become a seller. Absent such a decision, it was unlikely that any potentially interested party would incur the costs and risks of exploring a purchase of MFW.

Nevertheless, the Court of Chancery found, "this did not mean that the MFW Special Committee did not have the leeway to get advice from its financial advisor about the strategic options available to MFW, including the potential interest that other buyers might have *if MacAndrews & Forbes was willing to sell."* The undisputed record shows that the Special Committee, with the help of its financial advisor, did consider whether there were other buyers who might be interested in purchasing MFW, and whether there were other strategic options, such as asset divestitures, that might generate more value for minority stockholders than a sale of their stock to MacAndrews & Forbes.

The Special Committee Exercised Due Care

The Special Committee insisted from the outset that MacAndrews (including any "dual" employees who worked for both MFW and MacAndrews) be screened off from the Special Committee's process, to ensure that the process replicated arm's-length negotiations with a third party. In order to carefully evaluate M & F's offer, the Special Committee held a total of eight meetings during the summer of 2011.

From the outset of their work, the Special Committee and Evercore had projections that had been prepared by MFW's business segments in April and May 2011. Early in the process, Evercore and the Special Committee asked MFW management to produce new projections that reflected management's most up-to-date, and presumably most accurate, thinking. Consistent with the Special Committee's determination to conduct its analysis free of any MacAndrews influence, MacAndrews—including "dual" MFW/MacAndrews executives who normally vetted MFW projections—were excluded from the process of preparing the updated financial projections. Mafco, the licorice business, advised Evercore that all of its projections would remain the same. Harland Clarke updated its projections. On July 22, 2011, Evercore received new projections from HCHC, which incorporated the updated projections from Harland Clarke. Evercore then constructed a valuation model based upon all of these updated projections.

The updated projections, which formed the basis for Evercore's valuation analyses, reflected MFW's deteriorating results, especially in Harland's check-printing business. Those projections forecast EBITDA for MFW of $491 million in 2015, as opposed to $535 million under the original projections.

On August 10, Evercore produced a range of valuations for MFW, based on the updated projections, of $15 to $45 per share. Evercore valued MFW using a variety of accepted methods, including a discounted cash flow ("DCF") model. Those valuations generated a range of fair value of $22 to $38 per share, and a premiums paid analysis resulted in a value range of $22 to $45. MacAndrews & Forbes's $24 offer fell within the range of values produced by each of Evercore's valuation techniques.

Although the $24 Proposal fell within the range of Evercore's fair values, the Special Committee directed Evercore to conduct additional analyses and explore strategic alternatives that might generate more value for MFW's stockholders than might a sale to MacAndrews. The Special Committee also investigated the possibility of other buyers, *e.g.*, private equity buyers, that might be interested in purchasing MFW. In addition, the Special Committee considered whether other strategic options, such as asset divestitures, could achieve superior value for MFW's stockholders. Mr. Meister testified, "The Committee made it very clear to Evercore that we were interested in any and all possible avenues of increasing value to the stockholders, including meaningful expressions of interest for meaningful pieces of the business."

The Appellants insist that the Special Committee had "no right to solicit alternative bids, conduct any sort of market check, or even consider alternative transactions." But the Special Committee did just that, even though MacAndrews' stated unwillingness to sell its MFW stake meant that the Special Committee did not have the practical ability to market MFW to other buyers. The Court of Chancery properly concluded that despite the Special Committee's inability to solicit alternative bids, it *could* seek Evercore's advice about strategic alternatives, including *values that might be available if MacAndrews was willing to sell.*

Although the MFW Special Committee considered options besides the M & F Proposal, the Committee's analysis of those alternatives proved they were unlikely to achieve added value for MFW's stockholders. The Court of Chancery summarized the performance of the Special Committee as follows:

> [t]he special committee did consider, with the help of its financial advisor, whether there were other buyers who might be interested in purchasing MFW, and whether there were other strategic options, such as asset divestitures, that might generate more value for minority stockholders than a sale of their stock to MacAndrews & Forbes.

On August 18, 2011, the Special Committee rejected the $24 a share Proposal, and countered at $30 per share. The Special Committee characterized the $30 counteroffer as a negotiating position. The Special Committee recognized that $30 per share was a very aggressive counteroffer and, not surprisingly, was prepared to accept less.

On September 9, 2011, MacAndrews & Forbes rejected the $30 per share counteroffer. Its representative, Barry Schwartz, told the Special Committee Chair, Paul Meister, that the $24 per share Proposal was now far less favorable to MacAndrews & Forbes — but more attractive to the minority — than when it was first made, because of continued declines in MFW's businesses. Nonetheless, MacAndrews & Forbes would stand behind its $24 offer. Meister responded that he would not recommend the $24 per share Proposal to the Special Committee. Later, after having discussions with Perelman, Schwartz conveyed MacAndrews's "best and final" offer of $25 a share.

At a Special Committee meeting the next day, Evercore opined that the $25 per share *price was fair* based on generally accepted valuation methodologies, including DCF and comparable companies analyses. At its eighth and final meeting on *653 September 10, 2011, the Special Committee, although empowered to say "no," instead unanimously approved and agreed to recommend the Merger at a price of $25 per share.

Influencing the Special Committee's assessment and acceptance of M & F's $25 a share price were developments in both MFW's business and the broader United States economy during the summer of 2011. For example, during the negotiation process, the Special Committee learned of the underperformance of MFW's Global Scholar business unit. The Committee also considered macroeconomic events, including the downgrade of the United States' bond credit rating, and the ongoing turmoil in the financial markets, all of which created financing uncertainties.

In scrutinizing the Special Committee's execution of its broad mandate, the Court of Chancery determined there was no "evidence indicating that the independent members of the special committee did not meet their duty of care . . . ." To the contrary, the Court of Chancery found, the Special Committee "met frequently and was presented with a rich body of financial information relevant to whether and at what *price* a going private transaction was advisable." The Court of Chancery ruled that "the plaintiffs d[id] not make any attempt to show that the MFW Special Committee failed to meet its duty of care . . . ." Based on the undisputed record, the Court of Chancery held that, "there is no triable issue of fact regarding whether the [S]pecial [C]ommittee fulfilled its duty of care." In the context of a controlling stockholder merger, a pretrial determination that the *price* was negotiated by an empowered independent committee that acted with care would shift the burden of persuasion to the plaintiffs under the entire fairness standard of review.

Majority of Minority Stockholder Vote

We now consider the second procedural protection invoked by M & F — the majority-of-the-minority stockholder vote. Consistent with the second condition imposed by M & F at the outset, the Merger was then put before MFW's stockholders for a vote. On November 18, 2011, the stockholders were provided with a proxy statement, which contained the history of the Special Committee's work and recommended that they vote in favor of the transaction at a price of $25 per share.

The proxy statement disclosed, among other things, that the Special Committee had countered M & F's initial $24 per share offer at $30 per share, but only was able to achieve a final offer of $25 per share. The proxy statement disclosed that the MFW business divisions had discussed with Evercore whether the initial projections Evercore received reflected management's latest thinking. It also disclosed that the updated projections were lower. The proxy statement also included the five separate price ranges for the value of MFW's stock that Evercore had generated with its different valuation analyses.

Knowing the proxy statement's disclosures of the background of the Special Committee's work, of Evercore's valuation ranges, and of the analyses supporting Evercore's *fairness opinion,* MFW's stockholders—representing more than 65% of the minority shares—approved the Merger. In the controlling stockholder merger context, it is settled Delaware law that an uncoerced, informed majority-of-the-minority vote, without any other procedural protection, is itself sufficient to shift the burden of persuasion to the plaintiff under the entire fairness standard of review. The Court of Chancery found that "the plaintiffs themselves do not dispute that the majority-of-the-minority vote was fully informed and uncoerced, because they fail to allege any failure of disclosure or any act of coercion."

Both Procedural Protections Established

Based on a highly extensive record, the Court of Chancery concluded that the procedural protections upon which the Merger was conditioned—approval by an independent and empowered Special Committee and by a uncoerced informed majority of MFW's minority stockholders—had *both* been undisputedly established *prior to trial.* We agree and conclude the Defendants' motion for summary judgment was properly granted on all of those issues.

Business Judgment Review Properly Applied

We have determined that the business judgment rule standard of review applies to this controlling stockholder buyout. Under that standard, the claims against the Defendants must be dismissed unless no rational person could have believed that the merger was favorable to MFW's minority stockholders. In this case, it cannot be credibly argued (let alone concluded) that no rational person would find the Merger favorable to MFW's minority stockholders.

Questions

1. How does the Delaware Supreme Court justify its conclusion in *Kahn v. M&F Worldwide Corp.*? Do you agree with its assumptions?

2. Did the shareholders have a meaningful right to vote on the transaction? Was the independent committee truly independent (compare the court's analysis of independence in *Kahn* to the court's analysis of independence in *In re Oracle Corp. Derivative Litigation,* which we discussed in Part 2 of this casebook)?

3. After *Kahn,* how would you advise controlling shareholders (and boards of directors) to structure a freeze-out transaction?

Coggins v. New England Patriots Football Club, Inc.

492 N.E.2d 1112 (Mass. 1986)

Liacos, Justice.

On November 18, 1959, William H. Sullivan, Jr. (Sullivan), purchased an American Football League (AFL) franchise for a professional football team. The team was to be the last of the eight original teams set up to form the AFL (now the American Football Conference of the National Football League). For the franchise, Sullivan paid $25,000. Four months later, Sullivan organized a corporation, the American League Professional Football Team of Boston, Inc. Sullivan contributed his AFL franchise; nine other persons each contributed $25,000. In return, each of the ten investors received 10,000 shares of voting common stock in the corporation. Another four months later, in July, 1960, the corporation sold 120,000 shares of nonvoting common stock to the public at $5 a share.

[By 1974, Sullivan had acquired effective control of the Patriots, at which point he was ousted by the other voting shareholders. He then began his attempt to regain control, which he did by November, 1975, buying all 100,000 voting shares at a price of approximately $102 per share, renaming the corporation the New England Patriots Football Club, Inc. (Old Patriots). He ousted the hostile directors, put in his own people, and resumed control.]

. . . In order to finance this coup, Sullivan borrowed approximately $5,348,000 from the Rhode Island Hospital National Bank and the Lasalle National Bank of Chicago. As a condition of these loans, Sullivan was to use his best efforts to reorganize the Patriots so that the income of the corporation could be devoted to the payment of these personal loans and the assets of the corporation pledged to secure them. At this point they were secured by all of the voting shares held by Sullivan. In order to accomplish in effect the assumption by the corporation of Sullivan's personal obligations, it was necessary, as a matter of corporate law, to eliminate the interest of the nonvoting shares.

On October 20, 1976, Sullivan organized a new corporation called the New Patriots Football Club, Inc. (New Patriots). The board of directors of the Old Patriots and the board of directors of the New Patriots[5] executed an agreement of merger of the two corporations providing that, after the merger, the voting stock of the Old Patriots would be extinguished, the nonvoting stock would be exchanged for cash at the rate of $15 a share, and the name of the New Patriots would be changed to the name formerly used by the Old Patriots.[6] As part of this plan, Sullivan gave the New

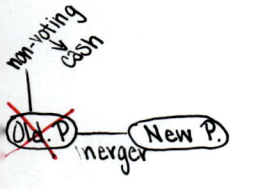

---

5. The two boards were identical. Each member of the board of directors of the Old Patriots (as constituted after Sullivan had regained control) was a member of the board of directors of the New Patriots. Each of the officers of the Old Patriots held the same position with the New Patriots.

6. Additional findings as to the purpose of this merger made by the Federal judge, as adopted by the trial judge, are: "Purported reasons for the merger [were] stated in the [proxy materials]. Three reasons are given: (1) the policy of the [National Football League] to discourage public ownership

Patriots his 100,000 voting shares of the Old Patriots in return for 100% of the New Patriots stock.

General Laws c. 156B, §78(c)(1)(iii), as amended through St. 1976, c. 327, required approval of the merger agreement by a majority vote of each class of affected stock. Approval by the voting class, entirely controlled by Sullivan, was assured. The merger was approved by the class of nonvoting stockholders at a special meeting on December 8, 1976.[7] On January 31, 1977, the merger of the New Patriots and the Old Patriots was consummated.

David A. Coggins (Coggins) was the owner of ten shares of nonvoting stock in the Old Patriots. Coggins, a fan of the Patriots from the time of their formation, was serving in Vietnam in 1967 when he purchased the shares through his brother. Over the years, he followed the fortunes of the team, taking special pride in his status as an owner.[8] When he heard of the proposed merger, Coggins was upset that he could be forced to sell. Coggins voted against the merger and commenced this suit on behalf of those stockholders, who, like himself, believed the transaction to be unfair and illegal. A judge of the Superior Court certified the class as "stockholders of New England Patriots Football Club, Inc. who have voted against the merger . . . but who have neither turned in their shares nor perfected their appraisal rights . . . [and who] desire only to void the merger."

The trial judge found in favor of the Coggins class but determined that the merger should not be undone. Instead, he ruled that the plaintiffs are entitled to rescissory damages, and he ordered that further hearings be held to determine the amount of damages. . . .

We conclude that the trial judge was correct in ruling that the merger was illegal and that the plaintiffs have been wronged. Ordinarily, rescission of the merger would be the appropriate remedy. This merger, however, is now nearly ten years old, and, because an effective and orderly rescission of the merger now is not feasible, we

---

of member football teams, (2) the difficulty in reconciling management's obligations to the NFL with its obligations to public stockholders, and (3) the cost and possible revelation of confidential information resulting from the obligations of publicly owned corporations to file reports with various public bodies. . . . I find, however, that while some of the stated reasons may have been useful by-products of the merger, the true reason for the merger was to enable Sullivan to satisfy his $5,348,000 personal obligation to the banks. The merger would not have occurred for the considerations stated as reasons in the Proxy Statement. . . . The Proxy Statement is an artful attempt to minimize the future profitability of the Patriots and to put a wash of corporate respectability over Sullivan's diversion of the corporation's income for his own purposes."

7. On the date of the meeting, 139,800 shares of nonvoting stock were outstanding, held by approximately 2,400 stockholders. The Sullivan family owned 10,826 shares. Of the remaining 128,974, a total of 71,644 voted in favor of the merger, 22,795 did not vote, and 34,535 voted against. The plaintiffs in this case are stockholders of 2,291 of the 34,535 voting against the merger.

Prior to the 1976 amendment of G. L. c. 156B, §78(c)(1)(iii), that section required a two-thirds vote of approval for a merger from each class of stock. The two-thirds requirement was reinstated in 1981 by St. 1981, c. 298, §4.

8. It was, in part, the goal of the Old Patriots, in offering stock to the public, to generate loyal fans.

remand the case for proceedings to determine the appropriate monetary damages to compensate the plaintiffs. . . .

Scope of Judicial Review. In deciding this case, we address an important corporate law question: What approach will a Massachusetts court reviewing a cash freeze-out merger employ? This question has been considered by courts in a number of other States.

The parties have urged us to consider the views of a court with great experience in such matters, the Supreme Court of Delaware. We note that the Delaware court announced one test in 1977, but recently has changed to another.[10] In *Singer v. Magnavox Co.*, the Delaware court established the so-called "business-purpose" test, holding that controlling stockholders violate their fiduciary duties when they "cause a merger to be made for the sole purpose of eliminating a minority on a cash-out basis." In 1983, Delaware jettisoned the business-purpose test, satisfied that the "fairness" test "long . . . applicable to parent-subsidiary mergers, *Sterling v. Mayflower Hotel Corp.*, Del. Ch., the expanded appraisal remedy now available to stockholders, and the broad discretion of the Chancellor to fashion such relief as the facts of a given case may dictate" provided sufficient protection to the frozen-out minority. *Weinberger v. UOP, Inc.*[11] "The requirement of fairness is unflinching in its demand that where one stands on both sides of a transaction, he has the burden of establishing its entire fairness, sufficient to pass the test of careful scrutiny by the courts." "The concept of fairness has two basic aspects: fair dealing and fair price." We note that the "fairness" test to which the Delaware court now has adhered is, as we later show, closely related to the views expressed in our decisions. Unlike the Delaware court, however, we believe that the "business-purpose" test is an additional useful means under our statutes and case law for examining a transaction in which a controlling stockholder eliminates the minority interest in a corporation. Cf. *Wilkes v. Springside Nursing Home, Inc.* This concept of fair dealing is not limited to close corporations but applies to judicial review of cash freeze-out mergers. See *Horizon House-Microwave, Inc. v. Bazzy*.

The defendants argue that judicial review of a merger cannot be invoked by disgruntled stockholders, absent illegal or fraudulent conduct. They rely on G.L. c. 156B, § 98 (1984 ed.).[12] In the defendants' view, "the Superior Court's finding of liability was premised solely on the claimed inadequacy of the offering price." Any dispute

---

10. We are not bound, of course, in our interpretation of Massachusetts law by decisions of the courts of our sister States interpreting their laws. We have said before, however, that we consider such decisions instructive. *Piemonte v. New Boston Garden Corp.*

11. See Note, *Delaware Improves Its Treatment of Freezeout Mergers: Weinberger v. UOP, Inc.*, 25 B.C.L. Rev. 685 (1984). That the new Delaware approach is not without its difficulties is illustrated by the opinion in *Rabkin v. Philip A. Hunt Chem. Corp.*

12. "The enforcement by a stockholder of his right to receive payment for his shares in the manner provided in this chapter shall be an exclusive remedy except that this chapter shall not exclude the right of such stockholder to bring or maintain an appropriate proceeding to obtain relief on the ground that such corporate action will be or is illegal or fraudulent as to him." G. L. c. 156B, § 98.

over offering price, they urge, must be resolved solely through the statutory remedy of appraisal.

We have held in regard to so called "close corporations" that the statute does not divest the courts of their equitable jurisdiction to assure that the conduct of controlling stockholders does not violate the fiduciary principles governing the relationship between majority and minority stockholders. "Where the director's duty of loyalty to the corporation is in conflict with his self-interest the court will vigorously scrutinize the situation." *American Discount Corp. v. Kaitz*. The court is justified in exercising its equitable power when a violation of fiduciary duty is claimed.

The dangers of self-dealing and abuse of fiduciary duty are greatest in freeze-out situations like the Patriots merger, where a controlling stockholder and corporate director chooses to eliminate public ownership.[14] It is in these cases that a judge should examine with closest scrutiny the motives and the behavior of the controlling stockholder. A showing of compliance with statutory procedures is an insufficient substitute for the inquiry of the courts when a minority stockholder claims that the corporate action "will be or is illegal or fraudulent as to him." G.L. c. 156B, §98. *Leader v. Hycor, Inc.* (judicial review may be had of claims of breach of fiduciary duty and unfairness).

A controlling stockholder who is also a director standing on both sides of the transaction bears the burden of showing that the transaction does not violate fiduciary obligations. . . . Judicial inquiry into a freeze-out merger in technical compliance with the statute may be appropriate, and the dissenting stockholders are not limited to the statutory remedy of judicial appraisal where violations of fiduciary duties are found.

Factors in judicial review. The defendants concentrate their arguments on the finding of the Superior Court judge that the offered price for nonvoting shares was inadequate. They claim that his conclusion that rescissory damages are due these plaintiffs is based wholly on a finding of price inadequacy. The trial judge, however, considered the totality of the circumstances, including the purpose of the merger, the accuracy and adequacy of disclosure in connection with the merger, and the fairness of the price. The trial judge correctly considered the totality of circumstances, even though he failed to attach adequate significance to each of these factors and to structure them correctly in his analysis.

Judicial scrutiny should begin with recognition of the basic principle that the duty of a corporate director must be to further the legitimate goals of the corporation. The result of a freeze-out merger is the elimination of public ownership in the corporation. The controlling faction increases its equity from a majority to 100%, using corporate processes and corporate assets. The corporate directors who benefit from this transfer of ownership must demonstrate how the legitimate goals of the

---

14. All freeze-out mergers are not alike. See Brudney & Chirelstein, *A Restatement of Corporate Freezeouts*, 87 Yale L.J. 1354, 1356, and sources cited (1978).

corporation are furthered. A director of a corporation violates his fiduciary duty when he uses the corporation for his or his family's personal benefit in a manner detrimental to the corporation. Because the danger of abuse of fiduciary duty is especially great in a freeze-out merger, the court must be satisfied that the freeze-out was for the advancement of a legitimate corporate purpose. If satisfied that elimination of public ownership is in furtherance of a business purpose, the court should then proceed to determine if the transaction was fair by examining the totality of the circumstances.

The plaintiffs here adequately alleged that the merger of the Old Patriots and New Patriots was a freeze-out merger undertaken for no legitimate business purpose, but merely for the personal benefit of Sullivan. While we have recognized the right to "selfish ownership" in a corporation, such a right must be balanced against the concept of the majority stockholder's fiduciary obligation to the minority stockholders. *Wilkes v. Springside Nursing Home, Inc.* Consequently, the defendants bear the burden of proving, first, that the merger was for a legitimate business purpose, and, second, that, considering the totality of the circumstances, it was fair to the minority.

The decision of the Superior Court judge includes a finding that "the defendants have failed to demonstrate that the merger served any valid corporate objective unrelated to the personal interests of the majority shareholders. It thus appears that the sole reason for the merger was to effectuate a restructuring of the Patriots that would enable the repayment of the [personal] indebtedness incurred by Sullivan. . . ." The trial judge considered the defendants' claims that the policy of the National Football League (NFL) requiring majority ownership by a single individual or family made it necessary to eliminate public ownership. He found that "the stock ownership of the Patriots as it existed just prior to the merger fully satisfied the rationale underlying the policy as expressed by NFL Commissioner Pete Rozelle. Having acquired 100% control of the voting common stock of the Patriots, Sullivan possessed unquestionable authority to act on behalf of the franchise at League meetings and effectively foreclosed the possible recurrence of the internal management disputes that had existed in 1974. Moreover, as the proxy statement itself notes, the Old Patriots were under no legal compulsion to eliminate public ownership." Likewise, the defendants did not succeed in showing a conflict between the interests of the league owners and the Old Patriots' stockholders. We perceive no error in these findings. They are fully supported by the evidence. Under the approach we set forth above, there is no need to consider further the elements of fairness of a transaction that is not related to a valid corporate purpose.

Remedy. The plaintiffs are entitled to relief. They argue that the appropriate relief is rescission of the merger and restoration of the parties to their positions of 1976. We agree that the normally appropriate remedy for an impermissible freeze-out merger is rescission. Because Massachusetts statutes do not bar a cash freeze-out, however, numerous third parties relied in good faith on the outcome of the merger. The trial judge concluded that the expectations of those parties should not be upset, and so chose to award damages rather than rescission.

We recognize that, because rescission is an equitable remedy, the circumstances of a particular case may not favor its employment. The goals of a remedy instituted after a finding that a merger did not serve the corporate purpose should include furthering the interests of the corporation. Ordinarily, we would remand with instructions for the trial judge to determine whether rescission would be in the corporation's best interests, but such a remedy does not appear to be equitable at this time. This litigation has gone on for many years. There is yet at least another related case pending (in the Federal District Court). Furthermore, other factors weigh against rescission. The passage of time has made the 1976 position of the parties difficult, if not impossible, to restore. A substantial number of former stockholders have chosen other courses and should not be forced back into the Patriots corporation. In these circumstances the interests of the corporation and of the plaintiffs will be furthered best by limiting the plaintiffs' remedy to an assessment of damages.

We do not think it appropriate, however, to award damages based on a 1976 appraisal value. To do so would make this suit a nullity, leaving the plaintiffs with no effective remedy except appraisal, a position we have already rejected. Rescissory damages must be determined based on the present value of the Patriots, that is, what the stockholders would have if the merger were rescinded. Determination of the value of a unique property like the Patriots requires specialized expertise, and, while the trial judge is entitled to reach his own conclusion as to value, the credibility of testimony on value will depend in part on the familiarity of the witness with property of this kind. On remand, the judge is to take further evidence on the present value of the Old Patriots on the theory that the merger had not taken place. Each share of the Coggins class is to receive, as rescissory damages, its aliquot share of the present assets.

The trial judge dismissed the plaintiffs' claims against the individual defendants based on waste of corporate assets. The remedy we order is intended to give the plaintiffs what they would have if the merger were undone and the corporation were put back together again. The trial judge's finding that the sole purpose of the merger was the personal financial benefit of William H. Sullivan, Jr., and the use of corporate assets to accomplish this impermissible purpose, leads inescapably to the conclusion that part of what the plaintiffs otherwise would have benefited by, was removed from the corporation by the individual defendants. We reverse the dismissal of the claim for waste of corporate assets and remand this question to the trial court. The present value of the Patriots, as determined on remand, should include the amount wrongfully removed or diverted from the corporate coffers by the individual defendants. . . .

Summary. The freeze-out merger accomplished by William H. Sullivan, Jr., was designed for his own personal benefit to eliminate the interests of the Patriots' minority stockholders. The merger did not further the interests of the corporation and therefore was a violation of Sullivan's fiduciary duty to the minority stockholders, and so was impermissible. In most cases we would turn to rescission as the appropriate remedy. In the circumstances of this case, however, rescission would be an inequitable solution. Therefore, we remand for a determination of the present value of the nonvoting stock, as though the merger were rescinded. The claim for waste of corporate assets brought against the individual defendants is reinstated. Those stockholders who voted against the merger, who did not turn in their shares, who did not perfect their appraisal rights, but who are part of the *Coggins* class, are to receive damages in the amount their stock would be worth today, plus interest at the statutory rate. . . .

The case is remanded to the Superior Court for further proceedings consistent with this opinion.

Questions

1. In *Weinberger v. UOP*, the Delaware Supreme Court, after going back and forth for years, eliminated the business purpose test in freeze-out mergers, reasoning that the entire fairness test was an adequate remedy. Do you agree?

2. Do the differences in approach between *Weinberger* and *Coggins v. New England Patriots Football Club, Inc.* suggest different underlying conceptions of the corporation and its role in society? Do they have different effects on the way that shareholders may view the corporation?

3. One of the problems in corporate governance stems from the "rational apathy" shareholders have with respect to participating in such things as shareholder votes. One reason for this apathy is the contemporary emphasis on diversifying shareholder portfolios and investor self-protection (see the reasoning in *Joy v. North* and our discussion of that case in Part 2). While it is true that many corporations do not conduct the kinds of businesses that engender peculiar loyalty, some, like the Patriots, do. More to the point, if it were not so easy for corporations to "dismiss" their shareholders, or if courts treated the corporation as something more than its stock price, perhaps shareholders would take a greater interest in governance matters in a way that might encourage long-term shareholding and patient capital, with the dual benefits of increased shareholder monitoring and insulation for managers to take a longer-term management perspective. The current system of market monitoring has its virtues but, as corporate scandals, like the ones of the early 2000s demonstrate, that model has its limitations.

The next case involves a type of transaction referred to as a short-form merger. Section 253 of the Delaware General Corporation Law provides that if a corporation owns at least 90% of all classes of stock of another corporation, it can, simply by resolution of the board of directors of the parent corporation and the filing of a certificate of ownership and merger with the secretary of state, merge the subsidiary corporation into the parent corporation, thereby eliminating the need for a shareholder vote. (If the parent corporation merges into the subsidiary, shareholder approval of the parent corporation is required (although not of the subsidiary corporation).) Other statutes have similar provisions. As *Glassman* illustrates, this type of transaction raises its own fiduciary issues.

Glassman v. Unocal Exploration Corp.
777 A.2d 242 (Del. 2001)

BERGER, Justice

. . .

I. Factual and Procedural Background

Unocal Corporation is an earth resources company primarily engaged in the exploration for and production of crude oil and natural gas. At the time of the merger at issue, Unocal owned approximately 96% of the stock of Unocal Exploration Corporation ("UXC"), an oil and gas company operating in and around the Gulf of Mexico. In 1991, low natural gas prices caused a drop in both companies' revenues and earnings. Unocal investigated areas of possible cost savings and decided that, by eliminating the UXC minority, it would reduce taxes and overhead expenses.

In December 1991 the boards of Unocal and UXC appointed special committees to consider a possible merger. The UXC committee consisted of three directors who, although also directors of Unocal, were not officers or employees of the parent company. The UXC committee retained financial and legal advisors and met four times before agreeing to a merger exchange ratio of .54 shares of Unocal stock for each share of UXC. Unocal and UXC announced the merger on February 24, 1992, and it was effected, pursuant to 8 Del. C. § 253, on May 2, 1992. The Notice of Merger and Prospectus stated the terms of the merger and advised the former UXC stockholders of their appraisal rights.

Plaintiffs filed this class action, on behalf of UXC's minority stockholders, on the day the merger was announced. They asserted, among other claims, that Unocal and its directors breached their fiduciary duties of entire fairness and full disclosure. The Court of Chancery conducted a two day trial and held that: (i) the Prospectus did not contain any material misstatements or omissions; (ii) the entire fairness standard does not control in a short-form merger; and (iii) plaintiffs' exclusive remedy in this case was appraisal. The decision of the Court of Chancery is affirmed.

II. Discussion

The short-form merger statute, as enacted in 1937, authorized a parent corporation to merge with its wholly-owned subsidiary by filing and recording a certificate evidencing the parent's ownership and its merger resolution. In 1957, the statute was expanded to include parent/subsidiary mergers where the parent company owns at least 90% of the stock of the subsidiary. The 1957 amendment also made it possible, for the first time and only in a short-form merger, to pay the minority cash for their shares, thereby eliminating their ownership interest in the company. . . .

[The court then reviewed the history of Delaware case law of remedies under the short-form merger statute.]

... In *Rabkin v. Philip A. Hunt Chemical Corp.*, however, the Court dispelled that view [articulated in *Weinberger* that appraisal was the exclusive remedy in cases of parent-subsidiary mergers] ... holding that ... appraisal is the exclusive remedy only if stockholders' complaints are limited to "judgmental factors of valuation."

Rabkin, through its interpretation of *Weinberger*, effectively eliminated appraisal as the exclusive remedy for any claim alleging breach of the duty of entire fairness. But *Rabkin* involved a long-form merger, and the Court did not discuss, in that case or any others, how its refinement of *Weinberger* impacted short-form mergers. . . .

Mindful of this history, we must decide whether a minority stockholder may challenge a short-form merger by seeking equitable relief through an entire fairness claim. Under settled principles, a parent corporation and its directors undertaking a short-form merger are self-dealing fiduciaries who should be required to establish entire fairness, including fair dealing and fair price. The problem is that § 253 authorizes a summary procedure that is inconsistent with any reasonable notion of fair dealing. In a short-form merger, there is no agreement of merger negotiated by two companies; there is only a unilateral act — a decision by the parent company that its 90% owned subsidiary shall no longer exist as a separate entity. The minority stockholders receive no advance notice of the merger; their directors do not consider or approve it; and there is no vote. Those who object are given the right to obtain fair value for their shares through appraisal.

The equitable claim plainly conflicts with the statute. If a corporate fiduciary follows the truncated process authorized by § 253, it will not be able to establish the fair dealing prong of entire fairness. If, instead, the corporate fiduciary sets up negotiating committees, hires independent financial and legal experts, etc., then it will have lost the very benefit provided by the statute — a simple, fast and inexpensive process for accomplishing a merger. We resolve this conflict by giving effect the intent of the General Assembly. In order to serve its purpose, § 253 must be construed to obviate the requirement to establish entire fairness.

Thus, we ... hold that, absent fraud or illegality, appraisal is the exclusive remedy available to a minority stockholder who objects to a short-form merger. In doing so, we also reaffirm *Weinberger's* statements about the scope of appraisal. The determination of fair value must be based on *all* relevant factors, including damages and elements of future value, where appropriate. So, for example, if the merger was timed to take advantage of a depressed market, or a low point in the company's cyclical earnings, or to precede an anticipated positive development, the appraised value may be adjusted to account for those factors. We recognize that these are the types of issues frequently raised in entire fairness claims, and we have held that claims for unfair dealing cannot be litigated in an appraisal. But our prior holdings simply explained that equitable claims may not be engrafted onto a statutory appraisal proceeding; stockholders may not receive rescissionary relief in an appraisal. Those decisions should not be read to restrict the elements of value that properly may be considered in an appraisal.

Although fiduciaries are not required to establish entire fairness in a short-form merger, the duty of full disclosure remains, in the context of this request for stockholder action. Where the only choice for the minority stockholders is whether to accept the merger consideration or seek appraisal, they must be given all the factual information that is material to that decision. The Court of Chancery carefully considered plaintiffs' disclosure claims and applied settled law in rejecting them. We affirm this aspect of the appeal on the basis of the trial court's decision. . . .

Questions

1. The court reasons that Unocal's board owed no fiduciary duties to the minority shareholder of UXC because, in effect, the statute required no action by the board other than to adopt a resolution of merger and file a certificate. As a result, the concept of fair dealing was inapplicable. Do you agree with this reasoning?

2. The short-form merger statute permits the parent's board to eliminate the subsidiary's minority shareholders, leaving the minority powerless except for an appraisal proceeding (which will only involve the issue of fair price). Recall our discussion of the origins of fiduciary duty—the need to restrain an actor with power from abusing that power at the expense of an actor without power. Does the appraisal action left by *Glassman* sufficiently create counterbalancing power in the minority shareholders of UXC to obviate the need for fiduciary duty? Is the court's conception of fair dealing really consistent with its expression of that concept in *Weinberger v. UOP*?

3. Why is there no claim against the UXC board? How does your answer to this question affect your answers to Question 2?

Mergers are not the only way to effectuate freeze-outs. Sometimes a freeze-out is hiding right in a corporation's capital structure. The following case, cited by the court in *Coggins v. New England Patriots Football Club, Inc.*, illustrates such an approach as well as the legal test applied to evaluate its equitable legitimacy.

Leader v. Hycor, Inc.
479 N.E.2d 173 (Mass. 1985)

NOLAN, Justice

The plaintiffs, former minority shareholders of the defendant corporation, appeal from a judgment entered against them after a trial before a judge of the Superior Court. Their suit challenged actions taken by the five majority shareholders, who also were named as defendants, which resulted in the forced redemption of all minority stock. On appeal, the plaintiffs argue that (1) the trial judge erred in ruling that the five majority shareholders, who also constituted the entire board of directors of Hycor, Inc., did not violate their fiduciary duty of loyalty to the minority shareholders when they effectuated a "recapitalization" of the corporation; and (2) the trial judge erred in ruling that the five dollar per share price, paid to former minority shareholders for their stock, was "consistent with various indicia used to determine the value of closely-held stock." For the reasons set forth below, we reverse and remand the case for further consideration of the price issue.

The relevant facts may be summarized as follows. Hycor, Inc. (Hycor), is a Massachusetts corporation that was organized in 1967 by the five individual defendants (the majority shareholders). Each of the majority shareholders has been a member of Hycor's board of directors, and an employee of the corporation, since its organization. Hycor's business primarily involves general scientific research and development in the field of military defense. Hycor specializes in the design and manufacture of electronic radar and optical countermeasure systems.

The majority shareholders and their family members owned all of Hycor's stock from May, 1967, when the corporation was organized, until February, 1969. At that time, Hycor made a public offering of 75,000 shares of stock, at four dollars a share, in an effort to raise capital. After the public offering, there were 525,000 shares of stock issued and outstanding. The majority shareholders and their families owned approximately 440,000 shares, or eighty-five percent, of the outstanding stock. The stock owned by the majority shareholders was not registered under the Federal Securities Act of 1933, and therefore, sale of this stock was restricted. A notation to this effect appeared on the stock certificates owned by the majority shareholders.

Between 1967 and 1980, Hycor was profitable in every fiscal year except one, 1971. In June of 1979, discussions took place between some of the majority shareholders and Hycor's corporate counsel. These discussions concerned the possibility of the defendants' acquiring 100 per cent ownership of the Hycor stock. On February 4, 1980, the majority shareholders, acting as directors of Hycor, mailed a written "Notice of Special Meeting of Stockholders" to be held at Hycor's offices on February 13, 1980. The notice stated that the purpose of the meeting was to vote on a recapitalization proposal. Under the terms of this proposal, Hycor's articles of organization would be amended to reduce the authorized capital stock from two million shares with a par value of one cent, to five hundred shares, with a par value of forty dollars. In effect, each "old" share would be reduced to 1/4,000 of a "new" share. Furthermore, no fractional shares of Hycor stock would be recognized after the recapitalization. Each holder of a fractional share would receive five dollars upon surrender of each "old" share certificate.

A letter from defendant Hyman, as president of Hycor, accompanied this notice. Hyman stated the reasons for the proposed recapitalization to be "the somewhat disappointing market history of the stock" and that "dividends . . . have not represented a significant return on a $4.00 investment." He indicated that the board of directors had no plans to increase dividends. Hyman also noted that there had been very limited trading in the stock.

On February 13, 1980, there were 517,000 shares of Hycor stock issued and outstanding. Approximately 81 per cent of these shares were owned by the majority shareholders and their families. The remaining shares were owned by 331 shareholders (the minority shareholders). Each minority shareholder owned less than 4,000 shares of stock. The special meeting of shareholders was held on this date. The four plaintiffs and one other minority shareholder appeared at the meeting and objected to the recapitalization proposal and the offer price of five dollars per share. Each of the named plaintiffs voted against the proposed recapitalization. The majority shareholders voted in favor of the plan; therefore, the change in the articles of organization was approved.

On April 24, 1980, the minority shareholders commenced this action. They alleged that the defendants had acted fraudulently, and had misrepresented the basis for the proposed amendment to the articles of organization in order to induce the plaintiffs to approve the change. The plaintiffs also alleged that the actions of the defendants constituted a breach of the fiduciary duty that the defendants owed to the corporation's minority shareholders, and that the defendants failed to give proper notice to the minority shareholders as required by G. L. c. 156B, § 87. The plaintiffs sought an appraisal of the fair market value of their shares in Hycor on the date that the amendments to the Articles of Organization became effective. They asked that damages be awarded to reflect accurately this value. Alternatively, the plaintiffs asked that the vote of the shareholders be declared a nullity and set aside, arguing that the actions of the majority constituted a breach of fiduciary duty and, furthermore, lacked a fundamental corporate purpose. The plaintiffs also asked the court to award punitive damages, costs, interest, and reasonable attorneys' fees. . . .

After trial, the judge ordered judgment entered for the defendants. He refused to find that "[t]here was no legitimate business purpose for the recapitalization," characterizing the plaintiffs' assertions to this effect as "[u]nsubstantiated by the evidence." The judge denied the plaintiffs' request for findings that the procedure used by the majority shareholders to effectuate the recapitalization was "unfair and a clear abuse of corporate power and control." Furthermore, he was not persuaded that "[a]ny arguable business purpose for the recapitalization could have been achieved by less drastic alternatives." Finally, he ruled that the five dollars per share price offered to the minority shareholders "was fair and reasonable and consistent with various indicia used to determine the value of closely held stock."

1. *Validity of the recapitalization.* The plaintiffs claim that the judge implicitly ruled that, as a matter of law, the recapitalization was fair and not an abuse of corporate power. They challenge this ruling, arguing that it constituted judicial approval of patently wrongful conduct by the majority shareholders, who violated their fiduciary duty of loyalty to the minority shareholders. Additionally, the plaintiffs argue that the ruling implies that the recapitalization was not a "freezing-out" of minority interests. The plaintiffs conclude that the judge's ruling was "manifest error."

A. *Statutory basis for recapitalization.* The minority shareholders characterize the actions of the majority shareholders as a "freeze out" of minority shareholders which lacked a legitimate business purpose. We turn first to the statutory provisions cited by the majority shareholders as authorizing the transaction at issue. General Laws c. 156B, § 71, as appearing in St. 1981, c. 298, § 1, provides, in relevant part, that "[a] corporation may . . . authorize, at a meeting duly called for the purpose, by vote of two-thirds of each class of stock outstanding and entitled to vote thereon or, if the articles of organization so provide, by vote of a lesser proportion but not less than a majority of each class of stock outstanding and entitled to vote thereon, any amendment of its articles of organization; provided, only, that any provision added to or changes made in its articles of organization by such amendment could have been included in, and any provision deleted thereby could have been omitted from, original articles of organization filed at the time of such meeting." Section 28 of that chapter permits a corporation to issue fractional shares of stock. The statute also authorizes the payment of cash in lieu of fractional share interests.

Pursuant to these statutory provisions, the majority shareholders amended the corporation's articles of organization, effectuating a recapitalization of Hycor and authorizing the payment of cash in exchange for fractional shares. This type of transaction, commonly described as a "reverse stock split," is one method employed by majority shareholders to eliminate public ownership in a company.

The defendants argue that they proceeded in accordance with the applicable corporate statutes in their attempt to return Hycor to private status. . . . Setting aside the issues of fairness of price and lack of corporate purpose, which we discuss below, we decide that the majority shareholders acted in compliance with the relevant portions of the Massachusetts corporation law when they effectuated the transaction at issue.

B. *Judicial review of the transaction.* Having decided that the transaction, on its face, was permissible under the provisions of the statute governing Massachusetts corporations, we turn to the plaintiffs' claims of breach of fiduciary duty and unfairness. Despite apparent compliance with statutory requirements, a transaction such as the one at issue is still subject to judicial scrutiny on these grounds. At this point, however, it is not enough for those challenging such a transaction merely to label it a "freezeout." . . . At the same time, however, we recognize that courts must avoid an "automatic stamp of approval of that which is manifestly inequitable."

We begin our analysis by considering the nature of the duty that the defendants owed to the plaintiffs under these circumstances. The plaintiffs contend that Hycor was a close corporation, and thus the defendants, as directors and majority shareholders, owed the plaintiffs a duty of "utmost good faith and loyalty." *Donahue v. Rodd Electrotype Co. of New England, Inc.* The defendants argue that Hycor was not a close corporation, and suggest that the defendants, as directors and stockholders of Hycor, were required to act in good faith and with inherent fairness. The defendants further state, however, that even if Hycor were a close corporation, the defendants met their burden of proving that they acted with the utmost good faith and loyalty.

In ruling on the fairness of the price that the defendants offered to the plaintiffs in exchange for their shares of stock, the judge referred to "indicia used to determine the value of closely held stock." It appears, therefore, that he considered Hycor to be a close corporation. We need not decide this issue.

[The court then reviewed *Donahue v. Rodd Electrotype* and *Wilkes v. Springside Nursing Home,* both of which are discussed in Part 3, Section II.C.]

In the case before us, the judge ruled that the evidence fell short of substantiating the plaintiffs' claim that the recapitalization was not designed to achieve a legitimate business purpose. We find no error in this ruling. The evidence presented by the defendants on this issue included the testimony of Hycor's president, Hyman, and its corporate counsel, Mr. Butterworth. Hyman testified that the main reason behind the recapitalization was not to eliminate all the public stockholders, but was related to the "dreadful market history of the stock." He stated that, while Hycor had the responsibilities of a public company, it did not enjoy the benefits of such status. Specifically, he noted the lack of a ready market for Hycor stock. Mr. Butterworth's testimony supported these assertions. We are satisfied that, based upon the evidence before him, the judge's decision was proper.

In the judge's opinion, the plaintiffs failed to establish that "[a]ny arguable business purpose for the recapitalization could have been achieved by less drastic alternatives." On appeal, the plaintiffs suggest that the "business purpose" at issue was avoiding the annoyance of telephone calls directed to the company's president concerning the purchase and sale of Hycor stock. They argue that less drastic means existed to eliminate this problem. However, the plaintiffs' argument ignores evidence that Hycor's status as a public company required the company to comply with various statutory duties, yet the company did not enjoy a ready market for its stock. We agree that the plaintiffs failed to carry their burden of establishing that less drastic alternatives were available to effectuate the defendants' legitimate business purpose.

2. *Fairness of price.* [The court held that the trial court's opinion contained inadequate information for it to judge the fairness of the price.]

. . . After reviewing the record before us, we deem it necessary to remand this case so that the judge may explicate the grounds for his conclusion that the price offered by the defendants was fair and reasonable. We are unable, on this record, to ascertain the basis for the judge's conclusion.

[Noting *Weinberger* and *Piemonte v. New Boston Garden*, the court nonetheless held that the Delaware block method of valuation remained good law in Massachusetts.]

We remand the case, solely with respect to the fairness of the price, for proceedings consistent with this opinion.

Questions

1. The Delaware Block Method of valuing stock is a stylized methodology in which each side presents expert evidence of the corporation's value in three different flavors: book value, earnings value (which is capitalized earnings), and market value

(which is the trading price of stock on the market and obviously cannot be used to value closely-held corporations). The judge has virtually complete discretion to choose these values (not bound by expert testimony) and takes a weighted average of them based upon her assessment of the relative reliability of each valuation measure in the context of the particular case. What are the advantages, and to whom, of this method of valuation over the open-ended approach of the Delaware Supreme Court in *Weinberger v. UOP*?

2. When valuing minority shares, whether in a freeze-out situation or an ordinary appraisal proceeding, two additional factors may come into play after fair value is established using the Delaware Block Method, the dividend discount method, or any other methodology. These are the questions of whether the value per share thus determined ought to be discounted for lack of marketability and for minority status. The first situation, marketability discount, applies where the corporation is closely held (and the shares of which are, by definition, not readily marketable) and where the trading market for the stock is very thin, which can occur when most of the stock is owned by a single person or entity or where, for a variety of reasons, only a small amount of stock has been publicly issued. Minority discounts, in one way of thinking, ought never to apply in the case of a public corporation because, by definition, all of the shares are minority shares (that is, there is no controlling interest). Minority discounts tend to be reserved for cases like those studied in Part 3, Section III, where there is a controlling stockholder or group of stockholders, or in the close corporation context where the same situation exists. While a minority discount ostensibly reflects a lack of control, the fact that courts discount the value of shares for that lack of control obviously implies an economic benefit to having control. Think back to the controlling stockholder cases as well as the close corporation cases we presented in Part 3. What is the economic benefit of control? Based on your answer, does it seem fair to discount a minority share for lacking control?

Section III
Tender Offers and Hostile Takeovers

Mergers and sales of assets are statutorily authorized transactions which require board approval before being submitted to shareholder vote. Tender offers, or takeovers as they are often called, while they can also result in changes in corporate control, are "deals" with the shareholders. Take, for example, Greenacres Corporation, a closely held corporation, the entire capital stock of which is owned by Jonathan. Jonathan would like to sell the company, and Michael is interested in acquiring it. Jonathan and Michael agree on a price, and it is easiest for Michael to purchase the stock of Greenacres. In selling Michael the stock, Jonathan is acting solely as a stockholder, not as a director or officer. After the sale, Greenacres as a corporation will remain unchanged, and all of the stock will be owned by Michael instead of Jonathan.

A tender offer is exactly the same thing only on a grander scale (and carefully regulated by the Securities Exchange Act of 1934). The difference is that in a tender offer, Greenacres is replaced by a publicly held corporation with shareholders who are, typically, more or less widely dispersed (although as you will see, in some of the cases that follow, the presence of a controlling shareholder or group of shareholders can affect the way in which the takeover is conducted. The presence of a large block of institutional investors can also make a difference). In order to acquire Greenacres' stock, Michael has several options:

(1) He could buy it on the open market. Once he reaches 5% ownership, Rule 13d-1, promulgated under section 13(d) of the Securities Exchange Act, requires him publicly to disclose that fact, as well as the purpose of the purchase and any plans he might have for corporate transactions involving Greenacres, by filing a Schedule 13D within 10 days of the acquisition. This might upset Greenacres' board and motivate them to take some sort of protective action. His large-scale buying, plus his ownership announcement and (under the circumstances) his stated intention to keep buying, will also drive up the price of Greenacres stock. Or,

(2) He could buy a few shares of Greenacres, obtain a copy of the shareholders' list, and go door to door, asking the Greenacres stockholders to commit to sell him their stock (and hope that his intended purchases remain secret). This, at a minimum and without regard to any possible legal difficulties, seems rather cumbersome. Or,

(3) He could take out an ad in *The New York Times, The Wall Street Journal*, and other papers of his choosing, announcing his intention to buy any and all shares of Greenacres and the price and form of consideration at which he is offering to buy the shares. Not only does this have the virtue of surprising Greenacres' board (although he must keep the offer open for twenty business days during which, as we shall see, the board, not to mention competing bidders, can cause their share of mischief), it also has the virtue of capping the price he's willing to pay for the stock. But it has the counterbalancing disadvantage of notifying other potential bidders that Greenacres might be worth buying at Michael's suggested price, thereby perhaps encouraging competing bids which will force Michael, if he really, really wants to buy Greenacres, to up his offering price.

When Michael engages in this last process, complying as he must with the various requirements of the securities laws, he is engaged in a tender offer. If the Greenacres board is happy with Michael's offer and encourages the shareholders to accept it, we call this a friendly takeover. If they're opposed and do their best to fight it, it is a hostile takeover. In this section, we focus on hostile takeovers because that is when the directors of Greenacres and state corporate governance law come into play.

The Delaware Chancery Court wrote, in *In re Siliconix*: "[U]nder the corporation law, a board of directors which is given the critical role of initiating and recommending a merger to the shareholders (see 8 Del. C. § 251) traditionally has been accorded no statutory role whatsoever with respect to a public tender offer for even a controlling number of shares." Consider this statement as you read the cases in this section.

A. *Unocal* / *Revlon* Duties

Unocal Corporation v. Mesa Petroleum Co.
493 A.2d 946 (Del. 1985)

MOORE, Justice

We confront an issue of first impression in Delaware—the validity of a corporation's self-tender for its own shares which excludes from participation a stockholder making a hostile tender offer for the company's stock.

The Court of Chancery granted a preliminary injunction to the plaintiffs, Mesa Petroleum Co., Mesa Asset Co., Mesa Partners II, and Mesa Eastern, Inc. (collectively "Mesa"),[1] enjoining an exchange offer of the defendant, Unocal Corporation (Unocal) for its own stock. The trial court concluded that a selective exchange offer, excluding Mesa, was legally impermissible. We cannot agree with such a blanket rule. The factual findings of the Vice Chancellor, fully supported by the record, establish that Unocal's board, consisting of a majority of independent directors, acted in good faith, and after reasonable investigation found that Mesa's tender offer was both inadequate and coercive. Under the circumstances the board had both the power and duty to oppose a bid it perceived to be harmful to the corporate enterprise. On this record we are satisfied that the device Unocal adopted is reasonable in relation to the threat posed, and that the board acted in the proper exercise of sound business judgment. We will not substitute our views for those of the board if the latter's decision can be "attributed to any rational business purpose." *Sinclair Oil Corp. v. Levien*, Del. Supr. Accordingly, we reverse the decision of the Court of Chancery and order the preliminary injunction vacated.

I

The factual background of this matter bears a significant relationship to its ultimate outcome.

On April 8, 1985, Mesa, the owner of approximately 13% of Unocal's stock, commenced a two-tier "front loaded" cash tender offer for 64 million shares, or approximately 37%, of Unocal's outstanding stock at a price of $54 per share. The "back-end" was designed to eliminate the remaining publicly held shares by an exchange of

---

1. T. Boone Pickens, Jr., is President and Chairman of the Board of Mesa Petroleum and President of Mesa Asset and controls the related Mesa entities.

securities purportedly worth $54 per share. However, pursuant to an order entered by the United States District Court for the Central District of California on April 26, 1985, Mesa issued a supplemental proxy statement to Unocal's stockholders disclosing that the securities offered in the second-step merger would be highly subordinated, and that Unocal's capitalization would differ significantly from its present structure. Unocal has rather aptly termed such securities "junk bonds".

Unocal's board consists of eight independent outside directors and six insiders. It met on April 13, 1985, to consider the Mesa tender offer. Thirteen directors were present, and the meeting lasted nine and one-half hours. The directors were given no agenda or written materials prior to the session. However, detailed presentations were made by legal counsel regarding the board's obligations under both Delaware corporate law and the federal securities laws. The board then received a presentation from Peter Sachs on behalf of Goldman Sachs & Co. (Goldman Sachs) and Dillon, Read & Co. (Dillon Read) discussing the bases for their opinions that the Mesa proposal was wholly inadequate. Mr. Sachs opined that the minimum cash value that could be expected from a sale or orderly liquidation for 100% of Unocal's stock was in excess of $60 per share. In making his presentation, Mr. Sachs showed slides outlining the valuation techniques used by the financial advisors, and others, depicting recent business combinations in the oil and gas industry. The Court of Chancery found that the Sachs presentation was designed to apprise the directors of the scope of the analyses performed rather than the facts and numbers used in reaching the conclusion that Mesa's tender offer price was inadequate.

Mr. Sachs also presented various defensive strategies available to the board if it concluded that Mesa's two-step tender offer was inadequate and should be opposed. One of the devices outlined was a self-tender by Unocal for its own stock with a reasonable price range of $70 to $75 per share. The cost of such a proposal would cause the company to incur $6.1–6.5 billion of additional debt, and a presentation was made informing the board of Unocal's ability to handle it. The directors were told that the primary effect of this obligation would be to reduce exploratory drilling, but that the company would nonetheless remain a viable entity.

The eight outside directors, comprising a clear majority of the thirteen members present, then met separately with Unocal's financial advisors and attorneys. Thereafter, they unanimously agreed to advise the board that it should reject Mesa's tender offer as inadequate, and that Unocal should pursue a self-tender to provide the stockholders with a fairly priced alternative to the Mesa proposal. The board then reconvened and unanimously adopted a resolution rejecting as grossly inadequate Mesa's tender offer. Despite the nine and one-half hour length of the meeting, no formal decision was made on the proposed defensive self-tender.

On April 15, the board met again with four of the directors present by telephone and one member still absent.[4] This session lasted two hours. Unocal's Vice President of Finance and its Assistant General Counsel made a detailed presentation of the proposed terms of the exchange offer. A price range between $70 and $80 per share was considered, and ultimately the directors agreed upon $72. The board was also advised about the debt securities that would be issued, and the necessity of placing restrictive covenants upon certain corporate activities until the obligations were paid. The board's decisions were made in reliance on the advice of its investment bankers, including the terms and conditions upon which the securities were to be issued. Based upon this advice, and the board's own deliberations, the directors unanimously approved the exchange offer. Their resolution provided that if Mesa acquired 64 million shares of Unocal stock through its own offer (the Mesa Purchase Condition), Unocal would buy the remaining 49% outstanding for an exchange of debt securities having an aggregate par value of $72 per share. The board resolution also stated that the offer would be subject to other conditions that had been described to the board at the meeting, or which were deemed necessary by Unocal's officers, including the exclusion of Mesa from the proposal (the Mesa exclusion). Any such conditions were required to be in accordance with the "purport and intent" of the offer.

Unocal's exchange offer was commenced on April 17, 1985, and Mesa promptly challenged it by filing this suit in the Court of Chancery. On April 22, the Unocal board met again and was advised by Goldman Sachs and Dillon Read to waive the Mesa Purchase Condition as to 50 million shares. This recommendation was in response to a perceived concern of the shareholders that, if shares were tendered to Unocal, no shares would be purchased by either offeror. The directors were also advised that they should tender their own Unocal stock into the exchange offer as a mark of their confidence in it.

Another focus of the board was the Mesa exclusion. Legal counsel advised that under Delaware law Mesa could only be excluded for what the directors reasonably believed to be a valid corporate purpose. The directors' discussion centered on the objective of adequately compensating shareholders at the "back-end" of Mesa's proposal, which the latter would finance with "junk bonds". To include Mesa would defeat that goal, because under the proration aspect of the exchange offer (49%) every Mesa share accepted by Unocal would displace one held by another stockholder. Further, if Mesa were permitted to tender to Unocal, the latter would in effect be financing Mesa's own inadequate proposal.

---

4. Under Delaware law directors may participate in a board meeting by telephone. Thus, 8 Del.C. § 141(i) provides:

> Unless otherwise restricted by the certificate of incorporation or by-laws, members of the board of directors of any corporation, or any committee designated by the board, may participate in a meeting of such board or committee by means of conference telephone or similar communications equipment by means of which all persons participating in the meeting can hear each other, and participation in a meeting pursuant to this subsection shall constitute presence in person at such meeting.

On April 24, 1985 Unocal issued a supplement to the exchange offer describing the partial waiver of the Mesa Purchase Condition. On May 1, 1985, in another supplement, Unocal extended the withdrawal, proration and expiration dates of its exchange offer to May 17, 1985.

Meanwhile, on April 22, 1985, Mesa amended its complaint in this action to challenge the Mesa exclusion. A preliminary injunction hearing was scheduled for May 8, 1985. However, on April 23, 1985, Mesa moved for a temporary restraining order in response to Unocal's announcement that it was partially waiving the Mesa Purchase Condition. After expedited briefing, the Court of Chancery heard Mesa's motion on April 26.

On April 29, 1985, the Vice Chancellor temporarily restrained Unocal from proceeding with the exchange offer unless it included Mesa. The trial court recognized that directors could oppose, and attempt to defeat, a hostile takeover which they considered adverse to the best interests of the corporation. However, the Vice Chancellor decided that in a selective purchase of the company's stock, the corporation bears the burden of showing: (1) a valid corporate purpose, and (2) that the transaction was fair to all of the stockholders, including those excluded.

Unocal immediately sought certification of an interlocutory appeal to this Court pursuant to Supreme Court Rule 42(b)....

On May 13, 1985 the Court of Chancery certified this interlocutory appeal to us as a question of first impression, and we accepted it on May 14. The entire matter was scheduled on an expedited basis.

II

The issues we address involve these fundamental questions: Did the Unocal board have the power and duty to oppose a takeover threat it reasonably perceived to be harmful to the corporate enterprise, and if so, is its action here entitled to the protection of the business judgment rule?

Mesa contends that the discriminatory exchange offer violates the fiduciary duties Unocal owes it. Mesa argues that because of the Mesa exclusion the business judgment rule is inapplicable, because the directors by tendering their own shares will derive a financial benefit that is not available to *all* Unocal stockholders. Thus, it is Mesa's ultimate contention that Unocal cannot establish that the exchange offer is fair to *all* shareholders, and argues that the Court of Chancery was correct in concluding that Unocal was unable to meet this burden.

Unocal answers that it does not owe a duty of "fairness" to Mesa, given the facts here. Specifically, Unocal contends that its board of directors reasonably and in good faith concluded that Mesa's $54 two-tier tender offer was coercive and inadequate, and that Mesa sought selective treatment for itself. Furthermore, Unocal argues that the board's approval of the exchange offer was made in good faith, on an informed basis, and in the exercise of due care. Under these circumstances, Unocal contends that its directors properly employed this device to protect the company and its stockholders from Mesa's harmful tactics.

III

We begin with the basic issue of the power of a board of directors of a Delaware corporation to adopt a defensive measure of this type. Absent such authority, all other questions are moot. Neither issues of fairness nor business judgment are pertinent without the basic underpinning of a board's legal power to act.

The board has a large reservoir of authority upon which to draw. Its duties and responsibilities proceed from the inherent powers conferred by 8 Del.C. § 141(a), respecting management of the corporation's "business and affairs."[6] Additionally, the powers here being exercised derive from 8 Del.C. § 160(a), conferring broad authority upon a corporation to deal in its own stock.[7] From this it is now well established that in the acquisition of its shares a Delaware corporation may deal selectively with its stockholders, provided the directors have not acted out of a sole or primary purpose to entrench themselves in office.

Finally, the board's power to act derives from its fundamental duty and obligation to protect the corporate enterprise, which includes stockholders, from harm reasonably perceived, irrespective of its source. Thus, we are satisfied that in the broad context of corporate governance, including issues of fundamental corporate change, a board of directors is not a passive instrumentality.[8]

Given the foregoing principles, we turn to the standards by which director action is to be measured. In *Pogostin v. Rice*, we held that the business judgment rule, including the standards by which director conduct is judged, is applicable in the context of a takeover. The business judgment rule is a "presumption that in making a business decision the directors of a corporation acted on an informed basis, in good faith and in the honest belief that the action taken was in the best interests of the company." *Aronson v. Lewis*. A hallmark of the business judgment rule is that a court will not

---

6. The general grant of power to a board of directors is conferred by 8 Del.C. § 141(a), which provides:
    (a) The business *and affairs* of every corporation organized under this chapter shall be managed by or under the direction of a board of directors, except as may be otherwise provided in this chapter or in its certificate of incorporation. If any such provision is made in the certificate of incorporation, the powers and duties conferred or imposed upon the board of directors by this chapter shall be exercised or performed to such extent and by such person or persons as shall be provided in the certificate of incorporation. (Emphasis added).
7. This power under 8 Del.C. § 160(a), with certain exceptions not pertinent here, is as follows:
    (a) Every corporation may purchase, redeem, receive, take or otherwise acquire, own and hold, sell, lend, exchange, transfer or otherwise dispose of, pledge, use and otherwise deal in and with its own shares; . . .
8. Even in the traditional areas of fundamental corporate change, i.e., charter amendments [8 Del.C. § 242(b)], mergers [8 Del.C. §§ 251(b), 252(c), 253(a), and 254(d)], sale of assets [8 Del.C. § 271(a)], and dissolution [8 Del.C. § 275(a)], director action is a prerequisite to the ultimate disposition of such matters.

substitute its judgment for that of the board if the latter's decision can be "attributed to any rational business purpose." *Sinclair Oil Corp. v. Levien.*

When a board addresses a pending takeover bid it has an obligation to determine whether the offer is in the best interests of the corporation and its shareholders. In that respect a board's duty is no different from any other responsibility it shoulders, and its decisions should be no less entitled to the respect they otherwise would be accorded in the realm of business judgment.[9] There are, however, certain caveats to a proper exercise of this function. Because of the omnipresent specter that a board may be acting primarily in its own interests, rather than those of the corporation and its shareholders, there is an enhanced duty which calls for judicial examination at the threshold before the protections of the business judgment rule may be conferred.

This Court has long recognized that:

> We must bear in mind the inherent danger in the purchase of shares with corporate funds to remove a threat to corporate policy when a threat to control is involved. The directors are of necessity confronted with a conflict of interest, and an objective decision is difficult.

In the face of this inherent conflict directors must show that they had reasonable grounds for believing that a danger to corporate policy and effectiveness existed because of another person's stock ownership. *Cheff v. Mathes.* However, they satisfy that burden "by showing good faith and reasonable investigation. . . ." Furthermore, such proof is materially enhanced, as here, by the approval of a board comprised of a majority of outside independent directors who have acted in accordance with the foregoing standards.

IV

A

In the board's exercise of corporate power to forestall a takeover bid our analysis begins with the basic principle that corporate directors have a fiduciary duty to act in the best interests of the corporation's stockholders. As we have noted, their duty of care extends to protecting the corporation and its owners from perceived harm whether a threat originates from third parties or other shareholders. But such powers are not absolute. A corporation does not have unbridled discretion to defeat any perceived threat by any Draconian means available.

The restriction placed upon a selective stock repurchase is that the directors may not have acted solely or primarily out of a desire to perpetuate themselves in office.

---

9. This is a subject of intense debate among practicing members of the bar and legal scholars. Excellent examples of these contending views are: Block & Miller, *The Responsibilities and Obligations of Corporate Directors in Takeover Contests*, 11 Sec. Reg. L.J. 44 (1983); Easterbrook & Fischel, *Takeover Bids, Defensive Tactics, and Shareholders' Welfare*, 36 Bus. Law. 1733 (1981); Easterbrook & Fischel, *The Proper Role of a Target's Management In Responding to a Tender Offer*, 94 Harv. L. Rev. 1161 (1981). Herzel, Schmidt & Davis, *Why Corporate Directors Have a Right To Resist Tender Offers*, 3 Corp. L. Rev. 107 (1980); Lipton, *Takeover Bids in the Target's Boardroom*, 35 Bus. Law. 101 (1979).

Of course, to this is added the further caveat that inequitable action may not be taken under the guise of law. The standard of proof established in *Cheff v. Mathes* . . . is designed to ensure that a defensive measure to thwart or impede a takeover is indeed motivated by a good faith concern for the welfare of the corporation and its stockholders, which in all circumstances must be free of any fraud or other misconduct. *Cheff v. Mathes*. However, this does not end the inquiry.

B

A further aspect is the element of balance. If a defensive measure is to come within the ambit of the business judgment rule, it must be reasonable in relation to the threat posed. This entails an analysis by the directors of the nature of the takeover bid and its effect on the corporate enterprise. Examples of such concerns may include: inadequacy of the price offered, nature and timing of the offer, questions of illegality, the impact on "constituencies" other than shareholders (i.e., creditors, customers, employees, and perhaps even the community generally), the risk of nonconsummation, and the quality of securities being offered in the exchange. While not a controlling factor, it also seems to us that a board may reasonably consider the basic stockholder interests at stake, including those of short term speculators, whose actions may have fueled the coercive aspect of the offer at the expense of the long term investor. Here, the threat posed was viewed by the Unocal board as a grossly inadequate two-tier coercive tender offer coupled with the threat of greenmail.

Specifically, the Unocal directors had concluded that the value of Unocal was substantially above the $54 per share offered in cash at the front end. Furthermore, they determined that the subordinated securities to be exchanged in Mesa's announced squeeze out of the remaining shareholders in the "back-end" merger were "junk bonds" worth far less than $54. It is now well recognized that such offers are a classic coercive measure designed to stampede shareholders into tendering at the first tier, even if the price is inadequate, out of fear of what they will receive at the back end of the transaction. Wholly beyond the coercive aspect of an inadequate two-tier tender offer, the threat was posed by a corporate raider with a national reputation as a "greenmailer."[13]

In adopting the selective exchange offer, the board stated that its objective was either to defeat the inadequate Mesa offer or, should the offer still succeed, provide the 49% of its stockholders, who would otherwise be forced to accept "junk bonds," with $72 worth of senior debt. We find that both purposes are valid.

---

13. The term "greenmail" refers to the practice of buying out a takeover bidder's stock at a premium that is not available to other shareholders in order to prevent the takeover. The Chancery Court noted that "Mesa has made tremendous profits from its takeover activities although in the past few years it has not been successful in acquiring any of the target companies on an unfriendly basis." Moreover, the trial court specifically found that the actions of the Unocal board were taken in good faith to eliminate both the inadequacies of the tender offer and to forestall the payment of "greenmail."

However, such efforts would have been thwarted by Mesa's participation in the exchange offer. First, if Mesa could tender its shares, Unocal would effectively be subsidizing the former's continuing effort to buy Unocal stock at $54 per share. Second, Mesa could not, by definition, fit within the class of shareholders being protected from its own coercive and inadequate tender offer.

Thus, we are satisfied that the selective exchange offer is reasonably related to the threats posed. It is consistent with the principle that "the minority stockholder shall receive the substantial equivalent in value of what he had before." *Sterling v. Mayflower Hotel Corp.* This concept of fairness, while stated in the merger context, is also relevant in the area of tender offer law. Thus, the board's decision to offer what it determined to be the fair value of the corporation to the 49% of its shareholders, who would otherwise be forced to accept highly subordinated "junk bonds," is reasonable and consistent with the directors' duty to ensure that the minority stockholders receive equal value for their shares.

V

Mesa contends that it is unlawful, and the trial court agreed, for a corporation to discriminate in this fashion against one shareholder. It argues correctly that no case has ever sanctioned a device that precludes a raider from sharing in a benefit available to all other stockholders. However, as we have noted earlier, the principle of selective stock repurchases by a Delaware corporation is neither unknown nor unauthorized. The only difference is that heretofore the approved transaction was the payment of "greenmail" to a raider or dissident posing a threat to the corporate enterprise. All other stockholders were denied such favored treatment, and given Mesa's past history of greenmail, its claims here are rather ironic.

However, our corporate law is not static. It must grow and develop in response to, indeed in anticipation of, evolving concepts and needs. Merely because the General Corporation Law is silent as to a specific matter does not mean that it is prohibited. In the days when *Cheff, Bennett, Martin* and *Kors* were decided, the tender offer, while not an unknown device, was virtually unused, and little was known of such methods as two-tier "front-end" loaded offers with their coercive effects. Then, the favored attack of a raider was stock acquisition followed by a proxy contest. Various defensive tactics, which provided no benefit whatever to the raider, evolved. Thus, the use of corporate funds by management to counter a proxy battle was approved. Litigation, supported by corporate funds, aimed at the raider has long been a popular device.

More recently, as the sophistication of both raiders and targets has developed, a host of other defensive measures to counter such ever mounting threats has evolved and received judicial sanction. These include defensive charter amendments and other devices bearing some rather exotic, but apt, names: Crown Jewel, White Knight, Pac Man, and Golden Parachute. Each has highly selective features, the object of which is to deter or defeat the raider.

Thus, while the exchange offer is a form of selective treatment, given the nature of the threat posed here the response is neither unlawful nor unreasonable. If the board of directors is disinterested, has acted in good faith and with due care, its decision in the absence of an abuse of discretion will be upheld as a proper exercise of business judgment.

To this Mesa responds that the board is not disinterested, because the directors are receiving a benefit from the tender of their own shares, which because of the Mesa exclusion, does not devolve upon *all* stockholders equally. However, Mesa concedes that if the exclusion is valid, then the directors and all other stockholders share the same benefit. The answer of course is that the exclusion is valid, and the directors' participation in the exchange offer does not rise to the level of a disqualifying interest. The excellent discussion in *Johnson v. Trueblood* of the use of the business judgment rule in takeover contests also seems pertinent here.

Nor does this become an "interested" director transaction merely because certain board members are large stockholders. As this Court has previously noted, that fact alone does not create a disqualifying "personal pecuniary interest" to defeat the operation of the business judgment rule.

Mesa also argues that the exclusion permits the directors to abdicate the fiduciary duties they owe it. However, that is not so. The board continues to owe Mesa the duties of due care and loyalty. But in the face of the destructive threat Mesa's tender offer was perceived to pose, the board had a supervening duty to protect the corporate enterprise, which includes the other shareholders, from threatened harm.

Mesa contends that the basis of this action is punitive, and solely in response to the exercise of its rights of corporate democracy. Nothing precludes Mesa, as a stockholder, from acting in its own self-interest. However, Mesa, while pursuing its own interests, has acted in a manner which a board consisting of a majority of independent directors has reasonably determined to be contrary to the best interests of Unocal and its other shareholders. In this situation, there is no support in Delaware law for the proposition that, when responding to a perceived harm, a corporation must guarantee a benefit to a stockholder who is deliberately provoking the danger being addressed. There is no obligation of self-sacrifice by a corporation and its shareholders in the face of such a challenge.

Here, the Court of Chancery specifically found that the "directors' decision [to oppose the Mesa tender offer] was made in the good faith belief that the Mesa tender offer is inadequate." Given our standard of review . . . we are satisfied that Unocal's board has met its burden of proof.

VI

In conclusion, there was directorial power to oppose the Mesa tender offer, and to undertake a selective stock exchange made in good faith and upon a reasonable investigation pursuant to a clear duty to protect the corporate enterprise. Further, the selective stock repurchase plan chosen by Unocal is reasonable in relation to the threat that the board rationally and reasonably believed was posed by Mesa's inadequate and coercive two-tier tender offer. Under those circumstances the board's action is entitled to be measured by the standards of the business judgment rule. Thus, unless it is shown by a preponderance of the evidence that the directors' decisions were primarily based on perpetuating themselves in office, or some other breach of fiduciary duty such as fraud, overreaching, lack of good faith, or being uninformed, a Court will not substitute its judgment for that of the board.

In this case that protection is not lost merely because Unocal's directors have tendered their shares in the exchange offer. Given the validity of the Mesa exclusion, they are receiving a benefit shared generally by all other stockholders except Mesa. In this circumstance the test of *Aronson v. Lewis* is satisfied. If the stockholders are displeased with the action of their elected representatives, the powers of corporate democracy are at their disposal to turn the board out.

With the Court of Chancery's findings that the exchange offer was based on the board's good faith belief that the Mesa offer was inadequate, that the board's action was informed and taken with due care, that Mesa's prior activities justify a reasonable inference that its principle objective was greenmail, and implicitly, that the substance of the offer itself was reasonable and fair to the corporation and its stockholders if Mesa were included, we cannot say that the Unocal directors have acted in such a manner as to have passed an "unintelligent and unadvised judgment". The decision of the Court of Chancery is therefore reversed, and the preliminary injunction is vacated.

Questions

1. What is the purpose of Unocal's exchange offer?

2. Why does the court disregard the Unocal board's fiduciary duties to Mesa?

3. As a doctrinal matter, where does the board get its power to intervene in hostile tender offers? Is the court's approach consistent with its jurisprudence in a case like *Arco v. Hariton*?

4. There has been a long debate in the scholarly literature over whether the board should have any power to block a hostile tender offer or whether it should be solely a matter of stockholder choice. What reasons can you see for allowing the directors to be involved? For leaving it to the shareholders? To what extent does your answer depend upon your view of the nature and the purpose of the public corporation?

5. Why does not the court apply the fairness standard? Isn't the Unocal board's response tainted with conflict of interest?

Unocal v. Mesa in context

In the 1970s, the corporate board was at the forefront of public and academic discussions. The social and political upheaval of the time led public-interest shareholder groups to use the SEC's proxy and shareholder proposal rules to address corporate practices related to the Vietnam War, environmental protection, occupational safety, and equal employment. Institutional investors became major players in corporate governance, raising new questions about the control of U.S. corporations. Several corporate bankruptcies, including the unexpected collapse of Penn Central, raised grave doubts about their boards' performance, while corporate scandals involving illegal political contributions revealed during the Watergate investigation exacerbated such doubts. A variety of studies concluded that the boards of directors of large and medium-sized corporations were no longer a significant check on the CEO. They also did not have much say in selecting the executives, because management controlled the proxy machinery. Outside directors were ineffective. Typically chosen from the same social networks as the top executives and sitting with them on other boards, they were unlikely to challenge the executives. Studies also revealed that most boards did not meet frequently enough to perform a meaningful role. (For a detailed examination of these developments and studies, see Joel Seligman, *A Sheep in Wolf's Clothing: The American Law Institute Principles of Corporate Governance Project*, 55 Geo. Wash. U. L. Rev. 325–381 (1987).)

Several proposals for reform followed. Some wanted more federal supervision and guidance (*see, e.g.*, William L. Cary, *Federalism and Corporate Law: Reflections Upon Delaware*, 83 Yale L.J. 663 (1974), Ralph Nader et al, Taming the Giant Corporation (1976)). Others focused on the composition of the board, calling for boards to be composed entirely of outside directors who would review the executives' decisions (*see, e.g.*, Harvey J. Goldschmid, *The Greening of the Board Room: Reflections on Corporate Responsibility*, 10 Colum. J.L. & Soc. Probs. 15 (1973)). Lawyers and business groups emphasized the importance of the board's structure. The American Bar Association's Committee on Corporate Laws, Section of Corporation, Banking and Business Law, published a *Corporate Director's Guidebook* in the fall of 1976 (32 Bus. L. 5 (1976)), and a revised edition early in 1978 (33 Bus. L. 1591 (1978)). The *Guidebook* described directors as "overseers of the corporation and monitors of corporate management" (1976 *Guidebook* at 31, 1978 *Guidebook* at 1619) and recommended that a significant number of outside directors serve on boards and that inside directors be prohibited from serving on the nominating, compensation, and audit committees (1976 *Guidebook* at 33–37, 1978 *Guidebook* at 1622–27). In 1978, the Business Roundtable published its recommendations for reform in *The Role and Composition of the Board of Directors of the Large Publicly Owned Corporation*, suggesting that the board had a monitoring role (although its responsibility extended beyond that role), and recommending that boards be composed of a majority of outside directors and that the audit and compensation committees be composed entirely of outside directors.

By the early 1980s, academics, lawyers, and businessmen agreed that the monitoring model was appropriate for the board's role. The idea was reinforced with the 1982 publication of the tentative draft of the American Law Institute's *Principles of Corporate Governance* (the final version was approved in 1992 after a decade-long heated debate). But consensus was limited to the fact that independent directors should play an important role in reviewing the activities of the executives, and that such review should focus on financial results. What that meant as far as the duties and liabilities of directors, and to whom directors owed them, remained contested issues throughout the 1980s. Some legal scholars wanted to use the monitoring model substantially to redefine directors' duties (*see*, e.g., Melvin A. Eisenberg, *Legal Models of Management Structure in the Modern Corporation: Officers, Directors, and Accountants*, 63 CAL. L. REV. 375 (1975)), but corporate lawyers and business groups were strongly opposed to any attempt to tinker with the very limited directorial duties. They focused on the monitoring role of non-management directors and suggested that good boards include a significant number of them (for more on the monitoring model of the board, see Lawrence E. Mitchell, *The Trouble with Boards*, in Scott F. Keiff and Troy A. Paredes eds., PERSPECTIVES ON CORPORATE GOVERNANCE (2010)).

During the 1980s, the Delaware courts brought the business community's emphasis on independent oversight to bear upon their analysis of directors' duties. Viewing the model as a structural rather than substantive one, the courts focused on the role of the independent directors (independence narrowly defined as lack of control or domination by an individual interested in the transaction). If a majority of independent, disinterested directors, following procedural requirements, approved the board's actions, the courts held such actions to be shielded from further judicial inquiry.

Take *Unocal*. When a hostile bidder makes an offer to the target corporation's shareholders, the decision of the target corporation's directors to adopt a defensive tactic, on its face, is tainted with a conflict of interest, because successful hostile bidders typically replace the board. Given the potential conflict of interest, a decision by a board to engage in a defensive tactic should have been analyzed under the fairness test just as any other form of self-dealing. But, beginning with *Unocal*, the Delaware courts adopted a more lenient test—a two prong test assessing, first, whether the directors "had reasonable grounds for believing that a danger to corporate policy and effectiveness existed" and, second, whether the defensive tactic the board adopted was "reasonable in relation to the threat posed." More important, as we will see in the following cases, the Delaware courts emphasized that if a majority of the independent directors endorsed the defensive tactic, then the board's action would likely meet the burden of the *Unocal* test (for more on the development of directors' duties in the 1980s, see Dalia T. Mitchell, *Status Bound: The Twentieth Century Evolution of Directors' Liability*, 5 NYU J. OF L. & BUS. 63 (2009)).

Moran v. Household International, Inc.
500 A.2d 1346 (Del. 1985)

MCNEILLY, Justice

This case presents to this Court for review the most recent defensive mechanism in the arsenal of corporate takeover weaponry—the Preferred Share Purchase Rights Plan ("Rights Plan" or "Plan"). The validity of this mechanism has attracted national attention. *Amici curiae* briefs have been filed in support of appellants by the Security and Exchange Commission ("SEC") and the Investment Company Institute. An *amicus curiae* brief has been filed in support of appellees ("Household") by the United Food and Commercial Workers International Union.

In a detailed opinion, the Court of Chancery upheld the Rights Plan as a legitimate exercise of business judgment by Household. We agree, and therefore, affirm the judgment below.

I

The facts giving rise to this case have been carefully delineated in the Court of Chancery's opinion. A review of the basic facts is necessary for a complete understanding of the issues.

On August 14, 1984, the Board of Directors of Household International, Inc. adopted the Rights Plan by a fourteen to two vote.[2] The intricacies of the Rights Plan are contained in a 48-page document entitled "Rights Agreement." Basically, the Plan provides that Household common stockholders are entitled to the issuance of one Right per common share under certain triggering conditions. There are two triggering events that can activate the Rights. The first is the announcement of a tender offer for 30 percent of Household's shares ("30% trigger") and the second is the acquisition of 20 percent of Household's shares by any single entity or group ("20% trigger").

If an announcement of a tender offer for 30 percent of Household's shares is made, the Rights are issued and are immediately exercisable to purchase 1/100 share of new preferred stock for $100 and are redeemable by the Board for $.50 per Right. If 20 percent of Household's shares are acquired by anyone, the Rights are issued and become non-redeemable and are exercisable to purchase 1/100 of a share of preferred. If a Right is not exercised for preferred, and thereafter, a merger or consolidation occurs, the Rights holder can exercise each Right to purchase $200 of the common stock of the tender offeror for $100. This "flip-over" provision of the Rights Plan is at the heart of this controversy.

Household is a diversified holding company with its principal subsidiaries engaged in financial services, transportation and merchandising. HFC, National Car Rental and Vons Grocery are three of its wholly-owned entities. . . .

III

. . .

A

While appellants contend that no provision of the Delaware General Corporation Law authorizes the Rights Plan, Household contends that the Rights Plan was issued pursuant to 8 Del.C. §§ 151 (g) and 157. It explains that the Rights are authorized by

---

2. Household's Board has ten outside directors and six who are members of management. Messrs. Moran (appellant) and Whitehead voted against the Plan. The record reflects that Whitehead voted against the Plan not on its substance but because he thought it was novel and would bring unwanted publicity to Household.

§ 157[7] and the issue of preferred stock underlying the Rights is authorized by § 151.[8] Appellants respond by making several attacks upon the authority to issue the Rights pursuant to § 157.

Appellants begin by contending that § 157 cannot authorize the Rights Plan since § 157 has never served the purpose of authorizing a takeover defense. Appellants contend that § 157 is a corporate financing statute, and that nothing in its legislative history suggests a purpose that has anything to do with corporate control or a takeover defense. Appellants are unable to demonstrate that the legislature, in its adoption of § 157, meant to limit the applicability of § 157 to only the issuance of Rights for the purposes of corporate financing. Without such affirmative evidence, we decline to impose such a limitation upon the section that the legislature has not.

As we noted in *Unocal:*

> [O]ur corporate law is not static. It must grow and develop in response to, indeed in anticipation of, evolving concepts and needs. Merely because the General Corporation Law is silent as to a specific matter does not mean that it is prohibited.

Secondly, appellants contend that § 157 does not authorize the issuance of sham rights such as the Rights Plan. They contend that the Rights were designed never to be exercised, and that the Plan has no economic value. In addition, they contend the preferred stock made subject to the Rights is also illusory, citing *Telvest, Inc. v. Olson.*

Appellants' sham contention fails in both regards. As to the Rights, they can and will be exercised upon the happening of a triggering mechanism, as we have observed during the current struggle of Sir James Goldsmith to take control of Crown Zellerbach. *See* Wall Street Journal, July 26, 1985, at 3, 12. As to the preferred shares, we agree with the Court of Chancery that they are distinguishable from sham securities

---

7. The power to issue rights to purchase shares is conferred by 8 Del.C. § 157 which provides in relevant part:
   > Subject to any provisions in the certificate of incorporation, every corporation may create and issue, whether or not in connection with the issue and sale of any shares of stock or other securities of the corporation, rights or options entitling the holders thereof to purchase from the corporation any shares of its capital stock of any class or classes, such rights or options to be evidenced by or in such instrument or instruments as shall be approved by the board of directors.

8. 8 Del.C. § 151(g) provides in relevant part:
   > When any corporation desires to issue any shares of stock of any class or of any series of any class of which the voting powers, designations, preferences and relative, participating, optional or other rights, if any, or the qualifications, limitations or restrictions thereof, if any, shall not have been set forth in the certificate of incorporation or in any amendment thereto but shall be provided for in a resolution or resolutions adopted by the board of directors pursuant to authority expressly vested in it by the provisions of the certificate of incorporation or any amendment thereto, a certificate setting forth a copy of such resolution or resolutions and the number of shares of stock of such class or series shall be executed, acknowledged, filed, recorded, and shall become effective, in accordance with § 103 of this title.

invalidated in *Telvest, supra*. The Household preferred, issuable upon the happening of a triggering event, have superior dividend and liquidation rights.

Third, appellants contend that § 157 authorizes the issuance of Rights "entitling holders thereof to purchase from the corporation any shares of *its* capital stock of any class...." (emphasis added). Therefore, their contention continues, the plain language of the statute does not authorize Household to issue rights to purchase another's capital stock upon a merger or consolidation.

Household contends, *inter alia*, that the Rights Plan is analogous to "anti-destruction" or "anti-dilution" provisions which are customary features of a wide variety of corporate securities. While appellants seem to concede that "anti-destruction" provisions are valid under Delaware corporate law, they seek to distinguish the Rights Plan as not being incidental, as are most "anti-destruction" provisions, to a corporation's statutory power to finance itself. We find no merit to such a distinction. We have already rejected appellants' similar contention that § 157 could only be used for financing purposes. We also reject that distinction here.

"Anti-destruction" clauses generally ensure holders of certain securities of the protection of their right of conversion in the event of a merger by giving them the right to convert their securities into whatever securities are to replace the stock of their company. The fact that the rights here have as their purpose the prevention of coercive two-tier tender offers does not invalidate them.

Fourth, appellants contend that Household's reliance upon § 157 is contradictory to 8 Del.C. § 203.[9] Section 203 is a "notice" statute which generally requires that timely notice be given to a target of an offeror's intention to make a tender offer.

---

9. 8 Del.C. § 203 provides in relevant part:
    (a) No offeror shall make a tender offer unless:
    (1) Not less than 20 nor more than 60 days before the date the tender offer is to be made, the offeror shall deliver personally or by registered or certified mail to the corporation whose equity securities are to be subject to the tender offer, at its registered office in this State or at its principal place of business, a written statement of the offeror's intention to make the tender offer....
    (2) The tender offer shall remain open for a period of at least 20 days after it is first made to the holders of the equity securities, during which period any stockholder may withdraw any of the equity securities tendered to the offeror, and any revised or amended tender offer which changes the amount or type of consideration offered or the number of equity securities for which the offer is made shall remain open at least 10 days following the amendment; and
    (3) The offeror and any associate of the offeror will not purchase or pay for any tendered equity security for a period of at least 20 days after the tender offer is first made to the holders of the equity securities, and no such purchase or payment shall be made within 10 days after an amended or revised tender offer if the amendment or revision changes the amount or type of consideration offered or the number of equity securities for which the offer is made. If during the period the tender offer must remain open pursuant to this section, a greater number of equity securities is tendered than the offeror is bound or willing to purchase, the equity securities shall be purchased pro rata, as nearly as may be, according to the number or shares tendered during such period by each equity security holder.

Appellants contend that the lack of stronger regulation by the State indicates a legislative intent to reject anything which would impose an impediment to the tender offer process. Such a contention is a *non sequitur*. The desire to have little state regulation of tender offers cannot be said to also indicate a desire to also have little private regulation. Furthermore, as we explain *infra*, we do not view the Rights Plan as much of an impediment on the tender offer process. . . .

Having concluded that sufficient authority for the Rights Plan exists in 8 Del.C. § 157, we note the inherent powers of the Board conferred by 8 Del.C. § 141(a), concerning the management of the corporation's "business and *affairs*" (emphasis added), also provides the Board additional authority upon which to enact the Rights Plan.

B

Appellants contend that the Board is unauthorized to usurp stockholders' rights to receive tender offers by changing Household's fundamental structure. We conclude that the Rights Plan does not prevent stockholders from receiving tender offers, and that the change of Household's structure was less than that which results from the implementation of other defensive mechanisms upheld by various courts.

Appellants' contention that stockholders will lose their right to receive and accept tender offers seems to be premised upon an understanding of the Rights Plan which is illustrated by the SEC *amicus* brief which states: "The Chancery Court's decision seriously understates the impact of this plan. In fact, as we discuss below, the Rights Plan will deter not only two-tier offers, but virtually all hostile tender offers."

The fallacy of that contention is apparent when we look at the recent takeover of Crown Zellerbach, which has a similar Rights Plan, by Sir James Goldsmith. The evidence at trial also evidenced many methods around the Plan ranging from tendering with a condition that the Board redeem the Rights, tendering with a high minimum condition of shares and Rights, tendering and soliciting consents to remove the Board and redeem the Rights, to acquiring 50% of the shares and causing Household to self-tender for the Rights. One could also form a group of up to 19.9% and solicit proxies for consents to remove the Board and redeem the Rights. These are but a few of the methods by which Household can still be acquired by a hostile tender offer.

In addition, the Rights Plan is not absolute. When the Household Board of Directors is faced with a tender offer and a request to redeem the Rights, they will not be able to arbitrarily reject the offer. They will be held to the same fiduciary standards any other board of directors would be held to in deciding to adopt a defensive mechanism, the same standard they were held to in originally approving the Rights Plan.

In addition, appellants contend that the deterrence of tender offers will be accomplished by what they label "a fundamental transfer of power from the stockholders to the directors." They contend that this transfer of power, in itself, is unauthorized.

The Rights Plan will result in no more of a structural change than any other defensive mechanism adopted by a board of directors. The Rights Plan does not destroy the assets of the corporation. The implementation of the Plan neither results in any outflow of money from the corporation nor impairs its financial flexibility. It does not dilute earnings per share and does not have any adverse tax consequences for the corporation or its stockholders. The Plan has not adversely affected the market price of Household's stock.

Comparing the Rights Plan with other defensive mechanisms, it does less harm to the value structure of the corporation than do the other mechanisms. Other mechanisms result in increased debt of the corporation. *See Whittaker Corp. v. Edgar* (sale of "prize asset"), *Cheff v. Mathes* (paying greenmail to eliminate a threat), *Unocal Corp. v. Mesa Petroleum Co.* (discriminatory self-tender).

There is little change in the governance structure as a result of the adoption of the Rights Plan. The Board does not now have unfettered discretion in refusing to redeem the Rights. The Board has no more discretion in refusing to redeem the Rights than it does in enacting any defensive mechanism. . . .

IV

Having concluded that the adoption of the Rights Plan was within the authority of the Directors, we now look to whether the Directors have met their burden under the business judgment rule. . . .

[The court concludes that the plan is authorized under the business judgment rule but that the board's behavior with respect to its exercise or redemption must be analyzed under *Unocal* when an actual takeover battle occurs.]

Questions

1. The poison pill at issue in *Moran* is an example of lawyerly creativity at its best, and the result in the case is a product of superb litigation. Note the court's understanding of the pill as in the nature of preferred stock (or debt) anti-destruction provisions. These provisions were created for an entirely different purpose. Often preferred stock or bonds are convertible into the common stock of the issuing corporation at a predetermined ratio (which ratio is protected by another set of provisions referred to as anti-dilution provisions). The issue facing these convertible security holders is that their conversion privilege only exists for as long as the issuing corporation is in existence. Having paid for their conversion rights (in the form of receiving a lower dividend or interest rate than is paid on non-convertible securities), they need to ensure that if the corporation is merged out of existence (at least in a stock-for-stock merger so that the preferred stock continues to exist in the surviving corporation), they have the right to convert into something, presumably the common stock of the surviving corporation. Anti-destruction provisions ensure the continuity of the conversion right by making the preferred convertible into the stock of the surviving corporation. Of course, this has a distinct economic purpose — to preserve the value of the conversion option. The rights at issue in *Moran* have no such economic purpose, since the intent is that they will never be exercised but instead serve to deter hostile bidders. Yet the court accepted the analogy. Note that this is not the first time that rights originally intended to have economic functions have

been used to serve a different purpose with the court's approval. Recall *Lehrman v. Cohen* in Part 3, in which the court sustained an arrangement of non-economic voting stock for the purpose of serving as a tiebreaker in disputes. The court similarly made a somewhat disingenuous economic case for the existence of the security.

2. In *Carmody v. Toll Bros, Inc.*, 723 A.2d 1180 (Del. Ch. 1998), a shareholder challenged "dead hand" rights plan prior to any potential takeover. The dead hand provision was created as a function of developments in takeover techniques adopted following *Moran*. *Moran* upheld the board's adoption of a poison pill in the absence of an offer on the table, but further noted that the issue of whether the pill could be maintained or would be required to be redeemed would be revisited in the face of an actual offer. The Delaware courts were generally willing to permit pills to remain in existence during takeover contests, because they frequently enabled the board to negotiate with other bidders and ultimately increase the takeover price to stockholders. Bidders began to develop techniques to evade poison pills, perhaps the most common of which was the proxy contest coupled with a tender offer. The purpose of the proxy contest was to replace the target board with directors elected by the bidder, who would then redeem or remove the poison pill and allow the takeover to proceed. "Dead hand" poison pills were the target's response. In a dead hand poison pill, the pill can only be redeemed or removed by the directors in place at the time the pill was adopted or their designated successors. In *Carmody v. Toll Bros, Inc.*, the shareholder plaintiff moved to invalidate the dead hand poison pill. The corporation and its directors moved to dismiss the complaint. Vice Chancellor Jacobs held that the shareholder's allegations were sufficient to state claims for the statutory invalidity of the pill and the directors' breach of fiduciary duty of loyalty. His reasoning included the observations that the dead hand provision distinguished among the voting rights of different directors, that it intentionally interfered with stockholder voting rights in the absence of any compelling reason to do so, and that it was "disproportionate" as a defensive measure because it effectively precluded stockholders from receiving takeover bids and participating in proxy contests.

3. In *Quickturn Design Systems, Inc. v. Shapiro*, 721 A.2d 1281 (Del. 1998), Mentor Graphics wanted to acquire Quickturn, because Quickturn held key patents to a business in which Mentor wanted to engage. Mentor had tried to enter the business on several occasions but was blocked by successful patent litigation pursued by Quickturn. At first, Mentor was unable to afford the acquisition, but due to a later slump in the market for its products, Quickturn's stock price plummeted, paving the way for Mentor to make a bid at a substantial premium but still well below Quickturn's previous stock price. Mentor launched a combined proxy contest and tender offer, the former to replace Quickturn's board and remove its defensive measures to allow the Mentor offer to proceed. In response, the Quickturn board (which consisted only of one inside director and seven independent directors) amended Quickturn's bylaws to allow the board to delay a special meeting called by stockholders (not at issue here) and to amend Quickturn's dead hand poison pill with a deferred redemption provision. This deferred redemption provision prohibited a newly elected board from

redeeming the poison pill for six months after taking office if the redemption was designed to permit a transaction with an "Interested Person." An "Interested Person" was defined to be one who "proposed, nominated or financially supported the election of the new directors to the board." The result was that Mentor would be prohibited from acquiring Quickturn for at least six months, by which time the stock price might have increased to a point where it was prohibitively expensive. The court held that in the absence of any authorizing provision for such restrictions in Quickturn's certificate of incorporation, the deferred redemption provision violated section 141(a) of the Delaware General Corporation Law by depriving newly elected directors of their power to manage the corporation. It also violated the directors' fiduciary duty by proscribing them from acting in their own best judgment as to the question of redemption.

4. What is the difference between protecting the interests of the corporation as an entity and the interests of the shareholders, and when is it appropriate to do one or the other? Corporate law recognizes statutorily only three constituent groups: stockholders, directors, and officers, while the entity theory of the corporation and simple reality recognize that there are many other groups such as workers and debtholders who have legitimate interests in the corporation, (During the 1980s and early 1990s, most states adopted some form of what is known as a constituency statute or stakeholder statute.) One of the longest-running battles in corporate law is the extent to which shareholder interests take precedence over other interests of the corporation—including the corporation's interest in its own independence, a strange concept that bears thinking about. Clearly, in the case of a takeover, when shareholders are being offered *en masse* an opportunity to sell the corporation and thus change its control group, the issue is squarely joined. The next cases grapple with this issue. As you read them (in addition to the foregoing cases), you have a unique opportunity to see a court attempting to fashion doctrine to address vital new issues that, particularly during the 1980s, came to it at a dizzying pace.

Revlon, Inc. v. MacAndrews & Forbes Holdings, Inc.
506 A.2d 173 (Del. 1986)

MOORE, Justice

In this battle for corporate control of Revlon, Inc. (Revlon), the Court of Chancery enjoined certain transactions designed to thwart the efforts of Pantry Pride, Inc. (Pantry Pride) to acquire Revlon.[1] The defendants are Revlon, its board of directors, and Forstmann Little & Co. and the latter's affiliated limited partnership (collectively,

---

1. The nominal plaintiff, MacAndrews & Forbes Holdings, Inc., is the controlling stockholder of Pantry Pride. For all practical purposes their interests in this litigation are virtually identical, and we hereafter will refer to Pantry Pride as the plaintiff.

Forstmann). The injunction barred consummation of an option granted Forstmann to purchase certain Revlon assets (the lock-up option), a promise by Revlon to deal exclusively with Forstmann in the face of a takeover (the no-shop provision), and the payment of a $25 million cancellation fee to Forstmann if the transaction was aborted. The Court of Chancery found that the Revlon directors had breached their duty of care by entering into the foregoing transactions and effectively ending an active auction for the company. The trial court ruled that such arrangements are not illegal *per se* under Delaware law, but that their use under the circumstances here was impermissible. We agree. Thus, we granted this expedited interlocutory appeal to consider for the first time the validity of such defensive measures in the face of an active bidding contest for corporate control. Additionally, we address for the first time the extent to which a corporation may consider the impact of a takeover threat on constituencies other than shareholders.

In our view, lock-ups and related agreements are permitted under Delaware law where their adoption is untainted by director interest or other breaches of fiduciary duty. The actions taken by the Revlon directors, however, did not meet this standard. Moreover, while concern for various corporate constituencies is proper when addressing a takeover threat, that principle is limited by the requirement that there be some rationally related benefit accruing to the stockholders. We find no such benefit here.

Thus, under all the circumstances we must agree with the Court of Chancery that the enjoined Revlon defensive measures were inconsistent with the directors' duties to the stockholders. Accordingly, we affirm.

I

The somewhat complex maneuvers of the parties necessitate a rather detailed examination of the facts. The prelude to this controversy began in June 1985, when Ronald O. Perelman, chairman of the board and chief executive officer of Pantry Pride, met with his counterpart at Revlon, Michel C. Bergerac, to discuss a friendly acquisition of Revlon by Pantry Pride. Perelman suggested a price in the range of $40–50 per share, but the meeting ended with Bergerac dismissing those figures as considerably below Revlon's intrinsic value. All subsequent Pantry Pride overtures were rebuffed, perhaps in part based on Mr. Bergerac's strong personal antipathy to Mr. Perelman.

Thus, on August 14, Pantry Pride's board authorized Perelman to acquire Revlon, either through negotiation in the $42–$43 per share range, or by making a hostile tender offer at $45. Perelman then met with Bergerac and outlined Pantry Pride's alternate approaches. Bergerac remained adamantly opposed to such schemes and conditioned any further discussions of the matter on Pantry Pride executing a standstill agreement prohibiting it from acquiring Revlon without the latter's prior approval.

On August 19, the Revlon board met specially to consider the impending threat of a hostile bid by Pantry Pride.[3] At the meeting, Lazard Freres, Revlon's investment banker, advised the directors that $45 per share was a grossly inadequate price for the company. Felix Rohatyn and William Loomis of Lazard Freres explained to the board that Pantry Pride's financial strategy for acquiring Revlon would be through "junk bond" financing followed by a break-up of Revlon and the disposition of its assets. With proper timing, according to the experts, such transactions could produce a return to Pantry Pride of $60 to $70 per share, while a sale of the company as a whole would be in the "mid 50" dollar range. Martin Lipton, special counsel for Revlon, recommended two defensive measures: first, that the company repurchase up to 5 million of its nearly 30 million outstanding shares; and second, that it adopt a Note Purchase Rights Plan. Under this plan, each Revlon shareholder would receive as a dividend one Note Purchase Right (the Rights) for each share of common stock, with the Rights entitling the holder to exchange one common share for a $65 principal Revlon note at 12% interest with a one-year maturity. The Rights would become effective whenever anyone acquired beneficial ownership of 20% or more of Revlon's shares, unless the purchaser acquired all the company's stock for cash at $65 or more per share. In addition, the Rights would not be available to the acquiror, and prior to the 20% triggering event the Revlon board could redeem the rights for 10 cents each. Both proposals were unanimously adopted.

Pantry Pride made its first hostile move on August 23 with a cash tender offer for any and all shares of Revlon at $47.50 per common share and $26.67 per preferred share, subject to (1) Pantry Pride's obtaining financing for the purchase, and (2) the Rights being redeemed, rescinded or voided.

The Revlon board met again on August 26. The directors advised the stockholders to reject the offer. Further defensive measures also were planned. On August 29, Revlon commenced its own offer for up to 10 million shares, exchanging for each share of common stock tendered one Senior Subordinated Note (the Notes) of $47.50 principal at 11.75% interest, due 1995, and one-tenth of a share of $9.00 Cumulative Convertible Exchangeable Preferred Stock valued at $100 per share. Lazard Freres opined that the notes would trade at their face value on a fully distributed basis.[4] Revlon stockholders tendered 87 percent of the outstanding shares (approximately 33 million), and the company accepted the full 10 million shares on a pro rata basis.

---

3. There were 14 directors on the Revlon board. Six of them held senior management positions with the company, and two others held significant blocks of its stock. Four of the remaining six directors were associated at some point with entities that had various business relationships with Revlon. On the basis of this limited record, however, we cannot conclude that this board is entitled to certain presumptions that generally attach to the decisions of a board whose majority consists of truly outside independent directors.

4. Like bonds, the Notes actually were issued in denominations of $1,000 and integral multiples thereof. A separate certificate was issued in a total principal amount equal to the remaining sum to which a stockholder was entitled. Likewise, in the esoteric parlance of bond dealers, a Note trading at par ($1,000) would be quoted on the market at 100.

The new Notes contained covenants which limited Revlon's ability to incur additional debt, sell assets, or pay dividends unless otherwise approved by the "independent" (non-management) members of the board.

At this point, both the Rights and the Note covenants stymied Pantry Pride's attempted takeover. The next move came on September 16, when Pantry Pride announced a new tender offer at $42 per share, conditioned upon receiving at least 90% of the outstanding stock. Pantry Pride also indicated that it would consider buying less than 90%, and at an increased price, if Revlon removed the impeding Rights. While this offer was lower on its face than the earlier $47.50 proposal, Revlon's investment banker, Lazard Freres, described the two bids as essentially equal in view of the completed exchange offer.

The Revlon board held a regularly scheduled meeting on September 24. The directors rejected the latest Pantry Pride offer and authorized management to negotiate with other parties interested in acquiring Revlon. Pantry Pride remained determined in its efforts and continued to make cash bids for the company, offering $50 per share on September 27, and raising its bid to $53 on October 1, and then to $56.25 on October 7.

In the meantime, Revlon's negotiations with Forstmann and the investment group Adler & Shaykin had produced results. The Revlon directors met on October 3 to consider Pantry Pride's $53 bid and to examine possible alternatives to the offer. Both Forstmann and Adler & Shaykin made certain proposals to the board. As a result, the directors unanimously agreed to a leveraged buyout by Forstmann. The terms of this accord were as follows: each stockholder would get $56 cash per share; management would purchase stock in the new company by the exercise of their Revlon "golden parachutes";[5] Forstmann would assume Revlon's $475 million debt incurred by the issuance of the Notes; and Revlon would redeem the Rights and waive the Notes covenants for Forstmann or in connection with any other offer superior to Forstmann's. The board did not actually remove the covenants at the October 3 meeting, because Forstmann then lacked a firm commitment on its financing, but accepted the Forstmann capital structure, and indicated that the outside directors would waive the covenants in due course. Part of Forstmann's plan was to sell Revlon's Norcliff Thayer and Reheis divisions to American Home Products for $335 million. Before the merger, Revlon was to sell its cosmetics and fragrance division to Adler & Shaykin for $905 million. These transactions would facilitate the purchase by Forstmann or any other acquiror of Revlon.

When the merger, and thus the waiver of the Notes covenants, was announced, the market value of these securities began to fall. The Notes, which originally traded near par, around 100, dropped to 87.50 by October 8. One director later reported (at

---

5. In the takeover context "golden parachutes" generally are understood to be termination agreements providing substantial bonuses and other benefits for managers and certain directors upon a change in control of a company.

the October 12 meeting) a "deluge" of telephone calls from irate noteholders, and on October 10 the Wall Street Journal reported threats of litigation by these creditors.

Pantry Pride countered with a new proposal on October 7, raising its $53 offer to $56.25, subject to nullification of the Rights, a waiver of the Notes covenants, and the election of three Pantry Pride directors to the Revlon board. On October 9, representatives of Pantry Pride, Forstmann and Revlon conferred in an attempt to negotiate the fate of Revlon, but could not reach agreement. At this meeting Pantry Pride announced that it would engage in fractional bidding and top any Forstmann offer by a slightly higher one. It is also significant that Forstmann, to Pantry Pride's exclusion, had been made privy to certain Revlon financial data. Thus, the parties were not negotiating on equal terms.

Again privately armed with Revlon data, Forstmann met on October 11 with Revlon's special counsel and investment banker. On October 12, Forstmann made a new $57.25 per share offer, based on several conditions.[6] The principal demand was a lock-up option to purchase Revlon's Vision Care and National Health Laboratories divisions for $525 million, some $100–$175 million below the value ascribed to them by Lazard Freres, if another acquiror got 40% of Revlon's shares. Revlon also was required to accept a no-shop provision. The Rights and Notes covenants had to be removed as in the October 3 agreement. There would be a $25 million cancellation fee to be placed in escrow, and released to Forstmann if the new agreement terminated or if another acquiror got more than 19.9% of Revlon's stock. Finally, there would be no participation by Revlon management in the merger. In return, Forstmann agreed to support the par value of the Notes, which had faltered in the market, by an exchange of new notes. Forstmann also demanded immediate acceptance of its offer, or it would be withdrawn. The board unanimously approved Forstmann's proposal because: (1) it was for a higher price than the Pantry Pride bid, (2) it protected the noteholders, and (3) Forstmann's financing was firmly in place.[7] The board further agreed to redeem the rights and waive the covenants on the preferred stock in response to any offer above $57 cash per share. The covenants were waived, contingent upon receipt of an investment banking opinion that the Notes would trade near par value once the offer was consummated.

---

6. Forstmann's $57.25 offer ostensibly is worth $1 more than Pantry Pride's $56.25 bid. However, the Pantry Pride offer was immediate, while the Forstmann proposal must be discounted for the time value of money because of the delay in approving the merger and consummating the transaction. The exact difference between the two bids was an unsettled point of contention even at oral argument.

7. Actually, at this time about $400 million of Forstmann's funding was still subject to two investment banks using their "best efforts" to organize a syndicate to provide the balance. Pantry Pride's entire financing was not firmly committed at this point either, although Pantry Pride represented in an October 11 letter to Lazard Freres that its investment banker, Drexel Burnham Lambert, was highly confident of its ability to raise the balance of $350 million. Drexel Burnham had a firm commitment for this sum by October 18.

Pantry Pride, which had initially sought injunctive relief from the Rights plan on August 22, filed an amended complaint on October 14 challenging the lock-up, the cancellation fee, and the exercise of the Rights and the Notes covenants. Pantry Pride also sought a temporary restraining order to prevent Revlon from placing any assets in escrow or transferring them to Forstmann. Moreover, on October 22, Pantry Pride again raised its bid, with a cash offer of $58 per share conditioned upon nullification of the Rights, waiver of the covenants, and an injunction of the Forstmann lock-up.

On October 15, the Court of Chancery prohibited the further transfer of assets, and eight days later enjoined the lock-up, no-shop, and cancellation fee provisions of the agreement. The trial court concluded that the Revlon directors had breached their duty of loyalty by making concessions to Forstmann, out of concern for their liability to the noteholders, rather than maximizing the sale price of the company for the stockholders' benefit.

II

To obtain a preliminary injunction, a plaintiff must demonstrate both a reasonable probability of success on the merits and some irreparable harm which will occur absent the injunction. Additionally, the Court shall balance the conveniences of and possible injuries to the parties.

A

We turn first to Pantry Pride's probability of success on the merits. The ultimate responsibility for managing the business and affairs of a corporation falls on its board of directors. In discharging this function the directors owe fiduciary duties of care and loyalty to the corporation and its shareholders. These principles apply with equal force when a board approves a corporate merger pursuant to 8 Del.C. §251(b); and of course they are the bedrock of our law regarding corporate takeover issues. While the business judgment rule may be applicable to the actions of corporate directors responding to takeover threats, the principles upon which it is founded—care, loyalty and independence—must first be satisfied.

If the business judgment rule applies, there is a "presumption that in making a business decision the directors of a corporation acted on an informed basis, in good faith and in the honest belief that the action taken was in the best interests of the company." *Aronson v. Lewis.* However, when a board implements anti-takeover measures there arises "the omnipresent specter that a board may be acting primarily in its own interests, rather than those of the corporation and its shareholders. . . ." *Unocal Corp. v. Mesa Petroleum Co.* This potential for conflict places upon the directors the burden of proving that they had reasonable grounds for believing there was a danger to corporate policy and effectiveness, a burden satisfied by a showing of good faith and reasonable investigation. In addition, the directors must analyze the nature of the takeover and its effect on the corporation in order to ensure balance—that the responsive action taken is reasonable in relation to the threat posed.

B

The first relevant defensive measure adopted by the Revlon board was the Rights Plan, which would be considered a "poison pill" in the current language of corporate takeovers—a plan by which shareholders receive the right to be bought out by the corporation at a substantial premium on the occurrence of a stated triggering event. By 8 Del.C. §§ 141 and 122(13),[11] the board clearly had the power to adopt the measure. *See Moran v. Household International, Inc.* Thus, the focus becomes one of reasonableness and purpose.

The Revlon board approved the Rights Plan in the face of an impending hostile takeover bid by Pantry Pride at $45 per share, a price which Revlon reasonably concluded was grossly inadequate. Lazard Freres had so advised the directors, and had also informed them that Pantry Pride was a small, highly leveraged company bent on a "bust-up" takeover by using "junk bond" financing to buy Revlon cheaply, sell the acquired assets to pay the debts incurred, and retain the profit for itself. In adopting the Plan, the board protected the shareholders from a hostile takeover at a price below the company's intrinsic value, while retaining sufficient flexibility to address any proposal deemed to be in the stockholders' best interests.

To that extent the board acted in good faith and upon reasonable investigation. Under the circumstances it cannot be said that the Rights Plan as employed was unreasonable, considering the threat posed. Indeed, the Plan was a factor in causing Pantry Pride to raise its bids from a low of $42 to an eventual high of $58. At the time of its adoption the Rights Plan afforded a measure of protection consistent with the directors' fiduciary duty in facing a takeover threat perceived as detrimental to corporate interests. Far from being a "show-stopper," as the plaintiffs had contended in *Moran*, the measure spurred the bidding to new heights, a proper result of its implementation.

Although we consider adoption of the Plan to have been valid under the circumstances, its continued usefulness was rendered moot by the directors' actions on October 3 and October 12. At the October 3 meeting the board redeemed the Rights conditioned upon consummation of a merger with Forstmann, but further acknowledged that they would also be redeemed to facilitate any more favorable offer. On October 12, the board unanimously passed a resolution redeeming the Rights in connection with any cash proposal of $57.25 or more per share. Because all the pertinent offers eventually equalled or surpassed that amount, the Rights clearly

---

11. The relevant provision of Section 122 is:
    "Every corporation created under this chapter shall have power to:
    "(13) Make contracts, including contracts of guaranty and suretyship, incur liabilities, borrow money at such rates of interest as the corporation may determine, issue its notes, bonds and other obligations, and secure any of its obligations by mortgage, pledge or other encumbrance of all or any of its property, franchises and income, . . .". 8 Del.C. § 122(13).

See Section 141(a). See also Section 160(a), n. 13.

were no longer any impediment in the contest for Revlon. This mooted any question of their propriety under *Moran* or *Unocal*.

C

The second defensive measure adopted by Revlon to thwart a Pantry Pride takeover was the company's own exchange offer for 10 million of its shares. The directors' general broad powers to manage the business and affairs of the corporation are augmented by the specific authority conferred under 8 Del.C. § 160(a), permitting the company to deal in its own stock.[13] However, when exercising that power in an effort to forestall a hostile takeover, the board's actions are strictly held to the fiduciary standards outlined in *Unocal*. These standards require the directors to determine the best interests of the corporation and its stockholders, and impose an enhanced duty to abjure any action that is motivated by considerations other than a good faith concern for such interests.

The Revlon directors concluded that Pantry Pride's $47.50 offer was grossly inadequate. In that regard the board acted in good faith, and on an informed basis, with reasonable grounds to believe that there existed a harmful threat to the corporate enterprise. The adoption of a defensive measure, reasonable in relation to the threat posed, was proper and fully accorded with the powers, duties, and responsibilities conferred upon directors under our law.

D

However, when Pantry Pride increased its offer to $50 per share, and then to $53, it became apparent to all that the break-up of the company was inevitable. The Revlon board's authorization permitting management to negotiate a merger or buyout with a third party was a recognition that the company was for sale. The duty of the board had thus changed from the preservation of Revlon as a corporate entity to the maximization of the company's value at a sale for the stockholders' benefit. This significantly altered the board's responsibilities under the *Unocal* standards. It no longer faced threats to corporate policy and effectiveness, or to the stockholders' interests, from a grossly inadequate bid. The whole question of defensive measures became moot. The directors' role changed from defenders of the corporate bastion to auctioneers charged with getting the best price for the stockholders at a sale of the company.

III

This brings us to the lock-up with Forstmann and its emphasis on shoring up the sagging market value of the Notes in the face of threatened litigation by their holders. Such a focus was inconsistent with the changed concept of the directors' responsibilities at this stage of the developments. The impending waiver of the Notes covenants had caused the value of the Notes to fall, and the board was aware of the

---

13. The pertinent provision of this statute is:

"(a) Every corporation may purchase, redeem, receive, take or otherwise acquire, own and hold, sell, lend, exchange, transfer or otherwise dispose of, pledge, use and otherwise deal in and with its own shares." 8 Del.C. § 160(a).

noteholders' ire as well as their subsequent threats of suit. The directors thus made support of the Notes an integral part of the company's dealings with Forstmann, even though their primary responsibility at this stage was to the equity owners.

The original threat posed by Pantry Pride—the break-up of the company—had become a reality which even the directors embraced. Selective dealing to fend off a hostile but determined bidder was no longer a proper objective. Instead, obtaining the highest price for the benefit of the stockholders should have been the central theme guiding director action. Thus, the Revlon board could not make the requisite showing of good faith by preferring the noteholders and ignoring its duty of loyalty to the shareholders. The rights of the former already were fixed by contract. The noteholders required no further protection, and when the Revlon board entered into an auction-ending lock-up agreement with Forstmann on the basis of impermissible considerations at the expense of the shareholders, the directors breached their primary duty of loyalty.

The Revlon board argued that it acted in good faith in protecting the noteholders because *Unocal* permits consideration of other corporate constituencies. Although such considerations may be permissible, there are fundamental limitations upon that prerogative. A board may have regard for various constituencies in discharging its responsibilities, provided there are rationally related benefits accruing to the stockholders. However, such concern for non-stockholder interests is inappropriate when an auction among active bidders is in progress, and the object no longer is to protect or maintain the corporate enterprise but to sell it to the highest bidder.

Revlon also contended that by *Gilbert v. El Paso Co.*, it had contractual and good faith obligations to consider the noteholders. However, any such duties are limited to the principle that one may not interfere with contractual relationships by improper actions. Here, the rights of the noteholders were fixed by agreement, and there is nothing of substance to suggest that any of those terms were violated. The Notes covenants specifically contemplated a waiver to permit sale of the company at a fair price. The Notes were accepted by the holders on that basis, including the risk of an adverse market effect stemming from a waiver. Thus, nothing remained for Revlon to legitimately protect, and no rationally related benefit thereby accrued to the stockholders. Under such circumstances we must conclude that the merger agreement with Forstmann was unreasonable in relation to the threat posed.

A lock-up is not *per se* illegal under Delaware law. Its use has been approved in an earlier case. Such options can entice other bidders to enter a contest for control of the corporation, creating an auction for the company and maximizing shareholder profit. Current economic conditions in the takeover market are such that a "white knight" like Forstmann might only enter the bidding for the target company if it receives some form of compensation to cover the risks and costs involved. However, while those lock-ups which draw bidders into the battle benefit shareholders, similar measures which end an active auction and foreclose further bidding operate to the shareholders' detriment. . . .

The Forstmann option had a . . . destructive effect on the auction process. Forstmann had already been drawn into the contest on a preferred basis, so the result of the lock-up was not to foster bidding, but to destroy it. The board's stated reasons for approving the transactions were: (1) better financing, (2) noteholder protection, and (3) higher price. As the Court of Chancery found, and we agree, any distinctions between the rival bidders' methods of financing the proposal were nominal at best, and such a consideration has little or no significance in a cash offer for any and all shares. The principal object, contrary to the board's duty of care, appears to have been protection of the noteholders over the shareholders' interests.

While Forstmann's $57.25 offer was objectively higher than Pantry Pride's $56.25 bid, the margin of superiority is less when the Forstmann price is adjusted for the time value of money. In reality, the Revlon board ended the auction in return for very little actual improvement in the final bid. The principal benefit went to the directors, who avoided personal liability to a class of creditors to whom the board owed no further duty under the circumstances. Thus, when a board ends an intense bidding contest on an insubstantial basis, and where a significant by-product of that action is to protect the directors against a perceived threat of personal liability for consequences stemming from the adoption of previous defensive measures, the action cannot withstand the enhanced scrutiny which *Unocal* requires of director conduct.

In addition to the lock-up option, the Court of Chancery enjoined the no-shop provision as part of the attempt to foreclose further bidding by Pantry Pride. The no-shop provision, like the lock-up option, while not *per se* illegal, is impermissible under the *Unocal* standards when a board's primary duty becomes that of an auctioneer responsible for selling the company to the highest bidder. The agreement to negotiate only with Forstmann ended rather than intensified the board's involvement in the bidding contest.

It is ironic that the parties even considered a no-shop agreement when Revlon had dealt preferentially, and almost exclusively, with Forstmann throughout the contest. After the directors authorized management to negotiate with other parties, Forstmann was given every negotiating advantage that Pantry Pride had been denied: cooperation from management, access to financial data, and the exclusive opportunity to present merger proposals directly to the board of directors. Favoritism for a white knight to the total exclusion of a hostile bidder might be justifiable when the latter's offer adversely affects shareholder interests, but when bidders make relatively similar offers, or dissolution of the company becomes inevitable, the directors cannot fulfill their enhanced *Unocal* duties by playing favorites with the contending factions. Market forces must be allowed to operate freely to bring the target's shareholders the best price available for their equity.[16] Thus, as the trial court ruled,

---

16. By this we do not embrace the "passivity" thesis rejected in *Unocal*. The directors' role remains an active one, changed only in the respect that they are charged with the duty of selling the company at the highest price attainable for the stockholders' benefit.

the shareholders' interests necessitated that the board remain free to negotiate in the fulfillment of that duty.

The court below similarly enjoined the payment of the cancellation fee, pending a resolution of the merits, because the fee was part of the overall plan to thwart Pantry Pride's efforts. We find no abuse of discretion in that ruling. . . .

V

In conclusion, the Revlon board was confronted with a situation not uncommon in the current wave of corporate takeovers. A hostile and determined bidder sought the company at a price the board was convinced was inadequate. The initial defensive tactics worked to the benefit of the shareholders, and thus the board was able to sustain its *Unocal* burdens in justifying those measures. However, in granting an asset option lock-up to Forstmann, we must conclude that under all the circumstances the directors allowed considerations other than the maximization of shareholder profit to affect their judgment, and followed a course that ended the auction for Revlon, absent court intervention, to the ultimate detriment of its shareholders. No such defensive measure can be sustained when it represents a breach of the directors' fundamental duty of care. In that context the board's action is not entitled to the deference accorded it by the business judgment rule. The measures were properly enjoined. The decision of the Court of Chancery, therefore, is affirmed.

Questions

1. Who were the noteholders that the Revlon board was trying to protect? What, if any, relevance should this have had to the court? Is there a reason why the initial identity of the noteholders shouldn't have made a difference?

2. Could the Revlon board legitimately have believed that protecting the noteholders and the Forstmann deal was better for the corporation than the Pantry Pride deal? If so, is the result in the case similar to that in *Dodge v. Ford* in that, had the directors of Revlon been less direct about their motives, the court might have seen the case differently?

3. Does *Revlon* suggest a different conception of the corporation in a control battle than generally exists under normal operating circumstances? Is the difference justifiable? Part of the wisdom of the *Unocal* test is the relatively judicious balance the court achieved between shareholder interests and the interests of the corporation as an entity. Does the fact that the *Revlon* directors evidently conceded a change in control justifiably change this balance?

4. The Revlon battle was as much a battle of personalities as it was a battle for corporate control. Connie Bruck, in her article on the struggle in *The American Lawyer* and later in her book, *The Predator's Ball*, wonderfully illustrates the contempt that Revlon's aristocratic French chair, Michel Bergerac demonstrated for the short, cigar chomping upstart, Ronald Perelman, whose claim to wealth and power rested on the back of Drexel Burnham's Michael Millken's famous junk

bond operation. As the story illustrates, even in large public corporations, human emotions and behavior are sometimes as critical a factor in corporate decisionmaking as sharp-eyed business planning, a reality we certainly saw in the case of close corporations.

With *Revlon* in place, the culture wars surfaced with a battle among Time Incorporated, Paramount Communications, and Warner Communications for dominance of the American media. While the following case was a victory for corporate values beyond simple stock price, one has to admit that the subsequent history of Time-Warner has been anything but brilliant. Following this deal, Time-Warner acquired Turner Broadcasting (parent company of CNN and Turner Movie Classics) and then in turn was merged with AOL to become AOL Time-Warner. In 2002, after the collapse of the Internet bubble, AOL Time Warner reported $54.24 billion loss. In 2003, AOL Time Warner changed its name back to Time Warner Inc. and, in 2009, split with AOL, which became an independent company. Moreover, while Time shareholders were offered a princely $200 a share by Paramount—an offer they were ultimately not permitted to accept—the closing price of Time Warner Inc. at the date of this writing (May 2018) was $94.17. Of course, this price is not adjusted for stock splits and for the mergers themselves, but it still doesn't look like a good deal for Time stockholders. As you read the case, consider whether these developments render the decision wrong.

Paramount Communications, Inc. v. Time Incorporated
571 A.2d 1140 (Del. 1989)

Horsey, Justice

Paramount Communications, Inc. ("Paramount") and two other groups of plaintiffs[1] ("Shareholder Plaintiffs"), shareholders of Time Incorporated ("Time"), a Delaware corporation, separately filed suits in the Delaware Court of Chancery seeking a preliminary injunction to halt Time's tender offer for 51% of Warner Communication, Inc.'s ("Warner") outstanding shares at $70 cash per share. The court below consolidated the cases and, following the development of an extensive record, after discovery and an evidentiary hearing, denied plaintiffs' motion. In a 50-page unreported opinion and order entered July 14, 1989, the Chancellor refused to enjoin Time's consummation of its tender offer, concluding that the plaintiffs were unlikely to prevail on the merits.

---

1. Plaintiffs in these three consolidated appeals are: (i) Paramount Communications, Inc. and KDS Acquisition Corp. (collectively "Paramount"); (ii) Literary Partners L.P., Cablevision Media Partners, L.P., and A. Jerrold Perenchio (collectively "Literary Partners"), suing individually; and (iii) certain other shareholder plaintiffs, suing individually and as an uncertified class.

On the same day, plaintiffs filed in this Court an interlocutory appeal, which we accepted on an expedited basis. Pending the appeal, a stay of execution of Time's tender offer was entered for ten days, or until July 24, 1989, at 5:00 p.m. Following briefing and oral argument, on July 24 we concluded that the decision below should be affirmed. We so held in a brief ruling from the bench and a separate Order entered on that date. The effect of our decision was to permit Time to proceed with its tender offer for Warner's outstanding shares. This is the written opinion articulating the reasons for our July 24 bench ruling.

The principal ground for reversal, asserted by all plaintiffs, is that Paramount's June 7, 1989 uninvited all-cash, all-shares, "fully negotiable" (though conditional) tender offer for Time triggered duties under *Unocal Corp. v. Mesa Petroleum Co.*, and that Time's board of directors, in responding to Paramount's offer, breached those duties. As a consequence, plaintiffs argue that in our review of the Time board's decision of June 16, 1989 to enter into a revised merger agreement with Warner, Time is not entitled to the benefit and protection of the business judgment rule.

Shareholder Plaintiffs also assert a claim based on *Revlon v. MacAndrews & Forbes Holdings, Inc.* They argue that the original Time-Warner merger agreement of March 4, 1989 resulted in a change of control which effectively put Time up for sale, thereby triggering *Revlon* duties. Those plaintiffs argue that Time's board breached its *Revlon* duties by failing, in the face of the change of control, to maximize shareholder value in the immediate term.

Applying our standard of review, we affirm the Chancellor's ultimate finding and conclusion under *Unocal*. We find that Paramount's tender offer was reasonably perceived by Time's board to pose a threat to Time and that the Time board's "response" to that threat was, under the circumstances, reasonable and proportionate. Applying *Unocal,* we reject the argument that the only corporate threat posed by an all-shares, all-cash tender offer is the possibility of inadequate value.

We also find that Time's board did not by entering into its initial merger agreement with Warner come under a *Revlon* duty either to auction the company or to maximize short-term shareholder value, notwithstanding the unequal share exchange. Therefore, the Time board's original plan of merger with Warner was subject only to a business judgment rule analysis.

I

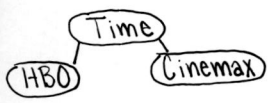

Time is a Delaware corporation with its principal offices in New York City. Time's traditional business is publication of magazines and books; however, Time also provides pay television programming through its Home Box Office, Inc. and Cinemax subsidiaries. In addition, Time owns and operates cable television franchises through is subsidiary, American Television and Communication Corporation. During the relevant time period, Time's board consisted of sixteen directors. Twelve of the directors were "outside," nonemployee directors. Four of the directors were also officers of the company. . . .

As early as 1983 and 1984, Time's executive board began considering expanding Time's operations into the entertainment industry. In 1987, Time established a special committee of executives to consider and propose corporate strategies for the 1990s. The consensus of the committee was that Time should move ahead in the area of ownership and creation of video programming. This expansion, as the Chancellor noted, was predicated upon two considerations: first, Time's desire to have greater control, in terms of quality and price, over the film products delivered by way of its cable network and franchises; and second, Time's concern over the increasing globalization of the world economy. Some of Time's outside directors, especially Luce and Temple, had opposed this move as a threat to the editorial integrity and journalistic focus of Time.[4] Despite this concern, the board recognized that a vertically integrated video enterprise to complement Time's existing HBO and cable networks would better enable it to compete on a global basis.

In late spring of 1987, a meeting took place between Steve Ross, CEO of Warner Brothers, and Nicholas of Time. Ross and Nicholas discussed the possibility of a joint venture between the two companies through the creation of a jointly-owned cable company. Time would contribute its cable system and HBO. Warner would contribute its cable system and provide access to Warner Brothers Studio. The resulting venture would be a larger, more efficient cable network, able to produce and distribute its own movies on a worldwide basis. Ultimately the parties abandoned this plan, determining that it was impractical for several reasons, chief among them being tax considerations.

On August 11, 1987, Gerald M. Levin, Time's vice chairman and chief strategist, wrote J. Richard Munro a confidential memorandum in which he strongly recommended a strategic consolidation with Warner. In June 1988, Nicholas and Munro sent to each outside director a copy of the "comprehensive long-term planning document" prepared by the committee of Time executives that had been examining strategies for the 1990s. The memo included reference to and a description of Warner as a potential acquisition candidate.

Thereafter, Munro and Nicholas held meetings with Time's outside directors to discuss, generally, long-term strategies for Time and, specifically, a combination with Warner. Nearly a year later, Time's board reached the point of serious discussion of the "nuts and bolts" of a consolidation with an entertainment company. On July 21, 1988, Time's board met, with all outside directors present. The meeting's purpose was to consider Time's expansion into the entertainment industry on a global scale. Management presented the board with a profile of various entertainment

---

4. The primary concern of Time's outside directors was the preservation of the "Time Culture." They believed that Time had become recognized in this country as an institution built upon a foundation of journalistic integrity. Time's management made a studious effort to refrain from involvement in Time's editorial policy. Several of Time's outside directors feared that a merger with an entertainment company would divert Time's focus from news journalism and threaten the Time Culture.

companies in addition to Warner, including Disney, 20th Century Fox, Universal, and Paramount.

Without any definitive decision on choice of a company, the board approved in principle a strategic plan for Time's expansion. The board gave management the "go-ahead" to continue discussions with Warner concerning the possibility of a merger. With the exception of Temple and Luce, most of the outside directors agreed that a merger involving expansion into the entertainment field promised great growth opportunity for Time. Temple and Luce remained unenthusiastic about Time's entry into the entertainment field.

The board's consensus was that a merger of Time and Warner was feasible, but only if Time controlled the board of the resulting corporation and thereby preserved a management committed to Time's journalistic integrity. To accomplish this goal, the board stressed the importance of carefully defining in advance the corporate governance provisions that would control the resulting entity. Some board members expressed concern over whether such a business combination would place Time "*in play.*" The board discussed the wisdom of adopting further defensive measures to lessen such a possibility.[5]

Of a wide range of companies considered by Time's board as possible merger candidates, Warner Brothers, Paramount, Columbia, M.C.A., Fox, MGM, Disney, and Orion, the board, in July 1988, concluded that Warner was the superior candidate for a consolidation. Warner stood out on a number of counts. Warner had just acquired Lorimar and its film studios. Time-Warner could make movies and television shows for use of HBO. Warner had an international distribution system, which Time could use to sell films, videos, books and magazines. Warner was a giant in the music and recording business an area into which Time wanted to expand. None of the other companies considered had the musical clout of Warner. Time and Warner's cable systems were compatible and could be easily integrated; none of the other companies considered presented such a compatible cable partner. Together, Time and Warner would control half of New York City's cable system; Warner had cable systems in Brooklyn and Queens; and Time controlled cable systems in Manhattan and Queens. Warner's publishing company would integrate well with Time's established publishing company. Time sells hardcover books and magazines, and Warner sells softcover books and comics.[6] Time-Warner could sell all of these publications and Warner's videos by using Time's direct mailing network and Warner's international

---

5. Time had in place a panoply of defensive devices, including a staggered board, a "poison pill" preferred stock rights plan triggered by an acquisition of 15% of the company, a fifty-day notice period for shareholder motions, and restrictions on shareholders' ability to call a meeting or act by consent.

6. In contrast, Paramount's publishing endeavors were in the areas of professional volumes and text books. Time's board did not find Paramount's publishing as compatible as Warner's publishing efforts.

distribution system. Time's network could be used to promote and merchandise Warner's movies.

In August 1988, Levin, Nicholas, and Munro, acting on instructions from Time's board, continued to explore a business combination with Warner. By letter dated August 4, 1988, management informed the outside directors of proposed corporate governance provision to be discussed with Warner. The provisions incorporated the recommendations of several of Time's outside directors.

From the outset, Time's board favored an all-cash or cash and securities acquisition of Warner as the basis for consolidation. Bruce Wasserstein, Time's financial advisor, also favored an outright purchase of Warner. However, Steve Ross, Warner's CEO, was adamant that a business combination was only practicable on a stock-for-stock basis. Warner insisted on a stock swap in order to preserve its shareholders' equity in the resulting corporation. Time's officers, on the other hand, made it abundantly clear that Time would be the acquiring corporation and that Time would control the resulting board. Time refused to permit itself to be cast as the "acquired" company.

Eventually Time acquiesced in Warner's insistence on a stock-for-stock deal, but talks broke down over corporate governance issues. Time wanted Ross' position as a co-CEO to be temporary and wanted Ross to retire in five years. Ross, however, refused to set a time for his retirement and viewed Time's proposal as indicating a lack of confidence in his leadership. Warner considered it vital that their executives and creative staff not perceive Warner as selling out to Time. Time's request of a guarantee that Time would dominate the CEO succession was objected to as inconsistent with the concept of a Time-Warner merger "of equals." Negotiations ended when the parties reached an impasse. Time's board refused to compromise on its position on corporate governance. Time, and particularly its outside directors, viewed the corporate governance provisions as critical for preserving the "Time Culture" through a pro-Time management at the top.

Throughout the fall of 1988 Time pursued its plan of expansion into the entertainment field; Time held informal discussions with several companies, including Paramount. Capital Cities/ABC approached Time to propose a merger. Talks terminated, however, when Capital Cities/ABC suggested that it was interested in purchasing Time or in controlling the resulting board. Time steadfastly maintained it was not placing itself up for sale.

Warner and Time resumed negotiations in January 1989. The catalyst for the resumption of talks was a private dinner between Steve Ross and Time outside director, Michael Dingman. Dingman was able to convince Ross that the transitional nature of the proposed co-CEO arrangement did not reflect a lack of confidence in Ross. Ross agreed that this course was best for the company and a meeting between Ross and Munro resulted. Ross agreed to retire in five years and let Nicholas succeed him. Negotiations resumed and many of the details of the original stock-for-stock exchange agreement remained intact. In addition, Time's senior management agreed to long-term contracts.

Time insider directors Levin and Nicholas met with Warner's financial advisors to decide upon a stock exchange ratio. Time's board had recognized the potential need to pay a premium in the stock ratio in exchange for dictating the governing arrangement of the new Time-Warner. Levin and outside director Finkelstein were the primary proponents of paying a premium to protect the "Time Culture." The board discussed premium rates of 10%, 15% and 20%. Wasserstein also suggested paying a premium for Warner due to Warner's rapid growth rate. The market exchange ratio of Time stock for Warner stock was .38 in favor of Warner. Warner's financial advisors informed its board that any exchange rate over .400 was a fair deal and any exchange rate over .450 was "one hell of a deal." The parties ultimately agreed upon an exchange rate favoring Warner of .465. On that basis, Warner stockholders would have owned approximately 62%[7] of the common stock of Time-Warner.

On March 3, 1989, Time's board, with all but one director in attendance, met and unanimously approved the stock-for-stock merger with Warner. Warner's board likewise approved the merger. The agreement called for Warner to be merged into a wholly-owned Time subsidiary with Warner becoming the surviving corporation. The common stock of Warner would then be converted into common stock of Time at the agreed upon ratio. Thereafter, the name of Time would be changed to Time-Warner, Inc. . . .

The resulting company would have a 24-member board, with 12 members representing each corporation. The company would have co-CEO's, at first Ross and Munro, then Ross and Nicholas, and finally, after Ross' retirement, by Nicholas alone. The board would create an editorial committee with a majority of members representing Time. A similar entertainment committee would be controlled by Warner board members. A two-thirds supermajority vote was required to alter CEO successions but an earlier proposal to have supermajority protection for the editorial committee was abandoned. Warner's board suggested raising the compensation levels for Time's senior management under the new corporation. Warner's management, as with most entertainment executives, received higher salaries than comparable executives in news journalism. Time's board, however, rejected Warner's proposal to equalize the salaries of the two management teams.

At its March 3, 1989 meeting, Time's board adopted several defensive tactics. Time entered an automatic share exchange agreement with Warner. Time would receive 17,292,747 shares of Warner's outstanding common stock (9.4%) and Warner would receive 7,080,016 shares of Time's outstanding common stock (11.1%). Either party could trigger the exchange. Time sought out and paid for "confidence" letters from various banks with which it did business. In these letters, the banks promised not to finance any third-party attempt to acquire Time. Time argues these agreements served only to preserve the confidential relationship between itself and the banks.

---

7. As was noted in the briefs and at oral argument, this figure is somewhat misleading because it does not take into consideration the number of individuals who owned stock in both companies.

The Chancellor found these agreements to be inconsequential and futile attempts to "dry up" money for a hostile takeover. Time also agreed to a "no-shop" clause, preventing Time from considering any other consolidation proposal, thus relinquishing its power to consider other proposals, regardless of their merits. Time did so at Warner's insistence. Warner did not want to be left "on the auction block" for an unfriendly suitor, if Time were to withdraw from the deal.

Time representatives lauded the lack of debt to the United States Senate and to the President of the United States. Public reaction to the announcement of the merger was positive. Time-Warner would be a media colossus with international scope. The board scheduled the stockholder vote for June 23; and a May 1 record date was set. On May 24, 1989, Time sent out extensive proxy statements to the stockholders regarding the approval vote on the merger. In the meantime, with the merger proceeding without impediment, the special committee had concluded, shortly after its creation, that it was not necessary either to retain independent consultants, legal or financial, or even to meet. Time's board was unanimously in favor of the proposed merger with Warner; and, by the end of May, the Time-Warner merger appeared to an accomplished fact.

On June 7, 1989, these wishful assumptions were shattered by Paramount's surprising announcement of its all-cash offer to purchase all outstanding shares of Time for $175 per share. The following day, June 8, the trading price of Time's stock rose from $126 to $170 per share. Paramount's offer was said to be "fully negotiable."[8]

Time found Paramount's "fully negotiable" offer to be in fact subject to at least three conditions. First, Time had to terminate its merger agreement and stock exchange agreement with Warner, and remove certain other of its defensive devices, including the redemption of Time's shareholder rights. Second, Paramount had to obtain the required cable franchise transfers from Time in a fashion acceptable to Paramount in its sole discretion. Finally, the offer depended upon a judicial determination that section 203 of the General Corporate Law of Delaware (The Delaware Anti-Takeover Statute) was inapplicable to any Time-Paramount merger. While Paramount's board had been privately advised that it could take months, perhaps over a year, to forge and consummate the deal, Paramount's board publicly proclaimed its ability to close the offer by July 5, 1989. Paramount executives later conceded that none of its directors believed that July 5th was a realistic date to close the transaction.

On June 8, 1989, Time formally responded to Paramount's offer. Time's chairman and CEO, J. Richard Munro, sent an aggressively worded letter to Paramount's CEO, Martin Davis. Munro's letter attacked Davis' personal integrity and called Paramount's offer "smoke and mirrors." Time's nonmanagement directors were not shown

---

8. Subsequently, it was established that Paramount's board had decided as early as March 1989 to move to acquire Time. However, Paramount management intentionally delayed publicizing its proposal until Time had mailed to its stockholders its Time-Warner merger proposal along with the required proxy statements.

the letter before it was sent. However, at a board meeting that same day, all members endorsed management's response as well as the letter's content.

Over the following eight days, Time's board met three times to discuss Paramount's $175 offer. The board viewed Paramount's offer as inadequate and concluded that its proposed merger with Warner was the better course of action. Therefore, the board declined to open any negotiations with Paramount and held steady its course toward a merger with Warner.

In June, Time's board of directors met several times. During the course of their June meetings, Time's outside directors met frequently without management, officers or directors being present. At the request of the outside directors, corporate counsel was present during the board meetings and, from time to time, the management directors were asked to leave the board sessions. During the course of these meeting, Time's financial advisors informed the board that, on an auction basis, Time's per share value was materially higher than Warner's $175 per share offer.[9] After this advice, the board concluded that Paramount's $175 offer was inadequate.

At these June meetings, certain Time directors expressed their concern that Time stockholders would not comprehend the long-term benefits of the Warner merger. Large quantities of Time shares were held by institutional investors. The board feared that even though there appeared to be wide support for the Warner transaction, Paramount's cash premium would be a tempting prospect to these investors. In mid-June, Time sought permission from the New York Stock Exchange to alter its rules and allow the Time-Warner merger to proceed without stockholder approval. Time did so at Warner's insistence. The New York Stock Exchange rejected Time's request on June 15; and on that day, the value of Time stock reached $182 per share.

The following day, June 16, Time's board met to take up Paramount's offer. The board's prevailing belief was that Paramount's bid posed a threat to Time's control of its own destiny and retention of the "Time Culture." Even after Time's financial advisors made another presentation of Paramount and its business attributes, Time's board maintained its position that a combination with Warner offered greater potential for Time. Warner provided Time a much desired production capability and an established international marketing chain. Time's advisors suggested various options, including defensive measures. . . . Time's board formally rejected Paramount's offer.[11]

At the same meeting, Time's board decided to recast its consolidation with Warner into an outright cash and securities acquisition of Warner by Time; and Time so informed Warner. Time accordingly restructured its proposal to acquire Warner as follows: Time would make an immediate all-cash offer for 51% of Warner's

---

9. Time's advisors estimated the value of Time in a control premium situation to be significantly higher than the value of Time in other than a sale situation.

11. Meanwhile, Time had already begun erecting impediments to Paramount's offer. Time encouraged local cable franchises to sue Paramount to prevent it from easily obtaining the franchises.

outstanding stock at $70 per share. The remaining 49% would be purchased at some later date for a mixture of cash and securities worth $70 per share. To provide the funds required for its outright acquisition of Warner, Time would assume 7–10 billion dollars worth of debt, thus eliminating one of the principal transaction-related benefits of the original merger agreement. Nine billion dollars of the total purchase price would be allocated to the purchase of Warner's goodwill.

Warner agreed but insisted on certain terms. Warner sought a control premium and guarantees that the governance provisions found in the original merger agreement would remain intact. Warner further sought agreements that Time would not employ its poison pill against Warner and that, unless enjoined, Time would be legally bound to complete the transaction. Time's board agreed to these last measures only at the insistence of Warner. For its part, Time was assured of its ability to extend its efforts into production areas and international markets, all the while maintaining the Time identity and culture. The Chancellor found the initial Time-Warner transaction to have been negotiated at arms length and the restructured Time-Warner transaction to have resulted from Paramount's offer and its expected effect on a Time shareholder vote.

On June 23, 1989, Paramount raised its all-cash offer to buy Time's outstanding stock to $200 per share. Paramount still professed that all aspects of the offer were negotiable. Time's board met on June 26, 1989 and formally rejected Paramount's $200 per share second offer. The board reiterated its belief that, despite the $25 increase, the offer was still inadequate. the Time board maintained that the Warner transaction offered a greater long-term value for the stockholders and, unlike Paramount's offer, did not pose a threat to Time's survival and its "culture." Paramount then filed this action in the Court of Chancery.

II

The Shareholder Plaintiffs first assert a *Revlon* claim. They contend that the March 4 Time-Warner agreement effectively put Time up for sale, triggering *Revlon* duties, requiring Time's board to enhance short-term shareholder value and to treat all other interested acquirors on an equal basis. The Shareholder Plaintiffs base this argument on two facts: (i) the ultimate Time-Warner exchange ratio of .465 favoring Warner, resulting in Warner shareholders' receipt of 62% of the combined company; and (ii) the subjective intent of Time's directors as evidenced in their statements that the market might perceive the Time-Warner merger as putting Time up "for sale" and their adoption of various defensive measures.

The Shareholder Plaintiffs further contend that Time's directors, in structuring the original merger transaction to be "takeover-proof," triggered *Revlon* duties by foreclosing their shareholders from any prospect of obtaining a control premium. In short, plaintiffs argue that Time's board's decision to merge with Warner imposed a fiduciary duty to maximize immediate share value and not erect unreasonable barriers to further bids. Therefore, they argue, the Chancellor erred in finding: that Paramount's bid for Time did not place Time "for sale"; that Time's transaction with Warner did not result in any transfer of control; and that the combined Time-Warner was not so large as to preclude the possibility of the stockholders of Time-Warner receiving a future control premium.

Paramount asserts only a *Unocal* claim in which the shareholder plaintiffs join. Paramount contends that the Chancellor, in applying the first part of the *Unocal* test, erred in finding that Time's board had reasonable grounds to believe that Paramount posed both a legally cognizable threat to Time shareholders and a danger to Time's corporate policy and effectiveness. Paramount also contests the court's finding that Time's board made a reasonable and objective investigation of Paramount's offer so as to be informed before rejecting it. Paramount further claims that the court erred in applying *Unocal's* second part in finding Time's response to be "reasonable." Paramount points primarily to the preclusive effect of the revised agreement which denied Time shareholders the opportunity both to vote on the agreement and to respond to Paramount's tender offer. Paramount argues that the underlying motivation of Time's board in adopting these defensive measures was management's desire to perpetuate itself in office.

The Court of Chancery posed the pivotal question presented by this case to be: Under what circumstances must a board of directors abandon an in-place plan of corporate development in order to provide its shareholders with the option to elect and realize an immediate control premium? As applied to this case, the question becomes: Did Time's Board, having developed a strategic plan of global expansion to be launched through a business combination with Warner, come under a fiduciary duty to jettison its plan and put the corporation's future in the hands of its shareholders?

While we affirm the result reached by the Chancellor, we think it unwise to place undue emphasis upon long-term versus short-term corporate strategy. Two key predicates underpin our analysis. First, Delaware law imposes on a board of directors the duty to manage the business and affairs of the corporation. 8 Del.C. § 141(a). This broad mandate includes a conferred authority to set a corporate course of action, including time frame, designed to enhance corporate profitability.[12] Thus, the question of "long-term" versus "short-term" values is largely irrelevant because directors, generally, are obliged to charter a course for a corporation which is in its best interest without regard to a fixed investment horizon. Second, absent a limited set of circumstances as defined under *Revlon*, a board of directors, while always required to act in an informed manner, is not under any *per se* duty to maximize shareholder value in the short term, even in the context of a takeover. In our view, the pivotal question presented by this case is: "Did Time, by entering into the proposed merger

---

12. Thus, we endorse the Chancellor's conclusion that it is not a breach of faith for directors to determine that the present stock market price of shares is not representative of true value or that there may indeed be several market values for any corporation's stock. We have so held in another context.

with Warner, put itself up for sale?" A resolution of that issue through application of *Revlon* has a significant bearing upon the resolution of the derivative *Unocal* issue.

A

We first take up plaintiffs' principal *Revlon* argument, summarized above. In rejecting this argument, the Chancellor found the original Time-Warner merger agreement not to constitute a "change of control" and concluded that the transaction did not trigger *Revlon* duties. The Chancellor's conclusion is premised on a finding that "[b]efore the merger agreement was signed, control of the corporation existed in a fluid aggregation of unaffiliated shareholders representing a voting majority—in other words, in the market." The Chancellor's findings of fact are supported by the record and his conclusion is correct as a matter of law. However, we premise our rejection of plaintiffs' *Revlon* claim on different grounds, namely, the absence of any substantial evidence to conclude that Time's board, in negotiating with Warner, made the dissolution or breakup of the corporate entity inevitable, as was the case in *Revlon*.

Under Delaware law there are, generally speaking and without excluding other possibilities, two circumstances which may implicate *Revlon* duties. The first, and clearer one, is when a corporation initiates an active bidding process seeking to sell itself or to effect a business reorganization involving a clear break-up of the company. However, *Revlon* duties may also be triggered where, in response to a bidder's offer, a target abandons its long-term strategy and seeks an alternative transaction also involving the breakup of the company.[13] Thus, in *Revlon*, when the board responded to Pantry Pride's offer by contemplating a "bust-up" sale of assets in a leveraged acquisition, we imposed upon the board a duty to maximize immediate shareholder value and an obligation to auction the company fairly. If, however, the board's reaction to a hostile tender offer is found to constitute only a defensive response and not an abandonment of the corporation's continued existence, *Revlon* duties are not triggered, though *Unocal* duties attach.[14]

The plaintiffs insist that even though the original Time-Warner agreement may not have worked "an objective change of control," the transaction made a "sale" of Time inevitable. Plaintiffs rely on the subjective intent of Time's board of directors

---

13. As we stated in *Revlon*, in both such cases, "[t]he duty of the board [has] changed from the preservation of... [the] corporate entity to the maximization of the company's value at a sale for the stockholder's benefit.... [The board] no longer face[s] threats to corporate policy and effectiveness, or to the stockholders' interests, from a grossly inadequate bid." *Revlon v. MacAndrews & Forbes Holdings, Inc.*, Del. Supr., 506 A.2d 173, 182 (1986).

14. Within the auction process, any action taken by the board must be reasonably related to the threat posed or reasonable in relation to the advantage sought, *see Mills Acquisition Co. v. Macmillan, Inc.*, Del. Supr., 559 A.2d 1261, 1288 (1988). Thus, a *Unocal* analysis may be appropriate when a corporation is in a *Revlon* situation and *Revlon* duties may be triggered by a defensive action taken in response to a hostile offer. Since *Revlon*, we have stated that differing treatment of various bidders is not actionable when such action reasonably relates to achieving the best price available for the stockholders. *Macmillan*, 559 A.2d at 1286–87.

and principally upon certain board members' expressions of concern that the Warner transaction *might* be viewed as effectively putting Time up for sale. Plaintiffs argue that the use of a lock-up agreement, a no-shop clause, and so-called "dry-up" agreements prevented shareholders from obtaining a control premium in the immediate future and thus violated *Revlon*.

We agree with the Chancellor that such evidence is entirely insufficient to invoke *Revlon* duties; and we decline to extend *Revlon's* application to corporate transactions simply because they might be construed as putting a corporation either "in play" or "up for sale." The adoption of structural safety devices alone does not trigger *Revlon*.[15] Rather, as the Chancellor stated, such devices are properly subject to a *Unocal* analysis.

Finally, we do not find in Time's recasting of its merger agreement with Warner from a share exchange to a share purchase a basis to conclude that Time had either abandoned its strategic plan or made a sale of Time inevitable.[16] The Chancellor found that although the merged Time-Warner company would be large (with a value approaching approximately $30 billion), recent takeover cases have proven that acquisition of the combined company might nonetheless be possible. The legal consequence is that *Unocal* alone applies to determine whether the business judgment rule attaches to the revised agreement. . . .

B

We turn now to plaintiffs' *Unocal* claim. We begin by noting, as did the Chancellor, that our decision does not require us to pass on the wisdom of the board's decision to enter into the original Time-Warner agreement. That is not a court's task. Our task is simply to review the record to determine whether there is sufficient evidence to support the Chancellor's conclusion that the initial Time-Warner agreement was the product of a proper exercise of business judgment.

We have purposely detailed the evidence of the Time board's deliberative approach, beginning in 1983–84, to expand itself. Time's decision in 1988 to combine with Warner was made only after what could be fairly characterized as an exhaustive appraisal of Time's future as a corporation. After concluding in 1983–84 that the corporation must expand to survive, and beyond journalism into entertainment, the board

---

15. Although the legality of the various safety devices adopted to protect the original agreement is not a central issue, there is substantial evidence to support each of the trial court's related conclusions. Thus, the court found that the concept of the Share Exchange Agreement predated any takeover threat by Paramount and had been adopted for a rational business purpose: to deter Time and Warner from being "put in play" by their March 4 Agreement. The court further found that Time had adopted the "no-shop" clause at Warner's insistence and for Warner's protection. Finally, although certain aspects of the "dry-up" agreements were suspect on their face, we concur in the Chancellor's view that in this case they were inconsequential.

16. We note that, although Time's advisors presented the board with such alternatives as an auction or sale to a third party bidder, the board rejected those responses, preferring to go forward with its pre-existing plan rather than adopt an alternative to Paramount's proposal.

combed the field of available entertainment companies. By 1987 Time had focused upon Warner; by late July 1988 Time's board was convinced that Warner would provide the best "fit" for Time to achieve its strategic objectives. The record attests to the zealousness of Time's executives, fully supported by their directors, in seeing to the preservation of Time's "culture," i.e., its perceived editorial integrity in journalism. We find ample evidence in the record to support the Chancellor's conclusion that the Time board's decision to expand the business of the company through its March 3 merger with Warner was entitled to the protection of the business judgment rule.

The Chancellor reached a different conclusion in addressing the Time-Warner transaction as revised three months later. He found that the revised agreement was defense-motivated and designed to avoid the potentially disruptive effect that Paramount's offer would have had on consummation of the proposed merger were it put to a shareholder vote. Thus, the court declined to apply the traditional business judgment rule to the revised transaction and instead analyzed the Time board's June 16 decision under *Unocal*. The court ruled that *Unocal* applied to all director actions taken, following receipt of Paramount's hostile tender offer, that were reasonably determined to be defensive. Clearly that was a correct ruling and no party disputes that ruling.

In *Unocal*, we held that before the business judgment rule is applied to a board's adoption of a defensive measure, the burden will lie with the board to prove (a) reasonable grounds for believing that a danger to corporate policy and effectiveness existed; and (b) that the defensive measures adopted was reasonable in relation to the threat posed. Directors satisfy the first part of the *Unocal* test by demonstrating good faith and reasonable investigation. We have repeatedly stated that the refusal to entertain an offer may comport with a valid exercise of a board's business judgment.

Unocal involved a two-tier, highly coercive tender offer. In such a case, the threat is obvious: shareholders may be compelled to tender to avoid being treated adversely in the second stage of the transaction. In subsequent cases the Court of Chancery has suggested that an all-cash, all-shares offer, falling within a range of values that a shareholder might reasonably prefer, cannot constitute a legally recognized "threat" to shareholder interests sufficient to withstand a *Unocal* analysis. In those cases, the Court of Chancery determined that whatever threat existed related only to the shareholders and only to price and not to the corporation.

From those decisions by our Court of Chancery, Paramount and the individual plaintiffs extrapolate a rule of law that an all-cash, all-shares offer with values reasonably in the range of acceptable price cannot pose any objective threat to a corporation or its shareholders. Thus, Paramount would have us hold that only if the value of Paramount's offer were determined to be clearly inferior to the value created by management's plan to merge with Warner could the offer be viewed—objectively—as a threat.

Implicit in the plaintiffs' argument is the view that a hostile tender offer can pose only two types of threats: the threat of coercion that results from a two-tier offer promising unequal treatment for nontendering shareholders; and the threat of inadequate value from an all-shares, all-cash offer at a price below what a target board in good faith deems to be the present value of its shares. Since Paramount's offer was all-cash, the only conceivable "threat," plaintiffs argue, was inadequate value.[17] We disapprove of such a narrow and rigid construction of *Unocal*, for the reasons which follow.

Plaintiffs' position represents a fundamental misconception of our standard of review under *Unocal* principally because it would involve the court in substituting its judgment as to what is a "better" deal for that of a corporation's board of directors. To the extent that the Court of Chancery has recently done so in certain of its opinions, we hereby reject such approach as not in keeping with a proper *Unocal* analysis.

The usefulness of *Unocal* as an analytical tool is precisely its flexibility in the face of a variety of fact scenarios. *Unocal* is not intended as an abstract standard; neither is it a structured and mechanistic procedure of appraisal. Thus, we have said that directors may consider, when evaluating the threat posed by a takeover bid, the "inadequacy of the price offered, nature and timing of the offer, questions of illegality, the impact on 'constituencies' other than shareholders, the risk of nonconsummation and the quality of securities being offered in the exchange." The open-ended analysis mandated by *Unocal* is not intended to lead to a simple mathematical exercise: that is, of comparing the discounted value of Time-Warner's expected trading price at some future date with Paramount's offer and determining which is the higher. Indeed, in our view, precepts underlying the business judgment rule militate against a court's engaging in the process of attempting to appraise and evaluate the relative merits of a long-term versus a short-term investment goal for shareholders. To engage in such an exercise is a distortion of the *Unocal* process and, in particular, the application of the second part of *Unocal's* test, discussed below.

In this case, the Time board reasonably determined that inadequate value was not the only legally cognizable threat that Paramount's all-cash, all-shares offer could present. Time's board concluded that Paramount's eleventh hour offer posed other threats. One concern was that Time shareholders might elect to tender into Paramount's cash offer in ignorance or a mistaken belief of the strategic benefit which a business combination with Warner might produce. Moreover, Time viewed the

---

17. Some commentators have suggested that the threats posed by hostile offers be categorized into not two but three types: "(i) *opportunity loss* . . . [where] a hostile offer might deprive target shareholders of the opportunity to select a superior alternative offered by target management [or, we would add, offered by another bidder]; (ii) *structural coercion*, . . . the risk that disparate treatment of non-tendering shareholders might distort shareholders' tender decisions; and . . . (iii) *substantive coercion*, . . . the risk that shareholders will mistakenly accept an underpriced offer because they disbelieve management's representations of intrinsic value." The recognition of substantive coercion, the authors suggest, would help guarantee that the *Unocal* standard becomes an effective intermediate standard of review. Gilson & Kraakman, *Delaware's Intermediate Standard for Defensive Tactics: Is There Substance to Proportionality Review?*, 44 The Business Lawyer, 247, 267 (1989).

conditions attached to Paramount's offer as introducing a degree of uncertainty that skewed a comparative analysis. Further, the timing of Paramount's offer to follow issuance of Time's proxy notice was viewed as arguably designed to upset, if not confuse, the Time stockholders' vote. Given this record evidence, we cannot conclude that the Time board's decision of June 6 that Paramount's offer posed a threat to corporate policy and effectiveness was lacking in good faith or dominated by motives of either entrenchment or self-interest.

Paramount also contends that the Time board had not duly investigated Paramount's offer. Therefore, Paramount argues, Time was unable to make an informed decision that the offer posed a threat to Time's corporate policy. Although the Chancellor did not address this issue directly, his findings of fact do detail Time's exploration of the available entertainment companies, including Paramount, before determining that Warner provided the best strategic "fit." In addition, the court found that Time's board rejected Paramount's offer because Paramount did not serve Time's objectives or meet Time's needs. Thus, the record does, in our judgment, demonstrate that Time's board was adequately informed of the potential benefits of a transaction with Paramount. We agree with the Chancellor that the Time board's lengthy pre-June investigation of potential merger candidates, including Paramount, mooted any obligation on Time's part to halt its merger process with Warner to reconsider Paramount. Time's board was under no obligation to negotiate with Paramount. Time's failure to negotiate cannot be fairly found to have been uninformed. The evidence supporting this finding is materially enhanced by the fact that twelve of Time's sixteen board members were outside independent directors.

We turn to the second part of the *Unocal* analysis. The obvious requisite to determining the reasonableness of a defensive action is a clear identification of the nature of the threat. As the Chancellor correctly noted, this "requires an evaluation of the importance of the corporate objective threatened; alternative methods of protecting that objective; impacts of the 'defensive' action, and other relevant factors." It is not until both parts of the *Unocal* inquiry have been satisfied that the business judgment rule attaches to defensive actions of a board of directors. As applied to the facts of this case, the question is whether the record evidence supports the Court of Chancery's conclusion that the restructuring of the Time-Warner transaction, including the adoption of several preclusive defensive measures, was a *reasonable response* in relation to a perceived threat.

Paramount argues that, assuming its tender offer posed a threat, Time's response was unreasonable in precluding Time's shareholders from accepting the tender offer or receiving a control premium in the immediately foreseeable future. Once again, the contention stems, we believe, from a fundamental misunderstanding of where the power of corporate governance lies. Delaware law confers the management of the corporate enterprise to the stockholders' duly elected board representatives. 8 Del.C. § 141(a). The fiduciary duty to manage a corporate enterprise includes the selection of a time frame for achievement of corporate goals. That duty may not be delegated to the stockholders. *Van Gorkom*. Directors are not obliged to abandon a deliberately conceived corporate plan for a short-term shareholder profit unless there is clearly no basis to sustain the corporate strategy.

Although the Chancellor blurred somewhat the discrete analyses required under *Unocal*, he did conclude that Time's board reasonably perceived Paramount's offer to be a significant threat to the planned Time-Warner merger and that Time's response was not "overly broad." We have found that even in light of a valid threat, management actions that are coercive in nature or force upon shareholders a management-sponsored alternative to a hostile offer may be struck down as unreasonable and nonproportionate responses.

Here, on the record facts, the Chancellor found that Time's responsive action to Paramount's tender offer was not aimed at "cramming down" on its shareholders a management-sponsored alternative, but ==rather had as its goal the carrying forward of a pre-existing transaction in an altered form==. Thus, the response was reasonably related to the threat. The Chancellor noted that the revised agreement and its accompanying safety devices did not preclude Paramount from making an offer for the combined Time-Warner company or from changing the conditions of its offer so as not to make the offer dependent upon the nullification of the Time-Warner agreement. Thus, the response was proportionate. We affirm the Chancellor's rulings as clearly supported by the record. Finally, we note that although Time was required, as a result of Paramount's hostile offer, to incur a heavy debt to finance its acquisition of Warner, that fact alone does not render the board's decision unreasonable so long as the directors could reasonably perceive the debt load not to be so injurious to the corporation as to jeopardize its well being. . . .

Questions

1. Is the opinion consistent with the balance the court has developed in previous cases between the role of directors and that of shareholders?

2. What are the significant differences between the transactions in *Revlon, Inc. v. MacAndrews & Forbes Holding, Inc.* and *Paramount Communications, Inc. v. Time, Inc.* that allowed the court to reach the result in *Time*?

3. Given the nature of Time Magazine, one can smile when we talk about preserving Time culture. But isn't the underlying justification an important one? After all, the 1990s and early twenty-first century have seen a dramatic consolidation in the book publishing industry, the periodical publishing industry, the broadcasting industry, and the movie industry. Isn't the court correct implicitly to recognize the significance of independent media, whether or not we happen to think the particular product is high quality? What does this suggest about the nature of the corporation? Is every solvent corporation unique and therefore deserving of preservation if the board has a vision of its products or services or way of doing business that it believes is special? Are there certain kinds of corporations (pharmaceuticals or managed care companies, or even football corporations, perhaps), that ought to be given special deference in their claims for independence because they serve uniquely important,

unquantifiable values in our society (and, in the case of media companies, values that touch upon constitutional concerns)? Or is every corporation an economic machine, existing to produce wealth for stockholders, regardless of the way in which that wealth is produced? How does this affect your view of the decision? Of the corporation? How would you design takeover law?

Paramount Communications Inc. v. QVC Network Inc.
637 A.2d 34 (Del. 1994)

Veasey, Chief Justice

In this appeal we review an order of the Court of Chancery dated November 24, 1993 (the "November 24 Order"), preliminarily enjoining certain defensive measures designed to facilitate a so-called strategic alliance between Viacom Inc. ("Viacom") and Paramount Communications Inc. ("Paramount") approved by the board of directors of Paramount (the "Paramount Board" or the "Paramount directors") and to thwart an unsolicited, more valuable, tender offer by QVC Network Inc. ("QVC"). In affirming, we hold that the sale of control in this case, which is at the heart of the proposed strategic alliance, implicates enhanced judicial scrutiny of the conduct of the Paramount Board under *Unocal Corp. v. Mesa Petroleum Co.,* Del.Supr., and *Revlon, Inc. v. MacAndrews & Forbes Holdings, Inc.,* Del.Supr. We further hold that the conduct of the Paramount Board was not reasonable as to process or result.

QVC and certain stockholders of Paramount commenced separate actions (later consolidated) in the Court of Chancery seeking preliminary and permanent injunctive relief against Paramount, certain members of the Paramount Board, and Viacom. This action arises out of a proposed acquisition of Paramount by Viacom through a tender offer followed by a second-step merger (the "Paramount-Viacom transaction"), and a competing unsolicited tender offer by QVC. The Court of Chancery granted a preliminary injunction. . . .

Under the circumstances of this case, the pending sale of control implicated in the Paramount-Viacom transaction required the Paramount Board to act on an informed basis to secure the best value reasonably available to the stockholders. Since we agree with the Court of Chancery that the Paramount directors violated their fiduciary duties, we have affirmed the entry of the order of the Vice Chancellor granting the preliminary injunction and have remanded these proceedings to the Court of Chancery for proceedings consistent herewith.

. . .

I. Facts

The Court of Chancery Opinion contains a detailed recitation of its factual findings in this matter. Only a brief summary of the facts is necessary for purposes of this opinion. The following summary is drawn from the findings of fact set forth in the Court of Chancery Opinion and our independent review of the record.

Paramount is a Delaware corporation with its principal offices in New York City. Approximately 118 million shares of Paramount's common stock are outstanding and traded on the New York Stock Exchange. The majority of Paramount's stock is publicly held by numerous unaffiliated investors. Paramount owns and operates a diverse group of entertainment businesses, including motion picture and television studios, book publishers, professional sports teams and amusement parks.

There are 15 persons serving on the Paramount Board. Four directors are officer-employees of Paramount: Martin S. Davis ("Davis"), Paramount's Chairman and Chief Executive Officer since 1983; Donald Oresman ("Oresman"), Executive Vice-President, Chief Administrative Officer, and General Counsel; Stanley R. Jaffe, President and Chief Operating Officer; and Ronald L. Nelson, Executive Vice President and Chief Financial Officer. Paramount's 11 outside directors are distinguished and experienced business persons who are present or former senior executives of public corporations or financial institutions.

Viacom is a Delaware corporation with its headquarters in Massachusetts. Viacom is controlled by Sumner M. Redstone ("Redstone"), its Chairman and Chief Executive Officer, who owns indirectly approximately 85.2 percent of Viacom's voting Class A stock and approximately 69.2 percent of Viacom's nonvoting Class B stock through National Amusements, Inc. ("NAI"), an entity 91.7 percent owned by Redstone. Viacom has a wide range of entertainment operations, including a number of well-known cable television channels such as MTV, Nickelodeon, Showtime, and The Movie Channel. . . .

QVC is a Delaware corporation with its headquarters in West Chester, Pennsylvania. QVC has several large stockholders, including Liberty Media Corporation, Comcast Corporation, Advance Publications, Inc., and Cox Enterprises Inc. Barry Diller ("Diller"), the Chairman and Chief Executive Officer of QVC, is also a substantial stockholder. QVC sells a variety of merchandise through a televised shopping channel. . . .

Beginning in the late 1980s, Paramount investigated the possibility of acquiring or merging with other companies in the entertainment, media, or communications industry. Paramount considered such transactions to be desirable, and perhaps necessary, in order to keep pace with competitors in the rapidly evolving field of entertainment and communications. Consistent with its goal of strategic expansion, Paramount made a tender offer for Time Inc. in 1989, but was ultimately unsuccessful.

Although Paramount had considered a possible combination of Paramount and Viacom as early as 1990, recent efforts to explore such a transaction began at a dinner meeting between Redstone and Davis on April 20, 1993. Robert Greenhill ("Greenhill"), Chairman of Smith Barney Shearson Inc. ("Smith Barney"), attended and helped facilitate this meeting. After several more meetings between Redstone and Davis, serious negotiations began taking place in early July.

It was tentatively agreed that Davis would be the chief executive officer and Redstone would be the controlling stockholder of the combined company, but the parties could not reach agreement on the merger price and the terms of a stock option to be granted to Viacom. With respect to price, Viacom offered a package of cash and stock (primarily Viacom Class B nonvoting stock) with a market value of approximately $61 per share, but Paramount wanted at least $70 per share.

Shortly after negotiations broke down in July 1993, two notable events occurred. First, Davis apparently learned of QVC's potential interest in Paramount, and told Diller over lunch on July 21, 1993, that Paramount was not for sale. Second, the market value of Viacom's Class B nonvoting stock increased from $46.875 on July 6 to $57.25 on August 20. QVC claims (and Viacom disputes) that this price increase was caused by open market purchases of such stock by Redstone or entities controlled by him.

On August 20, 1993, discussions between Paramount and Viacom resumed when Greenhill arranged another meeting between Davis and Redstone. After a short hiatus, the parties negotiated in earnest in early September, and performed due diligence with the assistance of their financial advisors, Lazard Freres & Co. ("Lazard") for Paramount and Smith Barney for Viacom. On September 9, 1993, the Paramount Board was informed about the status of the negotiations and was provided information by Lazard, including an analysis of the proposed transaction.

On September 12, 1993, the Paramount Board met again and unanimously approved the Original Merger Agreement whereby Paramount would merge with and into Viacom. The terms of the merger provided that each share of Paramount common stock would be converted into 0.10 shares of Viacom Class A voting stock, 0.90 shares of Viacom Class B nonvoting stock, and $9.10 in cash. In addition, the Paramount Board agreed to amend its "poison pill" Rights Agreement to exempt the proposed merger with Viacom. The Original Merger Agreement also contained several provisions designed to make it more difficult for a potential competing bid to succeed. We focus, as did the Court of Chancery, on three of these defensive provisions: a "no-shop" provision (the "No-Shop Provision"), the Termination Fee, and the Stock Option Agreement.

First, under the No-Shop Provision, the Paramount Board agreed that Paramount would not solicit, encourage, discuss, negotiate, or endorse any competing transaction unless: (a) a third party "makes an unsolicited written, bona fide proposal, which is not subject to any material contingencies relating to financing"; and (b) the Paramount Board determines that discussions or negotiations with the third party are necessary for the Paramount Board to comply with its fiduciary duties.

Second, under the Termination Fee provision, Viacom would receive a $100 million termination fee if: (a) Paramount terminated the Original Merger Agreement because of a competing transaction; (b) Paramount's stockholders did not approve the merger; or (c) the Paramount Board recommended a competing transaction.

The third and most significant deterrent device was the Stock Option Agreement, which granted to Viacom an option to purchase approximately 19.9 percent

(23,699,000 shares) of Paramount's outstanding common stock at $69.14 per share if any of the triggering events for the Termination Fee occurred. In addition to the customary terms that are normally associated with a stock option, the Stock Option Agreement contained two provisions that were both unusual and highly beneficial to Viacom: (a) Viacom was permitted to pay for the shares with a senior subordinated note of questionable marketability instead of cash, thereby avoiding the need to raise the $1.6 billion purchase price (the "Note Feature"); and (b) Viacom could elect to require Paramount to pay Viacom in cash a sum equal to the difference between the purchase price and the market price of Paramount's stock (the "Put Feature"). Because the Stock Option Agreement was not "capped" to limit its maximum dollar value, it had the potential to reach (and in this case did reach) unreasonable levels.

After the execution of the Original Merger Agreement and the Stock Option Agreement on September 12, 1993, Paramount and Viacom announced their proposed merger. In a number of public statements, the parties indicated that the pending transaction was a virtual certainty. Redstone described it as a "marriage" that would "never be torn asunder" and stated that only a "nuclear attack" could break the deal. Redstone also called Diller and John Malone of Tele-Communications Inc., a major stockholder of QVC, to dissuade them from making a competing bid.

Despite these attempts to discourage a competing bid, Diller sent a letter to Davis on September 20, 1993, proposing a merger in which QVC would acquire Paramount for approximately $80 per share, consisting of 0.893 shares of QVC common stock and $30 in cash. QVC also expressed its eagerness to meet with Paramount to negotiate the details of a transaction. When the Paramount Board met on September 27, it was advised by Davis that the Original Merger Agreement prohibited Paramount from having discussions with QVC (or anyone else) unless certain conditions were satisfied. In particular, QVC had to supply evidence that its proposal was not subject to financing contingencies. The Paramount Board was also provided information from Lazard describing QVC and its proposal.

On October 5, 1993, QVC provided Paramount with evidence of QVC's financing. The Paramount Board then held another meeting on October 11, and decided to authorize management to meet with QVC. Davis also informed the Paramount Board that Booz-Allen & Hamilton ("Booz-Allen"), a management consulting firm, had been retained to assess, *inter alia,* the incremental earnings potential from a Paramount-Viacom merger and a Paramount-QVC merger. Discussions proceeded slowly, however, due to a delay in Paramount signing a confidentiality agreement. In response to Paramount's request for information, QVC provided two binders of documents to Paramount on October 20.

On October 21, 1993, QVC filed this action and publicly announced an $80 cash tender offer for 51 percent of Paramount's outstanding shares (the "QVC tender offer"). Each remaining share of Paramount common stock would be converted into 1.42857 shares of QVC common stock in a second-step merger. The tender offer was conditioned on, among other things, the invalidation of the Stock Option Agreement, which was worth over $200 million by that point[5] QVC contends that it had to commence a tender offer because of the slow pace of the merger discussions and the need to begin seeking clearance under federal antitrust laws.

Confronted by QVC's hostile bid, which on its face offered over $10 per share more than the consideration provided by the Original Merger Agreement, Viacom realized that it would need to raise its bid in order to remain competitive. Within hours after QVC's tender offer was announced, Viacom entered into discussions with Paramount concerning a revised transaction. These discussions led to serious negotiations concerning a comprehensive amendment to the original Paramount-Viacom transaction. In effect, the opportunity for a "new deal" with Viacom was at hand for the Paramount Board. With the QVC hostile bid offering greater value to the Paramount stockholders, the Paramount Board had considerable leverage with Viacom.

At a special meeting on October 24, 1993, the Paramount Board approved the Amended Merger Agreement and an amendment to the Stock Option Agreement. The Amended Merger Agreement was, however, essentially the same as the Original Merger Agreement, except that it included a few new provisions. One provision related to an $80 per share cash tender offer by Viacom for 51 percent of Paramount's stock, and another changed the merger consideration so that each share of Paramount would be converted into 0.20408 shares of Viacom Class A voting stock, 1.08317 shares of Viacom Class B nonvoting stock, and 0.20408 shares of a new series of Viacom convertible preferred stock. The Amended Merger Agreement also added a provision giving Paramount the right not to amend its Rights Agreement to exempt Viacom if the Paramount Board determined that such an amendment would be inconsistent with its fiduciary duties because another offer constituted a "better alternative."[6] Finally, the Paramount Board was given the power to terminate the Amended Merger Agreement if it withdrew its recommendation of the Viacom transaction or recommended a competing transaction.

Although the Amended Merger Agreement offered more consideration to the Paramount stockholders and somewhat more flexibility to the Paramount Board than did the Original Merger Agreement, the defensive measures designed to make a competing bid more difficult were not removed or modified. In particular, there is no evidence in the record that Paramount sought to use its newly-acquired leverage to eliminate or modify the No-Shop Provision, the Termination Fee, or the Stock Option Agreement when the subject of amending the Original Merger Agreement was on the table.

---

5. By November 15, 1993, the value of the Stock Option Agreement had increased to nearly $500 million based on the $90 QVC bid.

6. Under the Amended Merger Agreement and the Paramount Board's resolutions approving it, no further action of the Paramount Board would be required in order for Paramount's Rights Agreement to be amended. As a result, the proper officers of the company were authorized to implement the amendment unless they were instructed otherwise by the Paramount Board.

Viacom's tender offer commenced on October 25, 1993, and QVC's tender offer was formally launched on October 27, 1993. Diller sent a letter to the Paramount Board on October 28 requesting an opportunity to negotiate with Paramount, and Oresman responded the following day by agreeing to meet. The meeting, held on November 1, was not very fruitful, however, after QVC's proposed guidelines for a "fair bidding process" were rejected by Paramount on the ground that "auction procedures" were inappropriate and contrary to Paramount's contractual obligations to Viacom.

On November 6, 1993, Viacom unilaterally raised its tender offer price to $85 per share in cash and offered a comparable increase in the value of the securities being proposed in the second-step merger. At a telephonic meeting held later that day, the Paramount Board agreed to recommend Viacom's higher bid to Paramount's stockholders.

QVC responded to Viacom's higher bid on November 12 by increasing its tender offer to $90 per share and by increasing the securities for its second-step merger by a similar amount. In response to QVC's latest offer, the Paramount Board scheduled a meeting for November 15, 1993. Prior to the meeting, Oresman sent the members of the Paramount Board a document summarizing the "conditions and uncertainties" of QVC's offer. One director testified that this document gave him a very negative impression of the QVC bid.

At its meeting on November 15, 1993, the Paramount Board determined that the new QVC offer was not in the best interests of the stockholders. The purported basis for this conclusion was that QVC's bid was excessively conditional. The Paramount Board did not communicate with QVC regarding the status of the conditions because it believed that the No-Shop Provision prevented such communication in the absence of firm financing. Several Paramount directors also testified that they believed the Viacom transaction would be more advantageous to Paramount's future business prospects than a QVC transaction.[7] Although a number of materials were distributed to the Paramount Board describing the Viacom and QVC transactions, the only quantitative analysis of the consideration to be received by the stockholders under each proposal was based on then-current market prices of the securities involved, not on the anticipated value of such securities at the time when the stockholders would receive them.[8]

The preliminary injunction hearing in this case took place on November 16, 1993. On November 19, Diller wrote to the Paramount Board to inform it that QVC had

---

7. This belief may have been based on a report prepared by Booz-Allen and distributed to the Paramount Board at its October 24 meeting. The report, which relied on public information regarding QVC, concluded that the synergies of a Paramount-Viacom merger were significantly superior to those of a Paramount-QVC merger. QVC has labelled the Booz-Allen report as a "joke."

8. The market prices of Viacom's and QVC's stock were poor measures of their actual values because such prices constantly fluctuated depending upon which company was perceived to be the more likely to acquire Paramount.

obtained financing commitments for its tender offer and that there was no antitrust obstacle to the offer. On November 24, 1993, the Court of Chancery issued its decision granting a preliminary injunction in favor of QVC and the plaintiff stockholders. This appeal followed.

II. Applicable Principles of Established Delaware Law

The General Corporation Law of the State of Delaware (the "General Corporation Law") and the decisions of this Court have repeatedly recognized the fundamental principle that the management of the business and affairs of a Delaware corporation is entrusted to its directors, who are the duly elected and authorized representatives of the stockholders. Under normal circumstances, neither the courts nor the stockholders should interfere with the managerial decisions of the directors. The business judgment rule embodies the deference to which such decisions are entitled.

Nevertheless, there are rare situations which mandate that a court take a more direct and active role in overseeing the decisions made and actions taken by directors. In these situations, a court subjects the directors' conduct to enhanced scrutiny to ensure that it is reasonable.[9] The decisions of this Court have clearly established the circumstances where such enhanced scrutiny will be applied. The case at bar implicates two such circumstances: (1) the approval of a transaction resulting in a sale of control, and (2) the adoption of defensive measures in response to a threat to corporate control.

A. The Significance of a Sale or Change[10] of Control

When a majority of a corporation's voting shares are acquired by a single person or entity, or by a cohesive group acting together, there is a significant diminution in the voting power of those who thereby become minority stockholders. Under the statutory framework of the General Corporation Law, many of the most fundamental corporate changes can be implemented only if they are approved by a majority vote of the stockholders. Such actions include elections of directors, amendments to the certificate of incorporation, mergers, consolidations, sales of all or substantially all of the assets of the corporation, and dissolution. Because of the overriding importance of voting rights, this Court and the Court of Chancery have consistently acted to protect stockholders from unwarranted interference with such rights.

In the absence of devices protecting the minority stockholders,[12] stockholder votes are likely to become mere formalities where there is a majority stockholder. For example, minority stockholders can be deprived of a continuing equity interest in their

---

9. Where actual self-interest is present and affects a majority of the directors approving a transaction, a court will apply even more exacting scrutiny to determine whether the transaction is entirely fair to the stockholders.

10. For purposes of our December 9 Order and this Opinion, we have used the terms "sale of control" and "change of control" interchangeably without intending any doctrinal distinction.

12. Examples of such protective provisions are supermajority voting provisions, majority of the minority requirements, etc. Although we express no opinion on what effect the inclusion of any such stockholder protective devices would have had in this case, we note that this Court has upheld,

corporation by means of a cash-out merger. Absent effective protective provisions, minority stockholders must rely for protection solely on the fiduciary duties owed to them by the directors and the majority stockholder, since the minority stockholders have lost the power to influence corporate direction through the ballot. The acquisition of majority status and the consequent privilege of exerting the powers of majority ownership come at a price. That price is usually a control premium which recognizes not only the value of a control block of shares, but also compensates the minority stockholders for their resulting loss of voting power.

In the case before us, the public stockholders (in the aggregate) currently own a majority of Paramount's voting stock. Control of the corporation is not vested in a single person, entity, or group, but vested in the fluid aggregation of unaffiliated stockholders. In the event the Paramount-Viacom transaction is consummated, the public stockholders will receive cash and a minority equity voting position in the surviving corporation. Following such consummation, there will be a controlling stockholder who will have the voting power to: (a) elect directors; (b) cause a break-up of the corporation; (c) merge it with another company; (d) cash-out the public stockholders; (e) amend the certificate of incorporation; (f) sell all or substantially all of the corporate assets; or (g) otherwise alter materially the nature of the corporation and the public stockholders' interests. Irrespective of the present Paramount Board's vision of a long-term strategic alliance with Viacom, the proposed sale of control would provide the new controlling stockholder with the power to alter that vision.

Because of the intended sale of control, the Paramount-Viacom transaction has economic consequences of considerable significance to the Paramount stockholders. Once control has shifted, the current Paramount stockholders will have no leverage in the future to demand another control premium. As a result, the Paramount stockholders are entitled to receive, and should receive, a control premium and/or protective devices of significant value. There being no such protective provisions in the Viacom-Paramount transaction, the Paramount directors had an obligation to take the maximum advantage of the current opportunity to realize for the stockholders the best value reasonably available.

B. The Obligations of Directors in a Sale or Change of Control Transaction

The consequences of a sale of control impose special obligations on the directors of a corporation.[13] In particular, they have the obligation of acting reasonably to seek the transaction offering the best value reasonably available to the stockholders. The courts will apply enhanced scrutiny to ensure that the directors have acted reasonably. The obligations of the directors and the enhanced scrutiny of the courts are

---

under different circumstances, the reasonableness of a standstill agreement which limited a 49.9 percent stockholder to 40 percent board representation. *Ivanhoe*, 535 A.2d at 1343.

13. We express no opinion on any scenario except the actual facts before the Court, and our precise holding herein. Unsolicited tender offers in other contexts may be governed by different precedent. . . .

well-established by the decisions of this Court. The directors' fiduciary duties in a sale of control context are those which generally attach.... As we held in *Macmillan*:

> It is basic to our law that the board of directors has the ultimate responsibility for managing the business and affairs of a corporation. In discharging this function, the directors owe fiduciary duties of care and loyalty to the corporation and its shareholders. *This unremitting obligation extends equally to board conduct in a sale of corporate control.*

In the sale of control context, the directors must focus on one primary objective—to secure the transaction offering the best value reasonably available for the stockholders—and they must exercise their fiduciary duties to further that end. The decisions of this Court have consistently emphasized this goal.

In pursuing this objective, the directors must be especially diligent. In particular, this Court has stressed the importance of the board being adequately informed in negotiating a sale of control....

... Some of the methods by which a board can fulfill its obligation to seek the best value reasonably available to the stockholders ... are designed to determine the existence and viability of possible alternatives. They include conducting an auction, canvassing the market, etc. Delaware law recognizes that there is "no single blueprint" that directors must follow.

In determining which alternative provides the best value for the stockholders, a board of directors is not limited to considering only the amount of cash involved, and is not required to ignore totally its view of the future value of a strategic alliance.... Instead, the directors should analyze the entire situation and evaluate in a disciplined manner the consideration being offered. Where stock or other non-cash consideration is involved, the board should try to quantify its value, if feasible, to achieve an objective comparison of the alternatives.[14] ... These considerations are important because the selection of one alternative may permanently foreclose other opportunities. While the assessment of these factors may be complex, the board's goal is straightforward: Having informed themselves of all material information reasonably available, the directors must decide which alternative is most likely to offer the best value reasonably available to the stockholders.

C. Enhanced Judicial Scrutiny of a Sale or Change of Control Transaction

Board action in the circumstances presented here is subject to enhanced scrutiny. Such scrutiny is mandated by: (a) the threatened diminution of the current stockholders' voting power; (b) the fact that an asset belonging to public stockholders (a control premium) is being sold and may never be available again; and (c) the

---

14. When assessing the value of non-cash consideration, a board should focus on its value as of the date it will be received by the stockholders. Normally, such value will be determined with the assistance of experts using generally accepted methods of valuation.

traditional concern of Delaware courts for actions which impair or impede stockholder voting rights. . . .

The key features of an enhanced scrutiny test are: (a) a judicial determination regarding the adequacy of the decisionmaking process employed by the directors, including the information on which the directors based their decision; and (b) a judicial examination of the reasonableness of the directors' action in light of the circumstances then existing. The directors have the burden of proving that they were adequately informed and acted reasonably.

Although an enhanced scrutiny test involves a review of the reasonableness of the substantive merits of a board's actions, a court should not ignore the complexity of the directors' task in a sale of control. There are many business and financial considerations implicated in investigating and selecting the best value reasonably available. The board of directors is the corporate decisionmaking body best equipped to make these judgments. Accordingly, a court applying enhanced judicial scrutiny should be deciding whether the directors made a *reasonable* decision, not a *perfect* decision. If a board selected one of several reasonable alternatives, a court should not second-guess that choice even though it might have decided otherwise or subsequent events may have cast doubt on the board's determination. Thus, courts will not substitute their business judgment for that of the directors, but will determine if the directors' decision was, on balance, within a range of reasonableness.

D. *Revlon* and *Time-Warner* Distinguished

The Paramount defendants and Viacom assert that the fiduciary obligations and the enhanced judicial scrutiny discussed above are not implicated in this case in the absence of a "break-up" of the corporation, and that the order granting the preliminary injunction should be reversed. This argument is based on their erroneous interpretation of our decisions in *Revlon* and *Time-Warner.*

In *Revlon,* we reviewed the actions of the board of directors of Revlon, Inc. ("Revlon"), which had rebuffed the overtures of Pantry Pride, Inc. and had instead entered into an agreement with Forstmann Little & Co. ("Forstmann") providing for the acquisition of 100 percent of Revlon's outstanding stock by Forstmann and the subsequent break-up of Revlon. Based on the facts and circumstances present in *Revlon,* we held that "[t]he directors' role changed from defenders of the corporate bastion to auctioneers charged with getting the best price for the stockholders at a sale of the company." We further held that "when a board ends an intense bidding contest on an insubstantial basis, . . . [that] action cannot withstand the enhanced scrutiny which *Unocal* requires of director conduct."

It is true that one of the circumstances bearing on these holdings was the fact that "the break-up of the company . . . had become a reality which even the directors embraced." It does not follow, however, that a "break-up" must be present and "inevitable" before directors are subject to enhanced judicial scrutiny and are required to pursue a transaction that is calculated to produce the best value reasonably available to the stockholders. In fact, we stated in *Revlon* that "when bidders make relatively similar offers, or dissolution of the company becomes inevitable, the directors cannot fulfill their enhanced *Unocal* duties by playing favorites with the contending factions." *Revlon* thus does not hold that an inevitable dissolution or "break-up" is necessary.

The decisions of this Court following *Revlon* reinforced the applicability of enhanced scrutiny and the directors' obligation to seek the best value reasonably available for the stockholders where there is a pending sale of control, regardless of whether or not there is to be a break-up of the corporation....

... [T]he Paramount defendants have interpreted our decision in *Time-Warner* as requiring a corporate break-up in order for that obligation to apply. The facts in *Time-Warner*, however, were quite different from the facts of this case, and refute Paramount's position here. In *Time-Warner*, the Chancellor held that there was no change of control in the original stock-for-stock merger between Time and Warner because Time would be owned by a fluid aggregation of unaffiliated stockholders both before and after the merger:

> If the appropriate inquiry is whether a change in control is contemplated, the answer must be sought in the specific circumstances surrounding the transaction. Surely under some circumstances a stock for stock merger could reflect a transfer of corporate control. That would, for example, plainly be the case here if Warner were a private company. But where, as here, the shares of both constituent corporations are widely held, corporate control can be expected to remain unaffected by a stock for stock merger. This in my judgment was the situation with respect to the original merger agreement. When the specifics of that situation are reviewed, it is seen that, aside from legal technicalities and aside from arrangements thought to enhance the prospect for the ultimate succession of [Nicholas J. Nicholas, Jr., president of Time], neither corporation could be said to be acquiring the other. *Control of both remained in a large, fluid, changeable and changing market.*
>
> The existence of a control block of stock in the hands of a single shareholder or a group with loyalty to each other does have real consequences to the financial value of "minority" stock. The law offers some protection to such shares through the imposition of a fiduciary duty upon controlling shareholders. *But here, effectuation of the merger would not have subjected Time shareholders to the risks and consequences of holders of minority shares. This is a reflection of the fact that no control passed to anyone in the transaction contemplated.* The shareholders of Time would have "suffered" dilution, of course, but they would suffer the same type of dilution upon the public distribution of new stock.

Paramount Communications Inc. v. Time Inc., Del. Ch. (emphasis added).

Moreover, the transaction actually consummated in *Time-Warner* was not a merger, as originally planned, but a sale of Warner's stock to Time.

In our affirmance of the Court of Chancery's well-reasoned decision, this Court held that "The Chancellor's findings of fact are supported by the record and *his conclusion is correct as a matter of law.*" Nevertheless, the Paramount defendants here have argued that a break-up is a requirement and have focused on the following language in our *Time-Warner* decision:

> However, we premise our rejection of plaintiffs' *Revlon* claim on different grounds, namely, the absence of any substantial evidence to conclude that Time's board, in negotiating with Warner, made the dissolution or break-up of the corporate entity inevitable, as was the case in *Revlon*.
>
> Under Delaware law there are, generally speaking and *without excluding other possibilities*, two circumstances which may implicate *Revlon* duties. The first, and clearer one, is when a corporation *initiates an active bidding process seeking to sell itself* or to effect a business reorganization involving a clear breakup of the company. However, *Revlon* duties may also be triggered where, in response to a bidder's offer, a target abandons its long-term strategy and seeks an alternative transaction involving the breakup of the company.

(Emphasis added).

The Paramount defendants have misread the holding of *Time-Warner*. Contrary to their argument, our decision in *Time-Warner* expressly states that the two general scenarios discussed in the above-quoted paragraph are not the *only* instances where "*Revlon* duties" may be implicated. The Paramount defendants' argument totally ignores the phrase "without excluding other possibilities." Moreover, the instant case is clearly within the first general scenario set forth in *Time-Warner*. The Paramount Board, albeit unintentionally, had "initiate[d] an active bidding process seeking to sell itself" by agreeing to sell control of the corporation to Viacom in circumstances where another potential acquiror (QVC) was equally interested in being a bidder.

The Paramount defendants' position that *both* a change of control *and* a break-up are *required* must be rejected. Such a holding would unduly restrict the application of *Revlon* . . . and has no basis in policy. There are few events that have a more significant impact on the stockholders than a sale of control or a corporate break-up. Each event represents a fundamental (and perhaps irrevocable) change in the nature of the corporate enterprise from a practical standpoint. It is the significance of *each* of these events that justifies: (a) focusing on the directors' obligation to seek the best value reasonably available to the stockholders; and (b) requiring a close scrutiny of board action which could be contrary to the stockholders' interests.

Accordingly, when a corporation undertakes a transaction which will cause: (a) a change in corporate control; *or* (b) a break-up of the corporate entity, the directors' obligation is to seek the best value reasonably available to the stockholders. This obligation arises because the effect of the Viacom-Paramount transaction, if consummated, is to shift control of Paramount from the public stockholders to a controlling stockholder, Viacom. Neither *Time-Warner* nor any other decision of this Court holds that a "break-up" of the company is essential to give rise to this obligation where there is a sale of control.

III. Breach of Fiduciary Duties by Paramount Board

We now turn to duties of the Paramount Board under the facts of this case and our conclusions as to the breaches of those duties which warrant injunctive relief.

A. The Specific Obligations of the Paramount Board

Under the facts of this case, the Paramount directors had the obligation: (a) to be diligent and vigilant in examining critically the Paramount-Viacom transaction and the QVC tender offers; (b) to act in good faith; (c) to obtain, and act with due care on, all material information reasonably available, including information necessary to compare the two offers to determine which of these transactions, or an alternative course of action, would provide the best value reasonably available to the stockholders; and (d) to negotiate actively and in good faith with both Viacom and QVC to that end.

Having decided to sell control of the corporation, the Paramount directors were required to evaluate critically whether or not all material aspects of the Paramount-Viacom transaction (separately and in the aggregate) were reasonable and in the best interests of the Paramount stockholders in light of current circumstances, including: the change of control premium, the Stock Option Agreement, the Termination Fee, the coercive nature of both the Viacom and QVC tender offers,[18] the No-Shop Provision, and the proposed disparate use of the Rights Agreement as to the Viacom and QVC tender offers, respectively.

These obligations necessarily implicated various issues, including the questions of whether or not those provisions and other aspects of the Paramount-Viacom transaction (separately and in the aggregate): (a) adversely affected the value provided to the Paramount stockholders; (b) inhibited or encouraged alternative bids; (c) were enforceable contractual obligations in light of the directors' fiduciary duties; and (d) in the end would advance or retard the Paramount directors' obligation to secure for the Paramount stockholders the best value reasonably available under the circumstances.

The Paramount defendants contend that they were precluded by certain contractual provisions, including the No-Shop Provision, from negotiating with QVC or seeking alternatives. Such provisions, whether or not they are presumptively valid in the abstract, may not validly define or limit the directors' fiduciary duties under Delaware law or prevent the Paramount directors from carrying out their fiduciary

---

18. Both the Viacom and the QVC tender offers were for 51 percent cash and a "back-end" of various securities, the value of each of which depended on the fluctuating value of Viacom and QVC stock at any given time. Thus, both tender offers were two-tiered, front-end loaded, and coercive. Such coercive offers are inherently problematic and should be expected to receive particularly careful analysis by a target board.

duties under Delaware law. To the extent such provisions are inconsistent with those duties, they are invalid and unenforceable.

Since the Paramount directors had already decided to sell control, they had an obligation to continue their search for the best value reasonably available to the stockholders. This continuing obligation included the responsibility, at the October 24 board meeting and thereafter, to evaluate critically both the QVC tender offers and the Paramount-Viacom transaction to determine if: (a) the QVC tender offer was, or would continue to be, conditional; (b) the QVC tender offer could be improved; (c) the Viacom tender offer or other aspects of the Paramount-Viacom transaction could be improved; (d) each of the respective offers would be reasonably likely to come to closure, and under what circumstances; (e) other material information was reasonably available for consideration by the Paramount directors; (f) there were viable and realistic alternative courses of action; and (g) the timing constraints could be managed so the directors could consider these matters carefully and deliberately.

B. The Breaches of Fiduciary Duty by the Paramount Board

The Paramount directors made the decision on September 12, 1993, that, in their judgment, a strategic merger with Viacom on the economic terms of the Original Merger Agreement was in the best interests of Paramount and its stockholders. Those terms provided a modest change of control premium to the stockholders. The directors also decided at that time that it was appropriate to agree to certain defensive measures (the Stock Option Agreement, the Termination Fee, and the No-Shop Provision) insisted upon by Viacom as part of that economic transaction. Those defensive measures, coupled with the sale of control and subsequent disparate treatment of competing bidders, implicated the judicial scrutiny of *Unocal, Revlon, Macmillan,* and their progeny. We conclude that the Paramount directors' process was not reasonable, and the result achieved for the stockholders was not reasonable under the circumstances.

When entering into the Original Merger Agreement, and thereafter, the Paramount Board clearly gave insufficient attention to the potential consequences of the defensive measures demanded by Viacom. The Stock Option Agreement had a number of unusual and potentially "draconian"[19] provisions, including the Note Feature and the Put Feature. Furthermore, the Termination Fee, whether or not unreasonable by itself, clearly made Paramount less attractive to other bidders, when coupled with the Stock Option Agreement. Finally, the No-Shop Provision inhibited the Paramount Board's ability to negotiate with other potential bidders, particularly QVC which had already expressed an interest in Paramount.[20]

---

19. The Vice Chancellor so characterized the Stock Option Agreement. Court of Chancery Opinion, 635 A.2d at 1272. We express no opinion whether a stock option agreement of essentially this magnitude, but with a reasonable "cap" and without the Note and Put Features, would be valid or invalid under other circumstances.

20. We express no opinion whether certain aspects of the No-Shop Provision here could be valid in another context. Whether or not it could validly have operated here at an early stage solely

Throughout the applicable time period, and especially from the first QVC merger proposal on September 20 through the Paramount Board meeting on November 15, QVC's interest in Paramount provided the *opportunity* for the Paramount Board to seek significantly higher value for the Paramount stockholders than that being offered by Viacom. QVC persistently demonstrated its intention to meet and exceed the Viacom offers, and frequently expressed its willingness to negotiate possible further increases.

The Paramount directors had the opportunity in the October 23–24 time frame, when the Original Merger Agreement was renegotiated, to take appropriate action to modify the improper defensive measures as well as to improve the economic terms of the Paramount-Viacom transaction. Under the circumstances existing at that time, it should have been clear to the Paramount Board that the Stock Option Agreement, coupled with the Termination Fee and the No-Shop Clause, were impeding the realization of the best value reasonably available to the Paramount stockholders. Nevertheless, the Paramount Board made no effort to eliminate or modify these counterproductive devices, and instead continued to cling to its vision of a strategic alliance with Viacom. Moreover, based on advice from the Paramount management, the Paramount directors considered the QVC offer to be "conditional" and asserted that they were precluded by the No-Shop Provision from seeking more information from, or negotiating with, QVC.

By November 12, 1993, the value of the revised QVC offer on its face exceeded that of the Viacom offer by over $1 billion at then current values. This significant disparity of value cannot be justified on the basis of the directors' vision of future strategy, primarily because the change of control would supplant the authority of the current Paramount Board to continue to hold and implement their strategic vision in any meaningful way. Moreover, their uninformed process had deprived their strategic vision of much of its credibility. When the Paramount directors met on November 15 to consider QVC's increased tender offer, they remained prisoners of their own misconceptions and missed opportunities to eliminate the restrictions they had imposed on themselves. Yet, it was not "too late" to reconsider negotiating with QVC. The circumstances existing on November 15 made it clear that the defensive measures, taken as a whole, were problematic: (a) the No-Shop Provision could not define or limit their fiduciary duties; (b) the Stock Option Agreement had become "draconian"; and (c) the Termination Fee, in context with all the circumstances, was similarly deterring the realization of possibly higher bids. Nevertheless, the Paramount directors remained paralyzed by their uninformed belief that the QVC offer was "illusory."

---

to prevent Paramount from actively "shopping" the company, it could not prevent the Paramount directors from carrying out their fiduciary duties in considering unsolicited bids or in negotiating for the best value reasonably available to the stockholders. . . .

This final opportunity to negotiate on the stockholders' behalf and to fulfill their obligation to seek the best value reasonably available was thereby squandered.[21]

IV. Viacom's Claim of Vested Contract Rights

Viacom argues that it had certain "vested" contract rights with respect to the No-Shop Provision and the Stock Option Agreement.[22] In effect, Viacom's argument is that the Paramount directors could enter into an agreement in violation of their fiduciary duties and then render Paramount, and ultimately its stockholders, liable for failing to carry out an agreement in violation of those duties. Viacom's protestations about vested rights are without merit. This Court has found that those defensive measures were improperly designed to deter potential bidders, and that such measures do not meet the reasonableness test to which they must be subjected. They are consequently invalid and unenforceable under the facts of this case.

The No-Shop Provision could not validly define or limit the fiduciary duties of the Paramount directors. To the extent that a contract, or a provision thereof, purports to require a board to act or not act in such a fashion as to limit the exercise of fiduciary duties, it is invalid and unenforceable. Despite the arguments of Paramount and Viacom to the contrary, the Paramount directors could not contract away their fiduciary obligations. Since the No-Shop Provision was invalid, Viacom never had any vested contract rights in the provision.

As discussed previously, the Stock Option Agreement contained several "draconian" aspects, including the Note Feature and the Put Feature. While we have held that lock-up options are not *per se* illegal, no options with similar features have ever been upheld by this Court. Under the circumstances of this case, the Stock Option Agreement clearly is invalid. Accordingly, Viacom never had any vested contract rights in that Agreement.

Viacom, a sophisticated party with experienced legal and financial advisors, knew of (and in fact demanded) the unreasonable features of the Stock Option Agreement. It cannot be now heard to argue that it obtained vested contract rights by negotiating and obtaining contractual provisions from a board acting in violation of its

---

21. The Paramount defendants argue that the Court of Chancery erred by assuming that the Rights Agreement was "pulled" at the November 15 meeting of the Paramount Board. The problem with this argument is that, under the Amended Merger Agreement and the resolutions of the Paramount Board related thereto, Viacom would be exempted from the Rights Agreement in the absence of further action of the Paramount Board and no further meeting had been scheduled or even contemplated prior to the closing of the Viacom tender offer. This failure to schedule and hold a meeting shortly before the closing date in order to make a final decision, based on all of the information and circumstances then existing, whether to exempt Viacom from the Rights Agreement was inconsistent with the Paramount Board's responsibilities and does not provide a basis to challenge the Court of Chancery's decision.

22. Presumably this argument would have included the Termination Fee had the Vice Chancellor invalidated that provision or if appellees had cross-appealed from the Vice Chancellor's refusal to invalidate that provision.

fiduciary duties.... Viacom's ... fate must rise or fall, and in this instance fall, with the determination that the actions of the Paramount Board were invalid.

V. Conclusion

The realization of the best value reasonably available to the stockholders became the Paramount directors' primary obligation under these facts in light of the change of control. That obligation was not satisfied, and the Paramount Board's process was deficient. The directors' initial hope and expectation for a strategic alliance with Viacom was allowed to dominate their decisionmaking process to the point where the arsenal of defensive measures established at the outset was perpetuated (not modified or eliminated) when the situation was dramatically altered. QVC's unsolicited bid presented the opportunity for significantly greater value for the stockholders and enhanced negotiating leverage for the directors. Rather than seizing those opportunities, the Paramount directors chose to wall themselves off from material information which was reasonably available and to hide behind the defensive measures as a rationalization for refusing to negotiate with QVC or seeking other alternatives. Their view of the strategic alliance likewise became an empty rationalization as the opportunities for higher value for the stockholders continued to develop.

It is the nature of the judicial process that we decide only the case before us—a case which, on its facts, is clearly controlled by established Delaware law. Here, the proposed change of control and the implications thereof were crystal clear. In other cases they may be less clear. The holding of this case on its facts, coupled with the holdings of the principal cases discussed herein where the issue of sale of control is implicated, should provide a workable precedent against which to measure future cases....

Questions

1. From *Unocal Corporation v. Mesa Petroleum Co.* through *Paramount Communications, Inc. v. Time, Inc.*, the Delaware Supreme Court, aided by the Chancery Court, developed a pragmatic approach to the new problem of hostile takeovers while creating well-reasoned doctrinal approaches consistent with the generally formalistic approach to corporate law that we have seen that court more or less consistently follow throughout the course. Does *Paramount Communications, Inc. v. QVC Network, Inc.* maintain that doctrinal formalism, or does it collapse into mere pragmatism? Is formalism possible in light of the complexity of takeover transactions and responses or is the court merely succumbing to necessity? Consider these questions not only in connection with *QVC* but also with *Unitrin, Inc. v. American General Corp.*, the following case. Do you think that the later cases (*QVC, Unitrin*) can be doctrinally reconciled with the court's earlier cases (*Unocal, Revlon, Time*) in a way that sustains a formally coherent approach?

2. Why does the ultimate ownership structure of Paramount matter so much to the court? Should it? Think back to the laws governing close corporations and

corporations with a controlling shareholder. What can you take from these in terms of understanding the court's conclusions in *QVC*?

Unitrin, Inc. v. American General Corp.
651 A.2d 1361 (Del. 1995)

HOLLAND, Justice

. . .

American General, which had publicly announced a proposal to merge with Unitrin for $2.6 billion at $50-3/8 per share, and certain Unitrin shareholder plaintiffs, filed suit in the Court of Chancery, *inter alia,* to enjoin Unitrin from repurchasing up to 10 million shares of its own stock (the "Repurchase Program"). On August 26, 1994, the Court of Chancery temporarily restrained Unitrin from making any further repurchases. After expedited discovery, briefing and argument, the Court of Chancery preliminarily enjoined Unitrin from making further repurchases on the ground that the Repurchase Program was a disproportionate response to the threat posed by American General's inadequate all cash for all shares offer, under the standard of this Court's holding in *Unocal Corp. v. Mesa Petroleum Co.,* ("Unocal"). . . .

This Court

Ultimate Disposition

This Court has concluded that the Court of Chancery erred in applying the proportionality review *Unocal* requires by focusing upon whether the Repurchase Program was an "unnecessary" defensive response. The Court of Chancery should have directed its enhanced scrutiny: first, upon whether the Repurchase Program the Unitrin Board implemented was draconian, by being either preclusive or coercive and; second, if it was not draconian, upon whether it was within a range of reasonable responses to the threat American General's Offer posed. Consequently, the interlocutory preliminary injunctive judgment of the Court of Chancery is reversed. This matter is remanded for further proceedings in accordance with this opinion.

The Parties

American General is the largest provider of home service insurance. On July 12, 1994, it made a merger proposal to acquire Unitrin for $2.6 billion at $50-3/8 per share. Following a public announcement of this proposal, Unitrin shareholders filed suit seeking to compel a sale of the company. American General filed suit to enjoin Unitrin's Repurchase Program.

Unitrin is also in the insurance business. It is the third largest provider of home service insurance. The other defendants-appellants are the members of Unitrin's seven person Board of Directors (the "Unitrin Board" or "Board"). Two directors are employees, Richard C. Vie ("Vie"), the Chief Executive Officer, and Jerrold V. Jerome ("Jerome"), Chairman of the Board. The five remaining directors are not and have never been employed by Unitrin. [Director Singleton owned more than 14% of Unitrin's stock, making him its largest shareholder. Director Sarofim owned 2.26% of the stock, and director Roberts owned 400,000 shares—a relatively small proportion of the outstanding stock.] . . .

The record reflects that the non-employee directors each receive a fixed annual fee of $30,000. They receive no other significant financial benefit from serving as directors. At the offering price proposed by American General, the value of Unitrin's non-employee directors' stock exceeded $450 million.

American General's Offer

In January 1994, James Tuerff ("Tuerff"), the President of American General, met with Richard Vie, Unitrin's Chief Executive Officer. Tuerff advised Vie that American General was considering acquiring other companies. Unitrin was apparently at or near the top of its list. Tuerff did not mention any terms for a potential acquisition of Unitrin. Vie replied that Unitrin had excellent prospects as an independent company and had never considered a merger. Vie indicated to Tuerff that Unitrin was not for sale.

According to Vie, he reported his conversation with Tuerff at the next meeting of the Unitrin Board in February 1994. The minutes of the full Board meeting do not reflect a discussion of Tuerff's proposition. Nevertheless, the parties agree that the Board's position in February was that Unitrin was not for sale. It was unnecessary to respond to American General because no offer had been made.

On July 12, 1994, American General sent a letter to Vie proposing a consensual merger transaction in which it would "purchase all of Unitrin's 51.8 million outstanding shares of common stock for $50-3/8 per share, in cash" (the "Offer"). The Offer was conditioned on the development of a merger agreement and regulatory approval. The Offer price represented a 30% premium over the market price of Unitrin's shares. In the Offer, American General stated that it "would consider offering a higher price" if "Unitrin could demonstrate additional value." American General also offered to consider tax-free "[a]lternatives to an all cash transaction."

Unitrin's Rejection

Upon receiving the American General Offer, the Unitrin Board's Executive Committee (Singleton, Vie, and Jerome) engaged legal counsel and scheduled a telephonic Board meeting for July 18. At the July 18 special meeting, the Board reviewed the terms of the Offer. The Board was advised that the existing charter and bylaw provisions might not effectively deter all types of takeover strategies. It was suggested that the Board consider adopting a shareholder rights plan and an advance notice provision for shareholder proposals.

The Unitrin Board met next on July 25, 1994 in Los Angeles for seven hours.[3] All directors attended the meeting. The principal purpose of the meeting was to discuss American General's Offer.

Vie reviewed Unitrin's financial condition and its ongoing business strategies. The Board also received a presentation from its investment advisor, Morgan Stanley & Co. ("Morgan Stanley"), regarding the financial adequacy of American General's proposal. Morgan Stanley expressed its opinion that the Offer was financially inadequate.[4] Legal counsel expressed concern that the combination of Unitrin and American General would raise antitrust complications due to the resultant decrease in competition in the home service insurance markets.

The Unitrin Board unanimously concluded that the American General merger proposal was not in the best interests of Unitrin's shareholders and voted to reject the Offer. The Board then received advice from its legal and financial advisors about a number of possible defensive measures it might adopt, including a shareholder rights plan ("poison pill") and an advance notice bylaw provision for shareholder proposals. Because the Board apparently thought that American General intended to keep its Offer private, the Board did not implement any defensive measures at that time.

On July 26, 1994, Vie faxed a letter to Tuerff, rejecting American General's Offer. . . .

Vie acknowledged during discovery that the latter portion of his letter referred, in part, to the Repurchase Program.

American General's Publicity

Unitrin's Initial Responses

On August 2, 1994, American General issued a press release announcing its Offer to Unitrin's Board to purchase all of Unitrin's stock for $50-3/8 per share. The press release also noted that the Board had rejected American General's Offer. After that public announcement, the trading volume and market price of Unitrin's stock increased.

At its regularly scheduled meeting on August 3, the Unitrin Board discussed the effects of American General's press release. The Board noted that the market reaction to the announcement suggested that speculative traders or arbitrageurs were acquiring Unitrin stock. The Board determined that American General's public announcement constituted a hostile act designed to coerce the sale of Unitrin at an

---

3. Prior to the meeting, Unitrin's outside counsel, Irell & Manella ("Irell"), sent Unitrin a draft press release and script for the meeting. These documents contemplated the adoption of the poison pill, advance notice provision and the Repurchase Program. American General argues that this shows that the Board action was a *fait accompli*. The Unitrin defendants argue that it was contingency planning.

4. Eric Daut, who prepared these materials for Morgan Stanley under extreme time pressure, had never prepared such information previously and did not rely on firm figures. Morgan Stanley, in turn, did not investigate these figures.

inadequate price. The Board unanimously approved the poison pill and the proposed advance notice bylaw that it had considered previously.

Beginning on August 2 and continuing through August 12, 1994, Unitrin issued a series of press releases to inform its shareholders and the public market: first, that the Unitrin Board believed Unitrin's stock was worth more than the $50-3/8 American General offered; second, that the Board felt that the price of American General's Offer did not reflect Unitrin's long term business prospects as an independent company; third, that "the true value of Unitrin [was] not reflected in the [then] current market price of its common stock," and that because of its strong financial position, Unitrin was well positioned "to pursue strategic and financial opportunities;" fourth, that the Board believed a merger with American General would have anticompetitive effects and might violate antitrust laws and various state regulatory statutes; and fifth, that the Board had adopted a shareholder rights plan (poison pill) to guard against undesirable takeover efforts.

Unitrin's Repurchase Program

The Unitrin Board met again on August 11, 1994. The minutes of that meeting indicate that its principal purpose was to consider the Repurchase Program. . . . [After a presentation involving written materials], Morgan Stanley recommended that the Board implement an open market stock repurchase. The Board voted to authorize the Repurchase Program for up to ten million shares of its outstanding stock.

On August 12, Unitrin publicly announced the Repurchase Program. . . . [The announcement noted the Board's belief that the market undervalued Unitrin's stock and that the directors were not participating in the Repurchase Program, as well as the fact that the Repurchase Program would increase the directors' share ownership percentage and that Unitrin's charter included a supermajority voting provision.]

. . . The following language from a July 22 draft press release revealing the antitakeover effects of the Repurchase Program was omitted from the final press release:

> Under the [supermajority provision], the consummation of the expanded repurchase program would enhance the ability of nonselling stockholders, including the directors, to prevent a merger with a greater-than-15% stockholder if they did not favor the transaction.

Unitrin sent a letter to its stockholders on August 17 regarding the Repurchase Program which stated . . . [the Board's belief that the program would increase liquidity for shareholders and increase the value of Unitrin's remaining, undervalued stock.]

Between August 12 and noon on August 24, Morgan Stanley purchased nearly 5 million of Unitrin's shares on Unitrin's behalf. The average price paid was slightly above American General's Offer price. . . .

Nature of Proceeding

Determines Judicial Review

In this case, before the Court of Chancery could evaluate the reasonable probability of the plaintiffs' success on the merits, it had to determine the nature of the proceeding. When shareholders challenge directors' actions, usually one of three levels of judicial review is applied: the traditional business judgment rule, the *Unocal* standard of enhanced judicial scrutiny, or the entire fairness analysis. "Because the effect of the proper invocation of the business judgment rule is so powerful and the standard of entire fairness so exacting, the determination of the appropriate standard of judicial review frequently is determinative of the outcome of [the] litigation."

[Plaintiffs did not appeal in this action the Chancery Court's ruling that the Repurchase Program did not put Unitrin up for sale. The Chancery Court had further held that the poison pill and Repurchase Program did not involve self-dealing sufficient to invoke entire fairness, and instead turned to a review of these actions under *Unocal*.]

Unitrin Board's Actions Defensive

Unocal is Proper Review Standard

. . .

The Court of Chancery held that all of the Unitrin Board's defensive actions merited judicial scrutiny according to *Unocal*.[9] The record supports the Court of Chancery's determination that the Board perceived American General's Offer as a threat and adopted the Repurchase Program, along with the poison pill and advance notice bylaw, as defensive measures in response to that threat. Therefore, the Court of Chancery properly concluded the facts before it required an application of *Unocal* and its progeny. The evolution of that jurisprudence is didactic.

---

9. We agree that the Court of Chancery properly applied a *Unocal* analysis to the Repurchase Program after it concluded the Repurchase Program was a component of Unitrin's defense, notwithstanding Unitrin's initial argument that its Board did not consider the Repurchase Program to be a part of its defensive response to American General's Offer. *Unocal's* standard of enhanced judicial scrutiny is proper whenever the record reflects that a board of directors took defensive measures in response to a "perceived 'threat to corporate policy and effectiveness which touches upon issues of control.'"

Unocal's Standard

Business Judgment Rule

Enhanced Judicial Scrutiny

. . .

The enhanced judicial scrutiny mandated by *Unocal* is not intended to lead to a structured, mechanistic, mathematical exercise.[13] Conversely, it is not intended to be an abstract theory. The *Unocal* standard is a flexible paradigm that jurists can apply to the myriad of "fact scenarios" that confront corporate boards.

Parties' Burdens Shift

Judicial Review Standards Differ

Business Judgment Rule and Unocal

The correct analytical framework is essential to a proper review of challenges to the decision-making process of a corporate Board. The ultimate question in applying the *Unocal* standard is: what deference should the reviewing court give "to the decisions of directors in defending against a takeover?" The question is usually presented to the Court of Chancery, as in the present case, in an injunction proceeding, a posture which is known as "transactional justification." To answer the question, the enhanced judicial scrutiny *Unocal* requires implicates both the substantive and procedural nature of the business judgment rule.

The business judgment rule has traditionally operated to shield directors from personal liability arising out of completed actions involving operational issues. When the business judgment rule is applied to defend directors against personal liability, as in a derivative suit, the plaintiff has the initial burden of proof and the ultimate burden of persuasion. In such cases, the business judgment rule shields directors from personal liability if, upon review, the court concludes the directors' decision can be attributed to any rational business purpose.

---

13. Efforts to relate *Unocal*'s inherently qualitative proportionality test to a quantitative formula have demonstrated the fallacy of such an exercise, *e.g.*, the reasonableness test:
> the reasonableness test requires a court to engage in a "calculus" of harms: a factual determination of what course of action is in the shareholders' best interests. Set forth in terms of an equation, an antitakeover device is in the shareholders' best interests if $(FV-TP)(pFV)-(TP-SV)(pSV) > 0$ where "FV" is a "full" value greater than the tender price, "TP" is the tender price, "pFV" is the probability of realizing this "full" value if the antitakeover device is maintained, "SV" is the subsequent value of the target's stock if the directors have not realized the "full" value and the tender offer is withdrawn or revised downwards, and "pSV" is the probability that SV shall occur. The only factor in the reasonableness equation which is precisely known is TP; the value of the other quantities may only be approximated.

George H. Kanter, Comment, *Judicial Review of the Antitakeover Devices Employed in the Noncoercive Tender Offer Context: Making Sense of the Unocal Test*, 138 U. Pa. L. Rev., 225, 254–55 (1989) (footnote omitted).

Conversely, in transactional justification cases involving the adoption of defenses to takeovers, the director's actions invariably implicate issues affecting stockholder rights. In transactional justification cases, the directors' decision is reviewed judicially and the burden of going forward is placed on the directors. If the directors' actions withstand *Unocal's* reasonableness and proportionality review, the traditional business judgment rule is applied to shield the directors' defensive decision rather than the directors themselves. . . .

In general, to effectively defeat the plaintiff's ability to discharge that burden, a board must sustain its burden of demonstrating that, even under *Unocal*'s standard of enhanced judicial scrutiny, its actions deserved the protection of the traditional business judgment rule. . . .

American General Threat

Reasonableness Burden Sustained

The first aspect of the *Unocal* burden, the reasonableness test, required the Unitrin Board to demonstrate that, after a reasonable investigation, it determined in good faith, that American General's Offer presented a threat to Unitrin that warranted a defensive response. This Court has held that the presence of a majority of outside independent directors will materially enhance such evidence. An "outside" director has been defined as a non-employee and non-management director, (*e.g.,* Unitrin argues, five members of its seven-person Board). Independence "means that a director's decision is based on the corporate merits of the subject before the board rather than extraneous considerations or influences."[15]

The Unitrin Board identified two dangers it perceived the American General Offer posed: inadequate price and antitrust complications. The Court of Chancery characterized the Board's concern that American General's proposed transaction could never be consummated because it may violate antitrust laws and state insurance regulations as a "makeweight excuse" for the defensive measure. It determined, however, that the Board reasonably believed that the American General Offer was inadequate and also reasonably concluded that the Offer was a threat to Unitrin's uninformed stockholders.

The Court of Chancery held that the Board's evidence satisfied the first aspect or reasonableness test under *Unocal.* The Court of Chancery then noted, however, that the threat to the Unitrin stockholders from American General's inadequate

---

15. American General argues that the Unitrin Board's investigation is not entitled to "material enhancement" under *Unocal* because the Board does not consist of a majority of outside, independent directors. According to American General, even if five of the seven Unitrin directors are "outside directors," they are not independent because they are dominated by Singleton. Although the Court of Chancery did not address the issue of domination in this pre-trial proceeding, its conclusion that the Board sustained its first *Unocal* burden of demonstrating reasonableness is an implicit rejection of American General's argument. Nevertheless, we recognize that final determinations regarding domination are usually made after a full trial.

opening bid was "mild," because the Offer was negotiable both in price and structure. The court then properly turned its attention to *Unocal's* second aspect, the proportionality test because "[i]t is not until both parts of the *Unocal* inquiry have been satisfied that the business judgment rule attaches to defensive actions of a board of directors."

Proportionality Burden

Chancery Approves Poison Pill

[The court reviewed the Chancery Court's approval of the poison pill under the reasonableness and proportionality tests of *Unocal*. Noting that this ruling was not at issue in this appeal, the court nonetheless stated that its effect on the Chancery Court's review of the Repurchase Program was "a factor to be considered on appeal. . . ."]

Proportionality Burden

Chancery Enjoins Repurchase Program

The Court of Chancery did not view either its conclusion that American General's Offer constituted a threat, or its conclusion that the poison pill was a reasonable response to that threat, as requiring it, *a fortiori*, to conclude that the Repurchase Program was also an appropriate response. The Court of Chancery then made two factual findings: first, the Repurchase Program went beyond what was "necessary" to protect the Unitrin stockholders from a "low ball" negotiating strategy; and second, it was designed to keep the decision to combine with American General within the control of the members of the Unitrin Board, as stockholders, under virtually all circumstances. Consequently, the Court of Chancery held that the Unitrin Board failed to demonstrate that the Repurchase Program met the second aspect or proportionality requirement of the initial burden *Unocal* ascribes to a board of directors.

The Court of Chancery framed the ultimate question before it as follows:

> This case comes down to one final question: Is placing the decision to sell the company in the hands of stockholders who are also directors a disproportionate response to a low price offer to buy all the shares of the company for cash?

The Court of Chancery then answered that question:

> I conclude that because the only threat to the corporation is the inadequacy of an opening bid made directly to the board, and the board has already taken actions that will protect the stockholders from mistakenly falling for a low ball negotiating strategy, a repurchase program that intentionally provides members of the board with a veto of any merger proposal is not reasonably related to the threat posed by American General's negotiable all shares, all cash offer.

In explaining its conclusion, the Court of Chancery reasoned that:

I have no doubt that a hostile acquiror can make an offer high enough to entice at least some of the directors that own stock to break ranks and sell their shares. Yet, these directors undoubtedly place a value, probably a substantial one, on their management of Unitrin, and will, at least subconsciously, reject an offer that does not compensate them for that value. . . . The prestige and perquisites that accompany managing Unitrin as a member of its Board of directors, even for the non-officer directors that do not draw a salary, may cause these stockholder directors to reject an excellent offer unless it includes this value in its "price parameter."

The Court of Chancery concluded that, although the Unitrin Board had properly perceived American General's inadequate Offer as a threat and had properly responded to that threat by adopting a "poison pill," the additional defensive response of adopting the Repurchase Program was unnecessary and disproportionate to the threat the Offer posed. . . . Therefore, the Court of Chancery held that the plaintiffs proved a likelihood of success on that issue and granted the motion to preliminarily enjoin the Repurchase Program.[18]

Proxy Contest

Supermajority Vote

Repurchase Program

Before the Repurchase Program began, Unitrin's directors collectively held approximately 23% of Unitrin's outstanding shares. Unitrin's certificate of incorporation already included a "shark-repellent"[19] provision barring any business combination with a more-than-15% stockholder unless approved by a majority of continuing directors or by a 75% stockholder vote ("Supermajority Vote"). Unitrin's shareholder directors announced publicly that they would not participate in the Repurchase Program and that this would result in a percentage increase of ownership for them, as well as for any other shareholder who did not participate.

The Court of Chancery found that by not participating in the Repurchase Program, the Board "expected to create a 28% voting block to support the Board's decision to reject [a future] offer by American General." From this underlying factual finding, the Court of Chancery concluded that American General might be "chilled" in its pursuit of Unitrin. . . .

The parties are in substantial disagreement with respect to the Court of Chancery's ultimate factual finding that the Repurchase Program was a disproportionate response under *Unocal*. Unitrin argues that American General or another potential

---

18. We note that the directors' failure to carry their initial burden under *Unocal* does not, *ipso facto*, invalidate the board's actions. Instead, once the Court of Chancery finds the business judgment rule does not apply, the burden remains on the directors to prove "entire fairness."

19. A "shark-repellent" is a provision in a company's by-laws or articles of incorporation that is intended to deter a bidder's interest in that company as a target for a takeover. . . .

acquiror can theoretically prevail in an effort to obtain control of Unitrin through a proxy contest. American General argues that the record supports the Court of Chancery's factual determination that the adoption of the Repurchase Program violated the principles of *Unocal*, even though American General acknowledges that the option of a proxy contest for obtaining control of Unitrin remained theoretically available. The stockholder-plaintiffs argue that even if it can be said, as a matter of law, that it is acceptable under certain circumstances to leave potential bidders with a proxy battle as the sole avenue for acquiring an entity, the Court of Chancery correctly determined, as a factual matter, that the Repurchase Program was disproportionate to the threat American General's Offer posed.

Proportionality Test

Shareholder Franchise

This Court has been and remains assiduous in its concern about defensive actions designed to thwart the essence of corporate democracy by disenfranchising shareholders. . . .

Nevertheless, this Court has upheld the propriety of adopting poison pills in given defensive circumstances. Keeping a poison pill in place may be inappropriate, however, when those circumstances change dramatically. Similarly, this Court has recognized the propriety of implementing certain repurchase programs (as in *Unocal* itself), as well as the unreasonableness and non-proportionality of responding defensively to a takeover bid with a coercive and preclusive partial self-tender offer.

More recently, this Court stated: "we accept the basic legal tenets," set forth in *Blasius Indus., Inc. v. Atlas Corp.*[21] that "[w]here boards of directors deliberately employ . . . legal strategies either to frustrate or completely disenfranchise a shareholder vote, . . . [t]here can be no dispute that such conduct violates Delaware law." *Stroud v. Grace*. . . .

This Court also specifically noted that boards of directors often interfere with the exercise of shareholder voting when an acquiror *launches both a proxy fight and a tender offer*. We then stated that such action "necessarily invoked both *Unocal* and *Blasius*" because "both [tests] recognize the inherent conflicts of interest that arise when shareholders are not permitted free exercise of their franchise." Consequently, we concluded that, "[i]n certain circumstances, [the judiciary] must recognize the special import of protecting the shareholders' franchise within *Unocal's* requirement that any defensive measure be proportionate and 'reasonable in relation to the threat posed.'"

---

21. In *Blasius*, the Court of Chancery held that board actions done primarily for the purpose of impeding the exercise of stockholder voting power are not invalid *per se*. "Rather, . . . in such a case, the board bears the heavy burden of demonstrating a compelling justification for such action." *Blasius Indus., Inc. v. Atlas Corp.*, Del. Ch., 564 A.2d 651, 661 (1988).

Takeover Strategy

Tender Offer/Proxy Contest

We begin our examination of Unitrin's Repurchase Program mindful of the special import of protecting the shareholder's franchise within *Unocal's* requirement that a defensive response be reasonable and proportionate. For many years the "favored attack of a [corporate] raider was stock acquisition followed by a proxy contest." *Unocal.* Some commentators have noted that the recent trend toward tender offers as the preferable alternative to proxy contests appears to be reversing because of the proliferation of sophisticated takeover defenses. Lucian A. Bebchuk & Marcel Kahan, *A Framework for Analyzing Legal Policy Towards Proxy Contests,* 78 Cal. L. Rev. 1071, 1134 (1990). In fact, the same commentators have characterized a return to proxy contests as "the only alternative to hostile takeovers to gain control against the will of the incumbent directors." *Id.*

The Court of Chancery, in the case *sub judice,* was obviously cognizant that the emergence of the "poison pill" as an effective [anti]takeover device has resulted in such a remarkable transformation in the market for corporate control that hostile bidders who proceed when such defenses are in place will usually "have to couple proxy contests with tender offers." Joseph A. Grundfest, *Just Vote No: A Minimalist Strategy for Dealing with Barbarians Inside the Gates,* 45 Stan. L. Rev. 857, 858 (1993).[25] The Court of Chancery concluded that Unitrin's adoption of a poison pill was a proportionate response to the threat its Board reasonably perceived from American General's Offer. Nonetheless, the Court of Chancery enjoined the additional defense of the Repurchase Program as disproportionate and "unnecessary."

The record reflects that the Court of Chancery's decision to enjoin the Repurchase Program is attributable to a continuing misunderstanding, i.e., that in conjunction with the longstanding Supermajority Vote provision in the Unitrin charter, the Repurchase Program would operate to provide the director shareholders with a "veto" to preclude a successful proxy contest by American General.[26] The origins of that

---

25. Another legal scholar states that, as a defensive tactic, the poison pill "warrants special attention chiefly because its preclusive effect frequently exceeds that of other takeover defensive tactics ... [and] make it effective even in circumstances where other defensive tactics may not work." Jeffrey N. Gordon, *Corporations, Markets, and Courts,* 91 Colum. L. Rev. 1931, 1946 (1991). *See also* Randall S. Thomas, *Judicial Review of Defensive Tactics in Proxy Contests: When is Using a Rights Plan Right?* 46 Vand. L. Rev. 503 (1993).

26. In reaching this result, the Court of Chancery described what it perceived to be the effect of the directors' increased percentage of stock ownership resulting from the Repurchase Program. The opinion of the Court of Chancery, as originally issued, stated:

> [I]t seems highly improbable that American General (or any other bidder) would view a proxy contest as a rational alternative once the repurchase program is completed. The repurchase program further reduces American General's incentive to undertake a proxy contest because a successful election will not provide American General with the power to combine the two companies. American General's directors will then control the

misunderstanding are three premises that are each without record support. Two of those premises are objective misconceptions and the other is subjective.

Directors' Motives

"Prestige and Perquisites"

Subjective Determination

The subjective premise was the Court of Chancery's *sua sponte* determination that Unitrin's outside directors, who are also substantial stockholders, would not vote like other stockholders in a proxy contest, *i.e.*, in their own best economic interests. At American General's Offer price, the outside directors held Unitrin shares worth more than $450 million. Consequently, Unitrin argues the stockholder directors had the same interest as other Unitrin stockholders generally, when voting in a proxy contest, to wit: the maximization of the value of their investments.

In rejecting Unitrin's argument, the Court of Chancery stated that the stockholder directors would be "subconsciously" motivated in a proxy contest to vote against otherwise excellent offers which did not include a "price parameter" to compensate them for the loss of the "prestige and perquisites" of membership on Unitrin's Board. The Court of Chancery's subjective determination that the *stockholder directors* of Unitrin would reject an "excellent offer," unless it compensated them for giving up the "prestige and perquisites" of directorship, appears to be subjective and without record support. It cannot be presumed.

It must be the subject of proof that the Unitrin directors' objective in the Repurchase Program was to forego the opportunity to sell their stock at a premium. In particular, it cannot be presumed that the prestige and perquisites of holding a director's office or a motive to strengthen collective power prevails over a stockholder-director's economic interest. Even the shareholder-plaintiffs in this case agree with the legal proposition Unitrin advocates on appeal: stockholders are presumed to act in their own best economic interests when they vote in a proxy contest.

---

company, but they still cannot implement a merger agreement without the consent of the former director stockholders.

The day after the original opinion was issued, American General's counsel wrote to the Court of Chancery to inform it of a factual error. According to American General's counsel, the original opinion was:

> technically not correct. If American General were to pursue and succeed in such a proxy contest when it owned less than 15% of Unitrin's stock, which, as the Court noted, are unrealistic assumptions, and the American General directors were then to approve a merger proposal, the supermajority provision would not apply.

The Court of Chancery acknowledged its mistake by sending out two corrected pages. Even with the two revised pages, the Court of Chancery's decision continues to reflect its initial misunderstanding of the Supermajority Vote provision.

Without Repurchase Program

Actual Voting Power Exceeds 25%

The first objective premise relied upon by the Court of Chancery, unsupported by the record, is that the shareholder directors needed to implement the Repurchase Program to attain voting power in a proxy contest equal to 25%. The Court of Chancery properly calculated that if the Repurchase Program was completed, Unitrin's shareholder directors would increase their absolute voting power to 25%. It then calculated the odds of American General marshalling enough votes to defeat the Board and its supporters.

The Court of Chancery and all parties agree that proxy contests do not generate 100% shareholder participation. The shareholder plaintiffs argue that 80–85% may be a usual turnout. Therefore, *without* the Repurchase Program, the director shareholders' absolute voting power of 23% would already constitute *actual voting power greater than* 25% in a proxy contest with normal shareholder participation below 100%.

Supermajority Vote

No Realistic Deterrent

The second objective premise relied upon by the Court of Chancery, unsupported by the record, is that American General's ability to succeed in a proxy contest depended on the Repurchase Program being enjoined because of the Supermajority Vote provision in Unitrin's charter. Without the approval of a target's board, the danger of activating a poison pill renders it irrational for bidders to pursue stock acquisitions above the triggering level.[30] Instead, "bidders intent on working around a poison pill must launch and win proxy contests to elect new directors who are willing to redeem the target's poison pill." Joseph A. Grundfest, *Just Vote No: A Minimalist Strategy for Dealing with Barbarians Inside the Gates,* 45 Stan. L. Rev. 857, 859 (1993).

As American General acknowledges, a less than 15% stockholder bidder need not proceed with acquiring shares to the extent that it would ever implicate the Supermajority Vote provision. In fact, it would be illogical for American General or any other bidder to acquire more than 15% of Unitrin's stock because that would not only trigger the poison pill, but also the constraints of 8 Del. C. § 203. If American General were to initiate a proxy contest *before* acquiring 15% of Unitrin's stock, it would need to amass only 45.1% of the votes assuming a 90% voter turnout. If it

---

30. The . . . flip-in and flip-over features [of a poison pill] stop individual shareholders or shareholder groups from accumulating large amounts of the target company's stock. No potential acquiror or other shareholder will risk triggering a [poison pill] by accumulating more than the threshold level of shares because of the threat of massive discriminatory dilution. The trigger level therefore effectively sets a ceiling on the amount of stock that any shareholder can accumulate before launching a proxy contest.

Randall S. Thomas, *Judicial Review of Defensive Tactics in Proxy Contests: When is Using a Rights Plan Right?,* 46 Vand. L. Rev. 503, 512 (1993).

commenced a tender offer at an attractive price contemporaneously with its proxy contest, it could seek to acquire 50.1% of the outstanding voting stock.

The record reflects that institutional investors own 42% of Unitrin's shares. Twenty institutions own 33% of Unitrin's shares. It is generally accepted that proxy contests have re-emerged with renewed significance as a method of acquiring corporate control because "the growth in institutional investment has reduced the dispersion of share ownership." Lucian A. Bebchuk & Marcel Kahan, *A Framework for Analyzing Legal Policy Towards Proxy Contests*, 78 Cal. L. Rev. 1071, 1134 (1990).[31] "Institutions are more likely than other shareholders to vote at all, more likely to vote against manager proposals, and more likely to vote for proposals by other shareholders." Bernard S. Black, *The Value of Institutional Investor Monitoring: The Empirical Evidence*, 39 UCLA L. Rev. 895, 925 (1992).

With Supermajority Vote

After Repurchase Program

Proxy Contest Appears Viable

The assumptions and conclusions American General sets forth in this appeal for a different purpose are particularly probative with regard to the effect of the institutional holdings in Unitrin's stock. American General's two predicate assumptions are a 90% stockholder turnout in a proxy contest and a bidder with 14.9% holdings, i.e., the maximum the bidder could own to avoid triggering the poison pill and the Supermajority Vote provision. American General also calculated the votes available to the Board or the bidder with and without the Repurchase Program:

> Assuming no Repurchase [Program], the [shareholder directors] would hold 23%, the percentage collectively held by the [directors] and the bidder would be 37.9%, and the percentage of additional votes available to either side would be 52.1%.
>
> Assuming the Repurchase [Program] is fully consummated, the [shareholder directors] would hold 28%, the percentage collectively held by the bidder and the [directors] would be 42.9%, and the percentage of additional votes available to either side would be 47.1%.

American General then applied these assumptions to reach conclusions regarding the votes needed for the 14.9% stockholder bidder to prevail: first, in an election of directors; and second, in the subsequent vote on a merger. With regard to the election of directors, American General made the following calculations:

---

31. Professor Grundfest has marshalled references to the literature discussing collective action problems for shareholder activity. Joseph A. Grundfest, *Just Vote No: A Minimalist Strategy for Dealing with Barbarians Inside the Gates*, 45 Stan. L. Rev. 857, 908 n.226 (1993).

> Assume 90% stockholder turnout. To elect directors, a plurality must be obtained; assuming no abstentions and only two competing slates, one must obtain the votes of 45.1% of the shares.
>
> The percentage of additional votes the bidder needs to win is: 45.1% - 14.9% (maximum the bidder could own and avoid the poison pill, §203 and supermajority) = 30.2%.

A merger requires approval of a majority of outstanding shares, 8 Del. C. §251, not just a plurality. In that regard, American General made the following calculations:

> Assume 90% stockholder turnout. To approve a merger, one must obtain the favorable vote of 50.1% of the shares.
>
> The percentage of additional votes the bidder needs to win is 50.1% - 14.9% = 35.2%.

Consequently, to prevail in a proxy contest with a 90% turnout, the percentage of additional shareholder votes a 14.9% shareholder bidder needs to prevail is 30.2% for directors and 35.2% in a subsequent merger. The record reflects that institutional investors held 42% of Unitrin's stock and 20 institutions held 33% of the stock. Thus, American General's own assumptions and calculations in the record support the Unitrin Board's argument that "it is hard to imagine a company more readily susceptible to a proxy contest concerning a pure issue of dollars."[33]

The conclusion of the Court of Chancery that the Repurchase Program would make a proxy contest for Unitrin a "theoretical" possibility that American General could not realistically pursue may be erroneous and appears to be inconsistent with its own earlier determination that the "repurchase program strengthens the position of the Board of Directors to defend against a hostile bidder, but will not deprive the public stockholders of the 'power to influence corporate direction through the ballot.'" Even a complete implementation of the Repurchase Program, in combination with the pre-existing Supermajority Vote provision, would not appear to have a preclusive effect upon American General's ability successfully to marshall enough shareholder votes to win a proxy contest. A proper understanding of the record reflects that American General or any other 14.9% shareholder bidder could apparently win a proxy contest with a 90% turnout.

The key variable in a proxy contest would be the merit of American General's issues, not the size of its stockholdings. If American General presented an attractive price as the cornerstone of a proxy contest, it could prevail, irrespective of whether the shareholder directors' absolute voting power was 23% or 28%. . . .

---

33. That institutions held a high percentage of Unitrin's stock is not as significant as the fact that the relatively concentrated percentage of stockholdings would facilitate a bidder's ability to communicate the merits of its position.

Consequently, a proxy contest apparently remained a viable alternative for American General to pursue notwithstanding Unitrin's poison pill, Supermajority Vote provision, and a fully implemented Repurchase Program.

Substantive Coercion

American General's Threat

This Court has recognized "the prerogative of a board of directors to resist a third party's unsolicited acquisition proposal or offer." *Paramount Communications, Inc. v. QVC Network, Inc.* The Unitrin Board did not have unlimited discretion to defeat the threat it perceived from the American General Offer by any draconian[34] means available. Pursuant to the *Unocal* proportionality test, the nature of the threat associated with a particular hostile offer sets the parameters for the range of permissible defensive tactics. Accordingly, the purpose of enhanced judicial scrutiny is to determine whether the Board acted reasonably in "relation . . . to the threat which a particular bid allegedly poses to stockholder interests." *Mills Acquisition Co. v. Macmillan, Inc.*

"The obvious requisite to determining the reasonableness of a defensive action is a clear identification of the nature of the threat." *Paramount Communications, Inc. v. Time, Inc.* Courts, commentators and litigators have attempted to catalogue the threats posed by hostile tender offers. Commentators have categorized three types of threats:

> (i) *opportunity loss* . . . [where] a hostile offer might deprive target shareholders of the opportunity to select a superior alternative offered by target management [or, we would add, offered by another bidder]; (ii) *structural coercion*, . . . the risk that disparate treatment of non-tendering shareholders might distort shareholders' tender decisions; and (iii) *substantive coercion*, . . . the risk that shareholders will mistakenly accept an underpriced offer because they disbelieve management's representations of intrinsic value.

This Court has held that the "inadequate value" of an all cash for all shares offer is a "legally cognizable threat." In addition, this Court has specifically concluded that inadequacy of value is *not* the only legally cognizable threat from "an all-shares, all-cash offer at a price below what a target board in good faith deems to be the present value of its shares." In making that determination, this Court held that the Time board of directors had reasonably determined that inadequate value was not the only threat that Paramount's all cash for all shares offer presented, but was *also*

---

34. *Draconian*, adj. Of or pert. to Draco, an archon and member of the Athenian eupatridae, or the code of laws which is said to have been framed about 621 B.C. by him as thesmothete. In them the penalty for most offenses was death, and to a later age they seemed so severe that they were said to be written in blood. Hence, barbarously severe; harsh; cruel. *Webster's New International Dictionary* 780 (2d ed. 1951).

reasonably concerned that the Time stockholders might tender to Paramount in ignorance or based upon a mistaken belief, *i.e.*, yield to substantive coercion.

The record reflects that the Unitrin Board perceived the threat from American General's Offer to be a form of substantive coercion. The Board noted that Unitrin's stock price had moved up, on higher than normal trading volume, to a level slightly below the price in American General's Offer. The Board also noted that some Unitrin shareholders had publicly expressed interest in selling at or near the price in the Offer. The Board determined that Unitrin's stock was undervalued by the market at current levels and that the Board considered Unitrin's stock to be a good long-term investment. The Board also discussed the speculative and unsettled market conditions for Unitrin stock caused by American General's public disclosure. The Board concluded that a Repurchase Program would provide additional liquidity to those stockholders who wished to realize short-term gain, and would provide enhanced value to those stockholders who wished to maintain a long-term investment. Accordingly, the Board voted to authorize the Repurchase Program for up to ten million shares of its outstanding stock on the open market.

In *Unocal,* this Court noted that, pursuant to Delaware corporate law, a board of directors' duty of care required it to respond actively to protect the corporation and its shareholders from perceived harm. In *Unocal,* when describing the proportionality test, this Court listed several examples of concerns that boards of directors should consider in evaluating and responding to perceived threats. Unitrin's Board deemed three of the concerns exemplified in *Unocal* relevant in deciding to authorize the Repurchase Program: first, the inadequacy of the price offered; second, the nature and timing of American General's Offer; and third, the basic stockholder interests at stake, including those of short-term speculators whose actions may have fueled the coercive aspect of the Offer at the expense of the long-term investor.

The record appears to support Unitrin's argument that the Board's justification for adopting the Repurchase Program was its reasonably perceived risk of substantive coercion, *i.e.*, that Unitrin's shareholders might accept American General's inadequate Offer because of "ignorance or mistaken belief" regarding the Board's assessment of the long-term value of Unitrin's stock. In this case, the Unitrin Board's letter to its shareholders specifically reflected those concerns in describing its perception of the threat from American General's Offer. The adoption of the Repurchase Program also appears to be consistent with this Court's holding that economic inadequacy is not the only threat presented by an all cash for all shares hostile bid, because the threat of such a hostile bid could be exacerbated by shareholder "ignorance or ... mistaken belief."

Range of Reasonableness

Proper Proportionality Burden

. . .

The Court of Chancery applied an incorrect legal standard when it ruled that the Unitrin decision to authorize the Repurchase Program was disproportionate because it was "unnecessary." The Court of Chancery stated:

> Given that the Board had already implemented the poison pill and the advance notice provision, the repurchase program was unnecessary to protect Unitrin from an inadequate bid.

In *QVC*, this Court recently elaborated upon the judicial function in applying enhanced scrutiny, citing *Unocal* as authority, albeit in the context of a sale of control and the target board's consideration of one of several reasonable alternatives. That teaching is nevertheless applicable here:

> a court applying enhanced judicial scrutiny should be deciding whether the directors made *a reasonable* decision, not *a perfect* decision. If a board selected one of several reasonable alternatives, a court should not second guess that choice even though it might have decided otherwise or subsequent events may have cast doubt on the board's determination. Thus, courts will not substitute their business judgment for that of the directors, but will determine if the directors' decision was, on balance, within a range of reasonableness.

Paramount Communications, Inc. v. QVC Network, Inc., Del. Supr., 637 A.2d 34, 45–46 (1994) (emphasis in original). The Court of Chancery did not determine whether the Unitrin Board's decision to implement the Repurchase Program fell within a "range of reasonableness."

The record reflects that the Unitrin Board's adoption of the Repurchase Program was an apparent recognition on its part that all shareholders are not alike. This Court has stated that distinctions among types of shareholders are neither inappropriate nor irrelevant for a board of directors to make, *e.g.,* distinctions between long-term shareholders and short-term profit-takers, such as arbitrageurs, and their stockholding objectives. In *Unocal* itself, we expressly acknowledged that "a board may reasonably consider the basic stockholder interests at stake, including those of short term speculators, whose actions may have fueled the coercive aspect of the offer at the expense of the long term investor."

The Court of Chancery's determination that the Unitrin Board's adoption of the Repurchase Program was unnecessary constituted a substitution of its business judgment for that of the Board, contrary to this Court's "range of reasonableness" holding in *Paramount Communications, Inc. v. QVC Network, Inc.* . . .

Draconian Defenses

Coercive or Preclusive

Range of Reasonableness

In assessing a challenge to defensive actions by a target corporation's board of directors in a takeover context, this Court has held that the Court of Chancery should evaluate the board's overall response, including the justification for each contested defensive measure, and the results achieved thereby. Where all of the target board's defensive actions are inextricably related, the principles of Unocal require that such actions be scrutinized collectively as a unitary response to the perceived threat. Thus, the Unitrin Board's adoption of the Repurchase Program, in addition to the poison pill, must withstand *Unocal's* proportionality review.

In Unocal, the progenitor of the proportionality test, this Court stated that the board of directors' "duty of care extends to protecting the corporation and its [stockholders] from perceived harm whether a threat originates from third parties or other shareholders." We then noted that "such powers are not absolute." Specifically, this Court held that the board "does not have unbridled discretion to defeat any perceived threat by any Draconian means available." Immediately following those observations in *Unocal,* when exemplifying the parameters of a board's authority in adopting a restrictive stock repurchase, this Court held that "the directors may not have acted *solely* or *primarily* out of a desire to perpetuate themselves in office" (preclusion of the stockholders' corporate franchise right to vote) and, further, that the stock repurchase plan must not be inequitable. (emphasis added). . . .

This Court also applied *Unocal's* proportionality test to the board's adoption of a "poison pill" shareholders' rights plan in *Moran v. Household Int'l, Inc.* After acknowledging that the adoption of the rights plan was within the directors' statutory authority, this Court determined that the implementation of the rights plan was a proportionate response to the theoretical threat of a hostile takeover, in part, because it did not "strip" the stockholders of their right to receive tender offers *and* did not fundamentally restrict proxy contests, *i.e.,* was not preclusive.

. . . As common law applications of *Unocal's* proportionality standard have evolved, at least two characteristics of draconian defensive measures taken by a board of directors in responding to a threat have been brought into focus through enhanced judicial scrutiny. In the modern takeover lexicon, it is now clear that since *Unocal,* this Court has consistently recognized that defensive measures which are either preclusive or coercive are included within the common law definition of draconian.

If a defensive measure is not draconian, however, because it is not either coercive or preclusive, the *Unocal* proportionality test requires the focus of enhanced judicial scrutiny to shift to "the range of reasonableness." Proper and proportionate defensive responses are intended and permitted to thwart perceived threats. When a corporation is not for sale, the board of directors is the defender of the metaphorical medieval corporate bastion and the protector of the corporation's shareholders. The fact that a defensive action must not be coercive or preclusive does not prevent a board from responding defensively before a bidder is at the corporate bastion's gate.[38]

The *ratio decidendi* for the "range of reasonableness" standard is a need of the board of directors for latitude in discharging its fiduciary duties to the corporation and its shareholders when defending against perceived threats. The concomitant requirement is for judicial restraint. Consequently, if the board of directors' defensive response is not draconian (preclusive or coercive) and is within a "range of reasonableness," a court must not substitute its judgment for the board's.

This Case

Repurchase Program

Proportionate With Poison Pill

In this case, the initial focus of enhanced judicial scrutiny for proportionality requires a determination regarding the defensive responses by the Unitrin Board to American General's offer. We begin, therefore, by ascertaining whether the Repurchase Program, as an addition to the poison pill, was draconian by being either coercive or preclusive.

A limited nondiscriminatory self-tender, like some other defensive measures, may thwart a current hostile bid, but is not inherently coercive. Moreover, it does not necessarily preclude future bids or proxy contests by stockholders who decline to participate in the repurchase. A selective repurchase of shares in a public corporation on the market, such as Unitrin's Repurchase Program, generally does not discriminate because all shareholders can voluntarily realize the same benefit by selling. Here, there is no showing on this record that the Repurchase Program was coercive.

We have already determined that the record in this case appears to reflect that a proxy contest remained a viable (if more problematic) alternative for American General even if the Repurchase Program were to be completed in its entirety. Nevertheless, the Court of Chancery must determine whether Unitrin's Repurchase Program would only inhibit American General's ability to wage a proxy fight and institute a merger or whether it was, in fact, preclusive because American General's success would either be mathematically impossible or realistically unattainable. If the Court of Chancery concludes that the Unitrin Repurchase Program was not draconian because it was not preclusive, one question will remain to be answered in

---

38. This Court's choice of the term draconian in *Unocal* was a recognition that the law affords boards of directors substantial latitude in defending the perimeter of the corporate bastion against perceived threats.... Stated more directly, depending upon the circumstances, the board may respond to a reasonably perceived threat by adopting individually or sometimes in combination: advance notice by-laws, supermajority voting provisions, shareholder rights plans, repurchase programs, etc.

its proportionality review: whether the Repurchase Program was within a range of reasonableness?

The Court of Chancery found that the Unitrin Board reasonably believed that American General's Offer was inadequate and that the adoption of a poison pill was a proportionate defensive response. Upon remand, in applying the correct legal standard to the factual circumstances of this case, the Court of Chancery may conclude that the implementation of the limited Repurchase Program was also within a range of reasonable additional defensive responses available to the Unitrin Board. In considering whether the Repurchase Program was within a range of reasonableness the Court of Chancery should take into consideration whether: (1) it is a statutorily authorized form of business decision which a board of directors may routinely make in a non-takeover context; (2) as a defensive response to American General's Offer it was limited and corresponded in degree or magnitude to the degree or magnitude of the threat (*i.e.,* assuming the threat was relatively "mild," was the response relatively "mild?"); (3) with the Repurchase Program, the Unitrin Board properly recognized that all shareholders are not alike, and provided immediate liquidity to those shareholders who wanted it. . . .

Remand to Chancery

In this case, the Court of Chancery erred by substituting its judgment, that the Repurchase Program was unnecessary, for that of the Board. The Unitrin Board had the power and the duty, upon reasonable investigation, to protect Unitrin's shareholders from what it perceived to be the threat from American General's inadequate all-cash for all-shares Offer. The adoption of the poison pill *and* the limited Repurchase Program was not coercive and the Repurchase Program may not be preclusive. Although each made a takeover more difficult, individually and collectively, if they were not coercive or preclusive the Court of Chancery must determine whether they were within the range of reasonable defensive measures available to the Board.

If the Court of Chancery concludes that individually and collectively the poison pill and the Repurchase Program were proportionate to the threat the Board believed American General posed, the Unitrin Board's adoption of the Repurchase Program and the poison pill is entitled to review under the traditional business judgment rule. The burden will then shift "back to the plaintiffs who have the ultimate burden of persuasion [in a preliminary injunction proceeding] to show a breach of the director's fiduciary duties." In order to rebut the protection of the business judgment rule, the burden on the plaintiffs will be to demonstrate, "by a preponderance of the evidence that the directors' decisions were *primarily* based on [(1)] perpetuating themselves in office or [(2)] some other breach of fiduciary duty such as fraud, overreaching, lack of good faith, or [(3)] being uninformed." . . .

Conclusion

We hold that the Court of Chancery correctly determined that the *Unocal* standard of enhanced judicial scrutiny applied to the defensive actions of the Unitrin defendants in establishing the poison pill and implementing the Repurchase

Program. The Court of Chancery's finding, that the Repurchase Program was a disproportionate defensive response, was based on faulty factual predicates, unsupported by the record. This error was exacerbated by its application of an erroneous legal standard of "necessity" to the Repurchase Program as a defensive response. . . .

Questions

1. What is the *Unocal* test in light of *Unitrin, Inc. v. American General Corp.*?

2. What does *Unitrin* tell you about the role and power of the board? How, if at all, does this affect your understanding or evaluation of the corporation's social role and obligations?

3. The court criticizes the Chancery Court's assumption that the shareholder directors of Unitrin would place a value on the prestige and other intangibles of their directorships so that they might be inclined to reject a good offer without adequate compensation for the loss of that prestige, noting its own view that shareholders are interested only in price. Do you agree?

4. Is the court's assumption regarding the shareholder directors consistent with *Unocal*, in which the court developed its proportionality review as a predicate to the application of the business judgment rule solely on the fear that directors might be acting to entrench themselves (and recall that in that case, directors owned shares as well), implying that the directorship itself had a value that transcended economics?

5. Is the court's analysis of the shareholder directors' interests consistent with its later discussion of the differences among different types of shareholders and the board's ability to take these differences into account? Is it consistent with the way the court has viewed the board in prior cases?

6. Is it wise for the court to assume that directors will seek to maximize their own self-interest? What does such a view suggest about the nature of the corporation itself? Assuming the court is correct in its assessment of the shareholder directors' interests, can directors be trusted to act in the best interests of the corporation? The shareholders?

B. Extending the *Unocal/Revlon* Approach

The following cases extend, with hindsight, the doctrine developed in the line of cases from *Unocal* to *Unitrin* to negotiated acquisitions and claims of shareholder disenfranchisement. As you read these cases, consider how they apply the doctrine we have discussed thus far. What aspects of the *Unocal/Revlon* approach remain intact? What aspects are changed, how, and why?

Hilton Hotels Corporation v. ITT Corporation

978 F. Supp. 1342 (Nev. 1997)

Pro, District Judge

. . .

I. FACTS

On January 27, 1997, Hilton announced a $55.00 per share tender offer for the stock of ITT, and announced plans for a proxy contest at ITT's 1997 annual meeting. This litigation commenced on the same date with the filing of Hilton's Complaint for Injunctive and Declaratory Relief seeking to enjoin ITT from impeding the shareholder franchise regarding the election of directors at ITT's annual meeting, and from taking other defensive measures in response to Hilton's announced tender offer and proxy contest.

On February 11, 1997, ITT formally rejected Hilton's tender offer. ITT proceeded to sell several of its non-core assets and opposed Hilton's takeover attempt before gaming regulatory bodies in Nevada, New Jersey and Mississippi.

When it became apparent that ITT would not conduct its annual meeting in May 1997, as it had customarily done in preceding years, Hilton filed a motion for a mandatory injunction to compel ITT to conduct the annual meeting in May. On April 21, 1997, this Court denied Hilton's Motion finding that Nevada law and ITT's by-laws did not require that ITT conduct its annual meeting within twelve months of the prior meeting, but rather that ITT had eighteen months within which to do so.

On July 15, 1997, ITT announced a Comprehensive Plan which, among other things, proposed to split ITT into three new entities, the largest of which would become ITT Destinations. ITT Destinations would be comprised of the current ITT's hotel and gaming business which account for approximately 93% of ITT's current assets. A second entity, ITT Educational Services, would consist of the current ITT's technical schools, and ITT's European Yellow Pages Division would remain with the current ITT as ITT World Directories.

Most significantly, under the Comprehensive Plan, the board of directors of the new ITT Destinations would be comprised of the members of ITT's current board with one important distinction. The new board would be a "classified" or "staggered" board divided into three classes with each class of directors serving for a term of three years, and with one class to be elected each year. Moreover, a shareholder vote of 80% would be required to remove directors without cause, and 80% shareholder vote would also be required to repeal the classified board provision or the 80% requirement to remove directors without cause.

Additionally, the record fairly supports Hilton's contention that the Comprehensive Plan contains a "poison pill" resulting in a $1.4 billion tax liability which would be triggered if Hilton successfully acquired more than 50% of ITT Destinations and that Hilton would be liable for 90% of the tax bill.

Finally, and critical to this Court's analysis, ITT seeks to implement the Comprehensive Plan prior to ITT's 1997 annual meeting and without obtaining shareholder approval.

II. THE PARTIES' CONTENTIONS AND APPLICABLE LEGAL STANDARDS

On July 16, 1997, ITT filed the Complaint for Declaratory Relief now before the Court, seeking two declarations:

1. That Hilton cannot show that ITT's board acted outside its powers or failed to exercise its powers in good faith and with a view to the interests of the corporation and its shareholders in adopting the Comprehensive Plan; and

2. That Hilton, as a would-be acquiror, is antagonistic to other ITT shareholders and thus lacks standing as a proper derivative plaintiff to pursue an injunction against the Comprehensive Plan based on alleged breach of fiduciary duty by ITT's board

Shortly after ITT's announcement of its Comprehensive Plan, Hilton announced an amended tender offer of $70.00 per share which was rejected by ITT. On August 26, 1997, Hilton filed its Motion for Injunctive and Declaratory Relief seeking:

1. A preliminary and permanent injunction enjoining ITT from proceeding with its Comprehensive Plan;

2. Declaring that by adopting the Comprehensive Plan, ITT's directors had breached their fiduciary duties to ITT and its shareholders;

3. Declaring that ITT may not implement its Comprehensive Plan without obtaining a shareholder vote; and

4. Requiring ITT to conduct its 1997 annual meeting for the election of directors not later than November 14, 1997.

. . .

III. DISCUSSION

This case involves consideration of the powers and duties of the board of directors of a Nevada corporation in responding to a hostile takeover attempt, and the importance of protecting the franchise of the shareholders of the corporation in the process.

Many courts have grappled with legal issues presented by the strategies employed by hostile bidders, such as Hilton, and the concomitant anti-takeover defensive measures utilized by target companies, such as ITT. Coupling an unsolicited tender offer with a proxy contest to replace the incumbent board is a favored strategy of would-be acquirors. A variety of sophisticated defensive measures, including "poison pill" plans have also evolved to frustrate a host of takeover attempts. As a result, "replacing the incumbent directors of the target corporation is viewed as an efficient way to eliminate the target company's ability to utilize these anti-takeover defenses."

Nevada state case law is virtually silent on the subject.... Where, as here, there is no Nevada statutory or case law on point for an issue of corporate law, this Court finds persuasive authority in Delaware case law.

A. Legal Framework for Board Action in Response to a Proxy Contest and Tender Offer.

As this case involves both a tender offer and a proxy contest by Hilton, the proper legal standard is a *Unocal/Blasius* analysis . . .

> In assessing a challenge to defensive actions by a target corporation's board of directors in a takeover context, this Court has held that the Court of Chancery should evaluate the board's overall response, including the justification for each contested defensive measure, and the results achieved thereby. Where all of the target board's defensive actions are *inextricably related*, the principles of *Unocal* require that such actions be scrutinized collectively as a unitary response to the perceived threat. *Unitrin*, 651 A.2d at 1386–87 (emphasis supplied).

> Where an acquiror launches both a proxy fight and a tender offer, it necessarily invoke[s] both *Unocal* and *Blasius*" because "both [tests] recognize the inherent conflicts of interest that arise when shareholders are not permitted free exercise of their franchise.... [I]n certain circumstances, [the judiciary] must recognize the special import of protecting the shareholders' franchise within *Unocal*'s requirement that any defensive measure be proportionate and 'reasonable in relation to the threat posed.'" *Unitrin*, 651 A.2d at 1379 . . .

> A board's unilateral decision to adopt a defensive measure touching "upon issues of control" that purposefully disenfranchises its shareholders is strongly suspect under *Unocal*, and cannot be sustained without a "compelling justification." *Stroud*, 606 A.2d at 92 n. 3.

These cases have drawn a distinction between the exercise of two types of corporate power: 1) power over the assets of the corporation and 2) the power relationship between the board (management) and the shareholders. Actions involving the first type of power invoke the business judgment rule, or *Unocal* if an action is in response to a reasonably perceived threat to the corporation. Actions involving the second power invoke a *Blasius* analysis. The issues raised in this case require the Court to focus on the power relationship between ITT's board and ITT shareholders, not on the ITT board's actions relating to corporate assets.

Several amicus briefs have been filed on behalf of ITT shareholders, urging that they be allowed to vote on the Comprehensive Plan and the board of directors at the 1997 annual meeting. This Court has found no legal basis mandating a shareholder vote on the adoption of ITT's Comprehensive Plan in its entirety. However, as the Court finds that the Comprehensive Plan would violate the power relationship between ITT's board and ITT's shareholders by impermissibly infringing on the shareholders' right to vote on members of the board of directors, it must be enjoined.

. . .

Delaware case law merely clarifies the basic duties established by the Nevada statutes. . . .

Thus, Delaware precedent establishes that a board has power over the management and assets of a corporation, but that power is not unbridled. That power is limited by the right of shareholders to vote for the members of the board. . . . This right underlies the concept of corporate democracy. This Court fully endorses the reasoning in . . . *Blasius* regarding the importance of the shareholder franchise to the entire scheme of corporate governance. This Court will, therefore, examine ITT's Comprehensive Plan under the *Unocal/Blasius* analysis.

Unocal requires the Court to consider the following two questions: 1) Does ITT have reasonable grounds for believing a danger to corporate policy and effectiveness exists? 2) Is the response reasonable in relation to the threat? If it is a defensive measure touching on issues of control, the court must examine whether the board purposefully disenfranchised its shareholders, an action that cannot be sustained without a compelling justification.

1. The Classified Board for ITT Destinations

The first defensive action this Court will analyze under the *Unocal* standard is the provision in the Comprehensive Plan for a classified board for ITT Destinations.

a. Reasonable grounds for believing a threat to corporate policy and effectiveness exists.

Nine of ITT's eleven directors are outside directors. Under *Unocal,* such a majority materially enhances evidence that a hostile offer presents a threat warranting a defensive response.

ITT argues strenuously that the Comprehensive Plan is better than Hilton's offer. This is not for the Court to decide, and it is not determinative under its analysis. Under *Unocal,* a court must first determine if there is a threat to corporate policy and effectiveness. ITT has failed to demonstrate such a threat.

ITT has made no showing that Hilton will pursue a different corporate policy than ITT seek to implement through its Comprehensive Plan. In fact, over the past few months, ITT has to a large extent adopted Hilton's proposed strategy of how it says it will govern ITT if its slate of directors is elected. There has also been no showing of Hilton's inability or ineffectiveness to run ITT if it does succeed in its takeover attempt. ITT cites to the fact that some Sheraton franchise owners will be unhappy if Hilton enters into certain management contracts, but this is not fundamental or pervasive enough to constitute a "threat" to ITT's corporate policy or effectiveness.

The ITT board has also failed to meet its burden of showing "good faith and reasonable investigation" of a threat to corporate policy or effectiveness which would meet the burden placed on the board under the first prong of the *Unocal* test. Since Hilton's tender offer was announced, the ITT board has not met with Hilton to discuss the offer. Moreover the overwhelming majority of ITT's evidence of good faith relates to its approval of the Comprehensive Plan, not to the inadequacy of Hilton's offer.

The sole "threat" ITT points to is that Hilton's offer of $70 a share is inadequate, primarily because this price does not contain a control premium. However, at the August 14, 1997, ITT board meeting, Goldman Sachs told the ITT board that the market valued ITT's plan at $62 to $64 dollars a share. This contradicts ITT's argument that there is no control premium over market price contained in Hilton's offer. That ITT itself was offering to buy back roughly 26% of its stock at $70 a share does not nullify this fact.

The only attempt ITT has made to satisfy the first prong of the *Unocal* analysis is to argue that Hilton's price is inadequate. However, while inadequacy of an offer is a legally cognizable threat, ITT has shown no real harm to corporate policy or effectiveness. The facts in *Unocal* illustrate this point well. *Unocal* involved a tender offer with a back-end offer of junk bonds. Junk bond financing could reasonably harm the future policy and effectiveness of a company. As ITT itself is offering only $70 a share, and the Comprehensive Plan involves greatly increasing the leveraging of ITT, its claim that Hilton's offer of $70 a share is a threat to policy or effectiveness is unpersuasive. In light of these facts, the alleged inadequacy of Hilton's offer is not a severe threat to ITT. Under the proportionality requirement, the nature of Hilton's threat will set the parameters for the range of permissible defensive tactics under the second prong of the *Unocal* test.

b. ITT's Response was Preclusive

Assuming Hilton's offer constitutes a cognizable threat under *Unocal*, ITT's response cannot be preclusive or coercive, and it must be within the range of reasonableness. As articulated in *Unitrin*, a board cannot "cram down" on shareholders a management sponsored alternative. The installation of a classified board for ITT Destinations, a company which will encompass 93% of the current ITT's assets and 87% of its revenues, is clearly preclusive and coercive under *Unitrin*. The classified board provision for ITT Destinations will preclude current ITT shareholders from exercising a right they currently possess—to determine the membership of the board of ITT. At the very minimum, ITT shareholders will have no choice but to accept the Comprehensive Plan and a majority of ITT's incumbent board members for another year. Therefore, the Comprehensive Plan is preclusive.

c. The Primary Purpose of the Comprehensive Plan is to Interfere with Shareholder Franchise

ITT's response to Hilton's tender offer touches upon issues of control, and this Court must determine whether the response purposefully disenfranchises ITT's shareholders. If so, under the analysis of *Stroud* and *Unitrin,* it is not a reasonable response unless a "compelling justification" exists. It is important to note that in *Blasius,* the board did something that normally would be entirely permissible under Delaware law and its own by-laws: it expanded the board from seven to nine individuals. It did this in the face of a hostile takeover by a company financed through "junk bonds" and two individuals who sought to substantially "cash out" many of the target corporation's assets. Still, while the board in *Blasius* had a good faith reason to act as it did, and it acted with appropriate care, the board could not lawfully prevent the shareholders from electing a majority of new directors.

Blasius' factual scenario is strikingly similar to the circumstances surrounding ITT's actions. Normally, a corporation is free to adopt a classified board structure. In fact many companies, including Hilton, have classified boards. As long as the classified board is adopted in the proper manner, whether through charter amendment, changes in the by-laws of a company or through shareholder vote, it is permissible. However, *Blasius* illustrates that even if an action is normally permissible, and the board adopts it in good faith and with proper care, a board cannot undertake such action if the primary purpose is to disenfranchise the shareholders in light of a proxy contest. Thus, while ITT could normally adopt a classified board or issue a dividend of shares creating ITT Destinations, it cannot undertake these actions if the primary purpose is to disenfranchise ITT shareholders in light of Hilton's tender offer and proxy contest.

As a board would likely never concede that its primary purpose was to entrench itself, this Court must look to circumstantial evidence to determine the primary purpose of ITT's action touching upon issues of control. While none of the following factors are dispositive, collectively they eliminate all questions of material fact, and demonstrate that the primary purpose of ITT's Comprehensive Plan was to disenfranchise its shareholders.

i. Timing

The intent evidenced by the timing of the Comprehensive Plan is transparent. Although ITT claims that a spin-off or sale was contemplated before Hilton's tender offer, it makes no mention of when the board determined to move from an annually elected board to a classified board. Moreover, all aspects of ITT's Comprehensive Plan were formulated against the backdrop of Hilton's tender offer and proxy contest, and the Plan was not announced until well after Hilton's initial tender offer. Finally, this major restructuring of ITT was announced and to be implemented in a little over two months, and designed to take effect less than two months before the annual meeting was to be held at which shareholders would have the opportunity to vote on an annually elected rather than a classified board.

ii. Entrenchment

The ITT directors who are approving the Comprehensive Plan are the same directors who will fill the classified board positions of ITT Destinations. ITT and its advisors recognized from the outset that they were vulnerable because they did not have a staggered board of directors. The members of ITT's board are appointing themselves to new, more insulated positions, and at least seven of the eleven directors are avoiding the shareholder vote that would otherwise occur at ITT's 1997 annual meeting. While companies may convert from annual to classified boards, as *Blasius* illustrates, the rub is in the details. It is the manner of adopting the Comprehensive Plan with its provision for a new certified board comprised of incumbent ITT directors which supports the conclusion that ITT's Plan is primarily designed to entrench the incumbent board.

iii. ITT's Stated Purpose

ITT has offered no credible justification for not seeking shareholder approval of the Comprehensive Plan. ITT simply claims that it wants to "avoid market risks and other business problems." Such vague generalizations do not approach the required showing of a reasonable justification other than entrenchment for the board's action. Simply stating that its "advisors" suggested a rapid implementation of the Comprehensive Plan, without pointing to a specific risk or problem, is insufficient to meet ITT's burden.

iv. Benefits of Comprehensive Plan

ITT argues that there are economic benefits to the Comprehensive Plan, and general benefits of the classified board provision for ITT Destinations, That may be true, but the additional benefits of a plan infringing on shareholder voting rights do not remedy the fundamental flaw of board entrenchment.

v. Effect of Classified Board

The classified board provision for ITT Destinations under ITT's Comprehensive Plan ensures that ITT shareholders will be absolutely precluded from electing a majority of the directors nominated under Hilton's proxy contest at the 1997 annual meeting. Such a Plan, coupled with ITT's vehement opposition to Hilton's tender offer, is inconsistent with ITT's earlier argument that a delay of the 1997 annual meeting from May to November would afford shareholders additional time to inform themselves and more fully consider the implications of their vote for directors at the 1997 annual meeting.

ITT's position is particularly anomalous given the fact that when ITT previously split the company in 1995, it sought shareholder approval. While shareholder approval may not be absolutely required to split ITT now anymore than it was in 1995, the fact that the ITT board decided to subject the 1995 split of the company to a shareholder vote is strong evidence that the primary purpose of its attempts to implement the Comprehensive Plan prior to the 1997 annual meeting is to entrench the incumbent ITT board.

vi. Failure to Obtain an IRS Opinion as to Effects of the Comprehensive Plan

ITT is not seeking an Internal Revenue Service opinion regarding the tax consequences of the three-way split of ITT under the Comprehensive Plan. . . . While obtaining a tax opinion from the Internal Revenue Service may not be mandatory, ITT's failure to seriously consider obtaining such an opinion provides additional evidence that ITT's primary intention in implementing the Comprehensive Plan at this time was to impede the shareholder franchise.

2. Other Provisions of the Comprehensive Plan

This Court's analysis regarding the threat to ITT under the first prong of *Unocal* is equally applicable to the remaining elements of the Comprehensive Plan. Whether the other aspects of ITT's Comprehensive Plan violate the second step of the *Unocal* analysis, that is whether they are preclusive or coercive, is problematic. Certainly the record before the Court supports Hilton's contention that the "tax poison pill" relating to its potential purchase of ITT Destinations is preclusive and coercive....

Serious questions exist as to whether the remaining provisions of the Comprehensive Plan are preclusive or coercive, or reasonable responses under *Unocal*. This Court finds it unnecessary, however, to undertake an exhaustive analysis of the laundry list of issues presented by both parties. The different provisions of the Comprehensive Plan are inextricably related, and this Court has already concluded that the staggered board provision is preclusive and was enacted for the primary purpose of entrenching the current board. Therefore, the entire Comprehensive Plan must be enjoined.

3. Duty to Maximize Value to Shareholders Under *Revlon*

Hilton further argues that injunctive relief is warranted based on an analysis of the Comprehensive Plan under the *Revlon* standard. The Court finds that Hilton has not extinguished all material facts as to whether the Comprehensive Plan involves: 1) an abandonment of the long-term strategy of ITT involving a breakup of the company or 2) a sale of control is contemplated in *Revlon* and *Paramount v. QVC*. Therefore, permanent injunctive relief on this basis is not warranted.

IV. CONCLUSION

. . .

Shareholders do not exercise day-to-day business judgments regarding the operation of a corporation — those are matters left to the reasonable discretion of directors, officers and the corporation's management team. Corporate boards have great latitude in exercising their business judgments as they should. As a result, shareholders generally have only two protections against perceived inadequate business performance. They may sell their stock or vote to replace incumbent board members. For this reason, interference with the shareholder franchise is especially serious. It is not to be left to the board's business judgment, precisely because it undercuts a primary justification for allowing directors to rely on their business judgment in almost every other context. Indeed, "one of the justifications for the business judgment rule's insulation of directors from liability for almost all of their decisions is that unhappy shareholders can always vote the directors out of office." . . .

As this Court has noted previously, "inquiries concerning fiduciary duties are inherently particularized and contextual. It is probably not possible to work out rules that will be perfectly predictive of future cases involving claimed impediments to the shareholder vote. It is sufficient to express a reasoned judgment on the facts presented." . . .

ITT strongly argues that its Comprehensive Plan is superior to Hilton's alternative tender offer. This argument should be directed to ITT's shareholders, not this Court.

. . .

Likewise, the good faith of the ITT board in implementing the Comprehensive Plan does not change this Court's analysis. . . . Simply put, there is no compelling justification for infringement of the shareholder franchise as proposed by the implementation of ITT's Comprehensive Plan before the 1997 annual meeting.

The ultimate outcome of the election of directors at ITT's 1997 annual meeting is not a relevant inquiry for this Court. That is something for the shareholders who own ITT to decide when they select the board who will lead the corporation. If a majority of the incumbent ITT board is re-elected after a fully-informed and fair shareholder vote, that board will be free to implement any business plan it chooses so long as that plan is consistent with ITT's charter and by-laws, and governing law.

This Court concludes that the structure and timing of ITT's Comprehensive Plan with its classified board provision for ITT Destinations, is preclusive and leaves no doubt that the primary purpose for ITT's proposed implementation of the Comprehensive Plan before the 1997 annual meeting is to impermissibly impede the exercise of the shareholder franchise by depriving shareholders of the opportunity to vote to re-elect or to oust all or as many of the incumbent ITT directors as they may choose at the upcoming annual meeting. It has as its primary purpose the entrenchment of the incumbent ITT board. As a result, the Court concludes that Hilton has prevailed on the merits of its claim for permanent injunctive relief.

IT IS THEREFORE ORDERED that Hilton's Motion for Permanent Injunctive Relief is granted to the extent that ITT is hereby enjoined from implementing its Comprehensive Plan announced July 15, 1997.

IT IS FURTHER ORDERED that ITT's annual meeting shall be held no later than November 14, 1997.

. . .

Questions

1. The court states: "Delaware case law merely clarifies the basic duties established by the Nevada statutes." If this is so, do we need corporation law statutes and, if so, why?

2. According to the court in *Hilton Hotels Corp. v. ITT*, what are potential threats to corporate policy? Does that accord with the doctrine as it developed in cases we

discussed in Subsection A (*Unocal, Revlon, Paramount v. Time, Paramount v. QVC, Unitrin*)?

3. According to the court in *Hilton Hotels Corp. v. ITT*, when are *Revlon* duties triggered?

4. Why didn't the board of ITT simply amend the corporation's bylaws to establish a staggered board? Why did it go through the trouble of splitting into 3 different entities?

5. Why wasn't the classified board a valid defensive tactic? In assessing it, which test did the court apply—*Unocal* or *Blasius*? Would the court have evaluated ITT's actions differently if Hilton only launched a tender offer rather than a tender offer combined with a proxy contest?

Omnicare, Inc. v. NCS Healthcare, Inc.
818 A.2d 914 (Del. 2003)

HOLLAND, Justice

NCS Healthcare, Inc. ("NCS"), a Delaware corporation, was the object of competing acquisition bids, one by Genesis Health Ventures, Inc. ("Genesis"), a Pennsylvania corporation, and the other by Omnicare, Inc. ("Omnicare"), a Delaware corporation. . . .

Overview of Opinion

The board of directors of NCS, an insolvent publicly traded Delaware corporation, agreed to the terms of a merger with Genesis. Pursuant to that agreement, all of the NCS creditors would be paid in full and the corporation's stockholders would exchange their shares for the shares of Genesis, a publicly traded Pennsylvania corporation. Several months after approving the merger agreement, but before the stockholder vote was scheduled, the NCS board of directors withdrew its prior recommendation in favor of the Genesis merger.

In fact, the NCS board recommended that the stockholders reject the Genesis transaction after deciding that a competing proposal from Omnicare was a superior transaction. The competing Omnicare bid offered the NCS stockholders an amount of cash equal to more than twice the then current market value of the shares to be received in the Genesis merger. The transaction offered by Omnicare also treated the NCS corporation's other stakeholders on equal terms with the Genesis agreement.

The merger agreement between Genesis and NCS contained a provision authorized by Section 251(c) of Delaware's corporation law. It required that the Genesis agreement be placed before the corporation's stockholders for a vote, even if the NCS board of directors no longer recommended it. At the insistence of Genesis, the NCS board also agreed to omit any effective fiduciary clause from the merger agreement. In connection with the Genesis merger agreement, two stockholders of NCS, who held a majority of the voting power, agreed unconditionally to vote all of their shares in favor of the Genesis merger. Thus, the combined terms of the voting agreements and merger agreement guaranteed, *ab initio,* that the transaction proposed by Genesis would obtain NCS stockholder's approval.

The Court of Chancery ruled that the voting agreements, when coupled with the provision in the Genesis merger agreement requiring that it be presented to the stockholders for a vote pursuant to 8 Del. C. § 251(c), constituted defensive measures within the meaning of *Unocal Corp. v. Mesa Petroleum Co.* After applying the *Unocal* standard of enhanced judicial scrutiny, the Court of Chancery held that those defensive measures were reasonable. We have concluded that, in the absence of an effective fiduciary out clause, those defensive measures are both preclusive and coercive. Therefore, we hold that those defensive measures are invalid and unenforceable.

The Parties

The defendant, NCS, is a Delaware corporation headquartered in Beachwood, Ohio. NCS is a leading independent provider of pharmacy services to long-term care institutions including skilled nursing facilities, assisted living facilities and other institutional healthcare facilities. NCS common stock consists of Class A shares and Class B shares. The Class B shares are entitled to ten votes per share and the Class A shares are entitled to one vote per share. The shares are virtually identical in every other respect.

The defendant Jon H. Outcalt is Chairman of the NCS board of directors. Outcalt owns 202,063 shares of NCS Class A common stock and 3,476,086 shares of Class B common stock. The defendant Kevin B. Shaw is President, CEO and a director of NCS. At the time the merger agreement at issue in this dispute was executed with Genesis, Shaw owned 28,905 shares of NCS Class A common stock and 1,141,134 shares of Class B common stock.

The NCS board has two other members, defendants Boake A. Sells and Richard L. Osborne. Sells is a graduate of the Harvard Business School. He was Chairman and CEO at Revco Drugstores in Cleveland, Ohio from 1987 to 1992, when he was replaced by new owners. Sells currently sits on the boards of both public and private companies. Osborne is a full-time professor at the Weatherhead School of Management at Case Western Reserve University. He has been at the university for over thirty years. Osborne currently sits on at least seven corporate boards other than NCS.

The defendant Genesis is a Pennsylvania corporation with its principal place of business in Kennett Square, Pennsylvania. It is a leading provider of healthcare and support services to the elderly. The defendant Geneva Sub, Inc., a wholly owned subsidiary of Genesis, is a Delaware corporation formed by Genesis to acquire NCS.

The plaintiffs in the class action own an unspecified number of shares of NCS Class A common stock. They represent a class consisting of all holders of Class A common stock. As of July 28, 2002, NCS had 18,461,599 Class A shares and 5,255,210 Class B shares outstanding.

Omnicare is a Delaware corporation with its principal place of business in Covington, Kentucky. Omnicare is in the institutional pharmacy business, with annual sales in excess of $2.1 billion during its last fiscal year. Omnicare purchased 1000 shares of NCS Class A common stock on July 30, 2002.

. . .

FACTUAL BACKGROUND

The parties are in substantial agreement regarding the operative facts. They disagree, however, about the legal implications. This recitation of facts is taken primarily from the opinion by the Court of Chancery.

NCS Seeks Restructuring Alternatives

Beginning in late 1999, changes in the timing and level of reimbursements by government and third-party providers adversely affected market conditions in the health care industry. As a result, NCS began to experience greater difficulty in collecting accounts receivables, which led to a precipitous decline in the market value of its stock. NCS common shares that traded above $20 in January 1999 were worth as little as $5 at the end of that year. By early 2001, NCS was in default on approximately $350 million in debt, including $206 million in senior bank debt and $102 million of its 5 3/4 % Convertible Subordinated Debentures (the "Notes"). After these defaults, NCS common stock traded in a range of $0.09 to $0.50 per share until days before the announcement of the transaction at issue in this case.

NCS began to explore strategic alternatives that might address the problems it was confronting. As part of this effort, in February 2000, NCS retained UBS Warburg, L.L.C. to identify potential acquirers and possible equity investors. UBS Warburg contacted over fifty different entities to solicit their interest in a variety of transactions with NCS. UBS Warburg had marginal success in its efforts. By October 2000, NCS had only received one non-binding indication of interest valued at $190 million, substantially less than the face value of NCS's senior debt. This proposal was reduced by 20% after the offeror conducted its due diligence review.

NCS Financial Deterioration

In December 2000, NCS terminated its relationship with UBS Warburg and retained Brown, Gibbons, Lang & Company as its exclusive financial advisor. During this period, NCS's financial condition continued to deteriorate. In April 2001, NCS received a formal notice of default and acceleration from the trustee for holders of the Notes. As NCS's financial condition worsened, the Noteholders formed a committee to represent their financial interests (the "Ad Hoc Committee"). At about that time, NCS began discussions with various investor groups regarding a restructuring in a "pre-packaged" bankruptcy. NCS did not receive any proposal that it believed provided adequate consideration for its stakeholders. At that time, full recovery for NCS's creditors was a remote prospect, and any recovery for NCS stockholders seemed impossible.

Omnicare's Initial Negotiations

In the summer of 2001, NCS invited Omnicare, Inc. to begin discussions with Brown Gibbons regarding a possible transaction. On July 20, Joel Gemunder, Omnicare's President and CEO, sent Shaw a written proposal to acquire NCS in a bankruptcy sale under Section 363 of the Bankruptcy Code. This proposal was for $225 million subject to satisfactory completion of due diligence. NCS asked Omnicare to execute a confidentiality agreement so that more detailed discussions could take place.

In August 2001, Omnicare increased its bid to $270 million, but still proposed to structure the deal as an asset sale in bankruptcy. Even at $270 million, Omnicare's proposal was substantially lower than the face value of NCS's outstanding debt. It would have provided only a small recovery for Omnicare's Noteholders and no recovery for its stockholders. In October 2001, NCS sent Glen Pollack of Brown Gibbons to meet with Omnicare's financial advisor, Merrill Lynch, to discuss Omnicare's interest in NCS. Omnicare responded that it was not interested in any transaction other than an asset sale in bankruptcy.

There was no further contact between Omnicare and NCS between November 2001 and January 2002. Instead, Omnicare began secret discussions with Judy K. Mencher, a representative of the Ad Hoc Committee. In these discussions, Omnicare continued to pursue a transaction structured as a sale of assets in bankruptcy. In February 2002, the Ad Hoc Committee notified the NCS board that Omnicare had proposed an asset sale in bankruptcy for $313,750,000.

NCS Independent Board Committee

In January 2002, Genesis was contacted by members of the Ad Hoc Committee concerning a possible transaction with NCS. Genesis executed NCS's standard confidentiality agreement and began a due diligence review. Genesis had recently emerged from bankruptcy because, like NCS, it was suffering from dwindling government reimbursements.

Genesis previously lost a bidding war to Omnicare in a different transaction. This led to bitter feelings between the principals of both companies. More importantly, this bitter experience for Genesis led to its insistence on exclusivity agreements and lock-ups in any potential transaction with NCS.

NCS Financial Improvement

NCS's operating performance was improving by early 2002. As NCS's performance improved, the NCS directors began to believe that it might be possible for NCS to enter into a transaction that would provide some recovery for NCS stockholders' equity. In March 2002, NCS decided to form an independent committee of board members who were neither NCS employees nor major NCS stockholders (the

"Independent Committee"). The NCS board thought this was necessary because, due to NCS's precarious financial condition, it felt that fiduciary duties were owed to the enterprise as a whole rather than solely to NCS stockholders.

Sells and Osborne were selected as the members of the committee, and given authority to consider and negotiate possible transactions for NCS. The entire four member NCS board, however, retained authority to approve any transaction. The Independent Committee retained the same legal and financial counsel as the NCS board.

The Independent Committee met for the first time on May 14, 2002. At that meeting Pollack suggested that NCS seek a "stalking-horse merger partner" to obtain the highest possible value in any transaction. The Independent Committee agreed with the suggestion.

Genesis Initial Proposal

Two days later, on May 16, 2002, Scott Berlin of Brown Gibbons, Glen Pollack and Boake Sells met with George Hager, CFO of Genesis, and Michael Walker, who was Genesis's CEO. At that meeting, Genesis made it clear that if it were going to engage in any negotiations with NCS, it would not do so as a "stalking horse." As one of its advisors testified, "We didn't want to be someone who set forth a valuation for NCS which would only result in that valuation . . . being publicly disclosed, and thereby creating an environment where Omnicare felt to maintain its competitive monopolistic positions, that they had to match and exceed that level." Thus, Genesis "wanted a degree of certainty that to the extent [it] w[as] willing to pursue a negotiated merger agreement . . . , [it] would be able to consummate the transaction [it] negotiated and executed."

In June 2002, Genesis proposed a transaction that would take place outside the bankruptcy context. Although it did not provide full recovery for NCS's Noteholders, it provided the possibility that NCS stockholders would be able to recover something for their investment. As discussions continued, the terms proposed by Genesis continued to improve. On June 25, the economic terms of the Genesis proposal included repayment of the NCS senior debt in full, full assumption of trade credit obligations, an exchange offer or direct purchase of the NCS Notes providing NCS Noteholders with a combination of cash and Genesis common stock equal to the par value of the NCS Notes (not including accrued interest), and $20 million in value for the NCS common stock. Structurally, the Genesis proposal continued to include consents from a significant majority of the Noteholders as well as support agreements from stockholders owning a majority of the NCS voting power.

Genesis Exclusivity Agreement

NCS's financial advisors and legal counsel met again with Genesis and its legal counsel on June 26, 2002, to discuss a number of transaction-related issues. At this meeting, Pollack asked Genesis to increase its offer to NCS stockholders. Genesis agreed to consider this request. Thereafter, Pollack and Hager had further conversations. Genesis agreed to offer a total of $24 million in consideration for the NCS common stock, or an additional $4 million, in the form of Genesis common stock.

At the June 26 meeting, Genesis's representatives demanded that, before any further negotiations take place, NCS agree to enter into an exclusivity agreement with it. . . . On June 27, 2002, Genesis's legal counsel delivered a draft form of exclusivity agreement for review and consideration by NCS's legal counsel.

The Independent Committee met on July 3, 2002, to consider the proposed exclusivity agreement. Pollack presented a summary of the terms of a possible Genesis merger, which had continued to improve. The then-current Genesis proposal included (1) repayment of the NCS senior debt in full, (2) payment of par value for the Notes (without accrued interest) in the form of a combination of cash and Genesis stock, (3) payment to NCS stockholders in the form of $24 million in Genesis stock, plus (4) the assumption, because the transaction was to be structured as a merger, of additional liabilities to trade and other unsecured creditors.

NCS director Sells testified, Pollack told the Independent Committee at a July 3, 2002 meeting that Genesis wanted the Exclusivity Agreement to be the first step towards a completely locked up transaction that would preclude a higher bid from Omnicare. . . .

After NCS executed the exclusivity agreement, Genesis provided NCS with a draft merger agreement, a draft Noteholders' support agreement, and draft voting agreements for Outcalt and Shaw, who together held a majority of the voting power of the NCS common stock. Genesis and NCS negotiated the terms of the merger agreement over the next three weeks. During those negotiations, the Independent Committee and the Ad Hoc Committee persuaded Genesis to improve the terms of its merger.

Omnicare Proposes Negotiations

By late July 2002, Omnicare came to believe that NCS was negotiating a transaction, possibly with Genesis or another of Omnicare's competitors, that would potentially present a competitive threat to Omnicare. Omnicare also came to believe, in light of a run-up in the price of NCS common stock, that whatever transaction NCS was negotiating probably included a payment for its stock. Thus, the Omnicare board of directors met on the morning of July 26 and, on the recommendation of its management, authorized a proposal to acquire NCS that did not involve a sale of assets in bankruptcy.

On the afternoon of July 26, 2002, Omnicare faxed to NCS a letter outlining a proposed acquisition. The letter suggested a transaction in which Omnicare would retire NCS's senior and subordinated debt at par plus accrued interest, and pay the NCS stockholders $3 cash for their shares. Omnicare's proposal, however, was expressly conditioned on negotiating a merger agreement, obtaining certain third party consents, and completing its due diligence.

Mencher saw the July 26 Omnicare letter and realized that, while its economic terms were attractive, the "due diligence" condition substantially undercut its strength. In an effort to get a better proposal from Omnicare, Mencher telephoned Gemunder and told him that Omnicare was unlikely to succeed in its bid unless it dropped the "due diligence outs." She explained this was the only way a bid at the last minute would be able to succeed. Gemunder considered Mencher's warning "very real," and followed up with his advisors. They, however, insisted that he retain the due diligence condition "to protect [him] from doing something foolish." Taking this advice to heart, Gemunder decided not to drop the due diligence condition.

Late in the afternoon of July 26, 2002, NCS representatives received voicemail messages from Omnicare asking to discuss the letter. The exclusivity agreement prevented NCS from returning those calls. In relevant part, that agreement precluded NCS from "engag[ing] or particpat[ing] [sic] in any discussions or negotiations with respect to a Competing Transaction or a proposal for one." The July 26 letter from Omnicare met the definition of a "Competing Transaction."

Despite the exclusivity agreement, the Independent Committee met to consider a response to Omnicare. It concluded that discussions with Omnicare about its July 26 letter presented an unacceptable risk that Genesis would abandon merger discussions. The Independent Committee believed that, given Omnicare's past bankruptcy proposals and unwillingness to consider a merger, as well as its decision to negotiate exclusively with the Ad Hoc Committee, the risk of losing the Genesis proposal was too substantial. Nevertheless, the Independent Committee instructed Pollack to use Omnicare's letter to negotiate for improved terms with Genesis.

Genesis Merger Agreement and Voting Agreements

Genesis responded to the NCS request to improve its offer as a result of the Omnicare fax the next day. On July 27, Genesis proposed substantially improved terms. First, it proposed to retire the Notes in accordance with the terms of the indenture, thus eliminating the need for Noteholders to consent to the transaction. This change involved paying all accrued interest plus a small redemption premium. Second, Genesis increased the exchange ratio for NCS common stock to one-tenth of a Genesis common share for each NCS common share, an 80% increase. Third, it agreed to lower the proposed termination fee in the merger agreement from $10 million to $6 million. In return for these concessions, Genesis stipulated that the transaction had to be approved by midnight the next day, July 28, or else Genesis would terminate discussions and withdraw its offer.

The Independent Committee and the NCS board both scheduled meetings for July 28. The committee met first. Although that meeting lasted less than an hour, the Court of Chancery determined the minutes reflect that the directors were fully informed of all material facts relating to the proposed transaction. After concluding that Genesis was sincere in establishing the midnight deadline, the committee voted unanimously to recommend the transaction to the full board.

The full board met thereafter. After receiving similar reports and advice from its legal and financial advisors, the board concluded that "balancing the potential loss of the Genesis deal against the uncertainty of Omnicare's letter, results in the conclusion that the only reasonable alternative for the Board of Directors is to approve the Genesis transaction." The board first voted to authorize the voting agreements with Outcalt and Shaw, for purposes of Section 203 of the Delaware General Corporation Law ("DGCL"). The board was advised by its legal counsel that "under the terms of the merger agreement and because NCS shareholders representing in excess of 50% of the outstanding voting power would be *required* by Genesis to enter into stockholder voting agreements contemporaneously with the signing of the merger agreement, and would agree to vote their shares in favor of the merger agreement, shareholder approval of the merger would be assured even if the NCS Board were to withdraw or change its recommendation. *These facts would prevent NCS from engaging in any alternative or superior transaction in the future.*" (emphasis added).

After listening to a *summary* of the merger terms, the board then resolved that the merger agreement and the transactions contemplated thereby were advisable and fair and in the best interests of all the NCS stakeholders. The NCS board further resolved to recommend the transactions to the stockholders for their approval and adoption. A definitive merger agreement between NCS and Genesis and the stockholder voting agreements were executed later that day. The Court of Chancery held that it was not a *per se* breach of fiduciary duty that the NCS board never read the NCS/Genesis merger agreement word for word.[4]

NCS/Genesis Merger Agreement

Among other things, the NCS/Genesis merger agreement provided the following:

NCS stockholders would receive 1 share of Genesis common stock in exchange for every 10 shares of NCS common stock held;

NCS stockholders could exercise appraisal rights under *8 Del. C. §262*;

NCS would redeem NCS's Notes in accordance with their terms;

NCS would submit the merger agreement to NCS stockholders regardless of whether the NCS board continued to recommend the merger;

NCS would not enter into discussions with third parties concerning an alternative acquisition of NCS, or provide non-public information to such parties, unless (1) the third party provided an unsolicited, *bona fide* written proposal documenting the terms of the acquisition; (2) the NCS board believed in good faith that the proposal was or was likely to result in an acquisition on terms superior to those contemplated by the NCS/Genesis merger agreement; and (3) before providing non-public information to that third party, the third party would execute a confidentiality agreement at least as restrictive as the one in place between NCS and Genesis; and

---

4. *See, e.g., Smith v. Van Gorkom,* 488 A.2d 858, 883 n. 25 (Del.1985).

If the merger agreement were to be terminated, under certain circumstances NCS would be required to pay Genesis a $6 million termination fee and/or Genesis's documented expenses, up to $5 million.

Voting Agreements

Outcalt and Shaw, in their capacity as NCS stockholders, entered into voting agreements with Genesis. NCS was also required to be a party to the voting agreements by Genesis. Those agreements provided, among other things, that:

Outcalt and Shaw were acting in their capacity as NCS stockholders in executing the agreements, not in their capacity as NCS directors or officers;

Neither Outcalt nor Shaw would transfer their shares prior to the stockholder vote on the merger agreement;

Outcalt and Shaw agreed to vote all of their shares in favor of the merger agreement; and

Outcalt and Shaw granted to Genesis an irrevocable proxy to vote their shares in favor of the merger agreement.

The voting agreement was specifically enforceable by Genesis.

The merger agreement further provided that if either Outcalt or Shaw breached the terms of the voting agreements, Genesis would be entitled to terminate the merger agreement and potentially receive a $6 million termination fee from NCS. Such a breach was impossible since Section 6 provided that the voting agreements were specifically enforceable by Genesis.

Omnicare's Superior Proposal

On July 29, 2002, hours after the NCS/Genesis transaction was executed, Omnicare faxed a letter to NCS restating its conditional proposal and attaching a draft merger agreement. Later that morning, Omnicare issued a press release publicly disclosing the proposal.

On August 1, 2002, Omnicare filed a lawsuit attempting to enjoin the NCS/Genesis merger, and announced that it intended to launch a tender offer for NCS's shares at a price of $3.50 per share. On August 8, 2002, Omnicare began its tender offer. By letter dated that same day, Omnicare expressed a desire to discuss the terms of the offer with NCS. Omnicare's letter continued to condition its proposal on satisfactory completion of a due diligence investigation of NCS.

On August 8, 2002, and again on August 19, 2002, the NCS Independent Committee and full board of directors met separately to consider the Omnicare tender offer in light of the Genesis merger agreement. NCS's outside legal counsel and NCS's financial advisor attended both meetings. The board was unable to determine that Omnicare's expressions of interest were likely to lead to a "Superior Proposal," as the term was defined in the NCS/Genesis merger agreement. On September 10, 2002,

NCS requested and received a waiver from Genesis allowing NCS to enter into discussions with Omnicare without first having to determine that Omnicare's proposal was a "Superior Proposal."

On October 6, 2002, Omnicare irrevocably committed itself to a transaction with NCS. Pursuant to the terms of its proposal, Omnicare agreed to acquire all the outstanding NCS Class A and Class B shares at a price of $3.50 per share in cash. As a result of this irrevocable offer, on October 21, 2002, the NCS board withdrew its recommendation that the stockholders vote in favor of the NCS/Genesis merger agreement. NCS's financial advisor withdrew its fairness opinion of the NCS/Genesis merger agreement as well.

Genesis Rejection Impossible

The Genesis merger agreement permits the NCS directors to furnish non-public information to, or enter into discussions with, "any Person in connection with an unsolicited bona fide written Acquisition Proposal by such person" that the board deems likely to constitute a "Superior Proposal." That provision has absolutely no effect on the Genesis merger agreement. Even if the NCS board "changes, withdraws or modifies" its recommendation, as it did, it must still submit the merger to a stockholder vote.

A subsequent filing with the Securities and Exchange Commission ("SEC") states: "the NCS independent committee and the NCS board of directors have determined to withdraw their recommendations of the Genesis merger agreement and recommend that the NCS stockholders vote against the approval and adoption of the Genesis merger." In that same SEC filing, however, the NCS board explained why the success of the Genesis merger had already been predetermined. "Notwithstanding the foregoing, the NCS independent committee and the NCS board of directors recognize that (1) the existing contractual obligations to Genesis currently prevent NCS from accepting the Omnicare irrevocable merger proposal; and (2) the existence of the voting agreements entered into by Messrs. Outcalt and Shaw, whereby Messrs. Outcalt and Shaw agreed to vote their shares of NCS Class A common stock and NCS Class B common stock in favor of the Genesis merger, ensure NCS stockholder approval of the Genesis merger." This litigation was commenced to prevent the consummation of the inferior Genesis transaction.

LEGAL ANALYSIS
Business Judgment or Enhanced Scrutiny

The "defining tension" in corporate governance today has been characterized as "the tension between deference to directors' decisions and the scope of judicial review." The appropriate standard of judicial review is dispositive of which party has the burden of proof as any litigation proceeds from stage to stage until there is a substantive determination on the merits. Accordingly, identification of the correct analytical framework is essential to a proper judicial review of challenges to the decision-making process of a corporation's board of directors.

[The court discusses the business judgment rule and enhanced scrutiny.]

Merger Decision Review Standard

The first issue decided by the Court of Chancery addressed the standard of judicial review that should be applied to the decision by the NCS board to merge with Genesis. This Court has held that a board's decision to enter into a merger transaction that does not involve a change in control is entitled to judicial deference pursuant to the procedural and substantive operation of the business judgment rule. When a board decides to enter into a merger transaction that will result in a change of control, however, enhanced judicial scrutiny under *Revlon* is the standard of review.

The Court of Chancery concluded that, because the stock-for-stock merger between Genesis and NCS did not result in a change of control, the NCS directors' duties under *Revlon* were not triggered by the decision to merge with Genesis. The Court of Chancery also recognized, however, that *Revlon* duties are imposed "when a corporation initiates an active bidding process seeking to sell itself." The Court of Chancery then concluded, alternatively, that *Revlon* duties had not been triggered because NCS did not start an active bidding process, and the NCS board "abandoned" its efforts to sell the company when it entered into an exclusivity agreement with Genesis.

After concluding that the *Revlon* standard of enhanced judicial review was completely inapplicable, the Court of Chancery then held that it would examine the decision of the NCS board of directors to approve the Genesis merger pursuant to the business judgment rule standard. After completing its business judgment rule review, the Court of Chancery held that the NCS board of directors had not breached their duty of care by entering into the exclusivity and merger agreements with Genesis. The Court of Chancery also held, however, that "even applying the more exacting *Revlon* standard, the directors acted in conformity with their fiduciary duties in seeking to achieve the highest and best transaction that was reasonably available to [the stockholders]."

The appellants argue that the Court of Chancery's *Revlon* conclusions are without factual support in the record and contrary to Delaware law for at least two reasons. First, they submit that NCS did initiate an active bidding process. Second, they submit that NCS did not "abandon" its efforts to sell itself by entering into the exclusivity agreement with Genesis. The appellants contend that once NCS decided "to initiate a bidding process seeking to maximize short-term stockholder value, it cannot avoid enhanced judicial scrutiny under *Revlon* simply because the bidder it selected [Genesis] happens to have proposed a merger transaction that does not involve a change of control."

The Court of Chancery's decision to review the NCS board's decision to merge with Genesis under the business judgment rule rather than the enhanced scrutiny standard of *Revlon* is not outcome determinative for the purposes of deciding this appeal. We have assumed arguendo that the business judgment rule applied to the decision by the NCS board to merge with Genesis. We have also assumed arguendo that the NCS board exercised due care when it: abandoned the Independent

Committee's recommendation to pursue a stalking horse strategy, without even trying to implement it; executed an exclusivity agreement with Genesis; acceded to Genesis' twenty-four hour ultimatum for making a final merger decision; and executed a merger agreement that was summarized but never completely read by the NCS board of directors.

Deal Protection Devices Require Enhanced Scrutiny

The dispositive issues in this appeal involve the defensive devices that protected the Genesis merger agreement. The Delaware corporation statute provides that the board's management decision to enter into and recommend a merger transaction can become final only when ownership action is taken by a vote of the stockholders. Thus, the Delaware corporation law expressly provides for a balance of power between boards and stockholders which makes merger transactions a shared enterprise and ownership decision. Consequently, a board of directors' decision to adopt defensive devices to protect a merger agreement may implicate the stockholders' right to effectively vote contrary to the initial recommendation of the board in favor of the transaction.

It is well established that conflicts of interest arise when a board of directors acts to prevent stockholders from effectively exercising their right to vote contrary to the will of the board. The "omnipresent specter" of such conflict may be present whenever a board adopts defensive devices to protect a merger agreement. The stockholders' ability to effectively reject a merger agreement is likely to bear an inversely proportionate relationship to the structural and economic devices that the board has approved to protect the transaction.

In *Paramount v. Time*, the original merger agreement between Time and Warner did not constitute a "change of control." The plaintiffs in *Paramount v. Time* argued that, although the original Time and Warner merger agreement did not involve a change of control, the use of a lock-up, no-shop clause, and "dry-up" provisions violated the Time board's *Revlon* duties. This Court held that "[t]he adoption of structural safety devices alone does not trigger *Revlon*. Rather, as the Chancellor stated, *such devices are properly subject to a Unocal analysis.*"

In footnote 15 of *Paramount v. Time*, we stated that legality of the structural safety devices adopted to protect the original merger agreement between Time and Warner were not a central issue on appeal. That is because the issue on appeal involved the "Time's board [decision] to recast its consolidation with Warner into an outright cash and securities acquisition of Warner by Time." Nevertheless, we determined that there was substantial evidence on the record to support the conclusions reached by the Chancellor in applying a *Unocal* analysis to each of the structural devices contained in the original merger agreement between Time and Warner.

There are inherent conflicts between a board's interest in protecting a merger transaction it has approved, the stockholders' statutory right to make the final decision to either approve or not approve a merger, and the board's continuing responsibility to effectively exercise its fiduciary duties at all times after the merger agreement is executed. These competing considerations require a threshold determination that board-approved defensive devices protecting a merger transaction are within the limitations of its statutory authority and consistent with the directors' fiduciary duties. Accordingly, in *Paramount v. Time,* we held that the business judgment rule applied to the Time board's original decision to merge with Warner. We further held, however, that defensive devices adopted by the board to protect the original merger transaction must withstand enhanced judicial scrutiny under the *Unocal* standard of review, even when that merger transaction does not result in a change of control.

Enhanced Scrutiny Generally

In *Paramount v. QVC,* this Court identified the key features of an enhanced judicial scrutiny test. The first feature is a "judicial determination regarding the adequacy of the decisionmaking process employed by the directors, including the information on which the directors based their decision." The second feature is "a judicial examination of the reasonableness of the directors' action in light of the circumstances then existing." We also held that "the directors have the burden of proving that they were adequately informed and acted reasonably."

In *QVC,* we explained that the application of an enhanced judicial scrutiny test involves a judicial "review of the reasonableness of the substantive merits of the board's actions." In applying that standard, we held that "a court should not ignore the complexity of the directors' task" in the context in which action was taken. Accordingly, we concluded that a court applying enhanced judicial scrutiny should not decide whether the directors made a perfect decision but instead should decide whether "the directors' decision was, on balance, within a range of reasonableness."

In *Unitrin,* we explained the "*ratio decidendi* for the 'range of reasonableness' standard" when a court applies enhanced judicial scrutiny to director action pursuant to our holding in *Unocal.* It is a recognition that a board of directors needs "latitude in discharging its fiduciary duties to the corporation and its shareholders when defending against perceived threats." "The concomitant requirement is for judicial restraint." Therefore, if the board of directors' collective defensive responses are not draconian (preclusive or coercive) and are "within a 'range of reasonableness,' a court must not substitute its judgment for the board's [judgment]." The same *ratio decidendi* applies to the "range of reasonableness" when courts apply *Unocal's* enhanced judicial scrutiny standard to defensive devices intended to protect a merger agreement that will not result in a change of control.

A board's decision to protect its decision to enter a merger agreement with defensive devices against uninvited competing transactions that may emerge is analogous to a board's decision to protect against dangers to corporate policy and effectiveness when it adopts defensive measures in a hostile takeover contest. In applying *Unocal's* enhanced judicial scrutiny in assessing a challenge to defensive actions taken by a target corporation's board of directors in a takeover context, this Court held that the board "does not have unbridled discretion to defeat perceived threats by any Draconian means available." Similarly, just as a board's statutory power with regard to a merger decision is not absolute, a board does not have unbridled discretion to defeat any perceived threat to a merger by protecting it with any draconian means available.

Since *Unocal*, "this Court has consistently recognized that defensive measures which are either preclusive or coercive are included within the common law definition of draconian." In applying enhanced judicial scrutiny to defensive actions under *Unocal*, a court must "evaluate the board's overall response, including the justification for each contested defensive measure, and the results achieved thereby." If a "board's defensive actions are inextricably related, the principles of *Unocal* require that such actions be scrutinized collectively as a unitary response to the perceived threat."

Therefore, in applying enhanced judicial scrutiny to defensive devices designed to protect a merger agreement, a court must first determine that those measures are not preclusive or coercive *before* its focus shifts to the "range of reasonableness" in making a proportionality determination. If the trial court determines that the defensive devices protecting a merger are not preclusive or coercive, the proportionality paradigm of *Unocal* is applicable. The board must demonstrate that it has reasonable grounds for believing that a danger to the corporation and its stockholders exists if the merger transaction is not consummated. That burden is satisfied "by showing good faith and reasonable investigation." Such proof is materially enhanced if it is approved by a board comprised of a majority of outside directors or by an independent committee.

When the focus of judicial scrutiny shifts to the range of reasonableness, *Unocal* requires that any defensive devices must be proportionate to the perceived threat to the corporation and its stockholders if the merger transaction is not consummated. Defensive devices taken to protect a merger agreement executed by a board of directors are intended to give that agreement an advantage over any subsequent transactions that materialize before the merger is approved by the stockholders and consummated. This is analogous to the favored treatment that a board of directors may properly give to encourage an initial bidder when it discharges its fiduciary duties under *Revlon*.

Therefore, in the context of a merger that does not involve a change of control, when defensive devices in the executed merger agreement are challenged *vis-à-vis* their effect on a subsequent competing alternative merger transaction, this Court's analysis in *Macmillan* is didactic.[54] In the context of a case of defensive measures taken against an existing bidder, we stated in *Macmillan*:

---

54. *Mills Acquisition Co. v. Macmillan Inc.*, 559 A.2d 1261, 1288 (Del.1988).

In the face of disparate treatment, the trial court must first examine whether the directors properly perceived that shareholder interests were enhanced. In any event the board's action must be reasonable in relation to the advantage sought to be achieved [by the merger it approved], or conversely, to the threat which a [competing transaction] poses to stockholder interests. If on the basis of this enhanced *Unocal* scrutiny the trial court is satisfied that the test has been met, then the directors' actions necessarily are entitled to the protections of the business judgment rule.[55]

The latitude a board will have in either maintaining or using the defensive devices it has adopted to protect the merger it approved will vary according to the degree of benefit or detriment to the stockholders' interests that is presented by the value or terms of the subsequent competing transaction.

Genesis' One Day Ultimatum

. . .

Genesis' twenty-four hour ultimatum was that, *unless both* the merger agreement and the voting agreements were signed with the terms it requested, its offer was going to be withdrawn. According to Genesis' attorneys, these "were unalterable conditions to Genesis' willingness to proceed." Genesis insisted on the execution of the interlocking voting rights and merger agreements because it feared that Omnicare would make a superior merger proposal. The NCS board signed the voting rights and merger agreements, without any effective fiduciary out clause, to expressly guarantee that the Genesis merger would be approved, even if a superior merger transaction was presented from Omnicare or any other entity.

Deal Protection Devices

Defensive devices, as that term is used in this opinion, is a synonym for what are frequently referred to as "deal protection devices." Both terms are used interchangeably to describe any measure or combination of measures that are intended to protect the consummation of a merger transaction. Defensive devices can be economic, structural, or both.

Deal protection devices need not all be in the merger agreement itself. In this case, for example, the Section 251(c) provision in the merger agreement was combined with the separate voting agreements to provide a structural defense for the Genesis merger agreement against any subsequent superior transaction. Genesis made the NCS board's defense of its transaction absolute by insisting on the omission of any effective fiduciary out clause in the NCS merger agreement.

Genesis argues that stockholder voting agreements cannot be construed as deal protection devices taken by a board of directors because stockholders are entitled to vote in their own interest. . . .

---

55. *Id.* (citation omitted).

In this case, the stockholder voting agreements were inextricably intertwined with the defensive aspects of the Genesis merger agreement. In fact, the voting agreements with Shaw and Outcalt were the linchpin of Genesis' proposed tripartite defense. Therefore, Genesis made the execution of those voting agreements a non-negotiable condition precedent to its execution of the merger agreement. . . .

With the assurance that Outcalt and Shaw would irrevocably agree to exercise their majority voting power in favor of its transaction, Genesis insisted that the merger agreement reflect the other two aspects of its concerted defense, i.e., the inclusion of a Section 251(c) provision and the omission of any effective fiduciary out clause. Those dual aspects of the merger agreement would not have provided Genesis with a complete defense in the absence of the voting agreements with Shaw and Outcalt.

These Deal Protection Devices Unenforceable

In this case, the Court of Chancery correctly held that the NCS directors' decision to adopt defensive devices to *completely* "lock up" the Genesis merger mandated "special scrutiny" under the two-part test set forth in *Unocal*. That conclusion is consistent with our holding in *Paramount v. Time* that "safety devices" adopted to protect a transaction that did not result in a change of control are subject to enhanced judicial scrutiny under a *Unocal* analysis. The record does not, however, support the Court of Chancery's conclusion that the defensive devices adopted by the NCS board to protect the Genesis merger were reasonable and proportionate to the threat that NCS perceived from the potential loss of the Genesis transaction.

Pursuant to the judicial scrutiny required under *Unocal's* two-stage analysis, the NCS directors must first demonstrate "that they had reasonable grounds for believing that a danger to corporate policy and effectiveness existed. . . ." To satisfy that burden, the NCS directors are required to show they acted in good faith after conducting a reasonable investigation. The threat identified by the NCS board was the possibility of losing the Genesis offer and being left with no comparable alternative transaction.

The second stage of the *Unocal* test requires the NCS directors to demonstrate that their defensive response was "reasonable in relation to the threat posed." This inquiry involves a two-step analysis. The NCS directors must first establish that the merger deal protection devices adopted in response to the threat were not "coercive" or "preclusive," and then demonstrate that their response was within a "range of reasonable responses" to the threat perceived. In *Unitrin*, we stated:

> A response is "coercive" if it is aimed at forcing upon stockholders a management-sponsored alternative to a hostile offer.
>
> A response is "preclusive" if it deprives stockholders of the right to receive all tender offers or precludes a bidder from seeking control by fundamentally restricting proxy contests or otherwise.

This aspect of the *Unocal* standard provides for a disjunctive analysis. If defensive measures are either preclusive or coercive they are draconian and impermissible. In this case, the deal protection devices of the NCS board were *both* preclusive and coercive.

This Court enunciated the standard for determining stockholder coercion in the case of *Williams v. Geier*. A stockholder vote may be nullified by wrongful coercion "where the board or some other party takes actions which have the effect of causing the stockholders to vote in favor of the proposed transaction for some reason other than the merits of that transaction." In *Brazen v. Bell Atlantic Corporation* (Del. 1997), we applied that test for stockholder coercion and held "that although the termination fee provision may have influenced the stockholder vote, there were 'no structurally or situationally coercive factors' that made an otherwise valid fee provision impermissibly coercive" under the facts presented.

In *Brazen*, we concluded "the determination of whether a particular stockholder vote has been robbed of its effectiveness by impermissible coercion depends on the facts of the case." In this case, the Court of Chancery did not expressly address the issue of "coercion" in its *Unocal* analysis. It did find as a fact, however, that NCS's public stockholders (who owned 80% of NCS and overwhelmingly supported Omnicare's offer) will be forced to accept the Genesis merger because of the structural defenses approved by the NCS board. Consequently, the record reflects that any stockholder vote would have been robbed of its effectiveness by the impermissible coercion that predetermined the outcome of the merger without regard to the merits of the Genesis transaction at the time the vote was scheduled to be taken. Deal protection devices that result in such coercion cannot withstand *Unocal*'s enhanced judicial scrutiny standard of review because they are not within the range of reasonableness.

Although the minority stockholders were not forced to vote for the Genesis merger, they were required to accept it because it was *a fait accompli*. The record reflects that the defensive devices employed by the NCS board are preclusive and coercive in the sense that they accomplished *a fait accompli*. In this case, despite the fact that the NCS board has withdrawn its recommendation for the Genesis transaction and recommended its rejection by the stockholders, the deal protection devices approved by the NCS board operated in concert to have a preclusive and coercive effect. Those tripartite defensive measures—the Section 251(c) provision, the voting agreements, and the absence of an effective fiduciary out clause—made it "mathematically impossible" and "realistically unattainable" for the Omnicare transaction or any other proposal to succeed, no matter how superior the proposal.

The deal protection devices adopted by the NCS board were designed to coerce the consummation of the Genesis merger and preclude the consideration of any superior transaction. The NCS directors' defensive devices are not within a reasonable range of responses to the perceived threat of losing the Genesis offer because they are preclusive and coercive. Accordingly, we hold that those deal protection devices are unenforceable.

Effective Fiduciary Out Required

The defensive measures that protected the merger transaction are unenforceable not only because they are preclusive and coercive but, alternatively, they are unenforceable because they are invalid as they operate in this case. Given the specifically enforceable irrevocable voting agreements, the provision in the merger agreement requiring the board to submit the transaction for a stockholder vote and the omission of a fiduciary out clause in the merger agreement completely prevented the board from discharging its fiduciary responsibilities to the minority stockholders when Omnicare presented its superior transaction. "To the extent that a [merger] contract, or a provision thereof, purports to require a board to act or not act in such a fashion as to limit the exercise of fiduciary duties, it is invalid and unenforceable."

In *QVC*, this Court recognized that "[w]hen a majority of a corporation's voting shares are acquired by a single person or entity, or by *a cohesive group acting together* [as in this case], there is a significant diminution in the voting power of those who thereby become minority stockholders." Therefore, we acknowledged that "[i]n the absence of devices protecting the minority stockholders, stockholder votes are likely to become mere formalities," where a cohesive group acting together to exercise majority voting powers have already decided the outcome. Consequently, we concluded that since the minority stockholders lost the power to influence corporate direction through the ballot, "minority stockholders must rely for protection solely on the fiduciary duties owed to them by the directors."

Under the circumstances presented in this case, where a cohesive group of stockholders with majority voting power was irrevocably committed to the merger transaction, "[e]ffective representation of the financial interests of the minority shareholders imposed upon the [NCS board] an affirmative responsibility to protect those minority shareholders' interests." (*McMullin v. Beran* (Del. 2000)). The NCS board could not abdicate its fiduciary duties to the minority by leaving it to the stockholders alone to approve or disapprove the merger agreement because two stockholders had already combined to establish a majority of the voting power that made the outcome of the stockholder vote a foregone conclusion.

The Court of Chancery noted that Section 251(c) of the Delaware General Corporation Law now permits boards to agree to submit a merger agreement for a stockholder vote, even if the Board later withdraws its support for that agreement and recommends that the stockholders reject it. The Court of Chancery also noted that stockholder voting agreements are permitted by Delaware law. In refusing to certify this interlocutory appeal, the Court of Chancery stated "it is simply nonsensical to say that a board of directors abdicates its duties to manage the 'business and affairs' of a corporation under Section 141(a) of the DGCL by agreeing to the inclusion in a merger agreement of a term authorized by § 251(c) of the same statute."

Taking action that is otherwise legally possible, however, does not *ipso facto* comport with the fiduciary responsibilities of directors in all circumstances. The synopsis to the amendments that resulted in the enactment of Section 251(c) in the Delaware corporation law statute specifically provides: "the amendments are not intended to address the question of whether such a submission requirement is appropriate in any particular set of factual circumstances." Section 251 provisions, like the no-shop provision examined in QVC, are "presumptively valid in the abstract." Such provisions in a merger agreement may not, however, "validly define or limit the directors' fiduciary duties under Delaware law or prevent the [NCS] directors from carrying out their fiduciary duties under Delaware law."

Genesis admits that when the NCS board agreed to its merger conditions, the NCS board was seeking to assure that the NCS creditors were paid in full and that the NCS stockholders received the highest value available for their stock. In fact, Genesis defends its "bulletproof" merger agreement on that basis. We hold that the NCS board did not have authority to accede to the Genesis demand for an absolute "lock-up."

The directors of a Delaware corporation have a continuing obligation to discharge their fiduciary responsibilities, as future circumstances develop, after a merger agreement is announced. Genesis anticipated the likelihood of a superior offer after its merger agreement was announced and demanded defensive measures from the NCS board that *completely* protected its transaction.[84] Instead of agreeing to the absolute defense of the Genesis merger from a superior offer, however, the NCS board was required to negotiate a fiduciary out clause to protect the NCS stockholders if the Genesis transaction became an inferior offer. By acceding to Genesis' ultimatum for complete protection *in futuro,* the NCS board disabled itself from exercising its own fiduciary obligations at a time when the board's own judgment is most important, i.e. receipt of a subsequent superior offer.

Any board has authority to give the proponent of a recommended merger agreement reasonable structural and economic defenses, incentives, and fair compensation if the transaction is not completed. To the extent that defensive measures are economic and reasonable, they may become an increased cost to the proponent of any subsequent transaction. Just as defensive measures cannot be draconian, however, they cannot limit or circumscribe the directors' fiduciary duties. Notwithstanding the corporation's insolvent condition, the NCS board had no authority to execute a merger agreement that subsequently prevented it from effectively discharging its ongoing fiduciary responsibilities. . . .

The NCS board was required to contract for an effective fiduciary out clause to exercise its continuing fiduciary responsibilities to the minority stockholders.[88] The

---

84. The marked improvements in NCS's financial situation during the negotiations with Genesis strongly suggests that the NCS board should have been alert to the prospect of competing offers or, as eventually occurred, a bidding contest.

88. *See Paramount Communications Inc. v. QVC Network Inc.,* 637 A.2d at 42–43. Merger agreements involve an ownership decision and, therefore, cannot become final without stockholder approval. Other contracts do not require a fiduciary out clause because they involve business

issues in this appeal do not involve the general validity of either stockholder voting agreements or the authority of directors to insert a Section 251(c) provision in a merger agreement. In this case, the NCS board combined those two otherwise valid actions and caused them to operate in concert as an absolute lock up, in the absence of an effective fiduciary out clause in the Genesis merger agreement.

In the context of this preclusive and coercive lock up case, the protection of Genesis' contractual expectations must yield to the supervening responsibility of the directors to discharge their fiduciary duties on a continuing basis. The merger agreement and voting agreements, as they were combined to operate in concert in this case, are inconsistent with the NCS directors' fiduciary duties. To that extent, we hold that they are invalid and unenforceable. . . .

VEASEY, Chief Justice, with whom STEELE, Justice, joins (dissenting)

. . .

The process by which this merger agreement came about involved a joint decision by the controlling stockholders and the board of directors to secure what appeared to be the only value-enhancing transaction available for a company on the brink of bankruptcy. The Majority adopts a new rule of law that imposes a prohibition on the NCS board's ability to act in concert with controlling stockholders to lock up this merger. The Majority reaches this conclusion by analyzing the challenged deal protection measures as isolated board actions. The Majority concludes that the board owed a duty to the NCS minority stockholders to refrain from acceding to the Genesis demand for an irrevocable lock-up notwithstanding the compelling circumstances confronting the board and the board's disinterested, informed, good faith exercise of its business judgment.

Because we believe this Court must respect the reasoned judgment of the board of directors and give effect to the wishes of the controlling stockholders, we respectfully disagree with the Majority's reasoning that results in a holding that the confluence of board and stockholder action constitutes a breach of fiduciary duty. The essential fact that must always be remembered is that this agreement and the voting commitments of Outcalt and Shaw concluded a lengthy search and intense negotiation process in the context of insolvency and creditor pressure where no other viable bid had emerged. Accordingly, we endorse the Vice Chancellor's well-reasoned analysis that the NCS board's action before the hostile bid emerged was within the bounds of its fiduciary duties under these facts.

. . . It is now known, of course, after the case is over, that the stockholders of NCS will receive substantially more by tendering their shares into the topping bid of Omnicare than they would have received in the Genesis merger, as a result of the post-agreement Omnicare bid and the injunctive relief ordered by the Majority of this Court. Our jurisprudence cannot, however, be seen as turning on such ex post

---

judgments that are within the *exclusive* province of the board of directors' power to manage the affairs of the corporation. *See Grimes v. Donald,* 673 A.2d 1207, 1214–15 (Del.1996).

felicitous results. Rather, the NCS board's good faith decision must be subject to a real-time review of the board action before the NCS-Genesis merger agreement was entered into.

An Analysis of the Process Leading to the Lock-up Reflects a Quintessential, Disinterested and Informed Board Decision Reached in Good Faith

... [T]he Majority has removed from their proper context the contractual merger protection provisions. The lock-ups here cannot be reviewed in a vacuum. A court should review the entire bidding process to determine whether the independent board's actions permitted the directors to inform themselves of their available options and whether they acted in good faith.

Going into negotiations with Genesis, the NCS directors knew that, up until that time, NCS had found only one potential bidder, Omnicare. Omnicare had refused to buy NCS except at a fire sale price through an asset sale in bankruptcy. Omnicare's best proposal at that stage would not have paid off all creditors and would have provided nothing for stockholders. The Noteholders, represented by the Ad Hoc Committee, were willing to oblige Omnicare and force NCS into bankruptcy if Omnicare would pay in full the NCS debt. Through the NCS board's efforts, Genesis expressed interest that became increasingly attractive. Negotiations with Genesis led to an offer paying creditors off and conferring on NCS stockholders $24 million—an amount infinitely superior to the prior Omnicare proposals.

But there was, understandably, a sine qua non. In exchange for offering the NCS stockholders a return on their equity and creditor payment, Genesis demanded certainty that the merger would close. If the NCS board would not have acceded to the Section 251(c) provision, if Outcalt and Shaw had not agreed to the voting agreements and if NCS had insisted on a fiduciary out, there would have been no Genesis deal! Thus, the only value-enhancing transaction available would have disappeared. NCS knew that Omnicare had spoiled a Genesis acquisition in the past, and it is not disputed by the Majority that the NCS directors made a reasoned decision to accept as real the Genesis threat to walk away.

When Omnicare submitted its conditional eleventh-hour bid, the NCS board had to weigh the economic terms of the proposal against the uncertainty of completing a deal with Omnicare. Importantly, because Omnicare's bid was conditioned on its satisfactorily completing its due diligence review of NCS, the NCS board saw this as a crippling condition, as did the Ad Hoc Committee. As a matter of business judgment, the risk of negotiating with Omnicare and losing Genesis at that point outweighed the possible benefits. The lock-up was indisputably a sine qua non to any deal with Genesis.

A lock-up permits a target board and a bidder to "exchange certainties." Certainty itself has value. The acquirer may pay a higher price for the target if the acquirer is assured consummation of the transaction. The target company also benefits from the certainty of completing a transaction with a bidder because losing an acquirer creates the perception that a target is damaged goods, thus reducing its value. ...

Our Jurisprudence Does Not Compel This Court to Invalidate the Joint Action of the Board and the Controlling Stockholders

The Majority invalidates the NCS board's action by announcing a new rule that represents an extension of our jurisprudence. That new rule can be narrowly stated as follows: A merger agreement entered into after a market search, before any prospect of a topping bid has emerged, which locks up stockholder approval and does not contain a "fiduciary out" provision, is per se invalid when a later significant topping bid emerges. As we have noted, this bright-line, per se rule would apply regardless of (1) the circumstances leading up to the agreement and (2) the fact that stockholders who control voting power had irrevocably committed themselves, *as stockholders,* to vote for the merger. Narrowly stated, this new rule is a judicially-created "third rail" that now becomes one of the given "rules of the game," to be taken into account by the negotiators and drafters of merger agreements. In our view, this new rule is an unwise extension of existing precedent. . . .

The Vice Chancellor held that the NCS directors satisfied *Unocal.* He even held that they would have satisfied *Revlon,* if it had applied, which it did not. Indeed, he concluded — based on the undisputed record and his considerable experience — that: "The overall quality of testimony given by the NCS directors is among the strongest this court has ever seen. All four NCS directors were deposed, and each deposition makes manifest the care and attention given to this project by every member of the board." We agree fully with the Vice Chancellor's findings and conclusions, and we would have affirmed the judgment of the Court of Chancery on that basis. . . .

. . . Moreover, to the extent a minority stockholder may have felt "coerced" to vote for the merger, which was already a *fait accompli,* it was a meaningless coercion — or no coercion at all — because the controlling votes, those of Outcalt and Shaw, were already "cast." Although the fact that the controlling votes were committed to the merger "precluded" an overriding vote against the merger by the Class A stockholders, the pejorative "preclusive" label applicable in a *Unitrin* fact situation has no application here. Therefore, there was no meaningful minority stockholder voting decision to coerce.

In applying *Unocal* scrutiny, we believe the Majority incorrectly preempted the proportionality inquiry. In our view, the proportionality inquiry must account for the reality that the contractual measures protecting this merger agreement were necessary to obtain the Genesis deal. The Majority has not demonstrated that the director action was a disproportionate response to the threat posed. Indeed, it is clear to us that the board action to negotiate the best deal reasonably available with the only viable merger partner (Genesis) who could satisfy the creditors and benefit the stockholders, was reasonable in relation to the threat, by any practical yardstick.

An Absolute Lock-up is Not a Per Se Violation of Fiduciary Duty

We respectfully disagree with the Majority's conclusion that the NCS board breached its fiduciary duties to the Class A stockholders by failing to negotiate a "fiduciary out" in the Genesis merger agreement. What is the practical import of a "fiduciary out?" It is a contractual provision, articulated in a manner to be negotiated, that would permit the board of the corporation being acquired to exit without breaching the merger agreement in the event of a superior offer.

In this case, Genesis made it abundantly clear early on that it was willing to negotiate a deal with NCS but only on the condition that it would not be a "stalking horse." Thus, it wanted to be certain that a third party could not use its deal with NCS as a floor against which to begin a bidding war. As a result of this negotiating position, a "fiduciary out" was not acceptable to Genesis. The Majority Opinion holds that such a negotiating position, if implemented in the agreement, is invalid per se where there is an absolute lock-up. We know of no authority in our jurisprudence supporting this new rule, and we believe it is unwise and unwarranted.

The Majority relies on our decision in *QVC* to assert that the board's fiduciary duties prevent the directors from negotiating a merger agreement without providing an escape provision. Reliance on *QVC* for this proposition, however, confuses our statement of a board's responsibilities when the directors confront a superior transaction and turn away from it to lock up a less valuable deal with the very different situation here, where the board committed itself to the *only* value-enhancing transaction available. The decision in *QVC* is an extension of prior decisions in *Revlon* and *Mills* that prevent a board from ignoring a bidder who is willing to match and exceed the favored bidder's offer. The Majority's application of "continuing fiduciary duties" here is a further extension of this concept and thus permits, wrongly in our view, a court to second-guess the risk and return analysis the board must make to weigh the value of the only viable transaction against the prospect of an offer that has not materialized....

Questions

1. What aspects of the agreement between NCS and Genesis most concern the court? Isn't the board of directors authorized to make decisions that commit the corporation to certain courses of action but not others? Why not in this case?

2. The majority concludes that an "effective fiduciary out clause" was necessary. What could have the NCS board negotiated for? Would Genesis have agreed? What would have happened if the controlling shareholders continued to insist on going through with the transaction?

Lyondell Chemical Company v. Ryan
970 A.2d 235 (Del. 2009)

BERGER, Justice

. . .

FACTUAL AND PROCEDURAL BACKGROUND

Before the merger at issue, Lyondell Chemical Company ("Lyondell") was the third largest independent, publicly traded chemical company in North America. Dan Smith ("Smith") was Lyondell's Chairman and CEO. Lyondell's other ten directors were independent and many were, or had been, CEOs of other large, publicly traded companies. Basell AF ("Basell") is a privately held Luxembourg company owned by Leonard Blavatnik ("Blavatnik") through his ownership of Access Industries. Basell is in the business of polyolefin technology, production and marketing.

In April 2006, Blavatnik told Smith that Basell was interested in acquiring Lyondell. A few months later, Basell sent a letter to Lyondell's board offering $26.50–$28.50 per share. Lyondell determined that the price was inadequate and that it was not interested in selling. During the next year, Lyondell prospered and no potential acquirors expressed interest in the company. In May 2007, an Access affiliate filed a Schedule 13D with the Securities and Exchange Commission disclosing its right to acquire an 8.3% block of Lyondell stock owned by Occidental Petroleum Corporation. The Schedule 13D also disclosed Blavatnik's interest in possible transactions with Lyondell.

In response to the Schedule 13D, the Lyondell board immediately convened a special meeting. The board recognized that the 13D signaled to the market that the company was "in play," but the directors decided to take a "wait and see" approach. A few days later, Apollo Management, L.P. contacted Smith to suggest a management-led LBO, but Smith rejected that proposal. In late June 2007, Basell announced that it had entered into a $9.6 billion merger agreement with Huntsman Corporation ("Huntsman"), a specialty chemical company. Basell apparently reconsidered, however, after Hexion Specialty Chemicals, Inc. made a topping bid for Huntsman. Faced with competition for Huntsman, Blavatnik returned his attention to Lyondell.

On July 9, 2007, Blavatnik met with Smith to discuss an all-cash deal at $40 per share. Smith responded that $40 was too low, and Blavatnik raised his offer to $44–$45 per share. Smith told Blavatnik that he would present the proposal to the board, but that he thought the board would reject it. Smith advised Blavatnik to give Lyondell his best offer, since Lyondell really was not on the market. The meeting ended at that point, but Blavatnik asked Smith to call him later in the day. When Smith called, Blavatnik offered to pay $48 per share. Under Blavatnik's proposal, Basell would require no financing contingency, but Lyondell would have to agree to a $400 million break-up fee and sign a merger agreement by July 16, 2007.

Smith called a special meeting of the Lyondell board on July 10, 2007 to review and consider Basell's offer. The meeting lasted slightly less than one hour, during which time the board reviewed valuation material that had been prepared by Lyondell management for presentation at the regular board meeting, which was scheduled for the following day. The board also discussed the Basell offer, the status of the Huntsman merger, and the likelihood that another party might be interested in Lyondell. The board instructed Smith to obtain a written offer from Basell and more details about Basell's financing.

Blavatnik agreed to the board's request, but also made an additional demand. Basell had until July 11 to make a higher bid for Huntsman, so Blavatnik asked Smith to find out whether the Lyondell board would provide a firm indication of interest in his proposal by the end of that day. The Lyondell board met on July 11, again for less than one hour, to consider the Basell proposal and how it compared to the benefits of remaining independent. The board decided that it was interested, authorized the retention of Deutsche Bank Securities, Inc. ("Deutsche Bank") as its financial advisor, and instructed Smith to negotiate with Blavatnik.

Basell then announced that it would not raise its offer for Huntsman, and Huntsman terminated the Basell merger agreement. From July 12–July 15 the parties negotiated the terms of a Lyondell merger agreement; Basell conducted due diligence; Deutsche Bank prepared a "fairness" opinion; and Lyondell conducted its regularly scheduled board meeting. The Lyondell board discussed the Basell proposal again on July 12, and later instructed Smith to try to negotiate better terms. Specifically, the board wanted a higher price, a go-shop provision, and a reduced break-up fee. As the trial court noted, Blavatnik was "incredulous." He had offered his best price, which was a substantial premium, and the deal had to be concluded on his schedule. As a sign of good faith, however, Blavatnik agreed to reduce the break-up fee from $400 million to $385 million.

On July 16, 2007, the board met to consider the Basell merger agreement. Lyondell's management, as well as its financial and legal advisers, presented reports analyzing the merits of the deal. The advisors explained that, notwithstanding the no-shop provision in the merger agreement, Lyondell would be able to consider any superior proposals that might be made because of the "fiduciary out" provision. In addition, Deutsche Bank reviewed valuation models derived from "bullish" and more conservative financial projections. Several of those valuations yielded a range that did not even reach $48 per share, and Deutsche Bank opined that the proposed merger price was fair. Indeed, the bank's managing director described the merger price as "an absolute home run." Deutsche Bank also identified other possible acquirors and explained why it believed no other entity would top Basell's offer. After considering the presentations, the Lyondell board voted to approve the merger and recommend it to the stockholders. At a special stockholders' meeting held on November 20, 2007, the merger was approved by more than 99% of the voted shares.

. . .

DISCUSSION

The class action complaint challenging this $13 billion cash merger alleges that the Lyondell directors breached their "fiduciary duties of care, loyalty and candor . . .

and . . . put their personal interests ahead of the interests of the Lyondell shareholders." Specifically, the complaint alleges that: 1) the merger price was grossly insufficient; 2) the directors were motivated to approve the merger for their own self-interest; 3) the process by which the merger was negotiated was flawed; 4) the directors agreed to unreasonable deal protection provisions; and 5) the preliminary proxy statement omitted numerous material facts. The trial court rejected all claims except those directed at the process by which the directors sold the company and the deal protection provisions in the merger agreement.

The remaining claims are but two aspects of a single claim, under *Revlon v. MacAndrews & Forbes Holdings, Inc.*, that the directors failed to obtain the best available price in selling the company. As the trial court correctly noted, *Revlon* did not create any new fiduciary duties. It simply held that the "board must perform its fiduciary duties in the service of a specific objective: maximizing the sale price of the enterprise." The trial court reviewed the record, and found that Ryan might be able to prevail at trial on a claim that the Lyondell directors breached their duty of care. But Lyondell's charter includes an exculpatory provision, pursuant to 8 Del. C. § 102(b)(7), protecting the directors from personal liability for breaches of the duty of care. Thus, this case turns on whether any arguable shortcomings on the part of the Lyondell directors also implicate their duty of loyalty, a breach of which is not exculpated. Because the trial court determined that the board was independent and was not motivated by self-interest or ill will, the sole issue is whether the directors are entitled to summary judgment on the claim that they breached their duty of loyalty by failing to act in good faith.

This Court examined "good faith" in two recent decisions. In *In re Walt Disney Co. Deriv. Litig.*, the Court discussed the range of conduct that might be characterized as bad faith, and concluded that bad faith encompasses not only an intent to harm but also intentional dereliction of duty:

> [A]t least three different categories of fiduciary behavior are candidates for the "bad faith" pejorative label. The first category involves so-called "subjective bad faith," that is, fiduciary conduct motivated by an actual intent to do harm. . . . [S]uch conduct constitutes classic, quintessential bad faith. . . .
>
> The second category of conduct, which is at the opposite end of the spectrum, involves lack of due care — that is, fiduciary action taken solely by reason of gross negligence and without any malevolent intent. . . . [W]e address the issue of whether gross negligence (including failure to inform one's self of available material facts), without more, can also constitute bad faith. The answer is clearly no.

* * *

That leaves the third category of fiduciary conduct, which falls in between the first two categories. . . . This third category is what the Chancellor's definition of bad faith — intentional dereliction of duty, a conscious disregard for one's responsibilities — is intended to capture. The question is whether such misconduct is properly treated as a non-exculpable, nonindemnifiable violation of the fiduciary duty to act in good faith. In our view, it must be. . . .

The *Disney* decision expressly disavowed any attempt to provide a comprehensive or exclusive definition of "bad faith."

A few months later, in *Stone v. Ritter*, this Court addressed the concept of bad faith in the context of an "oversight" claim. We adopted the standard articulated ten years earlier, in *In re Caremark Int'l Deriv. Litig.*:

> [W]here a claim of directorial liability for corporate loss is predicated upon ignorance of liability creating activities within the corporation . . . only a sustained or systematic failure of the board to exercise oversight—such as an utter failure to attempt to assure a reasonable information and reporting system exists—will establish the lack of good faith that is a necessary condition to liability.

The *Stone* Court explained that the *Caremark* standard is fully consistent with the *Disney* definition of bad faith. *Stone* also clarified any possible ambiguity about the directors' mental state, holding that "imposition of liability requires a showing that the directors knew that they were not discharging their fiduciary obligations."

The Court of Chancery recognized these legal principles, but it denied summary judgment in order to obtain a more complete record before deciding whether the directors had acted in bad faith. Under other circumstances, deferring a decision to expand the record would be appropriate. Here, however, the trial court reviewed the existing record under a mistaken view of the applicable law. Three factors contributed to that mistake. First, the trial court imposed *Revlon* duties on the Lyondell directors before they either had decided to sell, or before the sale had become inevitable. Second, the court read *Revlon* and its progeny as creating a set of requirements that must be satisfied during the sale process. Third, the trial court equated an arguably imperfect attempt to carry out Revlon duties with a knowing disregard of one's duties that constitutes bad faith.

. . . The Court of Chancery identified several undisputed facts that would support the entry of judgment in favor of the Lyondell directors: the directors were "active, sophisticated, and generally aware of the value of the Company and the conditions of the markets in which the Company operated." They had reason to believe that no other bidders would emerge, given the price Basell had offered and the limited universe of companies that might be interested in acquiring Lyondell's unique assets. Smith negotiated the price up from $40 to $48 per share—a price that Deutsche Bank opined was fair. Finally, no other acquiror expressed interest during the four months between the merger announcement and the stockholder vote.

Other facts, however, led the trial court to "question the adequacy of the Board's knowledge and efforts . . . ." After the Schedule 13D was filed in May, the directors apparently took no action to prepare for a possible acquisition proposal. The merger was negotiated and finalized in less than one week, during which time the directors met for a total of only seven hours to consider the matter. The directors did not seriously press Blavatnik for a better price, nor did they conduct even a limited market check. Moreover, although the deal protections were not unusual or preclusive, the trial court was troubled by "the Board's decision to grant considerable protection to a deal that may not have been adequately vetted under *Revlon*."

The trial court found the directors' failure to act during the two months after the filing of the Basell Schedule 13D critical to its analysis of their good faith. The court pointedly referred to the directors' "two months of slothful indifference despite *knowing* that the Company was in play," and the fact that they "languidly awaited overtures from potential suitors . . . ." In the end, the trial court found that it was this "failing" that warranted denial of their motion for summary judgment . . .

The problem with the trial court's analysis is that *Revlon* duties do not arise simply because a company is "in play." The duty to seek the best available price applies only when a company embarks on a transaction—on its own initiative or in response to an unsolicited offer—that will result in a change of control. Basell's Schedule 13D did put the Lyondell directors, and the market in general, on notice that Basell was interested in acquiring Lyondell. The directors responded by promptly holding a special meeting to consider whether Lyondell should take any action. The directors decided that they would neither put the company up for sale nor institute defensive measures to fend off a possible hostile offer. Instead, they decided to take a "wait and see" approach. That decision was an entirely appropriate exercise of the directors' business judgment. The time for action under *Revlon* did not begin until July 10, 2007, when the directors began negotiating the sale of Lyondell.

The Court of Chancery focused on the directors' two months of inaction, when it should have focused on the one week during which they considered Basell's offer. During that one week, the directors met several times; their CEO tried to negotiate better terms; they evaluated Lyondell's value, the price offered and the likelihood of obtaining a better price; and then the directors approved the merger. The trial court acknowledged that the directors' conduct during those seven days might not demonstrate anything more than lack of due care. But the court remained skeptical about the directors' good faith—at least on the present record. That lingering concern was based on the trial court's synthesis of the *Revlon* line of cases, which led it to the erroneous conclusion that directors must follow one of several courses of action to satisfy their *Revlon* duties.

There is only one *Revlon* duty—to "[get] the best price for the stockholders at a sale of the company." No court can tell directors exactly how to accomplish that goal, because they will be facing a unique combination of circumstances, many of which will be outside their control. As we noted in *Barkan v. Amsted Industries, Inc.,* "there is no single blueprint that a board must follow to fulfill its duties." That said, our courts have highlighted both the positive and negative aspects of various boards' conduct under Revlon. The trial court drew several principles from those cases: directors must "engage actively in the sale process," and they must confirm that they have obtained the best available price either by conducting an auction, by conducting a market check, or by demonstrating "an impeccable knowledge of the market."

The Lyondell directors did not conduct an auction or a market check, and they did not satisfy the trial court that they had the "impeccable" market knowledge that the court believed was necessary to excuse their failure to pursue one of the first two alternatives. As a result, the Court of Chancery was unable to conclude that the directors had met their burden under *Revlon*. In evaluating the totality of the circumstances, even on this limited record, we would be inclined to hold otherwise. But we would not question the trial court's decision to seek additional evidence if the issue were whether the directors had exercised due care. Where, as here, the issue is whether the directors failed to act in good faith, the analysis is very different, and the existing record mandates the entry of judgment in favor of the directors.

As discussed above, bad faith will be found if a "fiduciary intentionally fails to act in the face of a known duty to act, demonstrating a conscious disregard for his duties." The trial court decided that the *Revlon* sale process must follow one of three courses, and that the Lyondell directors did not discharge that "known set of [*Revlon*] 'duties'." But, as noted, there are no legally prescribed steps that directors must follow to satisfy their *Revlon* duties. Thus, the directors' failure to take any specific steps during the sale process could not have demonstrated a conscious disregard of their duties. More importantly, there is a vast difference between an inadequate or flawed effort to carry out fiduciary duties and a conscious disregard for those duties.

Directors' decisions must be reasonable, not perfect. "In the transactional context, [an] extreme set of facts [is] required to sustain a disloyalty claim premised on the notion that disinterested directors were intentionally disregarding their duties." The trial court denied summary judgment because the Lyondell directors' "unexplained inaction" prevented the court from determining that they had acted in good faith. But, if the directors failed to do all that they should have under the circumstances, they breached their duty of care. Only if they knowingly and completely failed to undertake their responsibilities would they breach their duty of loyalty. The trial court approached the record from the wrong perspective. Instead of questioning whether disinterested, independent directors did everything that they (arguably) should have done to obtain the best sale price, the inquiry should have been whether those directors utterly failed to attempt to obtain the best sale price.

Viewing the record in this manner leads to only one possible conclusion. The Lyondell directors met several times to consider Basell's premium offer. They were generally aware of the value of their company and they knew the chemical company market. The directors solicited and followed the advice of their financial and legal advisors. They attempted to negotiate a higher offer even though all the evidence indicates that Basell had offered a "blowout" price. Finally, they approved the merger agreement, because "it was simply too good not to pass along [to the stockholders] for their consideration." We assume, as we must on summary judgment, that the Lyondell directors did absolutely nothing to prepare for Basell's offer, and that they did not even consider conducting a market check before agreeing to the merger. Even so, this record clearly establishes that the Lyondell directors did not breach their duty of loyalty by failing to act in good faith. In concluding otherwise, the Court of Chancery reversibly erred.

CONCLUSION

Based on the foregoing, the decision of the Court of Chancery is reversed and this matter is remanded for entry of judgment in favor of the Lyondell directors. Jurisdiction is not retained.

Questions

1. When are *Revlon* duties triggered? Why were they triggered in *Lyondell Chemical Company v. Ryan*?

2. When are *Revlon* duties violated after *Lyondell*? What is the relevance of bad faith to the analysis of *Revlon* duties? Can directors acting in good faith ever breach their duties under *Revlon*?

C. Anti-Takeover Legislation

CTS Corporation v. Dynamics Corporation of America

107 S. Ct. 1637 (1987)

Justice POWELL delivered the opinion of the Court.

These cases present the questions whether the Control Share Acquisitions Chapter of the Indiana Business Corporation Law, Ind. Code § 23-1-42-1 *et seq.* (Supp.1986), is pre-empted by the Williams Act, 82 Stat. 454, as amended, 15 U.S.C. §§ 78m(d)–(e) and 78n(d)–(f) (1982 ed. and Supp. III), or violates the Commerce Clause of the Federal Constitution, Art. I, § 8, cl. 3.

I

A

On March 4, 1986, the Governor of Indiana signed a revised Indiana Business Corporation Law, Ind. Code § 23-1-17-1 *et seq.* (Supp.1986). That law included the Control Share Acquisitions Chapter (Indiana Act or Act). Beginning on August 1, 1987, the Act will apply to any corporation incorporated in Indiana, unless the corporation amends its articles of incorporation or bylaws to opt out of the Act. Before that date, any Indiana corporation can opt into the Act by resolution of its board of directors. The Act applies only to "issuing public corporations." The term "corporation" includes only businesses incorporated in Indiana. An "issuing public corporation" is defined as:

"a corporation that has:

"(1) one hundred (100) or more shareholders;

"(2) its principal place of business, its principal office, or substantial assets within Indiana; and

"(3) either:

"(A) more than ten percent (10%) of its shareholders resident in Indiana;

"(B) more than ten percent (10%) of its shares owned by Indiana residents; or

"(C) ten thousand (10,000) shareholders resident in Indiana." § 23-1-42-4(a).

The Act focuses on the acquisition of "control shares" in an issuing public corporation. Under the Act, an entity acquires "control shares" whenever it acquires shares that, but for the operation of the Act, would bring its voting power in the corporation to or above any of three thresholds: 20%, 33⅓%, or 50%. An entity that acquires control shares does not necessarily acquire voting rights. Rather, it gains those rights only "to the extent granted by resolution approved by the shareholders of the issuing public corporation." Section 23-1-42-9(b) requires a majority vote of all disinterested shareholders holding each class of stock for passage of such a resolution. The practical effect of this requirement is to condition acquisition of control of a corporation on approval of a majority of the pre-existing disinterested shareholders.

The shareholders decide whether to confer rights on the control shares at the next regularly scheduled meeting of the shareholders, or at a specially scheduled meeting. The acquiror can require management of the corporation to hold such a special meeting within 50 days if it files an "acquiring person statement," requests the meeting, and agrees to pay the expenses of the meeting. If the shareholders do not vote to restore voting rights to the shares, the corporation may redeem the control shares from the acquiror at fair market value, but it is not required to do so. Similarly, if the acquiror does not file an acquiring person statement with the corporation, the corporation may, if its bylaws or articles of incorporation so provide, redeem the shares at any time after 60 days after the acquiror's last acquisition.

B

On March 10, 1986, appellee Dynamics Corporation of America (Dynamics) owned 9.6% of the common stock of appellant CTS Corporation, an Indiana corporation. On that day, six days after the Act went into effect, Dynamics announced a tender offer for another million shares in CTS; purchase of those shares would have brought Dynamics' ownership interest in CTS to 27.5%. Also on March 10, Dynamics filed suit in the United States District Court for the Northern District of Illinois, alleging that CTS had violated the federal securities laws in a number of respects no longer relevant to these proceedings. On March 27, the board of directors of CTS, an Indiana corporation, elected to be governed by the provisions of the Act.

Four days later, on March 31, Dynamics moved for leave to amend its complaint to allege that the Act is pre-empted by the Williams Act, and violates the Commerce Clause. . . .

II

The first question in these cases is whether the Williams Act pre-empts the Indiana Act.

. . .

Because it is entirely possible for entities to comply with both the Williams Act and the Indiana Act, the state statute can be pre-empted only if it frustrates the purposes of the federal law.

A

Our discussion begins with a brief summary of the structure and purposes of the Williams Act. Congress passed the Williams Act in 1968 in response to the increasing number of hostile tender offers. Before its passage, these transactions were not covered by the disclosure requirements of the federal securities laws. The Williams Act, backed by regulations of the SEC, imposes requirements in two basic areas. First, it requires the offeror to file a statement disclosing information about the offer, including: the offeror's background and identity; the source and amount of the funds to be used in making the purchase; the purpose of the purchase, including any plans to liquidate the company or make major changes in its corporate structure; and the extent of the offeror's holdings in the target company.

Second, the Williams Act, and the regulations that accompany it, establish procedural rules to govern tender offers. For example, stockholders who tender their shares may withdraw them while the offer remains open, and, if the offeror has not purchased their shares, any time after 60 days from commencement of the offer. The offer must remain open for at least 20 business days. If more shares are tendered than the offeror sought to purchase, purchases must be made on a pro rata basis from each tendering shareholder. Finally, the offeror must pay the same price for all purchases; if the offering price is increased before the end of the offer, those who already have tendered must receive the benefit of the increased price.

B

The Indiana Act differs in major respects from the Illinois statute that the Court considered in *Edgar v. MITE Corp.*, 457 U.S. 624, 102 S.Ct. 2629, 73 L.Ed.2d 269 (1982). After reviewing the legislative history of the Williams Act, Justice White, joined by Chief Justice Burger and Justice Blackmun (the plurality), concluded that the Williams Act struck a careful balance between the interests of offerors and target companies, and that any state statute that "upset" this balance was pre-empted.

The plurality then identified three offending features of the Illinois statute. Justice White's opinion first noted that the Illinois statute provided for a 20-day pre-commencement period. During this time, management could disseminate its views on the upcoming offer to shareholders, but offerors could not publish their offers.

The plurality found that this provision gave management "a powerful tool to combat tender offers." This contrasted dramatically with the Williams Act; Congress had deleted express precommencement notice provisions from the Williams Act. According to the plurality, Congress had determined that the potentially adverse consequences of such a provision on shareholders should be avoided. Thus, the plurality concluded that the Illinois provision "frustrate[d] the objectives of the Williams Act." The second criticized feature of the Illinois statute was a provision for a hearing on a tender offer that, because it set no deadline, allowed management "to stymie indefinitely a takeover." The plurality noted that "delay can seriously impede a tender offer," and that "Congress anticipated that investors and the takeover offeror would be free to go forward without unreasonable delay." Accordingly, the plurality concluded that this provision conflicted with the Williams Act. The third troublesome feature of the Illinois statute was its requirement that the fairness of tender offers would be reviewed by the Illinois Secretary of State. Noting that "Congress intended for investors to be free to make their own decisions," the plurality concluded that "[t]he state thus offers investor protection at the expense of investor autonomy—an approach quite in conflict with that adopted by Congress."

C

As the plurality opinion in *MITE* did not represent the views of a majority of the Court, we are not bound by its reasoning. We need not question that reasoning, however, because we believe the Indiana Act passes muster even under the broad interpretation of the Williams Act articulated by Justice White in *MITE*. As is apparent from our summary of its reasoning, the overriding concern of the *MITE* plurality was that the Illinois statute considered in that case operated to favor management against offerors, to the detriment of shareholders. By contrast, the statute now before the Court protects the independent shareholder against the contending parties. Thus, the Act furthers a basic purpose of the Williams Act, "plac[ing] investors on an equal footing with the takeover bidder."

The Indiana Act operates on the assumption, implicit in the Williams Act, that independent shareholders faced with tender offers often are at a disadvantage. By allowing such shareholders to vote as a group, the Act protects them from the coercive aspects of some tender offers. If, for example, shareholders believe that a successful tender offer will be followed by a purchase of nontendering shares at a depressed price, individual shareholders may tender their shares—even if they doubt the tender offer is in the corporation's best interest—to protect themselves from being forced to sell their shares at a depressed price. As the SEC explains: "The alternative of not accepting the tender offer is virtual assurance that, if the offer is successful, the shares will have to be sold in the lower priced, second step." . . . In such a situation under the Indiana Act, the shareholders as a group, acting in the corporation's best interest, could reject the offer, although individual shareholders might be inclined to accept it. The desire of the Indiana Legislature to protect shareholders of Indiana corporations from this type of coercive offer does not conflict with the Williams Act. Rather, it furthers the federal policy of investor protection.

In implementing its goal, the Indiana Act avoids the problems the plurality discussed in *MITE*. Unlike the *MITE* statute, the Indiana Act does not give either management or the offeror an advantage in communicating with the shareholders about the impending offer. The Act also does not impose an indefinite delay on tender offers. Nothing in the Act prohibits an offeror from consummating an offer on the 20th business day, the earliest day permitted under applicable federal regulations. Nor does the Act allow the state government to interpose its views of fairness between willing buyers and sellers of shares of the target company. Rather, the Act allows *shareholders* to evaluate the fairness of the offer collectively.

D

The Court of Appeals based its finding of pre-emption on its view that the practical effect of the Indiana Act is to delay consummation of tender offers until 50 days after the commencement of the offer. As did the Court of Appeals, Dynamics reasons that no rational offeror will purchase shares until it gains assurance that those shares will carry voting rights. Because it is possible that voting rights will not be conferred until a shareholder meeting 50 days after commencement of the offer, Dynamics concludes that the Act imposes a 50-day delay. This, it argues, conflicts with the shorter 20-business-day period established by the SEC as the minimum period for which a tender offer may be held open. We find the alleged conflict illusory.

The Act does not impose an absolute 50-day delay on tender offers, nor does it preclude an offeror from purchasing shares as soon as federal law permits. If the offeror fears an adverse shareholder vote under the Act, it can make a conditional tender offer, offering to accept shares on the condition that the shares receive voting rights within a certain period of time. The Williams Act permits tender offers to be conditioned on the offeror's subsequently obtaining regulatory approval. There is no reason to doubt that this type of conditional tender offer would be legitimate as well.

Even assuming that the Indiana Act imposes some additional delay, nothing in *MITE* suggested that *any* delay imposed by state regulation, however short, would create a conflict with the Williams Act. The plurality argued only that the offeror should "be free to go forward without *unreasonable* delay." In that case, the Court was confronted with the potential for indefinite delay and presented with no persuasive reason why some deadline could not be established. By contrast, the Indiana Act provides that full voting rights will be vested—if this eventually is to occur—within 50 days after commencement of the offer. This period is within the 60-day period Congress established for restitution of withdrawal rights . . . We cannot say that a delay within that congressionally determined period is unreasonable.

Finally, we note that the Williams Act would pre-empt a variety of state corporate laws of hitherto unquestioned validity if it were construed to pre-empt any state statute that may limit or delay the free exercise of power after a successful tender offer. State corporate laws commonly permit corporations to stagger the terms of their directors. . . . By staggering the terms of directors, and thus having annual elections for only one class of directors each year, corporations may delay the time when a successful offeror gains control of the board of directors. Similarly, state corporation laws commonly provide for cumulative voting. By enabling minority shareholders to assure themselves of representation in each class of directors, cumulative voting provisions can delay further the ability of offerors to gain untrammeled authority over the affairs of the target corporation. . . .

In our view, the possibility that the Indiana Act will delay some tender offers is insufficient to require a conclusion that the Williams Act pre-empts the Act. The longstanding prevalence of state regulation in this area suggests that, if Congress had intended to pre-empt all state laws that delay the acquisition of voting control following a tender offer, it would have said so explicitly. The regulatory conditions that the Act places on tender offers are consistent with the text and the purposes of the Williams Act. Accordingly, we hold that the Williams Act does not pre-empt the Indiana Act.

III

As an alternative basis for its decision, the Court of Appeals held that the Act violates the Commerce Clause of the Federal Constitution. We now address this holding. On its face, the Commerce Clause is nothing more than a grant to Congress of the power "[t]o regulate Commerce . . . among the several States . . . ." But it has been settled for more than a century that the Clause prohibits States from taking certain actions respecting interstate commerce even absent congressional action. The Court's interpretation of "these great silences of the Constitution" has not always been easy to follow. Rather, as the volume and complexity of commerce and regulation have grown in this country, the Court has articulated a variety of tests in an attempt to describe the difference between those regulations that the Commerce Clause permits and those regulations that it prohibits.

A

The principal objects of dormant Commerce Clause scrutiny are statutes that discriminate against interstate commerce. . . . The Indiana Act is not such a statute. It has the same effects on tender offers whether or not the offeror is a domiciliary or resident of Indiana. Thus, it "visits its effects equally upon both interstate and local business."

Dynamics nevertheless contends that the statute is discriminatory because it will apply most often to out-of-state entities. This argument rests on the contention that, as a practical matter, most hostile tender offers are launched by offerors outside Indiana. But this argument avails Dynamics little. "The fact that the burden of a state regulation falls on some interstate companies does not, by itself, establish a claim of discrimination against interstate commerce." . . . Because nothing in the Indiana Act imposes a greater burden on out-of-state offerors than it does on similarly situated Indiana offerors, we reject the contention that the Act discriminates against interstate commerce.

B

This Court's recent Commerce Clause cases also have invalidated statutes that may adversely affect interstate commerce by subjecting activities to inconsistent regulations. . . . The Indiana Act poses no such problem. So long as each State regulates voting rights only in the corporations it has created, each corporation will be subject to the law of only one State. No principle of corporation law and practice is more firmly established than a State's authority to regulate domestic corporations, including the authority to define the voting rights of shareholders. See Restatement (Second) of Conflict of Laws § 304 (1971) (concluding that the law of the incorporating State generally should "determine the right of a shareholder to participate in the administration of the affairs of the corporation"). Accordingly, we conclude that the Indiana Act does not create an impermissible risk of inconsistent regulation by different States.

C

The Court of Appeals did not find the Act unconstitutional for either of these threshold reasons. Rather, its decision rested on its view of the Act's potential to hinder tender offers. We think the Court of Appeals failed to appreciate the significance for Commerce Clause analysis of the fact that state regulation of corporate governance is regulation of entities whose very existence and attributes are a product of state law. . . .

. . . Every State in this country has enacted laws regulating corporate governance. By prohibiting certain transactions, and regulating others, such laws necessarily affect certain aspects of interstate commerce. This necessarily is true with respect to corporations with shareholders in States other than the State of incorporation. Large corporations that are listed on national exchanges, or even regional exchanges, will have shareholders in many States and shares that are traded frequently. The markets that facilitate this national and international participation in ownership of corporations are essential for providing capital not only for new enterprises but also for established companies that need to expand their businesses. This beneficial free market system depends at its core upon the fact that a corporation — except in the rarest situations — is organized under, and governed by, the law of a single jurisdiction, traditionally the corporate law of the State of its incorporation.

These regulatory laws may affect directly a variety of corporate transactions. Mergers are a typical example. In view of the substantial effect that a merger may have on the shareholders' interests in a corporation, many States require supermajority votes to approve mergers. . . . By requiring a greater vote for mergers than is required for other transactions, these laws make it more difficult for corporations to merge. State laws also may provide for "dissenters' rights" under which minority shareholders who disagree with corporate decisions to take particular actions are entitled to sell their shares to the corporation at fair market value. By requiring the corporation to purchase the shares of dissenting shareholders, these laws may inhibit a corporation from engaging in the specified transactions.

It thus is an accepted part of the business landscape in this country for States to create corporations, to prescribe their powers, and to define the rights that are acquired by purchasing their shares. A State has an interest in promoting stable relationships among parties involved in the corporations it charters, as well as in ensuring that investors in such corporations have an effective voice in corporate affairs.

There can be no doubt that the Act reflects these concerns. The primary purpose of the Act is to protect the shareholders of Indiana corporations. It does this by affording shareholders, when a takeover offer is made, an opportunity to decide collectively whether the resulting change in voting control of the corporation, as they perceive it, would be desirable. A change of management may have important effects on the shareholders' interests; it is well within the State's role as overseer of corporate governance to offer this opportunity. The autonomy provided by allowing shareholders collectively to determine whether the takeover is advantageous to their interests may be especially beneficial where a hostile tender offer may coerce shareholders into tendering their shares.

Appellee Dynamics responds to this concern by arguing that the prospect of coercive tender offers is illusory, and that tender offers generally should be favored because they reallocate corporate assets into the hands of management who can use them most effectively.... Indiana's concern with tender offers is not groundless. Indeed, the potentially coercive aspects of tender offers have been recognized by the SEC, and by a number of scholarly commentators.... The Constitution does not require the States to subscribe to any particular economic theory. We are not inclined "to second-guess the empirical judgments of lawmakers concerning the utility of legislation"... In our view, the possibility of coercion in some takeover bids offers additional justification for Indiana's decision to promote the autonomy of independent shareholders.

Dynamics argues in any event that the State has "no legitimate interest in protecting the nonresident shareholders." Dynamics relies heavily on the statement by the *MITE* Court that "[i]nsofar as the ... law burdens out-of-state transactions, there is nothing to be weighed in the balance to sustain the law." But that comment was made in reference to an Illinois law that applied as well to out-of-state corporations as to in-state corporations. We agree that Indiana has no interest in protecting nonresident shareholders *of nonresident corporations*. But this Act applies only to corporations incorporated in Indiana. We reject the contention that Indiana has no interest in providing for the shareholders of its corporations the voting autonomy granted by the Act. Indiana has a substantial interest in preventing the corporate form from becoming a shield for unfair business dealing. Moreover, unlike the Illinois statute invalidated in *MITE*, the Indiana Act applies only to corporations that have a substantial number of shareholders in Indiana. Thus, every application of the Indiana Act will affect a substantial number of Indiana residents, whom Indiana indisputably has an interest in protecting.

D

Dynamics' argument that the Act is unconstitutional ultimately rests on its contention that the Act will limit the number of successful tender offers. There is little evidence that this will occur. But even if true, this result would not substantially affect our Commerce Clause analysis. We reiterate that this Act does not prohibit any entity—resident or nonresident—from offering to purchase, or from purchasing, shares in Indiana corporations, or from attempting thereby to gain control. It only provides regulatory procedures designed for the better protection of the corporations' shareholders. We have rejected the "notion that the Commerce Clause protects the particular structure or methods of operation in a . . . market." The very commodity that is traded in the securities market is one whose characteristics are defined by state law. Similarly, the very commodity that is traded in the "market for corporate control"—the corporation—is one that owes its existence and attributes to state law. Indiana need not define these commodities as other States do; it need only provide that residents and nonresidents have equal access to them. This Indiana has done. Accordingly, even if the Act should decrease the number of successful tender offers for Indiana corporations, this would not offend the Commerce Clause.

IV

On its face, the Indiana Control Share Acquisitions Chapter evenhandedly determines the voting rights of shares of Indiana corporations. The Act does not conflict with the provisions or purposes of the Williams Act. To the limited extent that the Act affects interstate commerce, this is justified by the State's interests in defining the attributes of shares in its corporations and in protecting shareholders. Congress has never questioned the need for state regulation of these matters. Nor do we think such regulation offends the Constitution. Accordingly, we reverse the judgment of the Court of Appeals.

It is so ordered.

. . .

Justice WHITE, with whom Justice BLACKMUN and Justice STEVENS join as to Part II, dissenting.

The majority today upholds Indiana's Control Share Acquisitions Chapter, a statute which will predictably foreclose completely some tender offers for stock in Indiana corporations. I disagree with the conclusion that the Chapter is neither pre-empted by the Williams Act nor in conflict with the Commerce Clause. The Chapter undermines the policy of the Williams Act by effectively preventing minority shareholders, in some circumstances, from acting in their own best interests by selling their stock. In addition, the Chapter will substantially burden the interstate market in corporate ownership, particularly if other States follow Indiana's lead as many already have done. The Chapter, therefore, directly inhibits interstate commerce, the very economic consequences the Commerce Clause was intended to prevent. The opinion of the Court of Appeals is far more persuasive than that of the majority today, and the judgment of that court should be affirmed.

Questions

1. According to the majority opinion in *CTS Corporation v. Dynamics Corporation of America*, which, if any, state antitakeover statutes would be preempted by the Williams Act?

2. Why would a state be concerned about takeovers? What are likely to be the concerns? Are they related to the goals of corporate law?

3. Section 203 of Delaware General Corporation Law, Delaware's anti-takeover statute, provides that if a bidder acquires 15 percent of a target's stock, the bidder is prohibited for a period of three years from engaging in a business combination, including merger, with the target. The provision does not apply if (1) the target board approves the combination before the bidder acquires 15 percent of the target's stock, (2) the bidder acquires 85 percent or more of the target's stock, or (3) both the board and 2/3 of the outstanding shares (not including those owned by the bidder) approve the combination. Corporations can opt out of section 203 in their charter or bylaws, provided that such opt out will not be effective for twelve months and cannot apply to a bidder that acquired 15 percent of the stock prior to the opt out.

Index

A

ACQUISITIONS. *See* Assets, Sales of; Close Corporations, Freeze-outs; Control, Sale of; Leveraged Buy-out; Mergers; Spin-offs; Tender Offers

ALIEN TORT STATUTE, 60, 61

APPRAISAL. *See* Mergers, Appraisal

ASSETS, SALES OF, 721, 722, 723, 724, 725, 726, 727, 728, 729, 730. *See also* Mergers; Spin-offs; Tender Offers

B

***BLASIUS* DUTIES,** 499, 500, 501, 502, 845, 860, 861, 862, 863, 864, 867. *See also* Proxy Contests; Shareholders, Voting; Tender Offers, *Unocal/Blasius*

BONDS. *See* Debt

BUSINESS JUDGMENT RULE, 92, 99, 132, 134, 149, 150, 154, 165, 169, 170, 171, 173, 174, 175, 181, 193, 207, 210, 211, 212, 213, 214, 223, 233, 234, 236, 237, 247, 261, 264, 297, 298, 299, 300, 301, 302, 305, 306, 318, 322, 323, 332, 340, 351, 372, 374, 375, 376, 379, 380, 397, 500, 501, 688, 691, 743, 744, 747, 748, 749, 750, 757, 777, 778, 779, 780, 782, 797, 802, 814, 815, 816, 817, 825, 840, 841, 842, 843, 857, 860, 865, 877, 879, 861. *See also* Care, Duty of; Good Faith; Loyalty, Duty of; Monitor, Duty to

BYLAWS, 63, 86, 87, 88, 89, 90, 137, 495, 529, 533, 554, 556, 558, 562, 563, 564, 565, 566, 567, 568, 569, 570, 571, 722, 724, 896, 905. *See also* Certificate of Incorporation

C

CAPITAL ASSET PRICING MODEL. *See* Valuation

CARE, DUTY OF
General, 89, 93, 127, 137, 138, 142, 193, 198, 199, 200, 201, 203, 207, 236, 237, 247, 249, 296, 297, 298, 299, 300, 301, 302, 303, 304, 305, 306, 307, 318, 322, 323, 325, 326, 328, 330, 333, 334, 343, 351, 352, 355, 363, 372, 374, 375, 376, 404, 500, 747, 750, 754, 756, 779, 782, 793, 797, 801, 802, 831, 852, 854, 863, 891, 892, 894, 895
Causation, 198, 202, 203, 204, 206, 208, 306
Duty to be Informed, 193, 199, 216, 223, 224, 225, 226, 227, 229, 231, 234, 236, 237, 238, 264, 294, 300, 301, 302, 305, 306, 322, 326, 327, 328, 329, 330, 331, 342, 350, 351, 352, 355, 357, 358, 361, 362, 363, 365, 367, 372, 374, 375, 380, 398, 783, 799, 812, 817, 831, 832, 886, 887, 892, 893
See also Business Judgment Rule; Derivative Actions; Directors;

Good Faith; Loyalty, Duty of; Monitor, Duty to; Officers

CERTIFICATE OF INCORPORATION
General, 5, 7, 21, 25, 38, 63, 86, 87, 88, 89, 90, 127, 128, 137, 239, 464, 564, 565, 572, 594, 595, 596, 825, 826
Reserved Power, 15, 16, 41
See also Bylaws

CHARITABLE CONTRIBUTIONS, 37, 38, 39, 40, 41, 42

CLOSE CORPORATIONS
General, 570, 571, 631, 632, 633, 638, 639, 640, 641, 642, 643, 644, 649, 654, 660, 679, 684
Buy-Sell Arrangements, 573, 604, 605, 613, 614, 665, 677, 678
Classified Stock, 571, 572
Cumulative Voting, 572, 574, 575, 581
Fiduciary Duties, 608, 613, 616, 617, 641, 642, 643, 644, 649, 650, 651, 654, 655, 658, 659, 665, 666, 670, 671, 672, 679, 680
Freeze-outs, 639, 640, 641, 649, 650, 656, 658, 659, 660. See also Mergers
Minority Shareholders, 25, 639, 640, 641, 642, 643, 649, 650, 651, 654, 655, 658
Oppression, 677, 678, 679, 682, 683, 684, 685, 686
Pooling Agreements, 573, 576, 577, 578, 579, 584, 586, 587, 588, 593, 602
Shareholder Power, 595, 596, 618, 619, 620, 621, 622, 623, 624, 626, 627, 631, 632
Voting, 571, 572
Voting Trusts, 572, 573, 578, 579, 581, 584, 585, 586, 587, 588, 592, 593, 594, 597, 598, 599, 600, 601, 602, 603.
See also Derivative Actions, Close Corporations, and

COMPENSATION, 142, 158, 159, 160, 163, 164, 165, 166, 211, 282, 283, 284, 285, 286, 287, 288, 291, 292, 293, 294, 295, 308, 309, 310, 311, 312, 313, 323, 324, 326, 327, 328, 329, 330, 331, 385, 537, 553, 808, 857. See also Waste

CONSTITUENCIES. See Stakeholders

CONTROL
Controlling Shareholders, Fiduciary Duties of, 641, 642, 643, 649, 650, 651, 654, 655, 658, 687, 688, 689, 691, 694, 695, 702, 703, 740, 761, 770, 771, 888
Sale of, 703, 704, 705, 706, 707, 708, 709, 710, 711, 712, 713, 714, 715, 819, 825, 826, 827, 828, 830, 831, 832, 835, 865
See also Assets, Sales of; Close Corporations; Mergers; Spin-offs; Tender Offers

CORPORATE OPPORTUNITY, 266, 270, 271, 272, 273, 274, 275, 276, 277, 279, 280, 281

CORPORATE PERSONALITY, 19, 20, 21

CORPORATE POWER, 21, 23, 35, 36, 41, 90, 91, 178, 180, 211, 704, 779, 860

CORPORATION, PURPOSE OF, 9, 10, 21, 23, 24, 31, 32, 34, 39, 40, 59, 60, 71

CORPORATION, THEORY OF, 3, 4, 8, 9, 14, 15, 17, 18, 19, 20, 21, 44, 45, 46, 47, 48, 49, 50, 91, 92, 504, 505, 506

CREDITORS' RIGHTS. See Debt

D

DEBENTURES. *See* Debt

DEBT
    General, 63, 69, 73, 81, 82, 84, 84, 85, 100, 101, 105, 106, 107, 108, 109, 110, 111, 112, 115, 120, 121, 133, 368, 369, 775, 794, 795
    Convertible Bonds, 101, 102, 103, 104, 119, 138, 790
    Exchange Offers, 116, 117, 118, 119, 120, 121
    Fiduciary Duties toward Debtholders, 103, 104, 112, 113, 119, 201, 799, 800. *See also* Stakeholders
    Junk Bonds, 105, 493, 775, 776, 780, 781, 862, 863
    Trust Indenture Act, 113, 114.
    See also Leveraged Buyout

DERIVATIVE ACTIONS
    General, 138, 152, 153, 246, 247, 395
    Close Corporations, and, 635fn4
    Demand Futility, 148, 149, 150, 152, 153, 154, 155, 156, 157, 163, 164, 165, 174, 178, 360, 371, 372, 374, 376, 377, 380, 381, 382, 383, 395, 396, 397, 398, 401, 402
    Demand on Directors, 148, 149
    Demand Refusal, 149, 150, 151, 153, 177, 178, 360, 371, 395
    Individual Actions, Different from, 140, 141, 143
    Security for Expenses, 144, 145, 146, 147
    Settlement, 343, 344, 350
    Special Litigation Committees, 167, 169, 170, 171, 172, 173, 178, 179, 180, 181, 182, 183, 185, 186, 187, 188, 189, 190, 191, 192

DIRECTORS
    Action by, 225, 227, 233, 234, 235, 236, 238, 247, 249, 251, 252, 268, 273, 274, 325
    Classified, 88, 89, 858, 861, 862, 863, 864
    Delegation of Power of, 86, 90, 91, 98, 178, 179, 324, 331, 336, 337, 595, 817
    Exculpation, 239, 295, 295, 322, 323, 333, 334, 335, 360, 374, 375, 403, 892
    Powers of, 29, 86, 87, 88, 89, 90, 91, 98, 99, 568, 569, 570, 626, 627, 778, 779
    Quorum, 87, 88, 90, 91, 253, 254, 474, 477, 483, 495, 566
    Removal of, 86, 88, 89, 90, 474, 475, 476, 477, 482, 558
    Role of, 86, 87, 88, 89, 90
    Sale of Office, 710, 711, 712, 713, 714, 715
    Special Committees, 324, 377, 394, 400, 402, 743, 744, 745, 746, 747, 748, 751, 752, 753, 754, 755, 756. *See also* Derivative Actions, Special Committees
    Structure of Board, 86, 87, 88, 775, 784, 785, 804, 820.
    See also Blasius Duties; Business Judgment Rule; Care, Duty of; Compensation; Corporate Opportunity; Disclosure, Duty of; Fairness; Good Faith; Loyalty, Duty of; Monitor, Duty to; Proxy Contests; *Revlon* Duties; Tender Offers

DISCLOSURE, DUTY OF, 216, 234, 253, 276, 277, 282, 283, 284, 285, 286, 287, 288, 295. 380, 381, 382, 404, 405, 406, 423, 424, 429, 430, 431, 432, 433, 434, 440, 441, 442, 443, 444, 445, 446, 447, 450, 451, 454, 507, 508, 511, 514, 515, 516, 517, 518, 519, 520, 525, 526, 528, 664, 666, 668, 670, 674, 675, 736, 737, 741, 761, 767

DIVIDENDS, 26, 27, 28, 29, 30, 31, 33, 34, 35, 53, 113, 572, 573, 626, 627,

630, 634, 640, 650, 652, 653, 654, 655, 656, 657, 658, 661, 676, 680, 681, 682, 684, 686, 688, 689, 690, 700

E

EFFICIENT CAPITAL MARKETS HYPOTHESIS, 215, 409, 410, 416, 417, 419, 421, 699. *See also* Valuation

EMPLOYEES
Duties Toward, 22, 23, 24, 665, 666, 667, 668, 669, 670, 671, 672, 673, 674, 675, 780
See also Stakeholders

ENTERPRISE LIABILITY, 66, 67, 68, 82, 85. *See also* Limited Liability; Veil Piercing

EQUAL DIGNITY RULE, 730

F

FAIRNESS, 221, 225, 241, 247, 248, 253, 254, 255, 257, 258, 259, 260, 261, 265, 283, 285, 288, 289, 290, 297, 298, 300, 301, 302, 303, 304, 305, 306, 307, 343, 403, 688, 689, 690, 691, 694, 706, 731, 740, 741, 742, 743, 744, 747, 749, 756, 757, 760, 761, 762, 764, 765, 766, 767, 770, 771, 781, 783, 785, 844. *See also* Loyalty, Duty of

FIDUCIARY DUTIES. *See* Blasius Duties; Business Judgment Rule; Care, Duty of; Close Corporations; Control; Debt, Fiduciary Duties toward Debtholders; Derivative Actions; Disclosure, Duty of; Employees, Duties toward; Fairness; Good Faith; Loyalty, Duty of; Mergers; Monitor, Duty to; Preferred Shareholders, Fiduciary Rights of; *Revlon* duties; Stakeholders; Tender Offers

FRAUD ON THE MARKET. *See* Securities Fraud

FREEZE-OUTS. *See* Assets, Sales of; Close Corporations; Mergers; Tender Offers

G

GOOD FAITH, 253, 295, 296, 300, 306, 322, 323, 330, 332, 333, 334, 335, 337, 342, 343, 351, 352, 353, 354, 355, 356, 362, 363, 365, 366, 373, 374, 378, 381, 383, 384, 386, 398, 401, 403, 404, 892, 893, 894, 895, 896

I

INSIDER TRADING
General, 405, 406, 423, 424, 450
Abstain or Disclose, 429, 432, 433, 434, 441, 443, 444, 445, 446, 447, 450, 454
Criminal sanctions, 449, 453, 454, 455, 456
Deceptive Device, 440, 450, 451, 452, 453, 456
In connection with, 435, 436, 437, 450, 451, 452, 453, 456
Insider, Definition of, 429, 441, 442, 444, 446
Materiality, 429, 430, 431
Misappropriation Theory, 448, 449, 450, 451, 452, 453, 456
Short-swing Trading, 457
Tipping, 432, 433, 441, 442, 443, 444, 445, 446
See also Securities Fraud

L

LEVERAGED BUYOUT, 105, 106, 107, 108, 109, 110, 111, 112, 113, 217, 218, 494, 795, 813

LIMITED LIABILITY, 63, 65. *See also* Corporation, Theory of; Enterprise Liability; Veil Piercing

LIMITED LIABILITY COMPANIES, 64, 65

LIMITED LIABILITY PARTNERSHIPS, 64

LIMITED PARTNERSHIPS, 64

LOYALTY, DUTY OF
General, 183, 184, 239, 240, 241, 242, 243, 244, 245, 247, 248, 250, 251, 270, 278, 281, 283, 287, 288, 290, 296, 301, 303, 305, 306, 307, 343, 363, 404, 452, 503, 739, 740, 797, 800, 892
Interested Director Transactions, 240, 241, 247, 248, 250, 251, 253, 254, 255, 257, 258, 259, 264, 265, 397
Psychology of, 240, 248
See also Business Judgment Rule; Care, Duty of; Close Corporations; Compensation; Control; Corporate Opportunity; Derivative Actions; Directors; Fairness; Good Faith; Mergers; Monitor, Duty to; Officers; Spin-offs

M

MERGERS
General, 721, 722, 730
Appraisal, 296, 301, 302, 508, 512, 528, 678, 679, 722, 724, 728, 729, 732, 742, 743, 759, 760, 761, 763, 764, 765, 766, 767, 769, 772, 874
Business Purpose Test, 732, 742, 743, 760, 762, 769, 770, 771
De facto, 722, 725, 726, 727
Freeze-outs, 730, 731, 739, 740, 741, 742, 743, 744, 747, 748, 749, 750, 760, 761, 762
Recapitalization, 767, 768, 769, 770

Rescission, 742, 762, 763
Short-form, 764, 765, 766, 767
See also Assets, Sales of; Close Corporations, Freeze-outs; Fairness; Tender Offers

MONITOR, DUTY TO, 99, 100, 199, 200, 344, 345, 350, 351, 352, 353, 354, 356, 357, 358, 361, 362, 363, 365, 366, 367, 372, 373, 374, 375, 376, 377, 378, 379, 380, 398, 404, 784, 785. *See also* Business Judgment Rule; Care, Duty of; Derivative Actions; Directors; Good Faith; Loyalty, Duty of

O

OFFICERS, 90, 319, 320, 321, 335, 336, 337, 338, 339

P

PARTNERSHIPS, 62, 64, 242, 243, 244

POISON PILLS. *See* Tender Offers

PREFERRED SHAREHOLDERS
General, 124, 125, 132, 133
Anti-destruction Clauses, 788, 789
Fiduciary Rights of, 127, 128, 133, 134. *See also* Stakeholders

PROXIES
General, 508, 509, 513, 514, 522
Causation, 508, 509, 510, 512, 526, 527, 531, 532
Materiality, 509, 510, 514, 515, 516, 520, 521, 522, 524, 525, 526
Reliance, 509, 522, 530, 531
See also Proxy Contests; Securities Fraud

PROXY CONTESTS
General, 461, 463, 464, 465, 466, 477, 478, 486, 487, 488, 489, 490, 491
Reimbursement for expenses, 467, 468, 470, 471, 472, 473, 478, 479
See also Proxies; Securities Fraud

R

REVLON DUTIES, 799, 800, 801, 802, 804, 811, 812, 813, 814, 825, 826, 827, 828, 829, 830, 831, 832, 865, 877, 878, 880, 888, 892, 893, 894, 895. *See also* Tender Offers

S

SECURITIES FRAUD
Fraud on the Market, 406, 408, 409, 411, 413, 414, 415, 416, 418, 419, 420, 421, 422, 423
Reliance, 405, 406, 407, 408, 409, 410, 411, 412, 413, 414, 415, 416, 417, 418, 420
Section 10(b), 405, 407, 423, 424
See also Insider Trading; Proxies; Proxy Contests

SHAREHOLDER PROPOSALS
General, 533, 534, 535, 536, 537, 538, 539, 543, 544, 545, 546, 554, 556, 562
Corporate Governance Proposals, 556, 557, 558, 559, 560, 562, 563, 564, 565, 566, 567, 568, 569, 570
No Action Letters, 544, 545, 546, 547, 548, 549, 550, 555, 562
Ordinary Business Proposals, 541, 542, 544, 545, 546, 547, 548, 549, 550, 551, 552, 553
See also Shareholders

SHAREHOLDERS
General, 461, 462, 463, 464
Ratification, 166, 285, 288, 289, 290, 291, 292, 293, 294, 469, 472
Voting, 100, 139, 234, 265, 283, 284, 462, 463, 464, 500, 501, 571, 572, 573, 748, 756, 757, 783, 845, 861
See also Assets, Sales of; Close Corporations; Control; Derivative Actions; Preferred Shareholders; Proxies; Proxy Contests; Shareholder Proposals; Stock

SOLE PROPRIETORSHIP, 62

SPIN-OFFS, 693, 694, 695, 696, 697

STAKEHOLDERS, 59, 60, 138, 504, 505, 780, 793, 799, 800, 816, 869, 874
See also Debt; Employees; Preferred Shareholders

STOCK
General, 100
Classified, 589, 590, 699, 700, 701, 702, 703, 821, 868, 876, 888
Options, 160, 161, 162, 163, 164, 165, 166, 282, 283, 284, 285, 286, 287, 288, 291, 292, 293, 294, 295, 309, 310, 311, 312, 313, 426, 434, 821, 822
Rights Plans, 785, 786, 787, 788, 789, 790, 791, 792, 794, 798, 821, 838, 839, 854
Treasury, 100, 118, 121, 230, 231, 644
See also Preferred Shareholders; Shareholders

T

TENDER OFFERS
General, 772, 773, 774, 777, 778, 779, 780, 789, 790, 815, 825, 835, 840, 841
Draconian Defenses, 779, 832, 834, 851, 854, 855, 862, 879, 880, 882, 883
Enhanced Scrutiny, 801, 825, 826, 827, 828, 829, 836, 853, 876, 878, 879, 880, 881
Fiduciary Out, 868, 881, 882, 883, 884, 885, 887, 888, 889, 891
Lockups, 793, 799, 800, 801, 802, 834, 878, 882, 885, 887, 889
No-Shop Provisions, 568, 796, 798, 801, 809, 814, 821, 823, 824, 831, 832, 833, 834, 878, 885, 891
Poison Pills, 568, 785, 786, 787, 788, 789, 790, 791, 792, 798, 811, 821, 838, 839, 840, 843, 844, 845, 846, 848, 849, 850, 851, 853, 854, 855, 856, 859

Repurchase Programs, 779, 839, 840, 843, 844, 845, 846, 847, 848, 849, 850, 852, 853, 854, 855, 856
Selective Tender Offer, 777, 778, 779, 780, 781, 782
Self-tender, 774, 775, 776, 845, 855
Shark Repellant, 844
State Antitakeover Laws, 896, 897, 898, 899, 900, 901, 902, 903, 904, 905
Supermajority Vote, 808, 825, 839, 844, 846, 847, 848, 849, 850, 902
Termination Fee, 821, 831, 832, 833, 873, 883
Unocal Duties, 779, 780, 781, 783, 784, 785, 789, 790, 797, 801, 812, 815, 816, 817, 818, 828, 840, 841, 845, 862, 865, 868, 878, 879, 880, 881, 882, 883, 888
Unocal Threats, 780, 781, 815, 816, 817, 842, 843, 851, 852, 861, 862
Unocal / Blasius, 860, 861, 862, 863, 864, 865
Unocal / Unitrin, 851, 852, 853, 854, 855, 856, 882, 883
See also Assets, Sales of; *Blasius* Duties; Control, Sale of; Insider Trading; Mergers; Proxy Contests; *Revlon* Duties; Stock, Rights Plans

V

VALUATION
General, 83, 84, 161, 162, 165, 225, 226, 227, 285, 286, 287, 327, 329, 524, 708, 732, 742, 745, 754, 755, 756, 757, 771, 890, 891
Book Value, 524, 526, 529, 604, 605, 606, 607, 608, 609, 610, 611, 614, 615, 616, 662, 668
Capital Asset Pricing Model, 214, 215
Delaware Block Method, 771, 772
Marketability Discount, 771, 772
Minority Discount, 771, 772
Portfolio Theory, 214, 438, 571, 764
See also Efficient Capital Markets Hypothesis

VEIL PIERCING
General, 65, 66, 67, 68, 73
Agency Liability, 66, 67, 68
Alter Ego, 66, 67, 68, 73, 74, 78, 79
Contracts, 73, 74, 75, 76, 78, 79, 80, 81
Parents-Subsidiary, 81, 82, 83, 84, 85
Reverse, 78, 79
See also Enterprise Liability; Limited Liability

W

WASTE, 21, 93, 150, 151, 158, 159, 208, 277, 282, 291, 292, 293, 294, 295, 307, 340, 341, 371, 372, 383, 384, 385, 386, 742, 763, 764. *See also* Compensation

WILLIAMS ACT, 896, 898, 899, 900, 901, 904, 905